G000093928

TOP INCOMES OVER THE TWENTIETH CENTURY

Top Incomes over the Twentieth Century

A Contrast Between Continental European and English-Speaking Countries

Edited by
A. B. ATKINSON,
Nuffield College, Oxford
and
T. PIKETTY
PSE, Paris

OXFORD
UNIVERSITY PRESS

OXFORD
UNIVERSITY PRESS

Great Clarendon Street, Oxford OX2 6DP

Oxford University Press is a department of the University of Oxford.
It furthers the University's objective of excellence in research, scholarship,
and education by publishing worldwide in

Oxford New York

Auckland Cape Town Dar es Salaam Hong Kong Karachi
Kuala Lumpur Madrid Melbourne Mexico City Nairobi
New Delhi Shanghai Taipei Toronto

With offices in

Argentina Austria Brazil Chile Czech Republic France Greece
Guatemala Hungary Italy Japan Poland Portugal Singapore
South Korea Switzerland Thailand Turkey Ukraine Vietnam

Oxford is a registered trade mark of Oxford University Press
in the UK and in certain other countries

Published in the United States
by Oxford University Press Inc., New York

© Oxford University Press, 2007

The moral rights of the authors have been asserted
Database right Oxford University Press (maker)

First published 2007

All rights reserved. No part of this publication may be reproduced,
stored in a retrieval system, or transmitted, in any form or by any means,
without the prior permission in writing of Oxford University Press,
or as expressly permitted by law, or under terms agreed with the appropriate
reprographics rights organization. Enquiries concerning reproduction
outside the scope of the above should be sent to the Rights Department,
Oxford University Press, at the address above

You must not circulate this book in any other binding or cover
and you must impose the same condition on any acquirer

British Library Cataloguing in Publication Data
Data available

Library of Congress Cataloging in Publication Data
Data available

Typeset by SPI Publisher Services, Pondicherry, India
Printed in Great Britain
on acid-free paper by
Biddles Ltd, King's Lynn, Norfolk

ISBN 978–0–19–928688–1

1 3 5 7 9 10 8 6 4 2

Preface

The origins of this volume, and the companion volume to follow, lie in the study of top incomes in France over the twentieth century published by one of us (TP) in 2001. The study used data from income tax and other sources to show the evolution of income inequality over a much longer continuous period than had previously been investigated (see Piketty 2001). This study, summarized in Chapter 3, inspired the other editor (ABA) to examine the same topic for the United Kingdom, and the results are presented in Chapter 4. Piketty and Emmanuel Saez extended the comparison further by making estimates for the United States (summarized in Chapter 5). Since then, the fruitfulness of income tax data in providing long run evidence about the top of the distribution has led to estimates being constructed for a sizeable number of countries (covered here in Chapters 6 to 12 and in a forthcoming second volume).

The aim of the project is to assemble in one place the studies of top incomes for a wide range of countries (ten in this volume). A number of the chapters are based on research that has already been published in journal articles (see the Bibliography, Chapters 1 and 2 in this volume), but the present versions contain more extensive accounts of the sources and methods as well as further and, in some cases, more recent results. Present journal editorial practice does not typically allow space for full documentation of methods, but we believe that it is important that these be recorded and discussed. The preparation of new economic data such as those presented here involves a large number of operations and recourse to a diversity of sources. Along the way, the data constructor has inevitably had to make assumptions and corrections; it is not simply a matter of copying tables. If this process is not documented in full, then the reader is unable to assess the validity of the final series. We have therefore encouraged authors to explain their methods in detail.

The volume is not intended to be a comparative study. Although a number of the chapters refer to evidence for other countries, it will be clear that each country studied has its own specificities with regard to systems of income taxation, to the ways in which data are collected, and to the wider processes of income determination. We cannot assume that the series are fully homogeneous across countries, and the literature on cross-country growth regressions warns us of the pitfalls in merging data without regard to the specificities of both data and reality. The emphasis is therefore on the historical experience of each of the ten countries. At the same time, as discussed in Chapter 1, the studies presented here represent a necessary first stage in any comparative analysis. The series were constructed by using the same raw data sources for all countries and applying the same methodology to derive the final series. Although fully homogenous, cross-country data sets do not exist, we have done our best to make our database as homogenous as possible, and to provide users with adequate guidance and technical information. We have therefore, in the final chapter (Chapter 13), assembled the key series for the ten countries. In the second volume, we hope to cover the Nordic countries, countries from Southern Europe, India, China, Brazil, and Indonesia, which will extend considerably the range of experience.

The bibliographic references for the first two chapters are grouped together, but we have kept separate bibliographies for the individual country chapters (even though this means some duplication), on the grounds that some readers may only be interested in one country, and wish to see the sources for that country collected together.

A number of the chapters were presented at a conference organized as part of the CHANGEQUAL network meeting at Nuffield College, Oxford, in September 2003. Atkinson worked on the final preparation of the manuscript while holding a Chaire Blaise Pascal at ENS-PSE. The editors would like to thank Lin Sorrell and Cathy Douglas for their help at Nuffield, and the authors for their contributions and patience.

A.B. Atkinson and T. Piketty

REFERENCE

Piketty, T. (2001). *Les hauts revenus en France au XXe siѐle: inégalités et redistributions, 1901–1998*. Paris: Grasset.

Contents

List of Figures, Tables, and Boxes

FIGURES

TABLES

BOXES

1

Top Incomes Over the Twentieth Century: A Summary of Main Findings[1]

T. Piketty

1.1 INTRODUCTION

This introductory essay presents some of the key findings and perspectives emerging from the detailed country chapters published in this volume. All chapters are part of a collective research project on the long-run dynamics of income and wealth distribution. The general objective of this project was to construct a high quality, long-run, international database on income and wealth distribution using historical tax statistics. The resulting database now includes annual series covering most of the twentieth century for over 20 (mostly Western) countries. The present volume focuses upon the contrast between continental European countries and English-speaking countries and includes ten case studies: France, UK, US, Canada, Australia, New Zealand, Germany, the Netherlands, Switzerland, and Ireland. A forthcoming volume will complete the study by covering Scandinavian and Northern Europe (including Sweden, Finland, and Norway), Southern Europe (including Italy, Spain, Portugal), as well as a number of Latin American (including Argentina, Brazil) and Asiatic countries (including India, China, and Indonesia).

The primary motivation for this project was a general dissatisfaction with existing income distribution databases. The international databases on inequality that existed were not high quality (they display little homogeneity over time or across countries),[2] they are not long-run (typically they cover only a couple of isolated years per country, generally restricted to the post-1970 or post-1980 period), and they almost never offer any decomposition of income inequality into a labour income and a capital income component. This latter feature of existing data sets is unfortunate, because the economic mechanisms at work can be very

[1] The references to this chapter are given at the end of Chapter 2.

[2] See, e.g., the Atkinson-Brandolini (2001) criticism of the World Bank (Deininger-Squire) secondary database. The database is 'secondary' in the sense that it is based on the collection of inequality measures computed by others using various income data sets and methodologies for different countries and time periods. In contrast, our inequality measures were computed by ourselves using the same primary data sources and methodology for all countries and time periods.

different for the distribution of labour income (demand and supply of skills, labour market institutions, etc.) and the distribution of capital income (capital accumulation, credit constraints, estate taxation, etc.), so that it is fairly heroic to test for any of these mechanisms using such data. The fact that existing databases are not long run is also most unfortunate, because structural changes in income and wealth distributions are relatively slow and very often span over several decades. In order to properly understand such changes, one needs to be able to put them into broader historical perspective.[3]

Our database also suffers from strong limitations (in particular, our long-run series are generally confined to top income and wealth shares and contain little information about bottom segments of the distribution), and fully homogenous, cross-country data sets do not exist. However, our database has the following advantages:

- we use the same raw data sources for all countries and apply the same methodology to derive the final series;
- the series are typically annual and cover a long-run of years;
- the data are mostly broken down by income source.

This means that they offer a unique opportunity to understand better the dynamics of income and wealth distribution and the two-way interaction between inequality and growth.

We should stress that the main objective of the chapters collected in this volume is to describe how the series were constructed, and to offer first cut analysis of the long-run dynamics of inequality in each individual country. Such analytical narratives and detailed case studies are useful, but in our view they should be seen as complements (rather than substitutes) to a more systematic statistical exploitation of the complete database, which we do not offer in this volume. We very much hope that future researchers will use our database to explore causal mechanisms in a more systematic way, and in particular that our data will contribute to renew the literature on cross-country inequality/growth regressions.[4]

The rest of this introductory essay is organized as follows. In section 1.2, we briefly present the basic data and methodology used to construct the database. Section 1.3 presents some of the main descriptive findings and conclusions, with particular emphasis to the Kuznets' curve debate. Section 1.4 attempts to illustrate how our database could potentially be used to renew the cross-country structural analysis of the interplay between inequality and growth, with better hopes of success than the previous literature. We then discuss some of the prospects for extending the database using additional published historical tax tabulations and collecting historical individual tax data (Section 1.5).

[3] This was first stressed by Kuznets (1955).

[4] One of the key reasons why the literature on cross-country inequality/growth regressions failed to deliver robust conclusions (see, e.g., Banerjee and Duflo (2003) for a critical appraisal) is the poor quality of existing databases.

1.2. CONSTRUCTING A NEW DATABASE: PRIMARY DATA AND METHODOLOGY

Household income surveys are a relatively recent venture: they virtually did not exist on a national basis prior to 1950, and in most countries they are not available in a homogenous, machine-readable format until the 1970s–1980s. The only data source that is consistently available on a long-run basis is tax data. Progressive income tax systems were set up in most Western countries at the beginning of the twentieth century (1913 in the US, 1914 in France, etc.), and in all countries with an income tax system the tax administration started compiling and publishing tabulations based on the exhaustive set of income tax returns.[5] These tabulations generally report for a large number of income brackets the corresponding number of taxpayers, as well as their total income and tax liability. They are usually broken down by income source: capital income, wage income, business income, etc.

In order to give a sense of what our primary data sources look like, we reproduce in Table 1.1 the raw top income tabulations for France in 1919, as they were originally published by the Finance Ministry. One can see for instance on this table that 181 French taxpayers reported tax income above one million francs in 1919 (a pretty large income at that time). We also reproduce on Table 1.2 the raw income composition tabulations for France in 1920. One can see that out of the 722 million French francs reported by French taxpayers with individual income above 1 million francs in 1920, 322 million francs took the form of '*revenus des valeurs et capitaux mobiliers*' (interest and dividend income), 356 million francs took the form of '*bénéfices industriels et commerciaux*' (business income), and only 16 million francs took the form of '*traitements publics et privés, salaires, etc.*' (wage income).

One can then use standard Pareto extrapolation techniques to compute top fractiles thresholds and average incomes using such data. This methodology is described in a detailed manner in Chapter 2. Here it is sufficient to recall that the Pareto law for top incomes is given by the following distribution function:

$$1 - F(y) = (k/y)^a \ (k > 0,\ a > 1) \qquad (1.1)$$

The corresponding density function is given by $f(y) = ak^a/y^{(1+a)}$. The key property of Pareto distributions is that the ratio between the average income $y^*(y)$ of individuals (or households or tax units) with income above y and y does not depend on the income threshold y:

$$\begin{aligned} y^*(y) &= \left[\int_{z>y} zf(z)dz\right] / \left[\int_{z>y} f(z)dz\right] \\ &= \left[\int_{z>y} dz/z^a\right] / \left[\int_{z>y} dz/z^{(1+a)}\right] = ay/(a-1) \qquad (1.2) \\ & i.e.\ y^*(y)/y = b,\ with\ b = a/(a-1) \end{aligned}$$

[5] Full details about the administrative publications where the raw tabulations were originally published are given in the country chapters.

Table 1.1 Raw top income tabulations, France 1919 (IMPÔT GÉNÉRAL SUR LE REVENU)

CATÉGORIES DE REVENUS.	NOMBRE de CONTRIBUABLES inscrits dans les rôles.	MONTANT des REVENUS imposés.	MONTANT DES DÉDUCTIONS pour SITUATION de famille.	MONTANT DES DÉDUCTIONS pour CHARGES DE FAMILLE 1,500 fr.	MONTANT DES DÉDUCTIONS pour CHARGES DE FAMILLE 5,000 fr.	MONTANT BRUT de l'impôt.	MONTANT des PÉNALITÉS et droits au sus.
1	2	3	4	5	6	7	8
		fr.	fr.	fr.	fr.	fr.	fr.
6,100 à 10,000 francs	130,787	1,170,324,800	123,915,000	7,110,000	34,406,000	3,805,400	170,500
10,100 à 20,000	193,679	2,851,910,400	417,507,000	25,410,000	194,082,000	21,056,000	759,100
20,100 à 30,000	58,894	1,477,045,800	137,517,000	8,983,500	97,740,000	18,687,300	755,300
30,100 à 50,000	39,974	1,529,512,700	93,711,000	6,235,500	79,134,000	40,061,400	1,025,200
50,100 à 100,000	23,882	1,592,572,500	62,733,000	3,354,000	46,894,000	94,486,600	1,907,700
100,100 à 200,000	9,487	1,517,031,000	21,768,000	1,513,500	50,530,000	142,413,800	2,820,500
200,100 à 300,000	2,289	556,396,900	6,651,000	315,000	5,456,000	99,524,900	965,900
300,100 à 500,000	1,388	527,734,800	3,204,000	138,000	3,080,000	126,024,700	1,228,500
500,100 à 1 million	576	387,082,900	1,380,000	46,500	1,318,000	130,956,900	1,680,800
Au-dessus de 1 million	181	451,968,100	420,000	13,500	336,000	206,785,300	883,400
TOTAUX	467,137	11,867,588,900	868,911,000	53,119,500	492,776,000	883,801,200	12,177,000

(contd.)

Table 1.1 (*Contd.*)

	MAJORATION DUE PAR LES CONTRIBUABLES CÉLÉBATAIRES. (25 p. 100.)			MAJORATION DUE PAR LES MÉNAGES SANS INFANTS. (10 p. 100.)				
	Nombre de contribuables supportant la majoration. 9	Montant des revenus des intéréssés 10	Produit de la majoration. 11	Nombre de contribuables supportant la majoration. 12	Montant des revenus des intéressés. 13	Produits de la majoration. 14	MONTANT des DÉDUCTIONS pour charges de famille. 15	PRODUIT NET TOTAL de l'impôt. 16
		fr.	fr.		fr.	fr.	fr.	fr.
	45,190	340,334,700	430,700	11,900	111,048,300	70,000	105,600	4,570,800
	21,602	301,518,900	875,600	29,401	413,678,300	354,800	727,800	22,518,600
	5,162	130,728,500	1,026,200	6,712	168,608,500	470,500	096,200	20,225,100
	3,398	132,038,600	1,073,900	4,225	168,148,800	431,000	1,801,200	40,777,300
	2,049	143,370,600	2,067,800	2,407	168,390,600	1,034,800	5,028,800	95,868,100
	746	99,947,600	3,173,800	904	125,934,300	1,557,000	10,161,500	139,805,600
	167	39,950,600	1,886,300	196	46,776,500	893,000	4,704,100	98,566,000
	114	33,245,200	2,153,300	123	45,315,200	1,137,000	3,080,000	127,403,800
	35	24,508,500	2,087,500	45	29,941,900	1,086,100	1,518,000	134,493,500
	23	49,247,600	5,993,800	17	33,763,300	1,506,700	336,000	214,833,200
TOTAUX	78,492	1,294,870,800	20,770,900	55,930	1,511,005,700	8,590,900	28,620,200	896,719,800

Note: TABLEAU *présentant, à la date du 30 avril 1922, la décomposition, par catégories de revenus, des résultats des rôles établis au titre de l'année 1920 (revenus de 1919)*

Source: Originally published in *Bulletin de statistique et de législation comparée*, March 1923: vol. 93.

Table 1.2 Raw income composition tabulations, France 1919 (IMPÔT GÉNÉRAL SUR LE REVENU.)

CATÉGORIES DE REVENUS.	MONTANT TOTAL des revenus globaux (A)	DÉCOMPOSITION DES REVENUS GLOBAUX SUIVANT LES DIVERSES SOURCES D'OÙ ILS PROVIENNENT (a).							
		REVENUS des propriétés bâties		REVENUS des propriétés non bâties		REVENUS des valeurs et capitaux mobiliers.		BÉNÉFICES de l'exploitation agricols.	
		Montant.	Proportion.	Montant.	Proportion.	Montant.	Proportion.	Montant.	Proportion.
1	2	3	4	5	6	7	8	9	10
	millions.	millions.	%	millions.	%	millions.	%	millions.	%
6,100 à 10,000 fr...	1,100	65	5.9	31	3.1	148	13.5	18	1.6
10,100 à 20,000	3,832	205	5.3	100	2.6	497	13.0	82	2.1
20,100 à 30,000	2,044	127	0.3	63	3.1	301	17.7	47	2.3
30,100 à 50,000	2,132	142	6.7	62	2.9	402	21.7	40	1.9
50,100 à 100,000	2,281	143	0.3	59	2.6	586	25.0	36	1.6
100,100 à 200,000	1,803	97	5.4	30	1.7	514	28.5	18	1.0
200,100 à 300,000	751	34	4.5	10	1.3	233	31.0	5	0.7
300,100 à 500,000	699	20	3.7	8	1.1	227	32.5	6	0.9
500,100 à 1 million......	530	17	3.2	4	0.7	186	35.1	4	0.8
Au-dessus de 1 million...	722	12	1.7	5	0.7	322	44.6	3	0.4
TOTAUX ET MOYENNES	16,897	868	5.5	375	2.4	3,536	22.2	259	1.6

(contd.)

Table 1.2 (*Contd.*)

	BÉNÉFICES Industriels et commerciaux.		BÉNÉFICES de l'exploitation minière.		TRAITEMENTS publics et privés, salaires, etc.		PENSIONS de rentes viagères		BÉNÉFICES des professions non commerciales.		REVENUS des charges et offices.	
	Montant. 11	Proportion. 12	Montant. 13	Proportion. 14	Montant. 15	Proportion. 16	Montant. 17	Proportion. 18	Montant. 19	Proportion. 20	Montant. 21	Proportion. 22
	millions.	%	millions.	%	millions.	%	millions.	%	millions.	%	millions.	%
	107	9.7	1	0.1	665	60.4	35	3.2	24	2.2	3	0.3
	820	21.6	3	0.1	1,873	48.9	72	1.9	148	3.8	26	0.7
	651	31.8	3	0.1	634	31.0	29	1.4	102	5.0	27	1.3
	705	35.0	2	0.1	502	23.5	22	1.0	101	4.7	34	1.6
	800	39.0	2	0.1	422	13.5	17	0.7	92	4.0	37	1.6
	800	44.4	3	0.2	257	14.2	8	0.4	50	3.1	20	1.1
	353	47.0	1	0.1	87	11.0	3	0.4	18	2.4	7	1.0
	314	49.2	1	0.1	68	9.7	3	0.3	14	2.0	3	0.5
	200	50.2	1	0.2	43	8.1	2	0.2	8	1.5.	"	"
	356	49.3	3	0.4	16	2.2	"	"	5	0.7	"	"
TOTAUX ET MOYENNES	5,358	33.7	20	9.1	4,567	28.7	189	1.2	568	3.6	167	1.0

Notes: IMPÔT ÉTABLI AU TITRE DE L'ANNÉE 1921,—BÉNÉFICES ET REVENUS RÉALISÉS AU COURS DE L'ANNÉE 1920. *Tableau présentant, pour les contribuables inscrits dans les rôles émis du 1st janvier 1921 au 30 avril 1922, la décomposition du revenu global* (Revenus déclarés seulement) les différentes sources de revenus.

(a) Avant toute déduction au titre des charges grovant le revenu global. (Contributions directes assimilées, pertes résultant d'un déficit d'exploitation, intérêts de *dellos*, etc.).

(b) Aucone concordance ne peut exister entre le montant de revenus indiqués au présent tableau et le montant des revenus quel servi de base aux impôts cédulaires pour l'anée 1921. Tous les contribuables assujettis aux impôts cédulaires ne sont pas, en effet, *possibles* de l'impôt général et, inversement, certains revenus entrant dans la composition du revenu global soumi à l'impôt général ne sont pas frappés par l'impôt cédulaire parce que leur montant ne déponse pas la somme affranchie de l'impôt dans la cédule correspondante.

Source: Originally published in *Bulletin de statistique et de législation comparée*, March 1923: vol. 93.

That is, if $b=2$, the average income of individuals with income above €100,000 is €200,000, and the average income of individuals with income above €1 million is €2 million. Although this law is only an asymptotic approximation (in practice, estimated b coefficients vary slightly with y), it works remarkably well for top incomes, as was first noted by Vilfredo Pareto (1896, 1896–97) in the 1890s using tax tabulations from Swiss cantons. In this volume, we do not address the interesting issue as to why this law holds, and we solely use is as an interpolation technique allowing us to compute top fractile thresholds and average incomes from grouped income data. It is important to note that although the b coefficient is (almost) invariant with y for a given country and a given year, it does vary substantially over time and across countries.[6] A higher b coefficient means a fatter upper tail of the income distribution, which generally implies higher inequality (for a constant mean). For instance, the b coefficient declined from about 2.3–2.4 to about 1.7–1.8 in France during the twentieth century, as top income shares dropped. The b coefficient went through a similar decline in all countries where inequality dropped, and it started rising again in countries where inequality rose since the 1970s, e.g. in the United States (where the b coefficient is now back to about 2.3–2.4).

Pareto extrapolation techniques are fairly powerful, but they do not allow extrapolation on income ranges for which we have no data. In that respect, one major limitation of tax data is that the income of individuals not subject to the tax is excluded from the data. Prior to the Second World War, the proportion of individuals subject to progressive income taxation hardly exceeded 10–15% in most countries, so that one can only compute top decile income series (and above) over the entire period. In order to construct top fractile income shares series from top fractile income data, one needs a total income denominator, which can be computed using aggregate income sources (national accounts and their ancestors). Constructing homogenous numerator and denominator series requires special care and raises a number of issues, many of which are addressed in Chapter 2.

1.3 BASIC DESCRIPTIVE FINDINGS: THE KUZNETS' CURVE, 50 YEARS LATER

The first economist to use these data sources and methodology in a systematic way was Kuznets (1953).[7] He exploited US income tax tabulations covering the

[6] Most authors refer to $a=b/(b-1)$ (rather than b) as the 'Pareto coefficient'. Note, however, that the b coefficient has a more intuitive economic meaning. One could for instance refer to $b-1$ as the 'income advantage of the rich' (IAR) coefficient. During the twentieth century the IAR coefficient declined from 130–140% to 70–80% in France, i.e. the income advantage of the rich nearly halved.

[7] Earlier authors (e.g. Bowley 1914 and Stamp 1916) used income tax data in a sophisticated way (see Chapter 4), but Kuznets was apparently the first scholar to use control totals to construct top income shares series.

1913–48 period and computed corresponding top decile and top percentile income shares series. These were the first long-run income distribution series ever produced (income distribution had been at the centre of speculative economic thought at least since the time of Ricardo and Marx, but few data were available). Unsurprisingly, these series had a major impact on economic thinking, especially after Kuznets (1955) proposed his famous 'Kuznets curve' theory in order to account for the 1913–48 decline in income inequality that he witnessed for the United States. According to this theory (which Kuznets himself viewed as highly speculative),[8] income inequality should follow an inverse U-shape along the development process, first rising with industrialization and then declining, as more and more workers join the high productivity sectors of the economy.

In a sense, all what we are doing in this project is to extend and generalize what Kuznets did in the early 1950s—except that we now have 50 more years of data, and over 20 countries instead of one. In addition, note that Kuznets had access to a fairly limited data processing technology, which probably explains why he did not use all available data as systematically as possible. In particular, Kuznets did not fully use the tabulations broken down by income source, and his top income shares series are only defined for total income (for instance, he did not compute separate series for wage income or capital income).

The fact that we have 50 more years of data, over 20 countries and series broken down by income source led us to adopt a fairly different perspective than Kuznets as to why income inequality dropped in Western countries during the first half of the twentieth century. First, as one can see on Figure 1.1, where we plot the basic series for the French case, the decline in top income shares witnessed by Kuznets for the US also took place in France, but it came to an end right after the Second World War. The secular decline in income inequality took place during a very particular and politically chaotic period, namely during the 1914–45 period (and especially during both World Wars and the early 1930s). This raises serious doubts about a gradual, Kuznets type explanation. If the decline in income inequality was due to a continuous reallocation process between from a low productivity to a high productivity sector (say, from rural to urban sector, as in Kuznets' original model), then it is hard to understand why the timing of the fall should be so particular.

Next, and most importantly, one can see from Figure 1.1 that the 1914–45 drop in top income shares is entirely due to the fall of top capital incomes: top wage shares actually did not decline at all. One gets the same picture by using other inequality measures, e.g. by looking at the top decile share rather than the top percentile share. In particular, the striking fact that the wage distribution in a country like France has been extremely stable in the long run during the twentieth century appears to be very robust, irrespective of how one measures wage inequality (for instance, the 90:10 ratio—and not only top wage shares—has also remained stable in the long run); see Piketty (2003) and Chapter 3. Labour

[8] 'This is perhaps 5% empirical information and 95% speculation, some of it possibly tainted by wishful thinking' (Kuznets 1955: 26).

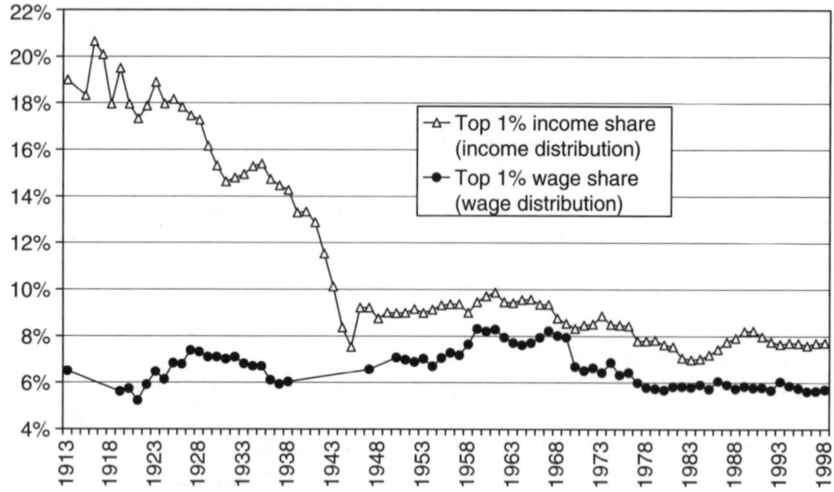

Figure 1.1 The fall of top capital incomes in France, 1913–98

Source: Piketty 2001, 2003, Chapter 3 this volume: Table 3A.1; authors' computations using income tax returns.

reallocation of the kind described by Kuznets did take place (the bottom 30% of the French wage distribution was made up almost exclusively of rural workers at the beginning of the twentieth century, and rural workers have virtually disappeared by the end of the twentieth century), but this did not lead to a compression of the wage distribution: low wage rural workers have been replaced by low wage urban workers, and the wage hierarchy remained more or less the same (in spite of the fact that real wages have been multiplied by five over the course of the century).

The fact that the drop in income inequality is solely due to the fall in top capital incomes, and that the fall took place mostly during wartime and the Great Depression, suggests an obvious explanation: for the most part, income inequality dropped because capital owners incurred severe shocks to their capital holdings during the 1914–45 period (destruction, inflation, bankruptcies, etc.) This interpretation is confirmed by available wealth and estate data. Note that the idea that capital owners incurred large shocks during the 1914–45 period and that this had a big impact on income distribution is certainly not new (Kuznets already mentioned this factor). What is new is that there is not much else going on.

The more challenging part that needs to be explained is the non-recovery of top capital incomes during the post-1945 period (see Figure 1.1). Here the proposed explanation is that the 1914–45 capital shocks had a permanent impact because the introduction of high income and estate tax progressivity (there was virtually no tax progressivity prior to 1914, and top rates increased enormously between 1914 and 1945) made it impossible for top capital holders to fully recover. Simple simulations (Piketty (2003) and Chapter 3) suggest that the long-run impact of tax progressivity on wealth concentration is indeed large enough to explain the magnitude of the observed changes.[9]

The French case depicted on Figure 1.1 is interesting, because it appears to be fairly representative of what happened in other OECD countries.[10] In all countries for which we have data, the secular decline in income inequality took place for the most part during the 1914–45 period, and most of the decline seems to be due to the fall of top capital incomes. The 1914–45 drop was larger in countries that were strongly hit by the war (e.g. France and Germany) than in the US, and there was no drop at all in countries not hit at all (such as Switzerland), which is consistent with the proposed explanation based on capital shocks. Moreover wealth concentration seems to have better recovered during the post-war period in countries with less tax progressivity (especially estate tax progressivity) such as Germany, which again seems broadly consistent with the tax explanation.

There are however important differences between rich countries. First, income inequality did keep declining during the 1950s–1960s in a number of countries (such as the UK), albeit at a lower pace than during the 1914–45 period.[11] Next, during the post-1970 period, one does observe a major divergence between rich countries. While top income shares have remained fairly stable in France and other continental European countries over the past three decades, they have increased enormously in the US, where they are now back to their interwar levels (see Figure 1.2). The UK and other Anglo-Saxon countries tend be somewhere in between the European pattern and the US pattern. Note that the rise of US top income shares is not due to the revival of top capital incomes, but rather to the very large increases in top wages (especially top executive compensation). As a consequence, top executives (the 'working rich') have replaced top capital owners (the 'rentiers') at the top of the US income hierarchy over the course of the twentieth century. This contrasts with the European pattern, where top capital incomes are still predominant at the top of the distribution (albeit at lower levels than at the beginning of the twentieth century).[12] This provides yet another example as to why it is vital to be able to break down income distribution series by income source (without such a decomposition, it is virtually impossible to understand the forces at play). Note however the new US pattern might not persist for very long: capital accumulation by the 'working rich' is likely to lead the revival of top capital incomes at the following generation, especially in a context of large cuts in US income and estate tax progressivity.

Although most countries covered in this volume do follow this general pattern (abrupt decline of top capital incomes during the 1914–45, sudden rise of top wages in Anglo-Saxon countries since the 1970s), a careful reading of the country chapters collected in this volume will reveal many interesting particularities.

[9] See Piketty (2003) and Chapter 3 in this volume.

[10] See the country chapters collected in this volume.

[11] This might be partly due to the steeply progressive tax structure applied in those countries (especially in the UK), but there are other explanations as well.

[12] See especially the striking contrast between the evolution of income composition patterns by fractile in the US (Saez 2005: fig. 4) and Germany (Dell 2005: fig. 5).

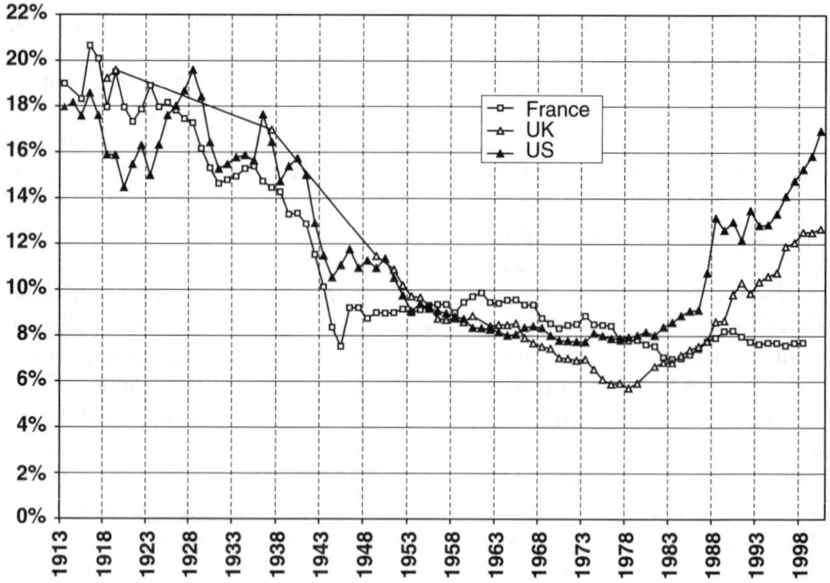

Figure 1.2 The top 1% income share in France, the UK, and the US, 1913–2000

Source: France: Piketty Chapter 3 (this volume): Table 3A.1; UK: Atkinson Chapter 4 (this volume): Table 4.1; US: Piketty and Saez Chapter 5 (this volume): Table 5A.1; authors' computations using income tax returns.

We already mentioned the very special case of Switzerland, where top shares have been basically flat in the long run. Countries like Ireland, Australia, and New Zealand, which were less strongly affected by the wars than other countries, also witnessed a limited inequality decline during the 1914–45 period (albeit less limited than in Switzerland, for reasons that probably have to do with differences in trade structures with countries at war). Top income shares in Canada have increased dramatically since the 1970s, thereby confirming the existence of a distinct Anglo-Saxon pattern, as opposed to continental Europe (e.g. France, Germany, and the Netherlands), where top shares hardly changed during the past 30 years. The case of Germany reveals another interesting pattern: although top German capital incomes were strongly hit by the Second World War, they seem to have recovered fairly quickly and to be structurally higher than in other Western countries, for reasons that might be related to the limited tax progressivity of the German fiscal system (more on this below).

1.4. NEW FRONTIERS (I): RETURN TO CROSS-COUNTRY STRUCTURAL ANALYSIS

So far, most of the effort in our collective project has been devoted to constructing homogenous series and producing consistent analytical narratives as to why income distribution evolved the way it did in the various countries. Although we believe one can learn a lot from carefully done case studies, the overall objective of the project is to provide a sufficiently rich database (with cross-country, temporal, and income source variations) so that one can conduct some rigorous cross-country testing of the various theoretical mechanisms at play. Although cross-country analysis will always suffer from severe identification problems, our hope is that richer data will allow a renewal of the analysis of the interplay between inequality and growth.

The first relationship that one might want to test in a systematic way is the impact of tax progressivity and other factors (such as fertility). Using standard stochastic models of capital accumulation, one can show that long run capital income or wealth concentration depends negatively on top income and estate tax rates and fertility:

$$b = G(t, n, \ldots)$$

Where $b = E(w|w > w_0)/w_0 = IAR$ (Pareto) coefficient, (1.3)
$t =$ top tax rate ($G_t < 0$),
$n =$ fertility ($G_n < 0$)

A high coefficient b means a fat upper tail of the distribution, i.e., high wealth concentration. Note that according to theoretical models, tax progressivity and fertility should have an impact on the concentration of wealth and capital income, but not on the concentration of labour income. One can then calibrate these theoretical formulae to see whether observed differences in tax progressivity and fertility across countries can account for observed differences in wealth concentration. By going through such a calibration exercise, Dell (2005) concludes that relatively small differences in top estate tax rates can have a large impact on long run wealth concentration. In particular, the difference in top estate tax rates between France and Germany appears to be large enough to account for the much higher concentration of wealth observed in Germany.

The other relationship that one might want to test using our data base is the impact of inequality on growth. Several theories (e.g. the theory of credit constraints) predict that inequality might have a negative impact on growth. However the testing of these theories has been plagued by serious data problems. One could think of using our data base to run standard cross-country regressions explaining the growth rate of country I at time t as a function of the inequality in country I at time t. If one tries to run such regressions using our long-run data base (say for France), then one would find a statistically significant, negative growth impact of inequality. The reason is simply that the pre-1914 period (and to a large extent the interwar period) is associated to high inequality and relatively low growth, whereas the post-1945 period is associated to low inequality and high growth. Although we believe that such regressions are more informative than standard cross-country regressions on inequality and growth (our regressions rely on high quality data and first order changes in inequality), it is fairly obvious that this very crude methodology raises serious identification problems. There are lots of reasons why post-1945 growth was higher than pre-1914 growth (including a simple catching-up effect following the 1914–45 shocks), and there is no way one can properly identify a causal impact of wealth concentration per se with such a crude regression. Using all countries in the data base might allow production of more convincing results.[13] In the meantime, one can safely conclude that the enormous decline in wealth concentration that took place between 1914 and 1945 did not prevent high growth from happening.

1.4 NEW FRONTIERS (II): EXTENDING THE INEQUALITY DATABASE

Although the international long-run inequality data base presented in this collective volume covers a large number of years and countries, it is far from being complete. First, historical income tax tabulations do exist for many more countries than the ten countries covered in the present volume, and the companion volume will include additional countries in Scandinavia and Northern Europe, Southern Europe, Latin America, and Asia. More countries are yet to be explored, both in the OECD and in the developing world. Note that our long-run data base is bound to be devoted for the most part to OECD countries. One reason is simply that a number of LDCs introduced a modern income tax only recently, so it is often impossible to construct long-run income distribution series for these countries. There are, however, some exceptions. For instance, a progressive income tax was introduced in 1922 in India, which allows the computation of the 1922–2000 top income share series for India (Banerjee and Piketty 2005). In addition to the countries covered in the companion volume, there probably exist a number of other non-OECD countries (especially ex-colonies) where tax data spanning reasonably long time periods are available. Note that even in LDCs where the income tax was introduced only recently, income tax returns data should probably be used more often as a useful supplement to standard income surveys.[14]

Next, the series constructed for the ten countries covered in the present volume are incomplete, in the sense that an exhaustive use of all published tax tabulations in these countries would allow the construction of a number of additional series. For all countries, we offer annual homogenous series on top income shares

[13] For a first attempt to use the data base to conduct panel cross-country regressions, see Atkinson and Leigh (2004) and Leigh (2006).

[14] For instance, it is only in 1980 that a modern progressive income tax was introduced in China (following the 1979 reforms), so that it is impossible to construct long-run Chinese inequality series. However, Chinese tax data available for the 1980s–90s offers a useful supplement to standard surveys, e.g. in order to compare inequality dynamics in China and India during the recent period (see Piketty and Qian 2004). In particular, one problem with standard surveys is that they severely under-estimate top incomes (this is true everywhere, but especially so in LDCs), and tax data allows us to address puzzling facts such as the Indian 'growth paradox' of the 1990s (see Banerjee and Piketty 2005).

covering most of the twentieth century. However, available tax tabulations also allow us to calculate effective income tax rates series for each top income fractile. This is a fairly tedious work (this requires collecting exhaustive information on tax law and taking into account all variations in family structure, children allowances, etc.), and such series have been constructed for only a handful of countries.[15] Available income composition data was used for most countries covered in this volume, albeit not always on an annual basis.[16] In countries with a progressive estate tax, there also exists a whole set of historical estate tax tabulations, which could be used to compute top estate shares series (wealth distribution among decedents), as well as top wealth shares series (wealth distribution among the living) using the estate multiplier.[17] In the context of this volume, we chose to concentrate on income tax tabulations and top income shares series, and we did not attempt to use estate tax tabulations in a systematic way.[18] Extending the data base in this direction raises technical difficulties but would be a useful step in order to enrich cross-country structural regressions.

Finally, and most importantly, one of the most exciting avenues for extending historical inequality data sets in the future probably consists of collecting micro-level tax data from individual tax returns available in national archives. As this volume attempts to illustrate, published tax tabulations are a useful date source and allow us to gain a better understanding of the long-run determinants and consequences of income inequality. However it is obvious that one could do a lot more if micro-level data sets were available. In most OECD countries, micro-level tax returns data sets are available only for the post-1970 or post-1980 period, and they usually cover a limited number of years and use a fairly low sampling rate.[19] The only way to construct micro-data sets for earlier periods and with adequate sampling rate is to go back to individual tax returns stored in national archives

[15] Note that available data on family structure, number of children, etc., for each income bracket could also be used to study marriage and fertility behaviour for each top income fractile and to analyse the behavioural impact of changing financial incentives.

[16] In some countries (e.g. France and the US), separate tabulations by wage brackets were also published and have been used to compute top wage shares series (and not only top income shares and top income composition series).

[17] In countries with a comprehensive tax on the wealth of the living (this is less common than a comprehensive estate tax), the corresponding data can also be used to compute top wealth shares series.

[18] Estate tax tabulations were used in a systematic way by Atkinson and Harrison (1978) for the UK (earlier authors did use estate tax data to produce top wealth shares estimates, albeit for shorter periods; official top wealth shares are now published every year by the UK Inland Revenue) and by Lampman (1962) (the resulting top wealth shares series have recently been extended until the present day for the US by Kopczuk and Saez (2004)). Similar series are also available for France (see Piketty 2001, 2003; Chapter 3; and Piketty et al. 2004). The chapter on Switzerland (Chapter 11) also uses wealth data, although not in a systematic way.

[19] One exception is the US, where the Internal Revenue Service (IRS) released annual micro-level data sets for income tax returns starting in 1960 and with large over-sampling at the top (see Piketty and Saez 2003 and Chapter 5 in this volume). In most countries, micro-level data sets with large over-sampling at the top (or sometime exhaustive date sets) have been used by tax authorities since the 1970s but are difficult to access for researchers.

(older returns were destroyed in some countries, but properly stored in others) and scan hundreds of thousands of them. Depending on technological evolution and financial resources made available for such projects, scholars working on historical changes in income distribution might throw away tax tabulations and start working on long run micro-level tax returns data set in ten years, 50 years, or more.

In order to illustrate what micro-level data sets could bring to the analysis of historical changes in inequality, we take the example of a recent study on wealth concentration in Paris and France over the 1807–1994 period. In France, a modern, universal estate tax was introduced in 1791, and individual estate tax returns have been stored and can be accessed in the local archives of each *département*. When the estate tax became progressive in 1902, the tax administration started compiling and publishing tabulations by estate brackets. No such tabulation was compiled between 1791 and 1902, when the estate tax was purely proportional. In order to put twentieth century top wealth shares series in perspective, Piketty et al. (2004) collected large samples of estate tax returns for all decedents with positive wealth in Paris every ten years between 1807 and 1887, as well as a similar sample for 1902, in order to ensure the consistency of the nineteenth-century series with the post-1902 tabulations based series. As one can see from Figure 1.3, the basic finding is that wealth concentration in Paris and France kept rising right until the First World War. This is important, since this confirms that there was no pre-existing, Kuznets-type trend in inequality prior to the 1914–45 capital shocks. If anything, the upward trend in wealth concentration appears to accelerate at the end of the nineteenth century and at the beginning of the twentieth century, which again

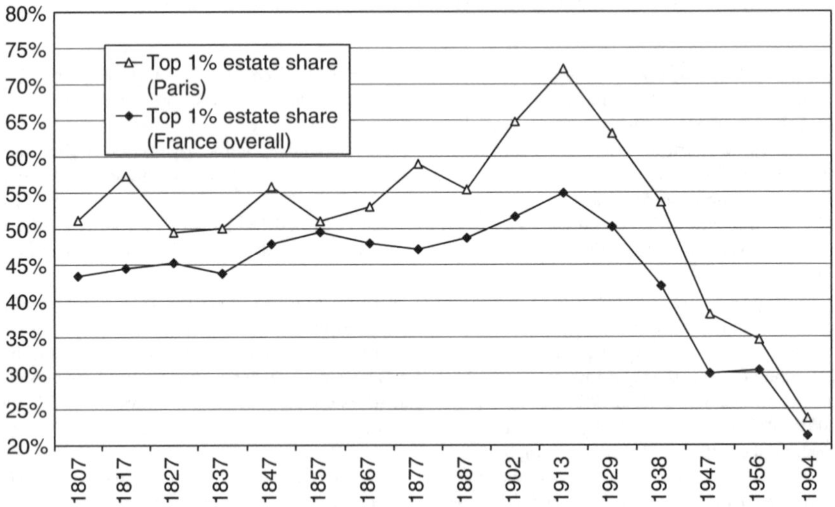

Figure 1.3 Wealth concentration in Paris and France overall, 1807–1994

Source: Piketty et al. 2004; authors' computations using estate tax returns.

Table 1.3 The age profile of wealth at death in Paris, 1817–1994

	20–29-yr-old	30–39-yr-old	40–49-yr-old	50–59-yr-old	60–69-yr-old	70–79-yr-old	80–89-yr-old	90–99-yr-old
1817	26	22	28	100	54	59	59	—
1827	44	50	53	100	88	87	60	—
1837	133	90	107	100	116	123	110	—
1847	87	73	102	100	117	204	132	—
1857	84	77	101	100	104	109	145	—
1867	67	58	136	100	141	125	154	—
1877	66	73	63	100	197	260	430	—
1887	45	33	63	100	152	233	295	—
1902	29	40	80	100	253	272	401	—
1947	31	51	73	100	113	105	105	109
1994	—	11	45	100	87	93	95	68

Note: Average estate left by 50–59-yr-old = 100.

Source: Piketty et al. 2004; authors' computations using estate tax returns.

contradicts the Kuznets view of a stabilization or a reversal of the inequality trend after the initial wave of industrialization.

Most importantly, the fact that we now have micro-samples of estate tax returns (with detailed information on age, occupation, types of assets, etc.) also allows us to shed some new light regarding the impact of inequality on growth. Per se, the existence of credit constraints does not necessarily imply that high wealth concentration is bad for growth. If most of the wealth is owned by active entrepreneurs who keep re-investing their assets in profitable projects, high wealth concentration is not necessarily bad. However if most of the wealth is owned by retired rentiers investing their wealth in low yield assets, then high wealth concentration can entail substantial efficiency costs. Here the striking finding is that wealth was getting older and older in France during the nineteenth century and until the First World War (see Table 1.3). There is also evidence that top wealth holders were investing a rising fraction of their wealth in low yield assets such as public bonds. Although this is not sufficient to prove that inequality had a negative growth impact, this shows that the very high levels of wealth concentration that prevailed in France at the eve of the First World War were associated with retired rentiers rather than with active entrepreneurs (with potential damaging growth effects). The data set also makes it possible to study the evolution of the share of aristocratic fortunes, to test hypothesis about the changing share of women in top wealth fractiles, etc.[20] With sufficient resources one could also construct panel data sets and follow the same individuals or dynasties over time. If and when such data sets become available for a large number of countries, both for income and estate tax returns, the scientific study of income distribution will take a new turn. But in the meantime, we very much hope that this volume will convince the reader that a systematic use of published tax tabulations allows us to make progress in this direction.

[20] See Piketty et al. (2004) for a detailed analysis.

2

Measuring Top Incomes: Methodological Issues

A. B. Atkinson

2.1 INTRODUCTION

There has been a marked revival of interest in the study of the distribution of top incomes using income tax data. Beginning with the research by Piketty of the long-run distribution of top incomes in France (Piketty 2001, 2003 and Chapter 3 this volume), there has been a succession of studies, as evidenced by the chapters contained in this volume. In using data from the income tax records, these studies use similar sources to the earlier work of Bowley (1914) and Stamp (1914, 1916, 1936) in the UK, and Kuznets (1953) in the US. The findings of recent research is, however, of added interest, since the data provide estimates covering nearly all of the twentieth century—a length of time series unusual in economics. The recent research covers a wide variety of countries, and opens the door to the comparative study of top incomes using income tax data.[1] Moreover, the techniques are considerably more developed.

This chapter is concerned with methodological issues. Its aim is to review certain aspects of the methodology underlying the new estimates and to make suggestions for its future development. In assessing the methods applied, it is helpful to begin by asking the question—why are we interested in the top of the distribution? Reasons for concern about the bottom of the distribution are more evident. Is interest in the rich just sensationalism? This question is addressed in Section 2.2. Section 2.3 takes up three methodological issues that arise in using the tabulated income tax data, which are all that is currently available for much of the early part of the period. How can we move from the limited information published by the tax authorities to the broad distributional statements in which we are interested? Section 2.4 turns to a subject already addressed in Chapter 1: the explanation of the observed patterns of difference across time and across countries, and the application of econometric modelling. The final section (2.5) summarizes briefly the issues raised for future research.

[1] For an early comparative study of the upper part of the distribution, using income tax data for Germany, France, Great Britain, the Netherlands, and the US, see Statistischen Reichsamt (1930).

2.2 WHY THE FUSS?

> Enthusiasm for redistributive policies is constantly kindled and fed by the conviction that income and wealth are drastically maldistributed, even if not as much so as in the distant past ... indeed these extremes are still visible, as between destitute vagrants and millionaire pop-stars or property speculators. Yet these extremes are obviously exceptions ... If the great bulk of incomes fell within some quite restricted range—as indeed they do—a reasonable observer might wonder what all the fuss was about (Letwin 1983: 58)

The share of the top income groups has risen significantly in recent decades in the UK, the US, and many other (but not all) countries. In the UK, the share of the top 1% in before tax income rose from 5.7% in 1978 to 8.7% in 1989, and by a further 3 percentage points in the next ten years. The share has effectively doubled. In the US, the share of the top 1% in before tax income (excluding capital gains) rose from 7.9% in 1976 to 16.9% in 2000. The share of an even wealthier group—the top 0.1%—has trebled in the US over this period.

Why do these increases at the top matter? Several answers can be given. The most general is that different parts of the distribution are interdependent. The outcome for one group is affected by the outcome for others; people interact in markets and in political decision making. The interdependence was well captured by Tawney when he referred to the fact that 'what thoughtful rich people call the problem of poverty, thoughtful poor people call the problem of riches'. Here I consider three more specific reasons why we should be interested in the top income groups: their command over resources, their command over people, and their global significance.

Income as Command over Resources

The textbook definition of income by economists refers to 'command over resources'. Are, however, the rich sufficiently numerous and sufficiently in receipt of income that they make an appreciable difference to the overall control of resources? If we ask how the rich fit into typical income distribution, then they may appear insignificant. The most commonly used summary measure of inequality, the Gini coefficient, is more sensitive to transfers at the centre of the distribution than at the tails. If we draw a Lorenz curve, the top 1% would be scarcely be distinguishable on the horizontal axis from the vertical endpoint, and the top 0.1% even less so. All of the action in the very top group would be lost in the last millimetre of the graph (on a standard sized book page).

This formulation nonetheless brings out the extent to which the increases in top shares described above are capable of impacting on overall inequality. If we treat the very top group as infinitesimal in numbers, but with a finite share S^* of total income, then the Gini coefficient can be approximated by $S^* + (1 - S^*)G$, where *G* is the Gini coefficient for the rest of the population. This means that, if the Gini coefficient for the rest of the population is 40%, then a rise of 8 percentage points in the top share causes a rise of 4.8 percentage points in the overall Gini. Given that the increase in the overall Gini recorded in the US between the 1970s and the 1990s was of the order of 5 percentage points, what is happening at the top is potentially important as an explanation. Figure 2.1 plots the overall Gini coefficient for the US over the post-war period, derived from the March income supplement of the Current Population Survey (see the footnotes for the way in which this has been spliced), alongside the share in before tax income estimated by Piketty and Saez (Chapter 5 in this volume). One should not read too much into the similarity of movement, but the picture is suggestive. (The relation between top shares and overall inequality is explored further by Leigh (2006).)

More concretely, we can ask whether increased taxes on the top income group would yield appreciable revenue that could be deployed to fund public goods or redistribution? The standard response by many economists in the past has been that 'the game is not worth the candle'. In the case of the UK, Prest, questioning the role of steeply progressive tax rates in the 1960s, noted that 'if the maximum poundage rate for income tax and surtax combined had been reduced to 75%, the loss of tax . . . would have been about £15 million out of a total of £2,929 million in 1963/64' (Prest 1967: 272). In other words, the share of the top income groups had become quantitatively unimportant.

The notion of 'taxable capacity' can be interpreted in different ways. Here I take as a simple measure of the additional taxable capacity of the top 1% in the UK

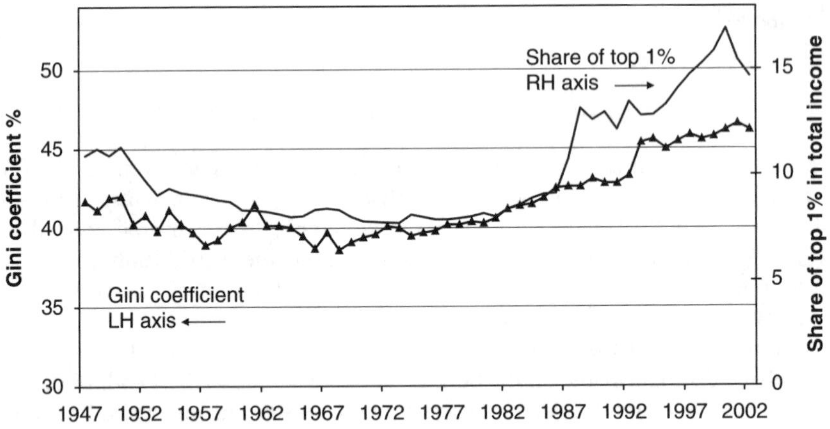

Figure 2.1 Share of top 1% and overall Gini coefficient in US, 1947–2002

Note: Different definitions of income and income unit.

Source: Top 1% from this volume, Chapter 5, Table 5.A2. Gini coefficient from US Department of Commerce, Bureau of the Census, Historical Income Tables: the series for families (Table F.4) from 1947 to 1967 is linked at 1967 to the series for households from 1967 to 2002. The latter is shown as a continuous series, but the footnotes indicate a number of significant changes in methods of estimation.

the excess over 1% of the net share multiplied by (1—average tax rate). In other words, this measures the income remaining in the hands of the top 1% after income tax that exceeds the mean income, expressed as a proportion of gross income (on which any extra tax would be levied). So that, taking rounded figures for 1977 in the UK, the total gross income was £100 billion and total net income was £80 billion, giving an average tax rate of 20%. The share of the top 1% in total net income was, in round terms, 4%, so that the 'excess' was 3%, or, expressed relative to gross income, $(1-0.2)^{*}3 = 2.4\%$. As is clear from Figure 2.2, which plots the 'excess share' in the UK from 1937 to 2000, the 1977 value represented a low point. Even with the high rates of tax in force after the Second World War, the excess share was more than 4%. Whereas a figure of some 2.5% in 1977 could perhaps be dismissed as quantitatively unimportant, subsequently the graph begins to rise sharply, and we are now talking about an excess share of more than 7.5% of total gross personal income. In budgetary terms, this cannot be ignored.

Income as Command over People

Income is important as a source of power. Such a statement is easily made, but less readily translated into a measurable construct. It is not evident for example whether it is absolute or relative income that matters. Is power associated with having more than £X million or with having more than some multiple of mean income? Nor is it clear whether it is the absolute number of people or the relative number. Do 10,000 millionaires have less power in a society of 100 million than in

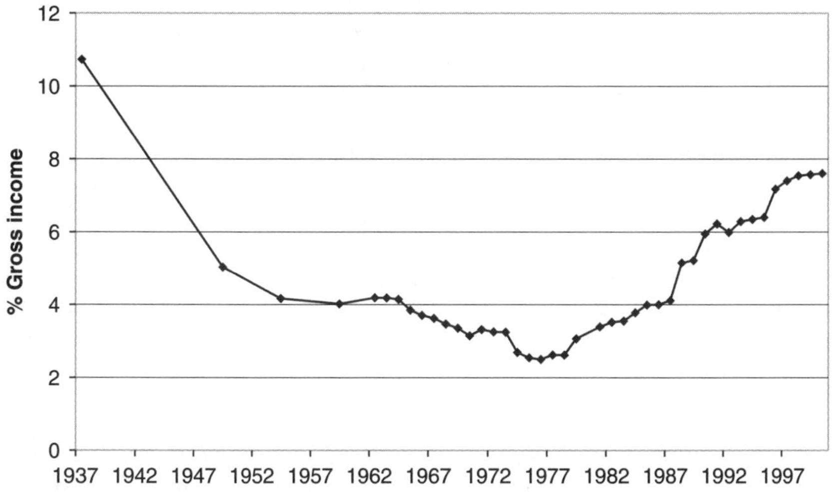

Figure 2.2 'Taxable capacity' of top 1% in the UK, 1937–2000

Source: Calculated from net income shares and average tax rates given in Tables 4.2 and 4B.1, Chapter 4, this volume.

a society of 1 million? Here I put forward one possible way of approaching the issue. It should be noted that I am concerned here with how far income conveys power, rather than vice versa. The converse role of power in determining the distribution of income is also important: see, for instance, Pen (1978).

The approach to measurement—only one of several that could be adopted—is based on the capacity of those with high incomes to opt out of communal provision. As Barry (2002) has argued, there are two forms of social exclusion, with two associated thresholds. In addition to the social exclusion most commonly studied, there is—at the other end of the scale—elite separation, in which the well off can choose to 'insulate themselves from the common fate and buy their way out of the common institutions' (Barry 2002: 16). Such voluntary isolation takes the concrete form of private provision of education and health care, and of gated communities. The ability to use 'exit' as a strategy is a clear manifestation of power. This in turn suggests that the capacity to opt out should be measured in relation to the cost of private provision, which is heavily influenced by the cost of labour. Services such as health and education are labour intensive. The same applies to the costs of policing and servicing a gated community. For this reason, I consider the purchasing power of income expressed in terms of number of people on average gross earnings that could be employed by a given income. Gross earnings may be too low a figure since it does not include social security taxes and other employment costs; it may be too high a figure to the extent that the costs of such employment can be set against tax. Whether the numbers should be relative or absolute is less clear. To the extent that those opting out have to finance public goods, then absolute numbers may be relevant. In terms of the impact on the rest of society, relative numbers may be relevant.

To illustrate this approach for the United Kingdom, suppose that we consider the number of people with gross income in excess of ten times the average earnings of a full-time worker.[2] Prior to the Second World War, there were some 100,000–150,000 tax units with an income of this level or higher. The number with an income in excess of ten times average earnings fell steadily after the Second World War and by 1979 was below 20,000. It is interesting to compare the fall with that in the number of indoor private domestic servants. In 1911, there were 1.4 million in Great Britain; by 1952 the number had fallen to 350,000 and by 1971 to 200,000 (Routh 1980: 35). Although the nature of the employment has changed, one suspects that the numbers have increased in the past two decades. Certainly the change in the income distribution has led to a reversal of the previous trend in the number with gross income in excess of ten times average earnings. The number is now broadly back to its 1949 level.

[2] Average weekly earnings of male manual workers from Feinstein (1972: table 65). For later years: 1965–68 from Department of Employment (1971: table 42, 1968; 1970–90), covering all workers, from Atkinson and Micklewright (1992: table BE1, 1991–2000), covering all workers, from Office for National Statistics (2001), New Earnings Survey (2001: table A30). The gross income data are described in Chapter 4.

Top Incomes in a Global Perspective

The analysis so far has considered the role of top incomes in a purely national context, but it is evident that the rich, or at least the super-rich, are global players. What however is their quantitative significance on a world scale? Does it matter if the share of the top 1% in the US doubles? The top 1% in the US constitutes 1.3 million tax units. How do they fit into a world of some 6 billion people?

To address this question, I take the estimates of the distribution of income among world citizens constructed by Bourguignon and Morrisson (2002), concentrating on the period since 1910 for which the underlying distributional data are better founded. Their method is to use evidence on the national distribution (or the distribution for a grouping of countries) about the shares of decile groups, and the top 5%. This is then combined with estimates of national GDP per head, expressed in constant purchasing power parity dollars. (I do not discuss here the issues raised by such a method.) The groups are treated as homogeneous, so that the highest income in each country is the mean income of the top 5%. Their results show that 'world inequality worsened . . . from 1820 to 1950, pausing only between 1910 and 1929 . . . [and then] continued to worsen . . . improving only between 1950 and 1960' (2002: 731). Over the twentieth century, the world Gini coefficient went from 61% in 1910 to 64% in 1950 and then to 65.7% in 1992.

Rightly, most attention has focused on the bottom of the world distribution, but what is happening at the top is also of interest. In particular, the pattern of change reported by Bourguignon and Morrisson for the twentieth century contrasts with the evidence provided in this volume of sharp falls in top income shares over the first three-quarters of the century in a number of OECD countries. Chapter 3 shows a fall in the share of the top 1% in before tax incomes in France from 18.3% in 1915 to 9.0% in 1950 and 7.6% in 1980 (Table 3A.1). Estimates for the UK show a fall from 19.2% in 1918, to 11.5% in 1949, and 5.9% in 1979 (Table 4.1). Estimates for the United States show the share falling from 18% in 1913, to 11.4% in 1950, and 8.2% in 1980 (Table 5A.1).

For the world as a whole, Bourguignon and Morrisson (2002: table 1) estimate the share of the top 5% in world income. Starting in 1910, this share was 36.7%. Over the next 50 years, it fell slightly to 34.1% in 1960, since when it has risen to 36.0% in 1992. There is little sign here of any dramatic effect at the world level of the sharp falls in top shares at a national level. However, the top 5% in the world distribution comprised in 1992 some 273 million people, with incomes in excess of US$22,000 (the eighth decile group in France was at the margin). The assumptions made in constructing the distribution mean that the richest group, the top 5% in the US, enter as all having incomes of US$88,000. No allowance is made for the inequality within this group. Yet there are large differences between, say, the top 1% and the 'next 4%'. Moreover, their shares have been changing in different ways. As Piketty (2001: 146) has emphasized, the income of the 'next 4%' in France is largely derived from salaries rather than from capital income, and different economic forces are likely to have been in operation.

In view of this, I have modified the Bourguignon-Morrisson calculations by assuming a continuous Pareto distribution of income for the top 5%—see Box 2.1. The coefficient of the Pareto distribution is estimated from the share of the top 5% in the total income of the top 10% (see equation (2.1) in Box 2.1). For example, for the US in 1992 the Bourguignon-Morrisson data show the share of the top 10% as 30.8% and that of the top 5% as 20.3%, which yields a Pareto coefficient of $1/(1-log(30.8/20.3)/log2) = 2.509$. This coefficient is changing over time, so that the modified procedure adopted here allows both for changes in the share of the top 5% and for changes in the distribution within that group.

Applied to each of the countries (or country groups) it is possible to calculate the number of people with incomes above a specified level, reflecting the different degrees of inequality at the top as well as the income required to enter the top 5% in each country. It should be noted that these figures relate to national income, not to household incomes—see Bourguignon and Morrisson (2002: 730). The population also includes everyone, not just adults. For the purposes of defining the 'globally rich' in Figure 2.3, I took those with more than 20 times mean world income, which in 1992 was essentially US$100,000. (In 1910, the figure was US$30,000, again in constant purchasing power parity dollars.) In 1992 there were an estimated 7.4 million people with incomes above this level, more than a third of them in the US. They constituted 0.14% of the world population, but received 5.4% of total world income, or rather more than the GDP of Germany. Clearly, it must be remembered that these estimates are the product of strong assumptions.

Box 2.1 Pareto distribution

The cumulative proportion of people with incomes y_i and higher is such that

$$H_i(y) = (k/y_i)^a$$

where a and k are constants, as in Chapter 1. The cumulative total income in range i and above, divided by the mean μ, is given by

$$\begin{aligned} G_i(y) &= k^a a/(a-1)y_i^{-(a-1)}/\mu \\ &= a/(a-1)k/\mu(H_i)^{(a-1)/a} \\ &= a/(a-1)(y_i/\mu)H_i \end{aligned}$$

The last of these implies that the mean income above y_i is a constant multiple $a/(a-1)$ of y_i. This multiple is called b in Chapter 1. The relative share of two groups, with H_i and H_j of the population, are given by

$$S_i/S_j = (H_i/H_j)^{(a-1)/a} \text{ or } \log(S_i/S_j) = ((a-1)/a)\log(H_i/H_j) \qquad (2.1)$$

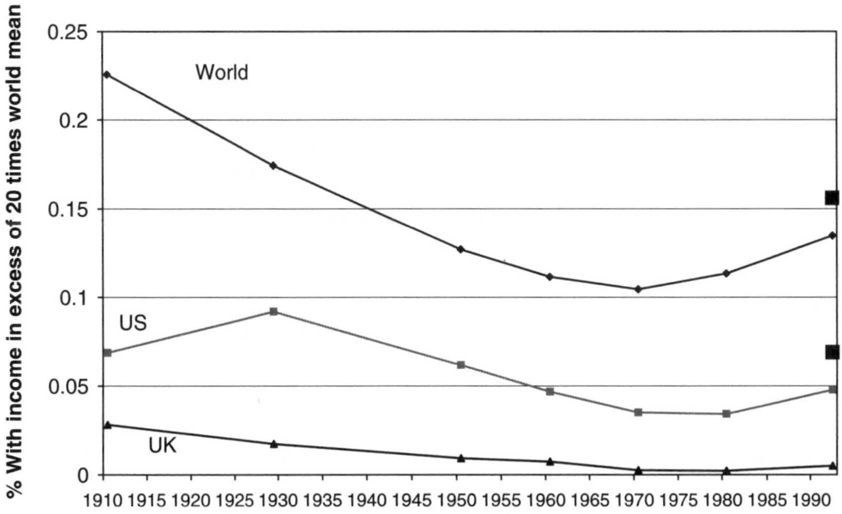

Figure 2.3 Globally rich as % world population, 1910–92

Source: Calculated from data on webesite listed in Bourguignon and Morrisson (2002) using the method described in this chapter.

What is interesting is the pattern of change over time revealed by Figure 2.3. As a proportion of the world population the globally rich fell from 1910 to 1970, mirroring the decline recorded in individual countries. The numbers from the UK fell consistently. Although those for the US were higher in 1929 than in 1910, by 1970 they too had fallen below 0.05% of the world population. But from 1970 we see a reversal, and a rise in the proportion of globally rich above the 1950 level. The number of globally rich doubled in the US between 1970 and 1992. Moreover, increased inequality at the top has a perceptible effect. The squares in Figure 2.3 for 1992 show the effect of a shift in the income distribution in just the US, where each of the nine lower decile groups gives up 0.5% of total income, to the advantage of the top 5%. In other words, the share of the top 5% rises by 4.5 percentage points (the distribution tilts within the top 10%, and indeed within the top 5%). According to the Piketty and Saez estimates in Chapter 5, the share of the top 5% in the US in fact increased by 4.3 percentage points between 1992 and 2000. As may be seen, this makes a perceptible difference to the world distribution.

Conclusion

In this section, I have suggested three ways of assessing the importance of changes at the top of the income distribution. While there may have been a time, a quarter of a century ago, when top incomes could be dismissed as quantitatively unimportant, the picture has been changed by the recent rise in inequality at the top in countries such as the US and UK.

2.3 MEASUREMENT ISSUES

> If a general Income Tax were established, such a Classification might be prepared periodically from the materials of it as would shew whether and in what degree the relative state of any Class had been changed. This constitutes the very important information which the Public should be constantly in possession of (Sayer 1833: appendix, p. 35).

The first progressive personal income tax was introduced in the UK more than 200 years ago, but the tax has had a chequered history. Introduced in 1799 as a war measure, Pitt's tax was abolished in 1802 with the Treaty of Amiens, and then reintroduced in a different—schedular—form by Addington in 1803. The tax remained in existence until 1816, when it was again abolished. It was not until the Budget of 1842 under Peel that the tax was introduced to stay. Hence the plea by Sayer in 1833 that recognized the value of the income tax records for statistical purposes. The history of the use of income tax records for distributional analysis is also a chequered one. For 1801, the income tax returns do indeed provide evidence on the distribution of total income, but the switch to a schedular system[3] meant that there was then a long gap until the introduction of super-tax in 1908, when information on total incomes began to be published regularly. Table 2.1 shows the typical form of the super-tax data. Piketty (2001: appendix A) gives the French data in full.

Table 2.1 Example of income tax data: UK super-tax 1911–12

Class	Number of persons	Total incomes assessed £
£5,000-	7,767	52,810,069
£10,000-	2,055	24,765,153
£15,000-	798	13,742,318
£20,000-	437	9,653,890
£25,000-	387	11,385,691
£35,000-	188	7,464,861
£45,000-	106	5,274,658
£55,000-	56	3,295,110
£65.000-	37	2,590,606
£75.000-	56	4,929,787
£100,000-	66	12,183,724
Total	11,953	148,095,867

Source: *Annual Report of the Inland Revenue for the Year 1913–14*: table 140, p. 135.

[3] The schedular system meant that people were taxed on different elements of their income under different schedules, and the same person may appear under different schedules, or indeed more than once under any particular schedule (as where he is carrying on distinct businesses in different parts of the country). Addington introduced the system in 1803 in response to political objections to total incomes being known (Sabine 1966: 38).

Table 2.1 illustrates the three methodological problems addressed in this section. The first is that we need to relate the number or persons to a control total. The early analyses of the super-tax data worked simply with the absolute numbers. Yet, as Bowley commented in his discussion of the analysis by Stamp (1936) of the absolute numbers in different income ranges, 'there is the difficulty that we did not know the number of incomes to divide [in order to calculate percentiles]. But why not guess?' The second issue concerns the definition of income and the relation to an income control total. The third problem is that, for much of the period, the only data available are tabulated by ranges. Micro-data only exist in recent years. The tabulated data vary considerably. The French tabulations vary from 24 ranges in 1944 to eight ranges in 1954. In the Netherlands, the annual *Statistiek der Rijksfinanciën* in the interwar period published very detailed tabulations, with nearly 40 intervals: in some higher ranges the numbers of incomes are in single figures. For some of the later years, however, there were only 15 intervals (see Chapter 10). This means that we have to interpolate to varying degrees.

Control Total for Population

In some countries, such as Australia, Canada, New Zealand from 1963, and the UK from 1990, the tax unit is the individual. The control total is therefore total individuals. For this purpose, Saez and Veall in Chapter 6 take the 'adult' Canadian population defined as those aged 20 and over. This definition excludes from the denominator those aged under 20 who are income receivers and who may be included in the income tax statistics. In the UK estimates in Chapter 4, the population is taken as those aged 15 and over. (The author first appeared in the UK income tax statistics at the age of 17, although his £8 a week salary hardly put him in the top 1%!) If taking an age cut-off of 20 gives a control total for population that is on the low side, and hence gives a lower bound on the share of the top 1%, taking a cut-off of 15 will give a control total on the high side, and hence gives an upper bound. It could be argued that the definition should vary over time, but it is not clear which direction the variation should take. Young people enter the labour force later today than a century ago, which is an argument for raising the cut-off age over time. On the other hand, young people have been becoming economically independent earlier, and in their estimates of the UK distribution of wealth over the twentieth century, Atkinson and Harrison (1978) took an age cut-off falling from 23 in 1923 to 18 in 1973.

How much difference is the population cut-off likely to make? In the UK in 1931 the population aged 15 and over was some 13% larger than that aged 20 and over (ONS 2003: 28). Suppose that the distribution is such that the upper tail is Pareto in form with exponent , as set out in Box 2.1. Armed with these formulae, we can see that the effect of taking a control total for population larger by $(1 + c)$ is that we have to go further down the distribution to locate the top X%, and, from equation (1*a*), the level of income falls by a factor $(1 + c)^{1/\alpha}$. From equation

(1b) we can see that this raises the estimated share by a factor $(1+c)^{1-1/\alpha}$. With $c = 13\%$ and $\alpha = 2$, this yields an adjustment of some 6% (not 6 percentage points). If the share of the top 1% were to be 10% with an assumed cut-off age of 20, then it would be 10.6% with a cut-off age of 15. The difference is rather modest; and may be even smaller if the income total is also increased when we move to a larger population, as would happen where for example a per capita allowance is made for the income of 'non-filers' (see below).

In other countries, the definition of the tax unit is less straightforward. In the UK, the tax unit until 1990 was defined as a married couple living together, with dependent children (without independent income), or as a single adult, with dependent children, or as a child with independent income.[4] The control total used in Chapter 4 for the UK population for this period is the total number of people aged 15 and over minus the number of married females. Similar procedures have been used in Germany (Chapter 9), Ireland (Chapter 12), the Netherlands (Chapter 10), New Zealand (Chapter 8) prior to 1953, and Switzerland (Chapter 11). In the United States, married women can file tax separate returns, but the number is 'fairly small (about 1% of all returns in 1998)' (Piketty and Saez 2001: 35).[5] Piketty and Saez therefore treat the data as relating to tax units, and take as a control total the number of people aged 20 and over minus the number of married females.

What difference does it make to use a different unit? If we treat all units as weighted equally (so couples do not count twice) and take total income, then the impact of moving from a couple based to an individual based system depends on the joint distribution of income. A useful special case is again that where the marginal distributions are such that the upper tail is Pareto in form. Suppose first that all rich people are either unmarried or have partners with zero income. The number of individuals with incomes in excess of £X is the same as the number of units and their total income is the same. The overall control total is unchanged, but the number of individuals exceeds the number of tax units (by a factor written as $(1+m)$). This means that to locate the top X%, we now need to go further down the distribution, and, given, the Pareto assumption, the share rises by a factor $(1+m)^{1-1/\alpha}$. With $\alpha = 2$ and $m = 0.4$, this equals 1.18. On the other hand, if all rich tax units consist of couples with equal incomes, then the same amount (and share) of total income is received by $2/(1+m)$ times the fraction of the population. In the case of the Pareto distribution, this means that the share of the top 1% is reduced by a factor $(2/(1+m))^{1-1/\alpha}$. With $\alpha = 2$ and $m = 0.4$, this equals 1.2. We have therefore likely bounds on the effect of moving to an individual basis. If the share of the top 1% is 10%, then this could be increased to 11.8% or reduced

[4] According to the Inland Revenue, 'there are not many children below the age of 15 who fall into this category' (Inland Revenue 1972: 1). For a small number of years, investment income of children was aggregated with that of their parents.

[5] Separate assessment also existed in the UK, but married couples were treated in the statistics as a unit even where the wife elected for separate assessment (see, for example, Inland Revenue 1963: 81, 1980: 6).

to 8.3%. The location of the actual figure between these bounds depends on the joint distribution, and this may well have changed over the century.

Control Total for Income

Our aim is to relate the amounts recorded in the tax data to a comparable control total. This is a matter that requires attention, since different methods are employed, which may affect comparability overtime and across countries. One approach starts from the income tax data and adds the income of those not covered (the 'non-filers'). This approach is used for the Netherlands (Chapter 10), the UK (Chapter 4), and the US (Chapter 5) for the years since 1944. The approach in effect takes the definition of income embodied in the tax legislation, and the resulting estimates will change with variations in the tax law. For example, short-term capital gains have been included to varying degrees in taxable income in the UK. A second approach starts from an external control total, typically derived from the national accounts. This approach is followed in Australia (Chapter 7), Canada (Chapter 6), France (Chapter 3), Germany (Chapter 9), except for the First World War years, Ireland (Chapter 12), New Zealand (Chapter 8), and the US for the years prior to 1944. The approach seeks to adjust the tax data to the same basis, correcting, for example, for missing income and for differences in timing. In this case, the income of non-filers appears as a residual. This approach has a firmer conceptual base, but there are significant differences between income concepts used in national accounts and those usually applied in income distribution analysis.[6]

The first approach estimates the total income that would have been reported if everybody had been required to file a tax return. Requirements to file a tax return vary across time and across countries. Typically most countries have moved from a situation at the beginning of the last century when a minority filed returns to a situation today where the great majority are covered. Canada is a good example. According to Saez and Veall, only some 2% of Canadians filed returns in 1930, whereas this figure was 97% in 2000: 'in Canada today, almost every adult, even if his or her income is below the exemption thresholds, has an incentive to file an income tax return' (2002: 37). In the US, 'before 1944, because of large exemption levels, only a small fraction of individuals had to file tax returns' (Piketty and Saez 2003: 4). In the case of the super-tax data for the UK in 1913, the non-filers were the great majority of the population; by the end of the century the income tax data cover all but a small number of adults. It should be noted that taxpayers might not need to make a tax return to appear in the statistics. Where there is tax collection at source, as with Pay-As-You-Earn (PAYE) in the UK, many people do not file a tax return, but are covered by the pay records of their employers. Estimates of the income of non-filers may be related to the average income of

[6] The theoretical relation between the definition of income in the national accounts and the control total for income appropriate for income distribution analysis has been examined in detail by the Canberra Expert Group on Household Income Statistics (2001).

filers. For the US, Piketty and Saez (Chapter 5) for the period 1944–98 impute to non-filers a fixed fraction of filers' average income (50% in 1944 and 1945, and 30% from 1945). In some cases, estimates of the income of non-filers already exist. Hartog and Veenbergen (1978) in the Netherlands used the estimates of the Central Bureau of Statistics. Atkinson (Chapter 4) makes use of the work of the Central Statistical Office.

The second approach starts from the national accounts totals for personal income. In the case of the US, Piketty and Saez use for the period 1913–43 a control total equal to 80% of (total personal income less transfers). In Canada, Saez and Veall (2005 and Chapter 6 in this volume) use this approach for the entire period 1920–2000. The estimates for Switzerland (Chapter 11) prior to 1971 take a total equal to 75% of (total personal income, including transfers, plus corporate savings), How do these national income based calculations relate to the totals in the tax data? In answering this question, it may be helpful to bear in mind the different stages set out schematically below:

Personal sector total income (PI)

minus Non-Household income (Non-profit institutions such as charities, life assurance funds)

equals Household sector total income

minus Items not included in tax base (e.g. employers' social security contributions and—in some countries—employees' social security contributions, imputed rent on owner-occupied houses, and non-taxable transfer payments)

equals Household Gross Income Returnable to Tax Authorities

minus Taxable income not declared by filers

minus Taxable Income of those not included in tax returns ('non-filers')

equals Declared Taxable Income of Filers.

The use of national accounts totals may be seen as moving down from the top rather than moving up from the bottom by adding the estimated income of non-filers. The percentage formulae can be seen as correcting for the non-household elements and for the difference between returnable income and the national accounts definition. Some of the items, such as social security contributions, can be substantial. Piketty and Saez base their choice of percentage for the US on the experience for the period 1944–98, when they applied estimates of the income of non-filers. In the case of Canada, Saez and Veall base the percentage on the experience since the mid-1970s when they feel that filing was close to complete. Given the increasing significance of some of the items (such as employers' contributions), and of the non-household institutions, such as pension funds, it is not evident that a constant percentage is appropriate. Since transfers were also smaller at the start of the twentieth century, total household returnable income was then closer to total personal income.

To illustrate these points, I take the case of the UK. Figure 2.4 shows the control totals for the UK derived by estimating the income of non-filers (the

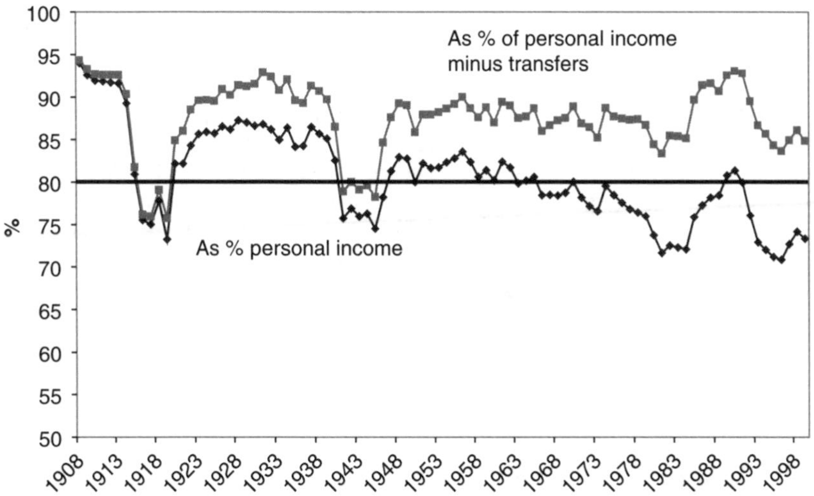

Figure 2.4 Personal income control totals for the UK, 1908–99

Sources: Tables 4c.1 and 4c.2, Chapter 4, this volume.

first approach described above). By expressing the UK totals as a percentage of total personal income from the national accounts, we can see the likely difference between the two approaches. The first obvious difference is in the war years, where the national accounts figures appear to be relatively higher. This means that use of the second approach would have caused an even larger fall of the top income shares during the First and Second World Wars. The second difference is that the UK totals are larger than 80% of the national accounts total (minus transfers) for all the rest of the period, but with a downward trend. The total expressed as a percentage of personal income minus transfers was around 92.5% before the First World War, which means that for the top 0.1% a share of 10% would become 11.6% if we applied the smaller control total of 80% of personal income minus transfers. This suggests that the UK shares would be rather higher, on the alternative basis, and that the downward trend would be less. The choice of control total is evidently important.

Whatever method is adopted, there seems a strong case for considering the link with the national accounts. The first reason is that it helps ensure consistency over time. Given that the construction of national accounts has historically made extensive use of the income tax data, the relation between the two series has typically been the subject of study. The first official national income estimate for the UK, for 1926, started from the income tax total. The link with national accounts takes on even greater significance when we turn to comparability across countries. As a result of the efforts of the United Nations Statistical Office and scholars such as Richard Stone, a broadly common approach has come to be adopted in the construction of national accounts, guided by successive versions of the UN System of National Accounts (SNA). This allows a direct link to be made across countries.

Need for a control total for income is of course avoided if, as in Chapters 4 and 7–12, we examine the 'shares within shares'. If we have a control total for population, we can calculate for example the share of the top 1% within the top 10%, without any requirement to estimate total incomes. This gives a measure of the degree of inequality among the top incomes that may be more robust. Moreover, as discussed further below, the shares within shares allow one to focus on factors affecting the distribution *among* the top income groups, rather than those affecting the distribution *between* the top groups and the rest of the population.

Interpolation

The basic data on which we are drawing are in the form of grouped tabulations, as in Table 2.1, where the intervals do not in general coincide with the percentage groups of the population with which we are concerned (such as the top 0.1%). We have therefore to interpolate in order to arrive at values for summary statistics such as the shares of total income. Moreover, some authors have extrapolated upwards into the open upper interval, and downwards below the lowest range tabulated. Thus, the French data shown by Piketty extend only as far as the top 3.591% in 1919, and the upper interval in 1998 contains 0.752% of the population (2001: tableau B1). These are extrapolated downwards to give estimates for the top 10% (in 1919) and upwards to give the share of the top 0.01% in 1998.

The standard practice for many years has been to assume that the distribution is Pareto in form, applying formulae similar to those used earlier in the paper. Feenberg and Poterba (1993, 2000) and Piketty (2001) have validated this method by comparing the results obtained using micro-data for recent years. This method has, however, the problem that the available information typically allows us to obtain more than one value for the exponent of the Pareto distribution, and hence different interpolated values. The Pareto distribution can, for example, be fitted to two points of the Lorenz curve, but there is then no assurance that the slopes at these points will be equal to the interval limits divided by the mean. In practice the method may work well, and the discrepancies may be small, but this depends on the nature of the distribution.

An alternative approach is based on placing upper and lower bounds. For any range, we know the number of people and their mean income. Bounds can be obtained by considering, on the one hand, carrying out the maximum mean-preserving transfers in an equalizing direction (putting everyone at the mean), and, on the other hand, the maximum dis-equalizing transfers (putting everyone at one or other limit of the range). Graphically, the resulting gross upper and lower bounds on the Lorenz curve can be obtained by joining the observed points linearly or by forming the envelope of lines drawn through the observed points with slopes equal to the interval endpoints divided by the mean (see Cowell 1995: 114). Where there are detailed ranges, the results for the lower bound of the top shares (linearized Lorenz curve) are normally very close to the upper bound, but in other cases the differences can be more marked, depending on where the ranges fall in relation to the shares in which we are interested. If, as seems reasonable in the case of top incomes, the frequency distribution can be assumed to be non-decreasing, then tighter, restricted bounds can be calculated (Gastwirth 1972). These restricted bounds are limiting forms of the split histogram, with one of the two densities tending to zero or infinity. Guaranteed to lie between these is the *mean-split histogram*, with sections of positive density on either side of the interval mean, as described by Cowell and Mehta (1982).

The impact of interpolation is illustrated in Figure 2.5 by the open top interval in the UK in 2000. The top range in the published data shows 88,000 people with incomes above £200,000. They constitute 0.19% of the population and their share of total income is 6.26%. We would like to extrapolate to calculate the share of the top 0.1%. The largest possible value for this share is obtained by assuming that the 0.09% who have to be excluded all received just enough to be in the range: i.e. £200,000. This gives the upper bound shown by the straight line, and an extrapolated share of 5%. A lower bound is obtained by assuming that everyone in the range has the mean income for the cell: i.e. £461,000. This is shown by the upper straight line and generates an extrapolated share of 3.4%. Such a range appears unacceptably large. If, however, we are willing to assume that the density is non-increasing, then we get the 'refined' lower bound shown by the quadratic marked by*. The lower bound for the share of the top 0.1% becomes 4.3%. The Pareto method, using the lower limit and the mean, which imply $b = 2.3$, yields an extrapolated figure of 4.8%. The mean split histogram method, assuming an upper limit of £5 million, gives an extrapolated figure of 4.6%.

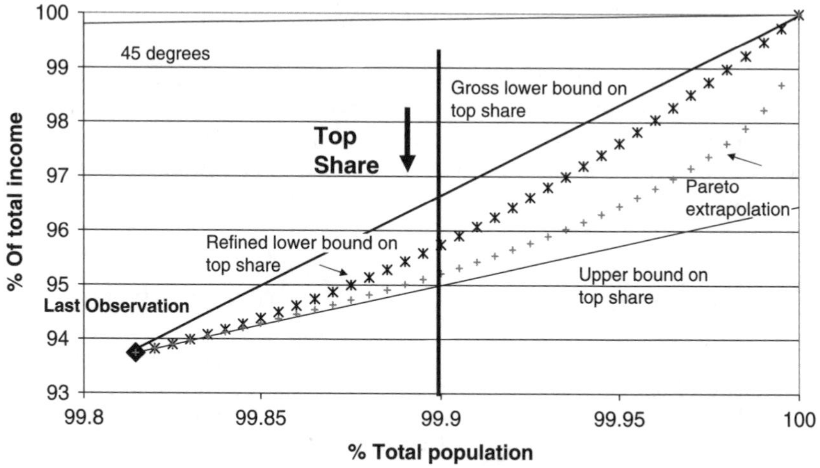

Figure 2.5 Interpolation into open upper interval, UK 2000 data

So far we have considered the share of the top X%, but we are also interested in the shares of intermediate groups, such as that of the 'next 4%' referred to earlier. This is more complex, since we can no longer use the fact that a mean-preserving equalising transfer reduces (or leaves unchanged) the share of the top X%. Such a transfer may raise the share of the next Y%. If we have to use the gross bounds, and have to take the minimum of the share of the top X% and the maximum of the top $(X + Y)$%, to calculate the upper bound on the share of the next Y%, then this may lead to wide bounds. (The lower bound takes the maximum of the share of the top X% and the minimum of the top $(X + Y)$%.) For the UK in 2000, such a calculation leads to bounds for the share of the next 4% of 13.5–16.2%. This may make it difficult to decide whether or not the share of this group is increasing: the bounds for 1990 are 14.0–14.7%. Finally, we should note the corresponding difficulties in obtaining bounds for the shares within shares.

The derivation of the bounds for the income shares is based on the argument that a mean-preserving equalizing transfer cannot raise the share of the top X%. The same argument does not apply to the *top percentiles*: an equalizing transfer from people inside the top X% to people at the boundary *raises* the x-percentile. Hence, the same bounds do not apply to percentiles. As is shown in Atkinson (2005), either the gross upper bound or the gross lower bound for a percentile is equal to the relevant income limit. This suggests that the resulting bounds are likely to be wide and that it is worthwhile seeking tighter bounds by making the assumption that the density function is non-increasing, as explained in Atkinson (2005). These refined bounds are used, for example, in Chapters 4 and 8. For the UK data in 1968, they yield a range for the top percentile from 4.08 to 4.51 times the mean (whereas the range limits £3000 and £5000 are 2.95 and 4.91 times the mean).

Conclusion

There are a number of methodological issues that warrant attention, notably the link with national accounts, particularly when we seek to make comparisons across countries and over time. The subject of interpolation may be regarded as passé, but there are a number of choices that need to be considered.

2.4 SPECIFICATION OF EXPLANATORY MODELS

> Consider the career of someone now retiring from a senior position on the board of one of Britain's 100 largest corporations... retiring with a peak salary of perhaps £80,000. Few people are as successful as this. Our hypothetical manager has fairly frugal tastes, and throughout his lifetime has reckoned to save around a quarter of his after-tax income. On retirement, the accumulated wealth of such a man would approach £200,000... he may

> be somewhat surprised to discover that there are in Britain at least 100,000 people richer than he is... There is a large number of very rich people in Britain, but the proportion of them who became rich as a result of personal savings from their own earnings is negligible. If the much lower maximum rates of tax introduced in 1979 [by Mrs Thatcher] persist for the next thirty years then the results will look very different. (Kay and King 1986: 63)

This passage was insightful with regard to the past and prescient with regard to the future. Chapter 1 has already identified a number of the key factors influencing top shares, including shocks to capital accumulation, the rise in executive remuneration, and the impact of progressive taxation. In this section, I consider the more technical issues of the specification of explanatory models and of data deficiencies.

Explaining Top Shares

In considering the explanation of the changes over time in top shares, there are two important elements that need to be taken into account. First, as emphasized in Chapter 1, in order to test different theories we need to break income down by source. In particular the explanations are likely to be different for earned and unearned income. In examining this aspect, a simple decomposition may be helpful. Taking for illustration the share of the top 1%, this can be broken down as follows:

Share of top 1% =
Proportion of earned income
X Share of top 1% of earners in earnings distribution
x Alignment coefficient for earnings
\+ (2.2)
Proportion of investment income
X Share of top 1% in investment income distribution
x Alignment coefficient for investment income

The 'alignment coefficient' is defined as follows: for earnings, it is the share in earnings of the top 1% of income recipients divided by the share of top 1% of earners. Since the top 1% of earners are not necessarily in the top 1% of income recipients, the coefficient is by definition less than or equal to 1. If none of the top 1% of income recipients have earned income, then the alignment coefficient is zero.

The decomposition (2.2) brings out the relation with the composition of incomes: the shares of earned and unearned income in total gross income. These shares are related to, but not identical to, factor shares in GNP. They are not the same, because the figures relate to households. Between households and the total economy stand various institutions, including the company sector, pension funds, and the government. The shares are affected by the re-allocation of income between persons and corporations, as where companies decide to retain a larger proportion of profits. They are affected by the growth of pension funds. These funds own shares in companies and hence receive dividend income. This dividend income is then paid to pensioners, in whose hands it is treated as deferred earnings, so that—in these statistics—it does not appear as unearned income.

The second key element is that there are two distinct sets of forces: those affecting the distribution *among* the top income groups and those affecting the distribution *between* the top groups and the rest of the population. In the case of wealth data for the share of the top 1%, Atkinson et al. (1989) estimated linear regressions covering the period 1923–81 for England and Wales. Among the significant explanatory variables were the impact of share prices (positive) and of the growth of 'popular wealth' (negative). The latter illustrates one of the forces affecting the distribution between the top 1% and the rest of the population, popular wealth being defined as the value of owner-occupied housing plus consumer durables. The former affects both the between and the within distributions.

In order to separate the between and within forces, it is suggested that we concentrate on the latter by looking at the 'shares within shares': i.e., investigating the determinants of the share of the top 1% within the top 10%. One advantage of this approach is that, where the distribution is approximately Pareto in form at the top, then the share of the top 1% within the top 10% is a linear function of $(1/\alpha)$—see equation (2.1) in Box 2.1. This allows us to make a direct link with theories that make predictions concerning the Pareto exponent. An example is provided by theories dealing with executive remuneration in a hierarchical structure. The model advanced by Simon (1957) and Lydall (1968: 129) leads to an approximately Pareto tail to the earnings distribution, where

$$1/\alpha = \log_e[1 + \textit{increment with promotion}] \textit{ divided by } \log_e [\textit{span of managerial control}] \qquad (2.3)$$

The theory suggests one approach to understanding the variation in α. Increments for promotion may have been influenced by the globalisation of the demand side of the market for top managers, one group for whom movement across national borders is significant. Corporations are now seeking to recruit globally to the upper echelons of their organization. Moreover, mobility may be less across language barriers, accounting for the differing experience of France and the Netherlands.

A second example is provided by the theories concerned with the accumulation of capital. Meade (1964) developed a model of individual wealth holding, allowing for accumulation and transmission of wealth via inheritance, and this model has been analysed in a general equilibrium setting by Stiglitz (1969). With equal division of estates at death, a linear savings process, and persistent differences in earnings, in the long-run the distribution of wealth mirrors the distribution of earnings (Atkinson and Harrison 1978: 211). In contrast, alternative assumptions about bequests can generate long-run equilibria where there is inequality of wealth even where earnings are equal. Stiglitz shows how the operation of primogeniture in passing on wealth can lead to a stable distribution with a Pareto upper tail, with

$$1/\alpha = log_e[1 + sr(1 - t)]/\log_e[1 + n] \tag{2.4}$$

where $sr(1-t)$ is the rate of accumulation out of wealth, r being the rate of return and t the tax rate, and n is the rate of population growth (Atkinson and Harrison 1978: 213). The model is highly stylized but again provides a direct link to explanatory variables. It suggests that we should begin by estimating a time-series relation of the form:

$$log(S_1/S_{10}) = a + br(1 - t) \tag{2.5}$$

where $r(1-t)$ is the rate of return taxed at the top marginal rate. In this way, we are bringing the specification of the econometric research closer to the underlying theoretical models than is often the case in economics.

Allowing for Data Deficiencies

In estimating a relation such as equation (2.5), standard practice introduces a stochastic term assumed to have certain properties, such as zero mean, constant variance, and independence over time. This stochastic term is intended to allow for sampling and other sources of error. In any specific application, however, we know more about the errors likely to occur and this information should be taken into account in the specification of the estimated relationship (see Atkinson 2001).

In the present case, we know quite a lot about the underlying income tax source. For example, the data for the early years may have been affected by the fact that the tax was being introduced, and that the administration would take time to become established. In the case of the UK super-tax, Stamp stated that he left out the first two years of the tax 'in order to give the statistics an opportunity to "get into their stride"'. (1936: 630). The operation of the income tax would have been perturbed by wartime and by occupation (in the case of France and Netherlands, for example). For these years, it seems reasonable to suppose that the error variance was larger. The income tax has been changed significantly over time, and this may have caused breaks in continuity. The introduction of independent taxation for husbands and wives in the UK in 1990 is an example. In the Netherlands, Hartog and Veenbergen (1978) describe three fiscal regimes: the 1914 Act, the 1941 Act, and 1964 Act. As they note, the 1914 legislation was in effect for a long period, allowing continuity in data collection. The 1941 Act changed, among other aspects, the treatment of 'new sources' of income. Under the initial legislation, existing sources of income were taxed on the basis of income in the preceding year, but a prediction was made of the income from new sources. After 1941 only past income was included. The form of the published statistics may have changed. For example, in the UK from 1975–76, the figures relate to total income. Prior to 1975–76, the distribution relates to *total net income*, which differs from *total income* in that it deducts allowable interest payments such as those for house purchase, alimony and maintenance payments, retirement annuity premiums, and other allowable annual payments.

The second source of error is the derivation of the control totals. The need to add to the totals reported in the income tax statistics depends on the extent of coverage of the tax, and this changed dramatically over the twentieth century. From the discussion in Section 2.2, it seems reasonable to suppose that the totals for income are subject to larger possible error than the totals for population. For this reason, the estimates of shares within shares may be less subject to error. For the absolute shares, on the other hand, the uncertainty surrounding the control total leads to expect the error variance to be higher when the proportion of filers is lower.

The third source of error arises when we are using tabulated data: the error of interpolation. Here again we can bring information to bear on the extent of the likely error. As described above, we can calculate bounds on the possible error. The difference between the bounds depends on the width of the ranges and on the location of the percentile cut-offs. More generally, there are likely to be differences as a result of changes in the form in which the data were published. As is noted earlier, the number of ranges can vary considerably over time.

There are several different ways in which we can seek to introduce this information about possible sources of error. The first, and perhaps the most common, is to introduce dummy variables for breaks in comparability. In analysing the wealth time series for the UK, Atkinson et al. (1989) included dummy variables allowing for two breaks, corresponding to reduced coverage of the data between 1938 and 1950 and to increased coverage from 1960. The latter (but not the former) proved to be statistically significant, and indicated a downward shift in 1960 of some 7 percentage points, which makes a considerable difference to the interpretation of the observed downward trend (often ignored by those who treat the data as a continuous series).

A second approach to known breaks is to use external information to estimate the impact of the change on the data series. For example, suppose it were possible using micro-data to calculate for an overlapping year the effect of moving from joint to independent taxation. This difference could be applied to all subsequent years. In this way we are in effect imposing a given coefficient on the dummy variable. This approach assumes that we have *more* information about the break. Going in the opposite direction, we might have *less* information. Suppose that we know only that there has been a succession of changes in tax law and practice that could affect the comparability of the series. We could then test for the robustness of any conclusion by examining how our estimate of a coefficient of interest, such as the impact of the net of tax rate of return, would be affected by the introduction of a dummy variable from any arbitrarily chosen year.

A third approach to data deficiencies is via the variance-covariance matrix for the stochastic terms. It would be possible to introduce prior information about the relative magnitude of the variances at different times. There are several sources for such information. There is the interpolation interval obtained from the upper and lower bounds. Or, as noted earlier, the sensitivity to the control totals depends on the proportion of non-filers, and the variance could be an increasing function of this percentage. Or use could be made of the error margins attached to national accounts totals. Feinstein (1972) gives a grading of B ('good') to many of the underlying national accounts series, indicating an error of ±(5–15%). For the war years, and 1918–20, the upper end of this possible range seems appropriate; for other years ±5% may be a reasonable guide. We can bring to bear judgment of the varying effectiveness of coverage of the tax statistics: for example, with a higher variance in earlier years of the tax.

Finally, we could treat the dependent variable in interval form. We could seek to estimate the relationship between the explanatory variables and the share of the top 1% expressed in terms of upper and lower bounds. This is rather different from the more usual interval estimation (see, for example, Stewart 1983), since the intervals are not fixed. For the kind of differences found with interpolation error, such an exercise does not seem warranted, but if allowance is made for different control totals in calculating the bounds, then the range could become wide enough for this approach to be necessary.

2.5 CONCLUSIONS: RESEARCH QUESTIONS FOR THE FUTURE

The three main sections of the chapter have all demonstrated the need for further research. To begin with, we should explore further the implications of rising inequality at the very top of the income distribution. This applies at the national level, where the rising share of the very rich is beginning to be significant in fiscal terms. Taxing the rich cannot now so easily be dismissed as a revenue source. The ability of those with high incomes to purchase labour services has increased, giving rise to concern about elite separation. The section on the construction of the estimates has highlighted the need for work on the control totals for income, particularly the link with national accounts. Interpolation may appear an old-fashioned topic but it is highly relevant to historical studies. Finally, we need to relate the explanatory models estimated to the underlying theories, and to make explicit allowance for data deficiencies.

REFERENCES (TO CHAPTERS 1 AND 2)

Atkinson, A. B. (2001). 'Data Matter', Cowles Lecture, Econometric Society, Auckland.

—— Brandolini, A. (2001). 'Promise and Pitfalls in the Use of ≪Secondary≫ Data-Sets : Income Inequality in OECD Countries as a Case Study', *Journal of Economic Literature*, 39: 771–99.

—— Harrison, A. J. (1978). *Distribution of Personal Wealth in Britain*. Cambridge: Cambridge University Press.

—— Leigh, A. (2004). 'The Distribution of Top Incomes in 5 Anglo-Saxon Countries over the Twentieth Century'. Discussion paper.

Atkinson, A. B. and Micklewright, J. (1992). *Economic Transformation in Eastern Europe and the Distribution of Income.* Cambridge: Cambridge University Press.

—— Gordon, J. P. F. and Harrison, A. J. (1989). 'Trends in the Shares of Top Wealth-Holders in Britain, 1923–81', *Oxford Bulletin of Economics and Statistics*, 51: 315–32.

Banerjee, A. and Duflo, E. (2003). 'Inequality and Growth: What Can the Data Say?', *Journal of Economic Growth*, 8: 267–99.

—— Piketty, T. (2005). 'Top Indian Incomes, 1922–2000', *World Bank Economic Review*, 19: 1–20.

Barry, B. (2002). 'Social Exclusion, Social Isolation, and the Distribution of Income', in J. Hills, J. Le Grand, and D. Piachaud (eds.) *Understanding Social Exclusion.* Oxford: Oxford University Press.

Bourguignon, F. and Morrisson, C. (2002). 'Inequality among World Citizens, 1820–1992', *American Economic Review*, 92: 727–44.

Bowley, A. L. (1914). 'The British Super-Tax and the Distribution of Income', *Quarterly Journal of Economics*, 28: 255–68.

Canberra Expert Group on Household Income Statistics (2001). *Final Report and Recommendations.* Ottawa: Canberra Expert Group on Household Income Statistics.

Cowell, F. A. (1995). *Measuring Inequality*, 2nd edn. London: Prentice Hall.

—— Mehta, F. (1982). 'The Estimation and Interpolation of Inequality Measures', *Review of Economic Studies*, 49: 273–90.

Dell, F. (2005). 'Top Incomes in Germany and Switzerland over the Twentieth Century', *Journal of the European Economic Association*, 3: 412–21.

Department of Employment (1971). *British Labour Statistics Historical Abstract, 1886–1968.* London: HMSO.

Feenberg, D. R. and Poterba, J. M. (1993). 'Income Inequality and the Incomes of Very High-Income Taxpayers: Evidence from Tax Returns', in J. Poterba (ed.) *Tax Policy and the Economy*, vol. 7. Cambridge: MIT Press, pp. 145–77.

—— —— (2000). 'The Income and Tax Share of Very High-Income Households, 1960–1995', *American Economic Review*, Papers and Proceedings, 90: 264–70.

Feinstein, C. H. (1972). *Statistical Tables of National Income, Expenditure and Output of the UK, 1855–1965.* Cambridge: Cambridge University Press.

Gastwirth, J. L. (1972). 'The Estimation of the Lorenz Curve and Gini Index', *Review of Economics and Statistics*, 54: 306–16.

Hartog, J. and Veenbergen, J. G. (1978). 'Long-Run Changes in Personal Income Distribution', *The Economist*, 126: 521–49.

Inland Revenue (1963). *Annual Report of the Commissioners, 1961–62.* London: HMSO.

—— (1972). *The Survey of Personal Incomes, 1969–70.* London: HMSO.

—— (1980). *The Survey of Personal Incomes, 1977–78.* London: HMSO.

Kay, J. A. and King, M. A. (1986). *The British Tax System*, 4th edn. Oxford: Oxford University Press.

Kopczuk, W. and Saez, E. (2004). 'Top Wealth Shares in the United States, 1916–2000: Evidence from Estate Tax returns', NBER Working Paper 10399.

Kuznets, S. (1953). *Shares of Upper Income Groups in Income and Savings.* New York: National Bureau of Economic Research.

—— (1955). 'Economic Growth and Income Inequality', *American Economic Review*, 45: 1–28.

Lampman, R. J. (1962). *The Share of Top Wealth-Holders in National Wealth, 1922–1956.* New Jersey: Princeton University Press, Princeton.

Leigh, A. (2006). 'Using Panel Data on Top Income Shares to Analyse the Causes and Effects of Inequality'. Discussion paper, Australian National University.
Letwin, W. (1983). 'The Case Against Equality', in W. Letwin (ed.) *Against Equality.* London: Macmillan.
Lydall, H. F. (1968). *The Structure of Earnings.* Oxford: Oxford University Press.
Meade, J. E. (1964). *Efficiency, Equality and the Ownership of Property.* London: Allen & Unwin.
Office for National Statistics (2001). *New Earnings Survey 2001.* London: Office for National Statistics.
Pareto, V. (1896). 'La courbe de la répartition de la richesse', *Ecrits sur la courbe de la répartition de la richesse* (edited by G. Busino, 1965). Paris: Librairie Droz pp. 1–15.
—— (1896–7). *Cours d'Economie Politique* (2 volumes) (edited by G. Busino, 1964). Paris: Librairie Droz.
Pen, J. (1978). 'The Role of Power in the Distribution of Personal Income: Some Illustrative Numbers', in W. Krelle and A. F. Shorrocks (eds.) *Personal Income Distribution.* Amsterdam: North-Holland, pp. 335–52.
Piketty, T. (2001). *Les hauts revenus en France au XXe siècle—Inégalités et redistributions, 1901–1998.* Paris: Grasset.
—— (2003). 'Income inequality in France, 1901–1998', *Journal of Political Economy,* vol. 111: 1004–42.
—— Qian, N. (2004). 'Income inequality and progressive income taxation in China and India (1986–2010)'. Discussion paper.
—— Saez, E. (2001). *Income Inequality in the United States, 1913–1998.* NBER Working Paper n° 8467.
—— —— (2003). 'Income Inequality in the United States, 1913–1998', *Quarterly Journal of Economics,* 118: 1–39.
—— Postel-Vinay, G. and Rosenthal, J-L. (2004). 'Wealth Concentration in a Developing Economy: Paris and France, 1807–1994'. CEPR Discussion Paper 4631 (forthcoming in *American Economic Review*).
Prest, A. R. (1967). *Public Finance,* 3rd edn. London: Weidenfeld & Nicolson.
Routh, G. (1980). *Occupation and Pay in Great Britain 1906–79,* 2nd edn. London: Macmillan.
Sabine, B. E. V. (1966). *A History of Income Tax.* London: Allen & Unwin.
Saez, E. (2005). 'Top Incomes in the United States and Canada over the Twentieth Century', *Journal of the European Economic Association,* 3: 402–11.
—— Veall, M. (2002). 'The Evolution of High Incomes in Canada, 1920–2000', Mimeo.
—— —— (2005). 'The Evolution of High Incomes in Northern America: Lessons from Canadian Evidence', *American Economic Review,* 95: 831–49.
Sayer, B. (1833). *An Attempt to Shew the Justice and Expediency of Substituting an Income or Property Tax for the Present Taxes, or a Part of Them.* London.
Simon, H. (1957). 'The Compensation of Executives', *Sociometry,* 20: 32–5.
Stamp, J. C., Lord (1914). 'A New Illustration of Pareto's Law', *Journal of the Royal Statistical Society,* 77: 200–4.
—— (1916). *British Incomes and Property.* London: P. S. King.
—— (1936). 'The Influence of the Price Level on the Higher Incomes', *Journal of the Royal Statistical Society,* 99: 627–73.
Statistischen Reichsamt (1930). 'Die Einkommenschichtung und die Heranziehung de einzelnen Einkommensklassen zur Einkommensteuer im Deutschen Reich, in

Frankreich, Grossbritannien, den Niederlanden und den Vereinigten Staaten von Amerika', *Wirtschaft und Statistik*, 10: 592–6.
Stewart, M. B. (1983). 'On Least Squares Estimation when the Dependent Variable is Grouped', *Review of Economic Studies*, 50: 737–53.
Stiglitz, J. E. (1969). 'Distribution of Income and Wealth Among Individuals', *Econometrica*, 37: 382–97.

3

Income, Wage, and Wealth Inequality in France, 1901–98[1]

T. Piketty

3.1 INTRODUCTION

The primary objective of this research is to document trends in income inequality in France during the twentieth century. Did income distribution become more unequal or more equal in France over the course of the 1901–98 period? What are the specific periods in which income inequality increased or declined, and what income deciles were most affected by these trends?

The second objective of this work is obviously to understand these facts. What are the economic mechanisms and processes that allow us to understand the way income inequality evolved in France over the course of the twentieth century? As we have seen in Chapter 1, according to Kuznets's influential hypothesis (Kuznets 1955), one should expect income inequality to decline spontaneously in advanced capitalist countries, as more and more workers join the high paying sectors of the economy. Can this model account for what happened in France during the 1901–98 period, or at least during the first half of the twentieth century?

One advantage of looking at France is that French data sources allow for a detailed analysis of inequality trends. In particular, I was able to construct fully homogeneous yearly series running from the First World War until the late 1990s for both income inequality and wage inequality, the first occasion on which (to my knowledge) this has been done for any country. I can therefore distinguish precisely between the trends that are due to changes in the wage structure and those that are due to changes in the concentration of capital income. This allows me not only to better understand the French experience, but also to re-interpret the experience of other countries. The main conclusion is that the decline in income inequality that took place during the first half of the twentieth century was mostly accidental. In France, and possibly in a number of other countries as well, wage inequality has actually been extremely stable in the long run, and the

[1] This chapter presents some of the results of Piketty (2001*a*). It is an extended version of Piketty (2003). I am grateful to seminar participants at Columbia, Harvard, MIT, Chicago, LSE, and Paris for lively discussions. I also thank an editor and two anonymous referees of Piketty (2003) for their helpful comments. I gratefully acknowledge financial support from the MacArthur Foundation.

secular decline in income inequality is for the most part a capital income phenomenon. Holders of large fortunes were badly hurt by major shocks during the 1914–45 period, and they were never able to fully recover from these shocks, probably because of the dynamic effects of progressive taxation on capital accumulation and pre-tax income inequality.

The rest of the chapter is organized as follows: Section 3.2 describes my data sources and outlines my methodology; Section 3.3 presents the basic facts that characterize my income inequality series and that need to be explained; Section 3.4 attempts to account for these facts; in Section 3.5, I briefly discuss whether my French conclusions can be applied to other developed countries; and Section 3.6 concludes.

3.2 DATA SOURCES

This work relies on three major types of data sources: data from income tax returns (1915–98), data from wage tax returns (1919–98), and data from the inheritance tax returns (1902–94).

Income Tax Returns (1915–98)

The most important data source is the income tax. A general income tax was enacted in France in 1914. It took effect for the first time in 1915 (that is, taxpayers reported their 1915 incomes at the beginning of 1916), and it has applied every year ever since. Most importantly, the French tax administration has been compiling every year since 1915 (including during the Second World War) summary statistics based upon the tabulation of all individual income tax returns. The raw materials produced by the tax administration have had the same general form since 1915: the tabulations indicate the number of taxpayers and the amount of their taxable income as a function of a number of income brackets (the number of brackets is usually very large, especially at the top of the distribution). This basic table is available for each single year of the 1915–98 period.[2]

One important limitation of these annual tables is that they only include those households whose income is high enough to be taxable under the general income tax system.[3] In France, less than 5% of the total number of households had to pay

[2] The complete technical characteristics of these raw statistical materials, as well as the exact references of the official statistical bulletins and administrative archives where these data were originally published by the French Ministry of Finance, are given in the book from which this paper is extracted (see Piketty 2001*a*: appendix A, pp. 555–91).

[3] For simplicity, I will always refer to tax units as 'households' in the context of this chapter. In actual fact, these are two different concepts: one non-married couple makes two tax units but one household, etc. All estimates reported here were computed in terms of tax units (i.e. the 'top decile income share' denotes the income share going to the top decile of the tax unit distribution of income per tax

the income tax during the first few years of the income tax system, and the percentage of taxable households fluctuated around 10–15% during the interwar period. This percentage then rose steadily from 10–15% in 1945 up to 50–60% in 1975, and finally stabilized around 50–60% since the 1970s. It is therefore impossible to use these data in order to produce estimates of the entire income distribution, and one needs to concentrate on top fractiles.

The methodology that I applied to the raw data can be described as follows:[4]

1. I used the basic tables produced by the tax administration in order to compute the Pareto coefficients associated with the top of the French income distribution for each year of the 1915–98 period. These structural parameters then allowed me to estimate for each single year of the 1915–98 period the average incomes of the top 10% of the income distribution (i.e., the top decile, which I denote P90–100), the top 5% of the income distribution (P95–100), the top 1% (P99–100), the top 0.5% (P99.5–100), the top 0.1% (P99.9–100) and the top 0.01% (P99.99–100), as well as the average incomes of the intermediate fractiles (P90–95, i.e. the bottom half of the top decile, P95–99, i.e. the next 4% etc.) and the income thresholds corresponding to the 90th percentile, the 95th percentile, etc. (P90, P95, etc.) For the years 1915–18, due to the small number of taxable households, I only estimated the incomes of fractiles P99–100 and above. The Pareto interpolation technique has been used by other researchers working with historical tax data,[5] and the estimates that I obtain for the French case appear to be as precise as those obtained in other countries (thanks to the large number of income brackets used by the tax administration).[6]
2. I then used French national income accounts in order to estimate total and average household income for the entire population (taxable and non-taxable), and I used these estimates to compute series for the share of fractile P90–100 in total income, the share of fractile P95–100 in total income, etc., and the share of fractile P99.99–100 in total income. This methodology

unit, etc., with no adjustment for the varying size of these tax units). The key point, however, is that the average number of tax units per household has been fairly stable since 1915 (around 1.3), and that the income profile of this ratio has been fairly stable since 1915 (as a first approximation). Tax data on the number of dependants and married couples per tax bracket also show that the income profile of average household size appears to have been relatively stable in the long run (in spite of a sharp fall of average household size).

[4] The methodology is fully described in the book (see especially Piketty 2001: appendix B, pp. 592–646). In particular, the book provides a detailed account of the many technical adjustments that were made to the tax data in order to take into account changes in tax law and to ensure homogeneity of the series. It includes all necessary information and intermediate computations to reproduce my estimates, from the raw data to my final series.

[5] See, e.g., Kuznets (1953) and Feenberg and Poterba (1993) (who applied Pareto interpolation techniques to US income tax returns data over the 1913–48 and 1950–89 periods).

[6] I used large micro-files of individual tax returns (including all taxpayers above a certain income threshold) available for the 1980s–1990s in order to make sure that my interpolation technique was indeed very reliable (see Piketty 2001*a*: appendix B, pp. 599–601).

(that is, using tax returns to compute the level of top incomes, and using national accounts to compute the average income denominator) is also standard in historical studies on income inequality (as in Kuznets 1953). The income concept that I have used both for the numerator and the denominator is pre-tax, pre-deductions taxable income.[7] Finally, note that I obtained average estimates of top income shares for the 1900–10 period by using the rough estimates of the income distribution that were made by the French tax administration prior to the First World War for revenue projection purposes (these estimates probably understate inequality a little bit).[8]

Wage Tax Returns (1919–98)

One important feature of the income tax system that was enacted in France in 1914–17 is that, in addition to the general income tax set up in 1914, it also included a number of taxes levied separately on each income source. In particular, there was a 'wage tax', i.e a progressive tax levied on individual wages, which was first applied in 1917. Individual wages were declared by employers, who had to file wage tax returns indicating the annual amount of wages paid to each individual employee. In 1919, the French tax administration started compiling summary statistics based on these wage returns. The basic statistical information is similar to that contained in the income tax tables: the wage tables indicate for a large number of earnings brackets the number of workers and the total amount of their wages (all sectors and occupations, including government employees, are included). The French tax administration stopped compiling these wage tables in 1939, so that these series only cover the 1919–38 period. In 1947, the French national statistical institute (INSEE) decided to use these wage tax returns to compile new series of annual statistical tables.[9] The INSEE tables look like the tax administration tables of the interwar period (they indicate for each wage bracket the number of wage earners and the total amount of wages), with the important difference that they cover the entire wage distribution, and not only top wages.[10]

I have used these raw data in the same way as the income tax data. Pareto interpolation techniques allowed me to compute the average wage of the top 10% of the wage distribution, the top 5%, the top 1%, etc. (fractiles were defined

[7] The adjustments that I made to national accounts series to ensure that I use the same income concept both at the numerator and at the denominator are described in Piketty (2001*a*: appendix G, pp. 693–720), where I also offer a detailed comparison of existing national accounts series. Official INSEE national accounts series start in 1949, and for earlier periods I have relied for the most part on the retrospective national accounts published by Villa (1994) and on the very well documented income accounts published by Dugé de Bernonville (1933–39).

[8] The adjustments that I made to these 1900–10 estimates on the basis of the data generated by the first few years of the income tax are described in Piketty (2001*a*: appendix I, pp. 738–41).

[9] The tax on wages was actually repealed in 1948, but the tax administration has kept using these returns to make sure that income tax taxpayers report the right wage.

[10] The 1919–38 tables only cover those wage earners whose wage is high enough to be taxable under the wage tax system (about 15–20% of all workers during the interwar period).

according to the total number of wage earners, taxable and non-taxable), and I have used independent estimates of the total wage bill (coming mostly from the national accounts) in order to compute top wage shares series.[11]

Inheritance Tax Returns (1902–94)

A progressive inheritance tax was enacted in France in 1901, and it has been in force every year ever since. Before 1901, the inheritance tax was purely proportional, so that the tax administration did not need information on total estates, and did not bother ranking individual estates and compiling statistical tables. In 1901, the tax administration started using inheritance tax returns to compile tables indicating the number of estates and the amount of these estates as a function of a number of estate brackets. These tables were compiled almost every year between 1902 and 1964 (with an interruption during the First World War and the early 1920s). Since 1964, similar tables have been compiled only in 1984 and in 1994. I have used these raw data in order to compute series for the average estate of the top 10% of the estate distribution, of the top 5%, of the top 1%, etc. (fractiles were defined according to the total number of adult decedents, taxable and non-taxable).[12]

3.3 THE BASIC FACTS

Consider first the evolution of the top decile income share (see Figure 3.1). The basic fact is that income inequality in France declined significantly over the course of the twentieth century. According to my estimates, the share of total household income received by the top decile dropped from about 45% at the beginning of the twentieth century to about 32–33% in the 1990s. In other words, the average income of the top 10% was about 4.5 times larger than the average income of the entire population at the beginning of the twentieth century, and it was about 3.2–3.3 times larger than the average income of the entire population in the 1990s.

Next, one can see immediately from Figure 3.1 that this secular decline has been far from steady. The top decile income share dropped during the First World War, and subsequently recovered during the 1920s and the first half of the 1930s.

[11] All technical details are given in Piketty (2001*a*: Appendix D, pp. 657–76). Unlike the annual income tables published by the tax administration (which had never been used to compute long-run inequality series until the present study), wage tables had already been used to produce series on interdecile ratios for the post-1950 period (see Baudelot and Lebeaupin 1979; Bayet and Julhès 1996). These authors did not compute top wage shares series, however. Most importantly, pre-Second World War wage tables had never been used until the present study (the very existence of these tables had probably been forgotten, just like the income tables).

[12] All technical details are given in Piketty (2001*a*: appendix J, pp. 744–71). These inheritance tables had never been used to construct long-run wealth inequality series until the present study.

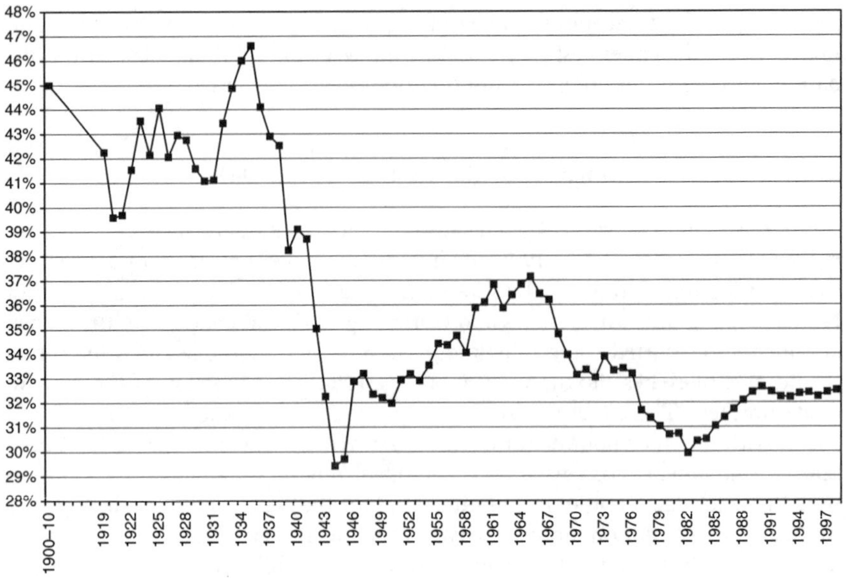

Figure 3.1 The top decile income share in France, 1900–98

Source: Author's computations based on income tax returns. See, Table 3A.1, col P90–100, and Piketty (2001*a*: appendix B, table B14, pp. 620–1).

In 1935 (i.e. at the height of the Great Depression in France) the top decile income share was slightly below 47%.[13] The income share received by the top decile then started to fall sharply in 1936, and even more so during the Second World War. The top decile income share fell to a nadir in 1944–45 (about 29–30%). As far as the post-war period is concerned, three sub-periods need to be distinguished. The top decile income share increased from 1945 (29–30%) to 1967–68 (36–7%). Then it declined until 1982–83, when it reached 30–31%. It has then increased somewhat since the early 1980s (32–33% in the 1990s). Note however that most of the action took place before 1945. Since the Second World War, income inequality in France (as measured by the top decile income share) appears to have been fluctuating around a constant mean value of about 32–33%, with no trend. In other words, most of the secular decline occurred during a specific time period (1914–45). These were times of crisis for the French economy, with two World Wars and the Great Depression of the 1930s. This definitely does not look like a gradual, Kuznets type process.

Moreover, and most importantly, my series show that the secular decline of the top decile income share is almost entirely due to very high incomes. The income share of fractile P90–95 has been extremely stable in the long-run: between 1900

[13] According to my estimates, the top decile income share has never been as high as in 1935 during the entire century. Note however that my average estimates for the 1900–10 decade probably understate inequality a little bit.

and 1998, that share has always been fluctuating around a mean value of about 11–11.5% of total household income (which means that these households always get about 2.2–2.3 times the average income) (see Figure 3.2). The income share of fractile P95–99 has experienced a modest secular decline, from about 15% of total household income at the beginning of the twentieth century to about 13–13.5% during the 1990s, i.e. a drop of about 10% (see Figure 3.2).

In contrast, the top percentile income share has dropped by more than 50%. The share of total income received by the top 1% was about 20% at the beginning of the twentieth century, and it was only about 7–8% during the 1990s (see Figure 3.2). In other words, the average income of the top 1% was about 20 times larger than the average income of the entire population at the beginning of the century, and it was about 7–8 times larger at the end of the century. Moreover, my series clearly show that the higher you go within the top percentile of the income distribution, the larger the secular decline (see Table 3.1). The most extreme case is that of the top 0.01%: their income share has dropped from about 3% at the beginning of the century to about 0.5–0.6% since 1945. In fact, the average real income of the top 0.01% has not increased at all during the entire twentieth century: expressed in 1998 French francs, it is about 15% lower in 1990–98 than what it was in 1900–10. During the same time period, the average real income of

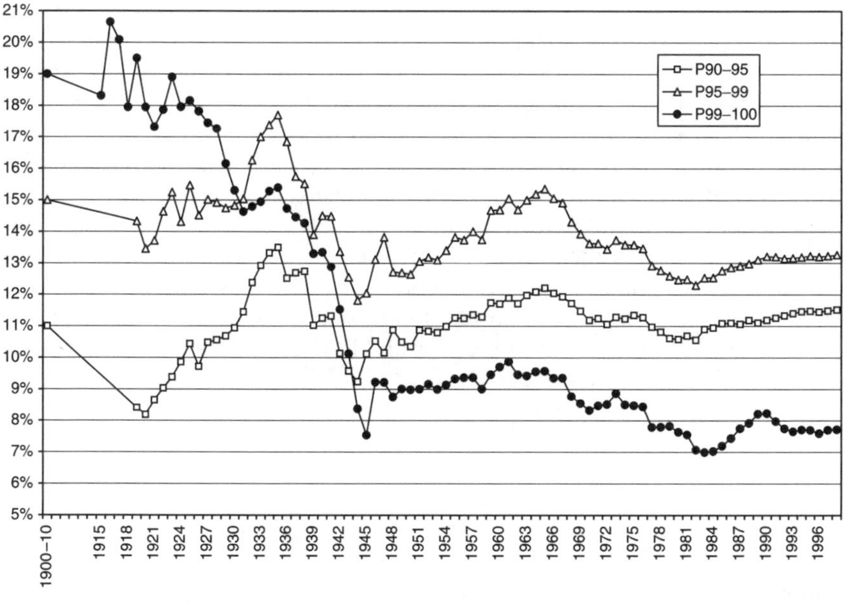

Figure 3.2 The income share of fractiles P90–95, P95–99, and P99–100 in France, 1900–98

Source: Author's computations based on income tax returns. See this chapter, Tables 3A.1 and 3A.2, and Piketty (2001*a*: appendix B, tables B14 and B15, pp. 620–2).

Table 3.1 Income growth and income shares in France, 1900–10 and 1990–98

Fractiles	Income growth	Income share (%) 1900–10	Income share (%) 1990–98	Difference (points) (%)	Share of total decline of top decile share corresponding to each fractile (%)	
P0–100	4.48	100.0	100.0	0.0	0.0	
P90–100	3.23	45.0	32.4	−12.6	−28.0	100.0
P95–100	2.77	34.0	21.0	−13.0	−38.3	103.2
P99–100	1.84	19.0	7.8	−11.2	−59.1	88.9
P99.5–100	1.54	15.0	5.2	−9.8	−65.6	78.1
P99.9–100	1.12	8.0	2.0	−6.0	−75.0	47.6
P99.99–100	0.83	3.0	0.6	−2.4	−81.6	19.4
P0–90	5.51	55.0	67.6	12.6	22.9	
P90–95	4.65	11.0	11.4	0.4	3.6	−3.2
P95–99	3.95	15.0	13.2	−1.8	−12.0	14.2
P99–99.5	2.94	4.0	2.6	−1.4	−34.4	10.9
P99.5–99.9	2.02	7.0	3.2	−3.8	−54.9	30.5
P99.9–99.99	1.30	5.0	1.4	−3.6	−71.1	28.2
P99.99–100	0.83	3.0	0.6	−2.4	−81.6	19.4

Note: 'Income growth' refers to the ratio between the average household incomes of 1990–98 and 1900–10 (both expressed in 1998 French Francs).

Source: Author's computations based on income tax returns (see Piketty 2001*a*: tables 2.1 and 2.2, pp. 128–9).

the entire population, as well as the average real income of fractile P90–95, has been multiplied by about 4.5 (see Table 3.1). According to my series, almost 90% of the secular decline of the top decile income share is due to the top percentile, and more than half of the top percentile drop is due to the top 0.1% (see Table 3.1).

The timing of the fall of very top incomes is also striking. Between 1945 and 1998, the income share of the top 1% has been fairly stable (see Figure 3.2). The secular fall took place exclusively during the 1914–45 period, and especially during the 1930s and the Second World War. It is interesting to note that that the deflationary years of the Great Depression had a very different impact on moderately high incomes and on very top incomes. While the income shares of fractiles P90–95 and P95–99 (the 'upper middle class') increased sharply during the early 1930s, the income shares of fractiles P99–100 and above (the 'rich') fell.[14] I will come back on this below.

3.4 ACCOUNTING FOR THE FACTS

The key facts that need to be explained are the following: the secular decline in the top decile income share took place during a specific time period (i.e. between 1914 and 1945, and mostly during the 1930s and the Second World War), and it is

[14] See Figure 3.2 and Tables 3A.1 and 3A.2.

due for the most part to the sharp drop in the top percentile income share (and, to a significant extent, to the sharp drop in the top 0.1% income share). How can one account for these facts?

Income Composition Patterns

One first needs to be aware of the large differences in income composition that have always characterized the various sub-fractiles of the top decile. Every single year of the 1915–98 period, tax returns tabulations show that the share of wage income declines continuously from fractile P90–95 to fractile P99.99–100, while the share of capital income (dividends, interest, and rents) rises continuously from fractile P90–95 to fractile P99.99–100. The shape of the self-employment income share is intermediate between the wage share and the capital share: it rises until fractile P99.5–99.9 (approximately), and declines afterwards. These variations in income composition within the top decile are truly enormous. Whereas the households of fractile P90–95 have very little capital or self-employment income (about 80–90% of their income is made of wages), the households of fractile P99.99–100 rely for the most part on their capital and self-employment income (typically, more than 60% of their income is made of capital income, and an extra 20% is made of self-employment income). Tax returns tabulations also distinguish between rents, dividend, and interest income, and my detailed series show that top capital incomes are mostly made of dividends (the share of interest and rents in total income is basically flat within the top decile, and the share of interest and rents in total capital income is steeply downward-sloping).[15] Large capital owners are predominantly shareholders, not bondholders or landlords.[16]

These composition patterns suggest that the secular decline of income inequality is primarily a capital income phenomenon. That is, the fractiles relying mostly on wage income did not experience any significant decline in the long run (or experienced a limited decline), whereas the fractiles relying mostly on their capital income experienced major shocks between 1914 and 1945 (wars, inflation, depression), from which they never fully recovered. This interpretation is consistent with the fact that the capital share at the level of fractile P99.99–100 was as small as 15% in 1945–46, and that the incomes of the top 0.01% were mostly made of self-employment income (more than 70% of total income) during those years. This is the only instance during the entire century when capital income is not the dominant source of income for very top incomes (capital income returned to its dominant position during the late 1940s and early 1950s, albeit at a somewhat lower level than during the interwar period). This clearly shows that the large drop in top income shares observed between 1914 and 1945 was due to a large extent to the fall of top capital incomes.

[15] For the detailled composition series, see Piketty 2001*a*: tables B16–B18, pp. 625–34.

[16] It is interesting to note that large capital owners were already predominantly shareholders (and to some extent bondholders, but very rarely landlords) at the beginning of the twentieth century.

The fact that the capital share is particularly low at the end of the Second World War is also consistent with macroeconomic data. Available series on factor shares do indeed show that the capital share in French corporate value-added has never been as low as in 1944–45 (see Figure 3.4 below). French GDP has never been as low as in 1944–45 during the twentieth century (fighting between the Germans and the Allies took place over significant portions of the French territory after D-Day, and firms were completely disorganized), and the big wage increase implemented by the provisional government implied that there was almost nothing left for profits.

The composition patterns derived from tax returns also allow me to account for the sharp divergence between moderately high incomes and very top incomes observed during the deflationary Great Depression of the early 1930s. Given that fractiles P90–95 and P95–99 mostly rely on wages, one should indeed expect these fractiles to benefit from the fall in prices : real wages did increase during the 1929–35 period (thanks to the nominal rigidity of wages and the fall in prices), at a time when real output was falling. Moreover, the high wage employees (and especially the government employees) of fractiles P90–95 and P95–99 were shielded from unemployment which hurt mostly low wage workers (such as low skill manufacturing or rural workers). Conversely, given that fractiles P99–100 and above mostly relied on capital income and business profits, one should indeed expect these fractiles to lose out in the recession (the capital share fell sharply during the early 1930s). This process reversed in 1936, when the Front Populaire decided to devalue the French franc and to put an end to the deflationary strategy. The high wage employees of fractiles P90–95 and P95–99 started to lose ground (inflation pushed their real wages down), while the fall of the profit holders of fractiles P99–100 and above was temporarily halted. This again shows that one needs to distinguish between the different sub-fractiles of the top decile in order to account properly for the inequality facts (this is true both for long run trends and for short run fluctuations).

The Long-Run Stability of Wage Inequality

Before I further explore the nature of the shocks suffered by capital owners during the 1914–45 period and the reasons why they never managed to fully recover from these shocks, it is important to make sure that the capital income view of the inequality facts is the right one. That is, I need to show that wage inequality did not play any significant role in the secular decline of the top decile income share.

My wage series demonstrate that wage inequality in twentieth century France has been extremely stable in the long run. The share of the total wage bill received by the top decile of the wage distribution has always fluctuated around a mean value of about 25–26%, and the share of the total wage bill received by the top 1% of the wage distribution has hovered near to 6–7% (see Figure 3.3). Note that the wage shares of the top decile and top percentile were substantially below their secular mean in 1919 (when my annual series start) and during the early 1920s.

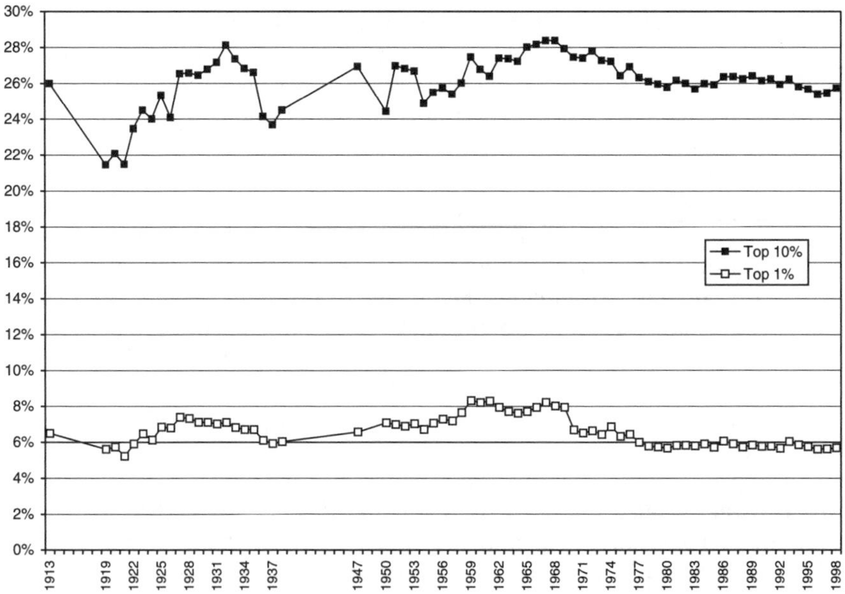

Figure 3.3 The top decile and top percentile wage shares in France, 1913–98

Source: Author's computations based on wage tax returns (see Piketty 2001*a*: appendix D, tables D7 and D16, col. P90–100 and P99–100, pp. 664 and 675).

But there is ample occupational and sector-specific evidence showing that this was not a 'normal' situation. The wage structure did narrow substantially during the First World War in France (low wage workers enjoyed nominal pay increases that were significantly higher than those obtained by high wage workers), and one can show that the top decile and top percentile wage shares were at the eve of the First World War very close to their secular mean.[17]

More generally, the fact that wage inequality has been extremely stable in the long run does not mean that the French history of wage inequality was smooth and steady during each single decade of the twentieth century. Both World Wars led to significant compressions of the wage structure. But the point is that, after each World War, the wage share received by high wage workers quickly recovered its pre-war level. My wage series also confirm that the deflationary depression of the early 1930s led to a widening of wage inequality: high-wage workers benefit from the nominal rigidity of their wages and from the fact that they are less exposed to unemployment than low wage workers. In the same way as with the income series, this process ends in 1936, when the Front Populaire decides to put an end to the deflationary strategy. The 1967–68 and 1982–83 turning points are also visible in

[17] See Piketty (2001*a*: pp. 188–91, 199–200). The estimates for 1913 reported on Figure 3.3 (26% for the top decile share, 6.5% for the top percentile share) were computed on the basis of this occupational and sector-specific data (and in particular on the basis of public sector data).

my wage series. Wage dispersion significantly widened between 1950 and 1967–68, and the sharp increases in the minimum wage implemented in the summer of 1968 and during the 1970s led to a significant decline in wage inequality until 1982–83, when the newly elected socialist government decided to freeze the minimum wage (wage dispersion has increased somewhat since then). In other words, wage inequality during the twentieth century in France has been going up and down for all sorts of reasons in the short and medium run, but it has always reverted back to its secular mean. No long run trend can be detected in the series.

The contrast between the long-run evolution of the share of total income received by the top percentile of the income distribution (Figure 3.2) and the long-run evolution of the share of the total wage bill received by the top percentile of the wage distribution (Figure 3.3) is particularly striking. While the top percentile income share has declined sharply from about 20% at the beginning of the century to about 7–8% in the 1990s, the top percentile wage share has always been near 6–7%.

My wage inequality series therefore confirm that the capital income interpretation of the inequality facts is the right one. The secular decline in the top percentile income share is due for the most part to the sharp drop in the level of the top capital incomes received by the affluent. Had this level remained constant (relative to the average income), there would have been no secular decline in the top percentile income share.[18]

Another advantage of looking at wages is that data are available on the entire distribution, and not only on the average and on the top decile. For the 1950–98 period, one can compute annual series for all percentile ranks of the wage distribution. By looking at the evolution of ratios such as P10 to the average wage, P50 to the average wage, and P90 to the average wage during this period, one can see that the entire distribution of wages has been extremely stable in the long run, and not only the top decile and top percentile shares.[19] Again, one does observe important fluctuations in the short run and medium run: the P90/P10 ratio rose sharply between 1950 and 1968, then declined sharply between 1968 and 1982–83, and finally rose somewhat since 1982–83.[20] But these short and medium run fluctuations cancel out in the longer run, in the same way as for top decile and percentile wage shares.

[18] Strictly speaking, this is more than the data can actually say: depending on the trends in family structure and correlations between the various types of incomes, a given trend in wage inequality can translate into various trends in income inequality. But the gap between Figure 3.2 and Figure 3.3 is simply too big to be undone by that kind of bias. Moreover, note that the correlation of wages between spouses has probably been trending upwards during the twentieth century (as a consequence of the upward trend in female participation), so that a stable level of wage concentration should actually give rise to an increasing level of income concentration (everything else equal).

[19] During the 1950–98 period, P10 has always been fluctuating around 45–50% of average wage, P50 around 80–85% of average wage, and P90 around 160–170% of average wage (see Piketty 2001*a*: appendix D, Table D12, p. 671).

[20] The fact that the turning points of post-war trends in wage inequality coincide with the breaks in French minimum wage policy was already apparent in the series compiled by Baudelot and Lebeaupin (1979) and Bayet and Julhès (1996).

The same phenomena seem to have occurred during the 1900–50 period. Available wage returns data do not allow me to estimate annual series for lower deciles prior to 1950, but occupational and sector-specific wage data can to some extent serve as a proxy. During the first half of the twentieth century, agricultural workers were very numerous (around 30% of all wage earners in 1900, down to 20% in 1930, 10% in 1950, and 1% in 1998), and very low wages were concentrated in this sector. By using the lowest wages observed in the agricultural sector as a proxy for P10, one finds that the P10/(average wage) was already around 45–50% in 1900 and 1930, i.e., around the same mean level as during the 1950–98 period.[21] That is, migration from the low wage rural sector to the high wage urban sector did not lead to a structural compression of wage inequality. Low wage rural workers disappeared, but they were replaced by low wage urban workers, so that the hierarchy did not change very much in the long run. This evidence stands in contrast with the theoretical predictions of Kuznets' two sector development model, according to which one should expect inequality to decline as more and more workers join the high paying, urban sector of the economy.

The Robustness of Wealth Levelling

As was already noted above, the fact that capital owners experienced major shocks during the 1914–45 period (and especially during the 1930s and the Second World War) is fully consistent with the general economic history of France during that period. In a sense, what happened between 1914 and 1945 period is just the normal consequence of an extraordinary recession. Capital income generally tends to be pro-cyclical, and it is natural to expect capital owners to suffer a lot from the Great Depression and the War and to be at their secular low in 1944–45, at a time when the French GNP was also at a century low.

In fact, what really needs to be explained is why capital owners never managed to fully recover from the shocks of the 1914–45 period. One explanation would simply be that capital owners were confronted during the 1914–45 with major shocks to their capital holdings (and not only to their capital income), and that it takes a long time to reconstitute the level of fortunes and capital income that capitalists enjoyed before these shocks. The shocks to capital holdings took three main forms: inflation, bankruptcies, and destructions.

First, one must bear in mind that inflation did act as a powerful capital tax. The French CPI was multiplied by a factor of more than 100 between 1914 and 1950, which means that bondholders were fully expropriated by inflation. The same process applied, in a less extreme way, to real estate owners and landlords. Rent

[21] See Piketty 2001*a*: 214–15, and appendix H, tables H2–H4, pp. 726–8. These P10 estimates for 1900 and 1930 were computed by using wages for low skill agricultural workers and rural female domestic workers as proxies. We only used money wages estimates, and we did not try to take into account in-kind payments (which were quite important for agricultural and domestic workers). The resulting estimates should therefore be considered as a lower bound for the true P10 in 1900 and 1930: the true P10/(average wage) ratio might have declined somewhat between 1900 and 1950, but it certainly did not rise.

control was severe during both World Wars, and the real value of rents was divided by 10 between 1913 and 1950.[22] Further the 1914–50 inflationary process was something entirely new for the economic agents of the time. There had been virtually no inflation since the Revolutionary and Napoleonic wars (the average annual inflation rate between 1815 and 1914 was 0.3%), and the government suddenly started to print vast quantities of money after 1914 to pay for the huge budget deficits brought on by the First World War.

Next, the 'recession' induced by the Great Depression of the 1930s and by the Second World War was not a 'normal' recession. Real GDP declined by 20% between 1929 and 1935, and by 50% between 1929 and 1944–5.[23] Many firms faded and disappeared during that time (much more than during a 'normal' recession). Bankruptcies were particularly numerous in manufacturing and in finance. Large fortunes have always comprised far more equity shares than bonds or real estate during the twentieth century. The impact of the bankruptcies of the 1930s and of the Second World War on top fortunes was therefore probably even larger than the impact of inflation.[24]

Finally, and most importantly, the physical destructions induced by both World Wars were truly enormous in France. According to the best available estimates, about one-third of the capital stock was destroyed during the First World War, and about two-thirds during the Second World War. This reflects the fact that the bombing technology was far more destructive during the Second World War than during the First World War. According to these estimates, the (capital stock)/(national income) ratio was around 5 at the eve of the First World War, and it then fell to 3.5 in 1934 and 1.2 in 1949.[25]

It is also important to recall that the French government enacted a broad nationalization program in 1945. The nationalization process often was straight expropriation: prices for shares were often set at an arbitrary low level, so as to punish the 'capitalists', who were often accused of 'collabouration' with the Vichy government. A leading example of this kind of punitive nationalization/expropriation process was the car company Renault.[26] At the same time, the provisional government decided to implement in 1945 a one-shot tax on capital holdings, with

[22] See Piketty 2001*a*: appendix F, table F1, pp. 690–1). On the history of rent control legislation in France since 1914, see Hirsch (1972) and Taffin (1993).

[23] See Piketty 2001*a*: appendix G, table G1, p. 695.

[24] It is unfortunately very difficult to quantify the impact of bankruptcies on the distribution of wealth. We know that the annual number of bankruptcies more than doubled between 1929 and 1935 (see INSEE 1966: 170–1), but we do not have systematic information about the individuals who own these firms and their rank in the wealth distribution.

[25] See Piketty 2001*a*: p. 137. These estimates are due to Sauvy (1965–75, 2: p. 442; 1984, 2: p. 323), who uses estimates of the capital stock computed by Cornut (1963: p. 399). These estimates are not fully homogenous (the 1949 capital stock is probably underestimated somewhat; see INSEE 1958: pp. 34–5), but they are broadly consistent with the independent computations by Divisia et al. (1956, 3: p. 62), who also find that the Second World War destructions were about twice as large as the first World War destructions.

[26] Unfortunately, there does not seem to exist any systematic, quantitative study of the 1945 nationalization process. Divisia et al. (1956, 3: pp. 73–6) describe a number of interesting examples of nationalization/expropriation, but they do not attempt to quantify the process at the national level.

rates up to 20% on top fortunes (and 100% on those fortunes which experienced substantial nominal increases during the war!).[27]

In other words, there are good reasons to believe that the accumulation process for large capital holdings was to a large extent set back to zero (or close to zero) in 1945. This interpretation is consistent with the composition patterns described above: in 1945, very top incomes were mostly made up of new entrepreneurs, simply because the old capitalists had disappeared.

But such an explanation cannot be the full story. More than 50 years have elapsed since 1945, and it would seem that this is a sufficiently long time period for capitalists to recover from the 1914–45 shocks (at least partly). The point is that the top percentile income share did not rise at all during the 1945–98 period (see Figure 3.2). Apparently, something important has changed over the course of the twentieth century: it just seems impossible to accumulate individual fortunes as large as those that were accumulated in the past.

It is also important to emphasize that the decline of top capital incomes is the consequence of a decreased concentration of capital income and not of a decline in the share of capital income in the economy as a whole. According to national accounts, the share of capital income (dividends, interest, and rent) in aggregate household income is approximately the same at the end of the twentieth century as at the beginning of the twentieth century, i.e. about 20% (see Figure 3.4). This is not too surprising, given the well-known long run stability of the capital share in corporate value-added. Note, however, that while it took only a few years for the capital share in corporate value-added to recover from the 1944–5 secular low, it is only in the 1980s–1990s that the capital share in aggregate household income reached the levels observed in the interwar and at the eve of the First World War (see Figure 3.4). This important time lag is due to a mixture of two factors. First of all, retained earnings were unusually high during the reconstruction period in France (1950s–1960s),[28] and the profit share was unusually low during the 1970s.[29] This explains why distributed dividends and interest income did not return to their pre-First World War and interwar levels (as a percentage of household income) until the 1980s–1990s. Next, several decades were needed for the real value of rents to recover from the 1914–50 inflation. Here again, one needs to wait until the 1980s–1990s to see the (rent index)/CPI ratio and the share

Similarly, Andrieu et al. (1987) offer a detailed analysis of the political context of the nationalization policies, but they do not try to quantify their importance. I return below to the complicated issue of the long run impact of the 1945 nationalizations.

[27] See Piketty (2001*a*: p. 138).

[28] High retained earnings during the 1950s–1960s were due primarily to the high investment needs of companies. This was exacerbated by the fact that retained earnings were close to zero during the 1930s (i.e. companies did not cut dividends as much as they should have during the Great Depression). See Malissen (1953) and Piketty (2001*a*: p. 62–3).

[29] The fall in the profit share was due primarily to the big wage push of the 1970s (the minimum wage was increased by 130% in real terms between 1968 and 1982–3, while GNP increased by only 40%!) The profit share started recovering when wages were frozen in 1982–3.

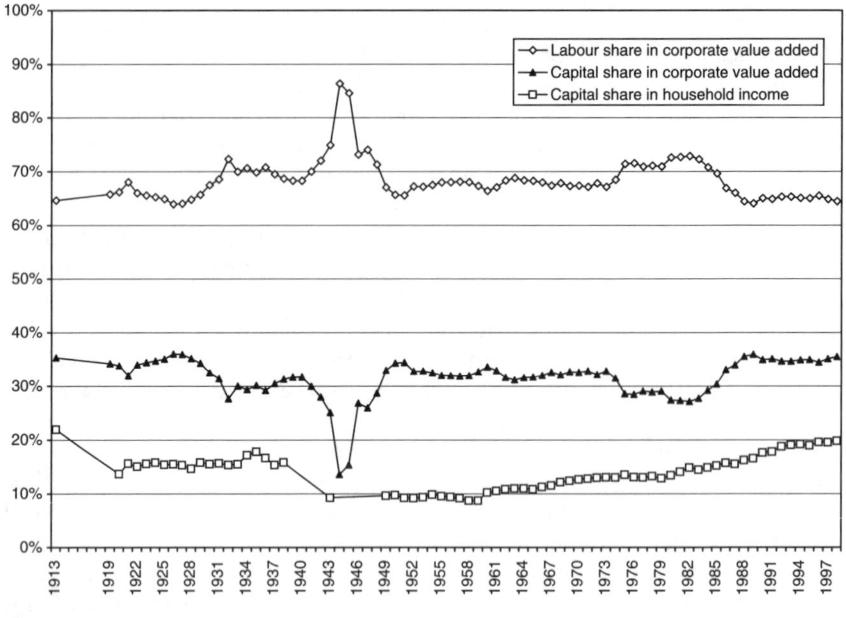

Figure 3.4 Factor shares in France, 1913–98

Source: Author's computations based on national accounts (see Piketty 2000*a*: appendix G, tables G3–G6 and G9, pp. 703–5 and 710–13).

of rents in household income returning to their pre-First World War level.[30] These time lags demonstrate the importance of the 1914–45 shocks. But the key point is that aggregate capital income has now fully recovered from these shocks, while top capital incomes did not recover.

One could also wonder whether the decline of top capital incomes could simply be the consequence of fiscal manipulation and tax evasion. I have performed two kinds of checks in order to make sure that fiscal manipulation and tax evasion can only be a small part of the story (at most), and that the observed trends do indeed describe a real economic phenomenon.

First, I have adjusted the capital income figures reported in tax returns so as to match the capital income totals coming from national accounts. The general conclusion is that the observed trends are simply too large to be explained by this kind of factor. Whatever the way one makes the adjustment, the trends are still very large.[31] In fact, all available information suggests that tax evasion in France has never been as high as in the interwar period, i.e. at the time when reported incomes at the very top of the distribution were much higher than what they were in

[30] One key reason why it took so long is because French landlords can (partially) adjust their rent to market conditions only when they have a new tenant. Note that high inflation (wage driven) during the 1970s temporarily halted this recovery process (in the same way as for dividends).

[31] For detailed computations, see Piketty 2001*a*: pp. 408–48.

the 1990s. If one looks at the (tax return capital income + legally tax exempt capital income)/(national accounts capital income) ratios, which can be viewed as a measure of tax evasion, then one finds ratios over 90% for the 1980–1990s, versus 60–70% for the interwar period. This is consistent with the fact that the tax administration had much less investigative power before the Second World War than it has today. Tax evasion therefore seems to amplify the trends rather than to reduce them.[32]

Next, I have used inheritance tax return data in order to test whether the leveling of fortunes is a real economic phenomenon. The results are spectacular (see Figure 3.5). Whereas the average estate left by the fractile P90–95 of the estate distribution has been multiplied by about 3.2 in real terms between 1900–10 and the 1990s, the average estate left by the fractile P99.99–100 of the estate distribution is nearly four times smaller during the 1990s than what it was in 1900–10. The decline in capital concentration seems truly astonishing. Inheritance tax returns are obviously subject to fiscal manipulation and tax evasion, but the trends are so enormous that these explanations can only be a small part of the story. One would need to assume that the reporting rate was 100% at the beginning of the twentieth century and less than 10% at the end of the twentieth century! This does not seem plausible. Moreover, in the same way as for income tax returns, it is likely that tax evasion was actually larger at the beginning of the twentieth century and during the interwar period than later in the century. It is also important to note that the inheritance tax and the gift tax were unified in France in 1942. One important consequence is that my pre-1942 top estates estimates exclude *inter vivos* gifts, while my post-1942 estimates do include inter-vivos gifts. This again tends to amplify the trend rather than to reduce it (inter-vivos gifts were already quite important at the beginning of the twentieth century).

Inheritance series show that the decline of top fortunes is the consequence of a decreased concentration of wealth and not of a decline in aggregate wealth in the economy as a whole. Top estates never recovered from the shocks, but lower estates did recover perfectly well and were able to compensate the fall in top estates. This is consistent with macroeconomic estimates showing that the (capital stock)/(national income) ratio was about 5 in the late 1990s, i.e., at about the same level as at the eve of the First World War.[33] In other words, both capital income and the capital stock have returned to their pre-First World War levels. The distribution has changed, not the aggregates.

Although the French tax administration did not compile inheritance tax tables until 1901, a number of inheritance series (based upon samples of tax returns

[32] I have also checked that legally tax exempt capital income (which has become more and more important over time) and capital gains (which were excluded from my basic series altogether) can only be a small part of the story. For instance, tax return data shows that capital gains represent an average income supplement of about 25% for fractile P99.99–100 (see Piketty 2001*a*: pp. 420–31, and Appendix A, pp. 586–8). This is a non-negligible amount in absolute terms, but this is not going to explain why the income share of fractile P99.99–100 has been divided by 5 during the twentieth century.

[33] For the 1999 figures, see INSEE 2001: pp. 34 and 38): 36583/6951= 5.2. The capital stock estimate for 1999 is not fully homogeneous with the estimates given above for 1913, 1934, and 1949, but the orders of magnitude seem right.

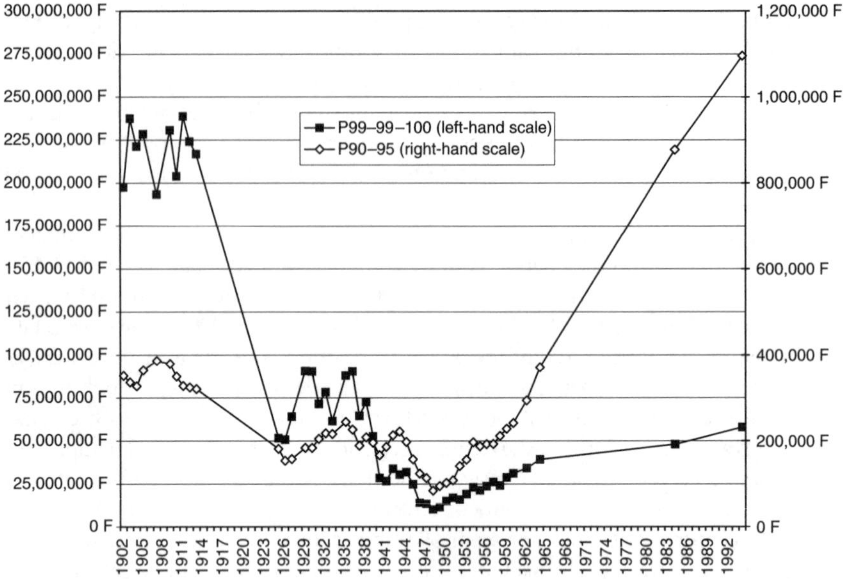

Figure 3.5 The average estate left by the fractiles P90–95 and P99.99–100 in France, 1902–94 (1998 French Francs)

Source: Author's computations based on inheritance tax returns (see Piketty 2001*a*: appendix J, table J–9, p. 763).

collected by historians) are available for the nineteenth century. Those series show that wealth concentration increased sharply in France between 1815 and 1914 (top estates rose more than lower estates), and that wealth inequality did not start declining until the First World War. This seems to confirm our 'accidental' interpretation of the inequality decline: no 'spontaneous' downward trend was taking place before the shocks.[34]

Finally, there is plenty of anecdotal evidence suggesting that the decline of top capital incomes is indeed a real economic and social phenomenon. Individuals living off large capital incomes were plentiful in the literature of the nineteenth century and the early twentieth century (see, e.g., the novels by Stendhal, Balzac, Proust, etc.), whereas they have virtually disappeared from the literary scene since the Second World War. It is also interesting to note that 'rentiers' have disappeared from French census questionnaires in 1946: since the 1946 census, one can no longer describe oneself as 'rentier' (this category was used in all censuses through 1936). Another interesting piece of evidence is the evolution of the number of household workers and domestic servants. At the eve of the First Word War,

[34] Inheritance series for the nineteenth century can be found in Daumard (1973) and Bourdieu et al. (2001). Morrisson (2000) reports top income shares estimates according to which income inequality declined somewhat in France between 1860 and 1900. But these estimates are based on macro-economic data alone and do not take into account the rise in wealth concentration that took place during this period. On these issues, see Piketty 2001*a*: pp. 535–42.

household workers and domestic servants were very numerous in France: about 0.9–1 million according to the censuses, i.e. around 5% of the labour force. This number fell suddenly in the aftermath of the First World War and during the 1930s (down to about 0.7 million, 3.5% of the labour force), and even more so in the aftermath of the Second World War. The number of household workers and domestic servants has stabilized around 0.2 million since 1950s–1960s, i.e. about 1% of the labour force, five times less than at the eve of the First World War.[35] The parallelism between this evolution and the evolution of top income shares is striking. It is particularly important to note that the number of household workers and domestic servants was relatively stable at the eve of the First World War. The obvious interpretation is that this number suddenly started falling together with the number of wealthy households who could afford having domestic servants.[36]

The Role of Progressive Taxation

How can one account for the fact that large fortunes never recovered from the 1914–45 shocks, while smaller fortunes did recover perfectly well? The most natural and plausible candidate for an explanation seems to be the creation and the development of the progressive income tax (and of the progressive inheritance tax). The large fortunes that generate the top capital incomes observed at the beginning of the twentieth century were accumulated during the nineteenth century, at a time when progressive taxation did not exist and capitalists could use almost 100% of their pre-tax income to consume and to accumulate.[37] The conditions faced by twentieth century capitalists to recover from the shocks incurred during the 1914–45 period were quite different. The top marginal rate of the income tax was set to only 2% in 1915 in France, but it quickly reached very high levels (over 60%) during the interwar period, and it stabilized around 60–70% after 1945. These high marginal rates applied only to a small fraction of incomes, but the point is that is they were to a large extent designed to hit the incomes of the top 1% (and even more so the top 0.1% and 0.01%) of the income distribution, i.e., the incomes that depend primarily on capital income and capital accumulation. Effective average tax rates have always been fairly moderate at the level of fractile P90–95: less than 1% during the interwar period, and

[35] For detailed series on the number of household workers and domestic servants since the 1901 census, see Piketty 2001*a*: appendix H, pp. 726–8.

[36] The labour cost of a domestic servant has increased at a slightly higher rate than per capita income in the long run (see Piketty 2001*a*: 86–7), but the gap seems far too small to explain why the number of domestic servants was divided by 5 across the century. In any case, labour costs cannot explain why the number of servants dropped so suddenly after the First World War (there was no sudden variation in labour costs).

[37] Before the creation of a progressive income tax in 1914, personal taxation relied on individual characteristics such as housing rents, the number of doors and windows, etc. Effective tax rates were roughly proportional and never exceeded 3–4% of income (see Caillaux 1910: 208–9 and Piketty 2001*a*: pp. 236–9). Note also that there did exist an inheritance tax during the nineteenth century, but it was purely proportional and the rate was only 1% (see below).

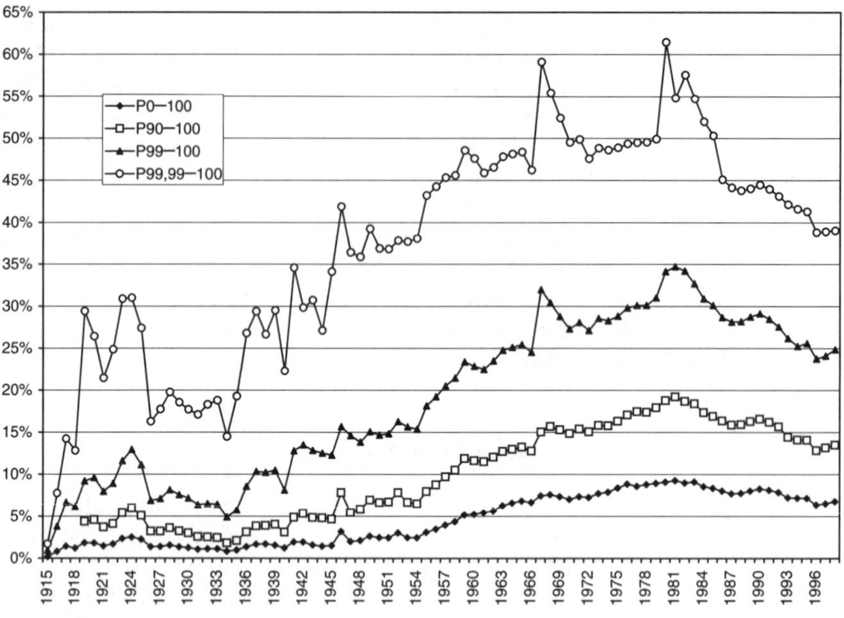

Figure 3.6 Effective average income tax rates in France, 1915–98

Source: Author's computations based on income tax returns and income tax laws (see Piketty (2001*a*: appendix B, table B-20, pp. 636–7).

between 5% and 10% since the Second World War. In contrast, effective average tax rates borne by fractile P99.99–100 reached 30% during the interwar period, and stabilized around 40–50% since the Second World War (see Figure 3.6).[38] It is therefore not surprising if progressive taxation had a substantial impact on capital accumulation at the very top and a negligible impact for smaller fortunes.

Needless to say, these numbers are not sufficient to prove in a rigorous way that the dynamic effects of progressive taxation on capital accumulation and pre-tax income inequality have the 'right' quantitative magnitude to account for the observed facts. One would need to know more about the savings rates of capitalists, how their accumulation strategies have changed since 1945 etc. Note however that the orders of magnitude do not seem unrealistic, especially if one assumes that the owners of large fortunes, whose pre-tax incomes and lifestyles were already severely hit by the 1914–45 shocks, were not willing to reduce their consumption down to very low levels and to increase their savings so as to counteract the rise in tax rates.[39]

[38] The large year-to-year variations on Figure 3.6 (especially for top incomes) show how chaotic the history of the income tax has been in France. For instance, the 1968 and 1981 spikes correspond to the large tax increases on the rich that were voted in the aftermath of the 1968 general strike and of the 1981 socialist electoral victory. I offer a detailed historical account of these politico-economic developments over the 1914–98 period in Piketty (2001*a*: chap. 4, pp. 233–334).

[39] Existing evidence shows that the negative shocks incurred between 1914 and 1945 and the rise in progressive taxation induced French wealthy families to reduce drastically their savings rate between

In fact, in the most standard economic models of capital accumulation, the behavioural response tends to amplify (and not to counteract) the rise in tax rates. That is, a rise in tax rates imposed on very top incomes leads wealthy taxpayers to increase their consumption and to reduce their savings. In the Barro-Becker dynastic model of capital accumulation, this behavioural effect is so large that large fortunes completely disappear in the long run. Progressive taxation leads to truncated wealth distribution in the long run, in the sense that there is nobody above the top marginal rate threshold.[40] In less extreme and more realistic models of capital accumulation, the impact of progressive taxation is smaller (large fortunes do not completely disappear). But the impact is still substantial. For instance, simple computations show that a capitalist will deplete his or her wealth at a very high rate if he or she keeps the same consumption after progressive taxation is introduced. In the absence of taxation (say, before the First World War), the capital stock of a capitalist consuming each year the full return (say, 5%) to his or her capital stock is stationary. But if an effective tax rate of 30% is suddenly introduced (say, in the interwar period), and if this capitalist keeps consuming the full before-tax return to his or her capital stock, then he or she will need to consume some his or her capital stock each year: 18% of the initial capital stock is destroyed after ten years, 42% after 20 years, etc., and there is no capital left after 35 years.[41]

Consider now the more interesting case of a capitalist (or a would-be capitalist) in 1945, and assume that this capitalist is ready to devote a large fraction of his or her income to capital accumulation. How much can he or she accumulate in 50 years? The point is that progressive taxation drastically reduces the assets that one can accumulate, including for capitalists adopting relatively low living standards (see Table 3.2). For instance, with a 5% before-tax return and for a consumption level equals to 40% of the before-tax return to the initial capital stock, one can accumulate in 50 years a fortune that is about 5 times as large with a 0% tax rate as with a 50% tax rate. That is, the initial capital stock is multiplied by 7.3 after 50 years in the absence of taxation, while the initial capital stock is multiplied by only 1.5 with a tax rate of 50%. This tax rate of 50% corresponds approximately to the average effective tax rates faced by fractile P99.99–100 in France since the Second World War, and the factor of 5 corresponds approximately to the secular decline in the income share of fractile P99.99–100.

Note also that these simple simulations do not take into account the impact of the progressive inheritance tax. During the nineteenth century, the French inheritance tax was strictly proportional, with a fixed 1% tax rate. A progressive

1873–1913 and 1946–53 (see Perrot 1961). Note however that this research by Perrot relies on a few hundred private account books from French wealthy families, and that it would need to be supplemented by extensive new research based on larger samples.

[40] For a formal proof of this result, see Piketty 2001*b*: pp. 30–2.

[41] This cumulative process would take place at an even faster pace in case of higher returns and/or higher tax rates (see Piketty 2001*b*: table 3). This mechanism is trivial, but I believe that it did contribute to amplify the shocks incurred by capital owners during the 1914–45 period.

Table 3.2 The impact of progressive taxation on capital accumulation

	r=5%, t=0%	r=5%, t=30%	r=5%, t=50%	r=10%, t=0%	r=10%, t=30%	r=10%, t=50%
c=100%	1.0	0.0	0.0	1.0	0.0	0.0
c=80%	3.1	0.3	0.0	24.3	0.0	0.0
c=60%	5.2	1.7	0.5	47.6	5.1	0.0
c=40%	7.3	3.0	1.5	70.8	13.2	3.1
c=20%	9.4	4.3	2.5	94.1	21.3	7.3
c=0%	11.5	5.6	3.4	117.4	29.5	11.5

Note: This table reads as follows: assume that a capitalist's consumption level is equal to a fixed fraction c (say, c=20%) of the full return r (say, r=5%) to his or her capital stock; in the absence of taxation (t=0%), his or her capital stock will be multiplied by 9.4 after 50 years; with an effective tax rate t=50%, his or her capital stock will be multiplied by 2.5 after 50 years (I assume that the capitalist keeps the same absolute consumption level during 50 years). The corresponding formula is given by: $x_n = c/(1-t) + [1+(1-t)r]^n x[1-c/(1-t)]$.

inheritance tax was introduced in 1901, but tax rates remained low until the First World War: at the eve of the war, top tax rates did not exceed 5%. In the same way as with the progressive income tax, the top rates of the progressive inheritance tax suddenly reached non-trivial levels in the aftermath of the First World War. One can compute that the effective tax rate faced by fractile P99.99–100 of the estate distribution was about 20–5% during the interwar period (or even 30–5% during the early 1920s), 30–5% during the 1950s, 15–20% during the 1960s–1970s and again 30–5% during the 1980s–1990s.[42] Note however that the long run impact of the progressive inheritance tax on capital accumulation, though important, has probably been less drastic than the impact of the progressive income tax. Because the income tax applies every year and has cumulative effects, an effective income tax rate of 50% can reduce by a factor of 5 the size of fortunes that one can accumulate in 50 years. In contrast, assuming the inheritance tax is paid once every 50 years (on average), an effective inheritance tax rate of 50% reduces by a factor of 2 the size of fortunes that one can accumulate in 50 years.

Finally, it is worth emphasizing that it is not that easy to find convincing explanations (other than the introduction of progressive taxation) that can account for the non-recovery of large fortunes. For instance, explanations based on hypothetical changes in before-tax returns to capital do not seem to work. All capital holders should have been hit by a reduction in before-tax asset returns. The point is that large fortunes were unable to recover from the 1914–45 shocks, while fortunes that were slightly smaller did recover perfectly well. One needs an explanation that applies only to the top of the distribution and nowhere else, and progressive taxation looks like an obvious candidate.

Another possible explanation would be the existence of a large public sector in France after the nationalizations of 1945. But the negative impact on private capital accumulation would seem to apply to all capital holders, or at least to broader segments of the wealth distribution than simply the very top. Moreover, one should not exaggerate the importance of the public sector in post-war France.

42 See Piketty 2001*a*: appendix J, pp. 767–71.

For instance, the output share of nationalized firms never went above 15–20% in the manufacturing sector.[43] This is a substantial share in absolute terms, but this does not seem sufficient to explain the magnitude of the observed trends. Although there was a public sector in postwar France, the point is that private capital accumulation could freely take place in at least 80–85% of the manufacturing sector. It is also interesting to note that Carré et al. (1972), in their standard account of post-war growth in France, have pointed out that the bulk of the growth performance came from manufacturing sub-sectors where there was almost no nationalized firm.[44] This suggests that there were plenty of economic opportunities to accumulate large fortunes with little interference with the public sector.

Assuming that the rise of progressive taxation is indeed the right explanation for the observed facts (or at least for a significant fraction of the observed facts), what was the economic impact of the non-recovery of large fortunes? More generally, what were the consequences for the performance of the French economy of the shocks incurred by capital owners during the 1914–45 period and the structural decline in the concentration of wealth? It is obviously very difficult to give a satisfactory answer to such a complex question. One could try to construct a historical micro data base on French firms so as to compare the growth performance of firms with different levels of capital dispersion and different levels of exposure to shocks during the 1914–45 period. In the meantime, one can make a number of simple remarks based on available macro-economic data.

First of all, the decline in wealth concentration does not seem to have been an obstacle to growth. Growth rates were extremely high from the late 1940s to the 1970s, and this period is now referred to as the '*Trente Glorieuses*' (the 'Thirty Glorious Years') in France.[45] Needless to say, these very high growth rates are to a large extent the consequence of the abysmal economic performance of the 1914–45 period (which was itself the consequence of the two World Wars and the Great Depression). During the '*Trente Glorieuses*', France was simply catching up with the most advanced capitalist countries, and in particular with the United States. According to Maddison's estimates, the ratio between US GDP per capita and French GDP per capita (both expressed in PPP terms) was about 1.4–1.5 at the eve of the First World War, up to 1.8 in 1950, and down to 1.2–1.3 in the late 1970s (this ratio has stabilized around 1.2–1.3 during the 1980s–90s).[46] Of course, one cannot rule out the possibility that French growth rates would have been even higher during the '*Trente Glorieuses*' if capital concentration had remained at the same level as in 1914. Note however that several macro-economic

[43] According to (incomplete) estimates given by Delion and Durupty (1982: p. 191), this output share was around 15–20% between 1945 and 1982, and it soon reached 30% between 1982 and 1986 (following the nationalizations of 1982), before being drastically reduced following the privatizations of 1986–87. Nationalized firms have been privatized one by one since 1986–87, and the public sector share is now converging toward 0%.

[44] See Carré, Dubois, and Malinvaud 1972: pp. 614–15.

[45] The idea of the '*Trente Glorieuses*' was coined by Fourastié (1979). Average real household income grew at about 5% per year between 1948 and 1978 in France (see Piketty 2001*a*: p. 72).

[46] See Maddison 1995: pp. 194–7.

historians have suggested that the decline in wealth concentration might have had a positive growth impact. For instance, Carré, Dubois and Malinvaud (1972) have pointed out that wealth redistribution during the 1914–45 period (in particular the inflation induced redistribution from creditors to debtors) might have favoured the development of new firms and new generations of entrepreneurs.[47] In presence of credit constraints, high capital concentration can indeed entail negative consequences for productive efficiency, and wealth redistribution can under certain conditions have positive efficiency effects. This is all very hypothetical however, and extensive research based on new micro-data sets would be necessary to test these hypotheses.

It is also important to emphasize that the rise of progressive taxation had apparently no negative impact on aggregate capital accumulation. As was already noted above, the (capital stock)/(national income) ratio seems to have fully recovered from the 1914–45 shocks, with a ratio around 5 both at the eve of the First World War and in the late 1990s. That is, the fall of large fortunes was compensated by rapid accumulation at intermediate and moderately high wealth levels, so that the structural decline in capital concentration seems to have had little impact on the average capital stock. It is interesting to note that this is exactly what the Barro-Becker dynastic model of capital accumulation would predict. In the presence of progressive taxation, dynastic preferences with a fixed rate of time preference imply that capital de-accumulation by the wealthy will be fully compensated by increased accumulation from individuals with lower wealth.[48] This does mean however that there is no efficiency cost: aggregate capital stock will recover in the long run, but it might well be inefficiently low during the transition. The analysis of the efficiency properties of progressive taxation in less extreme and more realistic models of capital accumulation is an issue that would deserve further research.

Finally, it is important to note that although progressive taxation seems to have had a substantial dynamic impact on capital concentration, its static impact on income inequality has been more moderate. During the 1990s, the after-tax top decile income share was quite close to the before-tax top decile share (30% vs. 33%). This reflects the fact that effective income tax rates have always been fairly moderate for the vast majority of top decile taxpayers (e.g. effective tax rates have never exceeded 5–10% at the level of fractile P90–95). Unsurprisingly, the impact is larger for higher incomes: during the 1990s, the after-tax top percentile income share is about 25% smaller than the before-tax top percentile income share (6% vs. 8%). At the level of fractile P99.99–100, after-tax income shares are more than 40% smaller than before tax income shares during the 1990s (0.35% vs. 0.6%).[49] It looks as if progressive taxation was designed to hit top capital incomes rather than to reduce drastically the top decile income share as a whole.[50]

[47] See Carré et al. 1972: 457–9 and 620.

[48] For a formal proof, see the Appendix to this chapter and Piketty 2001*b*: pp. 30–2.

[49] Series on after-tax income shares were computed by applying effective tax rates series to pre-tax income shares series (see Piketty 2001*a*: table B22, pp. 640–1).

[50] This conclusion would not be dramatically altered by the inclusion of non-taxable income transfers (most income transfers (pensions, unemployment benefits, etc.) are taxable and are therefore already taken into account in our before tax series).

3.5 HOW SPECIFIC IS THE FRENCH EXPERIENCE?

Estimates for other continental European countries (see Chapters 9, 10, and 11 in this volume) seem consistent with my French findings. First, the secular decline in the top decile income share seems to have occurred in all European countries during a specific time period, i.e. between 1914 and 1945 (and especially during the 1930s and the Second World War). Next, the substantial 1914–45 decline in the top decile share seems to be due for the most part to the top percentile share. Existing estimates also suggest that countries with larger war destructions experienced a larger decline of their top centile income share (for instance, total decline was apparently larger in Germany than in the UK), which again is consistent with my explanation. This would seem to imply that the 1914–45 inequality decline was in all European countries an accidental, capital-income phenomenon (for the most part).

The US case is particularly interesting. Kuznets (1953) used US tax returns statistics to construct annual 1913–48 top income shares series, and these series constitute a most valuable source of information on US inequality dynamics during the first half of the twentieth century (see also Chapter 5). Kuznets's series show that the significant decline in the top decile income share that took place between 1913 and 1948 is almost entirely due to the sharp decline of the top percentile income share. The total decline of the top percentile income share, though very significant, seems smaller than what I found in France. This is consistent with the capital-income explanation: the World Wars induced a much more severe shock on capital holders in France than in the US (unlike the Great Depression of the 1930s, which was more severe in the US). Kuznets's series also confirm that the inequality decline was not a linear, continuous process: the top percentile income share dropped during the First World War, recovered during the 1920s, and dropped again during the Great Depression and the Second World War.

Unfortunately, Kuznets did not construct separate series for wage inequality (there was no separate wage tax in the US, so the data are less rich than in France). It is therefore impossible to undertake the same kind of test than what I did for France. In particular, it is impossible to know whether US wage inequality declined significantly during the 1900–50 period (which would mean that what happened was not just an accidental capital-income phenomenon). (But see Chapter 5 below.) Since the time of Kuznets, several economists have collected long term, occupational wage data in order to shed light on this issue.[51] These data do show that there was significant wage compression during both World Wars (like in France). However, these data not allow any strong conclusion regarding the existence of a more general equalizing trend during the 1900–50 period.[52]

[51] See, e.g., Williamson and Lindert 1980; Goldin and Margo 1992; and Goldin and Katz 1999.

[52] Given the large changes in workforce composition, it is problematic to use occupational wage ratios to analyse long-run trends in wage inequality. In France, the ratio between average wage of managers and the average wage of production workers has declined enormously in the long run (both

It is interesting to note that Kuznets himself, in his 1955 article, started by proposing an interpretation of his 1953 series that was very much in line with the capital-income interpretation that I have advocated in this paper. Kuznets emphasized the shocks incurred by capital owners during the 1914–45 period, and he mentioned explicitly the dynamic impact of progressive taxation on capital accumulation and income inequality. But, by the end of his article (which was also his presidential address to the American Economic Asssociation), Kuznets formulated a completely different theory. Kuznets argued that there could well exist an endogenous mechanism forcing inequality to decline in advanced capitalist countries: in a two-sector model of economic development, one should indeed observe inequality to rise when only a small fraction of the population benefits from the incomes generated by the high-productivity sector, and to decline when most workers join the high-productivity sector.[53] Kuznets had basically no empirical evidence to support this theory: 'this is perhaps 5% empirical information and 95% speculation, some of it possibly tainted by wishful thinking'.[54] Although this optimistic theory quickly became popular, it is important to recall that the theory of the 'Kuznets' curve' is not supported by Kuznets' series. Kuznets' himself believed more strongly in the effect of shocks and progressive taxation than in the Kuznets' curve, and the first part of his theory seems to have been overly neglected by economists.

Regarding the more recent period, there exists one important divergence between US and French inequality dynamics. Top income shares have been increasing sharply in the US since the 1970s,[55] while my series show that they have been flat in France. The very steep rise in top incomes observed in the US since the 1970s seems to be due to large increases in high skill wages and executive compensation. The large decline in top tax rates observed in the US since the 1970s also provides a test for the theory of progressive taxation and capital accumulation. One should expect the decline in top tax rates to facilitate the accumulation of large fortunes and the resurgence of top capital incomes during the next few decades.

3.6 CONCLUDING COMMENTS

In this chapter I have presented new inequality series on France during the twentieth century. The main conclusion is that the decline in income inequality that took place during the first half of the twentieth century was mostly accidental.

during the 1900–50 and the 1950–98 periods), although the top decile and top percentile wage shares have been roughly constant (the explanation for this paradox is simply that the number of managerial jobs has increased a lot; see Piketty 2001*a*: pp. 203–10). To my knowledge, there does not exist any US wage inequality series expressed in terms of fractiles prior to 1940 (starting in 1940, censuses ask a question on wages).

[53] Kuznets also mentioned that with a higher variance of earnings in the urban sector it might take a long time before inequality starts declining (and it might not decline at all).

[54] See Kuznets 1955: 26.

[55] See Feenberg and Poterba 1993, 2000; and Chapter 5 in this volume.

In France, and possibly in a number of other developed countries as well, wage inequality has actually been extremely stable in the long run, and the secular decline in income inequality is for the most part a capital income phenomenon: holders of large fortunes were badly hurt by major shocks during the 1914–45 period, and they were never able to fully recover from these shocks, probably because of the dynamic effects of progressive taxation on capital accumulation and pre-tax income inequality.

More research is needed is order to better understand the determinants of long run inequality dynamics. The dynamic interplay between progressive taxation, capital accumulation and income inequality needs to be analyzed more carefully, both from an empirical and theoretical standpoint. I hope that the empirical findings presented in this chapter will contribute to stimulate future research in this area.

APPENDIX 3A: PROGRESSIVE TAXATION WITH DYNASTIC CAPITAL ACCUMULATION

I consider an infinite-horizon, discrete-time economy with a continuum *[0;1]* of dynasties. All dynasties maximize a standard dynastic utility function:

$$U_t = \sum_{t \geq 0} U(c_t)/(1+\theta)^t$$

$$(U'(c) > 0,\ U''(c) < 0)$$

All dynasties supply exactly one unit of (homogeneous) labour each period. Output per labour unit is given by a standard production function $f(k_t)(f'(k) > 0, f''(k) < 0)$, where k_t is the average capital stock per capita of the economy at period t. Markets for labour and capital are assumed to be fully competitive, so that the interest rate r_t and wage rate v_t are always equal to the marginal products of capital and labour:

$$r_t = f'(k_t)$$

$$v_t = f(k_t) - r_t k_t$$

For simplicity, I assume a two-point distribution of wealth. Dynasties can be of one of two types: either they own a large capital stock $k_t{}^A$, or they own a low capital stock $k_t{}^B (k_t{}^A > k_t{}^B)$. The proportion of high wealth dynasties is equal to λ (and the proportion of low wealth dynasties is equal to $1 - \lambda$), so that the average capital stock in the economy k_t is given by:

$$k_t = \lambda k_t{}^A + (1-\lambda) k_t{}^B$$

In such a dynastic capital accumulation model, it is well known that the long-run steady-state interest rate r^* and the long-run average capital stock k^* are uniquely determined by the utility function and the technology (irrespective of initial conditions): in steady-state, r^* is necessarily equal to θ, and k^* must be such that $f'(k^*) = r^* = \theta$ (if the interest rate is above the rate of time preference, then agents choose to accumulate capital indefinitely, and this cannot be a steady-state; conversely, if the interest rate is below the rate of time preference, agents dis-accumulate capital indefinitely and this cannot be a steady-state either). This does not mean however that convergence in individual wealth levels occurs in a such a model: in fact, any wealth distribution such that the average wealth is equal to k^* (the 'golden rule' capital stock) can be a long-run steady-state.

Proposition 1. In the absence of taxation taxation, all long-run steady-state wealth distributions $(k_\infty{}^A, k_\infty{}^B)(k_\infty{}^A > k_\infty{}^B)$ are characterized by the following condition:

(i) $\lambda k_\infty{}^A + (1-\lambda)k_\infty{}^B = k^*$ (with k^* such that $f'(k^*) = r^* = \theta$)

Consider now the effects of progressive taxation. Assume that individual capital stocks are taxed each period at a marginal tax rate $\tau > 0$ above some capital stock threshold k_τ.[56] In other words, the tax is equal to 0 if $k < k_\tau$, and the tax is equal to $\tau(k - k_\tau)$ if $k > k_\tau$. Further assume that the threshold k_τ is larger than the 'golden rule' capital stock k^* (defined by $f'(k^*) = r^* = \theta$). One can easily show that the only long-run effect of this progressive capital tax is to truncate the distribution of wealth. That is, the long-run distribution of wealth must be such that $k_\infty{}^A < k_\tau$, but long-run average wealth is unchanged (it is still equal to the 'golden rule' level k^*). Note that this truncation result holds no matter how small the tax rate τ: τ just needs to be strictly positive (say $\tau, = 0{,}0001\%$), and one gets the result according to which individual wealth levels above the threshold k_τ must completely disappear in the long-run. This illustrates how extreme the dynastic model really is.

Proposition 2. With progressive capital taxation at rate $\tau > 0$ levied on capital stocks above some threshold k_τ (with $k_\tau > k^*$), then all long-run steady-state wealth distributions $(k_\infty{}^A, k_\infty{}^B)(k_\infty{}^A > k_\infty{}^B)$ are characterized by the following two conditions:

(ii) $\lambda k_\infty{}^A + (1-\lambda)k_\infty{}^B = k^*$ (with k^* such that $f'(k^*) = r^* = \theta$)

(iii) $k_\infty{}^B < k_\infty{}^A < k_\tau$

Proof: In steady-state, after tax interest rates faced by both types of dynasties must be equal to the rate of time preference. This implies that both types of dynasties must be in the same tax bracket in the long run: either $k_\infty{}^B < k_\infty{}^A < k_\tau$, or $k_\tau < k_\infty{}^B < k_\infty{}^A$. Assume that $k_\tau < k_\infty{}^B < k_\infty{}^A$, and note k_∞ the average long-run capital stock ($k_\infty = \lambda k_\infty{}^A + (1-\lambda)k_\infty{}^B$). The long-run before tax interest rate r_∞ is given by $r_\infty = f'(k_\infty)$, and the long run after-tax interest rate $(1-\tau)r_\infty$ faced by both types of dynasties is such that $(1-\tau)r_\infty = \theta$. But $k_\tau > k^*$ implies that $k_\infty > k^*$, which in turn implies that $r_\infty = f'(k_\infty) < r^* = f'(k^*) = \theta$, which leads

[56] A similar result applies if one replaces the progressive capital tax by a progressive tax on capital income.

to a contradiction. Therefore $k_\infty{}^B < k_\infty{}^A < k_\tau$. This implies that the tax does not bind in the long-run and that $r_\infty = \theta$ and $k_\infty = k^*$, in the same way as in the absence of tax. *CQFD.*

APPENDIX 3B: DATA

Tables 3A.1, 3A.2, 3A.3, and 3A.4 present the data on top income shares in France, the sources for French income tax data, and income and population totals for France during the period of 1900–98.

Table 3A.1 Top income shares in France, 1900–98 (I)

	P90–100	P95–100	P99–100	P99.5–100	P99.9–100	P99.99–100
1900–10	45.00	34.00	19.00	15.00	8.00	3.00
1915			18.31	14.49	7.90	3.03
1916			20.65	16.52	9.39	3.79
1917			20.09	16.05	8.89	3.44
1918			17.95	14.28	7.67	2.87
1919	42.25	33.84	19.50	15.36	8.26	2.81
1920	39.59	31.41	17.95	14.12	7.63	2.86
1921	39.70	31.04	17.32	13.49	7.23	2.65
1922	41.54	32.50	17.87	13.84	7.26	2.51
1923	43.54	34.15	18.91	14.68	7.61	2.61
1924	42.14	32.27	17.96	13.91	7.05	2.39
1925	44.07	33.63	18.16	14.00	7.07	2.38
1926	42.06	32.34	17.82	13.73	6.98	2.41
1927	42.95	32.47	17.45	13.43	6.87	2.35
1928	42.75	32.19	17.27	13.24	6.77	2.33
1929	41.59	30.90	16.15	12.39	6.25	2.16
1930	41.08	30.14	15.31	11.59	5.79	1.93
1931	41.12	29.67	14.63	10.95	5.37	1.77
1932	43.44	31.06	14.80	10.89	5.22	1.67
1933	44.87	31.95	14.95	10.92	5.20	1.69
1934	46.01	32.68	15.28	11.17	5.31	1.71
1935	46.61	33.10	15.40	11.21	5.31	1.74
1936	44.10	31.58	14.74	10.77	5.17	1.74
1937	42.90	30.21	14.46	10.67	5.24	1.83
1938	42.52	29.79	14.27	10.49	5.05	1.75
1939	38.24	27.21	13.30	9.98	4.99	1.73
1940	39.11	27.85	13.35	9.89	4.90	1.65
1941	38.70	27.37	12.88	9.33	4.27	1.30
1942	35.04	24.90	11.53	8.26	3.64	1.06
1943	32.26	22.68	10.13	7.13	3.01	0.84
1944	29.42	20.18	8.37	5.75	2.32	0.61
1945	29.70	19.58	7.54	5.04	1.96	0.51
1946	32.87	22.34	9.22	6.35	2.61	0.72
1947	33.20	23.05	9.22	6.31	2.59	0.68
1948	32.35	21.46	8.75	6.00	2.43	0.63
1949	32.20	21.70	9.01	6.25	2.61	0.70
1950	31.97	21.62	8.98	6.23	2.60	0.70

(contd.)

Table 3A.1 (*Contd.*)

	P90–100	P95–100	P99–100	P99.5–100	P99.9–100	P99.99–100
1951	32.93	22.06	9.00	6.19	2.55	0.68
1952	33.19	22.35	9.16	6.27	2.53	0.65
1953	32.89	22.10	9.00	6.13	2.48	0.65
1954	33.53	22.55	9.14	6.20	2.45	0.64
1955	34.42	23.16	9.33	6.30	2.48	0.65
1956	34.36	23.11	9.37	6.29	2.46	0.65
1957	34.74	23.38	9.37	6.28	2.44	0.64
1958	34.05	22.76	9.01	6.02	2.34	0.60
1959	35.88	24.14	9.46	6.27	2.37	0.60
1960	36.11	24.40	9.71	6.48	2.45	0.62
1961	36.82	24.92	9.88	6.57	2.48	0.64
1962	35.88	24.16	9.46	6.25	2.34	0.58
1963	36.41	24.43	9.43	6.19	2.29	0.56
1964	36.84	24.75	9.56	6.28	2.30	0.56
1965	37.15	24.94	9.58	6.27	2.30	0.56
1966	36.46	24.41	9.36	6.14	2.26	0.57
1967	36.21	24.27	9.36	6.16	2.29	0.59
1968	34.80	23.08	8.77	5.76	2.15	0.56
1969	33.96	22.48	8.55	5.61	2.09	0.55
1970	33.14	21.95	8.33	5.45	2.02	0.53
1971	33.35	22.10	8.47	5.57	2.07	0.53
1972	33.03	21.97	8.52	5.63	2.11	0.55
1973	33.90	22.61	8.87	5.90	2.26	0.62
1974	33.33	22.09	8.50	5.60	2.09	0.53
1975	33.41	22.06	8.48	5.56	2.08	0.54
1976	33.19	21.91	8.44	5.53	2.08	0.54
1977	31.68	20.71	7.79	5.11	1.94	0.51
1978	31.38	20.56	7.80	5.11	1.93	0.50
1979	31.03	20.42	7.82	5.15	1.97	0.52
1980	30.69	20.11	7.63	5.01	1.91	0.50
1981	30.73	20.04	7.55	4.95	1.89	0.50
1982	29.93	19.37	7.07	4.61	1.72	0.44
1983	30.43	19.53	6.99	4.51	1.63	0.40
1984	30.52	19.57	7.03	4.51	1.65	0.41
1985	31.05	19.96	7.20	4.66	1.70	0.43
1986	31.39	20.30	7.44	4.85	1.81	0.46
1987	31.73	20.66	7.75	5.13	1.98	0.53
1988	32.09	20.90	7.92	5.28	2.06	0.57
1989	32.42	21.31	8.21	5.51	2.20	0.62
1990	32.64	21.45	8.23	5.52	2.20	0.62
1991	32.44	21.18	7.97	5.30	2.07	0.57
1992	32.23	20.90	7.75	5.12	1.97	0.54
1993	32.22	20.81	7.65	5.05	1.94	0.53
1994	32.37	20.90	7.71	5.10	1.98	0.55
1995	32.41	20.93	7.70	5.08	1.96	0.54
1996	32.25	20.79	7.59	5.01	1.92	0.53
1997	32.42	20.93	7.70	5.10	1.98	0.55
1998	32.50	20.98	7.72	5.10	1.97	0.55

Source: Author's computations based on income tax returns (see Piketty 2001*a*: appendix B. table B14, pp. 620–1).

Table 3A.2 Top income shares in France, 1900–1998 (II)

	P90–95	P95–99	P99–99.5	P99.5–99.9	P99.9–99	P99.99–100
1900–10	11.00	15.00	4.00	7.00	5.00	3.00
1915			3.82	6.59	4.87	3.03
1916			4.14	7.13	5.60	3.79
1917			4.04	7.16	5.45	3.44
1918			3.68	6.60	4.80	2.87
1919	8.41	14.33	4.15	7.10	5.45	2.81
1920	8.18	13.46	3.83	6.49	4.77	2.86
1921	8.66	13.72	3.83	6.26	4.58	2.65
1922	9.04	14.63	4.03	6.58	4.74	2.51
1923	9.38	15.25	4.22	7.08	4.99	2.61
1924	9.86	14.31	4.05	6.86	4.66	2.39
1925	10.44	15.47	4.16	6.93	4.69	2.38
1926	9.72	14.52	4.09	6.75	4.58	2.41
1927	10.48	15.02	4.02	6.56	4.52	2.35
1928	10.56	14.92	4.03	6.47	4.44	2.33
1929	10.69	14.75	3.77	6.13	4.09	2.16
1930	10.94	14.83	3.72	5.80	3.86	1.93
1931	11.45	15.04	3.69	5.57	3.61	1.77
1932	12.38	16.26	3.90	5.68	3.54	1.67
1933	12.92	17.00	4.02	5.72	3.51	1.69
1934	13.33	17.39	4.12	5.86	3.60	1.71
1935	13.50	17.71	4.19	5.90	3.57	1.74
1936	12.51	16.85	3.97	5.60	3.43	1.74
1937	12.69	15.75	3.79	5.44	3.41	1.83
1938	12.73	15.52	3.78	5.44	3.30	1.75
1939	11.03	13.91	3.32	4.99	3.26	1.73
1940	11.25	14.51	3.45	5.00	3.25	1.65
1941	11.32	14.49	3.55	5.06	2.97	1.30
1942	10.14	13.37	3.27	4.62	2.58	1.06
1943	9.58	12.55	3.00	4.12	2.18	0.84
1944	9.24	11.81	2.62	3.43	1.71	0.61
1945	10.12	12.04	2.50	3.08	1.45	0.51
1946	10.52	13.12	2.88	3.73	1.90	0.72
1947	10.16	13.83	2.91	3.72	1.91	0.68
1948	10.88	12.71	2.76	3.57	1.80	0.63
1949	10.50	12.69	2.76	3.64	1.91	0.70
1950	10.35	12.64	2.76	3.62	1.90	0.70
1951	10.87	13.05	2.82	3.63	1.88	0.68
1952	10.84	13.19	2.89	3.74	1.88	0.65
1953	10.80	13.10	2.86	3.65	1.83	0.65
1954	10.99	13.41	2.94	3.75	1.81	0.64
1955	11.26	13.83	3.02	3.82	1.83	0.65
1956	11.25	13.74	3.08	3.83	1.81	0.65
1957	11.36	14.01	3.09	3.84	1.80	0.64
1958	11.29	13.75	2.99	3.68	1.74	0.60
1959	11.74	14.68	3.19	3.90	1.77	0.60
1960	11.71	14.69	3.23	4.03	1.83	0.62
1961	11.90	15.05	3.31	4.09	1.84	0.64
1962	11.71	14.70	3.21	3.92	1.76	0.58
1963	11.98	15.00	3.24	3.90	1.73	0.56

(contd.)

Table 3A.2 (*Contd.*)

	P90–95	P95–99	P99–99.5	P99.5–99.9	P99.9–99	P99.99–100
1964	12.09	15.19	3.28	3.97	1.74	0.56
1965	12.21	15.36	3.31	3.97	1.74	0.56
1966	12.04	15.05	3.22	3.88	1.70	0.57
1967	11.93	14.92	3.20	3.86	1.70	0.59
1968	11.72	14.31	3.02	3.60	1.60	0.56
1969	11.48	13.94	2.94	3.52	1.54	0.55
1970	11.19	13.63	2.87	3.44	1.49	0.53
1971	11.25	13.63	2.90	3.50	1.54	0.53
1972	11.06	13.45	2.89	3.51	1.56	0.55
1973	11.29	13.74	2.98	3.64	1.63	0.62
1974	11.23	13.59	2.90	3.51	1.55	0.53
1975	11.35	13.59	2.92	3.48	1.54	0.54
1976	11.28	13.47	2.91	3.45	1.54	0.54
1977	10.97	12.92	2.68	3.17	1.43	0.51
1978	10.82	12.77	2.69	3.18	1.43	0.50
1979	10.62	12.59	2.67	3.18	1.45	0.52
1980	10.59	12.47	2.62	3.11	1.41	0.50
1981	10.69	12.49	2.61	3.06	1.39	0.50
1982	10.56	12.30	2.46	2.89	1.28	0.44
1983	10.91	12.53	2.49	2.88	1.23	0.40
1984	10.95	12.54	2.51	2.87	1.24	0.41
1985	11.09	12.76	2.54	2.95	1.28	0.43
1986	11.10	12.86	2.59	3.04	1.34	0.46
1987	11.07	12.91	2.62	3.15	1.44	0.53
1988	11.19	12.98	2.64	3.21	1.49	0.57
1989	11.11	13.10	2.70	3.31	1.57	0.62
1990	11.19	13.22	2.71	3.32	1.57	0.62
1991	11.26	13.20	2.67	3.23	1.50	0.57
1992	11.33	13.15	2.63	3.15	1.43	0.54
1993	11.40	13.16	2.60	3.11	1.41	0.53
1994	11.47	13.19	2.60	3.13	1.43	0.55
1995	11.48	13.23	2.61	3.13	1.42	0.54
1996	11.45	13.20	2.58	3.08	1.40	0.53
1997	11.49	13.23	2.60	3.12	1.43	0.55
1998	11.52	13.27	2.62	3.13	1.42	0.55

Source: Author's computations based on income tax returns (see Piketty 2001*a*: appendix B, table B15, pp. 621–2).

Table 3A.3 Sources for French income tax data, 1915–98

Income year	Sources
1915	BSLC mai 1920, tome 87, p. 766; BSLC octobre 1921, tome 90, p. 746
1916	BSLC mai 1920, tome 87, p. 767; BSLC octobre 1921, tome 90, p. 747
1917	BSLC mai 1920, tome 87, p. 767; BSLC octobre 1921, tome 90, p. 747
1918	BSLC avril 1921, tome 89, p. 629; BSLC octobre 1921, tome 90, p. 749
1919	BSLC octobre 1921, tome 90, p. 750
	BSLC mars 1923, tome 93, pp. 466–7
	BSLC janvier 1924, tome 95, pp. 106–7
	BSLC janvier 1925, tome 97, pp. 214–15
	BSLC novembre 1925, tome 98, pp. 732–3
1920	BSLC mars 1923, tome 93, pp. 472–3
	BSLC janvier 1924, tome 95, pp. 112–13
	BSLC janvier 1925, tome 97, pp. 220–1
	BSLC novembre 1925, tome 98, pp. 736–7
1921	BSLC janvier 1924, tome 95, pp. 118–9
	BSLC janvier 1925, tome 97, pp. 226–7
	BSLC novembre 1925, tome 98, pp. 740–1
1922	BSLC janvier 1925, tome 97, pp. 232–3
	BSLC novembre 1925, tome 98, pp. 744–5
1923	BSLC novembre 1925, tome 98, pp. 748–9
	RSRID 1926, pp. 234–5
1924	BSLC octobre 1926, tome 100, pp. 702–3
	RSRID 1927, pp. 250–1
1925	BSLC septembre 1927, tome 102, pp. 416–17
	RSRID 1928, pp. 266–7
1926	BSLC octobre 1928, tome 104, pp. 688–9
	RSRID 1929, pp. 230–231
1927	BSLC septembre 1929, tome 106, pp. 474–5
	RSRID 1930, pp. 256–7
1928	BSLC septembre 1930, tome 108, pp. 606–7
	RSRID 1931, pp. 270–1
1929	BSLC décembre 1931, tome 110, pp. 1020–1
	RSRID 1931–32, pp. 48–9
1930	BSLC octobre 1932, tome 112, pp. 720–1
1931	BSLC septembre 1933, tome 114, pp. 588–9
1932	BSLC septembre 1934, tome 116, pp. 618–19
1933	BSLC juillet 1935, tome 118, pp. 26–7
1934	BSLC juin 1936, tome 119, pp. 1046–7
1935	BSLC août 1937, tome 122, pp. 288–9
1936	BSLC juillet-août 1938, tome 124, pp. 36–7
1937	BSLC juillet-août 1939, tome 126, pp. 66–7
1938	BSMF n°3 (3ème trimestre 1947), pp. 676–7
1939	BSMF n°3 (3ème trimestre 1947), pp. 696–7
1940	BSMF n°3 (3ème trimestre 1947), pp. 714–15
1941	BSMF n°3 (3ème trimestre 1947), pp. 732–3
1942	BSMF n°3 (3ème trimestre 1947), pp. 750–1
1943	BSMF n°3 (3ème trimestre 1947), pp. 768–9
1944	BSMF n°6 (2ème trimestre 1948), pp. 310–11
1945	BSMF n°6 (2ème trimestre 1948), pp. 338–41
1946	S&EF n°3 (mars 1949), pp. 198–202; S&EF 'supplément Statistiques' n°4 (4ème trimestre 1949), pp. 610–15

(contd.)

Table 3A.3 (*Contd.*)

Income year	Sources
1947	S&EF n°8 (août 1949), pp. 624–627; S&EF 'supp. Statistiques' n°7 (3ème trimestre 1950), pp. 574–577
1948	S&EF n°20–1 (août–septembre 1950), pp. 628–631; S&EF 'supp. Stat.' n°14 (2ème trimestre 1952), pp. 204–207
1949	S&EF 'supp. Statistiques' n°14 (2ème trimestre 1952), pp. 244–247; S&EF n°31 (juillet 1951), pp. 636–639
1950	S&EF 'supp. Finances Françaises' n°18 (4ème trimestre 1953), pp. 346–349; S&EF n°46 (octobre 1952), pp. 882–885
1951	S&EF 'supp. Finances Françaises' n°21 (3ème trim. 1954), pp. 98–101; S&EF n°57 (septembre 1963), pp. 812–813
1952	S&EF n°67 (juillet 1954), pp. 630–633
1953	S&EF n°80 (août 1955), pp. 796–797
1954	S&EF 'supplément' n°96 (décembre 1956), pp. 1364–1367; S&EF n°93 (septembre 1956), pp. 936–937
1955	S&EF 'supplément' n°109 (janvier 1958), pp. 40–43; S&EF n°106 (octobre 1957), pp. 1096–1097
1956	S&EF 'supplément' n°121 (janvier 1959), pp. 42–45; S&EF n°116 (août 1958), pp. 920–921
1957	S&EF 'supplément' n°133 (janvier 1960), pp. 42–45; S&EF n°131 (novembre 1959), pp. 1372–1375
1958	S&EF 'supplément' n°145 (janvier 1961), pp. 44–47; S&EF n°143 (novembre 1960), pp. 1230–1233
1959	S&EF 'supplément' n°155 (novembre 1961), pp. 1622–1625; S&EF n°155 (novembre 1961), pp. 1386–1389
1960	S&EF 'supplément' n°170 (février 1963), pp. 386–389; S&EF n°168 (décembre 1962), pp. 1408–1411
1961	S&EF 'supplément' n°182 (février 1964), pp. 192–195; S&EF n°179 (novembre 1963), pp. 1378–1383
1962	S&EF 'supplément' n°196 (avril 1965), pp. 608–611; S&EF n°193 (janvier 1965), pp. 36–41
1963	S&EF 'supplément' n°209 (mai 1966), pp. 754–757; S&EF n°207 (mars 1966), pp. 270–275
1964	S&EF 'supplément' n°221 (mai 1967), pp. 566–569; S&EF n°221 (mai 1967), pp. 588–591 S&EF n°221 (mai 1967), pp. 534–537
1965	S&EF 'supplément' n°230 (février 1968), pp. 378–381; S&EF n°238 (octobre 1968), pp. 1038–1041 S&EF n°238 (octobre 1968), pp. 978–981
1966	S&EF 'supplément' n°245 (mai 1969), pp. 48–53 S&EF n°258 (juin 1970), pp. 68–71
1967	S&EF 'supplément' n°258 (juin 1970), pp. 46–51 S&EF n°263 (novembre 1970), pp. 28–31
1968	S&EF 'série bleue' n°270 (juin 1971), pp. 50–55 S&EF 'série rouge' n°271–272 (juillet–août 1971), pp. 74–77
1969	S&EF 'série bleue' n°280 (avril 1972), pp. 48–53 S&EF 'série rouge' n°283–284 (juillet–août 1972), pp. 84–87
1970	S&EF 'série bleue' n°297 (septembre 1973), pp. 46–51 S&EF 'série rouge' n°293 (mai 1973), pp. 98–101
1971	S&EF 'série bleue' n°304 (avril 1974), pp. 46–51 S&EF 'série rouge' n°309 (septembre 1974), pp. 24–27
1972	S&EF 'série rouge' n°319–320 (juillet–août 1975), pp. 22–25

1973	S&EF 'série rouge' n°328 (avril 1976), pp. 26–29
1974	S&EF 'série rouge' n°337 (janvier 1977), pp. 28–31
1975	S&EF 'série rouge' n°353 (mai 1978), pp. 28–31
1976	S&EF 'série rouge' n°363–364–365 (février 1980), pp. 160–163
1977	S&EF 'série rouge' n°371 (septembre 1980), pp. 96–99
1978	S&EF 'série rouge' n°380 (juin 1981), pp. 81–83
1979	S&EF 'série rouge' n°390 (1983), pp. 98–100
1980	S&EF 'série rouge' n°394 (1984), pp. 40–42
1981	S&EF 'série rouge' n°394 (1984), pp. 48–50
1982–86	Etats 1921 (situation au 31/3/n+2), tableaux IIA
1987–97	Etats 1921 (situation au 31/12/n+2), tableaux IIA
1998	Etat 1921 (situation au 31/12/n+1), tableau IIA

Notes: BSLC = Bulletin de Statistique et de Législation Comparée (Ministère des Finances, monthly publication, 1877–1940)

BSMF = Bulletin de Statistique du Ministère des Finances (Ministère des Finances, quarterly publication, 1947–8)

S&EF = Statistiques et Etudes Financières (Ministère des Finances, monthly publication, 1949–85)

RSRID = Renseignements Statistiques Relatifs aux Impôts Directs (Ministère des Finances, annual volumes, 1889–1975)

Etats 1921 = 'Etats statistiques' released by the Service d'Enquêtes Statistiques et de Documentation (SESDO) of the DGI (Ministère des Finances) (no formal publication)

Table 3A.4 Income and population totals for France, 1900–98

	(1) Total tax income (millions current french francs)	(2) Total number of tax units (thousands)	(3) (=(1)/(2)) Average tax income per tax unit (current FF)	(4) Average tax income per tax unit (1998 FF)	(5) Total number of tax units (thousands)	(6) (=(5)/(2)) Fraction of tax units subject to income tax (%)
1900	20.2	14,119	1,430	28,760		
1901	19.4	14,119	1,377	27,537		
1902	18.8	14,187	1,326	26,819		
1903	19.6	14,261	1,376	27,979		
1904	20.0	14,331	1,396	28,787		
1905	19.9	14,394	1,380	28,474		
1906	20.1	14,448	1,389	28,310		
1907	21.8	14,510	1,502	30,185		
1908	22.1	14,563	1,518	29,821		
1909	22.8	14,642	1,558	30,660		
1910	23.1	14,708	1,571	29,994		
1911	25.0	14,802	1,686	29,279		
1912	26.5	14,938	1,772	31,123		
1913	25.7	15,117	1,701	28,893		
1914	26.2	15,294	1,716	29,140		
1915	27.4	15,249	1,799	25,740	260	1.7%
1916	30.6	15,205	2,013	25,717	474	3.1%
1917	39.0	15,160	2,575	27,460	594	3.9%

(*contd.*)

Table 3A.4 (*Contd.*)

	(1) Total tax income (millions current french francs)	(2) Total number of tax units (thousands)	(3) (=(1)/(2)) Average tax income per tax unit (current FF)	(4) Average tax income per tax unit (1998 FF)	(5) Total number of tax units (thousands)	(6) (=(5)/(2)) Fraction of tax units subject to income tax (%)
1918	48.0	15,116	3,178	26,127	689	4.6%
1919	61.7	15,071	4,091	26,908	541	3.6%
1920	82.9	15,027	5,516	26,408	977	6.5%
1921	86.1	15,323	5,616	30,692	1,119	7.3%
1922	89.2	15,453	5,775	32,840	1,027	6.6%
1923	99.5	15,609	6,377	32,671	1,201	7.7%
1924	115.7	15,803	7,323	32,941	1,488	9.4%
1925	126.0	16,001	7,874	33,009	1,939	12.1%
1926	148.8	16,147	9,218	29,702	2,589	16.0%
1927	150.5	16,254	9,257	28,569	2,902	17.9%
1928	161.8	16,347	9,895	30,602	1,985	12.1%
1929	175.9	16,454	10,689	31,127	1,923	11.7%
1930	182.1	16,556	11,000	31,778	2,150	13.0%
1931	171.0	16,729	10,220	30,721	2,080	12.4%
1932	153.6	16,767	9,159	30,224	1,922	11.5%
1933	147.4	16,810	8,769	29,892	1,920	11.4%
1934	136.9	16,837	8,132	28,937	1,745	10.4%
1935	131.5	16,874	7,794	30,245	1,633	9.7%
1936	147.3	16,889	8,720	31,537	1,639	9.7%
1937	176.9	16,899	10,470	30,099	2,288	13.5%
1938	196.3	16,915	11,605	29,367	2,795	16.5%
1939	199.8	16,172	12,352	29,323	2,103	13.0%
1940	181.7	16,229	11,198	22,415	1,883	11.6%
1941	218.0	15,368	14,182	24,200	2,733	17.8%
1942	292.6	15,372	19,034	27,044	3,838	25.0%
1943	361.8	15,277	23,680	27,089	2,045	13.4%
1944	439.1	15,089	29,101	27,221	2,780	18.4%
1945	791.1	15,138	52,260	32,984	1,539	10.2%
1946	1343.5	16,536	81,249	33,605	4,149	25.1%
1947	1774.5	16,648	106,590	29,509	1,486	8.9%
1948	3015.1	16,818	179,285	31,315	2,690	16.0%
1949	3843.5	16,962	226,600	34,964	3,413	20.1%
1950	4489.1	17,077	262,870	36,873	2,982	17.5%
1951	5629.0	17,205	327,181	39,462	2,552	14.8%
1952	6621.6	17,302	382,705	41,250	3,370	19.5%
1953	6848.1	17,410	393,338	43,129	3,095	17.8%
1954	7319.2	17,497	418,299	45,683	3,142	18.0%
1955	7938.3	17,647	449,832	48,689	3,765	21.3%
1956	8792.4	17,820	493,392	51,251	4,401	24.7%
1957	9882.8	18,007	548,838	55,350	4,430	24.6%
1958	11382.3	18,223	624,607	54,727	4,984	27.4%
1959	12213.7	18,418	663,131	54,762	5,045	27.4%
1960	136.0	18,613	7,306	58,183	5,456	29.3%
1961	149.1	18,803	7,931	61,144	6,103	32.5%
1962	169.7	19,026	8,921	65,684	6,752	35.5%

1963	190.3	19,535	9,741	68,439	7,710	39.5%
1964	209.2	19,804	10,566	71,792	8,362	42.2%
1965	226.3	20,018	11,303	74,926	8,573	42.8%
1966	244.7	20,166	12,133	78,316	8,955	44.4%
1967	267.0	20,324	13,135	82,633	9,591	47.2%
1968	294.7	20,454	14,408	86,657	10,480	51.2%
1969	332.6	20,734	16,042	90,596	10,503	50.7%
1970	380.8	21,033	18,104	97,186	10,513	50.0%
1971	423.5	21,355	19,833	100,919	11,020	51.6%
1972	474.2	21,653	21,898	104,920	11,502	53.1%
1973	537.1	21,921	24,501	109,405	12,092	55.2%
1974	629.3	22,161	28,398	111,530	12,768	57.6%
1975	729.2	22,364	32,608	114,546	13,495	60.3%
1976	841.9	22,497	37,421	119,939	14,243	63.3%
1977	963.6	22,709	42,432	124,315	14,007	61.7%
1978	1103.8	22,939	48,118	129,214	14,564	63.5%
1979	1260.6	23,186	54,368	131,768	15,001	64.7%
1980	1446.4	23,457	61,661	131,552	15,290	65.2%
1981	1661.5	23,750	69,960	131,620	15,056	63.4%
1982	1899.9	24,043	79,024	132,981	15,309	63.7%
1983	2098.5	24,283	86,419	132,688	15,242	62.8%
1984	2256.8	24,572	91,844	131,301	15,210	61.9%
1985	2418.0	25,144	96,169	129,946	15,252	60.7%
1986	2556.5	25,534	100,121	131,731	13,314	52.1%
1987	2697.4	26,341	102,403	130,682	13,369	50.8%
1988	2836.0	26,791	105,854	131,534	13,470	50.3%
1989	3016.4	27,360	110,248	132,106	13,882	50.7%
1990	3215.5	28,029	114,718	132,943	14,297	51.0%
1991	3369.3	28,607	117,780	132,259	14,643	51.2%
1992	3478.4	29,052	119,729	131,296	14,754	50.8%
1993	3555.7	29,558	120,295	129,330	14,907	50.4%
1994	3634.7	30,038	121,003	127,917	14,990	49.9%
1995	3753.6	30,585	122,725	127,569	15,474	50.6%
1996	3878.3	31,134	124,569	126,946	15,181	48.8%
1997	3979.9	31,538	126,194	127,077	15,680	49.7%
1998	4163.1	32,251	129,085	129,085	17,007	52.7%

Sources: see Piketty 2001*a*: tables A1, G2, and H1).

REFERENCES

Andrieu, C., Le Van, L., and Prost, A. (1987). *Les nationalisations de la Libération—De l'utopie au compromis.* Paris: Presses de la FNSP.

Baudelot, C. and Lebeaupin, A. (1979). 'Les salaires de 1950 à 1975', *Economie et statistiques*, 113: 15–22.

Bayet, A. and Julhès, M. (1996). 'Séries longues sur les salaires', *INSEE-Résultats* 457, *série Emploi-revenus* 105.

Bourdieu, J., Postel-Vinay, G., and Suwa-Eisenman, A. (2001). 'Wealth Accumulation and Inequality in France, 1800–1940'. Unpublished manuscript. Fédération Paris-Jourdan, Paris.

Caillaux, J. (1910). *L'impôt sur le revenu.* Paris: Berger-Levrault.

Carré, J-J., Dubois, P., and Malinvaud, E. (1972). *La croissance française—Un essai d'analyse causale de l'après-guerre.* Paris: Éditions du Seuil.

Cornut, P. (1963). *Répartition de la fortune privée en France par département et par nature de biens au cours de la première moitié du XXe siècle.* Paris: Armand Colin.

Daumard, A. (1973). *Les fortunes françaises au XIXe siècle—Enquête sur le répartition et la composition des capitaux privées à Paris, Lyon, Lille, Bordeaux et Toulouse d'après l'enregistrement des déclarations de successions.* Paris: Mouton.

Delion, A. G. and Durupty, M. (1982). *Les nationalisations de 1982.* Paris: Economica.

Divisia, F., Dupin, J., and Roy, R. (1956). *A la recherche du franc perdu*, two volumes. Paris: Blanchard.

Dugé de Bernonville, L. (1933–39). 'Les revenus privés', *La France économique en 193..*: Special annual issues of *Revue d'Economie Politique* (May–June 1933/May–June 1939), pp. 47–53.

Feenberg, D. R. and Poterba, J. M. (1993). 'Income Inequality and the Incomes of Very High-Income Taxpayers: Evidence from Tax Returns', in J. Poterba (ed.), *Tax Policy and the Economy*, vol. 7. Cambridge: MIT Press, pp. 145–77.

—— —— (2000). 'The Income and Tax Share of Very High-Income Households, 1960–1995', *American Economic Review*, Papers and Proceedings, 90: pp. 264–70.

Fourastié, J. (1979). *Les Trente Glorieuses, ou la révolution invisible de 1946 à 1975.* Paris: Fayard.

Goldin, C. and Katz, L. (1999). 'The Returns to Skill across the Twentieth Century United States'. Unpublished manuscript, Department of Economics, Harvard University, Cambridge, MA.

—— and Margo, R. (1992). 'The Great Compression: The Wage Structure in the United States at Mid-Century', *Quarterly Journal of Economics*, 107: pp. 1–34.

Hirsch, A. (1972). 'Le logement', in *Sauvy (1965–1975)*, vol. 3 (1972): pp. 76–110 (2nd edn: *Sauvy (1984)*, vol. 2: 262–94).

INSEE (1958). 'Quelques données statistiques sur l'imposition en France des fortunes privées', *Etudes statistiques* (Quarterly supplement to *BMS*), 1 (January–March 1958): pp. 33–7.

—— (1966). *Annuaire statistique de la France 1966—Résumé rétrospectif.* Paris: INSEE.

—— (2001). 'Rapport sur les comptes de la Nation 2000', *INSEE-Résultats* 743, *série Economie générale* 189.

Kuznets, S. (1953). *Shares of Upper Income Groups in Income and Savings.* New York: National Bureau of Economic Research.

—— (1955). 'Economic Growth and Income Inequality', *American Economic Review*, 45: 1–28.

Lindert, P. (2000). 'Three Centuries of Inequality in Britain and America', in A. B. Atkinson and F. Bourguignon (eds.) *Handbook of Income Distribution.* Amsterdam: Elsevier Science, pp. 167–216.

Maddison, A. (1995). *Monitoring the World Economy.* Paris: OECD.

Malissen, M. (1953). *L'autofinancement des sociétés en France et aux Etats-Unis.* Paris: Dalloz.

Morrisson, C. (2000). 'Historical perspectives on income distribution: the case of Europe', in A. B. Atkinson and F. Bourguignon (eds.), *Handbook of Income Distribution.* Amsterdam: Elsevier Science, pp. 217–60.

Perrot, M. (1961). *Le mode de vie des familles bourgeoises, 1873–1953.* Paris: Armand Colin.

Piketty, T. (2001*a*). *Les hauts revenus en France au XXe siècle—Inégalités et redistributions, 1901–1998.* Paris: Grasset.

—— (2001*b*). 'Income Inequality in France, 1901–1998', CEPR Discussion Paper n°2876.

—— (2003). 'Income Inequality in France, 1901–1998', *Journal of Political Economy*, 111: pp. 1004–42.

Sauvy, A. (1965–75). *Histoire économique de la France entre les deux guerres*, four volumes. Paris: Fayard (2nd edn in 1984, three volumes, Paris: Economica).

Taffin, C. (1993). 'Un siècle de politique du logement', *Données sociales 1993*. Paris: INSEE, pp. 406–14.

Villa, P. (1994). 'Un siècle de données macroéconomiques', *INSEE-Résultats* 303–4, *série Economie générale*, pp. 86–7.

Williamson, J. and Lindert, P. (1980). *American Inequality—A Macroeconomic History*. New York: Academic Press.

4

The Distribution of Top Incomes in the United Kingdom 1908–2000[1]

A. B. Atkinson

4.1 INTRODUCTION

In 1909 the United Kingdom Government introduced 'super-tax', which was an additional income tax levied on top incomes. This event was important not only for its fiscal consequences, and the constitutional crisis generated by the initial rejection of the Budget by the House of Lords, but also because it provided information on total incomes that had not previously been available on a regular basis. Under the ordinary progressive income tax, with deduction at source and different schedules covering different sources of income, the authorities did not know the total income of individuals, which could be the subject of several separate assessments. (The first British income tax, Pitt's Act of 1799, did require an assessment of total income, but it was replaced in 1803 by a schedular system.) Super-tax, which was renamed 'surtax' in 1927, remained in existence until 1972, by which time another income tax source, the Survey of Personal Incomes, was in place. The tax information has shortcomings, but it provides a source of evidence about the distribution of top incomes covering virtually the whole of the twentieth century. In this respect, it is unique in the UK. No other source allows us to track the effect of the Depression; no other source allows a full comparison of the distributions before and after the World Wars. The super-tax/surtax statistics were studied by Bowley (1914), Stamp (1914 and 1936), Clark (1932), Champernowne (1936), among others, but they have not been used in recent years and their potential has not been fully exploited.

The aim of this chapter is to examine what can be said from the tax statistics about the evolution of top incomes in the United Kingdom over the twentieth

[1] I am most grateful to Thomas Piketty, whose work for France (1998, 2001, 2003, and Chapter 3 in this volume) stimulated me to put together the material I had been collecting for the UK for a number of years. I have benefited from valuable comments on earlier drafts by Fabien Dell, Chelly Halsey, Thomas Piketty, Emmanuel Saez, and Holly Sutherland. I have learned a lot from collabouration with Wiemer Salverda and Andrew Leigh. An account of the UK estimates, with a more detailed discussion of interpolation methods, appears as Atkinson (2005).

century.[2] Evidence for a century helps us put in perspective recent developments in income inequality. Attention has tended to focus on the rise in inequality in the 1980s (Atkinson 1993; Goodman and Webb 1994), but how far was this a reversal of the post-war equalization? How much equalization took place in the twentieth century as a whole? Did the equalization of incomes only begin after the First World War?

The nature of the income data in the UK is described on Section 4.2. As with all data from tax sources, they present the researcher with a number of problems, and these are considered in Section 4.3. The main features of the results are shown in Section 4.4, and a variety of alternative presentations set out in Section 4.5. The composition of top incomes, shown to be of great significance in France in the previous chapter, is investigated in Section 4.6. The final Section 4.7 summarizes the main conclusions.

4.2 THE INCOME TAX DATA

The published statistics give a classification of incomes by range of total before tax income, by the number of 'persons' and 'total income assessed'. This applies to both the super-tax/surtax data and the Survey of Personal Incomes (SPI) based on the income tax returns. To take an example, the Ninety-Eighth Annual Report of the Commissioners of Her Majesty's Inland Revenue shows that the total number of persons assessed to surtax in 1953–54 was 258,999 and the total assessed income was £1062 million. The published tables contain 17 ranges, the lowest being £2000–£2500 and the highest being £100,000 and upwards. (At that time, mean income was less than £450 a year.) The average assessed income of surtax payers was £4100 a year and 37 people had reported incomes in excess of £100,000 a year. The tables show the division by 'earned' and 'investment income'; earned income accounted for 62% of the total, but only 35% of total income in the range from £20,000 a year upwards.

The sources of the tabulated income data are listed in Appendix 4A. The income tax data relate to tax years, starting in April (currently on 6 April). The year is either identified in full (1953–54) or, where there is no risk of ambiguity, by the year in which the tax year started (1953). The income recorded in the surtax (and income tax) statistics are to a degree based on income at earlier dates, with the lag depending on the date, the kind of income, and the (varying) income tax treatment. In this study, to make some allowance for the lags, the data for the financial year (e.g. 1953–54) are related to the population in the calendar year (in this case, 1953). According to Bowley and Stamp, the income reviewed for

[2] In separate research, I consider the evidence for the nineteenth century, including the distribution for 1801, which is the only year in that century for which total income information is available, and re-examine the evidence about top earnings. For discussion of the evidence about the distribution of income in the nineteenth century—see Williamson (1985) and Feinstein (1988).

the fiscal year commencing in April of year *t* may be treated as 'virtually identical' with income for the calendar year *t*: 'it would be identical for Schedules A and B, and is closely similar for Schedules C and E' (1927: p. 16). This procedure brings the dating closer to the income actually covered, but the reader should bear in mind the timing issue in any investigation of the relation between top incomes and economic variables such as inflation or unemployment.

Nature of the Data

The data come from income tax records and suffer from potentially serious problems. There is a tendency to under-report certain types of income in order to evade tax; and avoidance has been possible through the use of close companies and trusts. The definitions of income and unit follow the tax law, and may not therefore correspond to those needed to study income distribution. There is little or no contextual data to help understand the determinants of the distribution, and in this respect the tax records compare unfavourably with micro-data from household surveys. At the same time, alternative sources such as household surveys are not immune from the problems just identified. Household surveys suffer from item non-reporting or under-reporting, and from differential complete non-response, which reduces the representativeness of the observed sample, and is especially likely to generate problems at the top end of the distribution. There are shortcomings that arise on account of failure to tailor questions asked to the chosen definitions, particularly when making use of surveys conducted for other purposes. Users of survey data may be constrained by its design: for example to using a household unit which does not throw light on the distribution among more narrowly defined units, such as the inner family (single person or couple, with or without dependant children).

The tax data for top incomes have to be used with caution, and are limited in their content, but they have a role to play, particularly when no other sources exist for the years in question.

Previous Studies of the Twentieth Century

As soon as distributional data from the super-tax returns became available, they were used by Stamp (1914 and 1916) and Bowley (1914). From the data for 1911–12 (the third year of operation), Stamp concluded that a Pareto distribution (see Box 2.1, Chapter 2 in this volume) with an exponent of 1.685 fitted well except at the top and bottom of the super-tax ranges, where the number of incomes was less than predicted. Using the same data, Bowley (1914) concluded that a Pareto exponent of 1.5 provided a good fit from £5000 to £55,000. The Pareto diagram for numbers plots the logarithm of the total number with incomes y or higher against the logarithm of income. The downward slope of the fitted line is the Pareto exponent, denoted here by α. To interpret the meaning of the Pareto exponent, we may note that a steeper Pareto curve, with a larger α, has less income above any particular level, y, the mean income above y being $\alpha/(\alpha - 1)$ times y. In this sense, there is less inequality as α increases, assuming that the rest of the distribution is adjusted to hold constant the mean.

The super-tax statistics were a natural tool to use in comparing inequality at the top before and after the First World War. In his study of the economic consequences of the First World War, Bowley noted, 'the only definite statistics existing in connection with the distribution of income [before and after the war] are those of incomes assessed for super-tax' (1930: 136). He compared the numbers with *net* incomes, applying the prevailing tax rates, above £3000, £10,000 and £50,000 per year, adjusted for inflation. He found that in each case a substantial reduction: for example the number in excess of £10,000 had fallen from 4000 in 1913–14 to 1300 in 1924–25. He concluded, 'there had been a very marked redistribution . . . the very rich have less than half their pre-war income' (1930: 160). The number with *gross* incomes in excess of £10,000 had fallen from 5000 in 1913–14 to 3500 in 1924–25.

The most extensive use of the super-tax data was by Stamp (1936) and by Champernowne (1936). Stamp took the super-tax data from 1911–12 to 1934–35, interpolating in each year to identify the gross income of the 10,000th person and the 25,000th person. He then examined the correlation between these income levels and indices of price levels. Champernowne in his Cambridge Prize Fellowship thesis (1936, published in 1973) employed both the Pareto diagram for numbers and a corresponding diagram for total income received by persons with incomes y or higher, referred to here as the Pareto diagram for amounts. Champernowne, using the super-tax data from 1912 to 1933, concluded, 'for each portion of the curve, steepness has been increasing fairly steadily since 1920 (except for the *very* rich), thus indicating increasing equality, whereas before 1920 this was not the case' (1973: 84). When his thesis was published in 1973, Champernowne added an appendix covering the period from 1913–14 to 1966–67, taking centred 3-year averages. This is the fullest run of years in any study using the super-tax/surtax data.[3] Described by the author as showing 'a very considerable reduction of the inequality', the Pareto exponents rose particularly between 1939–40 and 1951–52. These results are again based on absolute numbers: for example, the most extensive cover the range from the 200th richest person to the 51,200th richest. The Pareto exponent for this group, estimated using numbers, increased from 1.75 in 1927–28 to 1.82 in 1939–40, then jumped to 2.34 in 1951–52 and was 2.345 in 1963–64 (Champernowne 1973: 88). The findings are affected by the fact that the Pareto distribution is at best an approximation. The exponents estimated using the Pareto diagram for amounts are 1.64, 1.745, 2.28, and 2.34. Whereas the last of these values is virtually identical to that obtained from the distribution by numbers,

[3] After the Second World War, there were a number of studies of income levelling between 1938 and 1949, including Seers (1949 and 1956), Allen (1957), Lydall (1959) and Brittain (1960), but none of these used the surtax returns even where, like Allen, they were specifically concerned with higher incomes. An exception is Rhodes (1949 and 1951*a*), to whom reference is made below.

the values for earlier years are lower and tell a different story, indicating a continuing movement towards reduced inequality in the 1950s.

This review of previous uses of the super-tax/surtax data demonstrates the potential of the source, but also suggests that further exploration would be of value. A re-analysis is necessary to clarify what happened in the years that have been studied previously. The surtax data for more recent years have not been used. We can now use the data from the general income tax contained in the Survey of Personal Incomes. The analysis needs to be taken further by relating the absolute numbers and amounts of income to the total population and total income. This would allow us to calculate the income shares of top income recipients, providing an alternative to the Pareto exponent as a summary measure of inequality.

The Survey of Personal Incomes (SPI)

The schedular system of income taxation meant that only in the case of super-tax/surtax did the authorities assess the total income of individuals. However, the Inland Revenue has from time to time carried out special statistical exercises to combine the schedular income tax information to arrive at a distribution of income among taxpayers. In the days before computers, this was a substantial undertaking. One taxpayer may have been assessed under several different schedules, and may have appeared more than once under a particular schedule. These special statistical enquiries now take the form of the annual Survey of Personal Incomes, and I refer to earlier inquiries by the same title, abbreviated to SPI. The SPI figures are also published in the form of tabulations, but micro-data are available for recent years, and have been used from 1995–96 to 2000–01. The micro-data avoid the need for interpolation (see below), but the procedure for anonymizing the public use tapes involves the construction of composite records for people with high incomes (for this reason, we do not make estimates for the very top group—the top 0.01%).

Such a special investigation was first conducted for incomes assessed for the income tax year 1918–19, at the request of the Royal Commission on the Income Tax, repeated for 1919–20 and 1937–38. As described above, these surveys are taken here to refer to incomes in the calendar years 1918, 1919, and 1937, respectively, although this timing is only approximate.[4] The immediate post First World War SPI figures have tended to be dismissed. Lydall (1959) referred to the data for 1919–20 but discarded this year as 'abnormal'. Bowley said of the SPI data 'its utility was never great', since it related to a time of very rapid changes in income (1942: p. 113). In this regard, the availability of super-tax estimates on an annual basis helps us put the immediate post-war years in perspective. In contrast to the 1918 and 1919 surveys, the 1937 survey has been extensively used by scholars (such as Barna 1945).

[4] The timing is complicated by the fact that different types of income are assessed at different dates. Income returned for the tax year 1937–38 in part relates to income accruing in that year (e.g. the income of weekly wage-earners assessed half-yearly) and in part to income in the year 1936–37 (see the Inland Revenue Annual Report for the year 1939–40: p. 29 and Barna 1945: p. 254).

It provided for the first time tabulations of income by ranges of income after income tax and surtax.

The SPI as such officially began in 1949–50, when the Inland Revenue initiated a series of quinquennial inquiries (subsequently carried out for 1954–55, 1959–60, 1964–65, and 1969–79) based on the information contained in the income tax records for a sample of taxpayers. From 1963 to 1964 this was supplemented by smaller annual surveys with a sample size of around 125,000, and the annual surveys are now the sole source. The Central Statistical Office combined the SPI distribution with information from other sources to produce the distribution of income series published for many years annually in the national accounts Blue Book (hence referred to as the 'Blue Book' series). Data from the Family Expenditure Survey were used to add in non-taxable income not covered by the SPI and to augment the SPI sample for those tax units that are not included in the tax records. The Blue Book series was last published for 1984/85.

In that the SPI data cover a larger fraction of the population, they may be regarded as a superior source to the super-tax/surtax data for those years where we have both. Moreover, for those covered by both sources, the Inland Revenue expected the SPI figures to give more complete coverage, reflecting 'the deficiency [in the super-tax statistics] attributable to the leakage which is inherent in a system of direct assessment as opposed to a system of collection of duty at the source' (Inland Revenue (1920) *Annual Report*, p. 69; see also Stamp's discussion of Allen (1920: p. 122)). Operating in the opposite direction is the fact that the super-tax/surtax figures used here are, in general, based on the final assessment, whereas the SPI do not incorporate all adjustments (see below). In reality, the SPI and super-tax/surtax figures are close in almost all cases. Where there is an overlap (for 1918–19 and 1919–20, 1937–38, 1949–50, 1954–55, 1959–60 and from 1962–63 to 1972–73), I use the SPI figures, apart from the share of the top 0.01%, which is based on the super-tax/surtax data from 1959–60 to 1972–73 (since there is greater detail at the top).

4.3 PROBLEMS IN USE OF UK INCOME TAX DATA

There are several ways in which the income tax data depart from what would be desirable in measuring the annual distribution of income. There are several problems that have to be borne in mind when interpreting the findings.

Timing

In addition to the general issue of timing raised earlier, it should be noted that super-tax was initially assessed in tax year t on the income computed for income tax purposes in year (t–1), which itself was in part based on income of the preceding year (t–2) or of an average of the preceding years. Until 1926–27,

Schedule D assessments for income tax were based on a three-year average of profits, so that 'the profits of the years 1, 2 and 3 were averaged to make the [income tax] assessment for year 4, and this became the basis of the super-tax for the year 5' (Stamp 1936: p. 642). This meant, 'super-tax figures lag a long way behind the real profits' (Royal Commission on the Income Tax 1920: p. 124). The treatment changed in the Finance Act 1927, when the name changed to surtax, and the surtax levied in year t was based on income assessed to income tax in that year. To avoid confusion, the super-tax years have here been renumbered to refer to the income tax year, so that the year 1909–10, for example, is labelled 1908–9 (this is the reverse of the procedure used by Stamp (1936), who post-dated the surtax years).

In addition, the tax assessment could be levied up to six years after the date at which the income was received, the Inland Revenue having the power to assess, or adjust assessments, over that period. The Inland Revenue annual reports contain initial and revised figures. Clark studied the reports for a number of years and applied correcting factors (1937: p. 74): for example, for data four years before complete assessment due, he increases the number of taxpayers by 3.1%. Rhodes similarly compares the assessments for 1941–42 made four years apart and concludes that the distribution had 'changed materially' (1949: p. 54). In view of this, I use wherever possible the final figures, but in a few cases during the Second World War, and at the beginning of the 1960s, these were not published. No adjustment is made in these cases. (For 1961/62 we only have assessments up to 30 June 1964, and the figures were apparently substantially adjusted after that date. The final number of assessments is some 15,000 higher—see Inland Revenue, 110th Annual Report, p. 110. I have not used the data for this year.)

Part-Year Incomes

The underlying tax records refer to units receiving income at any point in the tax year in question. This includes people dying during the course of the year and people entering the relevant population, such as school-leavers. In the case of women marrying, becoming widowed, or divorced, they appear twice (once as single and once as part of the couple)—see Stark (1978: p. 53). The Royal Commission on the Distribution of Income and Wealth investigated the implications of 'part-year units' (1979: p. 36). Adjustments to the distribution of *before tax* income indicated that in 1975–76 the exclusion of such units reduced the Gini coefficient from 37.3% to 34.7%, but had a much smaller impact on the upper income groups, reducing the share of the top 10% by 0.3 percentage points. For our purpose, the key element is therefore the total of tax units, and this is designed to exclude part-year units (see below).

Definition of income

The tax base does not correspond to a comprehensive definition of income. Among the omissions are (most) capital gains and losses, and certain remuneration in kind. It cannot be assumed that these departures from a comprehensive definition have a constant effect over time. Incentives for tax avoidance were much less when the top tax rate was under 10% than when it was over 90%. Legislation has in some cases extended the tax base (for instance, surtax directions for close companies) and in others narrowed the base (for example, cessation of the taxation of imputed rents on owner-occupied houses). In the 1960s, the temporary rise in the income shares in 1965 is believed to be due to the payment of unusually large dividends in 1965–66 in anticipation of the introduction of Corporation Tax (*Inland Revenue Statistics* 1970: p. 61).

The definition of income appearing in the statistics has also changed. For instance, from 1985 employees' superannuation contributions (these are contributions to private pensions) were added back to earned income and this change may have contributed to an upward movement in the top income shares. From 1975–76, the figures relate to 'total income', but prior to that, the distribution relates to total net income, which differs from total income in that it deducts retirement annuity premiums, alimony and maintenance payments, and allowable interest payments such as those for house purchase. The Central Statistical Office (1978: tables D and E) analysed the distributional consequences of the change in definition in the overlap year 1975–76 showing that it particularly affected the highest percentile, which increased by 5.6%. The effect on top shares was, however, relatively modest: the share of the top 1% in before tax income was shown as rising from 5.6 to 5.7%. These changes need to be borne in mind when interpreting the findings. In the case of the US, Piketty and Saez (2003) apply adjustment factors to the threshold levels and mean incomes for the years 1913–43 (see Piketty and Saez 2001: p. 40). As they note, strictly the distribution needs to be re-ranked, but they conclude from examination of the micro-data for 1966–95 that this re-ranking has small effects.

Until 1937, the distributions relate only to ranges of income by income *before* tax, and do not show the distribution by ranges of income *after* tax, limiting what can be said about the distribution of disposable income. Although it would be possible to calculate for earlier years the distribution of *after tax* income by ranges of *before tax* income, this would not take account of the re-ranking of tax units as a result of taxation, and the interval ranges would be inapplicable, limiting the interpolation methods that can be applied. The re-ranking in this case can be significant, and attention is limited here to distributions ranked according to the variable under study.

Control Totals for Population

A key limitation of the earlier super-tax studies is the absence of a link to the aggregate population and aggregate total income. Here, I make estimates of the total population and total income (given in Table 4B.1), building on the foundation provided by the Blue Book distributional estimates constructed by the Central Statistical Office for a number of years from 1938 to 1984/85. This and the next sub-section describe the methods employed.

The unit to which the income tax data relate (up to 1989–90) is the married couple, or single adult, or single minor with income in his or her own right. We need, for a control total, the total number of such units in the whole population, whether tax-paying or not; this is referred to below as the total tax units (which should not be confused with the total number of actual taxpayers). Official estimates of the control total exist for most of the post-war period. For the earlier period, new estimates have been made for this study. Simplifying by ignoring minors aged under 15 with income, the method involves taking the total population of all males and females, aged 15 or over, less the number of married females. Such a breakdown of the population is available for Census years and from the National Register of September 1939. The procedure used, described in Appendix 4B, together with details of the underlying sources, is to express the constructed figures for tax units as a percentage of the total population and interpolate the percentage linearly. Appendix 4B compares the derived totals of tax units with evidence about total tax units for the pre-war period. Taken together, different ways of looking at the estimates do not suggest that our control totals for the population are obviously wrong in a particular direction.

From 1990, the tax unit became the individual and I have taken the total of all individuals aged 15 and over.

Control Totals for Income

As described in Chapter 2, the control total for income can be defined in two different ways. One can start from the national accounts figures for total personal income and work towards a definition closer to taxable income, or one can start from the income tax statistics and add the income of those tax units not covered. Here I adopt the latter approach. The starting point is the total 'actual' income assessed by the Inland Revenue for income tax purposes. The total refers to gross income assessed, from which I subtract the income of charities, colleges and other non-profit institutions, dividends paid to non-residents, allowances for depreciation, and that part of profits not distributed by companies. To the resulting figure are added, for the years up to 1944 (a) wages not assessed; (b) salaries below the exemption level; (c) self-employment income below the exemption level; (d) dividends and other capital income below the exemption level; and (e) contributory National Insurance retirement and widows' pensions. The sources are set out in Appendix 4C. For the years from 1945, when the income tax coverage had become much more extensive, the only allowance under (a) and (b) is for occupational pensions. The totals for wages and salaries for 1949–50, 1954–55, and 1959–60 suggest that the SPI figure is within 5% of the national accounts figure for wages and salaries, and the majority of that difference is likely to be attributable to under-recording of those covered. In the same way, in view of the lower exemption level post 1945, no adjustment is made under (c) and (d), but a sizeable addition is made under (e).

It should be emphasized that the resulting totals, both before and after 1945, have a significant error margin. Some periods are better covered than others by the necessary ingredient series and by contemporary estimates providing points of reference. The war periods and the years immediately following the First World War are particularly subject to error. Feinstein (1972) gives a grading of B ('good') to many of the underlying national accounts series, indicating a margin of error of $\pm$(5%–15%). For the war years and 1918–20 the upper end of this possible range seems appropriate; for recent years $\pm$5% may be a reasonable guide.

Interpolation

For the SPI years prior to 1995 and for all the super-tax/surtax information, the basic data are in the form of grouped distributions, showing the number of tax units, and the total amount of income, in each of a number of income ranges. An interpolation has to be made. It should be noted that I am referring here to closed intervals, with known upper and lower limits to the range. In no case in this chapter is any interpolation applied to the upper open interval.

As explained in Chapter 2, the standard interpolation method, adopted by Feenberg and Poterba (1993 and 2000) and Piketty (2001 and 2003), assumes that the distribution is Pareto in form. However, this method has the problem that, as was seen with the earlier UK studies by Champernowne and others, the information described above allows us to obtain more than one value for the exponent of the Pareto distribution, and hence different interpolated values. An alternative approach is based on placing upper and lower bounds. Gross upper and lower bounds on the Lorenz curve can be obtained by joining the observed points linearly or by forming the envelope of lines drawn through the observed points with slopes equal to the interval endpoints divided by the mean (see Cowell 1995: p. 114). Where there are detailed ranges, the results for the lower bound (linearized Lorenz curve) are normally very close to the upper bound, but in other cases the differences can be more marked, depending on where the ranges fall in relation to the shares in which we are interested. We have seen in Chapter 2 that for a top open interval the bounds could be particularly wide, since the upper bound on the top share is given by the line with slope equal to the starting point of the range (divided by the mean) all the way to the vertical axis. As noted above, no interpolation is applied here to an open upper interval. If there are more than X % of the population in the upper open interval, then no figure is given for the share of the top X %.

In Table 4.1 below, in order to give a single estimate, I have used the *mean-split histogram*. The rationale is as follows. Assuming, as seems reasonable in the case of top incomes, that the frequency distribution is non-decreasing, then tighter, restricted bounds can be calculated (Gastwirth 1972). These bounds are limiting forms of the split histogram, with one of the two densities tending to zero or infinity—see Atkinson (2005). Guaranteed to lie between these is the histogram split at the interval mean with sections of positive density on either side. In the tables, we show by shading the (very small) number of cases where the mean for the relevant range exceeded the midpoint, thus contradicting the non-increasing density assumption. In those cases, the gross lower bound is given. Percentiles are calculated using the bounds described in Atkinson (2005).

Conclusion

All of these problems in the use of the income tax data point to the need for careful interpretation of the results. Where possible, we give an indication of the possible sensitivity of the findings.

4.4 TOP INCOMES OVER THE TWENTIETH CENTURY

Table 4.1 summarizes the results obtained from the super-tax/surtax and SPI sources for the United Kingdom (figures for 1920 and earlier include what is now the Republic of Ireland). Together, these sources cover virtually the whole of the twentieth century. Figures 4.1 and 4.2 show graphically the shares in total gross income of a number of top percentile groups. Where there are missing years, the lines have been linearly interpolated. The break shown in the series in 1990 corresponds to the switch to independent taxation of husbands and wives. The switch from a net of deductions definition in 1975 is marked by a line in Table 4.1 but no break is shown in Figure 4.1 and 4.2. It should be noted that all the results in this section relate to the distribution of income before tax; evidence from 1937 concerning the after tax distribution is presented in Section 4.5.

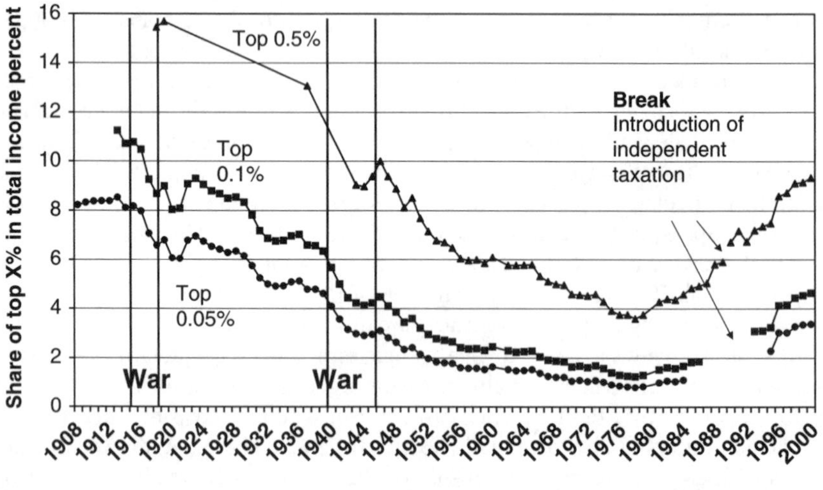

Figure 4.1 Share of total gross income of the top 0.05%, 0.1%, and 0.5% in the UK, 1908–2000

Source: See Table 4.1, this volume.

Table 4.1 Shares in total before tax income, UK 1908–2000

	Top 10%	Top 5%	Top 1%	Top 0.5%	Top 0.1%	Top 0.05%	Top 0.01%
1908						8.22	4.04
1909						8.31	4.12
1910						8.37	4.18
1911						8.38	4.19
1912						8.38	4.15
1913					11.24	8.53	4.25
1914					10.71	8.11	4.04
1915					10.77	8.17	4.07
1916					10.47	7.97	4.00
1917					9.26	7.06	3.52
1918	37.03	30.35	19.24	15.46	8.68	6.58	3.21
1919	38.73	31.48	19.59	15.69	8.98	6.79	3.32
1920					8.03	6.06	2.94
1921					8.08	6.04	2.90
1922					9.07	6.78	3.23
1923					9.29	6.95	3.34
1924					9.05	6.74	3.23
1925					8.79	6.53	3.13
1926					8.67	6.42	3.07
1927					8.49	6.28	3.01
1928					8.54	6.34	3.04
1929					8.33	6.15	2.93
1930					7.81	5.74	2.71
1931					7.17	5.24	2.44
1932					6.87	5.00	2.32
1933					6.75	4.91	2.24
1934					6.78	4.92	2.23
1935					6.96	5.08	2.35
1936					7.03	5.12	2.35
1937	38.37	29.75	16.98	13.07	6.59	4.78	2.18
1938					6.57	4.79	2.21
1939					6.35	4.61	2.13
1940					5.67	4.09	1.84
1941					5.00	3.57	1.57
1942					4.44	3.15	1.37
1943				9.04	4.23	2.98	1.28
1944				8.97	4.13	2.90	1.22
1945				9.38	4.23	2.95	1.23
1946				10.00	4.48	3.10	1.27
1947				9.38	4.10	2.81	1.14
1948				8.88	3.86	2.63	1.05
1949	32.25	23.39	11.47	8.12	3.45	2.34	0.94
1950				8.51	3.59	2.42	0.96
1951			10.89	7.69	3.21	2.15	0.85
1952			10.20	7.15	2.95	1.97	0.77
1953			9.72	6.78	2.77	1.84	0.70
1954	30.63	21.22	9.67	6.71	2.72	1.80	0.67
1955			9.30	6.48	2.65	1.77	0.68
1956			8.75	6.03	2.42	1.60	0.61
1957			8.70	5.96	2.37	1.57	0.59

(*contd.*)

Table 4.1 (*contd.*)

	Top 10%	Top 5%	Top 1%	Top 0.5%	Top 0.1%	Top 0.05%	Top 0.01%
1958			8.76	5.98	2.38	1.57	0.60
1959	29.96	20.26	8.60	5.85	2.30	1.52	0.60
1960			8.87	6.08	2.45	1.63	0.63
1961							
1962	29.37	19.72	8.43	5.76	2.29	1.52	0.58
1963	29.94	20.10	8.49	5.76	2.23	1.47	0.57
1964	29.91	20.07	8.48	5.77	2.26	1.49	0.58
1965	29.88	20.10	8.55	5.79	2.28	1.52	0.62
1966	28.94	19.22	7.92	5.32	2.04	1.37	0.52
1967	28.78	18.99	7.69	5.11	1.91	1.25	0.51
1968	28.55	18.76	7.54	5.00	1.87	1.21	0.47
1969	28.72	18.86	7.46	4.96	1.85	1.22	0.47
1970	28.82	18.65	7.05	4.59	1.64	1.05	0.42
1971	29.29	18.81	7.02	4.56	1.67	1.09	0.40
1972	28.90	18.48	6.94	4.52	1.61	1.04	0.37
1973	28.31	18.18	6.99	4.59	1.68	1.08	0.40
1974	28.10	17.77	6.54	4.29	1.58	1.02	0.37
1975	27.82	17.40	6.10	3.92	1.40	0.91	0.31
1976	27.89	17.33	5.89	3.75	1.30	0.86	0.30
1977	27.96	17.33	5.93	3.75	1.27	0.82	0.28
1978	27.78	17.11	5.72	3.60	1.24	0.79	0.28
1979	28.37	17.57	5.93	3.76	1.30	0.83	0.31
1980							
1981	31.03	19.45	6.67	4.27	1.53	0.99	
1982	31.23	19.65	6.85	4.40	1.61	1.07	
1983	31.76	19.98	6.83	4.36	1.58	1.04	
1984	32.52	20.67	7.16	4.59	1.67	1.10	
1985	32.65	20.75	7.40	4.83	1.82		
1986	32.94	21.04	7.55	4.92	1.86		
1987	33.27	21.38	7.78	5.04			
1988	34.21	22.37	8.63	5.80			
1989	34.15	22.51	8.67	5.90			
1990	36.90	24.43	9.80	6.72			
1991	37.65	25.13	10.32	7.18			
1992	37.64	24.89	9.86	6.74			
1993	38.34	25.51	10.36	7.20	3.09		
1994	38.33	25.62	10.60	7.36	3.10		
1995	38.51	25.80	10.75	7.49	3.24	2.28	
1996	39.30	26.85	11.90	8.59	4.13	3.03	
1997	38.94	26.78	12.07	8.72	4.15	3.02	
1998	39.47	27.42	12.53	9.11	4.44	3.27	
1999	38.97	27.18	12.51	9.15	4.54	3.35	
2000	38.43	27.04	12.67	9.33	4.64	3.37	

Note: [shaded] denotes non-decreasing density assumption not satisfied; gross lower bound used.

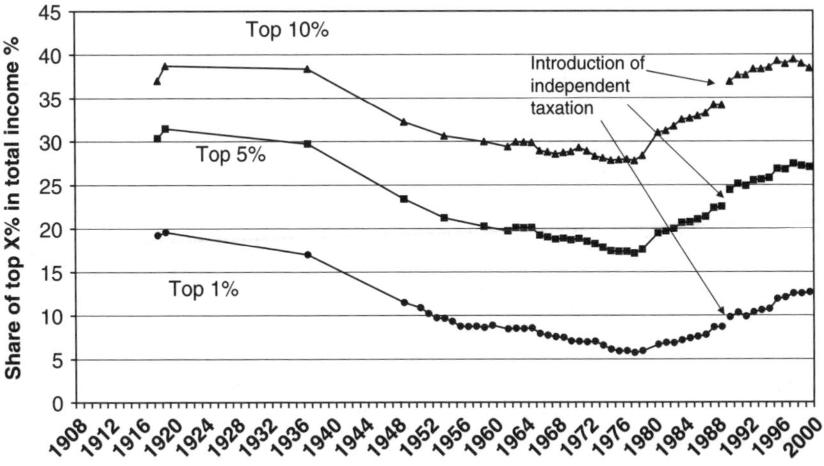

Figure 4.2 Share of total gross income of the top 1%, 5%, and 10% in the UK, 1908–2000

Source: Table 4.1, this volume.

Before and After the First World War

When super-tax began, those subject to tax coincided in size, if not in composition, with the 'Upper Ten Thousand'. This term originated in the United States, but has British resonance: for example the number of landowners listed as owning more than 1000 acres in 1880 was some 10,000 (Cannadine 1990: p. 9). There were many outside this class who were comfortably well off: for example, in August 1914 there were estimated to be 151,000 private motor cars in use (Bowley 1919: 22n). But the super-tax payers were more than comfortably off. The share of the top 0.05% was more than 8%, or 160 times their proportionate share. The share of the top 0.01%, an even smaller group (shown in the final column of Table 4.1), was 4%, or 400 times their proportionate share. Super-tax was only payable on incomes in excess of £5000 a year, which is estimated here to be some 70 times the average income of tax units, equivalent today to some £1.5 million a year. To give some idea of the position of those on the margin of being super-tax payers, we may note that Bonar Law, the businessman who became leader of the Conservative Party in the House of Commons in 1911, had an income of around £6000 a year, of which £4500 came from investments and the remainder from directorships (Blake 1955: p. 37). In 1913, the salary of High Court judges (Routh 1980: p. 64) was £5000 (their salaries remained at £5000 until 1954; in April 2001 they were £132,603, or some seven times the average income). On the same salary in 1913 was the Chancellor of the Exchequer (Routh 1980: p. 73). The Chancellor and judges were however soon to become liable to super-tax, as in the first war Budget of 1914 the threshold was lowered to £3000 and in 1918 to £2500, when 'a spirit of sacrifice was in the air' (Sabine 1966: p. 154). The lowering of the threshold more than doubled the number of super-tax payers and allows us to calculate the share of the top 0.1%. Initially this share was some 11% of total income, and the top thousandth began at some 40 times mean income. This addition to the series allows us to distinguish between the top 0.05% and the 'next 0.05%', a distinction that is of interest since at times their shares in total income have moved differently.

Before 1914 there is no apparent trend in the shares of the top 0.05% or the top 0.01%. The share of the top 0.01% in 1914 was identical to that in 1908. But by the end of the First World War, marked by the first set of vertical lines in Figure 4.1, there had been a significant fall in their share. The share of the top 0.05% fell from more than 8% in 1914 to 6% in 1920. The top 0.1 percentile fell in the same way from 40 times the mean to 30 times the mean. These are large changes. How far was the fall in the First World War temporary and how far a reflection of secular decline? The subsequent interwar period has been strangely neglected. In his historical study of UK income inequality, Soltow (1968) did not use any data for the interwar period, going direct from 1913 to 1962. Williamson's analysis (1985) stops in 1913; Lindert (2000) goes direct from 1911 to 1938. Table 4.1 and Figure 4.1 show that there was some recovery in the share of top incomes in the early 1920s as prices fell sharply, reflecting the fact that a significant source of income (rents) tended to remain unchanged in money terms. The lags in the income tax data may be important here, with the recovery partly reflecting the delayed entry of profits made during the war (a matter of considerable public concern at the time). War profits were subject to Excess Profits Duty, which further complicates the interpretation, since repayments of Duty were made where profits fell, and these repayments counted as income in the super-tax statistics (see the discussion of Allen 1920 by Bowley and Stamp).

Over the interwar period as a whole, top shares fell. The share of the top 0.05% went from 6% in 1920 to around 4.5% in 1939. The share of the top 0.01% fell from around 3% to around 2%. The decline was not, however, a steady one. There was broad stability over the 1920s: the shares in 1929 were essentially the same as those in 1920. The years 1929–32 then saw a rapid decline. The share of the top 0.05% fell from 6.2% in 1929 to 5.0% in 1932, a fall of a fifth in three years. The share was then broadly maintained until 1938. We have therefore a sequence of falls and plateaux. Second, the next 0.05 % saw little overall change over the interwar period: their share in 1937 was the same as that in 1917. The income required to be in the top 0.1 % was still some 30 times the mean at the end of the 1930s. This highlights the 'localised nature of redistribution', as was found by Brittain (1960) for a later period (1938–49), to which we now turn.

The Second World War and the Golden Age pre-1973

The year 1938 is the first for which there are official statistics for the income distribution as a whole. The official 'Blue Book' estimates show the share of the top 1% in before tax income as being sharply reduced from 16.6% in 1938 to 11.2% in 1949 (Royal Commission on the Distribution of Income and Wealth

1979: Table 2.4), with an even more dramatic change in after tax income. Our estimates show a similar picture for those higher up the scale. The share of the top 0.05% fell from 4.5% in 1939 to under 3% in 1945, and the decrease was not confined to this group: the share of the next 0.05% also fell. The 0.1 percentile fell from 30 times mean income to 20 times. The differences were still large: in 1944 the Duke of Wellington is reported to have had a gross income of £40,000 a year (Cannadine 1990: p. 630), or 135 times the mean income. At the same time, tax rates were then highly progressive: the Duke stated that he paid all but £4000 in tax (leaving him with some 16 times the mean disposable income).

This was not purely a step change. Figures 4.1 and 4.2 show that, post-war, the shares of the top groups fell steadily from 1948 for the next ten years. The share of the top 0.05% fell from 2.6% to 1.5% in 1959, another fall of over a third. The share of the top 0.5% fell from nearly 9% to under 6%. It should be noted that these figures all relate to before tax income; we discuss the after-tax distribution below.

From the later-1950s to 1965 there was a further plateau, as is shown most clearly by the share of the top 1%. It should be borne in mind that there were several changes in surtax in this period, which affected the lower ranges. The 1957 Budget allowed for 1956–57 and subsequent years the deduction against taxable income of the amount by which certain personal allowances exceeded the single allowance (Sabine 1966: 231 and Inland Revenue, 104th Annual Report, p. 89). (The Inland Revenue tables refer to 'total income' and 'assessed income', where the latter is equal to the former minus the deductible allowances. The statistics here are based on total income.) This excluded from the statistics people whose total income exceeded £2000 but who, because of allowances, were not liable to surtax. The numbers were estimated at 45,000 for 1956–57 with £95 million income (Inland Revenue, 101st Annual Report, p. 93). Since in this year the top 1% includes some people in this range, these numbers have been added back. In 1961–62 earned income relief was extended to surtax. For a person with only earned income, the surtax threshold was in effect doubled to £4000 for a single person. £4000 was more than five times the mean income, and about 0.6% had incomes in excess of this amount. The Inland Revenue estimated that the number excluded had risen by 1962–63 to 425,000 (Inland Revenue, 107th Annual Report, p. 98). The recorded share of the top 1% may therefore have been negatively affected. Allowance for these fiscal changes strengthens the conclusion of broad stability in this period.

Moving on to the mid-1960s, we may note the temporary rise in the income shares in 1965. This is believed to be due to the payment of unusually large dividends in 1965–66 in anticipation of the introduction of Corporation Tax (*Inland Revenue Statistics* 1970: 61). From 1966 to 1974 there was a further significant fall in the share of top incomes. By 1975, the share of the top 1% was 6%. The share of the top 0.1% was under 1.5%, or a third of its value immediately after the Second World War. To be in the top 0.1% in 1978, an income of eight times the mean would suffice.

The Final Quarter of the Twentieth Century

The year 1979, when Mrs Thatcher was elected, proved to be a turning point for the top income shares. In the next two decades, the shares of top income groups in the UK recovered the ground lost since the Second World War. In interpreting the rise shown in Figures 4.1 and 4.2, we need to bear in mind the introduction of independent taxation for husbands and wives. Until 1990, the incomes of husband and wife were aggregated in the SPI data (this applied even where they had elected for separate taxation). The data from 1990 relate to individuals, and the control total has been correspondingly adjusted. As may be seen from Figure 4.2, there was a distinct hiatus in 1990. But the upward trend continued at much the same rate. Between 1978 and 1989 the share of the top 1% rose by three percentage points; between 1990 and 2000 the share of the share of the top 1% rose by a further three percentage points. Even allowing for the break in 1990, the share of the top 1% has more than doubled since 1978. The share of the top 0.5% has increased by proportionately more. The share of the top 0.05%, the group with which we began in 1908, is 3.5% in 2000, or 70 times their proportionate share.

Taking into account the break in the series, it seems safe to conclude that the shares of top incomes are now broadly back where they were at the end of the Second World War. The last quarter of the twentieth century saw an almost complete reversal of the decline in observed inequality at the top that had taken place in the preceding 25 years.

Conclusions

We are considering here groups much smaller than those typically treated in distributional analyses. These are of particular interest since income change for the rich can be quite different from that evidenced by the rest of the distribution. Moreover, the groups may be small in size but they receive significant fractions of total income. The super-tax evidence shows that the top tenth of 1% had more than 10% of total income before the First World War. Since then, income shares at the very top fell dramatically for the first three-quarters of the century, but since 1979, they have recovered the ground lost since the Second World War. At the top of the distribution, we do appear to have a distinct U-shape of falling and then rising concentration of incomes.

4.5 ALTERNATIVE PRESENTATIONS

In seeking to understand the evolution of top income shares, we have first to ask how robust are the conclusions, in the light of the qualifications outlined in Section 4.3. In presenting the empirical evidence, I have emphasized changes over time. To this extent, the conclusions are robust to errors that are constant over time. If top incomes are consistently understated in the income tax data, the direction of movement is still correctly measured. But there may be good reasons to expect the errors to have changed in importance over time.

Robustness of the Conclusions

The results indicate that the shares of top income units in the UK have returned to broadly the level of 50 years ago, but that the degree of concentration is considerably reduced when compared with that before the First World War. At that time, a tenth of total income was received by the top 0.1% of tax units; in 2000 the group of recipients of the top tenth of income was at least some 5 times bigger (the top 0.5%).

How sensitive are the findings to the methods employed? It is evident that the estimated shares can be affected by the control totals. Our total income for 2000, for example, shows a rise of 11% over 1999. This rise is consistent with the recorded income of taxpayers, but is twice the growth of GDP. If the control total had only risen by the same amount as GDP, then the estimated share of the top 1% would have been 13.4%, rather than 12.7%, indicating a sharper upturn in 2000. The choice of control totals may therefore affect our view of the year-to-year changes. However, it seems unlikely that the conclusions about broad trends, or the U-turn, would be over-turned by variations in the control totals for total tax units or total income. The totals for the second half of the century are relatively well established. A variation of 20% or even 30% in the income shares in 1914 would not change the comparison of 1914 and 2000.

Where the conclusions about the century-long change, or the U-shape, may be most at risk is from an increasing departure of taxable income from total income. With the advent of high marginal tax rates, the decline in observed income shares may be in part a reflection of increasing conversion of income into forms that do not appear in the income tax statistics. In 1957, the *Economist* noted the small number of surtax payers and the low surtax yield, which 'offend the evidence of one's eyes' (9 February 1957: p. 490). Kaldor commented at the time that 'for a period of more than a decade not more than a few dozen taxpayers in the whole country had a taxed net income of more than £6,000, whilst the scale of living of the 'upper ten' has remained appreciably higher than this' (1955: p. 228). Titmuss argued that the income tax data are misleading in his book *Income Distribution and Social Change* (1962).

Retained Company Profits and Capital Gains

The conclusions regarding trends over time are particularly at risk on account of the retention of company profits. The retention of profits in private companies was a continuing matter of concern to the Inland Revenue, as in the celebrated William Morris surtax cases in 1926 and 1929 (Andrews and Brunner 1959: ch. IX). Investment in companies that paid low dividends but generated high capital growth allowed return to be converted into tax-free capital gains. In the 1940s and 1950s a number of studies examined the effect of imputing to persons the undistributed profits of businesses. Barna (1945: table 17) in his estimates for 1937 adds 22.6% to the incomes of those with £8000 a year or more (broadly the top 0.05%), and 5.9% to total income. This would imply adjusting the share of the top 0.05% upwards by a factor of 1.158, raising it from 4.78% to 5.54%.

Of particular potential importance is the increase in retained profits after the Second World War: they rose from 25% of corporate income in 1938 to 44% in 1950 (Feinstein 1972: table 11).[5] Seers (1949) examined the impact of allocating to individuals the undistributed profits of companies in his study of the levelling of incomes since before the Second World War. The effect on those with incomes above £2000 (broadly the top 0.5%) of his estimated allocations (1949: tables I and II) would be to raise the share by a factor of 1.24 in 1938 and 1.56 in 1947. As his results show, on this basis, the pre-tax share of the top income groups would be little different pre- and post-war. On the other hand, this calculation assumes that the top group retained the same share of equity as in 1937, whereas, as argued by Lydall (1959), the share of the top 1% in total equity had declined, in which case there would remain a fall in the income share compared with the pre-war level. An alternative approach is that adopted by Kaldor (1955), who compares the investment income recorded in the surtax returns with the wealth of top wealth-holders, assuming that these two groups can be equated. This approach was developed by Stark (1972) who made estimates of the accrued capital gains on all asset classes for 1954, 1959, and 1964. He concluded that 'if we compare the [distributions] before and after the inclusion of capital gains . . . there is little doubt that the shape of the distributions is changed substantially' (1972: p. 77). The Gini coefficient was estimated to be some 4–5% points higher in 1954 and 1959. These were years in which capital appreciation was large, but the size of the difference serves as a warning.

In order to test the robustness of our conclusion reached regarding the downward trend in top income shares from 1937, we can make an approximate adjustment for the impact on the share of the top 1% of the increase in retained earnings from 1937 to 1965, taking account of the changing pattern of share ownership. For certain benchmark years, information exists about the proportion of shares that are personally held (the sources used here are Barna (1945: pp. 72–3) and Atkinson (1972: p. 42)). The fraction of personally held shares owned by the top 1% is approximated using information for 1937 (Barna 1945: table 77) and *Inland Revenue Statistics 1973* (table 94). Retained earnings are from Feinstein (1972: table 11). Table 4.1 shows the share of the top 1% as virtually halving over the 20 years from 1937 to 1957; the adjusted share, shown in Figure 4.3, attributing to the top 1% their estimated share of retained earnings, falls from 20.7% to 13.9%, a fall of a third. The decline in the share is reduced but is still very substantial.

[5] See Chapter 3 for discussion of this phenomenon in France.

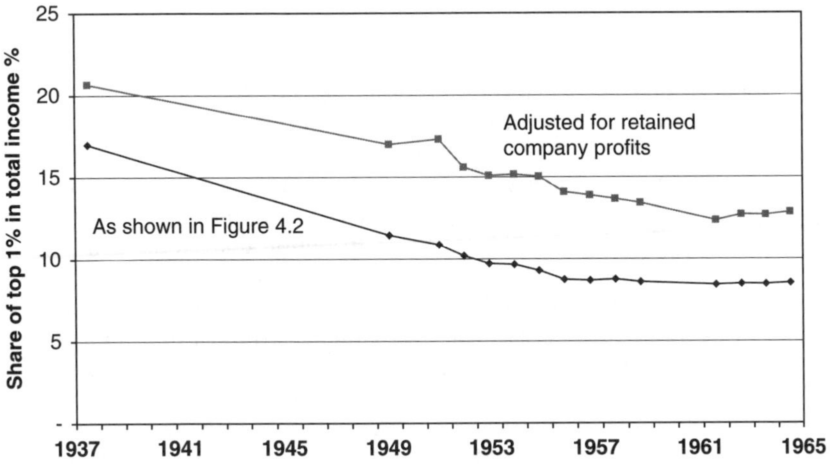

Figure 4.3 Effect on share of top 1% of adjustment for retained earnings, UK 1937–65

Recent Tax Cuts and their Effect on Reported Incomes

More recently, top tax rates have fallen. The top rate on investment income in the UK was reduced from 98% to 75% in 1979, from 75 % to 60% in 1984, and from 60% to 40% in 1988. Tax cuts may have reversed the previous tendency for top income shares to be under-recorded in the tax statistics. In the United States, a large increase in the top shares was observed after the Tax Reform Act of 1986. Feenberg and Poterba note that 'it might in part have been the result of high-income taxpayers responding to lower marginal tax rates by reporting more of their "true" income as taxable income... for example, through a decline in non-taxable employer-provided benefits or through a reduction in tax evasion' (2000: p. 267). Gordon and Slemrod argue, 'the jump in the observed income of the high-income individuals during the 1980s could in part reflect the effects of a reduction in income shifting [between corporate and personal tax bases] and an increased use of wage compensation in response to the drop in personal tax rates relative to corporate rates' (2000: p. 245). In their analysis of top income shares in the US, Piketty and Saez (2003, and Chapter 5 in this volume) note the surge that happened after 1986, but point out that the average increase from 1985 to 1994 is not significantly higher than the increase from 1978 to 1984 or from 1994 to 1998.

The same factors may have operated in the UK, although there are other reasons to expect the shares to be increasingly *understated*, including the replacement of earned income by stock options. From Table 4.1, there appears to have been something of a jump in the UK in 1988, when the top rate was cut to 40%, but this jump is modest in relation to the overall upward movement from 1979 to the end of the century. Income re-arrangement may have played a role, but it does not seem likely that it provides a full explanation.

Shares within Shares

The estimated shares of top income groups depend on the control totals for the total tax units and for total income. As noted earlier, the broad conclusions are not likely to be affected by errors in the control totals. At the same time, the more detailed year-on-year changes may be sensitive, as may comparisons across countries at a point in time. It is therefore interesting to consider the distribution *within* the top groups, since this relative distribution does not depend on the control total for income (it does depend on the control total for tax units).

Figure 4.4 shows the share of the top 1% within the top 10%, and the share of the top 0.1% within the top 1%. (The break with the introduction of independent taxation is not marked.) This demonstrates the concentration of income *within* the top groups: in 1937, for example, the top tenth of the top 1% had over a third of the total income of that select group. The time paths for the two groups are remarkably similar, and mirror those for the top income shares in Figure 4.1. Concentration within the top groups fell sharply over the first three-quarters of the century and then reversed.

As explained in Chapter 2, the behaviour of the shares within shares may be expressed in terms of the Pareto-Lorenz coefficient, or the Pareto coefficient derived from the Lorenz curve. Comparing distributions relative to the mean, a higher Pareto coefficient corresponds to less concentration. The Pareto-Lorenz coefficients calculated from two sets of relative income shares are shown in Figure 4.5. Before the First World War, the coefficient was stable over time, with values similar to that found by Stamp (1914). It rose, slowly, after 1918, and by 1934 it had reached a value close to 2. From 1939 to 1954, there was a sharper rise, followed by a period of broad constancy until the 1970s, when it increased again,

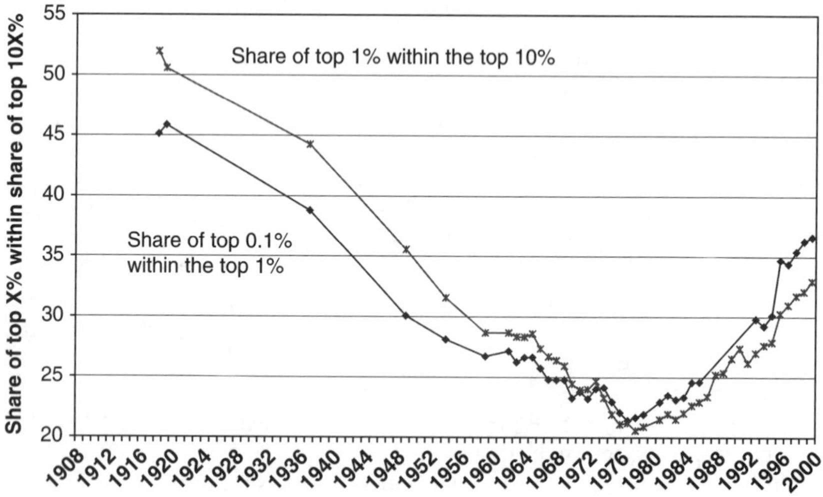

Figure 4.4 Shares within shares, UK 1918–2000

Source: Table 4.1, this volume.

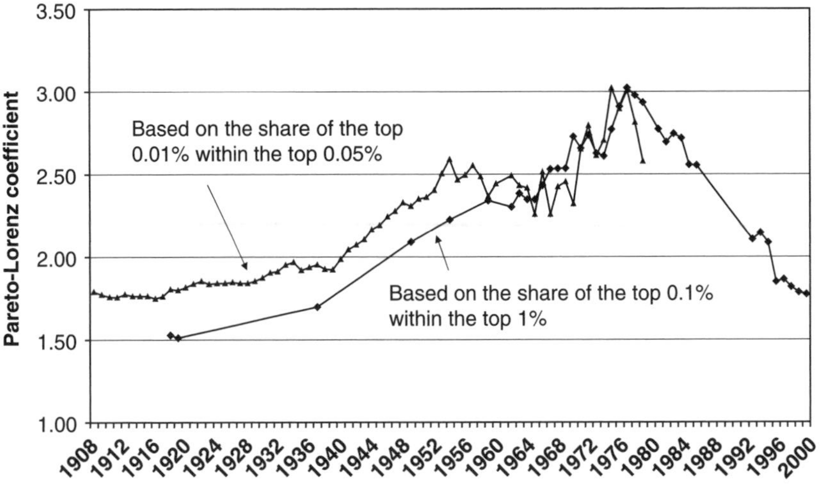

Figure 4.5 Pareto-Lorenz coefficients, UK 1908–2000

Source: Table 4.1, this volume.

reaching a value of 3. The coefficient then turned sharply down. By the end of the 1990s, it was around 1.8, not far from the values found at the beginning of the century. As far as the shape of the upper part of the income distribution is concerned, we appear to have come full circle.

Incomes after Tax

The evidence to this juncture refers to incomes before deduction of tax. While the data for 1918 show the amount of tax collected, they are classified by incomes before tax. Only from 1937 are there data classified by range of income after tax. The resulting estimates are given in Table 4.2 and graphed in Figures 4.6 and 4.7. The rise in after tax inequality is even more marked. Even subtracting 1 percentage point for the break in 1990, the share of the top 1% has risen from 4.2% in 1978 to 9.4% in 2000. The increase has continued after the election of the Blair Government in 1997, and if the trend continues the share will soon reach that observed in 1937. Indeed, in the case of the top 0.1%, we have precisely returned to the situation pre-Second World War.

The impact of income taxation on the top income shares is illustrated in Figure 4.8, which shows the percentage reduction in after tax shares compared with before tax shares. (These are not necessarily the same people.) The share of the top 0.1% in before tax income in 1937 was for example 6.59%, whereas the share in after tax income was 3.65%. This is shown in Figure 4.8 as a reduction by 45%. The reduction in the relative share of the top 10%, on the other hand, was less than 10%. The latter figure increased up to the early 1950s and then remained broadly constant. For the top 1% and 0.1%, in contrast, the arithmetic impact of

Table 4.2 Shares in total after tax income, UK 1937–2000

	Top 10%	Top 5%	Top 1%	Top 0.5%	Top 0.1%	Top 0.05%
1937	35.64	26.10	12.57	9.01	3.65	2.37
1938						
1939						
1940						
1941						
1942						
1943						
1944						
1945						
1946						
1947						
1948						
1949	28.75	18.75	6.76	4.17	1.23	0.68
1950						
1951						
1952						
1953						
1954	26.56	16.61	5.68	3.40	0.97	0.53
1955						
1956						
1957						
1958						
1959	25.91	16.21	5.51	3.33	0.95	0.54
1960						
1961						
1962	25.73	16.47	5.75	3.61	1.06	
1963	26.47	16.92	5.72	3.60	1.02	
1964	26.11	16.32	5.73	3.53	1.02	0.57
1965	25.75	15.95	5.47	3.32	0.93	0.54
1966	25.27	15.59	5.30	3.21	0.89	0.52
1967	25.19	15.55	5.23	3.16	0.87	0.50
1968	24.94	15.37	5.10	3.07	0.83	0.49
1969	25.07	15.38	5.03	2.99	0.81	0.44
1970	25.27	15.33	4.83	2.82	0.73	0.39
1971	26.16	15.89	5.00	2.94	0.80	0.45
1972	25.68	15.47	4.86	2.88	0.80	0.46
1973	25.28	15.32	4.89	2.91	0.81	0.46
1974	24.78	14.71	4.35	2.53	0.69	0.39
1975	24.81	14.64	4.23	2.45	0.66	0.37
1976	24.96	14.68	4.17	2.39	0.65	0.37
1977	25.15	14.77	4.24	2.45	0.66	0.38
1978	25.22	14.80	4.21	2.44	0.69	0.40
1979	26.18	15.61	4.71	2.82	0.86	0.53
1980						
1981	28.49	17.17	5.19	3.13	0.99	0.62
1982	28.52	17.27	5.32	3.20	1.02	0.64
1983	29.04	17.64	5.37	3.24	1.04	0.65
1984	29.64	18.20	5.63	3.43	1.10	0.67
1985	29.94	18.25	5.79	3.54	1.18	0.74
1986	30.03	18.40	5.80	3.56	1.21	0.77

1987	30.29	18.64	5.90	3.63	1.20	0.76
1988	31.54	19.84	7.05	4.65	1.83	
1989	31.29	19.92	7.14	4.66	1.81	
1990	33.92	21.73	8.02	5.41	2.21	
1991	34.52	22.20	8.35	5.67	2.35	
1992	34.47	21.96	8.01	5.37	2.13	
1993	34.94	22.48	8.45	5.75	2.37	1.61
1994	34.78	22.36	8.56	5.78	2.35	1.60
1995	34.88	22.52	8.66	5.89	2.46	1.72
1996	35.48	23.33	9.53	6.73	3.13	2.28
1997	35.24	23.33	9.75	6.92	3.25	2.38
1998	35.52	23.66	9.97	7.10	3.36	2.45
1999	34.95	23.38	9.96	7.13	3.44	2.53
2000	34.31	23.09	10.03	7.24	3.50	2.53

taxation increased during the Second World War and then declined in the post-war period. (I refer to 'arithmetic' impact, as I am not here considering the incidence of the tax.) The decline could be expected, even without any change in the tax schedule, as a result of the decline in top income shares. Equally, we would expect, other things equal, the pattern in Figure 4.8 to be reversed after 1979 as a result of the rise in the gross income shares. But other things were not equal, since the government cut income taxes. The impact of taxation on the top 0.1% fell from 44% in 1978 to 34% in 1979 as a result of the reduction in tax progressivity. There was a further fall, shown for the top 1%, in 1988, and this has been sustained. The convergence of the percentage reductions towards the right of Figure 4.8 illustrates the diminution of tax progression in the UK over the last two decades of the century.

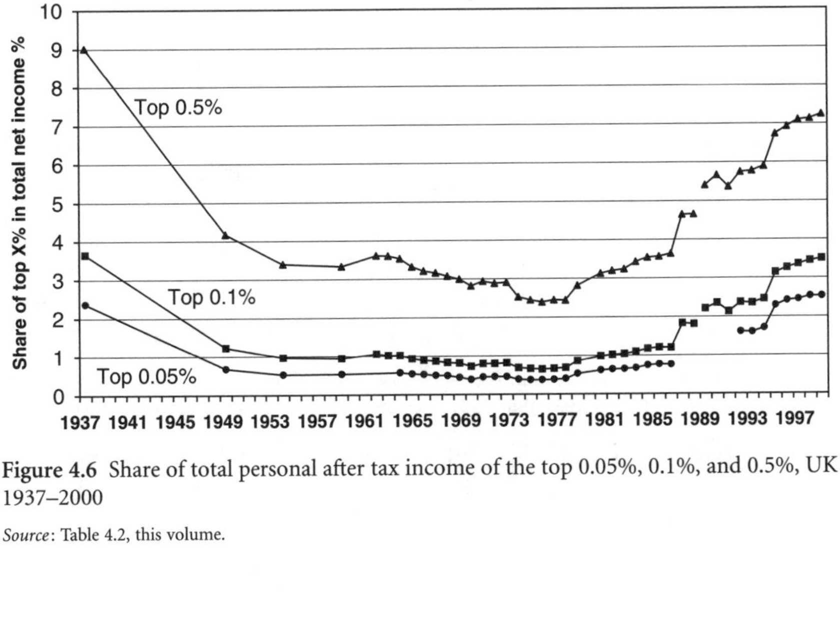

Figure 4.6 Share of total personal after tax income of the top 0.05%, 0.1%, and 0.5%, UK 1937–2000

Source: Table 4.2, this volume.

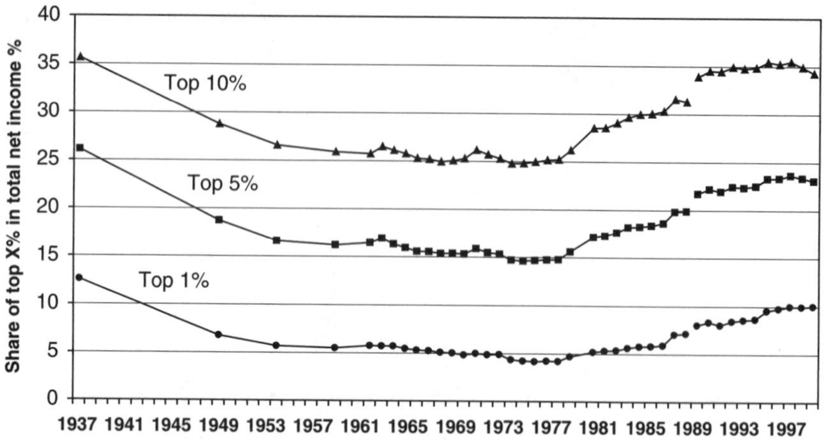

Figure 4.7 Share of total personal after tax income of the top 1%, 5%, and 10%, UK 1937–2000

Source: Table 4.2, this volume.

Conclusion

When presenting new evidence, it is clearly desirable to look at the findings from different directions, to help understand their significance. The evidence adduced in this section suggests:

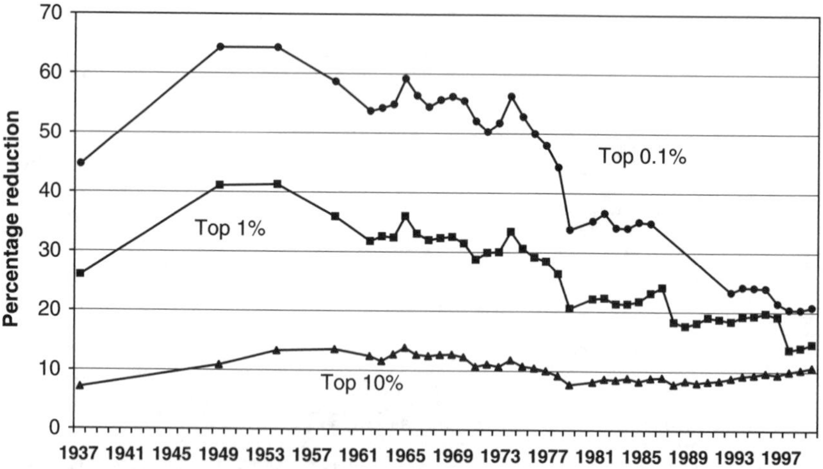

Figure 4.8 Percentage reduction in after tax shares compared with before tax shares, UK 1937–2000

Source: Tables 4.1 and 4.2, this volume.

- That the growth of retained profits did indeed reflect the conversion of income into capital gains, missing from the top income shares, but while income re-arrangement played a role, it cannot explain all the observed changes.
- That the distribution within top income groups exhibited a similar pattern of reduced concentration after 1914 and then increased concentration post-1978, with the implied Pareto coefficient rising and then falling over the century.
- Income after income tax shows the same U-pattern for top shares, and the reduction in tax progressivity post-1978 is most evident for the very top income groups.

4.6 COMPOSITION OF TOP INCOMES

When Crosland described the fall in personal income inequality in the UK over the first half of the twentieth century, he attributed it to a decline in capital income: 'the change has been almost entirely at the expense of property-incomes' (1964: p. 31). In Chapter 3, we have seen the importance of capital income in explaining the evolution of top income shares in France.

Composition of Total Household Income

The composition of income has indeed been long of interest in the United Kingdom. The Colwyn Committee (1927: appendix XV) asked the Inland Revenue to carry out a special analysis of the proportions of earned income and investment income in incomes in excess of £10,000 assessed for super-tax for the years 1913–14 and 1922–23, taken here to represent income in 1912 and 1921 respectively. These only covered a very small percentage of the population: 0.04% in 1921. It was only with the SPI of 1937 that we began to have regular information on income composition covering larger groups of the population. Study of income composition in the UK is, however, bedevilled by definitional problems. It may appear at first sight straightforward to identify the component of total income received by virtue of employment as a wage or salary earner. But the income tax statistics present a number of obstacles to such a calculation.

The first is that some of the distributional figures, such as those for 1937, relate to income net of deductions. I assume that we do not want to subtract deductions when considering the composition of income: we would like to know the salary received, not the salary net of interest paid for house purchase. In what follows, I take the gross income where this is available, and express the components as percentages of total gross income.

The second problem is that 'earned income' is a broad category. The variable available in the surtax statistics from 1946 (used by Rhodes 1951, 1952 and 1956) includes profits and professional earnings, pensions (occupational and National Insurance), and family allowances, in addition to employment income. This has long been recognized as a limitation. In 1916, Stamp noted,

> the official 'earned income' is swollen by the inclusion of so much profit as may be assigned to trade capital in ordinary business, where the capital belongs to the proprietor. The whole of the 'profits' of a draper are 'earned income', although he may have £2,000 invested in his business (1916: p. 314)

Stamp goes on to comment 'these considerations severely limit the value of the figures for economic purposes' (1916: p. 315). In 1912 for example incomes assessed to super-tax were 27.7% 'earned income', but only 4.3% were 'employment, directors' fees, etc.' We can therefore only make limited use of the surtax data. The SPI, on the other hand, is more detailed, providing information about employment income, wife's earned income, self-employment income, pensions (occupational and state, separately), family allowances, and rent, dividends, and interest. Even the SPI is not without problems. The figures for salaries and wages continue to include occupational pensions until 1959–60 (for men and single women; for wives they were included in that year with wife's earnings). Moreover, prior to 1972 the wife's self-employment income is included with her employment income.

In Figure 4.9 is shown the composition of total household income from 1949 to 2000. This covers the income of all households, including those not included in the tax statistics. The income is that reported in the SPI plus the pension income added as described in Appendix 4C. In considering the changes over time, we need to bear in mind the definitional changes noted above. Occupational pensions, for example, appear in employment income until 1959. The broad picture until 1979 is of stability in the share of employment income, and a decline in investment and self-employment income (both 10% in 1949) offset by a rise in transfers. If we add investment income and occupational pensions (to a significant degree funded), then, interestingly, the total in 1979 was close to that in

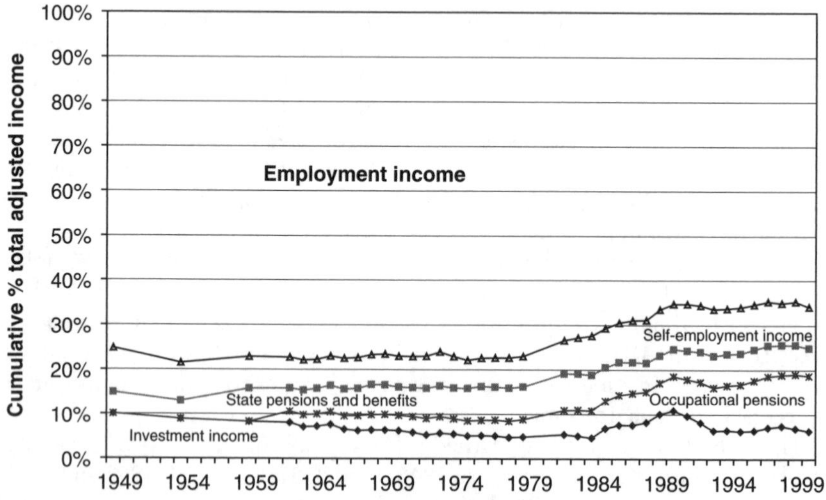

Figure 4.9 Composition of adjusted total income, UK 1949–2000

Source: Based on SPI data from sources listed in Table 4A.2 and pension income given in Table 4C.1.

1949. After 1979, the picture changes. The share of employment income (measured down from the top in Figure 4.9) fell by some 10 percentage points. There was an increase in investment and self-employment income and a large increase in transfer income. If we add investment income and occupational pensions, then they account for approaching a fifth of total income in 2000.

Composition of Top Incomes

How far are these changes mirrored in top incomes? Of course, the composition varies with income. In 1911, for example, investment income made up 72.3% of the income of those assessed to super-tax; and in 1921 the figure was virtually identical (71.3%). In Figures 4.10 and 4.11 are shown the estimated proportions from the SPI of gross income consisting of investment income (rent, dividends, and interest) and of earned income (including pensions before 1959, wife's self-employment income up to 1971). Both are net of deductions in 1937. The estimate is made as follows. For each range, the total earned (investment) income in all ranges above that level is expressed as a percentage of the total income above that level. A simple linear interpolation of the resulting percentages is then used to give the figure corresponding to the shares of particular percentile groups. So that the figure of X% for the top 1% in the graphs means that X% of the income of the top 1% consists of earnings (investment).

Figure 4.10 shows the proportion of gross income made up by employment income (dashed lines) and investment income (solid lines) in different top groups in a selection of years. In 1937, for example, investment income made up less than 40% of total income for the top 10%, but 70% of total income for the top

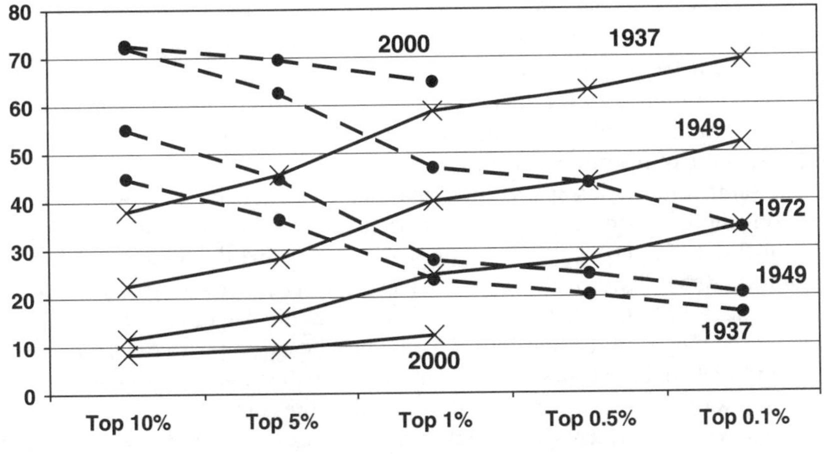

Figure 4.10 Composition of income for different groups, UK 1937–98

Notes: Investment income solid lines; employment income dashed lines.

Source: Based on SPI data from sources listed in Table 4A.2.

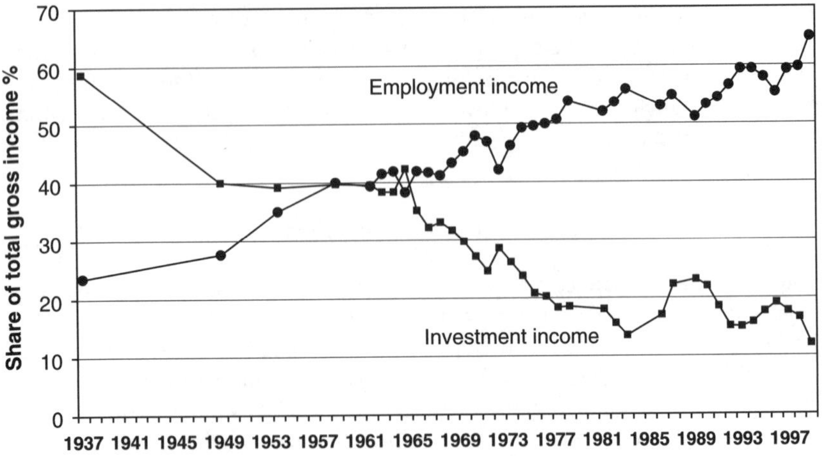

Figure 4.11 Composition of income of top 1%, UK 1937–2000

Source: Based on SPI data from sources listed in Table 4A.2.

0.1%—virtually the same figure as that found for super-tax payers in 1912 and 1921. The last observation suggests little change in composition over the interwar period, but since 1937 the investment income lines have shifted down consistently over time, and the employment lines have shifted upwards. By 1998, employment income accounted for nearly 60% of the income of the top 0.5%, whereas in 1937 the proportion had been only 20% and in 1949 only a quarter. As Piketty and Saez (Chapter 5 in this volume) note in the US, the income composition pattern has changed drastically at the top of the income distribution. The variation over time is shown for the top 1% in Figure 4.11. The proportion of investment income fell from 60% in 1937 to 40% in 1949, levelled off, and then fell sharply from 1965 to 1979. The 1980s and 1990s then saw cyclical variation but a less evident trend in the proportion of investment income. To the extent that employment income continued to increase its share, it was not at the expense of investment income.

The same information is presented another way in Figure 4.12, which shows the contribution of different components to the overall share of the top 1%. (The method of interpolation is linear, which means that the numbers shown in Figure 4.12 differ slightly from those in Table 4.1.) Over the first part of the post-war period, the contribution of investment income fell, as did that of the other components: self-employment income contributed 2 percentage points to the fall between 1949 and 1959 in the overall share. The further fall in the overall share between 1965 and 1979 was associated with a substantial fall in the contribution of investment income (some 2.5 percentage points), but there was also a modest contribution (around 0.75 percentage point reduction) from employment income. From 1979, however, the contribution of employment income to the overall share increased sharply and steadily over time. By the end of the century, employment income was

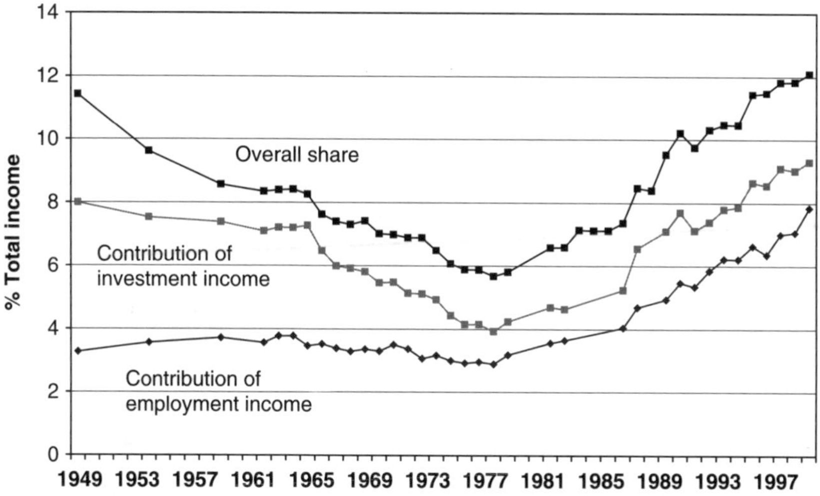

Figure 4.12 Contributions to share of top 1%, UK 1949–2000

Source: Based on SPI data from sources listed in Table 4A.2.

contributing nearly 8 percentage points to an overall share of 12%. Earnings appear to have become the dominant influence. At the same time, the fall in the contribution of investment income had come to an end, and there was a modest increase from the low point of 1979. The changing role of investment income may be summarized by saying that in 1979, if the top 1% had only investment income, then they would have their proportionate share of total income. Thirty years earlier, investment income alone would have given them five times their proportionate share; 20 years later, it would have given them twice their proportionate share.

Distribution of Top Earnings and Wealth

The contribution to top shares of employment, or other sources of income, depends on how that income is distributed and on the extent to which the top groups in overall income are also at the top for individual components (referred to as the 'alignment coefficients' in Chapter 2). Evidence about the former is provided by Figure 4.13, which shows the distribution of earnings among the employed and the distribution of wealth among individuals.

The earnings data from 1954 to 1979 are from the series on individual annual *principal source Schedule E income* published in the IR Annual Reports; the definition of earnings includes occupational pensions (but not National Insurance pensions) in addition to employment income. The earnings data from 1968 are from the New Earnings Survey, a survey of employers that provides information on earnings in the current pay period. The sample used excludes those whose pay was affected by absence during the survey period. The estimates from 1975 onwards are derived from micro-data. Further information is provided in Atkinson and

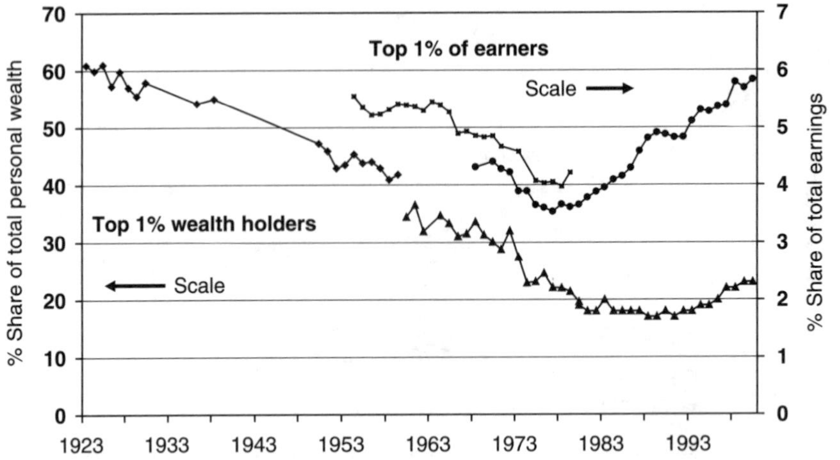

Figure 4.13 Shares of top earners and top wealth holders in UK, 1923–2000

Voitchovsky (2003). It is interesting to note that the share of top 1% of individual earners in Figure 4.13 exhibits broad stability from 1954 to 1965, in line with the contribution of earned income shown in Figure 4.12, and then a significant (1 percentage point) decline from 1965 to 1978. There is a U-shape for top earnings shares. The right hand arm of the U-shape (the rise of 2 percentage points in the share of the top 1%) is well known; the fact that there was a left hand arm, even if a little shorter, is less widely appreciated.

The wealth data are from the estate records, multiplied up by age and social class multipliers to give estimates of the wealth among the living population. The sources up to 1980 are Atkinson et al. (1989: table 1), from 1980 to 1985 from *Inland Revenue Statistics 1997*, Table 13.5, and from 1986 onwards from IR website (http://www.hmrc.gov.uk) Personal Wealth T13.5, 29 July 2003 (data for 1999 and 2000 provisional). There are potentially three breaks in the wealth series. The first is in 1938. The estimates up to 1938 relate to England and Wales; those from 1938 relate to Great Britain. The estimates for the year of overlap (1938) are identical, and the series have therefore been shown as continuous. The second break is in 1960, when the coverage of the underlying estate data was extended and more accurate estimates became possible of the wealth of the excluded population. The estimates of Atkinson and Harrison (1978: p. 166), suggest that the share of the top 1% was reduced by some 7 percentage points. The third break is in 1980, when the series switches to the official Inland Revenue estimates. The overlap for that year suggests little apparent difference. Even allowing for these breaks, it is clear that there was a long-run decline in the top wealth share from 1923 that continued until around 1979. The decline then stopped and, if anything, the shares increased in the 1990s. This is coherent with the evidence about the contribution of investment income to the share of the top 1%, and allows us to take the story back before 1949.

Conclusion

The major themes of the evolution of top shares over the twentieth century in the UK have been (1) the decline in the concentration of capital income over the first three-quarters of the century and (2) the rise in top earnings in the last two decades. Any explanation must be able to account for these striking developments. It is on these major themes that attention has focused. But there are also two accompanying minor themes that must not be forgotten. A contribution was made to the fall in the share of the top 1% by the reduction of the top earnings share between 1965 and 1978. Any theory of top earnings has to account for the U-shape for top earnings shares. Post-1979 there was some restoration of the contribution of investment income. The role of capital income was much more modest in the upswing of top income shares but it cannot be ignored.

4.7 CONCLUSIONS

The UK income tax statistics, neglected in recent years, can be used to generate new evidence about top incomes, providing for the first time a series that spans virtually the whole of the twentieth century. The new data paint a picture that, if blurred in places, allows us to draw broad conclusions about long run developments. Before the First World War, income in the UK was highly concentrated, with the top 0.1% having more than 10% of total gross income. There was no evident trend prior to 1914, but the position then changed. Top income shares fell markedly in both World Wars, but this was not the only factor at work. While there was some immediate post-war recovery, peace-time saw several periods of significant equalization. The magnitude of the change may be need to be qualified in the light of fiscal re-arrangement, but there have been distinct periods of equalisation, notably the period from 1923 to 1933 including the Great Crash, from 1946 to 1956, and from 1965 to 1978 (with a pause in the early 1970s).

Taking the period from 1908 to 1978 as a whole, we have seen that the top income shares in the UK fell dramatically. The share of the top 0.1% decreased from over 10% to 1.25%. Moreover, concentration within the top income group showed a similar decline. The year 1979 was however a turning point for the top income shares in the UK. In the next two decades, the shares of top income groups recovered the ground lost since the Second World War, and have continued to do so since 1997. The UK has not yet returned to the extent of inequality found before the Second World War, but if the trend of the 1990s continued for a further decade it would bring us close to the distribution of 1937. The same is true of the concentration within the top groups. Indeed, as far as the shape of the upper part of the income distribution is concerned, we are back to pre-war conditions.

Examination of the time series picture, and comparisons with other countries, suggest that explanations of the observed changes in the distribution of top incomes are likely to be complex and manifold. There is no steady trend. There have been episodes of equalisation, followed by plateaux. At the same time, certain elements stand out. Major themes have been the decline in the concentration of capital income over the first three-quarters of the century and the rise in top earnings, coupled with the reduction in tax progressivity, in the last two decades. Any explanation must be able to account for these striking developments. But there are also accompanying elements, including the reduction in the top earnings share prior to 1979 and the partial recovery of investment income after 1979.

APPENDIX 4A: SOURCES OF TABULATED INCOME DATA FOR THE UK

The super-tax/surtax are taken from published tabulations, mostly from the *Annual Reports of the Commissioners of Her Majesty's Inland Revenue*, referred to as *AR*, or in the more recent years from *Inland Revenue Statistics*, referred to as *IRS* (see Table 4A.1).

The SPI data are taken from *AR* or *IRS* or the special reports on the SPI, referred to as SPI, or one-off sources such as the report of the Colwyn Committee (1927) (see Table 4A.2).

APPENDIX 4B: CONSTRUCTION OF UK CONTROL TOTALS FOR POPULATION

This Appendix and the next one describe the sources of the control totals that are essential for the results. One of the major sources used in both are the national accounts, published in the 'Blue Book', known for much of the period as *National Income and Expenditure*, and referred to here as *NIE*. A second main source is the *Annual Abstract of Statistics*, referred to here as *AAS*. Unless otherwise stated, the figures relate to the United Kingdom, which up to 1920 included what is now the Republic of Ireland.

Total Population aged 15+ 1990–2000

Following the introduction of independent taxation for husbands and wives in 1990, the total used is that for all *individuals* aged 15 and over. The sources are *Population Trends (PT)*, Autumn 2004: 49 for 2000; Winter 2002: 47, for 1986, 1991, 1996–99; *PT*, Spring 2002: 59 for 1995; *PT*, Spring 2001: 59, for 1993 and 1994. The figures for 1990 and 1992 are linearly interpolated using the figures for 1986 and 1991, and 1991 and 1993, respectively. The figures are shown in Table 4B.1.

Table 4A.1 Sources for UK super-tax and surtax data, 1908–72

Income year	Super-tax/surtax year (where different)	Source
1908–09	1909–10	Royal Commission on the Income Tax, 1920a, p. 26
1909–10	1910–11	Royal Commission on the Income Tax, 1920a, p. 26
1910–11	1911–12	AR 1914–15: p. 134
1911–12	1912–13	AR 1914–15: p. 134
1912–13	1913–14	AR 1915–16: p. 49; Colwyn Committee (1927), Appendix XV contains information on composition of income
1913–14	1914–15	AR 1917–18: p. 19
1914–15	1915–16	AR 1918–19: p. 19
1915–16	1916–17	AR 1919–20: p. 85
1916–17	1917–18	AR 1920–21: p. 136
1917–18	1918–19	AR 1921–22: p. 145
1918–19	1919–20	AR 1922–23: p. 98
1919–20	1920–21	AR 1923–24: p. 110
1920–21	1921–22	Stamp 1936: p. 658
1921–22	1922–23	Stamp 1936: p. 658; Colwyn Committee (1927), Appendix XV contains information on composition of income
1922–23	1923–24	Stamp 1936: p. 658
1923–24	1924–25	Stamp 1936: p. 658
1924–25	1925–26	Stamp 1936: p. 659
1925–26	1926–27	Stamp 1936: p. 659
1926–27	1927–28	Stamp 1936: p. 659
1927–28	1928–29	Stamp 1936: p. 659
1928–29		Stamp 1936: p. 659
1929–30		AR 1934–35: p. 80
1930–31		AR 1935–36: p. 67
1931–32		AR 1936–37: p. 67
1932–33		AR 1937–38: p. 65
1933–34		AR 1938–39: p. 71
1934–35		AR 1939–40: p. 44
1935–36		AR 1940–41: p. 35
1936–37		AR 1941–42: p. 36
1937–38		AR 1942–43: p. 29
1938–39		AR 1942–43: p. 29
1939–40		AR 1942–43: p. 29
1940–41		AR 1943–44: p. 27
1941–42		AR 1946–47: p. 83
1942–43		AR 1947–48: p. 44
1943–44		AR 1948–49: p. 98
1944–45		AR 1949–50: p. 57
1945–46		AR 1950–51: p. 136
1946–47		AR 1951–52: p. 154
1947–48		AR 1953–54: p. 81
1948–49		AR 1954–55: p. 78
1949–50		AR 1955–56: p. 105
1950–51		AR 1956–57: p. 144

(*contd.*)

Table 4A.1 (*Contd.*)

Income year	Super-tax/surtax year (where different)	Source
1951–52		AR 1957–58: p. 96
1952–53		AR 1957–58: p. 96
1953–54		AR 1958–59: p. 82
1954–55		AR 1959–60: p. 84
1955–56		AR 1959–60: p. 84
1956–57		AR 1960–61: p. 92
1957–58		AR 1961–62: p. 207
1958–59		AR 1962–63: p. 99
1959–60		AR 1963–64: p. 101
1960–61		AR 1963–64: p. 101
1961–62		Not available
1962–63		AR 1964–65: p. 100
1963–64		AR 1965–66: p. 86
1964–65		AR 1966–67: p. 111
1965–66		AR 1967–68: p. 86
1966–67		IRS 1970: p. 48
1967–68		IRS 1971: p. 53
1968–69		IRS 1972: p. 53
1969–70		IRS 1973: p. 56
1970–71		IRS 1974: p. 24
1971–72		IRS 1975: p. 22
1972–73		IRS 1975: p. 22

Table 4A.2 Sources of UK SPI data, 1918–2000

Income tax assessment year	Nature of survey	Lower limit £ year (% mean tax unit income)	Source (s)	Composition data (changes marked by italics)
1918–19	Special exercise	130 (85%)	AR 1919–20: p. 70	—
1919–20	Special exercise	130 (82%)	Colwyn Committee 1927: appendix XIV	—
1937–38	Special exercise	200 (117%)	AR 1939–40: p. 30; income after tax from AR 1948–49: p. 83.	AR 1939–40: table 21, income net of deductions, earnings includes pensions.
1949–50	Quinquennial	135 (40%)	AR 1950–51: p. 97 before adjustment for wives' earnings deficiency; income after tax from AR 1950–51: p. 117, after adjustment for wives' earnings deficiency.	AR 1950–51: p. 97, income *gross of deductions*, earned income consists of wages and salaries, including pensions, not family allowances.
1954–55	Quinquennial	155 (34%)	AR 1955–56: p. 67 before adjustment for wives' earnings deficiency; income after tax from AR 1955–56: p. 94, after adjustment for wives' earnings deficiency.	AR 1955–56: p. 67 income gross of deductions, earned income consists of wages and salaries, including pensions, and wife's earnings, not family allowances.

1959–60	Quinquennial	180 (30%)	AR 1961–62: p. 93 before adjustment for wives' earnings deficiency; income after tax from AR 1962–63: p. 93, before adjustment for wives' earnings deficiency.	AR 1961–62: table 76 for earned income, consisting of wages and salaries, and wife's earnings, *not pensions* or family allowances; table 78 for total investment income (before deductions); table 79 for deductions to be added to net income to give gross income.
1962–63	Annual	180 (25%)	AR 1963–64: p. 83 before adjustment for wives' earnings deficiency and p. 88; income after tax from p. 83 after adjustment for wives' earnings deficiency.	AR 1963–64: table 73 for earned income, consisting of employment income and wife's earnings, not pensions or family allowances; table 74 for total investment income (before deductions); table 75 for total deductions.
1963–64	Annual	275 (37%)	AR 1964–65: p. 82 before adjustment for wives' earnings deficiency and p. 87; income after tax from p. 82 after adjustment for wives' earnings deficiency.	AR 1964–65: table 61 for earned income, consisting of employment income and wife's earnings, not pensions or family allowances; table 62 for total investment income (before deductions); table 63 for total deductions.
1964–65	Quinquennial	275 (34%)	AR 1965–66: p. 120 before adjustment for wives' earnings deficiency; income after tax from pp. 97, 135, and 137 and from IRS 1971: p. 71.	AR 1965–66: table 71 for earned income, consisting of employment income and wife's earnings, not pensions or family allowances; table 72 for total investment income (before deductions); table 73 for total deductions.
1965–66	Annual	275 (31%)	AR 1966–67: p. 174 before adjustment for wives' earnings deficiency; income after tax from p. 174.	AR 1966–67: table 103 for earned income, consisting of employment income and wife's earnings, not pensions or family allowances; table 104 for total investment income (before deductions); table 112 for total gross income.

(*contd.*)

Table 4A.2 (*Contd.*)

Income tax assessment year	Nature of survey	Lower limit £ year (% mean tax unit income)	Source (s)	Composition data (changes marked by italics)
			No correction made for investment income deficiency in SPI from 1966–67	
1966–67	Annual	275 (30%)	AR 1967–68: p. 96 before adjustment for wives' earnings deficiency; income after tax from p. 73.	AR 1967–68: table 66 for earned income, consisting of employment income and wife's earnings, not pensions or family allowances; table 67 for total investment income (before deductions); table 75 for total gross income.
1967–68	Annual	275 (29%)	IRS 1971: p. 73; income after tax from p. 73.	IRS 1970: table 52 for earned income, consisting of employment income and wife's earnings, not pensions or family allowances; table 53 for total investment income (before deductions); table 61 for total gross income.
1968–69	Annual	275 (27%)	IRS 1971: p. 73; income after tax from p. 73.	IRS 1971: table 59 for earned income, consisting of employment income and wife's earnings, not pensions or family allowances; table 60 for total investment income (before deductions); table 68 for total gross income.
1969–70	Quinquennial	330 (30%)	SPI 1969–70: p. 11; income after tax from p. 11.	SPI 1969–70: table 9 for earned income, consisting of employment income and wife's earnings, not pensions or family allowances; table 16 for total investment income (before deductions); table 2 for gross income.
1970–71	Annual	420 (34%)	IRS 1973: p. 81; income after tax from p. 81.	IRS 1973: table 64 for earned income, consisting of employment

				income and wife's earnings, not pensions or family allowances; table 65 for total investment income (before deductions); table 67 for gross income.
1971–72	Annual	420 (32%)	IRS 1974: p. 42; income after tax from p. 42.	IRS 1974: table 44 for earned income, consisting of employment income, not pensions or family allowances; table 49 for total investment income (before deductions); table 35 for gross income.
1972–73	Annual	595 (40%)	IRS 1975: p. 43; income after tax from p. 43.	IRS 1975: table 41 for earned income, consisting of employment income of husband and wife *(i.e. excluding her self-employment income)*, not pensions or family allowances; table 47 for total investment income (before deductions); table 39 for gross income.
1973–74	Annual	595 (34%)	IRS 1976: p. 36; income after tax from p. 36.	IRS 1976: table 38 for earned income, consisting of employment income of husband and wife (i.e. excluding her self-employment income), not pensions or family allowances; table 44 for total investment income (before deductions); table 39 for gross income.
1974–75	Annual	625 (29%)	IRS 1977: p. 43; income after tax from p. 43.	IRS 1977: table 43 for earned income, consisting of employment income of husband and wife (i.e. excluding her self-employment income), not pensions or family allowances; table 49 for total investment income (before deductions); table 37 for gross income.

(*contd.*)

Table 4A.2 (*Contd.*)

Income tax assessment year	Nature of survey	Lower limit £ year (% mean tax unit income)	Source (s)	Composition data (changes marked by italics)
			Data from now on relate to total income before deduction of allowable expenses such as mortgage interest.	
1975–76	Annual	675 (25%)	SPI 1975–76 and 1976–77: p. 16; income after tax from p. 16.	SPI 1975–76 and 1976–77: table 18 for earned income, consisting of employment income of husband and wife (i.e. excluding her self-employment income), not pensions or family allowances; table 24 for total investment income.
1976–77	Annual	735 (24%)	SPI 1975–76 and 1976–77: p. 86; income after tax from p. 86.	SPI 1975–76 and 1976–77: table 85 for earned income, consisting of employment income of husband and wife (i.e. excluding her self-employment income), not pensions or family allowances; table 91 for total investment income.
1977–78	Annual	810 (24%)	SPI 1977–78: p. 16; income after tax from p. 16.	SPI 1977–78: table 21 for earned income, consisting of employment income of husband and wife (i.e. excluding her self-employment income), not pensions; table 27 for total investment income.
1978–79	Annual	1000 (27%)	SPI 1978–79: p. 16; income after tax from p. 16.	SPI 1978–79: table 21 for earned income, consisting of employment income of husband and wife (i.e. excluding her self-employment income), not pensions; table 27 for total investment income.

1979–80	Annual	1000 (23%)	SPI 1979–80: p. 20; income after tax from p. 20.	SPI 1979–80: table 18 for earned income, consisting of employment income of husband and wife (i.e. excluding her self-employment income), not pensions; table 24 for total investment income.
1980–81	Annual	1350 (27%)	SPI 1982–83, frequencies by ranges from p. 8, p. 9 for after tax income, but no information available on amounts.	—
1981–82	Annual	1350 (25%)	SPI 1982–83, frequencies by ranges from p. 8, p. 9 for after tax income, and information on amounts by ranges supplied by Inland Revenue.	—
1982–83	Annual	1550 (27%)	SPI 1982–83: p. 10; income after tax from p. 10.	SPI 1982–83: table 14 for earned income, consisting of employment income of husband and wife (i.e. excluding her self-employment income), not pensions; table 4 for total investment income.
1983–84	Annual	1750 (29%)	SPI 1983–84: p. 10; income after tax from p. 10.	SPI 1983–84: table 14 for earned income, consisting of employment income of husband and wife (i.e. excluding her self-employment income), not pensions; table 4 for total investment income.
1984–85	Annual	2000 (31%)	SPI 1984–85: p. 10; income after tax from p. 10.	SPI 1984–85: table 14 for earned income, consisting of employment income of husband and wife (i.e. excluding her self-employment income), not pensions; table 4 for total investment income.

(contd.)

Table 4A.2 (*Contd.*)

Income tax assessment year	Nature of survey	Lower limit £ year (% mean tax unit income)	Source (s)	Composition data (changes marked by italics)
1985–86	Annual	2200 (30%)	IRS 1988: p. 23; income after tax from p. 23.	IRS 1988: table 2.4 for earned income, consisting of employment income of husband and wife (i.e. excluding her self-employment income), not pensions; table 2.3 for total investment income.
1986–87	Annual	2330 (29%)	IRS 1989: p. 24; income after tax from p. 24.	IRS 1989: table 2.4 for earned income, consisting of employment income of husband and wife (i.e. excluding her self-employment income), not pensions; table 2.3 for total investment income.
1987–88	Annual	2420 (28%)	IRS 1990: p. 28; income after tax from p. 28.	IRS 1990: table 2.5 for earned income, consisting of employment income of husband and wife (i.e. excluding her self-employment income), not pensions; table 2.4 for total investment income.
1988–89	Annual	2605 (27%)	IRS 1991: p. 25; income after tax from p. 25.	IRS 1991: table 2.5 for earned income, consisting of employment income of husband and wife (i.e. excluding her self-employment income), not pensions; table 2.4 for total investment income.
1989–90	Annual	2785 (26%)	IRS 1992: p. 29; income after tax from p. 29.	IRS 1992: table 2.9 for earned income, consisting of employment income of husband and wife (i.e. excluding her self-employment income), not pensions; table 2.8 for total investment income.

			Independent taxation introduced; data now relate to individuals.	
1990–91	Annual	3005 (35%)	IRS 1993: p. 34; income after tax from p. 34.	IRS 1993: table 3.4 for earned income, consisting of employment income of husband and wife (i.e. excluding her self-employment income), not pensions; table 3.3 for total investment income.
1991–92	Annual	3295 (37%)	IRS 1994: p. 36; income after tax from p. 36.	IRS 1994: table 3.5 for earned income, consisting of employment income of husband and wife (i.e. excluding her self-employment income), not pensions; table 3.4 for total investment income.
1992–93	Annual	3445 (39%)	IRS 1994: p. 36; income after tax from p. 36.	IRS 1994: table 3.5 for earned income, consisting of employment income of husband and wife (i.e. excluding her self-employment income), not pensions; table 3.4 for total investment income.
1993–94	Annual	3445 (39%)	IRS 1995: p. 34; income after tax from p. 34.	IRS 1995: table 3.6 for earned income, consisting of employment income of husband and wife (i.e. excluding her self-employment income), not pensions; table 3.5 for total investment income.
1994–95	Annual	3445 (38%)	IRS 1996: p. 35; income after tax from p. 35.	IRS 1996: table 3.6 for earned income, consisting of employment income of husband and wife (i.e. excluding her self-employment income), not pensions; table 3.5 for total investment income.

(contd.)

Table 4A.2 (*Contd.*)

Income tax assessment year	Nature of survey	Lower limit £ year (% mean tax unit income)	Source (s)	Composition data (changes marked by italics)
1995–96	Annual	3525 (37%)	IRS 1997: p. 34; income after tax from p. 34.	IRS 1997: table 3.6 for earned income, consisting of employment income of husband and wife (i.e. excluding her self-employment income), not pensions; table 3.5 for total investment income.
1996–97	Annual	3765 (37%)	IRS 1998: p. 34; income after tax from p. 34.	IRS 1998: table 3.6 for earned income, consisting of employment income of husband and wife (i.e. excluding her self-employment income), not pensions; table 3.5 for total investment income.
1997–98	Annual	4045 (37%)	IRS 1999: p. 36 for gross income (with top range from p. 32); income after tax from p. 32.	IRS 1999: table 3.6 for earned income, consisting of employment income of husband and wife (i.e. excluding her self-employment income), not pensions; table 3.5 for total investment income.
1998–99	Annual	4195 (36%)	IRS 2000: p. 41 for gross income (with top range from p. 37); income after tax from p. 37.	IRS 2000: table 3.6 for earned income, consisting of employment income of husband and wife (i.e. excluding her self-employment income), not pensions; table 3.5 for total investment income.
1999–2000	Annual	4335 (36%)	IR website: table 3.3.	IR website: table 3.6 for employment income, consisting of employment income of husband and wife (i.e. excluding her self-employment income), not pensions; table 3.5 for total investment

2000–01	Annual	4385 (32%)	IR website: table 3.3.	IR website: table 3.6 for employment income, consisting of employment income of husband and wife (i.e. excluding her self-employment income), not pensions; table 3.5 for total investment income.

Total Tax Units 1908–89

For the period 1908–89 we need to construct control totals for the total number of *tax units* in the population (taxpayers and non-taxpayers). The Blue Book (*NIE*) totals for the number of tax units are used where these exist: 1949, 1952–78, 1981, and 1984.[6] The source is Atkinson and Micklewright (1992: table BI1) except for 1952 from *NIE*, 1953: table 16; 1953 from *NIE* 1954: table 18; 1955 from *NIE* 1959: 26; 1956 and 1957 from *NIE* 1960: 20; 1958 from *NIE* 1961: 20; 1960 and 1961 from *NIE* 1962: 26. I have interpolated linearly to give figures for the years not covered between 1949 and 1984: i.e. 1950, 1951, 1979, 1980, 1982, and 1983.

For the years not covered in this way by Blue Book totals (1908–48 and 1985–89), we construct tax unit totals based on the total number of males aged 15 and over, plus the total number of females aged 15 and over, less married females. These constructed totals can be calculated directly for 1901, 1911, 1921, 1931, 1939, 1951, 1961, 1971, 1981, and 1991. The sources are:

- 1901: Mitchell (1988), Population and Vital Statistics, Table 4 for population by age, and Table 5 for proportion of females married for England and Wales and for Scotland; number of married females in Ireland from Census of Ireland 1901, General Report, p. 20.
- 1911: Mitchell (1988), Population and Vital Statistics, Table 4 for population by age, and Table 5 for proportion of females married for England and Wales and for Scotland; number of married females in Ireland from Census of Ireland 1911, General Report, p. 6.
- 1921: Mitchell (1988), Population and Vital Statistics Table 4 for population by age for England and Wales and for Scotland, and Table 5 for proportion of

[6] A figure for the total number of tax units in 1938 appears in the Report No 7 of the Royal Commission on the Distribution of Income and Wealth (1979: p. 23), but this is simply assumed to be equal to that in 1949 (see paragraph 2.26). For some years in the 1950s and early 1960s, the CSO extrapolated the distributional data from the most recent Survey of Personal Incomes. While the distributional data are open to question (Stark 1972: p. 19), the total numbers of tax units and total income (allocated and unallocated) contain independent information, and have been used here.

Table 4B.1 UK control totals for tax units (individuals) and income, 1908–2000

	Total tax units million	Total adult individuals million	Total Income £ million current prices	Tax deducted to give total net of tax income £ million current prices	Mean income per tax unit £ per year current prices	Mean income per individual £ per year current prices	Consumer price index 2000 = 100
1908	22.128		1,682		76		1.40
1909	22.361		1,689		76		1.41
1910	22.595		1,747		77		1.43
1911	22.805		1,817		80		1.43
1912	22.924		1,899		83		1.47
1913	23.063		1,966		85		1.46
1914	23.299		1,990		85		1.46
1915	23.480		2,164		92		1.64
1916	23.601		2,483		105		1.94
1917	23.686		2,982		126		2.43
1918	23.705		3,646		154		2.96
1919	23.714		3,773		159		3.26
1920	23.896		4,343		182		3.77
1921	22.525		3,770		167		3.44
1922	22.778		3,474		152		2.96
1923	22.997		3,434		149		2.78
1924	23.262		3,553		153		2.77
1925	23.436		3,635		155		2.77
1926	23.626		3,628		154		2.75
1927	23.812		3,761		158		2.68
1928	24.014		3,846		160		2.68
1929	24.164		3,896		161		2.65
1930	24.373		3,833		157		2.58
1931	24.583		3,694		150		2.47
1932	24.670		3,594		146		2.41
1933	24.710		3,584		145		2.35
1934	24.733		3,731		151		2.35
1935	24.782		3,780		153		2.37
1936	24.836		3,984		160		2.38
1937	24.889		4,243	306.5	170		2.47
1938	24.937		4,320		173		2.50
1939	25.141		4,436		176		2.58
1940	25.223		4,849		192		3.01
1941	25.174		5,382		214		3.33
1942	25.224		6,038		239		3.57
1943	25.383		6,384		252		3.69
1944	25.458		6,579		258		3.80
1945	25.497		6,502		255		3.90
1946	25.473		6,916		272		4.02
1947	25.583		7,674		300		4.30
1948	25.791		8,276		321		4.63
1949	25.900		8,730	1,098	337		4.76
1950	25.767		8,839		343		4.91
1951	25.633		9,844		384		5.36
1952	25.500		10,437		409		5.85
1953	25.300		11,090		438		6.03

1954	26.250		11,805	1,295	450		6.15
1955	26.200		12,874		491		6.42
1956	26.150		13,954		534		6.74
1957	26.100		14,495		555		6.98
1958	26.250		14,978		571		7.20
1959	26.500		16,019	1,735	604		7.23
1960	26.700		17,010		637		7.31
1961	26.900		18,894		702		7.56
1962	27.200		19,736	2,327	726		7.89
1963	27.400		20,446	2,314	746		8.04
1964	27.500		22,171	2,723	806		8.31
1965	27.600		24,225	3,352	878		8.69
1966	27.700		25,251	3,488	912		9.04
1967	27.800		26,568	3,796	956		9.27
1968	28.091		28,599	4,370	1,018		9.71
1969	28.161		30,898	5,146	1,097		10.23
1970	28.206		34,740	6,158	1,232		10.88
1971	28.240		37,400	6,356	1,324		11.91
1972	28.351		42,055	6,572	1,483		12.76
1973	28.123		48,655	8,045	1,730		13.92
1974	28.274		60,608	11,846	2,144		16.15
1975	28.341		75,798	16,000	2,675		20.07
1976	28.549		86,839	18,300	3,042		23.38
1977	28.892		95,588	18,200	3,308		27.09
1978	29.076		109,615	20,200	3,770		29.34
1979	29.390		129,022	22,300	4,390		33.27
1980	29.704		148,087		4,985		39.25
1981	30.018		159,543	30,300	5,315		43.91
1982	30.484		175,341	32,400	5,752		47.69
1983	30.950		188,572	35,300	6,093		49.88
1984	31.416		203,538	37,300	6,479		52.37
1985	31.743		232,962	38,800	7,339		55.55
1986	31.998		257,496	42,800	8,047		57.44
1987	32.249		280,949	45,300	8,712		59.84
1988	32.507		314,118	46,500	9,663		62.77
1989	32.788		356,688	53,400	10,879		67.65
1990		46.347	395,224	60,400		8,527	74.05
1991		46.455	413,204	63,500		8,895	78.40
1992		46.675	416,912	60,700		8,932	81.33
1993		46.894	417,668	65,100		8,907	82.63
1994		47.043	431,302	69,400		9,168	84.62
1995		47.249	452,844	74,434		9,584	87.56
1996		46.802	476,479	75,757		10,181	89.67
1997		46.919	514,729	79,512		10,971	92.48
1998		47.071	552,598	87,890		11,740	95.65
1999		47.347	601,932	93,200		12,713	97.13
2000		47.652	667,854	105,572		14,015	100.00

females married; figures adjusted to allow for Northern Ireland (NI) by multiplying by the ratio of the total NI population in 1922 to that for England and Wales and Scotland in 1921 from Mitchell (1988) Population and Vital Statistics, Table 3.

- 1931: *AAS* 1935–46, Table 9, Great Britain figures adjusted proportionately to UK using Northern Ireland totals (Table 6).
- 1939: *National Register 1939*, Table M, Great Britain figures adjusted proportionately to UK using Northern Ireland totals, p. ix.
- 1951: *AAS* 1981, table 2.8.
- 1961: *AAS* 1992, table 2.6.
- 1971, 1981 and 1991: *AAS* 2000, table 5.4.

The number of calculated units for these years is expressed as a percentage of total population (see below for the sources), and the percentages interpolated linearly for intermediate years, the results being multiplied again by total population to give figures for all years. Applying the resulting interpolated percentage to the total population gives a figure for 1984 that essentially coincides with the Blue Book figure; for 1949 the Blue Book figure is 97.7% of the constructed figure. We therefore apply an adjustment factor of 0.977 to the estimated totals for 1948 and earlier.

The sources for total population are:

- 1900–65: Feinstein 1972: Table 55, column 1, mid-year home population of Great Britain and Ireland (up to 1920) and Great Britain and Northern Ireland (from 1921), except years 1915–20 and 1939–45 when total population including those serving overseas;
- 1966–89: mid-year residential population from *AAS* 1997: table 2.1.

Control Total Units: Summary

To summarize, the final series is obtained as follows:

1. For 1908–48, constructed tax units adjusted proportionately in line with the 1949 Blue Book figure (i.e. multiplied by 0.977);
2. For 1949–84, Blue Book figures (interpolated linearly for 1950, 1951, 1979, 1980, 1982, and 1983);
3. For 1985–9, constructed tax units.

The resulting tax unit totals used in this chapter are shown in Table 4B.1.

Assessment

How do the derived totals of tax units compare with other evidence about total tax units for the pre-war period? For 1938 the figure of 24.9 million is rather higher (by some 4%) than the estimate of 24 million of Lydall (1959: p. 6), since he takes the population aged 18 or over (rather than 15 or over). Seers (1949:

p. 254) arrived at the still lower figure for 1938 of 23.5 million by a different route. He started with 10 million units above income tax exemption level from tax records, and added 11.5 million employees, excluding wives, earning below exemption level, 0.5 million self-employed below exemption limit, and 1.5 million rentiers, excluding wives, below exemption limit. The last of these numbers seems rather low for the total of units who are retired or unoccupied and below the exemption level (in 1939 there were aged 65 and over in Great Britain 1.845 million males and 1.572 million non-married females (National Register, September 1939, table M)). In contrast, the calculations given in the Beveridge Report show for Great Britain in 1939 a total of persons aged 15 and over, minus 'housewives', of 27.6 million (Beveridge 1942: p. 123), which is higher than our estimate. Our estimate is therefore bracketed by these earlier figures.

What about the earlier part of the period? In the 1920s and first half of the 1930s, there was considerable interest in deriving numbers for the total occupied population, as a basis for estimating national income. Clark (1934), for instance, describes the way in which he moves from numbers of taxpayers to the size of the occupied population. Here we are interested in what can be learned about the reverse process: working back from the occupied population to the number of tax units. For the 1920s, Clark (1932: p. 76) gives the number of incomes in the UK for 1924 as 19.065 million and for 1928 as 20.145 million. Our figures for tax units are 23.3 million and 24.0 million, but the Census of Population 1921 indicates an adjustment for the non-occupied of 4.4 million, so that there is close agreement. For the pre-First World War period, Bowley (1919: p. 11) gives a total of 20.15 million for the total number occupied in 1911 (this includes Southern Ireland). This is closely in line with our total of 22.8 million for all tax units in 1911, since calculations from the 1911 Census of Population suggests that the number of units exceeded the number occupied by 2.4 million.

APPENDIX 4C: CONSTRUCTION OF UK CONTROL TOTALS FOR INCOME

As described in the text, control totals for income can be defined in two different ways. One can start from the national accounts figures for total personal income and work towards a definition closer to taxable income, or one can start from the income tax statistics and add the income of those tax units not covered. Here I adopt the latter approach. As a result, the construction of the total personal income (before tax) series differs from that in Atkinson (2002), although it uses many of the same sources, notably Feinstein (1972) and the national accounts (NIE). In contrast, the estimates in Atkinson (2002) correspond to a more extensive definition; based on the estimates of 'allocated total income' made by the Central Statistical Office (CSO), which includes non-taxable income in kind and non-taxable social security benefits, of which the most important in the

1970s were social assistance, sickness/industrial injury benefits, NI disability pensions, invalidity pension and NI unemployment benefit (Ramprakash 1975: p. 82). (At that time, family allowances were taxable; child benefit, introduced in 1978, is tax-free.) In 1972–73, the total income covered by the *Survey of Personal Incomes* (*SPI*) was £40,778 million, to which the CSO estimated £2538 million should be added for the taxable income of non-filers and £2448 million for non-taxable income (Ramprakash 1972: p. 92). Here we make in principle the first, but not the second, of these additions in arriving at the control totals summarized in the final two columns of Table 4B.1. The control totals relate to tax years.

The detailed derivation of the control totals is shown in Table 4C.1 for the period from 1945 and Table 4C.2 for the period prior to 1945. The methods are described below. For the years 1969–75 we may compare them with the CSO estimates of added income. In four of the seven cases, the estimates made here are below those of the CSO, and in three above. The mean of the CSO estimates is 3.6% higher. Given that we were limited to materials available over throughout the 50-year period, this degree of agreement seems reassuring.

Adjustments from 1945

The starting point is (column 1) the total income reported in the SPI, which is 'total net income' until 1974 and then 'total income', with the sources given in Table 4A.2. The 1999 and 2000 totals relate only to taxpayers and have been increased by the ratio for all tax units in 1998 (an increase of 1.8%). The 1980 figure is interpolated logarithmically using personal sector gross income in 1979 and 1981. Where the SPI totals are not available, we take (column 2) the 'actual income' reported by the Inland Revenue less estimated undistributed profits. The sources are: 1945–51 from *AR* 1952–53: 46; 1952–60 from *AR* 1961–62: 43; 1961–62 from *AR* 1965–66: 50. Undistributed profits are taken as the average of those in year t and year (t–1) from Feinstein (1972: T30) (except years 1944 and 1945—see below).

To this must be added the adjustment for non-filers. The CSO estimates for 1972 show a total of £100 million adjustment for the under-coverage of earned income. This is less than a quarter of the difference between the *SPI* total and the national accounts figure for wages, salaries and pay of HM Forces, and is only 0.3% of the latter figure. It might be thought that the adjustment should be higher in the earlier post-war years, but the totals for 1949–50, 1954–55 and 1959–60 suggest that the *SPI* figure is within 5% of the national accounts figure, and the majority of that difference is likely to be attributable to under-recording of those covered. In view of this, we make no adjustment for earned incomes post-1945.

The elements allowed for in Table 4C.1 are therefore (a) NI retirement and widows' pensions and (b) occupational pensions, which together accounted for 94% of the adjustment for under-coverage in 1972/73. The two items are treated separately for all years where the SPI totals distinguish them: 1962–98, except 1980 and 1981. The adjustments are obtained by subtracting the totals recorded in the SPI from control totals. The sources of the control totals are:

- *National Insurance retirement pensions and widows' pensions*: 1945 from Minister of Reconstruction (1944: p. 52); 1946 and 1947 from *NIE* 1946–49: p. 43; 1948–57 from *NIE* 1958: p. 43; 1958–63 from *NIE* 1964: p. 43; 1964–68 from NIE 1969: p. 49; 1969–77 from *NIE* 1967–77: p. 59; 1978–85 from NIE 1987: p. 54; 1986–94 from *NIE* 1997: p. 102; 1995–2001 from *NIE* 2004: p. 201. The figures were converted to a tax year basis by taking 0.75 of the figure for year t and 0.25 of the figure for year $(t+1)$.
- *Occupational pensions*: Direct estimates of the total paid in occupational pensions are only available for a number of years. The NIE total refers to 'pensions and other benefits from life assurance and superannuation schemes', which includes items such as lump-sum payments on retirement or death, and refunds of contributions, which are not treated as part of taxable income. This total cannot therefore be used unadjusted. For the 1970s the CSO made estimates of the amounts of occupational pensions. The sources are (for tax years): 1972–73 from *NIE* 1975: p. 109; 1973–74 from *NIE* 1976: p. 111; 1974–75 from *NIE* 1977: p. 115; 1975–76 from *NIE* 1978: p. 119; 1976–77 from *NIE* 1979: p. 115; 1977–78 from *NIE* 1980: p. 110. The new system of national accounts SNA 1993 allows the total pensions in payment to be distinguished: sources (calendar years) 1990 and 1991 from *NIE* 1999: p. 209, 1995–2001 from NIE 2004: p. 223. The calendar year figures were converted to a tax year basis by taking 0.75 of the figure for year t and 0.25 of the figure for year $(t+1)$. Inspection of these figures showed that pensions in payment were around 55% of the national accounts total in the 1970s but had risen to around 70% in 1990, as would have been expected as pension schemes matured. A proportion of 55% was taken prior to 1978 and interpolated linearly between 55 and 70% between 1978 and 1990. The actual CSO figures were used for 1990–2000.
- *Remaining Years*: The *SPI* years 1949, 1954 and 1959 have totals for all pensions, and these were used with the sum of the control totals described above. The figures for 1945–48 were extrapolated backwards from 1949 using the total for NI retirement and widows' pensions. The adjustments in the SPI years were expressed as a percentage of the total NI and occupational pensions, and the percentages interpolated to give figures for 1950 to 1953, 1955 to 1958, and 1960 and 1961. The figures for 1980 and 1981, and for 1999, were interpolated using the total for NI retirement and widows' pensions.

It is interesting to compare the resulting totals with total personal sector gross income (final column in Table 4C.1). The adjusted total shows a distinct decline, from a figure in excess of 80% at the start of the 1950s to below 75% in the second half of the 1990s. The series is graphed in Figure 2.4 in Chapter 2.

Adjustments Prior to 1945

The estimates for the period prior to 1945 are set out in Table 4C.2. Figures for 1920 and earlier include what is now the Republic of Ireland. The starting point is

Table 4C.1 Derivation of control totals (£ million) for income in UK, 1945/46–2000/01

	1	2	3	4	5	6	7	8	9
Tax year starting in April	SPI income	Returned income (= IR actual income - undistributed profits)	Non-filers' NI retirement and widows' pensions	Non-filers' occupational pensions	All pensions (cols 3 and 4 combined)	Total added (col 3 + col 4) or col 5	CSO estimate of added income	ADJUSTED Total income (col 1 or 2 + col 6)	ADJUSTED Total as % Personal sector gross income
1945		6,379			123	123		6,502	74.5
1946		6,767			149	149		6,916	78.2
1947		7,367			307	307		7,674	81.3
1948		7,917			359	359		8,276	82.9
1949	8,359	8,280			371	371		8,730	82.7
1950		8,469			370	370		8,839	80.0
1951		9,468			377	377		9,844	82.2
1952		10,043			394	394		10,437	81.6
1953		10,693			397	397		11,090	81.7
1954	11,410	11,507			395	395		11,805	82.3
1955		12,432			442	442		12,874	82.8
1956		13,482			472	472		13,954	83.6
1957		13,983			512	512		14,495	82.4
1958		14,381			597	597		14,978	80.6
1959	15,391	15,014			628	628		16,019	81.4
1960		16,354			656	656		17,010	80.2
1961		18,178			716	716		18,894	82.4
1962	18,978	18,862	598	160		758		19,736	81.7
1963	19,601		682	163		845		20,446	79.9
1964	21,206		773	192		965		22,171	80.2
1965	23,166		851	208		1,059		24,225	80.6
1966	24,070		919	262		1,181		25,251	78.4
1967	25,272		971	325		1,296		26,568	78.5
1968	27,200		1,053	346		1,399		28,599	78.4
1969	29,344		1,115	439		1,554	1,328	30,898	78.7

1970	33,005	1,264	471		1,735	1,757	34,740	80.0
1971	35,600	1,330	471		1,800	2,094	37,400	78.2
1972	39,764	1,731	560		2,291	2,448	42,055	77.2
1973	45,907	2,024	725		2,748	2,531	48,655	76.6
1974	57,339	2,489	780		3,269	3,149	60,608	79.5
1975	72,196	2,944	658		3,602	4,310	75,798	78.4
1976	83,139	3,139	561		3,700		86,839	77.6
1977	91,198	3,896	494		4,390		95,588	76.8
1978	104,580	4,417	619		5,035		109,615	76.4
1979	123,252	4,867	904		5,770		129,022	76.0
1980	141,242			6,845	6,845		148,087	73.7
1981	151,633			7,910	7,910		159,543	71.6
1982	165,860	6,780	2,701		9,481		175,341	72.5
1983	178,045	7,316	3,211		10,527		188,572	72.3
1984	191,560	8,021	3,957		11,978		203,538	72.1
1985	218,910	8,569	5,483		14,052		232,962	75.9
1986	240,573	10,112	6,811		16,923		257,496	77.3
1987	261,336	10,443	9,170		19,613		280,949	78.2
1988	294,000	10,808	9,310		20,118		314,118	78.4
1989	332,250	11,346	13,092		24,438		356,688	80.8
1990	369,330	11,965	13,928		25,894		395,224	81.3
1991	384,470	13,078	15,655		28,734		413,204	79.9
1992	382,540	15,518	18,854		34,372		416,912	76.0
1993	382,200	16,275	19,194		35,468		417,668	72.9
1994	394,940	16,022	20,352		36,374		431,314	72.0
1995	414,980	15,662	22,202	37,864	37,864		452,844	71.2
1996	434,820	16,537	25,142	41,678	41,678		476,498	70.9
1997	469,700	17,100	27,929	45,029	45,029		514,729	72.7
1998	507,100	16,006	29,492	45,498	45,498		552,598	74.3
1999	542,594	21,883	37,455	59,338	59,338		601,932	76.8
2000	605,405	21,311	41,139	62,449	62,449		667,854	

the total 'actual' income assessed by the Inland Revenue for income tax purposes. It should be noted that, although the UK income tax administrative data at this time provided no distributional information, the totals can be used. The total in column 1 refers to gross income assessed less (a) the incomes of those below the exemption limit included in the assessments; (b) the income of charities, colleges, and other non-profit institutions; (c) dividends paid to non-residents; and (d) allowances for depreciation. From this we subtract that part of profits not distributed by companies (column 3) and add:

- wages not assessed (column 4-column 2)
- salaries below the exemption level (column 5)
- self-employment income below the exemption level (column 6)
- dividends and other capital income below the exemption level (column 7)
- contributory NI retirement and widows' pensions.

The sources for the different columns are described below.

1. *Column 1.* The sources are (years refer to income tax years commencing in April) 1908 from *AR* 1913–14: p. 100; 1909–18 from *AR* 1919–20: p. 62; 1919–23 from *AR* 1927–28: p. 73; 1924–28 from *AR* 1933–34: p. 63; 1929–35 from *AR* 1938–39: p. 56; 1936–42 from *AR* 1945–46: p. 52; 1945 from *AR* 1946–47: 65; 1943 and 1944 linearly interpolated.
2. *Column 2.* The wages included in the tax assessments are shown for most years in the sources given for column 1. (It should be noted that a distinction is drawn between 'wages' and 'salaries'.) 1943–45 calculated as same % of column 1 as 1942. Wages assessed prior to 1918 interpolated using the 1911 figure from Feinstein (1972: p. 173), and information on the exemption limit. Where the exemption limit was reduced by a factor $(1+x)$, the amount of wages assessed is assumed to rise according to the formula $(1+x)^4$.
3. *Column 3.* Post-1927 figure for year $(t-1)$, previously average of years $(t-1)$ and year $(t-2)$. 1920–38 from Feinstein 1972: T30; 1912 from Colwyn Committee 1927: p. 18; other years prior to 1920 interpolated using gross trading profits of companies and income from self-employment (undivided total) from Feinstein 1972: T5; 1939–44 taken as equal to the 1938 figure.
4. *Column 4.* Total wages from Feinstein 1972: T55. The figures are reduced by 5% to allow for the fact that some wage income would have escaped the attention of the Inland Revenue. The percentage deducted is a matter of judgment, but seems reasonable in the light of the post-1944 figures after the introduction of PAYE (collection at source).
5. *Columns 5–7.* The pre-1918 figures for salaries and self-employment income are based on the estimates for 1911 given by Bowley (1937: p. 81). The total of £264 million for salaries and self-employment earnings is close to the figure of £285 million given by Cannan et al. (1910: p. 64). They are extrapolated backwards to 1907 and forwards to 1917 using the series for salaries from Feinstein (1972: T55) and self-employment income from Feinstein (1972: T5

Table 4C.2 Derivation of control totals (£ million) for income in UK, 1908/09–1944/45

	1	2	3	4	5	6	7	8	9	10
Tax year starting in April	Assessed income inc wages	Wages assessed	Undistributed profits	Wages	Salaries below exemption level	Self employment income below exemption level	Dividends below exemption level	NI retirement and widows' pensions	ADJUSTED total income	ADJUSTED Total as % Personal sector gross income
1908	824	8	88	715	73	152	50		1,682	94.0
1909	822	8	89	721	74	154	50		1,688	92.6
1910	838	8	87	753	77	162	50		1,747	92.0
1911	866	8	86	781	80	174	50		1,817	91.9
1912	907	8	84	811	84	180	50		1,899	91.8
1913	951	8	90	835	89	180	50		1,966	91.6
1914	985	8	95	830	95	176	50		1,991	89.3
1915	1,050	23	103	910	99	227	50		2,164	80.9
1916	1,373	34	113	1,040	61	158	50		2,483	75.5
1917	1,631	58	137	1,310	70	181	50		2,982	75.0
1918	2,072	145	170	1,640	83	198	50		3,646	77.8
1919	2,547	826	200	1,970	110	221	50		3,773	73.2
1920	2,661	674	223	2,475	96	82	50		4,343	82.1
1921	2,462	490	240	1,933	85	67	50		3,770	82.1
1922	2,318	357	188	1,585	78	68	50		3,474	84.3
1923	2,303	301	195	1,510	76	66	50		3,434	85.6
1924	2,401	343	178	1,554	78	68	50		3,552	85.9
1925	2,337	243	226	1,579	101	89	77		3,635	85.7
1926	2,337	196	215	1,481	106	101	80	8	3,628	86.5
1927	2,416	285	209	1,624	104	101	80	11	3,761	86.2
1928	2,494	285	201	1,607	107	101	80	23	3,846	87.2
1929	2,531	290	217	1,638	106	103	80	26	3,896	87.0
1930	2,497	269	219	1,579	106	103	80	34	3,833	86.6
1931	2,826	620	167	1,495	49	66	80	39	3,694	86.8
1932	2,667	600	100	1,470	54	66	70	40	3,594	86.1

(*contd.*)

Table 4C.2 (*contd.*)

	1	2	3	4	5	6	7	8	9	10
Tax year starting in April	Assessed income inc wages	Wages assessed	Undistributed profits	Wages	Salaries below exemption level	Self employment income below exemption level	Dividends below exemption level	NI retirement and widows' pensions	ADJUSTED total income	ADJUSTED Total as % Personal sector gross income
1933	2,621	620	83	1,497	66	66	70	42	3,584	84.9
1934	2,747	650	103	1,568	68	66	70	43	3,730	86.4
1935	2,839	680	178	1,624	72	70	70	44	3,780	84.1
1936	3,015	725	216	1,724	76	74	79	44	3,984	84.2
1937	3,231	785	232	1,842	79	70	85	45	4,243	86.4
1938	3,341	804	291	1,888	81	68	84	46	4,319	85.6
1939	3,425	908	290	2,010	86	77	84	53	4,436	85.1
1940	4,056	1,382	290	2,270	82	83	84	60	4,849	82.5
1941	4,846	1,911	290	2,560	71	82	84	67	5,382	75.7
1942	5,625	2,286	290	2,810	74	88	84	74	6,038	76.9
1943	5,912	2,365	290	2,940	79	90	84	81	6,384	76.0
1944	6,198	2,479	290	2,950	84	91	84	88	6,579	76.3

and T6), reduced when the exemption limit changed using exponent of 3 for salaries and 1.5 for self-employment income, allowing a one year lag when the exemption limit was lowered from £160 a year to £130 in 1915–16. The figure of £50 million for 'Dividends and other capital income' below the tax threshold is taken from Bowley (1937: p. 81). It is identical to the figure given by Cannan et al (1910: p. 64) for 1911, and it is assumed to apply to all pre-First World War years.

8. *Column 8.* The figures relate to the contributory pensions first introduced in 1926. Figures up to 1934 from Clark (1937: p. 141); 1935–38 from *Hansard*, 14 December 1939: column 1316; 1939–44 interpolated from the figure of £95 million in Minister of Reconstruction (1944: p. 52).

Again, it is interesting to compare the resulting totals with total personal sector gross income (final columns in Table 4C.2). As a percentage of total personal gross income (with or without transfers), the adjusted total used here shows a sharp drop during the First and Second World Wars. (See Figure 2.4 in Chapter 2.) This means that use of a control total based on a constant percentage of the national accounts total would have shown an even larger fall of the top income shares during the First and Second World Wars, and a bigger subsequent recovery.

Net of Tax Incomes

From the totals for gross income are subtracted the figures for total income tax recorded in the sources listed in Appendix 4A.

REFERENCES

Allen, J. E. (1920). 'Some Changes in the Distribution of the National Income During the War', *Journal of the Royal Statistical Society*, 83: 86–115.

Allen, R. G. D. (1957). 'Changes in the Distribution of Higher Incomes', *Economica*, 24: 138–53.

Andrews, P. W. S. and Brunner, E. (1955). *The Life of Lord Nuffield.* Oxford: Basil Blackwell.

Atkinson, A. B. (1972). *Unequal Shares.* London: Allen Lane.

—— (1993). 'What is Happening to the Distribution of Income in the UK?', *Proceedings of the British Academy*, 82: 337–51.

—— (2002). 'Top Incomes in the United Kingdom over the Twentieth Century', Discussion Paper in Economic and Social History, No. 43, University of Oxford.

—— (2005). 'Top incomes in the UK over the twentieth century', *Journal of the Royal Statistical Society*, 168(2): 325–43.

—— and Harrison, A. J. (1978). *Distribution of Personal Wealth in Britain.* Cambridge: Cambridge University Press.

—— Micklewright, J. (1992). *Economic Transformation in Eastern Europe and the Distribution of Income.* Cambridge: Cambridge University Press.

Atkinson, A. B., and Voitchovsky, S. (2003). 'The Distribution of Top Earnings in the UK since the Second World War'. Discussion paper.

Atkinson, A. B. Gordon, J. P. F. and Harrison, A. J. (1989). 'Trends in the Shares of Top Wealth-Holders in Britain, 1923–81', *Oxford Bulletin of Economics and Statistics*, 51: 315–32.

Barna, T. (1945). *Redistribution of Incomes Through Public Finance in 1937.* Oxford: Clarendon Press.

Beveridge, W., Lord (1942). *Social Insurance and Allied Services.* London: HMSO.

Blake, R. (1955). *The Unknown Prime Minister.* London: Eyre and Spottiswode.

Bowley, A. L. (1914). 'The British Super-Tax and the Distribution of Income', *Quarterly Journal of Economics*, 28: 255–68.

—— (1919). *The Division of the Product of Industry.* Oxford: Oxford University Press.

—— (1930). *Some Economic Consequences of the Great War.* London: Butterworth.

—— (1937). *Wages and Income in the United Kingdom since 1860.* Cambridge: Cambridge University Press.

—— (1942). *Studies in the National Income, 1924–1938.* Cambridge: Cambridge University Press.

—— Stamp, J. C. (1927). *The National Income, 1924.* Oxford: Oxford University Press.

Brittain, J. A. (1960). 'Some Neglected Features of Britain's Income Levelling', *American Economic Review*, 50: 593–603.

Cannadine, D. (1990). *The Decline and Fall of the British Aristocracy.* New Haven: Yale University Press.

Cannan, E., Bowley A. L., Edgeworth, F. Y., Lees Smith, H. B., and Scott, W. R. (1910). 'The Amount and Distribution of Income (other than Wages) Below the Income Tax Exemption Limit in the United Kingdom', *Journal of the Royal Statistical Society*, 74: 37–66.

Census of Ireland (1901). *1901 Census Report.* Dublin: HMSO.

—— (1911). *1911 Census Report.* Dublin: HMSO.

Central Statistical Office (Office for National Statistics) (various years). *National Income and Expenditure.* London: HMSO.

Central Statistical Office (1978). 'The Distribution of Income in the United Kingdom, 1975/76', *Economic Trends*, No. 295.

Champernowne, D. G. (1936). *The Distribution of Income between Persons.* Prize Fellowship dissertation, King's College, Cambridge.

—— (1973). *The Distribution of Income, Between Persons.* Cambridge: Cambridge University Press.

Clark, C. (1932). *The National Income, 1924–1931.* London: Macmillan.

—— (1934). 'Further Data on the National Income', *Economic Journal*, 44: 380–97.

—— (1937). *National Income and Outlay.* London: Macmillan.

Colwyn Committee (1927). *Report of the Committee on National Debt and Taxation*, Cmd.2800. London: HMSO.

Cowell, F. A. (1995). *Measuring Inequality*, 2nd edn. London: Prentice Hall.

Crosland, C. A. R. (1964). *The Future of Socialism*, 2nd edn. London: Jonathan Cape.

Feenberg, D. R. and Poterba, J. M. (1993). 'Income Inequality and the Incomes of Very High-Income Taxpayers: Evidence from Tax Returns', in J. Poterba (ed.) *Tax Policy and the Economy*, vol. 7. Cambridge: MIT Press, pp. 145–77.

—— and —— (2000). 'The Income and Tax Share of Very High-Income Households, 1960–1995', *American Economic Review*, Papers and Proceedings, 90: 264–70.

Feinstein, C. H. (1972). *Statistical Tables of National Income, Expenditure and Output of the UK 1855–1965.* Cambridge: Cambridge University Press.

—— (1988). 'The Rise and Fall of the Williamson Curve', *Journal of Economic History*, 48: 699–729.

Gastwirth, J. L. (1972). 'The Estimation of the Lorenz Curve and Gini Index', *Review of Economics and Statistics*, 54: 306–16.

Goodman, A. and Webb, S. (1994). *For Richer, For Poorer*. Institute for Fiscal Studies, Commentary No. 42.

Gordon, R. H. and Slemrod, J. (2000). 'Are "Real" Responses to Taxes Simply Income Shifting Between Corporate and Personal Tax Bases?', in J. B. Slemrod (ed.) *Does Atlas Shrug?* New York: Russell Sage Foundation.

Inland Revenue (various years). *Annual Report of the Commissioners for the Year*. London: HMSO.

Inland Revenue (various years). *Inland Revenue Statistics*. London: HMSO.

Inland Revenue (various years). *Survey of Personal Incomes*. London: HMSO.

Kaldor, N. (1955). *An Expenditure Tax*. London: Allen & Unwin.

Lindert, P. (2000). 'Three Centuries of Inequality in Britain and America', in A. B. Atkinson and F. Bourguignon (eds.) *Handbook of Income Distribution*. Amsterdam: North-Holland.

Lydall, H. F. (1959). 'The Long-Term Trend in the Size Distribution of Income', *Journal of the Royal Statistical Society*, Series A, vol. 122: 1–46.

Minister of Reconstruction (1944). 'Social Insurance, Part I', Cmd 6550. London: HMSO.

Mitchell, B. R. (1988). *British Historical Statistics*. Cambridge: Cambridge University Press.

National Register (1939). *Statistics of Population on 29th September 1939*. London: HMSO.

Piketty, T. (1998). 'Les hauts revenus face aux modifications des taux marginaux supérieurs de l'impot sur le revenu en France, 1970–1996', Discussion Paper 9812. Paris: CEPREMAP.

—— (2001). *Les hauts revenus en France au 20ème siècle*. Paris: Grasset.

—— (2003). 'Income Inequality in France, 1901–1998', *Journal of Political Economy*, 111 (5): 1004–42.

—— Saez, E. (2001). *Income Inequality in the United States, 1913–1998*, Working Paper n°8467, NBER.

—— —— (2003). 'Income Inequality in the United States, 1913–1998', *Quarterly Journal of Economics*, 118: 1–39.

Ramprakash, D. (1975). 'Distribution of Income Statistics for the United Kingdom, 1972/73: Sources and Methods', *Economic Trends*, 262: 78–96.

Rhodes, E. C. (1949). 'The Distribution of Earned and Investment Incomes in the United Kingdom', *Economica*, 16: 53–63.

—— (1951). 'Distribution of Earned and Investment Incomes in the United Kingdom in 1937–38', *Economica*, 18: 18–34.

—— (1951*a*). 'The Distribution of Incomes and the Burden of Estate Duties in the United Kingdom', *Economica*, 18: 270–7.

—— (1952). 'The Inequality of Incomes in the United Kingdom', *Economica*, 19: 168–75.

—— (1956). 'Earned and Investment Income, UK, 1952–53', *Economica*, 23: 62–6.

Routh, G. (1980). *Occupation and Pay in Great Britain, 1906–79*. London: Macmillan.

Royal Commission on the Distribution of Income and Wealth (1979). *Report No.7, Fourth Report on the Standing Reference*, Cmnd. 7595. London: HMSO.

Royal Commission on the Income Tax (1920). *Report*, Cmd. 615. London: HMSO.

Royal Commission on the Income Tax (1920*a*). *Index to the Evidence & Appendices*, Cmd. 288. London: HMSO.

Sabine, B. E. V. (1966). *A History of Income Tax*. London: Allen & Unwin.

Seers, D. (1949). 'Income Distribution in 1938 and 1947', *Bulletin of the Oxford University Institute of Statistics*, 11: 253–68.
—— (1956). 'Has the Distribution of Income Become More Unequal?', *Bulletin of the Oxford University Institute of Statistics*, 18: 73–86.
Soltow, L. (1968). 'Long-run Changes in British Income Inequality', *Economic History Review*, 21: 17–29.
Stamp, J. C., Lord (1914). 'A New Illustration of Pareto's Law', *Journal of the Royal Statistical Society*, 77: 200–4.
—— (1916). *British Incomes and Property*. London: P. S. King.
—— (1936). 'The Influence of the Price Level on the Higher Incomes', *Journal of the Royal Statistical Society*, 99: 627–73.
Stark, T. (1972). *The Distribution of Personal Income in the United Kingdom, 1949–1963*. Cambridge: Cambridge University Press.
—— (1978). 'Personal Incomes' in W.F. Maunder (ed.) *Reviews of United Kingdom Statistical Sources*, vol. 6. Oxford: Pergamon Press.
Titmuss, R. M. (1962). *Income Distribution and Social Change*. London: Allen & Unwin.
Williamson, J. G. (1985). *Did British Capitalism Breed Inequality?* London: Allen & Unwin.

5

Income and Wage Inequality in the United States, 1913–2002[1]

T. Piketty and E. Saez

5.1 INTRODUCTION

According to Kuznets's influential hypothesis, income inequality should follow an inverse U-shape along the development process, first rising with industrialization and then declining, as more and more workers join the high productivity sectors of the economy (Kuznets 1955). Today, the Kuznets curve is widely held to have doubled back on itself, especially in the United States, with the period of falling inequality observed during the first half of the twentieth century being succeeded by a very sharp reversal of the trend since the 1970s. This does not imply however that Kuznets's hypothesis is no longer of interest. One could indeed argue that what has been happening since the 1970s is just a remake of the previous inverse-U curve: a new industrial revolution has taken place, thereby leading to increasing inequality, and inequality will decline again at some point, as more and more workers benefit from the new innovations.

To cast light on this central issue, we build new homogeneous series on top shares of pre-tax income and wages in the United States covering the 1913–2002 period. These new series are based primarily on tax returns data published annually by the Internal Revenue Service (IRS) since the income tax was instituted in 1913, as well as on the large micro-files of tax returns released by the IRS since 1960. First, we have constructed annual series of shares of total income accruing to various upper income groups fractiles within the top decile of the income distribution. For each of these fractiles, we also present the shares of each source of income such as wages, business income, and capital income. Kuznets (1953) did produce a number of top income shares series covering the 1913–48 period, but tended to under-estimate top income shares, and the highest group analysed by Kuznets is the top percentile.[2] Most importantly, nobody has

[1] This chapter is a longer and updated version of Piketty and Saez (2003). We thank Tony Atkinson for very helpful and detailed comments. We thankfully acknowledge financial support from the MacArthur Foundation, the Alfred P. Sloan Foundation, and NSF Grant SES-0134946.

[2] Analysing smaller groups within the top percentile is critical because capital income is extremely concentrated.

attempted to estimate, as we do here, homogeneous series covering the entire century.[3] Second, we have constructed annual 1927–2002 series of top shares of salaries for the top fractiles of the wage income distribution, based on tax returns tabulations by size of salaries compiled by the IRS since 1927. To our knowledge, this is the first time that a homogeneous annual series of top wage shares starting before the 1950s for the United States has been produced.[4]

Our estimated top shares series display a U-shape over the century and suggest that a pure Kuznets mechanism cannot account fully for the facts. We find that top capital incomes were severely hit by major shocks in the first part of the century. The post-First World War depression and the Great Depression destroyed many businesses and thus reduced significantly top capital incomes. The wars generated large fiscal shocks, especially in the corporate sector that mechanically reduced distributions to stockholders. We argue that top capital incomes were never able to fully recover from these shocks, probably because of the dynamic effects of progressive taxation on capital accumulation and wealth inequality. We also show that top wage shares were flat from the 1920s until 1940 and dropped precipitously during the war. Top wage shares have started to recover from the Second World War shock in the late 1960s, and they are now higher than before the Second World War. Thus the increase in top income shares in the last three decades is the direct consequence of the surge in top wages. As a result, the composition of income in the top income groups has shifted dramatically over the century: the working rich have now replaced the coupon-clipping rentiers. We argue that both the downturn and the upturn of top wage shares seem too sudden to be accounted for by technical change alone. Our series suggest that other factors, such as changes in labour market institutions, fiscal policy, or more generally social norms regarding pay inequality may have played important roles in the determination of the wage structure. Although our proposed interpretation for the observed trends seems plausible to us, we stress that we cannot prove that progressive taxation and social norms have indeed played the role we attribute to them. In our view, the primary contribution of this chapter is to provide new series on income and wage inequality.

One additional motivation for constructing long series is to be able to separate the trends in inequality that are the consequence of real economic change from those that are due to fiscal manipulation. The issue of fiscal manipulation has recently received much attention. Studies analysing the effects of the Tax Reform Act of 1986 (TRA86) have emphasized that a large part of the response observable in tax returns was due to income shifting between the corporate sector and the individual sector (Slemrod 1996; Gordon and Slemrod 2000). We do not deny that fiscal manipulation can have substantial short-run effects, but we argue that

[3] Feenberg and Poterba (1993, 2000) have constructed top income share series covering the 1951–95 period, but their series are not homogeneous with those of Kuznets. Moreover, they provide income shares series only for the top 0.5%, and not for other fractiles.

[4] Previous studies on wage inequality before 1945 in the United States rely mostly on occupational pay ratios (Williamson and Lindert 1980; Goldin and Margo 1992; and Goldin and Katz 1999).

most long-run inequality trends are the consequence of real economic change, and that a short-run perspective attributes improperly some of these trends to fiscal manipulation.

The chapter is organized as follows: Section 5.2 describes our data sources and outlines our estimation methods; in Section 5.3 we present and analyse the trends in top income shares, with particular attention to the issue of top capital incomes; Section 5.4 focuses on trends in top wages shares; and Section 5.5 offers concluding comments and proposes an international comparison. All series and complete technical details about our methodology are gathered in the appendices of the chapter.

5.2 DATA AND METHODOLOGY

Our estimations rely on tax returns statistics compiled annually by the Internal Revenue Service since the beginning of the modern US income tax in 1913. Before 1944, because of large exemptions levels, only a small fraction of individuals had to file tax returns and therefore, by necessity, we must restrict our analysis to the top decile of the income distribution.[5] Because our data are based on tax returns, they do not provide information on the distribution of individual incomes within a tax unit. As a result, all our series are for tax units and not individuals.[6] A tax unit is defined as a married couple living together (with dependents) or a single adult (with dependents), as in the current tax law. The average number of individuals per tax unit decreased over the century but this decrease was roughly uniform across income groups. Therefore, if income were evenly allocated to individuals within tax units,[7] the time series pattern of top shares based on individuals should be very similar to that based on tax units.

Tax units within the top decile form a very heterogeneous group, from the high middle class families deriving most of their income from wages to the super-rich living off large fortunes. More precisely, we will see that the composition of income varies substantially by income level within the top decile. Therefore, it is critical to divide the top decile into smaller fractiles. Following Piketty (2001), in addition to the top decile (denoted by P90–100), we have constructed series for a number of higher fractiles within the top decile: the top 5% (P95–100), the top

[5] From 1913 to 1916, because of higher exemption levels, we can only provide estimates within the top percentile.

[6] Kuznets (1953) decided nevertheless to estimate series based on individuals not tax units. We explain in Piketty and Saez (2001) why his method produced a downward bias in the levels (though not in the pattern) of top shares.

[7] Obviously, income is not earned evenly across individuals within tax units, and, because of increasing female labour force participation, the share of income earned by the primary earner has certainly declined over the century. Therefore, inequality series based on income earned at the individual level would be different. Our tax returns statistics are mute on this issue. We come back to that point when we present our wage estimates.

1% (P99–100), the top 0.5% (P99.5–100), the top 0.1% (P99.9–100), and the top 0.01% (P99.99–100). This also allows us to analyse the five intermediate fractiles within the top decile: P90–95, P95–99, P99–99.5, P99.5–99.9, P99.9–99.99. Each fractile is defined relative to the total number of potential tax units in the entire US population. This number is computed using population and family census statistics (US Department of Commerce, Bureau of Census 1975; and Bureau of Census 1999) and should not be confused with the actual number of tax returns filed. In order to get a more concrete sense of size of income by fractiles, Table 5.1 displays the thresholds, the average income level in each fractile, along with the number of tax units in each fractile all for 2000.

We use a gross income definition including all income items reported on tax returns and before all deductions: salaries and wages, small business and farm income, partnership and fiduciary income, dividends, interest, rents, royalties, and other small items reported as other income. Realized capital gains are not an annual flow of income (in general, capital gains are realized by individuals in a lumpy way) and form a very volatile component of income with large aggregate variations from year to year depending on stock price variations. Therefore, we focus mainly on series that exclude capital gains.[8] Income, according to our

Table 5.1 Thresholds and average incomes in top income groups in US, 2000

Percentile threshold (1)	Income threshold (2)	Income groups (3)	Number of tax units (4)	Average income in each group (5)
		Full population	133,589,000	$42,709
Median	$25,076	Bottom 90%	120,230,100	$26,616
Top 10%	$87,334	Top 10–5%	6,679,450	$100,480
Top 5%	$120,212	Top 5–1%	5,343,560	$162,366
Top 1%	$277,983	Top 1–0.5%	667,945	$327,970
Top .5%	$397,949	Top 0.5–0.1%	534,356	$611,848
Top .1%	$1,134,849	Top 0.1–0.01%	120,230	$2,047,801
Top .01%	$5,349,795	Top 0.01%	13,359	$13,055,242

Notes: Computations based on income tax return statistics. Income defined as annual gross income reported on tax returns excluding capital gains and all government transfers (such as social security, unemployment benefits, welfare payments, etc.) and before individual income taxes and employees' payroll taxes. Amounts are expressed in current 2000 dollars. Col. (2) reports the income thresholds corresponding to each of the percentiles in col. (1). For example, an annual income of at least $87,334 is required to belong to the top 10% tax units, etc.

Sources: Table 5A.0 and Table 5A.4, row 2000.

[8] In order to assess the sensitivity of our results to the treatment of capital gains, we present additional series including capital gains (see below). Details on the methodology and complete series are presented in appendix. The denominator for the series including capital gains in our first working paper Piketty and Saez (2001) included only capital gains going to the top 10% tax units. In this final version, we include instead all capital gains in the denominator for the series including capital (see Appendix 5A for a more detailed discussion).

definition, is computed before individual income taxes and individual payroll taxes but after employers' payroll taxes and corporate income taxes.[9]

The sources from which we obtained our data consist of tables displaying the number of tax returns, the amounts reported, and the income composition, for a large number of income brackets (US Treasury Department, Internal Revenue Service 1916–2002). As the top tail of the income distribution is very well approximated by a Pareto distribution, we use simple parametric interpolation methods to estimate the thresholds and average income levels for each of our fractiles. We then estimate shares of income by dividing the income amounts accruing to each fractiles by total personal income computed from National Income Accounts (Kuznets 1941, 1945; and US Department of Commerce 2000).[10] Using the published information on composition of income by brackets and a simple linear interpolation method, we decompose the amount of income for each fractile into five components: salaries and wages, dividends, interest income, rents and royalties, and business income.

We use the same methodology to compute top wage shares using published tables classifying tax returns by size of salaries and wages. In this case, fractiles are defined relative to the total number of tax units with positive wages and salaries estimated as the number of part-time and full workers from National Income Accounts (US Department of Commerce 2000) less the number of wives who are employees (estimated from US Department of Commerce, Bureau of Census 1975 and Bureau of Census 1999). The sum of total wages in the economy used to compute shares is also obtained from National Income Accounts (US Department of Commerce 2000).

The published IRS data vary from year to year and there are numerous changes in tax law between 1913 and 2002.[11] To construct homogeneous series, we make a number of adjustments and corrections. Individual tax returns micro-files are available since 1960.[12] They allow us to do exact computations of all our statistics for that period and to check the validity of our adjustments. Kuznets (1953) was not able to use micro-files to assess possible biases in his estimates due to his methodological assumptions.[13]

Our method differs from the recent important studies by Feenberg and Poterba (1993, 2000) who derive series of the income share of the top 0.5%[14] for 1951 to 1995. They use total income reported on tax returns as their denominator and the total adult population as their base to obtain the number of tax units

[9] Computing series after individual income taxes is beyond the scope of the present chapter but is a necessary step to analyse the redistributive power of the income tax over time, as well as behavioural responses to individual income taxation.

[10] This methodology using tax returns to compute the level of top incomes, and using national accounts to compute the total income denominator is standard in historical studies of income inequality. Kuznets (1953), for instance, adopted this method.

[11] The most important example is the treatment of capital gains and the percentage of these gains that are included in the statistics tables.

[12] These data are known as the Individual Tax Model files. They contain about 100,000 returns per year and largely oversample high incomes, providing a very precise picture of top reported incomes.

[13] In particular the treatment by Kuznets of capital gains produces a downward bias in the level of his top shares.

[14] They also present incomplete series for the top 1%.

corresponding to the top fractiles.[15] Their method is simpler than ours but cannot be used for years before 1945 when a small fraction of the population filed tax returns.

5.3 TOP INCOME SHARES AND COMPOSITION

Trends in Top Income Shares

The basic series of top income shares are presented in Table 5A1. Figure 5.1 shows that the income share of the top decile of tax units from 1917 to 2002 is U-shaped. The share of the top decile fluctuated around 40% to 45% during the interwar period. It declined substantially to about 30% during the Second World War, and then remained stable at 31% to 32% until the 1970s when it increased again. By the mid-1990s, the share had crossed the 40% level and is now at a level close to the pre-war level, although a bit lower. Therefore, the evidence suggests that the twentieth century decline in inequality took place in a very specific and brief time interval. Such an abrupt decline cannot easily be reconciled with a Kuznets type process. The smooth increase in inequality in the last three decades is more consistent with slow underlying changes in the demand and supply of factors, even though it should be noted that a significant part of the gain is concentrated in 1987 and 1988 just after the Tax Reform Act of 1986 which sharply cut the top marginal income tax rates (we will return to this issue).

Looking at the bottom fractiles within the top decile (P90–95 and P95–99) in Figure 5.2 reveals new evidence. These fractiles account for a relatively small fraction of the total fluctuation of the top decile income share. The drop in the shares of fractiles P90–95 and P95–99 during the Second World War is less extreme than for the top decile as a whole, and they start recovering from the World War shock directly after the war. These shares do not increase much during the 1980s and 1990s (the P90–95 share was fairly stable, and the P95–99 share increased by about 2 percentage points while the top decile share increased by about 10 percentage points).

In contrast to P90–95 and P95–99, the top percentile (P99–100 in Figure 5.2) underwent enormous fluctuations over the twentieth century. The share of total income received by the top 1% was about 18% before the First World War, but only about 8% from the late 1950s to the 1970s. The top percentile share declined during the First World War and the post-war depression (1916–20), recovered during the 1920s boom, and declined again during the Great Depression (1929–32, and 1936–38) and the Second World War. This highly specific timing for the pattern of top incomes, composed primarily of capital income (see below), strongly suggests that shocks to capital owners between 1914

[15] This method is not fully satisfactory for a long-run study as the average number of adults per tax unit has decreased significantly since the Second World War.

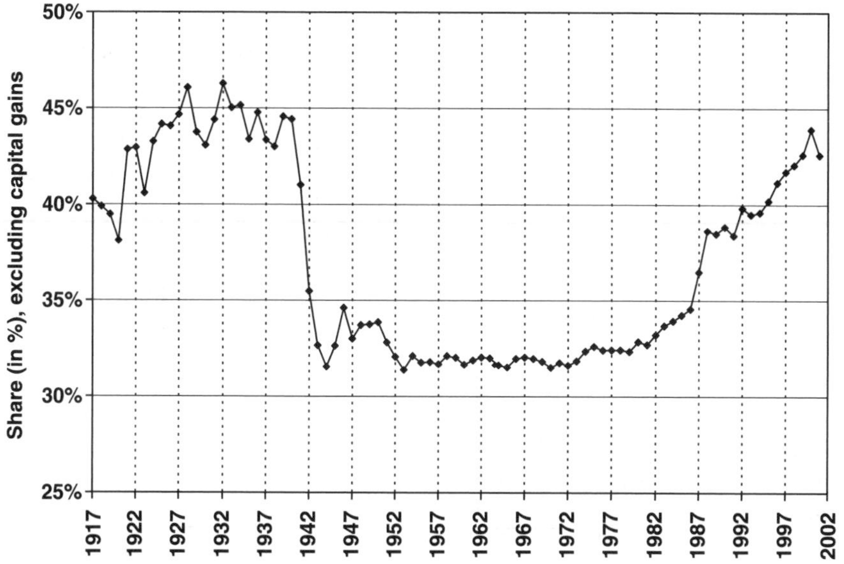

Figure 5.1 The top decile income share, US 1917–2002

Note: Income is defined as market income but excludes capital gains.
Source: Table 5A.1, col. P90–100.

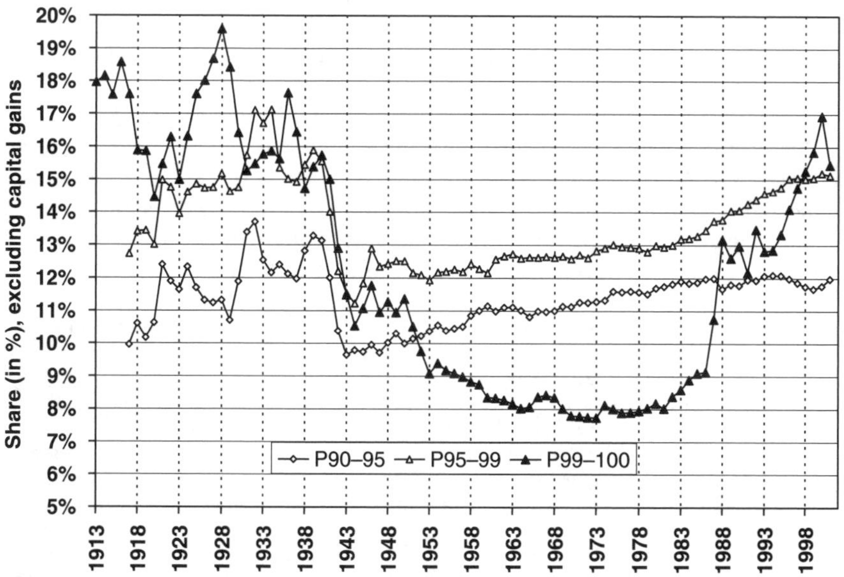

Figure 5.2 The income shares of P90–95, P95–99, and P99–100 in US, 1913–2002

Note: Income is defined as market income but excludes capital gains.
Source: Table 5A.1, col. P90–95, P95–99, P99–100.

and 1945 (Depression and Wars) played a key role. The depressions of the interwar period were far more profound in their effects than the post-Second World War recessions. As a result, it is not surprising that the fluctuations in top shares were far wider during the interwar period than in the decades after the war.[16]

Figure 5.2 shows that the fluctuation of shares for P90–95 and P95–99 is exactly opposite to the fluctuation for P99–100 over the business cycle from 1917 to 1939. As shown below, the P90–95 and P95–99 incomes are mostly composed of wage income while the P99–100 incomes are mostly composed of capital income. During the large downturns of the interwar period, capital income sharply fell while wages (especially for those near the top), which are generally rigid nominally, improved in relative terms. On the other hand, during the booms (1923–29) and the recovery (1933–6), capital income increased quickly, but as prices rose, top wages lost in relative terms.[17]

The negative effect of the wars on top incomes is due in part to the large tax increases enacted to finance them. During both wars, the corporate income tax (as well as the individual income tax) was drastically increased and this reduced mechanically the distributions to stockholders.[18] National Income Accounts show that during the Second World War, corporate profits surged, but dividend distributions stagnated mostly because of the increase in the corporate tax (who increased from less than 20% to over 50%) but also because retained earnings increased sharply.[19]

The decline in top incomes during the first part of the century is even more pronounced for higher fractiles within the top percentile, groups that could be expected to rely more heavily on capital income. As depicted in Figure 5.3, the income share of the top 0.01% underwent huge fluctuations during the century. In 1915, the top 0.01% earned 400 times more than the average; in 1970, the average top 0.01% income was 'only' 50 times the average; in 2002, they earned about 300 times the average income.

Our long-term series place the TRA 1986 episode in a longer term perspective. Feenberg and Poterba (1993, 2000), looking at the top 0.5% income shares series ending in 1992 (and 1995 respectively), argued that the surge after TRA86 appeared permanent. However, completing the series up to 2002 shows that the significant increase in the top marginal tax rate, from 31% to 39.6%, enacted in 1993 did not prevent top shares from increasing sharply up to year 2000.[20] From

[16] The fact that top shares are very smooth after 1945 and bumpy before is therefore not an artefact of an increase in the accuracy of the data (in fact, the data are more detailed before the Second World War than after), but reflects real changes in the economic conditions.

[17] Piketty (2001, 2003, Chapter 3 in this volume) shows that exactly the same phenomenon is taking place in France at the same period.

[18] During the First World War, top income tax rates reached 'modern' levels above 60% in less than two years. As was forcefully argued at that time by Mellon (1924), it is conceivable that large incomes found temporary ways to avoid taxation at a time where the administration of the Internal Revenue Service was still in its infancy.

[19] Computing top shares for incomes before corporate taxes by imputing corporate profits corresponding to dividends received is an important task left for future research (see Goldsmith et al. 1954 and Cartter 1954 for such an attempt around the Second World War period). See also the discussion of the UK case in Chapter 4.

[20] Slemrod and Bakija (2000) pointed out that top incomes have surged in recent years. They note that tax payments by taxpayers with AGI above US$200,000 increased significantly from 1995 to 1997.

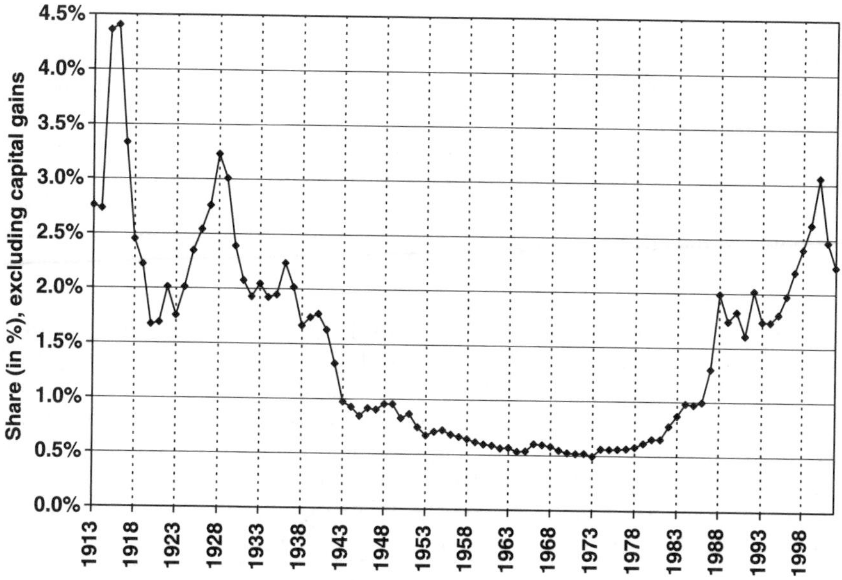

Figure 5.3 The top 0.01% income share, US 1913–2002

Note: Income is defined as market income but excludes capital gains.
Source: Table 5A.1, col. P99.99–100.

that perspective, looking at Figures 5.2 and 5.3, the average increase in top shares from 1985 to 1994 is not significantly higher than the increase from 1994 to 2000 or from 1978 to 1984. As a result, it is possible to argue that TRA86 produced no permanent surge in top income shares, but only a transitory blip. The analysis of top wage shares in Section 5.4 will reinforce this interpretation. In any case, the pattern of top income shares cannot be explained fully by the pattern of top income tax rates. Saez (2004) analyses in much more detail the links between top income shares and marginal tax rates for the period 1960–2000.

The drop in top incomes shares from 2000 to 2002, concentrated exclusively among the top 1% is also remarkable. This later phenomenon is likely due to the stock-market crash which reduced dramatically the value of stock-options and hence depressed top reported wages and salaries.[21] The series including realized capital gains display an even larger fall (see Figure 5A.2 in Appendix 5A).

The Secular Decline of Top Capital Incomes

To demonstrate more conclusively that shocks to capital income were responsible for the large decline of top shares in the first part of the century, we look at the composition of income within the top fractiles. Table 5A.7 reports the

[21] Because stock-options are reported as wage income only when exercised, our income measure (even excluding capital gains) is contaminated by stock-market fluctuations in the recent decades. Ideally, one would want to include in wage income only the Black-Scholes value of stock-options at the moment they are granted. The difference between the exercise profit and the Black-Scholes value (which is zero in expectation) should be conceptually considered as a capital gain.

composition of income in top groups for various years from 1916 and 1999. Figure 5.4 displays the composition of income for each fractile in 1929 (Panel A) and 1999 (Panel B). As expected, Panel A shows the share of wage income is a declining function of income and that the share of capital income (dividends, interest, rents, and royalties) is an increasing function of income. The share of entrepreneurial income (self-employment, small businesses, and partnerships) is fairly flat. Thus, individuals in fractiles P90–95 and P95–99 rely mostly on labour income (capital income is less than 25% for these groups) while individuals in the top percentile derive most of their income in the form of capital income. Complete series in Piketty and Saez (2001) show that the sharply increasing pattern of capital income is entirely due to dividends. This evidence confirms that the very large decrease of top incomes observed during the 1914–45 period was to a large extent a capital income phenomenon.

One might also be tempted to interpret the large upturn in top income shares observed since the 1970s as a revival of very high capital incomes, but this is not the case. As shown in Panel B, the income composition pattern has changed drastically between 1929 and 1999. In 1999, the share of wage income has increased significantly for all top groups. Even at the very top, wage income and entrepreneurial income form the vast majority of income. The share of capital income remains small (less than 25%) even for the highest incomes. Therefore, the composition of high incomes at the end of the century is very different from those earlier in the century. Before the Second World War, the richest Americans were overwhelmingly rentiers deriving most of their income from wealth holdings (mainly in the form of dividends).

Occupation data by income bracket were published by the IRS in 1916 only. Those statistics classified tax returns into 36 different occupations by brackets of income. We have combined these 36 occupations into four groups: salaried professions, independent professions, business owners, and capitalists and rentiers. The salaried professions are those who receive salaries such as teachers, civil servants, engineers, corporation managers, and officials. These individuals presumably derive an important part of their income in the form of wages and salaries. Independent professions are self-employed individuals or individuals working in partnerships such as lawyers, doctors, etc. Business owners are merchants, hotel proprietors, manufacturers, etc. These two groups presumably derive most of their incomes in the form of business income. Finally capitalists and rentiers are bankers, brokers, and those who classify themselves as 'capitalists: investors and speculators',[22] and presumably derive most of their income in the form of capital income. It is possible, especially at the very top, for some individuals to be classified in more than one group. We present in Table 5.2 the distribution of these four occupation groups by fractiles within the top percentile.[23] This table confirms

[22] At the very top, 'capitalists: investors and speculators' form the overwhelming majority of our capitalist and rentier group.

[23] We have added a fractile for the top 0.001% (top 400 taxpayers in 1916) to emphasize how the very top is composed overwhelmingly of 'capitalists'.

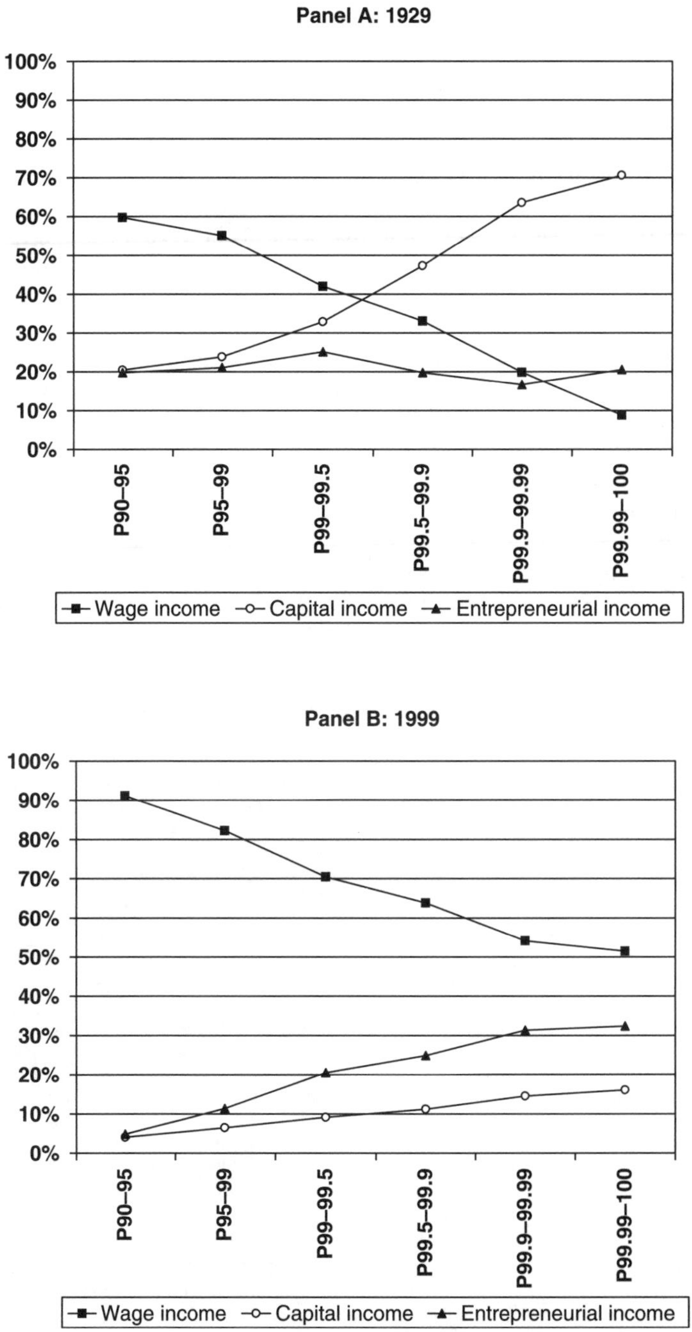

Figure 5.4 Income composition of top groups within the top decile in US, 1929 and 1999

Note: Capital income dose not include copital gains.

Source: Table 5A.7, rows 1929 and 1999.

our previous results: the share of the salaried occupation declines steadily within the top percentile from 28% to less than 10% at the very top. The share of independent professions also declines from 20% to 5%. The share of business owners is first increasing (from 30% to 40%) and declining slightly at the very top. The share of capitalists increases sharply especially at the very top where 95% of the top 400 taxpayers fall into this category. This table shows clearly that top corporate executives at the beginning of the century were only a tiny minority within the top taxpayers. In contrast, in 1999, more than half of the very top taxpayers derive the major part of their income in the form of wages and salaries. Thus, today, the 'working rich' celebrated by *Forbes Magazine* have overtaken the 'coupon-clipping rentiers'.

The dramatic evolution of the composition of top incomes appears robust and independent from the erratic evolution of capital gains excluded in Figures 5.1 to 5.4. Tables 5A.2 and 5A.3 display the top income shares including realized capital gains. In Table 5A.2, in order to get around the lumpiness of realizations, individuals are ranked by income *excluding* capital gains but capital gains are added back to income to compute shares. In Table 5A.3, individuals are ranked by income including capital gains and capital gains are added back to income to compute shares. The denominator for those series includes all realized capital gains.[24] As depicted for the top 1% on Figure 5A.2, these additional series show that including capital gains does not modify our main conclusion that very top

Table 5.2 Shares of each occupation within the top 1% in US, 1916

Fractiles (1)	Number of tax units (2)	Salaried professions (3)	Independent professions (4)	Business owners (5)	Capitalists and rentiers (6)
P99–99.5	198,950	30.5%	19.0%	30.3%	20.2%
P99.5–99.9	159,160	22.1%	14.0%	35.8%	27.9%
P99.9–99.99	35,811	16.2%	8.0%	39.7%	45.2%
P99.99–99.999	3,581	12.0%	5.1%	42.6%	65.4%
P99.999–100	398	8.0%	3.1%	33.2%	94.6%

Notes: Salaried professions defined as accounting profession (accountants, statisticians, actuaries, etc.), engineers, clergymen, public service: civil and military, teachers, corporation officials, and all other employees. Independent professions defined as architects, artists, authors, clergymen, lawyers and judges, medical profession, theatrical profession, all other professions, profession not stated, commercial travelers, and sportsmen. Business owners defined as farmers, hotel proprietors and restaurateurs, insurance agents, labour skilled and unskilled, lumbermen, manufacturers, merchants and dealers, mine owners and operators, saloon keepers, theatrical business owners, all other business, and business not stated. Capitalists and rentiers defined as bankers, real-estate brokers, stock and bond brokers, insurance brokers, all other brokers, and capitalists: investors and speculators.

Source: Computations based on interpolations from *Statistics of Income*, 1916. table 6c, pp. 126–37.

[24] In contrast, the first working paper Piketty and Saez (2001) included in the denominator for the series including capital gains, only realized capital gains going to the top 10% tax units. We have modified the denominator definition so that one can compute the concentration of realized capital gains (such as the fraction of all capital gains going to the top 10% or top 1% tax units) with our new series. The change in levels of the series are very small, however, because in general 75% to 90% of all realized capital gains go to the top 10% (see Appendix 5A for more details).

income shares dropped enormously during the 1914–1945 period before increasing steadily in the last three decades.[25]

The decline of the capital income share is a very long-term phenomenon and is not limited to a few years and a few thousands tax units. Figure 5.5 shows a gradual secular decline of the share of capital income (excluding again capital gains realizations) and dividends in the top 0.5% fractile from the 1920s to the 1990s: capital income made about 55% of total income in the 1920s, 35% in the 1950s–60s, and 15% in the 1990s. Sharp declines occurred during the First World War, the Great Depression, and the Second World War. Capital income recovered only partially from these shocks in the late 1940s and started a steady decline in the mid-1960s. This secular decline is entirely due to dividends: the share of interest, rent, and royalties has been roughly flat while the dividend share has dropped from about 40% in the 1920s, to about 25% in the 1950s and 1960s, to less than 10% in the 1990s.[26]

Most importantly, the secular decline of top capital incomes is due to a decreased concentration of capital income rather than a decline in the share of capital income in the economy as a whole. As displayed in Figure 5.6, the National

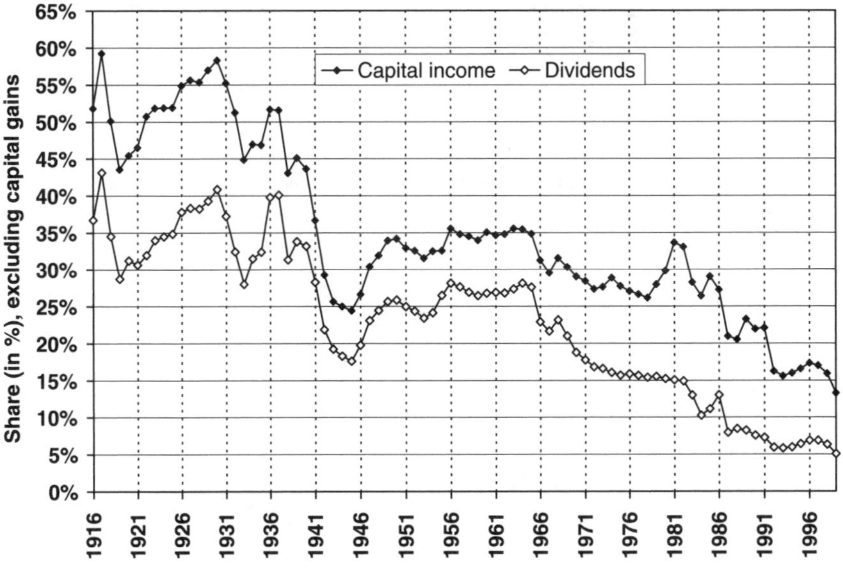

Figure 5.5 The capital income share in the top 0.5% in US, 1916–99

Note: Series display the share of capital income (excluding capital gains) and dividends in total income (excluding capital gains) for the top 0.5% income quantile.

Source: Table 5A.7, column P99.5–100

[25] It is interesting to note, however, that during the 1960s, when dividends were strongly tax disadvantaged relative to capital gains, capital gains do seem to represent a larger share in top incomes than during other periods such as the 1920s or late 1990s that also witnessed large increases in stock prices.

[26] Tax statistics by size of dividends analyzed in Piketty and Saez (2001) confirm a drastic decline of top dividend incomes over the century. In 1998 dollars, top 0.1% dividends earners reported on average about US$500,000 of dividends in 1927 but less than US$240,000 in 1995.

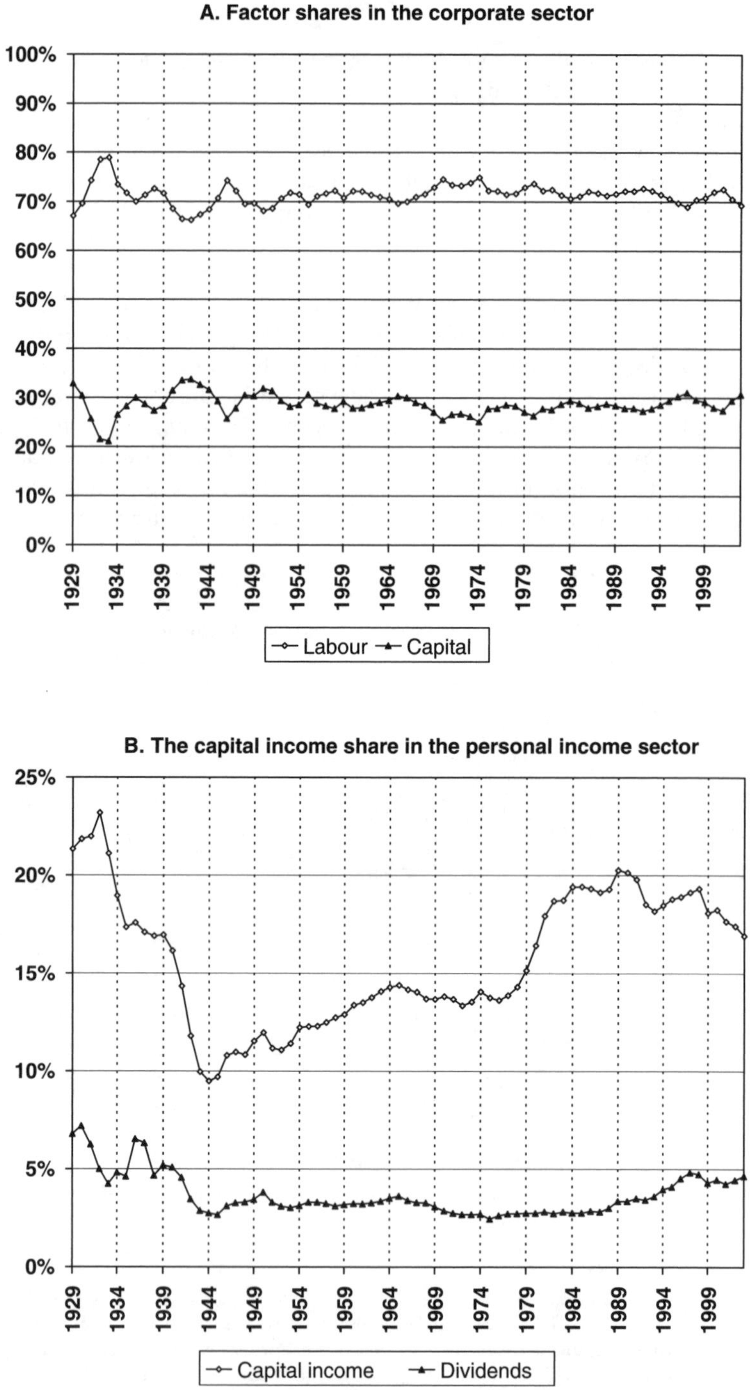

Figure 5.6 Capital income in the corporate and personal sector, US 1929–2003

Notes: Panel A from NIPA Table 1.14; consumption of fixed capital and net interest have been included in the capital share. Panal B from NIPA Table 2.1; capital income includes dividends, interest, and rents.

Source: Authors' computations based on National Income and Product Accounts.

Income Accounts series show that the aggregate capital income share has not declined over the century. As is well known, factor shares in the corporate sector have been fairly flat in the long-run with the labour share around 70%–75%, and the capital share around 25%–30% (Panel A). The share of capital income in aggregate personal income is about 20% both in the 1920s and in the 1990s (Panel B). Similarly, the share of dividends was around 5% in the late 1990s and only slightly higher (about 6%–7%) before the Great Depression. This secular decline is very small compared to the enormous fall of top capital incomes.[27] Contrarily to a widely held view, dividends as a whole are still well and alive.[28]

It should be noted, however, that the ratio of total dividends reported on individual tax returns to personal dividends in National Accounts has declined continuously over the period 1927–95, starting from a level close to 90% in 1927, declining slowly to 60% in 1988, and dropping precipitously to less than 40% in 1995. This decline is due mostly to the growth of funded pension plans and retirement saving accounts through which individuals receive dividends that are never reported as dividends on income tax returns. For the highest income earners, this additional source of dividends is likely to be very small relative to dividends directly reported on tax returns.

Estate tax returns statistics (available since the beginning on the estate tax in 1916) are an alternative important source of data to analyse the evolution of large fortunes.[29] Kopczuk and Saez (2004) used those data, recently compiled in electronic format by the IRS for most of the period, to construct top wealth shares for the period 1916–2000 using the estate multiplier method. Figure 5.7 displays the top 0.1% share series from Kopczuk and Saez (2004). It shows that the top 0.1% has indeed dropped drastically from over 20% in the early part of the century to around 7.5% in the 1970s. In contrast to top income shares, the increase in wealth concentration has been modest since the 1970s: the top 0.1% wealth share has increased modestly to around 9%–10% by 2000. This evidence is consistent with our previous results on the decline in top capital incomes over the century. There is a concern that estate tax avoidance and evasion might bias downward wealth concentration estimated using the estate multiplier technique. The most popular forms of estate tax avoidance involve setting up trusts whereby wealthy individuals can pass substantial wealth to the next generations with modest gift tax liability and while keeping some control over assets. Tax statistics on trusts, analysed in Kopczuk and Saez (2004), show, however, that capital income earned through all trusts is relatively modest and has actually declined in relative terms over the century. Thus, adding back all trust wealth to top wealth

[27] The share of dividends in personal income starts declining in 1940 because the corporate income tax increases sharply and permanently, reducing mechanically profits that can be distributed to stockholders.

[28] As documented by Fama and French (2000), a growing fraction of firms never pay dividends (especially in the new technology industries, where firms often make no profit at all), but the point is that total dividend payments continue to grow at the same rate as aggregate corporate profits.

[29] In particular, capital gains not realized before death are never reported on income tax returns, but are included in the value of assessed estates.

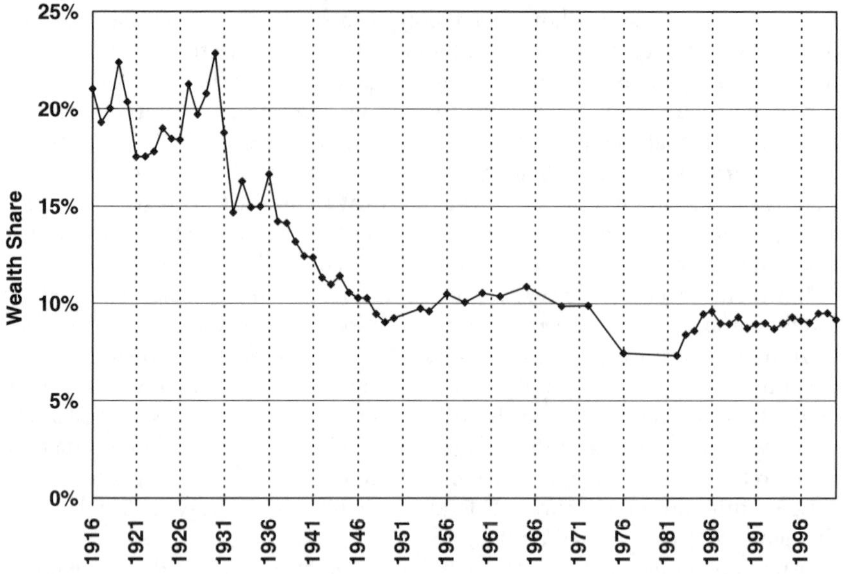

Figure 5.7 The top 0.1% wealth share in US, 1916–2000

Notes: Top wealth shares are estimated from estate tax returns using the estate multiplier method.
Source: Kopczuk and Saez 2004: Table 3, col. Top 0.1%.

holders would not affect the pattern of top wealth shares constructed in Kopczuk and Saez (2004).

Proposed Interpretation: The Role of Progressive Taxation

How can we explain the steep secular decline in capital income concentration? It is easy to understand how the macro-economic shocks of the Great Depression and the fiscal shocks of the World Wars have had a negative impact on capital concentration. The difficult question to answer is why large fortunes did not recover from these shocks. The most natural and realistic candidate for an explanation seems to be the creation and the development of the progressive income tax (and of the progressive estate tax and corporate income tax). The very large fortunes that generated the top 0.01% incomes observed at the beginning of the century were accumulated during the nineteenth century, at a time where progressive taxes hardly existed and capitalists could dispose of almost all their income to consume and to accumulate.[30] The fiscal situation faced by capitalists in the twentieth century to recover from the shocks incurred during the 1914–45 period has been substantially different. Top tax rates were very high from the end of the First World War to the early 1920s, and then continuously from 1932 to the

[30] During the nineteenth century, the only progressive tax was the property tax, but its level was low (see Brownlee 2000 for a detailed description).

mid-1980s. Moreover, the United States has imposed a sharply progressive estate tax since 1916, and a substantial corporate income tax ever since the Second World War.[31] These very high marginal rates applied to only a very small fraction of taxpayers, but created a substantial burden on the very top income groups (such as the top 0.1% and 0.01%) composed primarily of capital income. In contrast to progressive labour income taxation, which simply produces a level effect on earnings through labour supply responses, progressive taxation of capital income has cumulative or dynamic effects because it reduces the net-return on wealth which generates tomorrow's wealth.

It is difficult to prove in a rigorous way that the dynamic effects of progressive taxation on capital accumulation and pre-tax income inequality have the right quantitative magnitude and account for the observed facts. One would need to know more about the savings rates of capitalists, how their accumulation strategies have changed since 1945. The orders of magnitude do not seem unrealistic, especially if one assumes that the owners of large fortunes, whose pre-tax incomes were already severely hit by the pre-war shocks, were not willing to reduce their consumption to very low levels. Piketty (2001, 2003) provides simple numerical simulations showing that for a fixed saving rate, introducing substantial capital income taxation has a tremendous effect on the time needed to reconstitute large wealth holdings after negative shocks. Moreover, reduced savings in response to a reduction in the after-tax rate of return on wealth would accelerate the decrease in wealth inequality. Piketty (2003) shows that in the classic dynastic model with infinite horizon, any positive capital income tax rate above a given high threshold of wealth will eventually eliminate all large wealth holdings without affecting, however, the total capital stock in the economy.

We are not the first to propose progressive taxation as an explanation for the decrease in top shares of income and wealth. Lampman (1962) did as well and Kuznets (1955) explicitly mentioned this mechanism as well as the shocks incurred by capital owners during the 1913–48 period, before presenting his inverted U-shaped curve theory based on technological change. Explanations pointing out that periods of technological revolutions such as the last part of the nineteenth century (industrial revolutions) or the end of the twentieth century (computer revolution) are more favourable to the making of fortunes than other periods might also be relevant.[32] Our results suggest that the decline in income tax progressivity since the 1980s, the reduction in the tax rate for dividend income in 2003, and the projected repeal of the estate tax by 2011 might in a few decades produce again levels of wealth concentration similar to those of the beginning of the twentieth century.[33]

[31] From 1909 (first year the corporate tax was imposed) to the beginning of the Second World War, the corporate tax rate was low, except during the First World War.

[32] DeLong (1998) also points out the potential role of anti-trust law. According to DeLong, anti-trust law was enforced more loosely before 1929 and since 1980 than between 1929 and 1980.

[33] The tax cut on dividend income of 2003 generated a surge in dividend initiations among publicly traded companies (Chetty and Saez 2004). Microsoft, for example, started paying dividends in 2003 and made a huge special dividend distribution in 2004. William Gates, founder of the company and

5.4 TOP WAGE SHARES

Table 5B.2 displays top wage shares from 1927 to 2002 constructed using IRS tabulations by size of wages. There are three caveats to note about these long-term wage inequality series. First, self-employment income is not included in wages and therefore our series focus only on wage income inequality. As self-employment income has been a decreasing share of labour income over the century, it is conceivable that the pool of wage and salary earners has substantially evolved overtime, and that total labour income inequality series would differ from our wage inequality series. Second and relatedly, large changes in the wage force due to the business cycle and wars might affect our series through compositional effects because we define the top fractiles relative to the total number of tax units with *positive* wage income. As can be seen in column (1) of Table 5B.1, the number of tax units with wages declined during the Great Depression due to high levels of unemployment, increased sharply during the Second World War because of the increase in military personnel, and decreased just after the war. We show in Appendix 5B that these entry effects do not affect top shares when the average wage of the new entrants is equal to about 50% of the average wage. This condition is approximately satisfied for military personnel in the Second World War and thus top wage shares including or excluding military personnel during The Second World War are almost identical. Third, our wage income series are based on the tax unit and not the individual. As a result, an increase in the correlation of earnings across spouses, as documented in Karoly (1993), with no change in individual wage inequality, would generate an increase in tax unit wage inequality.[34]

Figure 5.8 displays the wage share of the top decile and Figure 5.9 displays the wage shares of the P90–95, P95–99, and P99–100 groups from 1927 to 2002. As for overall income, the pattern of top decile wage share over the century is also U-shaped. There are, however, important differences that we describe below. It is useful to divide the period from 1927 to 2002 into three sub-periods: the pre-Second World War period (1927–40); the war and post-war period (1941–69); and the last three decades (1970–2002). We analyse each of these periods in turn.

richest American person, earned US$3600 million from Microsoft dividends in 2004: by far the largest income ever earned in any single year in the United States. It remains to be seen whether this reform will affect significantly the composition of top reported incomes. It will certainly be a useful test of the magnitude of fiscal manipulation effects.

[34] This point can be analysed using the Current Population Surveys available since 1962 which allow the estimation of wage inequality series both at the individual and tax unit level. In Canada, it is possible to construct top income shares both at the family and individual level since 1982. Those series, presented in Saez and Veall (Chapter 4) show that the upward trend in top income shares is almost identical at the individual and family suggesting that the secondary earner effect cannot explain the surge in top income shares.

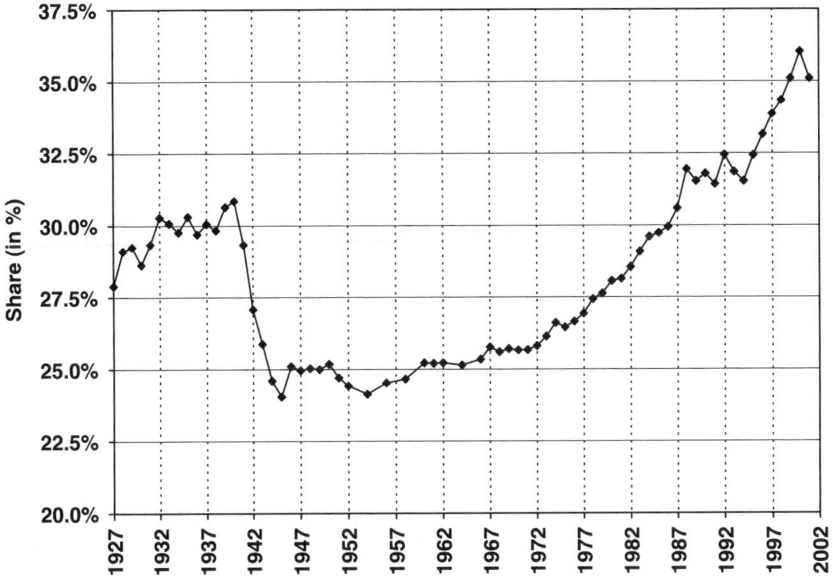

Figure 5.8 The top decile wage income share, US 1927–2002

Notes: Wage income includes bonuses, and profits from exercised stock options.

Source: Table 5B.2, col. P90–100.

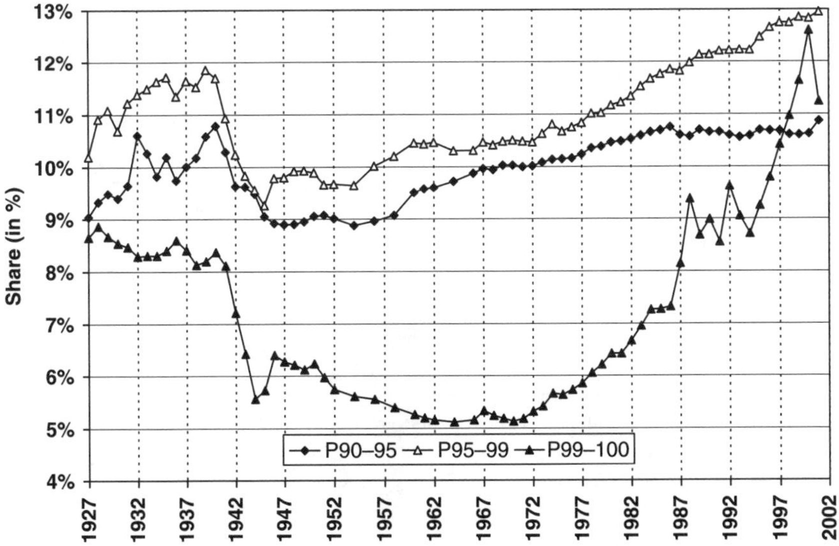

Figure 5.9 Wage income shares for P90–95, P95–99, and P99–100 in US, 1927–2002

Note: Wage income includes bonuses, and profits from exercised stock options.

Source: Table 5B.2, col. P90–95, 95–99, P99–100

Wage Inequality Stability Before the Second World War

Top wage shares display a striking stability from 1927 to 1940. This is especially true for the top percentile. In contrast to capital income, the Great Depression did not produce a reduction in top wage shares. On the contrary, the high middle class fractiles benefited in relative terms from the Great Depression. Even though the IRS has not published tables on wage income over the period 1913–26, we can use an indirect source of evidence to document trends in top wage shares. Corporation tax returns require each corporation to report separately the sum of salaries paid to its officers. This statistic, compensation of officers, is reported quasi-annually by the IRS starting in 1917. We report in Figure 5.10 the total compensation of officers reported on corporate tax returns divided by the total wage bill in the economy from 1917 to 1960 along with the shares of the P99.5–100 and P99–99.9 wage groups which are close in level to the share of officer compensation. From 1927 to 1960, officer compensation share and these fractiles shares track each other relatively closely. Therefore, the share of officer compensation from 1917 to 1927 should be a good proxy as well for these top wage shares. This indirect evidence suggests that the top share of wages was also roughly constant, or even slightly increasing from 1917 to 1926.

Previous studies have suggested that wage inequality has been gradually decreasing during the first half of the twentieth century (and in particular during the inter-war period) using series of wage ratios between skilled and unskilled

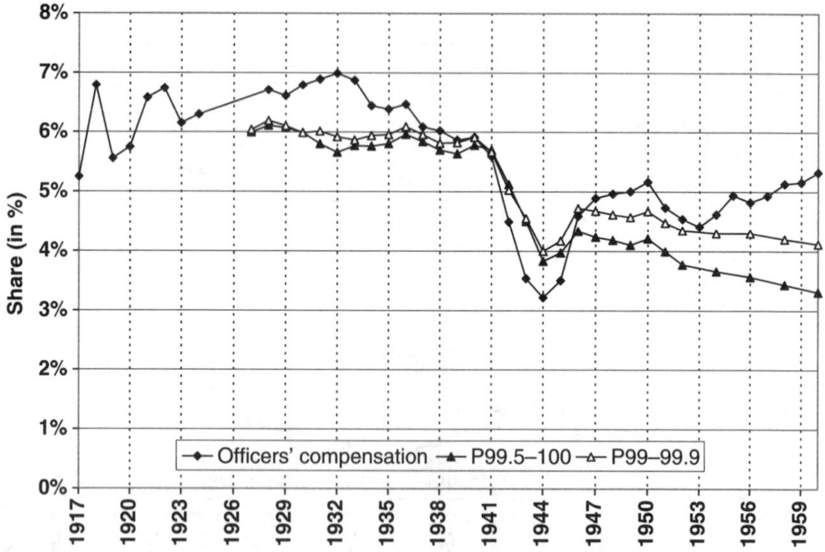

Figure 5.10 Shares of officers' compensation and wage shares, P99.5–100 and P99–99.9 in US, 1917–60

Source: Officers compensation from Authors' computations based on corporate income tax returns (Table 5B.1, col Officers compensation, and Table 5B.2, col. P99.5–100, and P99–99.5+P99.5–99.9)

occupations (see, e.g., Keat 1960; Williamson and Lindert 1980). However, it is important to recognize that a decrease in the ratio of skilled over unskilled wages does not necessarily imply an overall compression of wage income inequality, let alone a reduction in the top wage shares. Given the continuous rise in the numerical importance of white collar jobs, it is natural to expect that the ratios of high-skill wages to low-skill wages would decline over time, even if wage inequality measured in terms of shares of top fractiles of the complete wage distribution does not change.[35] Goldin and Katz (1999) have recently presented new series of white-collar to blue-collar earnings ratios from the beginning of the twentieth century to 1960, and they find that the decrease in pay ratio is concentrated only in the short periods of the two World Wars. Whether or not the compression of wages that occurred during the First World War was fully reversed during the 1920s in the United States is still an open question.[36]

Sharp Drop in Inequality During the Second World War with no Recovery

In all of our wage shares series, there is a sharp drop during the Second World War from 1941 to 1945.[37] The higher the fractile, the greater is the decrease. The share of P90–95 declines by 16% between 1940 and 1945, but the share of the top 1% declines by more than 30%, and the top 0.1% by almost 35% during the same period (Table 5B.2). This sharp compression of high wages can fairly easily be explained by the wage controls of the war economy. The National War Labour Board, established in January 1942 and dissolved in 1945, was responsible for approving all wage changes and made any wage increase illegal without its approval. Exceptions to controls were more frequently granted to employees receiving low wages.[38] Lewellen (1968) has studied the evolution of executive compensation from 1940 to 1963 and his results show strikingly that executive salaries were frozen in nominal terms from 1941 to 1945 consistent with the sharp drop in top wage shares that we find.

The surprising fact, however, is that top wage shares did not recover after the war. A partial and short-lived recovery can be seen for all groups, except the very top. But the shares never recover more than one third of the loss incurred during the Second World War. Moreover, after a short period of stability in the late 1940s,

[35] For instance, Piketty (2001) reports a long-run compression (both from 1900 to 1950 and from 1950 to 1998) of the ratio of the average wage of managers over the average wage of production workers in France, even though wage inequality (measured both in terms of top fractiles wage shares and in terms of P90/P10-type ratios) was constant in the long-run.

[36] Tax return data available for France make it possible to compute wage inequality series starting in 1913 (as opposed to 1927 in the United States). By using these data, Piketty (2001, 2003 and Chapter 3 in this volume) found that wage inequality in France (measured both in terms of top wage shares and in terms of P90/P10 ratios) declined during the First World War but fully recovered during the 1920s, so that overall wage inequality in 1930 or 1940 was the same as in 1913. Another advantage of the French wage data is that it always based upon individual wages (as opposed to total tax unit wages in the United States).

[37] Note that for fractiles below the top percentile, the drop starts from 1940 to 1941.

[38] See Goldin and Margo (1992) for a more detailed description.

a second phase of compression takes place in the top percentile. This compression phase is longer and most pronounced the higher the fractile. While the fractiles P90–95 and P95–99 hardly suffer from a second compression phase and start recovering just after the war, the top group shares experience a substantial loss from 1950 to the mid-1960s. The top 0.1% share for example declines from 1.6% in 1950 to 1.1% in 1964 (Table 5B.2).

The overall drop in top wage shares, although important, is significantly lower than the overall drop in top income shares. The top 1% income share dropped from about 18–19% before the First World War and in the late 1920s to about 8% in the late 1950s (Figure 5.2), while the top 1% wage share dropped from about 8.5% in the 1920s to about 5% in the late 1950s (Figure 5.9). This confirms that capital income played a key role in the decline of top income shares during the first half of the century.

The Increase in Top Shares Since the 1970s

Many studies have documented the increase in inequality in the United States since the 1970s (see, e.g., Katz and Murphy 1992). Our evidence on top shares is consistent with this evidence. After the Second World War compression, the fractiles P90–95 and P95–99 recovered slowly and continuously from the 1950s to the 1990s, and reached the pre-Second World War level in the beginning of the 1980s. As described above, the recovery process for groups within the top percentile did not begin until the 1970s and was much faster. In accordance with results obtained from the March Current Population Surveys (Katz and Murphy 1992; Katz and Autor 1999), we find that wage inequality, measured by top fractile wage shares, starts to increase in the early 1970s. This is in contrast with results from the May Current Population Surveys (DiNardo et al. 1996) suggesting that the surge in wage inequality is limited to the 1980s.

From 1970 to 1984, the top 1% share increased steadily from 5% to 7.5% (Figure 5.9). From 1986 to 1988, the top shares of wage earners increased sharply, especially at the very top (e.g. the top 1% share jumps from 7.5% to 9.5%). This sharp increase was documented by Feenberg and Poterba (1993) and is certainly attributable at least in part to fiscal manipulation following the large top marginal tax rate cuts of the Tax Reform Act of 1986 (see the discussion in Section 5.3 above). However, from 1988 to 1994, top wage shares stay on average constant,[39] but increase very sharply from 1994 to 2000 (the top 1% wage share increases from 8.7% to 12.6%). While everybody acknowledges that tax reforms can have large short-term effects on reported incomes due to retiming, there is a controversial debate on whether changing tax rates can have permanent effects on the level of reported incomes. Looking at long-time series up to 2001 casts doubts on the supply-side interpretation that tax cuts can have lasting effects on reported wages.

[39] One can note the surge in high wages in 1992 and the dip in 1993 and 1994 due to retiming of labour compensation in order to escape the higher rates enacted in 1993 (see Goolsbee 2000).

Part of the recent increase in top wages is due to the development of stock-options that are reported as wages and salaries on tax returns when they are exercised. Stock-options are compensation for labour services but the fact that they are exercised in a lumpy way may introduce some upward bias in our annual shares at the very top (top 0.1% and above). To cast additional light on this issue and on the timing of the top wage surge, we look at CEO compensation from 1970 to 2003 using the annual surveys published by *Forbes Magazine* since 1971. These data provide the levels and composition of compensation for CEOs in the 800 largest publicly traded US corporations. Figure 5.11 displays the average real compensation level (including stock-option exercised) for the top 100 CEOs from the Forbes list, along with the compensation of the CEO ranked 100 in the list, and the salary plus bonus level of the CEO ranked 10 (in terms of the size of salary plus bonus). As a comparison, we also report the average wage of a full-time worker in the economy from National Income Accounts. Consistent with the evolution of top wage shares, average CEO compensation has increased much faster than average wage since the early 1970s. Therefore, the increase in pay gap between top executives and the average worker cannot be attributed solely to the tax episodes of the 1980s.

Thus, by the end of the century, top wage shares are much higher than in the interwar period. These results confirm that the rise in top income shares and the dramatic shift of income composition at the top documented in Section 5.3 are mainly driven by the surge in top wages during the last three decades.

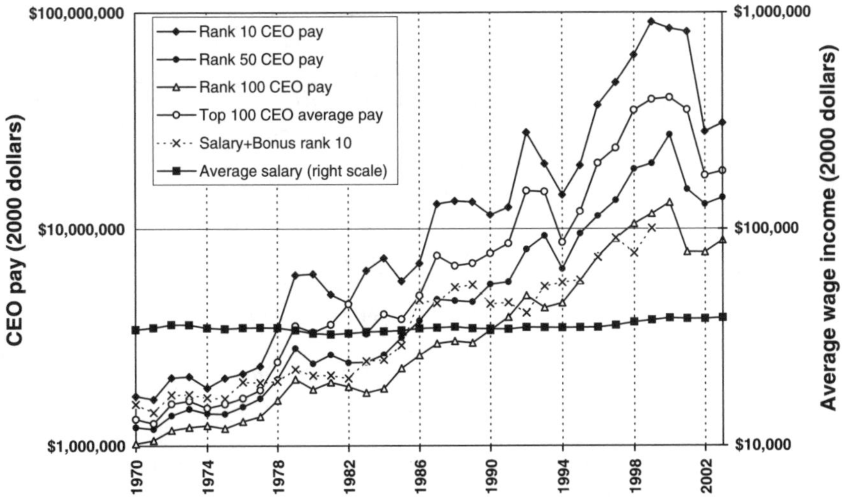

Figure 5.11 CEO pay vs. average wage income, US 1970–2003

Notes: The average wage income (right scale) is estimated as the total wages and salaries from National Income and Produts Accounts divided by the total number of full-time equivalent employees. CEO pay includes salary, bonus, and profits from exercised stock-options.All estimates are expressed in 2000 dollars using the official CPI.

Source: Table 5B.4, logarithmic scales.

Proposed Interpretation

The pattern of top shares over the century is striking: most of the decline from 1927 to 1960 took place during the four years of the Second World War. The extent of that decline is large, especially for very high wages. More surprisingly, there is no recovery after the war. We are of course not the first ones to document compression in wages during the 1940s. The Social Security Administration (US Bureau of Old-Age 1952) showed that a Lorenz curve of wages for 1949 displays much more equality than one for 1938. In a widely cited paper, Goldin and Margo (1992), using Census micro-data for 1940 and 1950, have also noted that the ratios P90/P10 and P50/P10 declined sharply during that decade. Our annual series allow us to conclude that most of the decline in top wage shares took place during the key years of the war with no previous decline in inequality before and no recovery afterwards.

The compression of wages during the war can be explained by the wage controls of the war economy, but how can we explain the fact that high wage earners did not recover after the wage controls were removed? This evidence cannot be immediately reconciled with explanations of the reduction of inequality based solely on technical change as in the famous Kuznets's process. We think that this pattern of evolution of inequality is additional indirect evidence that non-market mechanisms such as labour market institutions and social norms regarding inequality may play a role in the setting of compensation at the top. The Great Depression and the Second World War have without doubt had a profound effect on labour market institutions and more generally on social norms regarding inequality. During this period, the income tax acquired its modern form, and its top marginal tax rates were set very high, in excess of 80%. It is conceivable that such large income tax rates discouraged corporations from increasing top salaries. During that period, large redistributive programmes such as Social Security, and Aid for Families with Dependent Children were initiated. These strongly redistributive policy reforms show that American society's views on income inequality and redistribution greatly shifted from 1930 to 1945. It is also important to note that unionization increased substantially from 1929 to 1950 and that unions have been traditionally in favour of wage compression. In that context, it is perhaps not surprising that the high wages earners who were the most severely hit by the war wage controls were simply not able, because of social, fiscal, and union pressure, to increase their salaries back to the pre-war levels in relative terms.[40]

Similarly, the huge increase in top wage shares since the 1970s cannot be the sole consequence of technical change. First, the increase is very large, and concentrated among the highest income earners. The fractiles P90–95 and P95–99 experienced a much smaller increase than the very top shares since the 1970s. Second, such a large change in top wage shares has not taken place in most European countries and Japan which experienced the same technical change as the United States. For example, Piketty (2001, 2003) documents no change in top

[40] Emphasizing the role of social norms and unionization is of course not new and has been pointed out as important elements explaining the wage compression of the 1940s and 1950s by several studies (Phelps Brown 1977; Goldin and Margo 1992; and Goldin and Katz 1999). Moreover, as emphasized by Goldin and Margo (1992) and Goldin and Katz (1999), it is possible that the large increase in the supply of college graduates contributed to make the drop in top wage shares persistent.

wage shares in the last decades in France. DiNardo et al. (1996) argue that changes in institutions such as the minimum wage and unionization account for a large part of the increase in US wage inequality from 1973 to 1992. As emphasized by Acemoglu et al. (2001), it is possible that these changes in institutions have been triggered by previous technological changes making it impossible to sustain previous labour market arrangements (see also Acemoglu 2002). It seems unlikely, however, that changes in unionization or the minimum wage can explain the surge in very top wages. The marginal product of top executives in large corporations is notoriously difficult to estimate, and executive pay is probably determined to a significant extent by herd behaviour. Changing social norms regarding inequality and the acceptability of very high wages might partly explain the rise in US top wage shares observed since the 1970s.[41]

5.5 CONCLUSION

This chapter has presented new homogeneous series on top shares of income and wages from 1913 to 2002. Perhaps surprisingly, nobody had tried to extend the pioneering work of Kuznets (1953) to more recent years. Moreover, important wage income statistics from tax returns had never been exploited before. The large shocks that capital owners experienced during the Great Depression and the Second World War seem to have had a permanent effect: top capital incomes are still lower in the late 1990s than before the First World War. We have tentatively suggested that steep progressive taxation, by reducing the rate of wealth accumulation, has prevented the large fortunes to recover fully yet from these shocks. The evidence for wage series shows that top wage shares were flat before the Second World War and dropped precipitously during the war. Top wage shares have started recovering from this shock only since the 1970s but are now higher than before the Second World War.

To what extent is the US experience representative of other developed countries' long run inequality dynamics? It is interesting to compare the US top income share series with comparable series constructed for France by Piketty (2001 and Chapter 3 in this volume), and for the United Kingdom by Atkinson (Chapter 4).[42] There are important similarities between the American, French, and British pattern of the top 0.1 percent income share displayed on Figure 5.12.[43] In all three countries, top income shares fell considerably during the

[41] It is quite telling to read in the recent survey of Hall and Murphy (2004), two prominent and conservative researchers in this field, that their best explanation for the surge in stock-option compensation was that 'boards and managers falsely perceive stock options to be inexpensive because of accounting and cash-flow considerations'.

[42] See Lindert (2000) and Morrisson (2000) for recent surveys.

[43] Due to very high starting point of supertax in the United Kingdom, Atkinson was not able to compute top decile or even top percentile series covering the entire century (only the top 0.1% and higher fractiles series are available for the entire century for all three countries).

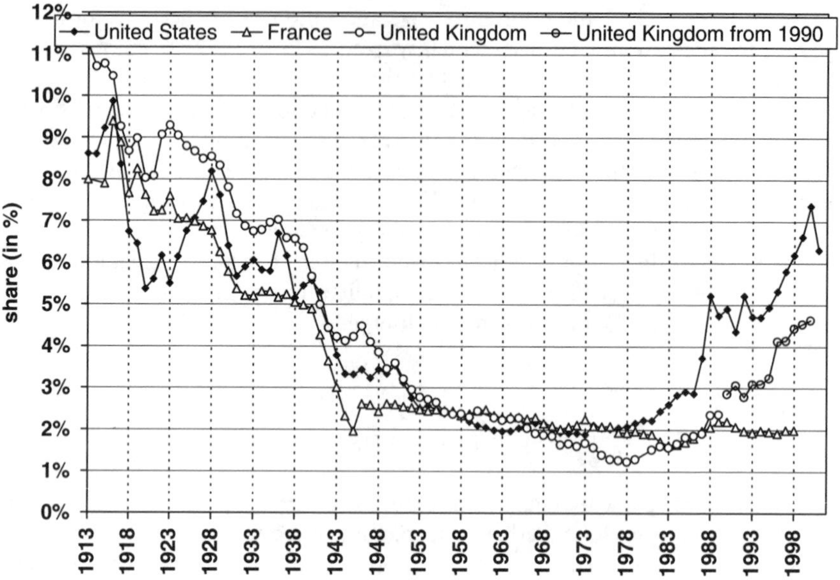

Figure 5.12 Top 0.1% income shares in the US, France, and the UK, 1913–98

Notes: In all three countries, income is defined berfore invdividual taxes and excludes capital gains. The unit is the in family as the current US tax law except for the UK from 1990.

Sources: US: Table 5A.1, column P99.9–100. France: computations based on income tax returns by Piketty 2001*b*: table A1, col. P.99.9–100. UK: computations based on income tax returns by Atkinson: chap. 4, table 4.1; values for 1987 to 1993 obtained by Pareto extrapolation. There is a discontinuity after 1989 in the UK series due to switch from tax unit to indivdual basis.

1914–45 period, and they were never able to come back to the very high levels observed at the eve of the First World War. It is plausible to think that in all three countries, top capital incomes have been hit by the depression and wars shocks of the first part of the century and could not recover because of the dynamic effects of progressive taxation on capital. Piketty (2001) also shows that in France, there was no spontaneous decline of top wage shares before the Second World War. In France, top wage shares declined during the First World War, but they quickly recovered during the 1920s and were stable until the Second World War.

Some important differences need however to be emphasized. First, the shock of the Second World War was more pronounced in France and in the United Kingdom than in the United States. This is consistent with the fact that capital owners suffered from physical capital losses during the war in Europe, while there was no destruction on US soil.[44] Second, the Second World War wage

[44] Estate tax data also show that the fall in top estates was substantially larger in France (see Piketty (2001).

compression was very short-lived in France, while it had long lasting effects in the United States. In France, wage inequality, measured both in terms of top wage shares and in terms of interdecile ratios appears to have been extremely stable over the course of the twentieth century. The US history of wage inequality looks very different from that in France: the war compression had long-lasting effects, and then wage inequality increased considerably since the 1970s, which explains the US upturn of top income shares since the 1970s.[45] The fact that France and the United States display such diverging trends is consistent with our interpretation that technical change alone cannot account for the US increase in inequality.

These diverging trends in top wages over the past 30 years explain why the income composition patterns of top incomes look so different in France and in the United States at the end of the century. In France, top incomes are still composed primarily of dividend income, although wealth concentration is much lower than what it was one century ago. In the United States, due to the very large rise of top wages since the 1970s, the coupon-clipping rentiers have been overtaken by the working rich. Such a pattern might not last for very long because our proposed interpretation also suggests that the decline of progressive taxation observed since the early 1980s in the United could very well spur a revival of high wealth concentration and top capital incomes during the next few decades.

APPENDIX 5A: INCOME INEQUALITY SERIES

This appendix describes the series of shares of top income fractiles that we have constructed using tax return data. The US income tax started in 1913 and 2002 is the most recent year for which data are available. Starting in 1916, the Internal Revenue Service (IRS) has published detailed statistical tables on tax returns in *Statistics of Income: Individual Income Tax Returns* (the tables for 1913–15 were published in the *Annual Reports of the Commissioner of Internal Revenue*). These annual 1913–2002 tables provide information on the number of tax returns, and the amounts reported for each source of income, for a large number of income brackets.[46] Starting in 1960, the IRS has constructed large micro-files of tax returns oversampling high incomes. These micro-files were constructed annually since 1966,[47] and they are publicly

[45] The United Kingdom also experienced an increase in top shares in the last two decades but more modest than in the United States.

[46] For 1913–15, the tables only provide information on the number of tax returns for a large number of income brackets.

[47] No micro-file is available for 1961, 1963, and 1965, and the micro-files for 1960, 1962, and 1964 do not include as many tax return variables as the files for the following years (this applies in particular to the 1960 file). Therefore we have mostly relied on published tables for the 1960–65 period (the 1960, 1962, and 1964 have been used for consistency checks only).

available until 1999. These annual 1966–99 micro-files allow us to check that our methods using published tables provide accurate results.

Computing Total Number of Tax Units and Total Income

The total number of tax units in the US population (had everybody been required to file a tax return), displayed in column (1) of Table 5A.0, has been computed using census data on the marital structure of the population: it is defined as the sum of the total number of married men; the total number of widowed and divorced men and women; and the total number of single men and women aged 20 or over.[48] Income fractiles are defined with respect to this total number of tax units. For instance, in 2002, with a total number of tax units equal to 139.703 million, there are 13.9703 million tax units in the top decile, 1.39703 million tax units in the top percentile, etc. Our theoretical definition of tax units implicitly assumes that married women never file separate returns (in practice, the number of married women filing separate returns is positive but fairly small (about 1% of all returns in 1998). Before 1948, however, married couples with two earners had interest in filing separately because there was a single schedule that applied to all tax units (married filing jointly, married filing separately, or singles). As a result, the number of returns for married women filing separately was higher (around 5%–6%). We did correct for this in our income series so as to make sure that there is no discontinuity between 1947 and 1948.[49]

Table 5A.0 also indicates the total number of tax returns actually filed (column (2)), as well as the fraction of tax units filing a tax return (column (3)). Since 1944, the vast majority of tax units have been filing tax returns, and the fraction of tax units actually filing has generally been around 90%–95%. But before the Second World War, due to large exemption levels, this fraction was usually around 10%–15%. The top decile is therefore the biggest fraction for which we can construct homogeneous estimates for the entire period, and this is why we limit our analysis to the top decile of the income distribution. In the early years of the income tax, from 1913 to 1916, the exemptions were even higher and we have to restrict the estimates to the top percentile.

[48] The marital structure data for pre-1970 censuses were taken from *Historical Statistics of the US—Colonial Times to 1970* (US Department of Commerce 1975); the marital structure data for 1980, 1990, 2000, estimated from Census data, are reported in *Statistical Abstract of the US*. Intercensal years were interpolated by assuming that the average size of tax units follows linear intercensal trends. We checked the accuracy of our procedure by computing the total number of individuals represented on tax returns and by dividing this number by total US population, and we found virtually the same pattern for this ratio as for the (total number of tax returns)/(total number of tax units) ratio.

[49] The magnitude of the correction was computed by using IRS tables by filling status. In effect, our 1913–47 top income levels and top shares series were adjusted upwards by about 2.5% in order to correct for this 'married women' bias. We made a similar correction for our wage series.

Total income for the entire population has been computed by using national accounts. We call tax return gross income the gross income definition reported on tax returns less capital gains realizations. Tax return gross income is defined as Adjusted Gross Income (AGI) plus adjustments less capital gains included in AGI. During the post-Second World War period, the ratio between total tax return gross income reported on tax returns and total personal income estimated in national accounts has been trending downward (from about 75%–80% in the late 1940s to about 65%–70% in the 1990s). This trend is due for the most part to the growth of non-taxable government transfers (non-taxable health care benefits, non-taxable and partially non-taxable social security benefits, etc.) because the ratio between total tax return gross income reported on tax returns and total personal income minus transfers estimated in national accounts has been fairly stable since the late 1940s (around 75%–80%).[50] The total income series (excluding capital gains) reported in Table 5A.0 (column (4)) was constructed as follows. For the 1944–2002 period, we have adjusted upwards the total tax return gross income series so as to take into account the fact that a small fraction of tax units did not file tax returns. We have imputed to non-filers a fixed fraction of filers' average income (50% in 1944–45, and 20% thereafter). The resulting series fluctuates between 77% and 83% of total personal income (minus transfers), and is about 2%–3% higher than total tax return gross income.[51, 52] For the 1913–43 period, our total income series (excluding capital gains) is equal to exactly 80% of total personal income (minus transfers).[53]

[50] In addition to non-taxable government transfers, non-taxable personal income includes imputed rent; interest and dividends received by pension plans, life insurance carriers and non-profit institutions; non-taxable employer and employee contributions to pension plans, health insurance, day care, etc.; capital and inventory adjustments (NIPA capital consumption is generally smaller than IRS capital consumption, so that NIPA entrepreneurial income is generally larger than IRS entrepreneurial income); etc. See Park (2000) for a detailed description of the differences between NIPA personal income and individual tax return income.

[51] Except in 1944–45, where it is about 11%–13% higher (because of the lower fraction of tax units actually filing).

[52] We chose not to take a fixed fraction of 1944–2002 personal income (minus transfers) for the following reason: although our resulting series is about 80% of personal income (minus transfers) all along the 1944–2002 period (with no trend), there exists a number of short-run fluctuations that cannot be fully accounted for by changes in the fraction of tax units actually filing (for instance, tax return gross income grows less than personal income in the mid-1980s, and catches up in the late 1980s).

[53] Official NIPA personal income series start in 1929 (we have used the latest NIPA series released on www.bea.doc.gov), and we have completed the NIPA series by linking it to the 1913–29 personal income series published by Kuznets (1941, 1945). Note that the total income series used by Kuznets (1953) to compute top income shares over the 1913–48 period is higher than ours: his only adjustment to personal income is imputed rent (see Kuznets 1953: 570–7), which seems insufficient to us. For instance, in 1948, Kuznets's total income denominator is equal to current US$202 billion, although total 1948 tax return gross income is equal to current US$161 billion (about 80% of US$202 billion), which seems implausible: this would imply that non-filers have higher average incomes than filers.

Average income per tax unit (Table 5A.0, column (5)) was computed by dividing our total income series (Table 5A.0, column (4)) by the total number of tax units (Table 5A.0, column (1)). (See also Figures 5A.0 and 5A.1 for further data on average income in the US.)

We have also computed a total income series (including capital gains) (Table 5A.0, column (6)) by adding to column (4) the total, pre-exclusion amount of all capital gains reported on tax returns. For the period 1944–2002, over 80% of tax units file so we assume that non-filers do not realize significant capital gains. For the period 1916 to 1943, as the fraction of filers is smaller, we assume that capital gains realized by the top 10% taxpayers (ranked by net taxable income) represents 90% of all realized capital gains in the US economy. The 90% fraction has been chosen based on 1944, year for which the top 10% realized 89% of all capital gains.[54] This denominator including capital gains differs slightly from the denominator used in the working paper version Piketty and Saez (2001). In the working paper version, we included in the denominator only realized capital gains reported by the top 10% taxpayers (ranked by income including the taxable portion of capital gains). The difference between the two denominators is small because capital gains are extremely concentrated, even today. For example, in 2000, the top 10% taxpayers reported almost 90% of all capital gains. We decided to change our denominator definition because including all capital gains is a more natural definition which does artificially inflates top income shares. Our new series

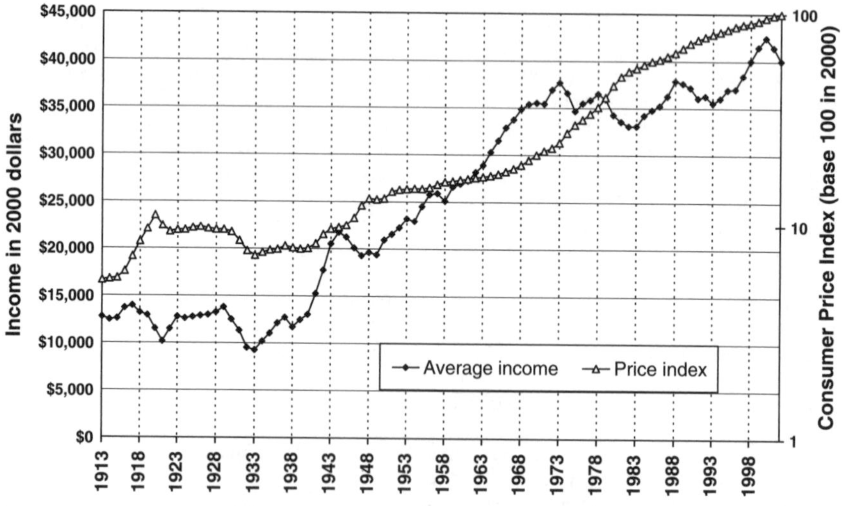

Figure 5A.0 Average real income and consumer price index, US 1913–2002

Source: Table 5A.0, col. average income (in real 2000 dollars) and CPI (base 100 in 2002)

[54] Note that we have no capital gains estimates for 1913–15 because capital gains are not reported separately in tax statistics for those years.

Table 5A.0 Reference totals for tax units and income, US 1913–2002

	Tax units			Income (excluding capital gains)		Income (including capital gains)		Inflation
Year	(1) N. tax units (thousands)	(2) N. tax returns (thousands)	(3) (2)/(1)(%)	(4) Total income (millions 2000 $	(5) Average income (2000 $)	(6) Total income (millions 2000 $	(7) Average income (2000 $)	(8) CPI (p(2000)/p(n))
1913	37,701	358	0.9	480,989	12,758	480,989	12,758	17.4076
1914	38,513	358	0.9	480,268	12,470	480,268	12,470	17.1843
1915	39,154	337	0.9	492,960	12,590	492,960	12,590	17.0141
1916	39,790	437	1.1	544,831	13,693	553,553	13,912	15.8124
1917	40,387	3,473	8.6	563,361	13,949	568,293	14,071	13.4688
1918	40,451	4,425	10.9	534,260	13,208	538,204	13,305	11.4726
1919	41,052	5,333	13.0	530,830	12,931	541,556	13,192	9.9848
1920	41,909	7,260	17.3	483,394	11,534	493,204	11,768	8.6225
1921	42,835	6,662	15.6	436,067	10,180	440,448	10,282	9.6556
1922	43,543	6,787	15.6	500,266	11,489	511,119	11,738	10.3048
1923	44,409	7,698	17.3	567,487	12,779	580,180	13,065	10.1226
1924	45,384	7,370	16.2	572,981	12,625	590,120	13,003	10.1024
1925	46,190	4,171	9.0	589,131	12,754	623,808	13,505	9.8560
1926	46,940	4,138	8.8	604,950	12,888	633,270	13,491	9.7584
1927	47,723	4,102	8.6	619,649	12,984	654,680	13,718	9.9474
1928	48,445	4,071	8.4	641,912	13,250	699,281	14,435	10.0785
1929	49,085	4,044	8.2	678,079	13,814	730,578	14,884	10.0785
1930	49,750	3,708	7.5	622,694	12,516	638,963	12,843	10.3369
1931	50,462	3,226	6.4	573,062	11,356	579,333	11,481	11.3343
1932	51,117	3,877	7.6	488,247	9,551	489,986	9,586	12.6358
1933	51,757	3,724	7.2	481,465	9,302	489,582	9,459	13.3148
1934	52,430	4,094	7.8	535,684	10,217	541,223	10,323	12.8770
1935	53,147	4,575	8.6	587,946	11,063	600,025	11,290	12.5630
1936	53,844	5,413	10.1	653,771	12,142	677,698	12,586	12.4386
1937	54,539	6,350	11.6	694,447	12,733	702,905	12,888	12.0063
1938	55,342	6,204	11.2	648,171	11,712	659,318	11,913	12.2389
1939	56,181	7,633	13.6	701,067	12,479	710,908	12,654	12.4127
1940	57,115	14,665	25.7	746,234	13,065	755,548	13,229	12.2898
1941	57,392	25,855	45.0	876,435	15,271	887,597	15,465	11.7045
1942	57,736	36,538	63.3	1,024,331	17,742	1,032,062	17,875	10.5732

(contd.)

Table 5A.0 (*contd.*)

	Tax units			Income (excluding capital gains)		Income (including capital gains)		Inflation
Year	(1) N. tax units (thousands)	(2) N. tax returns (thousands)	(3) (2)/(1)(%)	(4) Total income (millions 2000 $	(5) Average income (2000 $)	(6) Total income (millions 2000 $	(7) Average income (2000 $)	(8) CPI (p(2000)/p(n))
1943	58,250	43,602	74.9	1,195,041	20,516	1,212,209	20,811	9.9653
1944	58,656	46,920	80.0	1,274,511	21,728	1,291,884	22,025	9.7987
1945	58,997	49,933	84.6	1,252,872	21,236	1,292,804	21,913	9.5784
1946	59,297	52,817	89.1	1,191,811	20,099	1,246,245	21,017	8.8280
1947	60,118	55,099	91.7	1,159,544	19,288	1,192,865	19,842	7.7168
1948	60,825	52,072	85.6	1,193,880	19,628	1,225,113	20,141	7.1585
1949	61,537	51,814	84.2	1,193,117	19,389	1,215,829	19,758	7.2308
1950	62,446	53,060	85.0	1,306,832	20,927	1,348,169	21,589	7.1592
1951	63,060	55,447	87.9	1,359,720	21,562	1,398,741	22,181	6.6350
1952	63,684	56,528	88.8	1,416,803	22,247	1,448,725	22,749	6.4922
1953	64,273	57,838	90.0	1,492,937	23,228	1,518,893	23,632	6.4407
1954	64,928	56,747	87.4	1,489,846	22,946	1,532,226	23,599	6.4086
1955	65,589	58,250	88.8	1,608,893	24,530	1,669,241	25,450	6.4344
1956	66,257	59,197	89.3	1,709,657	25,803	1,765,867	26,652	6.3393
1957	66,947	59,825	89.4	1,734,734	25,912	1,776,949	26,542	6.1190
1958	67,546	59,085	87.5	1,697,095	25,125	1,748,198	25,882	5.9581
1959	68,144	60,272	88.4	1,813,114	26,607	1,886,603	27,686	5.9108
1960	68,681	61,028	88.9	1,850,218	26,939	1,911,403	27,830	5.8177
1961	69,997	61,499	87.9	1,907,985	27,258	1,995,257	28,505	5.7601
1962	71,254	62,712	88.0	2,008,327	28,185	2,072,856	29,091	5.6975
1963	72,464	63,943	88.2	2,095,244	28,914	2,167,476	29,911	5.6299
1964	73,660	65,376	88.8	2,231,772	30,298	2,320,506	31,503	5.5577
1965	74,772	67,596	90.4	2,356,222	31,512	2,468,342	33,011	5.4648
1966	75,831	70,160	92.5	2,494,332	32,893	2,601,147	34,302	5.3107
1967	76,856	71,652	93.2	2,594,491	33,758	2,736,936	35,611	5.1611
1968	77,826	73,729	94.7	2,713,379	34,865	2,893,175	37,175	4.9530
1969	78,793	75,834	96.2	2,789,058	35,397	2,928,049	37,161	4.6993
1970	79,924	74,280	92.9	2,840,171	35,536	2,921,141	36,549	4.4375
1971	81,849	74,576	91.1	2,900,416	35,436	3,012,203	36,802	4.2505

1972	83,670	77,573	92.7	3,088,464	36,913	3,229,936	38,603	4.1187
1973	85,442	80,693	94.4	3,220,561	37,693	3,351,334	39,224	3.8782
1974	87,228	83,340	95.5	3,190,566	36,577	3,286,127	37,673	3.4939
1975	89,127	82,229	92.3	3,089,082	34,659	3,179,647	35,675	3.2025
1976	91,048	84,670	93.0	3,230,625	35,482	3,343,465	36,722	3.0269
1977	93,076	86,635	93.1	3,335,715	35,839	3,455,478	37,125	2.8422
1978	95,213	89,771	94.3	3,476,330	36,511	3,602,376	37,835	2.6414
1979	97,457	92,694	95.1	3,502,365	35,938	3,673,430	37,693	2.3732
1980	99,625	93,902	94.3	3,412,997	34,258	3,568,200	35,816	2.0910
1981	101,432	95,396	94.0	3,403,601	33,555	3,550,100	35,000	1.8957
1982	103,250	95,337	92.3	3,415,200	33,077	3,569,826	34,574	1.7850
1983	105,067	96,321	91.7	3,476,227	33,086	3,689,704	35,118	1.7297
1984	106,871	99,439	93.0	3,658,188	34,230	3,887,076	36,372	1.6584
1985	108,736	101,660	93.5	3,783,643	34,797	4,059,326	37,332	1.6007
1986	110,684	103,045	93.1	3,901,038	35,245	4,424,003	39,970	1.5709
1987	112,640	106,996	95.0	4,084,958	36,266	4,294,283	38,124	1.5163
1988	114,656	109,708	95.7	4,343,915	37,887	4,570,601	39,864	1.4566
1989	116,759	112,136	96.0	4,392,120	37,617	4,596,001	39,363	1.3899
1990	119,055	113,717	95.5	4,423,995	37,159	4,576,567	38,441	1.3187
1991	120,453	114,730	95.2	4,343,984	36,064	4,471,262	37,120	1.2655
1992	121,944	113,605	93.2	4,424,533	36,283	4,566,536	37,448	1.2287
1993	123,378	114,602	92.9	4,383,859	35,532	4,551,275	36,889	1.1929
1994	124,716	115,943	93.0	4,493,765	36,032	4,655,489	37,329	1.1626
1995	126,023	118,218	93.8	4,655,920	36,945	4,845,250	38,447	1.1310
1996	127,798	120,351	94.2	4,731,676	37,025	5,005,670	39,169	1.0980
1997	129,532	122,422	94.5	4,976,817	38,421	5,357,449	41,360	1.0733
1998	131,720	124,771	94.7	5,274,544	40,044	5,744,141	43,609	1.0564
1999	133,233	127,075	95.4	5,531,113	41,514	6,070,064	45,560	1.0337
2000	134,473	129,374	96.2	5,712,243	42,479	6,326,982	47,050	1.0000
2001	137,088	130,255	95.0	5,684,503	41,466	6,000,676	43,772	0.9723
2002	139,703	130,201	93.2	5,594,026	40,042	5,822,191	41,675	0.9572

Notes: Tax units estimated as sum of married men, divorced and widowed men and women, and single men and women aged 20 and over. Before 1944, total income (excluding capital gains) is defined as 80% of personal income minus transfers from national accounts. From 1944 on, total income is defined as total adjusted gross income less realized capital gains, taxable SS and UI benefits and adding back all adjustments to gross income. Income of non-filers is imputed as 20% of average income (50% in 1944–45). Income including capital gains is defined as total income including 100% of capital gains reported on tax returns (from 1944 on) and assuming that the top 10% taxpayers earn 90% of all realized capital gains (before 1944). Piketty and Saez (2001) included only capital gains going to the top 10% in col. (7). Consumer Price Index (CPI-U) is the official CPI index from *Economic Report of the President*.

Source: Population and tax units estimates based on census and current population surveys (*Historical Statistics of the United States*, and *Statistical Abstract of the United States*).

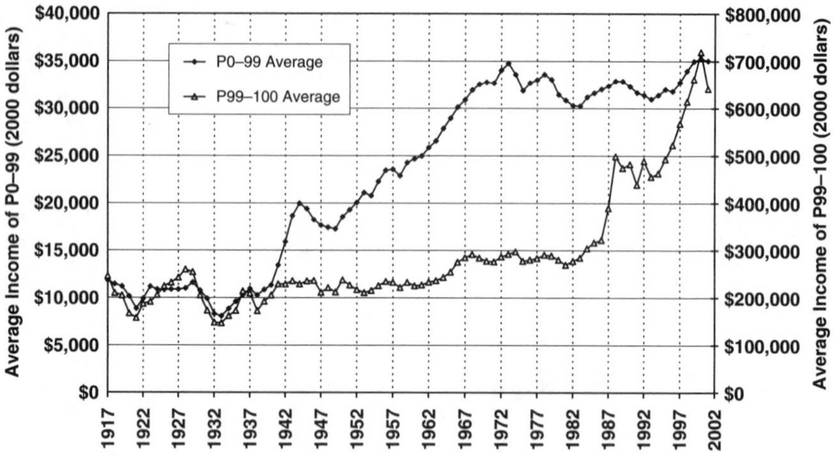

Figure 5A.1 Average real income of bottom 99% and top 1% in US, 1917–2002

Notes: Bottom 99% have stagnated from 1973 to 2000): (1) Income is defined as market income (excluding realized capital gains) and excludes all transfers such as Social Security benefits, unemployment insurance, welfare assistance etc. The importance of transfers has grown overtime. They represent in 2000 about 15% of personal income and aruond 10% in 1973, and only 1%–2% before 1930. (2) The unit is the tax unit (such as couple and dependets, or a head of household with dependents, or a single person). The number of invdividuals per tax unit has declined overtime from 2.5 in the 1973 to 2.1 in 2000 but the number of adults (aged 20 +) per tax unit has only declined from 1.6 to 1.5 from 1973 to 2000. A tax unit is smallar than a household (a household is defined as all individuals living in the same unit such as two roommates, etc.) In 2000, there were 134.5 million tax units but only 104.7 million households in the United States. Therefore, average household income is about 28% higher than average tax unit income. (3) All nominal income are deflated using the official Consumer Price Index (CPI-U). It has been recognized that the CPI-U understates inflation and new CPI series (CPI-U-RS) have been created for the period 1967–2002 displaying 15% less infaltion (and hence 15% more real income growth) for the period 1967 to 2002 and about 13% more real growth from 1973 to 2000.

In sum, from 1973 to 2000, the average income of the bottom 99% would have grown by about 40% in real terms insetead of stagnating (as displayed on the figure above) if we had included all transfers (+7% effect), used the CPI-V-RS (+13% effect) and especially defined income per capita (+20% effect). Under those assumptions, the average income of the top 1% would have grown by a factor 3.3 instead of a mere 2.5 (as in figure above).

The finding that top 1% incomes have done so much better than the bottom 99% since 1973 is therefore largely independent of those assumptions above.

Source: Table 5A.4, columns P0-90, P90–95, P95–99, and P99–100.

can also be used to estimate the evolution of capital gains concentration over time. The corresponding average income series is reported in column (7).

Note that all money amounts in current dollars were converted in 2000 dollars by using the CPI series reported on column (8) of Table 5A.0 (this series was used to convert all current dollars series computed in this chapter into 2000 dollars series, so that interested readers can easily compute current dollars series).[55]

We have made no adjustment for changes in the size of tax units. This is unlikely to affect our results in a significant way. The average size of tax units was

[55] This CPI series was constructed by linking the 1913–70 CPI series (all items) published in *Historical Statistics of the US—Colonial Times to 1970* (US Department of Commerce 1975) and the 1970–2002 CPI series (all items) published in the *Economic Report of the President* (US Government Printing Office 2004).

much larger in the 1910s (nearly 2.6) than in the 1990s (less than 2.1),[56] but published IRS tables and IRS micro-files show that this secular decline had approximately the same magnitude for all income brackets. Note that Kuznets (1953) did attempt to make adjustments for tax unit size: Kuznets' 1913–48 top income shares series are based on individuals and not tax units. As the published IRS tables are based on tax units and not individuals, Kuznets divided the total income reported in each income bracket by the total number of individuals represented by all tax returns in that bracket. This process would generate substantial re-ranking, as a tax return of a widow with no dependents reporting US$10,000 would be replaced by an individual with US$10,000 of income while a family of four with US$10,000 of income would be replaced by four identical individuals with US$2,500 of income each. However, Kuznets did not correct for the re-ranking and thus misclassified in the top shares large families with high total income but moderate income per capita. As a result, the shares estimated by

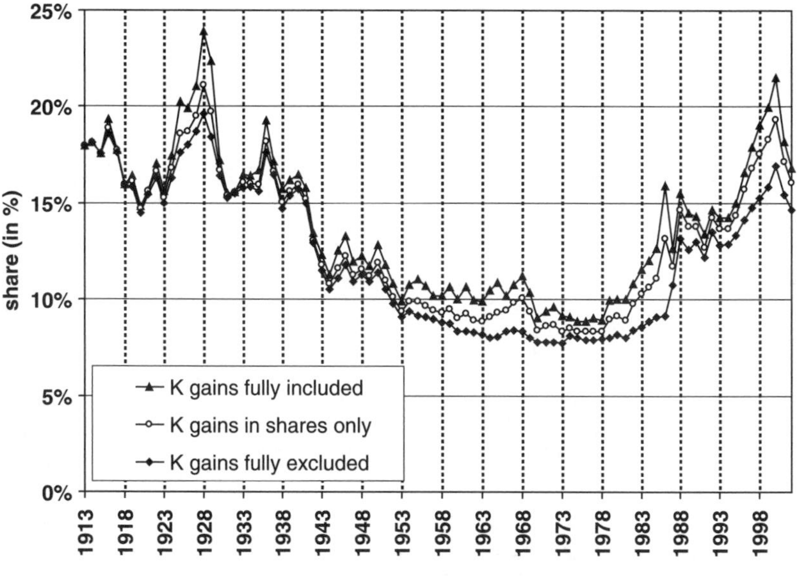

Figure 5A.2 Top 1% income shares in US: the role of capital gains, 1913–2002

Notes: The series K gains fully included are based on income including capital gains (both in ranking and for estimating top shares). The series K gains in shares only are based on ranking by income excluding capital gains but include capital gains in shares. The series K gains fully excluded are based on income excluding capital gains (both in ranking and for estimating top shares)

Sources: Table 5A.1, 5A.2, and 5A.3, column P99–100.

[56] Average tax unit size declined between the 1910s and the 1940s (from 2.6 to 2.3), increased between the 1940s and the 1960s (from 2.3 to 2.6), and declined between the 1960s and the 1990s (from 2.6 to 2.1).

Table 5A.1 Top fractiles income shares (excluding capital gains), US 1913–2002 (fractiles are defined by total income (excluding capital gains))

	P90–100 (1)	P95–100 (2)	P99–100 (3)	P99.5–100 (4)	P99.9–100 (5)	P99.99–100 (6)	P90–95 (7)	P95–99 (8)	P99–99.5 (9)	P99.5–99.9 (10)	P99.9–99.99 (11)
1913			17.96	14.73	8.62	2.76			3.23	6.11	5.86
1914			18.16	15.08	8.60	2.73			3.08	6.48	5.87
1915			17.58	14.58	9.22	4.36			3.00	5.36	4.86
1916			18.57	15.60	9.87	4.40			2.97	5.74	5.46
1917	40.29	30.33	17.60	14.23	8.36	3.33	9.95	12.74	3.37	5.88	5.03
1918	39.90	29.30	15.88	12.39	6.74	2.45	10.61	13.41	3.50	5.64	4.29
1919	39.48	29.31	15.87	12.23	6.45	2.22	10.17	13.44	3.63	5.78	4.23
1920	38.10	27.47	14.46	10.95	5.37	1.67	10.63	13.01	3.51	5.58	3.70
1921	42.86	30.46	15.47	11.60	5.60	1.69	12.40	14.98	3.87	6.00	3.91
1922	42.95	31.05	16.29	12.38	6.17	2.01	11.90	14.76	3.92	6.21	4.16
1923	40.59	28.95	14.99	11.32	5.50	1.75	11.64	13.96	3.67	5.82	3.75
1924	43.26	30.93	16.32	12.42	6.14	2.01	12.34	14.61	3.90	6.28	4.13
1925	44.17	32.47	17.60	13.41	6.75	2.35	11.70	14.86	4.19	6.66	4.41
1926	44.07	32.75	18.01	13.75	7.07	2.54	11.32	14.74	4.26	6.68	4.53
1927	44.67	33.43	18.68	14.33	7.47	2.76	11.23	14.75	4.35	6.86	4.71
1928	46.09	34.77	19.60	15.17	8.19	3.23	11.32	15.17	4.42	6.98	4.97
1929	43.76	33.05	18.42	14.21	7.62	3.01	10.71	14.63	4.20	6.59	4.62
1930	43.07	31.18	16.42	12.42	6.40	2.39	11.89	14.76	4.01	6.02	4.01
1931	44.40	31.01	15.27	11.32	5.68	2.07	13.39	15.74	3.95	5.65	3.60
1932	46.30	32.59	15.48	11.55	5.90	1.93	13.71	17.11	3.93	5.65	3.97
1933	45.03	32.49	15.77	11.78	6.05	2.04	12.54	16.72	3.99	5.72	4.01
1934	45.16	32.99	15.87	11.80	5.82	1.92	12.16	17.13	4.07	5.97	3.90
1935	43.39	30.99	15.63	11.67	5.80	1.95	12.40	15.36	3.96	5.87	3.85
1936	44.77	32.65	17.64	13.37	6.69	2.23	12.12	15.02	4.27	6.68	4.45
1937	43.35	31.38	16.45	12.42	6.16	2.02	11.97	14.93	4.04	6.25	4.15
1938	43.00	30.18	14.73	10.82	5.16	1.67	12.82	15.45	3.91	5.66	3.49
1939	44.57	31.29	15.39	11.37	5.45	1.74	13.28	15.89	4.03	5.91	3.71
1940	44.43	31.29	15.73	11.66	5.57	1.77	13.14	15.55	4.07	6.09	3.80
1941	41.02	29.02	15.01	11.15	5.29	1.63	12.00	14.01	3.86	5.86	3.66
1942	35.49	25.11	12.91	9.60	4.48	1.32	10.39	12.20	3.31	5.12	3.16
1943	32.67	23.02	11.48	8.43	3.78	0.97	9.65	11.54	3.06	4.65	2.81
1944	31.55	21.76	10.54	7.60	3.33	0.92	9.79	11.22	2.94	4.28	2.40

1945	32.64	22.90	11.07	7.87	3.32	0.84	9.74	11.83	3.20	4.55	2.47
1946	34.62	24.66	11.76	8.28	3.43	0.92	9.96	12.90	3.48	4.85	2.52
1947	33.02	23.30	10.95	7.71	3.24	0.90	9.72	12.35	3.25	4.47	2.33
1948	33.72	23.70	11.27	8.03	3.44	0.95	10.02	12.43	3.24	4.59	2.48
1949	33.76	23.46	10.95	7.77	3.34	0.95	10.30	12.52	3.18	4.43	2.38
1950	33.87	23.87	11.36	8.14	3.53	0.83	10.00	12.51	3.22	4.60	2.70
1951	32.82	22.67	10.52	7.41	3.12	0.87	10.15	12.15	3.11	4.29	2.25
1952	32.07	21.85	9.76	6.81	2.76	0.75	10.23	12.09	2.95	4.05	2.01
1953	31.38	21.01	9.08	6.26	2.51	0.67	10.37	11.93	2.82	3.76	1.83
1954	32.12	21.56	9.39	6.47	2.57	0.71	10.56	12.17	2.92	3.90	1.86
1955	31.77	21.38	9.18	6.28	2.49	0.72	10.39	12.20	2.90	3.80	1.77
1956	31.81	21.35	9.09	6.14	2.38	0.68	10.46	12.26	2.94	3.76	1.70
1957	31.69	21.17	8.98	6.08	2.36	0.66	10.52	12.19	2.90	3.72	1.70
1958	32.11	21.26	8.83	5.94	2.29	0.64	10.85	12.43	2.89	3.65	1.65
1959	32.03	21.02	8.75	5.90	2.19	0.62	11.01	12.28	2.85	3.71	1.58
1960	31.66	20.51	8.36	5.52	2.10	0.60	11.15	12.15	2.84	3.42	1.50
1961	31.90	20.91	8.34	5.41	2.05	0.59	10.99	12.57	2.93	3.36	1.47
1962	32.04	20.94	8.27	5.40	1.98	0.56	11.10	12.67	2.87	3.42	1.42
1963	32.01	20.90	8.16	5.33	1.96	0.57	11.11	12.73	2.83	3.37	1.40
1964	31.64	20.62	8.02	5.33	1.97	0.53	11.02	12.60	2.69	3.36	1.44
1965	31.52	20.70	8.07	5.42	2.04	0.54	10.82	12.63	2.64	3.38	1.50
1966	31.98	20.99	8.37	5.59	2.15	0.60	10.99	12.62	2.78	3.43	1.55
1967	32.05	21.07	8.43	5.63	2.16	0.60	10.97	12.65	2.80	3.47	1.56
1968	31.98	20.98	8.35	5.58	2.15	0.58	11.01	12.62	2.77	3.43	1.56
1969	31.82	20.68	8.02	5.30	2.00	0.55	11.14	12.66	2.71	3.30	1.45
1970	31.51	20.39	7.80	5.16	1.94	0.53	11.13	12.58	2.65	3.22	1.41
1971	31.75	20.50	7.79	5.12	1.91	0.52	11.26	12.71	2.66	3.21	1.40
1972	31.62	20.37	7.75	5.10	1.92	0.52	11.25	12.62	2.66	3.18	1.40
1973	31.85	20.57	7.74	5.07	1.89	0.50	11.28	12.83	2.67	3.18	1.39
1974	32.36	21.04	8.12	5.41	2.11	0.56	11.32	12.91	2.71	3.30	1.54
1975	32.62	21.03	8.01	5.31	2.04	0.56	11.60	13.02	2.70	3.27	1.48
1976	32.42	20.85	7.89	5.23	2.02	0.56	11.57	12.96	2.66	3.21	1.46
1977	32.43	20.83	7.90	5.25	2.04	0.57	11.60	12.93	2.65	3.21	1.48
1978	32.44	20.86	7.95	5.30	2.08	0.58	11.58	12.91	2.65	3.22	1.50
1979	32.35	20.83	8.03	5.38	2.16	0.62	11.52	12.80	2.65	3.23	1.54
1980	32.87	21.17	8.18	5.51	2.23	0.65	11.70	12.99	2.67	3.28	1.58

(*contd.*)

Table 5A.1 (*contd.*)

	P90–100 (1)	P95–100 (2)	P99–100 (3)	P99.5–100 (4)	P99.9–100 (5)	P99.99–100 (6)	P90–95 (7)	P95–99 (8)	P99–99.5 (9)	P99.5–99.9 (10)	P99.9–99.99 (11)
1981	32.72	20.97	8.03	5.42	2.23	0.66	11.75	12.94	2.60	3.20	1.57
1982	33.22	21.40	8.39	5.73	2.45	0.77	11.82	13.01	2.66	3.28	1.68
1983	33.69	21.79	8.59	5.94	2.61	0.87	11.91	13.19	2.66	3.33	1.74
1984	33.95	22.10	8.89	6.22	2.83	0.98	11.85	13.21	2.67	3.39	1.85
1985	34.25	22.38	9.09	6.39	2.91	0.97	11.87	13.28	2.70	3.48	1.94
1986	34.57	22.59	9.13	6.38	2.87	1.00	11.98	13.46	2.75	3.51	1.87
1987	36.48	24.49	10.75	7.76	3.73	1.30	11.99	13.74	2.98	4.04	2.43
1988	38.63	26.95	13.17	9.96	5.21	1.99	11.68	13.78	3.20	4.75	3.22
1989	38.47	26.66	12.61	9.37	4.74	1.74	11.81	14.05	3.24	4.63	3.00
1990	38.84	27.05	12.98	9.71	4.90	1.83	11.78	14.07	3.27	4.82	3.07
1991	38.38	26.43	12.17	8.90	4.36	1.61	11.95	14.26	3.27	4.54	2.75
1992	39.82	27.88	13.48	10.11	5.21	2.02	11.94	14.40	3.37	4.90	3.20
1993	39.48	27.41	12.82	9.45	4.72	1.74	12.07	14.59	3.37	4.74	2.98
1994	39.60	27.50	12.85	9.45	4.70	1.73	12.09	14.65	3.40	4.74	2.97
1995	40.19	28.11	13.33	9.87	4.94	1.80	12.08	14.77	3.47	4.93	3.14
1996	41.14	29.15	14.10	10.48	5.32	1.97	11.99	15.05	3.62	5.16	3.35
1997	41.70	29.83	14.77	11.12	5.80	2.19	11.87	15.07	3.65	5.31	3.61
1998	42.06	30.31	15.28	11.60	6.19	2.40	11.75	15.04	3.68	5.41	3.79
1999	42.59	30.91	15.85	12.14	6.63	2.63	11.68	15.06	3.71	5.51	4.00
2000	43.91	32.15	16.94	13.10	7.37	3.06	11.76	15.21	3.84	5.73	4.31
2001	42.58	30.61	15.46	11.76	6.31	2.47	11.98	15.15	3.70	5.45	3.84
2002	41.87	29.75	14.67	11.07	5.81	2.25	12.12	15.09	3.60	5.26	3.56

Notes: Taxpayers are ranked by gross income (excluding capital gains and government transfers). Income is defined as market income but excludes capital gains. The Table reports the percentage of total income accruing to each of the top groups. P90–100 denotes to top decile, P90–95 denotes the bottom half of the top decile, etc.

Source: Computations by authors on tax return statistics.

Table 5A.2 Top fractiles (defined excluding capital gains) income shares (including capital gains), US 1913–2002 (fractiles are defined by total income (excluding capital gains))

	P90–100 (1)	P95–100 (2)	P99–100 (3)	P99.5–100 (4)	P99.9–100 (5)	P99.99–100 (6)	P90–95 (7)	P95–99 (8)	P99–99.5 (9)	P99.5–99.9 (10)	P99.9–99.99 (11)
1913			17.96	14.73	8.62	2.76			3.23	6.11	5.86
1914			18.16	15.08	8.60	2.73			3.08	6.48	5.87
1915			17.58	14.58	9.22	4.36			3.00	5.36	4.86
1916			18.89	15.93	10.13	4.51			2.95	5.81	5.61
1917	40.43	30.57	17.72	14.32	8.39	3.33	9.87	12.85	3.40	5.93	5.06
1918	40.08	29.48	15.99	12.45	6.74	2.44	10.61	13.49	3.54	5.70	4.30
1919	39.92	29.79	16.15	12.42	6.51	2.22	10.13	13.64	3.74	5.91	4.29
1920	38.69	28.02	14.68	11.04	5.35	1.65	10.66	13.35	3.64	5.69	3.70
1921	43.08	30.72	15.62	11.68	5.61	1.68	12.37	15.10	3.94	6.07	3.93
1922	43.21	31.45	16.65	12.67	6.35	2.09	11.76	14.80	3.98	6.32	4.26
1923	40.98	29.32	15.28	11.57	5.65	1.83	11.65	14.04	3.72	5.91	3.83
1924	43.66	31.39	16.80	12.82	6.38	2.10	12.26	14.59	3.98	6.45	4.28
1925	44.55	33.24	18.62	14.33	7.37	2.63	11.32	14.62	4.29	6.96	4.74
1926	44.35	33.28	18.70	14.40	7.55	2.79	11.07	14.58	4.31	6.85	4.76
1927	44.96	34.02	19.49	15.13	8.08	3.05	10.94	14.53	4.36	7.05	5.04
1928	46.27	35.58	21.09	16.66	9.34	3.73	10.69	14.48	4.43	7.33	5.60
1929	43.97	33.78	19.76	15.55	8.77	3.61	10.20	14.02	4.20	6.78	5.16
1930	43.24	31.46	16.72	12.70	6.64	2.53	11.78	14.75	4.01	6.06	4.11
1931	44.40	31.10	15.39	11.44	5.77	2.13	13.31	15.70	3.95	5.67	3.64
1932	46.36	32.66	15.56	11.64	5.96	1.95	13.70	17.10	3.93	5.68	4.01
1933	45.17	32.76	16.09	12.09	6.29	2.14	12.41	16.67	4.00	5.80	4.15
1934	45.17	33.11	16.00	11.92	5.89	1.93	12.07	17.11	4.08	6.03	3.96
1935	43.54	31.34	15.97	11.97	5.96	1.98	12.20	15.37	3.99	6.01	3.99
1936	45.15	33.22	18.16	13.83	6.92	2.25	11.93	15.06	4.34	6.91	4.66
1937	43.54	31.59	16.67	12.58	6.23	2.03	11.95	14.93	4.08	6.35	4.21
1938	43.13	30.41	15.02	11.08	5.36	1.80	12.72	15.39	3.94	5.73	3.56
1939	44.75	31.53	15.64	11.57	5.56	1.77	13.23	15.89	4.07	6.01	3.78
1940	44.56	31.50	15.95	11.84	5.68	1.82	13.06	15.54	4.11	6.16	3.86
1941	41.17	29.25	15.23	11.34	5.43	1.71	11.92	14.02	3.89	5.91	3.72
1942	35.60	25.28	13.06	9.72	4.57	1.37	10.32	12.22	3.34	5.15	3.20

(*contd.*)

Table 5A.2 (*contd.*)

	P90–100 (1)	P95–100 (2)	P99–100 (3)	P99.5–100 (4)	P99.9–100 (5)	P99.99–100 (6)	P90–95 (7)	P95–99 (8)	P99–99.5 (9)	P99.5–99.9 (10)	P99.9–99.99 (11)
1943	32.98	23.38	11.78	8.67	3.93	1.03	9.60	11.60	3.12	4.73	2.90
1944	31.85	22.12	10.81	7.82	3.46	0.98	9.74	11.31	2.99	4.36	2.48
1945	33.24	23.63	11.61	8.32	3.59	0.95	9.61	12.02	3.30	4.72	2.65
1946	35.28	25.38	12.23	8.67	3.71	1.05	9.89	13.15	3.56	4.96	2.66
1947	33.38	23.73	11.25	7.97	3.44	1.00	9.65	12.48	3.29	4.53	2.44
1948	34.08	24.14	11.57	8.29	3.62	1.03	9.94	12.57	3.29	4.67	2.58
1949	34.00	23.77	11.19	7.98	3.48	1.02	10.23	12.58	3.21	4.50	2.46
1950	34.41	24.41	11.91	8.56	3.82	0.92	10.00	12.50	3.35	4.74	2.90
1951	33.18	23.17	10.98	7.79	3.37	0.97	10.00	12.20	3.19	4.43	2.40
1952	32.35	22.22	10.13	7.13	2.98	0.83	10.13	12.09	3.00	4.14	2.15
1953	31.60	21.31	9.37	6.53	2.69	0.75	10.28	11.94	2.85	3.83	1.95
1954	32.53	22.20	9.92	6.92	2.89	0.83	10.33	12.29	2.99	4.03	2.07
1955	32.52	22.21	9.92	6.92	2.93	0.88	10.31	12.28	3.00	3.99	2.05
1956	32.24	21.92	9.68	6.75	2.79	0.82	10.31	12.24	2.93	3.96	1.97
1957	32.03	21.65	9.42	6.52	2.66	0.77	10.37	12.24	2.90	3.86	1.89
1958	32.46	21.84	9.35	6.45	2.63	0.76	10.62	12.49	2.90	3.82	1.87
1959	32.56	21.95	9.49	6.62	2.66	0.78	10.61	12.45	2.87	3.96	1.88
1960	32.19	21.30	9.01	6.15	2.52	0.76	10.89	12.29	2.86	3.63	1.76
1961	32.56	21.84	9.24	6.32	2.65	0.82	10.73	12.59	2.93	3.66	1.84
1962	32.44	21.56	8.92	6.06	2.44	0.73	10.88	12.64	2.86	3.62	1.71
1963	32.48	21.56	8.86	6.00	2.41	0.73	10.92	12.70	2.87	3.59	1.67
1964	32.73	21.84	9.10	6.16	2.48	0.76	10.89	12.74	2.94	3.68	1.73
1965	32.85	22.00	9.30	6.33	2.62	0.82	10.85	12.70	2.97	3.71	1.80
1966	32.82	22.08	9.42	6.48	2.75	0.83	10.74	12.66	2.94	3.73	1.92
1967	33.39	22.66	9.83	6.81	2.87	0.84	10.73	12.83	3.02	3.94	2.04
1968	33.59	22.86	10.07	7.03	3.00	0.87	10.72	12.79	3.04	4.03	2.13
1969	32.92	22.08	9.40	6.54	2.79	0.87	10.84	12.68	2.86	3.75	1.92
1970	31.91	20.97	8.44	5.71	2.29	0.66	10.94	12.53	2.73	3.42	1.62
1971	32.42	21.39	8.65	5.86	2.38	0.69	11.03	12.73	2.79	3.48	1.69
1972	32.45	21.40	8.70	5.89	2.39	0.72	11.05	12.70	2.81	3.50	1.68
1973	32.27	21.22	8.34	5.59	2.19	0.60	11.05	12.88	2.75	3.40	1.59
1974	32.55	21.40	8.53	5.75	2.31	0.64	11.15	12.87	2.78	3.45	1.67

1975	32.75	21.33	8.37	5.61	2.23	0.64	11.42	12.96	2.75	3.38	1.59
1976	32.63	21.24	8.33	5.60	2.24	0.65	11.39	12.91	2.72	3.36	1.59
1977	32.69	21.27	8.36	5.63	2.27	0.65	11.42	12.91	2.73	3.37	1.62
1978	32.63	21.23	8.36	5.64	2.28	0.65	11.40	12.87	2.72	3.37	1.63
1979	33.01	21.77	9.00	6.24	2.74	0.90	11.24	12.77	2.76	3.50	1.85
1980	33.54	22.10	9.15	6.36	2.77	0.87	11.44	12.95	2.79	3.59	1.89
1981	33.32	21.82	8.93	6.22	2.72	0.86	11.50	12.89	2.71	3.49	1.86
1982	34.27	22.75	9.76	6.97	3.28	1.13	11.52	12.99	2.79	3.68	2.15
1983	34.98	23.46	10.28	7.41	3.54	1.24	11.53	13.17	2.88	3.87	2.30
1984	35.33	23.84	10.63	7.79	3.87	1.38	11.50	13.21	2.84	3.92	2.48
1985	35.97	24.46	11.09	8.17	4.07	1.42	11.51	13.36	2.92	4.10	2.65
1986	37.86	26.63	13.14	9.99	4.89	1.94	11.23	13.49	3.16	5.09	2.96
1987	37.30	25.57	11.75	8.64	4.25	1.50	11.74	13.82	3.11	4.39	2.74
1988	39.78	28.41	14.65	11.30	6.10	2.39	11.37	13.75	3.35	5.20	3.71
1989	39.34	27.80	13.81	10.44	5.47	2.10	11.55	13.98	3.38	4.97	3.37
1990	39.38	27.81	13.81	10.46	5.40	2.08	11.57	14.00	3.35	5.06	3.32
1991	38.78	26.98	12.72	9.38	4.67	1.72	11.80	14.26	3.34	4.71	2.95
1992	40.31	28.56	14.22	10.78	5.67	2.20	11.75	14.34	3.45	5.11	3.47
1993	40.05	28.22	13.68	10.25	5.27	1.97	11.83	14.54	3.43	4.98	3.30
1994	40.13	28.23	13.65	10.17	5.18	1.93	11.91	14.58	3.47	4.99	3.24
1995	40.94	29.09	14.35	10.76	5.51	2.00	11.85	14.74	3.59	5.25	3.50
1996	42.39	30.72	15.73	11.94	6.30	2.40	11.67	14.99	3.78	5.64	3.90
1997	43.34	31.89	16.82	12.96	7.08	2.66	11.45	15.07	3.86	5.88	4.42
1998	44.01	32.67	17.56	13.63	7.53	2.89	11.34	15.10	3.94	6.10	4.63
1999	44.80	33.52	18.29	14.28	7.96	3.08	11.28	15.23	4.01	6.31	4.88
2000	45.64	34.46	19.36	15.32	8.81	3.58	11.18	15.10	4.04	6.51	5.23
2001	43.91	32.27	17.17	13.32	7.37	2.90	11.63	15.10	3.85	5.95	4.47
2002	43.07	31.19	16.09	12.34	6.66	2.60	11.87	15.10	3.76	5.67	4.07

Notes: Taxpayers are ranked by gross income (excluding capital gains and government transfers).
Income to compute shares is defined as market income and includes capital gains. The Table reports the percentage of total income accruing to each of the top groups. P90–100 denotes to top decile, P90–95 denotes the bottom half of the top decile, etc. Those series differ slightly from Table A2 in Piketty and Saez (2001) because of the difference in the denominator: The denominator we use includes all capital gains while the denominator in Piketty and Saez (2001) included only capital gains going to the top 10%.

Source: Computations by authors on tax return statistics.

Table 5A.3 Top fractiles (defined including capital gains) income shares (including capital gains), US 1913–2002 (fractiles are defined by total income (including capital gains))

	P90–100 (1)	P95–100 (2)	P99–100 (3)	P99.5–100 (4)	P99.9–100 (5)	P99.99–100 (6)	P90–95 (7)	P95–99 (8)	P99–99.5 (9)	P99.5–99.9 (10)	P99.9–99.99 (11)
1913			17.96	14.73	8.62	2.76			3.23	6.11	5.86
1914			18.16	15.08	8.60	2.73			3.08	6.48	5.87
1915			17.58	14.58	9.22	4.36			3.00	5.36	4.86
1916			19.31	16.37	10.51	4.78			2.94	5.86	5.73
1917	40.51	30.64	17.74	14.34	8.40	3.37	9.87	12.90	3.39	5.94	5.04
1918	40.11	29.49	15.96	12.43	6.72	2.45	10.61	13.53	3.53	5.71	4.26
1919	40.32	30.17	16.41	12.64	6.63	2.29	10.15	13.76	3.77	6.01	4.34
1920	39.01	28.32	14.83	11.14	5.36	1.66	10.69	13.49	3.69	5.79	3.69
1921	43.18	30.80	15.64	11.70	5.60	1.69	12.38	15.17	3.94	6.10	3.91
1922	43.72	31.94	17.06	13.06	6.64	2.27	11.78	14.89	4.00	6.42	4.36
1923	41.46	29.78	15.64	11.91	5.91	2.00	11.68	14.13	3.73	6.00	3.91
1924	44.41	32.11	17.42	13.40	6.79	2.32	12.29	14.69	4.02	6.61	4.46
1925	46.35	35.01	20.24	15.86	8.52	3.31	11.34	14.77	4.38	7.34	5.21
1926	45.71	34.61	19.91	15.55	8.46	3.36	11.10	14.70	4.36	7.09	5.09
1927	46.67	35.69	21.03	16.60	9.25	3.75	10.98	14.67	4.43	7.34	5.50
1928	49.29	38.56	23.94	19.40	11.54	5.02	10.73	14.62	4.54	7.86	6.52
1929	46.71	36.48	22.35	18.07	10.91	4.99	10.23	14.13	4.29	7.15	5.92
1930	43.87	32.06	17.22	13.20	7.07	2.84	11.80	14.84	4.02	6.13	4.23
1931	44.54	31.23	15.50	11.57	5.89	2.25	13.31	15.73	3.93	5.67	3.64
1932	46.37	32.67	15.56	11.62	5.97	1.99	13.70	17.11	3.93	5.65	3.98
1933	45.60	33.19	16.46	12.46	6.61	2.34	12.42	16.73	4.00	5.86	4.26
1934	45.78	33.71	16.40	12.30	6.13	2.07	12.07	17.32	4.10	6.17	4.06
1935	44.49	32.28	16.68	12.63	6.39	2.19	12.21	15.61	4.04	6.24	4.20
1936	46.59	34.64	19.29	14.86	7.57	2.54	11.96	15.35	4.43	7.29	5.03
1937	44.23	32.27	17.15	13.02	6.49	2.17	11.96	15.12	4.13	6.53	4.32
1938	44.07	31.34	15.75	11.78	5.88	2.19	12.73	15.59	3.98	5.89	3.69
1939	45.52	32.28	16.18	12.06	5.87	1.96	13.24	16.10	4.12	6.19	3.91
1940	45.29	32.22	16.48	12.33	6.01	2.04	13.07	15.74	4.14	6.33	3.96
1941	41.93	29.99	15.79	11.86	5.81	1.98	11.94	14.21	3.92	6.06	3.83
1942	36.13	25.80	13.43	10.07	4.81	1.55	10.32	12.37	3.36	5.26	3.27

1944	32.51	22.77	11.28	8.26	3.76	1.16	9.75	11.48	3.02	4.50	2.59
1945	34.42	24.79	12.52	9.14	4.16	1.26	9.63	12.28	3.38	4.98	2.90
1946	36.70	26.77	13.28	9.61	4.39	1.47	9.93	13.49	3.66	5.22	2.92
1947	34.35	24.68	11.96	8.61	3.92	1.30	9.67	12.72	3.34	4.70	2.61
1948	35.01	25.06	12.24	8.90	4.06	1.31	9.96	12.81	3.34	4.85	2.75
1949	34.75	24.51	11.73	8.48	3.83	1.24	10.25	12.78	3.25	4.64	2.59
1950	35.56	25.53	12.82	9.37	4.39	1.22	10.03	12.71	3.45	4.98	3.17
1951	34.22	24.20	11.79	8.53	3.89	1.28	10.02	12.41	3.26	4.64	2.61
1952	33.21	23.07	10.79	7.74	3.43	1.09	10.14	12.28	3.05	4.31	2.34
1953	32.31	22.01	9.90	7.02	3.06	0.97	10.29	12.11	2.88	3.97	2.09
1954	33.64	23.30	10.77	7.71	3.49	1.17	10.34	12.52	3.06	4.22	2.32
1955	33.94	23.60	11.06	7.96	3.71	1.32	10.34	12.54	3.10	4.25	2.40
1956	33.46	23.13	10.67	7.70	3.49	1.20	10.34	12.45	2.97	4.22	2.29
1957	32.99	22.60	10.16	7.23	3.18	1.05	10.38	12.44	2.93	4.05	2.13
1958	33.56	22.93	10.21	7.27	3.22	1.08	10.63	12.72	2.94	4.05	2.14
1959	34.00	23.39	10.65	7.72	3.45	1.19	10.61	12.74	2.93	4.27	2.26
1960	33.48	22.57	10.03	7.13	3.25	1.17	10.90	12.54	2.91	3.88	2.07
1961	34.25	23.50	10.64	7.66	3.65	1.38	10.75	12.86	2.98	4.01	2.27
1962	33.70	22.81	9.95	7.06	3.19	1.16	10.90	12.86	2.89	3.86	2.03
1963	33.78	22.84	9.92	7.00	3.15	1.15	10.94	12.93	2.92	3.85	2.00
1964	34.42	23.50	10.48	7.39	3.37	1.30	10.92	13.02	3.09	4.01	2.07
1965	34.78	23.88	10.89	7.73	3.66	1.49	10.90	12.98	3.17	4.07	2.17
1966	33.67	22.92	10.18	7.22	3.39	1.29	10.75	12.74	2.96	3.83	2.10
1967	34.44	23.70	10.74	7.67	3.68	1.42	10.74	12.96	3.06	4.00	2.26
1968	34.85	24.15	11.21	8.14	4.02	1.61	10.70	12.94	3.07	4.12	2.41
1969	33.93	23.08	10.35	7.45	3.69	1.56	10.85	12.73	2.91	3.75	2.14
1970	32.63	21.66	9.03	6.25	2.78	1.00	10.96	12.64	2.77	3.48	1.78
1971	33.34	22.26	9.40	6.56	2.99	1.11	11.08	12.86	2.84	3.58	1.87
1972	33.59	22.52	9.64	6.78	3.13	1.18	11.07	12.88	2.86	3.65	1.95
1973	33.33	22.21	9.16	6.30	2.76	0.94	11.12	13.05	2.86	3.54	1.82
1974	33.31	22.12	9.12	6.31	2.73	0.88	11.19	13.00	2.82	3.58	1.85
1975	33.43	21.98	8.87	6.07	2.56	0.85	11.45	13.11	2.80	3.50	1.72
1976	33.41	21.97	8.86	6.07	2.59	0.86	11.44	13.11	2.79	3.47	1.73
1977	33.58	22.12	9.03	6.22	2.71	0.92	11.46	13.10	2.81	3.51	1.78
1978	33.49	22.04	8.95	6.16	2.65	0.86	11.45	13.09	2.79	3.51	1.79

(contd.)

Table 5A.3 (*contd.*)

	P90–100 (1)	P95–100 (2)	P99–100 (3)	P99.5–100 (4)	P99.9–100 (5)	P99.99–100 (6)	P90–95 (7)	P95–99 (8)	P99–99.5 (9)	P99.5–99.9 (10)	P99.9–99.99 (11)
1979	34.21	22.93	9.96	7.11	3.44	1.37	11.28	12.97	2.85	3.67	2.07
1980	34.63	23.17	10.02	7.15	3.41	1.28	11.47	13.15	2.87	3.74	2.13
1981	34.54	23.04	10.02	7.23	3.57	1.37	11.51	13.02	2.78	3.67	2.20
1982	35.33	23.83	10.80	7.97	4.18	1.73	11.50	13.04	2.83	3.79	2.44
1983	36.38	24.85	11.56	8.63	4.62	1.88	11.53	13.30	2.92	4.01	2.74
1984	36.74	25.29	11.99	9.04	4.98	2.15	11.45	13.30	2.95	4.06	2.83
1985	37.56	26.12	12.67	9.63	5.32	2.24	11.44	13.45	3.04	4.31	3.08
1986	40.63	29.49	15.92	12.62	7.40	3.34	11.14	13.57	3.30	5.22	4.05
1987	38.25	26.54	12.66	9.45	4.90	1.91	11.71	13.88	3.21	4.55	2.99
1988	40.63	29.29	15.49	12.09	6.80	2.86	11.34	13.80	3.40	5.29	3.94
1989	40.08	28.55	14.49	11.08	6.00	2.45	11.54	14.06	3.41	5.08	3.54
1990	39.98	28.41	14.33	10.94	5.82	2.33	11.57	14.08	3.39	5.12	3.49
1991	39.55	27.72	13.36	9.99	5.12	1.96	11.82	14.36	3.38	4.86	3.17
1992	40.82	29.06	14.67	11.20	6.03	2.46	11.76	14.39	3.47	5.17	3.57
1993	40.68	28.83	14.24	10.78	5.73	2.32	11.85	14.60	3.46	5.05	3.41
1994	40.78	28.89	14.23	10.73	5.70	2.29	11.89	14.66	3.50	5.03	3.41
1995	41.59	29.75	14.98	11.39	6.13	2.43	11.85	14.77	3.59	5.27	3.69
1996	43.19	31.54	16.57	12.82	7.19	3.04	11.65	14.97	3.75	5.63	4.15
1997	44.33	32.90	17.88	14.06	8.13	3.50	11.43	15.02	3.82	5.93	4.62
1998	45.25	33.99	19.03	15.13	8.97	3.91	11.26	14.96	3.89	6.16	5.06
1999	46.32	35.10	19.98	15.99	9.59	4.20	11.23	15.11	4.00	6.39	5.39
2000	47.61	36.61	21.52	17.46	10.88	5.07	11.00	15.08	4.07	6.58	5.80
2001	44.82	33.35	18.22	14.32	8.37	3.70	11.47	15.13	3.90	5.95	4.67
2002	43.67	31.96	16.81	12.99	7.32	3.13	11.71	15.15	3.81	5.68	4.18

Notes: Taxpayers are ranked by gross income including capital gains (excluding government transfers). Income to compute shares is defined as market income and includes capital gains. The Table reports the percentage of total income accruing to each of the top groups. P90–100 denotes to top decile, P90–95 denotes the bottom half of the top decile, etc. Those series differ slightly from Table A2 in Piketty and Saez (2001) because of the difference in the denominator: The denominator we use includes all capital gains while the denominator in Piketty and Saez (2001) included only capital gains going to the top 10%.

Source: Computations by authors on tax return statistics.

Table 5A.4 Top fractiles income levels (excluding capital gains), US 1913–2002 (fractiles are defined by total income (excluding capital gains)) (incomes are expressed in 2000 $)

	P90–100 (1)	P95–100 (2)	P99–100 (3)	P99.5–100 (4)	P99.9–100 (5)	P99.99–100 (6)	P0–90 (7)	P90–95 (8)	P95–99 (9)	P99–99.5 (10)	P99.5–99.9 (11)	P99.9–99.99 (12)	P90 (13)	P95 (14)	P99 (15)	P99.5 (16)	P99.9 (17)	P99.99 (18)
1913			229,136	375,763	1,099,313	3,514,871				82,509	194,875	830,918			65,620	107,611	340,199	1,430,935
1914			226,433	376,107	1,072,853	3,403,375				76,758	201,921	813,906			60,670	100,774	325,982	1,422,412
1915			221,308	367,086	1,160,746	5,489,423				75,528	168,665	679,759			51,143	97,313	358,638	1,819,678
1916			254,314	427,310	1,350,988	6,031,517				81,318	196,391	830,930			61,351	109,622	411,436	2,253,327
1917	56,197	84,628	245,496	397,107	1,165,846	4,646,110	9,642	27,766	44,411	93,885	204,923	779,150	22,138	30,659	75,688	122,701	425,860	1,942,778
1918	52,703	77,391	209,779	327,164	890,343	3,233,426	9,186	28,015	44,294	92,393	186,370	630,001	23,439	31,315	75,621	117,439	363,036	1,469,057
1919	51,052	75,793	205,175	316,384	834,536	2,870,852	9,054	26,310	43,447	93,965	186,846	608,278	22,180	30,634	76,851	119,524	381,136	1,356,444
1920	43,946	63,369	166,776	252,678	619,561	1,928,130	8,253	24,524	37,517	80,874	160,957	474,164	22,514	27,272	65,965	105,351	301,810	979,440
1921	43,632	62,011	157,516	236,155	570,306	1,719,633	6,746	25,252	38,135	78,877	152,617	442,603	22,085	27,548	64,994	100,286	281,703	901,008
1922	49,344	71,353	187,183	284,382	708,705	2,308,517	7,602	27,334	42,396	89,984	178,301	530,948	23,500	30,534	72,771	113,957	328,103	1,042,358
1923	51,869	73,986	191,567	289,392	703,327	2,238,328	8,790	29,751	44,590	93,742	185,908	532,771	25,251	34,368	75,142	119,098	335,753	1,025,279
1924	54,621	78,093	205,989	313,515	775,194	2,536,010	8,310	31,149	46,119	98,463	198,095	579,548	26,246	35,140	78,947	125,086	355,210	1,170,760
1925	56,332	82,816	224,515	342,164	861,187	2,991,027	8,267	29,849	47,392	106,865	212,409	624,538	26,908	35,107	84,772	133,296	371,004	1,234,448
1926	56,795	84,421	232,127	354,354	910,927	3,271,908	8,367	29,169	47,494	109,901	215,211	648,595	26,231	34,059	88,016	137,074	381,973	1,314,427
1927	57,995	86,817	242,533	372,209	970,267	3,581,252	8,344	29,173	47,889	112,856	222,695	680,158	26,717	34,930	90,013	139,501	391,000	1,461,038
1928	61,075	92,147	259,690	402,145	1,085,422	4,273,879	8,305	30,003	50,261	117,234	231,326	731,149	27,473	36,156	92,635	140,549	398,849	1,663,634
1929	60,450	91,309	254,433	392,693	1,052,917	4,152,319	9,016	29,591	50,528	116,173	227,637	708,540	26,821	35,783	93,212	141,408	375,522	1,497,802
1930	53,913	78,054	205,556	310,840	801,269	2,989,874	8,265	29,771	46,179	100,271	188,233	558,091	26,425	33,794	82,484	123,812	330,914	1,179,656
1931	50,428	70,437	173,419	257,194	644,492	2,355,785	7,331	30,419	44,692	89,643	160,370	454,348	26,121	32,777	74,729	110,152	275,828	972,445
1932	44,224	62,258	147,842	220,620	563,177	1,840,081	5,964	26,190	40,862	75,065	134,980	421,299	17,916	30,599	63,929	91,812	242,064	912,951
1933	41,885	60,440	146,707	219,140	563,212	1,901,983	5,940	23,330	38,874	74,275	133,122	414,460	17,426	28,102	62,184	89,323	233,920	875,641
1934	46,136	67,422	162,128	241,043	595,014	1,963,627	6,510	24,849	43,746	83,212	152,550	442,946	21,113	29,926	69,207	102,300	276,580	941,704
1935	48,004	68,567	172,890	258,213	641,286	2,153,159	7,265	27,441	42,486	87,567	162,445	473,300	23,187	32,904	72,540	106,916	290,011	1,026,737
1936	54,362	79,298	214,150	324,653	811,982	2,712,649	7,788	29,426	45,585	103,648	202,820	600,797	25,038	35,694	84,469	128,939	365,151	1,321,440
1937	55,195	79,910	209,463	316,165	784,504	2,566,386	8,369	30,479	47,522	102,762	199,081	586,517	26,534	35,625	84,458	129,458	362,903	1,238,572
1938	50,363	70,699	172,511	253,364	603,841	1,951,770	7,743	30,027	45,246	91,659	165,744	454,071	25,992	34,524	76,791	112,612	287,396	864,334
1939	55,616	78,083	192,084	283,647	680,206	2,172,855	8,032	33,149	49,583	100,521	184,508	514,356	29,310	38,703	84,011	123,701	322,147	1,060,151
1940	58,045	81,759	205,572	304,721	728,164	2,317,863	8,431	34,332	50,806	106,423	198,860	551,531	32,521	38,311	88,255	134,219	350,361	1,119,860
1941	62,657	88,624	229,185	340,492	807,738	2,487,704	10,508	36,657	53,483	117,879	223,680	621,075	33,642	41,539	96,381	149,724	394,831	1,228,466
1942	62,970	89,089	228,963	340,462	794,303	2,344,902	13,220	36,856	54,120	117,464	227,001	622,015	34,226	41,518	95,294	149,818	395,821	1,214,441
1943	67,025	94,458	235,618	345,851	776,171	1,995,521	15,918	39,592	59,168	125,385	238,271	640,688	34,952	45,285	101,798	160,607	409,838	1,063,653

(*contd.*)

Table 5A.4 (*contd.*)

	P90–100 (1)	P95–100 (2)	P99–100 (3)	P99.5–100 (4)	P99.9–100 (5)	P99.99–100 (6)	P0–90 (7)	P90–95 (8)	P95–99 (9)	P99–99.5 (10)	P99.5–99.9 (11)	P99.9–99.99 (12)	P90 (13)	P95 (14)	P99 (15)	P99.5 (16)	P99.9 (17)	P99.99 (18)
1944	68,551	94,555	228,989	330,430	722,999	2,007,911	17,130	42,547	60,946	127,548	232,288	580,231	38,163	45,257	104,782	158,588	388,225	1,077,031
1945	69,324	97,276	235,109	334,206	704,797	1,794,265	16,483	41,373	62,818	136,011	241,558	583,745	36,765	44,856	111,865	171,054	385,720	942,331
1946	69,575	99,119	236,412	332,868	689,817	1,841,828	15,160	40,032	64,795	139,956	243,630	561,816	35,841	45,834	115,557	172,562	384,820	933,052
1947	63,682	89,878	211,274	297,319	624,090	1,741,470	14,891	37,486	59,530	125,228	215,626	499,936	33,151	41,805	103,859	153,757	339,895	872,865
1948	66,187	93,021	221,205	315,070	674,642	1,872,216	14,455	39,353	60,975	127,339	225,177	541,578	34,872	45,541	105,841	159,286	362,917	982,569
1949	65,462	90,979	212,230	301,302	646,954	1,850,519	14,269	39,945	60,667	123,159	214,889	513,224	35,458	46,375	102,007	151,059	345,651	949,269
1950	70,883	99,913	237,737	340,503	739,114	1,730,493	15,377	41,854	65,457	134,970	240,850	628,961	38,315	47,664	109,696	169,176	382,547	850,449
1951	70,768	97,764	226,800	319,585	672,119	1,865,510	16,095	43,771	65,506	134,015	231,452	539,520	39,208	48,240	112,813	163,618	364,032	956,134
1952	71,356	97,207	217,097	302,911	613,117	1,659,022	16,791	45,505	67,235	131,282	225,360	496,906	41,885	51,443	111,623	164,547	341,772	854,558
1953	72,891	97,592	210,936	290,952	582,169	1,562,420	17,710	48,189	69,256	130,920	218,147	473,252	43,152	52,916	112,143	161,222	328,227	783,254
1954	73,701	98,946	215,474	296,887	588,872	1,619,721	17,307	48,456	69,815	134,061	223,890	474,334	43,389	52,952	114,157	163,664	330,869	793,588
1955	77,936	104,879	225,196	308,337	610,082	1,767,643	18,596	50,994	74,799	142,055	232,901	481,464	46,348	57,888	119,965	171,144	332,290	816,406
1956	82,070	110,168	234,474	317,071	614,872	1,757,602	19,551	53,973	79,091	151,877	242,621	487,902	48,280	60,403	128,267	174,215	344,427	822,401
1957	82,108	109,698	232,738	315,086	611,297	1,718,166	19,668	54,518	78,938	150,389	241,033	488,312	49,338	61,267	126,950	174,446	349,011	836,867
1958	80,682	106,832	221,944	298,599	576,050	1,614,126	18,952	54,533	78,054	145,288	229,237	460,708	49,353	61,550	123,540	166,936	329,444	790,031
1959	85,231	111,882	232,755	313,983	583,035	1,639,471	20,093	58,581	81,664	151,528	246,720	465,653	52,196	66,041	131,822	185,339	336,636	774,633
1960	85,283	110,513	225,121	297,463	564,770	1,606,587	20,457	60,053	81,861	152,779	230,636	449,013	53,145	60,897	130,664	171,842	322,380	760,141
1961	86,943	113,976	227,266	294,894	559,716	1,600,147	20,626	59,910	85,653	159,638	228,689	444,112	53,493	66,683	134,693	167,999	312,850	744,612
1962	90,316	118,056	233,196	304,353	559,229	1,582,943	21,282	62,577	89,271	162,038	240,635	445,483	56,466	69,202	138,709	180,559	326,335	735,796
1963	92,553	120,832	236,053	308,206	567,744	1,642,330	21,843	64,273	92,027	163,899	243,322	448,346	58,304	72,208	140,356	182,815	331,025	750,780
1964	95,862	124,969	243,016	323,177	596,572	1,609,724	23,014	66,755	95,458	162,856	254,828	484,000	60,834	72,836	141,138	190,541	337,960	723,597
1965	99,320	130,459	254,146	341,710	641,959	1,694,924	23,978	68,181	99,537	166,582	266,648	524,962	62,588	76,540	143,784	199,261	347,474	729,812
1966	105,198	138,099	275,257	367,448	708,577	1,983,286	24,859	72,296	103,810	183,066	282,165	566,943	65,302	80,616	156,320	215,278	388,463	901,232
1967	108,180	142,276	284,422	380,067	729,172	2,013,564	25,489	74,084	106,739	188,776	292,791	586,461	66,464	82,344	161,554	220,447	397,851	926,701
1968	111,507	146,267	291,189	388,989	748,008	2,027,641	26,349	76,747	110,037	193,389	299,234	605,827	69,149	85,095	166,653	222,221	409,986	897,699
1969	112,637	146,403	283,795	375,464	708,356	1,936,693	26,815	78,871	112,056	192,126	292,242	571,874	71,189	88,067	165,256	223,220	386,676	823,209
1970	111,987	144,899	277,317	366,451	688,605	1,866,840	27,041	79,074	111,795	188,182	285,913	557,690	71,352	88,771	162,919	220,267	394,825	885,756
1971	112,523	145,260	275,908	363,076	678,395	1,835,753	26,871	79,787	112,598	188,740	284,246	549,800	71,796	89,440	164,494	218,164	384,949	850,452
1972	116,730	150,377	286,225	376,433	707,106	1,921,141	28,044	83,083	116,415	196,017	293,765	572,213	75,074	92,513	170,935	226,166	399,314	879,542
1973	120,066	155,074	291,819	382,247	711,023	1,866,633	28,540	85,058	120,888	201,392	300,053	582,622	76,472	95,408	176,515	231,870	412,007	941,876
1974	118,363	153,893	297,141	395,705	770,643	2,059,178	27,490	82,834	118,080	198,577	301,970	627,472	74,726	95,148	173,514	230,550	452,041	1,084,508
1975	113,062	145,743	277,477	367,973	706,365	1,939,902	25,948	80,381	112,810	186,981	283,375	569,305	72,381	90,350	163,281	217,724	405,028	971,625
1976	115,026	147,933	279,928	371,201	716,457	1,993,880	26,644	82,119	114,934	188,656	284,887	574,521	74,006	92,112	164,832	218,316	406,247	993,887
1977	116,242	149,328	283,098	376,426	731,688	2,029,207	26,905	83,156	115,885	189,770	287,610	587,519	74,816	93,310	165,621	219,708	411,622	995,550

1978	118,443	152,340	290,359	387,171	759,157	2,119,679	27,408	84,547	117,835	193,547	294,175	607,988	76,053	94,588	169,213	224,190	426,111	1,080,089
1979	116,242	149,715	288,665	387,043	775,484	2,211,325	27,015	82,769	114,978	190,287	289,933	615,946	74,663	92,580	165,014	220,046	417,859	1,000,177
1980	112,592	145,047	280,121	377,266	764,353	2,243,291	25,555	80,137	111,278	182,977	280,494	600,027	72,337	89,561	159,550	211,339	407,446	1,073,110
1981	109,784	140,725	269,318	363,944	746,722	2,201,109	25,086	78,844	108,577	174,693	268,250	585,124	71,071	88,316	152,839	199,979	393,534	1,038,057
1982	109,875	141,540	277,513	379,191	810,478	2,562,559	24,544	78,209	107,547	175,835	271,369	615,803	70,568	86,910	152,699	199,288	396,572	1,156,024
1983	111,471	144,164	284,303	392,828	863,050	2,883,399	24,376	78,777	109,129	175,778	275,273	638,567	70,976	87,729	152,581	200,027	400,455	1,281,305
1984	116,201	151,274	304,179	425,592	968,648	3,357,544	25,122	81,128	113,048	182,767	289,828	703,215	72,799	90,755	158,720	208,356	426,435	1,464,608
1985	119,184	155,730	316,460	445,045	1,012,869	3,376,919	25,420	82,639	115,548	187,874	303,089	750,197	73,881	92,421	163,609	212,480	466,297	1,474,672
1986	121,837	159,226	321,762	449,732	1,010,667	3,513,740	25,624	84,447	118,592	193,792	309,498	732,548	75,332	93,779	165,738	215,503	413,283	1,446,071
1987	132,307	177,624	389,719	563,004	1,351,289	4,718,208	25,594	86,991	124,600	216,435	365,932	977,187	77,183	96,546	183,174	253,797	583,952	1,995,591
1988	146,343	204,197	498,794	754,884	1,975,094	7,540,601	25,836	88,489	130,548	242,704	449,831	1,356,704	78,167	99,541	201,118	292,472	760,032	2,990,710
1989	144,715	200,599	474,405	705,082	1,782,874	6,547,060	25,717	88,831	132,148	243,727	435,634	1,253,520	78,206	100,903	202,677	294,367	726,568	2,634,026
1990	144,315	201,061	482,388	721,904	1,820,223	6,784,079	25,253	87,569	130,729	242,872	447,325	1,268,683	77,162	99,591	201,580	297,867	741,897	2,779,977
1991	138,416	190,630	438,800	641,998	1,571,340	5,798,855	24,691	86,201	128,588	235,603	409,662	1,101,616	76,571	99,785	195,893	282,697	661,106	2,518,315
1992	144,472	202,320	489,090	733,778	1,891,764	7,317,678	24,262	86,625	130,627	244,402	444,281	1,288,884	76,215	98,895	202,907	300,790	744,084	2,998,135
1993	140,286	194,797	455,562	671,691	1,675,601	6,173,997	23,892	85,774	129,606	239,434	420,713	1,175,780	75,625	97,891	202,010	285,984	685,509	2,518,817
1994	142,676	198,198	463,088	680,867	1,695,219	6,241,652	24,183	87,153	131,975	245,309	427,279	1,190,060	76,477	99,872	206,507	292,539	696,932	2,591,735
1995	148,483	207,678	492,645	729,004	1,824,680	6,658,985	24,552	89,288	136,436	256,286	455,085	1,287,535	78,043	102,274	213,522	306,873	734,783	2,864,031
1996	152,456	216,066	522,516	776,977	1,972,879	7,314,462	24,214	88,847	139,453	268,055	478,002	1,379,369	77,137	104,412	225,096	330,718	827,931	3,335,778
1997	160,446	229,572	567,998	855,386	2,232,665	8,443,807	24,888	91,318	144,966	280,610	511,066	1,542,538	79,481	107,270	234,125	347,216	909,273	3,784,581
1998	169,153	243,830	614,527	932,992	2,491,037	9,664,282	25,781	94,477	151,156	296,061	543,481	1,694,009	81,980	111,576	247,662	367,829	968,584	4,299,189
1999	177,799	258,069	661,857	1,013,732	2,766,792	10,973,158	26,483	97,527	157,123	309,980	575,467	1,854,974	84,381	115,473	258,610	385,486	1,045,718	4,764,927
2000	186,525	273,121	719,642	1,112,934	3,130,905	12,984,220	26,474	99,930	161,490	326,358	608,445	2,036,067	86,855	119,567	276,476	395,987	1,128,348	5,318,430
2001	176,566	253,816	641,006	975,304	2,616,972	10,240,364	26,455	99,315	157,019	306,713	564,889	1,769,898	86,552	118,096	260,685	376,326	1,016,167	4,293,265
2002	167,661	238,267	587,339	886,198	2,326,405	8,995,161	25,862	97,056	150,998	288,479	526,146	1,585,453	84,550	114,341	245,807	355,883	925,821	3,834,838

Table 5A.5 Top fractiles (defined excluding capital gains) income levels (including capital gains), US 1913–2002 (fractiles are defined by total income (excluding capital gains)) (incomes are expressed in 2000 $)

	P90–100 (1)	P95–100 (2)	P99–100 (3)	P99.5–100 (4)	P99.9–100 (5)	P99.99–100 (6)	P0–90 (7)	P90–95 (8)	P95–99 (9)	P99–99.5 (10)	P99.5–99.9 (11)	P99.9–99.99 (12)	P90 (13)	P95 (14)	P99 (15)	P99.5 (16)	P99.9 (17)	P99.99 (18)
1913			229,136	375,763	1,099,313	3,514,871				82,509	194,875	830,918			65,620	107,611	340,199	1,430,935
1914			226,433	376,107	1,072,853	3,403,375				76,758	201,921	813,906			60,670	100,774	325,982	1,422,412
1915			221,308	367,086	1,160,746	5,489,423				75,528	168,665	679,759			51,143	97,313	358,638	1,819,678
1916			262,786	443,365	1,408,801	6,280,941				82,207	202,006	867,452			62,021	112,757	429,520	2,346,510
1917	56,895	86,025	249,334	402,963	1,180,335	4,682,948	9,690	27,766	45,198	95,706	208,619	791,156	22,138	31,203	77,156	124,915	432,422	1,958,182
1918	53,328	78,435	212,704	331,243	897,387	3,246,678	9,217	28,220	44,867	94,166	189,707	636,355	23,610	31,720	77,072	119,542	366,697	1,475,077
1919	52,668	78,609	213,105	327,650	858,958	2,930,300	9,142	26,728	44,985	98,559	194,824	628,809	22,531	31,718	80,608	124,628	394,000	1,384,532
1920	45,528	65,958	172,733	259,853	629,111	1,940,072	8,318	25,097	39,265	85,613	167,539	483,449	23,041	28,542	69,830	109,659	307,719	985,506
1921	44,301	63,169	160,582	240,218	577,044	1,726,455	6,777	25,433	38,816	80,945	156,011	449,332	22,243	28,040	66,698	102,517	285,986	904,582
1922	50,722	73,829	195,425	297,466	745,203	2,451,870	7,704	27,616	43,430	93,384	185,532	555,573	23,742	31,279	75,520	118,579	343,320	1,107,086
1923	53,535	76,618	199,690	302,267	738,738	2,385,736	8,898	30,452	45,850	97,114	193,149	555,738	25,846	35,339	77,844	123,737	350,226	1,092,800
1924	56,765	81,640	218,505	333,516	829,498	2,728,054	8,458	31,891	47,423	103,494	209,520	618,548	26,871	36,134	82,981	132,300	379,113	1,259,418
1925	60,171	89,779	251,458	387,140	995,396	3,552,963	8,610	30,563	49,359	115,775	235,076	711,222	27,552	36,565	91,840	147,521	422,499	1,466,369
1926	59,831	89,798	252,291	388,414	1,018,187	3,757,620	8,648	29,864	49,175	116,168	230,971	713,806	26,856	35,265	93,035	147,112	420,377	1,509,552
1927	61,682	93,340	267,435	415,119	1,108,836	4,179,841	8,687	30,024	49,816	119,752	241,689	767,613	27,496	36,337	95,513	151,400	441,275	1,705,243
1928	66,785	102,703	304,441	481,024	1,347,623	5,388,947	8,884	30,866	52,269	127,859	264,374	898,588	28,264	37,600	101,031	160,629	490,188	2,097,681
1929	65,450	100,543	294,042	463,021	1,305,723	5,372,428	9,557	30,357	52,168	125,063	252,345	853,867	27,516	36,944	100,344	156,757	452,545	1,937,914
1930	55,541	80,820	214,683	326,296	853,204	3,250,099	8,419	30,262	47,355	103,070	194,569	586,882	26,861	34,654	84,787	127,980	347,986	1,282,328
1931	50,975	71,398	176,743	262,752	662,523	2,447,354	7,397	30,552	45,062	90,735	162,809	464,209	26,236	33,049	75,639	111,827	281,815	1,010,244
1932	44,439	62,618	149,177	223,056	570,909	1,867,562	5,975	26,260	40,978	75,298	136,092	426,837	17,965	30,686	64,127	92,568	245,246	926,586
1933	42,726	61,980	152,222	228,722	594,944	2,027,035	6,008	23,472	39,419	75,723	137,167	435,823	17,532	28,496	63,396	92,037	245,977	933,213
1934	46,632	68,352	165,176	246,107	608,301	1,996,360	6,563	24,912	44,146	84,244	155,559	454,072	21,166	30,200	70,066	104,317	283,528	957,402
1935	49,162	70,768	180,273	270,387	673,349	2,230,319	7,370	27,555	43,392	90,160	169,646	500,353	23,284	33,606	74,688	111,655	306,587	1,063,531
1936	56,825	83,623	228,613	348,071	870,492	2,836,955	7,970	30,027	47,375	109,154	217,466	651,996	25,549	37,096	88,956	138,250	396,268	1,381,995
1937	56,118	81,437	214,823	324,377	803,412	2,610,920	8,425	30,800	48,091	105,270	204,618	602,578	26,813	36,051	86,520	133,059	372,841	1,260,064
1938	51,377	72,453	178,959	264,054	638,040	2,139,428	7,837	30,301	45,827	93,864	170,557	471,219	26,229	34,968	78,638	115,881	298,250	947,438
1939	56,631	79,792	197,895	292,688	703,164	2,244,365	8,099	33,470	50,267	103,103	190,069	531,920	29,594	39,237	86,168	127,430	333,148	1,095,041
1940	58,943	83,328	211,029	313,371	751,332	2,411,151	8,498	34,557	51,403	108,688	203,881	566,908	32,734	38,761	90,133	137,608	360,129	1,164,932
1941	63,674	90,468	235,526	350,735	839,401	2,638,071	10,596	36,832	54,203	120,317	228,568	639,548	33,803	42,098	98,374	152,996	406,575	1,302,719

1942	63,645	90,387	233,432	347,491	816,147	2,443,503	13,283	36,906	54,625	119,373	230,327	635,330	34,273	41,905	96,843	152,013	404,294	1,265,508
1943	68,633	97,318	245,192	360,655	818,068	2,147,117	16,042	39,947	60,350	129,730	246,302	670,396	35,266	46,189	105,325	166,020	428,842	1,144,457
1944	70,159	97,421	238,003	344,515	761,831	2,153,564	17,250	42,898	62,275	131,491	240,186	607,194	38,477	46,244	108,021	163,980	406,266	1,155,159
1945	72,838	103,559	254,423	364,421	787,418	2,074,565	16,731	42,116	65,844	144,426	258,672	644,402	37,425	47,017	118,785	183,173	425,799	1,089,541
1946	74,144	106,703	257,136	364,459	780,605	2,210,569	15,452	41,584	69,094	149,813	260,422	621,720	37,232	48,875	123,696	184,456	425,852	1,119,854
1947	66,231	94,177	223,300	316,211	682,534	1,981,598	15,068	38,284	61,897	130,388	224,630	538,193	33,856	43,467	108,139	160,178	365,905	993,223
1948	68,650	97,261	233,120	333,792	728,884	2,082,649	14,624	40,039	63,297	132,448	235,019	578,465	35,480	47,275	110,088	166,247	387,636	1,093,008
1949	67,182	93,931	221,142	315,417	688,036	2,013,332	14,395	40,432	62,128	126,868	222,262	540,781	35,890	47,492	105,078	156,243	364,211	1,032,788
1950	74,280	105,397	257,205	369,655	824,214	1,989,191	15,603	43,163	67,445	144,756	256,015	694,772	39,513	49,112	117,649	179,828	422,575	977,586
1951	73,587	102,805	243,521	345,663	746,698	2,145,234	16,312	44,369	67,627	141,378	245,404	591,305	39,744	49,802	119,012	173,481	398,973	1,099,502
1952	73,594	101,106	230,506	324,348	678,895	1,891,628	16,968	46,081	68,756	136,665	235,711	544,147	42,416	52,607	116,200	172,105	374,264	974,373
1953	74,665	100,724	221,513	308,479	636,377	1,766,505	17,856	48,606	70,526	134,548	226,505	510,808	43,526	53,886	115,250	167,398	354,274	885,563
1954	76,774	104,788	233,986	326,632	683,006	1,955,530	17,555	48,761	72,488	141,339	237,539	541,615	43,662	54,980	120,355	173,641	377,801	958,119
1955	82,753	113,031	252,560	352,224	746,255	2,243,984	18,954	52,474	78,149	152,895	253,716	579,841	47,694	60,480	129,120	186,439	400,187	1,036,409
1956	85,916	116,854	258,073	359,839	743,150	2,186,056	19,869	54,979	81,549	156,307	264,011	582,828	49,180	62,281	132,008	189,574	411,439	1,022,878
1957	85,004	114,945	249,968	345,867	705,712	2,032,352	19,898	55,063	81,190	154,069	255,906	558,307	49,832	63,015	130,056	185,210	399,039	989,898
1958	84,021	113,045	241,999	333,973	680,360	1,964,980	19,215	54,998	80,806	150,024	247,377	537,624	49,774	63,720	127,567	180,146	384,445	961,756
1959	90,134	121,517	262,825	366,559	736,362	2,145,675	20,473	58,751	86,190	159,091	274,108	579,771	52,348	69,701	138,401	205,914	419,136	1,013,809
1960	89,574	118,535	250,766	342,500	701,916	2,112,445	20,773	60,612	85,478	159,032	252,647	545,190	53,640	63,588	136,012	188,241	391,433	999,483
1961	92,823	124,481	263,510	360,035	756,007	2,327,714	21,085	61,165	89,723	166,986	261,042	581,373	54,614	69,852	140,892	191,765	409,541	1,083,179
1962	94,361	125,415	259,427	352,368	709,442	2,131,880	21,605	63,308	91,912	166,485	263,099	551,394	57,125	71,250	142,516	197,415	403,919	990,957
1963	97,159	128,985	265,033	358,674	719,554	2,187,492	22,187	65,333	94,974	171,392	268,454	556,450	59,265	74,520	146,773	201,698	410,841	999,998
1964	103,115	137,620	286,795	388,281	782,627	2,387,216	23,374	68,609	100,327	185,309	289,695	604,339	62,523	76,551	160,596	216,612	421,989	1,073,092
1965	108,435	145,255	307,132	417,929	864,793	2,710,798	24,445	71,614	104,786	196,335	306,213	659,681	65,739	80,576	169,465	228,828	436,645	1,167,233
1966	112,573	151,491	323,161	444,652	943,508	2,863,106	25,207	73,655	108,574	201,671	319,938	730,220	66,530	84,316	172,207	244,097	500,338	1,301,034
1967	118,903	161,401	350,115	485,353	1,023,385	2,985,831	25,938	76,406	114,222	214,877	350,845	805,335	68,547	88,117	183,890	264,157	546,333	1,374,167
1968	124,859	169,991	374,392	522,979	1,115,264	3,238,804	26,913	79,727	118,890	225,804	374,908	879,315	71,834	91,942	194,586	278,419	595,065	1,433,918
1969	122,328	164,123	349,332	485,940	1,035,337	3,224,924	27,265	80,534	117,820	212,724	348,591	792,050	72,689	92,598	182,974	266,261	535,549	1,370,784
1970	116,622	153,298	308,397	417,105	835,803	2,430,007	27,352	79,946	114,523	199,689	312,430	658,670	72,138	90,937	172,881	240,696	466,315	1,152,961
1971	119,310	157,403	318,454	431,555	875,425	2,550,252	27,267	81,217	117,141	205,354	320,587	689,333	73,082	93,049	178,974	246,057	482,645	1,181,460
1972	125,265	165,228	335,883	454,907	924,122	2,768,467	28,576	85,302	122,564	216,858	337,603	719,195	77,079	97,399	189,108	259,916	501,884	1,267,467
1973	126,587	166,466	327,157	438,208	858,315	2,346,731	29,044	86,707	126,293	216,107	333,181	692,935	77,955	99,673	189,413	257,471	490,017	1,184,127
1974	122,623	161,244	321,314	433,425	868,973	2,398,643	27,818	84,003	121,226	209,203	324,538	699,009	75,782	97,683	182,799	247,780	503,577	1,263,295
1975	116,836	152,159	298,475	400,436	795,491	2,294,180	26,244	81,513	115,580	196,514	301,672	628,970	73,400	92,569	171,606	231,782	447,476	1,149,070
1976	119,839	155,998	305,741	411,497	823,771	2,391,699	26,980	83,681	118,562	199,985	308,428	649,557	75,413	95,020	174,731	236,356	459,305	1,192,187

(*contd.*)

Table 5A.5 (*contd.*)

	P90–100 (1)	P95–100 (2)	P99–100 (3)	P99.5–100 (4)	P99.9–100 (5)	P99.99–100 (6)	P0–90 (7)	P90–95 (8)	P95–99 (9)	P99–99.5 (10)	P99.5–99.9 (11)	P99.9–99.99 (12)	P90 (13)	P95 (14)	P99 (15)	P99.5 (16)	P99.9 (17)	P99.99 (18)
1977	121,357	157,933	310,508	418,376	841,544	2,403,200	27,318	84,780	119,789	202,640	312,585	668,026	76,277	96,453	176,853	238,787	468,026	1,179,034
1978	123,457	160,631	316,292	427,097	861,066	2,449,179	27,797	86,283	121,716	205,487	318,604	684,609	77,615	97,703	179,652	242,808	479,812	1,247,986
1979	124,429	164,099	339,086	470,443	1,034,589	3,387,913	27,532	84,760	120,352	207,729	329,407	773,108	76,459	96,907	180,140	250,004	524,479	1,532,344
1980	120,141	158,320	327,843	455,823	991,654	3,130,942	25,951	81,962	115,940	199,863	321,865	753,955	73,984	93,313	174,274	242,509	511,971	1,497,730
1981	116,629	152,759	312,583	435,165	952,798	3,005,874	25,522	80,498	112,803	190,002	305,757	724,679	72,562	91,754	166,233	227,940	487,394	1,417,589
1982	118,494	157,328	337,350	481,632	1,134,852	3,917,846	24,900	79,660	112,323	193,068	318,327	825,631	71,877	90,770	167,665	233,773	531,700	1,767,423
1983	122,848	164,737	361,088	520,204	1,243,658	4,369,283	24,840	80,958	115,650	201,972	339,340	896,367	72,941	92,970	175,319	246,582	562,126	1,941,592
1984	128,514	173,391	386,610	566,365	1,406,602	5,036,777	25,619	83,637	120,086	206,854	356,306	1,003,249	75,051	96,406	179,638	256,147	608,378	2,197,114
1985	134,286	182,603	414,137	610,274	1,519,764	5,305,168	25,996	85,968	124,720	218,000	382,901	1,099,164	76,857	99,758	189,844	268,432	683,204	2,316,722
1986	151,341	212,872	525,308	798,253	1,955,294	7,737,890	26,740	89,809	134,763	252,363	508,993	1,312,783	80,115	106,566	215,830	354,412	740,636	3,184,510
1987	142,220	194,938	447,960	658,457	1,618,437	5,733,615	26,224	89,502	131,682	237,463	418,462	1,161,195	79,410	102,034	200,970	290,230	693,913	2,425,063
1988	158,574	226,475	584,131	900,815	2,431,659	9,521,255	26,432	90,673	137,061	267,448	518,104	1,643,926	80,097	104,507	221,622	336,861	920,934	3,776,266
1989	154,866	218,821	543,733	821,574	2,153,283	8,260,655	26,249	90,911	137,593	265,891	488,647	1,474,686	80,038	105,060	221,107	330,188	854,762	3,323,443
1990	151,379	213,819	530,859	804,110	2,075,261	7,996,387	25,674	88,939	134,559	257,608	486,322	1,417,358	78,369	102,508	213,810	323,835	828,838	3,276,756
1991	143,951	200,288	472,063	696,296	1,732,134	6,370,799	25,125	87,615	132,344	247,830	437,337	1,216,727	77,827	102,700	206,059	301,795	730,188	2,766,697
1992	150,967	213,915	532,672	807,265	2,122,134	8,235,400	24,626	88,020	134,226	258,079	478,547	1,442,883	77,442	101,619	214,262	323,989	832,989	3,374,136
1993	147,749	208,209	504,799	756,192	1,944,380	7,260,930	24,311	87,289	134,062	253,406	459,145	1,353,653	76,961	101,257	213,798	312,109	789,214	2,962,255
1994	149,810	210,736	509,356	759,299	1,932,148	7,213,916	24,607	88,884	136,082	259,413	466,087	1,345,285	77,996	102,980	218,379	319,109	787,836	2,995,451
1995	157,412	223,689	551,805	827,281	2,116,761	7,702,273	24,999	91,134	141,660	276,328	504,911	1,496,149	79,657	106,189	230,220	340,472	853,836	3,312,749
1996	166,032	240,637	615,949	935,674	2,468,155	9,387,860	24,747	91,435	146,800	296,225	552,553	1,529,369	79,342	108,649	242,587	373,377	987,042	4,193,838
1997	179,255	263,814	695,737	1,072,268	2,927,347	10,993,941	25,566	94,696	155,823	319,205	608,396	1,827,953	82,355	113,160	258,602	403,599	1,135,882	4,951,048
1998	191,922	284,932	765,980	1,188,385	3,282,773	12,619,715	26,670	98,921	164,680	343,575	664,680	2,020,368	85,646	118,869	277,803	437,293	1,229,557	5,644,573
1999	204,106	305,439	833,140	1,300,810	3,627,442	14,031,014	27,589	102,755	173,525	365,288	719,152	2,472,768	88,944	124,559	294,948	467,738	1,349,227	6,220,532
2000	214,745	324,311	910,985	1,441,728	4,145,448	16,848,012	27,875	105,179	177,642	380,246	765,803	2,734,013	91,417	128,686	313,128	479,886	1,467,650	6,901,066
2001	192,183	282,513	751,604	1,166,531	3,227,309	12,700,382	26,884	101,852	165,241	336,679	651,338	2,174,710	88,763	122,696	280,245	423,505	1,210,132	5,324,626
2002	179,479	259,994	670,767	1,028,267	2,777,336	10,821,981	25,925	98,964	157,301	313,266	590,999	1,883,509	86,211	117,851	261,498	393,105	1,069,905	4,613,653

Table 5A.6 Top fractiles (defined including capital gains) income levels (including capital gains), US 1913–2002 (fractiles are defined by total income (including capital gains)) (incomes are expressed in 2000 $)

	P90–100 (1)	P95–100 (2)	P99–100 (3)	P99.5–100 (4)	P99.9–100 (5)	P99.99–100 (6)	P0–90 (7)	P90–95 (8)	P95–99 (9)	P99–99.5 (10)	P99.5–99.9 (11)	P99.9–99.99 (12)	P90 (13)	P95 (14)	P99 (15)	P99.5 (16)	P99.9 (17)	P99.99 (18)
1913			229,136	375,763	1,099,313	3,514,871				82,509	194,875	830,918			65,620	107,611	340,199	1,430,935
1914			226,433	376,107	1,072,853	3,403,375				76,758	201,921	813,906			60,670	100,774	325,982	1,422,412
1915			221,308	367,086	1,160,746	5,489,423				75,528	168,665	679,759			51,143	97,313	358,638	1,819,678
1916			268,648	455,526	1,462,782	6,651,574				81,770	203,712	886,250			61,691	113,709	438,828	2,484,976
1917	56,999	86,233	249,583	403,634	1,182,195	4,735,238	9,678	27,766	45,395	95,531	208,994	787,413	22,138	31,339	77,015	125,139	430,377	1,980,047
1918	53,363	78,482	212,369	330,751	893,633	3,265,367	9,213	28,243	45,011	93,986	190,031	630,107	23,629	31,821	76,924	119,746	363,097	1,483,568
1919	53,184	79,593	216,488	333,444	874,581	3,016,350	9,085	26,774	45,370	99,532	198,160	636,606	22,571	31,989	81,404	126,762	398,886	1,425,190
1920	45,914	66,666	174,524	262,272	630,462	1,956,974	8,275	25,161	39,701	86,776	170,224	483,072	23,099	28,860	70,779	111,417	307,480	994,092
1921	44,400	63,348	160,795	240,569	576,014	1,736,074	6,765	25,453	38,986	81,021	156,707	447,118	22,260	28,163	66,760	102,974	284,577	909,622
1922	51,321	74,996	200,227	306,552	778,887	2,669,472	7,638	27,647	43,688	93,902	188,468	568,822	23,769	31,465	75,939	120,455	351,507	1,205,339
1923	54,167	77,805	204,363	311,143	771,649	2,610,263	8,828	30,530	46,165	97,583	196,016	567,358	25,912	35,581	78,221	125,574	357,549	1,195,646
1924	57,741	83,509	226,547	348,489	882,495	3,023,058	8,350	31,973	47,749	104,605	214,987	644,654	26,941	36,382	83,871	135,752	395,114	1,395,608
1925	62,602	94,562	273,407	428,404	1,151,173	4,471,377	8,340	30,642	49,851	118,410	247,711	782,261	27,623	36,929	93,930	155,450	464,699	1,845,415
1926	61,668	93,395	268,594	419,511	1,141,208	4,538,410	8,444	29,941	49,596	117,677	239,086	763,741	26,925	35,566	94,244	152,281	449,785	1,823,220
1927	64,021	97,924	288,429	455,365	1,269,489	5,150,164	8,427	30,118	50,298	121,493	251,834	838,302	27,582	36,688	96,902	157,755	481,912	2,101,104
1928	71,146	111,330	345,567	560,032	1,665,877	7,252,662	8,399	30,962	52,771	131,101	283,571	1,045,123	28,351	37,961	103,593	172,292	570,124	2,823,143
1929	69,523	108,603	332,700	537,804	1,624,393	7,427,510	9,105	30,442	52,578	127,597	266,156	979,602	27,593	37,235	102,378	165,336	519,184	2,679,212
1930	56,339	82,360	221,207	339,176	908,581	3,653,395	8,330	30,317	47,649	103,238	196,825	603,601	26,909	34,870	84,925	129,464	357,899	1,441,449
1931	51,139	71,710	177,932	265,565	676,601	2,583,034	7,379	30,567	45,155	90,299	162,807	464,775	26,248	33,116	75,276	111,826	282,158	1,066,251
1932	44,448	62,628	149,111	222,825	572,208	1,907,006	5,974	26,268	41,007	75,398	135,479	423,897	17,970	30,707	64,212	92,151	243,557	946,156
1933	43,136	62,784	155,700	235,812	625,148	2,217,493	5,962	23,487	39,555	75,587	138,478	448,221	17,544	28,595	63,283	92,917	252,975	1,020,897
1934	47,261	69,603	169,263	253,839	632,696	2,140,166	6,493	24,919	44,689	84,687	159,124	465,199	21,172	30,571	70,433	106,708	290,475	1,026,368
1935	50,233	72,898	188,273	285,276	721,682	2,470,168	7,251	27,568	44,054	91,271	176,174	527,406	23,294	34,119	75,609	115,952	323,163	1,177,904
1936	58,644	87,194	242,767	374,019	952,179	3,193,027	7,768	30,094	48,301	111,514	229,480	703,196	25,606	37,821	90,879	145,887	427,386	1,555,452
1937	57,006	83,176	221,022	335,700	837,012	2,802,363	8,326	30,835	48,715	106,345	210,372	618,640	26,844	36,520	87,403	136,801	382,779	1,352,457
1938	52,508	74,685	187,696	280,583	700,972	2,614,426	7,711	30,332	46,432	94,808	175,486	488,366	26,256	35,429	79,430	119,230	309,103	1,157,789
1939	57,597	81,690	204,681	305,153	742,985	2,484,501	7,992	33,505	50,942	104,209	195,695	549,483	29,625	39,765	87,093	131,202	344,148	1,212,205
1940	59,916	85,251	217,981	326,304	794,397	2,703,403	8,390	34,582	52,068	109,658	209,280	582,286	32,758	39,263	90,938	141,252	369,898	1,306,131

(contd.)

Table 5A.6 (*contd.*)

	P90–100 (1)	P95–100 (2)	P99–100 (3)	P99.5–100 (4)	P99.9–100 (5)	P99.99–100 (6)	P0–90 (7)	P90–95 (8)	P95–99 (9)	P99–99.5 (10)	P99.5–99.9 (11)	P99.9–99.99 (12)	P90 (13)	P95 (14)	P99 (15)	P99.5 (16)	P99.9 (17)	P99.99 (18)
1941	64,847	92,767	244,130	366,898	897,998	3,057,784	10,467	36,851	54,927	121,362	234,122	658,022	33,821	42,660	99,228	156,713	418,319	1,509,979
1942	64,580	92,248	240,044	359,896	860,095	2,763,140	13,179	36,912	55,299	120,191	234,847	648,646	34,279	42,422	97,507	154,996	412,768	1,431,050
1943	70,111	100,235	256,168	380,744	887,131	2,570,373	15,877	39,987	61,252	131,592	254,148	700,104	35,301	46,879	106,837	171,309	447,846	1,370,062
1944	71,608	100,279	248,459	363,737	827,161	2,564,195	17,089	42,937	63,234	133,181	247,881	634,157	38,512	46,956	109,409	169,233	424,306	1,375,419
1945	75,432	108,664	274,258	400,483	911,398	2,768,459	16,443	42,199	67,266	148,032	272,755	705,058	37,499	48,033	121,751	193,145	465,879	1,453,968
1946	77,131	112,505	279,042	404,047	923,006	3,095,444	15,120	41,757	70,871	154,038	274,307	681,625	37,386	50,131	127,184	194,290	466,884	1,568,123
1947	68,153	97,933	237,211	341,823	777,448	2,586,425	14,855	38,373	63,113	132,599	232,917	576,450	33,935	44,321	109,973	166,087	391,915	1,296,376
1948	70,522	100,930	246,584	358,530	816,764	2,629,464	14,416	40,115	64,516	134,637	243,971	615,353	35,548	48,186	111,907	172,580	412,355	1,379,985
1949	68,660	96,835	231,699	334,941	756,994	2,454,907	14,231	40,486	63,119	128,457	229,427	568,337	35,938	48,250	106,395	161,280	382,770	1,259,304
1950	76,779	110,250	276,766	404,582	947,870	2,633,441	15,326	43,308	68,621	148,949	268,760	760,584	39,646	49,968	121,058	188,780	462,602	1,294,201
1951	75,898	107,361	261,452	378,369	862,937	2,841,560	16,055	44,436	68,838	144,534	257,227	643,090	39,804	50,694	121,668	181,839	433,914	1,456,392
1952	75,552	104,958	245,477	351,983	779,860	2,476,115	16,751	46,145	69,828	138,971	245,014	591,388	42,475	53,427	118,161	178,898	406,757	1,275,440
1953	76,347	104,042	234,000	331,897	721,990	2,284,623	17,669	48,653	71,552	136,103	234,374	548,364	43,567	54,670	116,582	173,214	380,321	1,145,300
1954	79,377	109,959	254,243	364,027	823,817	2,758,102	17,266	48,795	73,888	144,458	249,080	608,896	43,692	56,042	123,011	182,078	424,732	1,351,342
1955	86,371	120,103	281,413	405,284	945,454	3,350,570	18,552	52,639	79,776	157,541	270,242	678,218	47,844	61,740	133,043	198,583	468,083	1,547,498
1956	89,182	123,274	284,429	410,653	929,161	3,191,824	19,506	55,090	82,986	158,205	281,026	677,754	49,280	63,378	133,611	201,792	478,451	1,493,488
1957	87,560	119,996	269,697	383,748	844,929	2,794,568	19,614	55,124	82,570	155,646	268,453	628,303	49,887	64,086	131,387	194,291	449,067	1,361,150
1958	86,863	118,676	264,141	376,228	832,986	2,799,000	18,899	55,049	82,309	152,053	262,039	614,540	49,821	64,906	129,292	190,823	439,446	1,369,966
1959	94,141	129,512	294,781	427,230	955,101	3,306,007	20,027	58,770	88,195	162,332	295,262	693,889	52,365	71,323	141,221	221,805	501,635	1,562,054
1960	93,162	125,649	279,264	396,817	904,214	3,269,832	20,374	60,674	87,246	161,711	269,967	641,368	53,695	64,903	138,303	201,146	460,486	1,547,089
1961	97,642	133,980	303,310	436,485	1,040,790	3,940,196	20,550	61,305	91,648	170,135	285,408	718,634	54,738	71,351	143,549	209,666	506,233	1,833,531
1962	98,039	132,689	289,452	410,512	929,244	3,376,697	21,196	63,389	93,498	168,391	280,829	657,305	57,198	72,479	144,147	210,718	481,503	1,569,582
1963	101,053	136,656	296,611	418,619	940,967	3,428,683	21,755	65,451	96,667	174,604	288,033	664,554	59,372	75,849	149,523	216,408	490,656	1,567,400
1964	108,444	148,072	330,124	465,317	1,062,433	4,102,226	22,782	68,815	102,559	194,931	316,038	724,678	62,711	78,255	168,936	236,310	506,017	1,844,017
1965	114,817	157,639	359,558	510,030	1,206,617	4,916,568	23,735	71,996	107,159	209,086	335,883	794,400	66,089	82,401	180,471	251,000	525,816	2,117,009
1966	115,501	157,240	349,030	495,244	1,161,215	4,424,520	24,881	73,763	109,292	202,816	328,751	798,626	66,627	84,874	173,185	250,821	547,209	2,010,562
1967	122,662	168,813	382,378	546,621	1,309,431	5,043,803	25,520	76,510	115,422	218,135	355,919	894,500	68,640	89,043	186,679	267,978	606,822	2,321,306
1968	129,545	179,562	416,838	605,136	1,495,501	6,003,507	26,393	79,527	120,243	228,540	382,545	994,611	71,654	92,988	196,944	284,091	673,091	2,657,937

1969	126,086	171,567	384,676	553,392	1,372,627	5,790,370	26,848	80,605	118,289	215,959	348,583	881,767	72,754	92,966	185,756	266,255	596,212	2,461,250
1970	119,249	158,351	329,865	456,938	1,014,360	3,641,285	27,060	80,148	115,472	202,792	317,582	722,480	72,320	91,691	175,568	244,666	511,490	1,727,674
1971	122,686	163,824	345,902	483,114	1,099,541	4,098,663	26,892	81,548	118,304	208,691	329,007	766,306	73,381	93,973	181,883	252,519	536,538	1,898,795
1972	129,653	173,859	372,049	523,469	1,206,681	4,548,099	28,089	85,448	124,311	220,629	352,666	835,412	77,211	98,787	192,397	271,513	582,985	2,082,224
1973	130,743	174,260	359,385	494,519	1,082,604	3,692,491	28,582	87,226	127,978	224,250	347,498	792,617	78,421	101,003	196,550	268,534	560,507	1,863,177
1974	125,484	166,649	343,669	475,196	1,027,806	3,310,904	27,500	84,319	122,394	212,142	337,043	774,129	76,066	98,624	185,367	257,328	557,694	1,743,756
1975	119,273	156,838	316,535	432,948	914,897	3,020,203	25,973	81,708	116,913	200,122	312,461	680,974	73,576	93,637	174,756	240,071	484,475	1,512,708
1976	122,701	161,389	325,388	445,722	952,837	3,157,853	26,662	84,013	120,389	205,054	318,943	707,836	75,712	96,485	179,159	244,414	500,515	1,574,091
1977	124,680	164,275	335,061	461,622	1,005,331	3,429,012	26,949	85,084	121,579	208,500	325,695	736,033	76,550	97,895	181,968	248,802	515,673	1,682,308
1978	126,694	166,746	338,643	466,224	1,001,858	3,240,098	27,437	86,643	123,772	211,062	332,315	753,164	77,939	99,354	184,526	253,257	527,859	1,651,001
1979	128,956	172,869	375,334	535,883	1,296,356	5,174,683	27,029	85,042	122,253	214,785	345,765	865,430	76,714	98,438	186,259	262,419	587,110	2,340,496
1980	124,043	165,957	358,916	512,105	1,221,163	4,571,874	25,518	82,129	117,717	205,728	334,840	848,862	74,135	94,744	179,387	252,285	576,417	2,187,021
1981	120,901	161,253	350,593	506,330	1,248,158	4,780,492	25,047	80,549	113,918	194,856	320,873	855,676	72,609	92,660	170,480	239,210	575,498	2,254,510
1982	122,159	164,788	373,259	550,773	1,443,749	5,994,492	24,493	79,530	112,670	195,744	327,530	938,111	71,760	91,050	169,989	240,531	604,136	2,704,242
1983	127,765	174,546	405,792	606,168	1,622,741	6,616,748	24,293	80,983	116,734	205,416	352,025	1,067,851	72,963	93,842	178,308	255,800	669,667	2,940,306
1984	133,613	183,942	436,072	657,538	1,811,708	7,832,766	25,053	83,284	120,910	214,606	368,996	1,142,701	74,734	97,067	186,370	265,270	692,943	3,416,764
1985	140,222	195,000	472,957	718,651	1,985,322	8,348,097	25,337	85,444	125,511	227,262	401,983	1,278,347	76,389	100,390	197,910	281,810	794,578	3,645,544
1986	162,393	235,722	636,202	1,009,000	2,956,924	13,367,774	25,512	89,064	135,602	263,403	522,019	1,800,163	79,450	107,230	225,272	363,483	1,015,602	5,501,476
1987	145,808	202,353	482,731	720,421	1,867,701	7,273,277	25,826	89,262	132,259	245,041	433,601	1,267,081	79,198	102,481	207,384	300,730	757,189	3,076,271
1988	161,961	233,516	617,620	964,018	2,710,338	11,411,233	26,056	90,405	137,490	271,222	527,438	1,743,572	79,860	104,834	224,750	342,930	976,756	4,525,859
1989	157,784	224,745	570,230	872,200	2,361,548	9,662,422	25,925	90,823	138,374	268,260	499,863	1,550,340	79,961	105,657	223,078	337,767	898,612	3,887,405
1990	153,670	218,391	550,843	841,413	2,238,989	8,970,255	25,420	88,948	135,278	260,273	492,019	1,491,070	78,378	103,056	216,021	327,628	871,943	3,675,827
1991	146,794	205,817	495,953	741,341	1,901,607	7,264,551	24,809	87,772	133,283	250,565	451,274	1,305,724	77,966	103,428	208,333	311,412	783,597	3,154,834
1992	152,872	217,681	549,391	838,760	2,258,666	9,223,700	24,414	88,062	134,754	260,021	483,784	1,484,773	77,479	102,020	215,875	327,535	857,173	3,779,053
1993	150,081	212,722	525,181	795,078	2,113,979	8,550,902	24,052	87,441	134,607	255,284	465,353	1,398,765	77,095	101,668	215,383	316,328	815,516	3,488,527
1994	152,234	215,705	531,261	801,392	2,129,232	8,565,994	24,338	88,763	136,816	261,129	469,432	1,414,036	77,890	103,536	219,824	321,399	828,098	3,556,878
1995	159,913	228,726	575,950	876,093	2,356,191	9,360,209	24,721	91,099	141,920	275,807	506,069	1,577,967	79,626	106,385	229,786	341,253	900,529	4,025,828
1996	169,185	247,078	649,082	1,004,351	2,816,838	11,905,656	24,398	91,291	146,577	293,814	551,229	1,806,969	78,689	107,271	243,771	368,390	1,006,194	4,851,818
1997	183,349	272,179	739,565	1,162,990	3,361,037	14,486,989	25,158	94,520	155,332	316,139	613,478	2,124,820	81,703	111,896	262,325	400,358	1,154,919	5,813,676
1998	197,309	296,436	829,725	1,319,827	3,910,927	17,052,937	26,141	98,181	163,115	339,623	672,053	2,450,704	84,589	117,054	276,921	433,208	1,289,992	6,819,331
1999	211,050	319,783	910,397	1,456,773	4,370,622	19,136,970	26,821	102,315	172,130	364,023	728,310	2,729,917	87,709	121,667	296,915	464,442	1,423,342	7,630,696
2000	223,991	344,460	1,012,584	1,642,549	5,117,680	23,869,868	26,848	103,522	177,429	382,619	773,766	3,034,104	89,977	127,532	313,698	482,906	1,547,553	8,752,114
2001	196,202	291,999	797,527	1,253,989	3,663,411	16,197,967	26,438	100,405	165,617	341,065	651,633	2,270,683	87,502	121,936	282,273	426,049	1,233,967	6,080,951
2002	181,991	266,374	700,436	1,082,943	3,048,937	13,048,843	25,646	97,608	157,859	317,928	591,445	1,937,837	85,030	117,230	263,800	396,027	1,083,908	5,086,546

Kuznets are lower than ours in levels.[57] Note however that the pattern over years is reassuringly almost identical.[58]

Finally, it is important to keep in mind that tax units are smaller than households. In 1998, there were approximately 1.3 tax units per household (on average), i.e 131 millions tax units vs. 101 millions households.[59] This means that incomes per household are in 1998 about 30% larger than incomes per tax units (on average). For instance, average income per tax unit was less than US$39,000 in 1998 (see Table 5A.0, column (5)), while average household income was about US$51,000.[60] Note, however, that this is unlikely to affect top shares in a significant way (assuming that the average number of households per tax units is approximately the same for all income brackets).

Computing Top Fractiles Income Shares

We have constructed three sets of top income shares series that treat differently realized capital gains. In variant 1 (Table 5A.1), we exclude completely capital gains: tax returns are ranked by income excluding capital gains, and top fractiles incomes exclude capital gains. Income shares were computed by using the total income (excluding capital gains series) series (Table 5A.0, column (4) and (5)). In variant 2 (Table 5A.2), tax returns are ranked by income excluding capital gains, but we add back the average capital gains accruing to each fractile when we compute top fractiles incomes. Income shares were computed by using the total income (including capital gains series) series (Table 5A.0, column (6) and (7)). Finally, in variant 3 (Table 5A.3), we include capital gains both when we rank tax returns and when we compute top fractiles incomes. Income shares were computed by using the total income (including capital gains series) series (Table 5A.0, column (6) and (7)). The concept of capital gains used to compute top

57 This is amplified by the fact that Kuznets's total income denominator is slightly higher than ours (see above), and by the way Kuznets treated capital gains (see below).

58 Our methodology also differs from that used by Feenberg and Poterba (1993, 2000) to compute their 1951–95 top income shares series: Feenberg and Poterba choose as base year 1989, and then compute the number of tax returns who are in the top 0.5% of the tax return distribution for that year, and use the US adult population series to compute the number of 'top income recipients' tax returns for other years. This methodology is innocuous in the short run, but can produce important biases in the long run because the average tax unit size declines over time, and this is also true if one looks at the average number of adults per tax unit. Note also that Feenberg and Poterba simply use total AGI as their total income denominator.

59 The average number of tax units per household declined from about 1.7 in the 1910s to about 1.2–1.3 in the early 1980s, and increased somewhat since then.

60 Average household income was about US$52,000 in 1998 according to the Current Population Survey (CPS) (cf. 'Money Income in the United States 1999', *Current Population Report P60–209* (September 2000). Note that total CPS income is virtually identical to our total income denominator (CPS income does include a number of cash transfers that are excluded by our tax income concept, but CPS income probably suffers from under-reporting at the top).

fractiles incomes in variants 2 and 3 and to rank tax returns in variant 3 is always 'full capital gains', i.e. total pre-exclusion capital gains (see below). Whether one should use variants 1, 2, or 3 is a matter of perspective. In the text of this chapter, we have focused on variant 1 series, so as to get rid of the very strong short-term volatility induced by capital gains. If one wants to include capital gains, then variant 2 series are probably the most meaningful series from an economic viewpoint: capital gains are typically very lumpy (they are realized once every few years), so that ranking tax returns by income including capital gains leads to artificially overestimate very top income levels. Note that variant 1 top income shares are always below variant 2 top income shares, and that variant 2 top income shares are always below variant 3 top income (see Figure 5A.2).

The top fractiles incomes series reported on Tables 5A.4, 5A.5, and 5A.6 were constructed as follows. For the 1966–99 period, the series were computed directly from the IRS micro-files. The micro-files easily allow us to rank tax returns by income excluding capital gains (variants 1 and 2) or by income including full capital gains (variant 3) and to compute top fractiles incomes without capital gains (variant 1) or with full capital gains (variants 2 and 3). For the 1913–65 and 2000–02 periods, the series were estimated from the published IRS tables using the Pareto interpolation technique described in Appendix 5C, according to the following methodology (all computations are available from the authors upon request):

1. Published IRS tables rank tax returns by net income (1913–43) or by AGI (1944–2002). These tables use a large number of income brackets (the thresholds P90, P95, P99, P99.5, P99.9, and P99.99 are usually very close to one of the income bracket thresholds), and one can use standard Pareto interpolation techniques in order to estimate the top fractiles income thresholds and income levels of the tax unit distribution of net income (1913–43) and AGI (1944–65 and 2000–2). We also did the same computations for the 1966–95 period in order to compare the series estimated from Pareto interpolation with the series computed from micro-files, and we found that both series never differ by more than 1% (the gap is usually less than 0.1%).
2. For a number of years before the Second World War, the filing threshold is so high that less than 10% of tax units actually file returns (see Table 5A.0, column (3)). However, the filing threshold for singles is substantially lower than the filing threshold for married households. Thus from 1917 on, it is always the case than more than 10% of single tax units are actually filing returns, although for some years less than 10% of married tax units are filing returns. As a result, the number of married tax units in the bottom brackets is too low for some years and needs to be adjusted upward. This problem of missing returns is especially acute for years 1925 to 1931. We adjusted for missing married returns using a simple extrapolation method, based on the assumption that marital ratios (i.e. ratios of married tax units to single men not head of households tax units) across income brackets is constant over

years.[61] We have done some sensitivity analysis using both years 1924 and 1932 as the base year. The alternative multipliers we obtain with year 1924 instead of year 1932 are close and the final series estimates of shares and income levels for the bottom fractile P90–95 are almost identical. Our final estimates are obtained using a moving average of the multipliers based on years 1924, and 1932.[62]

3. The 1913–65 and 2000–02 raw series obtained from Pareto interpolation were corrected in various ways. First, the raw series were adjusted upwards in order to include net income deductions (1913–43) and AGI adjustments (1944–65 and 2000–02) (AGI adjustments were also included in the 1966–99 micro-files computations). In practice, AGI adjustments (IRA contributions, moving expenses adjustment, self-employment tax, etc.) are pretty small (about 1% of AGI, up to 4% in the mid-1980s), and their importance declines with income within the top decile. Net income deductions for the period 1913–43 (charitable gifts, interest paid, local taxes, etc.) are higher (about 10% of net income), and their importance increases with income within the top decile (up to 15%–20% for fractile P99.99–100). We adjust our raw series for threshold levels and average income in each fractile using multiplicative factors so that our new series correspond to the level of gross income (before adjustment or deductions) reported in the published tables for each fractile.[63]
4. Next, and most importantly, corrections need to be made to the 1913–65 and 2000–02 raw series in order to ensure that capital gains are properly taken into account. The tax treatment of capital gains has changed many times since 1913: from 1913 to 1933, 100% of capital gains were included in net income (there was no capital gains exclusion); from 1934 to 1937, 70% of capital gains were included in net income (i.e. 30% of capital gains were excluded); from 1938 to 1941, 60% of capital gains were included in net income (i.e. 40% of capital gains were excluded); from 1942 to 1978, 50% of capital gains were included in net income (1942–43) or in AGI (1944–78) (i.e. 50% of capital gains were excluded); from 1979 to 1986, 40% of capital gains were included in AGI (i.e. 60% of capital gains were excluded); from 1987 on, 100% of capital gains were included in AGI (there

[61] More precisely, we assume that the ratio of marital ratios over two adjacent brackets is constant from year to year. We can successfully test this assumption comparing these ratios for years with low filing thresholds and where missing returns is not an issue. Thus we use the closest years for which the filing threshold is low enough so that all the married tax units with income in that particular income bracket file a return to compute these marital ratios. We then extrapolate the marital ratio for a year with high filing threshold in a low bracket using the bracket just above for that year and the marital ratios for the year with complete returns. We compute then the expected number of married tax units in each bracket in high filing threshold years. We obtain thus the missing number of returns in each bracket or equivalently a multiplier factor by which we must adjust the actual number of returns to obtain the real number of tax units. We use the same multiplier factors to adjust the dollar amounts reported in each bracket.

[62] For example, for year 1925, our multiplier is (6/7)*multiplier 1924 + (1/7)*multiplier 1932, etc.

[63] In principle, going from net income (or AGI) to gross income might induce reranking. However, using the micro-files for 1966–99, we have checked that this reranking has small effects on our final results and thus we do not attempt any correction for that re-ranking effect.

was again no capital gains exclusion).[64] In order to compute 'variant 1' series from the raw series, one could simply deduct for each fractile the share of capital gains estimated from IRS composition tables. This is the method Kuznets (1953) adopted in order to compute his 1913–48 series.[65] The problem is that IRS tables rank tax returns by net income or AGI (including the post-exclusion amount of capital gains), and that re-ranking can be substantial at the very top: in the extreme case where very top incomes of the net income or AGI distribution are only made of capital gains, then the deduction of capital gains would lead to the conclusion that the very top incomes of the distribution of income (excluding capital gains) are equal to 0. Kuznets did not try to correct for re-ranking, which means that his estimates of top income shares are biased downward.[66] The micro-files allowed us to compute the magnitude of the corrections that one needs to apply in order to obtain unbiased 'variant 1' series: the corrections are negligible for fractiles P90–95 and P95–99, but the income levels of fractiles P99–99.5 and P99.5–99.9 need to be increased by about 1%, the income level of fractiles P99.9–99.99 needs to be increased by about 2%. Most importantly, the top fractile P99.99–100 requires a more complicated correction method. We increase the income level of fractile P99.99–100 by about 40% of the capital gains share computed for that fractile.[67] These corrections coefficients were obtained from comparing micro-file unbiased estimates from the period 1966–99 to estimates obtained from published tables. For the period 1966–99, the correction coefficients are extremely stable (in spite of the huge variations in capital gains share), and it seems reasonable to use them for the 1913–65 and 2000–02 periods. Finally, one can compute 'variant 2' series from these unbiased 'variant 1' series using our capital gains shares series by fractiles of income excluding capital gains (see Table 5A.8 below; these capital gains series also illustrate the importance of re-ranking at the very top).

5. The construction of 'variant 3' series from raw series raises similar issues. For the 1913–33 and 2000–02 period (when there was no capital gain exclusion), there is no re-ranking issue. But for the 1934–65, one cannot simply add to the raw series the excluded amount of capital gains for each fractile: this addition alters the ranking of tax returns, and ignoring this re-ranking issue would lead to 'variant 3' series that are downwardly biased. The micro-files

[64] These exclusion rates actually applied to long term capital gains only, and the definition of 'long-term' capital gains (6 months, 12 months, or 18 months) has changed many times (from 1934 to 1941, there were several exclusion rates, and the 30% and 40% figures that we use for our estimation are the approximate average exclusion rates over all capital gains). We did use all the relevant information given in IRS tables and in the micro-files in order to compute the exact exclusion rates for each fractile. In practice however, the vast majority of capital gains always falls under the most favourable tax regime, so that the exclusion rates given above apply to most capital gains.

[65] Kuznets decided to exclude completely capital gains from his series, and he started by deducting capital gains from net income and AGI for each income bracket before applying Pareto interpolation techniques (Kuznets did not try to compute series including capital gains).

[66] See above for other problems explaining why Kuznets's estimates are biased downward.

[67] For instance, in 1995, when the capital gains share is 38.4% for fractile P99.99–100 (see Table 5A.8 below), the correction coefficient is about 15,4% ($0.4 \times 38.4 = 15.4$).

allowed us to compute the magnitude of the corrections that one needs to apply in order to obtain unbiased 'variant 3' series: the corrections are negligible for fractile P90–95, but the income levels of fractiles P95–99 and P99–99.5, need to be increased by about 1%, the income level of fractiles P99.5–99.9 and P99.9–99.99 need to be increased by about 2%, and the income level of fractile P99.99–100 need to be increased by about 4% (irrespective of the capital gains share). These corrections coefficients were again obtained from the analysis of micro-files over the period 1966–99. This analysis showed that applying the simple correction rule described above gave excellent results for all years 1966–99, and it seems reasonable to use the same rule for the 1913–65 and 2000–02 periods. Note that the corrections required are smaller than the corrections coefficients associated to 'variant 1' series (especially at the very top): that is, re-ranking is more important when one goes from ranking by income including post-exclusion capital gains to ranking by income excluding completely capital gains than when one goes from ranking by income including the taxable fraction of capital gains to ranking by income including full capital gains.

Computing Top Fractiles Income Composition

We have also constructed top fractiles income composition series (Table 5A.7 and Table 5A.8). The composition series reported in Table 5A.7 indicate for each income fractile the fraction of total income (excluding capital gains) that comes from the various types of income (excluding capital gains). We consider five types of income: wage income; entrepreneurial income; dividends; interest; and rents. Wage income includes wages and salaries as well as pensions and annuities.[68] Entrepreneurial income includes business, farm, partnerships and small corporations (S corporations) income. Dividends include general dividends and dividends received through partnerships and fiduciaries.[69] Interest includes taxable interest only.[70] Rents include rents, royalties, and fiduciary income. We have excluded from these composition series a number of small income categories such as alimony, taxable social security benefits, taxable unemployment insurance benefits, 'other income', etc. Taken all together, these small categories never make more 2% of the total income of the top decile (they usually make less than 1%),

[68] The share of pensions and annuities in total AGI has increased continuously from less than 1% in the 1960s to more than 6% in the late 1990s, but it has always been less than for 4% for the top decile and less than 2% for the top percentile.

[69] From 1936 to 1953, dividends from tax statistics do not include dividends distributed to partnerships and fiduciaries. This discontinuity was relatively easy to correct: dividends distributed to partnerships and fiduciaries display a very stable pattern (in particular, the 1936 downward jump in the pattern of dividend share by income fractile is virtually the same as the 1954 upward jump), and we simply added them back to the dividends total. Similarly, dividends and interest are lumped together by tax statistics in 1944–45, but this was easy to correct for because the pattern of interest share by income fractile was very stable at that time.

[70] Data on tax-exempt interest are scarce and incomplete, and we did not attempt to take tax-exempt interest into account.

Table 5A.7 Income composition by fractiles of total income, US 1916–1999 (wage income, entrepreneurial income, dividends, interest, and rents are expressed in % of total income (excluding capital gains) of each fractile)

	P90–100				
	Wage	Entrep.	Divid.	Interest	Rents
1916					
1917					
1918	46.1	25.8	14.4	8.0	5.6
1919	47.7	28.3	12.1	7.1	4.8
1920	52.0	22.4	13.8	7.4	4.4
1921	58.0	17.6	11.9	7.4	5.0
1922	54.3	19.1	12.6	7.7	6.3
1923	45.6	24.3	14.0	8.3	7.7
1924	44.3	25.1	13.8	8.6	8.3
1925	43.2	25.7	14.8	8.3	8.1
1926	43.2	23.7	16.7	8.6	7.8
1927	44.2	22.5	17.2	9.0	7.1
1928	45.5	20.9	18.2	8.9	6.4
1929	45.2	20.2	19.0	8.8	6.8
1930	49.1	15.8	19.1	9.4	6.6
1931	51.6	14.0	18.1	9.6	6.7
1932	58.1	11.3	15.4	8.9	6.3
1933	59.0	15.6	11.7	8.0	5.7
1934	60.2	15.4	12.4	6.5	5.5
1935	60.0	15.9	12.5	6.0	5.6
1936	56.5	17.0	15.7	4.7	6.1
1937	59.6	15.8	15.7	3.8	5.0
1938	63.1	16.6	11.5	3.9	4.9
1939	62.4	16.8	12.8	3.4	4.6
1940	63.4	16.8	12.7	2.8	4.3
1941	61.4	20.9	11.5	2.3	3.9
1942	60.1	25.4	8.9	1.8	3.7
1943	57.0	30.0	7.9	1.6	3.5
1944	61.1	27.6	6.9	1.5	2.9
1945	57.4	31.3	6.8	1.5	3.0
1946	54.0	33.6	7.8	1.5	3.1
1947	56.4	30.3	8.5	1.4	3.3
1948	59.7	27.0	8.6	1.4	3.3
1949	62.9	23.1	8.9	1.6	3.6
1950	63.1	23.0	8.9	1.5	3.5

	P95–100				
	Wage	Entrep.	Divid.	Interest	Rents
1916					
1917	31.4	31.4	23.5	7.7	5.9
1918	38.2	28.2	19.0	9.0	5.7
1919	39.4	31.7	15.8	8.2	5.0
1920	44.7	25.4	17.1	8.2	4.7
1921	49.0	20.5	16.4	8.7	5.4
1922	45.7	21.6	16.9	8.8	7.0
1923	39.6	25.4	17.8	9.1	8.0
1924	39.4	25.7	17.4	9.2	8.3
1925	39.3	26.0	18.3	8.6	7.9
1926	39.1	24.2	20.3	8.8	7.6
1927	39.8	22.8	21.0	9.4	7.0
1928	40.6	21.4	22.2	9.3	6.5
1929	40.4	20.7	23.0	9.1	6.8
1930	44.5	15.6	23.8	9.5	6.6
1931	47.2	13.8	22.4	9.9	6.7
1932	53.2	11.4	18.8	9.9	6.8
1933	53.8	15.7	15.1	8.8	6.6
1934	52.9	16.3	16.7	7.6	6.5
1935	52.4	17.3	16.9	6.8	6.6
1936	48.0	18.5	21.5	5.0	6.9
1937	53.8	16.8	20.3	3.9	5.2
1938	58.2	17.4	15.3	4.0	5.1
1939	56.4	18.4	16.6	3.7	5.0
1940	55.2	19.6	16.9	3.4	5.0
1941	52.2	24.7	15.6	2.8	4.7
1942	52.0	29.9	11.8	2.3	4.0
1943	47.7	36.2	10.6	2.0	3.6
1944	48.9	36.0	9.6	1.9	3.6
1945	45.2	39.8	9.4	1.9	3.6
1946	43.4	40.6	10.5	1.9	3.6
1947	45.9	36.6	11.7	1.8	4.0
1948	49.1	33.4	11.9	1.7	4.0
1949	53.0	28.5	12.3	1.9	4.3
1950	52.7	28.8	12.3	1.9	4.3

	P99–100				
	Wage	Entrep.	Divid.	Interest	Rents
1916	19.5	32.8	32.4	9.3	6.0
1917	24.4	22.2	37.3	11.4	4.6
1918	27.6	26.7	29.8	10.9	5.0
1919	28.7	31.8	24.9	10.2	4.4
1920	32.1	26.6	27.3	9.6	4.4
1921	35.5	22.5	26.4	10.2	5.4
1922	32.0	22.1	27.4	10.5	8.0
1923	32.2	20.9	29.0	9.9	8.0
1924	31.4	22.3	29.0	9.8	7.5
1925	29.7	23.7	29.5	9.5	7.5
1926	29.4	21.3	32.2	9.9	7.2
1927	29.2	20.7	32.8	10.3	7.0
1928	28.6	21.3	32.9	10.5	6.7
1929	28.4	20.3	33.8	10.4	7.0
1930	32.4	15.5	34.9	10.3	6.9
1931	37.0	14.3	31.4	10.5	6.9
1932	43.3	12.2	27.1	10.4	6.9
1933	44.3	16.6	23.2	9.5	6.5
1934	42.6	17.1	26.1	7.8	6.3
1935	41.7	18.4	26.6	6.8	6.4
1936	36.1	19.0	33.7	4.8	6.4
1937	36.3	18.4	34.0	4.9	6.4
1938	42.3	20.1	26.2	5.2	6.3
1939	39.5	21.2	28.2	4.7	6.3
1940	39.4	22.4	27.9	4.1	6.2
1941	38.4	28.9	24.3	3.2	5.3
1942	35.7	37.8	19.0	2.8	4.7
1943	30.0	46.6	16.8	2.5	4.1
1944	30.8	46.8	15.7	2.4	4.2
1945	29.7	48.7	15.0	2.4	4.2
1946	31.5	45.2	16.6	2.4	4.2
1947	34.4	39.4	19.2	2.2	4.8
1948	35.1	37.6	20.1	2.2	4.9
1949	37.6	33.3	21.1	2.5	5.5
1950	36.0	34.6	21.5	2.5	5.5

	P99.5–100				
	Wage	Entrep.	Divid.	Interest	Rents
1916	16.5	31.7	36.7	9.5	5.6
1917	21.7	19.0	43.1	12.0	4.1
1918	25.7	24.2	34.5	11.3	4.3
1919	26.0	30.4	28.7	10.8	4.0
1920	28.8	25.8	31.2	10.0	4.2
1921	31.5	22.0	30.7	10.7	5.2
1922	28.0	21.2	31.9	10.9	8.0
1923	28.1	20.0	34.0	10.1	7.8
1924	27.6	20.5	34.5	10.1	7.3
1925	25.9	22.2	34.8	9.8	7.3
1926	25.7	19.4	37.8	10.1	7.0
1927	25.3	19.1	38.3	10.5	6.8
1928	24.5	20.2	38.2	10.7	6.4
1929	24.2	18.9	39.3	10.8	6.9
1930	27.8	13.9	40.9	10.6	6.9
1931	31.6	13.1	37.2	10.9	7.1
1932	36.7	12.1	32.4	11.3	7.5
1933	37.9	17.2	28.0	10.1	6.8
1934	36.3	16.8	31.5	8.8	6.6
1935	35.7	17.4	32.4	7.7	6.7
1936	30.7	17.6	39.8	5.4	6.5
1937	31.7	16.8	40.1	5.0	6.5
1938	37.9	19.0	31.4	5.3	6.4
1939	35.1	19.8	33.8	4.9	6.4
1940	35.4	21.0	33.2	4.2	6.3
1941	35.2	28.1	28.3	3.1	5.3
1942	32.7	38.0	21.9	2.8	4.6
1943	27.3	47.0	19.2	2.5	3.9
1944	28.1	46.9	18.3	2.5	4.2
1945	27.4	48.2	17.7	2.6	4.2
1946	29.3	44.1	19.8	2.5	4.3
1947	31.9	37.7	23.1	2.3	5.0
1948	32.4	35.7	24.5	2.3	5.1
1949	34.4	31.6	25.7	2.6	5.7
1950	32.7	33.1	25.9	2.6	5.7

(contd.)

Table 5A.7 (*contd.*)

	P90–100				
	Wage	Entrep.	Divid.	Interest	Rents
1951	64.0	22.5	8.6	1.5	3.4
1952	65.7	21.6	8.0	1.5	3.2
1953	68.2	19.9	7.4	1.5	3.0
1954	67.0	20.5	7.7	1.5	3.3
1955	67.6	20.4	8.0	1.5	2.5
1956	67.0	20.8	7.9	1.5	2.8
1957	67.9	19.7	8.3	1.9	2.2
1958	68.9	19.1	7.8	2.0	2.2
1959	68.6	19.2	8.1	2.2	2.0
1960	70.1	17.7	7.8	2.3	2.1
1961	70.6	17.6	7.4	2.5	1.9
1962	70.7	17.5	7.2	2.7	1.8
1963	70.8	17.0	7.4	3.1	1.7
1964	69.0	18.4	8.0	3.3	1.3
1965	68.1	19.4	7.8	3.5	1.2
1966	69.9	18.0	6.9	3.4	1.7
1967	70.3	18.0	6.7	3.6	1.5
1968	70.8	17.3	6.7	3.8	1.4
1969	72.2	16.5	6.1	3.8	1.3
1970	73.7	15.2	5.6	4.2	1.3
1971	74.8	14.3	5.1	4.4	1.3
1972	74.6	14.5	5.1	4.4	1.4
1973	73.2	15.4	5.1	4.8	1.5
1974	72.7	14.9	5.2	5.4	1.8
1975	75.5	13.0	4.9	5.0	1.6
1976	76.1	12.4	4.9	5.1	1.5
1977	76.6	11.9	5.0	5.1	1.4
1978	76.9	11.9	4.9	5.0	1.4
1979	77.5	10.6	4.9	5.7	1.3
1980	78.1	8.3	5.1	7.2	1.3
1981	79.0	5.7	5.0	9.3	1.1
1982	79.4	5.1	5.3	9.0	1.2
1983	81.0	5.9	4.6	7.7	0.8
1984	80.6	6.2	4.1	8.6	0.6
1985	80.3	6.6	4.2	8.3	0.6

	P95–100				
	Wage	Entrep.	Divid.	Interest	Rents
1951	53.4	28.5	12.1	1.8	4.1
1952	55.7	27.3	11.2	1.9	3.9
1953	58.1	25.7	10.5	1.9	3.8
1954	58.3	25.1	10.9	1.8	3.9
1955	60.0	24.4	10.9	1.7	2.9
1956	58.6	25.3	11.1	1.9	3.2
1957	57.5	25.4	11.8	2.4	2.9
1958	58.5	24.7	11.3	2.6	2.9
1959	57.5	25.4	11.6	2.8	2.7
1960	59.0	23.7	11.4	3.0	2.8
1961	61.1	22.9	10.5	3.1	2.5
1962	61.0	22.9	10.3	3.3	2.4
1963	61.5	22.1	10.4	3.7	2.2
1964	59.8	23.6	11.0	3.9	1.7
1965	59.9	23.9	10.7	4.0	1.5
1966	60.2	23.7	9.9	4.0	2.2
1967	60.9	23.6	9.4	4.2	1.9
1968	61.2	22.8	9.5	4.5	1.9
1969	63.3	21.9	8.6	4.5	1.7
1970	65.2	20.2	7.9	5.0	1.8
1971	66.3	19.2	7.4	5.3	1.8
1972	66.2	19.3	7.2	5.3	2.0
1973	64.9	20.2	7.1	5.7	2.1
1974	64.8	19.5	7.0	6.3	2.4
1975	68.1	17.1	6.8	5.8	2.3
1976	69.2	16.2	6.8	5.8	2.0
1977	69.8	15.6	6.9	5.7	1.9
1978	70.5	15.2	6.7	5.7	1.9
1979	71.0	13.6	6.8	6.7	1.9
1980	72.3	10.3	7.0	8.4	1.9
1981	73.8	6.8	6.9	10.8	1.7
1982	73.9	6.5	7.2	10.5	1.9
1983	76.4	7.3	6.3	8.8	1.3
1984	75.5	7.7	5.6	10.1	1.1
1985	75.2	8.4	5.7	9.6	1.2

	P99–100				
	Wage	Entrep.	Divid.	Interest	Rents
1951	37.1	34.4	20.9	2.4	5.3
1952	37.7	34.4	20.0	2.5	5.4
1953	40.4	32.7	19.1	2.6	5.2
1954	39.4	32.9	19.8	2.9	5.0
1955	39.2	33.2	21.4	2.9	3.4
1956	39.3	32.0	21.6	2.9	4.2
1957	40.2	31.8	21.1	3.1	3.9
1958	40.8	31.6	20.2	3.3	4.0
1959	40.6	32.2	20.0	3.5	3.7
1960	42.5	30.1	19.7	3.8	4.0
1961	42.0	30.9	19.7	3.9	3.5
1962	42.1	30.8	19.4	4.3	3.4
1963	42.4	29.9	19.9	4.6	3.2
1964	42.7	28.5	21.8	4.7	2.4
1965	42.3	28.8	21.9	4.9	2.1
1966	40.9	32.6	18.5	4.9	3.2
1967	41.8	33.1	17.5	5.0	2.7
1968	42.0	31.5	18.3	5.4	2.7
1969	43.9	31.1	16.6	5.9	2.5
1970	45.6	30.0	14.9	6.5	2.9
1971	47.6	28.8	14.0	6.8	3.0
1972	49.3	27.2	13.6	6.6	3.2
1973	49.1	27.2	13.3	7.1	3.2
1974	49.4	26.2	12.9	7.9	3.6
1975	52.9	23.4	12.7	7.3	3.7
1976	54.7	22.0	12.8	7.0	3.6
1977	56.1	21.0	12.8	6.7	3.4
1978	58.1	19.6	12.4	6.5	3.4
1979	59.0	17.0	12.5	8.0	3.5
1980	60.5	13.3	12.5	10.0	3.6
1981	62.7	7.8	12.4	13.3	3.7
1982	62.6	8.2	12.3	12.9	3.9
1983	65.5	9.8	11.0	10.7	3.0
1984	66.1	9.9	8.9	12.4	2.7
1985	63.6	11.0	9.6	12.3	3.4

	P99.5–100				
	Wage	Entrep.	Divid.	Interest	Rents
1951	33.8	33.3	25.0	2.4	5.5
1952	34.7	32.7	24.4	2.6	5.6
1953	37.5	31.0	23.4	2.7	5.5
1954	36.4	31.1	24.1	3.0	5.3
1955	36.8	30.6	26.5	3.0	3.1
1956	36.4	28.1	28.1	3.0	4.4
1957	36.5	28.7	27.6	3.2	4.0
1958	37.1	28.3	26.9	3.5	4.1
1959	36.6	29.4	26.4	3.7	3.9
1960	38.2	26.7	26.8	4.0	4.3
1961	37.8	27.6	26.9	4.1	3.7
1962	38.1	27.1	26.8	4.4	3.6
1963	37.9	26.6	27.3	4.8	3.4
1964	37.6	27.0	28.1	4.8	2.5
1965	37.5	27.7	27.6	5.0	2.2
1966	37.2	31.6	22.9	4.9	3.5
1967	38.0	32.5	21.7	5.0	2.8
1968	37.3	31.1	23.2	5.6	2.8
1969	39.9	29.7	21.0	6.5	2.8
1970	41.0	30.0	18.8	7.0	3.2
1971	42.5	29.1	17.8	7.2	3.5
1972	46.2	26.4	16.9	7.0	3.5
1973	45.7	26.7	16.6	7.5	3.5
1974	45.6	25.5	16.1	8.6	4.2
1975	49.7	22.6	15.7	7.7	4.3
1976	52.0	20.9	15.9	7.0	4.2
1977	53.3	20.1	15.7	6.9	4.0
1978	55.0	18.9	15.4	6.7	4.0
1979	56.3	15.7	15.6	8.3	4.1
1980	57.7	12.5	15.3	10.3	4.3
1981	59.8	6.6	15.1	14.0	4.6
1982	59.3	7.6	14.9	13.1	5.0
1983	61.8	10.0	13.0	11.3	3.9
1984	63.5	10.0	10.3	12.9	3.2
1985	59.3	11.7	11.2	13.2	4.7

1987	79.5	9.7	4.0	6.7	0.1	1987	74.2	12.5	5.1	7.9	0.4	1987	63.9	17.2	7.2	10.4	1.4	1987	61.2	17.8	8.0	11.3	1.7
1988	76.3	12.3	4.3	6.8	0.3	1988	70.5	15.5	5.3	8.0	0.7	1988	59.8	21.2	7.6	10.0	1.5	1988	56.9	22.5	8.5	10.5	1.6
1989	75.0	12.5	4.2	7.9	0.5	1989	68.8	15.9	5.2	9.1	0.9	1989	56.7	22.3	7.4	11.8	1.8	1989	52.9	23.8	8.2	12.8	2.2
1990	75.6	12.3	3.9	7.6	0.6	1990	69.8	15.7	4.7	8.8	1.0	1990	57.9	22.3	6.8	11.1	2.0	1990	54.1	24.0	7.5	12.1	2.3
1991	76.2	12.5	3.7	7.0	0.7	1991	70.1	16.0	4.5	8.2	1.1	1991	57.4	23.0	6.6	11.0	2.1	1991	53.1	24.8	7.3	12.4	2.4
1992	78.1	13.0	3.3	4.8	0.9	1992	72.6	16.7	4.0	5.4	1.3	1992	61.6	23.6	5.4	7.1	2.3	1992	58.6	25.1	5.9	7.9	2.5
1993	78.8	13.1	3.2	3.9	1.0	1993	73.4	16.8	3.8	4.5	1.4	1993	62.1	23.8	5.3	6.2	2.6	1993	58.7	25.7	5.8	6.8	3.0
1994	77.9	14.1	3.2	3.7	1.1	1994	72.0	18.2	3.9	4.4	1.6	1994	59.1	26.8	5.3	6.1	2.7	1994	54.7	29.3	6.0	6.9	3.1
1995	77.3	13.7	3.5	4.3	1.2	1995	71.6	17.6	4.2	5.0	1.6	1995	59.6	25.5	5.8	6.6	2.5	1995	55.7	27.8	6.4	7.4	2.8
1996	77.6	14.4	3.1	3.8	1.1	1996	71.7	18.6	3.7	4.4	1.6	1996	59.2	27.3	5.1	5.9	2.4	1996	55.5	29.6	5.6	6.5	2.7
1997	77.1	14.7	3.2	3.8	1.2	1997	71.5	18.8	3.8	4.3	1.6	1997	59.7	27.1	5.2	5.7	2.4	1997	56.1	29.3	5.6	6.3	2.7
1998	76.9	14.7	3.4	3.7	1.3	1998	71.3	18.7	4.1	4.3	1.7	1998	60.3	26.7	5.1	5.4	2.5	1998	56.9	28.9	5.5	5.9	2.8
1999	77.0	15.1	3.1	3.5	1.2	1999	71.6	19.1	3.7	4.0	1.6	1999	61.1	26.6	4.8	5.2	2.4	1999	58.1	28.6	5.1	5.7	2.6

	P99.9–100						P99.9–100						P90–95						P95–99				
	Wage	Entrep.	Divid.	Interest	Rents		Wage	Entrep.	Divid.	Interest	Rents		Wage	Entrep.	Divid.	Interest	Rents		Wage	Entrep.	Divid.	Interest	Rents
1916	10.2	28.3	47.3	9.6	4.6	1916	5.6	24.3	56.8	9.3	4.0	1916						1916					
1917	15.4	16.0	52.7	12.9	3.1	1917	8.4	13.8	61.2	14.3	2.4	1917						1917	41.3	44.4	4.1	2.6	7.7
1918	19.2	22.5	42.7	12.4	3.2	1918	10.1	23.5	49.5	14.3	2.6	1918	67.9	18.5	2.5	5.6	5.5	1918	50.7	29.8	6.2	6.9	6.4
1919	19.0	30.7	35.4	11.6	3.3	1919	10.0	31.8	42.6	12.9	2.7	1919	71.2	18.2	2.2	4.0	4.4	1919	52.1	31.5	4.8	5.9	5.7
1920	21.1	25.5	39.2	10.5	3.7	1920	11.6	25.4	48.7	11.0	3.4	1920	73.2	15.3	2.6	5.3	3.6	1920	58.6	24.1	5.6	6.8	4.9
1921	23.1	21.7	39.9	10.9	4.5	1921	13.5	21.3	51.0	10.2	4.0	1921	79.0	10.8	1.4	4.6	4.1	1921	62.8	18.7	6.0	7.2	5.4
1922	20.0	20.0	41.4	10.9	7.6	1922	11.2	18.1	52.6	10.3	7.8	1922	75.7	12.9	1.8	4.9	4.7	1922	60.5	21.1	5.3	7.1	6.0
1923	20.2	17.7	44.7	10.1	7.3	1923	12.2	13.5	57.6	9.7	7.1	1923	61.8	21.8	2.8	6.5	7.1	1923	48.0	29.9	5.8	8.3	7.9
1924	20.1	17.2	45.8	10.2	6.6	1924	12.4	13.5	58.1	9.5	6.5	1924	58.1	23.5	3.0	7.2	8.2	1924	48.5	29.2	4.7	8.5	9.1
1925	18.7	20.2	45.3	9.5	6.4	1925	10.7	19.1	56.5	8.6	5.1	1925	56.0	24.6	3.4	7.4	8.6	1925	50.5	28.5	5.2	7.5	8.3
1926	18.1	16.3	49.8	9.7	6.1	1926	11.4	13.3	62.7	8.1	4.5	1926	56.9	22.2	4.6	7.8	8.5	1926	51.0	27.3	6.0	7.7	8.0
1927	17.6	16.9	49.8	9.8	5.8	1927	10.2	16.3	61.0	8.4	4.1	1927	59.0	21.3	4.5	7.8	7.4	1927	53.0	25.3	6.4	8.3	7.1
1928	16.6	20.3	47.9	10.1	5.1	1928	9.3	24.1	54.3	9.2	3.1	1928	61.2	20.2	4.5	7.8	6.3	1928	55.5	21.5	8.8	7.9	6.2
1929	15.9	18.0	49.6	10.6	5.8	1929	8.8	20.6	56.8	10.2	3.7	1929	59.7	19.8	5.8	7.7	7.0	1929	55.1	21.1	9.7	7.7	6.5
1930	19.1	10.7	53.8	10.1	6.2	1930	12.2	6.7	69.1	8.1	3.9	1930	61.2	18.1	5.4	8.8	6.4	1930	57.7	15.7	11.4	8.8	6.4
1931	21.8	10.4	50.4	10.6	6.8	1931	12.9	6.5	67.8	8.4	4.4	1931	62.6	16.4	5.6	8.7	6.7	1931	58.3	14.3	11.3	9.4	6.6
1932	25.7	10.4	44.9	11.4	7.6	1932	15.6	6.9	64.0	8.5	5.0	1932	71.4	12.1	4.7	6.6	5.1	1932	64.6	11.7	8.9	8.2	6.7
1933	27.0	16.6	39.5	10.2	6.6	1933	15.6	14.6	57.4	8.2	4.2	1933	71.5	16.2	2.3	5.9	4.1	1933	65.6	16.1	4.7	6.8	6.8
1934	26.0	13.6	45.4	8.6	6.3	1934	15.6	9.2	64.6	6.3	4.2	1934	74.5	15.0	3.4	3.8	3.4	1934	65.9	16.5	5.0	5.9	6.6
1935	25.3	14.9	46.0	7.4	6.4	1935	14.2	11.4	64.8	5.2	4.4	1935	73.8	15.0	3.2	4.2	3.8	1935	66.2	17.0	5.0	5.2	6.6
1936	21.1	14.5	53.5	4.9	6.0	1936	10.8	11.3	70.3	3.4	4.2	1936	72.2	15.9	3.3	4.0	4.6	1936	63.4	18.6	6.9	3.7	7.4
1937	22.6	12.5	54.3	4.4	6.2	1937	12.5	7.2	72.5	3.2	4.6	1937	74.0	13.6	4.3	3.5	4.6	1937	71.6	15.1	6.5	2.9	4.0

(contd.)

Table 5A.7 (*contd.*)

	P90–100						P95–100						P99–100						P99.5–100				
	Wage	Entrep.	Divid.	Interest	Rents		Wage	Entrep.	Divid.	Interest	Rents		Wage	Entrep.	Divid.	Interest	Rents		Wage	Entrep.	Divid.	Interest	Rents
1938	29.4	15.6	44.2	4.8	6.0	1938	18.9	9.5	63.6	3.4	4.6	1938	74.0	14.9	3.0	3.6	4.6	1938	72.1	15.0	5.8	3.1	4.0
1939	26.5	15.2	47.7	4.4	6.1	1939	16.3	8.1	67.8	3.1	4.7	1939	76.0	13.2	4.5	2.7	3.7	1939	71.3	15.8	6.2	2.8	3.8
1940	27.2	16.5	46.6	3.7	6.0	1940	16.3	9.4	66.9	2.7	4.6	1940	81.9	10.4	3.2	1.6	2.8	1940	69.9	17.0	6.5	2.7	3.9
1941	28.0	25.1	39.1	2.8	5.1	1941	16.8	19.4	57.4	2.2	4.2	1941	83.3	12.0	1.6	1.0	2.0	1941	65.7	20.6	7.1	2.5	4.1
1942	25.3	39.4	28.8	2.4	4.2	1942	13.3	42.3	39.3	1.9	3.2	1942	79.5	14.7	2.1	0.7	3.0	1942	68.4	21.9	4.6	1.8	3.3
1943	21.2	46.8	25.9	2.4	3.7	1943	11.5	44.8	38.3	2.3	3.1	1943	78.8	15.7	1.7	0.6	3.2	1943	65.0	26.0	4.4	1.5	3.2
1944	22.1	45.7	25.7	2.5	4.1	1944	12.5	39.6	41.8	2.5	3.6	1944	87.9	9.1	0.8	0.7	1.6	1944	65.6	26.0	4.0	1.5	3.0
1945	21.8	45.6	25.7	2.7	4.2	1945	13.4	35.0	44.5	3.1	3.9	1945	85.8	11.4	0.7	0.6	1.6	1945	59.5	31.6	4.4	1.5	3.1
1946	23.9	38.7	30.0	2.9	4.5	1946	15.1	24.4	52.5	3.6	4.4	1946	80.0	16.3	1.3	0.6	1.8	1946	54.0	36.4	5.0	1.5	3.1
1947	25.7	30.9	35.4	2.6	5.4	1947	15.0	17.1	59.6	3.0	5.3	1947	81.4	15.2	1.0	0.5	1.8	1947	56.0	34.2	5.1	1.4	3.3
1948	26.1	29.2	36.8	2.5	5.5	1948	15.6	17.1	59.4	2.7	5.2	1948	84.5	12.3	0.9	0.6	1.7	1948	61.5	29.5	4.6	1.3	3.1
1949	28.0	24.8	38.6	2.7	6.0	1949	17.0	13.6	61.4	2.7	5.4	1949	85.3	10.8	1.2	0.8	1.9	1949	66.3	24.3	4.7	1.4	3.3
1950	25.2	26.7	39.4	2.7	6.1	1950	11.9	15.0	64.7	2.6	5.8	1950	86.4	10.0	1.0	0.7	1.8	1950	66.6	24.0	4.7	1.4	3.3
1951	27.3	26.8	37.5	2.5	5.8	1951	15.4	15.0	61.6	2.3	5.6	1951	87.6	9.1	0.9	0.6	1.7	1951	67.2	23.5	4.7	1.4	3.1
1952	28.1	24.5	38.5	2.7	6.2	1952	16.3	11.5	63.5	2.7	6.0	1952	86.9	9.5	1.3	0.6	1.7	1952	70.1	21.7	4.2	1.4	2.7
1953	30.3	24.2	36.6	2.8	6.1	1953	17.2	11.3	62.5	2.8	6.2	1953	88.4	8.3	1.2	0.7	1.5	1953	71.4	20.4	4.1	1.4	2.8
1954	29.6	22.7	38.7	3.1	6.0	1954	18.2	11.5	61.0	3.0	6.3	1954	84.5	11.4	1.1	0.8	2.2	1954	72.7	19.2	4.1	1.0	3.0
1955	29.0	19.9	43.6	2.9	4.7	1955	17.1	9.3	67.1	2.7	4.0	1955	83.1	12.3	1.9	0.9	1.8	1955	75.4	18.0	3.2	0.9	2.5
1956	29.6	17.9	44.8	3.0	4.6	1956	17.7	6.7	68.7	2.9	4.0	1956	84.0	11.9	1.4	0.6	2.1	1956	72.6	20.4	3.4	1.2	2.4
1957	28.9	19.6	43.9	3.3	4.3	1957	17.6	7.3	67.3	3.3	4.4	1957	88.8	8.2	1.2	0.9	0.9	1957	70.0	20.7	5.1	1.9	2.2
1958	30.0	18.9	42.9	3.7	4.5	1958	18.1	7.5	66.1	3.7	4.6	1958	89.3	8.1	0.9	0.9	0.8	1958	70.8	19.8	5.2	2.0	2.2
1959	29.2	20.1	42.9	3.9	4.0	1959	17.8	8.6	65.9	3.8	3.8	1959	89.5	7.4	1.3	1.0	0.7	1959	69.4	20.6	5.7	2.2	2.1
1960	30.6	17.1	43.3	4.2	4.8	1960	18.1	5.4	68.4	4.2	3.8	1960	90.3	6.8	1.2	1.1	0.6	1960	70.3	19.4	5.8	2.4	2.1
1961	30.0	18.9	43.0	4.3	3.8	1961	17.0	7.8	67.5	4.3	3.4	1961	88.5	7.6	1.7	1.4	0.8	1961	73.6	17.7	4.5	2.5	1.8
1962	29.7	17.8	44.0	4.6	3.8	1962	17.4	5.4	68.7	4.7	3.8	1962	88.9	7.3	1.4	1.6	0.8	1962	73.1	17.9	4.5	2.7	1.7
1963	29.1	17.4	44.8	5.0	3.7	1963	16.6	4.9	69.9	4.9	3.6	1963	88.1	7.4	1.8	2.0	0.7	1963	73.6	17.1	4.4	3.2	1.6
1964	29.0	18.3	45.1	5.1	2.4	1964	12.6	3.2	78.0	4.7	1.5	1964	86.2	8.6	2.4	2.2	0.6	1964	71.6	19.1	4.5	3.5	1.3
1965	29.1	19.2	44.1	5.4	2.2	1965	13.1	5.7	74.0	5.3	1.9	1965	83.9	10.7	2.3	2.5	0.6	1965	72.0	19.3	3.9	3.6	1.2
1966	29.8	23.4	37.9	5.3	3.6	1966	15.9	11.3	62.9	5.8	4.0	1966	88.3	7.4	1.4	2.3	0.6	1966	72.7	17.9	4.3	3.5	1.6
1967	30.4	24.7	35.7	5.7	3.6	1967	17.8	13.6	58.0	6.4	4.1	1967	88.2	7.3	1.7	2.3	0.6	1967	73.3	17.4	4.1	3.7	1.4
1968	29.3	21.7	39.7	6.4	2.9	1968	18.2	11.3	58.8	8.2	3.6	1968	88.6	7.0	1.3	2.4	0.6	1968	73.7	17.2	3.9	3.9	1.3
1969	32.1	21.7	34.4	8.1	3.7	1969	18.4	8.3	57.2	11.2	4.8	1969	88.6	6.8	1.4	2.6	0.6	1969	75.3	16.1	3.7	3.7	1.2
1970	32.2	23.0	31.8	8.9	4.1	1970	18.1	10.6	55.0	11.2	5.0	1970	89.2	6.0	1.5	2.7	0.5	1970	77.1	14.1	3.5	4.1	1.1
1971	34.0	22.9	30.3	8.6	4.3	1971	19.0	13.6	51.5	10.8	5.1	1971	90.1	5.6	1.1	2.8	0.4	1971	77.6	13.4	3.5	4.4	1.2
1972	37.4	21.7	28.6	8.1	4.2	1972	24.5	12.3	48.3	9.9	4.9	1972	89.6	5.9	1.3	2.8	0.5	1972	76.4	14.6	3.3	4.5	1.2
1973	36.9	22.1	27.2	9.2	4.6	1973	23.3	12.8	46.2	11.8	5.8	1973	88.8	6.4	1.4	3.0	0.5	1973	74.2	16.0	3.4	4.8	1.5

1975	40.7	20.3	25.0	8.3	5.7	1975	25.8	16.7	40.1	9.7	7.6	1975	88.7	5.6	1.4	3.7	0.5	1975	77.4	13.3	3.2	4.8	1.4
1976	43.4	18.6	24.8	7.5	5.7	1976	27.9	16.4	38.9	8.4	8.3	1976	88.4	5.8	1.5	3.7	0.6	1976	77.9	12.7	3.3	5.1	1.0
1977	45.4	17.5	24.5	7.3	5.2	1977	29.2	15.6	39.4	8.1	7.7	1977	88.7	5.4	1.5	3.9	0.4	1977	78.1	12.4	3.4	5.2	1.0
1978	45.9	16.9	24.2	7.5	5.5	1978	30.7	16.3	37.7	7.9	7.4	1978	88.4	5.8	1.6	3.7	0.5	1978	78.0	12.6	3.3	5.2	1.0
1979	46.8	14.2	23.9	9.5	5.6	1979	31.3	13.7	36.2	11.5	7.3	1979	89.1	5.2	1.6	4.0	0.2	1979	78.4	11.5	3.3	5.8	1.0
1980	49.1	10.4	23.0	11.6	6.0	1980	33.7	10.7	34.7	13.3	7.6	1980	88.6	4.5	1.7	4.9	0.4	1980	79.7	8.5	3.6	7.4	0.9
1981	50.7	4.6	22.1	15.7	6.9	1981	35.4	3.5	32.5	18.9	9.7	1981	88.1	3.7	1.6	6.6	0.0	1981	80.6	6.1	3.5	9.2	0.5
1982	47.6	8.0	22.1	15.1	7.3	1982	30.3	12.1	30.8	18.6	8.3	1982	89.2	2.5	2.0	6.2	0.0	1982	81.2	5.4	3.9	9.0	0.6
1983	50.2	12.1	18.7	12.9	6.1	1983	34.0	21.4	23.9	14.6	6.1	1983	89.5	3.4	1.6	5.7	−0.1	1983	83.4	5.7	3.2	7.5	0.2
1984	53.9	12.1	13.1	15.6	5.3	1984	32.6	28.2	17.0	16.3	5.9	1984	89.9	3.2	1.4	5.8	−0.4	1984	81.8	6.3	3.3	8.5	0.1
1985	46.1	15.5	15.4	14.9	8.1	1985	34.5	26.5	15.9	17.1	6.0	1985	89.9	3.2	1.4	5.8	−0.4	1985	82.9	6.6	3.0	7.8	−0.3
1986	49.2	14.6	17.5	13.8	4.9	1986	38.8	24.1	18.0	15.7	3.4	1986	90.1	3.8	1.7	4.8	−0.5	1986	83.3	7.3	3.1	6.4	−0.2
1987	52.3	22.0	9.6	13.7	2.3	1987	36.2	31.3	12.2	17.9	2.5	1987	90.1	4.3	1.9	4.3	−0.6	1987	81.8	8.9	3.5	6.0	−0.2
1988	48.4	26.8	10.7	12.2	2.0	1988	38.7	30.3	14.7	14.3	2.0	1988	89.4	4.9	2.0	4.2	−0.5	1988	80.3	10.4	3.2	6.2	−0.1
1989	43.5	28.6	10.2	15.2	2.6	1989	30.8	35.3	13.2	17.9	2.7	1989	88.6	4.9	1.9	5.1	−0.5	1989	79.3	10.3	3.4	6.9	0.1
1990	45.7	27.4	9.6	14.4	2.8	1990	34.3	33.1	13.3	16.6	2.7	1990	88.7	4.7	2.0	4.9	−0.3	1990	80.5	9.8	2.9	6.7	0.1
1991	43.2	29.3	9.4	15.5	2.7	1991	29.9	36.4	11.8	19.3	2.6	1991	89.4	4.7	1.8	4.4	−0.3	1991	80.8	10.2	2.8	5.9	0.3
1992	53.2	27.6	7.3	9.3	2.7	1992	46.1	32.3	8.5	10.8	2.3	1992	90.9	4.3	1.7	3.3	−0.1	1992	82.6	10.5	2.6	3.9	0.4
1993	51.1	29.8	7.2	8.5	3.4	1993	41.0	36.2	8.7	10.4	3.8	1993	90.9	5.0	1.8	2.5	−0.1	1993	83.2	10.7	2.6	3.1	0.4
1994	44.4	35.9	7.2	8.9	3.5	1994	32.7	43.6	8.4	11.4	3.9	1994	91.1	5.0	1.6	2.2	0.1	1994	82.9	10.8	2.7	2.9	0.7
1995	46.7	32.7	8.0	9.3	3.3	1995	35.8	38.8	10.2	11.7	3.6	1995	90.4	4.9	1.8	2.8	0.1	1995	82.1	10.6	2.9	3.5	0.8
1996	46.6	35.0	7.1	8.0	3.3	1996	36.4	42.0	8.5	9.5	3.6	1996	91.7	4.4	1.6	2.3	0.1	1996	83.0	10.7	2.5	3.1	0.7
1997	48.0	34.6	6.8	7.6	3.1	1997	40.1	40.0	8.0	8.8	3.2	1997	90.8	4.6	1.8	2.6	0.2	1997	82.5	11.0	2.5	3.1	0.9
1998	50.4	33.3	6.3	7.0	3.0	1998	45.8	36.8	6.6	7.9	2.9	1998	91.1	4.7	1.9	2.1	0.2	1998	82.0	11.0	3.0	3.2	0.9
1999	53.1	31.8	5.7	6.7	2.7	1999	51.5	32.4	6.1	7.2	2.8	1999	91.2	4.8	1.7	2.2	0.2	1999	82.2	11.4	2.6	2.9	0.9

	P99–99.5						P99.5–99.9						P99.9–100						P95–99				
	Wage	Entrep.	Divid.	Interest	Rents		Wage	Entrep.	Divid.	Interest	Rents		Wage	Entrep.	Divid.	Interest	Rents		Wage	Entrep.	Divid.	Interest	Rents
1916	35.0	38.4	10.0	8.3	8.3	1916	26.9	37.4	19.0	9.4	7.2	1916	13.8	31.4	39.9	9.7	5.2	1916	5.6	24.3	56.8	9.3	4.0
1917	35.6	35.7	13.0	8.9	6.8	1917	30.6	23.4	29.6	10.9	5.5	1917	20.1	17.4	47.0	11.9	3.6	1917	8.4	13.8	61.2	14.3	2.4
1918	34.3	35.9	13.1	9.4	7.4	1918	33.5	26.1	24.8	10.0	5.6	1918	24.4	21.9	38.8	11.4	3.5	1918	10.1	23.5	49.5	14.3	2.6
1919	37.7	36.4	12.0	8.4	5.6	1919	33.7	30.2	21.3	9.9	4.9	1919	23.7	30.1	31.7	11.0	3.6	1919	10.0	31.8	42.6	12.9	2.7
1920	42.2	29.0	15.1	8.3	5.3	1920	36.1	26.1	23.7	9.5	4.6	1920	25.5	25.5	34.8	10.3	3.9	1920	11.6	25.4	48.7	11.0	3.4
1921	47.4	23.9	13.5	9.0	6.1	1921	39.4	22.3	22.1	10.4	5.8	1921	27.3	21.8	35.0	11.2	4.8	1921	13.5	21.3	51.0	10.2	4.0
1922	44.4	25.1	13.0	9.5	8.0	1922	35.7	22.4	22.8	10.8	8.3	1922	24.1	20.8	36.2	11.2	7.6	1922	11.2	18.1	52.6	10.3	7.8
1923	44.5	23.8	13.9	9.3	8.5	1923	35.4	22.1	24.1	10.1	8.3	1923	23.7	19.5	39.0	10.3	7.4	1923	12.2	13.5	57.6	9.7	7.1
1924	43.6	27.9	11.7	8.6	8.1	1924	34.6	23.7	23.7	10.1	7.9	1924	23.6	18.9	40.3	10.5	6.7	1924	12.4	13.5	58.1	9.5	6.5
1925	41.7	28.3	13.0	8.7	8.3	1925	32.8	24.1	24.8	10.1	8.1	1925	22.3	20.7	40.1	9.9	7.0	1925	10.7	19.1	56.5	8.6	5.1
1926	41.0	27.3	14.7	9.2	7.8	1926	33.3	22.6	25.7	10.5	7.9	1926	21.5	17.8	43.4	10.5	6.8	1926	11.4	13.3	62.7	8.1	4.5

(*contd.*)

Table 5A.7 (*contd.*)

	P90–100						P95–100						P99–100						P99.5–100				
	Wage	Entrep.	Divid.	Interest	Rents		Wage	Entrep.	Divid.	Interest	Rents		Wage	Entrep.	Divid.	Interest	Rents		Wage	Entrep.	Divid.	Interest	Rents
1927	41.7	25.8	15.0	9.8	7.7	1927	33.2	21.3	26.5	11.2	7.8	1927	21.3	17.3	44.1	10.6	6.7	1927	10.2	16.3	61.0	8.4	4.1
1928	42.1	25.2	15.4	9.7	7.5	1928	33.1	20.0	27.7	11.4	7.8	1928	20.5	18.3	44.3	10.6	6.3	1928	9.3	24.1	54.3	9.2	3.1
1929	42.0	25.1	16.2	9.3	7.4	1929	33.0	19.7	28.1	10.9	8.2	1929	19.8	16.6	45.7	10.9	7.0	1929	8.8	20.6	56.8	10.2	3.7
1930	46.5	20.4	16.9	9.3	6.8	1930	36.7	17.1	27.6	11.0	7.6	1930	22.9	13.0	45.4	11.2	7.5	1930	12.2	6.7	69.1	8.1	3.9
1931	52.1	17.6	14.7	9.3	6.3	1931	41.3	15.9	24.2	11.3	7.4	1931	26.9	12.5	40.7	11.7	8.2	1931	12.9	6.5	67.8	8.4	4.4
1932	62.6	12.7	11.8	7.7	5.3	1932	48.0	13.9	19.6	11.1	7.4	1932	30.5	12.0	35.7	12.9	8.9	1932	15.6	6.9	64.0	8.5	5.0
1933	63.0	14.6	9.1	7.7	5.7	1933	49.1	17.8	16.2	10.0	6.9	1933	32.5	17.6	30.9	11.1	7.8	1933	15.6	14.6	57.4	8.2	4.2
1934	60.9	18.0	10.5	4.9	5.6	1934	46.2	19.8	18.1	9.1	6.8	1934	31.2	15.8	35.9	9.7	7.4	1934	15.6	9.2	64.6	6.3	4.2
1935	59.3	21.2	9.8	4.1	5.7	1935	45.9	19.9	19.2	8.1	7.0	1935	30.8	16.6	36.7	8.5	7.4	1935	14.2	11.4	64.8	5.2	4.4
1936	52.9	23.4	14.7	2.8	6.2	1936	40.2	20.7	26.3	5.9	6.9	1936	26.1	16.1	45.3	5.6	6.9	1936	10.8	11.3	70.3	3.4	4.2
1937	50.4	23.5	15.3	4.6	6.2	1937	40.5	20.9	26.2	5.5	6.9	1937	27.5	15.1	45.4	5.1	6.9	1937	12.5	7.2	72.5	3.2	4.6
1938	54.2	23.0	12.0	4.7	6.1	1938	45.5	22.0	19.9	5.7	6.8	1938	34.1	18.4	35.5	5.5	6.6	1938	18.9	9.5	63.6	3.4	4.6
1939	52.1	25.0	12.5	4.3	6.0	1939	42.9	24.0	21.1	5.3	6.7	1939	31.3	18.6	38.3	5.0	6.8	1939	16.3	8.1	67.8	3.1	4.7
1940	50.8	26.3	13.0	3.9	6.0	1940	42.8	25.1	21.0	4.6	6.5	1940	32.2	19.7	37.3	4.2	6.6	1940	16.3	9.4	66.9	2.7	4.6
1941	47.3	31.2	12.9	3.2	5.4	1941	41.6	30.7	18.7	3.5	5.5	1941	32.8	27.6	31.2	3.0	5.4	1941	16.8	19.4	57.4	2.2	4.2
1942	44.4	37.0	10.8	2.9	5.0	1942	39.1	36.9	15.9	3.1	5.0	1942	30.2	38.1	24.4	2.7	4.5	1942	13.3	42.3	39.3	1.9	3.2
1943	37.3	45.4	10.3	2.5	4.6	1943	32.3	47.2	13.9	2.6	4.1	1943	24.5	47.4	21.8	2.5	3.9	1943	11.5	44.8	38.3	2.3	3.1
1944	37.7	46.6	9.0	2.3	4.3	1944	32.7	47.8	12.7	2.5	4.3	1944	25.7	47.9	19.7	2.5	4.2	1944	12.5	39.6	41.8	2.5	3.6
1945	35.3	49.9	8.5	2.2	4.1	1945	31.3	50.1	11.9	2.4	4.3	1945	24.5	48.9	19.7	2.6	4.3	1945	13.4	35.0	44.5	3.1	3.9
1946	36.8	47.9	9.2	2.0	4.0	1946	32.9	47.8	12.8	2.3	4.2	1946	26.8	43.5	22.4	2.6	4.6	1946	15.1	24.4	52.5	3.6	4.4
1947	40.2	43.4	10.0	2.0	4.3	1947	36.3	42.4	14.5	2.2	4.7	1947	29.6	35.9	26.5	2.5	5.4	1947	15.0	17.1	59.6	3.0	5.3
1948	41.9	42.4	9.4	2.0	4.4	1948	37.0	40.5	15.4	2.2	4.9	1948	29.9	33.6	28.6	2.4	5.6	1948	15.6	17.1	59.4	2.7	5.2
1949	45.2	37.5	10.2	2.2	4.9	1949	39.2	36.7	16.1	2.5	5.5	1949	32.2	29.1	29.8	2.7	6.2	1949	17.0	13.6	61.4	2.7	5.4
1950	43.9	38.1	10.8	2.2	5.0	1950	38.0	37.7	16.3	2.5	5.5	1950	30.0	30.9	30.1	2.7	6.2	1950	11.9	15.0	64.7	2.6	5.8
1951	44.8	37.1	11.1	2.2	4.8	1951	38.3	37.8	16.1	2.4	5.3	1951	31.6	31.1	28.9	2.5	5.9	1951	15.4	15.0	61.6	2.3	5.6
1952	44.4	38.2	10.1	2.4	4.9	1952	39.1	38.2	15.0	2.5	5.2	1952	32.2	29.0	29.8	2.7	6.3	1952	16.3	11.5	63.5	2.7	6.0
1953	47.0	36.6	9.6	2.3	4.5	1953	42.1	35.4	14.9	2.6	5.1	1953	34.9	28.7	27.6	2.8	6.0	1953	17.2	11.3	62.5	2.8	6.2
1954	46.0	36.8	10.3	2.6	4.4	1954	40.7	36.5	14.9	3.0	4.9	1954	33.5	26.6	30.9	3.1	5.9	1954	18.2	11.5	61.0	3.0	6.3
1955	44.2	38.6	10.5	2.6	4.0	1955	41.7	37.4	15.7	3.0	2.1	1955	33.3	23.7	35.1	2.9	4.9	1955	17.1	9.3	67.1	2.7	4.0
1956	45.4	39.9	8.0	2.8	3.8	1956	40.5	34.3	18.0	3.0	4.3	1956	33.9	22.0	36.2	3.1	4.8	1956	17.7	6.7	68.7	2.9	4.0
1957	47.4	38.3	7.7	2.8	3.8	1957	41.2	34.2	17.6	3.2	3.8	1957	33.0	24.0	35.5	3.3	4.2	1957	17.6	7.3	67.3	3.3	4.4
1958	48.0	38.5	6.7	3.1	3.7	1958	41.5	34.1	17.2	3.3	3.9	1958	34.2	23.0	34.7	3.7	4.5	1958	18.1	7.5	66.1	3.7	4.6
1959	48.2	38.2	7.1	3.3	3.3	1959	40.9	34.6	17.1	3.6	3.8	1959	33.1	24.0	34.9	4.0	4.0	1959	17.8	8.6	65.9	3.8	3.8
1960	50.5	36.1	6.4	3.5	3.5	1960	42.6	32.4	17.1	3.8	4.0	1960	34.9	21.2	34.4	4.2	5.2	1960	18.1	5.4	68.4	4.2	3.8
1961	50.3	35.7	7.1	3.7	3.3	1961	42.3	32.6	17.6	3.9	3.6	1961	34.5	22.7	34.5	4.3	4.0	1961	17.0	7.8	67.5	4.3	3.4
1962	50.5	36.2	6.0	4.1	3.1	1962	42.7	32.3	17.3	4.3	3.5	1962	34.0	22.1	35.4	4.6	3.9	1962	17.4	5.4	68.7	4.7	3.8

1964	52.6	31.4	9.5	4.4	2.1	1964	42.4	31.8	18.7	4.7	2.5	1964	34.2	23.0	34.8	5.3	2.7	1964	12.6	3.2	78.0	4.7	1.5
1965	52.0	31.2	10.3	4.6	1.9	1965	42.3	32.5	18.2	4.9	2.1	1965	34.0	23.2	35.1	5.4	2.3	1965	13.1	5.7	74.0	5.3	1.9
1966	48.2	34.6	9.8	4.8	2.7	1966	41.6	36.5	13.9	4.7	3.4	1966	34.5	27.5	29.4	5.2	3.5	1966	15.9	11.3	62.9	5.8	4.0
1967	49.1	34.3	9.3	5.0	2.3	1967	42.4	37.0	13.5	4.6	2.4	1967	34.5	28.3	28.4	5.5	3.4	1967	17.8	13.6	58.0	6.4	4.1
1968	51.1	32.3	8.9	5.0	2.7	1968	41.9	36.6	13.7	5.2	2.7	1968	32.7	24.9	33.8	5.9	2.7	1968	18.2	11.3	58.8	8.2	3.6
1969	51.3	33.7	8.2	4.9	1.9	1969	44.3	34.3	13.5	5.6	2.3	1969	36.3	25.8	27.5	7.1	3.4	1969	18.4	8.3	57.2	11.2	4.8
1970	54.5	30.2	7.5	5.5	2.3	1970	46.0	34.0	11.4	6.0	2.7	1970	36.8	27.1	24.1	8.1	3.8	1970	18.1	10.6	55.0	11.2	5.0
1971	57.2	28.1	6.8	6.0	2.0	1971	47.2	32.6	10.8	6.3	3.1	1971	38.9	25.9	23.4	7.9	4.0	1971	19.0	13.6	51.5	10.8	5.1
1972	54.9	28.7	7.7	6.0	2.7	1972	51.1	29.1	10.4	6.3	3.1	1972	41.5	24.7	22.3	7.6	4.0	1972	24.5	12.3	48.3	9.9	4.9
1973	55.5	28.2	7.3	6.4	2.6	1973	50.5	29.3	10.8	6.6	2.9	1973	41.2	25.0	21.2	8.3	4.2	1973	23.3	12.8	46.2	11.8	5.8
1974	56.7	27.3	6.9	6.6	2.5	1974	51.2	27.4	10.3	7.9	3.2	1974	40.8	24.0	20.7	9.3	5.2	1974	22.9	18.3	39.9	11.1	7.8
1975	59.0	25.0	6.8	6.6	2.6	1975	55.1	24.0	10.1	7.3	3.5	1975	45.9	21.6	19.6	7.8	5.0	1975	25.8	16.7	40.1	9.7	7.6
1976	60.0	24.0	6.7	6.8	2.5	1976	57.2	22.4	10.5	6.7	3.2	1976	48.9	19.3	19.7	7.2	4.8	1976	27.9	16.4	38.9	8.4	8.3
1977	61.5	22.8	7.2	6.4	2.1	1977	58.1	21.7	10.3	6.6	3.3	1977	51.1	18.2	19.3	7.1	4.4	1977	29.2	15.6	39.4	8.1	7.7
1978	64.2	21.0	6.4	6.1	2.2	1978	60.7	20.1	10.0	6.2	3.1	1978	51.4	17.1	19.3	7.3	4.9	1978	30.7	16.3	37.7	7.9	7.4
1979	64.4	19.6	6.4	7.4	2.2	1979	62.5	16.7	10.2	7.6	3.1	1979	52.3	14.4	19.5	8.7	5.0	1979	31.3	13.7	36.2	11.5	7.3
1980	66.3	15.0	7.0	9.5	2.2	1980	63.2	13.9	10.3	9.5	3.1	1980	54.9	10.3	18.5	10.9	5.4	1980	33.7	10.7	34.7	13.3	7.6
1981	68.6	10.4	7.0	12.1	1.9	1981	65.7	7.9	10.5	12.8	3.1	1981	56.5	5.0	18.2	14.5	5.9	1981	35.4	3.5	32.5	18.9	9.7
1982	69.6	9.5	6.8	12.6	1.5	1982	67.7	7.3	9.9	11.7	3.4	1982	54.7	6.3	18.5	13.6	6.9	1982	30.3	12.1	30.8	18.6	8.3
1983	73.7	9.5	6.6	9.4	0.9	1983	70.4	8.4	8.8	10.1	2.3	1983	57.6	7.8	16.3	12.1	6.1	1983	34.0	21.4	23.9	14.6	6.1
1984	71.9	9.6	5.9	11.3	1.3	1984	71.2	8.4	8.0	10.8	1.6	1984	64.1	4.4	11.3	15.2	5.0	1984	32.6	28.2	17.0	16.3	5.9
1985	73.9	9.4	6.1	10.3	0.4	1985	69.8	8.7	7.8	11.8	2.0	1985	51.2	10.6	15.2	14.0	9.0	1985	34.5	26.5	15.9	17.1	6.0
1986	75.1	10.9	5.7	8.2	0.1	1986	70.6	8.8	9.8	10.2	0.7	1986	53.9	10.4	17.2	12.9	5.6	1986	38.8	24.1	18.0	15.7	3.4
1987	70.4	15.9	5.2	8.1	0.4	1987	68.8	14.1	6.5	9.3	1.2	1987	59.9	17.7	8.4	11.7	2.2	1987	36.2	31.3	12.2	17.9	2.5
1988	68.3	17.2	5.1	8.5	0.9	1988	65.6	18.1	6.2	8.7	1.3	1988	53.9	24.8	8.4	10.9	2.0	1988	38.7	30.3	14.7	14.3	2.0
1989	67.4	18.2	4.9	8.8	0.7	1989	62.0	19.1	6.4	10.6	1.9	1989	50.1	25.1	8.6	13.7	2.5	1989	30.8	35.3	13.2	17.9	2.7
1990	68.8	17.4	4.5	8.2	1.0	1990	62.1	20.7	5.5	9.8	1.8	1990	52.1	24.3	7.6	13.2	2.8	1990	34.3	33.1	13.3	16.6	2.7
1991	68.9	18.0	4.7	7.1	1.3	1991	62.1	20.8	5.4	9.6	2.1	1991	50.3	25.4	8.0	13.4	2.8	1991	29.9	36.4	11.8	19.3	2.6
1992	70.4	19.1	4.0	5.0	1.6	1992	64.2	22.6	4.6	6.3	2.3	1992	57.4	24.8	6.6	8.5	2.9	1992	46.1	32.3	8.5	10.8	2.3
1993	71.3	18.7	4.0	4.4	1.6	1993	65.9	21.8	4.5	5.2	2.5	1993	56.5	26.4	6.5	7.5	3.2	1993	41.0	36.2	8.7	10.4	3.8
1994	71.1	20.0	3.5	3.7	1.6	1994	64.3	23.1	4.8	5.1	2.7	1994	50.7	31.9	6.6	7.5	3.3	1994	32.7	43.6	8.4	11.4	3.9
1995	70.6	19.2	4.0	4.5	1.7	1995	64.1	23.1	4.9	5.5	2.5	1995	52.2	29.6	6.9	8.1	3.1	1995	35.8	38.8	10.2	11.7	3.6
1996	69.7	20.7	3.7	4.3	1.7	1996	64.4	24.2	4.2	5.0	2.1	1996	52.4	31.0	6.2	7.2	3.2	1996	36.4	42.0	8.5	9.5	3.6
1997	69.8	20.6	4.1	4.0	1.6	1997	64.6	23.9	4.4	4.9	2.3	1997	52.6	31.3	6.1	6.9	3.1	1997	40.1	40.0	8.0	8.8	3.2
1998	70.7	19.9	4.0	3.8	1.7	1998	64.0	24.1	4.7	4.7	2.6	1998	53.1	31.3	6.1	6.5	3.0	1998	45.8	36.8	6.6	7.9	2.9
1999	70.4	20.5	3.7	3.6	1.9	1999	63.8	24.9	4.3	4.6	2.3	1999	54.2	31.3	5.5	6.3	2.7	1999	51.5	32.4	6.1	7.2	2.8

Notes: Groups ranked by income (AGI + adjustments) excluding realized capital gains and SS and UI benefits. Wages is defined as wages and salaries and pensions (and includes bonuses, stock-option exercises, etc.). Entrep. is profits from S-Corporations (entities not subject to corporate taxes and taxed only at the individual level) plus profits from Partnerships plus profits from sole proprietorship businesses (Schedule C income) plus farm income. Divid. is dividends distributed. Interest is interest income. Rents is rental income. The sums of all sources add up to 100% (other forms of income are very small and excluded from the decomposition).

and even less at the level of the top percentile, and excluding them simplifies the reading of our composition series (these small income categories were taken into account when computing top income levels and top income shares in total income).[71] For the 1966–99 period, the composition series were computed directly from the IRS micro-files. For the 1916–65 period,[72] the composition series were estimated from the published IRS tables indicating for each income bracket not only the number of taxpayers and the total amount of their taxable income but also the separate amounts for each type of income. The composition of income within each fractile was estimated from these tables using a simple linear interpolation method. Such a method is less satisfactory than the Pareto interpolation method used to estimate top income levels (no obvious law seems to fit composition patterns in a stable way), but micro-files show that the resulting estimates are still relatively precise: estimation errors are always less than 2 points, and they are usually much smaller (thanks to the fact that IRS tables are usually based on a very large number of income brackets).

The composition series reported in Table 5A.8 indicate for each income fractile the fraction of total income (including capital gains) that takes the form of capital gains. The concept of capital gains used to compute these series is again 'full capital gains', i.e., total pre-exclusion capital gains. We provide two sets of estimates in Table 5A.8: capital gains shares were computed both for fractiles of total income (excluding capital gains) (this corresponds to the 'variant 1' and 'variant 2' series described in section A2 above) and for fractiles of total income (including capital gains) (this corresponds to the 'variant 3' series described above). For the 1966–99 period, both capital gains shares series were computed directly from the IRS micro-files. For the 1916–65 and 2000–02 period, linear extrapolation from published IRS tables yields capital gains shares series for fractiles of net income or AGI (including the post-exclusion amount of capital gains), and one needs to correct these raw estimates in order to take re-ranking into account (see above). That is, capital gains shares are smaller for fractiles of income excluding capital gains than for fractiles of income including post-exclusion capital gains, and capital gains shares are smaller for fractiles of income including post-exclusion capital gains than for fractiles of income including pre-exclusion capital gains. Micro-files allowed us to compute the magnitudes of these corrections coefficients.[73] The capital gains shares series reported on Table 5A.8 demonstrate that re-ranking is substantial at the very top: in 1999, 53.8% of total income reported by the fractile P99.99–100 of the distribution of income including capital gains takes the form of capital gains, but the capital gains share

[71] The fact that these small income categories almost do not matter for top incomes implies that changes in tax law regarding those items (e.g. changes in the definition of taxable social security benefits) have negligible consequences for our income levels and shares series.

[72] We do not provide composition estimates for the 2000–02 period because better estimates will be obtained when the IRS micro-data become publicly available for those years. We do, however, compute the share of capital gains for years 2000–02 because this a necessary step to obtain variants 1 and 2 of the top income shares series presented earlier.

[73] The corrections formulas for capital gains shares that we inferred from micro-files are more complex than those applied to correct income levels, and they are available upon request.

Table 5A.8 Capital gains by fractiles of total income, US 1916–2002 (capital gains are expressed in % of total income (including capital gains) of each fractile)

	A. (fractiles are defined by total income (excluding capital gains))													B. (fractiles are defined by total income (including capital gains))											
	P90–100	P95–100	P99–100	P99.5–100	P99.9–100	P99.99–100	P90–95	P95–99	P99–99.5	P99.5–99.9	P99.9–99.99	P99.99–100		P90–100	P95–100	P99–100	P99.5–100	P99.9–100	P99.99–100	P90–95	P95–99	P99–99.5	P99.5–99.9	P99.9–99.99	P99.99–100
1916			3.2	3.6	4.1	4.0			1.1	2.8	4.2	4.0	1916			7.5	8.6	10.9	14.2			1.5	4.5	8.1	14.2
1917		1.6	1.5	1.5	1.2	0.8		1.7	1.9	1.8	1.5	0.8	1917		2.6	2.9	3.0	3.0	3.1		2.2	2.7	2.9	3.0	3.1
1918	1.2	1.3	1.4	1.2	0.8	0.4	0.7	1.3	1.9	1.8	1.0	0.4	1918	1.7	2.0	2.4	2.3	1.8	1.6	0.8	1.6	2.7	2.9	2.0	1.6
1919	3.1	3.6	3.7	3.4	2.8	2.0	1.6	3.4	4.7	4.1	3.3	2.0	1919	4.5	5.5	6.7	6.7	6.8	7.6	1.7	4.2	6.5	6.6	6.3	7.6
1920	3.5	3.9	3.4	2.8	1.5	0.6	2.3	4.5	5.5	3.9	1.9	0.6	1920	4.7	5.6	5.6	4.9	3.3	2.4	2.5	5.5	7.7	6.4	3.8	2.4
1921	1.5	1.8	1.9	1.7	1.2	0.4	0.7	1.8	2.6	2.2	1.5	0.4	1921	2.1	2.7	3.2	3.1	2.5	1.6	0.8	2.2	3.6	3.6	3.0	1.6
1922	2.7	3.4	4.2	4.4	4.9	5.8	1.0	2.4	3.6	3.9	4.4	5.8	1922	4.5	5.8	8.4	9.4	12.4	19.9	1.1	3.0	5.1	6.3	8.5	19.9
1923	3.1	3.4	4.1	4.3	4.8	6.2	2.3	2.7	3.5	3.7	4.1	6.2	1923	4.9	5.8	8.2	9.2	12.3	20.9	2.6	3.4	4.9	6.1	7.9	20.9
1924	3.8	4.3	5.7	6.0	6.5	7.0	2.3	2.7	4.9	5.5	6.3	7.0	1924	6.0	7.4	11.0	12.3	15.8	23.2	2.6	3.4	6.8	8.8	11.9	23.2
1925	6.4	7.8	10.7	11.6	13.5	15.8	2.3	4.0	7.7	9.6	12.2	15.8	1925	11.1	13.6	20.4	23.1	30.0	42.9	2.6	4.9	10.6	15.1	21.7	42.9
1926	5.1	6.0	8.0	8.8	10.5	12.9	2.3	3.4	5.4	6.8	9.1	12.9	1926	9.0	10.9	16.1	18.5	24.9	37.3	2.6	4.2	7.5	10.9	16.7	37.3
1927	6.0	7.0	9.3	10.3	12.5	14.3	2.8	3.9	5.8	7.9	11.4	14.3	1927	10.6	12.7	18.5	21.3	28.4	40.1	3.1	4.8	8.0	12.4	20.5	40.1
1928	8.5	10.3	14.7	16.4	19.5	20.7	2.8	3.8	8.3	12.5	18.6	20.7	1928	15.4	18.7	27.8	31.6	40.0	51.1	3.1	4.8	11.5	19.2	31.4	51.1
1929	7.6	9.2	13.5	15.2	19.4	22.7	2.5	3.1	7.1	9.8	17.0	22.7	1929	14.2	17.4	26.6	30.5	40.5	54.0	2.8	3.9	9.9	15.3	29.1	54.0
1930	2.9	3.4	4.3	4.7	6.1	8.0	1.6	2.5	2.7	3.3	4.9	8.0	1930	5.4	6.3	9.3	11.0	16.0	25.8	1.8	3.1	3.8	5.3	9.4	25.8
1931	1.1	1.3	1.9	2.1	2.7	3.7	0.4	0.8	1.2	1.5	2.1	3.7	1931	2.2	2.6	4.3	5.1	7.7	13.5	0.5	1.0	1.7	2.5	4.2	13.5
1932	0.5	0.6	0.9	1.1	1.4	1.5	0.3	0.3	0.3	0.8	1.3	1.5	1932	0.7	0.9	2.0	2.5	3.6	5.6	0.3	0.4	0.4	1.4	2.6	5.6
1933	2.0	2.5	3.6	4.2	5.3	6.2	0.6	1.4	1.9	2.9	4.9	6.2	1933	3.4	4.4	7.8	9.4	13.4	20.8	0.7	1.7	2.7	4.8	9.3	20.8
1934	1.1	1.4	1.8	2.1	2.2	1.6	0.3	0.9	1.2	1.9	2.5	1.6	1934	1.7	2.2	3.4	4.0	4.7	4.5	0.3	1.1	1.8	3.2	4.9	4.5
1935	2.4	3.1	4.1	4.5	4.8	3.5	0.4	2.1	2.9	4.2	5.4	3.5	1935	3.9	5.1	7.5	8.6	10.1	9.1	0.5	2.6	4.1	7.0	10.6	9.1
1936	4.3	5.2	6.3	6.7	6.7	4.4	2.0	3.8	5.0	6.7	7.9	4.4	1936	6.8	8.4	11.3	12.5	13.9	11.4	2.2	4.7	7.2	11.1	15.2	11.4
1937	1.6	1.9	2.5	2.5	2.4	1.7	1.0	1.2	2.4	2.7	2.7	1.7	1937	2.5	3.1	4.4	4.8	5.1	4.6	1.2	1.5	3.4	4.5	5.3	4.6
1938	2.0	2.4	3.6	4.0	5.4	8.8	0.9	1.3	2.3	2.8	3.6	8.8	1938	3.5	4.5	7.3	8.7	12.7	21.9	1.0	1.6	3.4	4.7	7.2	21.9
1939	1.8	2.1	2.9	3.1	3.3	3.2	1.0	1.4	2.5	2.9	3.3	3.2	1939	2.8	3.6	5.4	6.0	7.2	8.5	1.1	1.7	3.6	4.9	6.6	8.5
1940	1.5	1.9	2.6	2.8	3.1	3.9	0.7	1.2	2.1	2.5	2.7	3.9	1940	2.5	3.2	4.9	5.5	7.1	10.3	0.7	1.5	3.0	4.1	5.4	10.3
1941	1.6	2.0	2.7	2.9	3.8	5.7	0.5	1.3	2.0	2.1	2.9	5.7	1941	2.7	3.6	5.3	6.1	8.8	14.8	0.5	1.7	2.9	3.6	5.7	14.8
1942	1.1	1.4	1.9	2.0	2.7	4.0	0.1	0.9	1.6	1.4	2.1	4.0	1942	1.9	2.5	3.8	4.3	6.3	10.9	0.2	1.2	2.3	2.4	4.2	10.9
1943	2.3	2.9	3.9	4.1	5.1	7.1	0.9	2.0	3.3	3.3	4.4	7.1	1943	3.9	5.0	7.4	8.3	11.6	18.5	1.0	2.5	4.8	5.5	8.9	18.5
1944	2.3	2.9	3.8	4.1	5.1	6.8	0.8	2.1	3.0	3.3	4.4	6.8	1944	3.7	4.9	7.2	8.3	11.6	17.7	0.9	2.7	4.3	5.5	8.9	17.7

(*contd.*)

Table 5A.8 (*contd.*)

	A. (fractiles are defined by total income (excluding capital gains))											
	P90–100	P95–100	P99–100	P99.5–100	P99.9–100	P99.99–100	P90–95	P95–99	P99–99.5	P99.5–99.9	P99.9–99.99	P99.99–100
1945	4.8	6.1	7.6	8.3	10.5	13.5	1.8	4.6	5.8	6.6	9.4	13.5
1946	6.2	7.1	8.1	8.7	11.6	16.7	3.7	6.2	6.6	6.4	9.6	16.7
1947	3.8	4.6	5.4	6.0	8.6	12.1	2.1	3.8	4.0	4.0	7.1	12.1
1948	3.6	4.4	5.1	5.6	7.4	10.1	1.7	3.7	3.9	4.2	6.4	10.1
1949	2.6	3.1	4.0	4.5	6.0	8.1	1.2	2.4	2.9	3.3	5.1	8.1
1950	4.6	5.2	7.6	7.9	10.3	13.0	3.0	2.9	6.8	5.9	9.5	13.0
1951	3.8	4.9	6.9	7.5	10.0	13.0	1.3	3.1	5.2	5.7	8.8	13.0
1952	3.0	3.9	5.8	6.6	9.7	12.3	1.3	2.2	3.9	4.4	8.7	12.3
1953	2.4	3.1	4.8	5.7	8.5	11.6	0.9	1.8	2.7	3.7	7.4	11.6
1954	4.0	5.6	7.9	9.1	13.8	17.2	0.6	3.7	5.1	5.7	12.4	17.2
1955	5.8	7.2	10.8	12.5	18.2	21.2	2.8	4.3	7.1	8.2	17.0	21.2
1956	4.5	5.7	9.1	11.9	17.3	19.6	1.8	3.0	2.8	8.1	16.3	19.6
1957	3.4	4.6	6.9	8.9	13.4	15.5	1.0	2.8	2.4	5.8	12.5	15.5
1958	4.0	5.5	8.3	10.6	15.3	17.9	0.8	3.4	3.2	7.3	14.3	17.9
1959	5.4	7.9	11.4	14.3	20.8	23.6	0.3	5.3	4.8	10.0	19.7	23.6
1960	4.8	6.8	10.2	13.1	19.5	23.9	0.9	4.2	3.9	8.7	17.6	23.9
1961	6.3	8.4	13.8	18.1	26.0	31.3	2.1	4.5	4.4	12.4	23.6	31.3
1962	4.3	5.9	10.1	13.6	21.2	25.7	1.2	2.9	2.7	8.5	19.2	25.7
1963	4.7	6.3	10.9	14.1	21.1	24.9	1.6	3.1	4.4	9.4	19.4	24.9
1964	7.0	9.2	15.3	16.8	23.8	32.6	2.7	4.9	12.1	12.0	19.9	32.6
1965	8.4	10.2	17.3	18.2	25.8	37.5	4.8	5.0	15.2	12.9	20.4	37.5
1966	6.6	8.8	14.8	17.4	24.9	30.7	1.8	4.4	9.2	11.8	22.4	30.7
1967	9.0	11.8	18.8	21.7	28.7	32.6	3.0	6.6	12.1	16.5	27.2	32.6
1968	10.7	14.0	22.2	25.6	32.9	37.4	3.7	7.4	14.4	20.2	31.1	37.4
1969	7.9	10.8	18.8	22.7	31.6	39.9	2.1	4.9	9.7	16.2	27.8	39.9
1970	4.0	5.5	10.1	12.1	17.6	23.2	1.1	2.4	5.8	8.5	15.3	23.2
1971	5.7	7.7	13.4	15.9	22.5	28.0	1.8	3.9	8.1	11.3	20.2	28.0
1972	6.8	9.0	14.8	17.3	23.5	30.6	2.6	5.0	9.6	13.0	20.4	30.6
1973	5.2	6.8	10.8	12.8	17.2	20.5	1.9	4.3	6.8	9.9	15.9	20.5
1974	3.5	4.6	7.5	8.7	11.3	14.2	1.4	2.6	5.1	7.0	10.2	14.2
1975	3.2	4.2	7.0	8.1	11.2	15.4	1.4	2.4	4.9	6.1	9.5	15.4
1976	4.0	5.2	8.4	9.8	13.0	16.6	1.9	3.1	5.7	7.6	11.6	16.6

	B. (fractiles are defined by total income (including capital gains))											
	P90–100	P95–100	P99–100	P99.5–100	P99.9–100	P99.99–100	P90–95	P95–99	P99–99.5	P99.5–99.9	P99.9–99.99	P99.99–100
1945	7.9	10.2	14.4	16.6	23.2	33.3	2.0	5.8	8.5	11.1	18.8	33.3
1946	9.7	11.7	15.6	17.9	26.2	40.0	4.2	8.0	9.6	10.9	19.3	40.0
1947	6.2	7.7	10.6	12.6	19.6	30.3	2.3	4.8	5.7	6.7	14.2	30.3
1948	5.7	7.2	9.9	11.5	16.9	25.7	1.9	4.6	5.6	7.0	12.8	25.7
1949	4.1	5.3	7.8	9.2	13.7	20.9	1.3	3.0	4.2	5.6	10.2	20.9
1950	7.4	9.0	14.3	15.9	22.6	32.2	3.4	3.7	9.8	10.0	18.9	32.2
1951	6.4	8.5	13.2	15.4	22.4	32.3	1.5	4.0	7.6	9.6	17.5	32.3
1952	5.2	6.8	11.4	13.7	21.6	30.7	1.4	2.8	5.7	7.4	17.4	30.7
1953	4.1	5.5	9.5	11.9	19.2	29.0	1.0	2.3	3.9	6.2	14.7	29.0
1954	7.0	9.8	15.7	19.0	30.3	41.0	0.7	4.7	7.5	9.7	24.8	41.0
1955	10.0	12.9	21.4	25.7	39.3	49.0	3.2	5.4	10.3	13.9	33.9	49.0
1956	8.0	10.7	18.7	24.3	37.1	45.9	2.0	3.8	4.1	13.7	32.6	45.9
1957	6.0	8.2	14.0	18.3	29.2	37.5	1.1	3.5	3.4	9.8	25.1	37.5
1958	7.0	9.8	16.7	21.6	33.3	42.4	0.9	4.3	4.6	12.4	28.6	42.4
1959	9.8	14.1	23.0	29.1	44.2	53.4	0.3	6.7	6.9	16.9	39.4	53.4
1960	8.6	12.3	21.0	27.2	42.1	54.1	1.0	5.4	5.7	14.7	35.3	54.1
1961	11.7	16.0	28.5	37.1	54.6	66.7	2.3	5.8	6.4	21.1	47.2	66.7
1962	8.1	11.3	21.3	28.4	45.3	57.3	1.3	3.6	3.8	14.4	38.4	57.3
1963	8.6	11.9	22.3	29.0	45.1	55.9	1.8	3.9	6.3	15.9	38.9	55.9
1964	12.3	16.6	29.5	34.4	51.0	68.8	3.0	6.2	17.9	20.5	39.8	68.8
1965	14.5	18.7	33.4	37.8	55.3	76.3	5.4	6.4	22.6	22.0	40.8	76.3
1966	10.5	14.4	25.3	31.5	48.6	68.0	2.3	5.6	10.2	16.4	36.7	68.0
1967	13.6	18.3	30.7	36.1	53.3	72.8	3.3	7.9	17.2	20.3	41.1	72.8
1968	15.6	21.3	35.3	42.1	60.0	78.9	3.0	9.1	17.1	24.6	47.3	78.9
1969	12.2	17.0	31.1	38.5	58.4	79.7	2.1	5.5	12.2	18.9	42.8	79.7
1970	7.5	10.6	20.1	25.2	41.7	64.4	1.3	3.8	8.7	12.0	28.9	64.4
1971	9.9	13.9	25.1	31.3	49.0	71.0	1.9	5.6	10.7	16.6	35.8	71.0
1972	11.9	16.4	28.4	34.9	53.4	75.3	2.7	7.4	13.1	19.1	40.1	75.3
1973	10.2	13.9	24.9	30.0	46.5	68.5	2.8	6.2	13.7	17.1	35.0	68.5
1974	7.2	9.9	17.9	22.6	35.3	55.0	1.7	4.4	7.3	12.9	26.0	55.0
1975	6.5	9.1	16.3	20.1	31.7	51.2	1.5	4.2	8.2	11.6	22.0	51.2
1976	7.9	10.8	18.6	22.2	34.0	52.1	2.1	5.6	10.7	13.4	25.1	52.1

1977	4.2	5.4	8.8	10.0	13.1	15.6	1.9	3.3	6.4	8.0	12.1	15.6	1977	8.4	11.6	20.9	25.0	37.4	58.2	2.2	5.3	11.7	15.5	26.7	58.2
1978	4.1	5.2	8.2	9.3	11.8	13.5	2.0	3.2	5.8	7.7	11.2	13.5	1978	8.3	11.2	19.0	22.8	34.3	51.7	2.6	5.9	10.8	14.1	25.9	51.7
1979	6.6	8.8	14.9	17.7	25.0	34.7	2.3	4.5	8.4	12.0	20.3	34.7	1979	12.4	17.0	29.6	35.5	50.5	71.7	3.0	7.4	14.8	21.5	36.5	71.7
1980	6.3	8.4	14.6	17.2	22.9	28.4	2.2	4.0	8.4	12.9	20.4	28.4	1980	11.3	15.6	27.8	33.9	48.6	67.4	2.6	6.3	12.7	20.4	37.4	67.4
1981	5.9	7.9	13.8	16.4	21.6	26.8	2.1	3.7	8.1	12.3	19.3	26.8	1981	11.1	15.7	29.1	35.4	51.9	71.1	2.0	5.3	12.8	19.4	39.9	71.1
1982	7.3	10.1	17.8	21.3	28.6	34.6	1.8	4.3	8.9	14.8	25.4	34.6	1982	11.7	16.5	30.4	37.2	53.4	71.0	1.5	5.0	10.8	19.2	40.9	71.0
1983	9.3	12.6	21.3	24.5	30.6	34.0	2.7	5.6	13.0	18.9	28.8	34.0	1983	15.0	20.6	35.8	42.2	56.7	70.5	2.8	7.1	16.7	25.4	47.2	70.5
1984	9.6	12.8	21.4	24.9	31.1	33.3	3.0	5.9	11.6	18.7	29.9	33.3	1984	15.1	21.0	36.3	42.1	55.5	70.6	2.0	7.0	18.3	25.5	43.9	70.6
1985	11.3	14.8	23.6	27.1	33.4	36.3	3.9	7.4	13.8	20.8	31.7	36.3	1985	17.3	23.6	39.3	45.1	58.6	73.9	2.9	8.6	20.6	28.3	47.4	73.9
1986	19.6	25.3	38.8	43.7	48.3	54.6	6.0	12.0	23.2	39.2	44.2	54.6	1986	27.9	36.7	56.7	63.4	75.9	84.9	4.4	13.1	30.5	45.7	68.3	84.9
1987	7.0	8.9	13.0	14.5	16.5	17.7	2.8	5.4	8.9	12.6	15.8	17.7	1987	10.7	14.3	23.5	27.0	35.3	46.7	2.9	5.7	9.7	14.4	18.8	46.7
1988	7.7	9.8	14.6	16.2	18.8	20.8	2.4	4.8	9.3	13.2	17.5	20.8	1988	10.9	14.4	22.7	25.6	33.2	43.0	2.5	5.0	10.2	15.2	21.2	43.0
1989	6.6	8.3	12.8	14.2	17.2	20.7	2.3	4.0	8.3	10.8	15.0	20.7	1989	9.5	12.4	19.9	22.9	30.1	40.9	2.3	4.1	9.1	12.2	17.6	40.9
1990	4.7	6.0	9.1	10.2	12.3	15.2	1.5	2.8	5.7	8.0	10.5	15.2	1990	7.1	9.3	14.9	17.2	23.4	31.9	1.6	2.9	6.1	8.7	11.7	31.9
1991	3.8	4.8	7.0	7.8	9.3	9.0	1.6	2.8	4.9	6.3	9.5	9.0	1991	6.4	8.4	13.7	16.0	21.5	28.3	1.6	2.9	5.2	6.8	10.4	28.3
1992	4.3	5.4	8.2	9.1	10.9	11.1	1.6	2.7	5.3	7.2	10.7	11.1	1992	6.4	8.3	13.1	15.1	20.2	27.1	1.6	2.8	5.6	7.7	11.9	27.1
1993	5.1	6.4	9.8	11.2	13.8	15.0	1.7	3.3	5.5	8.4	13.1	15.0	1993	7.5	9.8	15.6	18.3	25.2	35.7	1.8	3.4	5.8	9.1	15.1	35.7
1994	4.8	6.0	9.1	10.3	12.3	13.5	1.9	3.0	5.4	8.3	11.5	13.5	1994	7.2	9.5	15.4	18.0	25.3	35.6	2.0	3.1	5.7	9.1	13.0	35.6
1995	5.7	7.2	10.7	11.9	13.8	13.5	2.0	3.7	7.3	9.9	13.9	13.5	1995	8.1	10.5	16.8	19.6	27.4	38.4	2.1	3.8	7.8	10.9	16.2	38.4
1996	8.2	10.2	15.1	16.9	20.1	22.1	2.8	5.0	9.4	13.5	18.8	22.1	1996	10.8	13.8	21.9	25.6	35.1	48.3	2.7	4.9	9.4	13.5	25.4	48.3
1997	10.4	12.9	18.3	20.2	23.7	23.2	3.5	6.9	12.0	15.9	24.0	23.2	1997	13.6	17.1	25.8	29.7	38.9	51.4	3.3	6.8	11.7	17.0	29.5	51.4
1998	11.7	14.2	19.6	21.3	24.0	23.3	4.3	8.0	13.7	18.1	24.4	23.3	1998	15.5	19.5	29.0	33.0	42.4	54.1	3.5	7.4	13.4	19.3	33.4	54.1
1999	12.9	15.5	20.6	22.1	23.8	21.8	5.1	9.5	15.2	20.0	25.0	21.8	1999	17.1	21.1	30.5	34.4	42.9	53.8	4.5	8.8	14.9	21.5	34.4	53.8
2000	13.1	15.8	21.0	22.8	24.5	22.9	5.0	9.1	14.2	20.5	25.5	22.9	2000	18.2	22.3	32.1	36.6	45.6	57.1	4.7	8.3	12.8	21.8	35.5	57.1
2001	8.1	10.2	14.7	16.4	18.9	19.4	2.5	5.0	8.9	13.3	18.6	19.4	2001	10.7	13.6	21.3	25.0	33.6	46.1	2.3	4.3	7.6	12.9	23.7	46.1
2002	6.6	8.4	12.4	13.8	16.2	16.9	1.9	4.0	7.9	11.0	15.8	16.9	2002	8.3	10.7	17.1	20.2	27.8	39.0	1.8	3.5	6.6	10.4	19.5	39.0

Notes: In Panel A, tax returns are ranked by total income excluding capital gains. Series report the additional income reported in the form of capital gains. The share of Capital gains reported are the share of total income including capital gains. For example, the top decile (defined by income excluding capital gains) in 1999 earned 12.9% of their total income (including capital gains) in the form of capital gains. In Panel B, average marginal tax rate on long-term capital gains (dollar weighted) are estimated from micro-files and using the TAXSIM calculator.

falls to 21.8% when one looks at the fractile P99.99–100 of the distribution of income excluding capital gains. Finally, note that the composition series (excluding capital gains) reported on Table 5A.7 were computed for fractiles of net income or AGI (including the post-exclusion amount of capital gains), but that the micro-files demonstrate that re-ranking has relatively small effects on non-capital gains income composition by fractile. For instance, in 1995, if one looks at the fractile P99.99–100 of the distribution of AGI (i.e., including 100% of capital gains), one can see that the wage share is 35.8%, the entrepreneurial income share is 38.8% and the dividend share is 10.2% (see Table 5A.7); with the fractile P99.99–100 of the distribution of income excluding capital gains, the wage share would be about 0.5 point higher, the entrepreneurial income share 1 point higher and the dividend share 1.5 points smaller. That is, shareholders are more likely than CEOs and entrepreneurs to have large capital gains, but the re-ranking is pretty small, and we therefore decided to compute all series reported in Table 5A.7 for fractiles of net income and AGI and to make no correction for re-ranking.

APPENDIX 5B: WAGE INEQUALITY SERIES

This appendix describes the series of shares of top fractiles salary earners that we have constructed using the tables published in *Statistics of Income* by size of salary since 1927.

Computing Total Number of Tax Units with Wages and Total Wages in the Economy

The sum of total wages in the economy used to compute shares is obtained from National Accounts 1929–2002, wages, and salaries, and does not include employers' health insurance and employers' social security contributions. Total wages for years before 1929 are obtained from Kuznets (1953) using a constant multiplier factor so that 1929 matches the NIPA figure. This total wage series includes both government employees and military personnel salaries. The total number of tax units with wage income in the full population is estimated as the number of part-time and full workers from National Accounts (which includes government and military employees) less the number of wives that are employees.[74] Military wages and workers

[74] The number of women employees is estimated as the number of women in the labour force (husband present) from the *Historical Statistics of the US* series D51 and D52 (before 1971) and *Statistical Abstract of the US*, No. 653 (after 1971) multiplied by the ratio of employees (from NIPA) over labour force for the full population (D29 and No. 646). The numbers of tax units with wages for years 1927 and 1928 are based on a simple extrapolation method using Lebergott (1964: tables A3, A4, and A5).

Table 5B.1 Aggregate series on wage income, US 1917–2002

	Total number of employees (1)	Married women employees (2)	Number of tax units with wage (3)	Total wage income (current mn$) (4)	Average wage income ($ 2000) (5)	Share of officer compensation (6)	CPI (base 2000) (7)
1917	29,042	1,354	27,689	26,174	12,139	5.25	7.425
1918	32,119	1,406	30,713	32,773	11,706	6.79	8.716
1919	31,441	1,404	30,036	35,858	11,388	5.56	10.015
1920	30,406	1,399	29,008	42,377	12,017	5.75	11.598
1921	28,041	1,446	26,595	34,311	11,814	6.58	10.357
1922	30,410	1,554	28,856	35,727	12,107	6.74	9.704
1923	33,285	1,677	31,608	41,845	12,726	6.15	9.879
1924	32,993	1,761	31,233	41,829	12,808	6.30	9.899
1925	34,619	1,864	32,756	43,467	12,375		10.146
1926	35,882	1,971	33,911	46,361	12,608		10.248
1927	36,017	2,064	33,953	46,763	12,915		10.053
1928	36,355	2,159	34,197	47,659	13,212	6.71	9.922
1929	37,699	2,274	35,425	50,460	13,490	6.61	9.922
1930	35,590	2,324	33,266	46,214	13,423	6.79	9.674
1931	32,724	2,338	30,386	39,157	13,562	6.89	8.823
1932	29,445	2,328	27,117	30,514	13,095	6.99	7.914
1933	30,940	2,449	28,491	29,027	12,492	6.87	7.510
1934	34,238	2,673	31,565	33,734	12,687	6.44	7.766
1935	35,577	2,787	32,790	36,722	12,967	6.39	7.960
1936	38,599	2,991	35,608	41,954	13,520	6.47	8.040
1937	39,701	3,047	36,654	46,139	13,953	6.09	8.329
1938	38,322	3,117	35,205	43,013	13,737	6.02	8.171
1939	39,633	3,220	36,413	45,985	14,402	5.86	8.056
1940	41,437	3,350	38,087	49,860	14,788	5.92	8.137
1941	45,785	3,896	41,889	62,085	15,871	5.59	8.544
1942	50,219	4,328	45,891	82,098	17,285	4.50	9.458
1943	55,995	4,887	51,108	105,786	18,827	3.54	10.035
1944	57,221	5,293	51,928	116,749	19,993	3.22	10.205
1945	55,548	5,338	50,210	117,493	20,260	3.50	10.440
1946	49,643	5,273	44,370	112,005	19,918	4.59	11.328
1947	49,936	5,354	44,582	123,097	19,023	4.90	12.959
1948	51,332	6,057	45,275	135,537	18,901	4.97	13.969
1949	50,358	6,270	44,088	134,719	19,344	5.01	13.830
1950	52,424	6,832	45,592	147,238	20,107	5.17	13.968
1951	56,415	7,557	48,858	171,591	20,181	4.73	15.072
1952	57,702	7,739	49,963	185,619	20,884	4.54	15.403
1953	58,918	8,227	50,691	198,970	21,751	4.41	15.526
1954	57,387	8,243	49,144	197,242	22,027	4.62	15.604
1955	59,080	8,615	50,465	212,129	23,103	4.94	15.542
1956	60,845	9,213	51,632	229,002	23,859	4.82	15.775
1957	61,308	9,583	51,725	239,926	23,946	4.93	16.343
1958	59,839	9,686	50,153	241,290	24,025	5.14	16.784
1959	61,587	10,072	51,515	259,814	24,936	5.16	16.918
1960	62,680	10,126	52,554	272,823	25,322	5.32	17.189
1961	62,881	10,935	51,946	280,483	25,693	5.48	17.361
1962	64,573	11,235	53,338	299,319	26,410	5.67	17.552
1963	65,619	11,726	53,893	314,809	27,010	5.74	17.762

(*contd.*)

Table 5B.1 (*contd.*)

	Total number of employees (1)	Married women employees (2)	Number of tax units with wage (3)	Total wage income (current mn$) (4)	Average wage income ($ 2000) (5)	Share of officer compensation (6)	CPI (base 2000) (7)
1964	67,275	12,059	55,216	337,742	27,901	5.70	17.993
1965	69,692	12,453	57,239	363,707	28,519	5.78	18.299
1966	73,516	13,158	60,358	400,265	28,915	5.70	18.830
1967	75,442	13,871	61,571	428,946	29,345	5.71	19.376
1968	77,602	14,766	62,836	471,904	30,120	5.62	20.190
1969	79,850	15,479	64,371	518,259	30,500	5.85	21.280
1970	79,750	15,972	63,778	551,472	30,685	5.96	22.535
1971	79,554	16,360	63,194	584,450	31,226	6.23	23.527
1972	81,583	16,833	64,750	638,671	32,243	6.47	24.280
1973	85,202	17,588	67,614	708,639	32,256	6.65	25.785
1974	86,573	18,055	68,518	772,150	31,162	6.87	28.621
1975	85,044	18,373	66,671	814,690	30,678	7.10	31.226
1976	87,402	18,943	68,459	899,580	31,154	7.11	33.037
1977	90,421	19,523	70,898	993,986	31,243	7.42	35.185
1978	94,785	20,282	74,503	1,121,020	31,240	7.59	37.859
1979	98,025	20,987	77,038	1,255,590	30,398	7.74	42.137
1980	98,379	21,466	76,913	1,377,416	29,276	7.91	47.825
1981	99,235	21,796	77,439	1,517,272	28,985	7.93	52.751
1982	97,762	21,991	75,771	1,593,395	29,094	8.13	56.022
1983	98,527	22,267	76,260	1,684,275	29,568	8.38	57.814
1984	103,119	23,111	80,008	1,854,793	29,829	8.47	60.300
1985	105,806	23,870	81,936	1,995,186	30,185	8.56	62.471
1986	107,735	24,395	83,340	2,114,392	30,830	8.77	63.658
1987	110,743	25,125	85,618	2,270,210	31,084	8.81	65.950
1988	113,896	25,775	88,121	2,452,699	31,367	8.29	68.654
1989	116,631	26,486	90,145	2,596,838	30,946	7.62	71.949
1990	118,127	26,779	91,348	2,754,605	30,750	7.46	75.834
1991	116,625	26,812	89,813	2,824,190	30,646	7.13	79.019
1992	117,110	27,227	89,883	2,966,813	31,126	7.45	81.390
1993	118,790	27,511	91,279	3,091,625	31,046	7.31	83.832
1994	121,708	28,438	93,270	3,254,312	31,087	8.66	86.011
1995	124,632	29,244	95,388	3,441,060	31,226	8.82	88.419
1996	127,009	29,671	97,338	3,630,142	31,384	8.79	91.072
1997	130,118	29,957	100,161	3,885,977	32,055	8.64	93.167
1998	133,456	30,387	103,069	4,192,775	33,190		94.657
1999	136,294	31,061	105,233	4,475,588	33,944		96.740
2000	139,207	31,514	107,693	4,836,329	34,742		100.000
2001	138,840	31,431	107,409	4,950,605	34,670		102.846
2002	137,262	31,074	106,188	4,976,266	34,702		104.472

Notes: Total number of part-time and full time employees from NIPA 1929–2001 (includes military). From 1917 to 1929. extrapolated using Lebergott series on employees. Married women employees from *Historical Statistics* and *Statistical Abstract*. Total wage bill is from NIPA 1929–1999 (line 1). Wage bill 1917–1927 extrapolated from Kuznets (1953: 570, (1)). Average wage is column (5) over column (2).Officer compensation share from corporate tax returns statistics.

form a substantial part of total wages and workers from 1943 to 1945.[75] However, excluding military wages and military personnel hardly changes the estimates of top shares, even during the war, because few military salaries are in the top fractiles and the average military salary is substantially smaller than average wage (see below).

Before 1948, as two wage earners had incentives to file separately (see Appendix 5A), the tax return statistics on wages reflects individual wages rather than family wages. As a result, using the same definition of tax units as described above produces a downward bias for top wage shares before 1947 and thus an artificial positive jump in top shares between 1947 and 1948. We correct for this discontinuity as follows. First, for years 1927–47, we temporarily redefine the total number of tax units with wages as the total number of part-time and full-time employees from National Accounts (that is, we add back the working wives). Second, we then compute top shares and levels using this alternative definition for the total number of tax units. The wage levels and thresholds that we obtain for 1927–47 correspond to individual wages (and not family wages) and thus are smaller than the levels and thresholds after 1948. But fortunately, shares computed at the individual level before 1948 and at the tax unit level after 1948 do not produce a discernible jump in the series. Third, in order to correct the discontinuity in levels and thresholds, we multiply the levels and thresholds that we obtain before 1948 by the ratio of the total number of individual tax units (new definition) to the total number of family tax units (old definition). This procedure produces levels and thresholds that are both continuous in 1947–48 and fully consistent with our share estimates. (See Table 5B.1)

Interpolations from IRS Tables

From 1927 to 1941, *Statistics of Income* provides tables by size of wages only for tax returns with net income above US$5000. The tables contain both the number of taxpayers and total wages reported by bracket from 1927 to 1935. The tables contain only the number of taxpayers (and not total wages reported) from 1936 to 1941. The number of returns and amounts of wage reported, even for brackets above US$5000, are underestimated because wages can be above US$5000 and net income below for some returns because of deductions (on average equal to 10% of gross income). Fortunately, the IRS publication for year 1928 provides the same table for returns filing Form 1040 with net income below US$5000. Taxpayers with relatively low income levels composed mostly of wages and salaries are allowed to file a shorter form called Form 1040A. In 1928 (as for most interwar years), Form 1040A could only be used for returns with *gross* income less than US$5000. As a result, combining the Tables by size of wages for net income above US$5000 and net income below US$5000 provides a complete distribution of wages reported on Form 1040 and thus a complete distribution of wages above US$5000.

[75] Military pay is about 15% of total wages in the US economy and slightly more than 20% of US wage earners from 1943 to 1945.

Assuming that for each bracket the ratio of the number of returns with net income below US$5000 to the number of returns with net income above US$5000 is constant from 1927 to 1941,[76] we can correct the tables and obtain a complete distribution of salaries above US$5000. These tables, however, allow only the estimation of series of top shares above US$5000. As US$5000 corresponds roughly to the threshold level P99, these truncated distributions allow the estimation of levels and shares only within the top percentile. After 1944, the IRS provides tables by size of wages for all returns (Forms 1040A and 1040) and thus covering the full tax return population.

From 1927 and 1941, estimation of salary distributions below US$5000 is done using the composition tables classified by net income brackets described in Appendix 5A. In these tables, the number of returns reporting wages, along with the total amount of those wages is reported for each bracket of net-income.[77] Average wage for wage earners and average net-income for each net-income bracket are computed. We then assume that each net-income bracket corresponds to a wage bracket with thresholds equal to the actual net-income thresholds multiplied by the ratio of average wage to average net-income in that bracket. In order to generate brackets fitting together, the final thresholds are taken as equal to the average of the corresponding top and bottom thresholds of two adjacent brackets. We therefore obtain a set of wage bracket thresholds where the number of returns and the wage amount reported for each bracket is the same as in the original composition table. This new distribution by size of wages is not perfectly accurate because ranking in terms of net-income is not identical to ranking in terms of wages. This method is therefore reliable only if wage income is close to net-income bracket by bracket. Fortunately, salaries constitute more than 90% of net-income reported in tax returns (with positive wage income) for brackets of net-income below US$5000. The ratio is above to 95% for brackets below US$3000. Shares and levels below the top percentile are obtained using these estimated wage distributions. This method can be tested using later years and is shown to give results extremely close to the direct method using tables distributed by wage size.[78] (See also Tables 5B.2 and 5B.3.)

Years 1942 and 1943 raise special problems because the IRS did not provide tables by size of wages for these two years. Fortunately, the IRS provided tables for returns reporting only salary income for each of the years 1942 to 1945. These tables are used to estimate wage distributions for 1942 and 1943 using a simple multiplier method. We take year 1944 as a benchmark and we assume that the ratios of returns with wages only to all returns with wages by wage

[76] This assumption can be successfully tested using the micro-files for the period 1966–95.

[77] Before 1937, the composition tables report only the amounts of wages and not the number of returns with positive wages in each bracket. We have estimated the number of returns in each bracket for these years assuming that the ratio of the number of returns with positive wages to the number of returns (with positive or zero wages) is the same as in 1937 for each bracket. We have checked that this assumption is reasonable by comparing these ratios for years 1937–40.

[78] As expected, this method provides estimates of levels and shares biased downward above the top percentile relative to the direct method using published tables by size of wages. We thus use the indirect estimates to compute thresholds, average levels, and shares for the fractiles P90–95 and P95–99 and then use the direct estimates for the fractiles within the top percentile.

Table 5B.2 Top wage income shares, US 1927–2002

(1)	P90–100 (2)	P95–100 (3)	P99–100 (4)	P99.5–100 (5)	P99.9–100 (6)	P99.99–100 (7)	P90–95 (8)	P95–99 (9)	P99–99.5 (10)	P99.5–99.9 (11)	P99.9–99.99 (12)	P99.99–100 (13)
1927	27.89	18.85	8.65	6.08	2.53	0.68	9.04	10.20	2.57	3.55	1.86	0.68
1928	29.11	19.78	8.87	6.20	2.59	0.69	9.33	10.91	2.66	3.61	1.91	0.69
1929	29.24	19.76	8.67	6.08	2.56	0.72	9.49	11.09	2.60	3.51	1.85	0.72
1930	28.63	19.23	8.54	5.99	2.56	0.73	9.40	10.69	2.55	3.43	1.82	0.73
1931	29.34	19.69	8.47	5.81	2.45	0.67	9.65	11.22	2.66	3.36	1.78	0.67
1932	30.28	19.68	8.29	5.66	2.37	0.62	10.61	11.39	2.63	3.29	1.75	0.62
1933	30.08	19.81	8.31	5.77	2.45	0.63	10.27	11.50	2.54	3.32	1.82	0.63
1934	29.77	19.94	8.31	5.76	2.37	0.59	9.83	11.64	2.55	3.38	1.78	0.59
1935	30.31	20.12	8.40	5.85	2.40	0.60	10.19	11.72	2.55	3.45	1.80	0.60
1936	29.70	19.95	8.60	6.02	2.45	0.59	9.75	11.35	2.58	3.57	1.86	0.59
1937	30.06	20.05	8.41	5.89	2.41	0.60	10.01	11.64	2.52	3.48	1.81	0.60
1938	29.83	19.66	8.13	5.74	2.36	0.59	10.18	11.53	2.38	3.39	1.77	0.59
1939	30.65	20.06	8.20	5.70	2.32	0.57	10.59	11.86	2.50	3.38	1.75	0.57
1940	30.85	20.07	8.37	5.84	2.39	0.58	10.78	11.70	2.53	3.45	1.81	0.58
1941	29.33	19.05	8.11	5.75	2.39	0.57	10.29	10.94	2.36	3.36	1.83	0.57
1942	27.08	17.45	7.21	5.12	2.18	0.51	9.63	10.24	2.09	2.94	1.67	0.51
1943	25.88	16.26	6.42	4.51	1.86	0.41	9.62	9.83	1.91	2.65	1.45	0.41
1944	24.61	15.13	5.56	3.84	1.56	0.36	9.48	9.56	1.73	2.28	1.20	0.36
1945	24.05	14.99	5.73	3.96	1.57	0.35	9.05	9.27	1.77	2.38	1.22	0.35
1946	25.10	16.18	6.40	4.33	1.68	0.37	8.92	9.79	2.06	2.66	1.31	0.37
1947	24.97	16.07	6.27	4.23	1.60	0.34	8.90	9.80	2.04	2.63	1.26	0.34
1948	25.03	16.13	6.21	4.20	1.58	0.35	8.90	9.92	2.01	2.62	1.23	0.35
1949	25.00	16.05	6.12	4.11	1.54	0.34	8.95	9.93	2.01	2.58	1.20	0.34
1950	25.18	16.13	6.24	4.21	1.57	0.34	9.06	9.89	2.03	2.64	1.23	0.34
1951	24.71	15.63	5.97	4.00	1.48	0.31	9.08	9.66	1.97	2.52	1.17	0.31
1952	24.43	15.41	5.74	3.78	1.39	0.30	9.01	9.67	1.96	2.40	1.09	0.30
1954	24.13	15.26	5.61	3.65	1.32	0.28	8.88	9.65	1.96	2.34	1.04	0.28
1956	24.53	15.57	5.56	3.57	1.26	0.25	8.96	10.02	1.99	2.31	1.00	0.25
1958	24.67	15.60	5.40	3.43	1.20	0.25	9.07	10.20	1.97	2.23	0.95	0.25
1960	25.23	15.72	5.26	3.31	1.14	0.23	9.51	10.46	1.95	2.17	0.91	0.23
1961	25.21	15.63	5.20	3.26	1.11	0.22	9.58	10.44	1.93	2.15	0.89	0.22
1962	25.22	15.62	5.16	3.24	1.09	0.21	9.60	10.47	1.92	2.15	0.88	0.21
1964	25.15	15.43	5.12	3.24	1.07	0.21	9.72	10.31	1.88	2.17	0.86	0.21
1966	25.34	15.47	5.16	3.27	1.11	0.22	9.87	10.31	1.89	2.16	0.88	0.22
1967	25.77	15.81	5.34	3.38	1.14	0.23	9.97	10.47	1.96	2.24	0.91	0.23
1968	25.60	15.66	5.24	3.32	1.12	0.23	9.95	10.42	1.92	2.20	0.89	0.23
1969	25.71	15.68	5.19	3.27	1.10	0.24	10.03	10.49	1.92	2.17	0.87	0.24
1970	25.67	15.64	5.13	3.21	1.06	0.21	10.03	10.51	1.92	2.15	0.85	0.21
1971	25.67	15.67	5.18	3.25	1.08	0.22	10.00	10.49	1.93	2.18	0.86	0.22
1972	25.81	15.80	5.32	3.38	1.14	0.24	10.02	10.47	1.94	2.24	0.90	0.24
1973	26.14	16.06	5.42	3.43	1.14	0.24	10.09	10.63	1.99	2.29	0.91	0.24
1974	26.61	16.48	5.66	3.63	1.26	0.27	10.14	10.81	2.04	2.37	0.99	0.27
1975	26.46	16.32	5.64	3.63	1.26	0.27	10.15	10.68	2.01	2.37	0.99	0.27
1976	26.66	16.49	5.74	3.70	1.30	0.29	10.16	10.76	2.03	2.40	1.02	0.29
1977	26.94	16.70	5.86	3.79	1.35	0.30	10.24	10.84	2.06	2.45	1.05	0.30
1978	27.43	17.07	6.06	3.93	1.40	0.31	10.36	11.02	2.13	2.53	1.09	0.31
1979	27.63	17.24	6.22	4.06	1.47	0.34	10.39	11.03	2.16	2.59	1.13	0.34

(contd.)

Table 5B.2 (*contd.*)

(1)	P90–100 (2)	P95–100 (3)	P99–100 (4)	P99.5–100 (5)	P99.9–100 (6)	P99.99–100 (7)	P90–95 (8)	P95–99 (9)	P99–99.5 (10)	P99.5–99.9 (11)	P99.9–99.99 (12)	P99.99–100 (13)
1980	28.06	17.60	6.43	4.23	1.57	0.38	10.47	11.17	2.20	2.66	1.19	0.38
1981	28.14	17.66	6.43	4.24	1.59	0.39	10.49	11.23	2.18	2.65	1.20	0.39
1982	28.55	18.02	6.67	4.42	1.67	0.41	10.53	11.35	2.25	2.75	1.26	0.41
1983	29.09	18.49	6.96	4.66	1.80	0.47	10.59	11.54	2.30	2.86	1.33	0.47
1984	29.61	18.95	7.27	4.93	1.99	0.52	10.66	11.68	2.34	2.94	1.47	0.52
1985	29.74	19.05	7.28	4.92	1.98	0.54	10.70	11.77	2.35	2.95	1.44	0.54
1986	29.94	19.19	7.33	4.96	2.02	0.58	10.76	11.86	2.37	2.94	1.44	0.58
1987	30.59	19.98	8.15	5.68	2.43	0.69	10.61	11.83	2.47	3.25	1.74	0.69
1988	31.95	21.37	9.39	6.79	3.16	1.10	10.58	11.99	2.59	3.64	2.06	1.10
1989	31.53	20.83	8.69	6.12	2.69	0.82	10.70	12.13	2.57	3.44	1.86	0.82
1990	31.79	21.13	8.99	6.41	2.87	0.91	10.66	12.14	2.59	3.54	1.96	0.91
1991	31.43	20.77	8.56	5.97	2.57	0.78	10.66	12.21	2.59	3.40	1.79	0.78
1992	32.45	21.85	9.63	6.97	3.33	1.22	10.60	12.22	2.66	3.64	2.11	1.22
1993	31.85	21.29	9.05	6.41	2.90	0.96	10.56	12.23	2.64	3.51	1.94	0.96
1994	31.54	20.94	8.72	6.07	2.63	0.83	10.59	12.22	2.65	3.44	1.80	0.83
1995	32.43	21.73	9.25	6.52	2.91	0.94	10.70	12.48	2.73	3.61	1.97	0.94
1996	33.15	22.46	9.80	6.98	3.21	1.11	10.69	12.66	2.82	3.77	2.10	1.11
1997	33.86	23.18	10.43	7.54	3.67	1.36	10.68	12.75	2.89	3.87	2.31	1.36
1998	34.34	23.72	10.97	8.08	4.12	1.65	10.61	12.75	2.89	3.96	2.48	1.65
1999	35.10	24.50	11.64	8.71	4.67	1.98	10.61	12.85	2.93	4.04	2.69	1.98
2000	36.03	25.42	12.61	9.64	5.44	2.45	10.62	12.84	2.99	4.24	3.03	2.45
2001	35.10	24.22	11.25	8.31	4.31	1.79	10.87	12.96	2.93	3.98	2.51	1.79
2002	33.89	22.89	10.28	7.43	3.70	1.45	10.99	12.62	2.84	3.75	2.27	1.45

Notes: Shares computed from tax returns statistics and total number of tax units and total wage bill from Table 5B.1. Wage income is wages, salaries, and tips on individual income tax form. It includes bonuses, and profits from exercised stockoptions.

brackets[79] are constant. This method can be successfully tested using 1945, where we can compute shares using direct complete tabulations. This methodology is reliable because the number of returns reporting wage only is large, even in the very top fractiles of wage earners. Below the top percentile, the method described above using composition tables can be used to compute alternative estimates for 1942 and 1943. We have checked that this method gives very similar results.[80]

[79] In fact, the ratio is assumed to be constant by fractiles of the distribution corresponding to each of the brackets of 1944. The multipliers for each of the 1942 and 1943 brackets are then obtained by using interpolated 1944 multipliers.

[80] In 1941, 1942, and 1943, an additional complication appears because returns for Forms 1040 and 1040A are tabulated separately in the composition tables by size of net-income. Wage distributions for returns corresponding to each of these forms are first estimated using the method described above. The two wage distributions thus obtained are then merged into a single wage distribution as follows: the distribution of wages within each bracket of the form 1040A distribution is assumed to be Paretian. Then we split each bracket of the form 1040A distribution so that each portion can be attributed fully to a given bracket of the form 1040 distribution. For each bracket of the form 1040 distribution, we add back the pieces coming from the form 1040A distribution.

Year (1)	P90–100 (2)	P95–100 (3)	P99–100 (4)	P99.5–100 (5)	P99.9–100 (6)	P99.99–100 (7)	P90–95 (8)	P95–99 (9)	P99–99.5 (10)	P99.5–99.9 (11)	P99.9–99.99 (12)	P90 (13)	P95 (14)	P99 (15)	P99.5 (16)	P99.9 (17)	P99.99 (18)
1927	38,215	51,652	118,536	166,708	347,050	925,207	24,777	34,930	70,362	121,620	282,803	21,443	27,627	56,710	87,533	198,830	550,891
1928	40,887	55,567	124,539	174,244	363,930	961,946	26,208	38,323	74,831	126,822	297,479	22,951	30,763	62,821	92,030	207,793	575,109
1929	41,983	56,722	124,481	174,441	367,972	1,027,358	27,242	39,782	74,520	126,056	294,703	23,489	30,772	62,659	91,435	206,950	592,717
1930	41,112	55,229	122,656	172,024	366,982	1,051,137	26,994	38,371	73,287	123,283	290,962	23,456	30,092	64,784	89,667	200,654	580,289
1931	42,853	57,521	123,686	169,703	357,469	980,702	28,185	40,980	77,670	122,764	288,229	25,280	32,152	64,558	91,827	198,533	565,938
1932	43,054	55,950	117,864	160,841	337,170	882,543	30,158	40,472	74,887	116,762	276,583	25,135	32,434	60,327	91,471	188,802	549,502
1933	40,799	53,735	112,715	156,415	331,759	854,043	27,864	38,990	69,015	112,574	273,716	23,888	30,541	57,089	85,329	185,957	533,810
1934	40,966	54,890	114,319	158,408	326,371	817,437	27,042	40,032	70,230	116,417	271,806	23,117	31,442	58,540	84,980	189,682	517,423
1935	42,644	56,608	118,188	164,529	338,014	845,873	28,679	41,214	71,849	121,155	281,579	24,673	32,824	60,877	85,482	194,641	533,486
1936	43,519	58,466	125,998	176,299	358,842	869,537	28,570	41,583	75,695	130,660	302,087	24,757	32,576	64,385	91,285	209,752	562,190
1937	45,432	60,602	127,054	178,006	363,853	903,217	30,262	43,988	76,102	131,544	303,923	27,049	34,683	65,062	93,425	211,844	570,288
1938	44,612	58,781	121,528	171,778	352,298	875,775	30,442	43,095	71,276	126,652	294,139	27,192	34,611	63,322	90,445	203,567	550,069
1939	48,040	62,884	128,498	178,608	363,796	894,731	33,196	46,479	78,388	132,312	304,803	29,723	37,654	66,891	95,343	211,398	561,199
1940	49,637	64,578	134,645	188,034	385,173	934,889	34,697	47,061	81,254	138,747	324,090	31,729	38,508	68,512	99,159	224,135	600,069
1941	50,889	66,084	140,712	199,651	415,380	983,947	35,693	47,428	81,774	145,718	352,209	32,789	39,326	68,367	101,373	241,957	657,542
1942	51,221	66,008	136,411	193,844	412,844	970,092	36,435	48,407	78,980	139,100	350,937	33,287	40,496	67,975	96,391	235,751	652,969
1943	53,379	67,070	132,515	186,091	384,029	852,490	39,687	50,709	78,938	136,604	331,972	36,729	43,564	68,228	95,687	232,822	583,703
1944	54,217	66,656	122,589	169,097	342,760	783,491	41,776	52,671	76,080	125,676	293,778	38,592	45,729	67,887	89,515	204,848	533,398
1945	53,898	67,207	128,352	177,279	352,386	781,071	40,585	51,919	79,422	133,497	304,743	37,513	44,529	69,495	95,352	216,509	542,010
1946	55,944	72,132	142,586	193,146	373,412	821,919	39,755	54,519	92,026	148,080	323,581	36,337	44,081	80,597	108,864	234,659	559,605
1947	53,202	68,502	133,676	180,377	341,177	725,857	37,902	52,207	86,972	140,177	298,431	35,136	41,585	76,333	103,293	220,354	504,750
1948	53,645	69,129	133,068	179,862	337,785	739,373	38,162	53,144	86,274	140,383	293,166	34,532	43,216	74,111	103,403	214,818	496,345
1949	55,245	70,921	135,204	181,649	339,167	744,006	39,567	54,849	88,758	142,266	294,178	35,757	44,738	76,619	105,804	215,953	498,378
1950	58,228	74,579	144,162	194,478	362,710	786,711	41,874	57,182	93,843	152,415	315,589	38,038	47,066	80,558	112,546	231,321	529,732
1951	57,573	72,847	139,125	186,546	345,005	717,680	42,298	56,277	91,702	146,929	303,593	38,835	46,850	79,926	108,896	223,563	506,975
1952	58,908	74,352	138,480	182,483	333,948	721,545	43,465	58,323	94,481	144,622	290,890	39,782	48,418	82,720	110,799	213,963	486,360
1954	62,072	78,485	144,300	187,994	338,292	712,914	45,662	62,032	100,609	150,421	296,673	41,706	50,980	88,771	116,949	219,952	487,834
1956	68,972	87,558	156,226	200,486	353,155	715,427	50,385	70,392	111,964	162,318	312,902	45,668	56,774	99,945	128,434	235,041	500,626
1958	70,712	89,420	154,644	196,649	343,768	702,092	52,002	73,113	112,638	159,868	303,952	46,706	59,212	101,432	127,880	229,640	487,353
1960	76,183	94,939	158,888	200,054	344,194	699,849	57,427	78,952	117,722	164,020	304,678	51,138	65,054	106,889	132,376	232,569	486,071
1961	78,411	97,247	161,620	203,028	346,498	697,859	59,577	81,155	120,215	167,165	307,466	53,274	67,087	109,330	134,922	236,068	487,193
1962	79,065	99,901	164,842	206,879	348,656	676,557	58,228	83,665	122,803	171,431	312,219	56,412	69,499	111,946	137,454	242,226	483,808
1964	84,920	103,727	174,053	220,075	363,349	699,295	66,114	86,146	128,032	184,258	326,026	60,734	73,060	115,404	146,459	261,112	494,731
1966	89,256	108,964	181,576	230,024	389,327	788,431	69,550	90,813	133,130	190,203	344,991	63,945	76,823	121,284	151,395	269,030	543,983
1967	92,669	113,675	191,815	243,066	408,920	829,613	71,662	94,138	140,562	201,599	362,169	65,615	79,472	126,531	160,977	285,129	569,252

(contd.)

Table 5B.3 (*contd.*)

Year (1)	P90–100 (2)	P95–100 (3)	P99–100 (4)	P99.5–100 (5)	P99.9–100 (6)	P99.99–100 (7)	P90–95 (8)	P95–99 (9)	P99–99.5 (10)	P99.5–99.9 (11)	P99.9–99.99 (12)	P90 (13)	P95 (14)	P99 (15)	P99.5 (16)	P99.9 (17)	P99.99 (18)
1968	95,233	116,477	194,968	246,831	417,381	856,447	73,989	96,854	143,103	204,193	368,594	67,847	81,859	129,473	163,877	287,095	581,679
1969	97,260	118,610	196,278	247,580	417,379	890,449	75,913	99,192	144,978	205,132	364,818	69,625	84,042	130,710	164,991	286,067	580,265
1970	98,491	120,009	196,956	246,332	405,546	803,374	76,972	100,771	147,578	206,526	361,338	70,543	85,391	133,472	167,583	286,229	560,330
1971	100,913	123,198	203,714	255,765	423,601	846,471	78,629	103,071	151,665	213,808	376,618	71,960	87,206	137,505	173,289	298,362	583,808
1972	104,857	128,346	216,230	274,740	464,056	988,640	81,368	106,374	157,720	227,411	405,767	74,713	90,022	142,605	181,209	318,815	642,457
1973	106,257	130,519	220,375	278,732	465,055	962,448	81,994	108,054	162,016	232,147	409,783	75,049	91,132	145,149	185,626	322,704	643,176
1974	104,788	129,742	223,024	285,683	495,305	1,071,241	79,835	106,421	160,366	233,279	431,313	72,750	89,044	144,755	183,516	331,935	707,418
1975	103,563	127,699	220,707	284,178	491,882	1,062,949	79,424	104,446	157,234	232,248	428,424	72,495	88,079	139,873	183,394	330,946	692,035
1976	106,022	131,188	228,103	294,430	518,305	1,144,439	80,858	106,960	161,776	238,463	448,737	74,028	89,925	144,552	187,215	341,868	739,757
1977	107,336	133,063	233,330	302,312	536,719	1,182,658	81,607	107,995	164,345	243,708	464,943	74,676	90,822	146,304	190,026	350,894	771,236
1978	109,025	135,706	240,713	312,207	556,635	1,245,071	82,343	109,454	169,220	251,098	480,138	75,257	91,684	150,240	196,784	364,111	798,532
1979	106,876	133,395	240,469	314,105	567,740	1,323,626	80,358	106,626	166,833	250,699	483,754	73,387	89,285	146,921	195,696	361,260	822,130
1980	105,078	131,771	240,610	316,542	586,607	1,425,231	78,384	104,560	164,677	249,023	493,424	71,405	87,131	145,289	192,259	368,215	850,885
1981	104,535	131,153	238,657	315,043	589,705	1,445,178	77,917	104,276	162,270	246,376	494,649	70,890	87,131	144,144	189,137	365,730	861,485
1982	107,166	135,274	250,469	332,136	627,511	1,546,478	79,059	106,475	168,799	258,290	525,398	71,777	88,406	147,737	198,032	383,588	926,808
1983	111,113	141,282	265,681	355,885	686,373	1,804,962	80,944	110,183	175,477	273,261	562,082	73,221	90,814	153,726	207,483	408,621	1,028,567
1984	113,835	145,686	279,403	378,743	764,663	2,009,879	81,983	112,259	180,065	282,264	626,309	74,084	92,078	157,989	212,542	439,327	1,129,789
1985	115,924	148,470	283,621	383,871	770,190	2,099,821	83,378	114,683	183,372	287,291	622,453	75,135	94,072	160,857	216,042	441,509	1,182,300
1986	119,335	152,929	291,979	395,395	803,952	2,303,756	85,740	118,167	188,562	293,257	637,308	77,051	96,747	166,023	219,820	447,968	1,232,562
1987	122,985	160,688	327,787	456,996	977,618	2,773,278	85,281	118,913	198,580	326,840	778,100	76,761	96,607	172,559	236,544	526,190	1,507,046
1988	129,511	173,278	380,482	550,884	1,280,874	4,450,505	85,746	121,477	210,081	368,389	928,699	76,678	97,668	179,662	257,709	615,076	1,984,933
1989	126,239	166,789	348,089	490,300	1,075,015	3,299,822	85,690	121,463	205,879	344,121	827,815	76,369	97,783	176,968	249,676	549,861	1,680,724
1990	126,429	168,060	357,614	509,408	1,139,996	3,609,764	84,798	120,670	205,819	351,758	865,572	75,671	96,665	176,942	250,847	581,084	1,758,639
1991	125,078	165,297	340,694	475,033	1,024,073	3,114,148	84,861	121,447	206,354	337,773	791,841	75,481	97,383	177,904	246,938	537,660	1,585,138
1992	131,600	177,199	390,393	565,338	1,351,362	4,939,105	86,000	123,902	215,450	368,834	952,728	76,380	98,189	184,492	262,476	608,713	2,124,462
1993	128,679	172,002	365,798	518,020	1,172,030	3,869,649	85,354	123,553	213,578	354,516	872,293	75,814	97,998	184,163	257,858	574,533	1,836,395
1994	127,926	169,924	353,746	492,597	1,066,342	3,353,820	85,929	123,969	214,896	349,161	812,180	76,325	98,483	184,699	257,938	551,860	1,686,746
1995	132,305	177,327	377,545	532,302	1,187,546	3,841,740	87,282	127,273	222,787	368,491	892,635	77,446	100,316	190,720	269,327	591,843	1,917,363
1996	135,755	183,985	401,303	571,454	1,314,026	4,527,854	87,525	129,656	231,152	385,811	956,934	77,009	101,360	196,579	281,009	618,575	2,149,578
1997	141,021	193,069	434,232	627,974	1,527,122	5,661,720	88,974	132,778	240,490	403,188	1,067,722	78,318	102,567	205,682	289,499	665,445	2,498,618
1998	147,556	203,913	471,589	694,714	1,772,298	7,078,684	91,199	136,994	248,464	425,318	1,182,699	80,019	105,887	211,327	302,138	707,276	2,949,712
1999	154,321	215,399	511,864	765,886	2,052,057	8,683,863	93,243	141,283	257,841	444,344	1,315,190	82,007	108,608	220,270	314,071	747,663	3,501,557
2000	161,801	228,277	566,234	865,771	2,441,640	10,998,522	95,410	144,132	268,592	475,823	1,510,943	83,221	110,859	228,869	328,104	818,391	3,983,756
2001	157,302	217,080	504,002	744,811	1,933,328	8,026,625	97,437	145,179	262,240	445,630	1,251,630	84,149	111,833	224,927	317,992	728,413	3,214,078
2002	152,030	205,396	461,043	667,017	1,657,166	6,487,565	98,612	141,470	255,094	420,827	1,131,260	82,721	110,169	219,928	304,324	688,949	2,737,121

Notes: Levels computed from tax returns statistics and total number of tax units and total wage bill from Table 5B.1. Wage income is wages, salaries, and tips on individual income tax

Finally, years 2000–02 require a specific method as micro-files are not available for these years.[81] We used the composition tables showing by brackets of Adjusted Gross Income (AGI), the number of returns with wage income and the total amount of wages reported. Using the same methodology we used for years 1927–41, we obtain a distribution of wages. We then compute shares and income levels from this distribution. Obviously, the levels and shares are underestimated using this method because ranking in terms of AGI and wages is not identical. However, using previous years 1991–99 where both the micro-files and the published composition tables are available, we can estimate by how much levels and shares estimated from published tables for each fractile should be adjusted to match estimates from the micro-files. Fortunately, these multiplier factors are extremely stable from 1991 to 1999 (the maximum variation between multipliers is always less than 5%). Therefore, we can use the multipliers from year 1999 to adjust the levels and shares for years 2000–02.[82]

The actual interpolation method used to obtain thresholds and average wage levels by fractiles is the same Pareto method as in Appendix 5A. In a number of years, however, the IRS only published the number of returns and not the amounts.[83] For these years, before applying the Pareto interpolation method, we estimated amounts using the approach described in Appendix 5C.[84]

All these steps involve a substantial number of computations that have not been described in full detail. Our computer programs are available upon request for readers interested in getting the full details of the estimation.

Entry Effects on Top Shares

The fractiles are defined relative to the total number of tax units with positive wages, and therefore our series measure inequality only among wage earners for each year. Entry or exit effects such as a rise of unemployment during depressions, or movements into the labour force such as military personnel during the wars, or a decline of self-employment and rise of wages workers, can affect our top shares measures through composition effects. Under one set of simple conditions that we now describe, shares of wages accruing to top fractiles are not affected by entry or exit effects. Suppose that the initial wage distribution density is $f(w)$ and that we add (or subtract) a new distribution $g(w)$ to the former distribution. The new distribution $g(w)$ represents a flow of entrants such as military personnel during the Second World War. Let us assume that the fraction of new entrants

[81] We do not report top wage shares for year 2002, because at the time this chapter was written, the complete composition table by income brackets was not yet available.

[82] Shares and levels are blown up by around 5% for fractiles P90–95 and P95–99, by around 10% for fractiles P99–99.5 and P99.5–99.9, and by around 20% for fractiles P99.9–99.99 and P99.99–100.

[83] For years 1935–41, and from 1944–61, the published tables report only the number of tax units in each bracket.

[84] We adopted the same method to compute top income shares in 1913–15 where only the number of tax units was available.

Table 5B.4 CEO pay vs. average wage, US 1970–2003

		CEO pay statistics (in thousands of 2000 dollars)					Composition of Pay of top 100 CEOs		
Year (1)	Average wage (in $ 2000) (2)	Total pay rank 10 (3)	Total pay rank 50 (4)	Total pay rank 100 (5)	Total pay average 100 (6)	Salary+bonus rank 10 (7)	Share salary+bonus (8)	Share stock options (9)	Share other (10)
1970	34,363	1,691	1,216	1,021	1,326	1,553	84.66	15.34	
1971	35,070	1,636	1,194	1,058	1,267	1,424	84.07	15.93	
1972	36,202	2,059	1,376	1,178	1,558	1,717	85.99	14.01	
1973	36,151	2,083	1,478	1,218	1,610	1,718	82.85	17.15	
1974	34,978	1,845	1,408	1,240	1,490	1,663	87.13	12.87	
1975	34,620	2,046	1,399	1,201	1,555	1,649	86.04	13.96	
1976	35,045	2,149	1,513	1,296	1,655	1,967	84.45	15.55	
1977	35,136	2,322	1,651	1,364	1,805	1,953	80.00	20.00	
1978	35,040	3,479	2,029	1,622	2,430	1,981	59.50	40.50	
1979	34,135	6,135	2,819	2,024	3,569	2,250	40.36	22.12	37.52
1980	33,023	6,204	2,390	1,815	3,337	2,106	43.44	38.10	18.46
1981	32,693	4,988	2,631	1,960	3,621	2,114	39.19	48.07	12.75
1982	32,997	4,545	2,413	1,871	4,500	2,044	32.66	55.29	12.06
1983	33,579	6,433	2,428	1,754	3,298	2,458	48.77	45.54	5.69
1984	33,732	7,330	2,633	1,836	4,045	2,488	42.68	15.76	41.56
1985	34,091	5,742	3,161	2,275	3,837	2,905	49.08	35.20	15.72
1986	34,822	6,932	3,776	2,609	4,928	4,697	52.44	30.53	17.04
1987	35,076	13,066	4,732	2,967	7,519	4,549	32.87	59.43	7.70
1988	35,362	13,476	4,671	3,043	6,754	5,389	38.32	51.90	9.78
1989	34,792	13,336	4,617	2,990	6,937	5,528	41.49	48.20	10.31
1990	34,631	11,628	5,554	3,417	7,701	4,511	35.68	38.56	25.76
1991	34,582	12,617	5,690	3,924	8,570	4,579	31.28	54.12	14.60
1992	35,228	27,835	8,039	4,933	15,018	4,101	17.29	67.55	15.16
1993	35,122	20,009	9,283	4,332	14,867	5,443	18.45	64.29	17.26
1994	35,085	14,364	6,535	4,553	8,656	5,666	41.23	34.22	24.54
1995	35,098	19,643	9,500	5,774	12,056	5,818	29.44	53.62	16.94
1996	35,233	37,299	11,493	7,459	20,126	7,386	22.37	58.28	19.35
1997	35,946	47,335	13,585	9,041	23,648	9,084	15.45	67.04	17.50
1998	37,188	63,700	18,925	10,564	35,316	7,725	9.24	78.72	12.04
1999	37,993	90,470	20,084	11,773	39,626	10,060	9.73	58.52	31.76
2000	38,846	84,449	27,207	13,292	40,378				
2001	38,562	81,672	15,270	7,831	35,499				
2002	38,593	28,098	13,046	7,810	17,693				
2003	38,900	30,809	13,975	8,880	18,500				

Notes: Average is the total wages and salaries divided by number of equivalent full-time employees (from National Income and Product Accounts) CEO pay statistics are computed from the top 100 CEOs (in term of total pay) from Forbes survey of 800 CEOs from 1970 to 2003.

within the top fractile is negligible (that is, the support of $g(w)$ is below the threshold of the top fractile of $f(w)$). This assumption is likely to be satisfied for top fractiles and movements in and out of the labour force due to wars or business cycles. Adding workers with the distribution $g(w)$ below the top increases the total wage income denominator which tends to reduce top shares but also increases the size of each fractile, which tends to increase top shares. Let us assume realistically that the top of the distribution $f(w)$ is Paretian with parameter a. Let us introduce $b = a/(a-1)$. Then, it is possible to show the following result:

If the average wage of the initial distribution $f(w)$ is b times larger than the average wage of distribution $g(w)$. Then, the two effects just described cancel out and adding $g(w)$ to the initial distribution $f(w)$ does not change top shares (up to a first degree of approximation). If the average wage of $f(w)$ is more (less) than b times the average wage of $g(w)$, then introducing $g(w)$ increases (decreases) top shares.

If we take the case of military personnel during the Second World War, b is about 1.5 and the average non-military salary during the Second World War is also about 1.5 times larger than the average military salary (see National Accounts). This explains why excluding military workers and wages hardly affects our top share estimates.

Let us consider the case of the very large increase in wage earners from a low level in 1938 (due to a very high unemployment rate) to 1948 (full employment). If we assume that the average wage of new entrants is 66% of the current average wage (which is perhaps a reasonable number), then excluding new entrants would not affect our top share estimates. If the average wage of new entrants is less that 66% of the average wage, then the entry effect biases our top shares upward, implying that the decline in top shares would be larger when eliminating the entry effect.

CEO Data

The CEO data are from the *Forbes Magazine* survey of 800 CEOs from the largest US corporations from 1970 to 2003. Total pay includes salary and bonus, stock options exercised during the year, the value of restricted stock awarded, and the value contingent pay. Average wage is the line wages and salaries from NIPA divided by the number of full-time equivalent employees from NIPA. (See Table 5B.4.).

APPENDIX 5C: PARETO METHOD OF INTERPOLATION

The Pareto interpolation technique used here and in Chapters 3, 6, 9, and 11 is that described in Piketty (2001). Iin order to estimate a given fractile threshold (P90, P95, ..., P99.99), we choose the income bracket threshold s such that the fraction p of tax units with income above s is as close as possible to the given fractile; we note b the ratio between the average income of all tax returns above s and s; we then compute $a = b/(b-1)$ and $k = sp^{(1/a)}$, which allows us to compute the given threshold income by using the Pareto formula

$$1-F(y) = (k/y)^a \tag{5C.1}$$

(where $F(y)$ is the cumulative distribution function). Top fractiles average incomes (P90–100, P95–100, ..., P99.99–100) are then obtained by multiplying the corresponding fractile threshold by b (in practice, the result barely depends on the interpolation threshold s, as long as s is not too far from the given fractile); intermediate fractiles average incomes (P90–95, P95–99, etc.) are obtained by difference. This interpolation technique is slightly different from the one used by Feenberg and Poterba (1993) and delivers more precise results (Feenberg and Poterba only use the slope between two consecutives thresholds s, and do not use the information embodied in the b coefficients).[85]

Where we have information only on the number of returns in a range, and not on the amounts, we estimate the amounts as follows. We assume that the distribution of income in each bracket (s, t) is Pareto distributed: i.e. follows the distribution (5C.1). The Pareto parameters a and k are obtained by solving the two equations: $k = sp^{(1/a)}$ and $k = tq^{(1/a)}$ where p is the fraction of tax returns above s and q the fraction of tax returns above t.[86] Note that the Pareto parameters k and a may vary from bracket to bracket. We then estimate the amount reported in bracket (s, t) simply as

$$Y = N \int_s^t y dF(y) \tag{5C.2}$$

where N is the total number of tax units (with positive wages). For the top bracket, this method cannot be applied and we therefore assume that the top bracket is Pareto distributed with Pareto parameters a and k equal to those of the bracket just below the top estimated by the method just described. When data on amounts reported are available, we can check that our estimated amounts Y are very close to the true reported amounts.

REFERENCES

Acemoglu, D. (2002). 'Technical Change, Inequality, and the Labour Market', *Journal of Economic Literature*, 40: 7–72.

—— Aghion, P. and Violante, G. (2001). 'Deunionization, Technical Change, and Inequality', Working paper, Harvard University.

[85] Atkinson (Chapter 2) notes that the estimation errors induced by Pareto interpolation techniques are sometimes non-negligible. But this is the case only when the raw data does not include sufficiently many income brackets. The only non-negligible (more than 1%) estimation error that we noticed over the 1966–95 period is related to fractile P99.99–100 during the 1990s: the top income bracket used in the IRS tables of the 1990s is not high enough (US$1 million and more, i.e., more than 0.1% of all tax units in the late 1990s), and this interpolation threshold yields estimates of P99.99–100 that are over-estimated by about 5% (in 1995). However, since 2000 (which is exactly the period for which micro-data are not yet available), the IRS has extended the top bracket to US$10 million and more. This top IRS bracket corresponds almost exactly to our top 0.01% group.

[86] This is the standard method of Pareto interpolation used by Kuznets (1953) and Feenberg and Poterba (1993).

Brownlee, W. E. (2000). 'Historical Perspective on US Tax Policy Toward the Rich', in J. Slemrod (ed.) *Does Atlas Shrug? The Economic Consequences of Taxing the Rich.* Cambridge: Cambridge University Press.

Bureau of Census (1999). *Statistical Abstract of the United States.* Department of Commerce, Washington DC: Hoover's Business Press.

Cartter, A. M. (1954). 'Income Shares of Upper Income Groups in Great Britain and the United States,' *American Economic Review*, 44: 875–83.

Chetty, R. and Saez, E. (2004). 'Dividend payments and Corporate Behaviour: Evidence from the 2003 Dividend Tax Cut', Working Paper, NBER.

Cooper, G. (1979). *A Voluntary Tax? New Perspectives on Sophisticated Estate Tax Avoidance.* Washington, DC: The Brookings Institution.

DeLong, J. B. (1998). 'Robber Barons', mimeo, Berkeley.

DiNardo, J., Fortin, N. and Lemieux, T. (1996). 'Labour Market Institutions and the Distribution of Wages, 1973–1992: A Semiparametric Approach,' *Econometrica*, 64: 1001–44.

Fama, E. and French, K. (2000). 'Disappearing Dividends: Changing Firm Characteristics or Lower Propensity to Pay?' Working Paper No. 509, Center for Research in Security Prices.

Feenberg, D. R. and Poterba, J. M. (1993). 'Income Inequality and the Incomes of Very High-Income Taxpayers: Evidence from Tax Returns', in J. Poterba, (ed.) *Tax Policy and the Economy*, vol 7. Cambridge, MA: MIT Press, pp. 145–77.

—— —— (2000). 'The Income and Tax Share of Very High-Income Households, 1960–1995', *American Economic Review*, Papers and Proceedings, 90: 264–70.

Goldin, C. and Margo, R. (1992). 'The Great Compression: The Wage Structure in the United States at Mid-Century', *Quarterly Journal of Economics*, 107: 1–34.

—— and Katz, L. (1999). 'The Returns to Skill across the Twentieth Century United States'. Manuscript, Harvard University, Department of Economics.

Goldsmith, S., Jaszi, G. Kaitz, H. and Liebenberg, M. (1954). 'Size Distribution of Income Since the Mid-Thirties', *Review of Economics and Statistics*, 36: 1–32.

Goolsbee, A. (2000). 'What Happens When You Tax the Rich? Evidence from Executive Compensation', *Journal of Political Economy*, 107: 352–78.

Gordon, R. and Slemrod, J. (2000). 'Are "Real" Responses to Taxes Simply Income Shifting Between Corporate and Personal Tax Bases', in J. Slemrod, (ed.) *Does Atlas Shrug? The Economic Consequences of Taxing the Rich.* Cambridge: Cambridge University Press.

Hall, B. and Murphy, K. J. (2004). 'The Trouble with Stock Options', *Journal of Economic Perspectives*, 17: 49–70.

Karoly, L. A. (1993). 'The Trend in Inequality among Families, Individuals, and Workers in the United States: A Twenty-five Year Perspective', in S. Danziger and P. Gottschalk (eds.) *Uneven Tides: Rising Inequality in America.* New York: Russell Sage Foundation, pp. 99–164.

Katz, L. and Autor (1999). 'Changes in the Wage Structure and Earnings Inequality', in O. Ashenfelter and D. Card (eds.) *Handbook of Labour Economics*, vol. 3A. Amsterdam: North-Holland.

—— Murphy, K. (1992). 'Changes in Relative Wages, 1963–1987: Supply and Demand Factors', *Quarterly Journal of Economics*, 107: 35–78.

Keat, P. (1960). 'Longrun Changes in Occupational Wage Structure, 1900–1956', *Journal of Political Economy*, 68: 584–600.

Kopczuk, W. and Saez, E. (2004). 'Top Wealth Shares in the United States, 1916–2000: Evidence from Estate Tax Returns', *National Tax Journal*, 57: 445–87.

Kuznets, S. (1941). *National Income and Its Composition, 1919–1938.* New York: National Bureau of Economic Research.

—— (1945). *National Product in Wartime.* New York: National Bureau of Economic Research.

—— (1953). *Shares of Upper Income Groups in Income and Savings.* New York: National Bureau of Economic Research.

—— (1955). 'Economic Growth and Income Inequality', *American Economic Review,* 45: 1–28.

Lampman, R. J. (1962). *The Share of Top Wealth-Holders in National Wealth, 1922–1956.* New Jersey: Princeton University Press, Princeton.

Lebergott, S. (1964). *Manpower in Economic Growth: The American Record since 1800.* New York: McGraw-Hill.

Lewellen, W. G. (1968). *Executive Compensation in Large Industrial Corporations.* New York: National Bureau of Economic Research.

Lindert, P. (2000). 'Three Centuries of Inequality in Britain and America', in A. B. Atkinson and F. Bourguignon (eds.) *Handbook of Income Distribution.* Amsterdam: Elsevier Science, pp. 167–216.

Mellon, A. (1924). *Taxation: The People's Business.* New York.

Morrisson, C. (2000). 'Historical perspectives on income distribution: The case of Europe', in A. B. Atkinson and F. Bourguignon (eds.) *Handbook of Income Distribution.* Amsterdam: Elsevier Science, pp. 217–60.

Park, T. S. (2000). 'Comparison of BEA Estimates of Personal Income and IRS Estimates of Adjusted Gross Income', *Survey of Current Business,* November, 7–13.

Phelps Brown, H. (1977). *The Inequality of Pay.* Oxford: Oxford University Press.

Piketty, T. (2001). *Les hauts revenus en France au 20eme siècle—Inégalités et redistributions, 1901–1998.* Paris: Editions Grasset.

—— (2003). 'Income Inequality in France, 1901–1998', Journal of Political Economy, *111: 1004–42.*

—— Saez, E. (2001). *Income Inequality in the United States, 1913–1998.* Working Paper n°8467, NBER.

—— —— (2003). 'Income Inequality in the United States, 1913–1998', *Quarterly Journal of Economics,* 118: 1–39.

Poterba, J. (2000). 'The Estate Tax and After-Tax Investment Returns', in J. Slemrod (ed.) *Does Atlas Shrug? The Economic Consequences of Taxing the Rich.* Cambridge: Cambridge University Press.

Saez, E. (2004). 'Reported Incomes and Marginal Tax Rates, 1960–2000: Evidence and Policy Implications', in J. Poterba (ed.) *Tax Policy and the Economy,* vol. 18. Cambridge, MA: MIT Press.

Slemrod, J. (1996). 'High Income Families and the Tax Changes of the 1980s: the Anatomy of Behavioural Response', in M. Feldstein and J. Poterba (eds.) *Empirical Foundations of Household Taxation.* Chicago: University of Chicago Press.

Slemrod, J. and Bakija, J. (2000). 'Does Growing Inequality Reduce Tax Progressivity? Should it?' Working Paper No. 7576, NBER.

US Bureau of Old-Age (1952). *Handbook of Old-Age and Survivors Insurance Statistics, 1949,* Washington, DC: US Bureau of Old-Age.

US Department of Commerce, Bureau of Census (1975). *Historical Statistics of the United States: Colonial Times to 1970.* Washington, DC: US Department of Commerce, Bureau of Census.

US Department of Commerce, Bureau of Economic Analysis (2000). *National Income and Product Accounts of the United States, 1929–97.* Washington DC: US Department of Commerce, Bureau of Economic Analysis. Available at: www.bea.doc.gov/bea/dn/nipaweb/

US Government Printing Office (2004). *Economic Report of the President.* Washington, DC: US Government Printing Office.

US Office of the Commissioner of Internal Revenue (1899–1916). *Annual Report of the Commissioner of Internal Revenue*, annual. Washington, DC: US Office of the Commissioner of Internal Revenue.

US Treasury Department, Internal Revenue Service (1916–2002*a*). *Statistics of Income: Individual Income Tax Returns*, annual. Washington, DC: US Treasury Department, Internal Revenue Service.

US Treasury Department, Internal Revenue Service (1916–2002*b*). *Statistics of Income: Corporate Income Tax Returns*, annual. Washington, DC: US Treasury Department, Internal Revenue Service.

Williamson, J. and Lindert, P. (1980). *American Inequality—A Macroeconomic History.* New York: Academic Press.

6

The Evolution of High Incomes in Canada, 1920–2000[1]

E. Saez and M. R. Veall

6.1 INTRODUCTION

The evolution of income inequality during the process of development has attracted enormous attention in the economics literature as well as in the political sphere. Understanding the relative roles of 'natural' economic progress such as technological change versus policy interventions such as taxation, redistribution, and regulation in shaping the distribution of income requires analysing long-term series on inequality. Income tax statistics are the only source of income distribution data available on a regular annual basis for extended periods of time, and are still the best source to study upper income groups. Recent studies, gathered in this volume, have used income tax statistics to construct inequality time series for various countries over the course of the twentieth century. All these studies have found dramatic declines in the top income shares in the first part of the century but the pattern has been different in the last two or three decades: an almost complete recovery in the United States, some recovery in the United Kingdom and no recovery at all in France. This divergence casts doubt on pure technological explanations, although other explanations are still tentative.

These 'high income' studies raise three important issues. First and most important, do tax statistics reveal real changes in income concentration rather than changes in tax reporting behaviour following tax changes? Many US

[1] This chapter is a longer version of 'The Evolution of High Incomes in Northern America: Lessons from Canadian Evidence' (Saez and Veall 2005). We thank Tony Atkinson, Tim Besley, David Card, Deb Fretz, Thomas Lemieux, Bruce Meyer, Thomas Piketty, and numerous seminar participants for helpful discussions and comments. We also thank Claude Bilodeau, Eric Olson, and Hélène Roberge of Statistics Canada for their assistance with computations from the Longitudinal Administrative Database; Emmanuel Manolikakis of Statistics Canada for additional national accounting data; Josée Begin, Gioia Campagna, Kevin Kennedy, and Ron Naylor of the Canada Customs and Revenue Agency for additional taxation data; and Simo Goshev, Alan Macnaughton, Mohammad Rahaman, Matthew Stewart, and the Canadian Tax Foundation library for assistance and expertise. Financial support from the Sloan Foundation, NSF Grant SES-0134946, and from the Social Sciences and Humanities Research Council of Canada to the SEDAP programme is gratefully acknowledged.

studies have shown, for example, that tax induced income shifting between the individual and corporate tax base can have dramatic effects on reported individual incomes (see, e.g., Gordon and Slemrod 2000 and Saez 2004). Second, an increase in cross-sectional income concentration over time, as in the United States and the United Kingdom in recent years, has very different welfare consequences depending on whether or not it is associated with increases in income mobility, and none of the previous studies has analyzed the mobility question for high income earners. Finally, there has been a substantial rise in married women's labour force participation in recent decades. To what extent is the increase in US top incomes (which must be calculated at a family level for the United States as the US has family based income taxation) due to increases in spousal income correlation rather than increased individual income concentration?

This study sheds new light on these three issues by using Canadian income tax statistics beginning in 1920 (the first year such statistics were produced) to estimate homogeneous series of income shares and income composition for various upper income groups within the top decile. Our series are based on individual income because personal income taxes in Canada are based on individual income (not on family income as in the United States). For more recent years, we use a micro-data set of a kind not available for the United States—a large panel covering 20% of all Canadian individual tax returns but also linked by family—to analyze wage income concentration, mobility within top income groups, and the differences between the patterns of individual and family income concentration.

Our estimated top shares series show that, similar to the French, British, and American experiences, top income shares in Canada fell sharply during the Second World War with no recovery during the next three decades. Over the last 20 years, top income shares in Canada have increased dramatically, almost as much as in the United States. This change has remained largely unnoticed because it is concentrated within the top percentile of the Canadian income distribution and thus can only be detected with tax return data covering very high incomes. As in the United States, the increase is largely due to a surge in top wages and salaries. As a result, the composition of income in the top income groups has also shifted in Canada since the Second World War: many more high income individuals derive their principal income from employment instead of as a return to capital.

The recent surge in Canadian top income shares does not seem to be mainly the consequence of tax induced changes in behaviour, including tax reporting behaviour. The Canadian reduction in marginal tax rates was much more modest than in the United States and did not induce shifting between the corporate and personal income tax base. Moreover, much of the Canadian surge occurred when there were no major tax changes. There is evidence (including a formal regression analysis we present) that the surge in Canadian top incomes has a US association, perhaps because many high income Canadians have the option to leave to work in the United States. If this brain drain threat explanation (or some other US related explanation) is correct, this would imply that the surge in top reported incomes in the United States has not just been a tax induced change in tax reporting behaviour. Otherwise it is difficult to reconcile the association between US and Canadian top incomes.[2]

Longitudinal micro-data show that income mobility for high income earners in Canada has been stable or has even decreased slightly since 1982. Similarly, top income shares based on three-or five-year averages display the same surge as those based on single year income. This suggests that the recent increase in cross-sectional income concentration is associated with a large increase in the concentration of lifetime resources and welfare. Using the family linkages in the Canadian micro-data, we also show that the increase in income concentration is identical at the family and individual levels.

To the best of our knowledge, this is the first time that Canadian income tax statistics have been exploited to construct long-term series on inequality in Canada. Blackburn and Bloom (1993) summarize a number of studies that examine both individual and family income inequality in Canada in the post-war period. The view that emerges from their summary is that changes in inequality from the late 1940s to the 1980s were modest. Heisz et al. (2001) summarize more recent Canadian inequality research which largely finds that Canadian earnings inequality has increased since 1980 but by much less than in the United States. Most of the studies discussed in these papers are based on survey data and none examine the war/pre-war period or focus on top shares.

The chapter is organized as follows. Section 6.2 describes our data sources and outlines our estimation methods. In Section 6.3, we present and analyse the trends in top income shares and their composition. Section 6.4 focuses on the recent increase in top income shares. Section 6.5 discusses the role of taxation. Finally, Section 6.6 offers a brief conclusion. All series and complete technical details of our methodology are gathered in the appendices.

6.2 DATA AND METHODOLOGY

Our estimates are from personal income tax return statistics compiled annually by the Canadian federal taxation authorities since 1920. Before the Second World War, because of high exemptions, only about 2% to 8% of individuals had to file tax returns and therefore, by necessity, we must restrict our analysis to the top 5% of the income distribution (denoted as P95–100).[3] Beginning with the Second World War we can extend our analysis to the top decile (P90–100). We also

[2] The question of whether the surge in top US incomes is due to supply side effects following tax cuts or to non-tax related effects is still debated (see Saez 2004 for a recent survey). The Canadian evidence could be consistent with either explanation of the US surge.

[3] All taxpayers with income above the exemption threshold are required to file a return. In the years when fewer than 5% of individuals file we interpolate from single persons to married couples. More than 5% of singles always file because of lower exemptions for singles. (See Appendix 6B for details of this procedure and its validation.)

construct series for a number of finer fractiles, e.g., P90–95, P95–99, P99–100 (the top 1%), P99.5–100 (the top 0.5%), P99.9–100 (the top 0.1%) and P99.99 (the top 0.01%). Each fractile is defined relative to the total number of adults (aged 20 and above) from the Canadian census (not the number of tax returns filed). Column (1) in Table 6A.1 reports the number of adult individuals in Canada from 1920 to 2000. The adult population has increased from about 5 million in 1920 to almost 23 million in 2000. In 2000, for example, there were 22.8 million adults and thus the top decile is defined as the top 2.28 million income earners, the top percentile as the top 228,000 income earners, etc. Column (2) in Table 6A.1 reports the actual number of returns filed. Table 6.1 gives thresholds and average incomes for a selection of fractiles for Canada in 2000.

We define income as gross market income before all deductions and including all income items reported on personal tax returns: salaries and wages, private pension income, self-employment and small business net income, partnership and fiduciary income, dividends, interest, other investment income, and other smaller income items. Realized capital gains are not an annual flow of income (in general, capital gains are realized infrequently in a lumpy way) and form a very volatile component of income with large aggregate variations from year to year depending on stock price variations. Moreover before 1972, capital gains were not taxable and hence not reported on tax returns. Therefore, we focus mainly on series excluding capital gains.[4] Our income definition is before personal income taxes and personal payroll taxes but after employers' payroll taxes and corporate income taxes. We exclude from our income definition all transfers such as unemployment insurance, welfare benefits, public retirement benefits, etc.

Table 6.1 Thresholds and average incomes in top groups within the top decile in 2000

Thresholds (1)	Income level (2)	Fractiles (3)	Number of tax units (4)	Average income (5)
		Full Population	22,807,585	$24,859
P90	$59,232	P90–95	1,140,379	$66,310
P95	$75,670	P95–99	912,303	$95,982
P99	$145,774	P99–99.5	114,038	$171,728
P99.5	$210,150	P99.5–99.9	91,230	$303,035
P99.9	$530,311	P99.9–99.99	20,527	$923,385
P99.99	$2,396,050	P99.99–100	2,281	$4,695,923

Notes: Computations based on income tax return statistics (see Appendix Section 6A). Income defined as annual gross income excluding capital gains and before individual taxes. Amounts are expressed in 2000 Canadian dollars. US$1 = CA$ 1.5.

Source: Table A and Table B3, row 2000.

[4] In the appendix, in order to assess the sensitivity of our results to the treatment of capital gains, for the period 1972–2000, we compute for each fractile (defined by ranking incomes excluding capital gains) the percentage of additional income reported in the form of realized capital gains. We also recompute our top income shares including realized capital gains in income (both for the ranking and the levels and shares computations). For the period 1972–2000, series with and without capital gains display about the same general pattern. See in particular Figure 6A.1.

Our principal data consist of tables of the number of tax returns, the amounts reported, and the income composition (since 1946) for a large number of income brackets. As the top tail of the income distribution is very well approximated by Pareto distributions, we can use simple parametric interpolation methods (as described earlier in Appendix 5C) to estimate the thresholds and average income levels for each fractile. For the years when micro-data are available, we check that the errors introduced by the interpolation method are negligible.

We then estimate shares of income by dividing the income amounts accruing to each fractile by 80% of Personal Income not including transfers from the National Accounts.[5,6] The total income and average income (per adult) series are reported in Columns (4) and (5) of Table 6A.1. These series are reported in real (2000) Canadian dollars. Our CPI deflator used to convert current incomes to real incomes is reported in Column (6).[7] The average income series along with the CPI deflator is plotted in Figure 6.1. Average real income per adult has increased by a factor of five from 1920 to 2000.[8] The Great Depression decreased real income by about one-third. The Second World War was a period of very high

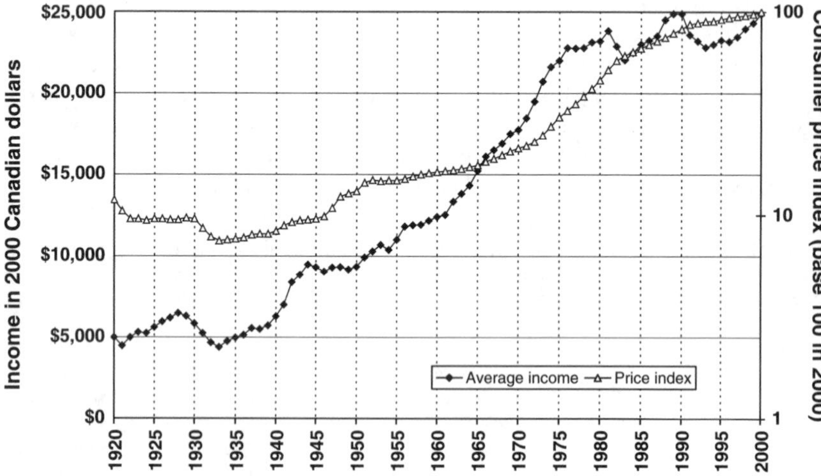

Figure 6.1 Average real income and consumer price index in Canada, 1920–2000

Source: Table A, Columns Average income (in real 2000 Canadian dollars) and CPI (base 100 in 2000).

[5] Using tax returns to compute the level of top incomes and national accounts to compute the total income denominator dates from the famous Kuznets (1953) study on American inequality.

[6] Personal Income is higher than total income from tax returns because it includes non-taxable items such as imputed rent, imputed interest, etc. In recent years in which virtually all adults with income file tax returns, total income from tax returns has always been very close to 80% of Personal Income net of transfers.

[7] Columns (7) and (8) report the average net tax (including both federal and provincial income taxes) and the average realized capital gain per adult.

[8] Average income during the same period in the United States has multiplied by a factor of four. Population in the United States has also grown more slowly.

growth in income. Average income grew steadily from 1950 to 1976. Since then, average income has increased very little with sharp downturns from 1981 to 1983 and from 1990 to 1993.

After analysing the top share data, we turn to the composition of income, concentrating on the period since 1946 when composition data were first published. Using this published information and a simple linear interpolation method, we decompose the amount of income for each fractile into six components: salaries and wages, professional income, business income, dividends, interest income, and other investment income.

We produce top wage share series for the period 1972 to 2000, using composition tables for 1972 to 1981[9] and longitudinal micro-files of tax returns (covering 20% of the total tax-filing population, over 4 million records in 2000) available beginning in 1982. In this case, fractiles are defined relative to the total number of individuals with positive wages. (Throughout this paper, 'wages' or 'wage income' includes salaries or any other type of employment earnings, including exercised stock options.) We also link married couples and re-compute top wage income shares at the family level. In that case, each fractile is defined relative to the total number of families (single adults and couples) with positive wage income. We also use the longitudinal structure of the micro-data to study income mobility. We compute mobility matrices for all our income groups for one, two, and three year lags and top income shares using real income averaged over three and five years instead of single year income.[10]

6.3 TOP INCOME SHARES

Trends

The basic series of top income shares are presented in Table 6B.1. Figure 6.2, Panel A displays the income share of the top 5% (P95–100) from 1920 to 2000 in Canada. The top 5% share displays sharp fluctuations up to the end of the Second World War (between 30% and 40% of total income) and is much more stable afterwards (around 25%). Before the Second World War, the fluctuations are strikingly counter-cyclical. The top share increases sharply during each downturn episode of the inter-war period: the sharp depression of 1920–21, the Great Depression from 1930 to 1933, and the pre-Second World War downturn of 1937–38. The top 5% share tends to decrease during the recoveries from the downturns (1921–23, 1933–5, and the Second World War), although the pattern is less pronounced than for the downturns. The top 5% share declines drastically during the Second

[9] Top wage shares for 1972–81 are estimated using the number of tax returns reporting wages and the amount of wages reported by income brackets. See Appendix 6D.

[10] In this case, our adult population and denominator are defined as the average across the relevant years.

World War years from almost 40% in 1938 to less than 25% in 1945.[11] This drastic reduction implies that the average income in the top 5% dropped from eight times the average income before the Second World War to just five times the average income in 1945. After the Second World War, the top 5% share declines very slowly (with very small fluctuations) from 25% to 22% by the mid-1980s. However, in the last 20 years, the top share has gone up substantially to about 29% in 2000, but is still substantially below its level just before the Second World War.

Therefore, the Canadian evidence suggests that the twentieth-century decline in inequality took place in a very specific and brief time interval, namely the Second World War years. This evidence is very much in line with the French (Piketty, Chapter 3 in this volume), and American (Piketty and Saez, Chapter 5 in this volume), findings. Moreover, the pattern of the sharp upturns and downturns in the pre-war period suggests that the business cycle was the main driving factor in these fluctuations. As a result, the traditional Kuznets inverted U-curve theory of inequality does not fit well with the Canadian experience over the century. The smooth increase in the top 5% share over the last 20 years seems to fit better with the skilled-biased technology explanations put forward in the case of the United States (see the survey by Acemoglu 2002). However, even for this later period, we will present further evidence that tends to contradict the technology explanation.

In order to understand the overall pattern of top income shares, it is useful to decompose the top decile into three groups, P90–95, P95–99, and the top percentile P99–100. The share of income accruing to these three groups is depicted in Figure 6.2, Panel B.. Three important facts should be noted. First, the counter-cyclical pattern before the Second World War appears to be stronger for P95–99 than for the top percentile. Second, the drop during the Second World War is much more substantial for the top percentile (from 18% in 1939 to 10% in 1945) than for the groups P90–95 and P95–99. Third, the upturn during the last two decades is concentrated in the top percentile (which increased from about 7.5% in the late 1970s to 13.5% in 2000). It is striking to note that the P90–95 share did not increase at all from the late 1970s and even the P95–99 share increased by less than one percentage point during the same period.

Examination of the very top groups (P99.9–100 and P99.99–100) in Figure 6.3 reinforces these three empirical findings. The higher the group, the sharper is the decline during the Second World War, and the sharper the recovery since the late 1970s. The very top group shares experience a drop of more than 50% from 1938 to 1945. Moreover, and in contrast to lower groups, the drop continues after the Second World War until the mid-1970s. As a result, the average individual in the top 0.01% had an income more than 200 times the average income in the adult population in 1920. In 1972, that individual had an income only 40 times higher than average. However, since the late 1970s, the very top groups have almost recovered their pre-Second World War levels. The top 0.01% share has been multiplied by almost five from 1972 to 2000. In 2000, average income in the

[11] In the United States, the fall in top income shares does not start before 1941, providing further evidence that the fall is closely related to the war.

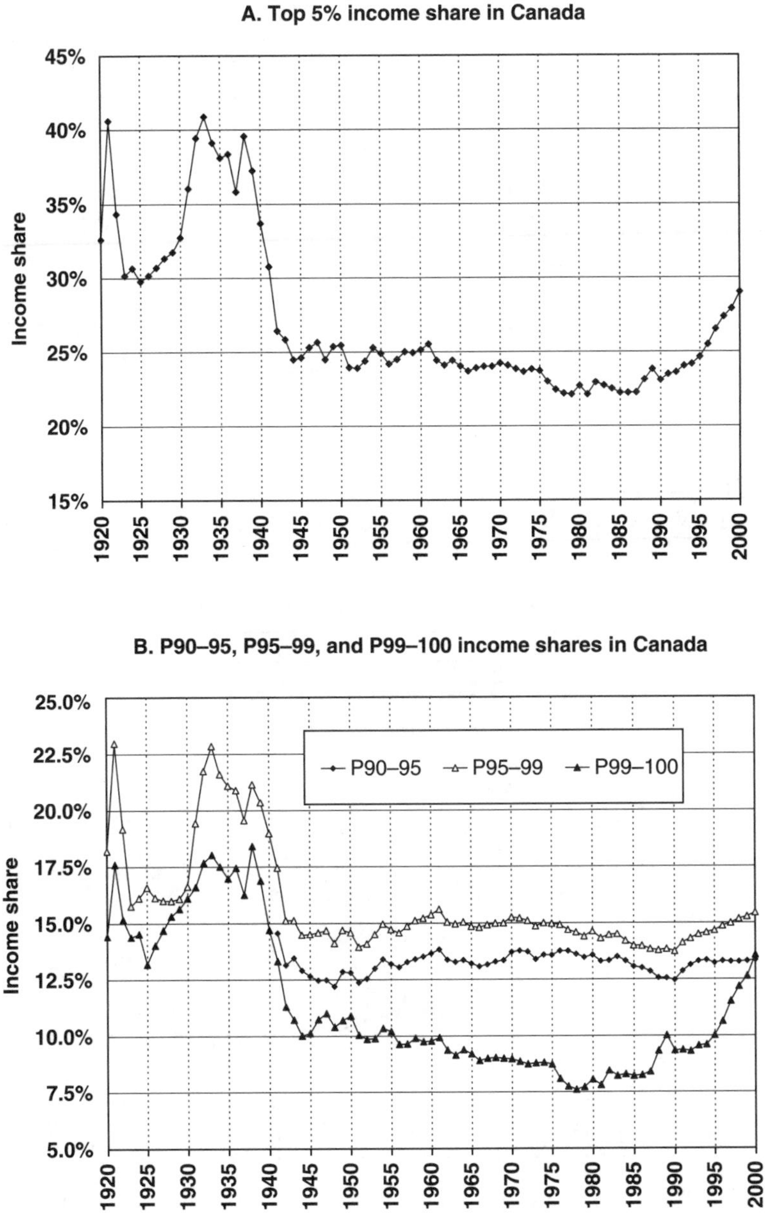

Figure 6.2 Top income shares in Canada, 1920–2000

Source: Table 6B.1, columns, P95–100, P90–95, P95–99, and P99–100.

top 0.01% is about 190 times the average income. We note, however, that this surge in top incomes is somewhat smaller than comparable estimates for the United States from Piketty and Saez (Chapter 5) also included in Figure 6.3. The fact that the rise in top shares is concentrated in the very top groups within

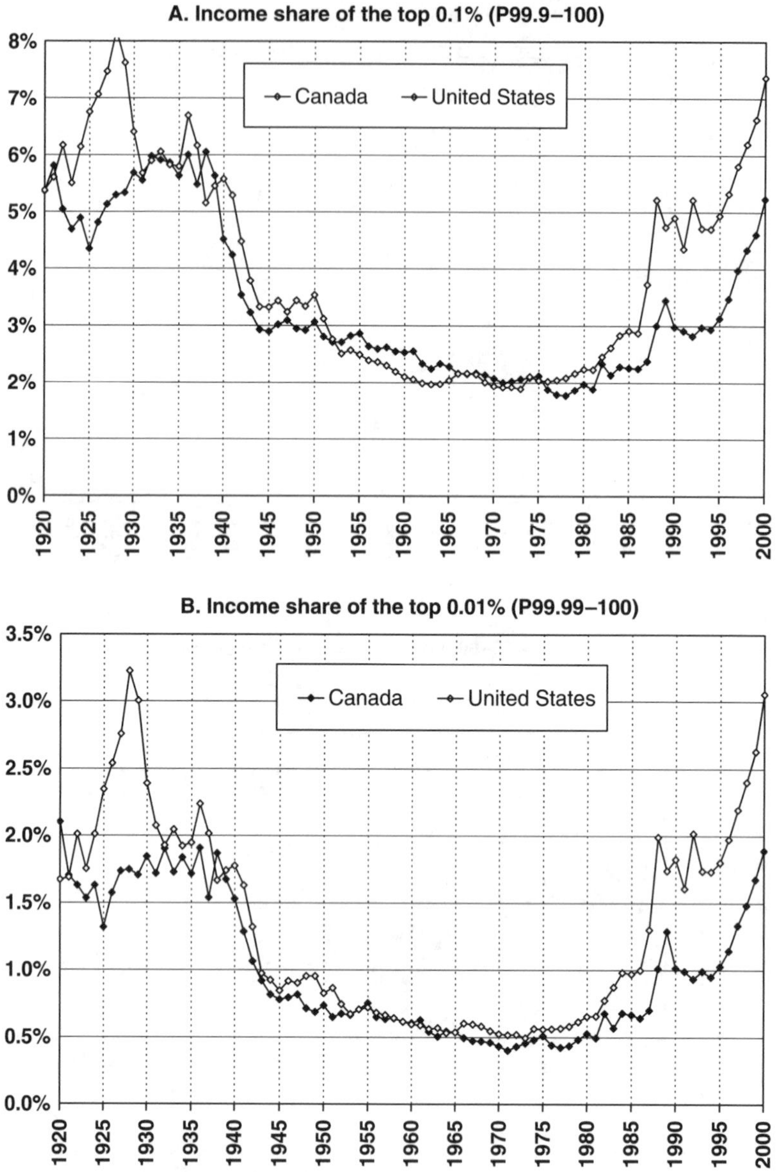

Figure 6.3 The income shares of the top income groups in Canada and US, 1920–2000

Source: Table 6B.1, this volume, and columns P99.9–100 and P99.99–100.United States, Piketty and Saez (chapter 5, this volume).

the top percentile explains why this surge in inequality at the top appears to have gone unnoticed in the literature on inequality in Canada. Tax returns are the only data that allow the analysis of groups within the top percentile. This surge in top incomes concentrated within the top groups, as opposed to gains spread more evenly across skilled workers, casts doubt on the skill-biased technology explanation. We will come back to this issue when we focus our analysis on the pattern of top employment income shares in the last two decades. We can also note that there is a short-term spike in top shares in 1989, and that this spike is bigger for the very top groups. We believe that this is evidence of a (transitory) response to the marginal tax rate flattening consistent with the findings of Sillamaa and Veall (2001). We will discuss in more detail the important issue of the effects of taxation on reported top incomes in Section 6.5. Finally, the very top groups do not display the same counter-cyclical behaviour as other high income groups. The top 0.01% share actually declined during the 1920–21 downturn and did not increase during the Great Depression.

The remainder of the chapter will be aimed at understanding the three key facts: the counter-cyclical pattern of top shares (except the very top share) in the pre-war period, the sharp fall of top shares during the Second World War (with the most dramatic decline at the very top) with no recovery after the war, and the surge in top income shares over the last 20 years (characterized by an extreme concentration at the top). In order to make progress in our understanding, we now turn to the analysis of the composition of incomes reported by the top groups.

The Composition of Top Incomes

Canada started publishing detailed information on the composition of incomes by income brackets in 1946. In the early period 1920 to 1945, only tables showing the distribution of occupations for all tax returns were published. Tax returns were classified according to the main source of income reported, such as employment income (employees), professional income (professionals), capital income (financial), and business income (merchants, manufacturers, etc.) These published tables display the number of tax returns in each occupation, and the total amount of taxes paid by each of these groups. The amount of taxes paid can be used to estimate roughly the average income in each category. Therefore, these tables are useful to cast light on the composition of incomes before the Second World War. Some of this evidence is summarized in Table 6C.1. Important findings emerge from this table.

First, at least two-thirds of tax filers are classified as employees during the interwar period. Therefore, it seems likely that group P95–99 is primarily composed of highly compensated employees during the pre-war period. This explains why the P95–99 share is so clearly counter-cyclical. The sharp downturns of the pre-war period were associated with sharp deflations (see Figure 6.1). Assuming wages are in general nominally rigid in the short-run, those who are able to keep their jobs during the recession experience a relative gain.[12] As we move up the income distribution, wage earners are replaced by businessmen and rentiers whose incomes are much more pro-cyclical. This explains why the very

[12] We provide further evidence on this point in the following section.

top shares within the top 1% do not display the same counter-cyclical pattern as the P95–99 share.

Second, the occupation tables also suggest that the very top of the income distribution in the pre-war period was formed of rentiers, as in the United States and France. In order to prevent personal income tax evasion through the accumulation of wealth within corporations (which were taxed at a flat rate substantially lower than the top personal income tax rate) and to provide some relief from double taxation, Canada issued a ruling creating Personal Corporations (see McGregor 1960) in 1925. Personal Corporations are defined as corporations controlled by a single individual or family and deriving at least a quarter of their profits from passive investments. Therefore personal corporations are clearly entities created by passive investors and not by owners-managers of businesses. Starting in tax year 1925, Personal Corporations were taxed directly at the personal level (as sub-chapter S corporations in the United States today). The occupation tables show that taxpayers classified as personal corporations had very large tax liabilities and hence very large incomes, and thus formed a substantial part of the top 0.01% group. Self-employed professionals and entrepreneurs form an intermediate category between the highly compensated employees and those with personal corporations.

Beginning in the tax year 1942, occupation tables were published by income brackets. Table 6C.2 reports the composition of occupations (employees, entrepreneurs, and rentiers) for each fractile. It shows that the fraction of employees is indeed very high for groups below the top percentile and that rentiers formed the majority at the very top. However, the important fact to note is that the fraction of employees remains substantial, even within the very top fractiles, explaining why even the top shares did not follow the downturns of the pre-war period. This is in contrast with the American and French experiences where the fraction of employees was very small at the top. In those two countries, the share of capital income was much more important at the very top and thus the very top income share dropped during the pre-war downturns.

Our Canadian top share series display a sharp drop during the Second World War, and that drop is larger for the very top groups. This fall can be in part explained by the fiscal shock in the corporate sector. As part of financing the war, Canada increased substantially taxes on corporations.[13] Moreover, corporations reduced their payout ratios during the war because of the high demand for investment, and perhaps also to avoid the personal income tax which imposed extremely high marginal tax rates (in excess of 90%) on the highest incomes. This is illustrated in Figure 6.4. Panel A displays the real aggregate value of profits before and after taxes, along with dividend distributions of Canadian corporations from the National Accounts for the period 1926 (the first year the data are available) to 1955. The figure shows that, in spite of a twofold increase in

[13] While during the war the corporation income tax itself increased modestly from 15% to 18%, an additional tax was introduced of the greater of 22% of total profits and 100% (part refundable after the war) of profit increases.

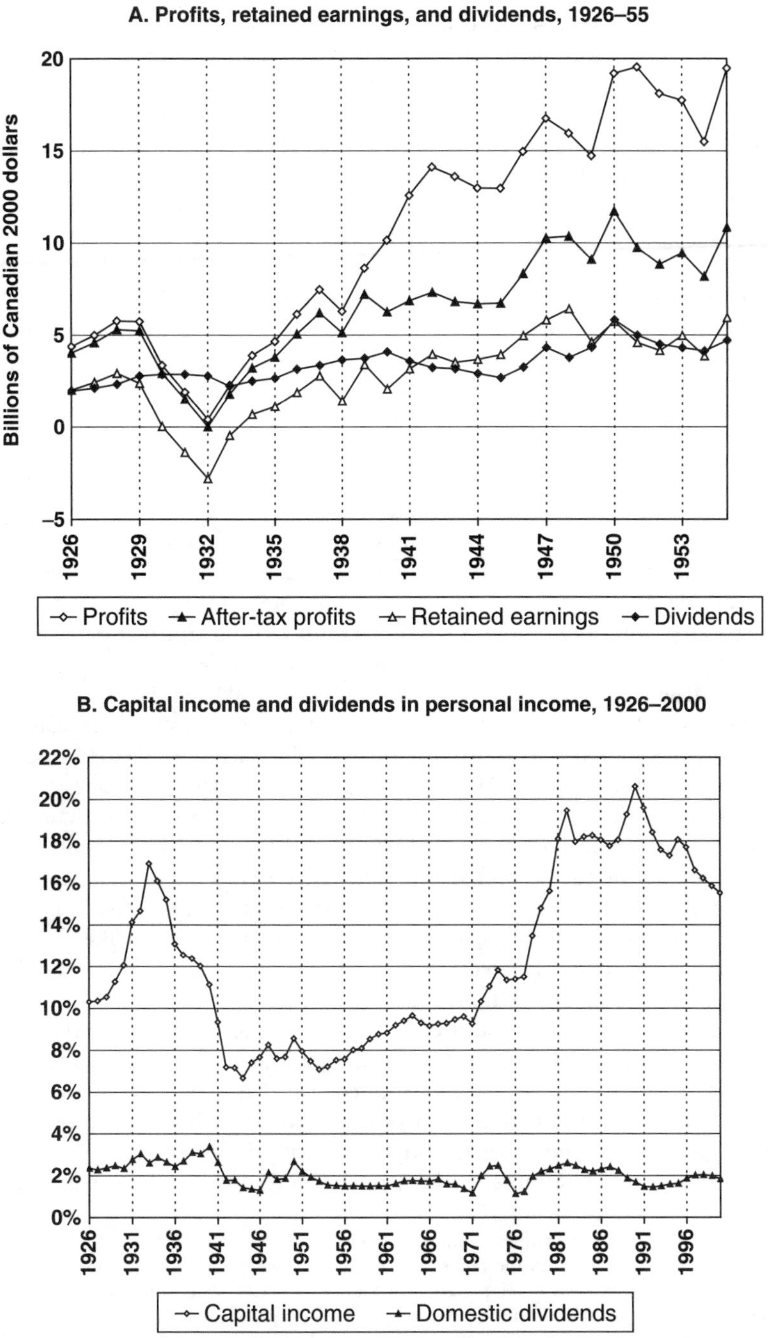

Figure 6.4 Capital income in the corporate and the personal sector in Canada, 1926–2000

Source: Authors' computations based on National Income and Expenditure Accounts.

profits from 1938 to 1945, real dividend payments actually decreased slightly. This explains why top income rentiers experienced a sharp drop relative to the fast growing average adult income during the the Second World War episode (see column 5 in Table 6A.1). Panel B in Figure 6.4 displays the share of total capital income (excluding capital gains), and the share of dividends from Canadian corporations in total personal income in the Canadian economy from 1926 to 2000. Consistent with the evidence in Panel A, the share of domestic dividends in personal income falls by more than 60% from 1938 to 1945. Moreover, the share of total capital income (including interest income and distributions from Canadian owned foreign stock) falls from over 12% in 1938 to about 6–7% at the end of the war. These figures show clearly that capital income accruing to individuals was sharply reduced during the war and this might explain why top incomes fell so much in relative terms.

However, the shares of income groups P90–95 and P95–99 also fell during the Second World War. The evidence from occupational tables in the pre-war period and from 1946 on (see below) shows that these groups are composed largely of employees. Therefore, it seems salaries of highly compensated employees must have fallen relative to average earnings in the economy. Indirect evidence confirms those results. Since 1915 for the Canadian manufacturing sector, data are available on the number and total employment income of salary earners (supervisory and office employees with a compensation contract determined at the annual level) and non-salaried employees (workers with a compensation contract determined either at the hourly, daily, or weekly level).

Figure 6.5 displays the ratio of the average compensation of salaried to non-salaried employees (left Y-axis), along with the fraction of salaried employees (right Y-axis) from 1915 to 1948. This figure shows that salary earners gained significantly relative to non-salaried employees in terms of employment and compensation during the downturns of 1920–21 and the Great Depression but lost significantly during the Second World War. These results are consistent with our other findings for this period and particularly support the hypothesis that a compression in wage income inequality took place in Canada during the war years.[14]

From 1946 on, detailed tables on the composition of income were published annually. Therefore, for each fractile within the top decile, we were able to construct series on the composition of incomes. These series are presented in Table 6C.3. Figure 6.6 shows the composition of income for each fractile in 1946 (Panel A) and 2000 (Panel B). As expected, Panel A shows the share of wage income is a declining function of income and that the share of capital income (dividends, interest, and other investment income) is an increasing function of income. The share of entrepreneurial income (professional and business income)

[14] The most direct explanation (Dominion Bureau of Statistics 1948) was that war labour regulations set strict bounds on the raises that corporations were able to give to their high salary employees. For example, raises for employees with salaries above CA$7,500 (corresponding roughly to percentile P99.5) required direct approval of the Minister (Department of National Revenue 1945). Similar evidence of wage compression has been found for the United States (Goldin and Margo 1992; Goldin and Katz 1999; and Piketty and Saez Chapter 5 in this volume).

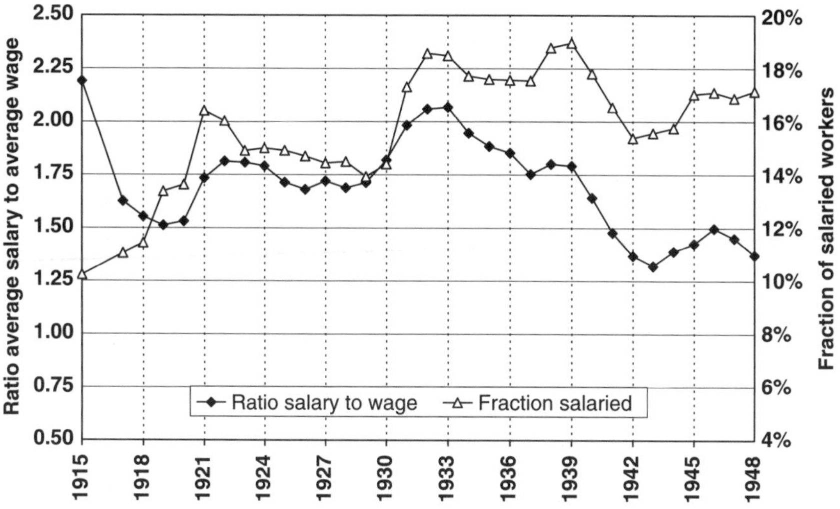

Figure 6.5 Salary vs. wage earners in manufacturing sector in Canada, 1915–48

Source: Series D280–287 in Urquhart and Buckley (1965) and The Canada Yearbook, various years.

Note: Number of wage workers for year 1925–30 has been reduced by 5% because of a change in the count of seasonal workers for these years.

presents an inverted U-shape, and peaks for fractile P99.5–99.9. Thus, individuals in fractiles P90–95 and P95–99 rely mostly on labour income (capital income is less than 25% for these groups) while individuals in the top percentile derive most of their income in the form of passive capital income (mostly dividend and estate income). However, as was found in the occupation tables for 1942, even within the very top groups, wage and salary income remains important. In France and the United States at that time, the share of wages and salaries was much lower at the top than in Canada.

Panel B shows that the income composition pattern has changed significantly from 1946 to 2000. In 2000, the share of wage income has increased for all groups, and this increase is larger at the very top. Entrepreneurial income (professional and business income) has fallen sharply, especially at the top. The share of capital income (dividends, interest, and other capital income, excluding capital gains) has slightly increased below the top 0.5% and fallen significantly for the very top groups. Therefore, both the self-employed or small business owners in the bottom of the top percentile, and the capital income earners in the very top, have been in large part replaced by highly compensated employees.

Figure 6.7 shows the evolution from 1946 to 2000 of the share of wage income for various fractiles. The wage share for the groups P90–95 and P95–99 has always been large (around 90% and 75% respectively). However, the wage share within the very top groups has steadily increased over the period. For example, the wage share in the top 0.1% has doubled from 34% to 72% over the period. Interestingly, there has been a reversal in the level of shares between the groups within the

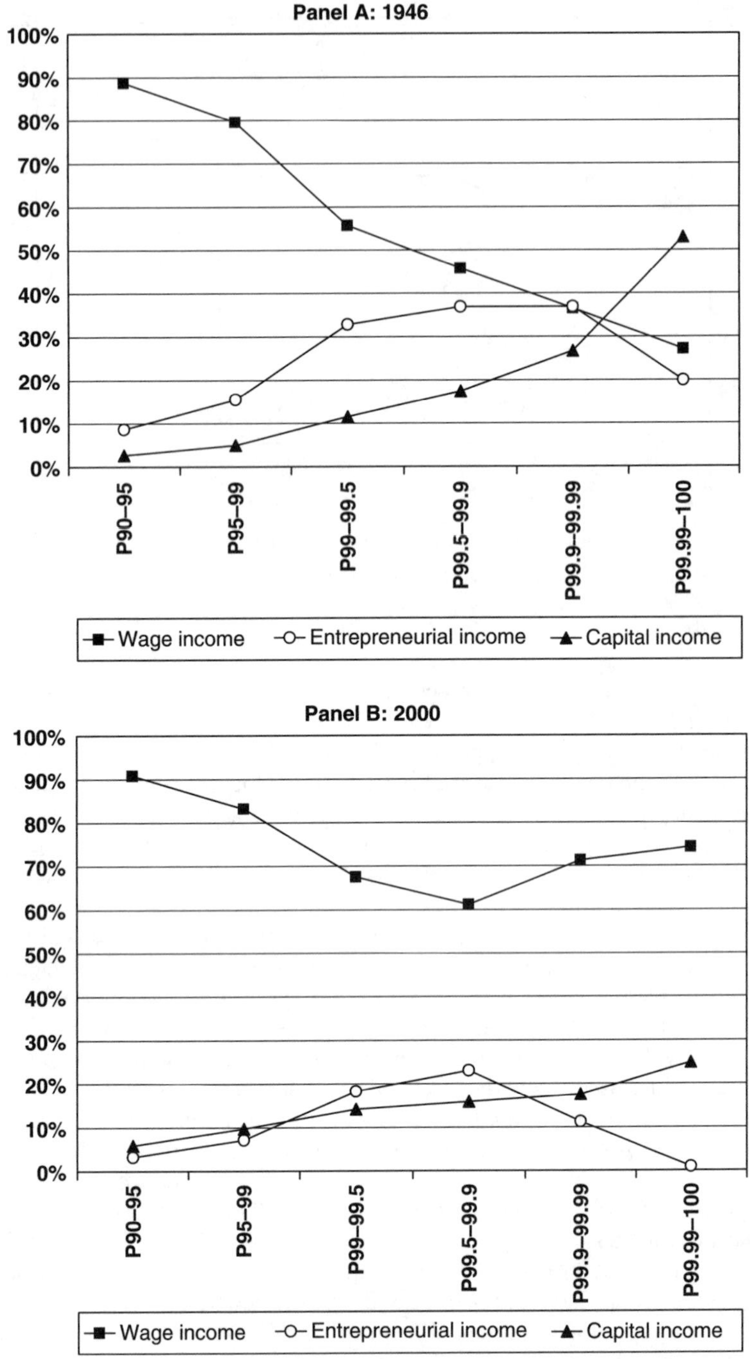

Figure 6.6 Income composition of top groups within the top decile in Canada, 1946 and 2000

Notes: Capital income does not include capital gains.

Source: Table 6C.3, rows 1946 and 2000.

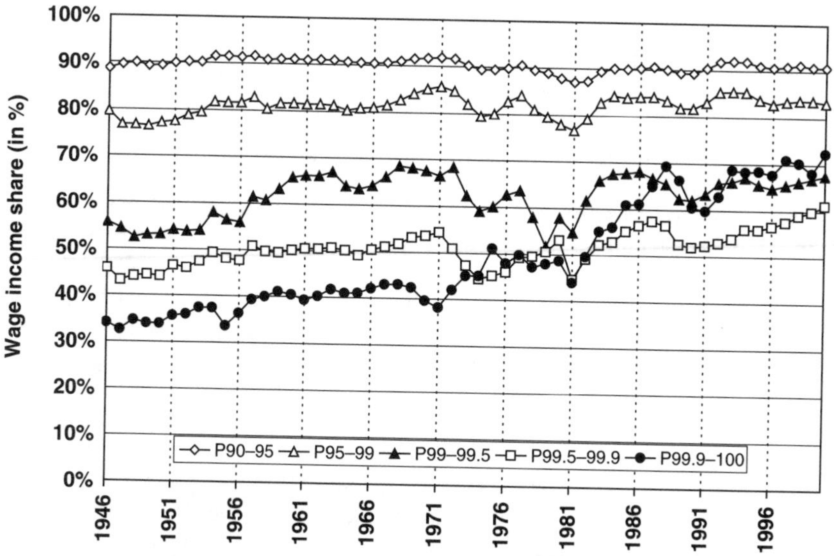

Figure 6.7 The share of wage income in upper income groups in Canada, 1946–2000

Source: Table 6C.3, cols. P90–95, P95–99, P99–99.5, P99.5–99.9, and P99.9–100.

top percentile. In 1946, the share of wages was lowest at the top while in 2000, the share of wages (within the top percentile) is higher for the top 0.1% group than for groups P99–99.5 and P99.5–99.9. In 2000, more than two-thirds of incomes reported by the top 0.01% individuals is composed of wages and salaries, showing that the working rich have become the main group at the very top and have to a large extent displaced individuals with large capital incomes.

Finally, two facts show that the decline of the share of capital income for the top 0.5% reflects a fall in large capital holdings (relative to the average) rather than a decline in the aggregate capital income in the economy. First, the share of capital income actually increases for the groups P90–95, P95–99, and P99–99.5, showing that top capital income earners have indeed lost relative to the other groups. Second, Panel B of Figure 6.4 shows clearly that the share of capital income and dividends in personal income from the National Accounts is not lower in 2000 than it was in the pre-war period. We saw earlier that top income shares have increased dramatically over the last 20 years in Canada, and that this increase was concentrated within the top 1%. At the same time, we have shown that the share of wages has also increased dramatically for groups within the top 1%. Therefore, there is a strong presumption that the recent upturn in top shares is the consequence of an unprecedented surge in the pay of the top compensated employees. In order to cast direct light on this issue, we analyse in the following section the top of the wage income distribution since 1972.

6.4 UNDERSTANDING THE SURGE IN TOP INCOMES IN RECENT DECADES

The Recent Surge in Top Wages and Salaries

The microfiles of tax returns, available from 1982, allow a detailed analysis of the wage income distribution where wage income is taken as the employment income of both wage and salary earners. We supplement these with extrapolations based on composition tables published for the years 1972–81 to estimate top wage shares by computing the share of total employment income accruing to various upper groups of the wage income distribution since 1972. Our top groups are now defined relative to the total number of individuals with positive wages. Table 6D.1 reports the total number of wage earners, the total wages reported, and the average wage per wage earner for the period 1972–2000. Table 6D.2 reports top wage income shares series for the same period and Table 6D.3 presents the average wage income and the income threshold for each fractile. We also report in Tables 6D.1, 6D.2, and 6D.3 the same statistics computed at the family level (instead of the individual level) for the period 1982–2000.[15]

Figure 6.8, Panel A displays the share of wages accruing to the P90–95, P95–99, and the top percentile of the wage income distribution. (We begin this figure in 1972 using extrapolations based on composition tables published for the 1972–81 period.) Our top groups are now defined relative to the total number of individuals with positive wage income. It shows that, exactly as with the total income shares, the increase is concentrated within the top percentile. The shares of P90–95 and P95–99 are almost flat while the P99–100 share doubles from around 5% in the late 1970s to over 10% in 2000. This extreme concentration probably explains why this dramatic increase in wage inequality has remained unnoticed in the literature on inequality in Canada. Survey data, on which almost all wage inequality studies in Canada have been based, do not allow analysis of the top percentile because of the top coding of reported earnings and because there are very few individuals in the top income groups. Therefore, this evidence shows that the surge in top wages led to a drastic shift in the composition of top incomes away from capital income and toward labour income, as well as to a dramatic increase in top income shares.

The fact that the rise in top wage shares is so concentrated is a problem for the simple skill-biased technology explanation. It suggests rather that the change in inequality is driven by a change in the compensation practice for highly ranked officers and executives. The comparison with the United States (Chapter 5) is instructive. The United States experienced a similar (both in timing and magnitude) surge in top wage incomes. However, the surge in top wage shares

[15] It is possible to compute those statistics with the microfiles. Families are defined as married couples or single individuals. In that case, the top groups are defined relative to the total number of families (reported in Table 6D.1, column (2)) with positive wages and salaries. The US wage series of Piketty and Saez (Chapter 5) are also defined at the family level.

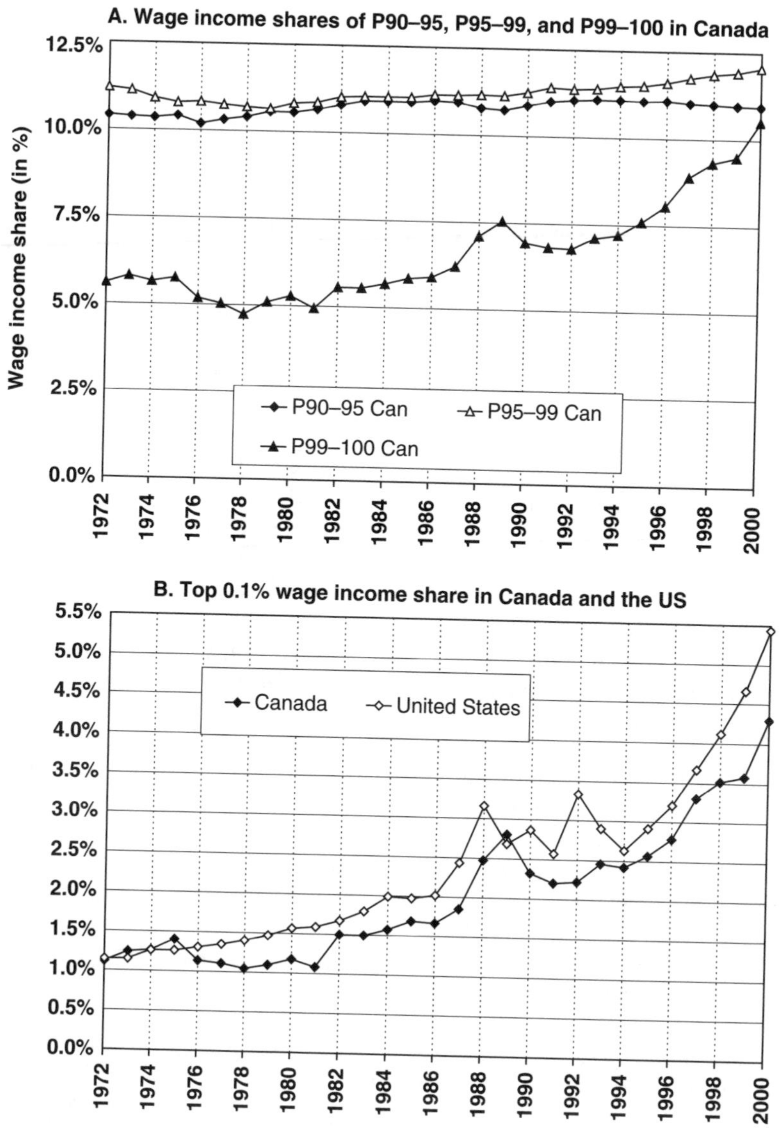

Figure 6.8 The top wage income shares in Canada, 1972–2000

Note: United Sates series are based on family earning while Canadian series are based on individual earnings.
Source: Table 6D.2, Panel A, columns P90–95, P95–99, P99–100, and P99.9–100. United States: Piketty and Saez (this volume).

in the United States started earlier (in the early 1970s), was not as concentrated as in Canada and was significant for the upper middle class P95–99 group as well. As a result, in contrast to the Canadian case, studies using survey data such as the Current Population Survey were able to document to a large extent the surge in high wages (see Katz and Autor 1999; and Acemoglu 2002 for recent surveys of these studies in the United States).[16]

There seem to be two direct explanations for the similar patterns in the United States and Canada. The first explanation relies on the fact that the two economies have experienced very similar technological change and thus we should expect the distributions of earnings in both countries to follow a similar path. This explanation, however, is not very useful, without defining more precisely what is meant by technology. The second explanation for the parallel pattern at the top might be competition for highly skilled executives driven by the surge in executive compensation in the United States. Top salaries have increased enormously over the last three decades in the United States. Moreover, Canadian executives can relatively easily move and find jobs in the United States as part of what is sometimes called the brain drain. Therefore, the only way for Canadian firms to retain their best executives might be to increase their salaries.[17]

The brain drain threat explanation seems more convincing to us than the technology explanation for a number of reasons. First, European countries experienced the same change in technology as did Canada and the United States. However, a number of these countries, such as France (see Chapter 3) have not experienced an increase in inequality at the top of the wage distribution.[18] Second, if the migration threat explanation is true, then groups with higher mobility costs (or smaller benefits from moving) should experience a smaller rise in their compensation. Three pieces of evidence suggest that this is the case.

First, the surge in inequality at the top is more concentrated in Canada than in the United States. The benefits from moving are clearly higher for the very top wage earners (who experienced the greatest increase in compensation in the United States, both in absolute and relative terms). Therefore, a model with fixed costs of moving would suggest that those at the very top in Canada are more likely to move than those in the upper middle class (below the top percentile). As a result, US driven competition should be stronger at the top, producing a more concentrated rise in inequality in Canada than in the United States, as we observed in the data. Finnie (2002) finds that international migration is in fact much more likely among those with high incomes.[19]

[16] Another very important difference between the United States and Canada is the pattern of inequality at the bottom. Low income earners have lost dramatically in the United States relative to Canada, explaining why overall inequality measures such as the Gini coefficient have increased much more in the United States than in Canada (see Blackburn and Bloom 1993; and Wolfson and Murphy 2000).

[17] Of course, this explanation does not help answering the question of why such a surge in top wages took place in the United States in the first place.

[18] British top income shares have increased significantly as well since 1980 (see Chapter 4), although less than in the United States or Canada. We expect higher mobility between the United Kingdom and the United States than between continental Europe and the United States.

[19] This is in contrast to the small and mixed income effects he finds for interprovincial migration (Finnie, 2004) but consistent with the bivariate comparisons in Graph 7 of Finnie (2001) where he reports that for 1996, 0.89% of Canadians with incomes in excess of CA$150,000 migrated internationally, compared to an average for all incomes of 0.12%. See Zhao et al. (2000) for similar evidence.

Second, the surge in top income shares started earlier in the United States than in Canada. Figure 6.8, Panel B displays the top 0.1% wage share for the United States (Chapter 5) and Canada since 1972. The top wage shares were very similar in the United States and Canada in the early 1970s. They started increasing almost ten years earlier in the United States and are slightly higher in the United States than in Canada today. Iqbal (1999) documents the brain-drain and notes that emigration of highly skilled Canadian workers to the United States increased during the 1980s and especially after 1995 when NAFTA (North American Free Trade Agreement) allowed high skilled workers to receive temporary work visa permits much more easily. The brain-drain pressures from the United States therefore correspond closely to the increase in top wage shares in Canada, suggesting that the latter might well have been driven by the former.

Third, the French speaking community in Quebec may be more reluctant to move to the United States because of language and perhaps also because of other cultural differences. Finnie (2002) finds that Quebec Francophones are much less likely to migrate internationally than residents of other provinces and than Quebec anglophones. This is consistent with earlier research (Finnie forthcoming), which finds a similar pattern in interprovincial migration. As a result, we would expect brain-drain pressures to be weaker for Quebec Francophones than for others in Canada. Figure 6.9 displays the top 1% wage share for francophones in Quebec and for Canadians in all other provinces from 1982 to 2000.[20] Figure 6.9 shows indeed that the rise in the top 1% share has been much more modest for francophones in Quebec (from about 4.5% to 6.5%) than for the rest of the provinces (from less than 6% to more than 11%). Complete series for each group within the top decile (reported in Table 6D.4) display similar patterns.[21] Even though top shares start at a higher level in 1982 for Canadians outside Quebec than for francophones in Quebec, the increase in top shares from 1982 to 2000 is larger, even in relative terms, for the former group than for the latter. Interestingly, in contrast to francophones, anglophones in Quebec as a group experience a surge in top wage shares as in the rest of the provinces.[22] Therefore, this evidence is consistent with the brain drain threat explanation and would be more difficult to reconcile with the pure technological change explanation as we would expect technological change to spread very quickly from province to province in Canada.

[20] Francophones are defined as those who complete their income tax returns in French.

[21] Very top incomes have also increased significantly for francophones (although much less than for non-Quebec residents). A model where francophones have a higher fixed cost of moving than anglophones on average would produce such results if the fixed cost (measured in dollars) is independent of income.

[22] Actually, the surge in top wage incomes for anglophones is even larger than for the rest of the provinces. The top 1% share increases from less than 7% to over 14%. However, part of this change is due to the fact that the fraction of anglophones within Quebec shrunk from 14.3% in 1982 to 11.5% in 2000. If lower income anglophones left disproportionately, then we would expect the top shares of anglophones to increase mechanically through a compositional effect.

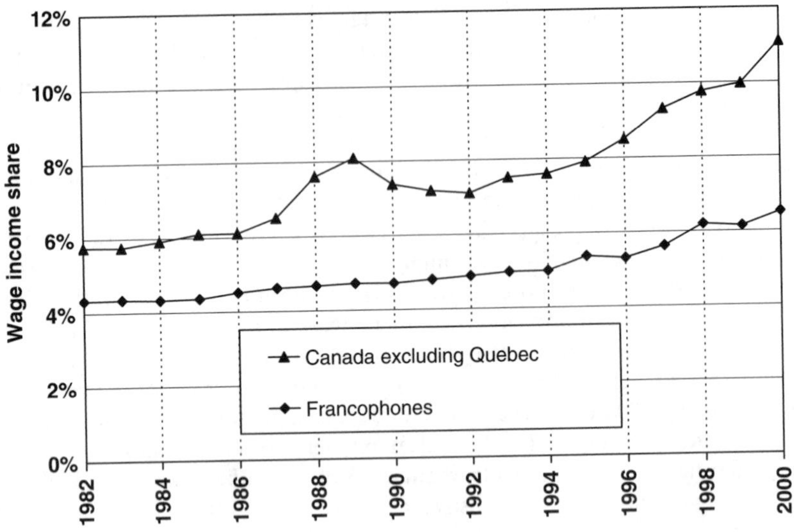

Figure 6.9 The top 1% wage income share of Quebec francophones vs. all filers from the rest of Canada, 1982–2000

Note: Francophones defined as those filing a tax return in French.

Source: Table 6D.4, Panels A and B, Column P99–100.

Family vs. Individual Units

Canadian income taxes are assessed at the individual level whereas US income taxes are based on family income (as US married couples almost always file a joint return).[23] Thus Canadian top income shares based on individual income and US top income shares based on family income might not be comparable. (See Chapter 2 for a formal discussion of this issue.) This question is particularly important given the recent large increase in married women's labour force participation. The Canadian tax return micro-data allow us to link the incomes of spouses and explore this issue. Table 6D.2, Panel B reports top wage income shares estimated at the family level. Figure 6.10 plots the top 1% wage income share estimated at the individual level (as reported above) and at the family level (as in the United States) for 1982–2000. Both the level and pattern of the two graphs are almost identical suggesting that changes in the correlation of earnings among spouses have had no effect on top income shares. Given this Canadian evidence, it seems likely that the recent dramatic increase in family income concentration documented in the United States is also due primarily to an increase in individual income concentration.

23 The Canadian personal income tax system in principle attributes capital income to the individual saver. Hence there are attempts to prevent tax evasion through transfers from high earning to low earning spouses.

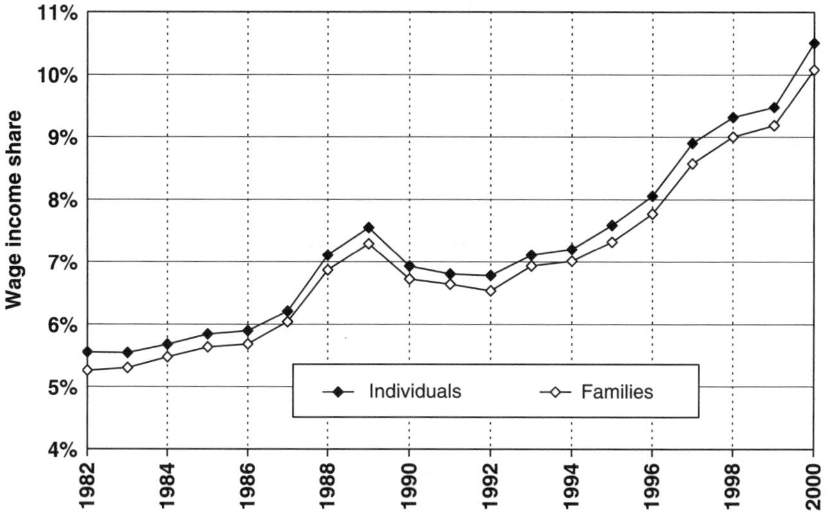

Figure 6.10 Top 1% wage income share for individuals and families in Canada, 1982–2000

Note: For families, top 1% defined relative to the total number of couples and single adults with positive wage income.

Source: Table 6D.2, Panels A and B, column P99–100.

The Development of Stock Options

The surge in top executive compensation in the United States is due in large part to the development of stock options. In Canada, the development of stock options has been slower because they do not receive a favored tax treatment (Klassen and Mawani 2000).[24] In contrast to the United States, profits from stock option exercises can be separated out from wages and salaries on Canadian income tax returns. In spite of the unfavorable tax treatment, evidence presented in Table 6D5 and Figure 6.11 shows the dramatic development of stock options since 1995.[25] Column (1) in Table 6D.5 shows that, in 1995, stock options represented only 0.26% of total employment income but this number has

[24] In the United States, profits from stock option exercise are treated like wage income (and hence are deductible from profits for the corporation and taxed like wage income for the individual). In Canada, stock options profits are not deductible for corporations and are in effect taxed very similarly to capital gains for most individuals upon exercise (but are fully reported and included in wages and salaries in the income tax statistics we have used). In effect, 75% of stock option exercise gains are taxable from 1990 to 1999 (50% before 1988, and 66.6% in 1988 and 1989). Over the course of 2000, the share of taxable stock-option gains was reduced to 50%.

[25] Published statistics in *Taxation Statistics* on aggregate stock options show that they represented less than 0.1% of total wages up to the year 1992. Hence stock options can clearly not explain the spike of 1987–89 when top wage shares increased by more than 1 percentage point. We present evidence only since 1995 because we have to rely on special computations prepared for this study directly by the Canadian Customs and Revenue Agency. Note also that one reason for the increase in the value of stock option exercises in the late 1990s is the increase in stock market prices at that time.

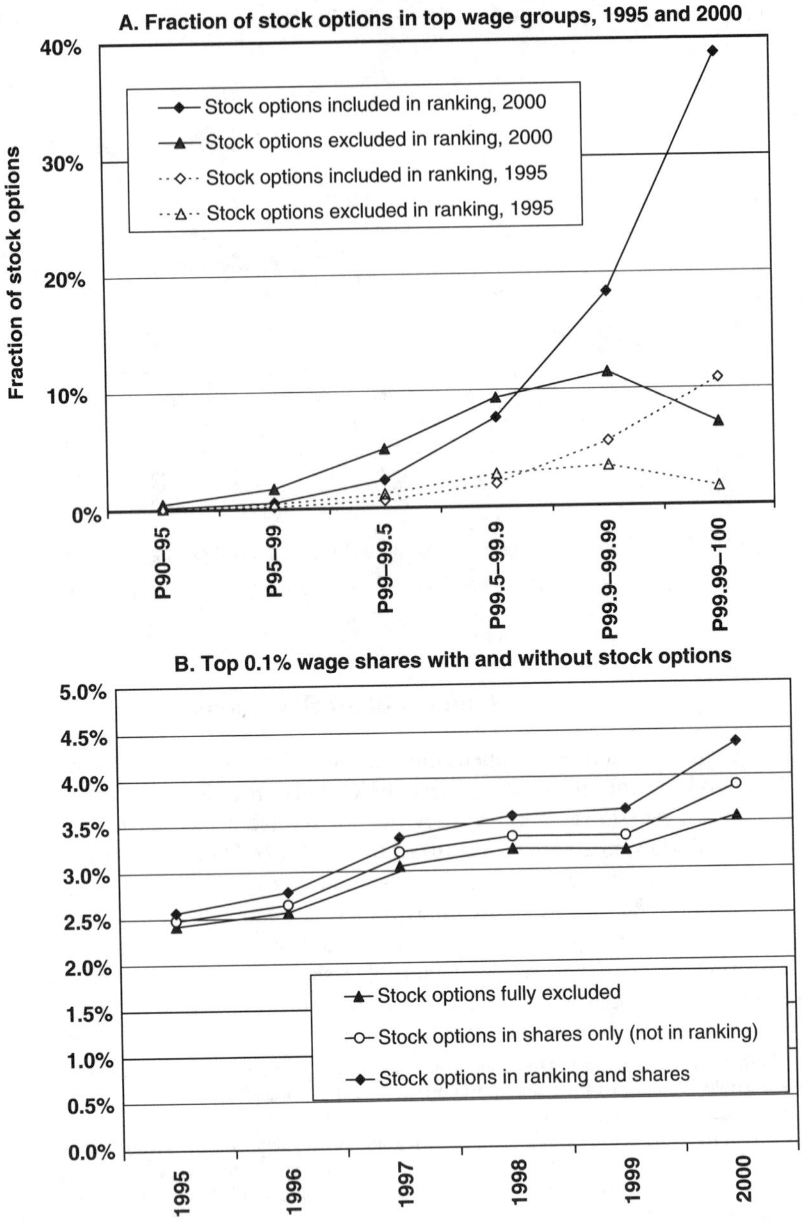

Figure 6.11 The role of stock options in the surge in top wage income shares in Canada, 1995–2000

Sources: For panel A: Table 6D.5, Panels A and D, rows 1995 and 2000. For Panel B: Table 6D.2, Panel A, col. P99.9–100, and Table 6D.5, Panels B and C, P.99.9–100.

increased to about 1.5% by 2000. Panel A in Table 6D.5 reports the fraction of the value of stock option exercises in total wages reported by top wage income groups (those fractions for years 1995 and 2000 are also depicted in Panel A of Figure 6.11). The evidence shows that the fraction of the value of stock option exercises in total wages reported by top wage groups has also increased dramatically since 1995. For example, the fraction of stock options in wages reported by the top 1% of wage earners increased from 3.3% in 1995 to over 13.5% in 2000.[26] It is also interesting to note the extreme concentration of stock options in the earnings distribution: the top 0.1% of wage earners exercise about two thirds of all stock options in each of the years from 1995 to 2000.

It is important to note, however, that stock options, like realized capital gains, are not an annual flow of income. As a result, top income and wage shares produced by ranking taxpayers including stock options might be upward biased as those with stock options have incomes that are unusually high in that particular year. As Canadian tax statistics report separately the value of stock option exercises, we can cast light on this phenomenon.[27] We can first re-compute top wage shares by excluding exercised stock options (both in the numerator and denominator). These top wage shares excluding stock options are reported in panel B of Table 6D.5. However, stock options do represent compensation for labour services and excluding them completely leads to an underestimation of top employment income shares. Therefore, the most satisfactory way to proceed is perhaps to exclude stock options in the ranking of individuals but add back stock options (both in the numerator and denominator) when computing shares. This method eliminates the upward bias due to lumpiness of stock option exercises while taking into account stock options. The top wage shares computed in this way are reported in Panel C of Table 6D.5 and the fraction of stock options for each group (groups defined by ranking of employment income excluding stock options) is reported in Panel D. The salient findings of Table 6D.5 are illustrated in Figure 6.11. Panel A of Figure 6.11 shows that the fraction of stock options in employment income is much lower when individuals are ranked by employment income excluding stock options. Even in 2000, the fraction of stock options is only around 10% for the top wage groups when ranked excluding stock options. Interestingly, the share of stock options peaks for group P99.9–99.99 and decreases at the very top. This is in stark contrast with the case where stock options are included in ranking. In the latter case, the share of stock options is steadily increasing as we move up toward the top. This shows that there is substantial re-ranking when stock options are excluded.[28] The

[26] It is therefore very likely that stock options in the United States, which receive a more favourable tax treatment than in Canada, also represent a large share of wages and salaries reported at the top.

[27] Such an analysis is unfortunately impossible for the United States where stock option exercises are never reported separately in tax or earnings statistics.

[28] The dotted lines in Panel A of Figure 6.11 show that the same phenomenon was present in 1995 even though stock options were a much smaller fraction of employment income, suggesting that the distributional characteristics of stock options have not changed much from 1995 to 2000, in spite of a dramatic increase in volume.

concentration of stock options, while still substantial, is less extreme when individuals are ranked excluding stock options. The top 1% wage earners (ranked excluding stock options) exercise about two-thirds of stock options.

Panel B of Figure 6.11 depicts the top 0.1% of wage income shares for the three treatments of options we discussed (fully included as in our previous analysis, included in shares but not in ranking, and fully excluded) from 1995 to 2000. As expected, the increase in the top 0.1% wage share is not as dramatic when ranking excludes stock options and even less so when stock options are completely excluded. However, the general pattern shows a steady increase in all three cases. Since 1978, the top 0.1% share would have increased by a factor of 3.5 if stock options were completely excluded instead of by a factor of 4.3 with stock options fully included. When stock options are included only in shares and not in ranking (perhaps the most meaningful economically), this factor is 3.85. Therefore, it is clear that the development of stock options can only explain a small fraction of the rise in top wage shares although it can explain a larger fraction of the surge since 1995. In any case, the re-ranking due to lumpiness in stock option exercises is only a minor element contributing to the surge in Canadian top wage shares over the last 25 years that we documented.

Mobility

Has the surge in top incomes been accompanied by an increase in mobility for the high income groups? Using 1982–2000 longitudinal tax return data, we explore this issue in two ways. First, we recompute top income shares based on average income over three or five years instead of a single year. If high incomes were relatively transitory, we would expect to see less concentration when incomes are measured over a longer time period. Those income shares are reported in Panel A of Table 6E.1. Figure 6.12, Panel A plots the top 0.1% income share using one year, three year and five year centred averages. The three curves match almost perfectly suggesting that income mobility has not increased significantly in recent years.

Second and more directly, Panel B reports that the probability of remaining in the top 0.1% group is about 60% one year later, about 50% two years later and between 40% and 50% three years later (such series for various top income groups are reported in Panel B of Table 6E.1). This suggests that mobility at the top is quite modest. Consistent with our Panel A results, there has been no increase in mobility since 1982, and perhaps even a slight decrease. Similar results apply to all top groups and strongly suggest that the surge in annual income concentration that we have documented is associated with a similar increase in longer term income concentration and welfare.[29] From the Canadian findings, it

[29] More generally, Baker and Solon (2003) and Beach et al. (2003) have used tax based data to conclude that the overall increase in annual earnings inequality in Canada was not due to increased earnings variability, although they do not consider top incomes specifically.

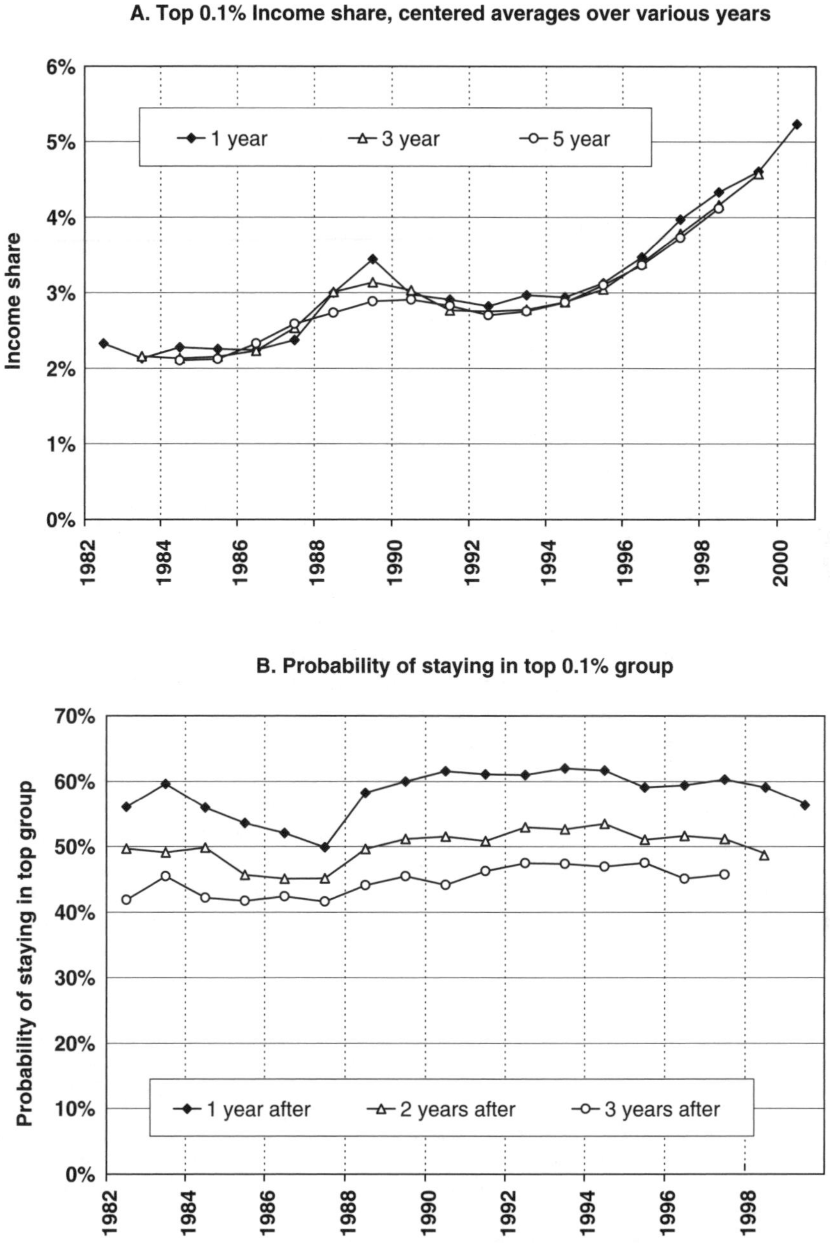

Figure 6.12 Mobility of high incomes in Canada, 1982–2000

Source: Table 6E.1: Computation details in Appendix Section E.

seems plausible that the surge in top US incomes is also not primarily due to increased mobility.[30]

6.5 THE ROLE OF TAXATION

As the empirical literature on behavioural responses to taxation has shown, income taxes can have a substantial impact on incomes reported for tax purposes, on which our top income and wage shares are based. Therefore, it is important to analyze, in parallel to the evolution of top income shares, the evolution of the income tax system. One key measure of the burden of the income tax system is given by the marginal rate of taxation. Such rates, at various percentiles of the income distribution, along with the top marginal tax rate, are reported in Figure 6.13 from 1920 to 2000.[31] A number of interesting findings emerge.

First, up to the early 1970s, the income tax in Canada had a very progressive structure, with many brackets and a very high top marginal income tax rate. However, the top marginal tax rate is a very imperfect measure of the burden of taxation, as extremely few taxpayers had incomes large enough to be in the top bracket. For example, in the early 1920s, the top marginal tax rate was in excess of 70% but the taxpayer at percentile P99.99 (approximately the 500th highest income in Canada at that time) faced a much more modest marginal rate of about 25%. Over the last 30 years, the top marginal tax rate has declined significantly to around 45%–50%, but, in the year 2000, a significant fraction of the population—around 5%—faced the top rate.[32]

Second, the upper middle class below the top percentile (from P90 to P99) has faced a continuously rising marginal tax rate (except the temporary surge of the Second World War), from negligible rates before the Second World War, to rates around 20% in the decades following the Second World War, up to around 35–45% in the last two decades. In comparison, percentile P99.9 faced a rate of about 45% in 1950 and about 48% in 2000. Over that same 50-year period,

[30] Because of lack of adequate data, top income mobility in the United States has not been examined in published work. However, a number of studies (e.g. Gottschalk 1997; and Buchinsky and Hunt 1999) have used survey data to find more generally that the increase in measured US inequality is not due to increased mobility. Bowlus and Robin (2004) use a lifetime model of wage/employment mobility to conclude that the US distribution of lifetime labour income has become more unequal over the last 20 years.

[31] In Canada, provincial income taxes represent a very significant portion of total income taxes. Therefore, Figure 6.13 displays marginal tax rates including both the federal and provincial income taxes (see Appendix 6F for details). Complete series on marginal and average income tax rates are reported in Tables 6F.1 and 6F.2 respectively.

[32] This evolution from many brackets extending very far into the distribution of incomes and a high nominal top rate toward a much smaller number of brackets with a lower top rate is a common pattern of most personal income tax systems of developed countries over the twentieth-century. Income tax systems in the United States, and the United Kingdom, among many others, have also followed the same path. It is an interesting political economy question as to the reasons for this change.

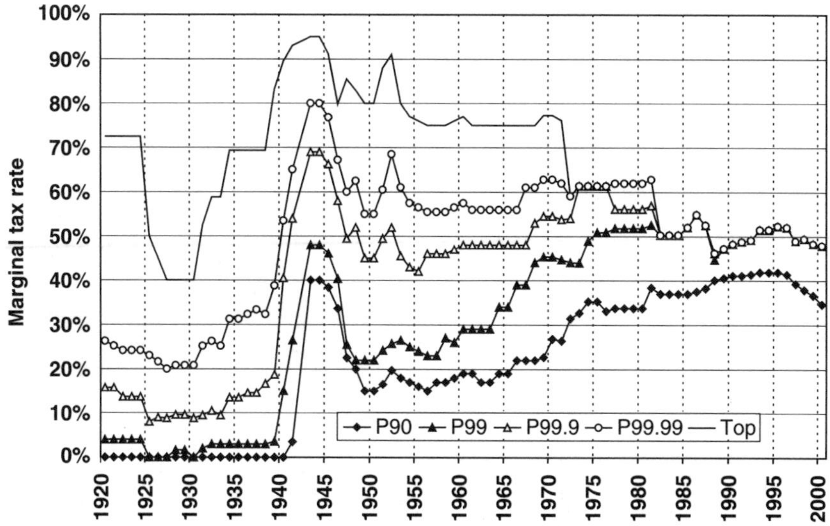

Figure 6.13 Marginal income tax rates in Canada for various percentiles, 1920–2000

Note: Year 1942 excluded because rates were reduced due to transition to a pay-as-you-earn system
Source: Table 6F.1, cols. P90, P99, P99.9, P99.99, and Top.

percentile P99.99 experienced a decline from 55% to 48% and only the super top (around 1000 individuals within the top 0.01%) had a decline in marginal tax rates of 10 percentage points or more. This stands in contrast to the US case where a much larger fraction of taxpayers experienced very large reductions in marginal tax rates from the 1960s and 1970s to the early 1990s.

For the United States, a number of studies have argued that the surge in top US incomes in the 1980s might not reflect actual income changes but rather changes in the way incomes are reported (see Saez 2004 for a recent survey). For example, a large fraction of the jump in US top income shares from 1986 to 1988 (see Figure 6.3) is due to shifts from the corporate sector to the personal sector (as the top personal tax rate became lower than the corporate tax rate after 1987). The Canadian experience casts new light on this issue in two ways.

First, the climb in Canadian top reported incomes is unlikely due to tax induced shifting from the corporate sector. Canadian corporate tax rates remained relatively stable until 1987, have since declined and in any case are offset in the personal income tax by a dividend tax credit which reduces the double taxation of dividends. Also, in contrast to the United States, for the Canadian top 0.01% income earners, the share of business income reported on personal income tax returns as a percentage of total income reported has been relatively stable and very low, between 1% and 3% of total income over the last 20 years (see Table 6C.3).

Second, Canadian changes in marginal tax rates have been different in both timing and degree. Figure 6.14 presents for 1960–2000 the average marginal

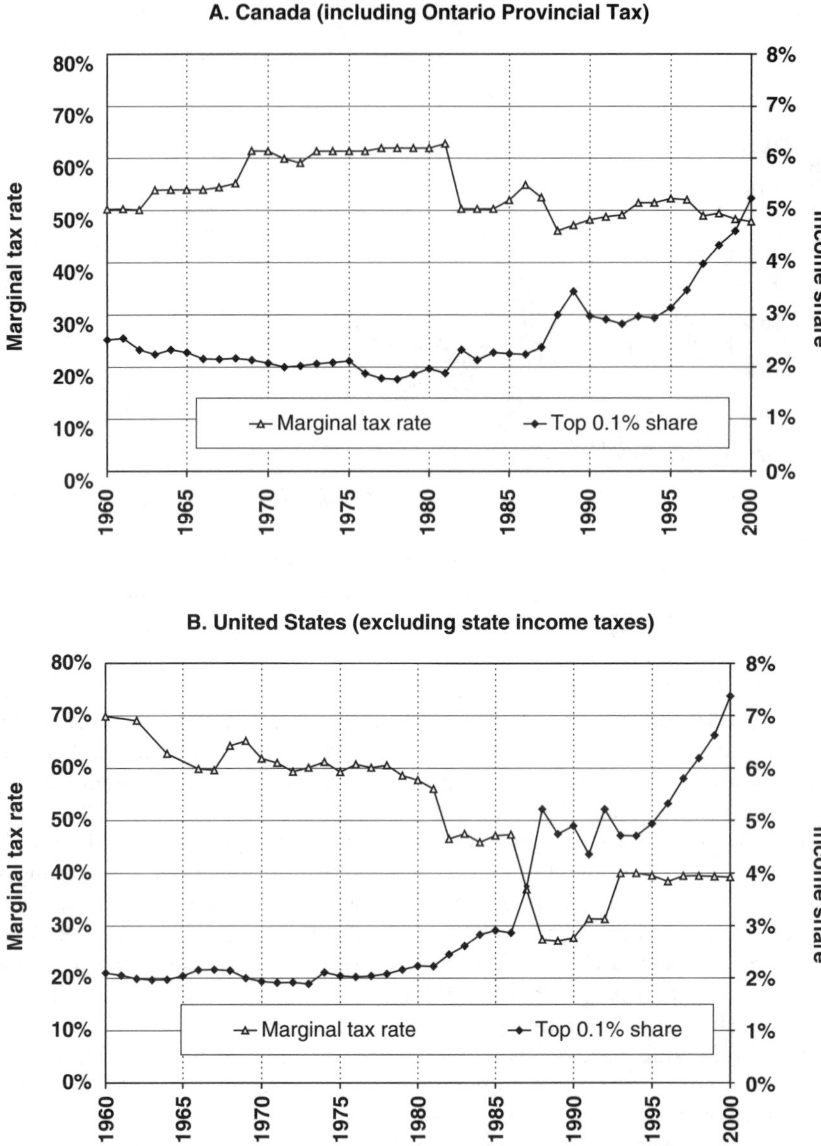

Figure 6.14 Marginal tax rates and income share for the top 0.1% in Canada and US, 1960–2000

Notes: Margainal tax rates in Canada include federal and Ontario provincial income taxes, as well as applicable surtaxes and credits. United Sates, Saez (2004) computations using micro-tax return data and TAXSIM calculator (does not include sate income taxes).

Source: Canada marginal tax rate computations based on Table 6F.1 (see Appendix Section 6F for details).

personal income tax rate (weighted by income) for those in the top 0.1% along with their income share, for Canada in Panel A, and the United States in Panel B (from Saez 2004). While marginal tax rates for the top 0.1% are about the same (around 50%) in the 1960s and the 1990s in Canada, US marginal tax rates dropped dramatically from about 70% in the early 1960s to less than 30% in the mid-1980s (and then increased to around 40% in the 1990s).

It is clear from Figure 6.14 that the US top 0.1% income share surge has so far been larger. There is perhaps also some indication that Canadian top shares started to increase during the 1980s at the time of some significant Canadian marginal tax rate cuts, although some of the effect was temporary (see below). But it is striking that between 1990 and 2000, top shares surged very similarly in both countries, particularly after 1995. This occurred even though there was very little further change in Canadian marginal tax rates facing these top income individuals and even though there was a substantial increase in the relevant US marginal personal income tax rates in 1993 (as emphasized by Piketty and Saez, Chapter 5 in this volume). Therefore, the dramatic climb in Canadian top reported incomes is unlikely to have been induced by changes in Canadian tax rates. If, as tentatively argued previously, some of the surge in Canadian top incomes is due to brain drain threats (or there is some other association with US factors), it must be the case that the surge in top US wage incomes is real and not entirely due to changes in the way US incomes are reported for tax purposes. Otherwise, those changes in the United States could not have increased incentives for Canadian top earners to move to the United States.

There are other things to learn from the Canada/United States comparison in Figure 6.14. First, as noted, there is clear evidence in Canada, as in the United States, of a short-term response to cuts in marginal tax rates. For example, there was a substantial tax cut in Canada in 1988 and Panel A shows a sharp increase in the 0.1% share between 1987 and 1989, which is partially reversed by 1990. Several other figures show similar spikes and it is particularly clear in the top wage series in Figure 6.8. This suggests that this short-term response was at least in part highly compensated employees shifting some of their compensation into the lower tax rate years. Goolsbee (2000) found similar effects for the US tax increase of 1993. Sillamaa and Veall (2001) analysed the Canadian tax cut of 1988 by comparing incomes in years 1986 and 1989. Consistent with our results, they found significant and large elasticities for high-income groups. However, our top share series shows that their elasticity estimates capture the short-term spike response but likely overstate the long-run response to the tax change.[33]

In order to test more formally that top income share movements in Canada are primarily due to US developments rather than to changes in marginal tax rates in Canada, we estimate simple regression models of the form:

[33] Sillamaa and Veall (2001) use four years of the same micro-data set used as part of this study. They find much lower tax responsiveness for low income groups, consistent with the US findings of Gruber and Saez (2002). Gagné et al. (2000) use provincial level aggregate data over 1972–96 and find a large tax responsiveness for high income individuals, but only for the 1988–96 period.

$$Log(\text{TOP1\% SHARE}_t) = \alpha + \varepsilon\ Log(1 - \text{MTR}_t) + \delta Log(\text{TOP1\%SHAREUS}_t) + v_t$$

where $TOP1\%SHARE_t$ is the share of income received by the top 1% of earners in Canada in year t, $TOP1\%SHAREUS_t$ is the equivalent US variable and MTR_t is the average (income weighted) marginal tax rate applicable to the top 1% group in Canada in year t. (We also estimate the corresponding regression for the top 0.1% share.) The central parameter is ε, the elasticity of top reported incomes (as a share of all reported incomes) with respect to the net of tax rate (defined as one minus the marginal tax rate). See Saez (2004) for a discussion of identification assumptions.

Results for these time series regressions are reported in Table 6.2. The Newey-West procedure (with eight lags) is used to correct the standard errors for possible heteroskedasticity and serial correlation. Panel A focuses on incomes for the full period 1920–2000 while Panel B focuses on wage incomes for the recent period 1972–2000. Columns (1) and (2) report results for the top 1% and columns (3) and (4) for the top 0.1%. Columns (1) and (3) exclude the US share variable. In that case, the estimated elasticities of income shares with respect to net of tax rates are around 0.8–1 for incomes and around 2.5–3 for wage incomes for the recent period. The reason these elasticity estimates are so enormous is that the entire surge in top wage income shares is attributed to the very modest decrease in Canadian marginal tax rates since 1972. Columns (2) and (4) use the full regression model with the log US income share as an additional independent variable. This has a dramatic effect on the estimated tax elasticities which drop to around 0.3–0.5 for incomes and around 0.2–0.3 (not significantly different from zero at the 5% level) for wage incomes. The coefficient on the US log income

Table 6.2 Marginal tax and US effects on Canadian top income shares, 1920–2000

	Top 1% No US control	US control	Top 0.1% No US control	US control
	(1)	(2)	(3)	(4)
A. Income Shares from 1920 to 2000				
Elasticity	0.826	0.476	0.961	0.299
	(0.126)	(0.130)	(0.294)	(0.168)
log (US top income share)		0.458		0.610
		(0.093)		(0.101)
Number of Observations	81	81	81	81
B. Wage Income Shares from 1972 to 2000				
Elasticity	2.550	0.177	3.023	0.278
	(0.762)	(0.345)	(0.544)	(0.258)
log (US top income share)		0.759		0.857
		(0.175)		(0.059)
Number of Observations	29	29	29	29

Notes: Estimates obtained by time-series regression of log (Canadian top income share) on a constant, log (1 - Canadian marginal tax rate). Results are from OLS regressions with standard errors corrected for heteroskedasticity and autocorrelation using the Newey-West procedure with eight lags. In col. 2 and 4, log (US top income share) is added as an additional right-hand side variable. Appendix Section 6F describes how the marginal tax rate series are estimated.

share is large and very significant and would imply that a 10% increase in the top US wage income share leads to a 8% increase in the top Canadian wage income share. Even if we do not accept such a causal interpretation, the results reinforce our informal analysis and make it clear that Canadian top income changes are much more strongly associated with similar US changes than with Canadian tax developments. This in turn is evidence that US changes are more than changes in US tax reporting behaviour.

6.6 CONCLUSION

This chapter has used personal income tax data to construct homogeneous series of top income shares in Canada over the course of the twentieth century. A number of important findings have emerged. First and most striking are the close parallels between the patterns and composition of top incomes in Canada and the United States. Both countries experienced a sharp drop in top shares during the Second World War with no recovery before the 1970s. However, during the last two decades, the top groups have largely recovered their pre-war levels. Interestingly, this recent increase in income concentration has not been associated with increased mobility at the top of the income distribution in Canada. Moreover both countries have experienced the same shift in the composition of top incomes. Today earners of employment income have, to a large extent, replaced rentiers at the top of the income distribution in both Canada and the United States.

The Canadian experience may help us understand the role of taxation in explaining the recent increase in top income shares in the United States. Although the drop in marginal tax rates since the 1960s has been much more modest in Canada than in the United States, the surge in top incomes has been almost as large in Canada as in the United States. The analysis of top Canadian incomes is more transparent because it is not plagued with shifts between the personal and corporate sectors, which have made the US results more difficult to interpret. Moreover, the concentration of the surge in the last decade and among only the very top income shares suggests that tax changes in Canada cannot be the sole cause. While clear evidence of short-term responses to taxation can be found in Canada, it could be very misleading to equate such responses to the permanent long-run effects of tax changes.

The surge in top wages in Canada is later and more concentrated within very top groups than in the United States and is much less pronounced for francophones in Quebec. We suggest that this is some evidence in favour of a brain drain explanation: the threat of migration to the United States by highly skilled Canadian executives or professionals may have driven the surge in top wage shares in Canada. This would be consistent with the smaller surge found for the United Kingdom (Chapter 4) and the lack of a surge in France (Chapter 3). These international differences are difficult to reconcile with a simple skill bias technological explanation. In any case, the relationship between the Canadian and US surges suggests strongly that the latter cannot be the consequence of changes in the way US incomes are reported for tax purposes. The remaining puzzle is why such a surge took place in the United States in the first place.

APPENDIX 6A

The appendices describe the construction of our top income share series based on tax return data. The Canadian federal income tax started in 1917 and 2000 is the most recent year for which data are available. Starting with the tax year 1920, the Taxation Division of the Department of National Revenue started publishing distributions of taxpayers. These statistics for years 1920–40 were published in *The Canada Yearbook* (Dominion Bureau of Statistics) and in *Incomes Assessed for War Income Tax in Canada* (Department of National Revenue) and in *Dominion Income Tax Statistics* (Department of Trade and Commerce). Many of these statistics, as well as a detailed overview of the income tax legislation for these years, are reproduced in *Canadian Fiscal Facts* (Canadian Tax Foundation 1957). After the Second World War, a much broader set of statistics was published in the annual publication *Taxation Statistics* (Canada Customs and Revenue Agency) covering the years 1948 to 2001. Finally, micro-files of tax returns, based on a 20% random sample of the Canadian population, are available from 1982. This micro-dataset of tax returns is known as the Longitudinal Administrative Databank (LAD). The microfiles allow the computation of a much broader set of inequality statistics than the published tables. Aggregate population and National Account statistics are from CANSIM (2003) (Canadian Socio-economic Information Matrix) as maintained by Statistics Canada.

Total Number of Individuals

The total number of individuals is computed as the number of individuals in the Canadian population aged 20 and above. These series are based on Census interpolations and provided by CANSIM. CANSIM provides two series for the size of population, one from 1920 to 1971 and a second one from 1971 to 2000. We paste these series using the recent series as the base. The series is reported in Table 6A.1, column (1). Upper income groups are defined with respect to this total adult population. For instance, in 2000, with a total adult population equal to 22.81 million, there are 2.281 million individuals in the top decile, 228,100 individuals in the top percentile, etc.

Table 6A.1 also indicates the total number of tax returns actually filed (column (2)), as well as the fraction of the adult population filing a tax return (column (3)). Before the Second World War, due to the high exemption levels, this fraction was low, usually around 5%. The top 5% is therefore the biggest fraction for which we can construct homogeneous estimates for the entire period. We can provide estimates for the top decile only after 1941. Exemptions were drastically reduced during and after the Second World War, and therefore the fraction filing has

Table 6A.1 Reference totals for population, income, and inflation in Canada, 1920–2000

	Adult population			Income		Inflation		
	(1) Population (aged 20+) ('000s)	(2) Number of tax returns ('000s)	(3) (2)/(1) (%)	(4) Total income (millions 2000 $)	(5) Average income (2000 $)	(6) CPI (2000 base)	(7) Average tax per adult (2000 $)	(8) Average capital gain per adult (2000 $)
1920	4,990	290.6	5.8	24,852	4,980	11.894	66	
1921	5,072	281.2	5.5	22,695	4,474	10.485	55	
1922	5,163	239.0	4.6	25,751	4,987	9.604	50	
1923	5,228	225.5	4.3	27,705	5,300	9.604	50	
1924	5,321	209.5	3.9	27,890	5,242	9.427	49	
1925	5,426	116.0	2.1	30,384	5,600	9.604	37	
1926	5,528	122.0	2.2	32,859	5,944	9.604	40	
1927	5,668	129.7	2.3	35,025	6,179	9.515	41	
1928	5,810	142.2	2.4	37,612	6,474	9.515	47	
1929	5,947	143.6	2.4	37,420	6,293	9.692	47	
1930	6,074	133.6	2.2	35,413	5,831	9.604	46	
1931	6,192	167.0	2.7	32,504	5,250	8.634	50	
1932	6,317	204.0	3.2	29,525	4,674	7.841	58	
1933	6,445	184.2	2.9	28,336	4,397	7.489	54	
1934	6,564	199.1	3.0	31,210	4,755	7.577	69	
1935	6,681	217.0	3.2	33,160	4,963	7.665	69	
1936	6,786	237.1	3.5	34,830	5,132	7.753	75	
1937	6,890	264.8	3.8	38,194	5,544	8.018	83	
1938	6,999	293.1	4.2	38,455	5,494	8.106	75	
1939	7,114	300.4	4.2	40,608	5,708	8.106	95	
1940	7,229	608.4	8.4	45,386	6,278	8.370	259	
1941	7,350	871.5	11.9	51,384	6,991	8.899	519	
1942	7,492	1,781	23.8	62,802	8,383	9.251	591	
1943	7,614	2,163	28.4	67,268	8,835	9.427	1,186	
1944	7,730	2,254	29.2	73,222	9,473	9.515	1,138	
1945	7,822	2,254	28.8	72,778	9,304	9.604	986	
1946	7,971	3,162	39.7	72,031	9,037	9.868	840	
1947	8,122	3,529	43.4	75,463	9,291	10.837	721	
1948	8,266	3,662	44.3	76,991	9,314	12.335	648	
1949	8,613	3,764	43.7	78,908	9,162	12.775	464	
1950	8,758	3,892	44.4	81,691	9,328	13.128	510	
1951	8,896	4,118	46.3	88,228	9,917	14.449	644	
1952	9,129	4,413	48.3	93,889	10,285	14.890	776	
1953	9,329	4,700	50.4	99,646	10,681	14.714	788	
1954	9,548	4,834	50.6	99,091	10,378	14.802	747	
1955	9,734	4,955	50.9	107,058	10,998	14.802	764	
1956	9,911	5,188	52.4	117,008	11,806	15.066	824	
1957	10,159	5,195	51.1	120,837	11,894	15.507	857	
1958	10,352	5,516	53.3	123,403	11,920	15.859	800	
1959	10,537	5,672	53.8	128,164	12,163	16.123	865	
1960	10,700	5,851	54.7	132,743	12,406	16.300	934	
1961	10,851	5,947	54.8	135,975	12,531	16.476	978	

(contd.)

Table 6A.1 (*contd.*)

	Adult population			Income		Inflation		
	(1) Population (aged 20+) ('000s)	(2) Number of tax returns ('000s)	(3) (2)/(1) (%)	(4) Total income (millions 2000 $)	(5) Average income (2000 $)	(6) CPI (2000 base)	(7) Average tax per adult (2000 $)	(8) Average capital gain per adult (2000 $)
1962	11,001	6,107	55.5	146,724	13,337	16.652	1,021	
1963	11,158	6,324	56.7	154,161	13,816	16.916	1,105	
1964	11,354	6,693	58.9	162,700	14,330	17.269	1,253	
1965	11,575	7,136	61.7	176,318	15,232	17.621	1,339	
1966	11,845	7,733	65.3	190,779	16,106	18.326	1,485	
1967	12,150	8,134	66.9	200,623	16,512	18.943	1,716	
1968	12,451	8,495	68.2	210,535	16,909	19.736	1,969	
1969	12,756	8,882	69.6	223,356	17,510	20.617	2,227	
1970	13,064	9,183	70.3	232,009	17,760	21.322	2,449	
1971	13,365	9,533	71.3	246,998	18,481	21.938	2,696	
1972	13,659	10,380	76.0	266,189	19,488	22.996	3,516	95
1973	13,983	11,004	78.7	289,654	20,715	24.758	3,700	142
1974	14,353	11,602	80.8	310,181	21,611	27.401	3,940	144
1975	14,737	12,002	81.4	324,154	21,996	30.396	3,909	181
1976	15,101	12,343	81.7	344,007	22,781	32.687	4,047	256
1977	15,454	12,586	81.4	351,688	22,757	35.242	3,998	284
1978	15,787	14,320	90.7	359,722	22,786	38.414	3,786	394
1979	16,129	14,682	91.0	372,951	23,123	41.938	3,970	605
1980	16,524	14,765	89.4	383,382	23,202	46.167	4,164	721
1981	16,919	15,179	89.7	403,154	23,829	51.894	4,324	540
1982	17,299	15,221	88.0	395,734	22,875	57.533	4,061	276
1983	17,654	15,303	86.7	389,172	22,045	60.881	3,819	379
1984	17,998	15,552	86.4	404,590	22,480	63.524	3,962	347
1985	18,321	15,864	86.6	421,517	23,007	66.079	4,196	468
1986	18,628	16,538	88.8	432,966	23,243	68.811	4,488	705
1987	18,966	17,071	90.0	446,054	23,518	71.806	4,868	1,075
1988	19,278	17,580	91.2	472,432	24,507	74.714	5,021	888
1989	19,690	18,132	92.1	489,777	24,875	78.414	5,416	1,102
1990	20,030	18,759	93.7	498,292	24,877	82.203	5,490	676
1991	20,313	19,051	93.8	478,939	23,578	86.784	5,221	611
1992	20,579	19,437	94.5	477,320	23,195	88.106	5,107	664
1993	20,843	19,829	95.1	475,314	22,804	89.692	5,055	1,017
1994	21,115	20,154	95.4	485,434	22,989	89.868	5,129	961
1995	21,394	20,515	95.9	497,433	23,252	91.806	5,240	507
1996	21,667	20,806	96.0	502,058	23,171	93.304	5,298	649
1997	21,971	21,124	96.1	515,341	23,455	94.802	5,470	839
1998	22,241	21,384	96.1	532,784	23,955	95.683	5,533	842
1999	22,517	21,882	97.2	547,416	24,312	97.357	5,611	867
2000	22,808	22,146	97.1	566,981	24,859	100.000	5,817	1,363

Notes: Population estimates based on census data, from CANSIM. Total income is 80% of personal income (less transfers) from National Accounts. Consumer Price Index (CPI) from CANSIM series. Average tax per capita includes both federal (and provincial) individual income taxes. Average capital gains per adult based on total capital gains (taxable and non-taxable) reported on tax returns since 1972.

increased dramatically and is around 95% today. Note that the fraction jumps from 80% to 90% in 1978 due a change in the rule for family allowances, which required spouses, even without any income, to file in order to claim the allowances. As a result, in Canada today, almost every adult, even if his or her income is below the exemption thresholds, has an incentive to file an income tax return.

It is important to note that many individuals in the population have no income (before transfers). The biggest group with no income is non-working spouses. The size of this group has shrunk over the century as female labour force participation has steadily increased. This secular phenomenon tends to reduce the size of top income shares over time as income is spread over a larger fraction of the population.

Total Income Denominator

In order to compute top income shares, we need to estimate total income that would have been reported on tax returns, had everybody been required to file a tax return. We call this total income measure Gross Tax Income (GTI). As only a fraction of the population was filing a tax return in the pre-war period, income tax statistics cannot be used to estimate the Gross Tax Income denominator. The natural way to compute such a denominator is to use the personal income series from the National Accounts. Personal income is a broader definition of income accruing to individuals than total Gross Tax Income (had everybody been required to file) for two main reasons. First, personal income includes all transfers from the government (such as welfare benefits, unemployment benefits, or family allowances) and many of these transfers are either partially or not at all reported on tax returns. Therefore, we first subtract transfers from the government (reported separately in National Account series) from the personal income series. Second, various forms of income such as in-kind labour income, imputed rental income of home owners, imputed interest on non-interest bearing bank accounts, etc., are not reported on tax returns but are included in personal income. As a result, it is not surprising that personal income less transfers is systematically higher than Gross Tax Income even in the recent period where practically all income earners file a tax return. Fortunately, the ratio of GTI over Personal Income less transfers has always been around 80% (there are relatively minor fluctuations between 78% and 82% with no trend) since the mid-1970s, when most individuals, even low income earners, started filing tax returns systematically. Before the mid-1970s, because exemptions were larger (in real terms), a number of individuals with small incomes were not required to file tax returns and therefore the ratio of GTI over Personal Income less transfers was smaller (the ratio increased smoothly from 50% in 1945 to around 80% in 1974).

Presumably, a small fraction of individuals with very small incomes do not file tax returns (as total tax returns account for only 96% of the adult population in 2000). On the other hand, a number of individuals below age 20 also file returns. Therefore, we assume that GTI for the total adult population (age 20 and above) had everybody filed a return would be around 80% of Personal Income less

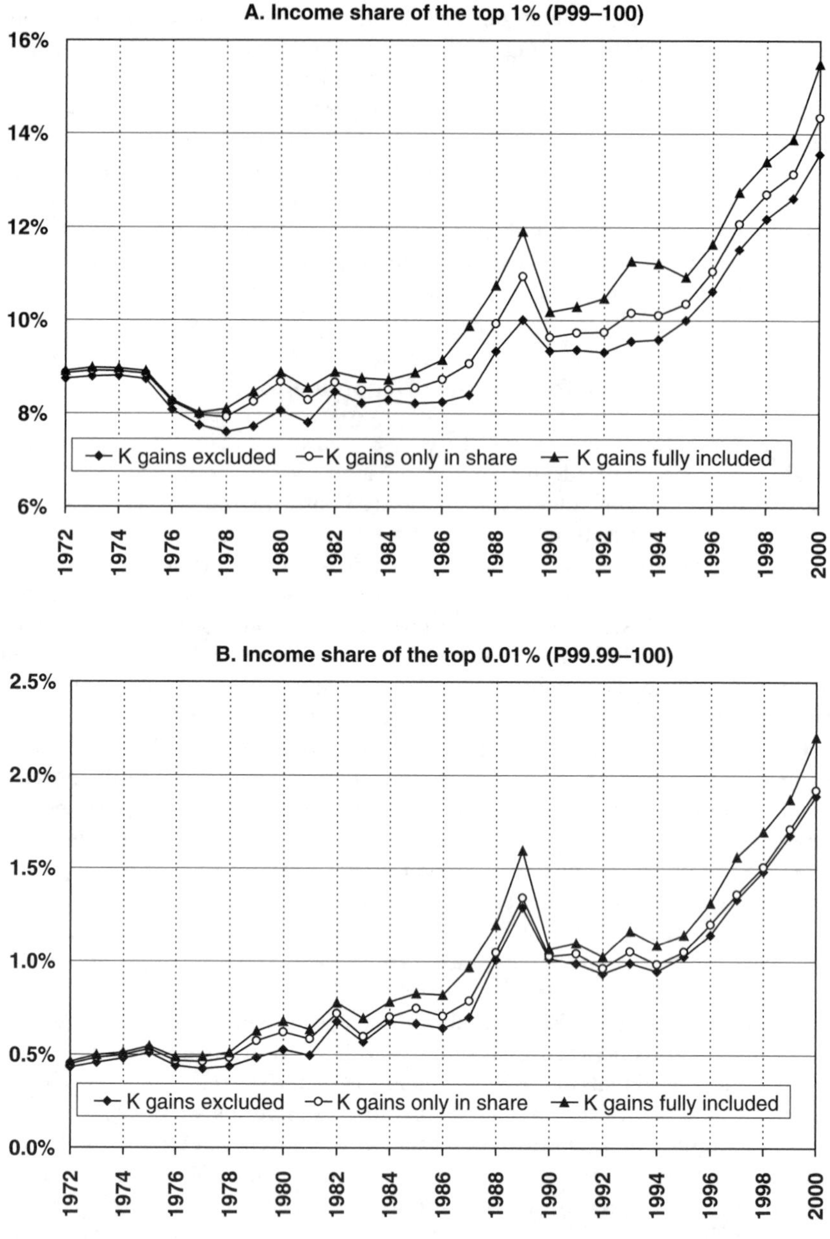

Figure 6A.1 Income shares with and without capital gains of top income groups in Canada, 1972–2000

Source: Tables 6B.1 and 6B.3, cols. P99–100 and P99.99–100.

transfers. Therefore, our total income denominator is defined uniformly over the period as 80% of Personal Income less transfers from the National Accounts.

The National Accounts provide series of Personal Income and Transfers only from 1926. Therefore, we have extrapolated the series of Personal Income (less transfers) for the period 1920–25 (from Urquhart and Buckley 1965), assuming that the ratio Personal Income over Gross National Product stays constant (and equal to 78% as in 1926). This assumption seems reasonable because the ratio Personal Income over GNP stays almost constant over the period 1926–39. Our total income denominator series (expressed in 2000 dollars) is reported in Column (4) of Table 6A.1. The average income per adult is reported in Column (5). The CPI index (base 100 in year 2000) is reported in Column (6).

(See Figures 6A.1, 6A.2, and 6A.3 for data on income shares and average income tax rates in Canada.)

APPENDIX 6B: TOP INCOME SHARES

Our income definition includes all sources of income reported on tax returns (except government transfers). With the exception of realized capital gains, which became taxable in 1972 (see below), and various government transfers (that are always negligible in the top decile), the definition of incomes reported on tax returns has been very stable since 1920. Since the introduction of the income tax, taxpayers have had to report incomes from all sources: wages and salaries for those employed, pensions for retired employees, self-employment income for the self-employed such as doctors or lawyers, profits from sole proprietorships and partnerships for owners of unincorporated businesses such as farmers or retail store owners. Capital income such as interest income, royalties, rents from real estate (as stated above, imputed rent from home ownership was never considered as taxable income), dividend distributions for shareholders of corporations, estate and trust income, and investment income on capital invested abroad were always taxable.

Since 1972, realized capital gains have been partially taxable. From 1972 to 1987, 50% of such gains were included in taxable income. In 1988 and 1989, 66.6% of gains were included in taxable income. From 1990 to 1999, 75% of gains were included in taxable income. Finally, over the course of tax year 2000, the amount of gains taxable was reduced back to 50%. The later 2000 reform was enacted retroactively and may explain why we do not observe a notable surge in realized capital gains in year 2000.

Most of our series exclude capital gains completely. Tax returns are ranked by income excluding capital gains, and top fractile incomes exclude capital gains. Income shares were computed by using the total income series (Table 6A.1, column (4)), as described in Appendix 6A. However, to assess the sensitivity of our income series to the exclusion of capital gains, for the period 1972–2000, we have also constructed series including full capital gains (i.e. not only the fraction reported on tax returns but the full amount of realized gains). For those series, we rank tax returns by income including full capital gains, and we compute total

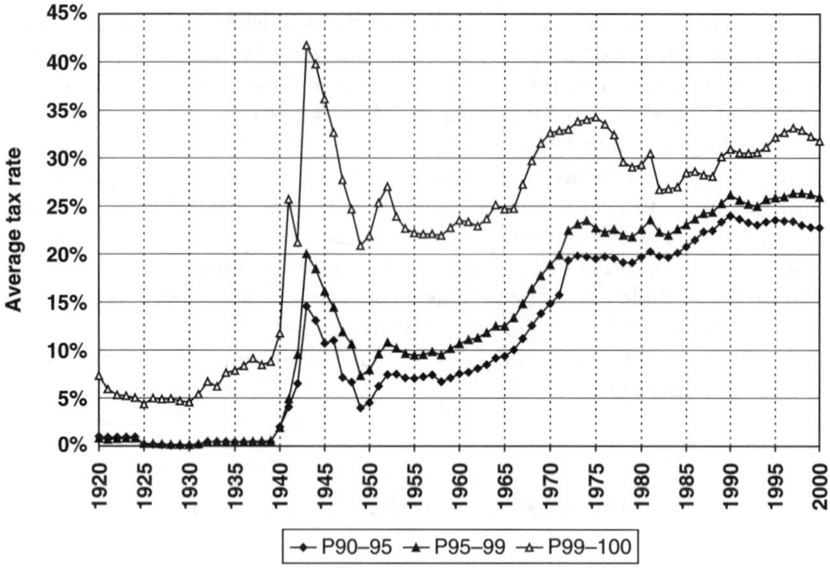

Figure 6A.2 Average income tax rates in Canada within top decile, 1920–2000

Notes: Average tax rates based on net taxes (including deductions and credits) divided by gross incomes. In 1942 tax rate lower due to transition to pay-as-you-earn system.

Source: Table 6F.2, cols. P90–95, P95–99, P99–100.

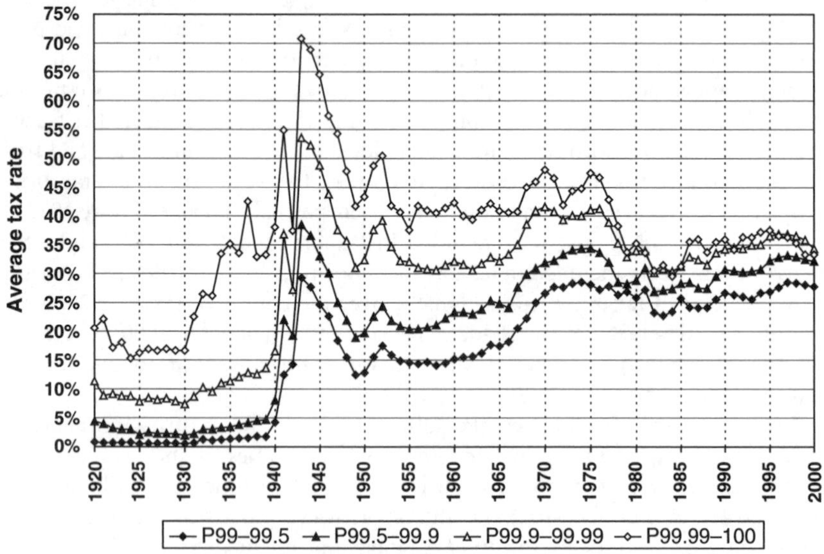

Figure 6A.3 Average income tax rates in Canada within top percentile, 1920–2000

Note: Average tax rates based on net taxes (including deductions and credits) divided by gross incomes.

Source: Table 6F.2, cols. P99–99.5, P99.5–99.9, P99.9–99.99, P99.99–100.

incomes (including capital gains) accruing to our top income groups. To compute income shares in that case, we add to the denominator described in Appendix 6A the full capital gains reported on tax returns.

In the text of this chapter, we have focused on series excluding capital gains because we cannot include capital gains before 1972. Excluding capital gains also allows getting rid of the very strong short-term volatility due to lumpiness in capital gains realizations. As a result, to analyse the role of capital gains, it is perhaps more useful to rank income excluding capital gains and see how much extra income accrues in the form of realized capital gains for each top income group. Therefore, we present three series. The first one (on which we focus in the text) excludes capital gains completely. The second series includes full capital gains both for ranking taxpayers and defining top income groups and in the amounts of income reported. The third series ranks taxpayers by income excluding capital gains (as in the first series) but adds back capital gains in the amount reported (both in the numerator and denominator) to compute top shares. The top fractile incomes series used to compute our top fractile income shares series are reported in real 2000 Canadian dollars in table B3 (for incomes excluding capital gains). For instance, Table 6B.3. indicates that the average top decile income was CA$105,262 in 2000, and the top decile income share reported in table 6B.1 for 2000 (42.34%) can be computed by dividing CA$105,262 by the average income reported in Table 6A.1 for 2000 (105,262/24,859=4.234). The top shares series including capital gains for the period 1972–2000 are reported in Table 6B.2. Panel A reports the series where capital gains are included both in the ranking and the amounts while Panel B reports the series where capital gains are excluded for the ranking but added back to compute the income shares.

The top fractile income series reported in tables 6B.1, 6B.2, and 6B.3 were constructed as follows: for the 1982–2000 period, the series were computed directly from the LAD microfiles (the microfiles allow us to rank tax returns by income excluding capital gains or by income including full capital gains and to compute average incomes without capital gains or with full capital gains for each of our top groups); for the 1920–81 period, the series were estimated from the published tax statistics tables, according to the following methodology (all computations are available from the authors upon request).

The published tables report the number of returns and tax paid by income brackets. Starting in 1938, the reported income amounts by income brackets are also available. In general, these tables display a large number of income brackets (the thresholds P90, P95, P99, P99.5, P99.9, and P99.99 are usually very close to one of the income bracket thresholds), and one can use standard Pareto interpolation techniques in order to estimate the income thresholds and income levels of the tax unit distribution of income.

Pareto Interpolation Technique

The general interpolation technique is that described in Appendix 5C. It is based on the well-known empirical regularity that the top tail of the income distribution

Table 6B.1 Top income shares in Canada, 1920–2000 (Groups are defined by total income (excluding capital gains))

	P90–100 (1)	P95–100 (2)	P99–100 (3)	P99.5–100 (4)	P99.9–100 (5)	P99.99–100 (6)	P90–95 (7)	P95–99 (8)	P99–99.5 (9)	P99.5–99.9 (10)	P99.9–99.99 (11)
1920		32.60	14.40	10.49	5.36	2.10		18.19	3.91	5.13	3.26
1921		40.58	17.60	12.55	5.81	1.70		22.98	5.05	6.74	4.10
1922		34.34	15.17	10.74	5.04	1.63		19.17	4.43	5.70	3.41
1923		30.15	14.38	10.22	4.69	1.53		15.77	4.17	5.52	3.16
1924		30.65	14.53	10.39	4.89	1.63		16.11	4.14	5.50	3.26
1925		29.76	13.18	9.48	4.34	1.32		16.59	3.70	5.14	3.02
1926		30.15	14.01	10.22	4.81	1.57		16.14	3.79	5.41	3.23
1927		30.70	14.69	10.78	5.13	1.74		16.01	3.91	5.65	3.40
1928		31.31	15.32	11.23	5.29	1.75		16.00	4.09	5.94	3.54
1929		31.73	15.64	11.47	5.34	1.71		16.09	4.17	6.14	3.63
1930		32.74	16.10	11.86	5.68	1.84		16.63	4.24	6.18	3.84
1931		36.03	16.60	12.00	5.55	1.72		19.42	4.61	6.44	3.84
1932		39.42	17.67	12.72	5.98	1.90		21.75	4.96	6.74	4.08
1933		40.88	18.03	12.89	5.91	1.73		22.84	5.14	6.99	4.18
1934		39.11	17.50	12.59	5.86	1.84		21.61	4.91	6.73	4.03
1935		38.09	16.99	12.19	5.63	1.72		21.10	4.79	6.56	3.91
1936		38.35	17.45	12.67	6.00	1.91		20.90	4.78	6.67	4.09
1937		35.81	16.26	11.79	5.48	1.54		19.55	4.46	6.32	3.94
1938		39.55	18.41	13.31	6.05	1.87		21.15	5.10	7.26	4.18
1939		37.23	16.88	12.23	5.63	1.67		20.34	4.66	6.60	3.96
1940		33.68	14.71	10.35	4.52	1.53		18.97	4.36	5.84	2.99
1941	45.31	30.74	13.30	9.46	4.24	1.29	14.56	17.45	3.84	5.22	2.95
1942	39.56	26.42	11.30	8.01	3.53	1.06	13.14	15.13	3.29	4.48	2.47
1943	39.29	25.84	10.72	7.51	3.23	0.92	13.45	15.12	3.21	4.29	2.31
1944	37.38	24.49	10.01	6.95	2.92	0.82	12.89	14.48	3.06	4.02	2.11
1945	37.27	24.63	10.12	6.99	2.89	0.78	12.64	14.51	3.13	4.10	2.11
1946	37.75	25.30	10.72	7.42	3.02	0.79	12.45	14.57	3.31	4.40	2.22
1947	38.14	25.66	10.99	7.61	3.09	0.82	12.47	14.67	3.38	4.53	2.27

1948	36.68	24.49	10.39	7.20	2.94	0.71	12.19	14.10	3.19	4.26	2.23
1949	38.22	25.37	10.69	7.38	2.91	0.69	12.84	14.69	3.31	4.46	2.23
1950	38.24	25.45	10.88	7.58	3.06	0.74	12.79	14.57	3.30	4.51	2.33
1951	36.31	23.96	10.03	6.94	2.80	0.65	12.35	13.93	3.09	4.14	2.15
1952	36.44	23.91	9.85	6.75	2.71	0.67	12.52	14.07	3.09	4.04	2.03
1953	37.36	24.37	9.88	6.75	2.70	0.66	12.98	14.50	3.12	4.05	2.04
1954	38.68	25.29	10.33	7.10	2.82	0.71	13.39	14.96	3.23	4.28	2.11
1955	38.08	24.90	10.19	7.00	2.86	0.75	13.18	14.71	3.19	4.14	2.11
1956	37.22	24.19	9.63	6.57	2.63	0.65	13.04	14.56	3.06	3.94	1.98
1957	37.76	24.50	9.64	6.54	2.59	0.64	13.26	14.86	3.10	3.95	1.95
1958	38.39	25.00	9.89	6.68	2.62	0.64	13.39	15.11	3.21	4.06	1.98
1959	38.44	24.94	9.74	6.55	2.54	0.61	13.50	15.21	3.19	4.01	1.93
1960	38.78	25.13	9.77	6.56	2.52	0.61	13.65	15.36	3.21	4.03	1.92
1961	39.35	25.53	9.93	6.63	2.55	0.63	13.82	15.61	3.29	4.08	1.92
1962	37.77	24.42	9.37	6.23	2.33	0.54	13.36	15.05	3.14	3.90	1.79
1963	37.37	24.11	9.14	6.06	2.24	0.51	13.26	14.96	3.08	3.82	1.73
1964	37.77	24.43	9.38	6.24	2.33	0.54	13.34	15.05	3.14	3.92	1.78
1965	37.23	24.04	9.20	6.12	2.28	0.54	13.19	14.84	3.08	3.84	1.74
1966	36.76	23.70	8.91	5.88	2.16	0.49	13.06	14.80	3.03	3.73	1.66
1967	37.06	23.91	9.00	5.93	2.15	0.47	13.15	14.91	3.07	3.78	1.68
1968	37.31	24.02	9.04	5.96	2.17	0.47	13.28	14.99	3.07	3.80	1.70
1969	37.34	24.01	9.01	5.91	2.13	0.46	13.33	15.00	3.09	3.78	1.67
1970	37.92	24.22	8.97	5.87	2.07	0.43	13.69	15.25	3.10	3.79	1.64
1971	37.83	24.08	8.87	5.79	2.00	0.40	13.76	15.21	3.08	3.79	1.60
1972	37.55	23.84	8.75	5.74	2.02	0.43	13.71	15.09	3.00	3.72	1.59
1973	37.02	23.65	8.80	5.78	2.06	0.46	13.37	14.85	3.02	3.72	1.60
1974	37.38	23.82	8.81	5.76	2.09	0.48	13.57	15.01	3.05	3.68	1.61
1975	37.28	23.71	8.74	5.73	2.11	0.51	13.56	14.97	3.01	3.62	1.60
1976	36.74	22.99	8.08	5.21	1.88	0.44	13.75	14.91	2.87	3.33	1.43
1977	36.18	22.43	7.74	4.98	1.79	0.43	13.75	14.69	2.76	3.20	1.36
1978	35.77	22.17	7.60	4.90	1.77	0.44	13.60	14.57	2.70	3.13	1.33
1979	35.57	22.11	7.72	5.06	1.86	0.48	13.46	14.40	2.65	3.20	1.38
1980	36.23	22.68	8.06	5.27	1.97	0.53	13.56	14.62	2.79	3.29	1.44
1981	35.39	22.10	7.80	5.08	1.88	0.50	13.29	14.30	2.72	3.20	1.39

(contd.)

Table 6B.1 (*contd.*)

	P90–100 (1)	P95–100 (2)	P99–100 (3)	P99.5–100 (4)	P99.9–100 (5)	P99.99–100 (6)	P90–95 (7)	P95–99 (8)	P99–99.5 (9)	P99.5–99.9 (10)	P99.9–99.99 (11)
1982	36.24	22.92	8.46	5.66	2.33	0.68	13.32	14.47	2.80	3.33	1.65
1983	36.19	22.71	8.21	5.44	2.13	0.57	13.48	14.49	2.78	3.30	1.56
1984	35.78	22.48	8.29	5.55	2.28	0.68	13.30	14.20	2.73	3.28	1.60
1985	35.25	22.20	8.21	5.51	2.26	0.67	13.04	13.99	2.70	3.26	1.59
1986	35.22	22.22	8.24	5.52	2.24	0.64	13.00	13.97	2.72	3.28	1.60
1987	35.05	22.22	8.40	5.69	2.38	0.70	12.83	13.82	2.71	3.31	1.68
1988	35.66	23.11	9.34	6.54	3.00	1.01	12.55	13.77	2.79	3.54	1.99
1989	36.36	23.83	10.01	7.15	3.44	1.29	12.53	13.82	2.86	3.71	2.15
1990	35.54	23.08	9.35	6.55	2.98	1.01	12.46	13.73	2.80	3.57	1.96
1991	36.31	23.47	9.37	6.51	2.91	0.99	12.84	14.11	2.86	3.60	1.92
1992	36.72	23.60	9.31	6.44	2.82	0.94	13.12	14.29	2.87	3.62	1.89
1993	37.31	24.03	9.56	6.64	2.97	0.99	13.28	14.48	2.91	3.67	1.98
1994	37.49	24.16	9.59	6.65	2.94	0.95	13.33	14.57	2.94	3.71	1.99
1995	37.85	24.65	10.00	6.99	3.13	1.03	13.21	14.64	3.02	3.86	2.10
1996	38.77	25.48	10.62	7.53	3.47	1.14	13.29	14.85	3.10	4.06	2.33
1997	39.78	26.51	11.52	8.32	3.97	1.33	13.26	14.99	3.20	4.35	2.64
1998	40.61	27.35	12.18	8.87	4.34	1.48	13.26	15.17	3.31	4.53	2.85
1999	41.17	27.89	12.62	9.25	4.61	1.68	13.29	15.27	3.37	4.64	2.93
2000	42.34	29.01	13.56	10.11	5.23	1.89	13.34	15.44	3.45	4.88	3.34

Notes: Computations by authors based on tax return statistics. Series for P90–95 are estimated only for the 1941–2000 period because the tax return population does not cover that group in the pre-war period.

	P90–100 (1)	P95–100 (2)	P99–100 (3)	P99.5–100 (4)	P99.9–100 (5)	P99.99–100 (6)	P90–95 (7)	P95–99 (8)	P99–99.5 (9)	P99.5–99.9 (10)	P99.9–99.99 (11)
Panel A: Groups ranked by income including full capital gains											
1972	37.81	24.11	8.92	5.85	2.08	0.46	13.70	15.19	3.07	3.76	1.62
1973	37.27	23.92	8.98	5.90	2.14	0.50	13.35	14.94	3.09	3.75	1.64
1974	37.61	24.07	8.97	5.86	2.15	0.51	13.54	15.10	3.11	3.71	1.64
1975	37.48	23.96	8.91	5.84	2.19	0.55	13.52	15.05	3.08	3.65	1.64
1976	36.90	23.23	8.29	5.36	1.98	0.49	13.67	14.94	2.93	3.39	1.49
1977	36.36	22.71	8.01	5.18	1.93	0.49	13.65	14.70	2.83	3.26	1.44
1978	36.49	22.95	8.10	5.17	1.96	0.51	13.53	14.85	2.94	3.21	1.45
1979	36.42	23.11	8.46	5.52	2.20	0.63	13.31	14.66	2.93	3.33	1.57
1980	37.23	23.84	8.88	5.84	2.39	0.68	13.39	14.96	3.04	3.45	1.71
1981	36.47	23.25	8.55	5.56	2.23	0.64	13.23	14.70	2.99	3.32	1.60
1982	36.58	23.35	8.89	6.05	2.59	0.78	13.22	14.46	2.85	3.46	1.81
1983	36.66	23.29	8.76	5.91	2.43	0.70	13.37	14.53	2.86	3.47	1.74
1984	36.11	22.92	8.73	5.94	2.54	0.78	13.19	14.20	2.79	3.40	1.75
1985	35.87	22.94	8.88	6.09	2.63	0.83	12.93	14.06	2.80	3.46	1.80
1986	36.22	23.35	9.15	6.26	2.67	0.82	12.87	14.20	2.90	3.58	1.85
1987	36.57	24.01	9.88	6.87	3.03	0.97	12.56	14.13	3.02	3.83	2.06
1988	37.07	24.72	10.74	7.70	3.66	1.20	12.35	13.97	3.04	4.05	2.46
1989	38.20	25.93	11.90	8.76	4.40	1.60	12.27	14.03	3.14	4.36	2.81
1990	36.33	24.03	10.18	7.21	3.30	1.07	12.30	13.85	2.97	3.91	2.23
1991	37.16	24.49	10.29	7.28	3.32	1.10	12.67	14.21	3.01	3.96	2.22
1992	37.80	24.87	10.47	7.40	3.32	1.03	12.94	14.40	3.07	4.08	2.29
1993	38.95	25.95	11.26	8.04	3.65	1.16	13.00	14.69	3.23	4.39	2.48
1994	38.56	25.64	11.21	8.07	3.61	1.09	12.93	14.43	3.14	4.46	2.52
1995	38.64	25.60	10.93	7.77	3.54	1.14	13.04	14.67	3.15	4.24	2.40
1996	39.63	26.53	11.64	8.40	3.97	1.31	13.10	14.89	3.24	4.43	2.65
1997	40.83	27.79	12.75	9.37	4.59	1.56	13.04	15.04	3.38	4.78	3.03
1998	41.63	28.61	13.40	9.91	4.92	1.70	13.02	15.21	3.49	4.99	3.23
1999	42.28	29.22	13.88	10.33	5.18	1.87	13.06	15.34	3.56	5.15	3.31
2000	44.04	31.07	15.50	11.76	6.16	2.20	12.98	15.56	3.75	5.60	3.95
Panel B: Groups ranked by income excluding capital gains											
1972	37.60	23.94	8.86	5.83	2.07	0.45	13.66	15.08	3.03	3.76	1.61
1973	37.09	23.76	8.92	5.87	2.12	0.48	13.33	14.83	3.05	3.75	1.63

(contd.)

Table 6B.2 (*contd.*)

	P90–100 (1)	P95–100 (2)	P99–100 (3)	P99.5–100 (4)	P99.9–100 (5)	P99.99–100 (6)	P90–95 (7)	P95–99 (8)	P99–99.5 (9)	P99.5–99.9 (10)	P99.9–99.99 (11)
1974	37.45	23.91	8.91	5.84	2.13	0.50	13.54	15.00	3.07	3.71	1.63
1975	37.34	23.81	8.86	5.81	2.16	0.53	13.53	14.95	3.04	3.65	1.63
1976	36.83	23.13	8.25	5.33	1.95	0.47	13.70	14.88	2.91	3.39	1.48
1977	36.30	22.62	7.97	5.14	1.89	0.46	13.68	14.65	2.82	3.25	1.42
1978	35.95	22.44	7.91	5.13	1.92	0.48	13.50	14.51	2.78	3.21	1.43
1979	35.89	22.57	8.25	5.45	2.11	0.57	13.31	14.28	2.80	3.33	1.54
1980	36.64	23.26	8.68	5.75	2.27	0.62	13.37	14.54	2.93	3.46	1.65
1981	35.68	22.52	8.28	5.49	2.14	0.58	13.14	14.21	2.79	3.33	1.56
1982	36.31	23.09	8.67	5.85	2.46	0.72	13.22	14.42	2.82	3.40	1.73
1983	36.32	22.96	8.49	5.68	2.27	0.60	13.36	14.47	2.81	3.41	1.67
1984	35.83	22.65	8.51	5.76	2.39	0.70	13.18	14.14	2.75	3.36	1.69
1985	35.45	22.53	8.55	5.80	2.43	0.75	12.92	13.98	2.75	3.36	1.68
1986	35.58	22.74	8.73	5.92	2.47	0.71	12.84	14.01	2.81	3.45	1.77
1987	35.51	22.91	9.07	6.22	2.66	0.79	12.60	13.84	2.85	3.57	1.87
1988	36.10	23.73	9.93	7.02	3.25	1.05	12.37	13.81	2.91	3.77	2.20
1989	37.13	24.81	10.94	7.92	3.86	1.34	12.33	13.87	3.01	4.07	2.51
1990	35.71	23.38	9.64	6.77	3.08	1.03	12.33	13.74	2.87	3.69	2.05
1991	36.54	23.84	9.73	6.80	3.05	1.04	12.70	14.10	2.93	3.75	2.01
1992	37.06	24.08	9.75	6.79	2.97	0.96	12.98	14.33	2.96	3.81	2.01
1993	37.78	24.71	10.16	7.10	3.18	1.05	13.07	14.55	3.06	3.92	2.13
1994	37.40	24.40	10.11	7.12	3.15	0.99	13.00	14.29	2.98	3.98	2.16
1995	38.09	25.01	10.36	7.27	3.27	1.05	13.08	14.66	3.08	4.00	2.22
1996	38.99	25.88	11.05	7.88	3.67	1.20	13.11	14.83	3.17	4.22	2.47
1997	40.09	27.03	12.07	8.75	4.15	1.36	13.05	14.96	3.32	4.60	2.79
1998	40.92	27.87	12.71	9.30	4.59	1.51	13.05	15.16	3.41	4.72	3.08
1999	41.50	28.42	13.14	9.63	4.77	1.71	13.08	15.28	3.50	4.87	3.06
2000	42.87	29.82	14.35	10.77	5.55	1.92	13.05	15.47	3.58	5.22	3.63

Notes: In Panel A, tax returns are ranked by total income including full capital gains, and shares are computed as total income and capital gains accruing to upper groups divided by total income plus total capital gains in the economy (from Table 6A.1). In Panel B, individuals are ranked by income excluding capital gains (as in Table 6B.1) but capital gains are added back (in both the numerator and the denominator) to compute top shares.

Table 6B.3 Top fractile income levels (excluding capital gains) in Canada, 1920–2000

	P90–100 (1)	P95–100 (2)	P99–100 (3)	P99.5–100 (4)	P99.9–100 (5)	P99.99–100 (6)	P90–95 (7)	P95–99 (8)	P99–99.5 (9)	P99.5–99.9 (10)	P99.9–99.99 (11)	P90 (12)	P95 (13)	P99 (14)	P99.5 (15)	P99.9 (16)	P99.99 (17)
1920		32,469	71,733	104,519	267,051	1,045,891		22,653	38,947	63,886	180,513		17,311	34,101	45,662	110,173	418,867
1921		36,311	78,753	112,300	259,766	761,937		25,700	45,206	75,433	203,969		19,390	39,351	53,371	128,898	418,693
1922		34,248	75,650	107,134	251,252	813,402		23,897	44,166	71,104	188,791		19,273	38,588	51,905	119,336	402,114
1923		31,957	76,231	108,273	248,609	812,975		20,889	44,189	73,189	185,902		18,232	38,120	52,707	121,158	394,127
1924		32,130	76,184	108,925	256,324	854,937		21,117	43,444	72,075	189,811		17,948	37,488	51,787	121,332	408,624
1925		33,331	73,783	106,138	243,143	738,052		23,218	41,427	71,887	188,153		17,899	34,715	51,062	119,211	389,900
1926		35,841	83,283	121,498	285,793	935,604		23,980	45,068	80,424	213,592		18,034	37,245	56,539	137,099	449,063
1927		37,939	90,778	133,260	317,177	1,072,086		24,729	48,296	87,281	233,298		18,329	39,758	60,525	149,795	503,521
1928		40,541	99,151	145,395	342,674	1,131,672		25,888	52,906	96,076	254,935		18,655	43,605	66,064	163,731	546,411
1929		39,930	98,428	144,389	335,707	1,072,879		25,305	52,467	96,559	253,729		18,242	43,149	65,631	166,663	529,034
1930		38,173	93,884	138,348	331,235	1,074,576		24,245	49,420	90,112	248,642		17,638	40,712	61,880	156,424	533,934
1931		37,825	87,161	125,951	291,516	902,424		25,491	48,360	84,560	223,696		18,856	40,688	59,347	142,159	471,635
1932		36,851	82,585	118,853	279,302	888,476		25,417	46,317	78,741	211,616		18,913	39,421	56,013	131,514	464,851
1933		35,944	79,284	113,361	259,662	759,290		25,109	45,206	76,786	204,148		18,761	38,670	54,947	126,986	440,499
1934		37,194	83,231	119,759	278,784	873,014		25,684	46,703	80,002	212,759		18,992	39,712	56,777	133,364	458,506
1935		37,805	84,311	121,034	279,382	851,694		26,179	47,588	81,447	215,846		19,426	40,300	57,873	135,930	450,137
1936		39,362	89,549	130,044	307,839	978,228		26,815	49,055	85,608	233,294		19,889	41,416	59,977	145,337	501,019
1937		39,705	90,125	130,756	303,688	853,743		27,099	49,495	87,522	242,633		20,167	41,818	60,664	149,065	543,315
1938		43,465	101,124	146,227	332,244	1,025,799		29,050	56,021	99,723	255,183		20,984	46,459	69,134	165,112	517,246
1939		42,495	96,366	139,581	321,411	955,500		29,027	53,152	94,109	251,020		21,145	44,905	64,643	159,339	516,173
1940		42,286	92,330	129,976	283,533	959,970		29,775	54,685	91,586	208,374		22,198	46,296	66,045	145,424	383,178
1941	31,671	42,983	92,953	132,247	296,050	898,984	20,359	30,491	53,645	91,297	229,057	17,429	23,935	45,837	65,019	150,140	477,795
1942	33,165	44,301	94,704	134,263	296,174	891,122	22,029	31,701	55,127	93,786	230,162	19,425	25,219	47,238	67,139	152,135	476,240
1943	34,709	45,659	94,690	132,714	284,918	811,023	23,760	33,399	56,666	94,664	226,560	21,258	26,944	48,891	68,590	151,055	459,722
1944	35,407	46,393	94,814	131,598	276,893	772,989	24,421	34,287	58,031	95,274	221,771	21,871	27,588	50,247	70,026	150,037	443,584
1945	34,678	45,831	94,164	130,030	268,973	724,766	23,526	33,747	58,298	95,294	218,226	21,064	26,749	50,396	70,283	148,844	430,675
1946	34,111	45,724	96,914	134,074	272,649	717,546	22,497	32,927	59,753	99,431	223,216	20,085	25,790	50,902	72,436	156,354	424,514
1947	35,435	47,689	102,140	141,433	286,732	757,247	23,180	34,076	62,847	105,109	234,452	20,799	26,410	52,727	76,313	163,025	454,757
1948	34,163	45,619	96,774	134,105	273,836	665,031	22,708	32,830	59,443	99,173	230,370	20,195	25,740	50,207	71,812	155,955	439,619
1949	35,013	46,496	97,897	135,177	266,891	629,434	23,530	33,645	60,616	102,249	226,608	20,994	26,685	51,530	74,059	160,900	422,834

(*contd.*)

Table 6B.3 (*contd.*)

	P90–100 (1)	P95–100 (2)	P99–100 (3)	P99.5–100 (4)	P99.9–100 (5)	P99.99–100 (6)	P90–95 (7)	P95–99 (8)	P99–99.5 (9)	P99.5–99.9 (10)	P99.9–99.99 (11)	P90 (12)	P95 (13)	P99 (14)	P99.5 (15)	P99.9 (16)	P99.99 (17)
1950	35,672	47,480	101,471	141,320	285,532	686,545	23,865	33,982	61,621	105,267	240,975	21,412	26,881	52,003	75,686	165,197	442,924
1951	36,009	47,524	99,490	137,692	278,081	644,625	24,494	34,532	61,289	102,595	237,354	22,209	27,587	51,962	74,234	166,579	421,316
1952	37,475	49,188	101,258	138,892	278,525	693,226	25,762	36,171	63,625	103,984	232,447	23,311	29,147	53,868	76,488	162,599	445,520
1953	39,901	52,067	105,489	144,284	288,824	708,175	27,735	38,712	66,694	108,149	242,230	25,024	31,297	57,082	79,659	169,329	446,235
1954	40,144	52,494	107,220	147,353	292,361	731,681	27,793	38,813	67,086	111,101	243,548	25,051	31,388	57,418	81,016	173,524	444,318
1955	41,886	54,777	112,063	153,978	314,335	827,081	28,996	40,455	70,148	113,889	257,363	26,165	32,665	59,918	84,225	176,429	487,650
1956	43,947	57,108	113,633	155,131	310,617	767,392	30,785	42,977	72,135	116,260	259,864	27,857	34,827	62,372	86,506	181,296	478,780
1957	44,910	58,284	114,649	155,458	307,943	756,477	31,537	44,193	73,840	117,337	258,106	28,374	35,745	64,094	87,896	181,157	469,872
1958	45,760	59,594	117,880	159,183	312,073	761,706	31,925	45,023	76,576	120,961	262,114	28,791	36,162	66,328	90,863	185,037	468,832
1959	46,758	60,675	118,404	159,332	309,177	746,792	32,842	46,243	77,477	121,871	260,553	29,678	37,226	67,438	91,478	185,716	465,186
1960	48,106	62,350	121,183	162,718	313,129	751,808	33,861	47,642	79,647	125,115	264,387	30,577	38,362	69,429	93,975	189,202	475,098
1961	49,309	63,991	124,384	166,238	319,418	785,701	34,626	48,893	82,530	127,943	267,609	31,197	39,209	71,899	96,886	192,280	482,447
1962	50,378	65,133	124,982	166,181	310,622	721,540	35,624	50,171	83,784	130,071	264,965	32,344	40,608	73,805	98,631	192,956	466,689
1963	51,625	66,605	126,302	167,417	309,469	699,068	36,644	51,681	85,187	131,904	266,180	32,998	41,546	75,166	99,965	194,910	460,322
1964	54,127	70,017	134,446	178,898	333,464	778,130	38,236	53,910	89,994	140,257	284,056	34,490	43,280	78,997	106,503	206,845	496,485
1965	56,705	73,242	140,151	186,533	347,294	816,445	40,167	56,515	93,769	146,343	295,166	36,207	45,378	81,806	109,948	213,399	507,094
1966	59,206	76,356	143,473	189,504	347,569	795,641	42,056	59,576	97,442	149,988	297,784	37,641	47,277	84,934	113,140	216,801	500,622
1967	61,195	78,959	148,563	195,739	355,183	779,389	43,431	61,559	101,387	155,878	308,049	39,091	49,332	89,051	119,179	227,947	517,421
1968	63,078	81,243	152,770	201,687	366,411	796,399	44,913	63,361	103,853	160,506	318,635	40,495	50,877	91,467	122,355	237,100	532,448
1969	65,384	84,076	157,730	207,108	373,664	805,461	46,692	65,663	108,352	165,470	325,686	42,072	52,787	94,383	126,371	246,253	535,568
1970	67,341	86,040	159,290	208,397	368,166	769,011	48,641	67,728	110,183	168,454	323,628	43,805	54,990	96,220	128,023	247,758	526,095
1971	69,919	88,985	163,851	214,008	369,433	744,779	50,852	70,269	113,694	175,152	327,727	45,888	57,394	99,184	132,204	253,542	523,234
1972	73,170	92,920	170,477	223,834	393,453	839,912	53,419	73,536	117,081	181,429	343,630	48,295	60,084	103,422	137,654	261,632	569,864
1973	76,683	97,975	182,211	239,302	426,940	946,684	55,392	76,915	125,078	192,392	369,191	50,024	62,420	109,872	147,169	277,333	613,789
1974	80,789	102,949	190,433	249,128	450,798	1,039,472	58,634	81,078	131,739	198,710	385,390	52,619	66,074	115,762	153,918	286,468	666,746
1975	81,990	104,318	192,266	252,029	464,774	1,119,592	59,662	82,331	132,503	198,898	392,016	53,892	67,160	116,966	154,912	286,913	695,411
1976	83,690	104,755	184,023	237,238	427,139	1,004,630	62,624	84,938	130,807	189,763	362,720	56,656	70,346	116,245	149,956	271,640	625,313
1977	82,325	102,085	176,188	226,710	406,221	967,192	62,565	83,560	125,667	181,832	343,891	56,736	69,939	112,408	144,101	257,338	600,746
1978	81,512	101,050	173,218	223,255	403,081	993,461	61,973	83,014	123,180	178,299	337,230	56,076	69,446	111,222	141,376	252,057	595,647
1979	82,252	102,257	178,397	234,194	430,559	1,116,863	62,248	83,216	122,647	185,045	354,303	56,128	69,550	110,773	143,486	268,957	633,595

1980	84,070	105,239	187,007	244,362	457,310	1,222,741	62,905	84,797	129,652	191,068	372,262	56,824	70,522	116,412	149,806	281,558	679,990
1981	84,328	105,329	185,866	242,245	447,984	1,181,916	63,328	85,200	129,486	190,810	366,701	57,186	70,877	116,010	149,484	276,425	666,223
1982	82,892	104,861	193,412	258,905	533,228	1,548,671	60,922	82,724	127,920	190,324	420,401	54,956	68,441	114,034	147,839	284,221	868,025
1983	79,779	100,120	181,078	239,629	470,000	1,254,361	59,438	79,880	122,526	182,037	382,848	53,606	66,602	109,279	141,709	267,553	741,082
1984	80,438	101,088	186,246	249,662	511,868	1,524,140	59,788	79,798	122,830	184,111	399,394	54,083	66,713	109,058	142,482	275,368	798,859
1985	81,091	102,161	188,980	253,584	518,810	1,532,272	60,021	80,456	124,376	187,278	406,203	54,335	67,156	110,273	144,762	280,133	836,173
1986	81,849	103,281	191,613	256,645	521,100	1,494,503	60,417	81,198	126,580	190,532	412,945	54,558	67,588	112,082	147,540	283,722	812,886
1987	82,441	104,520	197,483	267,450	558,558	1,646,277	60,362	81,279	127,516	194,672	437,701	54,541	67,544	112,595	149,078	295,924	888,355
1988	87,393	113,265	228,770	320,597	734,711	2,472,727	61,522	84,389	136,943	217,068	541,598	55,472	69,276	119,505	161,990	344,180	1,229,108
1989	90,447	118,548	248,996	355,908	856,437	3,208,841	62,346	85,936	142,084	230,775	595,059	56,194	70,133	123,433	169,449	371,951	1,390,897
1990	88,404	114,829	232,553	325,744	740,598	2,522,562	61,979	85,398	139,363	222,030	542,602	55,777	69,757	121,607	165,217	349,771	1,215,448
1991	85,622	110,681	220,811	306,754	686,128	2,331,894	60,563	83,149	134,868	211,910	503,266	54,383	68,269	117,966	159,102	329,009	1,109,688
1992	85,169	109,484	216,013	298,795	654,325	2,168,714	60,854	82,852	133,231	209,913	486,060	54,717	68,435	116,400	157,569	323,488	1,060,636
1993	85,092	109,602	217,895	302,932	677,059	2,259,905	60,582	82,529	132,858	209,400	501,188	54,346	68,179	116,215	156,774	326,131	1,105,608
1994	86,176	111,076	220,515	305,806	675,660	2,179,401	61,276	83,716	135,224	213,342	508,578	55,081	68,942	118,176	159,967	332,208	1,126,661
1995	88,010	114,607	232,562	324,871	727,543	2,387,939	61,412	85,118	140,254	224,204	543,054	55,202	69,470	122,149	166,491	355,236	1,210,910
1996	89,831	118,072	246,173	348,776	803,817	2,646,178	61,590	86,047	143,570	235,016	599,110	55,166	69,815	124,424	171,713	381,630	1,348,195
1997	93,299	124,377	270,296	390,338	931,868	3,128,899	62,221	87,898	150,253	254,956	687,753	55,641	70,646	129,178	182,008	428,509	1,634,284
1998	97,273	131,011	291,703	424,918	1,038,460	3,554,959	63,534	90,838	158,488	271,533	758,849	56,551	72,345	135,170	192,393	458,368	1,799,985
1999	100,093	135,586	306,740	449,765	1,119,794	4,074,630	64,601	92,798	163,715	282,258	791,479	57,483	73,638	139,473	198,915	478,918	1,931,959
2000	105,262	144,214	337,142	502,556	1,300,639	4,695,923	66,310	95,982	171,728	303,035	923,385	59,232	75,670	145,774	210,150	530,311	2,396,050

Notes: Groups are ranked by total income excluding capital gains. All amounts are reported in Canadian 2000 dollars (US$1 = CA$1.5 in 2000).
Computations by authors based on income tax return statistics.

is very closely approximated by a Pareto distribution. As described in earlier chapters, a Pareto distribution has the key property that the average income above a given threshold y is always exactly proportional to y. The coefficient of proportionality is equal to $b = a/(a-1)$, where a is the Pareto exponent.

For years before 1938, when the amounts by income brackets are not reported, we first estimate the amounts reported by bracket using the method described in Appendix 5C. When data on amounts reported are available (starting in 1938), we verify that our estimated amounts Y are very close to the true reported amounts (in general the true and estimated amounts differ by less than 2–3%).

Adjustments to Raw Pareto Interpolation

Published tax statistics tables rank tax returns by net income (1920–45) or by gross income (1946–2000). Gross tax income is defined as the sum of all sources of income before any deductions. Net income is gross tax income less deductions such as medical costs or charitable contributions allowed but before deducting personal and marital status exemptions. From 1920 to 1928, no deductions were allowed and net income is equal to gross tax income. From 1929 on, charitable deductions were allowed up to 10% of income, and medical expenses (in excess of 5% of income and up to a relatively modest maximum amount) were deductible from income. Starting in 1946, the level of deduction can be computed for each group using the composition tables. In the 1940s and 1950s, this amount fluctuates around 2% for all the income groups within the top decile.[34] Therefore, we increase our raw income thresholds, levels, and top shares (based on net income) by 2% for all groups in the period 1929–45.

Starting in 1946, in order to report statistics more quickly, the fiscal administration decided to compile tax statistics about one year after the filing deadline. Because of late filing, a small number of returns were not included in the statistics. To correct for this and based on the *Taxation Statistics* reports, we increase the number of returns and amounts reported by bracket by 2% from 1946 to 1957 and by 1% from 1958 to 1963. After 1963, the number of missing returns due to late filing is deemed to be extremely small and no correction is made.

For many of the pre-war years, the exemption levels were so high (especially in the period 1925–31) that less than 5% of adult individuals actually filed returns (see Table 6A.1, column (3)). However, the exemption level for singles is always half of the exemption level for married individuals. Thus from 1920 on, it is always the case than more than 5% of single individuals are actually filing returns, although for some years less than 5% of married tax units are filing returns. As a result, the number of taxpayers in the bottom brackets is too low for some years and needs to be adjusted upward. We adjusted for missing married returns using a simple extrapolation method, based on the assumption that marital ratios

[34] The level of deductions was much lower in Canada than in the United States at the top because the United States allowed unlimited charitable deductions as well as deductions for interest paid on debt.

(i.e. ratios of married individuals to single individuals) across income brackets is constant over those years.[35]

Starting in 1972, a fraction of capital gains is included in gross income and the dividend tax credit is introduced. From 1972 to 1987, 50% of realized gains were included in taxable income. In 1988 and 1989, 66.6% of gains were included in taxable income. From 1990 to 1999, 75% of gains were included in taxable income. Finally, over the course of tax year 2000, the amount of gains taxable was reduced back to 50%.[36] The dividend tax credit works as follows. First, dividends reported on tax returns are multiplied by a gross-up factor. This factor was 4/3 for 1972–77, 3/2 from 1978 to 1986, 4/3 in 1987, and 5/4 from 1988 to 2000. Second, a tax credit proportional to the grossed-up amount of dividends reported can be deducted from personal income tax liability. This dividend tax credit approximately offsets the corporate income tax paid on profits before distribution to shareholders in the form of dividends.[37] The important point for our study is that, after 1972, the income tax statistics rank individual taxpayers by gross income, which includes the taxable fraction of realized capital gains, as well as the grossed-up dividend amounts. The series we want to estimate are based on gross income excluding capital gains and including only the actual amount of dividends distributed.

The raw series we compute are based on the income definition reported in the income tax statistics, which includes capital gains and grossed-up dividends. Therefore, these raw series are an over-estimate of the income shares based on income excluding capital gains and dividend gross-up. In order to compute our series from the raw series, one could simply deduct for each group the share of capital gains and the grossed-up extra amount of dividends estimated from composition tables. The problem is that ranking according to the income tax statistics and ranking according to our income definition might be different, especially at the very top. For example, in the extreme case where very top incomes of the income tax statistics distributions consist only of capital gains, then the deduction of capital gains would lead to the conclusion that the very top incomes of the income (excluding capital gains) distribution are equal to zero. Therefore, deducting the full amount of capital gains and dividend gross-up would provide an

[35] More precisely, we assume that the ratio of marital ratios over two adjacent brackets is constant from year to year. We verify this assumption comparing these ratios for years with low filing thresholds and where missing returns is not an issue. We use the closest years for which the filing threshold is low enough so that all the married tax units with income in that particular income bracket file a return to compute these marital ratios. We then extrapolate the marital ratio for a year with high filing threshold in a low bracket using the bracket just above for that year and the marital ratios for the year with complete returns. We then compute the expected number of married tax units in each bracket in high filing threshold years. We thus obtain the missing number of returns in each bracket or equivalently a multiplier factor by which we must adjust the actual number of returns to obtain the real number of tax units.

[36] More precisely, 75% of capital gains realized before 28 February 2000, 66.6% of gains realized on or after 28 February and before 18 October and 50% of the gains realized on or after 18 October 2000 are included in taxable income. Under the present tax law, for years 2001 and after, 50% of realized gains are included in taxable income.

[37] The offset would be exact if the grossed-up factor and the dividend tax credit rate were equal to the corporate income tax rate. Before 1972, there was no dividend gross-up and the dividend tax credit was 10% of dividends from 1949 (the first year such a credit was introduced) to 1952, and 20% from 1953 to 1971. Since 1972, the dividend credit has fluctuated between 16.66% and 25%.

underestimate of the income shares we would like to estimate. However, the LAD micro-files available from 1982 allowed us to compute the magnitude of the corrections that one needs to apply in order to obtain unbiased series from the *Taxation Statistics* tables for the period 1972–81. More precisely, we computed the correction coefficients to be applied to the thresholds and average income levels for each fractile using the year 1982 for which we have both the imperfect published data and the micro-data, which allows to do exact computations. It turns out that those correction coefficients are reasonably stable over the years 1982–2000 (the correction coefficients are always in a plus or minus 5% range) and therefore we are confident that the extrapolations we make for years 1972–81 are fairly precise. The top income shares are reported in Table 6B.1 and the income thresholds and income averages for each of our top groups are reported in Table 6B.3.

From 1972 on, we have also computed two alternative series based on income including full realized capital gains. In the first series, we rank individuals by income including full capital gains and include capital gains in income. After 1982, we use the LAD micro-data to rank individuals by income including capital gains and we compute top income shares in that case by dividing the income amounts for each top group by our total income denominator from Table 6A.1, column (4) plus the total amount of realized capital gains corresponding to the amounts reported on tax returns. For the period 1972–81, we have again to deal with the re-ranking issue as only 50% of capital gains are included in gross income and as dividends included are grossed-up. Let us call the sum of the 50% of realized gains excluded from gross income net of the extra dividend gross-up the net missing amount.[38] Again, simply adding to the amounts estimated from the raw published series the net missing amount would lead to series that are downward biased because of re-ranking. We adopt the same methodology as above to make the corrections for years 1972–81. Namely, we use the year 1982 to compute correction coefficients for each of our fractiles, and we apply those correction coefficients to all years 1972–81. We have also checked carefully that the correction coefficients are stable over the period 1982 to 2000. The top income share series including capital gains are reported in Table 6B.2, Panel A.

In the second series, we rank individuals by income excluding capital gains (as in Table 6B.1), but we add back capital gains in incomes (both in the numerator and the denominator). Exact computations are possible from 1982 on using the LAD micro-data. For the period 1972–81, we adjust our raw series using correction coefficients from the year 1982 (as above). The results are reported in Table 6B.1, Panel B.

Notes on the Pre-War Published Statistics

Personal income taxation in Canada has always been assessed on a calendar year basis, meaning that income taxes were based on income earned during a calendar

[38] Note that the net missing amount could be negative if the dividend gross-up is larger than the capital gains exclusion.

year from 1 January to 31 December. From 1920 to 1940, however, the income tax statistics are reported by fiscal years (ending 31 March) and not by taxation year. Fiscal year means that the amounts and number of individuals were those for which income taxes were collected during the fiscal year 1 April of year t to 31 March of year $t+1$. However, because income tax returns and payments were due in mid-April of the following year, income taxes assessed and collected during fiscal year ending on 31 March of year $t+1$ corresponded almost entirely to incomes earned during calendar year $t-1$ (see Canadian Tax Foundation 1957: 190). Starting with tax year 1940, the exemptions were lowered significantly in order to increase revenues for the war. As a result the number of returns increased substantially and the fiscal administration was only able to assess 63.7% of all the returns filed for calendar tax year 1940 during fiscal year 1941/42. We assume that the returns assessed were drawn uniformly from all income classes and we simply multiply the number of individuals and amounts reported in the published table by a factor 1/0.637.

The year 1942 saw the transformation of the income tax from the old system with little or no withholding and where taxpayers paid their tax liability when they filed tax returns in the year following the calendar tax year to a new system of pay-as-you-earn where the government implemented widespread withholding as income was earned. In order to relieve taxpayers from having to pay taxes for two years in 1942 (both for year 1941 under the old system and for year 1942 under the new pay-as-you-earn system), the tax liability for tax year 1942 was reduced by 50% relative to the nominal tax schedule.[39]

APPENDIX 6C: COMPOSITION OF TOP INCOMES

Occupation Data from 1920 to 1945

From 1920 to 1945, the fiscal administration published in *The Canada Yearbook* tables dividing taxpayers into a number of occupational groups. A taxpayer was assigned to a group by major source of income. For example, those who reported wages and salaries as their major source of income were classified as employees. We report in Table 6C.1 the fraction of tax returns in each category as well as the fraction of the adult population filing tax returns for each year between 1920 and 1941. After 1941, the number of tax filers increased significantly and thus the figures cannot be compared with the pre-war years.

For tax year 1942, the fiscal administration first published occupation statistics by income brackets (Canada Customs and Revenue Agency 1947: 108–10). Using the income thresholds from our raw Pareto interpolations, we can estimate the fraction of taxpayers in each occupation for our top income groups. We have

[39] Higher incomes did not benefit fully from the 50% abatement as tax liabilities above a certain high threshold were to be paid at the time of death of the taxpayer. This deferral rule still made the tax burden for year 1942 much lower than the nominal rates.

Table 6C.1 Shares of total tax returns in each occupation in Canada, 1920–41

	Tax returns/adult population (1)	Employees (2)	Agrarians (3)	Professionals (4)	Merchants (5)	Manufacturers (6)	Financial (7)	Personal corporations (8)	All others (9)
1920	5.82%	71.33%	6.48%	5.90%	8.16%	0.56%			7.57%
1921	5.54%	74.10%	2.92%	6.77%	7.53%	0.62%			8.06%
1922	4.63%	73.67%	1.95%	8.60%	7.12%	0.54%			8.12%
1923	4.31%	74.89%	1.36%	8.60%	6.58%	0.50%			8.07%
1924	3.94%	75.52%	1.73%	8.38%	5.85%	0.43%			8.09%
1925	2.14%	70.20%	2.80%	5.50%	7.72%	0.74%	3.79%	0.11%	9.14%
1926	2.21%	68.14%	2.59%	4.99%	8.09%	0.74%	6.27%	0.39%	8.79%
1927	2.29%	67.46%	2.40%	5.22%	8.21%	0.77%	6.67%	0.50%	8.77%
1928	2.45%	67.06%	1.85%	5.23%	8.88%	0.80%	6.71%	0.64%	8.83%
1929	2.41%	69.40%	1.58%	5.19%	8.17%	0.66%	6.46%	0.42%	8.12%
1930	2.20%	72.05%	0.49%	4.87%	6.21%	0.62%	7.27%	0.43%	8.06%
1931	2.70%	79.49%	0.15%	3.60%	4.01%	0.32%	5.83%	0.31%	6.29%
1932	3.23%	82.24%	0.13%	2.91%	2.71%	0.23%	5.76%	0.30%	5.72%
1933	2.86%	81.12%	0.23%	3.15%	3.11%	0.24%	6.34%	0.32%	5.49%
1934	3.03%	80.35%	0.35%	3.30%	3.64%	0.27%	6.53%	0.27%	5.29%
1935	3.25%	80.69%	0.43%	3.24%	3.83%	0.28%	6.42%	0.25%	4.86%
1936	3.49%	80.03%	0.42%	3.25%	4.13%	0.29%	6.31%	0.24%	5.33%
1937	3.84%	81.33%	0.49%	2.95%	3.81%	0.30%	5.97%	0.25%	4.90%
1938	4.19%	77.54%	0.59%	4.04%	5.35%	0.58%	6.21%	0.31%	5.38%
1939	4.22%	77.44%	0.62%	3.68%	5.59%	0.56%	5.09%	0.26%	6.76%
1940	8.42%	87.44%	0.38%	2.00%	3.33%	0.26%	3.22%	0.13%	3.24%
1941	11.86%	86.60%	0.85%	1.82%	5.11%	0.28%	3.07%	0.11%	2.16%

Notes: Computations based directly on published tax return statistics Percentiles are based on average tax paid for each category.

Table 6C.2 Shares of each occupation within the top 10% in Canada, 1942

Fractile (1)	Number of individuals (2)	Employees (3)	Entrepreneurs (4)	Rentiers (5)
P90–95	361,443	91.8%	6.9%	1.3%
P95–99	289,154	83.2%	14.1%	2.8%
P99–99.5	36,144	59.4%	33.5%	7.1%
P99.5–99.9	28,915	52.0%	36.5%	11.5%
P99.9–99.99	6,506	46.7%	30.0%	23.3%
P99.99–99.999	651	38.3%	18.1%	43.6%
P99.999–100	72	27.3%	8.1%	64.6%

Notes: Computations based on interpolations from *Taxation Statistics*, 1947: 108–10. Category employees defined as employees and armed forces. Category entrepreneurs defined as agrarians, professionals, salesmen, and business proprietors. Category rentiers defined as financial and estates. Category All others excluded. Tax returns are classified in occupation categories by main source of income.

grouped occupations into three categories. The employees category is defined as employees and armed forces. The entrepreneurs category is defined as agrarians, professionals, salesmen, and business proprietors. The rentiers category is defined as financial and estates. The all others category is excluded. The results are reported in Table 6C.2.

Composition Data from 1946 to 2000

We have constructed income composition series for each of our top groups (Tables 6C.3 and 6C.4) for the post the Second World War period when tables reporting the composition of income, by income brackets, started to be published. The composition series reported in Table 6C.3 indicate for each upper income group the fraction of total income (excluding capital gains) that comes from the various types of income (excluding capital gains). We consider six types of income: wage income; professional income; business income; dividends; interest income; and other investment income. Wage income includes wages and salaries, commissions from employment, as well as pensions. Wage income also includes profits from exercised stock options (which are reported as employment income on Canadian tax returns). Professional income includes self-employment income from professions such as doctors, lawyers, etc. Business income includes income from sole proprietorships, partnership income, and farm income. Dividends include only dividends distributed by Canadian corporations (and not dividends distributed by foreign companies to individuals in Canada). Interest includes interest income from banks, mortgages, and annuity income. Other investment income includes rents, fiduciary income, investment income from foreign sources, as well as a number of smaller items. We have excluded from these composition series a number of minor income categories such as alimony, taxable social security benefits, taxable unemployment insurance

Table 6C.3 Income composition by fractiles of total income (excluding capital, gains) in Canada, 1946–2000

	P90–100							P95–100							P99–100							P99.5–100					
	Wage	Prof.	Busin.	Divid.	Interest	Invest.		Wage	Prof.	Busin.	Divid.	Interest	Invest.		Wage	Prof.	Busin.	Divid.	Interest	Invest.		Wage	Prof.	Busin.	Divid.	Interest	Invest.
1946	72.9	4.0	14.6	3.2	2.2	3.2	1946	65.2	5.5	17.9	4.5	2.7	4.2	1946	45.5	10.1	24.3	8.7	4.3	7.2	1946	41.0	11.3	23.8	10.9	4.8	8.3
1947	71.4	4.0	16.6	3.2	1.9	2.9	1947	62.6	5.6	21.0	4.5	2.5	3.9	1947	43.7	9.7	28.1	8.4	3.7	6.4	1947	38.9	10.7	28.6	10.5	4.1	7.3
1948	71.9	3.7	16.6	3.3	1.7	2.8	1948	62.8	5.3	21.1	4.7	2.2	3.8	1948	44.0	9.2	28.2	9.0	3.4	6.2	1948	40.2	9.8	28.1	11.2	3.7	7.0
1949	71.8	4.1	16.5	3.3	1.6	2.8	1949	62.9	5.8	20.8	4.7	2.1	3.7	1949	44.3	10.0	27.3	9.0	3.2	6.2	1949	40.3	10.9	26.9	11.3	3.6	7.2
1950	71.9	4.4	15.7	3.5	1.7	2.9	1950	63.0	6.2	19.7	5.0	2.2	3.9	1950	44.0	10.8	26.1	9.4	3.3	6.5	1950	40.0	11.7	25.8	11.6	3.5	7.4
1951	73.0	4.4	14.8	3.2	1.4	3.1	1951	64.3	6.3	18.7	4.6	1.9	4.2	1951	45.8	11.2	24.1	8.7	3.0	7.2	1951	42.1	12.3	23.5	10.5	3.2	8.4
1952	73.9	4.5	14.0	3.3	1.5	2.9	1952	65.2	6.4	17.7	4.7	2.1	3.9	1952	45.7	11.7	23.1	9.3	3.4	6.8	1952	42.0	12.6	22.4	11.5	3.8	7.8
1953	74.6	4.5	13.2	3.2	1.6	3.0	1953	66.3	6.4	16.6	4.6	2.1	4.1	1953	46.8	11.8	21.9	9.1	3.5	6.9	1953	43.4	12.7	21.0	11.2	3.9	7.8
1954	76.4	5.1	10.5	3.3	1.9	2.9	1954	68.3	7.4	13.2	4.7	2.5	3.9	1954	48.8	13.7	17.2	9.3	4.2	6.8	1954	44.6	15.2	16.2	11.5	4.7	7.7
1955	75.8	5.4	10.5	3.8	1.9	2.7	1955	67.3	7.7	13.4	5.5	2.4	3.7	1955	46.6	14.6	17.9	11.0	3.9	6.1	1955	42.2	16.0	17.1	13.7	4.3	6.7
1956	76.2	5.7	10.5	3.1	1.8	2.7	1956	68.0	8.2	13.2	4.5	2.3	3.8	1956	47.1	16.0	17.4	9.0	3.8	6.7	1956	43.1	17.6	16.4	11.0	4.3	7.7
1957	77.9	5.5	9.0	3.0	1.9	2.6	1957	70.4	8.0	11.2	4.3	2.5	3.6	1957	51.2	15.7	13.9	8.7	4.2	6.4	1957	46.3	17.9	12.8	10.7	4.8	7.5
1958	76.4	6.0	9.5	3.1	2.2	2.8	1958	68.6	8.7	11.6	4.5	2.9	3.8	1958	50.7	16.5	13.0	8.7	4.5	6.6	1958	45.9	18.9	11.6	10.7	5.1	7.7
1959	77.4	5.8	8.6	3.1	2.3	2.9	1959	70.0	8.4	10.4	4.4	3.0	3.9	1959	51.8	16.4	11.9	8.5	4.8	6.7	1959	46.2	19.3	10.5	10.6	5.4	8.1
1960	77.7	6.0	7.7	3.1	2.6	2.8	1960	70.4	8.8	9.1	4.4	3.4	3.9	1960	52.7	17.0	9.7	8.7	5.3	6.6	1960	46.4	20.4	8.4	10.9	6.1	7.9
1961	77.6	6.2	7.4	3.1	2.8	2.9	1961	70.3	9.0	8.6	4.4	3.7	4.0	1961	52.8	17.3	9.0	8.4	5.5	7.1	1961	46.2	20.6	7.9	10.5	6.3	8.6
1962	77.9	6.1	7.3	3.1	3.0	2.6	1962	70.7	8.9	8.5	4.5	3.8	3.6	1962	53.1	17.7	8.5	8.7	5.8	6.2	1962	46.6	21.3	7.2	10.8	6.7	7.4
1963	78.1	6.3	7.3	2.9	2.9	2.6	1963	71.0	9.2	8.5	4.2	3.7	3.5	1963	54.0	18.7	8.0	7.7	5.4	6.2	1963	47.4	22.9	6.6	9.4	6.1	7.6
1964	77.1	6.5	7.7	3.4	3.0	2.4	1964	69.7	9.6	8.9	4.9	3.8	3.3	1964	52.5	19.3	8.1	9.2	5.4	5.5	1964	46.8	23.1	6.5	11.2	6.0	6.5
1965	77.1	6.7	7.7	3.5	2.9	2.0	1965	69.8	9.9	9.0	5.0	3.6	2.7	1965	51.9	20.4	8.2	9.5	5.3	4.7	1965	46.1	24.5	6.5	11.5	5.9	5.5
1966	77.6	6.5	7.6	3.4	2.8	2.1	1966	70.5	9.6	8.8	4.8	3.6	2.8	1966	53.1	20.2	7.8	9.2	5.2	4.6	1966	47.4	24.2	6.0	11.1	5.7	5.5
1967	78.1	6.7	7.1	3.3	2.9	1.9	1967	71.3	9.9	8.1	4.7	3.5	2.6	1967	54.3	20.4	7.3	8.7	5.1	4.2	1967	48.2	24.9	5.8	10.6	5.7	4.9
1968	79.0	6.8	5.8	3.2	3.3	1.9	1968	72.4	10.0	6.6	4.5	4.1	2.5	1968	55.3	21.1	5.7	8.3	5.7	4.0	1968	48.6	26.1	4.5	10.0	6.2	4.6
1969	79.9	6.9	4.7	3.0	3.7	1.8	1969	73.5	10.2	5.3	4.3	4.4	2.4	1969	55.8	21.8	4.7	7.8	6.1	3.8	1969	49.3	26.3	3.9	9.4	6.7	4.5
1970	80.4	7.0	4.0	2.8	4.0	1.9	1970	74.1	10.4	4.4	3.9	4.8	2.5	1970	55.2	22.9	3.8	7.2	6.8	4.1	1970	48.7	27.4	3.2	8.6	7.5	4.7
1971	80.8	7.3	3.9	2.4	3.8	1.9	1971	74.4	11.0	4.3	3.3	4.5	2.5	1971	54.9	24.9	4.0	5.9	6.3	4.1	1971	48.8	29.6	3.5	6.8	6.8	4.6
1972	80.4	7.2	4.4	2.1	3.8	2.1	1972	73.9	10.8	5.0	3.0	4.6	2.8	1972	54.9	24.2	4.4	5.7	6.5	4.3	1972	47.8	29.9	3.6	6.8	7.1	4.8
1973	77.9	7.4	6.4	2.2	4.0	2.1	1973	70.9	11.2	7.4	3.1	4.8	2.7	1973	52.0	24.5	7.0	5.9	6.6	4.1	1973	46.5	29.0	5.7	7.0	7.1	4.7
1974	76.1	7.0	7.2	2.2	5.2	2.3	1974	68.5	10.5	8.8	3.1	6.3	2.9	1974	49.7	22.1	9.8	5.6	8.7	4.2	1974	44.7	25.8	8.5	6.8	9.5	4.8
1975	76.9	6.8	6.8	2.2	5.2	2.2	1975	69.7	10.2	8.2	3.0	6.2	2.7	1975	51.8	21.0	9.3	5.6	8.4	4.0	1975	47.3	24.1	8.4	6.6	9.1	4.5
1976	78.8	6.7	4.9	2.0	5.5	2.2	1976	72.1	10.0	5.8	2.9	6.5	2.7	1976	52.4	22.1	6.4	5.6	9.3	4.3	1976	46.7	25.9	5.5	6.7	10.2	5.0

1977	80.2	6.4	3.7	2.1	5.4	2.2	1977	73.9	9.7	4.3	3.0	6.5	2.7	1977	54.5	21.4	4.4	6.1	9.4	4.2	1977	49.4	24.6	3.8	7.3	10.1	4.9
1978	78.2	6.3	3.4	4.1	5.8	2.1	1978	71.2	9.5	3.7	6.1	6.9	2.5	1978	52.0	19.7	3.0	11.8	9.5	4.0	1978	48.7	20.8	2.5	13.4	10.1	4.6
1979	76.9	6.1	3.4	4.8	6.5	2.2	1979	69.6	9.2	3.8	7.1	7.7	2.7	1979	50.3	18.7	2.5	13.5	10.7	4.3	1979	49.6	17.6	1.8	14.8	11.2	5.0
1980	76.4	6.0	2.5	5.2	7.5	2.4	1980	69.5	8.9	2.4	7.5	8.8	2.9	1980	53.8	15.6	1.3	13.2	11.8	4.3	1980	51.5	15.3	0.5	15.1	12.6	5.1
1981	74.5	5.6	2.6	5.6	9.2	2.4	1981	66.9	8.3	2.9	8.1	10.9	2.9	1981	48.1	15.8	2.4	15.0	14.5	4.3	1981	44.4	16.2	1.4	17.2	15.6	5.1
1982	76.2	5.4	2.1	5.5	8.7	2.2	1982	69.7	7.9	2.3	7.4	10.0	2.7	1982	53.4	14.9	2.2	12.6	12.7	4.2	1982	49.3	15.9	1.7	14.8	13.3	5.1
1983	79.6	6.0	1.8	4.8	6.1	1.8	1983	73.7	9.0	1.9	6.5	7.0	2.0	1983	57.6	18.4	1.6	10.8	8.9	2.6	1983	53.4	20.9	1.1	12.3	9.3	3.1
1984	80.5	6.2	1.8	3.9	5.8	1.8	1984	74.8	9.3	1.9	5.3	6.7	2.1	1984	58.5	19.2	1.8	9.3	8.5	2.7	1984	54.2	21.5	1.5	11.0	8.8	3.1
1985	80.8	5.8	1.5	3.9	6.2	1.9	1985	75.4	8.6	1.5	5.3	7.1	2.2	1985	60.9	17.2	0.9	9.3	8.7	3.0	1985	57.5	19.0	0.4	10.8	8.9	3.4
1986	81.1	6.0	1.5	3.7	5.6	2.0	1986	75.8	8.9	1.5	5.1	6.4	2.4	1986	61.6	17.6	0.8	8.9	7.9	3.3	1986	58.4	19.0	0.3	10.4	8.2	3.7
1987	81.4	5.8	1.8	3.4	4.9	2.8	1987	76.0	8.5	1.8	4.5	5.6	3.5	1987	62.6	16.6	1.2	7.7	6.9	5.1	1987	60.6	17.6	0.8	8.9	7.1	5.1
1988	80.5	5.8	2.2	3.2	5.2	3.1	1988	75.3	8.3	2.3	4.3	5.9	3.9	1988	63.4	15.2	2.5	6.8	6.9	5.3	1988	62.5	15.3	2.4	7.5	6.9	5.4
1989	78.5	6.2	2.2	3.5	6.4	3.2	1989	72.7	8.9	2.4	4.6	7.4	4.0	1989	60.1	15.5	2.8	7.5	8.8	5.3	1989	59.2	15.4	2.7	8.4	9.0	5.4
1990	78.1	6.3	1.9	3.2	7.4	3.1	1990	72.1	9.0	2.1	4.3	8.7	3.9	1990	57.7	16.1	2.4	7.2	11.1	5.4	1990	55.9	16.6	2.3	8.1	11.7	5.4
1991	79.3	6.4	1.5	3.2	6.4	3.3	1991	73.1	9.2	1.7	4.3	7.5	4.2	1991	58.0	17.0	2.0	7.6	9.9	5.5	1991	55.7	17.8	2.0	8.9	10.5	5.0
1992	81.3	6.7	1.5	2.7	4.7	3.3	1992	75.4	9.7	1.7	3.6	5.6	4.1	1992	59.9	18.6	2.1	6.3	7.8	5.5	1992	57.3	19.9	2.1	7.1	8.4	5.2
1993	81.9	6.7	1.5	2.5	3.6	3.9	1993	76.2	9.6	1.6	3.4	4.2	4.9	1993	62.2	18.1	1.9	5.7	5.8	6.3	1993	60.5	19.4	1.9	6.4	6.2	5.7
1994	82.1	6.5	1.7	2.5	3.0	4.2	1994	76.6	9.4	1.9	3.4	3.6	5.1	1994	63.1	17.6	2.2	5.7	5.0	6.4	1994	61.4	18.6	2.2	6.4	5.4	5.9
1995	80.8	6.6	1.9	2.7	3.7	4.4	1995	75.2	9.4	2.1	3.5	4.3	5.5	1995	62.7	17.0	2.2	5.9	5.8	6.4	1995	61.5	17.9	2.2	6.8	6.2	5.5
1996	80.0	6.7	2.1	2.9	3.3	4.9	1996	74.5	9.4	2.4	3.9	3.9	6.0	1996	62.6	16.6	2.7	6.5	4.9	6.7	1996	61.7	17.0	2.6	7.5	5.2	5.9
1997	80.5	6.9	2.2	3.1	2.6	4.7	1997	75.2	9.6	2.5	4.2	2.9	5.6	1997	64.4	16.3	2.5	6.9	3.6	6.2	1997	64.0	16.3	2.4	7.9	3.8	5.7
1998	80.6	6.6	2.1	3.4	2.5	4.8	1998	75.4	9.1	2.3	4.5	2.9	5.8	1998	65.0	15.0	2.3	7.4	3.7	6.7	1998	64.5	14.6	2.0	8.6	3.9	6.4
1999	80.2	6.6	2.4	3.7	2.5	4.6	1999	75.1	9.1	2.6	4.9	2.9	5.4	1999	64.7	14.4	2.9	7.8	3.7	6.4	1999	64.0	14.1	2.8	9.0	4.0	6.2
2000	80.5	6.5	2.2	3.6	2.7	4.6	2000	75.7	8.8	2.4	4.6	3.1	5.4	2000	67.1	13.5	2.3	7.2	3.8	6.1	2000	67.0	12.9	2.1	8.2	3.9	5.9

	P99.9–100							P99.99–100							P90–95							P95–99					
	Wage	Prof.	Busin.	Divid.	Interest	Invest.		Wage	Prof.	Busin.	Divid.	Interest	Invest.		Wage	Prof.	Busin.	Divid.	Interest	Invest.		Wage	Prof.	Busin.	Divid.	Interest	Invest.
1946	34.0	10.2	22.2	16.7	6.0	10.9	1946	27.2	5.6	14.3	28.8	7.6	16.6	1946	88.7	0.8	7.8	0.7	1.0	1.1	1946	79.6	2.2	13.3	1.4	1.6	1.9
1947	32.6	9.7	26.6	16.6	4.9	9.6	1947	25.1	4.2	20.6	29.2	5.9	15.1	1947	89.7	0.6	7.5	0.5	0.8	0.9	1947	76.7	2.6	15.7	1.5	1.5	2.0
1948	34.6	9.3	25.5	17.6	4.3	8.7	1948	28.2	3.0	24.2	27.7	5.8	11.1	1948	90.0	0.6	7.4	0.5	0.7	0.9	1948	76.7	2.5	15.9	1.5	1.4	2.0
1949	34.0	10.2	25.0	17.7	4.0	9.1	1949	28.8	4.8	20.2	29.3	5.2	11.8	1949	89.3	0.7	7.9	0.5	0.6	0.9	1949	76.5	2.7	16.0	1.5	1.3	1.9
1950	34.0	10.4	25.2	17.6	3.6	9.3	1950	32.3	7.1	18.0	27.4	4.0	11.2	1950	89.5	0.8	7.6	0.6	0.7	0.9	1950	77.2	2.7	14.9	1.8	1.4	2.0
1951	35.6	11.4	22.1	15.5	3.5	11.9	1951	26.7	6.9	23.9	22.0	4.7	15.8	1951	90.0	0.8	7.3	0.5	0.5	0.8	1951	77.5	2.8	14.8	1.7	1.1	2.1
1952	36.0	11.0	19.7	18.7	4.7	9.9	1952	28.0	6.8	16.5	33.1	5.6	10.0	1952	90.3	0.8	6.8	0.6	0.5	1.0	1952	78.9	2.7	13.9	1.4	1.1	1.9
1953	37.4	10.8	18.6	17.7	4.9	10.6	1953	33.4	5.6	15.0	27.0	5.1	13.9	1953	90.2	0.8	6.7	0.6	0.6	1.1	1953	79.6	2.7	13.0	1.5	1.2	2.1
1954	37.4	14.8	13.4	18.4	6.2	9.9	1954	30.3	11.5	13.7	25.2	7.3	12.1	1954	91.6	0.9	5.4	0.6	0.7	0.9	1954	81.8	3.0	10.4	1.6	1.3	1.9

(*contd.*)

Table 6C.3 (*contd.*)

	P90–100							P95–100							P99–100							P99.5–100					
	Wage	Prof.	Busin.	Divid.	Interest	Invest.		Wage	Prof.	Busin.	Divid.	Interest	Invest.		Wage	Prof.	Busin.	Divid.	Interest	Invest.		Wage	Prof.	Busin.	Divid.	Interest	Invest.
1955	33.6	15.1	15.8	22.3	5.1	8.2	1955	25.9	11.1	16.3	32.7	5.7	8.3	1955	91.6	1.0	5.2	0.6	0.8	0.9	1955	81.6	3.0	10.3	1.6	1.4	2.0
1956	36.3	17.0	14.7	16.5	5.2	10.2	1956	26.2	11.5	18.4	23.8	5.9	14.2	1956	91.4	0.9	5.5	0.6	0.7	0.9	1956	81.6	3.2	10.5	1.6	1.3	1.8
1957	39.3	17.6	10.5	16.2	6.3	10.1	1957	29.4	12.7	10.4	24.8	8.4	14.3	1957	91.7	0.9	5.0	0.6	0.8	0.9	1957	82.9	3.0	9.4	1.5	1.4	1.8
1958	40.0	17.8	8.8	16.5	6.6	10.3	1958	30.0	11.9	7.3	26.3	9.3	15.2	1958	90.9	1.0	5.7	0.6	1.0	0.9	1958	80.4	3.6	10.6	1.7	1.8	2.0
1959	41.1	17.3	8.0	15.7	6.9	11.0	1959	32.0	9.8	7.6	24.8	8.9	17.0	1959	91.1	0.9	5.3	0.6	1.1	1.0	1959	81.6	3.2	9.5	1.7	1.9	2.1
1960	40.5	18.7	6.1	16.3	7.7	10.7	1960	31.0	10.1	5.7	26.8	10.2	16.2	1960	91.1	0.9	5.1	0.7	1.3	0.9	1960	81.6	3.6	8.8	1.8	2.1	2.1
1961	39.4	18.7	6.3	15.4	7.9	12.3	1961	28.4	9.8	6.4	25.5	10.2	19.7	1961	91.0	0.9	5.2	0.6	1.3	0.9	1961	81.5	3.7	8.3	1.9	2.5	2.1
1962	40.3	20.1	5.3	15.8	8.4	10.2	1962	30.3	12.8	4.2	25.4	11.5	15.7	1962	91.1	0.9	5.1	0.6	1.5	0.9	1962	81.6	3.5	8.5	1.9	2.6	2.0
1963	41.8	22.5	4.4	13.3	7.4	10.7	1963	35.4	14.4	3.0	20.7	9.0	17.6	1963	91.0	0.9	5.3	0.6	1.5	0.8	1963	81.3	3.4	8.7	2.0	2.7	1.9
1964	41.0	22.2	4.7	16.4	7.2	8.6	1964	32.5	13.2	4.3	27.6	9.3	13.1	1964	90.7	0.9	5.4	0.7	1.5	0.8	1964	80.3	3.5	9.4	2.2	2.7	1.9
1965	41.0	23.0	4.6	16.8	7.1	7.6	1965	32.0	14.0	5.7	28.4	8.5	11.5	1965	90.6	1.0	5.4	0.8	1.6	0.7	1965	80.8	3.4	9.4	2.3	2.6	1.6
1966	42.1	22.6	4.3	16.5	6.9	7.6	1966	31.8	12.8	4.6	30.4	8.7	11.8	1966	90.5	0.8	5.6	0.8	1.5	0.8	1966	81.0	3.2	9.4	2.2	2.6	1.6
1967	43.0	23.9	3.8	15.7	7.1	6.6	1967	34.0	13.2	3.1	30.2	9.2	10.3	1967	90.6	1.0	5.3	0.8	1.6	0.7	1967	81.5	3.5	8.5	2.3	2.6	1.6
1968	43.0	25.1	3.4	14.8	7.6	6.2	1968	35.0	13.6	4.6	27.1	10.3	9.4	1968	91.0	0.9	4.5	0.9	2.0	0.8	1968	82.7	3.3	7.1	2.2	3.1	1.6
1969	42.4	26.2	3.0	14.0	8.1	6.2	1969	35.7	13.5	5.5	24.9	10.3	10.0	1969	91.6	0.9	3.7	0.8	2.3	0.7	1969	84.1	3.3	5.7	2.1	3.4	1.5
1970	39.6	30.0	1.9	12.5	9.5	6.5	1970	33.0	17.9	1.9	22.7	13.6	10.9	1970	91.7	0.9	3.2	0.8	2.6	0.8	1970	85.2	3.0	4.7	1.9	3.6	1.6
1971	38.2	35.3	2.4	9.8	8.0	6.3	1971	31.9	23.3	3.2	18.6	11.2	11.8	1971	91.9	0.9	3.1	0.8	2.4	0.9	1971	85.7	3.0	4.5	1.8	3.5	1.6
1972	42.0	30.6	2.6	10.0	8.5	6.3	1972	40.5	16.8	2.6	18.2	11.9	10.1	1972	91.7	0.8	3.5	0.6	2.3	1.1	1972	84.8	3.1	5.3	1.5	3.5	1.9
1973	45.1	26.1	4.2	9.9	8.5	6.2	1973	45.1	14.2	4.0	16.1	11.4	9.4	1973	90.3	0.8	4.5	0.7	2.5	1.2	1973	82.0	3.4	7.6	1.5	3.7	1.8
1974	45.1	20.9	6.9	9.4	11.2	6.6	1974	45.4	9.0	6.1	14.4	13.8	11.2	1974	89.5	0.9	4.4	0.6	3.3	1.3	1974	79.4	3.8	8.3	1.6	4.9	2.1
1975	51.1	17.9	5.8	9.0	10.4	5.8	1975	58.3	8.2	3.3	12.1	11.1	6.9	1975	89.5	1.0	4.3	0.6	3.3	1.2	1975	80.0	3.9	7.6	1.6	4.9	2.0
1976	47.9	19.5	4.9	8.9	12.0	6.9	1976	49.5	8.9	6.4	11.6	14.3	9.3	1976	89.8	1.2	3.5	0.6	3.7	1.3	1976	82.7	3.6	5.4	1.4	5.1	1.8
1977	49.8	18.2	2.7	10.1	12.1	7.1	1977	53.6	6.8	3.1	13.6	13.5	9.5	1977	90.5	1.0	2.9	0.6	3.6	1.4	1977	84.0	3.5	4.2	1.4	5.0	1.9
1978	47.2	15.3	1.1	18.0	11.6	6.9	1978	49.7	6.8	1.4	21.0	12.1	9.0	1978	89.5	1.1	2.9	1.0	4.0	1.4	1978	81.0	4.3	4.1	3.2	5.6	1.8
1979	47.9	12.8	−0.4	19.2	13.1	7.4	1979	49.0	5.8	−1.1	21.8	14.4	10.1	1979	89.0	1.1	2.9	1.1	4.4	1.5	1979	79.5	4.3	4.4	3.7	6.2	1.9
1980	48.6	11.4	−1.3	19.2	14.5	7.7	1980	50.0	6.4	−1.9	20.6	15.4	9.5	1980	87.8	1.2	2.5	1.5	5.4	1.6	1980	77.9	5.4	3.0	4.4	7.2	2.1
1981	44.0	9.7	0.1	20.7	17.9	7.6	1981	44.7	6.0	−0.2	20.9	19.2	9.5	1981	87.1	1.2	2.1	1.5	6.5	1.6	1981	76.7	4.4	3.3	4.5	9.0	2.1
1982	49.6	8.7	0.5	19.1	14.1	8.0	1982	47.1	1.9	0.5	26.1	12.5	12.0	1982	87.4	1.1	1.7	2.1	6.3	1.4	1982	79.2	3.7	2.4	4.4	8.5	1.8
1983	55.1	14.1	0.3	15.4	10.3	4.8	1983	63.7	3.2	−0.7	18.1	9.6	6.0	1983	89.5	1.0	1.6	2.0	4.5	1.4	1983	82.8	3.6	2.1	4.0	5.9	1.6
1984	56.0	14.0	0.8	15.4	9.3	4.5	1984	59.8	2.0	−0.9	25.8	7.7	5.7	1984	90.2	1.1	1.6	1.6	4.2	1.4	1984	84.3	3.5	2.0	3.0	5.6	1.7
1985	60.9	11.1	−0.7	14.8	9.4	4.6	1985	64.3	1.2	−2.4	23.4	8.3	5.3	1985	90.1	1.1	1.5	1.5	4.6	1.3	1985	83.9	3.5	1.8	2.9	6.1	1.7
1986	61.1	11.6	−0.6	14.0	8.8	5.0	1986	65.9	2.0	−1.6	19.8	7.9	6.1	1986	90.3	1.1	1.6	1.4	4.1	1.4	1986	84.1	3.8	1.9	2.8	5.5	1.9
1987	65.0	10.2	−0.1	12.3	7.4	5.2	1987	68.9	1.9	−1.1	19.7	6.8	3.9	1987	90.7	1.1	1.8	1.3	3.6	1.6	1987	84.2	3.6	2.2	2.6	4.8	2.6

1989	66.5	6.4	3.0	10.0	8.8	5.6	1989	72.5	0.7	3.9	10.6	6.2	6.0	1989	89.4	1.3	1.7	1.2	4.6	1.8	1989	81.9	4.1	2.2	2.5	6.5	3.0
1990	60.5	8.7	2.5	9.9	12.7	5.8	1990	66.7	1.5	3.4	11.3	11.6	5.5	1990	89.4	1.3	1.4	1.1	5.1	1.6	1990	81.8	4.1	1.9	2.3	7.0	2.9
1991	59.8	9.7	2.0	12.2	12.2	4.1	1991	63.6	1.8	2.1	17.6	13.2	1.7	1991	90.5	1.3	1.1	1.1	4.3	1.8	1991	83.2	4.1	1.5	2.1	5.9	3.3
1992	62.9	11.2	2.5	8.8	9.9	4.7	1992	72.0	1.6	3.4	10.0	10.3	2.8	1992	91.9	1.2	1.1	1.0	3.0	1.8	1992	85.4	3.9	1.4	1.9	4.2	3.2
1993	68.7	10.0	1.6	7.7	7.2	4.8	1993	79.6	1.4	0.9	7.6	6.8	3.7	1993	92.1	1.3	1.2	1.0	2.4	2.1	1993	85.5	4.0	1.5	1.9	3.2	4.0
1994	68.3	9.5	2.3	7.9	6.4	5.6	1994	74.0	1.3	2.7	9.2	6.2	6.6	1994	92.0	1.3	1.4	1.0	2.0	2.4	1994	85.4	4.0	1.7	1.9	2.7	4.3
1995	68.4	8.9	2.0	9.1	7.3	4.3	1995	74.1	1.3	2.5	12.1	7.6	2.5	1995	91.1	1.4	1.5	1.0	2.5	2.6	1995	83.8	4.2	2.0	1.9	3.3	4.8
1996	67.8	8.4	2.7	10.4	5.7	5.1	1996	67.5	0.9	4.3	16.5	6.4	4.4	1996	90.7	1.4	1.6	1.1	2.3	2.9	1996	82.9	4.3	2.1	2.0	3.1	5.5
1997	70.9	8.1	1.8	11.0	3.7	4.5	1997	72.6	0.8	2.2	18.5	3.2	2.8	1997	91.0	1.4	1.7	1.0	1.8	3.0	1997	83.5	4.5	2.4	2.0	2.4	5.2
1998	70.3	6.5	1.5	11.9	3.9	5.9	1998	72.0	0.4	0.9	19.4	3.6	3.8	1998	91.3	1.4	1.8	1.1	1.6	2.8	1998	83.8	4.5	2.3	2.1	2.2	5.1
1999	68.1	6.6	2.5	12.7	4.1	6.0	1999	67.0	0.7	1.8	20.9	3.3	6.3	1999	90.9	1.5	1.9	1.4	1.6	2.8	1999	83.7	4.6	2.4	2.5	2.2	4.6
2000	72.4	5.8	1.7	10.9	4.0	5.3	2000	74.3	0.4	0.5	15.2	3.2	6.5	2000	90.9	1.5	1.8	1.2	1.9	2.8	2000	83.2	4.7	2.4	2.3	2.6	4.8

	P99–99.5							P99.5–99.9							P99.9–99.99							P99.99–100					
	Wage	Prof.	Busin.	Divid.	Interest	Invest.		Wage	Prof.	Busin.	Divid.	Interest	Invest.		Wage	Prof.	Busin.	Divid.	Interest	Invest.		Wage	Prof.	Busin.	Divid.	Interest	Invest.
1946	55.7	7.5	25.3	3.7	3.0	4.8	1946	45.8	12.0	24.9	6.9	4.0	6.5	1946	36.5	11.8	25.0	12.4	5.4	8.8	1946	27.2	5.6	14.3	28.8	7.6	16.6
1947	54.4	7.6	27.1	3.6	2.8	4.5	1947	43.2	11.4	29.9	6.4	3.5	5.7	1947	35.3	11.7	28.8	12.1	4.5	7.7	1947	25.1	4.2	20.6	29.2	5.9	15.1
1948	52.5	7.6	28.6	4.2	2.7	4.4	1948	44.1	10.2	29.9	6.7	3.2	5.9	1948	36.7	11.3	25.9	14.4	3.8	7.9	1948	28.2	3.0	24.2	27.7	5.8	11.1
1949	53.1	8.2	28.2	4.0	2.5	4.1	1949	44.4	11.3	28.1	7.1	3.3	5.9	1949	35.6	11.8	26.5	14.1	3.6	8.3	1949	28.8	4.8	20.2	29.3	5.2	11.8
1950	53.2	8.6	26.9	4.3	2.6	4.3	1950	44.1	12.5	26.2	7.6	3.5	6.1	1950	34.5	11.5	27.4	14.5	3.4	8.7	1950	32.3	7.1	18.0	27.4	4.0	11.2
1951	54.2	8.7	25.3	4.8	2.5	4.6	1951	46.4	13.0	24.5	7.1	3.0	6.0	1951	38.3	12.7	21.6	13.5	3.2	10.8	1951	26.7	6.9	23.9	22.0	4.7	15.8
1952	53.9	9.9	24.6	4.4	2.5	4.6	1952	46.0	13.6	24.2	6.7	3.1	6.4	1952	38.6	12.4	20.7	14.0	4.4	9.9	1952	28.0	6.8	16.5	33.1	5.6	10.0
1953	54.1	9.9	23.9	4.5	2.6	5.0	1953	47.4	14.0	22.6	6.8	3.2	6.0	1953	38.7	12.5	19.8	14.8	4.8	9.5	1953	33.4	5.6	15.0	27.0	5.1	13.9
1954	58.0	10.4	19.4	4.4	2.9	4.9	1954	49.4	15.5	18.1	6.9	3.8	6.3	1954	39.8	15.9	13.3	16.2	5.8	9.1	1954	30.3	11.5	13.7	25.2	7.3	12.1
1955	56.5	11.4	19.5	5.1	3.0	4.6	1955	48.1	16.6	18.1	7.7	3.8	5.7	1955	36.3	16.5	15.5	18.5	4.9	8.2	1955	25.9	11.1	16.3	32.7	5.7	8.3
1956	55.9	12.4	19.8	4.6	2.9	4.5	1956	47.7	18.0	17.4	7.2	3.7	6.0	1956	39.7	18.9	13.5	14.1	4.9	8.9	1956	26.2	11.5	18.4	23.8	5.9	14.2
1957	61.4	11.1	16.2	4.4	3.0	3.9	1957	50.8	18.1	14.4	7.0	3.9	5.8	1957	42.5	19.2	10.5	13.4	5.6	8.8	1957	29.4	12.7	10.4	24.8	8.4	14.3
1958	60.7	11.5	16.0	4.3	3.3	4.3	1958	49.8	19.6	13.5	7.0	4.2	6.0	1958	43.2	19.7	9.3	13.3	5.7	8.8	1958	30.0	11.9	7.3	26.3	9.3	15.2
1959	63.1	10.5	14.7	4.2	3.5	4.1	1959	49.5	20.5	12.0	7.3	4.5	6.2	1959	44.0	19.7	8.2	12.8	6.2	9.1	1959	32.0	9.8	7.6	24.8	8.9	17.0
1960	65.7	10.2	12.2	4.2	3.7	4.1	1960	50.1	21.4	9.8	7.5	5.1	6.1	1960	43.5	21.4	6.3	13.0	6.9	8.9	1960	31.0	10.1	5.7	26.8	10.2	16.2
1961	66.1	10.6	11.2	4.2	3.9	3.9	1961	50.5	21.7	8.9	7.3	5.2	6.4	1961	42.9	21.7	6.2	12.2	7.1	9.8	1961	28.4	9.8	6.4	25.5	10.2	19.7
1962	66.1	10.5	11.1	4.4	4.0	3.8	1962	50.4	22.0	8.4	7.8	5.7	5.7	1962	43.3	22.3	5.6	12.9	7.4	8.5	1962	30.3	12.8	4.2	25.4	11.5	15.7
1963	67.0	10.2	10.9	4.4	4.1	3.5	1963	50.7	23.2	7.9	7.2	5.3	5.7	1963	43.6	24.9	4.8	11.1	6.9	8.7	1963	35.4	14.4	3.0	20.7	9.0	17.6
1964	64.0	11.6	11.5	5.1	4.3	3.6	1964	50.2	23.7	7.5	8.2	5.2	5.2	1964	43.5	24.9	4.8	12.9	6.6	7.3	1964	32.5	13.2	4.3	27.6	9.3	13.1
1965	63.4	12.4	11.7	5.4	4.2	3.0	1965	49.2	25.3	7.6	8.4	5.2	4.3	1965	43.8	25.7	4.3	13.2	6.6	6.3	1965	32.0	14.0	5.7	28.4	8.5	11.5
1966	64.1	12.3	11.2	5.3	4.2	2.9	1966	50.5	25.1	7.0	8.1	5.0	4.3	1966	45.2	25.5	4.3	12.3	6.4	6.3	1966	31.8	12.8	4.6	30.4	8.7	11.8
1967	66.1	11.8	10.2	5.0	4.0	2.9	1967	51.1	25.4	6.9	7.6	5.0	3.9	1967	45.5	26.9	4.0	11.6	6.5	5.6	1967	34.0	13.2	3.1	30.2	9.2	10.3
1968	68.5	11.4	7.9	4.9	4.6	2.8	1968	51.8	26.6	5.2	7.3	5.4	3.7	1968	45.2	28.3	3.0	11.3	6.8	5.3	1968	35.0	13.6	4.6	27.1	10.3	9.4
1969	68.1	13.2	6.3	4.8	5.1	2.6	1969	53.2	26.3	4.3	6.8	5.9	3.5	1969	44.3	29.7	2.3	11.0	7.5	5.2	1969	35.7	13.5	5.5	24.9	10.3	10.0
1970	67.5	14.3	5.1	4.7	5.5	3.0	1970	53.6	26.0	3.8	6.4	6.4	3.7	1970	41.4	33.1	1.9	9.8	8.4	5.4	1970	33.0	17.9	1.9	22.7	13.6	10.9

(contd.)

Table 6C.3 (*contd.*)

	P90–100					
	Wage	Prof.	Busin.	Divid.	Interest	Invest.
1971	66.5	15.9	4.9	4.1	5.4	3.2
1972	68.4	13.5	6.1	3.5	5.3	3.2
1973	62.3	16.1	9.3	3.7	5.5	3.1
1974	59.0	15.1	12.0	3.5	7.2	3.2
1975	60.1	15.1	11.0	3.6	7.1	3.1
1976	62.6	15.2	8.0	3.5	7.7	2.9
1977	63.6	15.8	5.5	4.1	8.1	3.0
1978	57.9	17.8	4.0	9.0	8.5	2.9
1979	51.6	20.8	3.8	11.1	9.7	3.1
1980	57.9	16.2	2.8	9.8	10.4	3.0
1981	54.8	15.1	4.0	10.9	12.4	2.8
1982	61.6	13.1	3.2	8.4	11.4	2.4
1983	66.0	13.7	2.7	8.0	8.0	1.7
1984	67.5	14.3	2.5	5.8	7.9	2.0
1985	67.7	13.7	1.9	6.2	8.3	2.3
1986	68.1	14.6	1.8	5.7	7.4	2.4
1987	66.7	14.6	2.0	5.4	6.4	4.9
1988	65.5	14.8	2.7	5.2	6.8	5.1
1989	62.3	15.7	3.0	5.4	8.5	5.2
1990	62.0	15.1	2.5	5.2	9.8	5.4
1991	63.4	15.1	2.0	4.6	8.5	6.4
1992	65.7	15.5	1.9	4.3	6.4	6.2
1993	66.1	15.3	2.0	4.1	4.8	7.8
1994	67.0	15.1	2.3	3.9	4.2	7.5
1995	65.5	14.9	2.4	3.9	4.9	8.4
1996	64.8	15.5	2.8	4.1	4.4	8.5
1997	65.5	16.3	3.0	4.3	3.4	7.6
1998	66.2	15.9	3.0	4.3	3.2	7.4
1999	66.8	15.5	3.2	4.4	3.1	7.0
2000	67.6	15.4	2.9	4.3	3.3	6.6

	P95–100					
	Wage	Prof.	Busin.	Divid.	Interest	Invest.
1971	54.4	26.6	4.1	5.2	6.1	3.6
1972	50.9	29.5	4.1	5.1	6.3	4.0
1973	47.3	30.5	6.5	5.4	6.4	3.9
1974	44.5	28.5	9.5	5.3	8.5	3.8
1975	45.2	27.7	9.9	5.3	8.3	3.7
1976	46.0	29.5	5.9	5.5	9.2	4.0
1977	49.2	28.1	4.4	5.7	9.0	3.6
1978	49.5	23.9	3.2	10.8	9.3	3.3
1979	50.6	20.3	3.0	12.4	10.2	3.6
1980	53.1	17.5	1.6	12.7	11.5	3.7
1981	44.6	19.9	2.1	15.3	14.4	3.7
1982	49.1	20.9	2.5	11.7	12.8	3.1
1983	52.2	25.2	1.5	10.4	8.7	2.0
1984	52.9	26.8	1.9	7.9	8.5	2.1
1985	55.2	24.4	1.1	8.1	8.6	2.6
1986	56.5	24.1	0.9	8.0	7.8	2.8
1987	57.5	22.8	1.4	6.4	6.8	5.1
1988	56.6	22.5	2.4	6.5	6.9	5.2
1989	52.6	23.6	2.4	6.9	9.2	5.3
1990	52.0	23.2	2.2	6.7	10.9	5.1
1991	52.3	24.4	2.0	6.3	9.2	5.8
1992	53.0	26.7	1.9	5.8	7.1	5.5
1993	53.9	26.9	2.1	5.3	5.4	6.3
1994	55.9	25.8	2.1	5.3	4.6	6.2
1995	55.9	25.2	2.3	4.9	5.2	6.5
1996	56.6	24.4	2.6	5.1	4.7	6.7
1997	57.6	23.9	2.9	5.1	3.8	6.8
1998	59.0	22.3	2.6	5.4	3.9	6.9
1999	59.8	21.5	3.1	5.3	3.8	6.5
2000	61.2	20.5	2.6	5.3	3.9	6.7

	P99–100					
	Wage	Prof.	Busin.	Divid.	Interest	Invest.
1971	39.8	38.4	2.1	7.6	7.2	5.0
1972	42.4	34.2	2.6	7.8	7.6	5.3
1973	45.1	29.4	4.3	8.2	7.7	5.3
1974	45.0	24.4	7.1	7.9	10.4	5.2
1975	48.8	20.8	6.6	8.1	10.2	5.5
1976	47.4	22.7	4.4	8.1	11.3	6.1
1977	48.7	21.6	2.6	9.1	11.7	6.4
1978	46.4	17.9	1.0	17.0	11.5	6.3
1979	47.6	14.9	−0.2	18.4	12.7	6.6
1980	48.2	12.7	−1.1	18.8	14.3	7.2
1981	43.7	10.8	0.2	20.6	17.5	7.1
1982	50.7	11.4	0.5	16.3	14.8	6.4
1983	52.0	18.1	0.7	14.3	10.5	4.4
1984	54.4	19.0	1.6	11.0	10.0	4.0
1985	59.4	15.2	0.0	11.2	9.8	4.3
1986	59.2	15.4	−0.1	11.7	9.2	4.6
1987	63.4	13.6	0.3	9.2	7.7	5.8
1988	66.1	10.1	2.1	8.3	7.5	5.8
1989	62.6	9.9	2.4	9.6	10.3	5.3
1990	57.3	12.4	2.0	9.2	13.2	5.9
1991	57.8	13.8	2.0	9.4	11.7	5.3
1992	58.4	16.0	2.0	8.3	9.8	5.6
1993	63.2	14.3	1.9	7.8	7.4	5.4
1994	65.6	13.4	2.1	7.3	6.5	5.1
1995	65.7	12.7	1.8	7.6	7.1	5.2
1996	67.9	12.0	1.9	7.4	5.4	5.4
1997	70.1	11.7	1.5	7.3	4.0	5.4
1998	69.4	9.7	1.8	8.0	4.1	7.0
1999	68.7	9.9	2.9	8.0	4.6	5.8
2000	71.3	8.8	2.4	8.5	4.4	4.6

	P99.5–100					
	Wage	Prof.	Busin.	Divid.	Interest	Invest.
1971	31.9	23.3	3.2	18.6	11.2	11.8
1972	40.5	16.8	2.6	18.2	11.9	10.1
1973	45.1	14.2	4.0	16.1	11.4	9.4
1974	45.4	9.0	6.1	14.4	13.8	11.2
1975	58.3	8.2	3.3	12.1	11.1	6.9
1976	49.5	8.9	6.4	11.6	14.3	9.3
1977	53.6	6.8	3.1	13.6	13.5	9.5
1978	49.7	6.8	1.4	21.0	12.1	9.0
1979	49.0	5.8	−1.1	21.8	14.4	10.1
1980	50.0	6.4	−1.9	20.6	15.4	9.5
1981	44.7	6.0	−0.2	20.9	19.2	9.5
1982	47.1	1.9	0.5	26.1	12.5	12.0
1983	63.7	3.2	−0.7	18.1	9.6	6.0
1984	59.8	2.0	−0.9	25.8	7.7	5.7
1985	64.3	1.2	−2.4	23.4	8.3	5.3
1986	65.9	2.0	−1.6	19.8	7.9	6.1
1987	68.9	1.9	−1.1	19.7	6.8	3.9
1988	75.7	0.7	3.1	9.2	5.8	5.5
1989	72.5	0.7	3.9	10.6	6.2	6.0
1990	66.7	1.5	3.4	11.3	11.6	5.5
1991	63.6	1.8	2.1	17.6	13.2	1.7
1992	72.0	1.6	3.4	10.0	10.3	2.8
1993	79.6	1.4	0.9	7.6	6.8	3.7
1994	74.0	1.3	2.7	9.2	6.2	6.6
1995	74.1	1.3	2.5	12.1	7.6	2.5
1996	67.5	0.9	4.3	16.5	6.4	4.4
1997	72.6	0.8	2.2	18.5	3.2	2.8
1998	72.0	0.4	0.9	19.4	3.6	3.8
1999	67.0	0.7	1.8	20.9	3.3	6.3
2000	74.3	0.4	0.5	15.2	3.2	6.5

Notes: Wage is defined as wages and salaries, pensions, and other employment earnings (such as bonuses, stock-option exercises, etc.). Prof. is professional income defined as self-employment income from professions such as doctors, lawyers, etc. Busin. is business income defined as net profits from sole proprietorships, partnerships, and other small businesses (such as farm and fishing). Divid. defined as dividends from Canadian corporations. Interest includes bond and bank interest income as well as annuities. Invest. includes all other investment income such as estate and trust income, foreign investment income, etc. The sums of all sources add up to 100%. Capital Gains are excluded.

Table 6C.4 Share of capital gains in total income for upper groups in Canada, 1972–2000 (capital gains are expressed in % of total income (including capital gains) of each group)

A. Fractiles defined by total income excluding capital gains

	P90–100	P95–100	P99–100	P99.5–100	P99.9–100	P99.99–100	P90–95	P95–99	P99–99.5	P99.5–99.9	P99.9–99.99	P99.99–100
1972	0.6	0.9	1.7	2.0	2.8	4.7	0.2	0.4	1.3	1.5	2.2	4.7
1973	0.9	1.1	2.1	2.3	3.3	6.1	0.4	0.5	1.6	1.7	2.5	6.1
1974	0.8	1.0	1.7	1.9	2.6	4.2	0.4	0.6	1.5	1.5	2.0	4.2
1975	1.0	1.2	2.1	2.3	3.2	4.9	0.6	0.7	1.8	1.7	2.6	4.9
1976	1.4	1.7	3.1	3.5	4.7	6.8	0.8	0.9	2.5	2.7	4.1	6.8
1977	1.6	2.1	4.0	4.3	6.5	9.2	0.8	1.0	3.4	3.0	5.5	9.2
1978	2.2	2.9	5.6	6.1	9.2	11.5	1.0	1.3	4.6	4.1	8.4	11.5
1979	3.4	4.5	8.9	9.5	14.1	17.9	1.4	1.8	7.6	6.3	12.5	17.9
1980	4.1	5.4	9.9	11.1	15.9	17.6	1.7	2.5	7.5	7.6	15.2	17.6
1981	3.0	4.0	7.9	9.4	14.2	17.0	1.1	1.6	4.9	5.9	13.1	17.0
1982	1.4	1.9	3.7	4.4	6.2	7.2	0.5	0.9	2.0	3.2	5.8	7.2
1983	2.0	2.8	4.9	5.9	7.6	6.4	0.8	1.5	2.8	4.7	8.0	6.4
1984	1.7	2.3	4.1	5.0	6.2	4.8	0.6	1.1	2.3	4.1	6.8	4.8
1985	2.6	3.4	5.8	6.8	9.1	12.9	1.1	1.9	3.7	5.1	7.4	12.9
1986	3.9	5.2	8.4	9.5	12.0	11.9	1.8	3.2	6.0	7.7	12.1	11.9
1987	5.6	7.2	11.4	12.6	14.5	15.1	2.6	4.5	8.9	11.3	14.2	15.1
1988	4.7	6.0	9.2	10.1	10.9	7.2	2.1	3.7	7.2	9.4	12.7	7.2
1989	6.2	8.0	12.3	13.6	14.5	8.0	2.6	4.6	9.2	12.7	18.0	8.0
1990	3.1	3.9	5.6	5.8	5.8	4.0	1.6	2.7	5.1	5.9	6.6	4.0
1991	3.1	4.0	6.2	6.8	7.1	7.5	1.5	2.5	5.0	6.5	6.9	7.5
1992	3.7	4.7	7.1	7.7	7.8	5.7	1.7	3.1	5.7	7.7	8.8	5.7
1993	5.5	6.9	10.0	10.5	10.7	10.0	2.7	4.7	8.9	10.3	11.1	10.0
1994	3.8	5.0	8.9	10.4	10.4	7.7	1.6	2.2	5.4	10.4	11.6	7.7
1995	2.8	3.6	5.5	6.0	6.3	4.5	1.2	2.2	4.2	5.7	7.2	4.5
1996	3.3	4.2	6.5	7.1	8.0	7.5	1.4	2.6	4.8	6.4	8.2	7.5
1997	4.2	5.3	7.8	8.2	7.6	5.4	1.9	3.3	6.8	8.8	8.7	5.4
1998	4.1	5.2	7.4	7.9	8.7	4.9	1.8	3.4	6.2	7.1	10.5	4.9
1999	4.2	5.2	7.3	7.3	6.7	5.4	1.9	3.5	7.2	7.8	7.4	5.4
2000	6.4	7.8	10.4	11.0	10.6	6.7	3.1	5.4	8.5	11.4	12.7	6.7

B. Fractiles defined by total income including capital gains

	P90–100	P95–100	P99–100	P99.5–100	P99.9–100	P99.99–100	P90–95	P95–99	P99–99.5	P99.5–99.9	P99.9–99.99	P99.99–100
1972	1.2	2.7	3.8	4.6	7.5	17.2	0.2	0.5	2.1	3.0	4.7	17.2
1973	1.5	3.4	4.6	5.6	9.2	21.9	0.4	0.7	2.6	3.5	5.4	21.9
1974	1.4	2.9	3.8	4.5	7.0	15.4	0.5	0.8	2.4	3.1	4.4	15.4
1975	1.6	3.4	4.5	5.4	8.5	17.7	0.5	0.9	2.9	3.5	5.4	17.7
1976	2.3	4.9	6.6	8.0	12.4	23.9	0.8	1.2	4.1	5.5	8.6	23.9
1977	2.5	5.6	7.6	8.7	13.1	17.6	0.8	1.3	5.6	6.1	11.5	17.6
1978	3.4	7.6	10.4	12.1	18.3	21.4	1.0	1.7	7.5	8.3	17.2	21.4
1979	5.1	12.0	16.3	19.6	30.3	47.5	0.9	2.5	10.0	12.6	23.4	47.5
1980	6.1	14.2	18.4	22.8	33.8	46.9	1.0	3.4	9.9	15.2	28.6	46.9
1981	4.6	10.9	14.9	19.4	30.6	45.5	0.7	2.2	6.5	11.9	24.7	45.5
1982	2.6	5.9	7.8	10.0	14.8	20.4	0.4	1.2	3.3	6.4	12.4	20.4
1983	3.5	7.7	10.1	12.5	18.7	28.1	0.8	2.1	5.2	8.1	14.9	28.1
1984	2.9	6.4	8.3	10.2	15.0	21.7	0.7	1.7	4.1	6.7	12.0	21.7
1985	4.3	9.2	11.6	14.2	21.0	28.3	1.0	2.7	6.0	9.0	17.7	28.3
1986	6.7	13.5	16.1	18.2	24.3	31.7	1.6	5.2	11.6	13.7	21.0	31.7
1987	9.6	20.2	24.5	27.2	32.4	41.6	1.7	6.3	18.3	23.0	28.1	41.6
1988	8.2	17.1	20.8	23.5	28.7	26.7	1.4	4.6	14.1	18.8	29.7	26.7
1989	10.0	20.1	24.0	27.2	33.2	32.5	1.6	5.4	15.3	21.1	33.6	32.5
1990	5.5	11.5	14.0	15.9	18.2	10.3	1.1	3.3	9.4	14.1	21.9	10.3
1991	5.5	11.7	14.6	17.2	21.3	16.3	1.0	2.9	8.2	13.8	23.8	16.3
1992	6.4	13.8	17.4	20.6	26.8	16.5	1.1	3.2	9.5	15.6	31.4	16.5
1993	9.5	19.7	24.2	27.9	32.7	25.0	1.7	5.1	15.0	24.0	36.3	25.0
1994	6.6	14.2	21.6	27.7	31.6	19.3	1.0	2.3	9.1	24.3	38.0	19.3
1995	4.6	10.1	13.1	16.0	20.6	17.4	0.7	1.8	5.7	12.2	22.1	17.4
1996	5.4	11.1	13.9	16.5	20.8	22.8	1.1	2.6	7.2	12.6	19.7	22.8
1997	6.7	12.8	15.5	17.9	21.9	25.1	1.6	3.6	8.7	14.1	20.2	25.1
1998	6.4	12.2	14.9	17.2	19.9	22.1	1.4	3.2	8.4	14.4	18.8	22.1
1999	6.7	12.4	14.9	17.2	19.4	19.6	1.5	3.6	8.5	14.9	19.3	19.6
2000	9.9	17.5	20.6	23.2	24.9	26.6	2.4	5.7	12.3	21.3	24.0	26.6

Notes: In Panel A, tax returns are ranked by total income excluding capital gains. Series report the additional income reported in the form of capital gains. The share of capital gains reported is the share of total income including capital gains. For example, the top decile (defined by income excluding capital gains) in 2000 earned 6.4% of total income (including capital gains) in the form of capital gains. In Panel B, tax returns are ranked by total income including full realized capital gains. The series report the share of total income (including capital gains) accruing in the form of capital gains.

benefits, etc. Taken all together, these minor categories never make more than 2% of the total income of the top decile (they usually make less than 1%), and even less at the level of the top percentile, and excluding them simplifies the reading of our composition series (these minor income categories were taken into account when computing top income levels and top income shares in total income).[40] For the period after 1982, the composition series were computed directly from the LAD microfiles. For the 1946–81 period, the composition series were estimated from the published tables in *Taxation Statistics* indicating for each income bracket not only the number of taxpayers and the total amount of their total income but also the separate amounts for each type of income, as well as the deductions, and tax liability. The composition of income within each group was estimated from these tables using a simple linear interpolation method. Such a method is less satisfactory than the Pareto interpolation method used to estimate top income levels (no obvious law seems to fit composition patterns in a stable way), but microfiles show that the resulting estimates are still relatively precise: estimation errors are always less than 2 percentage points, and they are usually much smaller (thanks to the fact that published tables are usually based on a very large number of income brackets).

The composition series reported in Table 6C.4 indicate for each income group the fraction of total income (including capital gains) that takes the form of capital gains for the period 1972–2000. The concept of capital gains used to compute these series is again 'full capital gains', i.e. total pre-exclusion capital gains. We provide two sets of estimates in Table 6C.4 corresponding to the two ways we treated capital gains to compute top income shares (see Panel A and B in Table 6B.2). In the left panel, we report the fraction of capital gains for incomes ranked excluding capital gains (as in Panel B of Table B2). In the right panel, we report the fraction of capital gains for incomes ranked including full capital gains (as in Panel A of Table 6B.2). For the period starting in 1982, these series were computed using the LAD microfiles. For the period 1972–81, a direct linear extrapolation from published tables yields capital gains shares series for groups of income (including the post-exclusion amount of capital gains), and one needs to correct these raw estimates in order to take re-ranking into account (see Appendix 6B above). That is, capital gains shares are smaller for groups ranked by income excluding capital gains than for groups ranked by income including post-exclusion capital gains (as in the published tables), and capital gains shares are smaller for groups ranked by income including post-exclusion capital gains than for groups ranked by income including pre-exclusion capital gains. Microfiles allowed us to compute the magnitudes of these correction coefficients.[41] The capital gains shares series reported in Table 6C.4 demonstrate that re-ranking is substantial at the very top. For example, in 2000, 26.6% of total income reported by the fractile P99.99–100 of the distribution of

[40] The fact that these minor income categories almost do not matter for top incomes implies that changes in tax law regarding those items (e.g. changes in the definition of family allowances or unemployment benefits) have negligible consequences for our income levels and shares series.

[41] The correction formulas for capital gains shares that we inferred from microfiles are more complex than those applied to correct income levels, and they are available upon request.

income including capital gains takes the form of capital gains, but the capital gains share falls to 6.7% when one looks at the fractile P99.99–100 of the distribution of income excluding capital gains.

APPENDIX 6D: WAGES AND SALARIES SERIES

Top wage shares are estimated by Pareto interpolation from the LAD distribution tables from 1982 to 2000 and from *Taxation Statistics* published tables from 1972 to 1981. The total wage denominator is taken as equal to total employment reported on tax returns. Employment income on tax returns includes wages and salaries, commissions from employment, and other employment income. Wages and salaries include taxable allowances and benefits, bonuses and directors' fees as well as the value of stock option exercises. Total employment income on tax returns is always very close to 95% of wages and salaries (excluding supplementary labour income) from National Accounts with very little fluctuation over the period 1972–2000. The total number of wage earners is also estimated from LAD (1982–2000) and *Taxation Statistics* (1972–81) as the number of returns with positive wages and salaries. This statistic fluctuates around 100% of the National Accounts estimate of the number of full-time plus part-time employees with no trend over the period (the ratio is always between 98% and 102%). Total employment income and the total number of tax returns with positive wages and salaries are reported from 1972 to 2000 in Table 6D.1.

We estimate two series of top wage income shares. The first series, reported in Panel A of Table 6D.2, are estimated at the individual level (as is our income series). The second series, reported in Panel B, are wage income shares estimated at the family level whereby we add employment income of married couples. In that case, the total number of units (relative to which the upper groups are defined) is the total number of families with positive wage income in the LAD microfiles. The family series are limited to the period 1982–2000 when the LAD micro-data are available (as there is no information on earnings by couples in the published statistics). We use the same type of Pareto interpolation methods described in Appendix 6B to estimate these top wage shares from distribution tables by size of employment income obtained from the LAD microfiles beginning in 1982.

Using the composition tables published in *Taxation Statistics* from 1972 to 1981, we are able to extend our individual wage shares series back to 1972. Starting in 1972, the composition tables by brackets of total income give not only the amounts of wages and salaries reported but also the number of tax returns with positive wages and salaries. We use this information to obtain a preliminary distribution of wage income as follows.

Average wage income for wage earners and average gross income for each gross income bracket are computed. We then assume that each gross income bracket corresponds to a wage income bracket with thresholds equal to the actual gross income thresholds multiplied by the ratio of average wage income to average

Table 6D.1 Aggregate series on wages in Canada, 1972–2000

	Total number of employees (in thousands) (1)	Number of families with wage (in thousands) (2)	Total wage Income (in millions of 2000 dollars) (3)	Average individual wage (in 2000 dollars) (4)	Average family wage (in 2000 dollars) (5)	Consumer Price Index (CPI) (base 100 in 2000) (6)
1972	8,541		232,780	27,255		22.996
1973	8,955		250,139	27,933		24.758
1974	9,419		268,249	28,480		27.401
1975	9,648		281,100	29,135		30.396
1976	9,869		303,667	30,768		32.687
1977	10,014		309,893	30,945		35.242
1978	10,328		310,055	30,021		38.414
1979	10,772		319,123	29,625		41.938
1980	11,069		328,688	29,694		46.167
1981	11,420		333,827	29,232		51.894
1982	11,256	8,328	320,869	28,507	38,530	57.533
1983	11,185	8,290	314,970	28,160	37,996	60.881
1984	11,402	8,446	323,321	28,357	38,279	63.524
1985	11,582	8,548	330,655	28,549	38,682	66.079
1986	12,079	8,933	343,190	28,413	38,419	68.811
1987	12,312	9,001	351,459	28,547	39,046	71.806
1988	12,623	9,218	371,880	29,461	40,344	74.714
1989	12,962	9,389	386,737	29,836	41,189	78.414
1990	13,073	9,511	384,702	29,427	40,447	82.203
1991	12,916	9,476	370,462	28,683	39,097	86.784
1992	12,869	9,412	374,704	29,117	39,813	88.106
1993	12,903	9,460	374,313	29,011	39,568	89.692
1994	13,021	9,569	382,823	29,402	40,008	89.868
1995	13,195	9,718	388,505	29,443	39,979	91.806
1996	13,297	9,772	391,518	29,445	40,067	93.304
1997	13,615	9,989	407,506	29,932	40,797	94.802
1998	13,844	10,157	425,961	30,768	41,937	95.683
1999	14,233	10,432	443,824	31,183	42,543	97.357
2000	14,688	10,534	466,028	31,729	44,239	100.000

Notes: Total number of part-time and full time employees from number of tax returns reporting positive wages and salaries. Families defined as the sum of married couples and single individuals reporting positive wages and salaries. Total employment income reported on tax returns (sum of wages and salaries, commissions from employment and other employment income). Average individual wage in column (4) is column (3) divided by column (1). Average family wage in column (5) is column (3) divided by column (2). All amounts are reported in 2000 Canadian dollars.

gross income in that bracket. In order to generate brackets fitting together, the final thresholds are taken as equal to the average of the corresponding top and bottom thresholds of two adjacent brackets. We therefore obtain a set of wage bracket thresholds where the number of returns and the wage amount reported for each bracket is the same as in the original composition table. This new distribution by size of wages is not perfectly accurate because ranking in terms of gross income is not identical to ranking in terms of wages. From this con-

Table 6D.2 Shares of wage income for upper groups in Canada, 1972–2000

	P90–100 (1)	P95–100 (2)	P99–100 (3)	P99.5–100 (4)	P99.9–100 (5)	P99.99–100 (6)	P90–95 (7)	P95–99 (8)	P99–99.5 (9)	P99.5–99.9 (10)	P99.9–99.99 (11)
Panel A: Individuals											
1972	27.22	16.80	5.59	3.51	1.12	0.19	10.41	11.21	2.08	2.40	0.92
1973	27.31	16.93	5.79	3.69	1.24	0.23	10.38	11.14	2.11	2.45	1.00
1974	26.92	16.57	5.65	3.59	1.26	0.26	10.35	10.92	2.06	2.33	1.00
1975	26.97	16.56	5.76	3.70	1.40	0.32	10.41	10.80	2.06	2.30	1.08
1976	26.20	16.02	5.19	3.38	1.13	0.23	10.19	10.83	1.81	2.24	0.90
1977	26.10	15.79	5.04	3.25	1.10	0.23	10.31	10.75	1.78	2.15	0.87
1978	25.82	15.42	4.74	3.05	1.05	0.22	10.40	10.69	1.68	2.01	0.82
1979	26.30	15.74	5.09	3.25	1.10	0.23	10.56	10.65	1.84	2.16	0.87
1980	26.65	16.10	5.28	3.34	1.17	0.26	10.55	10.82	1.94	2.16	0.91
1981	26.44	15.79	4.94	3.10	1.08	0.24	10.65	10.85	1.84	2.02	0.84
1982	27.37	16.57	5.55	3.63	1.50	0.41	10.79	11.02	1.92	2.14	1.09
1983	27.52	16.59	5.54	3.63	1.49	0.42	10.92	11.05	1.92	2.14	1.07
1984	27.65	16.72	5.68	3.75	1.58	0.46	10.92	11.05	1.93	2.18	1.11
1985	27.80	16.89	5.84	3.91	1.68	0.51	10.91	11.05	1.94	2.22	1.18
1986	28.00	17.04	5.89	3.92	1.67	0.50	10.96	11.14	1.97	2.26	1.17
1987	28.28	17.35	6.21	4.21	1.85	0.55	10.94	11.14	2.00	2.36	1.30
1988	29.04	18.27	7.11	5.05	2.47	0.86	10.77	11.16	2.05	2.58	1.61
1989	29.43	18.70	7.55	5.47	2.80	1.10	10.73	11.15	2.08	2.67	1.71
1990	29.05	18.18	6.93	4.87	2.32	0.82	10.87	11.25	2.07	2.55	1.50
1991	29.22	18.21	6.80	4.73	2.20	0.75	11.01	11.41	2.07	2.53	1.45
1992	29.21	18.16	6.78	4.73	2.22	0.78	11.06	11.38	2.05	2.51	1.44
1993	29.59	18.51	7.11	5.04	2.46	0.86	11.08	11.41	2.07	2.58	1.60
1994	29.75	18.68	7.20	5.09	2.42	0.79	11.08	11.48	2.11	2.67	1.63
1995	30.15	19.10	7.59	5.38	2.57	0.84	11.06	11.51	2.21	2.81	1.73
1996	30.73	19.66	8.06	5.78	2.78	0.84	11.07	11.61	2.28	3.00	1.94
1997	31.66	20.64	8.90	6.56	3.30	1.08	11.02	11.74	2.34	3.26	2.22
1998	32.16	21.17	9.31	6.90	3.52	1.17	10.99	11.86	2.42	3.38	2.35
1999	32.35	21.40	9.48	7.02	3.58	1.21	10.95	11.92	2.45	3.44	2.37
2000	33.50	22.57	10.51	7.97	4.30	1.50	10.93	12.06	2.54	3.67	2.80

(contd.)

Table 6D.2 (*contd.*)

	P90–100 (1)	P95–100 (2)	P99–100 (3)	P99.5–100 (4)	P99.9–100 (5)	P99.99–100 (6)	P90–95 (7)	P95–99 (8)	P99–99.5 (9)	P99.5–99.9 (10)	P99.9–99.99 (11)
Panel B: Families											
1982	27.53	16.49	5.26	3.39	1.38	0.37	11.05	11.22	1.87	2.01	1.02
1983	27.84	16.66	5.30	3.41	1.39	0.39	11.19	11.36	1.89	2.02	1.00
1984	28.06	16.86	5.48	3.58	1.53	0.45	11.19	11.39	1.90	2.05	1.08
1985	28.29	17.08	5.64	3.74	1.60	0.48	11.20	11.45	1.90	2.13	1.12
1986	28.66	17.33	5.68	3.73	1.54	0.45	11.33	11.64	1.95	2.19	1.10
1987	28.99	17.68	6.04	4.06	1.78	0.53	11.31	11.64	1.98	2.29	1.24
1988	29.71	18.47	6.87	4.77	2.29	0.73	11.24	11.61	2.10	2.47	1.56
1989	30.11	18.91	7.29	5.17	2.62	0.99	11.20	11.62	2.12	2.55	1.64
1990	30.01	18.58	6.72	4.65	2.18	0.77	11.43	11.86	2.07	2.46	1.41
1991	30.39	18.76	6.64	4.56	2.09	0.72	11.63	12.12	2.09	2.47	1.37
1992	30.38	18.71	6.53	4.46	2.02	0.67	11.67	12.18	2.07	2.44	1.35
1993	30.80	19.14	6.93	4.85	2.29	0.79	11.67	12.20	2.09	2.56	1.50
1994	30.98	19.27	7.01	4.87	2.23	0.70	11.71	12.26	2.14	2.64	1.54
1995	31.40	19.66	7.32	5.13	2.37	0.74	11.74	12.34	2.19	2.76	1.63
1996	31.87	20.12	7.77	5.44	2.51	0.72	11.75	12.35	2.33	2.93	1.79
1997	32.70	20.99	8.57	6.16	2.99	0.93	11.71	12.42	2.42	3.17	2.06
1998	33.21	21.55	9.00	6.51	3.24	1.03	11.66	12.55	2.49	3.27	2.21
1999	33.46	21.80	9.19	6.65	3.30	1.06	11.67	12.61	2.53	3.35	2.24
2000	34.57	22.83	10.08	7.50	3.85	1.25	11.74	12.76	2.58	3.65	2.60

Notes: Shares computed from tax return statistics and total number of wage earners and total wage bill from Table 6D.1.
For example, in 2000, the top 10% individual wage and salary earners earned 33.50% of total wages and salaries in Canada.

structed wage income distribution, we compute average income levels and shares for each of our top income groups. The levels and shares are underestimated using this method because ranking in terms of total income is not identical to ranking in terms of wages and salaries. (See Table 6D.3.)

This method is therefore reliable only if wage income is a substantial fraction of income bracket by bracket. This is true below the top percentile but not for the top wage income groups. However, using years 1982–2000 where both the micro-files and the published composition tables are available, we can estimate by how much levels and shares estimated from published tables for each top income group should be adjusted to match estimates from the micro-files. Fortunately, these multiplier factors are extremely stable from 1982 to 2000 (the maximum variation between multipliers is always less than 10%). Therefore, we can use the multipliers from year 1982 to adjust the levels and shares for years 1972 to 1981.[42]

We repeat these computations for all provinces excluding Quebec and for Francophones in Quebec separately for years 1982–2000.[43] Each tax return identifies the province of residence, and francophones and anglophones within Quebec are identified according to the language of their tax returns. For these series, the total number of individuals is defined as the number of individuals in the LAD microfiles in that particular group with positive wages and salaries, and the total amount of employment income is defined as total employment income reported on tax returns for that particular group. Canadians are free to choose to file their tax returns in either English or French. Quebec is the only province with a strong majority of francophones. Quebec residents filing tax returns in French are almost certainly francophones. It might be the case, however, that some Quebec francophones may file tax returns in English. However, our conclusions on the differential trends for Quebec francophones and the rest of Canada remain valid as long as the share of top earner francophones who file tax returns in French does not decline over time. (See Table 6D.4.)

Data on stock options exercised for the period 1995–2000 have been provided by the Statistics Division of Canada Customs and Revenue Agency. The Agency provided us with two set of statistics.

First, wage earners were ranked by full employment income including stock options. The number of individuals, the amount of employment income they reported, as well as the amount of stock option they exercised was calculated for a range of full employment income brackets. From these statistics, we estimated, using the methods described above, the share of stock options in employment income for each of the top groups. Those statistics are reported in Panel A of Table 6D.5 (note that the share of employment income accruing to each of these groups has already been estimated and reported in Table 6D.2).

Second, wage earners were ranked by employment income excluding stock options. The number of individuals, the amount of employment income they

[42] Shares and levels are blown up by around 5% for groups P90–95 and P95–99, by around 10% for groups P99–99.5 and P99.5–99.9, and by around 20% for groups P99.9–99.99 and P99.99–100.

[43] Published tables in *Taxation Statistics* do not allow the estimation of these series for years when the LAD microfiles are not available.

Table 6D.3 Average wage income and threshold for each fractile (in 2000 Canadian dollars) in Canada, 1972–2000

Year (1)	P90–100 (2)	P95–100 (3)	P99–100 (4)	P99.5–100 (5)	P99.9–100 (6)	P99.99–100 (7)	P90–95 (8)	P95–99 (9)	P99–99.5 (10)	P99.5–99.9 (11)	P99.9–99.99 (12)	P90 (13)	P95 (14)	P99 (15)	P99.5 (16)	P99.9 (17)	P99.99 (18)
Panel A: Individuals																	
1972	74,176	91,592	152,435	191,436	303,889	528,735	56,758	76,379	113,428	163,307	278,701	51,874	62,946	101,161	133,067	214,059	437,850
1973	76,281	94,602	161,842	205,975	345,806	654,217	57,961	77,792	117,699	171,003	311,103	52,940	64,541	104,693	138,521	230,334	516,617
1974	76,672	94,396	160,915	204,376	358,854	729,138	58,954	77,768	117,514	165,731	317,373	53,921	64,965	105,230	137,210	229,652	550,330
1975	78,574	96,477	167,729	215,365	407,596	917,144	60,669	78,666	120,177	167,272	351,050	55,050	65,334	108,021	139,696	243,226	647,177
1976	80,619	98,551	159,565	207,809	348,605	706,510	62,689	83,301	111,353	172,512	309,004	57,974	68,783	109,466	137,948	222,599	535,335
1977	80,757	97,699	155,807	201,203	341,321	715,802	63,824	83,172	110,516	166,171	299,232	58,572	70,512	107,085	131,525	217,644	534,030
1978	77,520	92,609	142,210	183,368	314,320	669,860	62,436	80,212	101,088	150,599	274,651	57,372	68,577	98,633	123,275	197,969	483,615
1979	77,903	93,237	150,822	192,623	324,693	675,700	62,576	78,837	109,056	159,593	285,627	57,366	68,236	97,408	127,710	209,745	497,139
1980	79,142	95,616	156,757	198,121	348,019	768,976	62,672	80,338	115,401	160,697	301,085	57,487	69,177	104,232	133,374	215,907	546,180
1981	77,274	92,308	144,288	181,003	315,995	693,354	62,244	79,322	107,592	147,198	274,089	57,167	68,540	100,434	120,704	197,776	486,721
1982	78,017	94,494	158,269	207,072	426,459	1,165,309	61,540	78,555	109,461	152,210	344,313	56,437	67,681	100,687	121,961	227,231	703,728
1983	77,481	93,450	156,117	204,382	419,860	1,186,896	61,509	77,786	107,869	150,525	334,548	56,563	67,404	99,036	120,412	225,013	672,182
1984	78,392	94,841	160,952	212,674	446,616	1,313,681	61,940	78,314	109,217	154,176	350,345	57,111	67,798	100,184	122,610	231,121	745,186
1985	79,365	96,448	166,752	223,021	480,757	1,446,320	62,282	78,873	110,487	158,583	373,550	57,321	68,265	100,926	124,586	240,070	834,990
1986	79,553	96,808	167,465	222,984	473,927	1,423,370	62,303	79,140	111,944	160,288	368,343	57,425	68,284	101,769	126,768	242,726	768,191
1987	80,742	99,047	177,191	240,480	528,405	1,581,208	62,439	79,515	113,904	168,452	411,561	57,488	68,550	103,185	129,889	265,343	881,177
1988	85,561	107,639	209,351	297,675	727,984	2,526,101	63,483	82,208	121,004	190,117	528,183	58,247	70,091	108,699	141,153	314,450	1,260,222
1989	87,816	111,586	225,231	326,405	836,300	3,267,809	64,047	83,174	124,075	198,944	566,097	58,793	70,615	111,099	146,353	334,945	1,404,351
1990	85,489	106,992	203,931	286,327	682,712	2,416,870	63,989	82,753	121,558	187,241	489,947	58,480	70,428	109,342	141,919	300,906	1,167,181
1991	83,809	104,470	195,160	271,400	631,891	2,147,467	63,151	81,794	118,892	181,280	463,632	58,045	69,965	107,479	138,763	287,629	1,037,253
1992	85,055	105,731	197,387	275,276	646,407	2,266,611	64,377	82,812	119,539	182,469	466,393	59,092	71,028	108,223	140,358	287,814	1,090,105
1993	85,852	107,404	206,122	292,430	713,087	2,504,019	64,303	82,719	119,847	187,253	514,107	58,906	70,938	108,147	141,307	310,116	1,225,954
1994	87,478	109,832	211,662	299,131	711,517	2,326,451	65,126	84,371	124,214	196,030	532,074	59,633	71,901	111,112	146,848	324,963	1,221,657
1995	88,774	112,444	223,415	316,574	755,220	2,462,685	65,104	84,704	130,255	206,866	565,625	59,473	72,029	114,458	152,136	345,237	1,311,880
1996	90,496	115,783	237,178	340,323	818,861	2,477,941	65,212	85,433	134,039	220,685	634,507	59,483	72,255	117,457	157,049	383,280	1,393,046
1997	94,758	123,552	266,302	392,405	987,746	3,236,470	65,962	87,866	140,189	243,567	737,868	60,089	73,387	123,931	168,319	436,280	1,715,679
1998	98,945	130,279	286,515	424,418	1,082,738	3,590,101	67,607	91,218	148,659	259,790	804,247	61,433	75,430	130,746	179,725	462,914	1,882,364
1999	100,864	133,432	295,520	438,057	1,116,347	3,764,928	68,294	92,913	152,976	268,471	822,131	62,124	76,422	134,367	186,407	474,949	2,071,545
2000	106,300	143,214	333,382	505,704	1,364,367	4,773,356	69,385	95,677	161,000	291,071	985,623	63,102	77,836	138,825	197,300	537,560	2,512,359

Panel B: Families																	
1982	101,672	121,763	194,309	250,309	511,079	1,349,561	81,581	103,627	138,310	185,116	417,915	74,526	89,830	129,074	151,821	273,478	846,293
1983	101,255	121,163	192,781	248,161	506,639	1,415,197	81,347	103,258	137,401	183,542	405,688	74,435	89,440	128,252	150,448	270,782	816,125
1984	103,166	124,019	201,423	263,091	561,297	1,652,549	82,312	104,668	139,755	188,540	440,047	75,186	90,596	130,231	153,572	285,697	915,816
1985	104,710	126,476	208,625	276,533	592,585	1,781,916	82,943	105,939	140,716	197,520	460,437	76,085	91,851	132,476	158,725	296,556	992,748
1986	105,736	127,841	209,679	275,335	569,604	1,643,210	83,631	107,382	144,022	201,769	450,314	76,271	92,548	135,127	164,394	300,509	939,486
1987	108,912	132,844	226,832	305,163	666,990	2,007,646	84,979	109,347	148,502	214,706	518,029	77,375	94,098	138,089	171,512	331,688	1,119,115
1988	115,606	143,741	267,153	370,777	892,020	2,854,513	87,471	112,889	163,530	240,466	673,965	79,704	96,964	148,122	184,410	399,648	1,563,466
1989	120,026	150,726	290,581	412,451	1,045,693	3,937,357	89,326	115,762	168,711	254,140	724,397	81,303	99,157	153,470	189,299	431,098	1,783,381
1990	117,668	145,697	263,420	364,268	855,408	3,010,609	89,640	116,266	162,572	241,483	615,941	81,377	99,669	151,938	184,294	384,250	1,460,320
1991	115,876	143,067	253,166	347,359	796,625	2,757,097	88,686	115,541	158,974	235,042	578,795	80,498	98,743	149,486	182,022	366,742	1,326,439
1992	117,979	145,318	253,709	346,453	784,457	2,599,814	90,641	118,220	160,965	236,952	582,751	82,194	101,141	152,066	186,483	367,555	1,314,715
1993	120,065	149,183	270,201	377,743	892,534	3,081,161	90,948	118,928	162,660	249,045	649,354	82,380	101,535	153,312	191,940	402,448	1,537,901
1994	122,019	151,817	276,086	383,744	880,033	2,748,987	92,221	120,750	168,428	259,672	672,371	83,446	102,866	156,909	199,646	420,980	1,463,066
1995	123,535	154,694	287,821	403,626	930,949	2,915,317	92,377	121,411	172,016	271,796	710,463	83,517	103,158	158,597	206,114	444,955	1,584,672
1996	125,466	158,421	305,788	428,399	989,484	2,847,768	92,512	121,579	183,176	288,127	783,008	83,638	103,420	160,787	214,211	482,484	1,657,332
1997	131,161	168,399	343,931	493,801	1,199,195	3,746,988	93,922	124,517	194,060	317,452	916,107	84,916	105,403	169,861	227,671	552,238	2,081,551
1998	137,032	177,878	371,382	537,101	1,334,955	4,236,519	96,185	129,502	205,662	337,637	1,012,559	86,863	108,431	180,598	240,394	595,741	2,279,223
1999	140,577	183,137	385,853	559,047	1,386,464	4,440,136	98,018	132,458	212,660	352,192	1,047,167	88,274	110,355	187,208	247,866	621,701	2,391,342
2000	148,136	195,663	431,773	642,584	1,648,036	5,359,561	100,609	136,635	220,962	391,221	1,235,644	90,315	112,950	197,153	266,105	709,700	2,917,182

Notes: Levels computed from tax return statistics and total number of tax units and total employment income from Table 6D.1. For example, in 2000, the threshold P90 of the top decile of the wage and salaries distribution was $63,102 for individuals.

Table 6D.4 Top wage income shares, francophones in Quebec vs. all filers from rest of Canada, 1982–2000

	# Wage Earners ('000s) (1)	Average wage income ($ 2000) (2)	P90–100 (3)	P95–100 (4)	P99–100 (5)	P99.5–100 (6)	P99.9–100 (7)	P99.99–100 (8)	P90–95 (9)	P95–99 (10)	P99–99.5 (11)	P99.5–99.9 (12)	P99.9–99.99 (13)
Panel A: Francophones in Quebec													
1982	2,355	26,613	26.08	15.24	4.33	2.56	0.82	0.19	10.85	10.91	1.77	1.74	0.63
1983	2,347	25,937	25.95	15.11	4.34	2.58	0.83	0.17	10.85	10.77	1.76	1.75	0.66
1984	2,412	26,465	25.99	15.08	4.33	2.58	0.83	0.17	10.92	10.75	1.75	1.75	0.66
1985	2,456	26,566	25.97	15.10	4.36	2.60	0.84	0.17	10.87	10.75	1.76	1.76	0.67
1986	2,586	26,256	26.24	15.31	4.51	2.74	0.94	0.21	10.93	10.80	1.77	1.80	0.73
1987	2,675	26,585	26.40	15.44	4.62	2.84	1.01	0.24	10.96	10.82	1.78	1.83	0.77
1988	2,729	26,895	26.37	15.51	4.66	2.86	1.02	0.25	10.86	10.84	1.80	1.85	0.77
1989	2,766	26,904	26.42	15.57	4.72	2.91	1.03	0.25	10.85	10.85	1.81	1.88	0.78
1990	2,827	26,888	26.65	15.68	4.71	2.89	0.99	0.22	10.97	10.97	1.83	1.89	0.77
1991	2,797	26,285	27.11	15.94	4.80	2.95	1.03	0.24	11.17	11.15	1.85	1.92	0.79
1992	2,781	26,685	27.19	15.98	4.88	3.04	1.13	0.33	11.21	11.11	1.84	1.91	0.81
1993	2,788	26,519	27.37	16.12	4.97	3.13	1.19	0.36	11.25	11.15	1.84	1.94	0.83
1994	2,831	26,755	27.40	16.14	4.98	3.13	1.16	0.31	11.27	11.16	1.85	1.97	0.85
1995	2,869	26,691	27.66	16.54	5.37	3.50	1.47	0.54	11.12	11.17	1.87	2.04	0.93
1996	2,889	26,494	27.80	16.62	5.31	3.41	1.32	0.36	11.19	11.31	1.90	2.09	0.97
1997	2,952	26,419	28.15	16.99	5.62	3.67	1.46	0.39	11.16	11.37	1.95	2.21	1.08
1998	3,014	26,973	28.89	17.71	6.20	4.18	1.84	0.63	11.19	11.51	2.02	2.34	1.21
1999	3,082	27,327	28.65	17.59	6.14	4.10	1.74	0.50	11.06	11.46	2.03	2.36	1.24
2000	3,184	27,878	29.23	18.01	6.51	4.44	1.98	0.67	11.22	11.50	2.08	2.45	1.31

Panel B: Canada excluding Quebec

1982	8,509	28,915	27.55	16.79	5.76	3.82	1.61	0.44	10.77	11.03	1.94	2.20	1.17
1983	8,468	28,669	27.74	16.83	5.75	3.82	1.62	0.46	10.91	11.07	1.94	2.20	1.16
1984	8,617	28,843	27.89	16.98	5.91	3.96	1.72	0.50	10.91	11.07	1.95	2.23	1.22
1985	8,755	28,983	28.12	17.19	6.10	4.13	1.83	0.54	10.93	11.09	1.97	2.30	1.29
1986	9,099	28,896	28.28	17.30	6.11	4.10	1.78	0.55	10.98	11.19	2.01	2.33	1.23
1987	9,233	29,027	28.64	17.71	6.51	4.47	2.02	0.61	10.93	11.21	2.04	2.46	1.41
1988	9,498	30,123	29.56	18.80	7.60	5.48	2.77	0.97	10.76	11.20	2.12	2.72	1.80
1989	9,785	30,591	29.99	19.27	8.08	5.93	3.12	1.20	10.71	11.19	2.15	2.82	1.92
1990	9,824	30,135	29.47	18.64	7.37	5.24	2.58	0.92	10.83	11.27	2.12	2.66	1.66
1991	9,703	29,361	29.57	18.60	7.18	5.06	2.44	0.84	10.97	11.42	2.12	2.63	1.60
1992	9,684	29,780	29.54	18.50	7.11	5.00	2.40	0.83	11.04	11.40	2.10	2.60	1.57
1993	9,711	29,733	29.96	18.91	7.52	5.39	2.69	0.94	11.05	11.39	2.12	2.70	1.75
1994	9,789	30,163	30.14	19.09	7.60	5.43	2.63	0.85	11.05	11.49	2.18	2.80	1.78
1995	9,929	30,198	30.54	19.49	7.91	5.66	2.71	0.84	11.05	11.59	2.24	2.95	1.87
1996	10,016	30,307	31.20	20.17	8.50	6.21	3.02	0.93	11.03	11.67	2.30	3.19	2.09
1997	10,271	30,901	32.11	21.13	9.31	6.92	3.47	1.07	10.98	11.82	2.40	3.44	2.41
1998	10,438	31,821	32.61	21.70	9.77	7.29	3.73	1.19	10.91	11.93	2.48	3.56	2.54
1999	10,749	32,222	32.89	21.98	9.97	7.44	3.81	1.23	10.91	12.00	2.54	3.62	2.59
2000	11,080	32,970	34.02	23.21	11.10	8.48	4.57	1.54	10.82	12.11	2.62	3.90	3.03

Notes: Francophones in Quebec defined as Quebec residents filing tax return in French Canada excluding Quebec defined as residents from Canadian provinces excluding Quebec.

Table 6D.5 The role of stock options in top wage income shares in Canada, 1995–2000

	P0–100 (1)	P90–100 (2)	P95–100 (3)	P99–100 (4)	P99.5–100 (5)	P99.9–100 (6)	P99.99–100 (7)	P90–95 (8)	P95–99 (9)	P99–99.5 (10)	P99.5–99.9 (11)	P99.9–99.99 (12)	P99.99–100 (13)
Panel A: Fraction of stock options in total wage income and top wage income groups (ranked including stock options) (in percent)													
1995	0.261	0.89	1.39	3.33	4.45	7.23	10.82	0.03	0.13	0.58	1.92	5.47	10.82
1996	0.429	1.43	2.19	5.06	6.64	10.25	16.43	0.08	0.21	0.96	3.22	7.33	16.43
1997	0.648	2.06	3.10	6.72	8.55	12.33	16.00	0.09	0.30	1.39	4.35	10.03	16.00
1998	0.669	2.09	3.14	6.77	8.67	13.03	19.04	0.07	0.30	1.31	4.04	9.92	19.04
1999	0.880	2.68	4.01	8.61	11.05	16.82	25.69	0.08	0.36	1.59	5.05	12.21	25.69
2000	1.538	4.44	6.55	13.56	17.16	25.58	38.79	0.10	0.49	2.34	7.58	18.30	38.79
Panel B: Top wage income shares excluding stock options (both in ranking and in wage income) (in percent)													
1995		29.97	18.89	7.37	5.17	2.42	0.78	11.08	11.52	2.20	2.75	1.64	0.78
1996		30.46	19.34	7.72	5.46	2.56	0.75	11.11	11.62	2.26	2.90	1.81	0.75
1997		31.26	20.18	8.41	6.10	2.99	0.97	11.08	11.77	2.31	3.11	2.02	0.97
1998		31.72	20.67	8.78	6.40	3.16	1.03	11.05	11.89	2.39	3.23	2.14	1.03
1999		31.78	20.75	8.79	6.38	3.14	1.00	11.03	11.96	2.41	3.23	2.14	1.00
2000		32.49	21.44	9.33	6.85	3.50	1.13	11.05	12.11	2.48	3.35	2.37	1.13
Panel C: Top wage income shares excluding stock options in ranking but including stock options in wage income (in percent)													
1995		30.12	19.06	7.52	5.30	2.48	0.79	11.06	11.53	2.22	2.82	1.69	0.79
1996		30.65	19.57	7.94	5.64	2.64	0.76	11.08	11.63	2.30	3.00	1.88	0.76
1997		31.61	20.58	8.79	6.43	3.14	1.00	11.03	11.79	2.36	3.29	2.14	1.00
1998		32.08	21.08	9.17	6.72	3.30	1.05	11.00	11.91	2.44	3.42	2.25	1.05
1999		32.23	21.26	9.25	6.76	3.29	1.03	10.97	12.01	2.49	3.46	2.26	1.03
2000		33.17	22.22	10.06	7.48	3.84	1.20	10.95	12.16	2.57	3.65	2.64	1.20
Panel D: Fraction of stock options in top wage income groups ranked excluding stock options (in percent)													
1995		0.74	1.13	2.29	2.76	2.79	1.53	0.09	0.38	1.14	2.73	3.38	1.53
1996		1.08	1.61	3.22	3.59	3.36	1.94	0.13	0.52	2.31	3.79	3.99	1.94
1997		1.77	2.61	5.01	5.80	5.46	3.95	0.18	0.79	2.75	6.16	6.38	3.95
1998		1.79	2.61	4.85	5.53	4.81	3.11	0.21	0.89	2.99	6.24	5.63	3.11
1999		2.28	3.27	5.83	6.46	5.43	3.40	0.35	1.30	4.10	7.45	6.38	3.40
2000		3.31	4.74	8.46	9.66	10.02	7.01	0.42	1.68	5.00	9.28	11.43	7.01

Notes: Stock options are reported as wage income on tax returns when exercised. In Panel A, wage earners are ranked by wage income including stock option exercises (as in Table D2), and fraction of stock options (in total wage income) are reported in percent. In Panel B, wage earners are ranked by wage income excluding stock options and wage income shares are computed excluding stock options (in both numerator and denominator). In Panel C, wage earners are ranked by wage income excluding stock options but wage income shares are computed including stock options (in both numerator and denominator). In Panel D, wage earners are ranked by wage income excluding stock options and the share of stock options (in percent) in total wage income (including stock options) are reported.

reported, as well as the amount of stock options they exercised was calculated for a range of employment income (excluding stock options) brackets. From these statistics, we estimated the shares of employment income (excluding stock options) accruing to each of the top wage groups (ranked by employment income excluding stock options). These statistics are reported on Panel B of Table 6D.5. Keeping the ranking by employment income excluding stock options, we estimated the share of employment income (including stock options) accruing to each of these top groups (ranked by employment income excluding stock options) by adding back the amount of stock options reported both in the numerator for each group and the denominator. Those top wage shares are reported in Panel C of Table 6D.5. Finally, for each of these groups, we estimated the fraction of stock options they reported (computed as the amount of stock options divided by the amount of employment income including stock options). Those statistics are reported in Panel D of Table 6D.5.

APPENDIX 6E: INCOME MOBILITY SERIES

We have used the longitudinal structure of the micro-data available for the period 1982–2000 to analyse mobility of high incomes.

First, we have estimated top income shares based on three and five consecutive years of income instead of just one year of income as we did previously. To compute such top income shares, we have ranked individuals according to the sum of real market incomes over the corresponding years (missing individuals in one or more years are counted as zero income). The total number of adults is taken as the average over the corresponding years (from Table 6A.1). The total income for the denominator is taken as the sum of total real incomes (from Table 6A.1). Table 6E.1, Panel A reports those top income shares results.

Second, we have computed direct measures of mobility for high income groups. We report in Panel B of Table 6E.1, the probability of an individual in a top income group in year *t* remaining in this top income group one, two, and three years later. This probability is estimated unconditional of whether the individual files an income tax return in the later year. Complete matrices of mobility across those top income groups are available from the authors upon request.

APPENDIX 6F: ESTIMATING MARGINAL TAX RATES AND AVERAGE TAX RATES, 1920–2000

The Canadian income tax structure has gone through many reforms over the course of the century. Perry (1955, 1989) provides a comprehensive description of the development and evolution of taxation in Canada during the pre-war and post-war periods respectively.

Table 6E.1 High income mobility in Canada, 1982–2000

Panel A: Top Income Shares, averages over various years	One year average						Three-year average						Five-year average				
	P90–100	P95–100	P99–100	P99.5–100	P99.9–100		P90–100	P95–100	P99–100	P99.5–100	P99.9–100		P90–100	P95–100	P99–100	P99.5–100	P99.9–100
1982	36.24	22.92	8.46	5.66	2.33												
1983	36.19	22.71	8.21	5.44	2.13	1982–1984	35.72	22.41	8.13	5.40	2.16						
1984	35.78	22.48	8.29	5.55	2.28	1983–1985	35.52	22.26	8.10	5.38	2.13	1982–1986	35.21	22.08	8.02	5.32	2.11
1985	35.25	22.20	8.21	5.51	2.26	1984–1986	35.21	22.09	8.09	5.39	2.16	1983–1987	35.12	22.04	8.06	5.35	2.12
1986	35.22	22.22	8.24	5.52	2.24	1985–1987	35.15	22.16	8.23	5.51	2.23	1984–1988	35.17	22.26	8.37	5.64	2.33
1987	35.05	22.22	8.40	5.69	2.38	1986–1988	35.42	22.58	8.70	5.94	2.54	1985–1989	35.40	22.63	8.78	6.01	2.59
1988	35.66	23.11	9.34	6.54	3.00	1987–1989	35.97	23.27	9.41	6.59	3.01	1986–1990	35.40	22.76	8.99	6.21	2.74
1989	36.36	23.83	10.01	7.15	3.44	1988–1990	35.89	23.35	9.58	6.76	3.14	1987–1991	35.66	23.03	9.23	6.43	2.88
1990	35.54	23.08	9.35	6.55	2.98	1989–1991	35.88	23.28	9.46	6.64	3.03	1988–1992	35.78	23.14	9.31	6.49	2.91
1991	36.31	23.47	9.37	6.51	2.91	1990–1992	35.84	23.07	9.12	6.31	2.77	1989–1993	35.92	23.16	9.23	6.41	2.82
1992	36.72	23.60	9.31	6.44	2.82	1991–1993	36.45	23.39	9.18	6.33	2.76	1990–1994	36.04	23.15	9.10	6.27	2.70
1993	37.31	24.03	9.56	6.64	2.97	1992–1994	36.83	23.61	9.26	6.40	2.78	1991–1995	36.64	23.53	9.27	6.39	2.76
1994	37.49	24.16	9.59	6.65	2.94	1993–1995	37.24	23.96	9.50	6.59	2.88	1992–1996	37.16	23.97	9.55	6.62	2.87
1995	37.85	24.65	10.00	6.99	3.13	1994–1996	37.77	24.48	9.88	6.90	3.05	1993–1997	37.82	24.57	10.01	7.00	3.10
1996	38.77	25.48	10.62	7.53	3.47	1995–1997	38.60	25.31	10.56	7.47	3.39	1994–1998	38.56	25.29	10.57	7.47	3.37
1997	39.78	26.51	11.52	8.32	3.97	1996–1998	39.59	26.26	11.30	8.10	3.78	1995–1999	39.43	26.16	11.25	8.04	3.73
1998	40.61	27.35	12.18	8.87	4.34	1997–1999	40.45	27.13	11.98	8.68	4.16	1996–2000	40.38	27.10	11.99	8.67	4.12
1999	41.17	27.89	12.62	9.25	4.61	1998–2000	41.37	28.04	12.71	9.31	4.57						
2000	42.34	29.01	13.56	10.11	5.23												

Panel B: Probability of staying in top group in next years

	One year						Two years						Three years				
	P90–100	P95–100	P99–100	P99.5–100	P99.9–100		P90–100	P95–100	P99–100	P99.5–100	P99.9–100		P90–100	P95–100	P99–100	P99.5–100	P99.9–100
1982	78.93%	74.60%	66.94%	63.90%	56.07%	1982	73.63%	68.67%	61.07%	58.03%	49.71%	1982	69.57%	63.64%	55.13%	51.68%	41.91%
1983	80.78%	76.75%	70.09%	67.12%	59.63%	1983	75.30%	70.10%	61.72%	58.00%	49.15%	1983	71.24%	65.69%	57.07%	53.75%	45.47%
1984	80.70%	76.08%	68.90%	65.68%	55.97%	1984	75.29%	70.08%	62.16%	58.96%	49.86%	1984	70.65%	64.62%	55.52%	51.63%	42.22%
1985	80.17%	75.41%	67.08%	63.84%	53.62%	1985	74.30%	68.43%	58.77%	54.91%	45.70%	1985	70.43%	64.50%	54.89%	51.23%	41.75%
1986	79.73%	74.62%	65.72%	62.00%	52.08%	1986	74.03%	68.78%	60.05%	55.82%	45.10%	1986	70.62%	65.10%	56.95%	52.98%	42.42%
1987	78.90%	73.67%	64.40%	60.08%	49.93%	1987	73.77%	68.40%	59.81%	55.87%	45.19%	1987	69.66%	64.10%	55.40%	51.33%	41.63%
1988	79.57%	75.09%	68.45%	65.64%	58.24%	1988	73.50%	68.63%	61.22%	58.30%	49.68%	1988	69.42%	64.17%	56.32%	53.55%	44.10%
1989	79.59%	75.41%	70.12%	68.03%	59.97%	1989	73.55%	68.86%	62.89%	60.49%	51.21%	1989	68.98%	63.88%	57.54%	55.13%	45.49%
1990	80.01%	76.29%	70.68%	68.87%	61.55%	1990	73.95%	69.57%	63.32%	60.88%	51.56%	1990	70.03%	64.73%	57.21%	54.62%	44.19%
1991	80.54%	76.60%	70.70%	68.79%	61.08%	1991	75.22%	70.21%	62.76%	60.74%	50.86%	1991	70.95%	65.13%	57.29%	55.35%	46.31%
1992	82.08%	77.83%	70.99%	69.19%	61.00%	1992	76.31%	71.02%	63.88%	61.83%	52.98%	1992	72.45%	66.06%	58.71%	56.54%	47.51%
1993	82.08%	77.17%	70.29%	69.13%	61.99%	1993	76.66%	70.23%	63.19%	61.89%	52.64%	1993	72.53%	65.53%	58.37%	56.20%	47.36%
1994	81.85%	76.54%	70.15%	68.84%	61.66%	1994	76.37%	70.13%	63.36%	61.28%	53.49%	1994	71.95%	64.80%	58.10%	55.51%	46.98%
1995	81.55%	76.17%	69.29%	67.89%	59.11%	1995	75.73%	69.27%	62.66%	60.97%	51.05%	1995	71.26%	64.70%	58.06%	56.02%	47.55%
1996	80.85%	75.17%	69.78%	68.29%	59.40%	1996	75.11%	68.92%	63.15%	61.30%	51.67%	1996	70.68%	64.31%	58.23%	55.71%	45.10%
1997	80.64%	75.63%	70.01%	68.23%	60.30%	1997	75.01%	69.73%	63.26%	60.67%	51.19%	1997	69.75%	64.17%	58.06%	55.28%	45.73%
1998	80.82%	76.24%	70.56%	68.17%	59.10%	1998	74.13%	69.01%	63.15%	60.25%	48.99%						
1999	79.55%	75.07%	69.37%	66.38%	56.60%												

Note: Panel A displays top income shares estimated using income averaged over 1, 3, and 5 years. The one year average is identical to Table 6B.1 estimates. In the case of multiple year estimates, individuals are ranked according to the sum of real market incomes over the corresponding years (missing individuals in one or more years are counted as zero income). The total number of adults is taken as the average over the corresponding years (from Table 6A.1). The total income for the denominator is taken as the sum of total real incomes (from Table 6A.1). Panel B reports the probability of individuals in a top group in a given year remaining in that top group in the next year, after two years, and after three years.

Marginal tax rates reported in Table 6F.1 have been computed as follows. We consider each of the raw income thresholds P90, P95, etc. estimated from the interpolation methods described in Appendix 6B. We then assume that the taxpayer at each of these income thresholds is a married taxpayer (who can claim the married exemption level) with two dependents (for example, a married couple with two children under 18). We therefore subtract from raw income the married exemption and two dependent exemptions. We also subtract the average level of deductions claimed on top of marital and personal exemptions at the corresponding percentiles to obtain net taxable income.[44] Tax liability is then obtained from taxable income from a standard tax schedule with increasing marginal tax rates by income brackets, from which the marginal tax rate for any taxable income level can be easily obtained. The marginal tax rate we report includes all surtaxes, as well as the provincial tax rate (see below).

For some years, surtaxes apply only to some forms of income such as investment income. Similarly, dividends from Canadian corporations often face a lower marginal tax rate. In those cases, we have assumed that the marginal dollar earned by the taxpayer has the same composition as total income for the average taxpayer in that percentile.[45] For the period 1949–71, we have taken into account the dividend credit to reduce the marginal tax rate according to the share of dividend income accruing at each percentile. Starting in 1972, in addition to the dividend tax credit, dividends were grossed-up before being included in income. As a result, for high income earners in a high tax bracket, the net marginal tax on received dividends was very close to the marginal tax on ordinary income and therefore we assume that dividends are taxed as normal income when computing our marginal tax rates.

Before 1942, some provinces and municipalities levied personal income taxes. The two biggest provinces, Ontario and Quebec, did not introduce provincial income taxes before 1935 and 1941 respectively.[46] Therefore, we do not try to add these provincial taxes in our computations of marginal tax rates and tax liability in the pre-war period. During the Second World War, the provinces agreed to stop raising income taxes and let the federal government collect all income taxes. After the Second World War and up to 1961, all provinces (except Quebec) worked on a tax rental agreement whereby the federal government would collect all income taxes and redistribute part of income tax collections to each province. Therefore before 1962, the federal income tax liability includes both federal and provincial income taxes. Starting in 1962 and up to 1971, tax collection

[44] For years 1920–28, no additional deductions were allowed. For 1929–45, we have assumed that deductions amounted to 2% of gross income at all percentiles (which is true on average for year 1946, the first year these details are available). From 1946 to 2000, the level of deductions increases slightly over time and we have made approximate computations for each year and percentile threshold using the available tables from *Taxation Statistics*.

[45] For example, if the taxpayer in percentile P99.9 reports on average 30% investment income, and 70% labour income, and the marginal tax rate for investment and labour income are $t1$ and $t2$ respectively, we estimate the marginal tax rate as $t = 0.3^{*}t1 + 0.7^{*}t2$.

[46] Some large cities in these provinces had modest income taxes since the beginning of the century or even before.

Table 6F.1 Marginal income tax rates in Canada, 1920–2000

	P90 (1)	P95 (2)	P98 (3)	P99 (4)	P99.5 (5)	P99.9 (6)	P99.95 (7)	P99.99 (8)	P99.999 (9)	Top (10)
1920	0.0	0.0	4.0	4.0	4.2	15.8	20.0	26.3	44.1	72.5
1921	0.0	0.0	4.0	4.0	4.2	15.8	21.0	25.2	39.9	72.5
1922	0.0	0.0	0.0	4.0	4.2	13.7	16.8	24.2	39.9	72.5
1923	0.0	0.0	0.0	4.0	4.2	13.7	16.8	24.2	39.9	72.5
1924	0.0	0.0	0.0	4.0	3.2	13.7	16.8	24.2	39.9	72.5
1925	0.0	0.0	0.0	0.0	2.0	8.0	14.0	23.0	38.0	50.0
1926	0.0	0.0	0.0	0.0	1.8	9.0	14.4	21.6	36.9	45.0
1927	0.0	0.0	0.0	0.0	1.6	8.8	13.6	20.0	32.0	40.0
1928	0.0	0.0	0.0	1.6	2.4	9.6	15.2	20.8	33.6	40.0
1929	0.0	0.0	0.0	1.6	2.4	9.6	15.2	20.8	33.6	40.0
1930	0.0	0.0	0.0	0.0	1.6	8.8	14.4	20.8	33.6	40.0
1931	0.0	0.0	0.0	2.0	3.2	9.5	15.8	25.2	39.9	52.5
1932	0.0	0.0	0.0	3.0	4.0	10.5	15.8	26.3	41.0	58.8
1933	0.0	0.0	0.0	3.0	4.0	9.5	14.7	25.2	36.8	58.8
1934	0.0	0.0	0.0	3.0	4.0	13.5	19.8	31.3	47.9	69.3
1935	0.0	0.0	0.0	3.0	4.0	13.5	19.8	31.3	47.9	69.3
1936	0.0	0.0	0.0	3.0	4.0	14.6	20.8	32.3	50.0	69.3
1937	0.0	0.0	0.0	3.0	5.0	14.6	21.9	33.4	47.9	69.3
1938	0.0	0.0	0.0	3.0	5.0	16.7	22.9	32.3	51.1	69.3
1939	0.0	0.0	0.0	3.6	6.0	18.7	27.5	38.8	60.0	83.2
1940	0.0	3.0	8.0	15.0	19.0	40.5	43.5	53.5	68.5	89.5
1941	3.5	5.0	21.0	26.5	37.0	54.0	57.0	65.0	75.0	93.0
1942	18.0	18.0	20.0	22.0	29.0	43.1	43.4	50.0	59.4	59.4
1943	40.0	40.0	44.0	48.0	58.0	69.0	69.5	80.0	95.0	95.0
1944	40.0	40.0	44.0	48.0	58.0	69.0	69.5	80.0	95.0	95.0
1945	38.4	38.4	42.2	46.1	55.7	66.2	66.7	76.8	91.2	91.2
1946	33.6	33.6	37.0	40.3	48.7	58.0	62.6	67.2	79.8	79.8
1947	22.5	24.0	24.0	25.5	35.0	49.5	55.0	60.0	75.5	85.5
1948	20.0	20.0	20.0	22.0	31.0	52.0	57.5	62.5	73.0	83.0
1949	15.0	17.0	19.0	22.0	26.0	45.0	50.0	55.0	65.0	80.0
1950	15.0	17.0	19.0	22.0	26.0	45.0	50.0	55.0	70.0	80.0
1951	16.5	18.7	20.9	24.2	33.0	49.5	55.0	60.5	77.0	88.0
1952	19.7	22.4	22.4	25.7	35.5	52.0	57.5	68.5	79.5	91.0
1953	18.0	20.5	23.5	26.5	31.0	45.5	50.0	61.0	72.0	80.0
1954	17.0	19.0	21.5	25.0	28.5	43.0	47.5	57.5	67.0	77.0
1955	16.0	18.0	21.0	24.0	32.5	42.0	46.5	56.5	66.0	76.0
1956	15.0	17.0	20.0	23.0	31.5	46.0	45.5	55.5	65.0	75.0
1957	17.0	17.0	20.0	23.0	31.5	46.0	45.5	55.5	65.0	75.0
1958	17.0	17.0	20.0	27.0	31.5	46.0	45.5	55.5	65.0	75.0
1959	18.0	18.0	25.0	26.0	32.5	47.0	46.5	56.5	66.0	76.0
1960	19.0	19.0	22.0	29.0	33.5	48.0	46.5	57.5	67.0	77.0
1961	19.0	19.0	26.0	29.0	38.5	48.0	47.0	56.0	65.0	75.0
1962	17.0	22.0	26.0	29.0	38.5	48.0	47.0	56.0	65.0	75.0
1963	17.0	22.0	26.0	29.0	38.5	48.0	52.0	56.0	65.0	75.0
1964	19.0	22.0	26.0	34.0	43.5	48.0	52.0	56.0	65.0	75.0
1965	19.0	22.0	30.0	34.0	43.5	48.0	52.0	56.0	65.0	75.0
1966	22.0	22.0	30.0	39.0	43.5	48.0	52.0	56.0	65.0	75.0
1967	22.0	26.0	35.0	39.0	43.5	48.0	52.0	61.0	65.0	75.0
1968	22.0	26.0	35.0	44.0	44.0	53.0	53.0	61.0	65.0	75.0

(contd.)

Table 6F.1 (*contd.*)

	P90 (1)	P95 (2)	P98 (3)	P99 (4)	P99.5 (5)	P99.9 (6)	P99.95 (7)	P99.99 (8)	P99.999 (9)	Top (10)
1969	22.7	30.9	41.2	45.3	45.3	54.6	59.7	62.8	72.1	77.3
1970	26.8	30.9	41.2	45.3	45.3	54.6	59.7	62.8	72.1	77.3
1971	26.4	30.5	40.6	44.7	49.7	53.8	58.9	61.9	66.0	76.1
1972	31.4	33.9	44.0	44.0	49.0	54.0	59.1	59.1	59.1	59.1
1973	32.6	38.9	43.9	43.9	48.9	61.3	61.3	61.3	61.3	61.3
1974	35.2	38.9	43.9	48.9	50.9	61.3	61.3	61.3	61.3	61.3
1975	35.2	38.0	42.9	50.9	50.9	61.3	61.3	61.3	61.3	61.3
1976	33.1	38.0	45.7	50.9	50.9	61.3	61.3	61.3	61.3	61.3
1977	33.8	37.8	46.1	51.8	51.8	56.2	61.9	61.9	61.9	61.9
1978	33.8	37.8	46.1	51.8	51.8	56.2	61.9	61.9	61.9	61.9
1979	33.8	37.8	46.1	51.8	51.8	56.2	61.9	61.9	61.9	61.9
1980	33.8	46.1	46.1	51.8	51.8	56.2	61.9	61.9	61.9	61.9
1981	38.4	46.7	46.7	52.6	52.6	56.9	62.8	62.8	62.8	62.8
1982	37.0	37.0	44.4	50.3	50.3	50.3	50.3	50.3	50.3	50.3
1983	37.0	37.0	44.4	50.3	50.3	50.3	50.3	50.3	50.3	50.3
1984	37.0	37.0	44.4	50.3	50.3	50.3	50.3	50.3	50.3	50.3
1985	37.0	37.6	45.2	52.0	52.0	52.0	52.0	52.0	52.0	52.0
1986	37.5	38.8	47.0	54.9	54.9	54.9	54.9	54.9	54.9	54.9
1987	38.3	45.9	46.4	52.5	52.5	52.5	52.5	52.5	52.5	52.5
1988	40.0	40.0	44.7	44.7	46.1	46.1	46.1	46.1	46.1	46.1
1989	40.6	40.6	45.2	47.2	47.2	47.2	47.2	47.2	47.2	47.2
1990	41.1	41.1	45.8	48.2	48.2	48.2	48.2	48.2	48.2	48.2
1991	41.1	41.1	47.3	48.8	48.8	48.8	48.8	48.8	48.8	48.8
1992	41.3	41.3	47.6	49.1	49.1	49.1	49.1	49.1	49.1	49.1
1993	41.9	41.9	50.1	51.5	51.5	51.5	51.5	51.5	51.5	51.5
1994	41.9	44.4	51.5	51.5	51.5	51.5	51.5	51.5	51.5	51.5
1995	41.9	44.9	52.3	52.3	52.3	52.3	52.3	52.3	52.3	52.3
1996	41.3	44.3	52.0	52.0	52.0	52.0	52.0	52.0	52.0	52.0
1997	39.3	41.8	49.0	49.0	49.0	49.0	49.0	49.0	49.0	49.0
1998	37.9	40.1	49.4	49.4	49.4	49.4	49.4	49.4	49.4	49.4
1999	36.7	48.3	48.3	48.3	48.3	48.3	48.3	48.3	48.3	48.3
2000	34.6	46.4	47.9	47.9	47.9	47.9	47.9	47.9	47.9	47.9

Notes: Marginal tax rates are calculated assuming exemptions for a married person with two dependents and average deductions by gross income level. Before 1972, only the federal income tax rates are reported as these included provincial income tax rates in most cases. Beginning in 1972, the reported income rates include then-applicable provincial income tax, assuming residence in the largest province, Ontario. All rates include applicable surtaxes and credits.

Source: Computations by authors based on gross income interpolations (reported in Table 6B.4) and tax law for each year.

agreements were passed whereby the federal government granted abatements from federal income taxes and provinces would receive in provincial taxes amounts equal to the abatement from federal income taxes. Therefore for years before 1972, we simply use the federal income tax structure to compute marginal tax rates, as well as tax liabilities reported in *Taxation Statistics*.

Starting in 1972, the nominal federal tax rate was lowered but each province defined a given percentage that the federal tax administration would collect on behalf of the province on top of the nominal federal income tax. In Table 6F.1, we have used the case of Ontario (the largest province containing more than half of the highest incomes in Canada) to compute marginal tax rates. Over the years, the Ontario provincial tax has changed many times and special provincial surtaxes have been introduced as well that have in part offset the decline in progressivity of the federal tax system. All these surtaxes have been included in the estimation of marginal tax rates reported in Table 6F.1. Marginal tax rates for other provinces have followed a very similar time pattern as rates for Ontario. Quebec in particular has almost always had marginal rates slightly higher than Ontario (by 2 to 4 percentage points in general).

Average tax rates have been computed as the sum of federal and provincial tax liability (after surtaxes and net of all credits) paid by each group divided by total gross income (including only the taxable portion of capital gains for the 1972–2000 period) reported by each group. We have decided to include the taxable portions of capital gains in the income denominator so that our average tax rate measures reflect the average tax on ordinary income. For years 1982–2000, we have used the LAD micro-files to do these computations. In the period 1920–81, we have used the distribution tables, which always report the amount of taxes paid by income brackets. Average tax rates are reported in Table 6F.2 and depicted in Figures 6F.2 and 6F.3 for various top income groups.

We have estimated the (income weighted) marginal tax rate for the top 1% and top 0.1% groups in Canada for the regression analysis of Table 6.2 and the graphical analysis in Figure 6.14 as follows. The top 0.1% marginal tax rate is estimated as:

$$[\mathit{Share}\ P99.9\text{–}99.99^{*}\ \mathit{MTR}\ 99.95 + \mathit{Share}\ P99.99\text{–}100^{*}(\mathit{MTR}\ 99.99 + \mathit{MTR}99.999)/2)]/(\mathit{Share}\ P99.9\text{–}99.99 + \mathit{Share}\ P99.99\text{–}100)$$

where Share P99.9–99.99 denotes the income share of group P99.9–99.99 from Table 6B.1 and MTR 99.95 denotes the marginal tax rate at percentile 99.95 from Table 6F.1, etc.

Similarly, the top 1% marginal tax rate is estimated as:

$$(\mathit{Share}\ P99\text{–}99.9^{*}\ \mathit{MTR}\ 99.5 + \mathit{Share}\ P99.9\text{–}100^{*}\ \mathit{MTR}\ \mathit{Top}\ 0.1\%)/(\mathit{Share}\ P99\text{–}99.9 + \mathit{Share}\ P99.9\text{–}100)$$

where Share P99–99.9 is the income share of P99–99.5 plus P99.5–99.9 from Table 6B.1 and MTR Top 0.1% is the marginal tax rate for the top 0.1% group estimated above.

Table 6F.2 Average tax rates in upper groups in Canada, 1920–2000

	P90–100 (1)	P95–100 (2)	P99–100 (3)	P99.5–100 (4)	P99.9–100 (5)	P99.99–100 (6)	P90–95 (7)	P95–99 (8)	P99–99.5 (9)	P99.5–99.9 (10)	P99.9–99.99 (11)
1920	2.90	3.69	7.34	9.77	14.92	20.50	1.00	0.80	0.82	4.39	11.33
1921	2.35	2.95	5.92	8.03	12.76	22.14	0.91	0.68	0.68	3.96	8.87
1922	2.18	2.77	5.32	7.22	11.72	17.11	0.93	0.75	0.71	3.24	9.14
1923	2.26	2.91	5.22	7.05	11.78	18.01	0.92	0.80	0.74	3.03	8.75
1924	2.21	2.81	5.02	6.72	10.91	15.31	0.95	0.82	0.76	2.99	8.71
1925	1.47	2.06	4.36	5.88	10.38	16.22	0.18	0.24	0.47	2.07	7.84
1926	1.77	2.44	4.97	6.60	11.21	16.90	0.17	0.25	0.58	2.50	8.44
1927	1.77	2.43	4.86	6.42	10.97	16.59	0.12	0.20	0.56	2.29	8.10
1928	1.82	2.49	4.93	6.49	11.20	16.93	0.07	0.15	0.64	2.29	8.37
1929	1.74	2.38	4.68	6.15	10.66	16.62	0.05	0.15	0.63	2.23	7.86
1930	1.67	2.30	4.55	5.98	10.37	16.62	0.03	0.12	0.55	1.95	7.37
1931	1.87	2.59	5.39	7.21	12.98	22.57	0.14	0.20	0.65	2.24	8.68
1932	2.40	3.25	6.72	8.85	15.41	26.47	0.43	0.43	1.25	3.03	10.25
1933	2.21	2.99	6.21	8.25	14.42	26.19	0.43	0.45	1.09	3.03	9.56
1934	2.70	3.67	7.65	10.15	18.03	33.45	0.43	0.45	1.24	3.29	11.00
1935	2.75	3.75	7.87	10.44	18.60	35.17	0.42	0.43	1.33	3.44	11.34
1936	2.98	4.06	8.37	10.97	18.89	33.56	0.42	0.47	1.48	3.85	12.05
1937	3.23	4.42	9.16	12.06	21.17	42.51	0.42	0.48	1.50	4.16	12.82
1938	3.11	4.21	8.47	11.03	18.83	32.91	0.38	0.50	1.79	4.53	12.54
1939	3.17	4.30	8.82	11.51	19.48	33.28	0.45	0.55	1.76	4.70	13.64
1940	4.93	6.21	11.76	14.93	23.84	38.07	2.01	1.91	4.23	8.04	16.55
1941	10.74	13.90	25.71	31.10	42.30	54.88	4.07	4.90	12.42	22.02	36.81
1942	11.89	14.55	21.24	24.12	30.31	37.42	6.54	9.55	14.23	19.23	27.25
1943	24.08	29.03	41.74	47.06	58.50	70.81	14.57	20.02	29.28	38.45	53.60
1944	22.31	27.17	39.80	45.14	56.92	68.85	13.08	18.44	27.69	36.58	52.30
1945	19.73	24.35	36.16	41.32	53.04	64.52	10.73	16.11	24.65	33.05	48.81
1946	18.48	22.16	32.65	37.12	47.36	57.39	11.00	14.44	22.62	30.10	43.78
1947	14.92	18.68	27.73	31.89	41.97	54.30	7.18	11.90	18.37	25.02	37.54
1948	13.29	16.58	24.68	28.77	38.63	47.81	6.68	10.61	15.45	21.96	35.69

1949	9.99	13.04	20.89	24.69	33.56	41.68	3.96	7.33	12.42	18.90	31.05
1950	10.77	13.92	21.91	25.88	35.02	43.30	4.50	7.95	12.81	19.68	32.40
1951	12.81	16.18	25.34	29.71	40.19	48.72	6.27	9.58	15.52	22.61	37.62
1952	14.05	17.50	27.04	31.43	41.99	50.46	7.46	10.82	17.46	24.36	39.18
1953	12.90	15.77	23.94	27.68	36.41	41.75	7.51	10.21	15.85	21.85	34.68
1954	12.25	14.96	22.68	26.24	34.33	40.63	7.13	9.63	14.86	20.92	32.23
1955	12.05	14.68	22.22	25.72	33.50	37.57	7.08	9.46	14.54	20.35	32.04
1956	11.97	14.52	22.10	25.71	33.67	41.71	7.24	9.51	14.34	20.39	31.03
1957	12.13	14.67	22.13	25.68	33.29	40.96	7.44	9.83	14.66	20.69	30.79
1958	11.74	14.43	21.96	25.76	33.02	40.49	6.72	9.50	14.06	21.08	30.61
1959	12.28	15.07	22.75	26.77	33.88	41.36	7.13	10.15	14.48	22.26	31.50
1960	12.82	15.68	23.54	27.64	34.56	42.28	7.55	10.68	15.16	23.31	32.12
1961	13.00	15.87	23.38	27.29	33.64	39.95	7.70	11.09	15.50	23.33	31.58
1962	13.05	15.76	22.94	26.62	32.65	39.35	8.10	11.29	15.64	23.02	30.62
1963	13.55	16.33	23.69	27.51	33.82	41.01	8.50	11.83	16.18	23.81	31.72
1964	14.46	17.35	25.14	28.92	35.00	42.12	9.17	12.50	17.63	25.31	32.83
1965	14.40	17.16	24.69	28.34	34.22	40.87	9.37	12.49	17.43	24.85	32.18
1966	14.94	17.64	24.73	28.11	35.03	40.58	10.04	13.37	18.16	24.10	33.38
1967	16.56	19.50	27.27	30.77	36.26	40.72	11.21	14.81	20.51	27.64	35.00
1968	18.24	21.38	29.70	33.52	39.95	44.98	12.56	16.36	22.28	29.85	38.56
1969	19.64	22.89	31.51	34.91	41.97	45.97	13.79	17.72	25.01	30.92	40.87
1970	20.66	23.95	32.61	35.79	42.93	48.04	14.84	18.86	26.60	31.89	41.58
1971	21.40	24.64	32.84	35.58	41.92	46.56	15.73	19.86	27.68	32.24	40.75
1972	23.82	26.37	32.95	35.69	39.91	41.90	19.33	22.47	27.65	33.34	39.33
1973	24.52	27.15	33.80	36.63	41.07	44.33	19.81	23.13	28.31	34.09	40.05
1974	24.64	27.42	33.99	36.83	41.14	44.74	19.70	23.49	28.56	34.33	40.00
1975	24.32	27.04	34.26	37.47	42.64	47.47	19.50	22.74	28.09	34.37	41.03
1976	23.85	26.28	33.51	36.92	42.58	46.70	19.72	22.26	27.23	33.63	41.24
1977	23.61	26.05	32.39	34.89	39.86	42.81	19.55	22.59	27.80	31.98	38.87
1978	22.62	24.70	29.59	31.35	36.05	38.27	19.10	21.98	26.33	28.49	35.27
1979	22.50	24.48	29.05	30.16	33.14	33.74	19.08	21.81	26.88	28.24	32.90
1980	23.15	25.10	29.30	31.05	34.37	35.24	19.70	22.57	25.86	28.84	33.97
1981	24.01	26.14	30.46	32.12	33.90	33.66	20.28	23.57	27.20	30.97	33.99
1982	22.49	24.01	26.73	28.36	30.29	30.52	19.76	22.28	23.26	26.87	30.18

(contd.)

Table 6F.2 (*contd.*)

	P90–100 (1)	P95–100 (2)	P99–100 (3)	P99.5–100 (4)	P99.9–100 (5)	P99.99–100 (6)	P90–95 (7)	P95–99 (8)	P99–99.5 (9)	P99.5–99.9 (10)	P99.9–99.99 (11)
1983	22.32	23.83	26.80	28.76	31.05	31.48	19.65	21.97	22.77	27.13	30.85
1984	22.82	24.33	26.98	28.62	30.19	29.55	20.13	22.60	23.44	27.38	30.42
1985	23.64	25.21	28.45	29.65	31.30	31.30	20.81	23.07	25.72	28.32	31.30
1986	24.15	25.63	28.59	30.69	33.69	35.53	21.48	23.67	24.17	28.49	32.90
1987	24.63	25.88	28.23	30.12	33.51	35.98	22.35	24.24	24.10	27.54	32.42
1988	24.84	26.04	28.09	29.75	32.30	33.73	22.46	24.37	24.13	27.46	31.51
1989	26.16	27.53	30.12	31.92	34.37	35.48	23.36	25.28	25.59	29.51	33.60
1990	26.85	28.28	30.92	32.69	34.88	35.92	24.01	26.15	26.68	30.71	34.26
1991	26.39	27.78	30.55	32.34	34.44	34.16	23.67	25.63	26.36	30.49	34.52
1992	26.05	27.49	30.51	32.46	35.06	36.32	23.29	25.21	26.01	30.28	34.36
1993	25.92	27.41	30.59	32.75	35.45	36.29	23.06	24.99	25.58	30.41	34.96
1994	26.45	28.05	31.13	33.05	35.78	37.20	23.37	25.69	26.67	30.74	35.04
1995	26.95	28.65	32.17	34.43	36.91	37.51	23.56	25.86	26.90	32.25	36.54
1996	27.20	29.02	32.68	34.75	36.81	36.52	23.46	25.97	27.62	32.82	36.88
1997	27.62	29.58	33.13	34.92	36.69	36.31	23.41	26.34	28.50	33.14	36.82
1998	27.54	29.57	32.88	34.58	36.15	35.31	23.02	26.36	28.37	32.93	36.52
1999	27.29	29.26	32.24	33.78	34.97	33.32	22.81	26.23	28.08	32.44	35.85
2000	27.14	29.00	31.77	33.18	34.00	33.31	22.77	25.92	27.77	32.16	34.32

Notes: Computations by authors based on tax return statistics. Average tax rate defined as ratio of total net taxes paid to total gross income reported (including taxable capital gains) for each group. Average tax rates reported include both Provincial and Federal taxes and surtaxes as well as all income tax credits and deductions.

REFERENCES

Acemoglu, D. (2002). 'Technical Change, Inequality, and the Labour Market', *Journal of Economic Literature*, 40: 7–72.

Baker, M. and Solon, G. (2003). 'Earnings Dynamics and Inequality among Canadian Men, 1976–1992: Evidence from Longitudinal Income Tax Records', *Journal of Labour Economics*, 21: 267–88.

Beach, C., Finnie, R., and Gray, D. (2003). 'Earnings Variability and Earnings Instability of Women and Men in Canada', *Canadian Public Policy*, 29 (Supplement): S41–S63.

Blackburn, M. L. and Bloom, D. E. (1993). 'The Distribution of Family Income: Measuring and Explaining Changes in the 1980s for Canada and the United States', in D. Card and R. Freeman (eds.) *Small Differences that Matter*. Chicago: University of Chicago Press.

Bowlus, A. and Robin, J-M. (2004). 'Twenty Years of Rising Inequality in US Lifetime Labour Income Values', *Review of Economic Studies*, 71: 709–42.

Buchinsky, M. and Hunt, J. (1999). 'Wage Mobility in the United States', *Review of Economics and Statistics*, 81: 351–68.

Canada Customs and Revenue Agency (formerly Revenue Canada, formerly Department of National Revenue), Taxation Division (1948–2001). *Taxation Statistics*. Ottawa: Queens' Printer.

Canadian Tax Foundation (1957), *Canadian Fiscal Facts*, Canadian Tax Foundation.

CANSIM, 2003, Canadian Socio-economic Information Matrix, Statistics Canada: Ottawa.

Department of National Revenue (Taxation Division), (1924–38). *Incomes Assessed for War Income Tax in Canada*. Ottawa: Department of National Revenue.

—— (1945). *The Wartime Salaries Order*. Ottawa: E Cloutier, printer to the King.

Department of Trade and Commerce (1942–44). *Dominion Income Tax Statistics*. Ottawa: Dominion Bureau of Statistics.

Dominion Bureau of Statistics (1905–48). *The Canada Yearbook*. Ottawa: Dominion Bureau of Statistics.

Feenberg, D R and Poterba, J M, 1993, 'Income Inequality and the Incomes of Very High-Income Taxpayers: Evidence from Tax Returns', in J Poterba, editor, *Tax Policy and the Economy*, vol 7, MIT Press, Cambridge, 145–77.

Finnie, R. (2001). 'The Brain Drain: Myth and Reality—What It Is and What Should be Done', *Choices*, 7: 3–29.

—— (2002). 'Leaving and Coming Back to Canada: Evidence from Longitudinal Data'. Unpublished *manuscript, School of Policy Studies, Queen's University* (cited with permission).

—— (2004). 'Who Moves?—A Panel Logit Model Analysis of Inter-Provincial Migration In Canada', *Applied Economics*, 36: 1759–79.

Gagné, R., Nadeau J-F. and Vaillancourt, F. (2000). 'Taxpayers' Response to Tax-Rate Changes: A Canadian Panel Study', *CIRANO Scientific Series 2000s-59*, Université de Montréal.

Goldin, C. and Margo, R. (1992). 'The Great Compression: The Wage Structure in the United States at Mid-Century', *Quarterly Journal of Economics*, 107: 1–34.

—— and Katz, L. (1999). 'The Returns to Skill across the Twentieth Century United States'. Unpublished manuscript, Department of Economics, Harvard University.

Goolsbee, A. (2000). 'What Happens When You Tax the Rich? Evidence from Executive Compensation', *Journal of Political Economy*, 108: 352–78.

Gordon, R. and Slemrod, J. (2000). 'Are "Real" Responses to Taxes Simply Income Shifting Between Corporate and Personal Tax Bases?', in J. Slemrod (ed.) *Does Atlas Shrug? The Economic Consequences of Taxing the Rich.* Cambridge, MA: Harvard University Press.

Gottschalk, P. (1997). 'Inequality, Income Growth and Mobility: The Basic Facts', *Journal of Economic Perspectives*, 11: 21–40.

Gruber, J. and Saez, E. (2002). 'The Elasticity of Taxable Income: Evidence and Implications', *Journal of Public Economics*, 84: 1–32.

Heisz, A., Jackson, A., and Picot, G. (2001). 'Distributional Outcomes in Canada in the 1990s', in K. Banting, A. Sharpe, and F. St-Hilaire (eds.) *The Review of Economic Performance and Social Progress. The Longest Decade: Canada in the 1990s.* Montreal: McGill-Queen's University Press.

Iqbal, M. (1999). 'Are We Losing Our Minds? Trends, Determinants and the Role of Taxation in Brain Drain to the United States', Paper No. 265–99, The Conference Board of Canada.

Katz, L. and Autor, D. (1999). 'Changes in the Wage Structure and Earnings Inequality', in O. Ashenfelter and D. Card (eds.) *Handbook of Labour Economics*, volume 3A. Amsterdam: North Holland.

Klassen, K. and Mawani, A. (2000). 'The Impact of Financial and Tax Reporting Incentives on Option Grants to Canadian CEOs', *Contemporary Accounting Research*, 17: 227–62.

Kuznets, S. (1953). *Shares of Upper Income Groups in Income and Savings.* New York: National Bureau of Economic Research.

McGregor, G. (1960). 'Personal Corporations', *Canadian Tax Papers No. 18*, Toronto: Canadian Tax Foundation.

Perry, J. H. (1955). *Taxes, Tariffs, and Subsidies: A History of Canadian Fiscal Development*, 2 Volumes. Toronto: University of Toronto Press.

—— (1989). *A Fiscal History of Canada—The Post War Years.* Canadian Tax Paper No. 85, Canadian Tax Foundation.

Saez, E. (2004). 'Reported Incomes and Marginal Tax Rates, 1960–2000: Evidence and Policy Implications', in J. Poterba (ed.) *Tax Policy and the Economy.* Cambridge, MA: MIT Press, pp. 113–73.

—— and Veall, M. (2005). 'The evolution of high incomes in Northern America: Lessons from Canadian evidence', *American Economic Review*, 95: 831–49.

Sillamaa, M-A. and Veall, M. R. (2001). 'The Effect of Marginal Tax Rates on Taxable Income: A Panel Study of the 1988 Tax Flattening in Canada', *Journal of Public Economics*, 80: 341–56.

Urquhart, M. C. and Buckley, K. A. H. (1965). *Historical Statistics of Canada.* Cambridge: Cambridge University Press.

Vaillancourt, F. (1985). 'Income Distribution and Economic Security in Canada: An Overview', in F. Vaillancourt (research coordinator) *Income Distribution and Economic Security in Canada.* Toronto: University of Toronto Press.

Wolfson, M. and Murphy, B. (2000). 'Income Inequality in North America: Does the 49th Parallel Still Matter?', *Canadian Economic Observer*, August.

Zhao, J., Drew, D., and Murray, T. S. (2000). 'Brain Drain or Brain Gain: The Migration of Knowledge Workers from and to Canada', *Education Quarterly Review*, 6: 8–44.

7

The Distribution of Top Incomes in Australia[1]

A. B. Atkinson and A. Leigh

7.1 INTRODUCTION

Visiting Australia at the end of the nineteenth century, commentator Francis Adams observed that: 'In England the average man feels that he is an inferior; in America he feels that he is superior; in Australia he feels that he is an equal' (Adams 1892). Income inequality in Australia a century ago may therefore have been less than in the UK and the US.[2] This chapter takes a long-run perspective of the Australian income distribution, asking what can be learned from the income tax returns, particularly about top incomes. How far has Australia differed from the pattern in other Anglo-Saxon OECD countries, such as the United States and the United Kingdom, where income inequality declined over the first three-quarters of the century, and then increased in the final decades?

One major reason for making use of the income taxation statistics is that they do provide a quantitative basis for measuring the trends. Prior to federation in 1901, each of the six Australian colonies levied income tax, and from 1914 onwards, the federal government had its own income tax (it was not until 1941 that the state income taxes were abolished). The federal income tax returns were tabulated separately for individuals and corporations from 1921 onwards, and provide a rich source of information about individual incomes. It is these data that provide the basis for our estimate of top income shares in Australia from

[1] We are most grateful to those who have helped us secure access to the necessary data and publications. Specific thanks are due to Carl Obst of the Australian Bureau of Statistics, Dan Andrews, and Michael Plumb of the Reserve Bank of Australia, and Lisa Cox of the Department of Employment and Workplace Relations. We have also benefited from comments and advice from Harry Greenwell, Thomas Piketty, John Quiggin, Emmanuel Saez, Peter Saunders, Michael Schneider, and seminar participants at the Australian National University, Harvard University, Nuffield College, Oxford, and the University of Melbourne. None of the above is responsible for the conclusions reached in the chapter. Parts of this chapter appeared in a different form in Atkinson and Leigh (2007).

[2] For earlier references to the study of income and wealth in Australia, see Maddock et al. (1984) and Saunders (1993).

1921 to 2002. (Note that the Australian tax year begins on 1 July. Throughout this chapter, any reference to a tax year should be taken to refer to the start of the tax year—for example, the 1980 tax year is the tax year starting 1 July 1980 and ending 30 June 1981.)

In using the income tax data, we are not, however, under-estimating their shortcomings (see, e.g. Brown 1957). As a source of information about the distribution as a whole, taxation data suffer from the fact that the figures relate only to taxpayers; Butlin (1983) emphasizes the importance of the exclusion of zero incomes. For this reason, most studies of the income distribution as a whole have employed other sources. Butlin (1983) uses variation in minimum wages across industries, and finds a fall in inequality (skilled: unskilled wage ratio) between 1901 and 1968. Jones (1975) and McLean and Richardson (1986) compare censuses conducted during the First World War and the Great Depression with more recent surveys, and conclude that inequality fell from 1915 to 1968 and 1933 to 1980 respectively. In recent years, the major source has been household surveys, notably the Survey of Income and Housing Costs (SHIC) (previously the Income Distribution Survey): see, for example, Australian Bureau of Statistics (1997, 1999, and 2001).[3] At the same time, we should also note that household surveys too have shortcomings, particularly when it comes to investigating the top of the distribution. They are affected by differential non-response and by incomplete response; the sample sizes often limit what can be said about groups such as the top 0.1%. The official results from the SIHC, for example, are typically presented in terms of the share of the top 20%. Moreover, surveys (and, of course, population censuses) in Australia have tended to be conducted periodically, not annually, which means that considerable reliance may be placed on a single, not necessarily typical, year.

One major attraction of income tax data is that they allow a long time perspective. The long period covered has been exploited by Berry (1977), who used data for 1922/23, 1932/33, 1942/43, 1952/53, 1962/63, and 1972/73, and by Smith (2001), who used data from 1916/17 to 1996/97 to measure tax progressivity. Others have used taxation data for particular years. Hancock (1971) uses data from 1950–51 to 1966–67 (see Ingles 1981: p. 17) for actual income, taxable income, and after tax income. Harris (1970) used income tax data to examine the distribution for 1955–56 and 1965–66; Ternowetsky (1979) used data from 1955–56 to 1974–75. Our focus here is on the top of the income distribution, as in other chapters in this volume. To establish estimates of the shares of top income groups, we need information on the total number of individuals and the total personal income, but we do not need to know the full shape of the distribution below the top ranges. (Indeed, as explained in Chapter 2, we can estimate the Pareto-Lorenz coefficients without information on total income.)

[3] Studies of trends in Australian inequality in the 1980s and 1990s include Bradbury et al. (1990), Saunders et al. (1991), Saunders (1997, 1998), Harding (1997), and Harding and Greenwell (2002).

The methods used here are described in Section 7.2; the findings are presented in Section 7.3; and the conclusions are summarized in Section 7.4.

7.2 INCOME TAX DATA AND ESTIMATION METHODS

The tax unit in Australia is the individual. In what follows we take as the principal case that where the control population is that aged 15 and over, but also show the effects of taking those aged 20 and over. If taking an age cut-off of 20 gives a control total for population that is on the low side, and hence gives a lower bound on the share of the top X%, taking a cut-off of 15 will give a control total on the high side, and hence gives an upper bound. It could be argued that the definition should vary over time, but it is not clear which direction the variation should take. Young people enter the labour force later today than a century ago, which is an argument for raising the cut-off age over time. On the other hand, young people have been becoming economically independent earlier, and in their estimates of the UK distribution of wealth over the twentieth century, Atkinson and Harrison (1978) took an age cut-off falling from 23 in 1923 to 18 in 1973. We have therefore followed other authors in this volume and applied a constant age cut-off in determining the 'adult' population.

The coverage of the tax returns has varied greatly over the century. The fraction of Australians aged 15 and over who filed a tax return was around 11–12% in 1921–22. The figure then dropped to 5–7% in 1923–38, but the general trend was upwards. By the end of the Second World War, one-third of the adult population paid tax. Between 1950 and 2000, the fraction of the Australian population paying tax fluctuated between 50% and 62%.

Control Total for Income

In order to calculate the income shares, we need a control total for income. We are interested in the total *returnable* income that would enter the tax-base if there were no exemptions (income after subtracting the exemptions is referred to as taxable income): 'total income that would have been reported on tax returns, had everybody been required to file a tax return' (Saez and Veall 2003: 38). Our concept corresponds to their Gross Tax Income, with the qualification that we do not at this stage exclude realized capital gains.

The most straightforward approach to arriving at a control total is to start from the total gross income in the tax returns and add an estimate of the total gross income of non-filers. This method was used by Piketty and Saez (Chapter 5) for the US for the period 1944–98: they impute to non-filers a fixed fraction of filers' average income (50% in 1944 and 1945 and 30% from 1945). The aim is to take account of the year-to-year variation in the proportion of filers. The different fractions are intended to take account of the larger percentage of non-filers in the first two years.[4] These imputations for non-filers are closely linked with the early studies of national accounts, to which we now turn.

A different approach to the control total for income, and that followed here, starts from the national accounts totals for personal income. As explained in Chapter 2, it is not appropriate to take simply the personal sector total income. We have to exclude non-household elements, such as charities, life assurance funds, and universities. We have to exclude items not included in the tax base, such as employers' social security contributions, and non-taxable transfer payments. The exclusion of these items follows the practice in studies in other countries, but their significance is likely to differ across countries, and the appropriate adjustment may well be different. In the case of the US, Piketty and Saez (Chapter 5) use for the period 1913–43 a control total equal to 80% of (total personal income less transfers). In Canada, Saez and Veall (2005) use the constant percentage approach, applied to 'total personal income less transfers', for the entire period 1920–2000, basing the percentage (80%) on the experience since the mid-1970s when they feel that filing was close to complete.

Here, rather than apply a percentage adjustment to another series, we have attempted to construct a household income series from the national accounts—see Appendix 7B. There are official series for total household income for recent decades, but we have had to construct our own series for much of the period. This has involved assembling different elements from the official statistics and from academic sources. For the years 1913–27, we have resorted to use of GDP to extrapolate backwards. Our treatment also differs with respect to social security transfers. In Australia, transfers have been taxed to a significant degree since 1944. We therefore switch our personal income denominator to include transfers from this point onwards. (Throughout the total excludes imputed rent.) Using the calculated total income series, we find that the total recorded in the tax data is some 80% in the mid-1960s, when the number of calculated tax units was 60% of the population aged 15+ and 69% of the population aged 20+. The former figure, and our constructed total income, implies that non-taxpayers had on average an income of less than 40% of those filing. This appears reasonable, but, while we take the constructed total as our central case, we experiment with taking 90% of the constructed total.

Deductions

Income tax systems differ in the extent of their provisions allowing the deduction of such items as interest paid, depreciation, pension contributions, alimony

[4] An alternative approach would use the exemption levels. If the lower tail of the distribution can be approximated by a reverse Pareto distribution, such that By^{β} gives the proportion with income below y, then the average income of those below the exemption is $\beta/(1+\beta)$ times the exemption level.

payments, and charitable contributions. (We are not referring here to personal exemptions.) Income from which these deductions have been subtracted is referred to in this chapter as 'taxable income'; we refer to total income before deductions as 'actual income'. As in other studies, our preferred variable is actual income, but the available published information is not always in this form. This difficulty arises both on account of the variable measured and on account of the variable according to which individuals are classified. These two are not always identical, in that we may have the distribution of variable Y_1 by ranges of variable Y_2.

In Australia, the statistics from 1958 onwards are in our preferred form, relating to the distribution of actual income by ranges of actual income. From 1947–48 to 1957–58, the published figures give the distribution of taxable income by range of actual income; from 1944–45 to 1946–47, there are distributions of both actual and taxable income by range of actual income; prior to 1944–45 the figures related to the distribution of taxable income by range of taxable income. In order to create a continuous series, we use the ratio of the actual and taxable income top income shares in 1944–46 to adjust the shares in the years 1921–43 and 1947–57.[5] However, it is possible that our adjustment procedure understates the effect on the top 10% and top 5% shares for the later years. Even in the adjusted series, both show a sharp jump between 1957 and 1958.

Capital Gains and Imputation

Another issue is the treatment of capital gains. The basic series presented for the US by Piketty and Saez (Chapter 5) excludes capital gains, but they also present series including capital gains. In Australia, as with the UK (Chapter 4), the approach has been different, with certain gains brought under the regular income tax (and therefore included in the estimates), but other gains taxed, such as those taxed since 1986 under a separate Capital Gains Tax, excluded.

Related is the imputation system, under which part of any corporation tax paid is treated as a pre-payment of personal income tax. Payment of dividends can be made more attractive by the introduction of an imputation system, in place of a 'classical' system where dividends are subject to both corporation and personal income tax. Insofar as capital gains are missing from the estimates but dividends are covered, a switch towards (away from) dividend payment will

[5] The ratio of the top income shares produced using actual income to those produced using taxable income in these years is 1.016 for the 10% share, 1.020 for the 5% share, 1.033 for the 1% share, 1.042 for the 0.5% share, 1.073 for the 0.1% share, 1.091 for the 0.05% share, and 1.126 for the 0.01% share. Two things should be noted about this adjustment procedure. First, the years 1944 to 1946 are not necessarily typical. Second, the adjustment for the earlier period makes no allowance for the re-ranking necessary to give the distribution by ranges of actual income.

increase (reduce) the apparent shares. The effect of the introduction of imputation in Australia in 1987 is evident in the statistics.

7.3 TOP INCOME SHARES IN AUSTRALIA

Australian tax data are published in the annual Reports of the Commissioner of Taxation (see Appendix 7C). Table 7.1 shows the estimated shares of the top income groups for the period 1921–2000. As explained above, the figures for the earlier part of the period relate to taxable income. Since taxable income is less than total income, the estimated shares will be lower on this account (the fact that we are using external control totals means that the estimated share of the top X% is affected only via the numerator). Appendix Table 7A.1 shows the top income shares, with the estimated shares from 1921–43 and 1947–57 adjusted to make some allowance for this break. As noted in Section 7.1, census of population or, in Australia, household survey data, are only collected in certain years, which means that we may be placing a great deal of reliance on a single observation. It is a considerable advantage of the income tax statistics that we have observations for every year over a 80 year span.

We cannot go back to the start of the century, but in 1921 the share of the top 5% in total gross income was around 18–19%. (It should be noted that this relates to gross income among individuals, and is therefore not comparable with today's figures for disposable income among households.) The share of the top 1% was around 12%, and that of the top 0.1% (a group much smaller than those usually considered) was around 4%. If we compare these figures with those of other countries studied in this volume (see Chapter 13), then the shares of top income groups in Australia do indeed appear lower. There are a number of reasons for being cautious in making such cross-country comparisons, but the shares of the top 5% were typically around 30% in other countries. Even in New Zealand, the nearest both geographically and in its share of the top 5%, that share was around 25%. The very top shares, like that of the top 0.1%, were lower in New Zealand. But in Canada, the US, and particularly the European countries, the shares of the top 1% and top 0.1% were noticeably higher than in Australia. There may therefore have been some foundation for the view recounted at the start of this chapter.

Has this been maintained? In fact, top shares fell. Figure 7.1 shows that the top shares in Australia fell significantly over the period from 1921 to 1980. The share of the top 1%, which began at more than 10%, had fallen to under 5% by 1980. The share of the top 0.1% was nearly 4% in 1921 but had fallen to 1% in 1980. At the same time, the fall was far from steady. There were periods, such as the 1920s and 1933–43, when the top shares were broadly constant.

How far has this decline been attributable to major shocks? McLean and Richardson, for example, note that 'for the purpose of establishing trends in the income distribution over time, the fact that 1933 was a year of deep depression is a distinct drawback' (1986: p. 73), but the impact of the Depression is itself of considerable interest (see also McLean 1988). They adjust for unemployment

Table 7.1 Top income shares, Australia 1921–2002

	10%	5%	1%	0.5%	0.1%	0.05%	0.01%
1921	—	19.43	11.63	8.55	3.97	2.80	1.24
1922	—	17.65	10.68	7.91	3.57	2.45	—
1923	—	—	11.76	9.08	3.98	2.80	—
1924	—	—	11.67	8.84	4.25	—	—
1925	—	—	11.31	8.58	3.99	2.81	—
1926	—	—	11.07	8.42	3.88	2.72	—
1927	—	—	11.68	8.56	3.86	2.64	—
1928	—	—	11.85	8.92	4.26	3.16	—
1929	—	—	10.67	7.91	3.58	2.50	—
1930	—	—	9.75	7.15	3.20	2.22	—
1931	—	—	9.34	6.93	3.07	2.11	0.85
1932	—	—	9.27	6.91	3.08	2.14	0.90
1933	—	—	10.32	7.73	3.53	2.46	—
1934	—	—	10.36	7.79	3.49	2.44	—
1935	—	—	10.54	7.77	3.49	2.42	—
1936	—	—	11.28	8.25	3.71	2.56	—
1937	—	—	9.83	7.17	3.19	2.20	0.89
1938	—	—	10.39	7.61	3.41	2.36	0.97
1939	—	20.71	10.73	7.81	3.50	2.44	1.04
1940	—	20.57	10.30	7.48	3.37	2.35	0.99
1941	34.61	23.67	10.78	7.68	3.34	2.32	0.94
1942	34.12	23.26	10.43	7.34	3.11	2.12	0.85
1943	34.23	23.42	10.45	7.32	3.09	2.12	0.86
1944	31.25	21.09	9.03	6.22	2.49	1.66	0.64
1945	28.75	19.56	8.44	5.79	2.31	1.55	0.62
1946	31.61	21.76	9.51	6.52	2.59	1.72	0.66
1947	33.10	23.41	10.62	7.31	2.92	1.94	0.73
1948	32.77	23.35	10.80	7.40	2.89	1.96	0.73
1949	32.82	23.66	11.26	7.89	3.31	2.23	—
1950	31.53	25.56	14.13	10.22	4.47	—	—
1951	26.65	18.87	9.08	6.23	2.53	1.67	—
1952	26.31	19.51	8.99	6.11	2.44	1.57	0.55
1953	26.10	18.70	8.71	5.97	2.43	1.58	0.58
1954	25.77	18.10	8.06	5.48	2.19	1.42	0.52
1955	25.53	17.49	7.54	5.10	2.01	1.29	0.48
1956	25.69	17.84	7.91	5.42	2.16	1.39	0.51
1957	23.99	16.33	7.04	4.75	1.84	1.19	0.43
1958	29.77	19.41	7.44	4.86	1.76	1.14	0.41
1959	29.85	19.44	7.39	4.82	1.75	1.12	0.41
1960	29.60	19.14	7.09	4.58	1.62	1.04	0.37
1961	29.71	19.20	7.10	4.58	1.65	1.06	0.40
1962	30.22	19.62	7.23	4.64	1.64	1.04	0.38
1963	30.35	19.84	7.36	4.72	1.65	1.05	0.37
1964	29.45	18.95	6.84	4.37	1.52	0.96	0.34
1965	29.22	18.68	6.69	4.27	1.46	0.92	0.31
1966	28.51	18.19	6.47	4.12	1.41	0.89	0.31
1967	28.66	18.29	6.58	4.23	1.51	0.98	0.38
1968	28.36	17.99	6.38	4.06	1.40	0.89	0.32
1969	27.85	17.61	6.25	4.00	1.42	0.92	0.36
1970	27.65	17.30	5.92	3.74	1.26	0.79	0.27

(contd.)

Table 7.1 (*contd.*)

	10%	5%	1%	0.5%	0.1%	0.05%	0.01%
1971	28.24	17.59	5.92	3.70	1.25	0.78	0.27
1972	27.80	17.50	6.06	3.81	1.29	0.81	0.28
1973	26.74	16.73	5.67	3.54	1.17	0.73	0.24
1974	25.87	15.87	5.22	3.24	1.06	0.65	0.21
1975	25.54	15.65	5.13	3.22	1.10	0.68	0.23
1976	25.20	15.35	4.99	3.11	1.05	0.65	0.21
1977	25.15	15.25	4.92	3.08	1.06	0.67	—
1978	25.01	15.14	4.87	3.02	1.03	0.65	—
1979	25.17	15.20	4.83	2.97	1.02	0.65	—
1980	25.39	15.31	4.79	2.95	1.02	0.66	—
1981	25.31	15.15	4.61	2.83	0.96	0.62	—
1982	25.82	15.44	4.67	2.87	1.00	0.63	—
1983	25.32	15.16	4.68	2.89	1.02	0.66	—
1984	25.50	15.25	4.75	2.96	1.03	—	—
1985	25.93	15.63	5.02	3.19	1.14	0.75	0.35
1986	26.61	16.17	5.39	3.48	1.29	0.85	0.36
1987	28.66	17.94	6.67	4.53	1.89	1.41	0.60
1988	30.28	19.84	8.41	6.04	2.99	2.13	0.98
1989	27.64	17.46	6.43	4.29	1.79	1.31	0.51
1990	27.66	17.37	6.34	4.24	1.79	1.33	0.55
1991	28.22	17.70	6.41	4.28	1.81	1.35	0.57
1992	28.52	17.95	6.55	4.38	1.87	1.37	0.57
1993	29.40	18.66	6.96	4.69	2.08	1.46	0.61
1994	29.42	18.87	7.13	5.10	2.56	1.65	0.71
1995	29.13	18.76	7.23	4.95	2.14	1.52	0.73
1996	29.16	18.77	7.24	4.93	2.07	1.44	0.65
1997	30.41	19.73	7.81	5.38	2.32	1.64	0.75
1998	30.11	19.63	7.84	5.43	2.37	1.67	0.76
1999	31.48	20.95	8.84	6.29	3.04	2.15	—
2000	31.28	20.98	9.03	6.44	3.06	2.24	—
2001	30.61	20.33	8.31	5.75	2.51	1.75	—
2002	31.34	20.90	8.79	6.11	2.68	1.87	—

Note: Figures are for tax years (e.g. 1921 denotes the tax year 1 July 1921–30 June 1922).
Source: Authors' calculations.

and under-employment, which has the effect of reducing the Gini coefficient substantially. At the same time, they note that the effect of declining capital income would operate in the opposite direction. From Figure 7.1, we can see that the top shares fell from 1928 to 1932, but then recovered about half of their loss. The Depression left only a limited permanent effect.

Nor is the Second World War associated with a permanent fall in the share of the top 1%: the shares in 1947 were similar to those in 1939 (although the top 0.5% and 0.1% did show a decline). This stands in contrast to several other Anglo-Saxon nations: in Britain, Canada, and the United States (though not in New Zealand) top income shares fell significantly during the Second World War. The immediate post Second World War period saw the effects of the commodity price boom. There is a clear spike in 1950, mainly due to the peak wool prices which sheep farmers received in that year. Jones (1975: 31, n.26) noted this spike, comparing the figures for 1949–50 and 1950–1. This illustrates again how one

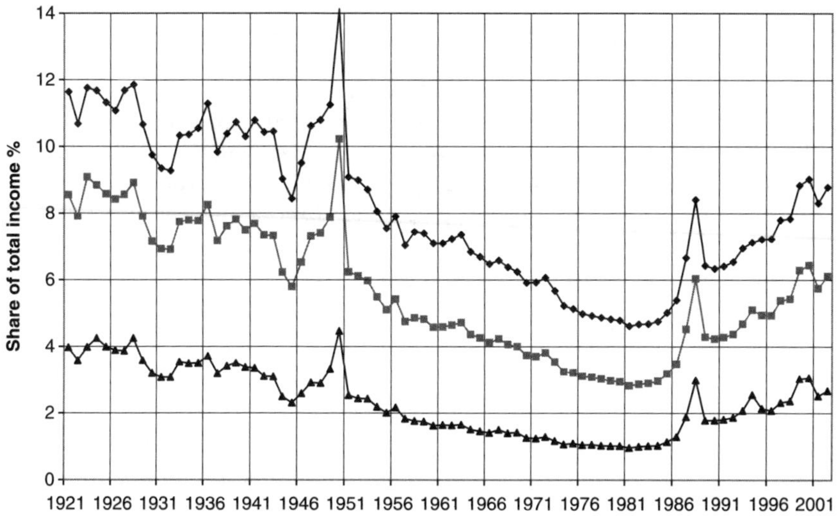

Figure 7.1 Shares of top 1%, 0.5%, and 0.1% Australia, 1921–2002

Source: Table 7.1, this volume.

could be misled by relying on a single observation. If we just compared 1921 and 1950, we might conclude that top shares had significantly increased. (The same pattern can be seen in New Zealand top incomes—see Chapter 8.)

Recent Years

The 60 years from 1921 as a whole were apparently a period of major decline at the top of the distribution. From 1980, however, the pattern reversed. By 1998 the top shares were back well above their 1958 levels. The share of the top 1%, which had fallen to under 5%, by the end of the 1990s was back to 8%. The share of the top 0.1%, which had been 1% at the end of the 1970s, has more than doubled. Again round this trend there is year-to-year variation. There is a distinct spike in 1988, following a large reduction in the top marginal tax rate (from 60% in 1985–86 to 49% in 1987–88) and the property price boom of the late-1980s.

As documented by Saunders (2004), there has been considerable debate as to whether income inequality in Australia continued to increase in the second half of the 1990s. He studied this issue with the aid of data from the Survey of Income and Housing Costs, concluding that the share of the top 20% increased between 1995–96 and 2000–01. Our estimates provide additional evidence, which differs in that it relates to gross individual incomes, but which is complementary in that it gives detail about the very top. At the same time, the sharp fall in the top shares in 2001 warns against drawing conclusions from short-term changes about longer term developments. But even if we discount the higher observations for 1999 and 2000, the direction of change seems clearly upwards. The share of the top 1% is about 1 percentage point higher in 2001 than in 1996.

Top Income Shares in the State of Victoria, 1912–21

Because our series for Australia as a whole starts only in 1921, it is interesting to examine the evidence for the state of Victoria that covers the earlier period 1912–21—see Table 7.2. Alone among the Australian states, Victorian income tax statistics in the 1910s separated individual taxpayers from corporations. Comparing the two series in overlapping years (1921–23) in Figure 7.2, we can

Table 7.2 Top income shares, Victoria, Australia, 1912–23

	10%	5%	1%	0.5%	0.1%	0.05%	0.01%
1912	—	—	12.69	9.48	—	—	—
1913	—	—	11.65	8.64	—	—	—
1914	—	—	—	8.17	3.87	—	—
1915	—	—	—	7.70	—	—	—
1916	—	—	—	6.62	3.28	—	—
1917	—	—	—	6.88	—	—	—
1918	—	—	—	7.06	—	—	—
1919	—	—	12.55	9.70	—	—	—
1920	—	—	10.15	7.43	—	—	—
1921	—	—	9.85	7.10	—	—	—
1922	—	—	—	—	—	—	—
1923	—	19.04	11.42	8.13	3.49	2.40	—

Note: Figures for 1912 and 1913 are for calendar years. Figures for 1914 onwards are for tax years (e.g. 1914 denotes the tax year 1 July 1914–30 June 1915).

Source: Authors' calculations.

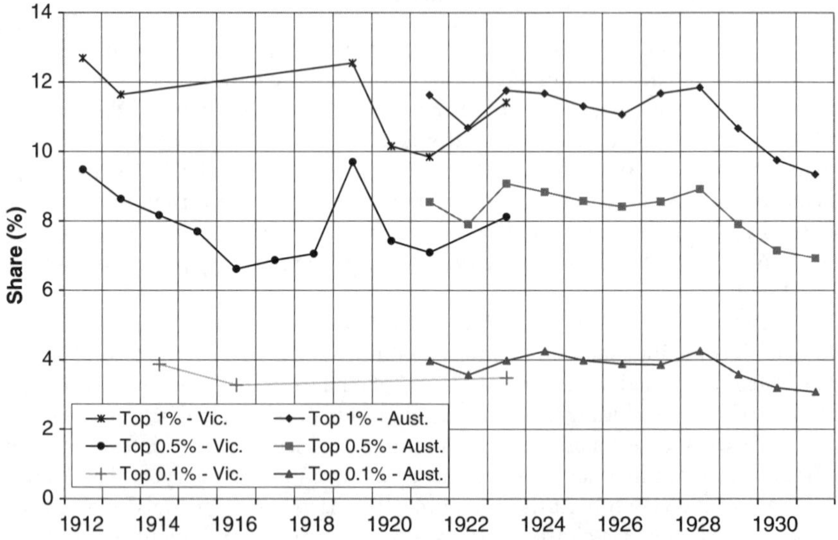

Figure 7.2 Comparing Victoria, 1912–23, with Australia, 1921–31

Source: Tables 7.1 and 7.2, this volume.

see that Victorian top income shares are very close to those in Australia as a whole. Assuming therefore that the Victorian series was representative of Australia as a whole during the 1910s, this suggests that Australian top income shares fell, though only modestly, during the First World War.

Inequality Within the Top 10%

Earlier chapters have shown how the rise in income shares of the 1980s and 1990s in the US was concentrated at the top. The evidence of Piketty and Saez for the US (Figure 5.2, Chapter 5) shows that, whereas the share of the top 10% as a whole increased by some 10 percentage points, that of the second vintile (i.e. those in the top 10% but not the top 5%) was essentially stable. Figure 7.3 shows for Australia the second vintile and the shares of those in the top 5% but not the top 1% (referred to as the 'next 4%'). It should be noted that the Australian tax data do not allow us to estimate the share of the top 5% between 1923 and 1938. In the graphs, where there are missing data, we interpolate the series linearly, but this is clearly unsatisfactory, as may be seen by considering what would have been missed in the case of the share of the top 1% (see Figure 7.1).

The scale on Figure 7.3 is the same as that for Figure 7.1, making apparent that in 1945 the top 1% had approximately the same amount of income as the second vintile. There is very considerable inequality within the top 10%. Leaving aside the limited data for the 1920s and 1930s, we can see that these 'next' shares were declining from 1941 to 1957. It may be observed that the Korean War wool boom had a positive effect only at the very top: the share of the second vintile in Australia actually fell in 1950. After the switch in definition in 1958, which added at least 2 percentage points

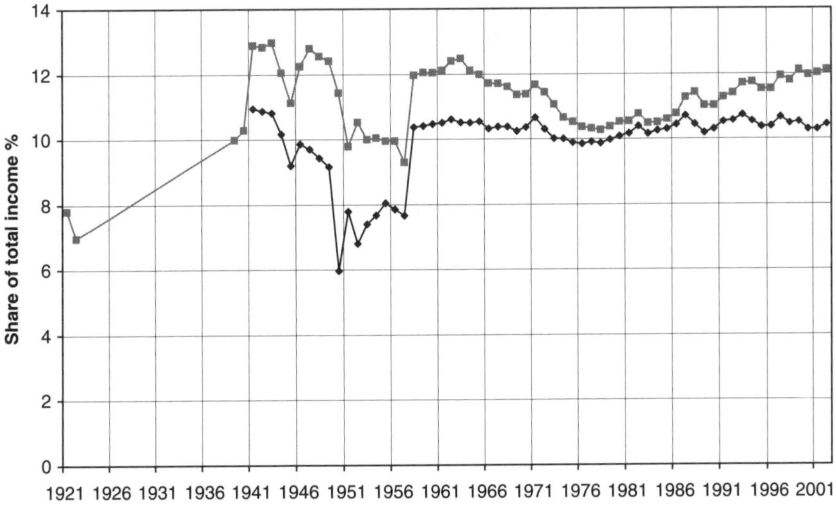

Figure 7.3 Share of next 4% and second vintile in Australia, 1921–2002

Source: Table 7.1, this volume.

to the share of the top 10%, the downward trend continued for the next 4% but not for the second vintile. Equally, after 1980, there is little increase for the second vintile. For the next 4%, the share rose from 10.5% in 1980 to 11.8% in 1998.

As has been noted in Chapter 2, looking at the distribution *within* the top 10% has the advantage that the estimates do not depend on the control total for income. Figure 7.4 shows the share of the top 1% within the top 10% and the share of the top 0.1% within the top 1%. Also shown for reference, as a solid line without markers, is the share of the top 10% in total income (which does depend on the control total). It appears that in the 1940s and again in the 1990s the distribution within the top 1% is as relatively unequal as the overall distribution: the top 10% of the top 1% have a similar share to the top 10% overall. The 'within' distribution got steadily less unequal from 1921 to 1982, and then returned: by 1998 the share of the top 0.1% within the top 1% was similar to the level at the end of the 1930s.

Figure 7.5 shows the shares within shares in the form of Pareto-Lorenz coefficients.[6] The Pareto-Lorenz coefficient for the share of the top 0.1% within the top 1% peaks in 1974 at 3.2, before declining to 1.9 in 2000—approximately the same level as in 1921. The coefficient for the share of the top 1% within the top 10% peaks in 1982 at 3.9, before declining to 2.2 in 2000, only slightly higher than in 1941, the first year for which it can be calculated.

Sensitivity of the Results

How sensitive are these results to changes in the control totals? On average, changing the population control to those aged 20 and over (a lower bound

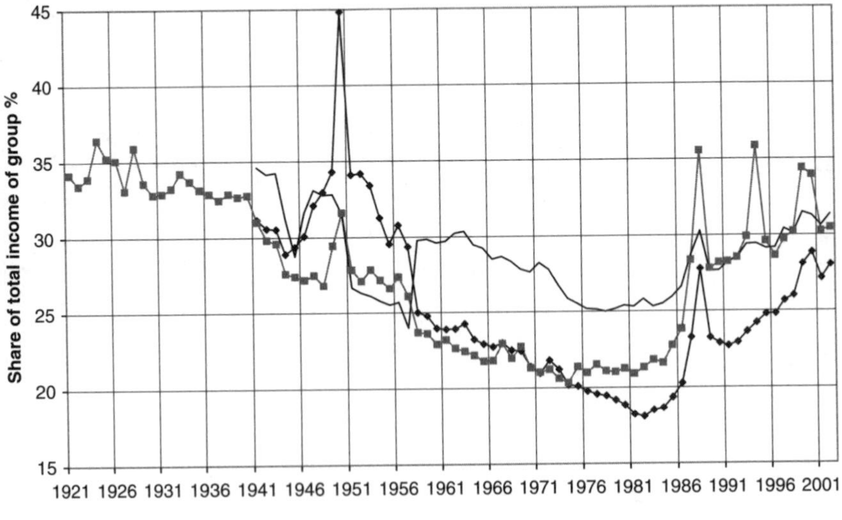

Figure 7.4 Shares within shares in Australia, 1921–2002

Source: Table 7.1, this volume.

[6] Defined as $1/[1 + Log_{10}[S_1/S_{10}]]$

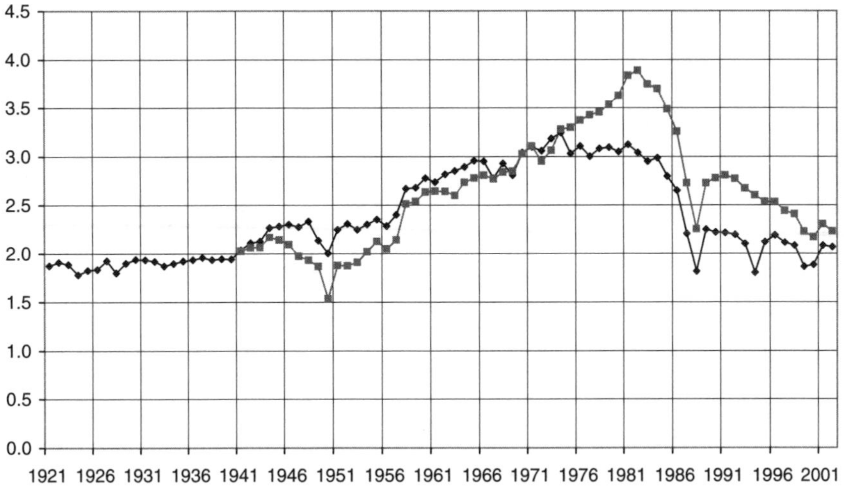

Figure 7.5 Pareto-Lorenz coefficients, Australia 1921–2002

for the population total) reduces our estimate of the share of the top percentile group by 0.5 percentage points, and the share of the top decile group by 1.9 percentage points. Going in the opposite direction, maintaining a population control total of those aged 15 and over, but reducing the personal income denominator to 90% of personal income increases our estimate of the top percentile group share by an average of 0.7 percentage points, and the share of the top decile group by 3.1 percentage points. The second of these changes would mean that the share of the top 10% in 1921 became 21.6% in place of 19.4%, and that the share of the top 0.1% became 4.4%% in place of 4.0%. These changes do not affect the conclusions we drew regarding the relative position of Australia.

Sources of Top Incomes

The findings for France, the US and other countries have demonstrated the importance of examining the sources of top incomes. From 1954–55 onwards, it is possible to separate salary and wage income from other income sources. Figure 7.6 charts the fraction of income that came from salary and wages earnings for three top income groups—the top 10%, 1%, and 0.1%. From the mid-1950s until the end of the 1970s, the proportion of income derived from salary and wages grew for all three top income groups.[7] Over the last two decades of the

[7] Unfortunately, during the earlier period (1929–30 to 1953–54), Australian taxation statistics were only separated into income from 'personal exertion' (wages, salaries, and self-employment income) and 'property'. Also, because the Australian taxation statistics do not contain information on the number of taxpayers reporting wage income, it is not possible to use these data to compile a separate series on the distribution of wage income, as has been done for a number of other countries, including Canada and the US.

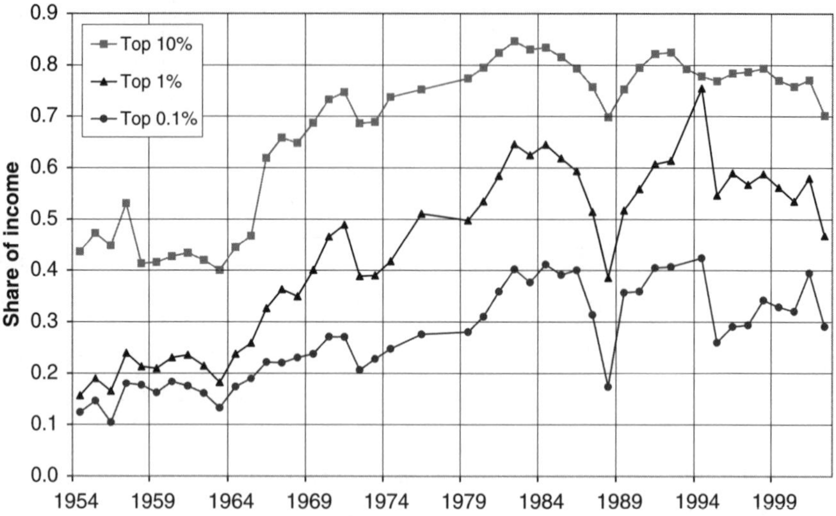

Figure 7.6 Fraction of income from salary and wages, Australia 1954–2002

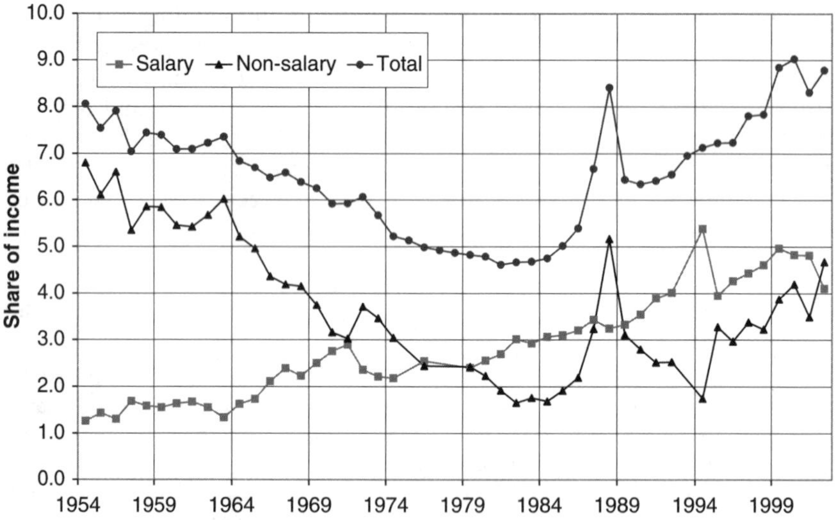

Figure 7.7 Contributions to share of top 1%, Australia 1954–2002

twentieth century, salary and wage income fluctuated somewhat, but the proportion of salary and wage income for top income groups in 2000 was quite similar to the proportion in 1980.

Figure 7.7 breaks down the income of the top 1% into salary and non-salary components. The decline in top income shares that occurred from the mid-1950s until the late-1970s was due entirely to a reduction in non-salary income accruing to the top 1%.[8] During the 1980s and 1990s, both salary and non-salary income have contributed towards the rising share of the top 1%, though salary income has accounted for slightly more of the growth than has non-salary income.

7.4 CONCLUSIONS

The estimates for Australia presented in this chapter run parallel to those for the other nine countries. Insofar as they are comparable (see Chapter 13), they indicate that the top shares in 1921 were less concentrated than in the Northern Hemisphere. Even so, the estimated share of the top 0.1% was around 4%, or 40 times their proportionate share.

Since the 1920s, top income shares in Australia have fallen considerably. Their path has much in common with four other Anglo-Saxon countries: Canada (Chapter 6), New Zealand (Chapter 8), the UK (Chapter 4), and the US (Chapter 5). As we show in our comparison of these five Anglo-Saxon countries (Atkinson and Leigh 2004), each saw a decline in top income shares in the three decades after the Second World War, followed by a sharp rise from the mid-1970s onwards. In 2000, the income share of the richest 1% of Australians was higher than it had been at any point since 1951, while the share of the richest 10% was higher than it had been since 1949. The top 0.1% still have some 25 times their proportionate share.

APPENDIX 7A: SOURCES OF POPULATION AND TAX UNIT TOTALS

Australian population data are from Australian Bureau of Statistics, Australian Historical Population Statistics, Cat No 3105.0.65.001, table 18. Figures are provided on an annual basis for 1921 onwards, and are converted into a tax-year basis by simply averaging the figures for the two calendar years covered by a tax year. Since the tax unit in Australia is the individual, no further conversion is required.

Population data for the state of Victoria are from Australian Bureau of Statistics, Australian Historical Population Statistics, Cat No 3105.0.65.001, table 23. Figures are available from the censuses of 1911, 1921, and 1933, and are linearly interpolated for intervening years.

Our population data are provided in Table 7A.1.

[8] Using taxation statistics, Lydall (1965) noted that the ratio of wages for those in the top percentile group to median wages grew during the 1950s. But as Figure 7.8 shows, this trend was swamped by the fall in non-salary income for those in the top percentile group.

Table 7A.1 Population totals for Australia, 1912–2002

Tax year starting 1 July	Australia: individuals 15 and over	Australia: individuals 20 and over	Australia: taxpayers	Victoria: individuals 15 and over	Victoria: individuals 20 and over	Victoria: taxpayers
1912	3,094,463	2,643,721	—	925,733	790,701	40,976
1913	3,164,345	2,711,396	—	942,060	807,520	44,172
1914	3,234,227	2,779,072	—	958,387	824,338	40,581
1915	3,304,109	2,846,747	—	974,714	841,157	45,084
1916	3,373,991	2,914,423	—	991,041	857,975	43,424
1917	3,443,873	2,982,098	—	1,007,368	874,793	49,889
1918	3,513,754	3,049,774	—	1,023,695	891,612	50,626
1919	3,583,636	3,117,449	—	1,040,022	908,430	73,548
1920	3,653,518	3,185,125	—	1,056,349	925,249	87,486
1921	3,723,400	3,252,800	457,632	1,072,676	942,067	97,470
1922	3,809,400	3,327,200	433,144	1,095,189	962,091	—
1923	3,907,800	3,410,500	193,605	1,117,702	982,114	127,818
1924	4,005,000	3,492,500	215,693	—	—	—
1925	4,110,100	3,580,300	225,398	—	—	—
1926	4,207,200	3,661,500	245,107	—	—	—
1927	4,319,300	3,755,500	257,939	—	—	—
1928	4,427,600	3,847,600	260,500	—	—	—
1929	4,519,700	3,921,700	322,799	—	—	—
1930	4,598,000	3,986,400	296,765	—	—	—
1931	4,668,600	4,052,200	230,749	—	—	—
1932	4,737,400	4,119,200	221,867	—	—	—
1933	4,805,200	4,191,200	220,240	—	—	—
1934	4,866,900	4,263,300	248,508	—	—	—
1935	4,934,100	4,336,900	245,349	—	—	—
1936	5,010,700	4,403,600	290,224	—	—	—
1937	5,085,300	4,470,100	332,380	—	—	—
1938	5,163,100	4,536,600	346,441	—	—	—
1939	5,238,900	4,602,300	623,375	—	—	—
1940	5,319,800	4,677,400	785,019	—	—	—
1941	5,390,000	4,753,600	1,493,053	—	—	—
1942	5,446,700	4,819,400	1,962,756	—	—	—
1943	5,496,600	4,874,700	2,049,694	—	—	—
1944	5,544,700	4,926,900	2,038,465	—	—	—
1945	5,594,100	4,985,300	2,051,248	—	—	—
1946	5,638,600	5,038,900	2,438,498	—	—	—
1947	5,675,200	5,090,400	2,643,440	—	—	—
1948	5,734,100	5,165,800	2,833,415	—	—	—
1949	5,847,000	5,290,000	3,051,476	—	—	—
1950	6,002,800	5,451,100	3,263,373	—	—	—
1951	6,135,600	5,587,200	3,420,265	—	—	—
1952	6,252,700	5,692,200	3,474,922	—	—	—
1953	6,336,200	5,762,800	3,549,137	—	—	—
1954	6,417,200	5,825,500	3,685,644	—	—	—
1955	6,528,200	5,914,800	3,811,004	—	—	—
1956	6,655,600	6,019,100	3,901,094	—	—	—
1957	6,782,800	6,118,700	3,921,292	—	—	—
1958	6,891,000	6,206,100	4,037,862	—	—	—
1959	7,027,200	6,303,200	4,199,374	—	—	—

1960	7,171,400	6,402,400	4,357,805	—	—	—
1961	7,323,200	6,512,900	4,406,628	—	—	—
1962	7,485,100	6,605,900	4,555,447	—	—	—
1963	7,643,900	6,706,300	4,460,472	—	—	—
1964	7,805,400	6,832,000	4,632,025	—	—	—
1965	7,980,900	6,967,900	4,771,504	—	—	—
1966	8,179,788	7,124,349	4,927,072	—	—	—
1967	8,343,833	7,294,605	5,001,174	—	—	—
1968	8,522,217	7,456,171	5,204,042	—	—	—
1969	8,716,454	7,629,999	5,372,500	—	—	—
1970	8,901,723	7,799,368	5,570,720	—	—	—
1971	9,319,988	8,183,692	5,691,431	—	—	—
1972	9,510,934	8,347,141	5,076,252	—	—	—
1973	9,691,778	8,507,292	5,420,004	—	—	—
1974	9,898,311	8,685,640	5,551,322	—	—	—
1975	10,073,371	8,839,661	5,179,359	—	—	—
1976	10,245,988	8,985,211	5,527,309	—	—	—
1977	10,428,589	9,139,068	5,568,298	—	—	—
1978	10,616,188	9,310,408	5,538,132	—	—	—
1979	10,797,294	9,483,735	5,662,971	—	—	—
1980	10,984,362	9,676,805	5,973,373	—	—	—
1981	11,197,720	9,900,675	6,199,831	—	—	—
1982	11,439,261	10,150,267	6,104,878	—	—	—
1983	11,642,452	10,361,571	6,306,340	—	—	—
1984	11,843,586	10,556,177	6,546,544	—	—	—
1985	12,062,771	10,758,065	6,966,074	—	—	—
1986	12,318,832	10,971,610	7,181,864	—	—	—
1987	12,576,530	11,190,263	7,629,453	—	—	—
1988	12,833,133	11,425,459	7,906,142	—	—	—
1989	13,089,498	11,676,326	8,033,918	—	—	—
1990	13,310,134	11,907,731	7,800,273	—	—	—
1991	13,498,506	12,134,432	7,422,503	—	—	—
1992	13,678,327	12,355,556	7,661,794	—	—	—
1993	13,829,567	12,535,922	7,609,311	—	—	—
1994	13,994,701	12,718,015	7,861,134	—	—	—
1995	14,183,640	12,914,400	8,165,642	—	—	—
1996	14,399,399	13,120,280	8,239,600	—	—	—
1997	14,604,610	13,310,687	8,251,106	—	—	—
1998	14,810,586	13,496,995	8,019,205	—	—	—
1999	15,016,967	13,685,995	8,592,521	—	—	—
2000	15,234,957	13,886,215	8,473,317	—	—	—
2001	15,463,445	14,101,339	8,534,329	—	—	—
2002	15,656,801	14,296,696	8,665,443	—	—	—

Note: The estimates presented in this paper use the population denominator of individuals aged 15 and over. Estimates using a population denominator of individuals aged 20 and over are presented only as a robustness check.

APPENDIX 7B: DERIVATION OF PERSONAL INCOME SERIES

In this chapter, two personal income series are presented—one with social transfers, and another without transfers. Until tax year 1943, transfers were largely untaxed. From 1944 onwards, transfers were taxed. We therefore switch our personal income denominator to include transfers from 1944 onwards, but include both series for the entire period. Australia switched from pounds to dollars in the mid-1960s, at the ratio of £1 = $2. While some of our original sources are in pounds, we present all our tables in millions of dollars.

Starting from the most recent period, for the years 1959–2001, we use Australian Bureau of Statistics, *National Accounts, 5204.0,* Table 46. We include compensation of employees (which does not include imputed interest on pension funds), interest, dividends, and gross mixed income, less other interest payable and consumption of fixed capital. For the series with transfers, we add workers' compensation and social assistance benefits. We are grateful to Carl Obst of the ABS for assistance in determining the correct series to use.

Working back in time, for the period before 1959 we have used household national accounts data supplied by the Australian Government to the United Nations. Years from 1946 to 1950 are from United Nations (1955: series H7, table 4, p. 50). For 1951–52, and 1954, we use United Nations (1958: table 2, p. 5). For 1953 and 1955–59, we use United Nations (1966: table 3, p. 10). We use the same line items from the 1955, 1958, and 1966 publications: compensation of employees (subtracting 4% to account for imputed interest from pension funds), income from unincorporated enterprises, rent and interest, and dividends. None of these publications includes social transfers, so we use figures on Commonwealth social spending, from Barnard (1986: table 5, p. 25, column D. The series are linked together as follows. The Australian Bureau of Statistics data are set at a ratio of one, and linked to the United Nations (1966) data using the ratio of the two series during the overlap period. The United Nations (1958) figures are then linked to the *adjusted* 1966 series using the overlapping years between the 1958 and 1966 series. The source for 1938–46 is the United Nations (1950: table 5, p. 32). We use wages and salaries (subtracting 4% to account for imputed interest from pension funds), pay of forces, income from unincorporated businesses and farms, rent and interest, dividends, and deferred pay of members of forces. For the series with transfers, we include cash social service benefits. The series is linked in the way described above. Prior to the Second World War, data on personal income are contained in Clark and Crawford (1938: p. 13). (See also Mauldon et al. 1938.) Clark and Crawford provide figures for 1928–33, and we use rows A–I of their table. We have also used their 'tentative' estimate for 1934 in Appendix A. This leaves a 'gap' from 1935 to 1937. The figure for 1938 derived from UN (1950) is 29.4% higher than that for 1934 derived from Clark and Crawford. The 'net national product at market prices' series from Butlin (1962: table 1), shows a rise of 30.8%. We therefore use the Butlin series to interpolate. Finally, for the period 1913–27, we extrapolate backwards using the Butlin series. Our personal income series are provided in Table 7B.1.

We also present a series on personal income (excluding transfers) for the state of Victoria for the years 1912–21. For the years 1913–14 onwards, we use as our base the Australian personal income series without transfers, as derived above. This is compared against GDP data from Butlin (1977: 41) to calculate a ratio of personal income to GDP (72.3%). We then use Cashin (1995: table 1, p. 26), and compare Cashin's Victorian GDP figures for 1900, 1910, and 1920 with data for

Table 7B.1 Personal income totals for Australia, 1912–2002

Tax year starting 1 July	Australia: Including Transfers ($M)	Australia: Excluding Transfers ($M)	Victoria, Australia: Excluding Transfers ($M)
1912			189
1913	621	601	204
1914	600	579	198
1915	682	659	229
1916	683	659	241
1917	640	616	251
1918	678	653	270
1919	1,082	1,038	296
1920	1,063	1,015	326
1921	1,037	999	325
1922	1,123	1,085	356
1923	1,210	1,165	370
1924	1,307	1,260	—
1925	1,332	1,283	—
1926	1,410	1,357	—
1927	*1,437*	*1,382*	—
1928	1,382	1,327	—
1929	1,354	1,299	—
1930	1,107	1,057	—
1931	1,017	971	—
1932	*1,026*	*978*	—
1933	1,117	1,069	—
1934	1,167	1,116	—
1935	1,257	1,201	—
1936	1,412	1,351	—
1937	*1,485*	*1,419*	—
1938	1,525	1,458	—
1939	1,622	1,555	—
1940	1,745	1,678	—
1941	2,048	1,957	—
1942	2,340	2,238	—
1943	2,460	2,350	—
1944	2,430	2,316	—
1945	*2,668*	*2,524*	—
1946	2,715	2,572	—
1947	3,339	3,146	—
1948	3,946	3,705	—
1949	4,578	4,307	—
1950	*5,973*	*5,678*	—
1951	6,638	6,260	—
1952	7,123	6,756	—
1953	*7,351*	*6,960*	—
1954	*7,893*	*7,474*	—
1955	8,556	8,081	—
1956	9,145	8,650	—
1957	9,059	8,514	—
1958	*9,771*	*9,160*	—
1959	10,843	10,165	—
1960	11,585	10,838	—

(*contd.*)

Table 7B.1 (*contd.*)

Tax year starting 1 July	Australia: Including Transfers ($M)	Australia: Excluding Transfers ($M)	Victoria, Australia: Excluding Transfers ($M)
1961	11,912	11,076	—
1962	12,607	11,741	—
1963	13,971	13,017	—
1964	15,070	14,072	—
1965	15,925	14,865	—
1966	17,831	16,689	—
1967	18,766	17,580	—
1968	20,929	19,648	—
1969	23,109	21,672	—
1970	25,641	24,105	—
1971	28,637	26,832	—
1972	32,866	30,548	—
1973	41,074	38,159	—
1974	50,902	46,760	—
1975	59,135	53,659	—
1976	68,113	61,109	—
1977	74,498	66,315	—
1978	82,990	74,200	—
1979	92,124	82,555	—
1980	104,630	93,467	—
1981	120,459	107,675	—
1982	132,515	116,700	—
1983	146,104	127,738	—
1984	158,817	138,596	—
1985	174,633	152,589	—
1986	189,421	165,583	—
1987	205,912	180,550	—
1988	230,688	204,394	—
1989	257,389	229,361	—
1990	264,479	232,624	—
1991	268,041	230,657	—
1992	277,365	237,676	—
1993	287,510	243,463	—
1994	306,060	260,743	—
1995	331,797	282,558	—
1996	349,967	297,854	—
1997	361,404	309,423	—
1998	383,311	328,799	—
1999	404,179	346,018	—
2000	437,877	369,629	—
2001	457,891	388,724	—
2002	475,331	402,570	—

Note: The estimates presented in this paper use the income denominator 'personal income excluding transfers' until 1943, and 'personal income including transfers' from 1944 onwards (reflecting the fact that most transfers were taxed from 1944). Years marked in italics (e.g. 1958) correspond to changes in national accounts sources (see text).

total Australian GDP from Butlin (1962: 460–1) and Butlin (1977: 41). Across this period, we find that Victorian GDP is a constant 33% of Australian GDP. We therefore calculate that Victorian personal income is 23.8% (*0.723*0.33*) of Australian GDP, and accordingly construct the Victorian personal income series from Butlin's Australian GDP figures. This series is also provided in Appendix Table 7B.1.

APPENDIX 7C: SOURCES OF INCOME TAX DATA

The chapter relies solely on tabulated data, which means that we have to interpolate. Typically, for each income range, there is information on the number of

Table 7C.1 Sources of income tax data for Australia, 1921–2002

Year	Source
1921–35	Schedule 1
1936	Schedule 1B
1937	Schedule 1A
1938–40	Schedule No 6
1941–42	Schedule No 7
1943	Schedule No 6
1944–47	Schedule No 11
1948–49	Schedule No 10
1950	Schedule No 97
1951	Schedule No 98
1952	Schedule No 99
1953–54	Schedule No 1
1955	Schedule No 1(1)
1956–61	Schedule 1(1)
1962–79	Schedule 1.1
1980	Schedule 1.1(e)
1981	Schedule 1.1(a)
1982–84	Table 1.3(e)
1985	Tables 1.3(e) & 1.25
1986–88	Tables 1.3(e) & 1.24
1989	Tables 1.3(c) & 1.24
1990–91	Tables 1.3(f) & 1.24
1992	Tables 1.3(f) & 1.22
1993	Tables 1.6(i) & 1.13
1994	Tables P16 & C5
1995	Tables I4 & I14
1996	Tables I4 & I15
1997	Tables I2 & I14
1998	Tables I4 & I14
1999	Personal Tax Tables 6A, 6B & 9
2000–02	Personal Tax Tables 5A, 5B & 9

Note: All references are to the annual *Report of the Commissioner of Taxation*. References to years denote tax years (e.g. 1921 denotes the tax year 1 July 1921–30 June 1922).

taxpayers and the total amount of taxable income. In order to calculate the shares of specified percentages of the population, we have used the *mean-split histogram.* Assuming, as seems reasonable in the case of top incomes, that the frequency distribution is non-decreasing, then upper and lower bounds can be calculated that are limiting forms of the split histogram, with one of the two densities tending to zero or infinity—see Atkinson (2005). Guaranteed to lie between these is the histogram split at the interval mean with sections of positive density on either side. We have not interpolated shares that lie in the top open interval. In the case of Australia, Saunders (1998: 28) checked using micro-data from income distribution surveys in 1989 and 1995, and concluded that use of grouped data made 'very little difference'. Micro-data samples of taxpayers are not presently available in Australia, as they are in some other countries.

Data on individual taxpayers are available from 1921 (prior to that date, the data included companies as well as individuals). Estimates are taken from the annual *Report of the Commissioner of Taxation* (see Table 7C.1). Tabulations have typically been published with a three year lag from the end of the financial year. From tax year 1994–95 onwards, data are available in electronic form from the Australian Taxation Office. Until 1957, the Australian taxation statistics presented tabulations of taxable income. From 1958 onwards, this switched to actual income.

Data for the state of Victoria is derived from the state yearbook (see Appendix Table 7C.2). From 1912 onwards, figures are tabulated for Personal Exertion, Property, Combined, and Companies. We sum the first three categories to derive a consistent series for the top incomes of individuals. In the calendar years 1912, 1913, and 1914, Victorian figures were presented on a calendar year basis, before switching to a standard Australian financial year (1 July to 30 June) from the 1914 tax year onwards.

Table 7C.2 Sources of income tax data for Victoria, Australia, 1912–23

Year	Source for incomes data	Notes
1912	*VY* 1913–14: 132	4 income bands; calendar year basis.
1913	*VY* 1914–15: 138	4 income bands; calendar year basis.
1914	*VY* 1915–16: 144	4 income bands; calendar year basis.
1914–15	*VY* 1916–17: 150	Switch to financial year (starting 1 July) from this point onwards; 5 income bands.
1915–16	*VY* 1917–18: 50	5 income bands.
1916–17	*VY* 1918–19: 50	5 income bands.
1917–18	*VY* 1919–20: 48	5 income bands.
1918–19	*VY* 1920–21: 58	5 income bands.
1919–20	*VY* 1921–22: 52	5 income bands.
1920–21	*VY* 1922–23: 44	5 income bands.
1921–22	*VY* 1923–24: 45	5 income bands.
1922–23	—	
1923–24	*VY* 1925–26: 50	16 bands.

Note: *VY* denotes the *Victorian Yearbook*, various years. 1912–14 are calendar years, 1914–15 to 1923–24 are tax years.

REFERENCES

Adams, F. (1892). *Australian Life.* London: Chapman & Hall.

Atkinson, A. B. (2005). 'Top incomes in the UK over the 20th century', *Journal of the Royal Statistical Society,* 168(2): 325–43.

——Harrison, A. (1978). *Distribution of Personal Wealth in Britain.* Cambridge: Cambridge University Press.

——Leigh, A. (2004). 'The Distribution of Top Incomes in Anglo-Saxon Countries over the Twentieth Century', discussion paper.

—— (2007). 'The Distribution of Top Incomes in Australia', *Economic Record,* forthcoming.

Australian Bureau of Statistics (1997). *Income Distribution in Australia, 1995–6,* ABS Catalogue 6523.0. Canberra: ABS.

——(1999). *Income Distribution in Australia, 1997–8,* ABS Catalogue 6523.0. Canberra: ABS.

——(2001). *Income Distribution Australia, 1999–2000,* ABS Catalogue 6523.0. Canberra: ABS.

Barnard, A. (1986). 'Some Government Financial Data', *Australian National University Source Papers in Economic History,* No 13.

Berry, M. J. (1977). 'Inequality', in A. F. Davies, S. Encel, and M. J. Berry (eds.) *Australian Society: A Sociological Introduction.* Cheshire, Melbourne: Longman.

Bradbury, B., Doyle, J., and Whiteford, P. (1990). 'Trends in the Disposable Incomes of Australian Families 1982–83 to 1989–90'. SPRC Discussion Paper No. 16, University of New South Wales.

Brown, H. P. (1957). 'Estimation of Income Distribution in Australia', in M. Gilbert and R. Stone (eds.) *Income and Wealth,* Series VI. London: Bowes & Bowes, pp. 202–38.

Butlin, N. G. (1962). *Australian Domestic Product, Investment and Foreign Borrowing, 1861–1938/39.* Cambridge: Cambridge University Press.

Butlin, M. W. (1977). 'A Preliminary Annual Database 1900–01 to 1973–74'. Research Discussion Paper 7701, Reserve Bank of Australia, Sydney.

Butlin, N. G. (1983). 'Trends in Australian Income Distribution: A First Glance'. Working Paper No. 17, Department of Economic History, Australian National University.

Cashin, P. A. (1995). 'Real GDP in the Seven Colonies of Australasia 1861–1991', *Review of Income and Wealth,* 41(1): 19–39.

Clark, C. and Crawford, J. G. (1938). *The National Income of Australia.* Sydney: Angus & Robertson.

Hancock, K. (1971). 'The economics of social welfare in the 1970s', in H. Weir (ed.) *Social Welfare in the 1970s.* Sydney: Australian Council of Social Service.

Harding, A. (1997). 'The Suffering Middle: Trends in Income Inequality in Australia. 1982 to 1993–94'. Discussion Paper No. 21, NATSEM, Canberra.

——Greenwell, H. (2002). 'Trends in Income and Expenditure Inequality in the 1980s and 1990s—A Re-Examination and Further Results'. Discussion Paper No 57, NATSEM, Canberra.

Harris, C. P. (1970). 'Income Tax and Income Distribution in Australia 1955–6 and 1965–6', in C. P. Harris (ed.) *Selected Readings for Economic Behaviour,* McCutchan, Berkeley.

Ingles, D. (1981). 'Statistics on the Distribution of Income and Wealth in Australia'. Research Paper No. 14, Development Division, Department of Social Security, Canberra.

Jones, F. L. (1975). 'The changing shape of the Australian income distribution, 1914–15 and 1968–69', *Australian Economic History Review*, 15: 21–34.

Leigh, A. (2004). 'Deriving Long-Run Inequality Series from Tax Data', Discussion Paper 476, Australian National University Centre for Economic Policy Research.

Lombard, M. (1991). 'Income Distribution in Australia, 1983–89', *Economic Papers*, 10: 52–63.

McLean, I. W. (1988). 'Unequal Sacrifice: Distributional Aspects of Depression and recovery in Australia', in R. G. Gregory and N. G. Butlin (eds.) *Recovery from the Depression: Australia and the World Economy in the 1930s*. Cambridge: Cambridge University Press, pp. 335–56.

McLean, I. and Richardson, S. (1986). 'More or less equal?', *Economic Record*, 62: 67–81.

Maddock, R., Olekalns, N., Ryan, J., and Vickers, M. (1984). 'The Distribution of Income and Wealth in Australia, 1914–1980: An Introduction and Bibliography', Source Paper No. 1, Department of Economic History, Australian National University.

Mauldon, F. R. E., Giblin, L. F., and Clark, C. (1938). 'Australia's National Income', *Economic Record*, 14: 204–19.

Piketty, T. and Saez, T. (2001). 'Income Inequality in the United States, 1913–1998'. Working Paper 8467, NBER.

—— —— (2003). 'Income Inequality in the United States, 1913–1998', *Quarterly Journal of Economics*, 118(1): 1–39.

Saez, E. and Veall, M. (2003). 'The Evolution of High Incomes in Canada, 1920–2000', Working Paper 9607, NBER.

—— —— (2005). 'The Evolution of High Incomes in Northern America: Lessons from Canadian Evidence', *American Economic Review*, 95: 831–49.

Saunders, P. (1993). 'Longer run changes in the distribution of income in Australia', *Economic Record*, 69: 353–66.

—— (1997). 'Economic Adjustment and Distributional Change: Income Inequality and Poverty in Australia in the 1980s', in P. Gottschalk, B. Gustaffson, and E. Palmer (eds.) *Changing Patterns in the Distribution of Economic Welfare*. Cambridge: Cambridge University Press.

—— (1998). 'Household Budgets and Income Distribution over the Longer Term: Evidence for Australia'. SPRC Discussion Paper No 89, University of New South Wales.

—— (2004). 'Examining Recent Changes in Income Distribution in Australia', *Economic and Labour Relations Review*, 15: 51–73.

—— H. Stott and G. Hobbes (1991). 'Income Inequality in Australia and New Zealand: International Comparisons and Recent Trends', *Review of Income and Wealth*, 37: 63–79.

Smith, J. P. (2001). 'Progressivity of the Commonwealth Personal Income Tax, 1917–97', *Australian Economic Review*, 34: 263–78.

Ternowetsky, G. W. (1979). 'Taxation Statistics and Income Inequality in Australia: 1955–56 to 1974–75', *A.N.Z.J.S.*, 15: 16–24.

United Nations (1950). *National Income Statistics of Various Countries, 1938–48*. New York: United Nations.

United Nations (1955). *National Income Statistics*. New York: United Nations.

United Nations (1958). *Yearbook of National Accounts Statistics*. New York: United Nations.

United Nations (1966). *Yearbook of National Accounts Statistics*. New York: United Nations.

8

The Distribution of Top Incomes in New Zealand[1]

A. B. Atkinson and A. Leigh

8.1 INTRODUCTION

In 1900, New Zealanders were richer than the citizens of any other country except Britain. Yet over the course of the century, living standards in New Zealand steadily slipped behind many other developed nations, particularly after the Second World War. The immediate post-war decades saw government policies that maintained low unemployment, but did not lead to high levels of economic growth. These policies changed radically in the last two decades of the twentieth century, as New Zealand experienced substantial free market reforms. Tariff reductions, privatisations, deregulation of the labour market, and welfare cuts were notable features of this period (see Evans et al. 1996). At the same time, as has been widely reported, in these recent years income inequality has increased in New Zealand. According to *The Social Report 2005*, 'income inequality rose between 1988 and 1991, then plateaued, and has been rising since 1994' (Ministry of Social Development 2005: 62). Such conclusions are based on the Household Economic Surveys[2] (see, for example, Snively 1990; Dixon 1998; Statistics New Zealand 1999; Bakker and Creedy 1999; O'Dea 2000; Hyslop and Maré 2001 and 2005; Podder and Chatterjee 2002;) and on Census of Population data (for example, Easton 1996; Martin 1997).

[1] We are most grateful to those who have helped us secure access to the necessary data and publications. Specific thanks are due to Sandra Watson of Te Tari Taake/Inland Revenue, Michael Dunn, formerly with Te Tari Taake/Inland Revenue, Claire Stent, Lisa Hampl and Stephen Flanagan of Te Tari Tatau/Statistics New Zealand, David Rea of Te Manatū Whakahiato Ora/Ministry of Social Development, Patricia Gordon of the Remuneration Authority, Malcolm Macaskill of the State Services Commission, Corrine Cromar and Ruth Graham of the Parliamentary Library, and Sherry Maier of Sheffield Consulting. Thanks to Stephen Waldegrave for giving us a copy of his unpublished review of the literature on income distribution in New Zealand, on which we have drawn heavily. We have also benefited from comments and advice from Simon Chapple, Brian Easton, Nick Carroll, David Haugh, Gary Hawke, Dave Maré, Thomas Piketty, Emmanuel Saez, Suzanne Snively, Charles Waldegrave, and seminar participants at the Australian National University, Harvard University, Nuffield College, Oxford, and the University of Melbourne. None of the above is responsible for the conclusions reached in the chapter.

[2] Previously known as the Household Expenditure and Income Survey, this survey samples approximately 3000 households annually.

The top of the income distribution has been particularly affected. *The Social Report* goes on to say, 'Most of the observed increase in inequality has been due to a larger overall rise in incomes for those in the top 20 percent.' It is with the top of the distribution that the present chapter is concerned. It uses tabulated data from New Zealand's personal income tax to study the long-run evolution of the income distribution, focusing on the top income groups, not just the top 20% but the top 1% and even smaller groups at the very top. The personal income tax was first introduced in 1892. From 1921 onwards, taxation statistics were tabulated separately for individuals, excluding companies, and thus allowing estimates of the personal distribution. We present estimates from that year to 2002.[3] Our data cover, therefore, over three-quarters of a century.

In using the income tax data, we are following in the steps of Easton (1983), who employed annual income tax data from 1945–46 to 1976–77 to calculate a Pareto coefficient for the upper tail, the income shares of different decile groups, and the Gini coefficient. We have followed a similar method, in that we use as a control total the total population aged 15+, but we differ in that we have constructed an independent control total for income, rather than use that reported in the tax statistics. The latter was affected by the introduction of PAYE on 1 April 1958, and Easton shows a break in the series in that year.

The methods used here are described in Section 8.2, and in Section 8.3 we consider a number of caveats that have to be entered regarding the use of income tax data. The findings are presented in Section 8.4, and assessed in Section 8.5.

8.2 DATA DESCRIPTION

The basic data from the personal income tax statistics consist of tabulations of incomes by income ranges, giving the total number of taxpayers and the total amount of income declared. The sources for each year from 1921 to 2002 are given in Appendix 8A; the Appendix also explains why no data are available for 1931, 1932, 1941–44 and 1961. Even with these omissions, we have 75 annual observations, which is a long series and one that spans much of the century with the exception of the period before and during the First World War.

Definition of the Tax Unit and Control Total

To what do the data relate? Until 1953, the tax unit in New Zealand was defined as a single adult or a married couple living together. Dependent children were treated as being in the same tax unit as their parents, unless the children had an

[3] The New Zealand tax year begins on 1 April. Throughout this paper, any reference to a tax year should be taken to refer to the start of the tax year—for example, the 1980 tax year is the tax year starting 1 April 1980, and ending 31 March 1981.

independent income, in which case they formed their own tax unit. We use as our control total for 1921–52 the total adult population, defined as number of people aged 15 and over, and from this subtract the number of married females. The sources are given in Appendix 8B. This total is too high to the extent that people aged 15 and over are still dependent, and too low to the extent that children aged under 15 have an independent income. The use of a control total for a fixed date means that we ignore people who appear in the tax statistics for part of the year: those entering the labour force, those dying, and those migrating. Part-year incomes are by definition less likely to appear in the top income groups.[4]

From the tax year 1953–54 onwards, the tax unit became the individual, and the control total used from that point onwards is simply the total number of people aged 15 and over. There is therefore a break in comparability in 1953: the series before that date relates to tax units, and the figures from 1953 relate to individuals. Consideration of different assumptions about the joint distribution of income suggests that the switch to independent assessment may either raise or lower the top shares. As shown in Chapter 2, where all rich people are either unmarried or have partners with zero income, the share rises on moving to independent assessment, since we have to include a larger number of observations in order to arrive at a given percentage of the population. But if, at the other extreme, all rich tax units consist of couples with equal incomes, then the same amount (and share) of total income is received by a larger fraction of the population (since not everyone is married), so that the measured share falls. It is not therefore easy to suggest a correction, and the necessary adjustment may well have changed over the century. In earlier parts of the century, the former assumption may have been more appropriate. In accounting for a change in the filing rules that occurred in the US in 1948, Piketty and Saez (2003) adjust the US estimates, increasing the recorded income shares by 'about 2.5%' for the earlier period 1913–47 (Piketty and Saez 2001: 35n). Towards the end of the century, incomes may have been less unequally distributed within the tax unit. In particular, increasing female labour force participation is likely to have had a major impact. Female labour force participation increased from 29.6% in 1961 to 57.9% in 1996 (Statistics New Zealand 1999: figure 1.9). We return to the change in unit of analysis in Section 8.4.

In 1999, New Zealand implemented an overhaul of its tax system, extending the process under which, with the longstanding PAYE for wages and salaries, only those taxpayers who receive unusual forms of income (such as self-employment earnings, rental income, or overseas dividends) are required to file a tax return. This reduced substantially the number of returns filed: fewer than 1 million of New Zealand's 3 million taxpayers now file a tax return.[5] However, non-filers

[4] For a discussion of part-year incomes in the UK, see Chapter 4.

[5] The figure of less than one million is those who are required to file an IR3 return. Additionally, about two-thirds of a million New Zealanders are required to verify information on a Personal Tax Summary which is sent to them by the Inland Revenue Department.

remain within the taxation statistics, since their incomes are now reported by their employers or other government agencies. Thus, while the 1999 reforms reduced the number of New Zealanders who file tax returns, the total number of people included in the taxation statistics has expanded significantly. As a result, the ratio of the number of taxpayers to the over-15 population is virtually 1. Indeed in some years it exceeds 1 (see Appendix Table 8B.1). The New Zealand Inland Revenue Department explains this on the basis that the taxpaying population includes a small number of children, as well as any migrant who works in New Zealand at any point in the tax year. Anyone dying in the year is recorded as having a part-year income, as is anyone who enters the taxpaying population mid-way through the year. By contrast, the population statistics are based on calendar year means, and so will invariably miss some migrants, some who die during the year, and some who turn 15 during the year.[6] Where the number of taxpayers is larger than the adult population, we use the number of taxpayers as our population denominator.

The resulting series for the population control totals is given in Appendix Table 8B.1; the series used in our central estimates is shown in bold.

Control Total for Income

What income is covered? How does the total relate to the national accounts aggregates? As in the previous chapter, we are interested in the incomes of *households*, not the wider personal sector, which typically includes non-profit bodies serving persons (such as charities and trade unions) and life assurance and pension funds. We want to use income tax data that relate to persons and not to limited companies. Prior to 1921, individuals and companies cannot be separated in the New Zealand tax tabulations, and we are therefore unable to use data for the first two decades of the century. We are interested in *Gross* income, in the sense of income before tax. We are interested in the total *returnable* income that would enter the tax-base if there were no exemptions (income after subtracting the exemptions is referred to as taxable income).

With this aim in mind, our approach to the control total for income starts from the national accounts totals for household income: i.e. excluding non-household elements, such as charities, life assurance funds, and universities. We then exclude items not included in the tax base, such as imputed rent, and employers' social security contributions. Transfer payments pose particular problems, as they became progressively taxable, beginning with the universal superannuation benefit (a payment to high income aged not eligible for the income tested Age Benefit) from 1951, what is now called New Zealand Superannuation (which combined the universal benefit and Age Benefit) in 1976, the unemployment benefit for single persons in 1979, and then all social security benefits from 1986 (at which time they were grossed up, to leave the net value unchanged for

[6] Email from Sandra Watson, Inland Revenue Department, 7 October 2004.

a person with no other income). We have adopted the simplest procedure in that we have included transfers in the control total throughout the period. This is not entirely satisfactory, but is unlikely to generate any major discontinuity in the estimated top shares.

The method adopted here pre-supposes the existence of national accounts totals for household income. In the case of New Zealand, these exist for recent decades, but we have had to construct our own series for much of the period. This has involved assembling different elements from the official statistics and from academic sources, as described in Appendix 8C. For the earliest years (1921–30) we have resorted to use of GDP to extrapolate backwards. In view of the volatility of GDP at that time,[7] this potentially introduces considerable error, and the estimates of the top shares prior to 1931 should be regarded with particular caution.

The procedure we have adopted is that of working back from the national accounts, rather than forward from the income tax totals, adding an estimated amount for those not covered. (See Chapter 2 for discussion of these two approaches.) It is therefore probable that the totals are too inclusive. Grounds for believing this to be the case are provided by the fact that our New Zealand constructed total, expressed as a percentage of the UN SNA total for household current receipts, is larger than for four other Anglo-Saxon countries: for example, in 1996, the figure was 86%, compared with 83% (Australia), 75% (UK), 72% (Canada), and 62% (US). Earlier we noted that, following the 1999 changes in tax administration, the coverage of people should be virtually 100%. For the four years 1999–2000 to 2002–03, the total income reported in the income tax data was some 90–95% of the national accounts total. In the light of these considerations, we have reduced our calculated totals for all years (1921–2002) by multiplying by 0.95. The resulting series is shown in Appendix Table 8C.1.

8.3 CAVEATS SURROUNDING THE USE OF TAX SOURCES[8]

Changes in taxation legislation occur frequently. It was well put by the New Zealand Census and Statistics Department: 'income-tax law is dynamic rather than static and there are few years in which amendments, some major and others minor, to the law have not affected the statistics' (1953: p. 4).[9] They go on to reassure the reader that 'while a comparison of the results for one particular year with those for another year may be uncertain without an examination of the law applying to those years, the broad picture presented by the tables is significant'.

[7] The estimates of Easton (1997: Appendix 5) show nominal GDP as falling from $366m in 1928–29 to $235m in 1932–33.

[8] The limitations of the income tax data are discussed by Easton (1983: pp. 14–16).

[9] For a description of tax changes up to 1968, see the Ross Committee on Taxation (1968). We are grateful for Brian Easton for this reference.

We have already referred to three important changes in the New Zealand income tax system: the change from joint to individual filing in 1953, the decision to tax Universal superannuation payments in 1951, and the taxation of other benefits in 1986. However, there are other potential differences and these can affect the comparability of the estimates across time.

Some changes extend the tax base. For example in 1940, the New Zealand Government brought within returnable income the proprietary income received by the shareholders in closely held companies (not more than five shareholders). This was partially reversed in 1953, from which date only dividends paid were included. With respect to capital gains, New Zealand is unusual among developed nations for not having a separate capital gains tax. Instead, the extent to which capital gains are brought within the scope of taxable income has evolved steadily over time—leading to some anomalous results.[10] A further source of difference, important in the present context, is the tax treatment of farming and other primary producers.

Many of the changes in tax law affected the coverage of the population. Some reduced coverage. For example, in 1959 a special exemption from social security income tax was introduced that had the effect of eliminating the liability for those with small incomes to file tax returns; this mainly affected those in receipt of purely investment income (New Zealand Department of Statistics 1968: 8). However, most changes have expanded the coverage of the statistics, such as the move to PAYE taxation in 1958. This led the coverage of individuals to jump from 53% to 68% (see the final column of Appendix Table 8B.1). This may have caused a discontinuity in our series, although the top incomes are less likely to have been affected,[11] and our control totals do not jump. With the reduction in the tax threshold relative to average incomes, the income tax has become a mass tax. In 1924, only 9% of New Zealanders aged 15 and over filed a tax return, but since the 1999 tax filing reforms, the coverage has been close to 100%.

The coverage of the statistics is also affected by changes in administrative practice, particularly the form in which information is published. Most importantly for our purposes, the statistics for 1921–40 are based upon assessable income, which excludes certain income that is not included in the tax base but is taken into account in determining the tax rate. The statistics are then unavailable from 1941–44, and from 1945 onwards, our estimates relate to total income.

The interpretation of the data not only depends on the *personal* tax law. Of particular significance are changes in the taxation of *corporations*. For shareholders, the relative attractions of dividend income and capital gains can be

[10] Robin Oliver of the Inland Revenue Department, gives the following example:

An entity holding a portfolio of shares, such as a mutual fund, is usually taxed on profits on realisation. The rationale is that shares held in a portfolio are on revenue account because selling shares is a normal part of the business of such an entity. A small investor holding shares directly, on the other hand, can realise a tax-free capital gain. (Oliver 2000)

[11] It may be noted that many of those entering the statistics in 1958 were women: the percentage of women rose from 23.9% to 32.8% according to Easton (1983: table 10.3).

significantly affected by the company tax regime. One key feature is the extent to which there is an imputation system, under which part of any corporation tax paid is treated as a pre-payment of personal income tax. Payment of dividends can be made more attractive by the introduction of an imputation system, in place of a 'classical' system where dividends are subject to both corporation and personal income tax. Insofar as capital gains are missing from the estimates but dividends are covered, a switch towards (away from) dividend payment will increase (reduce) the apparent shares. The effect of the introduction of imputation in New Zealand in 1989 is very evident—see below.

Similarly, when it was announced that the marginal tax rate on earnings over $60,000 would be raised from 33% to 39% in the 2000 tax year, many taxpayers took the opportunity to realize business earnings in the 1999 tax year, significantly boosting top income shares in that year, and perhaps to a lesser extent also in the 1998 tax year. Although the increase was not legislated until 2000, the Labour Party had made clear in late 1998 that if elected, it planned to raise the top marginal tax rate from 33% to 39% (for an example of commentary on Labour's plans during that period, see Main 1998). The Labour Party easily beat the incumbent National Party in November 1999, a result that was widely predicted by political pundits (see Bennett 2000).

The caveats above suggest that these findings should be interpreted carefully, and that the figures for individual years may be particularly affected by fiscal and other changes. Notwithstanding this, a number of these changes do not affect the shares of top incomes. The extension of coverage for example may bring new taxpayers into the statistics, changing total recorded income, but the purpose of using control totals is to ensure that such changes do not affect the identification of the top X% (assuming that they are already covered) or their calculated share.

8.4 TOP INCOMES IN NEW ZEALAND

Table 8.1 shows the estimated shares of the top income groups for the full period 1921–2002, while Figures 8.1 and 8.2 present the results graphically. The table gives the shares of the top 20%, 10%, 5%, 1%, 0.5%, and 0.1%. The last of these groups is small: 3000 people or fewer. For this reason, we do not give estimates for any smaller group. Moreover, from 1989 the top 0.1% falls within the open top interval of the available tabulations, and we do not here make any attempt at extrapolation. Figure 8.1 shows the shares for the top 1%, 0.5%, and 0.1%. Figure 8.2 is different in that it shows the shares of the 'next 4%' and 'second vintile': i.e. those in the top 5% but not the top 1%, and those in the top 10% but not the top 5%, respectively. This allows us to see the extent to which experience differed within the top 10%. It is important to note that there are two major breaks in continuity, marked by heavy vertical lines in Figures 1 and 2. The estimates for 1921 to 1940 relate to assessable income, which excludes certain income not included in the tax base but taken into account in determining the tax rate; those

Table 8.1 Top income shares, New Zealand 1921–2002

	20%	10%	5%	1%	0.5%	0.1%
1921	—	—	25.39	11.34	7.82	3.13
1922	—	—	23.84	10.47	7.22	2.89
1923	—	—	24.72	10.94	7.54	2.96
1924	—	33.73	24.47	10.89	7.51	2.91
1925	—	34.97	25.16	11.08	7.60	2.92
1926	—	35.73	25.18	10.84	7.36	2.79
1927	—	35.69	24.99	10.64	7.20	2.69
1928	—	35.85	25.42	11.47	7.98	3.17
1929	—	36.54	25.48	10.99	7.48	2.88
1930	—	38.38	26.17	10.57	7.06	2.60
1931	—	—	—	—	—	—
1932	—	—	—	—	—	—
1933	—	38.13	25.99	10.86	7.39	2.81
1934	—	37.97	25.64	10.42	6.96	2.49
1935	—	—	24.65	10.36	6.93	2.77
1936	49.98	34.49	24.15	10.66	7.28	2.81
1937	45.03	30.36	20.51	8.33	5.48	1.91
1938	41.74	27.64	18.47	7.32	4.79	1.66
1939	44.55	29.72	19.92	7.85	5.15	1.86
1940	43.42	28.67	19.16	7.42	4.83	1.67
1941	—	—	—	—	—	—
1942	—	—	—	—	—	—
1943	—	—	—	—	—	—
1944	—	—	—	—	—	—
1945	38.00	25.26	17.08	6.88	4.49	1.60
1946	40.12	27.10	18.54	7.50	4.90	1.76
1947	41.75	28.44	19.54	7.72	5.03	1.77
1948	42.50	28.80	19.67	7.74	5.09	1.87
1949	43.21	29.56	20.32	8.02	5.26	1.92
1950	43.77	31.32	22.59	9.44	6.17	2.23
1951	43.17	29.32	20.11	7.88	5.11	1.85
1952	44.33	30.14	20.59	7.94	5.11	1.83
1953	53.17	35.93	24.83	9.90	6.41	2.33
1954	52.90	35.40	24.29	9.54	6.15	2.20
1955	51.98	34.13	22.89	8.76	5.61	1.98
1956	52.99	35.04	23.53	8.91	5.74	2.10
1957	51.63	33.94	22.69	8.65	5.61	2.00
1958	49.87	31.93	20.66	7.26	4.51	1.48
1959	50.44	32.65	21.37	7.60	4.77	1.63
1960	50.01	32.17	20.93	7.44	4.71	1.66
1961	—	—	—	—	—	—
1962	50.15	31.97	20.59	7.25	4.60	1.61
1963	50.08	31.98	20.67	7.29	4.63	—
1964	50.66	32.32	20.85	7.42	4.82	1.80
1965	49.37	31.06	19.69	6.72	4.23	1.43
1966	49.19	30.72	19.30	6.56	4.12	1.38
1967	49.43	30.91	19.39	6.59	4.14	1.41
1968	49.73	31.15	19.59	6.72	4.23	1.44
1969	49.69	31.02	19.47	6.70	4.23	1.45
1970	49.69	30.76	19.11	6.64	4.21	1.48

1971	49.47	30.66	19.01	6.43	4.00	1.31
1972	49.61	31.29	19.90	7.08	4.47	1.52
1973	50.35	31.84	20.35	7.47	4.79	1.69
1974	50.84	32.02	20.38	7.55	4.95	1.68
1975	48.40	29.98	18.70	6.56	4.20	1.45
1976	47.82	31.10	20.36	7.48	4.74	1.55
1977	46.58	28.86	17.89	6.13	3.86	1.31
1978	46.89	29.10	17.99	6.12	3.85	1.29
1979	45.69	28.22	17.29	5.77	3.62	1.21
1980	46.80	28.83	17.51	5.65	3.52	1.18
1981	46.53	28.48	17.15	5.50	3.44	1.14
1982	47.03	28.70	17.24	5.49	3.41	1.14
1983	47.09	28.92	17.52	5.68	3.56	1.22
1984	45.97	28.19	17.09	5.60	3.53	1.22
1985	44.90	27.57	16.74	5.51	3.48	1.19
1986	43.45	26.51	15.85	4.88	3.01	1.00
1987	42.87	26.61	16.29	5.48	3.52	1.27
1988	42.16	26.26	16.08	5.35	3.38	1.16
1989	44.34	28.34	17.97	6.59	4.33	—
1990	47.42	31.12	20.41	8.21	5.66	—
1991	48.13	31.48	20.53	7.96	5.37	—
1992	49.51	32.49	21.32	8.40	5.71	—
1993	49.87	32.99	21.86	8.76	5.94	—
1994	49.19	32.86	22.06	9.00	6.12	—
1995	48.68	32.62	21.97	8.98	6.11	—
1996	48.00	32.18	21.69	8.92	6.12	—
1997	48.39	32.57	22.03	9.16	6.32	—
1998	50.40	34.39	23.58	10.21	7.23	—
1999	54.90	38.68	27.74	13.77	—	—
2000	48.97	32.26	21.20	8.25	5.50	—
2001	49.55	32.79	21.76	8.76	5.98	—
2002	49.86	32.86	21.79	8.86	6.09	—

Note: Estimates upto 1940 relate to assessable income, afterwards to total income. Estimates upto 1952 relate to tax units, afterwards to individuals.

from 1945 relate to total income. The estimates before 1953 relate to tax units, whereas those from 1953 onwards are for individuals only.

Beginning with the inter-war period, we can see that the share of the top 1% is estimated to be in excess of 10% from 1921 to 1936. In other words, the members of the top 1% had on average more than ten times their proportionate share of total income. The top 0.5% had 7% or more, and the top 0.1% an estimated share of 2.5% or more, giving them at least 25 times their proportionate share. These shares were broadly stable over the 1920s and the first half of the 1930s, but fell sharply in 1937–38, leaving the share of the top 1% at around 7.5% in 1940. For those below the top 1%, in the next 4%, there appears to be an inverse-U shape (see Figure 8.2), with a rise at the beginning of the 1930s and a sharper fall starting in 1935. No figure can be given for the second vintile until 1924, but its share shows a similar pattern to that of the next 4%.

The immediate post Second World War period saw the effects of the commodity price boom. According to those tabulating the statistics at the time, 'the increases in the higher income groups in 1950–51 and the decreases in the

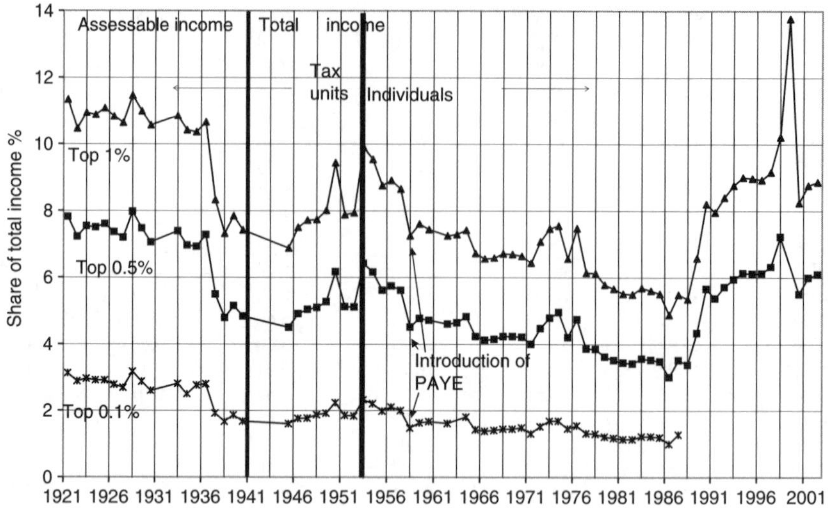

Figure 8.1 Shares of top 1%, 0.5%, and 0.1% in New Zealand, 1921–2002

Source: Table 8.1, this volume.

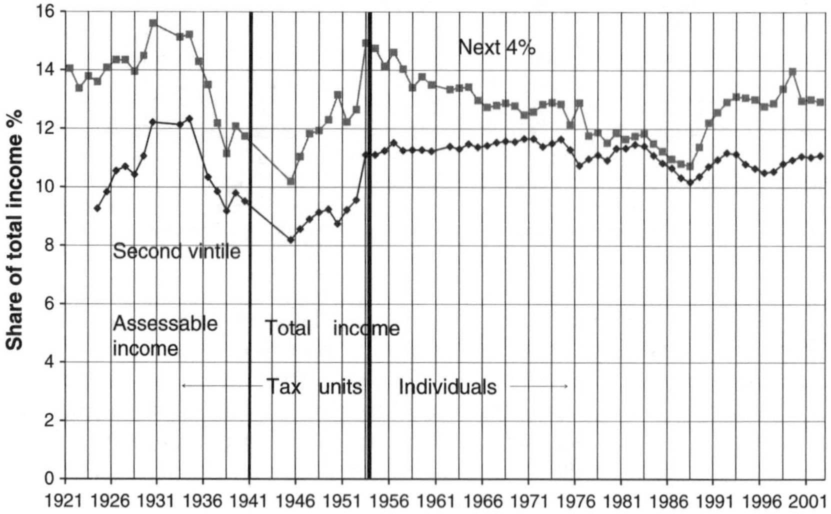

Figure 8.2 Shares of next 4% and second vintile in New Zealand, 1921–2002

Source: Table 8.1, this volume.

same groups in 1951–52 were mainly due to the peak wool prices which sheep farmers received in 1950–51' (*Monthly Abstract of Statistics*, August 1954: 3).[12] (The same pattern can be observed in Australian top incomes—see Chapter 7.)

[12] Although account must be taken of the income smoothing provisions.

It may be noted that the 1950 boom had a more marked impact on the share of the top 1% than on the share of either the top 0.1% or the next 4%, and that the share of the second vintile actually fell in 1950.

The introduction of individual taxation was associated with a jump in the top shares: the share of the top 1% rose by some 2 percentage points, and the share of the top 5% by 4 percentage points. After 1953, the share of the top 1% fell substantially: it nearly halved in the next 30 years. The share of the top 0.1% similarly halved. As noted earlier, the introduction of PAYE in 1958 may have affected the estimates, but if we subtract the difference between 1958 and 1957, this still leaves a sharp reduction in the top shares. The share of the next 4% was reduced less proportionately than the share of the top 1%, although it still fell by 3–4 percentage points (allowing for the possible 1958 break). In contrast, the share of the next vintile was not much reduced, remaining broadly constant before falling a little in the 1980s: it remained in excess of 10%. There was a change in the shape of the distribution, not just a uniform scaling-down of all shares. In this connection, it is interesting to look at Figure 8.3, which charts the top 1% share against two comparison groups—the salary earned by a judge on the High Court (the Supreme Court until 1980) and the basic salary paid to a Member of Parliament—both expressed as a fraction of average earnings. More detail on these measures is set out in Appendix 8D. The judges' pay would have placed them in the top 1% and the salary shows some, but not all, of the same changes as the share of the top 1%. In contrast, parliamentary salaries as a percentage of average earnings showed little variation over this period. This is consistent with MPs being in the 'next 4%'. The changes recorded in Figure 8.1 for the top 1% and above appear to reflect specific factors affecting the very top of the income distribution, rather than a more general reduction in income differentials.

After 1986, the top shares recovered the ground lost since 1953. This is clearly the case for the top 1% and top 0.5%. In the mid-1980s, the top 1% had on average around 5 times their proportionate share of total income; by the mid-1990s this figure had become more like 9 times, and it remains around that value in 2002. From 1986 to 2002, the top 0.5% doubled its share, which in 2002 was virtually the same as that in 1953. We have been unable to locate data on salaries at the very top, but a survey by Sheffield Remuneration Survey found that CEO salaries rose by 29% from 1996–2002, while labour costs across the economy rose only 20% over the same period.[13] This rise in CEO salaries might have been part of the explanation for the increased income share of the richest. For the next 4% there was also a recovery in the share of income, although it ended up some 2 percentage points lower than in 1953. For the second vintile, in contrast, the series is virtually flat, as is the relative wage of MPs in Figure 8.3.

[13] CEO salary data provided by Sherry Maier of Sheffield Consulting. Average hourly earnings figures from Quarterly Employment Survey, downloaded from the website of Te Tari Tatau/Statistics New Zealand.

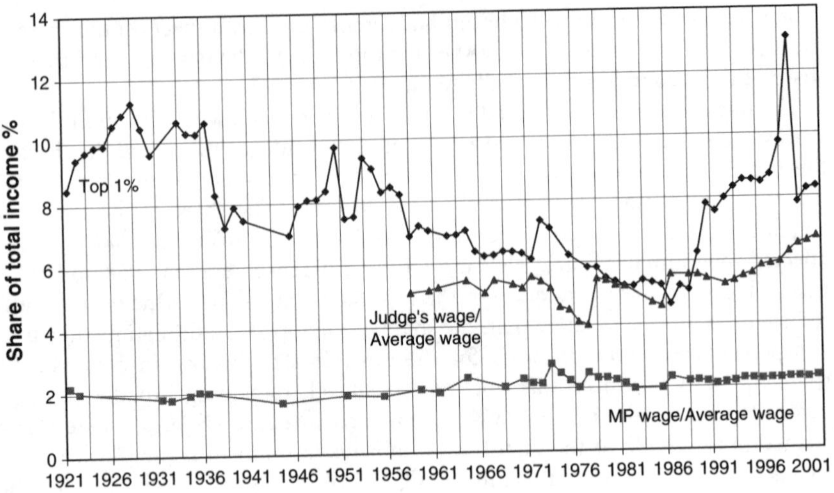

Figure 8.3 Comparison with other top income groups in New Zealand, 1921–2002

Source: Table 8.1 and 8A.4, this volume.

A number of important tax changes occurred in the 1980s and 1990s, which may explain some of the variation in the data. A fringe benefits tax was put in place in 1985 (initially at a rate of 45%), which resulted in executive remuneration that was previously paid in the form of low interest loans, company vehicles or retirement income schemes being switched to being paid as salary. Another change was the introduction of dividend imputation in 1989, allowing income to be released in the form of dividends without the risk of double taxation. It was also pre-announced that the top individual rate would be reduced to the company tax rate in 1990, causing a postponement of payments out of company income until 1990. As we have explained in the previous section, similar anticipation of tax changes is likely to have caused the sharp spike in top income shares is observed in 1998–9, and may have caused the 2000 figure to be depressed. Since these observations are clearly misleading, in some of the following analysis we omit the years 1998, 1999, and 2000.

In their analysis of changes in income distribution over the tax years 1983–97, Hyslop and Maré (2001) conclude that most of the increase in inequality across New Zealand households occurred in the 1980s, with only a modest rise taking place in the 1990s. Our data are consistent with that pattern, in the sense that there has been little rise in top income shares since 1994. If we ignore the three years from 1998–2000, the top income shares in New Zealand did not change a great deal around the turn of the century. The shares of the top 1% and top 0.5% in 2002 were little different from those in 1994.

The conclusions for percentiles, shown in Table 8.2, largely mirror the findings for income shares. In the 1920s, to belong to the top 1%, one needed an income of at least 5.5 times the mean. To belong to the top 0.1%, some 700 taxpayers, one needed an income about 18 times the mean. These numbers had fallen to 4.5 and

Table 8.2 Top income percentiles (% mean), New Zealand 1921–2002

	20%	10%	5%	1%	0.5%	0.1%
1921	—	—	2.59	5.40	9.06	17.78
1922	—	—	2.41	5.45	7.92	17.44
1923	—	—	2.49	5.67	8.20	18.53
1924	—	0.79	2.46	5.67	8.02	18.31
1925	—	1.06	2.53	5.83	8.22	18.38
1926	—	1.75	2.64	5.86	8.25	17.89
1927	—	1.85	2.61	5.81	8.16	17.25
1928	—	1.80	2.54	5.84	8.21	19.50
1929	—	1.91	2.67	5.94	8.23	17.91
1930	—	2.25	2.93	6.03	8.49	17.01
1931	—	—	—	—	—	—
1932	—	—	—	—	—	—
1933	—	2.10	2.85	5.91	8.41	17.84
1934	—	2.14	2.86	5.95	8.28	17.01
1935	—	—	2.65	5.69	8.38	12.44
1936	1.25	1.84	2.44	5.68	7.98	17.52
1937	1.30	1.77	2.29	4.83	6.81	12.99
1938	1.35	1.65	2.13	4.33	6.02	11.38
1939	1.38	1.74	2.28	4.71	6.11	11.70
1940	1.33	1.70	2.22	4.62	5.72	11.33
1941	—	—	—	—	—	—
1942	—	—	—	—	—	—
1943	—	—	—	—	—	—
1944	—	—	—	—	—	—
1945	1.14	1.46	1.90	3.97	5.60	10.51
1946	1.15	1.50	2.01	4.54	6.06	11.36
1947	1.18	1.53	2.14	4.80	6.33	11.72
1948	1.21	1.60	2.16	4.73	6.28	11.67
1949	1.20	1.60	2.25	4.77	6.54	12.12
1950	1.08	1.48	2.17	5.67	7.65	14.26
1951	1.22	1.61	2.20	4.85	6.47	11.63
1952	1.26	1.65	2.29	5.01	6.55	11.69
1953	1.54	1.97	2.65	6.13	8.11	14.55
1954	1.57	1.99	2.59	6.05	7.86	14.01
1955	1.60	2.03	2.60	5.60	7.26	12.57
1956	1.60	2.03	2.70	5.67	7.29	12.71
1957	1.58	2.00	2.61	5.42	7.04	12.83
1958	1.61	2.04	2.58	4.97	6.20	10.30
1959	1.59	2.02	2.61	5.13	6.44	10.78
1960	1.60	2.02	2.58	4.95	6.20	10.47
1961	—	—	—	—	—	—
1962	1.63	2.06	2.60	4.81	6.01	10.34
1963	1.63	2.05	2.58	4.80	5.96	—
1964	1.64	2.08	2.62	4.69	5.94	10.83
1965	1.64	2.07	2.57	4.48	5.66	9.50
1966	1.66	2.08	2.59	4.38	5.55	9.31
1967	1.66	2.09	2.61	4.43	5.55	9.32
1968	1.67	2.10	2.62	4.48	5.69	9.49
1969	1.67	2.11	2.59	4.38	5.67	9.45
1970	1.69	2.14	2.58	4.30	5.55	9.38

(contd.)

Table 8.2 (*contd.*)

	20%	10%	5%	1%	0.5%	0.1%
1971	1.68	2.13	2.60	4.36	5.51	9.15
1972	1.63	2.08	2.56	4.66	5.99	9.46
1973	1.64	2.10	2.57	4.73	6.20	11.39
1974	1.68	2.12	2.65	4.62	5.93	11.48
1975	1.64	2.07	2.51	4.08	5.47	9.65
1976	1.52	1.91	2.50	4.53	6.49	10.44
1977	1.57	2.01	2.44	4.06	5.18	8.72
1978	1.57	2.03	2.48	4.04	5.19	8.77
1979	1.54	2.00	2.43	3.87	4.90	8.26
1980	1.58	2.07	2.52	3.88	4.81	7.96
1981	1.58	2.07	2.50	3.73	4.70	7.75
1982	1.60	2.10	2.53	3.77	4.67	7.71
1983	1.59	2.09	2.53	3.84	4.77	8.09
1984	1.55	2.04	2.45	3.75	4.68	8.09
1985	1.51	1.99	2.39	3.66	4.66	7.79
1986	1.48	1.94	2.37	3.48	4.11	6.79
1987	1.42	1.87	2.30	3.55	4.49	8.08
1988	1.39	1.84	2.28	3.55	4.48	7.74
1989	1.39	1.87	2.33	3.99	5.19	—
1990	1.41	1.92	2.43	4.50	6.10	—
1991	1.44	1.96	2.50	4.55	6.17	—
1992	1.46	2.00	2.54	4.77	6.32	—
1993	1.45	1.99	2.55	4.92	6.63	—
1994	1.40	1.92	2.49	4.96	6.84	—
1995	1.38	1.89	2.48	5.00	6.81	—
1996	1.37	1.86	2.44	4.86	6.69	—
1997	1.36	1.86	2.45	4.92	6.74	—
1998	1.36	1.90	2.53	5.15	7.13	—
1999	1.41	1.92	2.57	5.70	—	—
2000	1.45	1.98	2.52	4.86	6.41	—
2001	1.44	1.98	2.52	4.86	6.54	—
2002	1.47	2.00	2.52	4.81	6.58	—

Note: See note to Table 8.1.

12 by 1940. (It should be noted that the errors of interpolation may be quite large, and that there is considerable year-to-year variation.) The figures for 1959 were not dissimilar, but they fell to 3.5 and 7 by the mid-1980s, only to increase again, so that at the end of the century, one needs around 5 times mean income to belong to the top 1%.

8.5 ASSESSMENT

In assessing the validity of these estimates, we begin with a comparison with other studies of income inequality in New Zealand. We then consider the 'shares within shares', which do not depend on control totals for income, and the associated 'Pareto-Lorenz' coefficients.

Comparison with Other Studies

How do our estimates compare with those of earlier studies? Using data from the census of population, Martin (1997: 30) concluded that the period 1951 to 1991 could be divided into four sub-periods. From the early 1950s to the mid-1970s, the dispersion of income was decreasing slowly; from the mid-1970s to the early 1980s, dispersion was increasing slowly; there then followed a period in the early to mid-1980s when dispersion decreased slowly; finally, from the mid-1980s to the early 1990s, dispersion increased rapidly. The estimates presented in Figure 8.1 follow broadly this pattern, but place the temporary increase in the early rather than the late 1970s. Indeed for the share of the top 0.1%, 0.5%, and 1% our findings are better described as a steady downward trend from 1953 to 1985, with a brief hiatus in the first half of the 1970s. As already noted, the distribution at the very top was moving in a different way from lower parts of the distribution. This is brought out in Figure 8.4 where we show our estimates of the shares of the top 10% (previously shown in components in Figures 8.1 and 8.2) and top 20%.

As explained at the outset, we have followed Easton (1983) in using the income tax data, but our method differs in that we have applied independent control totals for income. As may be seen from Appendix Table 8C.1, in 1953 when Easton's series begins, our control total was some 20% larger than the total reported in the tax statistics (and used by Easton). Over the ensuing 20 years, the proportion fell to under 10%. As a result, our estimates of the top shares are lower than those of Easton, but the difference narrows over the 1950s and 1960s.

The main source used today is the Household Economic Survey (HES). In the right hand part of Figure 8.4, we show the results for the period 1981 to 1997 from the work of Mowbray (2001).[14] These relate to a quite different concept of income: household total income, after taxes, and adjusted for household composition. It is not therefore surprising that both level and time patterns are different. For example, the HES series is virtually flat from 1981 to 1987, whereas our series shows the share of the top 10% falling by some 2 percentage points. Nonetheless, the two sources show the same pattern of a sharp rise at the end of the 1980s.

Podder and Chatterjee (2002) make a comparison between their estimates of the share of the top 5% based on the HES and those derived from the income tax returns, referring to the study by Chatterjee and Srivastav (1992), which gave a figure for the share of the top 5% of income-tax payers of 14.3% in 1983/4. They cite evidence from the tax data supplied by Statistics New Zealand that shows the share increasing to 21.1% by 1991/92 and 22.7% by 1995/96. As they comment,

[14] Easton (1999) explains that the March 1996 HES, or the HES 1995/6, covers households interviewed between April 1995 and March 1996, and that they reported their income for the previous year. The observations are therefore intermediate in timing between those reported from the tax data. Easton notes that the HES procedure 'gives an average of the incomes for the year ended September 1995' (1999: 56, n. 1), and we have therefore allocated the HES observation to the year 1995 on the basis that the greater part of this average lies in this year.

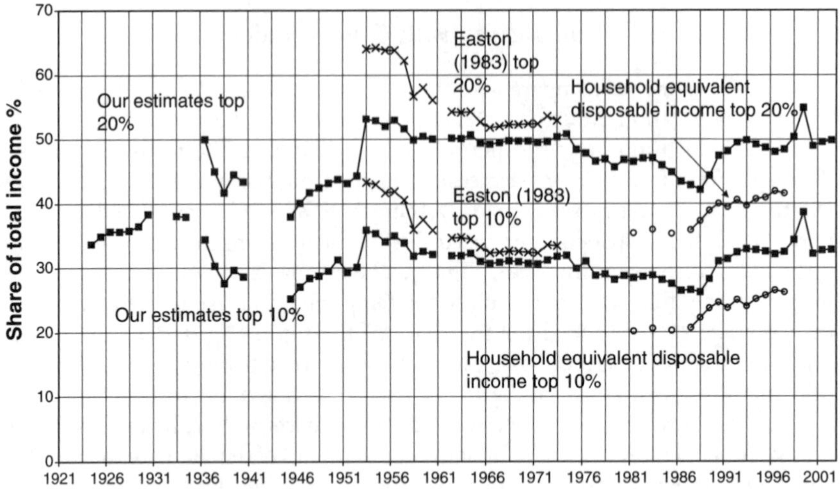

Figure 8.4 Comparison with other studies of New Zealand: shares of top 10% and 20%, 1921–2002

Source: Table 8.1, this volume; Easton 1983; Mowbray 2001.

'this represents an increase of nearly 59% over the 12-year period—more than double the increase when measured with Survey data' (2002: p. 14). Their own data shows the share of the top 5% rising from 15.3% in 1983/84 to 17.0% in 1991/92 and 19.0% in 1995/96. The estimates both relate to gross income, but the Podder and Chatterjee figures take the household unit, whereas the tax data relate to individuals. We should not therefore expect the figures or the trends to be the same, but this cannot explain the large discrepancy. In fact, the difference lies in the fact that the income tax estimates cited are based on the total number of taxpayers, not the total adult population, and on the total income reported in the tax returns, not on total incomes. Our estimates in Table 8.1 show the share of the top 5% rising from 17.5% in 1983 to 20.5% in 1991 and 22.0% in 1995, a rise of 26%, which is close to that recorded in the HES estimates of Podder and Chatterjee (2002: table 1).

Shares Within Shares

We have suggested above that there was a change in the shape of the distribution, not simply redistribution between rich and poor. This can be investigated further by looking at the 'shares within shares': for example, the share of the top 1% within the total income of the top 10%. This is shown in Figure 8.5, together with the overall share of the top 10% (shown without year markers). One advantage of this calculation is that it does not involve the control total for income, allowing some test of the sensitivity of the findings. As we stressed in Section 8.2, the control totals must be regarded with considerable caution, particularly those for

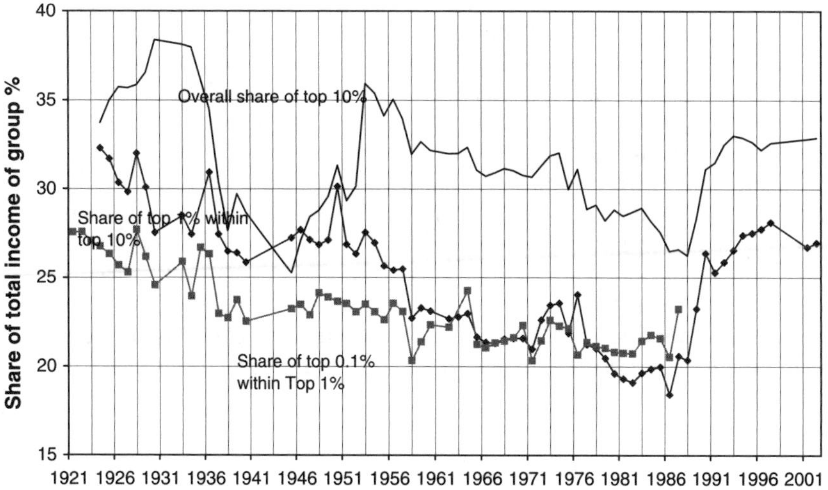

Figure 8.5 Shares within shares in New Zealand, 1921–2000

Source: Table 8.1, this volume.

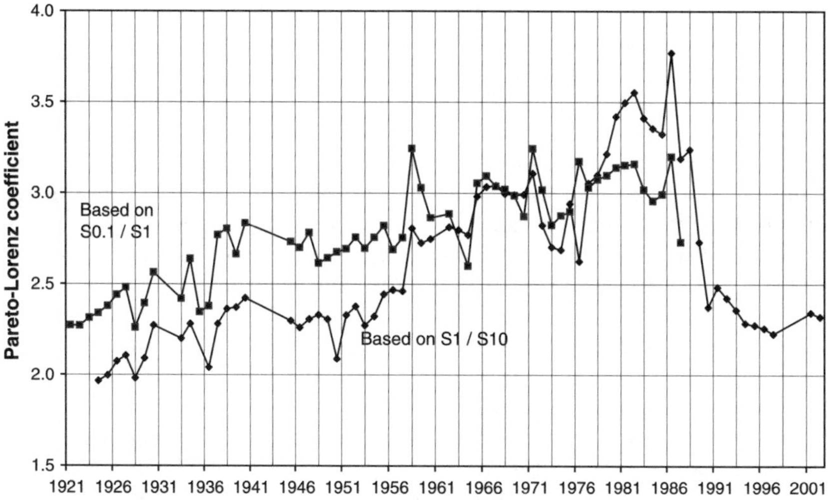

Figure 8.6 Pareto-Lorenz coefficients, New Zealand 1921–2002

Source: Table 8.1, this volume.

the earlier years. We have not shown the estimates for 1998, 1999, and 2000 for the reason discussed above.

The value of the share within share is similar in magnitude, at both the beginning and end of the period, to that of the overall share, but the time path is definitely different. In 1924, the top 1% had some third of the total income of the top 10%. The percentage trended downwards to reach a little more than a quarter in 1940. In

1953, the percentage was 27.5% and then fell, with some ups and downs, to 18% in 1986. The fall was then reversed, the figure reaching 27% again in the 1990s and remaining at around that level—back as it was at the time of the Coronation. The share of the top 0.1% within the top 1% was initially a little lower, and the decline less rapid, so that by the late 1950s the values were similar.

An alternative formulation of the shares within shares is shown in Figure 8.6 in the form of Pareto-Lorenz coefficients, which rise as the shares become less concentrated[15] The Pareto-Lorenz coefficient for the share of the top 0.1% within the top 1% trended fairly steadily upwards from 1921 (2.3) until 1986 (3.2). In 1987, it dropped to 2.7, and the taxation statistics do not allow us to calculate it for subsequent years. The Pareto-Lorenz coefficient for the share of the top 1% within the top 10% peaked in 1986 at 3.8, before declining to 2.3 in 2002, about the same value as in 1930.

8.6 CONCLUSIONS

The research reported in this chapter allows us to place in historical perspective the recent rise in income inequality in New Zealand. The tax data used have evident shortcomings, but they allow us to cover a period of 80 years and to give estimates for individual years. The recent rise in top shares followed a 60 year period in which the income share of the rich had occasionally risen, but had mostly been on a downwards trajectory. There had been a distinct change in the shape of the distribution at the top of the scale, reflected in the rise of the estimated Pareto-Lorenz coefficient from around 2 to around 3.5, a rise that was reversed much more sharply after 1986. The reversal appears, however, to have been a step change, rather than a continuing trend, and top shares in 2002 were little different from those in 1994.

In seeking to understand the underlying causal mechanisms, the reader can readily identify a number of factors specific to the situation of New Zealand. These include the heavy dependence of the economy on agriculture, and the impact of changes in the farm sector, such as its increasingly corporate nature. The recent policy experiments in New Zealand have received much attention (see, for example, Evans et al. 1996). These include, in the late-1980s and early-1990s, the rapid deregulation of the economy. In considering the relative importance of policy changes, as against the structural factors emphasised, for example, by Hyslop and Maré (2005), it is helpful to separate those factors that specifically affect the shares of the top income groups, and those that affect directly the incomes of the rest of the population (and indirectly the to shares). In the latter group would come for instance increased female labour force participation, which is likely to have increased total income without adding proportionately to the top income shares. In the former group come changes in top income tax

[15] Defined as $1/[1 + Log_{10}[S_1/S_{10}]]$

rates. Progressive taxation may have contributed to the fall in top income shares over the 1930s and 1940s, with the top marginal tax rate rising from 25% in 1930 to 65% in 1940, peaking at 77% from 1942–45. Likewise, top tax rates may have been a factor in the growth in top income shares during the late-1980s. Between 1985 and 1989, the top marginal tax rate was halved from 66% to 33%. Lower tax rates have several possible effects—they may induce the rich to work more, they may increase their investment returns, thus boosting the amount they could invest in subsequent years, and they may induce companies to increase top salaries. We have also noted the impact of the taxation of fringe benefits.

The evolution of top income shares in New Zealand over the century is likely to have been affected by what is happening elsewhere—see Atkinson and Leigh (2004). As an English-speaking country, New Zealand CEO salaries were most likely affected by the internationalization of the market for executives. And just as a rapid rise in top US salaries placed upward pressure on top salary income in neighbouring Canada (Saez and Veall in Chapter 6), so the rise in top incomes in Australia, which continued through the 1980s and 1990s, is likely to also have been a factor in the rise of top incomes in New Zealand. The combination of long time series, and of data broadly comparable across countries, promises to provide a valuable source of evidence about the underlying determinants of top income shares.

APPENDIX 8A: SOURCES OF INCOME TAX DATA FOR NEW ZEALAND

The chapter relies solely on tabulated data, which means that we have to interpolate. Typically, for each income range, there is information on the number of taxpayers and the total amount of income declared to the taxation authorities. In order to calculate the shares of specified percentages of the population, we have used the *mean-split histogram*, as discussed in Chapter 2. Gross bounds on the top income shares are obtained by assuming that all of the density is located at the interval mean (lower bound) or that the density is concentrated at the end points (upper bound). Assuming, as seems reasonable in the case of top incomes, that the frequency distribution is non-increasing, then more refined upper and lower bounds for the shares can be calculated; these are limiting forms of the split histogram, with one of the two densities tending to zero or infinity. Guaranteed to lie between these is the histogram split at the interval mean with sections of positive density on either side. We check for each interval whether the non-increasing density assumption is consistent with the interval mean; in the cases where this is not satisfied, and there is a significant difference between the gross bounds, we substitute the lower gross bound. In our main series, we have not interpolated shares that lie in the top open interval. For the percentiles, the same mean-split histogram technique is used, although it should be noted that the refined bounds do not apply in this case (an equalizing mean-preserving transfer can raise the top percentile).

The publications and sources used here are shown in Table 8A.1 Estimates for 1980–2002 are based on data supplied by Te Tari Taake/Inland Revenue, and

Table 8A.1 Sources of income tax data for New Zealand, 1921–2002

Year	Source	Notes
1921–22	*SRPWH* 1922: 150	Total assessable income by range. Data until 1949–50 refer to the assessment year: data for the assessment year 1922–23 is taken to relate mainly to incomes in year 1921–22.
1922–23	*SRPWH* 1923: 154	Assessable income.
1923–24	*SRPWH* 1924: 184	Assessable income.
1924–25	*SRPWH* 1925: 126	Assessable income.
1925–26	*SRPWH* 1926: 122	Assessable income.
1926–27	*SRPWH* 1927: 124	Assessable income.
1927–28	*SRPWH* 1928: 132	Assessable income.
1928–29	*SRPWH* 1929: 132	Assessable income.
1929–30	*SRPWH* 1930: 108	Assessable income.
1930–31	*SRPWH* 1931: 75	Assessable income.
1931–32 & 1932–33	Unavailable	
1933–34	*MAS* Jan 1936: xx	Assessable income.
1934–35	*MAS* Jan 1937: xxvi	Assessable income.
1935–36	*OY* 1940: 774–5	Assessable income; calculated using information on increases; Only 6 ranges.
1936–37	*MAS* Sept 1938: xviii	Assessable income.
1937–38	*MAS* Feb 1940: xi	Assessable income.
1938–39	*MAS* April 1941: 12	Assessable income.
1940–41	*MAS* April 1942: 9	Assessable income.
1941–42 to 1944–45	Unavailable	
1945–46	*IITS* for 1946–47, 1947–48, 1948–49, and 1949–50: 16	Total (returnable) income; assessable income in *OY* 1950: 681; from 1940–41 assessment year, proprietary income of closely held companies included.
1946–47	*MAS* Nov 1949: 2	Total (returnable) income; assessable income in *OY* 1950: 681.
1947–48	*MAS* Aug 1950: 4–5	Total (returnable) income; assessable income in *OY* 1950: 681.
1948–49	*MAS* Oct 1951: 7	Total (returnable) income and assessable income.
1949–50	*IITS* for the Income Year 1949–50: 15	From this year, the data refer to the income year; previous data refer to the assessment year (data for the assessment year T was taken to relate mainly to incomes in year (T-1).
1950–51	*MAS* Sep 1953: 12	
1951–52	*MAS* Aug 1954: 3	
1952–53	*MAS* Sep 1955: 5	
1953–54	*IITS* for the Income Year 1953–54: 16	From this year, aggregated assessments of husband and wife now counted as two assessments; increase for 1952–53 from 612.7k to 641.3k; from this year, company proprietary income excluded and company dividends received included.
1954–55	*IITS* for the Income Year 1954–55: 17	
1955–56	*IITS* for the Income Year 1955–56: 17	
1956–57	*IITS* for the Income Year 1956–57: 17	

1957–58	*IITS* for the Income Year 1957–58: 15	Year of transition to PAYE. All tax for 1957–58 income year remitted in full. Figures for 1957–58 estimated.
1958–59	*IITS* for the Income Year 1958–59: Table 2	
1959–60	*IITS* for the Income Year 1959–60: Table 2	
1960–61	*IITS* or the Income Years 1960–61 and 1961–62: Table 2	
1961–62	Unavailable	
1962–63	*IITS* to 1965–66, Table 8	
1963–64	Supplement to MAS Oct 1967, p 3	First published in $.
1964–65	*IITS* to 1966–67, Table 1	
1965–66	*IITS* to 1967–68, Table 1	
1966–67	*IITS* to 1968–69, Table 1	
1967–68	*IITS* to 1969–70, Table 1	
1968–69	*IITS* to 1970–71, Table 1	
1969–70	*IITS* to 1971–72, Table 1	
1970–71	*IITS* to 1972–73, Table 1	
1971–72	*IITS* for the Income Year 1971–72, Table 1	
1972–73	*IITS* to 1975–76, Table 1	
1973–74	*IITS* to 1977, Table 1	
1974–75	*OY* 1979, page 692	
1975–76	*IITS* to 1979, Table 1	
1976–77	*OY* 1979, page 692	
1977–78	*IITS* 1977–78, Table 1	
1978–79	*IITS* 1978–79, Table 1	
1979–80	*IITS* 1979–80, Table 1	
1980–81 to 2002–03	Computer file supplied by Inland Revenue	Data supplied on 30 September 2004.

Note: SRPWH denotes the *Statistical Report on Prices, Wage-Rates and Hours.* OY denotes *The New Zealand Official Yearbook*; MAS denotes *Monthly Abstract of Statistics*; IITS denotes *Income(s) and Income Tax Statistics for the Income Year.*

show the distribution of income broken down into some 40–60 ranges, with the top interval in 2002 starting at an annual income of $200,000 (0.4 percent of taxpayers were in this band). Figures for 2002 are progress totals, based only on data available to the Inland Revenue Department as at 16 September 2004.

Prior to 1980, information on the distribution of persons by total income was published regularly in the publication *Income(s) and Income Tax Statistics for the Income Year*, referred to here as IITS. The year in the title referred either to the year covered by the full survey (e.g. *(Report on the) Income(s) and Income Tax Statistics for the Income Year 1957–58)*, or the year to which the data had been projected using a preliminary set of returns (e.g. *Incomes and Income Tax Statistics to 1966–67)*. The latter type of publication, which included information on income trends, is illustrated by *Incomes and Income Statistics to 1972–73*, containing final data for the 1970–71 income year. The next publication was in fact *Statistics of Incomes and Income Tax for the Income Year 1971–2*, containing data for that year (1971–72). The data were also published in Supplements to the *Monthly Abstract of Statistics* or the *Monthly Abstract of Statistics* (MAS) itself: for example, the final estimates for 1964–65 were published in the MAS for November–December 1968. Figures for 1921–30 were published in the *Statistical Report on Prices, Wage-Rates and Hours* (SRPWH).

The statistics are based on a sample of 5% (10% from 1945–46 to 1967–68) with a complete enumeration of all persons with incomes above a certain level ($8,000 in 1968–69—see IITS to 1970–71, 9). There are no data for 1961 (information not processed or published), 1941–44 (not collected on account of staff shortages during the war), or for 1931–32 (not collected as an economy measure during economic depression). The data for 1974 and 1976 are taken from provisional estimates made on the basis of a restricted sample (the regular statistics were not processed for these years).

In using the resulting estimates, the following needs to be borne in mind:

1. The estimates from 1945 to 2002 relate to total income. Total income is before deduction of exemptions and includes non-assessible income. Examples of non-assessable income include certain types of overseas income, and certain types of tax-exempt government security.
2. The estimates from 1921 to 1940 relate only to assessible income.
3. Independent taxation was introduced in 1953.
4. Dividend imputation was introduced in 1989, allowing income to be released in the form of dividends without the risk of double taxation; it was also pre-announced that the top individual rate would be reduced to the company tax rate in 1990, causing a postponement of payments out of company income until 1990.
5. In 1999, New Zealand implemented a substantial overhaul of its tax system. Under the present system, residents whose only income is wage earnings, welfare benefits or superannuation are not required to file a tax return. However, wage and salary earners, and welfare and superannuation recipients, remain within the taxation statistics, since their incomes are now reported by their employers or other government agencies.
6. When it was announced that the marginal tax rate on earnings over $60,000 would be raised from 33% to 39% in the 2000–01 tax year, many taxpayers took the opportunity to realize business earnings in the 1999–2000 tax year, significantly boosting top income shares in that year.

APPENDIX 8B: SOURCES OF POPULATION AND TAX UNIT TOTALS

The estimated resident population of New Zealand relates to all people who usually live in New Zealand at a given date. It includes all residents present in New Zealand and counted by the census, residents who are temporarily overseas (who are not included in the census), and an adjustment for residents missed or counted more than once by the census (net census undercount). Visitors from overseas are excluded. The census count of the usually resident population of New Zealand at a given census date is used to derive the base population for post-censal population estimates.

From 1953, the data relate to individuals aged 15+. The figures for 1953 to 1957 are linearly interpolated from the Census figures for 1951 and 1961 (source: Mitchell 1995: 64 and 65). The sources from 1958 are listed below (where *MAS* denotes *Monthly Abstract of Statistics*): December 1958 from *MAS* October 1959: 19; December 1959 from *MAS* April 1961: 19; December 1960 from *MAS* February 1963: 9; December 1961 from *MAS* November 1963: 13; December 1962 from *MAS* May 1964: 15; December 1963 from *MAS* January 1965: 11; December 1964 from *MAS* January 1966: 14; December 1965 from *MAS* April 1967: 9; December 1966 from *MAS* 1968: 9; December 1968 from *MAS* February 1970: 9; December 1969 from *MAS* August 1970: 15; December 1970 from *MAS* May 1972: 7; December 1971 from *MAS* December 1973: 9; December 1972 from *MAS* May 1974: 11; December 1973 from *MAS* January/February 1975: 8; December 1974 from *MAS* December 1975: 8; December 1975 from *MAS* May 1978: 7; December 1976 from *MAS* August 1978: 7; December 1977 from *MAS* July 1979: 5; December 1978 from *MAS* April 1980: 8; December 1979 from *MAS* November-December 1981: 10; March 1981 from *MAS* August 1982: 10; December 1981 from *MAS* April 1983: 10; March 1983 from *MAS* March 1984: 10; December 1983 from *MAS* June 1984: 10; December 1984 from *MAS* June 1985: 10; December 1985 from *MAS* April 1986: 10. The figures from 1986 to 1990 are interpolated linearly between 1985 and 1991. The data for the population by age from 1991 onwards are from the Statistics New Zealand website (www.stats.govt.nz).

Prior to 1953 the figures relate to tax units, calculated by subtracting the estimated number of married women from the adult population. The population by age is available for the Census years 1921, 1926, 1936, 1941, 1951, and 1961 (Mitchell 1995: 64 and 65). We have linearly interpolated these figures to give an annual series. The number of married women in Census years is from United Nations, 1954: 192 (for 1945 and 1951) and New Zealand Census and Statistics Department 1940: table 16. We then expressed the number of tax units in Census years as a percentage of the population aged 15+ and interpolated the percentages linearly (for 1952 we took the percentage in 1951).

Our population series are set out in Table 8B.1. As noted in the text, for the years 2000–02 we take the total number of taxpayers, since this exceeds the calculated total.

APPENDIX 8C: DERIVATION OF PERSONAL INCOME SERIES

The New Zealand financial year runs from 1 April to 31 March.

Working backwards in time, for the period 1971–72 to 2002–03, we use tables headed '8.8 Household Income and Outlay Account' helpfully provided by

Table 8B.1 New Zealand population totals (thousands) 1921–2002

Tax year starting 1 April	Total tax units aged 15 and over	Total individuals aged 15 and over	Total taxpayers	Total taxpayers as % total tax units (italics) or total individuals
1921	**669**	—	89	*13.3*
1922	**688**	—	71	*10.3*
1923	**704**	—	75	*10.7*
1924	**721**	—	76	*10.5*
1925	**741**	—	80	*10.7*
1926	**761**	—	99	*13.1*
1927	**779**	—	104	*13.3*
1928	**793**	—	109	*13.7*
1929	**806**	—	113	*14.1*
1930	**822**	—	126	*15.3*
1931	**838**	—	—	—
1932	**850**	—	—	—
1933	**862**	—	121	*14.0*
1934	**873**	—	134	*15.3*
1935	**883**	—	149	*16.9*
1936	**896**	—	188	*21.0*
1937	**893**	—	214	*24.0*
1938	**891**	—	257	*28.9*
1939	**891**	—	298	*33.5*
1940	**884**	—	315	*34.8*
1941	**869**	—	—	—
1942	**862**	—	—	—
1943	**849**	—	—	—
1944	**848**	—	—	—
1945	**856**	—	392	*45.8*
1946	**882**	—	463	*52.5*
1947	**894**	—	519	*58.0*
1948	**905**	—	546	*60.3*
1949	**917**	—	585	*63.8*
1950	**927**	—	605	*65.3*
1951	**939**	—	585	*62.3*
1952	**958**	—	613	*64.0*
1953	—	**1,432**	661	46.1
1954	—	**1,459**	649	44.5
1955	—	**1,487**	663	44.6
1956	—	**1,514**	689	45.5
1957	—	**1,541**	814	52.9
1958	—	**1,568**	1,058	67.5
1959	—	**1,589**	1,050	66.1
1960	—	**1,611**	1,085	67.4
1961	—	**1,649**	—	—
1962	—	**1,690**	1,157	68.5
1963	—	**1,728**	1,189	68.8
1964	—	**1,765**	1,228	69.6
1965	—	**1,804**	1,274	70.6
1966	—	**1,827**	1,309	71.6
1967	—	**1,853**	1,343	72.5

1968	—	1,878	1,368	72.8
1969	—	1,908	1,414	74.1
1970	—	1,947	1,461	75.0
1971	—	1,984	1,517	76.5
1972	—	2,036	1,574	77.3
1973	—	2,094	1,650	78.8
1974	—	2,157	1,673	77.5
1975	—	2,196	1,577	71.8
1976	—	2,231	1,710	76.7
1977	—	2,253	1,649	73.2
1978	—	2,273	1,686	74.2
1979	—	2,291	1,716	74.9
1980	—	2,327	1,664	71.5
1981	—	2,356	1,712	72.7
1982	—	2,401	1,763	73.4
1983	—	2,445	1,748	71.5
1984	—	2,484	1,772	71.3
1985	—	2,507	1,810	72.2
1986	—	2,537	1,848	72.9
1987	—	2,567	1,855	72.3
1988	—	2,597	1,795	69.1
1989	—	2,628	1,809	68.9
1990	—	2,658	1,865	70.2
1991	—	2,688	1,896	70.5
1992	—	2,717	2,002	73.7
1993	—	2,748	2,085	75.9
1994	—	2,785	2,139	76.8
1995	—	2,826	2,139	75.7
1996	—	2,873	2,054	71.5
1997	—	2,913	2,001	68.7
1998	—	2,939	1,915	65.1
1999	—	2,958	2,937	99.3
2000	—	2,980	3,011	101.0
2001	—	3,007	3,075	102.3
2002	—	3,061	3,125	102.1

Notes: 1. The estimates presented in this paper use the population denominator of tax units aged 15 and over until 1952, and individuals aged 15 and over from 1953 onwards (reflecting the change from joint to individual taxation in 1953). 2. As noted in the text, for the years 2000–02 we take the total number of taxpayers.

Stephen Flanagan of Statistics New Zealand. We have taken the total of compensation of employees, entrepreneurial income, actual interest, and dividends, social security benefits in cash and social assistance benefits in cash (termed 'Social Assistance Grants-Social Welfare' in the 1971–72 to 1985–86 table), and pension fund benefits. The last of these categories is only distinguished in the tables covering the period from 1986–87 onwards, and this may cause a minor break in comparability between the estimates up to 1985 and those from 1986 onwards. As explained in the text, we have reduced all figures by multiplying by a factor of 0.95.

For the preceding period 1938–39 to 1970–71, a series on Private Income was published regularly in the *Monthly Abstract of Statistics* (*MAS*). The sources are in the Supplement to *MAS* March 1975: table 5, except for 1939–40, 1940–41, and 1945–46 from the Supplement to *MAS* January 1973: table 5. This source gives salary and wage payments, pay, and allowances of Armed Forces, social security benefits, and pensions, and other personal income (excluding company dividends). The element missing compared with later years is company dividends. These have been interpolated using the series for company income (before distribution). There is reason to suppose that the proportion distributed has fallen since the immediate post-war period, when the total company income was some $100 m. Inspection of the value for 1971–72 (see previous paragraph) and the dividends reported in the income tax statistics led us to assume that 50% were distributed as dividends to New Zealand households up to NZ$100 m and that 10% was distributed on income in excess of that amount. This generates a percentage of around 15% for 1971–72, which is in line with the observed figure. The 'private income' series may include some income of non-household institutions, which we allow for by linking the series to that from 1971–72 (which involves a reduction of some 0.7%). We have not included the rental value of owner-occupied houses. Again, as explained in the text, we have reduced all figures by multiplying by a factor of 0.95.

For the period 1931–32 to 1938–39, we used the figures on total private income published regularly in *MAS*: 1938–39 from *MAS* 13 June 1941 applying the same assumption about dividends as above, 1931–32 to 1937–38 from *MAS* June 1939, where no assumption about dividends is required. The figures cover wages, salary, pensions, investment income, and the net income of the self-employed. Undistributed company income is excluded. The series is linked, using the 1938–39 observation to give figures comparable with those for later years. For the period prior to 1931–32, we linked the series at 1931–32 to that for nominal GDP constructed by Easton (1997: appendix 5). As explained in the text, we have reduced all figures by multiplying by a factor of 0.95.

Our personal income series are set out in Table 8C.1. It should be noted that New Zealand switched from pounds to dollars on 10 July 1967, at the ratio of £1 = $2. While some of our original sources are in pounds, we present all our tables in millions of dollars. For the years 2000 to 2002, the mean income is calculated using the number of taxpayers.

APPENDIX 8D: COMPARISON GROUPS FOR NEW ZEALAND TOP INCOME SHARES

To calculate average wages, we use the average wage of a full-time employee, published annually by Statistics New Zealand since 1998 (*New Zealand Income Survey*, Table 11). That publication shows average weekly wages, and we multiply these by 52 to obtain average annual wages. From 1921 to 1997, we calculate average wages using a nominal wage index kindly supplied by Claire Stent, Librarian at Statistics New Zealand, and link this to the 1998 average wage.

Table 8C.1 New Zealand personal income totals and coverage, 1921–2002

Tax year starting 1 April	Personal income $ million	Total covered by tax data $ million	Total covered as % personal income	Mean annual income per tax unit (italics) or individual $
1921	192	75	39.0	*288*
1922	203	67	33.0	*295*
1923	214	74	34.6	*304*
1924	231	79	34.2	*321*
1925	233	83	35.6	*315*
1926	232	93	40.1	*305*
1927	240	97	40.4	*308*
1928	254	104	40.9	*320*
1929	247	105	42.6	*306*
1930	211	99	46.9	*257*
1931	189	—	—	*226*
1932	175	—	—	*205*
1933	192	87	45.3	*223*
1934	199	94	47.3	*227*
1935	231	110	47.7	*261*
1936	289	146	50.5	*322*
1937	318	158	49.7	*356*
1938	350	182	52.0	*393*
1939	372	225	60.5	*418*
1940	405	244	60.3	*458*
1941	—	—	—	—
1942	—	—	—	—
1943	—	—	—	—
1944	—	—	—	—
1945	618	372	60.2	*722*
1946	663	453	68.3	*752*
1947	750	558	74.4	*839*
1948	789	614	77.8	*872*
1949	888	712	80.2	*969*
1950	1,104	857	77.6	*1,191*
1951	1,138	911	80.1	*1,212*
1952	1,208	1,003	83.0	*1,261*
1953	1,333	1,110	83.3	931
1954	1,444	1,189	82.3	990
1955	1,520	1,243	81.8	1,022
1956	1,622	1,352	83.4	1,071
1957	1,735	1,448	83.5	1,126
1958	1,754	1,523	86.9	1,118
1959	1,891	1,650	87.3	1,190
1960	2,046	1,813	88.6	1,270
1961	2,110	—	—	—
1962	2,225	2,025	91.0	1,317
1963	2,406	2,190	91.0	1,392
1964	2,599	2,394	92.1	1,472

(*contd.*)

Table 8C.1 (*contd.*)

Tax year starting 1 April	Personal income $ million	Total covered by tax data $ million	Total covered as % personal income	Mean annual income per tax unit (italics) or individual $
1965	2,799	2,569	91.8	1,552
1966	2,926	2,772	94.7	1,601
1967	3,017	2,821	93.5	1,628
1968	3,138	2,945	93.9	1,671
1969	3,445	3,226	93.6	1,806
1970	4,011	3,764	93.8	2,060
1971	4,696	4,422	94.2	2,367
1972	5,482	5,089	92.8	2,693
1973	6,391	6,052	94.7	3,052
1974	7,211	7,047	97.7	3,343
1975	8,593	7,908	92.0	3,913
1976	9,978	9,343	93.6	4,472
1977	11,393	10,223	89.7	5,057
1978	13,198	11,832	89.6	5,807
1979	15,693	13,788	87.9	6,850
1980	18,332	15,904	86.8	7,878
1981	21,988	19,138	87.0	9,333
1982	24,521	21,758	88.7	10,213
1983	25,773	22,455	87.1	10,541
1984	28,612	24,346	85.1	11,519
1985	33,697	28,122	83.5	13,441
1986	40,303	32,611	80.9	15,886
1987	46,980	36,969	78.7	18,302
1988	50,108	37,350	74.5	19,294
1989	53,114	40,352	76.0	20,211
1990	54,657	43,861	80.2	20,563
1991	54,179	43,926	81.1	20,156
1992	54,554	45,921	84.2	20,079
1993	57,023	48,826	85.6	20,751
1994	61,084	51,496	84.3	21,933
1995	65,632	54,571	83.1	23,224
1996	69,888	54,996	78.7	24,326
1997	72,279	55,819	77.2	24,813
1998	73,677	56,226	76.3	25,069
1999	77,520	76,837	99.1	26,207
2000	79,226	75,128	94.8	26,312
2001	84,160	80,389	95.5	27,371
2002	86,529	83,767	96.8	27,691

Remuneration of judges refers to a puisne judge on New Zealand's highest court. This was the Supreme Court until 1980, when that body was renamed the High Court. Our period of analysis stops at 2002, so does not encompass the creation of a new Supreme Court in 2004 (following abolition of appeals to the Privy Council). Figures supplied by Patricia Gordon of the New Zealand Remuneration Authority.

Salaries of members of parliament are the base salary for an MP, excluding allowances. Figures for 1921–2001 were supplied by Ruth Graham of the New Zealand Parliamentary Library. Recent years were obtained from the annual *Parliamentary Salaries and Allowances Determination.*

Table 8D.1 New Zealand comparison groups for top income shares, 1921–2002

Year	Average annual wage	Basic salary of a member of parliament	Annual wage of a judge on the High Court
1921	453	1,000	—
1922	445	900	—
1923	438	—	—
1924	444	—	—
1925	451	—	—
1926	458	—	—
1927	467	—	—
1928	481	—	—
1929	482	—	—
1930	482	—	—
1931	446	810	—
1932	409	729	—
1933	395	—	—
1934	398	765	—
1935	407	823	—
1936	450	900	—
1937	491	—	—
1938	512	—	—
1939	521	—	—
1940	535	—	—
1941	554	—	—
1942	579	—	—
1943	598	—	—
1944	604	1,000	—
1945	654	—	—
1946	680	—	—
1947	703	—	—
1948	751	—	—
1949	795	—	—
1950	846	—	—
1951	966	1,800	—
1952	1,013	—	—
1953	1,081	—	—
1954	1,164	—	—
1955	1,204	2,200	—
1956	1,228	—	—
1957	1,284	—	—
1958	1,277	—	6,500
1959	1,385	2,800	—
1960	1,554	—	8,000

(*contd.*)

Table 8D.1 (*contd.*)

Year	Average annual wage	Basic salary of a member of parliament	Annual wage of a judge on the High Court
1961	1,623	3,100	8,500
1962	1,688	—	—
1963	1,742	—	—
1964	1,816	4,300	9,900
1965	1,938	—	—
1966	2,013	—	10,170
1967	2,129	—	11,600
1968	2,246	4,650	—
1969	2,372	—	12,620
1970	2,637	6,100	13,688
1971	3,144	6,832	17,456
1972	3,518	7,604	19,002
1973	3,974	11,000	20,590
1974	4,618	11,440	21,130
1975	5,304	11,933	23,799
1976	6,033	12,121	24,744
1977	6,882	17,088	27,512
1978	7,772	18,000	42,500
1979	9,144	21,187	49,452
1980	10,817	24,326	56,779
1981	13,201	28,145	68,978
1982	15,058	29,552	—
1983	15,606	—	—
1984	16,128	—	75,741
1985	17,716	34,976	81,043
1986	21,323	49,500	118,800
1987	23,665	—	—
1988	26,072	57,000	145,000
1989	27,588	61,000	153,500
1990	29,310	63,500	159,500
1991	30,421	63,500	—
1992	31,006	66,000	163,000
1993	31,085	67,500	166,500
1994	31,517	71,000	173,500
1995	32,270	72,500	180,500
1996	33,413	74,500	195,000
1997	34,671	78,000	204,000
1998	35,640	80,000	212,200
1999	36,552	83,000	229,200
2000	37,289	85,000	243,000
2001	38,532	87,000	253,900
2002	39,208	90,500	264,100

Data on salaries of top public servants are not included, since deregulation of public service salaries makes it difficult to discern an appropriate comparison group.

Each of these series is presented in Table 8D.1.

REFERENCES

Atkinson, A. B. and Leigh, A. (2004). 'Understanding the Distribution of Top Incomes in Anglo-Saxon Countries over the Twentieth Century'. Discussion paper.

—— —— (2007) 'The Distribution of Top Incomes in Australia', *Economic Record*, vol. 83.

Bakker, A. and Creedy, J. (1999). 'Macroeconomic Variables and Income Inequality in New Zealand', *New Zealand Economic Papers*, 33: 59–80.

Bennett, T. (2000). 'New Zealand Election 1999'. Research Note 26, 1999–2000, Australian Parliamentary Library, Canberra, ACT.

Chatterjee, S. and Srivastav, N. (1992). *Inequalities in New Zealand's Personal Income Distribution 1983/84: Measurements and Patterns*, Income Distribution Series No 1, Social Policy Research Unit, Massey University, Palmerston North.

Dixon, S. (1998). 'Growth in the dispersion of earnings: 1984–97', *Labour Market Bulletin*, 1&2: 71–107

Easton, B. (1983). *Income distribution in New Zealand.* Wellington: New Zealand Institute of Economic Research.

—— (1996). 'Income Distribution', in B. Silverstone, A. Bollard, and R. Lattimore (eds.) *A Study of Economic Reform: The Case of New Zealand.* Amsterdam: Elsevier.

—— (1997). *In Stormy Seas: The Post-War New Zealand Economy.* Otago: Otago University Press.

—— (1999). 'What has Happened in New Zealand to Income Distribution and Poverty Levels?', in S. Shaver and P. Saunders (eds.) *Social Policy for the 21st Century: Justice and Responsibility.* Social Policy Research Centre Reports and Proceedings No. 142, pp. 55–66.

Evans, L., Grimes, A., Wilkinson, B., and Teece, D. (1996). 'Economic reform in New Zealand: The Pursuit of Efficiency', *Journal of Economic Literature*, 34: 1856–902.

Hyslop, D. and Maré, D. (2001). 'Understanding Changes in the Distribution of Household Incomes in New Zealand Between 1983–86 and 1995–98'. Treasury Working Paper Series 01/21, New Zealand Treasury, Wellington.

—— —— (2005). 'Understanding New Zealand's Changing Income Distribution, 1983–1998', *Economica*, 72: 469–95.

Main, V. (1998). 'National resorts to "taxometer" gimmick', *The Dominion (Wellington)*, 4 November, p. 2

Martin, B. (1997). 'Income Trends Among Individuals and Families, 1976 to 1996'. Briefing Paper prepared for the Population Conference, Wellington.

Ministry of Social Development (2005). *The Social Report 2005.* Wellington: Ministry of Social Development.

Mitchell, B. R. (1995). *International Historical Statistics: Africa, Asia and Oceania, 1750–1988*, 2nd rev. edn. London: Stockton.

Mowbray, M. (2001). *Distributions and Disparity: New Zealand Household Incomes.* Wellington: Ministry of Social Policy.

New Zealand Census and Statistics Department (1940). *Population Census, Vol IV: Ages and Marital Status.* Wellington: Government Printer.

New Zealand Department of Statistics (1953). *Incomes and Income-Tax Statistics for the Year 1949–50.* Wellington: Government Printer.

—— (1968). *Incomes and Income-Tax to 1966–67.* Wellington: Government Printer.

O'Dea, D. (2000). 'The Changes in New Zealand's Income Distribution'. Treasury Working Paper 00/13.

Oliver, R. (2000). 'Capital Gains Tax—The New Zealand case'. Paper presented at the Fraser Institute 2000 Symposium on Capital Gains Taxation, Vancouver BC, Canada. 18 September. Available at:http://www.goodreturns.co. nz/article/976485506.html

Piketty, T. and Saez, T. (2001). 'Income Inequality in the United States, 1913–1998'. National Bureau of Economic Research Working Paper 8467, NBER.

—— —— (2003). 'Income Inequality in the United States, 1913–1998', *Quarterly Journal of Economics*, 118(1): 1–39.

Podder, N. and Chatterjee S. (2002). 'Sharing the national cake in post reform New Zealand: income inequality trends in terms of income sources', *Journal of Public Economics*, 86: 1–27.

Ross Committee on Taxation (1968). *Report of the Committee on Taxation.* Wellington: Government Printer.

Saez, E. and Veall, M. (2003). 'The Evolution of High Incomes in Canada, 1920–2000'. Working Paper 9607, NBER.

Snively, S. (convenor) (1990). *Who Gets What? The Distribution of Income and Wealth in New Zealand.* Wellington: New Zealand Planning Council.

Statistics New Zealand (1999). *New Zealand Now: Incomes.* Wellington: Statistics New Zealand.

Stephens, F. B. (1936). 'National Income of New Zealand', *Economic Record*, 12(23): 231–56.

United Nations (1954). *Demographic Yearbook, 1954.* New York: United Nations.

United Nations (1983). *Yearbook of National Accounts, 1981.* New York: United Nations.

Waldegrave, S. (2000). 'New Zealand's Income Distribution Literature'. Unpublished manuscript.

9

Top Incomes in Germany Throughout the Twentieth Century: 1891–1998

F. Dell[1]

9.1 INTRODUCTION

This chapter aims at providing for the first time homogenous top income shares for Germany over the whole twentieth century. Using income tax data, we are able to trace top income shares back into the past as far off as 1891, when the first modern income tax was put into effect in Prussia. We can thus study top income shares series for a period longer than a century, beginning at a time when Germany was still in a phase of late industrialization.[2]

Being very similar to France (and indeed all continental European countries documented in this volume), Germany constitutes an appropriate comparison point to deepen our understanding of how top incomes distribution changes. Like France, Germany was deeply shaken by the two World Wars. Like France (and the Netherlands), Germany built a comprehensive Welfare State after the Second World War. Like France, Germany did not experience sharp tax cuts in the 1980s.

Indeed, one (still tentative) explanatory factor of the evolution of top income share is the (progressive) income tax system. As Piketty and Saez (2003) put it, 'top capital incomes were never able to recover from these [World Wars and Great Depression] shocks probably because of the dynamic effects of progressive taxation on capital accumulation and wealth inequality'. The German experience could thus enlighten us on this issue because of the proximity and similarity between German and French economies, associated with different tax systems.[3]

[1] PSE, Paris, and DIW, Berlin. I would like to thank my PhD adviser, Thomas Piketty, for helpful discussions and constant support. I also would like to thank Nicole Buschle and Markus Zwick of the German Federal Statistical Office for helping me working with contemporary German income tax micro-data. I am also most grateful to Anthony Atkinson, Stefan Bach, Pierre-Cyrille Hautcoeur, Albrecht Ritschl, and Emmanuel Saez for helpful comments. Previous drafts have been presented at a seminar at Nuffield College in Oxford (September 2003); at the UCLA (April 2004); and the EEA Conference in Madrid (August 2004); I thank participants for comments.

[2] The First Industrial Revolution came relatively late in Germany (later than in France and, of course, later than in the UK).

[3] The German tax system differs from the French system in various ways but the most striking and constant element is the very low effective rates of inheritance taxes throughout the century, which were already noticed by Schumpeter in the early 1920s.

Nevertheless, Germany is also a country whose path through the twentieth century was strewn with more exogenous shocks than any other industrialized country. Several episodes deserve special attention. First, the First World War years and the subsequent inflation period, which fundamentally transformed the structure of top incomes. Then the Third Reich, when Nazi power led to skyrocketing top income shares in the context of an ever more centrally administered economy. After the Second World War, the second inflationary episode and the monetary reform of 1948 drastically shifted the burden of the defeat off the top of the wealth distribution and onto the lower groups. Lastly, the years since the Reunification saw two radically different income distributions being merged in the course of an outside driven transition process. Our series, beginning very early,[4] cast light on the 1891–1913 period, usually too remote to be documented, and nevertheless very interesting since it gives insight in how income inequalities might have looked like during the end of the industrialization process.

Among former attempts to estimate income shares (or simply assess income distribution in Germany before the Second World War), one should cite, Geisenberger and Müller (1972) (pre-First World War years) and Procopovitch (1926) (for Prussia) and Sweezy (1939) (for the Third Reich).[5] These attempts are not as comprehensive as the present work in terms of the range of income shares they estimate as well as in terms of the time periods they study. Moreover, the methodology used is often very elusively described, thus preventing us to assess the reasons of some discrepancies with our results in terms of levels. Geisenberger and Müller (1972) calculate income shares for Prussia (1873–1913), Saxony (1881–1913), Hessen (1886–1913) and Baden (1891–1913). The results for Prussia are very similar to ours (see Figure 9.1).[6] Procopovitch estimates top income shares for (among others) Prussia for the tax years 1875, 1896, 1913, and 1919 as well as for Saxony for 1912.[7] Procopovitch pinpoints the decisive importance of urban areas in income

[4] Equivalent data are only available on a regular basis after 1915 for France; after 1914 for the Netherlands; after 1913 for the US; and after 1908 for the UK.

[5] Grumbach (1957), quoted by Hoffmann (1965: 510sq.) estimated Pareto coefficients for a very wide time span (1822–1939), for various parts of the German Empire (including Prussia) before 1918. Unfortunately, only one Pareto coefficient was estimated each year for the whole income distribution and no attempt was made at deriving income shares. Moreover, the methodology used is discussed in general and abstract terms preventing the reader from knowing the detail of the estimation methods adopted (in particular, one would like to know how Grumbach bridged the frequent gaps resulting from pre-1891 changes in the 'income-related-taxes' of that time).

[6] Prussia was by far the biggest component of the German Empire. Nonetheless, aggregating Prussian data with data of other German States could render our picture of top income evolution in Germany before the First World War more complete. The fact that the tax unit definition is not homogenous across states (Saxony, for instance, had a income tax based on individuals) is an important obstacle.

[7] Procopovitch's figure seem at first sight significantly higher than ours (for instance: top 1% share in 1913: 24.3% whereas we estimate only 17.5%). But Procopovitch's top income groups are relative to the entire population and not to a total of tax units. In 1913 for instance, his top 1% represent more than 400,000 Prussian tax payers whereas ours represent only 160,000. Adapted to our total of tax units, Procopovitch's top income shares are similar to ours: for instance, the top 1% in the tax year 1913 is 18.2% and the top 10% is 38.9% (ours is 37.7%).

concentration dynamics. He concludes stating 'It would be extremely interesting to compare the distribution of incomes at the beginning of the present century with that of a century ago'. Sweezy (1939) uses earlier version of the tabulations which we call 'synthetic' (see Statistisches Reichsamt 1939) published in the late 1930s by the German Statistical Office and which merge tax data (at the top) and social insurance data (at the bottom). The conclusion is that 'the general picture of the distribution of individual income shows that inequality has increased during the Hitler regime' and also points to a rise in wealth inequality at the same time.

From 1969 to 1998, Becker and Hauser (2003) systematically documented equivalized market and disposable income inequality using the German *Income and Consumption Survey* (EVS), but without addressing specifically the issue of top incomes: standard surveys are problematic for estimating top income shares, particularly for smaller percentile groups.

Our main results are the following: top income shares fell in Germany over the twentieth century following the very chaotic period of 1914–45. This decline is mostly due to the fall of the top percentile, and within the top percentile to the fall of the highest group (top 0.01%). Although the First World War and Nazi government of Germany had a very positive impact on top income shares, the pre-First World War levels were never reached again after the Second World War. Nevertheless top income shares grew again in the 1950s and 1960s, reaching levels largely superior to those which could be observed at the same time in France, the United States or Britain (see Chapters 3, 4, and 5 in this volume). This partial recovery not only happened at the very top of the distribution, but also in the

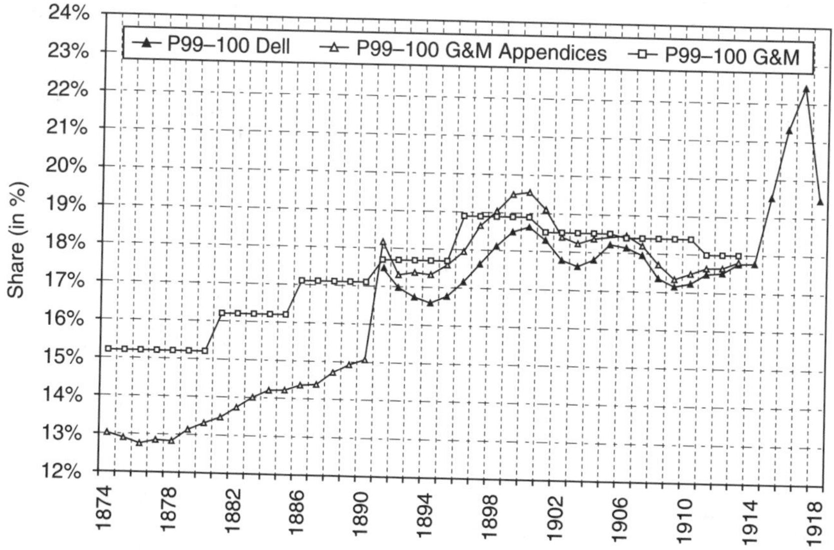

Figure 9.1 Series of Müller and Geisenberger (1972) for Prussia

Source: Author's computation on Prussion income tax data; Mueller and Geisenberger 1972: 44–5, appendix 1: 59–60.

lower groups of the top decile thus leading to a sensible de-concentration of the top decile. However, throughout the second half of the century, the German top decile exhibits an original physiognomy: the gap between the top one percent and the following nine percentiles is much wider than in any other developed country (since the mid-1980s however, Anglo-Saxon countries present a comparable concentration).

The present chapter is organized as follows: Section 9.2 presents our data sources and explains our estimation methods and Section 9.3 presents top income shares series over the century.

9.2 DATA AND METHODOLOGY USED

This section briefly presents the different data we use in this work and the methodology used to estimate top income shares. More details on this topic can be found in appendices 9.A to 9.I.

Our data rely on tax returns statistics compiled by the successive German fiscal administrations over the twentieth century. The raw data we use consist of tables containing, for a large number of income brackets, the number of taxpayers and the amounts declared. Other such tabulations are available (unfortunately only after 1926) to assess composition by income sources.

Unlike other developed countries, the German state did encounter numerous breaks over the twentieth century. So did the data we use. Three major periods have thus to be distinguished: before 1920, the Interwar Years, and the Federal Republic period.

Before 1920, there was no central fiscal administration: in the Wilhelmine Empire, direct tax collection was conducted at the level of the member states of the federation (the most prominent exception to this federalism was the introduction of an imperial inheritance tax in 1906). Direct income taxes did not exist everywhere in the Reich at the end of the nineteenth century. Nevertheless around 1900 all major states (Saxony, Bavaria, Hessen, and most notably Prussia) had brought modern income taxes into operation. The present version of this paper only uses Prussian data to document the pre-1920 period.[8] Income tax was introduced in Prussia in 1891 and the first data we use relate to the tax year 1891. It should nonetheless be noted that there exists from 1873 onward a Prussian income tax which mixes features of the old *Classensteuer* with features of a properly modern income tax. The *Classensteuer* categorized people according

[8] It is important to bear in mind that before the First World War, Prussia accounted for two-thirds of the total German population. Moreover, Prussian territory encompassed low density rural areas (e.g. *Ostpreußen*) as well as high density industrial regions (e.g. *Ruhrgebiet*) with numerous cities. The capital of the empire, Berlin, was also part of it. Prussian high incomes are therefore probably a good proxy of German high incomes for the pre-1920 period. Nevertheless, data from other member states such as Saxony and Bavaria are available and are currently exploited in order to complete the Prussian data.

to their status (classes) and not to the extent of their income. Although the status was largely positively correlated with income, the publications before 1891 do not tabulate a distribution of income by size stricto sensu. The period 1873–91 can thus be seen as the last transition stage toward modern income tax. For former (and unfortunately undocumented) use of these data, see Geisenberger and Müller (1972);[9] for more recent use, see Grant (2002) who also gives a good summary of the evolution of Prussian income-related-taxes throughout the nineteenth century.

After the First World War and the German Revolution, the Weimar Republic saw the institution of a federal income tax. Together with the development of a modern and centralized Statistical Office,[10] this new tax system led to the first all-German income tax statistics. However, the coexistence of an ex-post declaration-based income tax (*Einkommensteuer*, henceforward *ES*) with a ex-ante pay-as-you-earn tax system on wages and salaries (*Lohnsteuer*, henceforward *LS*) led to two series of statistical publications (see Appendix 9.A) which must be dealt with caution in order to reconstruct the top of the income distribution. Moreover, data for the hyperinflation years (1919–24), the Second World War (1939–45) and the Allied Occupation Years (1945–49) were never gathered. Nevertheless, available data give us the opportunity to relate the puzzling evolution of high incomes in the Interwar Period, as well as their composition.

After the Second World War, income tax in the Federal Republic of Germany was organized along the same lines as before the war. Tabulations were published regularly at a three year interval. Although the double taxation system of the Interwar Years continued to apply (it still exists), statistics were unified progressively from 1961 onward. The publications available for the nineties (1992, 1995, and 1998) also account for the ex-Democratic Republic of Germany, known as the *neue Bundesländer*. For the nineties, we have been able to use micro-data from the German Federal Statistical Office to asses the precision of our interpolation method. No data is available after 1998. To summarize, we have data for 1891–1918 (on a yearly basis), 1925–38 (on a yearly basis or every two years) and 1950–98 (every three years).

Incomes considered in the various publications used for this paper are total 'net incomes (i.e. minus expenses necessarily incurred in obtaining these incomes, the so-called *Werbungskosten*), before social transfers and taxes, but after employers' payroll taxes and corporate income tax.

[9] Geisenberger and Müller calculated income shares of the top 5, 1, and 0.1% for the 1873–1913 period. Unfortunately, the precise sources used are not given extensively (as the same years are sometimes documented in different publications, with different level of detail), and the interpolation method as well as the control totals used are not documented either. Moreover, the construction of homogeneous series bridging the 1891 gap obviously entails the use of corrective factors (pre-1891 top incomes were systematically underestimated) which are not documented at all. The appendices are very poor, note for instance the discrepancies between series for P99–100 corrected in the body of the text and still exhibiting a huge blip in 1891 in the appendices. For a comparison of those estimates with our results, see Figure 9.1.

[10] The *Statistisches Reichsamt*, see Tooze (2001) on this issue.

Because our data rely on tax returns, they only provide information on incomes at the tax unit level. We cannot assess intra-tax unit income distribution with our data. The fractiles we estimate are defined relative to the total number of potential tax units derived from population and family census statistics. Following Piketty (2001), we focus on the top decile and on smaller fractiles within it that are of crucial interest to understand with finesse the evolution of top incomes. We thus built series for the top decile (denoted by P90–100), the top 5% (P95–100), the top 1% (P99–100), the top 0.5% (P99.5–100), the top 0.1% (P99.9–100) and the top 0.01% (P99.99–100). As the top tail of income distributions is generally well approximated by Pareto distribution, we use simple parametric methods to estimate thresholds and average income for all of our fractiles (for more details on the Pareto method, see Appendix 5C; see Chapter 2 for discussion of the issue of the precision and reliability of such interpolation methods). In order to control, within the top decile, for the (heavy) effect of the top fractiles, we systematically analyse intermediate fractiles P90–95, P95–99, P99–99.5, P99.5–99.9, and P99.9–99.99.

We then estimate the shares of each fractile in the overall personal income by dividing the amounts accruing to each fractile by a homogeneous total personal income series derived from national accounts (after 1950) and from reliable series built by Hoffman and Müller for the Pre-Second World War years.

9.3 TOP INCOMES IN GERMANY

Trends in Top Income Shares: General Pattern

Series of top incomes shares are presented in Figures 9.2 to 9.8.[11] One immediately notices the two basic facts that characterize top income evolution in Germany: a long-run decrease combined with short-term jerky variations.

Figure 9.2 shows the evolution of the income share of the top decile over the century. Before the First World War, the top decile share varied between 38% and 42% of total income. After the Second World War, it has been oscillating between 30% and 35%. The decline thus took place between 1914 and 1945. The top percentile (see Figure 9.4) experienced the same kind of evolution. Before the First World War, its share was about 17–20% of total income. The two World Wars brought this share down under 12% and since the 1970s the share even remained under 11%. In other words, since 1891, the share of the top percentile was divided by two in Germany. If we look at the upper percentile of this top percentile (see Figure 9.6), we see that its share was ranging between 3% and 4% at the beginning of the century and now remains below 2%.

[11] These new series may differ slightly from those in Dell (2005) due to refinements in the estimates. Nonetheless, the basic secular pattern is unchanged and the levels compared to other countries still exhibit the differences highlighted.

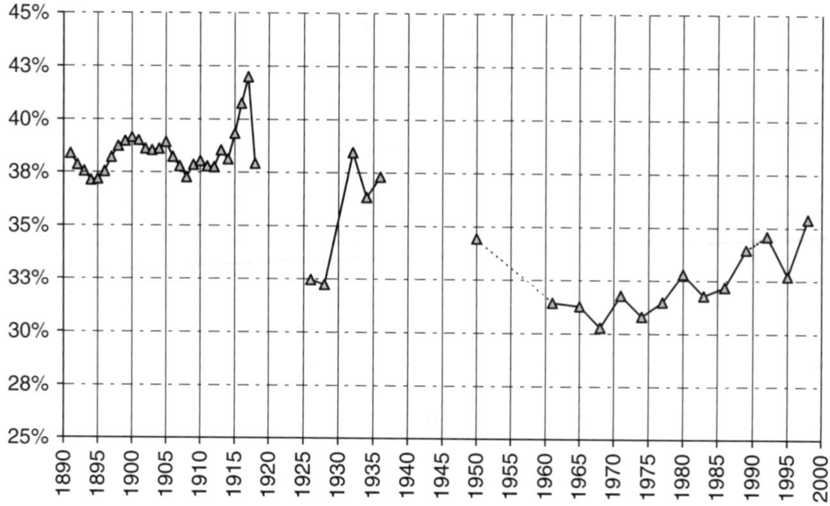

Figure 9.2 Share of the top decile, Germany, 1891–1998

Source: Author's computation on German income tax data; Table 9I.5, this volume.

We can thus say that in the course of the twentieth century, the share of top incomes was dramatically reduced in Germany, and all the more than one looks further right in the tail of the distribution. At the same time one notices two sudden surges in the share of top incomes which took place during the First World War and just before the Second World War, the two moments in the history of twentieth century when Germany saw an authoritarian government take control. Before the First World War and after the Second World War, income shares of the higher groups (top 1% and above) are highly pro-cyclical: boom of the late 1890s when the crisis of the late 1870s comes to an end; downs of 1953–54, 1966–67, 1973–74, 1983, and 1993 can be found in the data.

The evolution of top income shares is driven by the highest income groups. Looking at intermediate fractiles thus enables us to have a more differentiate picture of top incomes evolution. The lower part of the top decile (see Figure 9.3) exhibits a very different pattern: the first half of the top decile (P90–95) saw its share of total income growing over the century. From about 8% at the end of the nineteenth century, it has remained since the late 1970s above 10%. As far as the P95–99 is concerned, one can see that its share actually remained quasi-unchanged in the course of the century.

Pre-First World War Years and the War itself

Once these basic facts set, one can look more precisely at short-term variations. They are of great magnitude, reflecting the chaotic history of Germany over the century. During the Pre-First World War years, top incomes grew to reach their secular maximum (this is even more clear looking at the rough evolution before

1891 documented in Figure 9.1). The years of the war saw a rapid rise of the top incomes but the Revolution of 1918 and the subsequent institutional and economic chaos of the early Weimar Republic constituted a brutal shock from which top incomes never recovered until today.

The growth of top incomes at the beginning of the period studied is easily understandable since it corresponds to the final phase of the late industrialization of the German economy. The pattern of accelerated growth observed during the First World War can be accounted for with two factors. First, the war did not take place on German soil and no physical capital destruction occurred (in contrast to what happened for France). Second, the quick organization of a consensus with the Unions to guaranty a United Front in German society (*Zentrale Arbeitsgemeinschaft*) and the progressive establishment of a military dictatorship closely related to the heavy industrial sector may have been a favorable context for huge profits to be realized at the top of the distribution. Clearly, financing the war led the Kaiser to resort to huge loans, the interests of which were (partly) paid thanks to new taxes on capital. But these were quite modest and the effects of unsustainable deficit spending were to be felt only later on. The war also caused huge disruptions in the productive sector but these were probably offset at the top by the growing demand for military equipment (Germany, contrary to France, was at war on two fronts). Clearly, the war did not mean benefits for all, even in the top decile. The group immediately following the top percentile (P95–99) experienced a steep decline during the war (from 12.6% in 1913 to 10.6% in 1918) symmetrical to the rise of the top percentile, and the second vintile remained unaffected. One tentative explanation of this pattern is that the P95–99 income group may reflect the fate of small businesses which experienced most negatively the reorganizations linked to the war (redirection of labor force and inputs toward defense relevant activities). Further down the distribution, high wages of civil servants and other white collars of the Wilhelmine Reich may have remained unaffected by the war. Unfortunately, the absence of composition data before the First World War prevents us from assessing more precisely this explanation.

Once the war was over, the monetary instability it had launched plunged the German economy into chaos until 1924–25.

Interwar Period

The global impact of Hyperinflation Years (1920–24) on top incomes (and on income distribution in general) is a highly disputed issue of German economic history. However, comparing the end of the War (1918) with the first year of economic stability (1925) enables us to draw conclusions on this topic. Once again, dividing the top decile into smaller fractiles proves to be absolutely necessary in order to have a precise picture of what happened. The top percentile's share dropped brutally during these years (from 19% to about 11%) and the share of the top 0.01% was even more negatively affected (falling from more than

3.5% to less than 1.5%). On the other hand, lower fractiles within the top decile (P90–95 and P95–99) experienced a much more enviable fate: the share of the second vintile was in the late 1920s at a very high level (around 10% compared to some 8% before the war) and that of the following 4% seems to have been unaffected by the chaos of 1920–24. Thus, according to our data, the German hyperinflation of the 1920s led to an unprecedented de-concentration of top incomes. This phenomenon is illustrated in Figure 9.7 which graphs the share P99–100 within P90–100. Such a measure only describes the shape of the upper part of the distribution and is thus independent of our income denominator. In 1918 incomes accruing to the upper percentile represented more than the half the total income earned within the top decile. Ten years later, the share had fallen down to less than 35%. These results are perfectly in-line with the diagnostic of Holtfrerich (1980)[12] who sees in the *Mittelstand* the main and only winner of the redistribution process which took place at the time. On the other hand, Peukert (1987) argues in favour of a global stability of top incomes over the hyperinflation years, combined with a complete modification of the structure of the top decile.[13]

One can anyway assert that as the Weimar Republic finally enjoyed a stable economy (and as we at last enjoy tax data), top income shares above the top percentile were substantially under their pre-war levels. As far as the (lower) rest of the top decile is concerned, the pre-war shares had been regained or improved.

The second half of the 1920s and the 1930s were the theatre of the most dramatic variation of top income shares in the twentieth century. The stable years of the Weimar Republic (1925–29) let top income shares unchanged and can thus be described as a short stabilization period before the rapid changes of the 1930s.[14] The Great Depression, indeed, had a sharp and differentiated effect on the top decile. Between 1927 and 1933, the top percentile's share did not decrease much, and remained at its low level at about 11% of total income. At the same time, however, P90–95 and P95–99 experienced a sharp rise: P90–95 even reached its all century maximum at about 12% in 1932. This contrasting situation can be understood as follows: on the one hand, the higher part of the top decile did not significantly suffer of the Depression and of the deflationary measures imposed by the Brüning government at the time, and on the other hand, the lower part of the top decile, being mainly composed of (short-term downward

[12] The position of Holtfrerich is based on the same raw data as those used in the present chapter (p.271sq.) Note however that Holtfrerich draws conclusions on the whole 1913–28 period, without trying to disentangle the effect of the War and that of Hyperinflation, his assumption being that Germany actually experienced one single large inflation period from 1914 to 1924. This perspective is not necessarily accurate to study income distribution as our data show that the two sub-periods (1913–18 and 1919–25) saw completely different evolutions of top incomes.

[13] Persons of private means were badly hurt whereas businessmen keen on bold investments were largely rewarded. This is not necessarily contradictory with our results: it depends a lot on the limits of the period studied. Data concerning income composition for this period are sorely lacking to asses more in-depth such questions.

[14] The late Weimar Republic is actually subject to very controversial debate (among others about the question of overvalued wages). See Bochardt (1990) and Ritschl (1990) for a recent econometric testing attempt of this assumption.

rigid) wages (see the section on income composition), deflation did not hit them and even made their relative weight grow.

The pattern followed by the top 1% share during the Depression is surprising but casts new light on the way the turmoil of the early 1930s impacted German society. As in any other developed country at the time, the corporate sector in Germany experienced a huge negative shock between 1929 and 1932 (see, for instance, Sweezy (1940) and Spoerer (1996)). Real levels of income earned in the top groups fell significantly. For instance, an average of 1.38 million 1995 marks accrued to the top 0.01% in 1928, whereas only 926 thousand marks were earned by the same group in 1932.[15] Compared to the dramatic contraction of national income, however, the drop did not lead to a fall of more than 10% in terms of shares (in France for instance the 1928–32 drop of the top 0.01% share is of 34%). This, added to the growing share of the P90–99 group, means that compared to other countries, the bottom of the distribution in Germany might have suffered more under the Depression relative to the top. The skyrocketing German unemployment rates of the time are consistent with this analysis (see Figure 9H.3). In such a context, pretending, with aggressive anticapitalist rhetoric, that they would take care of the 'small people', the Nazis were in a good position to win democratic elections in 1932.

When the Nazis came to power in 1933, the top decile had been thoroughly equalized: (P99–100, P95–99, P90–95) had moved from a (18%, 13%, 8%) pattern in 1913 to a (11%, 14%, 11%) pattern in 1934. The effect of Nazi economic administration changed radically this outcome of 20 years of inequality evolution. In a period of time of only five years, the pre-First World War shares were nearly recovered and levels were noticeably improved. From 1933 to 1938, the share of the top percentile grew from 11% to 16%; the share of the top 0.01% grew by more than 100% from less than 1.25% to more than 2.5% thus almost recovering its levels of the end of the nineteenth century. P90–95 and P95–99 went down respectively to 10% and 13%.

This evolution can be easily accounted for by the consequences of the Nazis coming to power. Two distinct periods can be highlighted. The first phase (1933–34), consisting of strengthening their grasp on power (among others by bringing back full employment thanks to civil building works), trickled down to the whole economy. Once the country was brought into line (*Gleichschaltung*), the second phase began after 1934–35, and aimed at preparing the economy to the coming war (*Wehrhaftmachung*). This preparation was institutionalized by the Four Year Plan (from 1936 onward) under which Germany definitely ceased to be a market economy. Domestic consumption was curbed (though maintained at levels guaranteeing social stability) and wages growth was soon stopped (so-called *Lohnstop*). A hidden deficit spending policy was organized using parallel currencies. Since the deficit was meant to finance investment in heavy industries and consumption prices were controlled by law, this expansionist

[15] It means a −49% decrease comparable to the −41% observed in France for the same group between the same dates, see Piketty (2001).

policy remained largely unnoticed (the existence of the most widespread of these currencies, the 'MEFO' bonds, named after the firm which emitted them, were only revealed at the Nuremberg Trial against Schacht, the *Reichsbank* president during the war). Systematically exploiting the accounts of German corporations before the war, Spoerer (1996) shows that virtually all armament related industries saw their profits boom in the late 1930s. Contrary to Sweezy (1940), who uses less comprehensive data, Spoerer (1996) shows that not only big corporations but also smaller one gained from these policies. Both authors agree that final consumption related industries were excluded of the process. Spoerer argues that these profits may have been the price Nazis paid to the corporate sector to have them follow their political and military objectives, a kind of compensation for the loss of autonomy of corporations on the road to war. To what precise extent the Nazi regime helped a new category of 'Nazi entrepreneurs' to thrive is nevertheless hard to assess as well as the question whether these entrepreneurs were junior partners of the Nazis or only opportunistic profiteers. Our data nevertheless clearly show that high income group objectively gained from the new regime. The progressive expropriation of Jewish businesses probably accelerated the quick concentration of top incomes.

Unfortunately, we do not have data on the Second World War and its aftermath. As for the hyperinflation years, we can only compare the situation before 1938 with the outcome in 1950. It is nonetheless important to remember that the allied bombings of Germany were mostly directed at cities and communication infrastructure. Thus the amount of productive capital stock destroyed during the war was relatively small, and the investments realized under the Nazi power were not lost for the German economy of the 1950s.[16]

The Years of the Federal Republic

The Federal Republic of Germany, from 1950 to 1998, witnessed an original pattern. The share of the top decile oscillated between 30% and 35% over the whole period. However there seems to be a downward trend in the 1950s and 1960s followed by an upward trend in the 1970s, 1980s, and even 1990s. Once again, one should differentiate the picture at the very top of the distribution from that beneath.

The top percentile exhibits a striking stability throughout the period at about 11%. This level is similar to that observed during the Weimar Republic and much lower than the level of the early twentieth century. The war and the allied occupation thus seems to have undone what the Nazis did at the top of the distribution.[17] Looking further into the top percentile at the top 0.01%, one is

[16] For a detailed assessment of the economic result of the war, see Abelshauser (2004).

[17] It should be recalled here that the data we have do no permit to trace individuals. Top income groups may experience mobility and therefore rich individuals may change as top income groups remain stable.

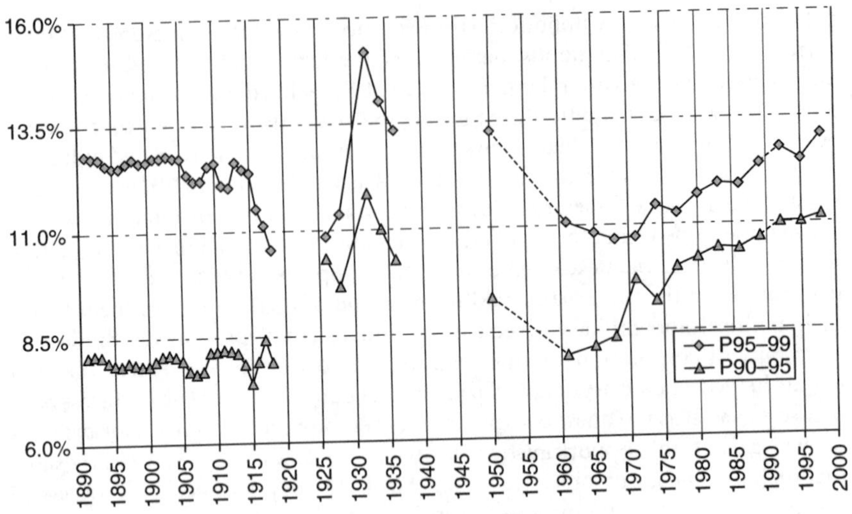

Figure 9.3 Share of P90–95 and P95–99, Germany 1891–1998

Source: Author's computation on German income tax data, Table 9I.5

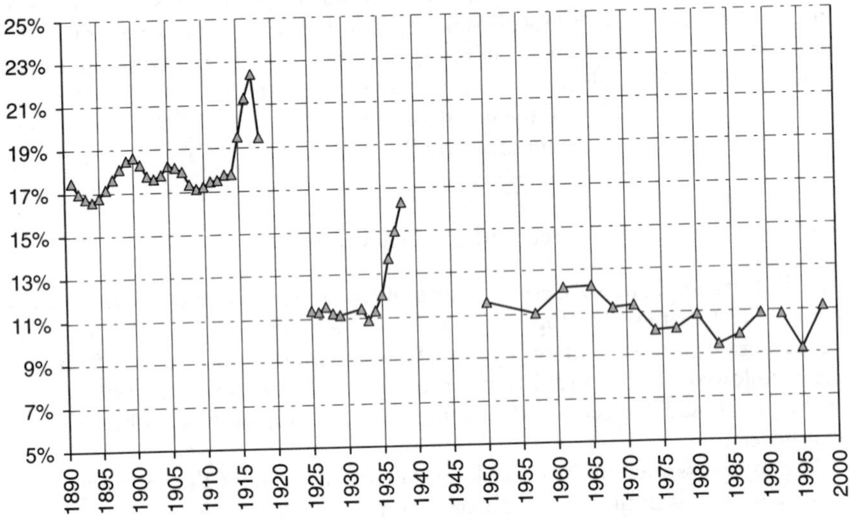

Figure 9.4 Share of the top percentile, Germany 1891–1998

Source: Author's computation on German income tax data, Table 9I.5

nonetheless led to nuance that judgement since the share of very high income groups remained in the years after the war at higher levels than before, notably in the 1960s and in the late 1980s and 1990s. A robust confirmation of this fact is given by shares within shares (see Figure 9.8). The share of the top 0.01% within the top percentile was about 12% before the war, it was in the 1960s and in the late 1980s and 1990s about 15%.

Compared to other developed countries studied in this book like France or the United States, the top 0.01% income share is much higher throughout the post-war period. For instance, the French and American top 0.01% income share remained around 0.5% after the Second World War and until the late 1980s (in the case of France, until today). The German top 0.01% income share is always twice to thrice higher, fluctuating between 1% and 1.5%. Note that this difference is not as striking at the top 1% level. This means that top incomes are structurally more concentrated in Germany than in France or the United States in the immediate after war, and until today in the case of France. Looking once again at shares within shares, one can have a confirmation of this phenomenon, which is robust to differences which could exist between income total denominators. The share of the top 1% within the top 10% (see Figure 9.7) fluctuates in Germany between 30% and 40% with a downward trend since 1961. The same share has been fluctuating (with a downward trend also in France and in the US between 20% and 30% only since the Second World War. In the recent years, however, the US reached German-style levels. The same kind of pattern can be observed when looking at the share of the top 0.01% with the top percentile. Thus the higher concentration of top incomes in Germany is linked to the higher weight of very top income groups: the super-rich German were richer than the super-rich Americans until the late 1980s (see Figures 9.7, 9.9, and 9.10 for illustration of these comparisons).

Note, last, that the pattern followed be the top percentile's share is very pro-cyclical after the war. The recessions of 1966–67, 1973–74, and of the early 1980s are periods of drop in the shares.[18]

The bottom part of the top decile does not exhibit the same stability as the upper part (see Figures 9.3 and 9.9). Although it is comparable with levels observed in other developed countries after the war, the point for P90 and P95 for 1950 should be considered with caution (see Appendices for more on this issue) and may be significantly overestimated. From the early 1960s onward, however, the share of the bottom 9% of the top decile has been constantly growing following a trend comparable to that followed by the US (or France in the more recent years, see Figure 9.9). At last, Reunification, does not seem to have impacted significantly top income shares at least at the all-German level.

Evolution of Top Incomes Composition

Information on sources of income enables us to estimate the share of various income sources at different levels of the income distribution, using simple linear interpolation methods. Unfortunately, such information is not available

[18] The drop for 1995 may be related to the aftermath of the 1993 recession but is also at least partly a blip linked to the surge of tax avoidance based on fictional real estate losses which followed the Reunification and the huge real estate investment in the new *Länder*.

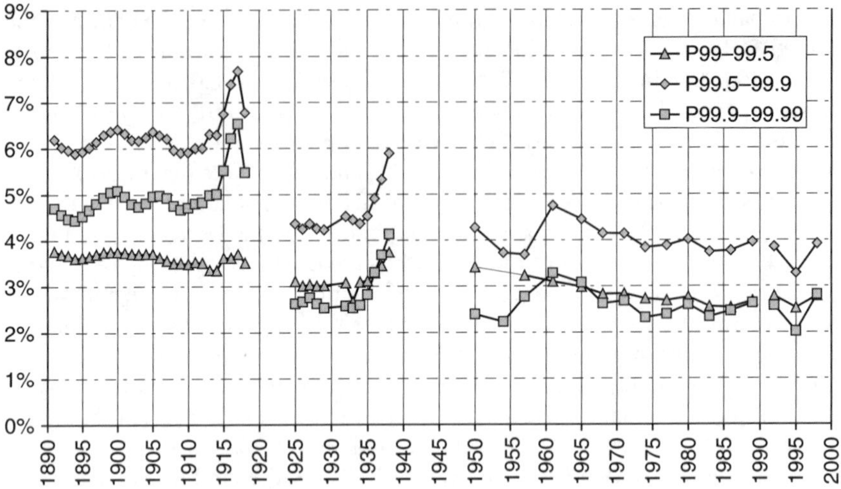

Figure 9.5 Share of P99–99.5, P99.5–99.9, and P99.9–99.9, Germany 1891–1998

Source: Author's computation on German income tax data, Table 9I.5

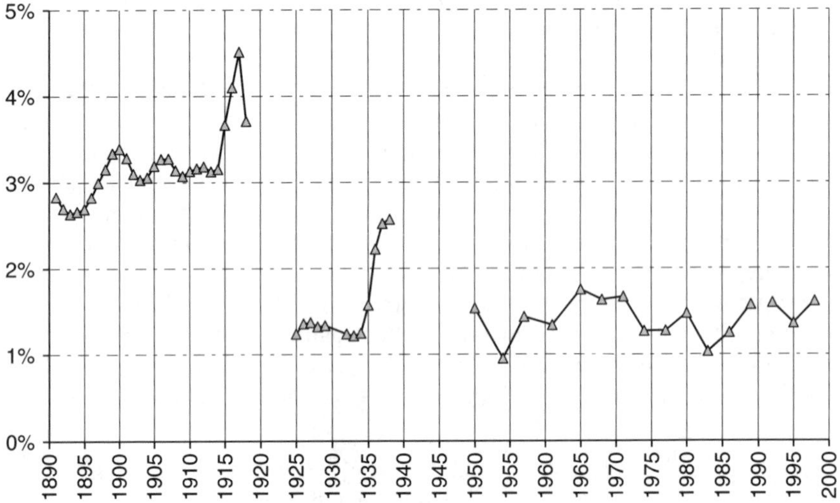

Figure 9.6 Share of the top 0.01%, Germany 1891–1998

Source: Author's computation on German income tax data, Table 9I.5

before 1926. We present here estimates concerning the interwar period (see Figures 9.11–9.13) and the recent years (see Figures 9.14–9.15). The basic fact about the composition of top incomes is, as in France or the US, the share of capital income is growing with income. In 1928 as in 1936, 70–80% of the P90–95

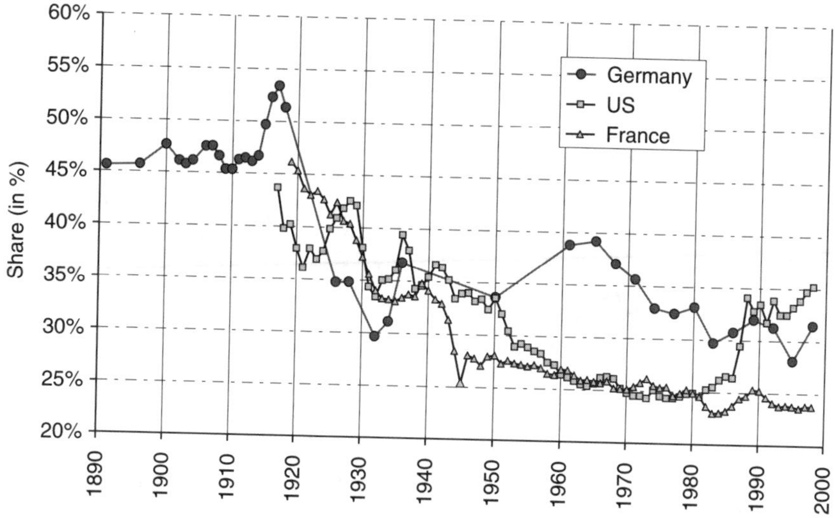

Figure 9.7 Share of the top percentile within the top decile, France, US, and Germany 1891–1998

Source: Author's computations on German income tax data; France—Chapter 3, this volume; US—Chapter 4, this volume.

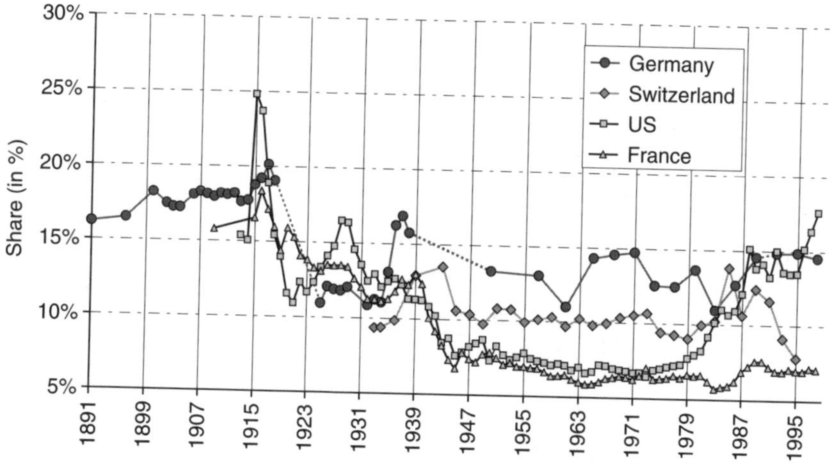

Figure 9.8 Share of P99.99–100 in top percentile, Germany 1891–1998

Source: Author's computations on German income tax data; France—Chapter 3, this volume; US—Chapter 4, this volume.

percentile is made of wages. The rest being capital and business income, and self-employment income. The top 0.1%[19] is on the contrary basically made of capital income and wages only represent a mere 10–20% of this fractile. The same

[19] We do not give estimates for the top 0.01% because it would most of the time entail linear extrapolations, which are obviously not robust.

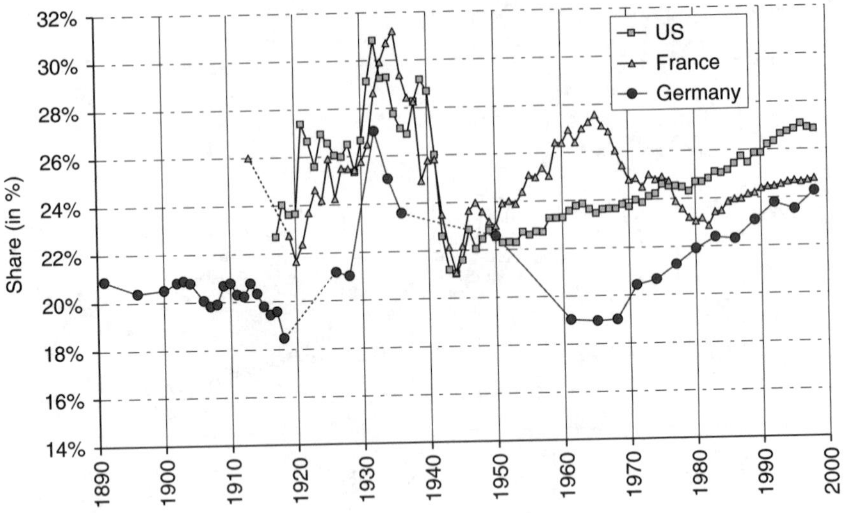

Figure 9.9 Share of the bottom part of the top decile (P90–99), France, US, and Germany 1891–1998

Source: Germany—author's computations on German income tax data; France—Chapter 3, this volume; US—Chapter 4, this volume.

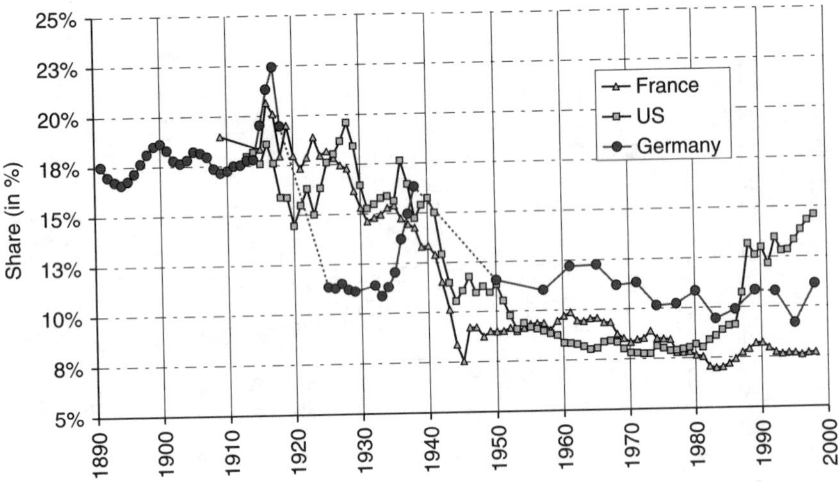

Figure 9.10 Share of the top part of the top decile (P99–100), France, US, and Germany 1891–1998

Source: Germany—author's computations on German income tax data; France—Chapter 3, this volume; US—Chapter 4, this volume.

pattern can be observed during the last decade of the twentieth century. It should be noted here that German tax law registers as 'business income' (*Einkünfte aus dem Gewerbebetrieb*) incomes that would, for example in France, be recorded as capital income. This phenomenon still exists today and is related

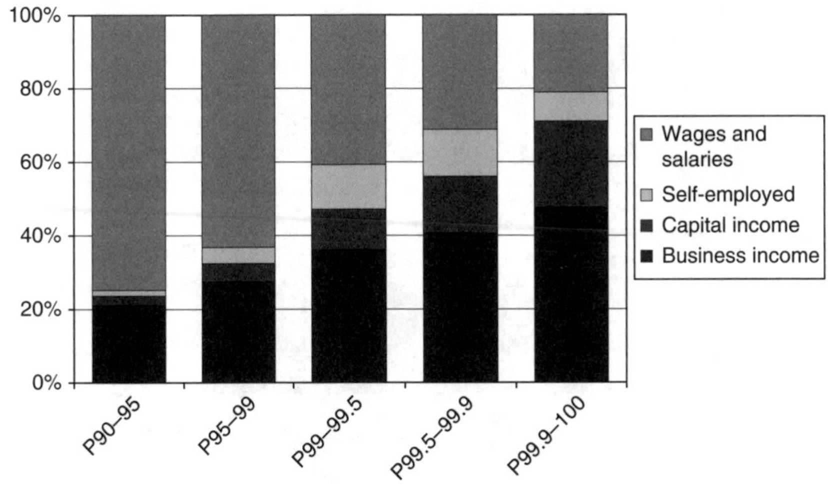

Figure 9.11 Sources of income in top income groups in Germany, 1928

Source: Author's computation on German income tax data, Table 9I.5.

to the fact that public corporations (*Aktiengesellschaften*) which pay dividends which are in turn taxed under the category 'capital income' was until recently quite rare in Germany. Other legal forms for societies (*Kommanditengesellschaft* or *Offene Handelsgesellschaft*) seem to have been much more widespread and even encouraged by corporate and business tax law. The structure of top incomes appears to be very similar to that of other countries (with also a local maximum of self-employment incomes about the P99 threshold). Thus top income shares decline in the first half of the century is a capital income phenomenon as well as the striking concentration of top German incomes after the Second World War. Further study of the effective impact of German direct income and wealth taxes on the dynamics of capital accumulation could cast light on these facts.[20]

Income composition estimates also cast an interesting light on economic shocks such as the Great Depression. Not only did the Great Depression lower all top incomes: as already said, the top decile was fundamentally transformed during the Depression with lower percentiles weighting more whereas the share of the top centile was only slightly negatively affected. Composition estimates for 1932 confirm very clearly our former assumption that this phenomenon was the result of real wages having become relatively more important within the top decile thanks to deflation. In 1932 indeed, wages are more present higher in the distribution: they still represent about 35% of incomes in the top

[20] See Dell (2005) for an preliminary attempt at understanding the German originality using German inheritance tax. Top income tax rates in Germany have remained at 40% before the Second World War and fluctuated between 50% and 60% after the war. These rates were thus smaller than those experienced in France until very recently, and in Anglo-Saxon countries until the beginning of the 1980s. On the top of that, inheritance tax rates have been significantly lower, and exemption brackets much larger, than in France after 1945.

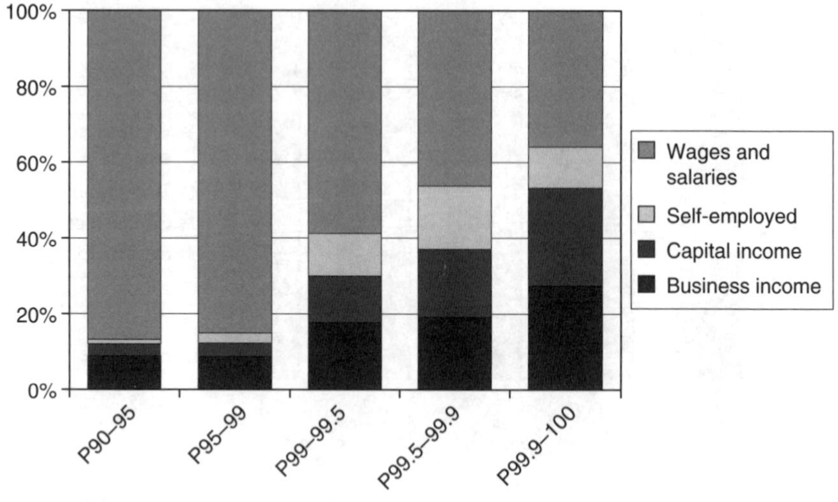

Figure 9.12 Sources of income in top income groups in Germany, 1932

Source: Author's computation on German income tax data, Table 9I.5.

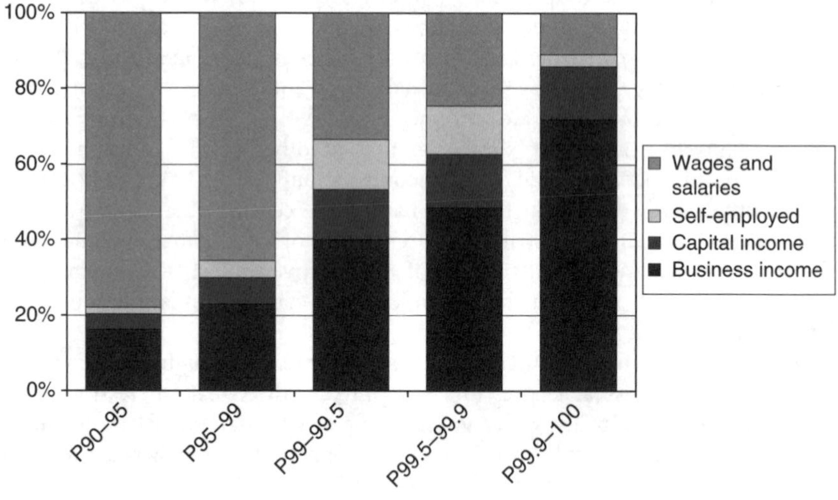

Figure 9.13 Sources of income in top income groups in Germany, 1936

Source: Author's computation on German income tax data, Table 9I.5.

0.1 percentile whereas four years before, as four years later, they represent a maximum of 20%.

9.4 CONCLUSION

In this chapter we display for the first time complete patterns of evolution for top incomes in Germany throughout the twentieth century. We show that top income

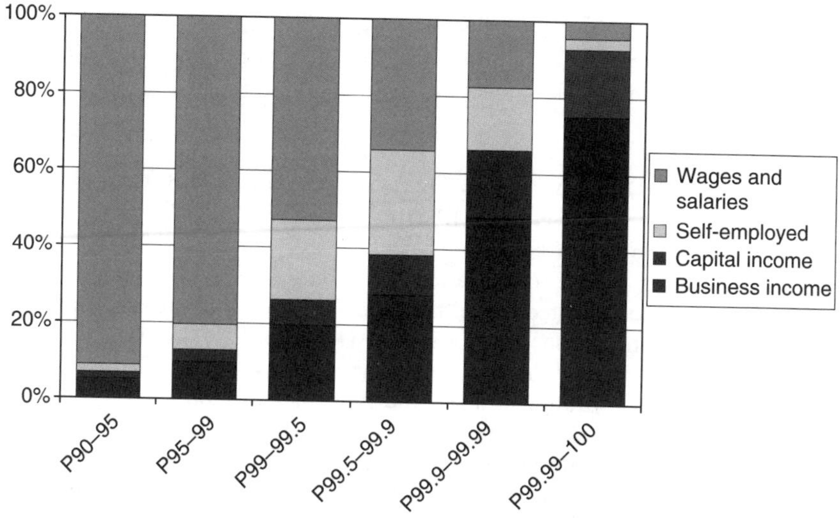

Figure 9.14 Sources of income in top income groups in Germany, 1992

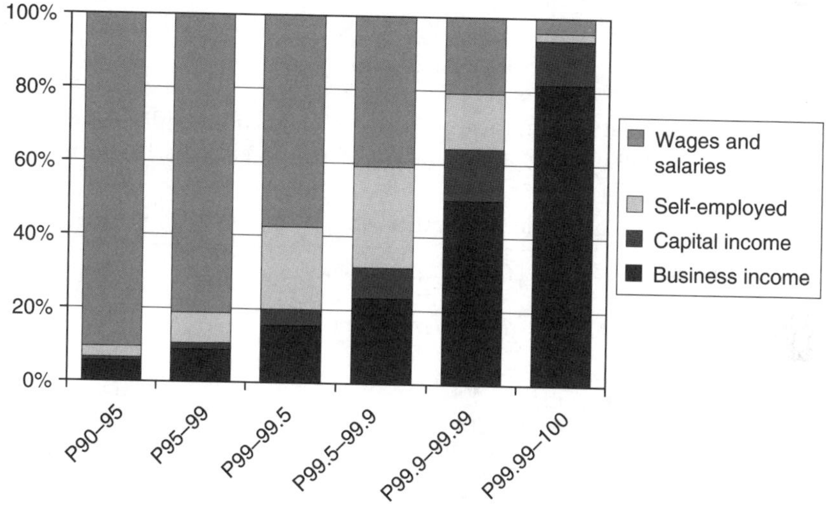

Figure 9.15 Sources of income in top income groups in Germany, 1998

Source: Author's computation on German income tax data, Table 9I.5.

shares decreased over the century largely because of the shocks of the 1914–45 period. We also highlight an original evolution during the interwar years: Nazi power helped top incomes to recover part of their pre-1913 shares. Further, we pinpoint a specific structure of the top decile of the German income distribution after the Second World War, characterized by high stability and high concentration: super-rich Germans were richer than super-rich Americans until the late 1980s.

Using (partial) estimates of income sources we show that these top incomes which were hit hard in the course of the century were basically capital incomes. Thus understanding the pattern observed should encourage us to look more precisely at wealth distributions and the effect of progressive taxation on wealth accumulation dynamics over the century.

APPENDIX 9A: DATA FOR GERMANY OVER THE TWENTIETH CENTURY

See Table 9A.1 for precise references to the publications used. Sometimes, the same tax year is documented more than once; we only indicate here the most detailed publication used for one given year. The years 1920 and 1949 were not used in this work because their robustness was not assured. Indeed, 1920 and 1949 were years of institutional, fiscal, and monetary turmoil which render the interpretation of the income shares we could estimate quite dubious.

In order to estimate thresholds and average income of top income groups, we assume that the tail of the income distribution is Pareto shaped. The detail of this estimation strategy is given in the next section.

APPENDIX 9B: INTERPOLATION TECHNIQUE USING PARETO'S LAW

With the German data, we have at our disposal tabulations with fiscal income brackets containing amounts and numbers of tax payers. The Pareto method

Table 9A.1 Income tax publications used, Germany

Years	Name of the main publication	Volume
1891–1918	*Statistisches Jahrbuch für den preußischen Staat*	17(1921)
1920	*Statistik des deutschen Reichs*	312 (ES)
1925	*Statistik des deutschen Reichs*	348 (ES)
1926	*Statistik des deutschen Reichs*	375 (ES) & 359 (LS)
1927	*Statistik des deutschen Reichs*	375 (ES)
1928	*Statistik des deutschen Reichs*	391 (ES) & 378 (LS)
1929	*Statistik des deutschen Reichs*	430 (ES)
1932	*Statistik des deutschen Reichs*	482 (ES) & 492 (LS)
1933	*Statistik des deutschen Reichs*	482 (ES)
1934	*Statistik des deutschen Reichs*	499 (ES) & 492 (LS)
1935	*Statistik des deutschen Reichs*	534 (ES)
1936	*Statistik des deutschen Reichs*	534 (ES) & 530 (LS)
1937–1938	*Statistik des deutschen Reichs*	580
1949	*Statistisches Jahrbuch der Bundesrepublik Deutschland*	–
1950	*Statistik der Bundesrepublik Deutschland*	125 (ES) & 107 (LS)
1954	*Fachserie L: Finanzen und Steuern*	Reihe 6.1 (ES)
1955	*Statistik der Bundesrepublik Deutschland*	– (LS)
1957	*Fachserie L: Finanzen und Steuern*	Reihe 6.1 (ES)
1961–1968	*Fachserie L: Finanzen und Steuern*	Reihe 6.1 (ES)
1971–1998	*Fachserie L: Finanzen und Steuern*	Reihe 7.1 (ES)

used to interpolate has been described in Appendix 5C. The accuracy of our estimates relies on the assumption that the income distributions observed are indeed Pareto tailed, as well as on the number of top brackets published in tax statistics. The first issue has received various theoretical justifications (Champernowne 1953; Mandelbrot 1960; Gabaix 1999, for instance) and is thus more than as simple empirical regularity. As far as the second issue is concerned, German tax statistics most of the time produced tabulations with very numerous top brackets, and the P99.99 fractile is most of the time larger than the top bracket published (see Appendix 9I where years for which this is not the case are indicated). Nevertheless we checked with micro-data the accuracy of our estimates for the 1990s, for which micro data are available—see Appendix 9C.

APPENDIX 9C: CHECKS OF INTERPOLATION ASSUMPTIONS USING MICRO-DATA IN THE 1990s

We completed the extensive use of tax data tabulations published by the German Statistical Offices by working on income tax micro-data. These were provided by the German Federal Statistical Office, for the first time to a non-German, under strong anonymization conditions. There are available data for the years 1992, 1995, and 1998. Original data-sets contain about 30 million observations. Table 9C.1 summarizes these figures. We worked on a 10% stratified random sampling set with an over-representation (sampling rate of 70%) of the top centile. This enabled us to check the validity of the Pareto assumption made when using tabulations for years before 1990.

Since the micro-data we used rely on a sample, we reproduced the type of tabulation used before 1992 to distinguish sampling error and estimation error. Results are given in Table 9C.2 and show that most of the time, the relative estimation error is smaller than 1%. Higher errors arise in 1995 but remain under 2%.

APPENDIX 9D: TAX UNIT DEFINITION OVER THE TWENTIETH CENTURY

The first German income tax was introduced in Prussia in 1891. Tax units were the married couple plus children if any. In comparison with other European

Table 9C.1 Tax units in the micro-data set for Germany in the 1990s

	1992	1995	1998
TU in the file	29,478,994	29,478,994	28,672,912
Total TU	43,972,179	44,618,987	45,172,545
Share	67.00%	66.50%	63.50%

Note: Tax units (TU) with cut-off age at 20.

Source: Author's computation on micro data provided by the *Statistisches Bundesamt.*

Table 9C.2 The accuracy of quantile estimation for Germany in the 1990s

1992	Micro Data Sample	Tabulation Sample	Tabulation Total	Sampling Error	Estimation Error
P90–100	148,992	148,563	148,540	−0.02%	−0.29%
P95–100	203,773	202,759	202,717	−0.02%	−0.50%
P99–100	473,216	469,014	468,763	−0.05%	−0.89%
P99,5–100	708,984	703,592	703,083	−0.07%	−0.76%
P99,9–100	1,894,885	1,881,457	1,878,210	−0.17%	−0.71%
P99,99–100	7,742,969	7,791,919	7,756,572	−0.45%	0.63%
1995	Micro Data Sample	Tabulation Sample	Tabulation Total	Sampling Error	Estimation Error
P90–100	152,952	152,249	152,173	−0.05%	−0.46%
P95–100	204,398	202,677	202,494	−0.09%	−0.84%
P99–100	445,741	438,526	437,807	−0.16%	−1.62%
P99,5–100	656,363	648,114	646,656	−0.22%	−1.26%
P99,9–100	1,734,253	1,702,345	1,694,440	−0.46%	−1.84%
P99,99–100	7,430,870	7,424,250	7,379,744	−0.60%	−0.09%
1998	Micro Data Sample	Tabulation Sample	Tabulation Total	Sampling Error	Estimation Error
P90–100	174,949	174,644	175,015	0.21%	−0.17%
P95–100	242,577	240,338	240,835	0.21%	−0.92%
P99–100	586,814	585,152	587,232	0.36%	−0.28%
P99,5–100	909,658	907,564	911,298	0.41%	−0.23%
P99,9–100	2,700,748	2,694,098	2,709,431	0.57%	−0.25%
P99,99–100	12,819,136	12,798,031	12,895,617	0.76%	−0.16%

Note: Yearly fiscal income of tax units, in DM.
Source: Author's computation on micro data provided by the *Statistisches Bundesamt*.

countries like France, who introduced income taxes only during or after the First World War, Prussia was thus quite ahead of its time. The broad basis of Prussia's income tax was a mark of modernity: whereas France's first income tax (1914/15) applied to less than 5% of the entire French population, Prussia's income tax basis represented from 20% (1891) to about 50% (1914) of the total tax units (see Figure 9G.1).[21]

After 1920, tax units remained based on couples but the introduction of a pay-as-you-earn tax on wages, relying on individual-based tax units, makes the reconstitution of an homogenous income distribution more complex: the vast majority of tax payers only paid the so-called *Lohnsteuer* (*LS*) and were therefore recorded in specific statistics. Above a given income threshold, one had to file a tax return, and one thus entered the 'classical' income tax (*Einkommensteuer*: *ES*) statistics.[22] This fiscal dichotomy still exists today. It entails that one has to merge

[21] For a precise account of the genesis of Prussia's fiscal modernity at the turn of the century, see Ketterle (1994).

[22] The threshold has been existing until 1995. After this date (and notably for 1998), there was no obligation of filing tax returns for wage earners with no other income source. 'Pure' wage earners are nonetheless still present in the statistics via PAYE records.

income tax data coming from two different kinds of tabulations in order to estimate fractiles bigger than the top 1% of the income distribution.[23]

This problem is particularly significant for the Interwar period and just after the Second World War. After 1961 (included) indeed, the German Statistical Office published income tabulations which already contained agglomerate data and could therefore be used without further treatment (this is why table sources does not document the specific *Lohnsteuer* publications which continued to be issued by the Federal Statistical Office until 1992). Before 1961, one has to merge the various tabulations on its own. For the years 1925, 1927, 1929, 1933, 1935, and 1937–38, the lack of PAYE statistics made it impossible for us to estimate fractiles P90 and P95. Two kinds of problem arise due to this merging process.

First, the merging of *LS* and *ES* tabulation can lead to double counting. Fortunately, the *LS* statistics only record the PAYE tax payers who do not earn more than the '*ES*-threshold', which suppresses most potential cases of double counting. Nonetheless, for the years 1926, 1928, and 1932, some double counting exists because people with mixed activity may be present in both statistics: small wages lead them to appear in the *LS* statistics (with their wage) and other incomes make them pay the *ES* (on these other incomes). These tax payers are thus split in two. The number of tax units affected by these double counts is modest (in 1928 they were less than 300,000, which is less than 1% of all tax units) and probably lead to a slight underestimation of our top income groups around P90 and P95. Clearly, the problem cannot impact significantly higher income groups because if the wage component exceeds the '*ES*-threshold' then the tax unit disappears from the LS statistics. The *ES*-threshold is thus the upper bound of the possible under-estimation.

Second, the heterogeneity of tax units (married couple based at the top, but individual based at the bottom, since PAYE tax was collected on an individual basis) may lead to some bias in the estimates of the fractiles beneath and around the *ES*-threshold. For the years 1950, 1954, and 1957 the merging of the two sets of tabulations rely would rely on too many ad hoc hypotheses and we are thus able to estimate robustly only top groups above P99. We nonetheless produce estimates of P90 and P95 for 1950 using a synthetic tabulation published in Statistisches Bundesamt (1954*b*). This tabulation is comparable to the synthetic tabulations existing for the interwar years Statistisches Reichsamt (1939) and which lead to estimates identical to ours. From 1968 onward, the German Statistical Office issued tabulations matching 'whenever the necessary information was at hand' the married individuals taxed separately by the PAYE wage tax. We use these tabulations, but unfortunately the Statistical Office did not document properly the extent to which the matching it implemented did solve the problem.

In conclusion, the reader should keep in mind that the robustness of the P90 and P95 estimates between 1919 and 1968 is not guaranteed. After 1968, one still

[23] The threshold indeed guarantees that higher fractiles (top 1% and higher) are only constituted of '*ES* income tax' payers.

cannot exclude a upward bias for these fractiles. This bias would nevertheless be conservative with regard to our findings, namely that, compared with other developed countries, P90 and P95 are low relative to P99 and the other fractiles further up the distribution.

APPENDIX 9E: FISCAL INCOME DEFINITION: INCOME AND THE GERMAN TAX STATISTICS OVER THE TWENTIETH CENTURY

The Prussian income tax was a 'modern' income tax because of its very broad definition of taxable income: wages and salaries, capital income, self-employed incomes were part of the taxable basis. Capital gains were not taxable under the income tax. Apart from an exemption threshold (*Existenzminimum*), every income had to be taxed. Dependent children were taken into account by 'moving' tax payers one, two, or three brackets down the tax schedule. Published statistics, however, most of the time record incomes before application of this system (at least as far as the 'top' incomes are concerned, i.e. those for which a tax return was effectively filed).[24] Prussian income tax statistics can therefore be used without any specific treatment.

After the First World War, however, the simplicity of the Prussian system was lost and the income tabulated in the tax statistics varied over time. As far as *ES* statistics are concerned, the income concept used was slightly more restrictive and law dependant than the one we used before 1920. Incomes (*Einkommen*) are tabulated after deductions of the costs incurred by earning them. These costs are of two kinds: those which can be related to one specific income source (*Werbungskosten*) and those which cannot be related to a specific income source (*Sonderleistungen* before 1934 and *Sonderausgaben* after 1934 and until today). We corrected for the latter but not for the former.[25] The correction was realized by adding the minimal lump sum deduction allowed by law. We therefore adopted a conservative correction which cannot be likely to overestimate our top income groups. As far as the LS statistics are concerned, the lump sum deductions for wage and salaries (equivalent of *Werbungskosten* and *Sonderleistungen* and *-ausgaben*) were all deducted in the 1920s but not anymore in the 1930s a well as after the Second World War: in the process of merging *ES* and *LS* statistics we thus had to

[24] Indeed, for smaller incomes, the Prussian income tax relied heavily on estimation of tax payers' incomes by a local commission. The threshold above which a return had to be filed has remained that of 3000m throughout the period.

[25] The latter is often more variable across time and of less economic significance than the former. For instance, when the Nazi came to power, contribution to unions (which were part of the *Sonderleistungen*) stopped to be deductible, and purchases of *Ersatz* became tax deductible. Clearly, we do not want such variation to impact our income definition. As far as *Werbungskosten* are concerned, on the contrary, their deduction seems necessary, at least for the self-employed, and business income. Moreover, the post-Second World War incomes are also after deductions of these *Werbungskosten*.

translate the wage distribution to the right in the 1920s (add the *Sonderleistungen*) and to the left in the 1930s (subtract the *Werbungskosten*).

Note that from the Interwar years onward, capital gains are taxable in Germany (with a specific treatment, however, see Appendix 9F). Pensions are also fully taxable at the time (in the course of the 1950s, most of them became tax exempt) but unemployment benefits are tax exempt. From 1932 onward, most of agricultural income was tax exempt. We did not corrected the series for this exemption first because the German economy encountered too heavy a shock between 1929 and 1932 to correct the post-crisis years using pre-crisis year data, and, second, because agricultural income is anyway a very small portion of incomes at the top of the distribution.

The post-1949 German tax law is based on a set decreasing series of income concepts, which was already in part, although unsystematically, used in the 1930s. Each concept is based on the previous one, new deductions being operated. Estimates of top incomes shares in this paper are based on the 'overall amount of incomes' (*Gesamtbetrag der Einkünfte*, or *GdE*). This fiscal income is the more upstream concept available, i.e. the one from which fewer law dependant deductions were subtracted (it, however, contains compensations of losses between various sources at the taxpayer's level). What it measures is thus relatively close to an economically relevant concept of primary income containing all wages and salaries, business, and self-employment income as well as financial capital and real estate incomes. Payroll taxes paid by employees are included but those paid by employers are not. A small part of the pensions (from 1955 onward, the so-called *Ertragsanteil* which varies across individuals but represent about 30% of the pension) is included but unemployment benefits are not. Most importantly, wage and salary incomes are taken into account after deduction of the costs incurred by earning those incomes, which is often a lumpy deduction.[26] This makes wages and salaries homogenous to other income sources. No correction is made for these deductions in the series presented here.

Overall, thus, the raw fiscal income which is the material of our series is a fairly wide income notion, which is moreover homogenous over the century (at least for the top income groups we are focusing on).

APPENDIX 9F: CAPITAL GAINS AND THE GERMAN TAX LAW

The Taxation of Capital Gains in the Late 1980s and the Reforms of the 1990s

Capital gains on productive capital (*Betriebsvermögen*) are subject to the income tax in Germany under the category of 'extraordinary incomes'. They therefore

[26] These are the *Werbungskosten* which are deducted of the *Bruttolohn* to produce the *Einkünfte aus unselbständiger Arbeit* which is taken into account in ES tax statistics, in a setting which was already functioning before the war.

enjoy a tax reduction of 50%. Capital gains on personal capital (*Privatvermögen*) are tax exempt if they are not realized within a 'speculation period' of one year. Moreover, part of the capital gains on productive capital enjoy exemption brackets. The determination of the exemption bracket is complex and depends on the absolute level of the capital gain as well as on the age of the tax payer. Moreover, and more importantly, capital gains from financial capital are tax exempt if they represent less than 1% of the firm sold or if the shareholder had no 'significant participation' in the firm during the five years preceding the realization of the gains. 'Significant participation' (*wesentliche Beteiligung*) means holding 25% of the firm.

In 1990, a Tax Reform Act had a huge impact on capital gain realization, although the part of the reform concerning capital gain taxation was ultimately considerably weakened. It originally restricted to the first DM2 million of capital gains the 50% tax reduction. The following DM3 million still enjoyed a 33% tax reduction but capital gains in excess of DM5 million were to be taxed at full rate. This restriction was subject to discussion within the ruling coalition[27] and finally in the new income tax law for 1990, the 50% reduction still applied to the first DM30 million (sic). This episode and its impact on income tax statistics is documented in Rosinus (2000: 461, n. 24) and can be seen in Figure 9F.3.

The tax reforms of the late 1990s also changed the conditions under which capital gains are taxed: the 'significant participation' criterion has been tightened up progressively. Thus the 25% of the total firm capital threshold was reduced to 10% after 1998 and to 1% (which led the concept of 'significant participation' to disappear) from 2001 onward. This may have led to lumpy capital gain realizations in 1998 (last years at 25%) and 2000 (last year at 10%).

Capital Gains Taxation

As already mentioned, capital gains were not taxable in Prussia before the First World War. After the First World War, they became taxable under conditions similar to those existing at the end of the century ('significant participation' of 25% and reduced taxation rates).

Assessing the Importance of Capital Gains in the 1990s

The raw micro-data we use include 100% of taxable capital gains. Top incomes shares estimated on raw data are thus based on the capital gains included (CGI) income distribution. Since micro-data enable us to identify capital gains for each tax payer, we can estimate series of capital gain excluded (CGE) top income shares. Last, we can use the fractiles of the CGE distribution to identify to groups for which we calculate total including capital gains.

[27] 'Schwarz-Gelbe' Coalition of Christian Democrats and Liberals under H. Kohl.

To stick to the habitual notations, let P^0XX be the threshold of the XXth percentile for the CGI distribution. $P^0XX{-}100$ is the average CGI income above this threshold and $T^0XX{-}100$ is the total CGI income above this threshold. Similarly let P^1XX be the threshold of the XXth percentile for the CGE distribution. Then $P^1XX{-}100$ (resp. $T^1XX{-}100$) is the average (resp. the total) GCE income above that threshold. Finally we define $P^2XX{-}100$ (resp. $T^2XX{-}100$), the average (resp. total) CGI income of individuals above P^1XX.[28]

Tables 9F.1–9F.3 give these three income series for 1992, 1995, and 1998.

Columns 9 and 10 show that capital gains affect mostly the top of the distribution. Comparing columns 12 and 14 give an idea of the magnitude of the re-ranking which takes place when including capital gains: amounts along the F_0 distributions of CGI incomes are clearly concentrated at the top (showing that to a certain extent, capital gains 'make' top income earners). Opposite, capital gains in the F_1 distributions of CGE incomes are much more uniformly distributed. The fact that column 10 may be smaller than one also reflect the consequences of this re-ranking.

When comparing the different years documented, two scenarios can be pointed out, these scenarios can be easily related to the stock market activity in the 1990s in Germany (Figures 9F.1 and 9F.2 show the evolution of the German DAX from 1988 to 2002).

The 1992–95 scenario is a scenario of low growth of assets, which corresponds to capital gains of modest magnitude. Looking at column 10 and 13 in Tables 9F.1 and 9F.2, one sees that the capital gain issue become significant (entails variations of more than 1% of the quantities of interest) only above P99.

The 1998 scenarios a scenario of rapid growth of assets with, on the top of it, a tax law reform which may have encouraged lumpy capital gain realization. Capital gains in 1998 are still very concentrated at the top but the order of magnitude of the 'overestimation' implied by taking them into account is much greater than in the previous years (they represent more than 50% of total income in P99.99–100 whereas only 20% in 1992 and 1995).

These results are consistent with what Piketty and Saez (2003) found for the US: capital gain realization takes place at the very top of the distribution. In Germany, it seems to be a phenomenon of smaller magnitude (e.g. column 10 for P99.99–100 is 126% in 1992 and 176% in 1998 in the US against 113% and 164% in Germany) and, most of all, even more concentrated at the top of the GCI-income distribution (e.g. column 10 for P99–99.5 is 106% in 1992 and 115% in 1998 in the US against 99.9% and 98.0% in Germany).

Correcting for Capital Gains Before 1990

Two main factors can explain the amount of capital gains realized a given year. The growth of the value of capital in the previous years is the first obvious factor which

[28] For the sake of symmetry we could define P^3 resp. T^3 being average resp. total CGE incomes above CGI distribution based thresholds, but this has not much economic significance.

Table 9F.1 Capital gains and the various aggregates, Germany 1992

	Capital gains fully included				Capital gains fully excluded				Ratios		
PXX	P^0XX 1	T^0XX 2	P^0XX−XX+1 3	P^0XX−100 4	P^1XX 5	T^1XX 6	P^1XX−XX+1 7	P^1XX−100 8	1/5 9	3/7 10	4/8 11
P90	83,731	207,132,984,174	94,211	148,992	83,616	207,292,385,041	>94,283	148,055	100.1%	99.9%	100.6%
P95	107,994	239,932,965,755	136,412	203,773	107,752	240,377,773,514	136,665	201,827	100.2%	99.8%	101.0%
P99	202,904	52,205,547,718	237,448	473,216	200,838	52,274,981,774	237,764	462,477	101.0%	99.9%	102.3%
P99.5	287,839	72,555,563,393	412,508	708,984	282,597	72,551,729,341	412,487	687,191	101.9%	100.0%	103.2%
P99.9	716,457	49,274,714,617	1,245,098	1,894,885	682,761	48,369,766,571	1,222,232	1,786,008	104.9%	101.9%	106.1%
P99.99	3,235,910	34,047,520,812	7,742,969	7,742,969	2,847,350	30,164,912,024	6,859,999	6,859,999	113.6%	112.9%	112.9%

	Share of CG when ranking takes CG into account		Share of CG when ranking does not take CG in to account			Hybrid series		Ratios	
PXX	CinF_0 12	C/T_0 13	CinF_1 14	C/(T_1+C) 15	T_1+C 16	P^2XX−XX+1 17	P^2XX−100 18	17/7 19	18/8 20
P90	335,749,965	0.2%	520,208,727	0.3%	207,812,593,767	94,520	150,168	100.3%	101.4%
P95	977,020,679	0.4%	1,539,560,975	0.6%	241,917,334,489	137,540	205,815	100.6%	102.0%
P99	618,746,469	1.2%	797,852,072	1.5%	53,072,833,846	241,393	478,915	101.5%	103.6%
P99.5	2,001,710,546	2.8%	2,170,908,665	2.9%	74,722,638,006	424,829	716,438	103.0%	104.3%
P99.9	3,817,529,626	7.7%	2,904,399,538	5.7%	51,274,166,109	1,295,621	1,882,872	106.0%	105.4%
P99.99	7,284,721,114	21.4%	1,354,924,553	4.3%	31,519,836,577	7,168,132	7,168,132	104.5%	104.5%
Totals above P50	16,046,308,271		11,146,705,254						

Note: Yearly fiscal income of tax units, in DM.

Source: Author's computation on micro data provided by the *Statistisches Bundesamt*.

Table 9F.2 Capital gains and the various aggregates, Germany 1995

	Capital gains fully included				Capital gains fully excluded				Ratios		
PXX	P^0XX 1	T^0XX 2	P^0XX−XX+1 3	P^0XX−100 4	P^1XX 5	T^1XX 6	P^1XX−XX+1 7	P^1XX−100 8	1/5 9	3/7 10	4/8 11
P90	90,340	226,454,996,524	101,506	152,952	90,206	226,028,805,748	101,315	150,245	100.1%	100.2%	101.8%
P95	116,014	257,117,314,453	144,063	204,398	115,747	255,990,668,168	143,431	199,176	100.2%	100.4%	102.6%
P99	206,199	52,454,030,913	235,120	445,741	204,377	51,816,345,137	232,261	422,153	100.9%	101.2%	105.6%
P99.5	278,517	69,050,551,193	386,890	656,363	274,014	67,205,627,306	376,553	612,045	101.6%	102.7%	107.2%
P99.9	647,793	44,224,817,761	1,101,295	1,734,253	620,765	41,314,129,519	1,028,813	1,554,012	104.4%	107.0%	111.6%
P99.99	2,815,634	33,155,790,429	7,430,870	7,430,870	2,540,775	28,024,312,771	6,280,804	6,280,804	110.8%	118.3%	118.3%

	Share of CG when ranking takes CG into account		Share of CG when ranking does not take CG in to account			Hybrid series		Ratios	
PXX	CinF_0 12	C/T_0 13	CinF_1 14	C/(T_1+C) 15	T_1+C 16	P^2XX−XX+1 17	P^2XX−100 18	17/7 19	18/8 20
P90	363,316,725	0.2%	494,997,565	0.2%	226,523,803,313	101,537	151,913	100.20%	101.1%
P95	1,157,095,038	0.5%	1,106,158,220	0.4%	257,096,826,388	144,051	202,290	100.40%	101.6%
P99	647,657,083	1.2%	670,280,759	1.3%	52,486,625,896	235,266	435,243	101.30%	103.1%
P99.5	1,896,794,928	2.7%	1,468,603,096	2.1%	68,674,230,402	384,781	635,221	102.20%	103.8%
P99.9	3,255,794,541	7.4%	1,976,074,562	4.6%	43,290,204,081	1,078,022	1,636,977	104.80%	105.3%
P99.99	6,804,235,939	20.5%	1,725,731,020	5.8%	29,750,043,791	6,667,575	6,667,575	106.20%	106.2%
Totals above P50	15,455,480,235		9,283,422,266						

Note: Yearly fiscal income of tax units, in DM.

Source: Author's computation on micro data provided by the *Statistisches Bundesamt*.

Table 9F.3 Capital gains and the various aggregates, Germany 1998

	Capital gains fully included				Capital gains fully excluded				Ratios		
PXX	P^0XX 1	T^0XX 2	P^0XX-XX+1 3	P^0XX-100 4	P^1XX 5	T^1XX 6	P^1XX−XX+1 7	P^1XX−100 8	1/5 9	3/7 10	4/8 11
P90	94,624	242,399,291,651	107,322	174,949	94,284	243,618,900,129	107,861	170,859	100.40%	99.5%	102.4%
P95	123,876	282,812,836,888	156,518	242,577	123,198	285,350,632,137	157,923	233,857	100.60%	99.1%	103.7%
P99	228,674	59,620,985,602	263,970	586,814	223,465	60,840,025,721	269,367	537,592	102.30%	98.0%	109.2%
P99.5	318,469	83,458,193,056	461,886	909,658	303,578	85,449,974,320	472,909	805,817	104.90%	97.7%	112.9%
P99.9	827,490	64,092,377,558	1,576,483	2,700,748	710,841	61,278,431,906	1,507,268	2,137,451	116.40%	104.6%	126.4%
P99.99	4,716,607	57,907,298,189	12,819,136	12,819,136	3,042,628	35,275,678,446	7,809,097	7,809,097	155.00%	164.2%	164.2%

	Share of CG when ranking takes CG into account		Share of CG when ranking does not take CG in to account			Hybrid series		Ratios	
PXX	CinF_0 12	C/T_0 13	CinF_1 14	C/(T_1+C) 15	T_1+C 16	P^2XX−XX+1 17	P^2XX−100 18	17/7 19	18/8 20
P90	801,394,485	0.3%	1,830,682,567	0.8%	245,449,582,696	108,672	178,383	100.80%	104.4%
P95	2,337,027,670	0.8%	4,550,026,641	1.6%	289,900,658,779	160,441	248,093	101.60%	106.1%
P99	1,636,173,880	2.7%	2,805,462,352	4.6%	63,645,488,073	281,788	598,702	104.60%	111.4%
P99.5	6,057,015,428	7.3%	8,400,633,185	9.8%	93,850,607,504	519,401	915,616	109.80%	113.6%
P99.9	14,792,602,346	23.1%	11,953,249,358	19.5%	73,231,681,264	1,801,283	2,500,475	119.50%	117.0%
P99.99	29,510,089,865	51.0%	4,445,463,594	12.6%	39,721,142,040	8,793,204	8,793,204	112.60%	112.6%
Totals above P50	57,295,647,727		40,025,609,630						

Note: Yearly fiscal income of tax units, in DM.

Source: Author's computation on micro data provided by the *Statistisches Bundesamt*.

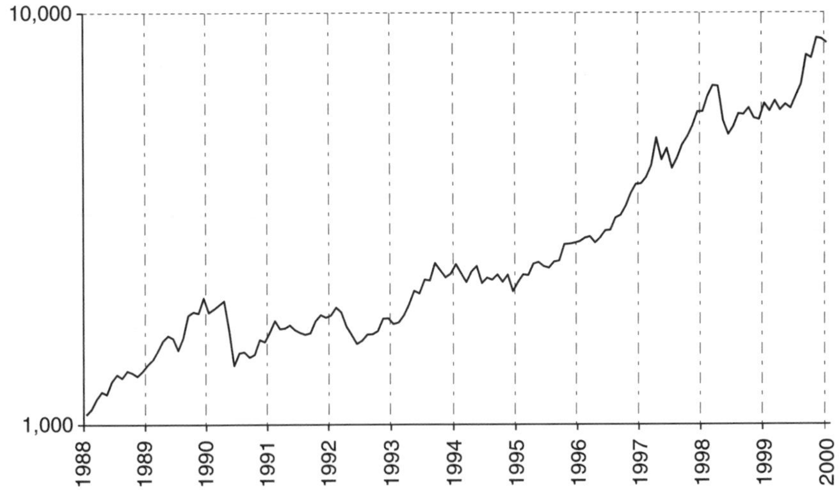

Figure 9F.1 German DAX index, 1988–2000

Source: DAX, log scale.

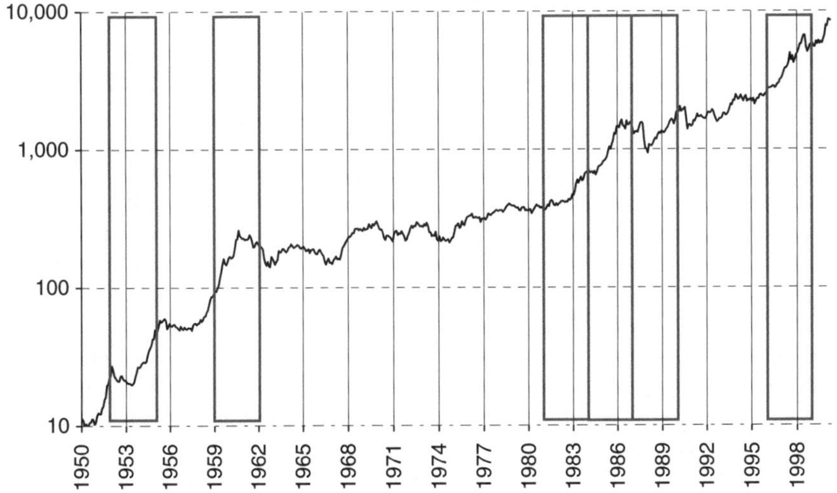

Figure 9F.2 German DAX index, 1950–2002

Note: The 3 year (taxation year + 2 preceding years) periods outlined identify the years when, according to the evolution of the stock market, high capital gain realizations may have been taking place.

Source: The DAX Index is continued from 1987 backward to 1959 with the Index of the *Börsenzeitung* and then retropolated back to 1948 by Stehle (1999).

drives the size of potential capital gains. The timing of the realization is driven by various factors among which anticipated tax reforms can play an important role. 1989, for instance, is a singular episode illustrating this phenomenon: bullish stock market conjuncture and anticipated tax reform combined and led to obviously huge capital gain realizations (which would probably have spread over time

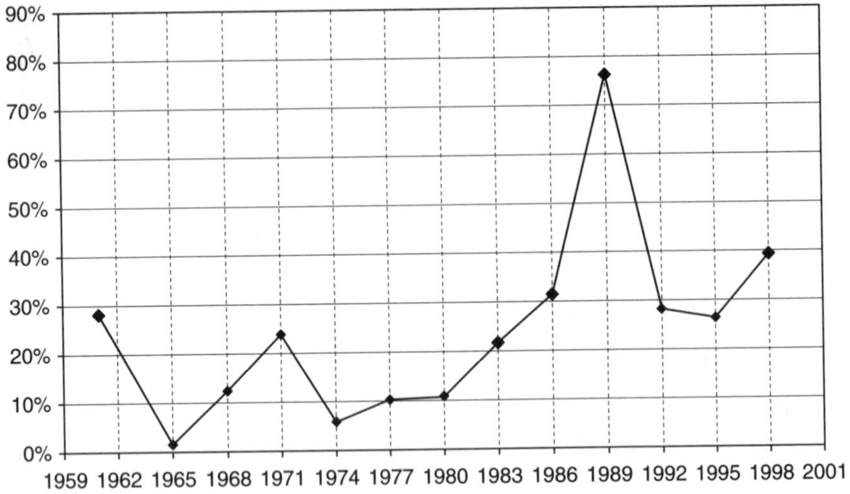

Figure 9F.3 Implicit capital gains in the last bracket, German tax data, 1961–98

Note: Share of implicit capital gains in total taxable income filed in bracket DM10 million +. Bigger rectangles denote years for which the 1998 scenario-correction was applied.

Source: German tax data, various years.

otherwise). These two determinants are of totally different nature. If the former is of fundamental economic nature, the latter is pure noise. The P^0 series should ideally be corrected of this second effect whereas they should not be corrected for the first one.

After the Second World War, we focus on the growth of capital value (proxied by the evolution of the stock market) to correct our series for capital gains. We use correction factors of 1992 for all years where the stock market was rather bearish, and correction factors of 1998 for all years where the stock market was bullish (see Figure 9F.2). The years we classify as bullish 1961, 1983, 1986, and 1989. The value for 1989 has nevertheless to be corrected further. Figure 9F.3 gives for years after 1961 the 'implicit capital gains' in the top bracket of income tax statistics. Knowing that capital gains are taxed at half the rate of other incomes, the gap between the tax effectively paid by tax payers in the top bracket and the tax they should have paid if their taxable income had been entirely subject to the 'normal' tax rates of the schedule give an indication of the size of capital gains declared in the top bracket. This measure is too rough an indication to be used to correct the series for standard years but it clearly shows the specific status of 1989 and confirm that the years 1961, 1983, and 1986 were years of higher capital gain realizations (implicit capital gains above 20%, like in the 1990s).[29] We therefore first corrected the data for 1989 in order for them to exhibit potential capital gains of the same magnitude as those observed in 1998.

[29] Clearly, according to Figure 9F.3, 1971 could also be a candidate for higher capital gains correction. Nevertheless the German stock market in the first half of the 1970s does not support such correction. Conversely, 1954 may have been a year of heavy capital gain realizations (see Figure 9F.2), but since correcting it according to the 1998 scenario leads to huge blips downward in our series, we preferred not taking the risk to over-correct and we treated it like 1950 and 1957.

During the Interwar years, although capital gains were taxable, we did not correct the series. Indeed, we do not have any indication to assess the importance of capital gains before 1945 (implicit capital gains cannot be calculated because the treatment of capital gains was at the time more complex than after the war) and applying corrections estimated in the 1990s is likely to add more noise than signal to the series. Thus the shares for 1925–28 may be slightly over-estimated (which would be a conservative bias with regard to our findings for these years, namely that top income shares were at the lowest level of the century). For the 1932–38 years, a correction based on stock-market fluctuations does not make much sense since the German economy departed more and more from a free market economy under the Nazi rule, and both the value of the capital stock and the decision to sell assets probably responded more and more to political factors while the stock market was loosing a lot of its economic relevance.

APPENDIX 9G: TOTAL TAX UNIT SERIES (CONTROL TOTALS FOR POPULATION)

In order to calculate top income shares, we need to know the total number of tax units in the population. This total number is most of the time considerably higher than the number of actual taxpayers and should not be confused with the total number of households.

In order to build such control totals for the population, we use the simple formula:

$$Tax\ Units = \frac{Married\ couples}{2} + Bachelors - Children$$

The accuracy of this total depends on two questions. First, the definition of children should be chosen in a such way that all children are dependant and all adults are either separate tax units or part of a couple (population cut-off problem). Second, the formula relies on the assumption that all married couple are treated as single tax units by tax law and fiscal statistics.

The first problem is difficult to tackle without very precise information about occupational status in different age groups, and its evolution over time. Such information being not at our disposal, we decided to define children as individuals aged 20 or less from 1925 until 1998.[30] For the years before 1918, Prussian data provide us with the exact total number of tax units (broken down in tax paying and tax exempt, see Table 9G.1). (See Table 9G.2 for the same information for Germany, 1891–1998.)

[30] Two remarks should be added here. First, under the assumption that the upper tail of the distribution is Pareto, one can estimate the difference in terms of top income shares entailed by the choice of a cut-off at 15 rather than 20. As shown in Chapter 2, this difference is 'rather modest'. Second, the problem of cut-off population is, at least in the German case, linked to the law-dependant tax unit definition problem. Individuals under the cut-off age and nonetheless economically independent can be expected to be most of the time wage-earners. They therefore enter 'tax return' statistics as p-a-y-e contributors, who are anyway treated as individual tax units (see below).

The second question is more complex. As noted in Chapter 2, 'the impact of moving from household based to individual based tax units depends on the joint distribution of income'. As far as the *ES* is concerned, couples are most of the time treated as a single tax unit.[31] Conversely, the *LS* PAYE system is based on individual tax units. Thus the use of control totals for population relying on married couples being counted only once could bias our top income fractiles where *LS* data matters, that is around P90 to P95. (See Figures 9G.1, 9G.2, and 9G.3.)

APPENDIX 9H: TOTAL HOUSEHOLD INCOME SERIES (CONTROL TOTALS FOR TOTAL INCOME)

As we have seen in the previous sections, we use an income concept originating from tax system and fiscal law to estimate top income quantiles. Top income shares should therefore be calculated with the total income which would have been reported on tax return statistics, 'had every single tax unit been required to declare its income' as Saez and Veall (2005) put it. Various strategies have been adopted by authors who dealt with long series of top income shares (see Chapter 2). Suffice here to say that a 'bottom-up' strategy competes with a 'top–down' strategy.

The 'bottom–up' strategy adds missing income elements to the total fiscal income recorded in tax statistics (income of non filers, exonerated income components). This is the strategy we use to construct our denominator for the pre-First World War years. The 'top–down' strategy uses national accounts as a starting point to calculate the total income denominator by subtracting income components in order to stick as much as possible to the income concept on which tax law relies. As argued in Atkinson (Chapter 2, this volume), this approach guaranties historical continuity as well as a link between countries.[32] This is the methodology we use for the rest of our series. Most of the time, one needs at least one reference point to calibrate a '(total fiscal income) on (chosen national accounts total income aggregate) ratio'. Unfortunately, we do not have a clear benchmark for Germany since the number of tax filers never exceeded 80% of all tax units in the course of the twentieth century (see Figures 9G.1–3). In the following, we describe how we solved this problem and the potential bias the solutions adopted may entail. Three periods should be addressed independently: before, between and after the two World Wars.

[31] Tax payers can choose between common declaration (*Zusammenveranlagung*) and separate declaration (*getrennte Veranlagung*). Common taxation most of the time leads to less taxes (specially for high incomes) thanks to the *Splittingstabelle* system. For recent years where we have micro data, the number of married couples choosing a separate taxation is less than 0.5%. Given that there were no additional incentives in the past to choose *getrennte Veranlagung*, we can thus ignore this possibility.

[32] The SNA (United Nations System of National Accounts) provides a common framework which makes comparisons easier. Most importantly, the ESA95 (European System of Accounts, base-year 1995), which should be used everywhere in the European Union since 1999, imposes a normalized use of fully equivalent aggregates. Thanks to retropolation works led by the national institutes, we can thus have fully comparable income aggregates inside the Union, from 1980, sometimes 1970, onward.

Table 9G.1 Tax units control total for Prussia, 1891–1918

		Overall population			Tax-exempt						Tax filers			Tax paying				
Tax year	Income year	Total population	Total tax units	Share of tax units in total population	Population	Tax units	Among which: *Freigestellte*	Share of *Freigestellte* in Tax-exempt tax units	Share of tax units in population (tax-exempt domain)	Share of tax-exempt tax units in total tax units	Tax units	Share of tax-payers among tax filers	Population	Tax units	Tax units in tabulations	Difference	Share of tax units in population (tax-payers domain)	Share of paying tax units in total tax units
1	2	3	4	5	6	7	8	9	10	11	12	13	14	15	16	17	18	19
1892	1891	29,895,224	*10,921,508*	36.5%	20,952,059	*8,544,043*	158,996	1.9%	*40.8%*	78.2%	2,594,854	93.9%	8,943,165	2,435,858	2,435,858	0.0%	27.2%	22.3%
1893	1892	30,080,017	*10,989,017*	36.5%	21,055,068	*8,590,931*	164,659	1.9%	*40.8%*	78.2%	2,644,437	93.8%	9,024,949	2,479,778	2,479,778	0.0%	27.5%	22.6%
1894	1893	30,387,331	*11,101,287*	36.5%	21,239,905	*8,677,776*	177,532	2.0%	*40.9%*	78.2%	2,696,540	93.4%	9,147,426	2,519,008	2,519,008	0.0%	27.5%	22.7%
1895	1894	30,812,583	11,256,643	36.5%	21,143,299	8,653,351	191,769	2.2%	40.9%	*76.9%*	2,795,061	93.1%	9,669,284	2,603,292	2,603,292	0.0%	26.9%	23.1%
1896	1895	31,349,283	11,473,418	36.6%	21,066,453	8,819,803	205,809	2.3%	41.9%	76.9%	2,859,424	92.8%	10,282,830	2,653,615	2,652,515	0.0%	25.8%	23.1%
1897	1896	31,849,116	11,723,457	36.8%	21,204,796	8,958,683	220,156	2.5%	42.2%	76.4%	2,984,960	92.6%	10,644,320	2,764,804	2,763,995	0.0%	26.0%	23.6%
1898	1897	32,348,765	11,936,695	36.9%	21,215,115	9,028,480	236,850	2.6%	42.6%	75.6%	3,145,065	92.4%	11,133,650	2,908,215	2,907,279	0.0%	26.1%	24.4%
1899	1898	32,908,839	12,165,125	37.0%	21,160,676	9,072,399	252,570	2.8%	42.9%	74.6%	3,345,296	92.4%	11,748,163	3,092,726	3,092,166	0.0%	26.3%	25.4%
1900	1899	33,469,818	12,447,933	37.2%	20,890,102	9,070,375	265,254	2.9%	43.4%	72.9%	3,642,812	92.7%	12,579,716	3,377,558	3,377,091	0.0%	26.8%	27.1%
1901	1900	34,056,414	12,656,746	37.2%	20,590,178	9,009,479	285,820	3.2%	43.8%	71.2%	3,933,087	92.7%	13,466,236	3,647,267	3,646,527	0.0%	27.1%	28.8%
1902	1901	34,551,274	12,812,985	37.1%	20,613,249	9,052,142	303,391	3.4%	43.9%	70.6%	4,064,234	92.5%	13,938,025	3,760,843	3,759,377	0.0%	27.0%	29.4%
1903	1902	35,114,667	13,033,565	37.1%	20,686,670	9,136,579	320,344	3.5%	44.2%	70.1%	4,217,330	92.4%	14,427,997	3,896,986	3,895,184	0.0%	27.0%	29.9%
1904	1903	35,629,139	13,249,695	37.2%	20,540,902	9,117,137	327,833	3.6%	44.4%	68.8%	4,460,391	92.6%	15,088,237	4,132,558	4,130,956	0.0%	27.4%	31.2%
1905	1904	36,269,439	13,567,150	37.4%	20,483,263	9,174,914	332,699	3.6%	44.8%	67.6%	4,724,935	92.9%	15,786,176	4,392,236	4,390,608	0.0%	27.8%	32.4%
1906	1905	36,829,724	13,848,209	37.6%	20,297,174	9,175,055	339,789	3.7%	45.2%	66.3%	5,012,943	93.2%	16,532,550	4,673,154	4,672,429	0.0%	28.3%	33.7%
1907	1906	37,467,246	14,203,497	37.9%	18,842,470	8,817,655	351,178	4.0%	46.8%	62.1%	5,737,020	93.9%	18,624,776	5,385,842	5,384,556	0.0%	28.9%	37.9%
1908	1907	38,026,556	14,560,767	38.3%	17,957,848	8,682,413	352,061	4.1%	48.3%	59.6%	6,230,415	94.3%	20,068,708	5,878,354	5,876,741	0.0%	29.3%	40.4%
1909	1908	38,598,423	14,771,359	38.3%	17,676,308	8,670,077	367,810	4.2%	49.0%	58.7%	6,469,092	94.3%	20,922,115	6,101,282	6,099,422	0.0%	29.2%	41.3%
1910	1909	39,145,535	15,048,290	38.4%	16,768,154	8,805,397	606,216	6.9%	52.5%	58.5%	6,849,109	91.1%	22,377,381	6,242,893	6,241,494	0.0%	27.9%	41.5%
1911	1910	39,773,029	15,443,627	38.8%	16,382,969	8,887,448	635,741	7.2%	54.2%	57.5%	7,191,920	91.1%	23,390,060	6,556,179	6,551,705	−0.1%	28.0%	42.5%

(*contd.*)

Table 9G.1 (*contd.*)

		Overall population			Tax-exempt						Tax filers		Tax paying				
Tax year	Income year	Total population	Total tax units	Share of tax units in total population	Population	Tax units	Among which: *Freigestellte*	Share of *Freigestellte* in Tax-exempt tax units	Share of tax units in population (tax-exempt domain)	Share of tax-exempt tax units in total tax units	Tax units	Share of tax-payers among tax filers	Population	Tax units	Tax units in tabulations	Difference	Share of tax units in population (tax-payers domain)	Share of paying tax units in total tax units
1912	1911	40,236,830	15,700,613	39.0%	16,004,537	8,790,398	631,473	7.2%	54.9%	56.0%	7,541,688	91.6%	24,232,293	6,910,215	6,906,497	−0.1%	28.5%	44.0%
1913	1912	40,751,635	16,017,048	39.3%	15,545,529	8,694,855	608,382	7.0%	55.9%	54.3%	7,930,575	92.3%	25,206,106	7,322,193	7,318,382	−0.1%	29.0%	45.7%
1914	1913	41,228,784	16,254,480	39.4%	15,136,123	8,565,554	578,920	6.8%	56.6%	52.7%	8,267,846	92.9%	26,092,661	7,688,926	7,684,062	−0.1%	29.4%	47.3%
1915	1914	41,036,081	15,832,483	38.6%	15,230,399	8,460,486	591,887	7.0%	55.5%	53.4%	7,963,884	91.7%	25,805,682	7,371,997	7,300,619	−1.0%	28.3%	46.6%
1916	1915	41,052,718	15,914,623	38.8%	15,386,644	8,368,766	521,556	6.2%	54.4%	52.6%	8,067,413	93.1%	25,666,074	7,545,857	7,508,529	−0.5%	29.3%	47.4%
1917	1916	40,682,389	15,855,343	39.0%	16,623,104	8,623,871	365,103	4.2%	51.9%	54.4%	7,596,575	93.9%	24,059,285	7,231,472	7,130,655	−1.4%	29.6%	45.6%
1918	1917	40,115,914	16,097,364	40.1%	16,380,850	8,208,122	243,678	3.0%	50.1%	51.0%	8,132,920	95.6%	23,735,064	7,889,242	7,777,358	−1.4%	32.8%	49.0%
1918	1917	38,073,380	15,463,273	40.6%	15,256,982	7,773,894	221,492	2.8%	51.0%	50.3%	7,910,871	95.8%	22,816,398	7,689,379	7,579,154	−1.4%	33.2%	49.7%
1919	1918	37,806,233	15,815,749	41.8%	11,454,110	6,251,706	164,867	2.6%	54.6%	39.5%	9,728,910	97.4%	26,352,123	9,564,043	9,477,139	−0.9%	36.0%	60.5%

Notes: Second occurrence of 1917: without the *Regierungsbezirke* Posen and Bromberg, which were not recorded in 1918. For the years 1892–94 (*emphasized* values), 4 has been constructed using 3 and assuming that 5 in 1892–94 was equal to its 1895 value. For the years 1892–94 (*emphasized* values), 7 has been constructed the same way, assuming constant (7–8)/6. The (always small) discrepancy between 15 (tax-paying population according to the handbooks) and 16 (tax-paying units effectively recorded in the tabulations) for the years 1914 and 1916–18 remains unaccounted for (described as *Einkommensteuerpflichtige deren Veranlagung ausgesetzt war*).

Source: *Statistisches Jahrbuch für den preußischen Staat* 1921(17): p. 218.

Table 9G.2 Tax units (TU) control total, Germany 1891–1998

Year	TU total	Territorial changes/reference
1891	10,921,508	Prussia
1892	10,989,017	
1893	11,101,287	
1894	11,256,643	
1895	11,473,418	
1896	11,723,457	
1897	11,936,695	
1898	12,165,125	
1899	12,447,933	
1900	12,656,746	
1901	12,812,985	
1902	13,033,565	
1903	13,249,695	
1904	13,567,150	
1905	13,848,209	
1906	14,203,497	
1907	14,560,767	
1908	14,771,359	
1909	15,048,290	
1910	15,443,627	
1911	15,700,613	
1912	16,017,048	
1913	16,254,480	
1914	15,832,483	
1915	15,914,623	
1916	15,855,343	
1917	16,097,364	
1918	15,815,749	– Posen & Bromberg
1925	27,077,500	Republic of Weimar
1926	27,579,348	
1927	28,054,998	
1928	28,525,419	
1929	28,987,601	
1930	29,451,244	
1931	29,916,752	
1932	30,361,630	
1933	30,822,000	
1934	30,713,242	
1935	31,021,052	+ Saarland
1936	30,949,636	
1937	30,875,878	
1938	30,908,380	
1950	21,924,508	Federal Republic of Germany
1951	22,108,509	
1952	22,263,231	
1953	22,539,301	
1954	22,709,548	
1955	22,910,718	
1956	23,112,187	

(contd.)

Table 9G.2 (*contd.*)

Year	TU total	Territorial changes/reference
1957	23,360,650	
1958	23,753,607	
1959	25,619,052	
1960	26,053,847	+ West-Berlin and Saarland
1961	26,558,730	
1962	26,773,185	
1963	26,966,456	
1964	27,206,775	
1965	27,438,278	
1966	27,499,648	
1967	27,402,490	
1968	27,467,500	
1969	27,827,930	
1970	27,767,969	
1971	28,024,378	
1972	28,318,630	
1973	28,607,551	
1974	28,711,788	
1975	28,773,815	
1976	28,901,211	
1977	29,080,847	
1978	29,429,724	
1979	29,850,430	
1980	30,322,201	
1981	30,806,346	
1982	31,179,142	
1983	31,512,050	
1984	31,877,877	
1985	32,360,735	
1986	32,923,250	
1987	33,179,362	
1988	33,642,946	
1989	34,376,745	
1990	34,835,678	
1991	43,737,103	Reunification
1992	43,972,179	
1993	44,232,219	
1994	44,404,071	
1995	44,618,987	
1996	44,869,739	
1997	45,039,120	
1998	45,172,545	

Federal Republic Years

As seen in the previous section, even in recent years, the total number of tax returns filed is much lower than the tax unit total. Figure 9G.3 shows the evolution of the total number of filers. Note that the expression 'filers' does not

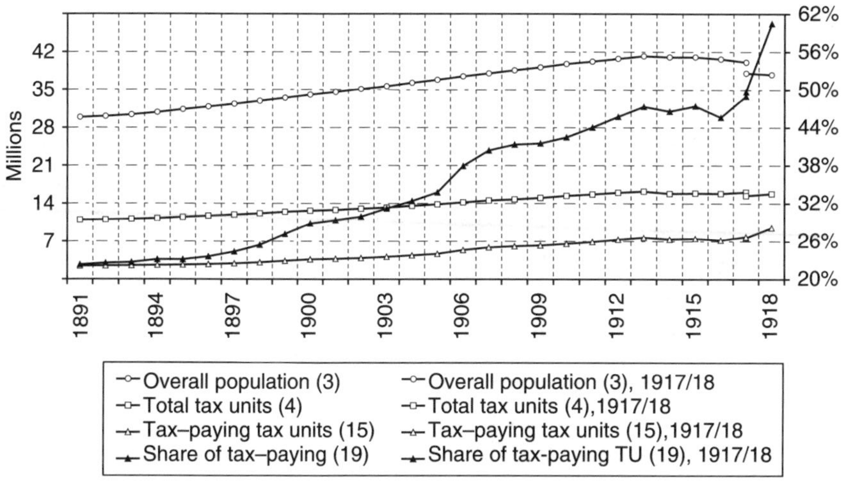

Figure 9G.1 Evolution of the overall Prussian population; evolution of the share of tax units actually filing tax returns, 1891–1918

Note: Numbers in brackets refer to columns in Table 9G.1 Solid triangles should be read on the right scale (%).

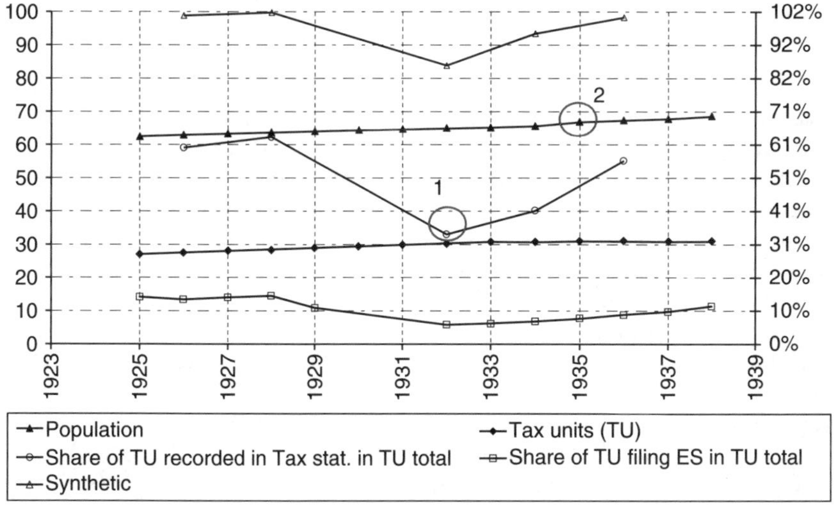

Figure 9G.2 Overall population, tax units, Weimar Republic, and Third Reich, 1925–38

Notes: 'Synthetic' series refer to *Statistisches Reichsamt* (1939). The blip (1) is linked to the gigantic rise in unemployment in the Depression (see Figure 94.3). The (very slight) blip (2) is linked to the reintegration unemployment in the Depression (see *Statistisches Reichsamt* 1939). This blip is also linked to the reintegration of Saarland in the Reich (less than 2% additional population).

Source: German income tax statistics, German statistical handbooks, various years, and *Statistisches Reichsamt.*

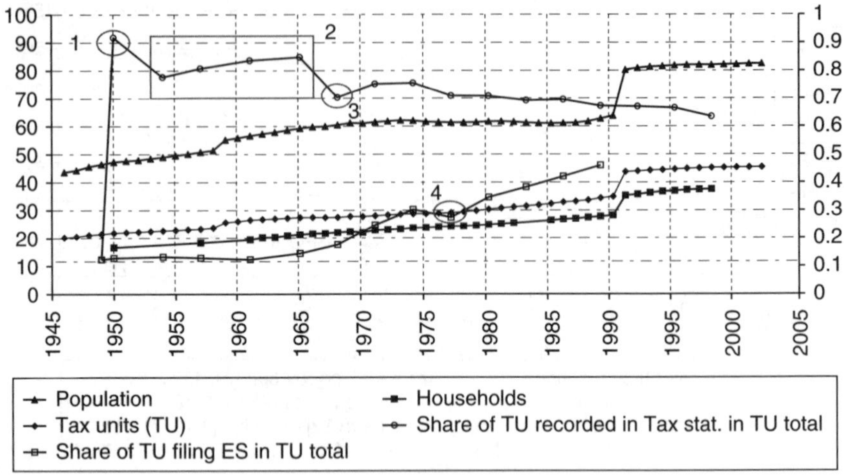

Figure 9G.3 Overall population, households, and tax units, Federal Republic of Germany, 1946–2002

Notes: The full dots read on the left scale (million) and the empty dots on the right scale(%); 1950 relies on rough estimates of the whole distribution by the German Federal Statistical Office (see *Statistisches Bundesamt) (1954a*); 1954–65 rely on attempts to merge ES and LS statistics; 1954 and 1957 are rough units (from CS) and family tax units (from ES) where the two statistics mesh (around DM 25,000); 1968 is the first homogenous estimate of the German Federal Statistical Office, using only family based tax units (even for LS); the 1977 blip for the share of filed returns of the ES is linked to the Tax Reform of 1975, which led to arise of the threshold above which filing an income tax return was required.

Source: German income tax statistics, various years.

precisely fit the German reality (nor the British one for instance) since only a fraction (about 3 million in 1950, about 15 million in the 1990s) of all tax payers do effectively file an income tax return every year. The remaining part of German tax payers never file tax return: they pay the pay-as-you-earn tax.

During the postwar years, the share of tax filers in the tax unit total has then been stable around 70%. Thus, we do not have a precise estimation of the structural gap between national accounts aggregates of personal income and the total fiscal income for recent years (contrary to, for instance, France).

The total income series we computed for 1950–98 is based on the ESA95 concept of Net Primary Income of Private Households.[33] This aggregate is available back to 1980 thanks to retropolations operated on a ESA95 basis by the *Statistisches Bundesamt* (see Statistisches Bundesamt (2005)). This NPIPH aggregate is the sum of gross wages and salaries paid to the households by the firms (including payroll taxes),[34] pre-tax net wealth income,[35] pre-tax net

[33] Thereafter NPIPH, in German *Nettonationaleinkommen der privaten Haushalte*. Unfortunately, this aggregate is most of the time published for two 'Institutional Sectors' together: Households (*private Hauhalte*) (S.14) and 'non-profit oriented private Organizations' *private Organisationen ohne Erwerbszweck*. The calibration strategy we use should solve this problem, provided that the income share of these organizations has been constant over time. Note that net means that capital depreciation is taken into account. NPIPH remains a pre-tax, pre-transfers income.

[34] Code: D1; *Arbeitsnehmerentgelt* in German.

[35] Code: D4; *Vermögenseinkommen* in German.

profits,[36] pre-tax net self-employment income.[37] For the years 1950 to 1980 we constructed homogenous series of primary income using retropolated series from 1950 to 1990 published by the German Federal Statistical Office in the 1990s (see Statistisches Bundesamt (1991)): since 'primary income' was not a aggregate of the German National Accounts system at the time, we take the *Volkseinkommen* of the private households, which is very close income concept.[38] We then adjust this NPIPH series to fiscal income by subtracting payroll taxes paid by employers, which are not part of the taxable income base. The adjusted NPIPH is approximately equal to disposable income of the national accounts throughout the period. Figure 9H.2 graphs the various aggregates of the German National Accounts after 1945 and the adjusted NPIPH we constructed.

The adjusted aggregate is calculated before taxes and social transfers but after deduction of social contributions paid by employers and is thus roughly homogenous to the gross fiscal income (GdE) we use after 1945 to estimate top income groups. Figure 9H.1 shows which share of this aggregate is contained in income tax statistics from 1950 to 1998. The share is stable between 70% and 80% throughout the period. We take 90% of the adjusted NPIPH series for total fiscal income denominator for the whole period 1950–98. This adjusts for the small differences which remain between numerator (GdE) and denominator (adjusted NPIPH) namely (i) the presence of approximately 30% of the pensions in the GdE (so called *Ertragsanteil*, which should lead to an adjustment upward of the denominator);[39] and (ii) the absence of the *Werbungskosten* in the GdE (which should lead to an adjustment downward of the denominator).[40] Finally, our total fiscal income series is about 87% of NPIPH just after the Second World War and decreases until it reaches 78% of NPIPH in the 1980s and remains stable afterward. This trend mainly reflects the continuous increase of employers' social contributions in Germany from 1950 to 1980. The share is significantly higher than in France (Piketty 2001) because French fiscal income does not include social contributions paid by the employees.[41] The share is comparable to the one found for the US by Piketty and Saez (2003).

The gap between our denominator and the total gross fiscal income registered by the tax administration can either be related to income of non-filers or to the existence of tax exempt capital income, systematic underreporting of business

[36] Code: B2n; *Nettobetriebsüberschuss* in German.

[37] Code: B3n; *Selbstständigeneinkommen* in German.

[38] A little bit tighter though. We thus adjust it upward by 4%. In the 1980s we can compare both aggregates, and the augmented Volkseinkommen of the private households is always within 2% of the NPIPH.

[39] This correction is negligible. In 1983 for instance, pensions represent less than 1.5% of the total taxable income.

[40] This is the dominating effect, for instance in 1983, the wage and salaries incomes subject to LS and included in the GdE were reduced by DM 70 billion by Werbungskosten and other similar deductions. Correcting would lead to an increase of slightly more than 8% of the GdE.

[41] Part of the gap is filled by the fact that our German series are after deduction of the Werbungskosten, whereas the series for France are corrected for the corresponding 'abattements' for wage and salary incomes (which are much higher at about 30%).

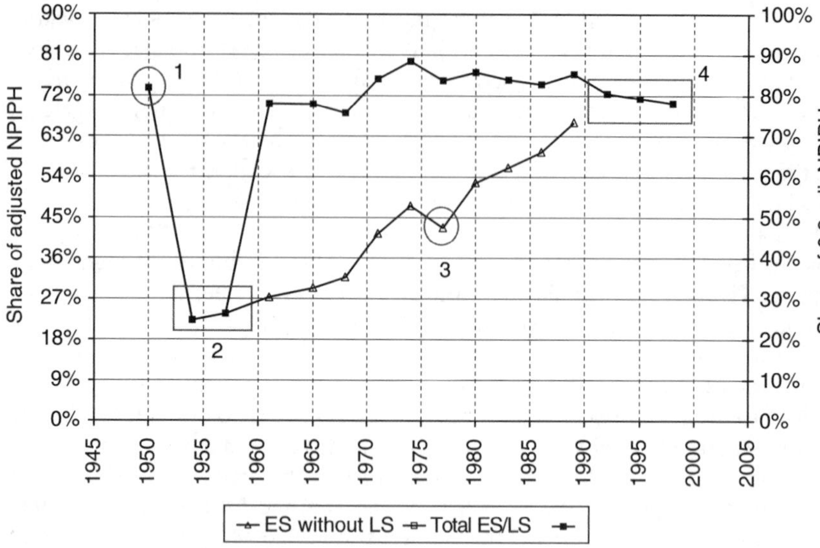

Figure 9H.1 Net personal income of private households and total taxable income Federal Republic of Germany, 1950–98

Notes: 1950 relies on rough estimates of the whole distribution by the German Federal Statistical Office (see *Statistisches Bundesamt* 1954*a*); for 1954–57 there is no simple way to merge ES and LS statistics. The figures here only refer to the ES Statistics (roughly the top 10% of the distribution); the 1977 blip for the share of filed returns the ES is linked to the Tax Reform of 1975 which led to a rise of the thershold above which filing an income tax return was required; from 1992 onward, the ES and LS statistics are integrated.

Source: German income tax statistics and national accounts (various years).

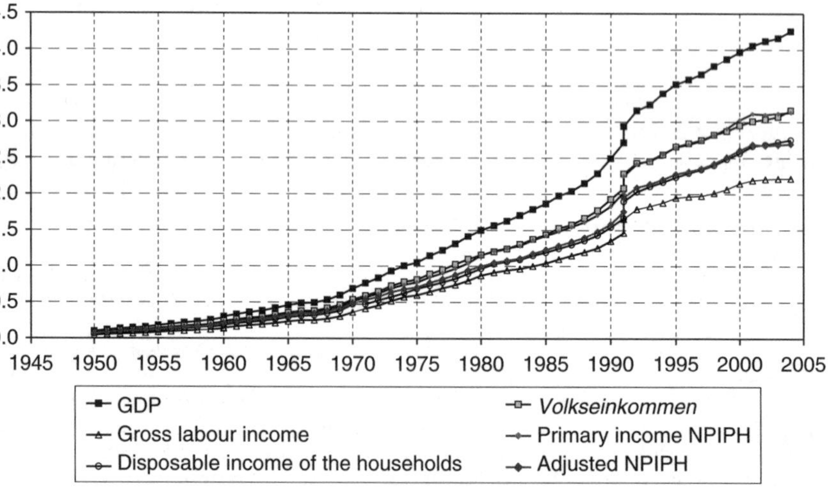

Figure 9H.2 Aggregates of the German national accounts after the Second World War and adjusted net personal income of private households, 1950–2004

Source: German national accounts from *Statistisches Bundesamt 1991 and 2005.*

and agricultural income and systematic tax optimization on incomes from real estate.[42] We now review the consistency of the denominator with other available sources on incomes of non-filers after the Second World War. Those sources are however too heterogenous to be used as benchmarks, which is why we adopted the 'top–down' approach.

A starting point is, for 1950, a rough attempt of the *Statistisches Bundesamt* to estimate the 'whole fiscal' income distribution (Statistisches Bundesamt 1954*a*; and Statistisches Bundesamt 1954*c*). The middle and the top of the distribution are estimated thanks to income tax data for 1950, and the bottom is unfortunately estimated with unspecified methodology, obviously using social security statistics. Ninty-one percent of our tax units total is present in these tabulations (see Figure 9G.3, point 1).[43]

The total amount of gross fiscal income recorded in tax returns in Germany in 1950 amounts to some 82% of our income total (see Figure 9H.1, point 1). The gap cannot be explained only by the missing income of the bottom 10%.[44] However, the numerous tax exemptions (*Sondervergünstigungen*) which were enacted after 1949 by the newly founded Federal Republic, and which stood in stark contrast with the very severe taxation during the allied occupation, as well as a probably high level of tax avoidance and evasion can explain part of the missing share. The rough estimate for 1950 is compatible with our series, although it may hint at a slight over-estimation of our denominator at the beginning of the period. The poor documentation of this estimate and the very low confidence displayed by the statisticians of the time in their own attempt to reconstruct the whole income distribution dissuaded us to use this attempt to correct our series.

For more recent years, the share of tax units recorded is stable at about 70% of all tax units, for an income share of all returns of about 75–80% of NPIPH: around 80–90% of our income total is contained in fiscal statistics.

[42] Large scale exploitation of the loopholes of the German tax law has been very popular in the late 1970s and early 1980s, as well as in the 1990s. In 1980 for instance, 'income from real estate' is negative throughout the distribution and losses offset gains by more than 300% in some brackets. Correcting for this kind of tax avoidance is very tricky and we preferred keeping our series uncorrected. One should therefore keep in mind that some of our estimates may be slightly biased downward in the late 1970s, early 1980s and in the 1990s. If we corrected for this major kind of tax avoidance at the end of the period, our top income shares would be even higher.

[43] This does not hint at an overestimation of our tax unit total since pensioners are not included (because tax exempt for most of them) in the reconstitution. We do not try to correct our series using this 1950 estimate. Once again, the methodology on which this estimate relies is unknown, and the statistics of the following years (1954–65) indicate that this estimate does not rely on an homogenous (family based) definition of tax units. We thus prefer to keep a clear cut and robust tax units series which only rely on population statistics.

[44] The primary income share of the bottom 10% is extremely small. Rough estimates for Germany in 1950 are 1% (see Statistisches Bundesamt 1954*b*). Piketty and Saez (2003) impute 1% of their income total (1/20 of the average income) to the missing bottom 5% of the distribution after 1945. In any case, 5% is an upper bound to the share of the bottom 10%.

Data sources which document the bottom of the income distribution in Germany in the recent years most of the time rely on measures of the distribution of disposable income of households. They are thus of little use to calibrate our total fiscal income denominator. The two main data sources are the Income and Expenditure Survey (EVS *Einkommens und Verbrauchsstichprobe*)—conducted by the German Federal Statistical Office in 1962, 1969, and from 1973 onward, every five years—and the German Socio-Economic Panel (SOEP) conducted by the German Institute for Economic Research (DIW) on a yearly basis since 1984.

Hauser and Becker (2003) estimate deciles of equivalized disposable income from 1969 to 1998 using the EVS. They find a share of the bottom three deciles at about 17% throughout the period. Disposable income at the bottom of the distribution is significantly higher than fiscal income, all the more when, like in Germany, unemployment benefits and most pensions are tax exempt. This is coherent with our series.

Systematic estimates of bottom shares of disposable equivalized income relying on SOEP data can be used to estimate a bottom 30% income share of a at least 14% in the late 1980s and in the 1990s.[45]

Matching EVS data and data from the National Accounts, the DIW has been estimating disposable income distributions throughout the postwar period.[46] The quality of these estimates is hard to assess and they contain few details about how they were realized. For 1983, a distribution of gross income has been estimated together with a distribution of disposable income (Bedau 1985). The share of the bottom 30% is of less than 5% for gross income, and of about 19% for disposable income.[47]

Thus, it seems unlikely that the bottom 30% of the income distribution earns the 10–20% missing from our income total. One has to assume that a significant part of the gap between our income denominator and total fiscal income from tax statistics is not due to income of the non-filers but much more to non-taxable or hidden income of the filers. No significant trend being observed in the (implicit) share of these non taxable or hidden incomes, we preferred to keep a clear-cut income denominator. Taking these income components into account (by either shrinking our denominator, or correcting up our top income groups) could only concentrate further the income distribution as long as most of the avoidance/evasion does not take place at the bottom of the distribution, which is very unlikely because this bottom is mostly made of wages and salaries which cannot avoid taxation easily.

[45] See Wagner and Krause (2001), $PO - 30 \leq PO - 20 + PO - 20 - PO - 10$. Moreover, comparing equivalized income shares and and income shares relying on tax units is not straightforward.

[46] We are most grateful to A.B. Atkinson for drawing our attention to those series.

[47] Note that the concept of gross income used by the DIW is very different from what our series contain. Indeed it is the primary income of the households without any adjustment, which is more than 30% higher than our total fiscal aggregate. This difference nonetheless does not impact much the bottom of the distribution.

Interwar Years

The interwar years saw the development of 'modern' national accounting in Germany (see Tooze 2001). In their seminal work, Hoffmann and Mueller (1959) provide us with series of personal income (*Einkommen der privaten Haushalte*), which are homogenous to the NPIPH used after the Second World War. We adjust these series downward for social contributions paid by employers and take once again 90% of this adjusted aggregate to build our income denominator. Throughout the interwar years, we have a lower share of tax units present in our sources than after the Second World War. Figure 9G.2 shows that this share is between 55% and 65% at the beginning and at the end of the period, with a huge blip downward in 1932 (35%) and 1934 (42%) due to the Great Depression and the sudden rise of unemployment (see Figure 9H.3) which made millions of tax units exit the income tax statistics. During the same period, the total fiscal income recorded fluctuated between 70% and 80% or our total income denominator (with a low at 62% in 1932), see Figure 9H.4. It means that (excepted for 1932) 20–30% of total primary income was accruing to the bottom 35–45% of the income distribution which is an acceptable assumption consistent with what we assume after the Second World War.

Like for 1950, there were some attempts of the Statistical Office (at that time, *Statistisches Reichsamt*) to build comprehensive income tabulations, using not only fiscal data but also data from social benefits (see *Statistisches Reichsamt* 1939). We thus have 'reference' points of the total income (for 1926, 1928, 1932,

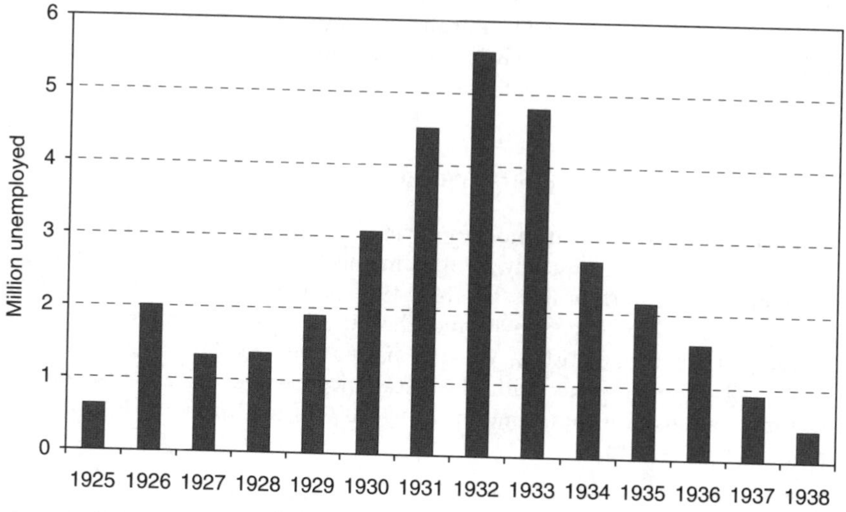

Figure 9H.3 Unemployment in Germany, 1925–38

Source: *German Statistical Handbook* 1939/40.

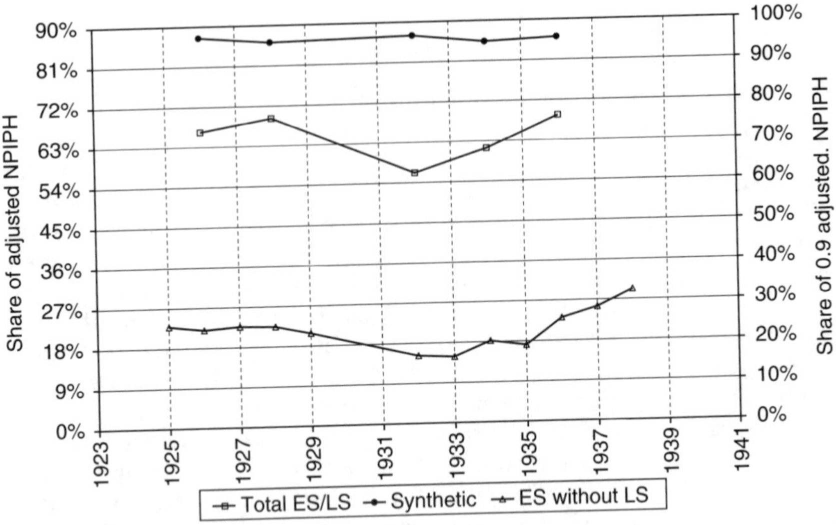

Figure 9H.4 Net personal income of private households and total taxable income, Weimar Republic and Third Reich 1925–38

Note: The 'synthetic' series originates from *Statistisches Reichsamt* (1939).

Source: German income tax statistics and National accounts (Various years).

1934, and 1936). The share of these income aggregates is given in Figure 9H.4 (series 'synthetic') and amounts to more than 95% of our income total for the whole period. It does not include the unemployed and thus the missing 5% can de interpreted as both the residual incomes of the unemployed and the income evading or avoiding taxation. Once again, these exogenous sources are consistent with our data, but we do not rely on them to calibrate our income control total because of their unspecified methodology.[48]

Pre-First World War period

National accounts in their modern form did not exist at the time of the Wilhemine Empire. Fortunately, Hoffmann and Mueller (1959) did reconstruct series of personal income for the 1891–1913 period. The series are based on fiscal sources with precise estimation of the part of personal income that do not appear in tax return statistics. We thus have at our disposal series which are intrinsically homogeneous with the fiscal incomes we use to estimate the fractiles. Total fiscal income amount to 85–90% of total personal income over the period 1891–1913.

48 Note moreover that these 'ready to use' distributions were published for a larger readership than the raw income tax tabulations, and one cannot exclude the possibility that they were manipulated. Inequalities were indeed a very sensitive issue for the Nazi power who meant to be socialist as well as nationalist.

Income year	Total taxable income Million mark	Tax filers					Tax free			Overall population		
		Exonerated incomes of tax-filers Million mark	Among which 900M of the *Freigestellte* Million mark	Rest: family deductions above DA 900m Million mark	Share of the rest in total taxable income Million mark	Total income of tax filers Million mark	Share of exonerated incomes in total income Mark	Estimated income Million mark	Mean income Million mark	Wage index	Income total	Income of private household series
1	2	3	4	5	6	7	8	9	10	11	12	13
1891	5,704	297	143	154	2.7%	6,001	4.9%	5,148	634	65	11,149	12,446
1892	5,725	308	148	160	2.8%	6,033	5.1%	5,241	634	65	11,274	12,580
1893	5,785	327	160	167	2.9%	6,112	5.4%	5,315	633	65	11,427	12,756
1894	5,937	347	173	174	2.9%	6,284	5.5%	5,340	631	65	11,624	12,997
1895	6,086	368	185	183	3.0%	6,454	5.7%	5,461	634	65	11,915	13,329
1896	6,375	389	198	191	3.0%	6,764	5.8%	5,558	636	68	12,322	13,811
1897	6,775	417	213	204	3.0%	7,192	5.8%	5,627	640	68	12,819	14,400
1898	7,258	446	227	219	3.0%	7,704	5.8%	5,689	645	71	13,393	15,075
1899	7,841	472	239	233	3.0%	8,313	5.7%	5,732	651	73	14,045	15,854
1900	8,376	507	257	250	3.0%	8,883	5.7%	5,714	655	75	14,597	16,536
1901	8,560	533	273	260	3.0%	9,093	5.9%	5,748	657	74	14,841	16,831
1902	8,709	559	288	271	3.1%	9,268	6.0%	5,801	658	74	15,069	17,092
1903	9,123	578	295	283	3.1%	9,701	6.0%	5,810	661	75	15,511	17,634
1904	9,668	595	299	296	3.1%	10,263	5.8%	5,898	667	77	16,161	18,422
1905	10,332	616	306	310	3.0%	10,948	5.6%	5,964	675	80	16,912	19,321
1906	11,748	731	316	415	3.5%	12,479	5.9%	5,799	685	84	18,278	21,000
1907	12,795	775	317	458	3.6%	13,570	5.7%	5,773	693	89	19,343	22,304
1908	13,219	981	331	650	4.9%	14,200	6.9%	5,795	698	88	19,995	23,095
1909	13,711	1,342	546	796	5.8%	15,053	8.9%	5,756	702	89	20,809	24,097
1910	14,487	1,409	572	837	5.8%	15,896	8.9%	5,842	708	91	21,738	25,064
1911	15,240	1,441	568	873	5.7%	16,681	8.6%	5,842	716	91	22,523	26,190
1912	16,262	1,456	548	908	5.6%	17,718	8.2%	5,870	726	95	23,588	27,519
1913	17,560	1,458	521	937	5.3%	19,018	7.7%	5,870	735	100	24,888	29,173
1914	16,550	1,410	533	*877*	5.3%	17,959	7.9%	*5,870*	746	100	23,829	—
1915	18,247	1,436	469	*967*	5.3%	19,683	7.3%	*6,140*	782	105	25,823	—
1916	19,165	1,344	329	*1,016*	5.3%	20,510	6.6%	*6,680*	809	114	27,190	—
1917	23,484	1,464	219	*1,245*	5.3%	24,948	5.9%	*7,490*	940	128	32,438	—
1918	29,524	1,713	148	*1,565*	5.3%	31,237	5.5%	*8,570*	1,408	146	39,807	—

Notes: for 1891–1913: 2 = Hoffmann and Mueller 1959: table 34, p.73, col. 3 corrected for 1910; 3 = *id.*, col. 4; 4 = Table 9G.1, col. 8 × 900M; 5 = 3 − 4; 6 = 5/2; 7 = 2 + 3; 8 = 3/7; 9 = Hoffmann and Mueller 1959: tab. 35, p.74, col. 5; 10 = 9 / ([Table 9G.1]: 7 + 8); 11 = see Kuczinsky 1960; and Hoffmann and Mueller 1959: 6; 12 = 7 + 9; 13 = Hoffmann and Mueller 1959: table 37, 76–77, col; 5 *Einkommen der Haushalte*; for 1913–18: the missing information (*emphasized values*) is 5 and 9. 5 is completed assuming constant 6 over the period; 9 is completed using 11 (which for the 1914–18 years is a very partial index of *Ruhrgebiet* coal miners, see Bry 1960: table A-2 part II, p.330.

Source: Statistisches Reichsamt 1932: 21–27; Hoffmann and Mueller 1959: tables 34 to 37, pp.73–77.

Table 9H.2 Income control total, 1891–1998

Year	Income control	Territorial change/reference
1891	11,149	Prussia
1892	11,274	
1893	11,427	
1894	11,624	
1895	11,915	
1896	12,322	
1897	12,819	
1898	13,393	
1899	14,045	
1900	14,597	
1901	14,841	
1902	15,069	
1903	15,511	
1904	16,161	
1905	16,912	
1906	18,278	
1907	19,343	
1908	19,995	
1909	20,809	
1910	21,738	
1911	22,523	
1912	23,588	
1913	24,888	
1914	23,829	
1915	25,823	
1916	27,190	
1917	32,438	
1918	39,807	−Posen & Bromberg
1925	48,387	Republic of Weimar
1926	49,894	
1927	55,450	
1928	59,719	
1929	59,910	
1930	55,035	
1931	46,193	
1932	36,293	
1933	37,142	
1934	42,075	
1935	46,949	+ Saarland
1936	51,809	
1937	57,902	
1938	64,517	
1950	63,526	Federal Republic of Germany
1951	77,222	
1952	87,680	
1953	93,596	
1954	100,091	
1955	114,263	

(contd.)

Table 9H.2 (*contd.*)

Year	Income control		Territorial change/reference
1956	126,265		
1957	137,291		
1958	149,320		
1959	161,545		
1960	183,353		
1960	193,741	+ Saarland	West-Berlin
1961	209,899		
1962	228,692		
1963	241,071		
1964	266,231		
1965	291,096		
1966	309,265		
1967	311,878		
1968	339,025		
1969	372,412		
1970	433,689		
1971	478,547		
1972	518,799		
1973	576,623		
1974	613,612		
1975	635,994		
1976	693,273		
1977	739,950		
1978	790,686		
1979	850,010		
1980	895,913		
1981	944,883		
1982	968,277		
1983	994,892		
1984	1,055,955		
1985	1,105,805		
1986	1,154,916		
1987	1,204,203		
1988	1,254,053		
1989	1,333,387		
1990	1,425,378		
1991	1,584,258		
1991	1,757,114	Reunification	
1992	1,881,862		
1993	1,925,657		
1994	1,984,767		
1995	2,050,265		
1996	2,081,598		
1997	2,118,264		
1998	2,181,034		

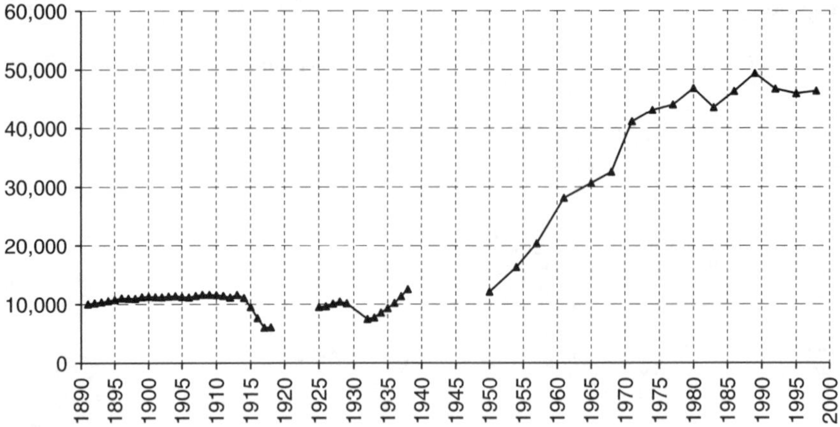

Figure 9H.5 Average tax unit income over the twentieth century in Germany

Note: 1995 Deutsche Mark.

For the 1913–18 years, these series are unfortunately not available. Following the same methodology, we extended the series of Hoffmann and Mueller (1959) to 1918 (see Tables 9H.1 and 9H.2).

Figure 9H.5 graphs the evolution of the real average fiscal income per tax unit over the twentieth century in Germany. The last years of the nineteenth century and the first decade of the twentieth century are years of great stability of this average income in Prussia. The First World War, however, led to a sharp decline. The Weimar Republic witnessed a rapid decline during the Great Depression which was more than offset by the growth which occurred at the beginning of the Third Reich. The average tax unit income was in 1950 back at its 1938 level and rose constantly during the three following decades. The 1980s marked the end of this continuous rise (depression of the early 1980s, compensated by the boom of the late 1980s). The 1990s are years of great stability, at a lower level however, following the Reunification which brought more population than income to the pre-1989 Federal Republic of Germany.

APPENDIX 9I: FRACTILES AND SHARES

This Appendix gives the detailed results in Tables 9I.1–9I.8:

Table 9I.1 Nominal thresholds and nominal average income of top income groups, Prussia 1891–1918

	P90	P95	P99	P99.5	P99.9	P99.99	P90–100	P95–100	P99–100	P99.5–100	P99.9–100	P99.99–100	P90–95	P95–99	P99–99.5	P99.5–99.9	P99.9–99.99 \\
1891	1,326	2,095	6,209	9,745	30,110	126,364	3,896	6,154	17,756	27,869	76,513	287,524	1,638	3,254	7,643	15,708	53 067 \\
1892	1,339	2,105	6,127	9,585	29,369	122,262	3,854	6,058	17,292	27,052	73,877	274,438	1,650	3,250	7,531	15,346	51 593 \\
1893	1,339	2,102	6,103	9,528	29,008	119,391	3,832	6,014	17,079	26,663	72,528	268,828	1,649	3,248	7,494	15,197	50 717 \\
1894	1,332	2,093	6,060	9,485	29,059	121,303	3,834	6,027	17,132	26,814	73,303	274,551	1,641	3,251	7,451	15,192	50 942 \\
1895	1,327	2,092	6,122	9,597	29,674	124,352	3,861	6,084	17,420	27,307	74,982	279,529	1,637	3,250	7,532	15,388	52 254 \\
1896	1,337	2,115	6,228	9,804	30,561	130,974	3,945	6,238	18,031	28,385	78,665	296,883	1,652	3,290	7,678	15,815	54 419 \\
1897	1,376	2,181	6,433	10,167	31,912	138,860	4,101	6,501	18,941	29,936	83,775	322,006	1,702	3,391	7,946	16,476	57 305 \\
1898	1,400	2,229	6,647	10,552	33,261	145,841	4,263	6,790	19,940	31,652	89,034	347,456	1,735	3,503	8,228	17,307	60 321 \\
1899	1,425	2,277	6,819	10,874	34,662	155,782	4,397	7,024	20,867	33,274	94,622	376,365	1,770	3,563	8,459	17,937	63 317 \\
1900	1,457	2,330	6,969	11,132	35,620	159,221	4,513	7,216	21,487	34,321	97,704	390,963	1,810	3,649	8,652	18,475	65 120 \\
1901	1,486	2,366	6,966	11,092	35,058	157,024	4,516	7,190	21,186	33,737	95,511	380,643	1,842	3,691	8,635	18,294	63 829 \\
1902	1,510	2,388	6,929	10,970	34,109	150,924	4,462	7,058	20,558	32,550	91,245	358,588	1,866	3,683	8,566	17,876	61 540 \\
1903	1,535	2,425	7,003	11,070	34,397	149,988	4,509	7,122	20,637	32,624	90,938	355,107	1,896	3,743	8,651	18,046	61 585 \\
1904	1,551	2,456	7,138	11,306	35,394	153,838	4,598	7,279	21,214	33,603	93,671	364,411	1,918	3,795	8,826	18,585	63 589 \\
1905	1,570	2,497	7,307	11,639	37,108	162,254	4,752	7,559	22,253	35,446	99,502	389,803	1,945	3,885	9,060	19,432	67 246 \\
1906	1,600	2,554	7,502	12,008	38,707	172,170	4,916	7,847	23,347	37,371	106,092	421,069	1,986	3,972	9,323	20,191	71 094 \\
1907	1,637	2,612	7,603	12,191	39,403	176,673	5,019	8,007	23,854	38,252	108,860	435,105	2,031	4,045	9,457	20,600	72 610 \\
1908	1,686	2,675	7,642	12,199	39,083	174,913	5,043	8,001	23,496	37,508	106,872	425,352	2,086	4,127	9,485	20,167	71 485 \\
1909	1,830	2,872	7,813	12,436	39,271	174,970	5,232	8,211	23,718	37,753	107,117	425,279	2,253	4,334	9,683	20,412	71 766 \\
1910	1,867	2,932	7,916	12,627	39,940	179,384	5,351	8,402	24,263	38,705	110,315	440,630	2,299	4,436	9,821	20,803	73 614 \\
1911	1,914	2,997	8,148	13,010	41,488	185,320	5,419	8,483	25,080	40,046	114,206	453,550	2,354	4,334	10,114	21,506	76 501 \\
1912	1,958	3,068	8,330	13,319	42,567	190,593	5,557	8,705	25,804	41,260	117,928	469,038	2,409	4,430	10,347	22,094	78 916 \\
1913	2,015	3,181	8,863	16,122	51,338	198,122	5,898	9,309	27,205	44,137	124,153	479,128	2,488	4,834	10,274	24,133	84 711 \\
1914	1,912	3,035	8,539	15,668	50,682	195,890	5,735	9,103	26,765	43,468	122,764	474,491	2,367	4,687	10,063	23,644	83 683 \\
1915	1,923	3,121	9,025	16,998	59,360	237,026	6,379	10,352	31,688	51,638	148,884	594,501	2,406	5,018	11,738	27,326	99 372 \\
1916	2,178	3,509	9,887	19,700	70,871	281,670	6,988	11,261	36,556	60,714	176,855	702,890	2,715	4,938	12,397	31,679	118 407 \\
1917	2,802	3,387	11,317	22,712	86,389	353,335	8,460	13,522	45,175	75,436	222,496	910,024	3,398	5,608	14,915	38,670	146 104 \\
1918	2,832	3,421	11,432	22,891	86,929	357,068	8,543	13,666	45,671	76,224	224,964	924,059	3,421	5,664	15,119	39,039	147 286 \\
1919	3,604	4,067	13,186	25,144	90,955	367,554	9,544	15,113	49,003	80,329	231,140	934,049	3,975	6,640	17,677	42,626	153 039 \\

Notes: Capital gains excluded.

Table 9I.2 Nominal thresholds and nominal average income of top income groups, Germany 1925–38

	P90	P95	P99	P99.5	P99.9	P99.99	P90–100	P95–100	P99–100	P99.5–100	P99.9–100	P99.99–100	P90–95	P95–99	P99–99.5	P99.5–99.9	P99.9–99.99
1925			8,983	13,553	33,714	110,958			20,271	29,429	69,097	222,156			11,114	19,512	52,090
1926	2,907	3,251	8,781	13,340	33,912	**118,251**	5,871	8,006	20,417	29,965	72,886	**246,492**	3,736	4,903	10,870	19,234	**53,597**
1927			10,014	14,924	38,054	132,973			22,779	33,568	81,594	271,115			11,991	21,561	60,536
1928	3,348	3,859	10,557	15,564	38,462	**133,740**	6,747	9,453	23,490	34,381	82,698	**277,476**	4,042	5,944	12,599	22,301	**61,056**
1929			10,454	15,367	36,783	128,058			22,976	33,498	80,044	276,718			12,454	21,862	58,191
1932	2,442	3,379	6,171	9,018	22,035	74,912	4,594	6,355	13,629	19,915	45,563	148,377	2,832	4,537	7,343	13,503	34,139
1933			4,775	8,944	21,864	74,356			13,081	19,751	45,210	147,275			6,411	13,387	33,869
1934	2,591	3,613	7,133	10,538	25,039	84,630	4,977	6,939	15,481	22,488	52,629	171,611	3,016	4,803	8,475	14,952	39,408
1935			7,834	11,807	29,371	103,314			18,216	27,005	66,438	238,321			9,428	17,147	47,340
1936	2,945	4,013	9,095	13,810	36,519	**145,267**	6,245	9,050	22,946	34,898	92,361	**372,072**	3,440	5,576	10,995	20,532	**61,282**
1937			10,576	16,400	45,519	183,335			28,070	43,208	116,325	472,739			12,931	24,929	76,724
1938			12,656	20,190	56,264	223,815			34,077	52,555	139,894	536,046			15,599	30,720	95,877

Notes: Capital gains included; **bold values** are extrapolated, i.e. the last bracket contains more than the quantile.

Table 9I.3 Nominal thresholds and nominal average income of top income groups, Federal Republic of Germany 1950–98 (1)

	P90	P95	P99	P99.5	P99.9	P99.99	P90–100	P95–100	P99–100	P99.5–100	P99.9–100	P99.99–100	P90–95	P95–99	P99–99.5	P99.5–99.9	P99.9–99.99
1950	4422*	6067*	13914*	24,909	49,814	**211,142**	10039*	14550*	34319*	48,860	120,635	**502,891**	5397*	9588*	19,744	30,948	**78,479**
1954				27,745	72,733	233,607				62,352	147,458	473,613				41,076	111,219
1957			25,846	38,403	105,590	429,208			66,279	95,608	261,191	954,598			37,949	54,198	184,197
1961	10,723	14,978	39,267	60,627	175,935	762,828	25,427	38,373	105,169	162,375	445,311	1,742,753	12,481	21,674	47,962	91,642	301,150
1965	14,332	19,157	51,568	79,558	213,726	923,293	33,375	49,493	132,979	202,802	541,738	2,098,300	17,257	28,621	63,157	118,068	368,787
1968	19,434	23,466	56,079	88,244	215,087	923,120	37,597	54,590	141,748	213,892	557,496	2,277,192	20,603	32,801	69,603	127,991	366,418
1971	28,906	31,251	78,964	121,306	306,537	1,330,633	54,604	76,059	197,891	299,102	788,460	3,218,338	33,149	45,601	96,681	176,762	518,474
1974	33,596	47,275	95,446	142,249	341,301	1,399,859	66,237	93,206	221,693	326,824	812,483	3,073,013	39,267	61,084	116,563	205,409	561,313
1977	44,101	60,365	113,937	171,817	417,865	1,725,457	80,609	110,336	265,869	395,296	986,278	3,664,635	50,881	71,453	136,442	247,551	688,683
1980	55,401	64,684	135,315	203,315	514,990	2,133,601	97,463	134,574	327,956	492,766	1,275,803	4,936,219	60,352	86,229	163,146	297,006	869,090
1983	58,895	74,043	130,536	197,698	499,155	2,177,607	102,728	139,824	325,409	492,838	1,307,773	5,370,825	65,632	93,428	157,981	289,104	856,323
1986	65,521	85,146	142,711	219,814	569,586	2,620,037	115,576	158,532	378,729	583,344	1,625,245	7,226,706	72,619	103,483	174,113	322,869	1,002,860
1989	73,024	91,103	166,351	258,878	642,178	3,589,998	134,809	187,206	459,588	715,220	2,074,823	10,063,533	82,412	119,110	203,957	375,319	1,187,188
1992	83,731	107,994	202,904	287,839	716,457	3,235,910	148,992	203,773	473,216	708,984	1,894,885	7,742,969	94,211	136,412	237,448	412,508	1,245,098
1995	90,340	116,014	206,199	278,517	647,793	2,815,634	152,952	204,398	445,741	656,363	1,734,253	7,430,870	101,506	144,063	235,120	386,890	1,101,295
1998	94,624	123,876	228,674	318,469	827,490	4,716,607	174,949	242,577	586,814	909,658	2,700,748	12,819,136	107,322	156,518	263,970	461,886	1,576,483

Notes: Capital gains included; **bold values** are extrapolated, i.e. the last bracket contains more than the quantile; <*> means than the value has been estimated on the basis of 'synthetic' tabulations constructed with tax statistics but with unspecified mthodology as far as the merging of ES and LS statistics are concerned.

Table 9I.4 Nominal thresholds and nominal average income of top income groups, Federal Republic of Germany 1950–98 (2)

	P90	P95	P99	P99.5	P99.9	P99.99	P90–100	P95–100	P99–100	P99.5–100	P99.9–100	P99.99–100	P90–95	P95–99	P99–99.5	P99.5–99.9	P99.9–99.99
1950	4,416*	6,053*	13,772*	24,455	47,471	**185,789**	9,976*	14,411*	33,540*	47,358	113,704	**445,544**	5,402*	9,605*	19,770*	30,947	**77,037**
1954				27,240	69,312	205,556				60,436	138,986	419,604				41,074	109,176
1957			25,582	37,703	100,624	377,669			64,775	92,669	246,184	845,741			38,000	54,195	180,814
1961	10,684	14,896	38,373	57,792	151,134	492,092	24,833	36,994	96,347	143,840	352,432	1,061,641	12,544	21,869	48,943	93,829	287,929
1965	14,312	19,114	51,043	78,109	203,674	812,427	33,165	49,020	129,962	196,568	510,611	1,859,020	17,270	28,674	63,241	118,061	362,014
1968	19,407	23,413	55,508	86,637	204,971	812,274	37,360	54,069	138,531	207,318	525,463	2,017,512	20,619	32,862	69,695	127,985	359,689
1971	28,866	31,181	78,160	119,097	292,120	1,170,853	54,261	75,333	193,400	289,908	743,157	2,851,335	33,175	45,686	96,809	176,753	508,952
1974	33,549	47,169	94,474	139,659	325,249	1,231,767	65,820	92,316	216,662	316,778	765,799	2,722,582	39,297	61,198	116,718	205,398	551,004
1977	44,041	60,230	112,777	168,688	398,212	1,518,268	80,102	109,283	259,836	383,145	929,608	3,246,738	50,921	71,585	136,624	247,538	676,035
1980	55,325	64,539	133,937	199,612	490,769	1,877,404	96,850	133,289	320,514	477,619	1,202,497	4,373,317	60,398	86,389	163,363	296,990	853,129
1983	58,684	73,638	127,562	188,454	428,791	1,404,749	100,326	134,797	298,114	436,579	1,035,010	3,271,772	65,962	94,266	161,211	296,004	818,727
1986	65,286	84,680	139,461	209,536	489,293	1,690,155	112,874	152,833	346,961	516,753	1,286,266	4,402,329	72,985	104,412	177,673	330,575	958,830
1989	72,761	90,605	162,561	246,773	551,652	2,315,866	131,657	180,476	421,038	633,575	1,642,075	6,130,453	82,826	120,179	208,127	384,276	1,135,065
1992	83,616	107,752	200,838	282,597	682,761	2,847,350	148,055	201,827	462,477	687,191	1,786,008	6,859,999	94,283	136,665	237,764	412,487	1,222,232
1995	90,206	115,747	204,377	274,014	620,765	2,540,775	150,245	199,176	422,153	612,045	1,554,012	6,280,804	101,315	143,431	232,261	376,553	1,028,813
1998	94,284	123,198	223,465	303,578	710,841	3,042,628	170,859	233,857	537,592	805,817	2,137,451	7,809,097	107,861	157,923	269,367	472,909	1,507,268

Notes: Capital gains excluded; **bold values** are extrapolated, i.e. the last bracket contains more than the quantile; <*> means than the value has been estimated on the basis of 'synthetic' tabulations constructed with tax statistics but with unspecified mthodology as far as the merging of ES and LS statistics are concerned.

Table 9I.5 Nominal thresholds and nominal average income of top income groups, Federal Republic of Germany 1950–98 (3)

	P90	P95	P99	P99.5	P99.9	P99.99	P90–100	P95–100	P99–100	P99.5–100	P99.9–100	P99.99–100	P90–95	P95–99	P99–99.5	P99.5–99.9	P99.9–99.99
1950	4,416*	6,053*	13,772*	24,455	47,471	**185,789**	9,898*	14,268*	33,141*	46,865	114,429	**481,274**	5,384*	9,527*	19,447*	30,049	**74,033**
1954				27,240	69,312	205,556				59,807	139,872	453,254				39,882	104,919
1957			25,582	37,703	100,624	377,669			64,004	91,705	247,754	913,564			37,379	52,623	173,763
1961	10,684	14,896	38,373	57,792	151,134	492,092	24,355	36,171	94,434	142,904	380,660	1,547,709	12,388	21,334	45,848	83,439	251,995
1965	14,312	19,114	51,043	78,109	203,674	812,427	32,905	48,534	128,415	194,523	513,869	2,008,102	17,214	28,439	62,207	114,637	347,897
1968	19,407	23,413	55,508	86,637	204,971	812,274	37,068	53,533	136,882	205,161	528,815	2,179,303	20,551	32,592	68,556	124,273	345,663
1971	28,866	31,181	78,160	119,097	292,120	1,170,853	53,836	74,585	191,099	286,891	747,898	3,079,994	33,066	45,311	95,227	171,626	489,105
1974	33,549	47,169	94,474	139,659	325,249	1,231,767	65,305	91,400	214,084	313,482	770,685	2,940,915	39,169	60,696	114,810	199,441	529,517
1977	44,041	60,230	112,777	168,688	398,212	1,518,268	79,475	108,198	256,744	379,159	935,539	3,507,105	50,754	70,998	134,391	240,359	649,673
1980	55,325	64,539	133,937	199,612	490,769	1,877,404	96,092	131,967	316,699	472,650	1,210,169	4,724,028	60,200	85,680	160,693	288,377	819,861
1983	58,684	73,638	127,562	188,454	428,791	1,404,749	98,395	131,800	292,195	433,738	1,117,908	4,769,739	65,142	91,961	151,017	263,226	716,550
1986	65,286	84,680	139,461	209,536	489,293	1,690,155	110,701	149,435	340,072	513,391	1,389,288	6,417,916	72,078	101,859	166,438	293,969	839,168
1989	72,761	90,605	162,561	246,773	551,652	2,315,866	129,123	176,463	412,678	629,452	1,773,596	8,937,255	81,797	117,241	194,967	341,724	993,409
1992	83,616	107,752	200,838	282,597	682,761	2,847,350	150,168	205,815	478,915	716,438	1,882,872	7,168,132	94,520	137,540	241,393	424,829	1,295,621
1995	90,206	115,747	204,377	274,014	620,765	2,540,775	151,913	202,290	435,243	635,221	1,636,977	6,667,575	101,537	144,051	235,266	384,781	1,078,022
1998	94,284	123,198	223,465	303,578	710,841	3,042,628	178,383	248,093	598,702	915,616	2,500,475	8,793,204	108,672	160,441	281,788	519,401	1,801,283

Notes: Capital gains included but ranking according to distribution of incomes exluding capital gains excluded; **bold values** are extrapolated, i.e. the last bracket contains more than the quantile; <*> means than the value has been estimated on the basis of 'synthetic' tabulations constructed with tax statistics but with unspecified mthodology as far as the merging of ES and LS statistics are concerned.

Table 9I.6 Top income shares, Germany 1891–1998 (1)

	P90–100	P95–100	P99–100	P99.5–100	P99.9–100	P99.99–100	P90–95	P95–99	P99–99.5	P99.5–99.9	P99.9–99.99	P90–99	P99–100/P90–100	P99.99–100/P99–100
1891	38.4%	30.3%	17.5%	13.7%	7.5%	2.8%	8.1%	12.8%	3.8%	6.2%	4.7%	20.9%	45.6%	16.2%
1892	37.8%	29.7%	17.0%	13.3%	7.3%	2.7%	8.1%	12.8%	3.7%	6.0%	4.6%	20.9%	44.9%	15.9%
1893	37.5%	29.5%	16.7%	13.1%	7.1%	2.6%	8.1%	12.7%	3.7%	6.0%	4.5%	20.8%	44.6%	15.7%
1894	37.1%	29.2%	16.6%	13.0%	7.1%	2.7%	7.9%	12.6%	3.6%	5.9%	4.4%	20.5%	44.7%	16.0%
1895	37.2%	29.3%	16.8%	13.1%	7.2%	2.7%	7.9%	12.5%	3.6%	5.9%	4.5%	20.4%	45.1%	16.0%
1896	37.5%	29.7%	17.2%	13.5%	7.5%	2.8%	7.9%	12.5%	3.7%	6.0%	4.7%	20.4%	45.7%	16.5%
1897	38.2%	30.3%	17.6%	13.9%	7.8%	3.0%	7.9%	12.6%	3.7%	6.1%	4.8%	20.6%	46.2%	17.0%
1898	38.7%	30.8%	18.1%	14.4%	8.1%	3.2%	7.9%	12.7%	3.7%	6.3%	4.9%	20.6%	46.8%	17.4%
1899	39.0%	31.1%	18.5%	14.7%	8.4%	3.3%	7.8%	12.6%	3.7%	6.4%	5.1%	20.5%	47.5%	18.0%
1900	39.1%	31.3%	18.6%	14.9%	8.5%	3.4%	7.8%	12.7%	3.8%	6.4%	5.1%	20.5%	47.6%	18.2%
1901	39.0%	31.0%	18.3%	14.6%	8.2%	3.3%	8.0%	12.7%	3.7%	6.3%	5.0%	20.7%	46.9%	18.0%
1902	38.6%	30.5%	17.8%	14.1%	7.9%	3.1%	8.1%	12.7%	3.7%	6.2%	4.8%	20.8%	46.1%	17.4%
1903	38.5%	30.4%	17.6%	13.9%	7.8%	3.0%	8.1%	12.8%	3.7%	6.2%	4.7%	20.9%	45.8%	17.2%
1904	38.6%	30.6%	17.8%	14.1%	7.9%	3.1%	8.0%	12.7%	3.7%	6.2%	4.8%	20.8%	46.1%	17.2%
1905	38.9%	30.9%	18.2%	14.5%	8.1%	3.2%	8.0%	12.7%	3.7%	6.4%	5.0%	20.7%	46.8%	17.5%
1906	38.2%	30.5%	18.1%	14.5%	8.2%	3.3%	7.7%	12.3%	3.6%	6.3%	5.0%	20.1%	47.5%	18.0%
1907	37.8%	30.1%	18.0%	14.4%	8.2%	3.3%	7.6%	12.2%	3.6%	6.2%	4.9%	19.8%	47.5%	18.2%
1908	37.3%	29.6%	17.4%	13.9%	7.9%	3.1%	7.7%	12.2%	3.5%	6.0%	4.8%	19.9%	46.6%	18.1%
1909	37.8%	29.7%	17.2%	13.7%	7.7%	3.1%	8.1%	12.5%	3.5%	5.9%	4.7%	20.7%	45.3%	17.9%
1910	38.0%	29.8%	17.2%	13.7%	7.8%	3.1%	8.2%	12.6%	3.5%	5.9%	4.7%	20.8%	45.3%	18.2%
1911	37.8%	29.6%	17.5%	14.0%	8.0%	3.2%	8.2%	12.1%	3.5%	6.0%	4.8%	20.3%	46.3%	18.1%
1912	37.7%	29.6%	17.5%	14.0%	8.0%	3.2%	8.2%	12.0%	3.5%	6.0%	4.8%	20.2%	46.4%	18.2%
1913	38.5%	30.4%	17.8%	14.4%	8.1%	3.1%	8.1%	12.6%	3.4%	6.3%	5.0%	20.8%	46.1%	17.6%
1914	38.1%	30.2%	17.8%	14.4%	8.2%	3.2%	7.9%	12.5%	3.3%	6.3%	5.0%	20.3%	46.7%	17.7%
1915	39.3%	31.9%	19.5%	15.9%	9.2%	3.7%	7.4%	12.4%	3.6%	6.7%	5.5%	19.8%	49.7%	18.8%
1916	40.8%	32.8%	21.3%	17.7%	10.3%	4.1%	7.9%	11.5%	3.6%	7.4%	6.2%	19.4%	52.3%	19.2%
1917	42.0%	33.6%	22.4%	18.7%	11.0%	4.5%	8.4%	11.1%	3.7%	7.7%	6.5%	19.6%	53.4%	20.1%
1918	37.9%	30.0%	19.5%	16.0%	9.2%	3.7%	7.9%	10.6%	3.5%	6.8%	5.5%	18.4%	51.3%	19.1%

1925			11.3%	8.2%	3.9%	1.2%			3.1%	4.4%	2.6%			11.0%
1926	32.5%	22.1%	11.3%	8.3%	4.0%	1.4%	10.3%	10.8%	3.0%	4.3%	2.7%	21.2%	34.8%	12.1%
1927			11.5%	8.5%	4.1%	1.4%			3.0%	4.4%	2.8%			11.9%
1928	32.2%	22.6%	11.2%	8.2%	4.0%	1.3%	9.7%	11.4%	3.0%	4.3%	2.6%	21.0%	34.8%	11.8%
1929			11.1%	8.1%	3.9%	1.3%			3.0%	4.2%	2.5%			12.0%
1932	38.4%	26.6%	11.4%	8.3%	3.8%	1.2%	11.8%	15.2%	3.1%	4.5%	2.6%	27.0%	29.7%	10.9%
1933			10.9%	8.2%	3.8%	1.2%			2.7%	4.4%	2.5%			11.3%
1934	36.3%	25.3%	11.3%	8.2%	3.8%	1.3%	11.0%	14.0%	3.1%	4.4%	2.6%	25.0%	31.1%	11.1%
1935			12.0%	8.9%	4.4%	1.6%			3.1%	4.5%	2.8%			13.1%
1936	37.3%	27.0%	13.7%	10.4%	5.5%	2.2%	10.3%	13.3%	3.3%	4.9%	3.3%	23.6%	36.7%	16.2%
1937			15.0%	11.5%	6.2%	2.5%			3.4%	5.3%	3.7%			16.8%
1938			16.3%	12.6%	6.7%	2.6%			3.7%	5.9%	4.1%			15.7%
1950	34.4%	24.9%	11.6%	8.2%	3.9%	1.5%	9.3%	13.3%	3.4%	4.3%	2.4%	22.6%	33.6%	13.3%
1954				6.9%	3.2%	1.0%				3.7%	2.2%			
1957			11.0%	7.9%	4.2%	1.4%			3.2%	3.7%	2.8%			13.1%
1961	31.4%	23.4%	12.2%	9.1%	4.5%	1.3%	7.9%	11.1%	3.1%	4.7%	3.3%	19.0%	38.8%	11.0%
1965	31.3%	23.1%	12.2%	9.3%	4.8%	1.8%	8.1%	10.8%	3.0%	4.5%	3.1%	19.0%	39.2%	14.3%
1968	30.3%	21.9%	11.2%	8.4%	4.3%	1.6%	8.4%	10.6%	2.8%	4.1%	2.6%	19.0%	37.1%	14.6%
1971	31.8%	22.1%	11.3%	8.5%	4.4%	1.7%	9.7%	10.7%	2.8%	4.1%	2.7%	20.4%	35.6%	14.7%
1974	30.8%	21.6%	10.1%	7.4%	3.6%	1.3%	9.2%	11.5%	2.7%	3.8%	2.3%	20.6%	32.9%	12.6%
1977	31.5%	21.5%	10.2%	7.5%	3.7%	1.3%	10.0%	11.3%	2.7%	3.9%	2.4%	21.3%	32.4%	12.5%
1980	32.8%	22.6%	10.8%	8.1%	4.1%	1.5%	10.2%	11.7%	2.8%	4.0%	2.6%	21.9%	33.1%	13.6%
1983	31.8%	21.3%	9.4%	6.9%	3.3%	1.0%	10.4%	11.9%	2.6%	3.8%	2.3%	22.4%	29.7%	11.0%
1986	32.2%	21.8%	9.9%	7.4%	3.7%	1.3%	10.4%	11.9%	2.5%	3.8%	2.5%	22.3%	30.7%	12.7%
1989	33.9%	23.3%	10.9%	8.2%	4.2%	1.6%	10.7%	12.4%	2.7%	4.0%	2.6%	23.1%	32.0%	14.6%
1992	34.6%	23.6%	10.8%	8.0%	4.2%	1.6%	11.0%	12.8%	2.8%	3.9%	2.6%	23.8%	31.2%	14.8%
1995	32.7%	21.7%	9.2%	6.7%	3.4%	1.4%	11.0%	12.5%	2.5%	3.3%	2.0%	23.5%	28.1%	14.9%
1998	35.4%	24.2%	11.1%	8.3%	4.4%	1.6%	11.2%	13.1%	2.8%	3.9%	2.8%	24.3%	31.5%	14.5%

Note: Excluding capital gains excepted for 1925–38.

Table 9I.7 Top income share, Germany 1950–98 (2)

	P90–100	P95–100	P99–100	P99.5–100	P99.9–100	P99.99–100	P90–95	P95–99	P99–99.5	P99.5–99.9	P99.9–99.99
1950	34.6%	25.1%	11.8%	8.4%	4.2%	1.7%	9.3%	13.2%	3.4%	4.3%	2.4%
1954				7.1%	3.3%	1.1%				3.7%	2.3%
1957			11.3%	8.1%	4.4%	1.6%			3.2%	3.7%	2.8%
1961	32.2%	24.3%	13.3%	10.3%	5.6%	2.2%	7.9%	11.0%	3.0%	4.6%	3.4%
1965	31.5%	23.3%	12.5%	9.6%	5.1%	2.0%	8.1%	10.8%	3.0%	4.5%	3.1%
1968	30.5%	22.1%	11.5%	8.7%	4.5%	1.8%	8.3%	10.6%	2.8%	4.1%	2.7%
1971	32.0%	22.3%	11.6%	8.8%	4.6%	1.9%	9.7%	10.7%	2.8%	4.1%	2.7%
1974	31.0%	21.8%	10.4%	7.6%	3.8%	1.4%	9.2%	11.4%	2.7%	3.8%	2.4%
1977	31.7%	21.7%	10.4%	7.8%	3.9%	1.4%	10.0%	11.2%	2.7%	3.9%	2.4%
1980	33.0%	22.8%	11.1%	8.3%	4.3%	1.7%	10.2%	11.7%	2.8%	4.0%	2.6%
1983	32.5%	22.1%	10.3%	7.8%	4.1%	1.7%	10.4%	11.8%	2.5%	3.7%	2.4%
1986	32.9%	22.6%	10.8%	8.3%	4.6%	2.1%	10.4%	11.8%	2.5%	3.7%	2.6%
1989	34.8%	24.1%	11.8%	9.2%	5.3%	2.6%	10.6%	12.3%	2.6%	3.9%	2.8%
1992	34.8%	23.8%	11.1%	8.3%	4.4%	1.8%	11.0%	12.7%	2.8%	3.9%	2.6%
1995	33.3%	22.2%	9.7%	7.1%	3.8%	1.6%	11.0%	12.5%	2.6%	3.4%	2.2%
1998	36.2%	25.1%	12.2%	9.4%	5.6%	2.7%	11.1%	13.0%	2.7%	3.8%	2.9%

Note: Including capital gains.

Table 9I.8 Top income shares, Germany 1950–98 (3)

	P90–100	P95–100	P99–100	P99.5–100	P99.9–100	P99.99–100	P90–95	P95–99	P99–99.5	P99.5–99.9	P99.9–99.99
1950	34.2%	24.6%	11.4%	8.1%	3.9%	1.7%	9.3%	13.2%	3.4%	4.1%	2.3%
1954				6.8%	3.2%	1.0%				3.6%	2.1%
1957			10.9%	7.8%	4.2%	1.6%			3.2%	3.6%	2.7%
1961	30.8%	22.9%	11.9%	9.0%	4.8%	2.0%	7.8%	10.8%	2.9%	4.2%	2.9%
1965	31.0%	22.9%	12.1%	9.2%	4.8%	1.9%	8.1%	10.7%	2.9%	4.3%	3.0%
1968	30.0%	21.7%	11.1%	8.3%	4.3%	1.8%	8.3%	10.6%	2.8%	4.0%	2.5%
1971	31.5%	21.8%	11.2%	8.4%	4.4%	1.8%	9.7%	10.6%	2.8%	4.0%	2.6%
1974	30.6%	21.4%	10.0%	7.3%	3.6%	1.4%	9.2%	11.4%	2.7%	3.7%	2.2%
1977	31.2%	21.3%	10.1%	7.5%	3.7%	1.4%	10.0%	11.2%	2.6%	3.8%	2.3%
1980	32.5%	22.3%	10.7%	8.0%	4.1%	1.6%	10.2%	11.6%	2.7%	3.9%	2.5%
1983	31.2%	20.9%	9.3%	6.9%	3.5%	1.5%	10.3%	11.7%	2.4%	3.3%	2.0%
1986	31.6%	21.3%	9.7%	7.3%	4.0%	1.8%	10.3%	11.6%	2.4%	3.4%	2.2%
1989	33.3%	22.7%	10.6%	8.1%	4.6%	2.3%	10.5%	12.1%	2.5%	3.5%	2.3%
1992	35.1%	24.0%	11.2%	8.4%	4.4%	1.7%	11.0%	12.9%	2.8%	4.0%	2.7%
1995	33.1%	22.0%	9.5%	6.9%	3.6%	1.5%	11.0%	12.5%	2.6%	3.3%	2.1%
1998	36.9%	25.7%	12.4%	9.5%	5.2%	1.8%	11.3%	13.3%	2.9%	4.3%	3.4%

Note: Including capital gains (ranking according to distribution excluding capital gains).

REFERENCES

Abelshauser, W. (2004). *Deutsche Wirtschaftsgeschichte seit 1945*. Bonn: C. H. Beck.

Atkinson, A. B. (2005). 'Top incomes in the UK over the 20th century', *Journal of the Royal Statistical Society*, 168(2): 325–43.

Becker, I. and Hauser, R. (2003). *Anatomie der Einkommensverteilung*. Berlin: Sigma Editions.

Bedau, K-D. (1985). 'Das Einkommen sozialer Haushaltsgruppen in der Bundesrepublik Deutschland im Jahr 1983', *DIW Wochenbericht*, 14: 177–87.

Borchardt, K. (1990). *Economic Crisis and Political Collapse. The Weimarer Republic, 1924–1933*. Oxford: Berg.

Bry, G. (1960). *Wages in Germany, 1871–1945*. Princeton: Princeton University Press.

Champernowne, D. G. (1953). 'A model of income distribution', *Economic Journal*, 63: 318–51.

Dell, F. (2005). 'Top Incomes in Germany and Switzerland over the Twentieth Century', *Journal of the European Economic Association*, 3: 412–21.

Gabaix, X. (1999). 'Zipf's law for cities: an explanation', *Quarterly Journal of Economics*, 114: 739–67.

Geisenberger, S. and Müller, J. H. (1972). *Die Einkommenstruktur in verschiedenen deutschen Länder, 1874–1914*. Berlin: Duncker & Humblot.

Grant, O. W. (2002). 'Does industrialization push up inequality ? New evidence on the Kuznets curve from nineteenth century Prussian tax statistics'. Discussion Papers in Economic and Social History, University of Oxford.

Grumbach, F. (1957). 'Statistische untersuchungen über die entwicklung der einkommenverteilung in deutschland'. Unpublished PhD thesis, University of Münster.

Hoffmann, W. G. (1965). *Das Wachstum der deutschen Wirtschaft seit der Mitte des 19.* Berlin: Jahrhunderts.

—— Muller, J. H. (1959). *Das deutsche Volkseinkommen, 1851–1957*. Tübingen: Mohr Verlag.

Holtfrerich, C. L. (1980). *Die deutsche Inflation*. Berlin: de Gruyter Verlag.

Ketterle, J. (1994), *Die Einkommensteuer in Deutschland, Modernisierung und Anpassung einer direkten Steuer von 1890–91 bis 1920*. Köln: Botermann & Botermann Verlag.

Kuczinsky, J. (1960–72). *Die Geschichte der Lage der Arbeiter unter dem Kapitalismus*. Berlin: AkademiVerlag.

Mandelbrot, B. (1960). 'The pareto-levy law and the distribution of income', *International Economic Review*, 1: 79–106.

Peukert, D. (1987). *Die Weimarer Republik: Krisenjahren der klassischen Moderne*. Frankfurt: Surhkamp.

Piketty, T. (2001). *Les hauts revenus en France au 20ème siècle*. Paris: Grasset.

—— Saez, E. (2003). 'Income Inequality in the United States, 1913–1998', *Quarterly Journal of Economics*, 118: 1–39.

Procopovitch, S. N. (1926). 'The distribution of national income', *Economic Journal*, 26: 69–82.

Ritschl, A. (1990). 'Zu hohe Löhne in der Weimarer Republik? Eine Auseinandersetzung mit Holtfrerichs Berechnungen zur Lohnposition der Arbeiterschaft 1925–1932', *Geschichte und Gesellschaft*, pp. 375–402.

Rosinus, W. (2000). 'Die steuerliche Einkomensverteilung', *Wirtschaft und Statistik*, (6): 456–63.

Saez, E. and Veall, M. (2005). 'The evolution of high incomes in Northern America: Lessons from Canadian evidence', *American Economic Review*, 95: 831–49.

Spoerer, M. (1996). *Von Scheingewinnen zum Rüstungsboom, Eigenkapitalrentabilität der deutschen Industrieaktiengesellschaften, 1925–1941*. Stuttgart: Steiner Verlag.

Statistische Reichsamt (1932). 'Das deutsche Volkseinkommen vor und nach dem Kriege', *Einzelschriften zur Statistik des deutschen Reichs*, vol. 24. Berlin: Reimar Hobbing.

—— (1939). 'Die Einkommenschichtung im Deutschen Reich', *Wirtschaft und Statistik*, 660sq. Berlin: Reimar Hobbing.

Statistische Bundesamt (1954). 'Zur Frage der Einkommeschichtung', *Wirtschaft und Statistik*, (6), 265–73.

—— (1954*a*). 'Nochmals Zur Frage der Einkommeschichtung', *Wirtschaft und Statistik*, (10): 457–60.

—— (1954*b*). 'Versuch eines Vergleiches der Einkommensteuerschichtung in der Bundesrepublik Deutschland 1950 und im Deutschen Reich 1936', *Wirtschaft und Statistik*, (10): 460–4.

—— (1991). 'Volkswirtschaftliche Gesamtrechnungen, Revidierte Ergebnisse, 1950 bis 1990', Fachserie 18, vol. S. 15.

—— (2005). 'Volkswirtschaftliche Gesamtrechnungen, Revidierte Ergebnisse, 1970 bis 2004', Fachserie 18, vol. S. 21.

Stehle, R. (1999). 'Renditenvergleich von Aktien und festverzinslichen Wertpapiere auf Basis des DAX and des REXP'. Mimeo, Humboldt-Universität zu Berlin.

Sweezy, M. Y. (1939). 'Distribution of wealth and income under the Nazis', *Review of Economic Statistics*, 21: 178–84.

—— (1940). 'German corporate profits: 1926–1938', *Quarterly Journal of Economics*, 54: 384–98.

Tooze, A. (2001). *Statistics and the German State, 1900–1945*. Cambridge: Cambridge University Press.

Wagner, G. and Krause, P. (2001). *Lebenslagen in Deutschland: Forschungsprojekt Einkommensverteilung und Einkommensmobilität*. Technical report, Bundesministerium für Arbeit und Sozialordnung.

10

Top Incomes in the Netherlands over the Twentieth Century[1]

W. Salverda and A. B. Atkinson

10.1 INTRODUCTION

As a contrast to the rising income inequality in Anglo-Saxon countries (Chapters 4 to 8), the Netherlands (NL) is of particular interest.[2] After attaining very high levels of unemployment in the early 1980s, it has seen an impressive growth of employment, and its unemployment rate has become closer to that of the US than to the EU average. It is natural to ask how far this change has involved increased inequality in market incomes. The developments of the past two decades have moreover to be seen in the light of the longer run evolution of the personal income distribution in OECD countries. For much of the first three-quarters of the twentieth century the dominant tendency had been for a decline in inequality. Pen (1979) summarized the experience of the Netherlands as 'a clear case of levelling'. It is interesting to ask how far changes in the 1980s and 1990s have reversed the long-run tendency towards reduced inequality. How different was the end of the twentieth century from the beginning?

Taking a long-run and, in this book as a whole, a cross-country perspective on income distribution is important if we are to understand the underlying determinants, but implementing such an approach poses major problems in terms of data availability. As in the other chapters we draw here on the income tax returns, a source that has been relatively under-utilized. Its pros and cons have been discussed in earlier chapters. We use published tabulations for earlier years and the micro-data from tax records for more recent years. In the Netherlands, Schultz (1968) and Hartog and Veenbergen (1978) (see also Hartog 1983) constructed a long time series of income distribution estimates from 1914–1972 using the published income tax statistics. As we will see, the results they present

[1] We are most grateful to Emiel Afman in particular and also to Cees Nierop for carrying out the calculations for the Dutch micro-data and to Statistics Netherlands for making the data available. We thank Joop Hartog, both for valuable comments on an earlier version and for his considerable assistance by supplying working sheets from his earlier study, Emmanuel Saez, Thomas Piketty, and Fabien Dell for their most helpful comments.

[2] See Atkinson and Salverda (2005) for a direct comparison of the Netherlands and the UK.

regarding top shares are less detailed and differ slightly because of a different determination of the population of tax payers that provided the basis for estimating the percentiles at the top.

The first aim of this chapter is to depict the development of the top part of the distribution of income over time. As other European countries, the Netherlands lost its important colonies during the twentieth century; in particular, Indonesia obtained independence quickly after the Second World War. The Netherlands also had significant incomes policies for part of the post-war period, and considerations of income inequality and protection still play a considerable role in present day policy making. The Dutch wartime experience differed because of neutrality in 1914–18 and occupation up to 1945 during the last war. Top shares are considered and compared for two distributions, those of gross incomes and disposable incomes. Second, the chapter aims to inquire into the composition of top income by its two major types: from capital and from labour, distinguishing on the capital side between income from activity in enterprise and pure property income from interest, dividend, etc. Wage moderation can be considered one of the hallmarks of the Dutch economy and it is interesting to find out whether this had any effect on the evolution of top shares. In addition, the chapter discusses the rate of taxation on top shares in gross incomes.

In Section 10.2, we describe the data and methods, building on the work of Schultz, Hartog and Veenbergen, but bringing the series up to date by using the Income Panel Survey micro-data from 1977. Section 10.3 portrays the evolution of the top shares of gross incomes and disposable income including the 'shares within shares', which do not rely on control totals for income, and which provide a direct link to the theoretical literature on the Pareto distribution. In Section 10.4, we present the results for the composition of top incomes by source of income that enables the cross-country comparison, but which allows the reader to draw conclusions about the Netherlands separately. In Section 10.5, we summarize the findings regarding the evolution of top incomes over the twentieth century, discuss what seems specific to the Netherlands and suggest questions for further research.

10.2 DATA AND METHOD

In this section, we first describe the sources of data on gross and net incomes and types of incomes for the Netherlands. These are (a) the income tax tabulations; (b) the income distributions based on the income tax data published by Statistics Netherlands, that is the *Centraal Bureau voor de Statistiek* (*CBS*); and (c) the Income Panel Survey (or *Inkomenspanelonderzoek*: *IPO*), a source of microdata that is also maintained by *CBS* for the period starting in 1977. All data are based on the administrative records of the tax authorities. Next, we present the method used to approach the data focusing on additions to the general discussion of Chapter 2.

Data Sources

The income tax was introduced in the Netherlands on 1 May 1915, and the first data relate to the tax year 1915/16, taken as corresponding to incomes in 1914. We make use of the same sources as Hartog and Veenbergen (1978)—see Appendix 10A for a detailed list. The distribution of taxable (gross) incomes was initially published in *Jaarcijfers voor het Koninkrijk der Nederlanden* or (from 1925) *Jaarcijfers voor Nederland* (both referred to as *JC*), and then from 1931 in the annual *Statistiek der Rijksfinanciën* (*SR*). In the latter source, the tabulations are very detailed; in some higher ranges the numbers of incomes are in single figures. Statistics Netherlands published a less detailed distribution in a volume *Statistiek der Inkomens en Vermogens in Nederland* in the 1930s, containing distributional data classified by local communities. Notably, up to 1946 we used the more detailed data that Hartog and Veenbergen had gathered from Statistics Netherlands, in particular for the amount of income tax paid. The data relate to tax units, combining the incomes of husbands and wives, and including the non-labour income of under-age children. The tables show the amounts of tax deducted, enabling the computation of net of tax income by range of gross income (not by range of net income) and therefore the effective tax rate on gross income. The detailed data of Hartog and Veenbergen, which have not been published systematically before, are available on the Oxford University Press website.[3]

According to the explanatory notes to the tables in early years, the assessment was based on income sources existing at 1 May of each year, but later the notes refer to income in the preceding year. According to *JC* (1937: 196) 'in general the figures relate to the preceding year'. The notes to *JC* (1943–46), say (in English) 'These figures relate in general to the incomes received in the calendar year preceding the fiscal year' (p. 342). This indicates that the figures for, say, 1938/39 relate to the calendar year 1937. This is the procedure followed by us from 1915/16, taken to represent 1914, to 1940/41, taken to represent 1939. Corroborative evidence is provided by the footnote attached to the figure for 1938/39 (*SR* 1940: table XVL, n. 12) attributing the rise from 1937/38 to the effect of the devaluation of 28 September 1936. It also is consistent with Hartog and Veenbergen (1978). It appears that the timing of the statistical observation then changed with the introduction of a new income tax regime from 1 January 1941. Data for 1941 and 1946 are taken as relating to those years.

From 1950, the income tax data formed the basis for an official analysis of income distribution covering in principle the whole population, published as *Inkomens-en Vermogensverdeling* (*IenV*). Results are also published in *JC*. As described, for example, in *Inkomenverdelings 1959 en vermogensverdeling 1960*, the estimates of the distribution are derived from tax forms (income and

[3] Hartog had gathered this information for Hartog and Veenbergen (1978). We are immensely grateful to him for keeping these data for such a long period, for making them available to us, and allowing us to publish them on the Oxford University Press website.

property tax) and are based on a sample for incomes below 30,000 guilders and property below 300,000 guilders, with complete coverage above these limits. The *CBS*, with access to the individual data, was able to carry out detailed analyses. Tabulations are given, for example, by 'total income' (*totaalinkomen*), by 'typical income' (*kerninkomen*), and by 'spendable income' (*besteedbaar inkomen*). Total income is gross income before deduction of tax or social contributions for both primary and secondary incomes, i.e. income from labour, pension, unincorporated enterprise, capital, property as well as social security, including benefits paid to the employee by the employer, minus expenses necessarily incurred in obtaining this income minus losses not already deducted, fiscal deductions (except those related to private houses), and certain personal obligations (but not pension contributions). Information on spendable income by range of spendable income, is available from 1959. Spendable income includes imputed rent on owner occupied houses, with the exception of 1970–79 when no information on housing is available,[4] and deducts income tax and social security contributions, interest paid and deductions for private houses (e.g. the interest on mortgages). The data are taken to refer to the year indicated: i.e. the *Inkomensverdeling 1958* figures relate to 1958. This is again consistent with Hartog and Veenbergen (1978).[5]

The methods of analysis and presentation by *CBS* have varied over the years. For example, in 1964, there was a change in the treatment of part year incomes (including part year tax units). Whereas part year income had previously been converted to an annual equivalent, the 'assessment to time proportion' was introduced in that year. Subsequently, tax units were allocated to intervals on the basis of their annual income but only actual income was added to the amounts. The treatment of part year incomes affects the distribution as a whole, but has only a modest impact on top shares, so no break is shown in the diagrams.[6] Changes were made in the unit of analysis. The unit of analysis up to 1979 is the tax unit, or '*inkomenstrekker*', as in the tax data. After 1979 the *CBS* analysis was carried out in terms of households, and the published tables provided less detail at the top, although a special analysis was made for 1980–84 that gave the distribution by disposable income for full year tax units (Kleijn and Van de Stadt 1987: p. 12). Households are defined in economic terms meaning that people live and spend their incomes together though they may be taxed separately, e.g. old parents or adult children living with the family. For this reason, we have used micro-data from the Income Panel Survey for the period from 1977, since those data, though also primarily aimed at the analysis of households, allowed us to reconstruct the concept of the tax unit for these years. In 1979 the *IenV* data give only full year incomes, so that there is in fact no overlap (the *IenV* series for total income ending in 1975).

[4] Note that the addition of imputed rent goes together with the subtraction of tax-deductible costs related to housing (particularly interest paid on mortgages). Usually the latter is quantitatively much more important than the former resulting in lower incomes where housing is taken into account.

[5] Although they do not give a figure for 1941 (from *JC* 1947–50: 268).

[6] The impact on the top shares was downward and amounted to 0.53, 0.26, 0.06, and 0.02 for the top 10%, 5%, 1%, and 0.5% respectively.

The Income Panel Survey (IPO)

The *IPO* is a set of micro-data based on the annual income tax files, combined with other administrative sources such as those covering rent subsidies, student grants, and child allowances. The survey comprises detailed personal and demographic information that is combined to form household incomes. Instead of using the household concept of *IPO*, which has the economic rationale of joint spending, we combined the personal data into tax units following our consistent definition over the long period. The dataset does not include information on the educational attainment of individuals, nor on the number of their working hours. The survey was originally set up as a random sample of the population aged 15 and over based on house address leaving out people on boats or in mobile homes. In that form, it covered the years 1977, 1981, and 1985. The legal shifting of student grants from parents to the students in 1986 induced an increase in the number of households with an income. In 1989 the restriction on boats and mobile homes was dropped and since then *IPO* has been available for all individual years and taken the characteristics of a panel survey with some 200,000 respondents, including approximately 75,000 'core persons' who are supplemented by the members of their households (*CBS* 2000: 5). Nevertheless numbers at the very top can become so small that some year-on-year volatility cannot be excluded as substantial individual settlements with the tax inspector will gain more weight (the Dutch data will be more sensitive because of the smaller numbers compared to larger countries). The *IPO* panel has been corrected for immigration flows since 1990. The respondents are re-weighted to make the survey nationally representative in terms of household incomes (this does not necessarily hold for the years preceding 1990). Total income and disposable income are defined as above. Both income concepts exclude realized capital gains or compensation in the form of stock options as these were not subject to income taxation. *IPO* also distinguishes between various sources of income including labour income, income from business activity, from property and from social transfers and pensions.

Changes in Tax Legislation and Statistical Presentation

The form of tax legislation affects the comparability of the figures both across countries and internally across time in the Netherlands. Hartog and Veenbergen (1978) describe three fiscal regimes: the 1914 Act, the 1941 Act, and 1964 Act. As they note, the 1914 legislation was in effect for a long period, allowing continuity in data collection. The 1941 Act changed, among other aspects, the treatment of 'new sources' of income. Under the initial legislation, existing sources of income were taxed on the basis of income in the preceding year, but a prediction was made of the income from new sources. After 1941 only past income actually received was included. The 1964 Act legally endorsed the changes of 1941 which had been introduced under German occupation.

The tax treatment of households evolved as follows (see Pott-Buter and Tijdens 2002). From the start in 1914–72, the basic principle was to tax the incomes of married persons as one income, although some changes were made to the way they were added together, initially (1941) to influence the level of taxation between couples and singles and later (1962) to also stimulate the employment participation of women.[7] From 1973 on, the income from labour of married women was taxed individually (from 1976 extended to disability benefit) while all other types of income as well as tax deductions not related to labour still had to be declared by the man or, later, the highest earner in the household. During the period 1973–99, several important changes were made to the practice of applying the principle with important effects, on the one hand, on female (part-time) employment participation—which is outside the scope of this contribution—and, on the other hand, also on the demarcation of the household. Under certain conditions, people living together without formal marriage can nowadays opt for 'fiscal partnership' and be treated on the same basis as married couples. The number of such new partnerships, however, remained very limited during the period under study and started to increase only after the major revision of the tax system in 2001,[8] which is after the end of the period covered here.

Summary of Data

The main features of the data are summarized in Table 10.1 and the years of coverage are illustrated in Figure 10.1. The main differences over time may be summarized as follows:

- *1914–46*: From tabulated income tax data, published in *JC* and *SR*; information on gross income and net of tax income (by range of gross income), presented in a rather uniform format, with break in continuity in 1941; as we effectively came to use the data provided by Hartog and Veenbergen because of their greater detail, the source is best indicated as *HV*.
- 1950–75: From tabulated data in *IenV* with a slight break in continuity in 1964; information on gross income and, from 1959, on spendable income; various changes in the format of the presentation;
- 1977–99: Information on gross income and spendable income from *IPO* micro-data, apparently with better coverage since 1989.

We have therefore a three-part series, as in the UK but in contrast to the unified series for France constructed by Piketty (2001).

[7] In 1962 a change was made to stimulate female employment participation: a man would still pay the income tax on both incomes but could deduct one-third of his wife's labour income up to a certain maximum (2000 guilders in 1962) (Pott-Buter and Tijdens 2002: p. 21).

[8] The new system enables tax optimisation across partners in a household as partners can now decide to spread tax deductions.

Table 10.1 Overview of income tax data sources for the Netherlands

Geographical coverage	Kingdom of the Netherlands; does not include (ex-)colonies, European territory only.
Unit of analysis	Tax unit, essentially married couple or single adult (though nowadays people may choose 'fiscal partnership' without marriage but this seems quantitatively unimportant up to 1999).
Coverage of population	Tax data (up to 1946) restricted to taxpayers; *IenV* and *IPO* seek to cover whole population.
Definition of income	Total gross income and total disposable income.
Processing delays	Generally based on final figures as agreed by the tax authorities; publication usually 5–6 years after T.
Number of ranges	In *HV* data typically around 27 ranges, increasing to 38 in 1930, in *IenV* the number of ranges varies from 15 to 44. *IPO* has micro-data.
Limit on numbers in cell	No limit in income-tax tabulations, lowest positive number 1 taxpayer. Results from *IPO* cannot be published for less than 100.
Information on tax unit composition	Distribution classified by married/single from 1930. The *IPO* surveys present more detail such as age and other members of the household except the couple.
Information on net incomes	(1) Distribution of spendable income by range of spendable income available for 1959–84 in tabulations (based on *IenV*) but for full-year incomes only, and for 1977–1999 from *IPO*; (2) Net of tax income by range of gross income available from 1914 with few missing years.
Information on source of income	*IenV* for the years presented here and *IPO*.

Methods

The use of the income tax data to study the distribution of income raises a number of methodological problems, as has been described in Chapter 2. As will be evident below, our approach involves compromises between what would be the best measure of the income distribution at a point in time and the desire to compare with quite distant periods in the past (the beginning of the twentieth century).

The basic limitation is that, for many years, the tax data give only partial coverage of the population. Here we follow two approaches, which we can associate with Kuznets and with Pareto. The approach of Kuznets (1953) was to compare the income tax data with countrywide estimates of the total population and of the total income. In the case of the Netherlands this means that we take the 679,110 tax units in 1914 and express them as a percentage (23%) of the estimated total number of tax units. Similarly we take their total income of *f* 1309 million and express it as a percentage of estimated total income, which gives 60%. The key issue here is then the derivation of the control totals for total tax units and total income. These reference totals are discussed below.

The second method focuses on the distribution within the top group. If we have a control total for population, we can calculate for example the share of the top 1% within the top 10%. This gives a measure of the degree of inequality among the top incomes. As explained in Chapter 2, this method can be associated

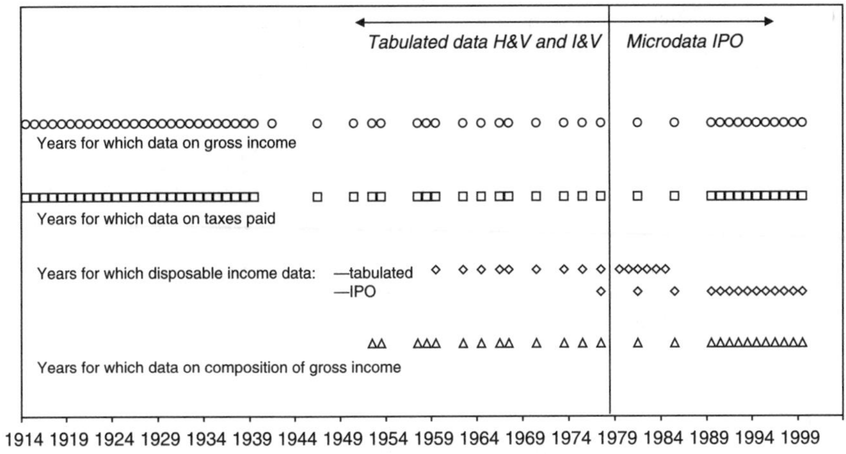

Figure 10.1 Years for which data in the Netherlands, 1914–99

with Pareto. Suppose that the upper tail of the distribution approaches the Pareto form: i.e. that the cumulative distribution F is such that $(1-F)$ is proportional to $y^{-\alpha}$, where y is income. If we assume that this holds exactly within the top income group, then this implies (see Box 2.1) that the share of the top 1% within the top 10% is $(0.1)^{(1-1/\alpha)}$. The same value would be obtained if we took the share of the top 0.1% in the top 1%. By taking the share within the taxpaying population, we do not need to estimate the total income, although we still need a total for the population. This method uses information on all ranges above (via the cumulative income share), in contrast to methods of calculating the Pareto exponent that use adjacent points on the cumulative distribution. For this reason, we shall refer to it as the Pareto-Lorenz coefficient, since it is the Pareto coefficient derived from the Lorenz curve without resort to the income cut-off level.

Control Totals for Population

The first control total we are seeking is that for the total of tax units in the population. It should be stressed that the total number of tax units should not be confused with the total number of actual taxpayers, which may be considerably smaller. Tax units are defined by two principles: first, the potential of receiving one or more incomes which are in principle subject to taxation, and, second, the way incomes are considered as interrelated in taxation. Consequently, tax units are all married couples, with or without under-age children, and all single 'adult' persons over the age of 15. This differs from households in an economic sense to the extent that adult children living with their parents or old-age single parents living with their married children are considered separate tax units. In 1935 for example there were 1.3 million taxpaying units, whereas our estimated control

Table 10.2 Top shares in gross income, Netherlands. 1914–99

	Top 10%	2nd vintile	Top 5%	Next 4%	Top 1%	Top 0.5%	Top 0.1%	Top 0.05%	Top 0.01%
1914	45.87	9.36	36.51	15.55	20.96	16.34	8.63	6.34	
1915	51.21	9.14	42.07	16.49	25.58	20.31	11.44	8.58	
1916	53.31	9.13	44.18	16.30	27.88	22.53	13.02	9.84	
1917	52.47	9.69	42.78	16.27	26.51	21.34	12.39	9.53	
1918	48.50	10.30	38.20	16.25	21.95	17.18	9.65	7.40	
1919	49.48	10.14	39.34	15.60	23.74	19.07	10.79	8.17	
1920	46.23	10.30	35.92	15.34	20.59	16.30	8.92	6.65	
1921	44.03	10.69	33.35	15.06	18.29	14.23	7.60	5.65	
1922	43.19	11.05	32.13	15.31	16.82	12.79	6.57	4.83	
1923	43.08	11.15	31.93	15.48	16.45	12.40	6.30	4.61	
1924	43.84	11.01	32.84	15.50	17.34	13.22	6.88	5.09	
1925	43.87	10.83	33.04	15.29	17.75	13.64	7.19	5.37	
1926	43.87	10.69	33.18	15.19	17.99	13.82	7.26	5.39	
1927	44.33	10.61	33.72	15.35	18.37	14.13	7.39	5.47	
1928	44.58	10.57	34.01	15.38	18.63	14.38	7.57	5.64	
1929	43.85	10.51	33.34	15.24	18.09	13.86	7.10	5.21	
1930	43.02	10.62	32.41	15.26	17.15	12.97	6.47	4.69	2.09
1931	42.18	11.07	31.11	15.52	15.59	11.51	5.47	3.90	1.70
1932	41.33	11.29	30.04	15.61	14.43	10.46	4.79	3.37	1.44
1933	41.19	11.28	29.91	15.71	14.20	10.24	4.63	3.24	1.38
1934	40.82	11.21	29.62	15.60	14.02	10.09	4.53	3.17	1.34
1935	40.69	11.15	29.54	15.53	14.00	10.10	4.55	3.18	1.33
1936	41.10	10.92	30.18	15.35	14.83	10.89	5.15	3.70	1.68
1937	41.92	10.69	31.23	15.18	16.05	12.06	6.13	4.57	2.41
1938	41.60	10.67	30.93	15.26	15.68	11.63	5.60	4.02	1.81
1939	42.02	10.73	31.28	15.49	15.79	11.64	5.54	3.93	1.71
1940									
1941	45.07	10.82	34.25	16.61	17.64	13.06	6.36	4.55	
1942									
1943									
1944									
1945									
1946	40.82	11.74	29.08	16.22	12.86	8.93	3.74	2.56	1.03
1947									
1948									
1949									
1950	36.74	10.58	26.16	14.11	12.05	8.59	3.80	2.65	
1951									
1952	36.95	10.50	26.45	13.83	12.61	9.13	4.22	2.94	
1953	36.76	10.62	26.14	14.15	11.99	8.44	3.69	2.57	
1954									
1955									
1956									
1957	33.98	10.23	23.75	13.36	10.39	7.20	2.98		
1958	34.88	10.27	24.61	13.32	11.29	8.03	3.62		
1959	34.20	10.31	23.89	13.46	10.43	7.23	3.05		
1960									
1961									
1962	34.12	10.18	23.93	13.36	10.58	7.39			

1963									
1964	33.25	10.12	23.13	13.09	10.07	7.00			
1965									
1966	33.05	10.36	22.69	13.24	9.46	6.44			
1967	32.64	10.34	22.30	13.04	9.26	6.29			
1968									
1969									
1970	31.34	10.09	21.25	12.61	8.64	5.76	2.12	1.39	0.57
1971									
1972									
1973	28.37	9.97	18.40	11.49	6.90	4.48	1.59	1.02	0.36
1974									
1975	27.47	10.16	17.40	11.37	6.12	3.95	1.38	0.88	0.33
1976									
1977	27.81	10.46	17.35	11.34	6.01	3.81	1.26	0.77	
1978									
1979									
1980									
1981	28.46	10.89	17.57	11.73	5.85	3.66	1.28	0.81	
1982									
1983									
1984									
1985	29.10	11.09	18.00	12.09	5.92	3.65	1.21	0.77	
1986									
1987									
1988									
1989	28.48	10.86	17.62	11.92	5.70	3.52	1.19	0.78	
1990	28.20	10.87	17.33	11.76	5.56	3.42	1.09	0.68	
1991	28.11	10.85	17.25	11.71	5.54	3.41	1.14	0.73	
1992	27.99	10.86	17.13	11.62	5.50	3.39	1.14	0.73	
1993	27.96	10.98	16.97	11.73	5.24	3.15	0.98	0.60	
1994	28.28	11.10	17.18	11.85	5.33	3.21	1.00	0.63	
1995	28.45	11.13	17.32	11.95	5.37	3.23	1.00	0.61	
1996	28.24	11.02	17.22	11.83	5.39	3.28	1.06	0.69	
1997	28.21	10.98	17.23	11.77	5.46	3.34	1.11	0.72	
1998	28.03	10.97	17.06	11.76	5.29	3.21	1.00	0.61	
1999	28.09	10.96	17.13	11.75	5.38	3.28	1.08	0.69	

Note: Shading indicates violation of non-increasing density assumption. Series upto 1946 based on tabulated income tax data; series from 1950 to 1975 based on data produced by Central Bureau of Statistics; series from 1977 based on IPO micro-data.

total is some 4 million. To calculate total tax units, treating husbands and wives as a unit, we take the total population aged 15+ at a specified date and subtract the number of married females or the number of married men where this is smaller. (See Appendix 10B for the details.) This 'constructed total' would be a correct control total for tax units if all children under the age of 15 were dependent and all children aged 15+ and all adults (e.g. parents) living with a married couple formed separate tax units. This total is then compared with official estimates available for certain years. The total for tax units is typically less than the constructed total. Among the reasons for the difference is that the number of children under the age of 15 with their own income (for example from investments) is smaller than the number of children aged 15+ who have no independent income. Though independent taxation of income from labour was introduced for husbands and wives, the married household has been the basic unit of income taxation until the very end of the period considered here.

We show in Table 10B.1 the constructed total and the number of income units recorded in the *HV*, *IenV*, and *IPO* estimates. *IenV* is systematically closer to the control total than *HV*, and while in the early years of *IPO* we notice a substantial shortfall, the total converged towards 95% of the constructed total at a time that the coverage was believed to be virtually complete. We have therefore taken as our *control total* a fixed proportion (95%) of the constructed total for all years (including *IPO*)—see Appendix 10B.

It should be noted that this approach does not allow for the existence in the tax data of part year incomes. Part year units (not to be confounded with part-time units comprising persons working less than full-time working hours) may arise for several reasons. People reach the age of 15 or die in the course of the tax year, people marry in the course of the tax year and cease to be separate units, or they may emigrate or immigrate. Official studies using the tax data often make corrections for such units. The *IenV* studies in a number of years converted part year incomes into annual equivalents.[9] A comparison of all incomes covered here with full-year incomes from the *IPO* data for 1999 shows a reduction of the number of tax units by no less than 10%, and of total gross income of *f* 18 billion or 3%. Between the two distributions the top-decile share shifts downward by 1.4 percentage points from 28.1 to 26.7.

Control Totals for Income

There are a number of reasons why the definition of income in the tax data does not coincide with that preferred for distributional analysis. Typical tax laws do not allow full deduction of all interest paid; on the other hand, social security payments may not be taxable in all countries—they are, however, in the Netherlands. The taxable income may refer to an earlier time period (which is why national account figures may include a reference period adjustment). The recorded taxable income may, moreover, differ from the true value on account of understatement. Finally, as already stressed, there are people not included ('non-filers').

The income tax statistics in the Netherlands have been relatively extensive in their coverage of the population for most of the period. Starting at about one-quarter of the control total in 1914, the percentage of taxpayers is about half for 1920–30, when a decline to one-third sets in. Since 1945 the coverage has increased from three-quarters to more than 90% from 1957 on. For the pre-Second World War period, the *CBS* has made estimates of the income of non-filers

[9] This may be done in at least two ways: we could treat a person present with an income of *Y* for half the year as 1 person with income 2*Y* or as half a person with income *Y*. *CBS* applied both methods in different years.

(*CBS* 1941: 14, 1948: 21), and these have been used directly. We are following here Hartog and Veenbergen (1978). For the interim period (1946–75), we allocate to each non-filing tax unit a percentage (20%) of the mean income of filers, a method used by Piketty and Saez (Chapter 5) in the US. We continue this use for the *IPO* period though admittedly it applies to small numbers only. The resulting totals are shown in Table 10B.2.

Composition of Income

The composition of income in the top shares refers to the source of income. Various sources can be distinguished in principle, though not always in the actual practice of income statistics. First, income can be earned as a wage or salary in exchange for the efforts of labour, as income from own enterprise as a self-employed owner or as a professional. It can also be property income arising as rent, interest or divided from the ownership of houses, savings or shares, or it can be a based on a social benefit.[10] Pensions and life insurance receipts have a complicated position in this respect, as they could be considered proceeds from property, which when put in a collective pension fund they are not in a formal sense. In the Dutch tax system such savings as well as their proceeds are tax deductible and often not even observed by the tax authorities; the receipts as pensions at later age are taxed as income. Ideally, one would focus on at least four types: labour, enterprise, property, and transfers (including pensions) as these relate directly to clear economic functions. It should be noted that the distinction by source of income is not identical to that by socio-economic category of the person receiving the income though they overlap to a large extent. For example, employees can have income from property or the self-employed can have some income from dependent labour, and both can receive a transfer.

No information on sources is available before *IenV*, starting 1946. Moreover, data are not available for all individual years; presentations vary and are more or less detailed. Importantly, for a long time dependent labour and (occupational) pensions were taken together in one category, both formally being proceeds from labour as far as income taxation is concerned. The distinction of pensioners as a socioeconomic category, offers some help but only very incidentally. It is no problem, however, to distinguish all sources in *IPO*. Consequently, we cover the post-war period incompletely up to 1977 but virtually completely since—naturally, as far as the observations of the tax system go.

Gross and Disposable Income Distributions and the Tax Rate

We are interested in both gross and disposable income distributions, in the sense that the former embodies the implications of the market economy for

[10] Some social transfers are tax exempt, e.g. student grants.

individuals and that the latter represents disposable resources. Official statistics of 'spendable' income start in 1959, the concept referring to income after deduction of income tax and social security contributions, interest paid and mostly excluding additions and deductions related to owner-occupied houses. It should be stressed that we will focus on spendable income by ranges of that type of income, not by gross income. Consequently, when comparing gross and disposable incomes, we will be considering two different distributions and persons found in the top shares in one are not necessarily found in the top shares of the other.

In addition, we will consider income tax paid. For virtually all years since the start in 1914 information is available on the amount of tax paid by ranges of gross income. This enables us to estimate the effective tax rate paid by the top shares. Here we consistently compare for the same type of distribution total gross income on the one hand and taxes paid on the other. This disregards contributions to social security, which were non-existent before 1939. We focus on the tax rate because of its possible economic significance and do not consider after tax income shares, as the concept of income differs greatly from disposable income for most of the period. The calculated tax rate is the ratio of the tax paid to the income received by those in the top X%, and therefore corresponds to the average for the tax units found in the share disregarding the evolution within the share.

Interpolation Methods

Where the basic data on which we are drawing are in the form of grouped tabulations, then, since the intervals do not in general coincide with the percentage groups of the population with which we are concerned (such as the top 0.1%), we have to interpolate in order to arrive at values for summary statistics such as the percentiles and shares of total income. The distributions typically show the number of tax units, and the total amount of income, or tax, in each of a number of specified ranges of income (e.g. 1000–1500 guilders), with an open-ended top interval. The standard practice, adopted by Piketty (2001), is to assume that the distribution is Pareto in form. This method has however the problem that, as discussed in Chapter 2, the information described above allows us to obtain more than one value for the exponent of the Pareto distribution, and hence different interpolated values. An alternative approach is based on placing upper and lower bounds. Gross upper and lower bounds on the Lorenz curve can be obtained by joining the observed points linearly or by forming the envelope of lines drawn through the observed points with slopes equal to the interval endpoints divided by the mean (see Chapter 2). Where there are detailed ranges, as in much of the early Dutch data, the results for the lower bound (linearized Lorenz curve) are normally very close to the upper bound (indistinguishable on the graphs drawn), but in other cases the differences can be more marked, depending on where the ranges fall in relation to the shares in which we are interested. In order to give a single estimate, we have used the mean-split histogram. The rationale is as follows. Assuming, as seems reasonable in the case of top incomes, that the frequency distribution is non-increasing, then tighter, restricted bounds can be calculated (Gastwirth 1972). These bounds are limiting forms of the split histogram, with one of the two densities tending to zero or infinity—see Atkinson (2005). Guaranteed to lie between these is the histogram split at the interval mean with sections of positive density on either side, and this is the method applied in this chapter.[11]

This above approach has been applied to both gross and disposable income. For determining compositional shares or tax rates, however, this approach could not be applied. Though tax rates usually increase with income they do so in discontinuous steps following from the rules of the tax system and at each level they are linear in principle. Also deviations can happen because tax units will differ with respect to tax deductible amounts. Also, for composition not all types of income can show increasing importance with rising incomes; instead they have to sum up to 100%. As the best way to deal with this we simply choose a linear interpolation within the boundary class. The result may slightly underestimate the tax rate and the compositional shares of the types of income that tend to increase with income.

Summary of Methods

Box 10.1 summarizes the approach adopted in this chapter, illustrating it with the first and last year of the period covered (Tax units are measured in thousands, incomes are measured in millions of guilders).

10.3 THE EVOLUTION OF TOP SHARES

In this section, we present the main findings for the top shares in the distributions of gross income and disposable income respectively. To provide a proper background to the developments at the very top of the income distribution Figure 10.2 depicts the evolution of the average income of all tax units on the basis of the same data. The income was deflated and the figure also shows the development of consumer prices. Real income declined during the two wars but more surprisingly it also showed a strong decline during the first half of the 1980s which was followed by an equally strong increase during the second half and a stagnation in the 1990s.

[11] We show by shading the (very small) number of cases where the mean for the relevant range exceeded the midpoint, thus contradicting the non-increasing density assumption. Only a few years (of the 1960s) seem to pose a problem

Box 10.1 Summary of approach adopted in Netherlands estimates

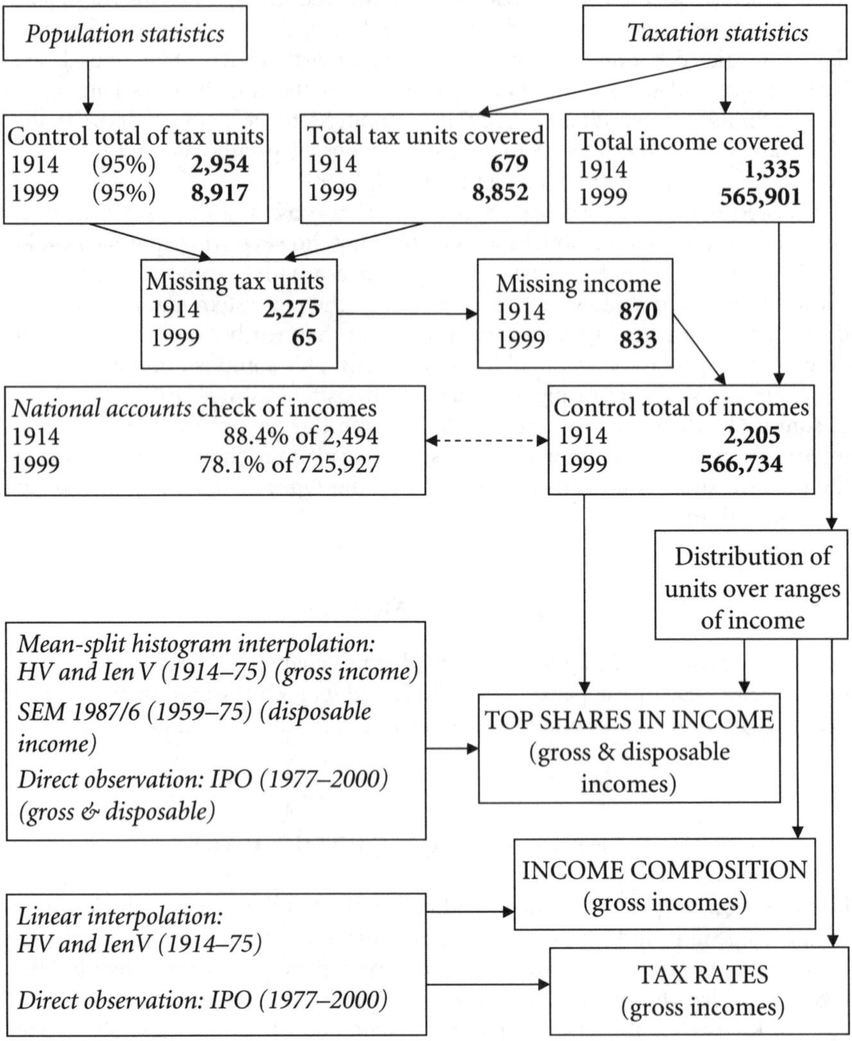

Gross Income

Table 10.2 and Figures 10.3A and B summarize the results for the percentile shares of gross income covering the following groups: top 10%, top 5%, top 1%, 0.5%, and 0.1% (for the sake of clarity we show the top 0.05% and top 0.01% in the

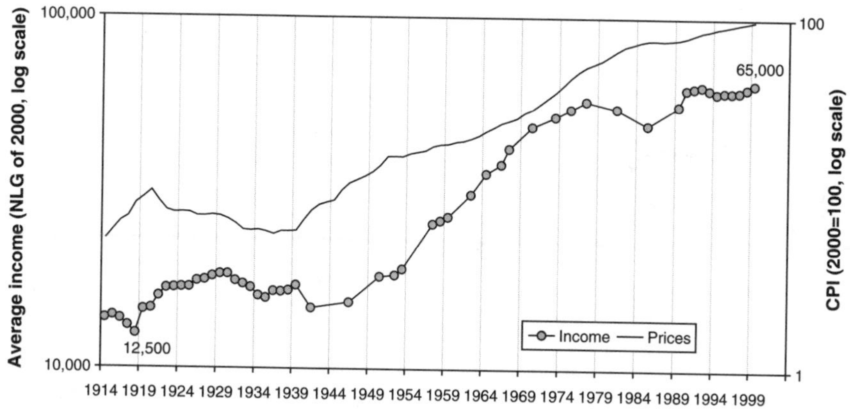

Figure 10.2 Real gross average tax unit income and consumer prices Netherlands, 1914–99

table only). For the first three-quarters of the century, the share of top income groups fell sharply. The top 1% began with some 20% of total gross income, but by 1981 this share had fallen to under 6%. The share of the top 0.1% fell from around 10% to 1.3%. The two World Wars seem to play a role, with initial upward movements followed by a steep decline. The country was fully involved in the Second World War while during the first war it was caught between the belligerent countries, which led to strong and continuous inflation (tripling of wholesale prices) and an initial surge of unemployment that was followed by an adaptation process (Lubbers 1926: 175–9). Exorbitant profits were an important issue at the time and may have contributed to the initial increase in the top shares and relatively high level of the Dutch top shares compared to other countries.

There is considerable similarity in the rate of fall compared to the UK (see Chapter 4), even the annual movements mirror each other to a remarkable degree and the levels reached in the 1970s are virtually identical. In the interwar period, for instance, the very top shares recovered during the 1920s, fell sharply in 1929–31, and then began to recover after the mid-1930s. Turning to the shares of the top 5% and top 10%, we see that the shares for the Netherlands tended to be relatively high compared to other countries, but it should be noted that the statistical coverage was already much more extensive from the start. It also appears that the fall in the 1950s and early 1960s was less, but sharper from 1970. The parallel movements found in Figure 10.3A suggest that the fall was concentrated particularly in the top 1% and above, a point which is illustrated by Figure 10.3C. This makes it all the more interesting that from 1977 to 1999 the *IPO*-based estimates show a remarkable stability in the share of the top 10%.

How far are these conclusions likely to be sensitive to data problems? The break for 1964 mentioned above appears to have a small effect only: 0.56% for the share of the top 10%, which was some 34%. The switch from the *IenV* to *IPO* estimates does not allow any overlap year, but the first *IPO* figures, for 1977, are mostly

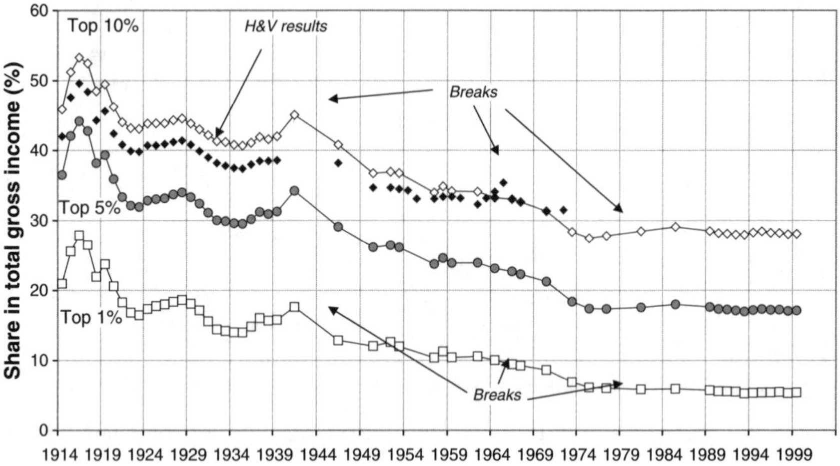

Figure 10.3A Gross income shares of top 10%, 5%, and 1%, Netherlands 1914–99

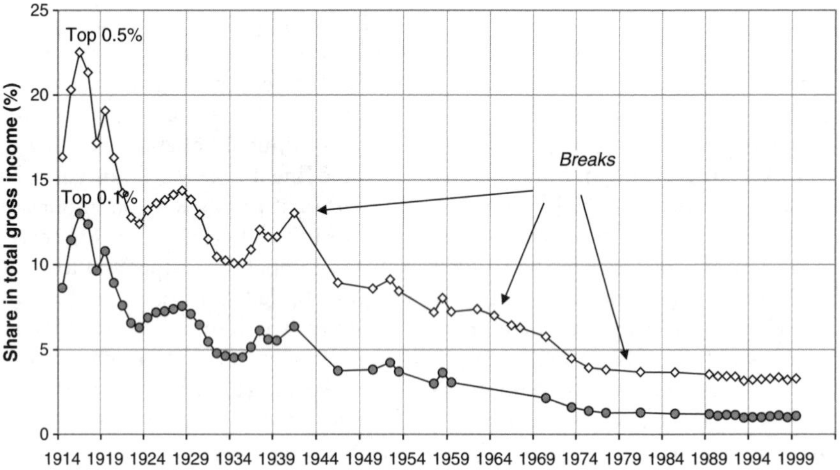

Figure 10.3B Gross income shares of top 0.5% and 0.1%, Netherlands 1914–99

closer to the *IenV* figures for 1975 than the latter are to the *IenV* figures for 1973. The estimates of the shares of the top 10% for the Netherlands differ from those of Hartog and Veenbergen (1978), shown by separate dots in Figure 3A, in that, to maintain comparability with the other chapters, we have used our own control totals and a different method of interpolation. The two series do, however, move closely together. Their estimates cover the period 1914–72. At the end of the period, the estimates are very close (less than half a percentage point apart).

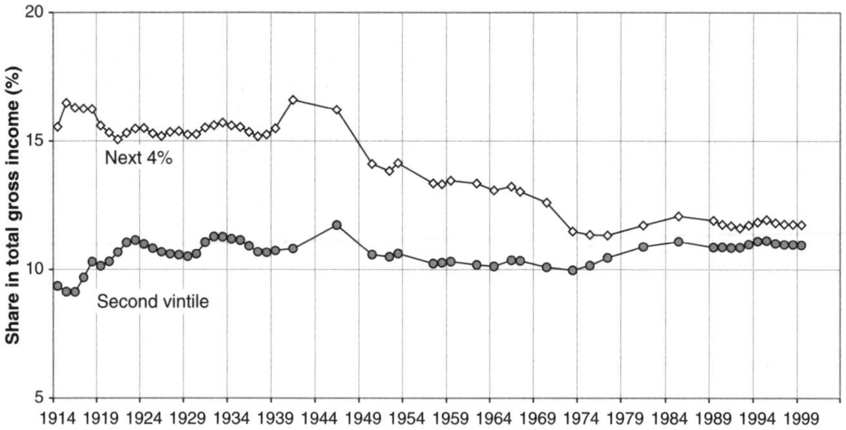

Figure 10.3C Gross income shares of next 4% and second vintile group, Netherlands 1914–99

Initially our estimates are about 3.5 percentage points higher, with the difference declining between 1939 and 1950 to around 2 percentage points and then narrowing. On this basis, we show a modestly larger fall in the share of the top 10% over the period as a whole. Hartog and Veenbergen did not disaggregate the top 10%, but they show (Table 2) the percentage of income recipients per income decile. For 1914 they show 1% of tax units receiving 20% of total income, which is very close to our figure; for 1972 they show 1% receiving 10% of total income, which is again very close to our figure.

The 'Next' Groups

The changing distribution within the top 10% can be looked at another way: in terms of the shares of the 'next 4%' (of those in the top vintile group but not in the top percentile) and of the second vintile (those in the top 10% but not in the top 5%). Piketty (2001: 146) has emphasized that the income of these groups is largely derived from salaries rather than from capital income; different economic forces may therefore have been in operation. He shows that in France the share of the next 4%, which he labels the 'upper middle class', was around 15% at the beginning of the century and around 13–13.5% in the 1990s—a relatively modest reduction. The share of the second vintile was, if anything, higher at the end of the century than at the beginning. The evidence of Piketty and Saez for the US (Chapter 5) shows that the rise of the 1980s and 1990s was concentrated at the top. Whereas the share of the top 10% increased by some 10 percentage points, that of the second vintile was essentially stable.

In Figure 10.3C we show the shares of the 'next 4%' and the second vintile (here, and in subsequent graphs, we do not show series breaks explicitly). The share of the next 4% started off around 16%, was around 14% in the period after the Second World War, but fell in the late 1960s and early 1970s, and is currently around 12%. The share of the second vintile group is remarkably stable, leaving aside a rise during the first ten years. Apparently, most of the inter-war decline of the top 10% is restricted to the top-1%, while its post-war decline is broader and covers the upper vintile as a whole.

Shares Within Shares

Clearly, changes in the shares of top income groups can come about in part because of redistribution between them and the rest of the population and in part on account of alterations in the distribution within the top income groups. The within-distribution is shown in Figure 10.4A; and the corresponding Pareto-Lorenz coefficient in Figure 10.4B. We should note again that these 'shares within shares' do not depend on the control totals for income; they are therefore not affected by errors in the derivation of these totals. The movements for the two groups are strikingly similar, with a steady decline that levels off after the mid-1970s, continuing very slowly (better visible in Figure 10.4B). The early 1920s, the Depression years and the Second World War can be recognized as clear dips in the movement—these were also years with decreasing total income in the country. Examination of the shares within shares shows that what we are observing is not just redistribution from the top income groups to the rest of the population. The upper tail is changing in shape. The rise in the Pareto-Lorenz coefficient from around 1.5 in 1914 to around 3.5 in 1999 provides a direct link to the theoretical models that contain predictions about the evolution of this coefficient (see Chapter 2).

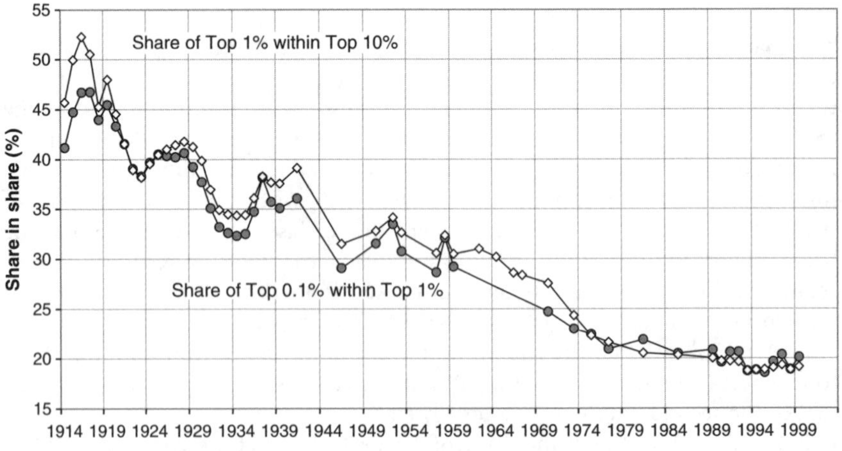

Figure 10.4A Gross income shares within shares, Netherlands 1914–99

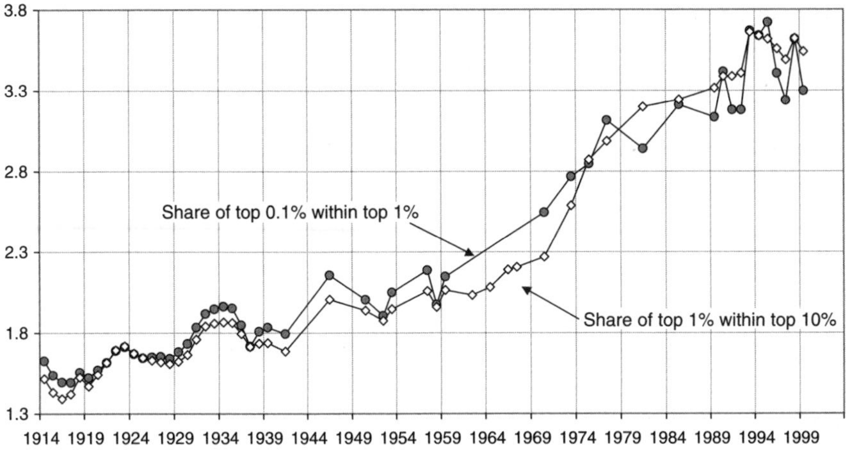

Figure 10.4B Gross income Pareto-Lorenz coefficients of gross incomes, Netherlands 1914–99

Disposable Income

Evidence about the distribution of disposable income is more limited in time and detail. We focus on what Statistics Netherlands calls disposable or 'spendable' income. It represents income after deducting tax and social security contributions paid by the employee and adding social benefits including the public pension. It should be noted, however, that the above concept of gross incomes already includes social transfers, implying a higher level compared to spendable income than would be found in a comparison to primary or market incomes only, which do not comprise transfers. A ranking of disposable income by ranges of disposable income is available from 1959 on. It has been revisited by CBS in the 1980s to enhance consistency of the approach (Kleijn and Van de Stadt 1987)

Top shares in the distribution of disposable incomes are shown in Table 10.3, based on *IenV* and *IPO* with a clear break between the two, which is apparent in 1977 and 1981. The *CBS* figures relate only to full year incomes and as a consequence the same selection was chosen for *IPO* but applying the same shares of the control total of the population to arrive at similar groups for gross and disposable income.[12] There are two smaller breaks in comparability in the *IenV* period because of exclusion or inclusion of owner-occupied housing incomes and costs. From the start of the period a decline is found until the mid-1970s, followed by stable levels for each of the top shares. Figure 10.5 depicts the two shares within shares. Again both change very closely together, but now the decline

[12] Likewise the total of disposable income was complemented with missing incomes in the same way as was used for for non-filers of gross incomes. For *IenV* this was done on the basis of full year incomes, thus including part year incomes in the non-filers, while for *IPO* the basis was all incomes.

Table 10.3 Top shares in disposable income by range of disposable income, full year incomes only, Netherlands 1959–99

	Top 10%	2nd vintile	Top 5%	Next 4%	Top 1%	Top 0.5%	Top 0.1%	Top 0.05%
1959 (incl)*	30.20	10.78	19.42	12.79	6.63	4.12	1.35	0.84
1960								
1961								
1962 (incl.)	30.03	10.60	19.43	12.62	6.81	4.27	1.44	0.92
1963								
1964 (incl.)	29.50	10.73	18.77	12.39	6.38	3.97	1.31	0.83
1965								
1966								
1967 (incl.)	28.52	10.46	18.06	11.94	6.12	3.81	1.28	0.81
1968								
1969								
1970 (excl.)	27.45	10.20	17.25	11.48	5.77	3.58	1.19	0.76
1971								
1972								
1973 (excl.)	25.34	9.96	15.38	10.65	4.73	2.84	0.92	0.59
1974								
1975 (excl.)	24.54	9.87	14.67	10.29	4.38	2.61	0.81	0.50
1976								
1977 (excl.)	24.77	9.97	14.80	10.35	4.45	2.65	0.79	0.47
1977 *IPO*	24,56	9,98	14,58	10,33	4,26	2,49	0,71	0,42
1978								
1979 (excl.)	25.32	10.06	15.26	10.54	4.72	2.85		
1979 (incl.)	24.38	9.74	14.64	10.10	4.54	2.75	0.85	0.51
1980 (incl.)	23.99	9.73	14.26	9.98	4.28	2.55	0.61	0.31
1981 (incl.)	24.18	9.82	14.36	10.05	4.31	2.60	0.86	0.55
1981 *IPO*	24,68	10,13	14,55	10,40	4,14	2,41	0,71	0,43
1982 (incl.)	24.00	9.85	14.15	10.09	4.06	2.34		
1983 (incl.)	23.59	9.60	13.99	9.87	4.12	2.42	0.72	0.43
1984 (incl.)	23.87	9.67	14.20	10.02	4.18	2.47		
1985 *IPO*	25,16	10,24	14,92	10,63	4,29	2,49	0,72	0,44
1986								
1987								
1988								
1989	24,96	10,22	14,74	10,56	4,18	2,43	0,73	0,45
1990	25,57	10,59	14,98	10,42	4,57	2,74	0,88	0,56
1991	25,36	10,24	15,11	10,60	4,51	2,70	0,87	0,56
1992	24,97	10,18	14,79	10,46	4,33	2,56	0,78	0,48
1993	24,84	10,25	14,59	10,43	4,16	2,42	0,70	0,43
1994	24,95	10,28	14,67	10,46	4,22	2,47	0,74	0,45
1995	24,95	10,23	14,72	10,45	4,27	2,51	0,77	0,48
1996	24,99	10,28	14,72	10,47	4,25	2,50	0,76	0,48
1997	24,78	10,17	14,61	10,31	4,30	2,58	0,86	0,58
1998	24,58	10,19	14,39	10,30	4,09	2,38	0,71	0,43
1999	24,73	10,22	14,51	10,33	4,18	2,48	0,78	0,49

Note: See note to Table 10.2 .* excluding and including income and costs from self-owned housing.

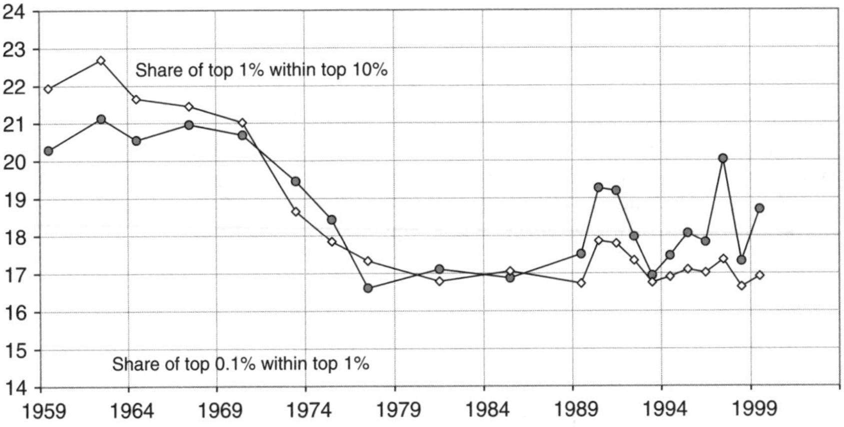

Figure 10.5 Disposable income shares within shares, Netherlands 1959–99

stops at the end of the 1970s while before for gross incomes it continued at a slow pace until the end of the period. The level breaks between *IenV* and *IPO* do not seem to affect the within-shares.

By dividing the top shares in the disposable distribution by those in the gross or before tax distribution, we get a ratio that measures the arithmetic impact of taxation (and social contributions) on inequality as measured by top shares—see Figure 10.6. It can be referred to as the 'implicit tax rate' relative to the overall situation though it should be clear that the persons involved are not necessarily identical. The ratios for the higher shares tend to move upward at a very slow pace during most of the period; those for the top 10% remain basically unchanged. We come back to the tax issue in the next section.

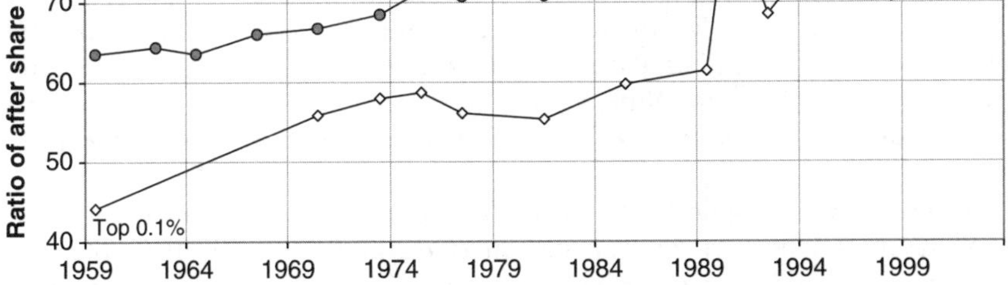

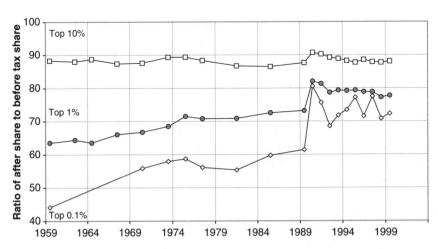

Figure 10.6 Ratio of disposable income to gross income top shares, Netherlands 1959–99

Summary

Summarizing the section as a whole, we can say that gross income top shares shrunk very substantially up to the mid-1970s and have largely remained at a stable level since. The two World Wars seem to have acted as turning points in this evolution. No recent increase is found for the Netherlands, unlike the Anglo-Saxon countries. Disposable income top shares show a similar movement over the shorter period since 1959 for which information is available.

10.4 COMPOSITION AND TAXATION

Now we turn to the income composition of the top shares and the incidence of taxation.

Contributions of Capital and Labour Incomes

Compositional data by source of income are available since 1952. For the period since 1977 we could use the micro-data from *IPO*, for the earlier years most but not all *IenV* publications contain relevant information. Table 10.4 details the changing composition for four types of income: from labour, enterprise, other property (rents, dividends, and interest), and other incomes (pensions, transfers). It should be noted that definitions of types of income are not entirely unchanged over the period. Particularly, pensions were not distinguished from labour income initially and shifted to other incomes from 1967 onward. Wages are defined as much as possible as including the income from labour received as a director, professional or freelance worker.

Figure 10.7 presents the most striking finding: the evolution for the total and the three top shares of the contribution of capital income, which comprises income from enterprise as well as from property—labour income, pensions, and transfers complement this. Capital shares are much higher for the top shares but a dramatic decline is found, as in other countries studied in this volume. Over a period of almost 50 years the capital share in total income plummeted from 34% to 8%. The decline affected all top shares though the time pattern shows interesting differences. For the total as well as the top decile and top vintile the decline is concentrated in the first 25 years and it is relatively limited during the second half. The pattern is different for the very top shares. They do show some decline during the first half of the period but most of it seems to occur in the second half.

Figure 10.8 shows the shifting composition at the very top in more detail. Apparently, first property income was squeezed and then income from enterprise and wages traded places; other incomes managed to maintain their share. At the turn of the century wage earnings are the predominant category of income in

	1952	1955	1957	1958	1959	1962	1964	1966	1967	1970	[illegible]	[illegible]	1977	1981	1985	1989	1990	[illegible]	[illegible]	[illegible]	[illegible]	[illegible]	[illegible]	[illegible]	[illegible]	[illegible]
Top 0.1%																										
Wages*	26.1	27.8	33.7	25.8	29.7					21.4	25.7	28.4	25.9	33.7	33.8	36.9	38.4	32.8	37.7	53.0	56.9	60.9	63.8	65.8	60.0	62.2
Enterprise	40.9	47.4	42.5	37.0	44.3					47.5	53.3	53.5	54.9	40.5	37.7	37.0	38.9	40.4	36.9	25.0	26.0	25.3	22.8	19.1	28.8	25.3
Property**	30.1	22.5	21.2	34.6	23.3					18.5	14.3	15.0	12.5	20.7	20.3	21.7	13.1	12.0	14.3	13.1	9.0	9.3	9.0	11.8	7.1	4.0
Other***	2.9	2.3	2.6	2.6	2.7					12.5	6.6	3.1	6.7	5.1	8.2	4.4	9.6	14.8	11.1	8.9	8.1	4.5	4.3	3.2	4.1	8.5
Top 0.5%																										
Wages	25.9	27.4	30.8	26.1	27.9	26.2	24.8	26.7	24.0	23.1	30.6	36.1	36.4	42.5	46.1	45.6	48.5	48.0	49.4	59.2	62.5	64.0	62.5	62.7	65.2	66.1
Enterprise	47.0	51.6	48.7	44.2	50.6	56.6	59.7	54.7	53.4	51.6	51.8	47.6	48.5	36.3	35.1	36.9	33.6	33.1	31.5	24.0	23.6	24.4	25.3	25.4	25.1	24.0
Property	24.8	18.3	17.9	27.0	18.7	16.2	14.4	12.9	15.8	15.6	10.5	11.4	9.5	15.0	11.7	12.3	9.6	9.1	10.7	9.1	6.4	6.4	6.8	7.2	5.1	4.2
Other	2.3	2.7	2.5	2.7	2.8	0.9	1.1	5.8	6.8	9.7	7.1	4.9	5.6	6.2	7.1	5.2	8.3	9.9	8.4	7.7	7.5	5.2	5.5	4.6	4.6	5.8
Top 1%																										
Wages	26.1	27.8	31.1	27.6	28.5	27.9	27.7	29.8	27.3	26.8	35.8	41.8	45.0	49.7	51.5	50.6	53.4	53.2	55.9	64.0	65.6	65.7	65.9	67.0	66.7	69.0
Enterprise	49.2	52.9	50.1	46.2	51.7	56.6	58.7	53.9	51.7	49.3	47.1	41.7	40.8	31.5	31.5	33.5	30.7	29.6	26.7	21.4	21.8	22.8	22.9	22.6	24.2	21.5
Property	22.3	16.6	16.2	23.5	16.7	14.7	13.0	11.7	15.2	14.7	9.1	10.3	8.2	12.3	10.0	10.0	8.1	8.1	8.8	7.5	5.7	5.6	5.7	5.7	4.6	3.9
Other	2.4	2.7	2.5	2.7	3.0	0.9	0.6	4.6	5.9	9.2	8.0	6.2	6.0	6.5	6.9	5.9	7.7	9.1	8.6	7.1	7.0	5.9	5.5	4.7	4.6	5.7
Top 5%																										
Wages	32.8	35.3	39.0	37.3	37.0	39.2	40.7	43.6	40.6	40.3	49.6	54.8	63.0	65.2	64.5	63.7	65.8	66.9	68.8	72.6	74.0	73.2	73.8	75.1	74.9	76.4
Enterprise	49.1	50.3	47.2	45.2	48.4	49.2	48.6	44.8	41.3	37.7	34.8	28.5	24.3	19.3	20.5	22.5	20.4	19.3	16.8	14.3	14.4	15.7	15.5	14.6	15.3	14.4
Property	15.7	12.1	11.6	15.1	11.8	10.9	9.4	8.4	12.0	11.9	5.8	7.1	5.4	7.6	6.3	6.1	5.7	5.5	5.9	5.0	3.7	4.1	3.9	3.9	3.6	3.3
Other	2.4	2.3	2.2	2.4	2.8	0.7	1.3	3.2	6.1	10.0	9.8	9.7	7.4	7.9	8.6	7.7	8.2	8.2	8.6	8.0	7.9	7.0	6.8	6.4	6.2	5.9
Top 10%																										
Wages	39.0	41.3	45.2	44.4	43.7	46.6	48.5	51.2	48.0	47.7	56.2	60.8	69.6	70.8	69.8	69.2	70.9	71.8	73.0	76.1	77.2	76.5	77.1	77.9	77.8	78.8
Enterprise	45.9	46.7	43.2	41.9	44.0	43.7	42.2	38.8	35.3	31.7	28.6	22.8	18.4	14.7	15.7	17.2	15.7	14.6	12.8	11.0	11.1	12.3	11.9	11.5	12.1	11.6
Property	12.8	10.0	9.5	11.9	9.7	9.1	7.7	7.0	10.3	10.0	4.2	5.8	4.1	6.0	5.0	4.9	4.6	4.7	4.9	4.2	3.2	3.6	3.3	3.3	3.1	2.9
Other	2.4	2.0	2.1	1.7	2.7	0.7	1.6	3.0	6.5	10.6	11.0	10.8	7.9	8.6	9.4	8.7	8.7	8.8	9.3	8.7	8.6	7.6	7.7	7.3	7.0	6.7
Total																										
Wages	61.3	62.0	68.2	66.9	67.4	70.9	70.2	72.3	66.5	60.4	63.3	62.6	67.5	65.8	63.5	63.8	64.7	65.0	64.8	65.9	66.4	66.9	67.6	68.1	69.1	70.3
Enterprise	26.9	27.2	23.6	23.5	23.6	22.1	21.2	19.0	16.9	15.0	12.5	10.3	8.6	6.9	7.1	7.4	7.1	6.8	6.1	5.5	5.9	6.4	5.9	5.9	5.7	5.6
Property	6.6	5.7	4.8	6.0	5.2	4.7	4.1	3.7	5.8	5.9	1.9	2.9	2.5	3.6	3.2	3.3	3.3	3.3	3.5	3.2	2.8	2.9	2.8	2.7	2.5	2.4
Other	5.2	5.1	3.4	3.7	3.8	2.2	4.5	5.0	10.7	18.7	22.3	24.2	21.4	23.6	26.3	25.5	25.0	24.9	25.6	25.3	25.0	23.8	23.8	23.4	22.7	21.6

* Wages include occupational pensions in 1953–66 (estimated at 4 % in 1952 and 6% in 1966), later these are included in other incomes ('Other'). In 1952–75 and 1989–91 and 1993–99 directors' incomes are included in wages; this type of income shows great annual volatility. ** Property income includes income from interest, real estate etc.; these incomes are extremely volatile at the very top. *** Other incomes balance wages, enterprise and property income to arrive at 100%.

Sources: 1952–1975: *IenV*; 1977–99: *IPO*

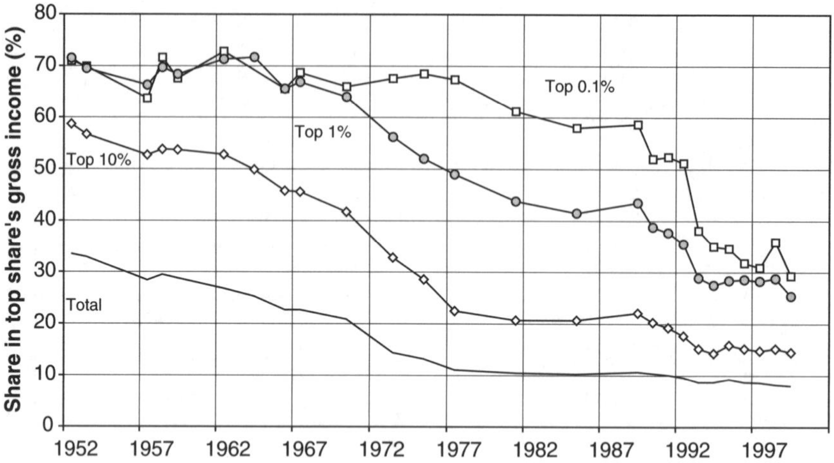

Figure 10.7 Capital income shares within gross income of top 10%, 1%, and 0.1%, Netherlands 1952–99

each and every top share. As changes in the rest of the distribution were much less extensive, the compositional disparity of the top shares compared to the rest of the distribution is greatly reduced. The divergence in wage shares between the total and the top 1% declined from 35 percentage points in 1952 via 23% in 1977 to no more than 2% in 1999. Evidently, the steep compositional gradient within the top 10% largely disappeared at the same time.

It is important to note again that the composition by source of income is not identical to that by socio-economic category. The former puts together all

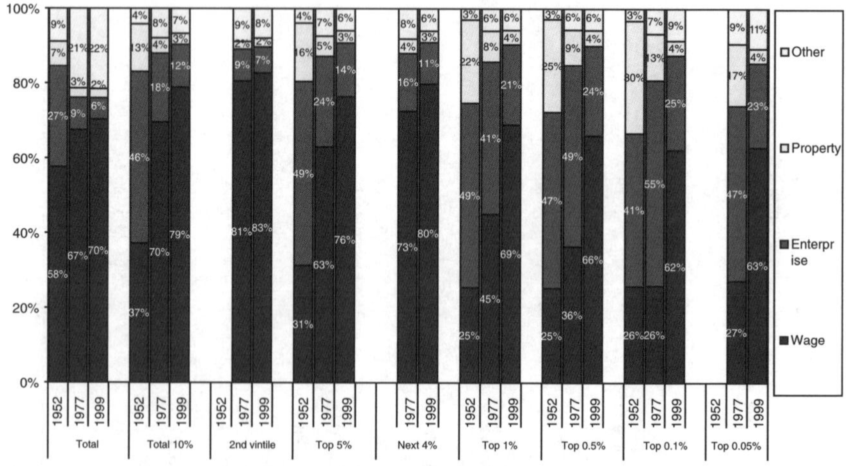

Figure 10.8 Composition of top shares by source of income, Netherlands 1952, 1977, and 1999

incomes for one type of source irrespective of the nature of the recipient. The composition by socio-economic category, however, starts from the latter. It focuses on tax units and categorizes them by the most important source of income. The essential difference[13] is that the tax units, and individual persons for that matter, may have income from other sources than the typifying one. Persons characterized as employees because wage earnings are their most important income, may also receive income from property, e.g. interest or dividend. Table 10.5 indicates that over the period, particularly for the self-employed, these other incomes have become more important.[14] For the self-employed tax units this concerns primarily wages, which grew from 3% to 26% of their tax unit's total income. The table also shows the impact of the initial categorization of pensions as labour income and the shift away from property income to other incomes, as the main income from the 'other' socio-economic category.

The switch between the two types of income up to the very top seems very striking. It certainly seems important, particularly if it helps explain the near stability of the Dutch top shares since 1977. Various candidates for an explanation suggest themselves. An important potential explanation for the shift between both may be the strong decline in self-employment which will have taken away income from enterprise. Self-employment fell from 18% of tax units in 1952 via

Table 10.5 Composition of aggregate gross income by socio-economic category of receiving tax unit, Netherlands 1952, 1977, and 1999

	Self-employed	Employees	Pensioners	Other	Total
1952					
profits from enterprise	90	1	0	0	28
income from labour	3	95	74	0	64
income from property	5	4	22	83	7
other income	1	0	3	17	1
total	100	100	100	100	100
1977					
profits from enterprise	73	0	0	−2	9
income from labour	13	93	4	7	67
income from property	4	1	9	3	3
other income	79	6	88	92	21
total	100	100	100	100	100
1999					
profits from enterprise	62	0	0	−2	6
income from labour	26	94	6	16	70
income from property	3	1	6	4	2
other income	9	4	88	82	22
total	100	100	100	100	100

[13] Another difference is that for a tax unit comprising more than one person, the categorization depends on the person with the most important income.

[14] In the *IenV* period, the total income concepts may sometimes differ from that used for sources of income.

8% in 1977 to 6% in 1999, and their income share fell from 30% via 12% to 9%. This may be more relevant during the first half of the period.

Though capital and wage incomes have traded places within the top shares, the increased role of the latter has not been able to prevent the decline or the stability of the top shares. Figure 10.9 shows the share of top share wages in total income: i.e., the lines show what the shares of the different groups would have been if they had received only wage income. The impact of wages remained largely unchanged at the very top. It did increase, however, for the top decile as a whole. The well known moderation of wages in the Netherlands, which extended over much of the last decades, and the corresponding limited increase in wage inequality may have contributed. The growing role of wages that remains may partly rest on the strong growth of two-income households (as a consequence of increased female employment participation). The dotted line in Figures 10.9 A, B, and C serves to illustrate this for the top 10%. It shows the wage share if we take only the wages of the first earner. It indicates the share of top 10% wages when the second wage income is not taken into account. Unfortunately the information is not systematically available before the *IPO* period, but the growing difference after 1977 brings out the impact of second earners. The second income seems to explain the rise of the 1990s.[15] For the top 1% the effect (not shown) is also substantial but does not take away the full increase over the 1990s. For the top 0.1% the effect is negligible.

These are real economic phenomena, but the shift may also relate to tax shifting, which means that capital incomes may increasingly be moved outside the reach of income taxation. Apart from voluntary re-arrangement by individual

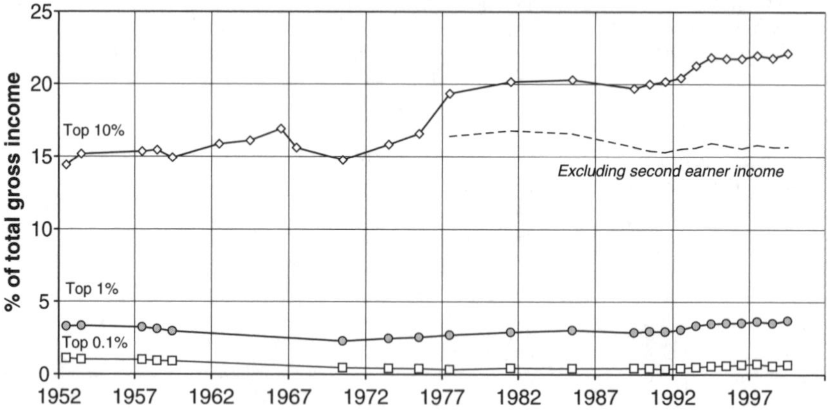

Figure 10.9A Wage income contributions to gross income of top 10%, 1%, and 0.1%, Netherlands 1952–99

[15] Between 1977 and 1999 the number of two-earners almost doubled and their share among tax units increased from 14% to 17%. In the top decile their population share grew more strongly from 33% to 58%. The rise of second incomes does not apply to the top 0.1%.

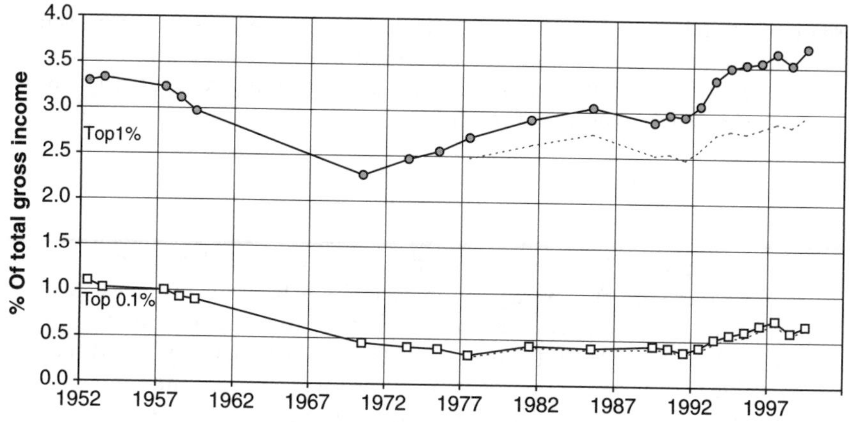

Figure 10.9B Wage income contributions to gross income of top 1% and 0.1%, Netherlands 1952–99

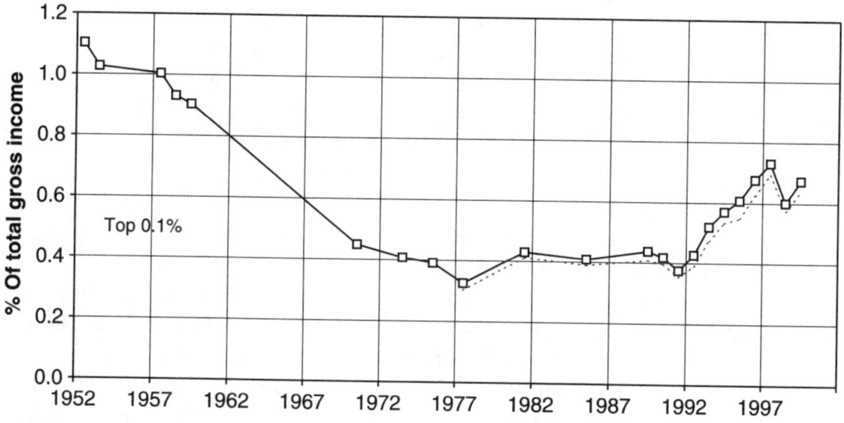

Figure 10.9C Wage income contributions to gross income of top 0.1%, Netherlands 1952–99

tax units it is important to realize that savings via pensions funds or life insurance companies are tax exempt including the income from property received by these institutions.[16] Occupational-pension fund savings in the Netherlands grew from 19% of GDP in 1952 via 50% in 1981 to 119% in 1999, a much higher level than in other countries.[17] Counting those proceeds as capital income would uplift the

[16] The pension payments, however, are subject to income taxation. Normally, they will be received at a later stage in life when incomes are lower and tax progression is less (the so-called 'reversal rule').

[17] Only Switzerland has larger savings. The UK has 75%, US and Canada have around 50%, and many other EU countries are below 10% (OECD 2004: 734)

share of capital incomes and mitigate its decline (1981–99: 14.1–13.3 as against 10.1–8.1 in Table 10.4). However, this would not necessarily increase the top shares.[18] Both issues, real economic factors and tax shifting, need further scrutiny beyond what will be said about taxation below.

Taxation of Income

The Dutch data also allow estimation of the actual amounts of tax paid by the top shares and therefore the average effective rates of taxation on gross incomes across the tax units comprised in the top shares. From the start in 1914 to the end in 1999 the amounts of tax paid—i.e. income tax to national government—are available with the exception of some of the interwar years and some years in the *IenV* period. In Section 10.3 we discussed disposable income, but this is a second way to approach after tax income. It differs in two respects from the first: only tax is deducted and not social contributions, and tax payments are now specified by ranges of gross income and can therefore be related directly to the top shares in gross incomes, thus we remain within the same type of distribution.

Table 10.6 gives the results and Figure 10.10 presents the effective tax rates for the three top shares and the national average.[19] We find very low levels of taxation at the start of the observation period, of between 3% and 6% of income, which soon—at the end of the First World War—increase to a range of 5–13%. This was followed by a significant decline during the Depression years. A huge leap upward is found subsequent to the Second World War: in 1946 effective tax rates range from 21% for the top 10% to 50% for the top 0.1%. The figure also shows that the national average of taxation followed a rather similar pattern to the top shares with a substantial increase in 1946.

After a further increase a maximum rate was reached in the mid-1960s at 27% for the top 10% as a whole and 64% for the top 0.1%. A gradual decline followed between the mid-1970s and 1990, which was the year of the *Oort*-revision of income taxation, named after the preparatory Government Commission's chair *Oort*. The revision brought down formal marginal rates and clearly also effective taxation for the highest top shares but not for the top decile as a whole, as a nine-band tax rate structure ranging from 14% to 72% was replaced with a three-band structure ranging from 13% to 60%. In 1994 tax rates fell across the board, including the top 10% which now came to a level below 20%, the lowest for the post-war period. However, behind this was a change in the structure of the tax system which may lead us astray. The compulsory contributions to social insurance,[20] which used to be levied separately, were integrated into the structure of

[18] This is shown by a tentative estimation using annual pension contributions of tax units in *IPO* to allocate the proceeds.

[19] Assuming that all tax payments are recorded in the income statistics; the total is related to the control total of income to find the average tax rate.

[20] Old age: AOW; surviving relatives: AWW; and exceptional health expenditures: AWBZ.

Table 10.6 Effective top share tax rates, Netherlands 1914–99

	Average	Top 10%	Top 5%	Top 1%	Top 0.5%	Top 0.1%	Top 0.05%	Top 0.01%
1914	1.1	2.4	2.7	3.5	3.8	4.5	4.6	
1915	1.4	2.7	3.1	3.8	4.1	4.6	4.7	
1916	1.6	2.8	3.1	3.8	4.1	4.4	4.8	
1917	1.5	2.7	3.1	3.9	4.2	4.7	4.8	
1918	2.3	4.4	5.2	7.3	8.4	11.2	12.4	
1919	2.8	5.2	6.0	8.3	9.4	12.2	13.1	
1920	2.7	4.9	5.7	8.0	9.1	11.9	12.9	
1921	2.4	4.4	5.2	7.3	8.5	11.3	12.4	
1922	2.1	4.0	4.7	6.7	7.8	10.5	11.7	
1923	2.1	3.9	4.6	6.5	7.6	10.3	11.6	
1924	2.1	4.0	4.8	6.7	7.8	10.5	11.7	
1925	2.2	4.1	4.9	6.9	8.0	10.7	11.9	
1926	2.2	4.1	4.9	6.9	8.0	10.7	11.9	
1927	1.8	3.4	4.0	5.6	6.4	8.7	9.6	
1928	1.8	3.4	4.1	5.7	6.6	8.8	9.7	
1929	1.8	3.5	4.1	5.9	6.9	9.4	10.6	
1930	1.7	3.3	3.9	5.6	6.5	9.4	11.0	
1931	1.4	2.9	3.4	4.9	5.7	8.1	9.4	11.9
1932	1.2	2.5	3.0	4.4	5.1	7.2	8.3	10.7
1933	1.2	2.5	3.0	4.3	5.0	7.2	8.4	11.2
1934	1.1	2.4	2.9	4.2	4.9	6.9	8.1	11.0
1935	1.1	2.3	2.8	4.1	4.8	6.8	7.9	10.8
1936	1.2	2.5	3.0	4.4	5.2	7.5	8.8	12.1
1937	1.3	2.8	3.4	5.1	6.0	8.8	10.4	14.9
1938	1.2	2.7	3.2	4.7	5.5	8.0	9.5	14.2
1939	1.3	2.7	3.3	4.8	5.6	8.0	9.4	12.5
1940								
1941								
1942								
1943								
1944								
1945								
1946	12.6	21.2	24.7	34.8	39.7	50.0	53.0	56.2
1947								
1948								
1949								
1950	13.8	25.5	30.8	43.5	48.6	58.6	61.7	67.4
1951								
1952	12.4	23.9	29.2	42.0	46.4	55.2	59.6	
1953	12.5	23.7	28.8	41.5	46.0	55.6	60.3	
1954								
1955								
1956								
1957	11.8	22.8	27.9	40.1	45.2	54.5	57.5	
1958	12.0	22.8	27.5	37.7	41.4	46.7	48.0	
1959	12.4	23.5	28.5	40.0	44.7	52.5	54.7	
1960								
1961								
1962	13.2	24.8	30.2	42.7	44.0	49.7		
1963								

(*contd.*)

Table 10.6 (*contd.*)

	Average	Top 10%	Top 5%	Top 1%	Top 0.5%	Top 0.1%	Top 0.05%	Top 0.01%
1964	14.1	25.9	31.1	41.6	44.6	46.9		
1965								
1966	14.6	27.1	32.5	44.0	48.1	51.8		
1967	14.4	25.3	30.3	41.3	44.9			
1968								
1969								
1970	13.9	26.0	30.9	41.6	45.2	50.7	53.3	54.9
1971								
1972								
1973	15.9	27.7	33.0	44.6	49.0	56.8	58.7	60.8
1974								
1975	16.0	27.8	33.1	45.4	50.0	58.7		
1976								
1977	14.9	24.7	29.4	40.8	45.1	52.6	55.6	
1978								
1979								
1980								
1981	13.8	21.9	26.1	37.0	41.6	50.6	53.0	
1982								
1983								
1984								
1985	12.1	20.0	24.1	35.1	39.9	50.2	54.4	
1986								
1987								
1988								
1989	12.2	20.9	25.0	35.4	39.7	49.6	54.0	
1990	13.7	22.1	25.8	34.2	37.4	41.5	42.6	
1991	14.0	22.5	26.3	35.1	38.4	44.1	44.9	
1992	14.2	22.8	26.7	35.3	38.9	44.7	46.1	
1993	14.0	22.4	26.2	34.5	37.8	43.1	45.5	
1994	10.3	19.4	23.4	32.2	35.8	41.9	45.0	
1995	9.7	18.9	22.8	31.4	34.6	38.6	38.1	
1996	9.2	18.2	22.2	31.2	34.6	39.8	42.1	
1997	8.6	17.8	21.8	30.8	34.3	39.0	40.1	
1998	8.4	17.0	20.9	29.8	33.1	36.6	38.1	
1999	8.7	17.8	21.9	31.7	35.5	42.1	45.6	

Notes: Calculated by linear interpolation in boundary ranges. Income in 1946 and 1950 is called 'fiscal income' by CBS.

income taxation to facilitate the levying process whilst social security remained legally independent. Contributions (levied at a flat rate up to a given level of income—about the modal wage) and entitlements were unchanged. To enable the integration the tax rate for the first band of income taxation (applying to all tax units) was roughly halved, from 13% to 7%. With stronger declines at the top over the last two decades the picture seems slightly more favourable to after tax income than the (inverse) ratio that was found above for the ratio of disposable to gross income (Figure 10.6).

The drastic post-war increase in the tax rates will likely overestimate the increase in actual taxation experienced by households, to the extent that local

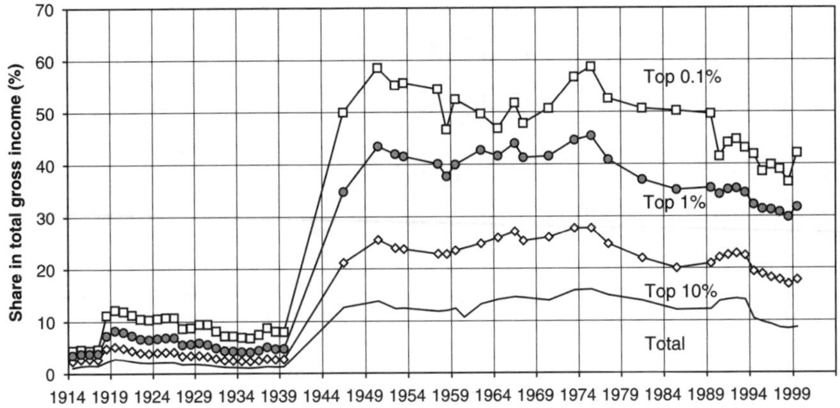

Figure 10.10 Effective tax rates on gross income of top 10%, 1%, and 0.1%, Netherlands 1914–99

taxes (municipalities, provinces) which were levied separately before became integrated into national taxation.[21] The rise of tax rates looks impressive, particularly at the high end of the distribution. However, when comparing top share rates relative to the average rate (total taxation of the control total of gross income), the evolution is strikingly different, see Figure 10.11. Soon after the introduction of income taxation in 1914 levels of relative taxation were reached for the top 10% which were basically kept unchanged for the rest of the century. The upsurge of 1946 previously found in Figure 10.11 leaves no trace at all; apparently, it touched tax units across the distribution in equal measure. During the 1930s, relative tax rates of the top 1% and 0.1% were actually higher than in the post-war period.

The favourable change that the *Oort* revision of 1990 made to the top rates is clearly visible, as is the effect of the 1994 integration of social contributions change that we just discussed. It seems to have a larger effect for those on lower incomes with an increase in relative taxation of the top shares as a consequence. However, the net effect of relative income taxation taken together with relative social security contributions, which affect lower incomes more,[22] remained basically unchanged.

In a *ceteris paribus* world the declining tax rates would give little reason to expect increasing tax shifting or evasion but there is also little reason to assume that the world has not changed, e.g. because of the liberalization of capital movements in recent decades.

[21] An indication of their importance is, e.g., that in 1920/21, depending on the municipality, a family with an annual income of 5000 guilders would pay a total tax rate including local taxes of between 4% and 19% (about 8% in the median municipality). At the same level of income the average national tax rate in our estimations would amount to no more than 1.3%. At an income level of 2000 guilders the total would range from 2% to 10% as against our national estimation of 2.6% (*CBS* 1925: 1).

[22] Notably, the rate of taxation including social contributions for the top 0.1% is only about twice as high as the average during the 1990s.

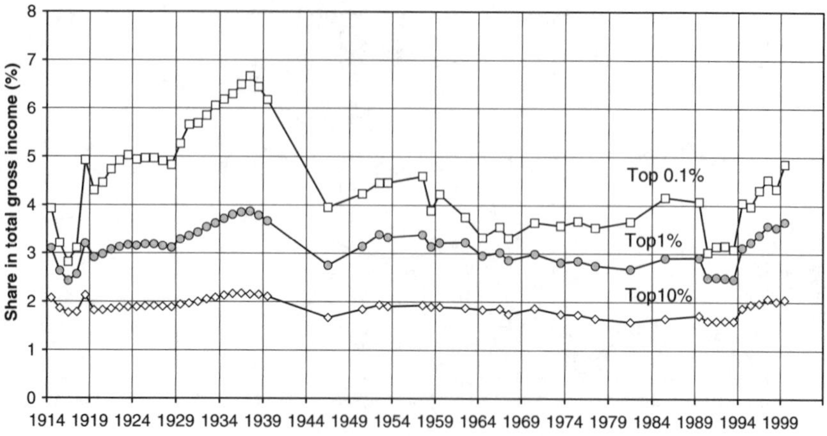

Figure 10.11 Relative effective tax rates on gross income of top 10%, 1%, and 0.1% (average = 1), Netherlands 1914–99

10.5 CONCLUSIONS

The aim of this chapter is to detail the evidence from income tax data about the distribution of top incomes in the Netherlands over the twentieth century. For reasons given in the text, the estimates may not be fully comparable over time, or to other countries for that matter. Nevertheless, we feel confident that the main conclusions are sufficiently robust to be taken as a starting point for a search for explanations.

The main findings relate to:

- the top shares in the distribution of all gross incomes over the full period (1914–99);
- the composition by income source of these shares for part of the period (1952–99);
- the income-tax rates of these top shares, again for the full period; and
- the top shares in the distribution of disposable income (after tax and social contributions), for full year incomes only, also for part of the period only (1959–99).

The results first mentioned show a strong decline in the gross income top shares, influenced by the aftermath of the two World Wars, down to a low point in the mid-1970s. At the start nearly half of all incomes were concentrated in the top 10% and around one-quarter in the top 1%; since the 1970s these shares have been around 28% and 6% respectively. Within the top decile it is the upper groups that fell, while the second vintile remained roughly stable. There was a change in the shape of the distribution: the Pareto–Lorenz coefficient rose from around 1.5 to 3.5. A long and steady decline runs parallel to other countries but, strikingly, the Dutch top shares have remained virtually flat since the 1970s and do not show the U-turn of a new rise that is found for Britain, the US, or other Anglo-Saxon countries. A major question for further research it is what can explain this near stability of the last 25 years.

The compositional results provide an equally intriguing picture as during the last decades incomes from capital and labour have rapidly traded places within the top shares and wage earnings now are the predominant source of income up to the very top, while previously this role was played by capital incomes. Capital income shares fell from one-third of all incomes in the early 1950s to well below 10%. In terms of shares in total income, wage earnings roughly made for the decline of capital incomes in the top shares with their virtual stability as a result. A major question for research is whether the change in composition, particularly the decline in capital incomes, hangs together with the stability of the top shares.

It exceeded our expectation that we were able to estimate income tax rates for the top shares for the entire period. They show a quick development after the start and a huge level upswing after the Second World War, reaching unprecedented levels as in many other countries, followed by some decline over the last two decades. However, the increase was so general, touching the entire population, that *relative* tax rates at the top appear to have remained largely unchanged since the 1920s, apart from a higher intermezzo during the Depression years. The evolution of the tax rates as such provides no clear motive for a possible tax shifting that could help to explain the first two observations. Nevertheless, in a changing world top income units may have migrated their income to other forms of taxation or to other countries, e.g. Luxembourg, or they may even have migrated themselves, e.g. to just across the Belgian border. The small geographical size of the country may facilitate this and given the small absolute numbers in the top share brackets the effects may be considerable.[23]

Fourth, the top shares in disposable income distribution mirror the development of gross top shares albeit with a smaller amplitude. Disposable top shares have essentially also been flat since the 1970s. Interestingly, the ratio of disposable to gross shares remained stable for the top decile as a whole but increased for the higher top shares.

APPENDIX 10A: SOURCES OF TABULATED INCOME TAX DATA FOR THE NETHERLANDS

The tabulated income data come from a variety of sources. The first is the series of annual statistical yearbooks: *JC* denotes *JaarCijfers voor het Koninkrijk der*

[23] At first sight, however, the published income tax data for Belgium do not suggest a marked increase in top income shares: the share of the top 1% in 1998 was 6.7%, compared with 6.3% in 1990, but the data warrant closer examination. These figures relate only to those covered by the income tax statistics, and need to be adjusted using control totals. The sources are Institut National de Statistique (1992: tableau 1 and 2000: tableau 1).

Nederlanden and *SY* denotes *Statistical Yearbook of the Netherlands* (in English). The second main source is the series of publications on the public finances: *SR* denotes *Statistiek der Rijksfinancien*. All pre-war data were found in more detail in the base material of Hartog and Veenbergen (1978)—see the OUP website. This was then replaced for this purpose by the regular studies of income distribution referred to in the text as *IenV*: *Inkomens- en Vermogensverdeling* (sometimes *Inkomens T en Vermogensverdeling T+1*). (See Tables 10A.1 and 10A.2.)

Table 10A.1 Sources for data on total gross income and summary statistics, Netherlands 1915–99

Tax year	Assumed income year (if different)	Lower limit (NLG)	Number of taxpayers (x 1000)	Total income (Million NLG)	Source	Notes
1915/16	1914	650	679.1	1334.5	JC 1921, p 147	Tax introduced 1 May 1915.
1916/17	1915	650	757.5	1724.7	JC 1918, p 154	
1917/18	1916	650	876.0	2064.8	JC 1921, p 147	Including payments in arrears.
1918/19	1917	650	897.2	2140.2	JC 1920, p 145	Suspension of interest payments on Russian national debt; including payments in arrears.
1919/20	1918	800	966.0	2431.9	JC 1921, p 147	Increase in tax threshold; Including payments in arrears.
1920/21	1919	800	1368.3	3638.9	JC 1921, p 147	Large increase in prices; 1 May 1919 considerable increase in tax introduced.
1921/22	1920	800	1638.5	4291.7	JC 1923, p 139	
1922/23	1921	800	1690.2	4138.3	JC 1923, p 139	Influence of fall in prices and economic crisis.
1923/24	1922	800	1632.0	3848.3	JC 1925, p 141	Influence of fall in prices and economic crisis.
1924/25	1923	800	1624.6	3761.3	JC 1925, p 141	Influence of fall in prices and economic crisis.
1925/26	1924	800	1657.9	3863.9	JC 1927, p 145	
1926/27	1925	800	1694.0	3902.8	JC 1929, p 150	
1927/28	1926	800	1719.4	3932.3	JC 1929, p 150	
1928/29	1927	800	1746.1	4028.6	SR 1933, p 18	1 May 1928 tax rate reduced (SR 1933, note 11).
1929/30	1928	800	1830.9	4284.9	SR 1933, p 18	1929 economic crisis had little effect on the figures for 1929/30 (SR 1929–31, p. 25, n. 16).

1930/31	1929	800	1892.6	4367.2	SR 1933, p 18	
1931/32	1930	800	1867.2	4206,4	SR 1933, p 18	First year when married/single split given; expansion of number of income brackets from 28 to 39.
1932/33	1931	800	1668.2	3657.2	SR 1936, p 22	
1933/34	1932	800	1484.6	3156.8	SR 1936, p 22	
1934/35	1933	800	1445.0	3042.0	SR 1936, p 22	
1935/36	1934	800	1355.1	2828.0	SR 1938, p 22	
1936/37	1935	800	1284.6	2666.0	SR 1938, p 22	
1937/38	1936	800	1304.2	2738.1	SR 1939, p 22	
1938/39	1937	800	1364.4	2933.8	SR 1940, Table XVL	Reference to effect of devaluation of 28 September 1936.
1939/40	1938	800	1409.2	3009.9	SR 1941	
1940/41	1939	800	1536.4	3295.9	JC 1943–1946, p 342	Refers to timing.
1941		—	2838.4	4645.3	JC 1947–1950, p 268	No figures available for 1942–45
1946		—	3605.4	7696.2	JC 1951–1952, p 270	New tax law: all income is now total past nominal income, whereas in earlier years the notion 'income source' still played a minor role (Hartog and Veenbergen, 1978. p. 547). Further increase in number of brackets from 39 to 44.Very detailed at top.
1950		—	3994.4	12100.0	JC 1963–1964, p 308; see also JC 1953–1954, p 272 where slightly different figures for total (also given in *IenV* 1952, p 10)	= income after revisions, also for following years. (Inkomensverdeling 1950, Table 4, p. 35 gives NLG 12102.3 as total income.)
1952		—	4011.8	13878.3	*IenV* 1952, p 10	Reduction in number of income classes from 44 to 15.
1953		—	4078.6	14539.3	*IenV* 1955, p 9	
1957		—	4566.9	23565.2	*IenV* 1957, Table 3	
1958		—	4606.2	24933.8	*IenV* 1958, Table 3	
1959		—	4689.9	26136.6	*IenV* 1959, Table 3	
1962			5099.6	34699.3	*IenV* 1962, Table 3	Change in method of allocating to income classes; increase in number of classes from 15 to 30.
1964		—	5316.6	42780.2	*IenV* 1964, Table 3	

(contd.)

Table 10A.1 (*contd.*)

Tax year	Assumed income year (if different)	Lower limit (NLG)	Number of taxpayers (x 1000)	Total income (Million NLG)	Source	Notes
1964		—	5316.6	45495.5	*IenV* 1966, p 18	
new basis						
1966		—	5776.3	56002.1	*IenV* 1966, p 28	
1967		—	5734.6	64478.1	*IenV* 1967, p 20	
1970		—	5631,0	88821.2	*IenV* 1970, Table 3	
1973		—	5889.4	123814.3	*IenV* 1973, part 2, p 77	
1975		—	5679.9	160741.2	Personele Inkomensverdeling 1975, part 1, p. 29 and part 2, p. 199–200	Part-year tax units fully counted.
1977			6352,03	206683,9	Inkomens-panel-onderzoek *IPO*	Change to microdata.
1981			6842,26	262741,1		
1985			7461,44	291083,3		
1989			7961,685	351414,1		
1990			8105,432	407289,2		
1991			8221,719	431711,3		
1992			8308,599	456141,5		
1993			8401,439	460075,3		
1994			8484,282	464977,2		
1995			8538,224	480660,2		
1996			8613,567	493609,2		
1997			8698,122	510375,6		
1998			8757,897	535214		
1999			8851,797	565900,6		

APPENDIX 10B: TOTAL POPULATION AND INCOME DATA FOR THE NETHERLANDS

The initial total number of tax units is calculated from *CBS* population statistics by age and gender (*Maandstatistiek Bevolking* and data specially provided by *CBS* from its archives) for the total population aged 15 and over. From this has been subtracted the minimum of the number of men and women married. For 1950–99 this is obtained directly from the above *CBS* population statistics. For 1920 and 1930 it is obtained from the census data (specially provided by *CBS*) and for other years from 1914 to 1946 it is obtained by linear inter- and extra-polation of the percentages of married persons for 1920 and 1930 applying this to the absolute numbers from the population statistics.

Table 10B.1 shows the resulting figures in the first column. The third and fourth columns show the reported totals in the tax statistics. As may be seen, over

Table 10A.2 Sources for data on disposable income, Netherlands 1959–99

Year	Total tax units	Total disposable income	Source	Notes
1959	4,257.7	20,166.3	*SEM* 1987: 6, table 1.1	Full year incomes
1962	4,567.4	26,977.7	*SEM*, 1987: 6, table 1.2	Full year incomes
1964	4,678.6	34,559.3	*SEM*, 1987: 6, table 1.3	Full year incomes
1967	4,972.0	45,362.9	*SEM*, 1987: 6, table 1.4, *IenV* 1967: 20	Full year incomes
1970	5,240.6	62,271.0	*SEM* 1987: 6, table 1.5	Full year incomes; excludes imputed rent and costs of owner-occupied housing
1973	5,573.4	89,144.5	*SEM* 1987: 6, table 1.6	Full year incomes; excludes imputed rent on owner-occupied housing
1975	5,699.2	115,636	*SEM* 1987: 6, table 1.7	Full year incomes; excludes imputed rent on owner
1977	5,771.4	138,694.4	*SEM* 1987: 6, table 1.8	Full year incomes; excludes imputed rent on owner
1979	5,877.2	162,192.8	*SEM* 1987: 6, table 1.9	Full year incomes; excludes imputed rent on owner
1979	5,877.2	155,587.2	*SEM* 1987: 6, table 1.10	Full year incomes
1980	5,977.5	165,611	*SEM* 1987: 6, table 1.11	Full year incomes
1981	6,014.8	171,033.3	*SEM* 1987: 6, table 1.12	Full year incomes
1982	6,025.6	175,816.8	*SEM* 1987: 6, table 1.13	Full year incomes
1983	6,399.3	184,717.2	*SEM* 1987: 6, table 1.14	Full year incomes
1984	6,553.5	187,949.9	*SEM* 1987: 6, table 1.15	Full year incomes
1977	6352,03	134,923	*Inkomenspanelonderzoek* (*IPO*)	Includes imputed rent for owner-occupied housing. All incomes.
1981	6842,26	171,365		
1985	7461,44	192,620		
1989	7961,685	231,484		
1990	8105,432	251,742		
1991	8221,719	264,665		
1992	8308,599	274,318		
1993	8401,439	281,968		
1994	8484,282	292,009		
1995	8538,224	305,420		
1996	8613,567	314,998		
1997	8698,122	328,803		
1998	8757,897	343,465		
1999	8851,797	358,009		

Notes: Data on disposable (*besteedbaar*) income is published in *IenV* (see Table A1) and the monthly *SEM* (*Sociaal Economische Maandstatistiek*).

time the total has converged towards the constructed total—see Figure 10B.1. By 1999 the *IPO* total was fairly stable at around 95% of the constructed total, and the coverage was believed to be complete. We have therefore taken a fixed proportion (95%) of the constructed total for all years. The difference between the reported figure and the 95% figure (the estimated number of 'non-filers') is shown in the final column.

Table 10B.1 Population totals (thousands), Netherlands 1914–99

	Tax units calculated from population 15+ minus married 1	TOTAL USED (95% of column 1) 2	Reported taxpayers in JC and SR 3	Numbers reported in IenV 4	Numbers reported in IPO 5	Difference between column 2 and reported numbers 6
1914	3,109	2,954	679			2,274
1915	3,159	3,001	758			2,244
1916	3,209	3,048	876			2,172
1917	3,259	3,096	897			2,199
1918	3,297	3,132	966			2,166
1919	3,348	3,181	1,368			1,812
1920	3,400	3,230	1,638			1,591
1921	3,456	3,283	1,690			1,593
1922	3,509	3,334	1,632			1,702
1923	3,570	3,391	1,625			1,766
1924	3,631	3,450	1,658			1,792
1925	3,690	3,506	1,694			1,812
1926	3,747	3,560	1,719			1,841
1927	3,808	3,617	1,746			1,871
1928	3,871	3,677	1,831			1,846
1929	3,929	3,733	1,893			1,840
1930	3,987	3,788	1,867			1,921
1931	4,062	3,859	1,668			2,190
1932	4,130	3,923	1,485			2,438
1933	4,187	3,978	1,445			2,533
1934	4,245	4,033	1,355			2,678
1935	4,308	4,093	1,285			2,808
1936	4,368	4,149	1,304			2,845
1937	4,426	4,204	1,364			2,840
1938	4,485	4,261	1,409			2,852
1939	4,536	4,309	1,536			2,773
1940						
1941	4,637	4,405	2,838			1,567
1942						
1943						
1944						
1945						
1946	4,890	4,646	3,605			1,040
1947	4,925	4,679				
1948	4,965	4,717				
1949	4,994	4,745				
1950	5,041	4,789		3,994		
1951	5,071	4,817				
1952	5,090	4,836		4,012		
1953	5,123	4,867		4,079		789
1954	5,164	4,906				
1955	5,213	4,952				
1956	5,253	4,990				
1957	5,301	5,036		4,567		469
1958	5,376	5,107		4,606		501

1959	5,446	5,174	4,750		484
1960	5,505	5,229			
1961	5,646	5,364			
1962	5,776	5,487	5,100		387
1963	5,880	5,586	,		
1964	5,966	5,667	5,317		357
1965	6,066	5,763			
1966	6,151	5,843	5,776		67
1967	6,210	5,900	5,735		165
1968	6,278	5,964			
1969	6,359	6,041			
1970	6,442	6,120	5,631		489
1971	6,524	6,198			
1972	6,604	6,274			
1973	6,702	6,367	5,889		478
1974	6,812	6,471			
1975	6,950	6,603	#5,680		839
1976	7,070	6,716			
1977	7,198	6,838		6,352	486
1978	7,336	6,969			
1979	7,492	7,117			
1980	7,642	7,260			
1981	7,778	7,389		6,842	547
1982	7,892	7,497			
1983	8,028	7,626			
1984	8,173	7,764			
1985	8,315	7,899		7,461	438
1986	8,430	8,008			
1987	8,552	8,124			
1988	8,641	8,209			
1989	8,661	8,228		7,962	266
1990	8,780	8,341		8,105	236
1991	8,852	8,410		8,222	188
1992	8,921	8,475		8,309	166
1993	8,992	8,542		8,401	141
1994	9,049	8,597		8,484	113
1995	9,119	8,663		8,538	125
1996	9,185	8,726		8,614	112
1997	9,252	8,789		8,698	91
1998	9,319	8,853		8,758	95
1999	9,386	8,917		8,852	65

Note: # full-year incomes only, consequently the control total of incomes may be somewhat overestimated and the top shares underestimated.

Source: Population (column 1) from *CBS, Bevolkingsstatistiek*, other numbers (columns 3 and 4) from income distribution sources mentioned in text.

The starting point for the total income series is provided by the tax statistics. As explained in the text, for the period from 1977 we take the *IPO* totals, shown in column 3 of Table 10B.2. In order to determine the top income shares, we have enlarged the population share of the top groups correcting for the difference between our constructed total of population and the *IPO* total of tax units. For

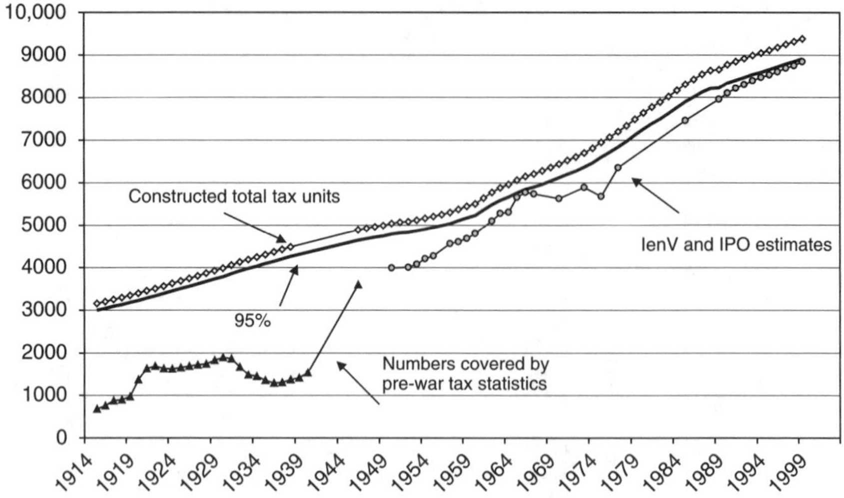

Figure 10B.1 Tax units (×1000), Netherlands 1914–99

the period 1941 and earlier, we take the totals reported in *JC/SR* (see Table 10A.1) and add the estimated income of those below the tax threshold, shown in column 4. The sources of the latter are 1914–20 from *CBS* (1941: 14), 1921–39 from *CBS* (1948: 21), 1941 from CBS (1950: 41). The missing income is divided by the estimated number of non-filers (column 5 in Table 10B.1) to give the mean income of non-filers. This is expressed in column 4 as a percentage of the mean income of filers (obtained by dividing column 1 in Table 10B.2 by column 3 in Table 10B.1). This percentage appears to be close to 20% in the 1930s, and this proportion is assumed to apply in the period 1946–99 as well. Multiplying the resulting mean income by the estimated number of non-filers yields the estimates in column 6 of Table 10B.2. In 1968, the data only cover people with incomes above 15,000 guilders, a percentage of the national accounts figure (see below) has therefore been assumed.

The resulting estimates may be compared with the personal sector gross income totals in the national accounts. (These figures are close to those for the 'current receipts of households and non-profit institutions' contained in the *United Nations Yearbook of National Accounts Statistics.*) The sources are 1914–20 from *CBS* (1941: 14), 1921–39 from *CBS* (1948: 21), 1941 from *CBS* (1950: 41), and years up to 1977 from the national accounts (*NR*), various years (for example, 1950–59 from *NR* 1960, published by *CBS* in 1961). Data for 1977–99 are from *CPB* Netherlands Bureau of Economic Policy Analysis, or Centraal Plan Bureau (*CPB*) (1999) that was the last publication presenting the data according to the pre-1993 *SNA*, which serves to improve consistency with the previous data. *CPB* data follow *CBS* as closely as possible and offer the advantage of including the data for 1977–86 that has been revised in 1995 (although the data for 1998

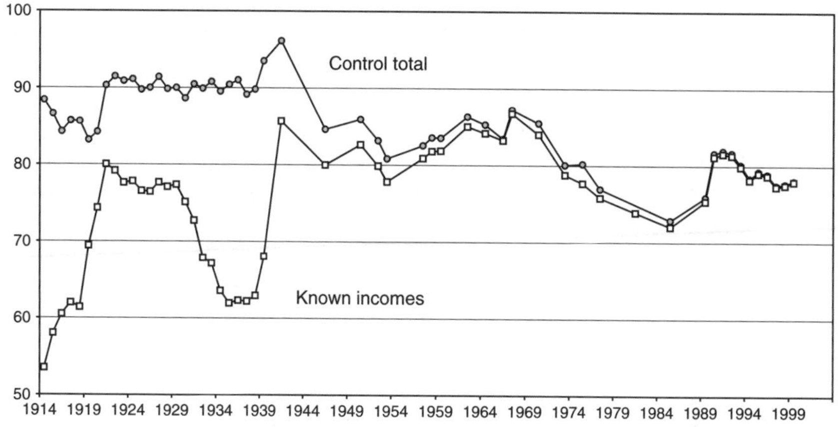

Figure 10B.2 Control totals of gross income and known gross income as % of national accounts personal income total, Netherlands 1914–99

and 1999 are provisional). Thus the series in column 8 of Table 10B.2 comes as close as possible to standardization on a pre-1977 basis, but a precise linking for that year has not been pursued here as the tax-based income data changed at the same time with the use of *IPO* as a source. The totals used here are compared with the national accounts totals for personal income in Figure 10B.2.

The series for disposable income is obtained by subtracting from the gross income totals described above the difference between the gross and disposable income in the *IenV* estimates, shown in the penultimate column of Table 10B.2. Column 10 shows the *IPO* totals for disposable income.

ENGLISH TITLES OF DATA SOURCES

Jaarcijfers voor het Koninkrijk der Nederlanden, from 1925 *Jaarcijfers voor Nederland* (both referred to as *JC*), Statistical Yearbook of Netherlands, published by the Central Bureau of Statistics (Centraal Bureau voor de Statistiek, Statistics Netherlands), referred to as CBS.

Statistiek der Rijksfinanciën (referred to as *SR*), Statistics of Public Finances.

IenV: Inkomens- en Vermogensverdeling (sometimes *Inkomens T en Vermogensverdeling T+1*), Income and Wealth Distribution, published by *CBS.*

Inkomenspanelonderzoek, referred to as *IPO,* Income Panel Study conducted by CBS.

Nationale Rekeningen (referred to as NR), National Accounts, published by the CBS.

Table 10B.2 Reference income totals (million guilders) and prices, Netherlands 1914–99

	JC and SR 1	IenV 2	IPO gross incomes 3	Missing income: below threshold 4	Income of non-filers as % filers' income 5	Assumed missing income (based on 20% of filers' mean) 6	TOTAL GROSS INCOME USED 7	National accounts figure 8	Total as % national account 9	TOTAL DISPOSABLE INCOME USED 10	Consumer price index 11
1914	1334			870	19.5		2205	2494	88.4		116
1915	1725			850	16.7		2575	2973	86.6		131
1916	2065			810	15.8		2875	3412	84.3		147
1917	2140			820	15.6		2960	3453	85.7		156
1918	2432			960	17.6		3392	3961	85.6		186
1919	3639			720	14.9		4359	5241	83.2		201
1920	4292			570	13.7		4862	5772	84.2		219
1921	4138			532	13.6		4670	5172	90.3		191
1922	3848			598	14.9		4446	4860	91.5		170
1923	3761			643	15.7		4404	4846	90.9		165
1924	3864			660	15.8		4524	4965	91.1		166
1925	3903			673	16.1		4576	5098	89.8		165
1926	3932			697	16.6		4629	5143	90.0		158
1927	4029			713	16.5		4742	5187	91.4		158
1928	4285			709	16.4		4994	5558	89.9		160
1929	4367			713	16.8		5080	5644	90.0		158
1930	4206			756	17.5		4962	5598	88.6		152
1931	3657			892	18.6		4549	5028	90.5		143
1932	3157			1026	19.8		4183	4652	89.9		132
1933	3042			1072	20.1		4114	4531	90.8		131
1934	2828			1155	20.7		3983	4448	89.5		132
1935	2666			1225	21.0		3891	4303	90.4		129
1936	2738			1262	21.1		4000	4394	91.0		125
1937	2934			1270	20.8		4204	4715	89.2		130
1938	3010			1285	21.1		4295	4781	89.8		130
1939	3296			1232	20.7		4528	4842	93.5		131

1942								184
1943								190
1944								195
1945								223
1946	7696		444	8141	9621	84.6		244
1947								256
1948								268
1949								284
1950		12100	481	12581	14644	85.9		309
1951								347
1952		13878	570	14448	17374	83.2		348
1953		14539	562	15101	18684	80.8		347
1954								361
1955								368
1956								375
1957		23565	485	24050	29136	82.5		397
1958		24934	541	25475	30482	83.6		406
1959		26137	540	26677	31930	83.5	21034	409
1960		\	491	28176	35327	79.8		421
1961								426
1962		34699	528	35227	40809	86.3	28064	440
1963								458
1964		45495	612	46108	54062	85.3	36020	486
1965								510
1966		56002	130	56132	67279	83.4		540
1967		64478	370	64848	74345	87.2	47056	557
1968								578
1969								621
1970		88821	1542	90363	105714	85.5	64360	648
1971								697
1972								752
1973		123814	2008	125822	157140	80.1	91684	812
1974								890
1975		#160741	5222	165963	206870	80.2	119302	982
1976								1067

(contd.)

Table 10B.2 (*contd.*)

	JC and SR 1	IenV 2	IPO gross incomes 3	Missing income: below threshold 4	Income of non-filers as % filers' income 5	Assumed missing income (based on 20% of filers' mean) 6	TOTAL GROSS INCOME USED 7	National accounts figure 8	Total as % national account 9	TOTAL DISPOSABLE INCOME USED 10	Consumer price index 11
1977			206684			3160	209844	272610	77.0	136987	1138
1978											1185
1979											1235
1979inc											
1980											1316
1981			262741			4200	266,941	355441	75.1	174104	1405
1982											1488
1983											1529
1984											1579
1985			291083			3420	294504	403856	72.9	194880	1615
1986											1617
1987											1609
1988											1621
1989			351414			2344	353758	466034	75.9	233032	1638
1990			407289			2376	409665	501681	81.7	253205	1679
1991			431711			1970	433681	529167	82.0	265877	1744
1992			456142			1822	457963	560641	81.7	275417	1808
1993			460075			1546	461621	575904	80.2	282911	1846
1994			464977			1234	466212	594675	78.4	292785	1897
1995			480660			1403	482064	608087	79.3	306313	1931
1996			493609			1283	494892	627018	78.9	315820	1972
1997			510376			1071	511447	660097	77.5	329490	2015
1998			535214			1160	536373	690592	77.7	344211	2053
1999			565901			833	566734	725927	78.1	358537	2098

Sources: National accounts incomes (col. 8) from UN, *National Accounts* (1914–75) and *CPB, Macro-economische Verkenning* 1999: Table A.12 (1977–99). Consumer price index numbers (col.

REFERENCES

Atkinson, A. B. (2005). 'Top Incomes in the United Kingdom over the Twentieth Century', *Journal of the Royal Statistical Society*, A(168): 325–43.

—— Salverda, W. (2005). 'Top Incomes in the Netherlands and the United Kingdom over the Twentieth Century', *Journal of the European Economic Association*, 3: 883–913.

CBS (*Centraal Bureau voor de Statistiek*, Statistics Netherlands) (1925). *Rangschikkinglijst der gemeenten naar den belastingdruk op het inkomen over de belastingjaren 1923/1924 en 1924/1925.*

—— (1941). *Berekeningen over het nationale inkomen van Nederland voor de periode 1900–1920*, speciale onderzoekingen van de Nederlandse conjunctuur, no. 4.

—— (1948). *Het nationale inkomen van Nederland, 1921–1939*, Monografieën van de Nederlandse conjunctuur, deel 8. Utrecht: W. de Haan.

—— (1950). 'Het nationale inkomen van Nederland, 1940–1945', *Statistische en econometrische onderzoekingen*, 5(1): 31–45.

—— (1999). *Makroeconomische Verkenning 1999.* The Hague: CPB.

—— (2000). *Documentatie Inkomenspanelonderzoek on-site basisbestanden, 1977–1998*, versie 2.

Gastwirth, J. L. (1972). 'The Estimation of the Lorenz Curve and Gini Index', *Review of Economics and Statistics*, 54: 306–16.

Hartog, J. (1983). 'Inequality reduction by income taxes: Just how much? An investigation for the Netherlands, 1914–1973', *Empirical Economics*, 8: 9–13.

—— Veenbergen, J. G. (1978). 'Dutch Treat: Long-Run Changes in Personal Income Distribution', *De Economist*, 126: 521–49.

Institut National de Statistique (1992). 'Statistique Fiscale des Revenus, Exercice 1991', *Statistiques financières*, numéro 58. Brussels: Ministère des Affaires Economiques.

—— (2000). 'Statistique Fiscale des Revenus, Exercice 1999, b. Distribution par fractions', *Niveau de Vie.* Brussels: Ministère des Affaires Economiques.

Kleijn, J. P. de, and van de Stadt, H. (1987). 'Inkomensniveau en inkomensongelijkheid 1959–1984', Supplement bij de *Sociaal-Economische Maandstatistiek*, 6: 11–38.

Kuznets, S. (1953). *Shares of Upper Income Groups in Income and Savings.* New York: National Bureau of Economic Research.

Lubbers, G. (1926) *De Statistiek van het arbeidsloon en van de werkloosheid.* Amsterdam: H. J. Paris.

OECD (2004). *Financial Markets Trends*, October, 87.

Pen, J. (1979). 'A Clear Case of Levelling: Income Equalization in the Netherlands', *Social Research*, 46: 682–94.

Piketty, T. (2001). *Les hauts revenus en France au XXe siècle—Inégalités et redistributions, 1901–1998.* Paris: Grasset.

Piketty, T. and Saez, E. (2003). 'Income Inequality in the United States, 1913–1998', *Quarterly Journal of Economics*, 118: 1–39.

Pott-Buter, H. A. and Tijdens, K. G. (2002). *Emancipatie-effectrapportage belasting en premies, een verkenning naar nieuwe mogelijkheden vanuit het belastingstelsel 2001.* AIAS Research Report 12, Amsterdam Institute for Advanced Labour Studies, Universiteit van Amsterdam

Schultz, T. P. (1968). 'Secular Equalization and Cyclical Behavior of Income Distribution', *Review of Economics and Statistics*, 50: 259–67.

11

Income and Wealth Concentration in Switzerland over the Twentieth Century[1]

F. Dell, T. Piketty, and E. Saez

11.1 INTRODUCTION

The evolution of income and wealth inequality during the process of development has attracted enormous attention in the economics literature. Liberals have blamed income and wealth concentration because of concerns for equity and in particular for tilting the political process in the favour of the wealthy. They have proposed progressive taxation as an appropriate counter-force against wealth concentration. For conservatives, concentration of income and wealth is considered as a natural and necessary outcome of an environment that provides incentives for work, entrepreneurship, and wealth accumulation, key elements of macro-economic success. Progressive taxation may redistribute resources away from the rich and wealthy and reduce wealth concentration but it might also weaken those incentives and generate large efficiency costs. Therefore, it is of great importance to understand the forces driving income and wealth concentration over time and understand whether government interventions through taxation are effective and/or harmful to curb wealth inequality. This task is greatly facilitated by the availability of long and homogeneous series of income or wealth concentration.

A number of recent studies, gathered in this volume, have constructed series for shares of income accruing to upper income groups (such as the top decile, top percentile, etc.) for various countries: Piketty (2001, 2003, and Chapter 3 in this volume) for France, Atkinson (2005 and Chapter 4 in this) for the United Kingdom, Piketty and Saez (2003 and Chapter 5) for the United States and Dell (Chapter 9) for Germany. Shares of wealth accruing to top wealth groups have also been constructed for some countries: Atkinson and Harrison (1978), and Atkinson, Gordon and Harrison (1989) for the United Kingdom,[2] Kopczuk

[1] We thank Tony Atkinson and seminar participants at the CHANGEQUAL conference on Inequality at Nuffield College in Oxford for helpful comments and discussions. Financial support from the Sloan foundation, NSF Grant SES-0134946, and the MacArthur foundation are thankfully acknowledged.

[2] Lindert (2000) presents these UK wealth concentration series as well as more recent estimates prepared by the British fiscal administration.

and Saez (2004) for the United States, Piketty, Postel-Vinay, and Rosenthal (2004) for France. All these series share two important and striking characteristics. First, in all those countries, a dramatic reduction in top income and wealth shares is observed from the early part of the century to the decades following the Second World War. In virtually all cases, the share of income or wealth accruing to the top 1% has been divided by a factor two and sometimes by a much greater factor. For example, in the United Kingdom, the top 1% income share falls from almost 20% in 1918 to 6% in the 1970s (Atkinson, Chapter 4 in this volume). Second, in all those countries as well, those dramatic decreases are concentrated in the very top groups of the income or wealth distribution. There are relatively little secular changes for the bottom part of the top decile or even the bottom of the top percentile, and the majority of the decrease is actually concentrated in the top 0.1%.

In contrast, the evolution of top income shares in the recent decades has been different across countries: the United States, Canada, and the United Kingdom have experienced a large increase in top income shares while France, and the Netherlands display hardly any change in top income shares. For the United States (Piketty and Saez 2003 and Chapter 5 in this volume) and Canada (Saez and Veall 2005 and Chapter 6 in this volume), and the United Kingdom (Atkinson 2005 and Chapter 4 in this volume), this dramatic increase has been due to a dramatic increase in top wages and salaries. Kopczuk and Saez (2004) and Atkinson et al. (1989) show that in both the United States and the United Kingdom, the increase in top wealth shares has been very small and almost negligible relative to the dramatic increase in top income shares. This suggests that, although income concentration has increased sharply in the United States and the United Kingdom, it has not yet translated into a significant increase in wealth concentration.[3]

Following Piketty (2001, 2003), most authors have argued that the dramatic increase in tax progressivity—which took place during the First World War and the interwar period in all the countries studied and which remained in place after the Second World War period at least until the recent decades—has been the main factor preventing top income and wealth shares from coming back to the very high levels observed at the beginning of the century.[4] Indeed, with marginal income tax rates in excess of 60%, and sometimes reaching even 90% for very high incomes, a wealthy individual has to pay in taxes a very large fraction of its returns on capital, and accumulating or sustaining a fortune requires much higher saving rates.

[3] However, a spread of popular wealth could account for these flat shares, reconcentration at the top nonetheless taking place. This is for instance what happened in the UK, accentuated in the 1980s and 1990s by privatization and more recently by the house price boom.

[4] Earlier studies of income and wealth concentration in the United States (Kuznets 1953 and Lampman 1962) also mentioned the development of progressive taxation as a factor explaining the decline of US income and wealth concentration in the first half of the twentieth century.

However, because the effects of taxes on wealth concentration are a long-term process, it is nearly impossible to provide a rigorous proof of this hypothesis. The goal of the present chapter is to provide a simple test of this hypothesis by examining the case of Switzerland, a country which did not experience the shocks of the two World Wars and never established a very progressive tax structure. For most of the century, and it is still true today, the majority of income taxes in Switzerland are levied at the local level (county (Canton) level and municipal level). These local income and wealth taxes present a relatively flat rate structure with low top marginal tax rates. Today, the combined county and municipal income tax rates are around 25% in general, and the top local wealth tax rate are in general less than 0.5% (see *Charge Fiscale en Suisse*). Switzerland has also imposed federal income and wealth taxes (starting during the First World War in 1915). However, the top marginal income tax rates have been around 10% for most of the period and the top wealth tax rates have in general been less than 0.5%, except for a very few years during the World Wars (see *Charge Fiscale en Suisse*). There is no federal inheritance and estate taxes and most counties do not levy inheritance taxes between spouses and between parents and children, or levy only a very modest tax of below 10% for bequests to children. Thus over the twentieth century, the marginal tax rate in Switzerland on capital income of the very wealthy including federal and local income, wealth, and inheritance taxes has been very low relative to other OECD countries.[5]

Therefore, if the development of progressive taxation is the main factor which drove and kept top income and wealth shares at a much lower level than in early part of century, then we should not observe such a drop in Switzerland, a country which never experienced sustained progressive taxation. In order to answer this question, the present chapter uses Swiss income and wealth tax statistics to construct homogeneous series of income and wealth shares for various upper income and wealth groups within the top decile. As personal income and wealth taxes in Switzerland are based on family income (and not individual income), our series measure inequality among families (which may be different from inequality among individuals). Our top wealth shares series start in 1913 and cover a large number of years up to year 1957, the last year a federal wealth tax was implemented. Since 1957, we have to rely on wealth surveys compiled by the federal administration from county wealth tax statistics. Unfortunately, such surveys were only made about once every ten years, and the latest year available is 1997. Our top income share series start in 1933[6] and end in 1996, the latest year available (due to a fundamental income tax reform starting in 1997 in some counties and with a long transition period, see below). Because

[5] This statement should be carefully evaluated by estimating the average and marginal tax rates that top income and wealth groups face in Switzerland using the detailed statistics published in *Charge Fiscale en Suisse*. We leave establishing rigorously this key first stage point for future work.

[6] Before 1933, Switzerland imposed federal income taxes but those taxes were based on labour income only and excluded capital income. As a result, these income tax statistics cannot be compared to the tax statistics starting in 1933 where all sources of income, both labour and capital, are reported.

federal income taxes in Switzerland have been assessed every two years on the average income of the two preceding years, our top income shares series are bi-annual. In contrast to the wealth share series, the income series are quasi-continuous and cover almost all the years in the period 1933–97.

Our results strongly support the tax explanation discussed above: top wealth and income shares in Switzerland fell during the shocks of the World Wars and the Great Depression (although much less than in other countries) but, most importantly, top wealth and income shares fully recovered from those shocks in the post Second World War period. As a result, by 1969, the top wealth shares are about as high as they were before the First World War, and top income shares are higher in the early 1970s than in the pre-Second World War period. As we mentioned above, these results offer a striking contrast with the experiences of France, the United Kingdom, the United States, and Canada. Thus, although Switzerland had relatively less income and wealth concentration in the early part of the century than those countries, by the 1960s, Switzerland displays significantly more income and especially wealth concentration than other countries. Interestingly, Switzerland does display a reduction in income and wealth concentration since the 1970s, suggesting that non-tax factors such as the aging of the population and the development of pensions might have reduced wealth concentration.

Finally, we investigate the issue of tax evasion through relocation to Switzerland or through Swiss bank accounts investments. We obtain upper bounds on the fraction of income taxpayers in Switzerland with income abroad or non-resident taxpayers. Although the fraction of such taxpayers has increased in recent decades, it still remains below 20% even at the very top of the income distribution suggesting that the phenomenon of migration toward Switzerland of wealthy individuals is a very limited phenomenon relative to the number of high income individuals actually living in European high tax countries.

Similarly, we can estimate an upper bound on the total amount of capital income earned through Swiss accounts, which is never reported (either to the Swiss fiscal administration for Swiss residents or to foreign fiscal administrations in the case of non-residents). This amount is at most around $5 billion in recent years and is negligible relative to total incomes earned by high income individuals in the United States. This amount is also relatively small relative to high incomes earned in large European countries such as France and clearly cannot account for the gap in top income shares that has taken place between continental Europe and Anglo-Saxon countries in recent decades. Clearly, Switzerland is only but one of the potential destination for investors trying to evade taxes in their home country. Trying to estimate systematically amounts of capital income earned and evaded in all tax havens would be a useful project that we leave for future work.

The paper is organized as follows. Section 11.2 describes our data sources and outlines our estimation methods. In Section 11.3, we present and analyse the trends in top income shares since 1933. Section 11.4 presents the evolution of top wealth shares since 1913. Section 11.5 discusses the evidence on capital income earned in Switzerland by non-residents. Finally, Section 11.6 offers a brief conclusion.

11.2 DATA AND METHODOLOGY

Income and Wealth Federal Taxation and Statistical Sources

Switzerland has imposed a Federal individual income tax irregularly in the first part of the twentieth century. The first two federal income taxes were the *Impôt de Guerre* (based on incomes earned from 1911 to 1914) and the *Nouvel Impôt Federal de Guerre Extraordinaire* (based on incomes earned in 1917 to 1928). Statistics on these income taxes were published in *Statistique du 1er impôt fédéral de guerre 1916/17* and in *Statistique concernant le nouvel impôt fédéral de guerre extraordinaire (périodes I, II, et III)*, respectively. Unfortunately, those early income taxes were based only on labour income and excluded capital income and therefore are not analysed in this study.[7]

Starting with the third federal income tax from 1933 to 1937 (*Contribution Fédérale de Crise*), the income tax was assessed on total income (both income from labour and capital). The fourth federal income tax (*Impôt Fédéral pour la Défense Nationale*) started in 1939 and has been imposed regularly ever since. This study is based on statistics by size of income published by the Swiss fiscal administration covering those two federal income taxes for the periods 1933–37 and 1939–96 (except 1941–42 for which no statistics were published).

A striking feature of the federal income tax in Switzerland is that, except for 1933, it is not imposed on annual incomes as in most other countries but on the average of two consecutive annual incomes. Column (0) in Table 11.2 shows the bi-annual periods corresponding to the federal income tax in Switzerland since 1933. For example, for the last period of analysis 1995–96, the income tax is assessed on average (nominal) income earned in 1995 and 1996. The income tax corresponding to those years is paid twice in the two following years (1997 and 1998). Therefore, there is a substantial lag between the moment when the incomes are earned and the moment when the income tax is paid. The distribution statistics have been published in *Contribution Fédérale de Crise* (for years 1933–37), *Impôt Fédéral pour la Defense Nationale* (for years 1939–80), and in *Impôt Fédéral Direct* (for years 1981–92). (For years after 1992, the paper publication is no longer available but statistics have been made available online at http://www.estv.admin.ch). Many of these income distributions are also been published in the annual statistical yearbook for Switzerland, *Annuaire Statistique de la Suisse.*

After 1995/96, some counties in Switzerland start to switch to a standard annual tax system instead of the bi-annual tax. By 2003, all counties have switched to the new annual system. Unfortunately, during the transition period, no uniform statistics for the full country exist and hence estimates would require merging data from different counties and different years. That is why we do not try to estimate top income shares after 1995/96, the last uniform bi-annual

[7] Those taxes also included a wealth tax on individuals. We exploit those early wealth statistics to estimate top wealth shares early in the twentieth century (see below).

tax period. We leave for future research estimates covering the transition period and subsequent years. Such estimates are important to assess the effect on top income shares of averaging income over two years instead of considering annual incomes as in all other countries.

Our estimates are based on tabulation by size of income before deductions (this is called Revenu net or net income).[8] The income definition is stable over time and includes employment income, business income, and capital income. It always excludes realized capital gains. Before 1971, income distributions are presented by size of income after personal exemption deductions (this is called Revenu imposable or taxable income). However, information on the amounts and levels of those deductions is provided and we add back those amounts in our estimation to obtain consistent series over time based on income before deductions. We can check with statistics for 1971–72 (as well as later years) presented both by size of income before deductions and income after deductions that adding back deductions does not introduce any significant error in our estimates.

Federal wealth taxes have been levied irregularly over the twentieth century in Switzerland. At the same time the federal income taxes were levied, Switzerland imposed a federal wealth tax. Those wealth taxes were based on family net worth as of 1 January 1915 (for the first federal wealth tax, *Impôt de Guerre*), as of 1 January 1921, 1925, and 1929 (for the second federal wealth tax, *Nouvel Impôt Fédéral de Guerre Extraordinaire*), and as of 1 January 1934, 1936, and 1938 (for the third federal wealth tax, *Contribution Fédérale de Crise*). Special federal wealth taxes were also levied on net worth as of 1 January of 1940 and 1945 (*Sacrifice de Guerre*). Finally, a more regular wealth tax (*Impôt Fédéral pour la Défense Nationale*) was imposed every two years from 1947 to 1957 (always based on family net worth as of 1 January of the corresponding years). After 1957, the federal wealth tax was eliminated.

All these federal wealth taxes were progressive with an exemption level (which depended on family structure). As a result, families below the exemption thresholds are not included in the statistics. For 1940, however, statistics on wealth for families below the taxable threshold were collected for the county of Thurgovia. We extrapolate the distribution of wealth in this county to Switzerland to obtain a complete wealth distribution for 1940.

In addition to federal wealth taxes, counties have levied on a regular basis (and often since the beginning of the twentieth century or even earlier) wealth and income taxes. Unfortunately, statistics on county wealth and income taxes displaying distributions of income and wealth have not been officially published, although some counties (such as the largest and wealthiest county of Zurich) have compiled such statistics for internal use.[9] However, for a number

[8] Note that this purely statistical nomenclature is somewhat misleading and corresponds more to a 'gross income' notion than to a 'net income' notion (as frequently stated in the Swiss statistical publications).

[9] Income and wealth tax statistics for the county of Zurich have been made available to us for a number of years from 1934 to 1999. Such county statistics could be used to expand our series estimates. They moreover feature tabulations of the joint income/wealth distribution.

of years (1913, 1919, 1969, 1981, 1991, and 1997), Switzerland has compiled such statistics based on the wealth tax statistics of all counties to construct wealth distributions as of 1 January of those years. In contrast to the federal wealth tax statistics, those distributions cover the universe of families with positive net worth. The wealth distributions for 1913 and 1919 have been published in *Annuaire Statistique de la Suisse* (1914: 222–6 and 1921: 378, respectively). The wealth distributions for 1969, 1981 were not officially published but have been made available to us by the federal fiscal administration. The wealth distributions for 1991 and 1997 have published in *Annuaire Statistique de la Suisse* (1997 and 2003, respectively). The Swiss administration plans to construct such wealth distributions every six years and the next one should be produced for wealth held as of 1 January 2003 (but is not yet available).

The concept of wealth used for tax purposes (at the federal or county levels) is very broad and includes all assets (tangible assets such as land, buildings, residences, furniture, vehicles, jewellery, business assets, and intangible assets such as stocks, bonds, cash, and also some pension rights) net of all liabilities. Taxpayers were assessed at the same time for wealth and income taxes so a number of tables showing wealth (respectively income) by size of income (respectively wealth) are also available, although we have not used them in the present study.

As discussed in introduction, Swiss income and wealth taxes are levied both at the federal and local (county and city) levels. There is some variation in the level of local income and wealth taxes. The Swiss fiscal administration has published regularly summaries showing the level of income and wealth taxes by size of income and wealth and by locality in the publication *Charge Fiscale en Suisse.* Interestingly, this publication describes not only federal taxation but also county and local level taxation and hence can provide a very accurate picture of the fiscal environment for high income, high wealth families in Switzerland. This publication is available since the beginning of the twentieth century and could be used to estimate average income and wealth tax rates of each of our top income and wealth groups in every year. We have not yet exploited those statistics on taxation but plan to do so in the future to establish rigorously our claim that the tax burden on high income, high wealth individuals in Switzerland has been substantially lower than in other countries such as the United States or France.

Total Number of Tax Units and Total Income

The individual income and wealth taxes in Switzerland have always been assessed at the family level (married couples with children dependents if any or single taxpayers with children dependents if any). Therefore, our total number of tax units is defined as the total number of adults (aged 20 and above) less half the number of married men and women. The total number of adults in Switzerland is obtained from *Annuaire Statistique de la Suisse* (1993: 47) which reports population totals in Switzerland by age ranges for each of the decennial census from 1900 to 1990. The estimate for year 2000 is obtained from the same source (available online at http://www.statistik.admin.ch). Those statistics also report for every census the total number of married individuals. We have interpolated linearly our estimates between two consecutive censuses to create an annual series for the total number of adults and total number of tax units in Switzerland. Those series are reported in columns (1) and (2) in Table 11.1.

Our total income denominator is estimated as follows. For the period 1971–96, between 75% and 95% of families are filing tax returns (see columns (3) and (4) in Table 11.1), therefore in that case, we estimate the denominator starting from total income (called Revenu net) reported on tax returns (before personal deductions and exemptions) and we assume that non-filers earn on average 20% of average income. Our denominator is not very sensitive to the exact assumption we are making about non-filers average income as this group is small relative to filers for the period 1971–96. For the period before 1971, the fraction of filers is smaller and therefore we rely on National Accounts to estimate our total income denominator. We simply take the denominator as 75% of National Income. National Income is defined as the sum of personal income (including government transfers) and corporate savings (after tax profits of corporations after distribution of dividends). In 1971, our method starting from total income reported from tax returns generates a total equal to 74.9% of National Income so there is no discontinuity in our denominator estimation. National Accounts are published in *Annuaire Statistique de la Suisse* (various years) and also compiled in Siegenthaler (1996). Unfortunately, the breakdown of National Income into personal income, government transfers, and corporate savings is not available for all years and therefore we decided to adopt the simple uniform 75% of National Income rule.[10] Those National Income figures are available starting in 1929. For the period 1901–28 (reported on Table 11.1 but not used in our estimates which start in 1933, we have used Maddison (1995) GDP estimates which we have pasted to year 1929). Column (5) reports our denominator (in real 2000 Swiss Francs) and column (6) reports the average real income per tax unit. Our Consumer Price Index (CPI) series, reported on column (7) of Table 1 is obtained from Global Financial Data (available online at http:// www.globalfindata.com). We estimate the CPI in any given year as the average of maximum and minimum value for the CPI reported in the corresponding year. As described above, income tax in Switzerland is based on the average of the incomes earned in two consecutive years. Therefore, we average in the same way our tax unit totals, denominator totals (for the pre-1971 period), and Consumer Price Index series. Those estimates are presented in Table 11.2.

National Accounts in Switzerland do not report personal wealth estimates. Therefore, we have estimated our total wealth denominator starting from

[10] This approach assumes that there has not been any significant trend prior to the 1970s in the share of government transfers plus corporate savings within national income. We do not have data to assess this assumption. However, as far as government transfers are concerned this assumption is conservative with regard to our main findings. Indeed, one might expect the trend (if any) to be increasing over time. This would mean that our total income denominator is under-estimated at the beginning of the period, and thus that our top income share are over-estimated. The secular decline of top income shares in Switzerland would then be even smaller. For instance if the 'real' income total in 1933 were 90% of national income (small transfers, no savings during the Depression), the top 1% income share would be 8.3% and not 10%, compared with 8.0% in 1995–96.

Table 11.1 Reference totals for population, income, and inflation in Switzerland, 1901–2002

	Adult population		Tax years and tax returns		Personal income		Inflation
	(1) Adult population (aged 20+) ('000s)	(2) Tax units ('000s)	(3) Tax returns ('000s)	(4) Fraction filing (percent)	(5) Total income (millions Fr.)	(6) Average income per tax unit (2000 Fr.)	(7) CPI (2000 base)
1901	1,997	1,447	—		24,214	16,732	8.848
1902	2,022	1,464	—		24,611	16,813	8.848
1903	2,047	1,481	—		24,989	16,879	8.955
1904	2,072	1,497	—		25,359	16,938	8.955
1905	2,097	1,514	—		26,134	17,264	9.061
1906	2,123	1,530	—		26,073	17,036	9.275
1907	2,148	1,547	—		26,417	17,075	9.701
1908	2,173	1,564	—		26,761	17,113	9.914
1909	2,198	1,580	—		27,091	17,142	10.021
1910	2,224	1,597	—		27,407	17,161	10.234
1911	2,242	1,611	—		27,744	17,217	10.554
1912	2,261	1,626	—		28,054	17,255	10.767
1913	2,279	1,640	—		28,344	17,280	10.660
1914	2,298	1,655	—		28,128	16,999	10.660
1915	2,317	1,669	—		28,506	17,078	11.845
1916	2,335	1,684	—		28,418	16,880	13.706
1917	2,354	1,698	—		25,278	14,887	17.091
1918	2,373	1,712	—		25,238	14,738	21.490
1919	2,391	1,727	—		26,976	15,622	23.352
1920	2,410	1,741	—		28,667	16,464	23.774
1921	2,440	1,761	—		27,960	15,876	20.872
1922	2,469	1,781	—		30,688	17,231	17.841
1923	2,499	1,801	—		32,386	17,984	17.131
1924	2,528	1,821	—		33,484	18,391	17.690
1925	2,558	1,841	—		35,802	19,452	17.580
1926	2,587	1,860	—		37,385	20,095	17.063
1927	2,616	1,880	—		39,151	20,822	16.734
1928	2,646	1,900	—		41,003	21,579	16.828
1929	2,675	1,920	—		43,121	22,459	16.812
1930	2,705	1,940	—		43,487	22,418	16.551
1931	2,730	1,955	—		42,110	21,539	15.694
1932	2,755	1,970	—		40,154	20,379	14.529
1933	2,780	1,986	272.4	13.7	42,638	21,475	13.787
1934	2,806	2,001	264.1	13.1	42,817	21,401	13.573
1935	2,831	2,016			42,790	21,225	13.390
1936	2,856	2,031	271.5	13.3	41,885	20,620	13.662
1937	2,881	2,046			44,419	21,706	14.174
1938	2,906	2,062	—		44,382	21,527	14.320
1939	2,931	2,077	677.2	32.5	44,339	21,349	14.519
1940	2,956	2,092			43,943	21,004	15.887
1941	2,982	2,107	no statistics		42,924	20,369	18.139
1942	3,014	2,125			41,465	19,517	20.161
1943	3,047	2,142	1,139.5	53.0	42,528	19,857	21.216

1944	3,080	2,159			43,569	20,182	21.650
1945	3,113	2,176	1,366.5	62.6	46,148	21,208	21.796
1946	3,145	2,193			50,697	23,116	21.781
1947	3,178	2,210	1,203.0	54.2	54,426	24,623	22.752
1948	3,211	2,228			54,905	24,648	23.450
1949	3,244	2,245	963.1	42.7	53,443	23,809	23.199
1950	3,277	2,262			57,108	25,248	22.819
1951	3,322	2,287	1,092.0	47.5	59,670	26,094	23.887
1952	3,367	2,312			61,672	26,678	24.489
1953	3,412	2,337	1,146.7	48.8	64,824	27,742	24.310
1954	3,457	2,362			68,499	29,006	24.539
1955	3,502	2,386	905.3	37.7	72,551	30,401	24.740
1956	3,547	2,411			76,517	31,731	25.084
1957	3,592	2,436	955.9	39.0	79,609	32,676	25.607
1958	3,637	2,461			81,591	33,150	26.044
1959	3,682	2,486	1,185.4	47.4	87,619	35,242	25.908
1960	3,727	2,511			93,289	37,151	26.223
1961	3,790	2,546	1,285.2	50.1	101,494	39,859	26.904
1962	3,852	2,582			108,828	42,156	27.864
1963	3,915	2,617	1,299.1	49.3	114,578	43,786	28.882
1964	3,977	2,652			122,438	46,169	29.742
1965	4,040	2,687	1,530.6	56.6	127,209	47,339	30.824
1966	4,102	2,722			130,534	47,948	32.357
1967	4,165	2,758	1,784.0	64.3	133,842	48,535	33.594
1968	4,228	2,793			140,118	50,170	34.516
1969	4,290	2,828	1,817.7	63.9	148,192	52,400	35.326
1970	4,353	2,863			158,323	55,294	36.734
1971	4,381	2,890	2,036.9	70.2	169,477	58,650	39.017
1972	4,409	2,916			178,891	61,348	41.656
1973	4,437	2,942	2,288.2	77.4	178,997	60,835	45.703
1974	4,465	2,969			180,570	60,825	49.816
1975	4,493	2,995	2,420.6	80.5	172,611	57,632	52.714
1976	4,521	3,021			172,890	57,222	53.798
1977	4,549	3,048	2,542.3	83.1	178,523	58,575	54.447
1978	4,577	3,074			183,150	59,579	54.974
1979	4,605	3,100	2,665.6	85.6	184,980	59,662	56.666
1980	4,633	3,127			188,947	60,428	59.341
1981	4,699	3,181	2,790.1	87.0	192,181	60,424	62.835
1982	4,766	3,234			192,601	59,550	66.574
1983	4,832	3,288	2,904.5	87.6	195,565	59,478	68.752
1984	4,899	3,342			201,526	60,306	70.676
1985	4,965	3,395	3,106.1	90.8	198,472	58,452	73.057
1986	5,032	3,449			207,395	60,129	73.593
1987	5,098	3,503	3,112.5	88.2	209,033	59,674	74.809
1988	5,164	3,557			218,325	61,385	76.120
1989	5,231	3,610	3,227.1	88.7	222,919	61,744	78.895
1990	5,297	3,664			228,669	62,408	82.978
1991	5,322	3,685	3,272.6	88.6	231,186	62,739	87.533
1992	5,346	3,706			226,798	61,202	91.088
1993	5,370	3,727	3,495.4	93.5	225,319	60,464	93.743
1994	5,394	3,747			227,158	60,619	94.899
1995	5,419	3,768	3,401.9	90.0	216,562	57,472	96.384
1996	5,443	3,789			217,253	57,339	97.465
1997	5,467	3,810			226,274	59,394	97.972
1998	5,491	3,831	Transition to annual system		232,159	60,608	98.005

(*contd.*)

Table 11.1 (*contd.*)

	Adult population		Tax years and tax returns		Personal income		Inflation
	(1)	(2)	(3)	(4)	(5)	(6)	(7)
	Adult population (aged 20+) ('000s)	Tax units ('000s)	Tax returns ('000s)	Fraction filing (percent)	Total income (millions Fr.)	Average income per tax unit (2000 Fr.)	CPI (2000 base)
1999	5,515	3,851			236,379	61,376	98.783
2000	5,540	3,872			247,376	63,886	100.341
2001					239,564		101.367
2002					237,895		101.951

Notes: All details in the text. Tax units defined as adult individuals (aged 20+) less half of married individuals. Population, adults, married individuals from decennial census from *Annuaire Statistique de la Suisse*, (1993: 47) and linear interpolation. Year 2000 from http://www.statistik.admin.ch/stat_ch/ber01/fufr01.htm Col. (3) reports the number of tax returns for the Federal Income Tax and column (4) the fraction of filers. Starting in 1934, each tax year corresponds to two calendar year. For tax period 1934/35, income taxation is based on average income earned in 1934 and 1935, etc. Total income computed as total income on tax returns before deductions (*Revenu Net*) plus 20% of average income imputed to non-filers for period 1971–on. From 1929 to 1970, total income defined as 75% of net National Income. Total income in 1901–20 imputed from Madison series on GDP per capita (pasted to 1929, 75% of National Income). Consumer Price Index from http:// www.globalfindata.com (1) (average of maximum and mininum value for each year).

total wealth reported on tax returns. Fortunately, for a number of years (1913, 1919, 1940, 1969, 1981, 1991, 1997), the tabulations are based on the full population (with positive net worth) and hence the total net worth reported is equal to total personal net worth in the economy.[11] For the remaining years, the fraction of families covered is not complete but is over 10% (except for years 1934, 1936, 1938). As wealth is so concentrated, we estimate that the wealth of filers is over 80% of total wealth. From the wealth of filers, we estimate total wealth using the closest years with complete coverage and assuming that the non-filers in the non-complete year have the same wealth share as in the closest complete years. More precisely, for year 1915, we use 1913 as the reference. For 1921, we use 1919 as the reference. For 1925, 1929, 1932, 1934, and 1936, we use the mean of 1919 and 1940 as the reference. For years 1941, 1945, and 1947, we use 1940 are the reference. For years 1949, 1951, 1953, 1955, and 1957, we use the mean of 1940 and 1969 as the reference. Again, as wealth is very concentrated, even in the years where relatively few families are covered by the statistics, we estimate that over 60% of total wealth (and over 80% except in the 1930s) is reported in the statistics so that our top wealth shares results are not very sensitive to our denominator estimations. Our total wealth estimates are presented in Table 11.3.[12]

[11] We have no information on negative worth but we assume that total negative worth is negligible compared to total positive worth.

[12] The average wealth levels in the first two years 1913 and 1915 are much higher than from 1919 on. Both years 1913 and 1919 have full coverage and the inflation index more than doubles between 1913 and 1919, so nominal wealth levels actually increase by 30% from 1913 and 1919 (see *Annuaire Statistique de la Suisse* (1921: 378), which presents both wealth distributions side to side). So it might

Estimating Top Income and Wealth Shares

Top income and wealth shares are estimated using the standard Pareto interpolation method (see Appendix 5C). For recent years, the top bracket may contain more than 0.01% of tax units. In that case, we impute the very top shares assuming that the distribution has a constant Pareto parameter in the top bracket and this Pareto parameter is estimated using the ratio of average incomes in the top bracket to the top bracket threshold. Table 11.2 presents the top income shares (along with the reference totals) in Switzerland from 1933 to 1996 and Table 11.3 presents the top wealth shares (along with the reference totals) from 1913 to 1997.

Non-Residents and Capital Income earned in Switzerland

Switzerland is a renowned place for bank secrecy and therefore is believed to host large accounts on behalf of wealthy foreign individuals or businesses interested in evading taxes in their own countries. Indeed, the secrecy banking rules make it very difficult for foreign fiscal administrations to assess whether residents from their countries are evading capital income taxes through Swiss accounts. Related, because Switzerland imposes moderate tax rates on high incomes and high wealth Swiss residents, a number of celebrities such as Sport stars and other wealthy individuals, most of them Europeans, have chosen to live in Switzerland and become Swiss residents (for tax purposes) in order to flee the high tax rates from their home countries. Swiss income tax statistics can cast interesting light on both of these aspects of tax avoidance and tax evasion.

First, in contrast to the popular view that returns on wealth invested through Swiss accounts can escape completely taxation, the Swiss administration imposes a flat 35% tax at source (called advance tax or *Impôt Anticipé*) on all returns earned through Swiss accounts. The fiscal administration states clearly that this tax is very well enforced and that virtually all Swiss financial institutions comply carefully with this rule. At the same time, the fact that this tax is a flat rate tax allows Swiss financial institutions to keep the identity and levels of each individual account secret. The 35% advance tax is refunded to Swiss residents when they file their income tax (individual or corporate).[13]

For non-residents, the advance tax is refunded only if they show evidence that they have reported those incomes for tax purposes in their country of residency. The Swiss fiscal administration publishes every year in *Recettes fiscales*

be the case that the price indexes reported by Global Financial Data are narrow indices and provide a very imperfect measure of the general price increases. It seems hard to believe that wealth would increase only by 30% in nominal terms while all prices in the economy are doubling. Fortunately, wealth concentration estimates are completely independent of price indices.

[13] Paying the advance tax does not free Swiss residents from reporting those incomes on their tax returns. This, together with the fact that combined federal and local income tax rates in Switzerland very rarely reach 35%, implies that virtually all income earned by Swiss residents and subject to the advance tax will be reported on their tax returns and hence be included in the statistics we are using.

Table 11.2 Top income shares in Switzerland, 1933–95/96

	Aggregate series					Top groups shares					Intermediate groups shares					Shares within shares			
(0)	Consumer price index (1)	Number of tax units ('000s) (2)	Total real income (millions Fr.) (3)	Real income per tax unit (2000 Fr.) (4)	% Tax units covered in statistics (5)	10% (6)	5% (7)	1% (8)	0.5% (9)	0.10% (10)	0.01% (11)	10–5% (12)	5–1% (13)	1–0.5% (14)	0.5–0.1% (15)	0.1–0.1% (16)	0.01% (17)	top 1 within top 10% (18)	top 0.1 within top 1% (19)
1933	13.787	1,986	42,638	21,475	13.7	31.16	21.92	9.98	7.19	3.27	0.94	9.24	11.94	2.79	3.92	2.33	0.94	32.02	32.74
1934–35	13.573	2,008	42,515	21,169	13.2	30.92	21.59	9.69	6.94	3.14	0.91	9.33	11.90	2.75	3.80	2.23	0.91	31.34	32.44
1936–37	13.662	2,039	43,984	21,573	13.3	30.47	21.46	9.94	7.21	3.35	0.98	9.01	11.52	2.73	3.86	2.37	0.98	32.61	33.71
1939–40	14.519	2,085	46,212	22,169	32.5	32.94	23.77	11.78	8.78	4.36	1.52	9.17	11.99	3.00	4.42	2.84	1.52	35.77	36.99
1943–44	21.216	2,150	43,494	20,227	53.0	32.59	22.70	10.54	7.67	3.71	1.43	9.89	12.17	2.87	3.96	2.29	1.43	32.32	35.22
1945–46	21.796	2,185	48,404	22,157	62.6	33.24	23.36	10.49	7.50	3.44	1.10	9.89	12.87	2.98	4.06	2.34	1.10	31.54	32.83
1947–48	22.752	2,219	55,507	25,015	54.2	31.58	21.95	10.01	7.15	3.26	1.03	9.63	11.94	2.86	3.89	2.23	1.03	31.70	32.57
1949–50	23.199	2,253	54,808	24,324	42.7	32.29	22.22	9.99	7.13	3.23	0.96	10.07	12.23	2.85	3.90	2.27	0.96	30.93	32.37
1951–52	23.887	2,299	61,448	26,726	47.5	31.29	21.65	9.94	7.18	3.37	1.07	9.64	11.71	2.76	3.81	2.30	1.07	31.77	33.87
1953–54	24.310	2,349	66,984	28,515	48.8	30.33	21.16	9.80	7.08	3.30	1.05	9.17	11.36	2.73	3.78	2.25	1.05	32.32	33.65
1955–56	24.740	2,399	75,066	31,291	48.8	29.72	20.92	9.81	7.06	3.24	0.97	8.80	11.11	2.75	3.82	2.28	0.97	32.99	33.07
1957–58	25.607	2,449	81,297	33,199	38.2	30.99	21.79	10.11	7.24	3.31	1.03	9.20	11.69	2.87	3.93	2.28	1.03	32.61	32.73
1959–60	25.908	2,499	91,022	36,429	46.5	31.47	22.35	10.54	7.58	3.51	1.09	9.11	11.82	2.95	4.08	2.42	1.09	33.48	33.27
1961–62	26.904	2,564	107,103	41,773	48.9	31.56	22.70	10.87	7.85	3.62	1.06	8.87	11.83	3.02	4.23	2.56	1.06	34.43	33.28
1963–64	28.882	2,634	120,331	45,677	48.0	31.72	22.83	10.91	7.88	3.64	1.12	8.90	11.92	3.04	4.24	2.52	1.12	34.39	33.32

1965–66	30.824	2,705	132,118	48,845	55.7	31.60	22.60	10.67	7.67	3.50	1.05	9.01	11.92	3.00	4.17	2.45	1.05	33.77	32.78
1967–68	33.593	2,775	138,905	50,051	63.1	32.29	23.01	10.86	7.81	3.58	1.08	9.27	12.15	3.05	4.23	2.50	1.08	33.63	32.96
1969–70	35.326	2,846	156,414	54,965	62.8	32.70	23.32	11.00	7.92	3.66	1.14	9.38	12.32	3.09	4.26	2.52	1.14	33.65	33.25
1971–72	39.017	2,903	180,234	62,089	69.0	32.49	23.03	10.81	7.79	3.62	1.14	9.47	12.22	3.02	4.16	2.48	1.14	33.26	33.51
1973–74	45.703	2,956	187,907	63,578	76.0	30.96	21.51	9.77	6.98	3.20	1.04	9.45	11.75	2.79	3.78	2.16	1.04	31.55	32.75
1975–76	52.714	3,008	174,529	58,017	78.9	30.29	20.47	8.79	6.15	2.68	0.83	9.82	11.68	2.64	3.47	1.85	0.83	29.01	30.49
1977–78	54.447	3,061	181,723	59,369	81.4	29.93	20.12	8.49	5.90	2.56	0.79	9.80	11.63	2.59	3.34	1.77	0.79	28.38	30.13
1979–80	56.666	3,114	191,423	61,479	83.6	29.89	20.06	8.40	5.82	2.51	0.76	9.83	11.66	2.58	3.31	1.75	0.76	28.09	29.88
1981–82	62.835	3,207	198,122	61,770	86.9	29.87	20.02	8.40	5.85	2.58	0.84	9.85	11.62	2.55	3.27	1.75	0.84	28.12	30.73
1983–84	68.752	3,315	201,365	60,746	87.5	29.88	20.00	8.39	5.85	2.62	0.86	9.88	11.61	2.54	3.23	1.76	0.86	28.07	31.25
1985–86	73.057	3,422	203,694	59,519	90.7	30.35	20.64	9.05	6.48	3.16	1.25	9.72	11.59	2.57	3.32	1.91	1.25	29.82	34.91
1987–88	74.809	3,530	215,591	61,078	88.1	30.78	20.93	9.07	6.41	2.94	0.96	9.85	11.86	2.67	3.47	1.97	0.96	29.47	32.39
1989–90	78.895	3,637	231,711	63,705	88.6	30.78	20.96	9.22	6.59	3.15	1.15	9.81	11.74	2.63	3.44	2.01	1.15	29.95	34.20
1991–92	87.533	3,695	233,597	63,215	86.4	29.99	20.14	8.60	6.09	2.85	1.00	9.85	11.54	2.51	3.24	1.85	1.00	28.68	33.18
1993–94	93.743	3,737	227,639	60,916	90.8	29.65	19.87	8.48	6.01	2.82	0.98	9.78	11.39	2.47	3.19	1.84	0.98	28.61	33.27
1995–96	96.384	3,779	218,126	57,728	84.0	29.22	19.27	8.03	5.67	2.67	0.87	9.95	11.24	2.36	3.00	1.80	0.87	27.47	33.23

Notes: Computations by authors based on wealth tax return statistics. See text for details. Consumer Price Index from http://www.globalfindata.com (mean from Table 11.1 over corresponding years). Total income based on means from Table 11.1. Percentage of tax units covered by tax statistics reported on column (5). Col. (6) to (17) display the top of total income accruing to each upper income group for corresponding years. Top 0.1% and above estimates for years 1993–94, 1995–96 not precise because top bracket contains more than 1% of tax units.

Table 11.3 Top wealth shares in Switzerland, 1913–97

	Aggregate wealth					Top groups shares						Intermediate groups shares					
	Consumer Price Index (1)	Total real wealth (millions Fr.) (2)	Real wealth per family (2000 Fr.) (3)	Tax returns with positive wealth/total tax units (4)	% Wealth Covered in statistics (5)	10% (6)	5% (7)	1% (8)	0.5% (9)	0.10% (10)	0.01% (11)	10–5% (12)	5–1% (13)	1–0.5% (14)	0.5–0.1% (15)	0.1–0.01% (16)	0.01% (17)
1913	10.660	123,457	75,264	40.72	100.0	84.81	73.57	46.65	37.15	19.13	5.43	11.24	26.92	9.50	18.03	13.70	5.43
1915	11.845	138,587	83,028	16.57	90.6	80.46	68.62	42.25	33.56	17.68	5.50	11.84	26.37	8.69	15.89	12.18	5.50
1919	23.351	77,263	44,743	53.84	100.0	76.25	62.29	36.42	28.33	14.25	4.12	13.96	25.88	8.08	14.09	10.13	4.12
1921	22.538	90,548	51,415	16.59	85.8	77.02	63.98	38.05	29.44	14.56	4.26	13.04	25.93	8.61	14.88	10.29	4.26
1925	17.732	116,670	63,388	16.07	87.3	75.83	64.55	40.68	32.48	16.49	5.09	11.28	23.87	8.19	15.99	11.41	5.09
1929	16.854	133,760	69,667	15.07	88.3	76.71	66.50	41.95	32.93	17.14	5.96	10.20	24.56	9.02	15.79	11.18	5.96
1934	13.698	147,470	73,707	3.85	62.7	—	67.96	40.43	31.16	15.49	4.57	—	27.53	9.27	15.67	10.92	4.57
1936	13.552	142,804	70,305	3.67	61.8	—	68.14	40.10	30.81	15.24	4.42	—	28.04	9.29	15.56	10.82	4.42
1938	14.399	136,655	66,284	3.79	62.4	—	73.30	44.43	34.57	17.54	5.20	—	28.87	9.86	17.02	12.35	5.20
1940	15.067	156,472	74,791	42.05	100.0	80.84	67.58	40.39	31.20	15.73	4.82	13.26	27.19	9.19	15.47	10.91	4.82
1941	17.021	130,795	62,066	15.92	89.3	81.91	69.31	41.45	31.85	15.90	5.22	12.61	27.85	9.61	15.95	10.68	5.22
1945	21.786	145,357	66,800	22.43	93.3	78.25	64.31	37.14	28.40	14.35	4.92	13.94	27.17	8.74	14.05	9.44	4.92
1947	22.183	153,294	69,353	22.74	93.5	79.04	65.38	38.30	29.47	15.08	5.49	13.66	27.08	8.83	14.39	9.59	5.49
1949	23.378	155,046	69,072	23.66	94.0	78.77	65.06	37.82	29.10	14.99	5.22	13.71	27.23	8.73	14.11	9.77	5.22
1951	23.263	157,976	69,082	10.59	80.9	79.89	66.22	38.97	30.16	15.65	5.47	13.67	27.25	8.80	14.52	10.18	5.47
1953	24.353	164,779	70,520	10.89	81.4	79.85	66.63	39.99	31.23	16.46	5.78	13.22	26.64	8.76	14.77	10.68	5.78
1955	24.711	182,995	76,680	11.37	82.2	79.94	67.32	41.50	32.67	17.50	6.16	12.62	25.82	8.83	15.17	11.33	6.16
1957	25.385	202,305	83,037	12.46	83.8	79.90	67.35	41.85	33.05	17.89	6.36	12.55	25.50	8.80	15.16	11.52	6.36
1969	35.002	389,835	137,844	54.45	100.0	78.91	66.71	41.56	32.79	17.92	6.66	12.21	25.15	8.77	14.87	11.26	6.66
1981	61.142	508,318	159,822	66.99	100.0	69.58	56.63	33.04	25.56	13.45	5.18	12.96	23.59	7.48	12.11	8.27	5.18
1991	85.553	619,626	168,153	68.72	100.0	69.94	56.58	33.57	26.51	14.93	6.48	13.36	23.01	7.05	11.58	8.46	6.48
1997	97.980	765,423	200,913	70.23	100.0	71.31	57.98	34.80	27.64	15.98	7.29	13.33	23.19	7.16	11.66	8.69	7.29

Notes: Computations by authors based on wealth tax return statistics. See text for details. Number of tax units define fractiles same as in Table 11.1. Wealth tax assessed on total family net worth (wealth - liabilities) as of January 1st of each tax year. Consumer Price Index from globalfindata.com (as of 1 January of corresponding years). Total real wealth extrapolated using years with complete coverage. Col. (4) reports the ratio of the number of tax returns with positive wealth to the total number of tax units (including non-filers). The percentage of total personal net worth in the economy covered by tax statistics reported on column (5) (estimated using years with 100% wealth coverage). Col. (6) to (17) display the top of total net-worth accruing to each upper wealth group on 1 January of each year. Top 0.01% estimates for years 1981, 1991, and 1997 not precise because top bracket contains more than 0.1% of tax units.

de la Confédération the total amount of advance tax paid, and the amounts refunded broken down by categories such as Swiss individual residents (personnes physiques), Swiss corporations (personnes morales), and non-residents (individuals or corporations). The difference between payments and refunds corresponds to capital income earned through Swiss accounts by non-residents and presumably never reported for tax purposes. Thus, we can use those statistics to estimate how much capital income is earned by non-residents, what fraction is reported in their countries and what fraction is never reported in their countries. We also estimate by how much top income shares in France would be increased if we added back to the French top income groups all the capital income evaded through Swiss accounts. In reality, the French are not the only foreigners to use Swiss accounts and there are many other tax haven jurisdictions which are actively used to evade taxes on capital income (such as Luxembourg, Monaco, Andorra, and Monte-Carlo, to name a few along the French border). However, our estimates are still instructive to get a sense of the magnitudes and dissipate the myth that the sums earned through those secret Swiss accounts are gigantic.

Second, the tabulations by size of income we use also provide a breakdown of taxpayers that allows us to estimate an upper bound on the number of non-residents filing income taxes in Switzerland or the number of Swiss residents getting income from abroad. Presumably, all the wealthy foreigners relocating in Switzerland for fiscal reasons will fall into those categories. More precisely, the Swiss income tax statistics divide taxpayers into normal cases and special cases. Special cases are: (1) those taxpayers who did not have regular incomes over the two year period taken into account for tax purposes (and which are subject to different rules to compute average income for tax purposes); or (2) taxpayers who are non-residents or residents with income from abroad. This second category is called special cases (others) (*cas spéciaux, autres*) and is the category of interest for us. From 1957 to 1992, this category is tabulated by size of income, allowing us to compute the fraction of taxpayers (income weighted) in each top income group, which falls in this special cases (others) category. For years 1949 to 1956, only the total number of special cases (others) is reported with no breakdown by size of income.

11.3 TOP INCOME SHARES

Figure 11.1 displays the average real income per tax unit (from our denominator measure) and the Consumer Price Index in Switzerland from 1901 to 2000. Figure 11.1 shows that real incomes grew slowly before the Second World War, rapidly from the Second World War to the early 1970s, and have stagnated since then. This broad pattern is quite similar to the French experience (see Piketty in Chapter 3 of this volume). Since the beginning of the century, Switzerland has always been among the very richest countries in the World. It should be noted that the business cycles and in particular the Great Depression have been mild in Switzerland. Price inflation has been moderate over the century, with sustained

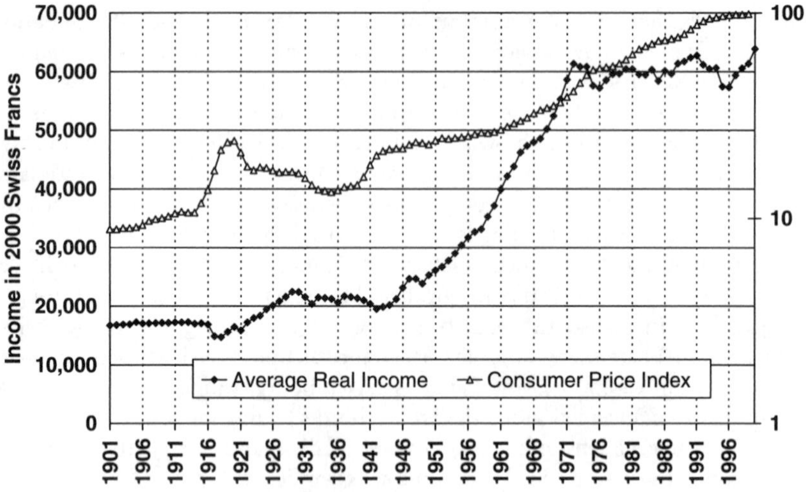

Figure 11.1 Average real income and consumer price index in Switzerland, 1901–2000

Source: Table 11.1, col. (6) and (7).

inflation only during the First World War and to a lesser extent during the Second World War and the 1970s.

Figure 11.2 displays the top 10% and top 5% income shares in Switzerland from 1933 to 1996. Those top income shares are very stable over the period, with the top 10% share varying between 30% and 33% and the top 5% share between 20% and 24%. Figure 11.3 decomposes the top 10% into three groups: the top 1%, the next 4% (top 5–1%), and the second vintile (top 10–5%). The two bottom groups are remarkably stable over the period. The top 1% income share experiences somewhat

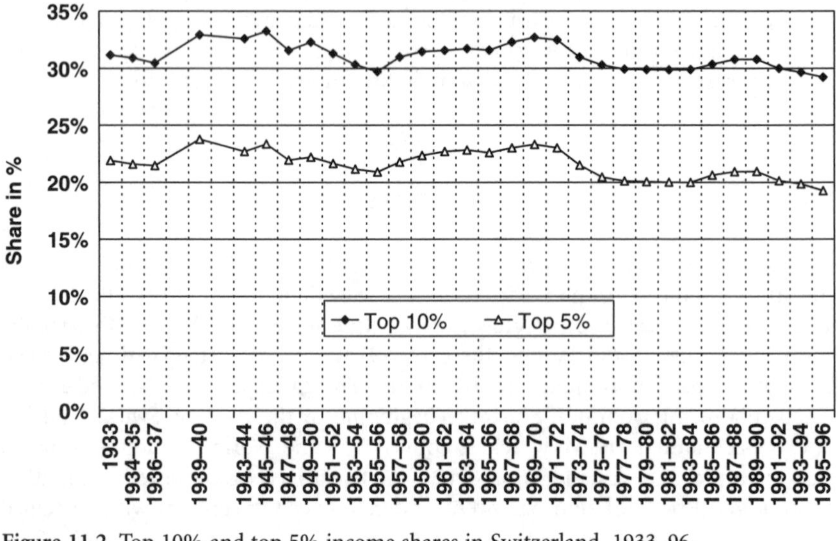

Figure 11.2 Top 10% and top 5% income shares in Switzerland, 1933–96

Source: Table 11.2: col. top 10% and top 5%.

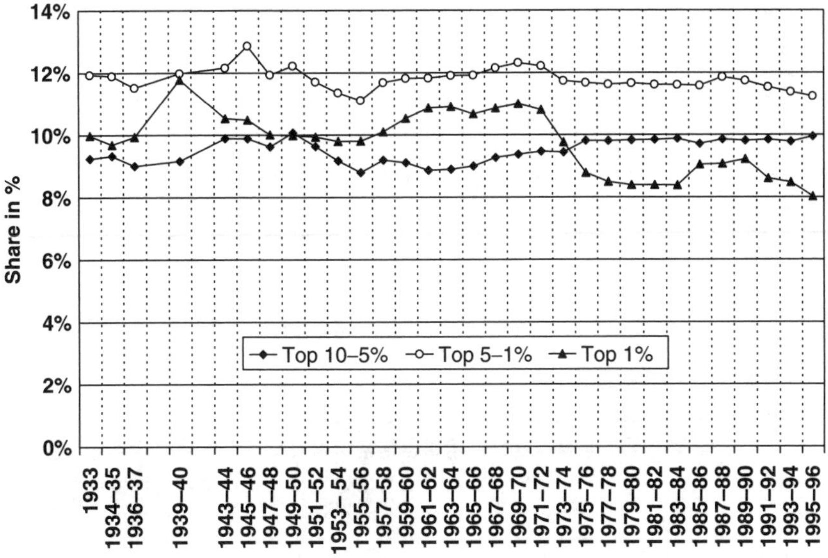

Figure 11.3 Top 1%, top 5–1%, and top 10–5% income shares in Switzerland, 1933–96

Source: Table 11.2: col. top 1%, 5–1% and top 10–5%.

larger fluctuations but never falls below 8% or goes above 12%. Three elements should be noted. First, there is spike in top 1% income share (but not in the other two groups) for years 1939–40, just at the eve of the Second World War. It is conceivable that such a spike is due to an influx of wealthy immigrants fleeing from the Nazis. Second, the top 1% income share does not fall during the Second World War or in the decades following the war. Quite to the contrary, the top 1% income share is the 1960s is actually slightly higher than in the 1930s. Finally, the top 1% income share falls in the early 1970s and again in the 1990s, so that it is a its lowest point in 1995–96, the last year we construct those estimates.

Figure 11.4 decomposes the top 1% group into three groups: the bottom half to the top percentile (top 1–0.5%), the next 0.4% percent (top 0.5–0.1%), and the top 1%. The figure shows that even the top 0.1% income share did not experience large fluctuations over the century (except for a temporary spike in 1939–40). Figure 11.5 shows the evolution of shares within shares, namely the share of the top percentile within the top decile, and the share of the top 0.1% within the top percentile. Shares within shares only rely on income tax data and are thus immune against any biases in income control totals. The two series exhibit a striking stability and similarity throughout the century fluctuating between 30% and 35% almost over the entire period confirming the pattern observed with simple income shares.

Figure 11.6 contrasts the experience of the top 0.1% income group in Switzerland with the French (Piketty, Chapter 3 in this volume) and the American (Piketty and Saez, Chapter 5 in this volume) experiences. In contrast to France and the United States, there is no decline in the top income share from the pre-war period to the decades following the Second World War. As a result, although the top 0.1%

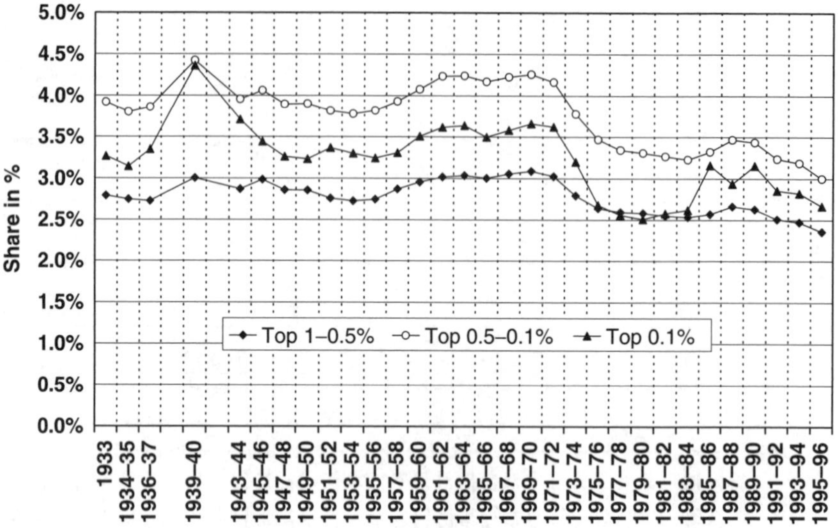

Figure 11.4 Top 0.1%, top 0.5–0.1%, and top 1–0.5% income shares in Switzerland, 1933–96

Sources: Table 11.2: col. top 0.1%, top 0.5–0.1%, and top 1–0.5%.

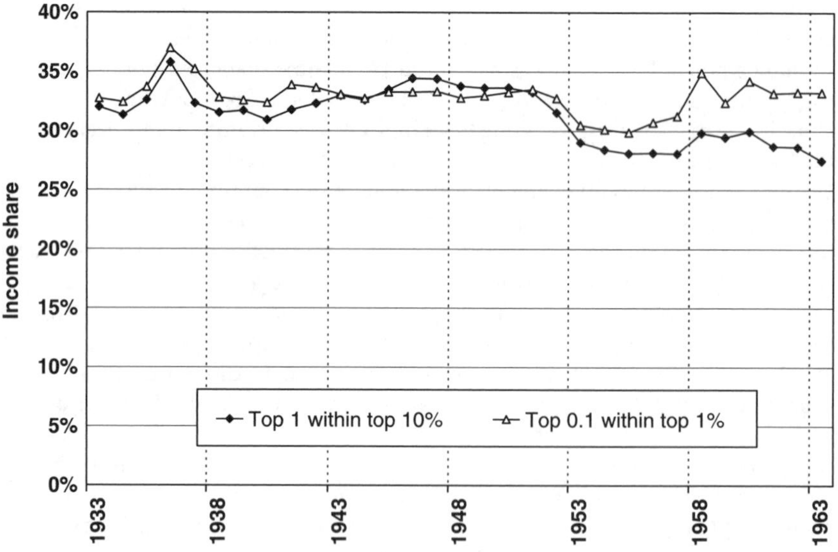

Figure 11.5 Shares within shares in Switzerland, 1933–63

Sources: Table 11.2: col. 18 and 19.

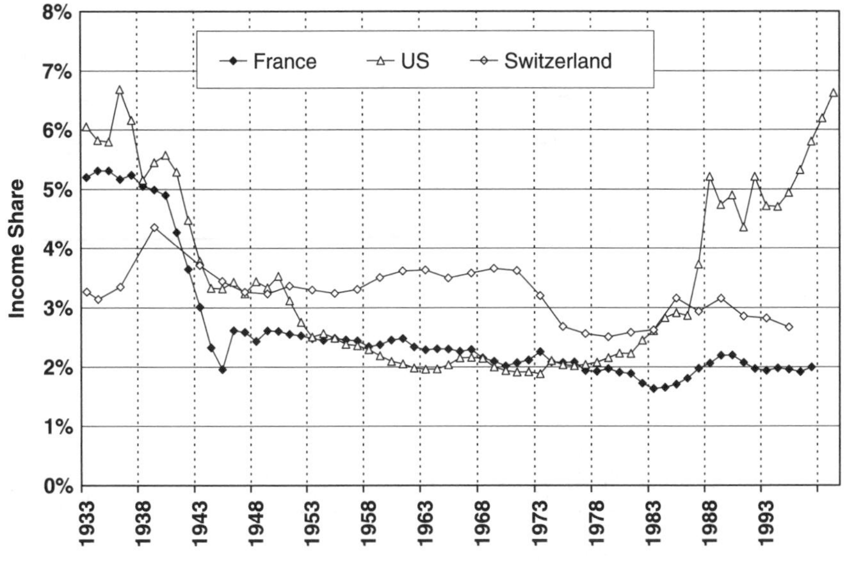

Figure 11.6 The top 0.1% income share in France, the US, and Switzerland 1933–97

Sources: US: Piketty and Saez (Chapter 5, this volume): table A1, col. top 0.1%; France: Piketty (2003, and Chapter 3, this volume); Switzerland: Table 11.2, column Top 0.1% income share.

income share in Switzerland was lower (around 3–4%) than in France or US (5–6%) in the 1930s, the top 0.1% income share was substantially higher in Switzerland in the 1960s (around 3.5%) than in the France and the United States (2–2.5%).

Therefore, the Swiss income share results show clearly that the large decline in very top income shares from the pre-war period to the post-war decades that has been found in all other countries studied in this volume did not take place in Switzerland. There are two limitations in those income concentration estimates for Switzerland. First, they start only in 1933, at a time where top income shares in other countries (such as France, the United States, or the United Kingdom) had already fallen significantly relative to their pre-First World War levels, therefore it would important to know whether Switzerland experienced substantial wealth and income deconcentration in the early part of the twentieth century. Second, the dramatic fall in very top income shares in other countries was primarily a capital income phenomenon due to a drastic fall in top fortunes. However, the Swiss income tax statistics do not provide information on the composition of top incomes and therefore do not allow us to look separately at the capital and labour income components.

Therefore, in order to overcome those two limitations, we now turn to wealth statistics which are available since 1913 and allow us to focus directly on the capital component of inequality.

11.4 TOP WEALTH SHARES

Table 11.3 presents our top wealth shares estimates for Switzerland. Figure 11.7 displays the wealth shares of the top 1%, the next 4% (top 5–1%), and the second

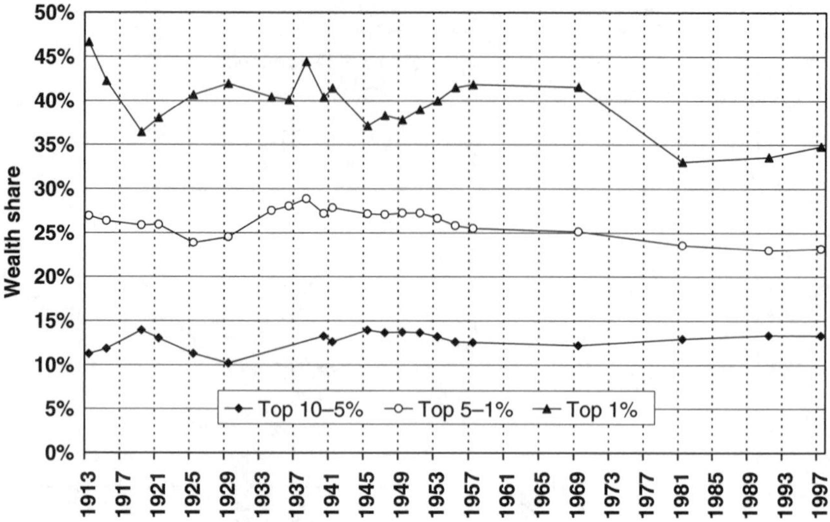

Figure 11.7 Top 10–5%, top 5–1%, and top 1% wealth shares in Switzerland, 1913–97

Source: Table 11.3, col. top 10–5%, top 5–1% and top 1%.

vintile (top 10–5%). Those groups are defined relative to all families in Switzerland (as for income shares) ranked according to net worth (gross wealth minus liabilities). Figure 11.7 shows that top wealth shares have also been remarkably stable over the full twentieth century in Switzerland. In particular, the top 1% income share is about the same in 1969 and in 1915 (around 42%). Thus, although the levels of income concentration were relatively low in Switzerland, this evidence shows that wealth in Switzerland is actually quite concentrated. It is notable that there was some reduction in wealth concentration from 1969 to 1981 with the top 1% wealth share falling from 42% to 33%.

Figure 11.8 decomposes the top percentile of wealth holders into the top 0.1%, the next 0.4% (top 0.5–0.1%), and the bottom half of the top percentile (top 1–0.5%). The figure shows that even very top wealth holders groups do not experience a secular decline, at least not before the 1970s. The top 0.1% wealth share stands at about 17% both in 1915 and in the 1960s.

Figure 11.9 compares Switzerland with the United States by displaying the top 1% wealth share series in both countries since 1915. The estimates for the United States are from Kopczuk and Saez (2004) and are estimated from estate tax statistics using the estate multiplier technique (and hence are based on individual wealth as opposed to family wealth in Switzerland). The figure shows that wealth concentration was similar in the United States and Switzerland at the beginning of the century, with the top 1% holding about 40% of total wealth. However, wealth concentration declined drastically in the United States to about 25% by the 1960s while it remained above 40% in Switzerland as late as 1969.

This evidence, together with our previous results on top income shares, shows that the reduction in income and wealth concentration documented for most

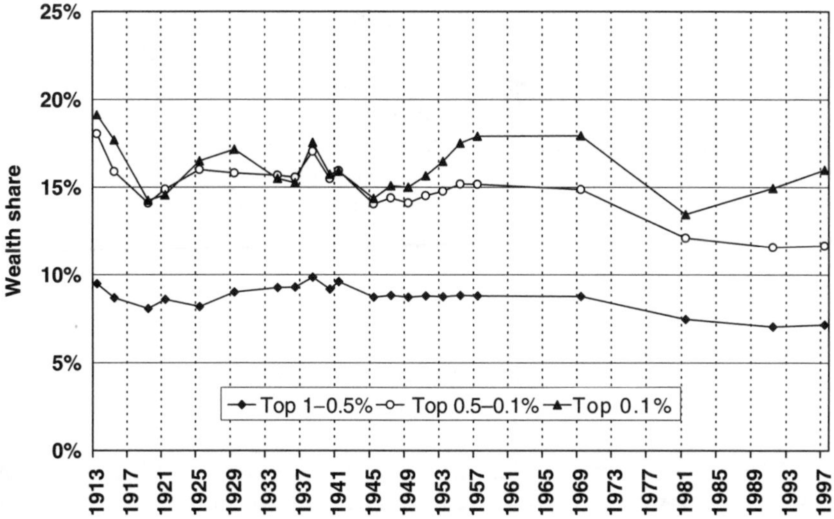

Figure 11.8 Top 1–0.5%, top 0.5–0.1%, and top 0.1% wealth shares in Switzerland, 1913–97

Source: Table 11.3, col. top 1–0.5%, top 0.5–0.1% and top 0.1%

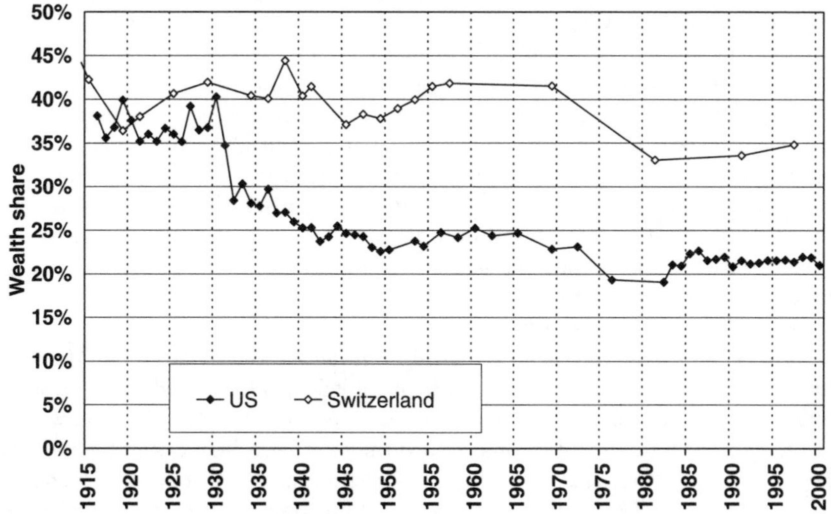

Figure 11.9 The top 1% wealth share in the US and Switzerland, 1915–2000

Note: US wealth shares are based on individual adults while Swiss shares are based on the family level.

Sources: US: Kopczuk and Saez (2004): table B1, col. top 1%; Switzerland: Table 11.3, top 1% wealth share.

countries did not happen in Switzerland and hence is not a necessary outcome of the development process of economically advanced countries. As we discussed in the introduction, the finding that wealth concentration did not decrease in Switzerland, a country which never imposed very high tax rates on top income earners and top wealth holders, is consistent with the explanation that progressive taxation is the main reason which prevented large fortunes from recovering to the pre-First World War levels in other countries in the second part of the twentieth century.

11.5 FOREIGN CAPITAL INCOME AND FOREIGNERS IN SWITZERLAND

Table 11.4 presents the fraction of special cases (others) which contains all non-resident taxpayers filing income taxes in Switzerland as well as all Swiss residents with income abroad among our top income groups. Figure 11.10 depicts those fractions for three tax periods, 1957–58, 1973–74, and 1991–92. First, the fraction of such returns increases sharply as we move up the income distribution, starting from negligible levels in the second vintile to significant fractions at the very top. Second, those fractions increase substantially over time. By 1991–92, at the very top 0.01% group, such taxpayers represent 20% of taxpayers while they were only 8% of taxpayers in 1957–58. This suggests that the number of wealthy foreigners living in Switzerland has probably increased sharply since the 1950s. However, the important point to note is that they remain a minority even in recent years and at the very top. Switzerland is a small country with moderate income concentration in recent decades. As a result, the view that a very large fraction of the wealthy in Europe and around the world relocate to Switzerland to escape high taxation in their countries is clearly contradicted by the tax statistics. Obviously, one would need to produce the same statistics for all potential tax havens and not only Switzerland, to assess to what extent wealthy individuals in high tax countries relocate to lower tax countries.

Table 11.5 displays the results obtained from the aggregate statistics on the 35% flat advance tax withheld at source on all capital income earned through Swiss financial institutions. Those statistics are averaged by decades. They show that the fraction of total capital income earned through Swiss financial institutions by non-residents but reported to the fiscal administration in their country of residency (and hence refunded by the Swiss fiscal administration) has indeed increased substantially since the 1950s from 1% to about 20% in recent years. The fraction of capital income whose advance tax is never refunded is an upper bound on capital earned by non-residents and never reported for tax purposes in their home countries (and hence presumably evaded). Table 11.5 show that this upper bound is relatively modest and is lower than 10% of total capital income earned in Switzerland in recent decades. It stands at around SF7.25 billion (around US$5

Table 11.4 Fraction of non-residents and residents with income abroad in top income groups in Switzerland, 1949/50–1991/92

	Aggregate series		Fraction special in top groups						Fraction special in intermediate groups					
	Number of special taxpayers (1)	Fraction special (percent) (2)	10% (5)	5% (6)	1% (7)	0.5% (8)	0.10% (9)	0.01% (10)	10–5% (11)	5–1% (12)	1–0.5% (13)	0.5–0.1% (14)	0.1–0.01% (15)	0.01% (16)
1949–50	4,644	0.21												
1951–52	5,234	0.23												
1953–54	6,427	0.27												
1955–56	6,964	0.29												
1957–58	8,187	0.33	2.34	3.01	4.61	5.26	6.41	8.11	0.64	1.54	2.93	4.27	5.64	8.11
1959–60	10,231	0.41	2.42	3.08	4.7	5.23	6.52	9.65	0.69	1.56	3.31	4.1	5.11	9.65
1961–62	13,235	0.52	2.54	3.18	4.61	4.97	5.79	8.06	0.8	1.81	3.65	4.26	4.85	8.06
1963–64	15,569	0.59	2.91	3.61	5.21	5.54	6.63	9.38	0.98	2.06	4.33	4.59	5.4	9.38
1965–66	20,722	0.77	3.28	4.08	5.93	6.36	7.66	8.85	1.14	2.34	4.81	5.25	7.15	8.85
1967–68	25,630	0.92	3.73	4.56	6.28	6.6	8.3	11.5	1.55	2.95	5.45	5.14	6.91	11.5
1969–70	33,679	1.18	4.44	5.43	7.47	8.08	10.32	12.78	1.86	3.54	5.88	6.13	9.2	12.78
1971–72	44,359	1.53	4.85	5.94	8.13	8.94	11.95	14.19	2.2	4.00	6.04	6.32	10.92	14.19
1973–74	55,235	1.87	5.23	6.49	9.21	10.28	13.25	15.64	2.36	4.23	6.54	7.76	12.09	15.64
1975–76	64,950	2.16	5.4	6.86	10.19	11.41	15.15	20.38	2.36	4.36	7.35	8.52	12.81	20.38
1977–78	70,449	2.30	5.18	6.59	9.85	11.1	14.51	19.52	2.29	4.21	7.01	8.49	12.28	19.52
1979–80	81,731	2.62	5.57	7.08	10.58	12.08	16.42	22.03	2.49	4.56	7.2	8.79	13.98	22.03
1981–82	94,279	2.94	5.86	7.5	11.18	12.69	16.58	19.8	2.53	4.84	7.72	9.62	15.04	19.8
1983–84	94,615	2.85	5.56	7.08	10.89	12.55	16.46	20.1	2.48	4.33	7.06	9.38	14.69	20.1
1985–86	93,517	2.73	5.89	7.48	11.45	13.21	17.13	19.9	2.51	4.38	7.01	9.48	15.31	19.9
1987–88	71,160	2.02	4.1	5.33	8.46	9.84	12.86	14.41	1.49	2.94	5.14	7.28	12.1	14.41
1989–90	81,983	2.25	5.99	7.69	11.75	13.48	16.9	18.39	2.36	4.5	7.41	10.34	16.05	18.39
1991–92	88,072	2.38	6.35	8.18	12.35	14.11	18.06	20.07	2.61	5.07	8.08	10.63	16.98	20.07

Notes: Computations by authors based on wealth tax return statistics. See text for details. Table displays the fraction of taxpayers residents with income abroad and non-residents with income in Switzerland (called special cases, others in statistics). Col. (1) report the total number of special cases (others) and column (2) the fraction of special cases (others) (relative to all tax units, col. (2) in Table 2). Col. (3) to (13) report the fraction of special cases (others) (income weighted) in all top income groups. Information not available after 1991/92.

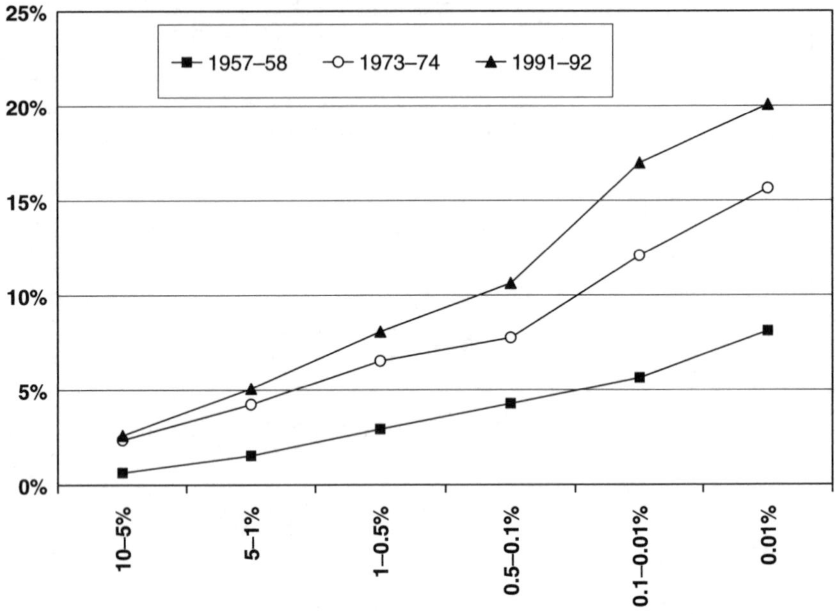

Figure 11.10 The fraction of foreign income earners and non-residents in top income groups Switzerland, 1957–91

Notes: The figure display for three tax years the fraction of special cases (others) defined as tax returns filed by non-residents (with income in Switzerland) or tax returns filed by Swiss residents with income from foreign (non Swiss) sources.

Sources: Table 11.4.

billion) per year in recent years. This is extremely small relative to total incomes reported by very top groups in the United States.[14]

Table 11.5 shows how this upper bound on capital income evaded through Swiss accounts compares with total income reported in top income groups in France. The table shows that those numbers are small relative to the top 1% (around 7% in recent decades) or even the top 0.1% (around 30%), although they are comparable in magnitude to total incomes reported by the top 0.01% taxpayers (the top 2000 French taxpayers). Therefore, if all this capital income were added back to the top 0.01% French incomes, the top 0.01% French income share would at most double from 0.5% to about 1% of total French income. That would still be a modest level of top income concentration relative to the almost 3% share of total income earned by the top 0.01% income earners in the United States in 2000.

[14] For example, as noted in Chapter 5, Bill Gates, the richest person in the United States, will earn almost US$4 billion in 2004 due to extraordinary dividends from Microsoft. The top 0.01% US taxpayers (about 13,400 taxpayers) in 2000, earned in total about US$175 billion even excluding realized capital gains (see Piketty and Saez, Chapter 5 this volume). Those amounts clearly dwarf the at most US$5 billion in capital income earned through Swiss accounts by wealthy foreigners who evade taxes in their country.

Table 11.5 Capital Income earned through Swiss accounts and tax evasion, 1950–2002

Period	Capital income		Percent of capital income accruing to							
			Based on advance tax refunds					As a percent of top income groups in France		
	Total in (millions of (2000 CH Fr.) (1)	As a % of total personal income (from Table 1) (2)	Swiss corporations (3)	Swiss individual residents (4)	Foreigners (5)	Advance tax never refunded (6)	Total capital income with no advance tax refund (mn 2000 CH Fr.) (9)	top 1% (10)	top 0.1% (11)	top 0.01% (12)
1950–59	6,516	9.18	40.40	38.11	1.11	20.37	1,327	4.1	15.1	57.8
1960–69	13,347	10.94	41.61	36.89	2.66	18.83	2,514	4.3	17.4	68.9
1970–79	28,070	15.96	43.07	35.58	4.80	16.55	4,644	7.1	28.8	110.2
1980–89	40,464	19.96	50.12	29.17	8.55	12.16	4,919	7.3	29.8	114.6
1990–98	66,588	29.50	53.47	25.72	12.02	8.80	5,860	7.7	30.0	108.8
1999–02	85,826	35.72	57.40	13.62	20.53	8.46	7,258			

Notes: Col. (1) displays the average annual real value of capital income earned through Swiss financial institutions (all subject to 35% withholding advance tax, except minor exemptions). Col. (2) shows the amount as a percentage of personal income in Switzerland from Table 11.1, col. (5). Col. (3)–(5) show the fraction of capital income earned by Swiss corporations (personnes morales), Swiss individual residents (personnes physiques), and non-residents based on refunds of the advance tax. Col. (6) displays the fraction of capital income whose advance tax is never refunded and hence presumably evaded. Col. (7) shows the average annual real amount of capital income (in 2000 million of Swiss Francs) whose tax is not refunded (col. (6) times col. (1)). This is an upper bound of capital income evaded by non-residents through Swiss accounts. Col. (7)–(9) show by what percentage would the top 1%, 0.1%, and 0.01% income shares in France would be increased if all the capital income whose advance tax is never refunded was allocated fully to those top income groups.

Source: *Recettes fiscales de la Confédération 2002* (*Administration fédérale des contributions, Division Statistique fiscale et documentation, Berne, avril* 2003).

Therefore, evasion through secret Swiss accounts can clearly not account for the gap in top income shares documented in this volume between continental European countries and Anglo-Saxon countries. However, as we mentioned above, it would be extremely useful to try to compile similar estimates of total capital income evaded not only through Switzerland but through all other potential tax havens.

11.6 CONCLUSION

This chapter has shown that in contrast to other countries studied in the volume, Switzerland did not experience a reduction in income and wealth concentration from the pre-First World War period to the decades following the Second World War. We have tentatively argued that the absence of progressive income and wealth taxation in Switzerland is the main factor explaining the discrepancy of the Swiss experience, although more work is clearly needed to establish to what extent taxation of top income and top wealth holders was lower in Switzerland than in other countries. Interestingly, the pattern of economic growth in Switzerland is very close to the French or American experience, albeit less tumultuous. This suggests that the high concentration of wealth and low levels of top tax rates that Switzerland experienced in the post-Second World War period did not provide a boost to its economic performance relative to other countries such as France or the United States (which also grew very quickly after the Second World War). It also suggests that the high wealth concentration levels were not an impairment to achieve high growth in the period after the Second World War.[15]

APPENDIX 11: REFERENCES ON DATA SOURCES FOR SWITZERLAND

Virtually all statistical publications in Switzerland are bilingual, published in French and German (we give both titles wherever possible)

General Statistics about Switzerland

Siegenthaler, H. (1996). *Statistique Historique de la Suisse/Historische Statistik der Schweiz.* Zurich: Chronos.

[15] The experience from Latin America suggests that high wealth concentration might impair growth through political instability and subsequent poor government management of the economy. The high wealth concentration levels in Switzerland obviously did not generate political instability in that country.

Statistical Yearbook (1891–2004). *Annuaire Statistique de la Suisse/Statistisches Jahrbuch der Schweiz.* Zurich. Verlag des Art.

Tax Burden Statistics

Statistisches Bureau (1919–1929) 'Les Impots sur le Produit du travail et le capital dans les principales communes de la Suisse', *Bulletin de Statistique Suisse.* Bern: Eidgenossisches Statistisches Amt.

Statistisches Bureau (1929–2004) *Charge Fiscale en Suisse/Steuerbelastung in der Schweiz.* Bern: Eidgenossisches Statistisches Amt (published in the series *Statistiques de la Suisse/Statistische Quellenwerke der Schweiz* up to 1960).

Income and Wealth Tax Statistics (by Size of Income and Wealth)

Administration fédérale des contributions (1920) *Statistique du 1er Impôt Fédéral de Guerre 1916/1917.* Bern: Eidgenossisches Steuerverwaltung.

Administration fédérale des contributions (1926, 1930, 1934) *Statistique Concernant le Nouvel Impôt Fédéral de Guerre Extraordinaire/Statistik der Neuen Ausserordentlichen Eidgenossischen Kriegssteuer* volumes I, II, and III. Bern: Eidgenossisches Steuerverwaltung.

—— (1937, 1939, 1941) *Contribution Fédérale de Crise/Eidgenossische Krisenabgabe* (Periods I, II, and III published in series *Statistiques de la Suisse/Statistische Quellenwerke der Schweiz*). Bern: Eidgenossisches Steuerverwaltung.

—— (every two years 1941–80) *Impôt Fédéral pour la Defense Nationale/Eidgenossische Wehrsteuer: Statistik*, periods I to XX. Bern: Eidgenossisches Steuerverwaltung (published in the series *Statistiques de la Suisse/Statistische Quellenwerke der Schweiz*).

—— (biannual 1982–95) *Impôt Fédéral Direct. Statistique de la Periode de Taxation/Direkte Bundessteuer. Statistik der Veranlagungsperiode.* Bern: Eidgenossisches Steuerverwaltung.

For years after 1992, the paper publication is no longer available but statistics have been made available online at http://www.estv.admin.ch

Statistics on advanced flat tax on capital income (Impôt Anticipé)

Administration fédérale des contributions (Division Statistique fiscale et documentation) (2003). *Recettes fiscales de la Confédération 2002.* Berne: Administration fédérale des contributions.

REFERENCES

Atkinson, A. B. (2005). 'Top incomes in the UK over the 20th century', *Journal of the Royal Statistical Society*, 168(2): 325–43.

—— Harrison, A. J. (1978). *Distribution of Personal Wealth in Britain.* Cambridge: Cambridge University Press.

—— Gordon, J. P. F., and Harrison, A. J. (1989). 'Trends in the Shares of Top Wealth-Holders in Britain, 1923–81', *Oxford Bulletin of Economics and Statistics*, 51: 315–32.

Kopczuk, W. and Saez, E. (2004). 'Top Wealth Shares in the United States, 1916–2000: Evidence from Estate Tax Returns', *National Tax Journal*, 57: 445–87.

Kuznets, S. (1953). *Shares of Upper Income Groups in Income and Savings.* New York: National Bureau of Economic Research.

Lampman, R. J. (1962). *The Share of Top Wealth-Holders in National Wealth, 1922–1956.* New Jersey: Princeton University Press, Princeton.

Lindert, P. (2000). 'Three Centuries of Inequality in Britain and America', in A. B. Atkinson and F. Bourguignon (eds.) *Handbook of Income Distribution.* Amsterdam: Elsevier Science, pp. 167–216.

Maddison, A. (1975). *Monitoring the World Economy.* Paris: OECD.

Piketty, T. (2001). *Les hauts revenus en France au 20eme siècle—Inégalités et redistributions, 1901–1998.* Paris: Editions Grasset.

—— (2003). 'Income Inequality in France, 1901–1998', *Journal of Political Economy*, 111: 1004–42.

—— Saez, E. (2003). 'Income Inequality in the United States, 1913–1998', *Quarterly Journal of Economics*, 118: 1–39.

—— Postel-Vinay, G. and Rosenthal, J-L. (2004). 'Wealth Concentration in a Developing Economy: Paris and France, 1807–1994'. Mimeo EHESS and UCLA.

12

Long-Term Trends in Top Income Shares in Ireland

B. Nolan

12.1 INTRODUCTION

As earlier chapters have highlighted, there has been an upsurge of interest in rich countries in the incomes of those at the top of the income distribution. Evidence for some countries, notably the US and the UK, has fuelled a general perception that those at the top have done particularly well in the last quarter century or so, with the remuneration of top executives a source of particular comment. From an analytic point of view, a key contribution has been the use of data from income tax records to investigate these trends over the long term, notably Piketty (2001), Piketty and Saez (2003), and Atkinson (2005) for France, the US, and the UK respectively. This has encouraged others to exploit the potential of data from this source, and in that spirit this chapter uses this type of information to look for the first time at long-run trends in top income shares in Ireland from the 1920s up to the end of the twentieth century.

The serious problems in using and interpreting data from income tax records have been long recognized, as discussed in earlier chapters. What is reported will depend on how income is defined in the tax code, and both this and the tax unit may change over time. Income from different sources may well be treated differently, reported incomes are affected by tax avoidance in response to the way the tax code is framed, and people may not report honestly in order to evade tax—probably the single most important factor undermining confidence in the use of income tax data in some countries. These are issues that cannot be ignored, but on the other hand other sources of income data also have their problems and tax data have some important advantages, particularly in looking at top income shares. Household surveys for example are subject to response bias and mis-measurement of incomes, and they have particular problems in capturing the top of the income distribution. As in many other countries, for Ireland tax data are in any case 'the only game in town' for studying income shares in the long term since representative national household survey data only became available from the 1970s.

The chapter is structured as follows: Section 12.2 describes the information available for Ireland from income tax records; Section 12.3 details how the estimates of top income shares are derived from this information, and how the methodological issues that arise are addressed; Section 12.4 presents the key results, showing how the estimated shares have evolved over time; Section 12.5 discusses these trends, both in terms of their robustness from a measurement perspective and their substantive interpretation; Finally, Section 12.6 summarizes the conclusions and points to the many remaining gaps in our knowledge.

12.2 INCOME TAX DATA ON TOP INCOMES FOR IRELAND

Up until 1922, the entire island of Ireland formed part of the United Kingdom of Britain and Ireland. At that date, the island was divided into 'the Irish Free State', comprising 26 out of a total of 32 counties, and 'Northern Ireland', each with their own parliament but with the Free State in large measure independent of Britain. Its remaining tenuous links with Britain were broken in 1949 when the Republic of Ireland was formally established, but financially the state was in effect a separate unit from 1922. The first Annual Report of the Revenue Commissioners for the new state (which for convenience we will simply call 'Ireland' from here on) was published in 1924, for the financial year 1923–24—the tax year at that point, and for many years subsequently, ran from April to the following March. The material it presented included figures derived from the administration of what was then called super-tax, a special tax levied on incomes in excess of £2000 per annum.[1] (The currency of the new state remained linked one-for-one with Sterling for many years, up to the end of the 1970s.)

Super-tax became surtax at the end of the 1920s, levied on incomes in excess of £1500 per annum from the early 1930s, and similar figures in relation to surtax were presented in the Annual Reports of the Revenue Commissioners up until the mid-1950s. The figures given are the numbers assessed for super/surtax categorized by income range, and the total income assessed in each of those categories—to illustrate, Table 12.1 reproduces the figures published in relation to 1936–37. The relevant table was then dropped from the Annual Reports of the Revenue Commissioners (with the Reports from 1957–58 up to 1963–64 not presenting it). It was re-instated in the Annual Report from 1964–65 (at which stage surtax applied to incomes in excess of £3000), and then presented each year up to 1973–74, at which point surtax itself was phased out. The number of tax units covered by the published tables ranges from 1519 in 1923–24 to 7381 in 1954–55, 4897 in 1964–65 and 8675 in 1973–74.[2] Note that surtax was charged on income in the

[1] Note that it may be possible to derive estimates for the period before 1921–22 from tax statistics published by the United Kingdom authorities, but these would relate to the island of Ireland as a whole and not allow the series we present here to be extended.

[2] Note that most of the Annual Reports provide figures covering the previous five years, and the figures published for any year changed from one Report to the next as further information was processed, so we have used the last figures published for each year—for example, the 1944–45 figures are taken from the Report for the year ended March 1951.

Table 12.1 Surtax payers classified by income ranges, Ireland 1936–37

Class	Total number of assessments	Total incomes assessed £
Over £1,500 and not over £2,000	860	1,496,366
Over £2,000 and not over £3,000	772	1,844,250
Over £3,000 and not over £4,000	272	909,890
Over £4,000 and not over £5,000	140	610,993
Over £5,000 and not over £6,000	99	534,455
Over £6,000 and not over £8,000	87	589,141
Over £8,000 and not over £10,000	46	403,314
Over £10,000 and not over £20,000	45	627,742
Over £20,000	22	1,658,101
Total	2,343	8,674,352

Source: Fourteenth Annual Report of the Revenue Commissioners, Year ended 31 March 1937, Table 126, p. 177.

previous year up to the early 1960s, when introduction of PAYE meant that tax was charged on current rather than previous year's income (except for income from self-employment, which was taxed on a previous year basis right up to the 1990s).

These super-tax or surtax figures relate only to the very top of the income distribution, covering less than half of 1% on all tax units. In addition, however, some very valuable figures were collated and published in connection with the production of the first official national accounts figures for Ireland, covering much more of the income distribution and relating to the years 1938 and 1943 only. These were presented in the White Paper on National Income and Expenditure that contained the first official Irish national accounts estimates (Minister for Finance 1946). The estimation of national accounts aggregates relied primarily on the income approach, and for this purpose information available to the Revenue Commissioners was recognized as a key resource. This served as the basis for the estimation of aggregate earned income other than income from agriculture of persons earning more than £150 per year, and of all income from dividends and rent. Since the basic records were not centralized or mechanized, this involved work in each income tax district to extract figures from individual records. Crucially for present purposes, it was also decided that information on personal income classified by income range would be produced.[3]

The figures this produced for 1938 and 1943 are shown in Table 12.2. A number of features should be noted. The figures relate to income other than that from agriculture, forestry and fishing, and to those with (such) incomes over £150 per year. The figures for incomes over £1500 were derived from surtax statistics, while those in the £150–1500 range seem to have relied on income tax information and on regular and special statistical enquiries into wages in industry, with such enquiries also providing the basis for estimates of the aggregate income of

[3] The nature of this exercise has been discussed in a paper by Linehan and Lucey (2000). They note that Revenue staff had to return to individual assessments to produce these tabulations, that extensive use of overtime was needed, and that the Revenue found the exercise to be a very disruptive one and were reluctant to repeat it.

Table 12.2 Personal income classified by income ranges, Ireland 1938 and 1943

	1938	1943	1938	1943
	Number		Aggregate income £ million	
Not exceeding £150	Not known		52.7	69.1
Over £150 and not over £200	46,452	53,364	8.2	9.4
Over £200 and not over £250	38,504	49,778	8.7	11.1
Over £250 and not over £300	22,635	28,482	6.2	7.7
Over £300 and not over £400	20,536	24,364	7.1	8.4
Over £400 and not over £500	10,447	12,272	4.6	5.4
Over £500 and not over £750	12,034	15,255	7.2	9.2
Over £750 and not over £1,000	4,318	5,659	3.7	4.8
Over £1,000 and not over £1,500	3,165	4,486	3.8	5.4
Over £1,500 and not over £2,000	1,170	1,840	2.0	3.2
Over £2,000 and not over £200	1,751	2,692	6.1	8.9
Over £10,000	79	109	1.8	1.7
Income from agriculture, forestry, and fishing			39.3	84.6
Total personal income			151.4	228.9

Source: *National Income and Expenditure, 1938–1944*, Minister for Finance 1946; table: 6, p. 18.

those below £150. The accompanying text and notes state that it was not possible to classify agricultural incomes by size, but that most such incomes were probably under £150 per year. A total of over 160,000 incomes are classified in the figures for 1938, at a time when the total number at work was about 1.2 million. Only about 4,600 out of this total were in the surtax net, with incomes above £1500. So for these two years and these two only, over the period from 1922 to 1973 where we otherwise have to rely on the surtax series, we will be able to estimate the shares of a much wider range of top income groups.

While the final published figures based on surtax relate to 1973–74, an entirely new series of figures was initiated in the Annual Report of the Revenue Commissioners for 1976, derived from the administration of general income tax (with which surtax had by then been integrated). The numbers covered were now very much larger, amounting to almost 750,000 tax units in the first set published, relating to 1974–75. These figures have been continued in subsequent years, with the amount of detail presented increasing in more recent years, notably since the late 1980s when the figures were hived off to a separate Statistical Report rather than the Annual Report itself. By 2000–01, the details presented took 18 tables (compared with the single table published for surtax in earlier years) and the number of tax units covered exceeded 1.7 million. Table 12.3 shows an example of the key figures for current purposes, relating to the year 2000. Unfortunately, the much wider coverage in the income tax statistics compared with those from surtax comes at a price when we are most interested in the very top. This is because the income range categories employed in presenting the income tax figures are much broader. In the last year that surtax figures were published, the top income range showing incomes over £10,000 per annum contained only about 1500 tax units. The same top income range

Table 12.3 Income tax payers classified by income ranges, Ireland 2000

Lower income IR£	Upper income IR£	Number of tax units	Total income IR£ m.
0	3,000	218,063	307.55
3,000	4,000	63,458	222.92
4,000	5,000	65,547	294.61
5,000	6,000	58,984	324.12
6,000	7,000	59,215	385.12
7,000	8,000	63,377	475.79
8,000	9,000	64,925	551.75
9,000	10,000	66,303	630.18
10,000	12,500	148,394	1666.19
12,500	15,000	132,676	1819.07
15,000	17,500	102,385	1659.09
17,500	20,000	85,418	1598.23
20,000	25,000	124,102	2773.45
25,000	30,000	89,947	2459.56
30,000	35,000	58,024	1874.35
35,000	40,000	37,645	1405.55
40,000	50,000	41,917	1860.96
50,000	60,000	20,273	1103.65
60,000	75,000	13,080	866.04
75,000	100,000	7,777	664.54
100,000	—	9,146	1779.011
Total		1,530,656	24721.75

Source: *Statistical Report of the Revenue Commissioners*, year ended 31 December 2002: table IDS8, p. 81.

was used initially when the income tax statistics were introduced, but this has not kept pace with incomes subsequently so that by 2000 a total of over 11,000 tax units were in the top category. As we shall see, this constrains our ability to distinguish income groups at the very top.

The definition of income used in these statistics should be noted. In the figures based on income tax from the mid-1970s, the income concept on which tax units are categorized is referred to as 'total income'. This is the total income of taxpayers from all sources 'as estimated in accordance with the provisions of the Income Tax Acts'. It is thus net of such items as capital allowances, allowable interest paid, losses, allowable expenses, retirement annuities, and superannuation contributions. In more recent years, as well as 'total income', figures have also been published using a concept referred to as 'gross income', which includes all those items except superannuation contributions. These are available for the years from 1989–90 onwards (commencing in the Statistical Report for 1991); for consistency with the figures available up to that date we focus most of our attention here on 'total income', though we look below at whether it makes any difference if 'gross income' is used instead. The definition underlying the surtax statistics is less clear but seems likely to be similar to 'total income'. (Since the figures produced for 1938 and 1943 in the national accounts exercise rely on income tax and surtax for the top of the distribution, the income concept employed there seems also to be similar.)

12.3 USING IRISH INCOME TAX DATA TO ESTIMATE TOP INCOME SHARES

We now describe how this information is used to produce estimates of top income shares for Ireland from 1922 to 2000. To do so we must tackle the methodological issues discussed in Chapter 2:

1. In terms of recipients the tax data cover only those with incomes over a threshold or likely to have some tax liability, so we need to derive control totals for the total number of tax units in the population; we must then use these to convert the number of tax units in different income ranges in the tax data into percentages of all income recipients in the population;
2. The incomes reported in the tax data will only be a sub-set of total income accruing to households, again because some income recipients are not covered but also not all income accruing to those in the tax data may necessarily be covered; so we need to derive control totals for total income, and then use these to convert the income accruing to those in different ranges in the tax data into percentages of total income; and finally,
3. We need to interpolate/extrapolate to arrive at the shares for the specific groups of interest, for example the top 1%.

Focusing first on the total number of income recipients, in the Irish case the unit of tax for surtax and income tax purposes throughout most of the period was the single adult or married couple with dependent children if any. From the 1980s married persons could submit separate returns if they so wished (though their total tax liability would not be affected), but only a relatively small number do so. We treat the single adult or married couple with dependent children as the unit throughout for the purpose of our estimates, and thus require a control total for the aggregate number of such units in the population as a whole (rather than the total appearing in the tax statistics).

We can derive this directly for each year in which there was a Census of Population, by taking the total number of adults (aged 18 or over) and subtracting the total number of married women. With the Census carried out only every five or ten years, we then have to interpolate to produce figures for intercensal years. We do so by taking the total number of tax units for each Census year and simply using linear interpolation to arrive at figures for the other years.[4] The number of tax units in each year which this produces is shown in Table 12.4A.

To estimate shares in total income we also need a control total for aggregate income. As discussed in earlier chapters one way to do so is to estimate the income of those not covered in the tax statistics, coming as close as possible to the

[4] There was no Census of Population between 1911 and 1926, so to derive the number of tax units for 1922–25 inclusive we assume the year-to-year change was the same as that between the Census of 1926 and that of 1936.

Table 12.4A Control totals for number of tax units, Ireland 1922–2000

Year	Total tax units	Year	Total tax units
1922	1,494,898	1961	1,317,780
1923	1,499,323	1962	1,320,531
1924	1,503,748	1963	1,323,282
1925	1,508,173	1964	1,326,032
1926	1,512,598	1965	1,328,783
1927	1,517,023	1966	1,331,534
1928	1,521,448	1967	1,336,702
1929	1,525,873	1968	1,341,869
1930	1,530,298	1969	1,347,037
1931	1,534,723	1970	1,352,204
1932	1,539,147	1971	1,357,372
1933	1,543,572	1972	1,377,099
1934	1,547,997	1973	1,396,825
1935	1,552,422	1974	1,416,552
1936	1,556,847	1975	1,436,279
1937	1,553,822	1976	1,456,005
1938	1,550,797	1977	1,475,732
1939	1,547,773	1978	1,495,458
1940	1,544,748	1979	1,515,185
1941	1,541,723	1980	1,554,631
1942	1,538,698	1981	1,594,077
1943	1,535,673	1982	1,606,670
1944	1,532,649	1983	1,619,264
1945	1,529,624	1984	1,631,857
1946	1,526,599	1985	1,644,451
1947	1,519,608	1986	1,657,044
1948	1,512,617	1987	1,668,307
1949	1,505,625	1988	1,679,570
1950	1,498,634	1989	1,690,834
1951	1,491,643	1990	1,702,097
1952	1,474,257	1991	1,713,360
1953	1,456,870	1992	1,745,193
1954	1,439,484	1993	1,777,026
1955	1,422,098	1994	1,808,860
1956	1,404,712	1995	1,840,693
1957	1,387,325	1996	1,872,526
1958	1,369,939	1997	1,923,468
1959	1,352,553	1998	1,974,411
1960	1,335,166	1999	2,025,353
		2000	2,076,295

Source: Tax units estimated from Census of Population as described in text.

same definition of income, and add this to the reported incomes of those who are covered. While this would have some attractions for recent years when most of the population is within the tax net, it would be a very different proposition for 50 or 60 years ago when only a small minority was covered. The alternative is to take aggregate personal sector income as estimated in the national accounts, and subtract certain elements in order to align it more closely with incomes as they would be reported in the tax statistics. There are significant differences in the definition and coverage of income in the national accounts versus income tax statistics, most obviously in that national accounts personal sector income includes not only individuals but also non-profit institutions such as charities and life assurance funds. In addition, some national accounts income attributable to households is not included in the tax base, such as in the Irish case employers' social security contributions and imputed rent of owner-occupiers. The national accounts figures are not independent of the income tax ones, since the latter are one of the sources used in deriving the national accounts estimates in the first place, but reconciling the two is often difficult. This is certainly the case for Ireland, where the National Accounts do not disaggregate personal sector income into household and non-household components even for the most recent years.

A particularly important consideration in the current context is producing figures for Ireland that, insofar as possible, are reasonably comparable with the figures presented for other countries in the other chapters of this volume. We therefore seek to follow the approach adopted in producing estimates for the US and Canada (Chapters 5 and 6). Where available, we take aggregate income of the personal sector, and subtract transfers paid by the state to households, and social insurance contributions paid by employers. We then take 80% of that figure, to take account of other elements of personal sector income not included in incomes returned for tax, and use this as control total for income in deriving top income shares. This control total for each year is shown in Table 12.4B.

This procedure is straightforward over the years for which official national accounts estimates are available for Ireland. This is the case for years from 1938 onwards (though some approximation is required to derive the required control total for the years 1939–43). However, prior to 1938 no official national income data were produced, and thus no official series on national income, much less personal sector income, exists. Estimates of national income for certain years from 1926 to 1938 were produced in the late 1930s by Duncan (1939, 1940); while these have been criticized by subsequent scholars (see Kennedy et al. 1988; O'Rourke 1995), no alternative series has been produced. For each of the years 1922–37 we therefore had to first estimate national income, by amending Duncan's estimates in the light of subsequent studies and then interpolating the years he did not cover. We then derive from those national income figures estimates of total personal sector income and then of the lower control total we are seeking for current purposes. The figures for 1922–37 shown in Table 12.4B are estimated in this manner, as described in more detail in Appendix 12B. They clearly have to be taken as rough approximations, without placing much confidence in the pattern from year to year, but do allow us to push back the series another 15 years and get some sense of what the level of top income shares might have been in the 1920s.

With the tax data showing numbers of taxpayers classified by income range and their total income, we then use the control totals for tax units and income to convert these into shares, of all tax units and of total income respectively.[5] The

[5] In doing so we take into account the fact that the surtax figures for the 1920s, 1930s, 1940s, and 1950s actually relate to incomes in the previous year.

Table 12.4B Control totals for income, Ireland 1922–2000

	Aggregate personal sector income £/IR £ m.	Income control total (80% of personal sector income minus transfers and employers' social insurance) £/IR £ m
1922	146.50	116.00
1923	147.00	116.42
1924	148.00	117.22
1925	148.50	117.61
1926	149.60	118.48
1927	151.00	119.59
1928	152.50	120.78
1929	153.76	121.78
1930	146.00	115.63
1931	133.37	105.63
1932	129.00	102.17
1933	125.52	99.41
1934	132.00	104.54
1935	138.00	109.30
1936	145.92	115.57
1937	152.00	120.38
1938	165.70	122.72
1939	175.00	129.68
1940	192.00	143.12
1941	207.00	154.56
1942	230.00	172.80
1943	253.00	190.80
1944	263.60	200.12
1945	286.00	217.19
1946	297.70	226.41
1947	308.10	233.00
1948	326.70	246.68
1949	340.40	253.61
1950	356.50	267.25
1951	387.70	290.26
1952	417.50	305.70
1953	442.60	327.68
1954	445.40	329.44
1955	470.80	348.80
1956	473.90	349.44
1957	495.40	363.92
1958	501.90	369.28
1959	533.40	393.68
1960	602.87	431.62
1961	653.82	468.92
1962	707.47	508.77
1963	746.35	535.15
1964	853.73	613.63
1965	905.24	648.18
1966	965.64	687.58
1967	1,034.27	732.01

(contd.)

Table 12.4B (*contd.*)

	Aggregate personal sector income £m.	Income control total (80% of personal sector transfers employers' social insurance) £m
1968	1,169.78	821.53
1969	1,326.57	926.72
1970	1,528.01	1061.78
1971	1,761.67	1221.71
1972	2,118.58	1474.54
1973	2,600.50	1799.30
1974	3,057.95	2064.27
1975	3,987.07	2649.90
1976	4,718.69	3115.98
1977	5,627.76	3742.94
1978	6,647.60	4445.68
1979	7,812.30	5220.98
1980	9,495.08	6260.72
1981	11,709.38	7648.13
1982	13,125.84	8256.13
1983	14,477.43	9024.18
1984	16,024.35	9985.49
1985	17,081.60	10578.02
1986	18,241.42	11251.02
1987	19,421.66	12027.68
1988	20,698.32	12930.34
1989	22,204.71	14133.70
1990	23,528.68	15013.66
1991	24,932.83	15723.66
1992	26,303.53	16578.91
1993	28,644.34	18117.64
1994	29,679.42	18696.83
1995	31,954.14	20105.18
1996	34,436.87	21782.64
1997	38,055.83	24140.37
1998	42,718.51	27406.17
1999	48,029.29	31092.15
2000	54,266.96	35382.31

Source: Personal sector income, transfers and employers social insurance contributions from *National Income and Expenditure*, various issues, for 1938 and from 1944 onwards; for earlier years see text and Appendix 1.

numbers in a particular income range will vary from one year to the next, and the boundaries of those ranges will also change over time, which means that interpolation then has to be used in order to arrive at estimates of income shares for a specific group such as the top 1% or 10%. The standard practice in analysis focusing on the top of the income distribution, as discussed in earlier chapters (see Appendix 5C), has been to assume that the distribution is Pareto in form, and here we interpolate within closed ranges making that assumption. (An alternative approach is based on placing upper and lower bounds on the Lorenz curve, as discussed in Atkinson 2005 and Chapter 2 this volume.)

Ideally, we would like to be able to produce estimates for the top 10%, top 1%, top 0.5%, and top 0.1% of tax units, on which recent studies and the contributions to this volume have focused where possible. It turns out that, given the nature of the published tax data, we are only able to do so reliably for the two years 1938 and 1943, covered by the special exercise associated with the first Irish national accounts. For the years before that and from 1944 to 1973 where we have to rely on surtax data, only the very top shares can be estimated—the top 0.1% and occasionally the top 0.5%—because so few tax units were covered by those statistics. For the later years from 1975 when we rely on data from the income tax statistics, on the other hand, we can estimate the share of the top 10%, top 1%, and often the top 0.5%, but the open-ended income range at the top generally contains much more than 0.1% of all tax units. One can extrapolate into the open range, again assuming a Pareto distribution, and this is done by, for example, Piketty (2001, 2003) and Piketty and Saez (2003). Here we do so to produce estimates for the share of the top 0.5% for several years in the 1990s when the open-ended range in the published statistics contained marginally more than 0.5%, and also to estimate the share of the top 1% for most of the period from 1975 to 1989. We do not do so when the open-ended range contains a group much larger than the one of interest—for example, we do not extrapolate to arrive at an estimate for the share of the top 0.1% when we have already had to do so to estimate the share of the top 0.5%.

12.4 ESTIMATES OF TOP INCOME SHARES FOR IRELAND

Having described the data and methods employed, we now present our estimates of top income shares for Ireland from 1922 to 2000, shown in Table 12.5. Where available, estimates of the share going to the top 10%, top 1%, top 0.5%, and top

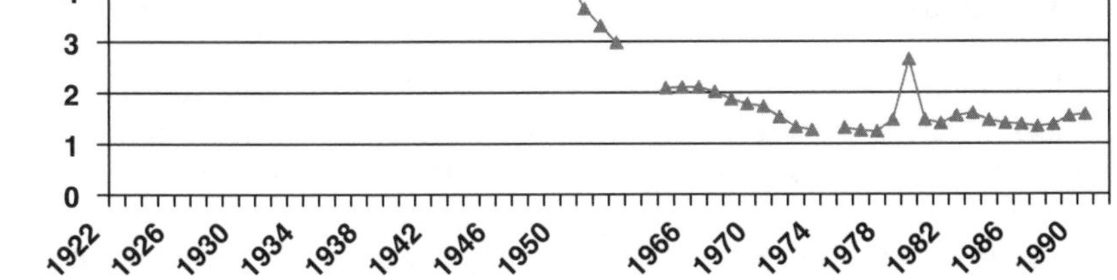

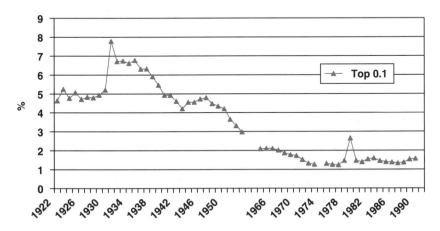

Figure 12.1 Share of top 0.1% in total income Ireland, 1922–90

Source: Table 12.5.

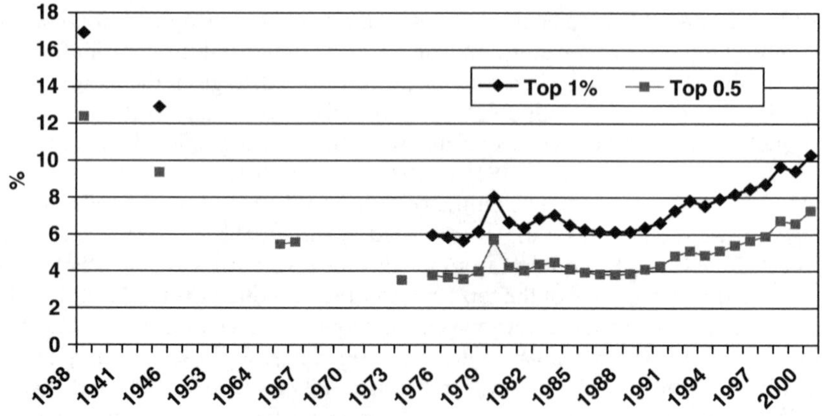

Figure 12.2 Shares of top 1% and top 0.5% in total income, Ireland 1938–2000

Source: Table 12.5.

0.1% are presented. Figure 12.1 graphs the share of the top 0.1% from 1922 to 1990, while Figure 12.2 graphs the shares of the top 0.5% and top 1% from 1938 to 2000—the different time-periods reflecting their differing availability.

Over the period from 1922 all the way up to 1973, since we have to rely in most years on the sur-tax figures we can estimate only the share going to the very top, the top 0.1%. The share of this small group is estimated to have been 4.6% in 1922. We then see it fluctuating between that figure and about 5% through the 1920s. This share rose sharply in the early 1930s, peaking at 7.8% in 1931 and staying well over 6% until 1938–39 when it fell sharply. It was below 5% by the early 1940s, showed some very modest increase from 1944 to 1946–47, and subsequently fell substantially to reach about 3% by the early/mid-1950s. With a gap in the data series until 1964 we see it at about 2% by that date, continuing to fall until the early 1970s when it was as low as 1.3%. We then have estimates for the top 0.1% derived from the income tax statistics until 1990, albeit with extrapolation into the open range often required. We see that the long-term decline in the share of this group did not continue, with a modest increase to about 1.6% by 1990 (and a peak in 1979 when it hit 2.6% but then fell back immediately).

Throughout the entire period from 1922 to 1973 we can produce estimates for broader income groups at the top only for 1938 and 1943, because of the special exercise carried out in connection with the first national accounts. We see from Table 11.5 that in 1938 these show almost half of the income control total going to the top 10% of tax units. About 17% was going to the top 1%, while the top 0.5% is estimated to have had about 10%. (The estimate for the share of the top 0.1% derived from this source is very close to that derived from the sur-tax statistics, which is not surprising since those statistics were the key source for this part of

Table 12.5 Shares of top income groups, Ireland 1922–2000

	Income groups			
	Top 10%	Top 1%	Top 0.5%	Top 0.1%
	% of total income			
1922				4.64
1923				5.25
1924				4.77
1925				5.07
1926				4.72
1927				4.83
1928				4.80
1929				4.94
1930				5.21
1931				7.78
1932				6.71
1933				6.74
1934				6.61
1935				6.77
1936				6.31
1937				6.32
1938				5.91
1938b	47.61	16.93	12.38	5.95
1939				5.46
1940				4.93
1941				4.93
1942				4.61
1943				4.21
1943b	35.68	12.92	9.36	4.00
1944				4.56
1945				4.56
1946				4.73
1947				4.80
1948				4.48
1949				4.35
1950				4.21
1951				3.65
1952				3.31
1953				2.98
1954				
1955				
1956				
1957				
1958				
1959				
1960				
1961				
1962				
1963				
1964				2.09
1965			5.46	2.11

(*contd.*)

Table 12.5 (*contd.*)

	Income groups			
	Top 10%	Top 1%	Top 0.5%	Top 0.1%
1966			5.57	2.11
1967				2.02
1968				1.87
1969				1.78
1970				1.73
1971				1.52
1972				1.33
1973			3.51	1.27
1974				
1975	28.62	5.96	3.76	1.31*
1976	27.96	5.83	3.66	1.26
1977	27.29	5.64	3.56	1.24*
1978	28.20	6.16	3.98	1.47*
1979	31.32	8.03	5.68	2.65*
1980	31.50	6.65	4.21	1.47*
1981	30.85	6.37	4.02	1.40
1982	32.57	6.87	4.36	1.55*
1983	33.29	7.05	4.48	1.60*
1984	31.57	6.50	4.10	1.46*
1985	31.28	6.27	3.93	1.40*
1986	31.03	6.15	3.83	1.38
1987	31.16	6.14	3.81	1.34*
1988	30.51	6.15	3.85	1.37*
1989	30.52	6.38	4.10	1.54*
1990	31.05	6.64	4.28	1.57*
1991	32.46	7.30	4.82*	
1992	34.00	7.83	5.09*	
1993	33.39	7.55	4.85*	
1994	34.84	7.93	5.10*	
1995	35.33	8.19	5.39	
1996	35.55	8.48	5.65	
1997	35.51	8.73	5.90	
1998	35.89	9.67	6.75	
1999	34.93	9.44	6.60	
2000	36.07	10.30	7.28*	

Note: * indicates based on extrapolation into top open income category in published statistics.
Sources: Derived from: (1) Income control totals from Table 12.4B; (2) Number of tax units control totals from Table 12.4A; (3) Distribution of tax units by total income range from: (a) 1922–53 and 1964–73 *Surtax Statistics*; 1938b and 1943b from Table 12.2. (b) 1975–2000 *Income Tax Statistics*. Full details on these sources are given in the Appendices.

the distribution in the national accounts exercise.) By 1943, this had changed quite markedly. The share of the top 10% was down to 36%, that of the top 1% was down to 13%, and the share of the top 0.5% had also declined by 4 percentage points—with the top 0.1% also having fallen sharply over this period. This period, for which we happen to have a broader distributional picture, is obviously a very particular one with 1943 being in the middle of the Second World War, which although Ireland remained neutral still had very a substantial economic impact—issues to which we return in the next section.

After 1943, apart from the top 0.1% the sur-tax figures allow us to estimate shares for the top 0.5% only for a few years in the mid-1960s and for 1973. The pattern is once again a very marked decline from 1943, from a share of over 9% down to about 3.5% by 1973. The figures available for the mid-1960s suggest that this share had reached about 5.5% by that point, once again suggesting that the decline took place throughout the period.

Once the income tax figures become available, we then have estimates from the mid-1970s all the way to 2000 for the shares of the top 10%, top 1% and top 0.5%.[6] Compared with 1943, by 1975 the share of the top 1% had fallen from 13% to 6%, consistent with the decline in the shares of the top 0.5% and 0.1%. The share of the top 10% had also fallen, though much more modestly in proportionate terms, from 36% to 29%.

From 1975 up to 1990 the share of the top 0.5% was about 3.5–4.5% and that of the top 1% about 6–7% of total income, with the exception of 1979 when (like the top 0.1%) they saw a once-off jump. The share of the top 10% fluctuated in the 28–33% range. In the 1990s, however, there was a substantial increase in the shares of the top 0.5%, top 1%, and top 10%. By 2000 the share of the top 0.5% had risen to over 7%; that of the top 1% had risen to over 10%; and the share of the top 10% was up to 36%. In proportionate terms this represents a much sharper rise the higher one goes up the distribution, with the percentage increase from 1990 to 2000 being 16% for the top 10%, 55% for the top 1%, and 70% for the top 0.5%.

So the figures we have derived from published tax statistics on top income shares for Ireland show some quite dramatic trends over the period from the foundation of the State: we explore these further in the next section.

12.5 INTERPRETATION AND RELIABILITY

Having described the trends in top income shares implied by Irish tax data, we now come to the questions of interpretation and reliability. What causal forces could have produced such dramatic changes in top income shares over time? Can we in fact believe that these changes actually took place, or does the nature of the underlying data fatally undermine our confidence in the measured trends as a reflection of reality?

The studies for other countries presented in this volume of course pay considerable attention to these fundamental issues. In doing so they have the advantage, compared with Ireland, of having additional data on the composition of top

[6] For the top 0.5% extrapolation into the open range was required for some years in the 1990s and for 2000.

incomes by source and how that evolved over time, going back to the first half of the twentieth century. Piketty (Chapter 3, this volume) is thus able to show in the French case that the very pronounced fall in top income shares up to the late 1940s reflected a fall in income from capital, in particular in the form of dividends, and links these to shocks in the form of inflation, bankruptcies and physical destruction. Similarly Piketty and Saez (Chapter 5, this volume) are able to show that in the US shocks to capital incomes during the depression and the Second World War played the major role in the sharp fall in the share of top income groups. Across the US, Canada, France, and the UK the similarity in the scale of the fall in top income shares between about 1914 and mid-century is indeed striking. However the exact timing of that fall differs across these countries, and one is left searching for specific shocks operating in varying ways during the World Wars and the intervening Great Depression but leading to a similar overall trend.

Adding Ireland as an observation adds to the complexity. After stability in the 1920s we see a substantial rise in the share of income going to the very top in the early to mid-1930s, as the Depression hit. This was followed by a decline in top income shares from the late 1930s to the mid-1940s, similar to that in the other countries listed above. But Ireland differs from those countries in many respects. Ireland was a predominantly agricultural country at the time, unlike the industrial leaders others have studied, and was not a participant in the Second World War. There was no nationalization, and Ireland was less affected by the Depression of the 1930s than countries relying more heavily on industry, trade and finance—though it was deeply affected by the 'Economic War' with Britain during the 1930s, when exports of Irish agricultural output to Britain were very severely restricted and subject to duties, and when retaliatory duties were placed on imports from Britain.[7] In addition, the Irish government pursued a more broadly based protectionist strategy from the early 1930s, via a range of tariffs and quotas. The result was a squeeze on farm incomes but a rapid increase in domestic industrial production during the period from 1932 to 1938.[8] This may have contributed to the sharp increase in the share of income going to the top 0.1%, but that is highly speculative—and the level of uncertainty about the level of national income and how it evolved over that period has to be emphasized once again.

The comparison between 1938 and 1943 can be made with somewhat greater confidence, since official national income figures were produced and we can go beyond the share of the top 0.1%. The sharp fall in top income shares observed between these two years could perhaps be associated with the operation of wage and price controls and unavailability of raw materials during the Second World War, both of which may well have reduced profits (see, e.g. O'Grada 1997).

[7] This stemmed from a dispute about annuity payments in relation to loans made for land purchase, which the Irish government stopped paying to Britain when the government changed in 1932.

[8] See for example Kennedy et al. 1988: chap. 2 and O'Rourke 1995.

Unfortunately, a detailed decomposition of top incomes by source is not possible with the data available for Ireland for that period. However, the role of income from agriculture versus other incomes bears some consideration. The figures on incomes by income range for 1938 and 1943 produced in the course of the first national accounts exercise did not in fact allocate income from agriculture across the income categories—total income from agriculture is simply given separately. The national accounts exercise states that 'It has not been possible to classify agricultural incomes by size . . . In any case, most personal incomes from agriculture alone, even at the present time of comparative prosperity, are probably in the under £150 class' (Minister for Finance 1946: p. 20). A footnote to the table does state however that 'an appreciable number of farmers (if only a minute proportion of the large total) are in the "over £150" income class' (Minister for Finance 1946: table 6, p. 18, n. a). Since £150 is close to the bottom cut-off for the top decile at that time, it is worth trying to make some assessment of the sensitivity of the results to alternative assumptions about incomes from agriculture at the top.

About half the workforce was in agriculture at the time, and while 26% of total personal income came from agriculture in 1938 this had risen to 37% by 1943. It is interesting first to exclude agricultural income from the income control total and recalculate the shares going to top groups in non-agricultural income instead. Shares of top income groups in non-agricultural income are of course higher in both years, but also more stable: the share of the top 1%, for example, falls from 23%% to 20.5%, compared with the decline from 17% to 13% seen in Table 12.5. This greater stability is because agricultural income doubled between 1938 and 1943, with none of that increase accruing to the top income groups in Table 12.5 but with the income control total being affected. So the rise in agricultural income accounts for about half the measured reduction in our estimates of top income shares, which may be misleading if some agricultural income does in fact accrue to the top of the distribution.

It is clearly unsatisfactory to have to focus on non-agricultural incomes, and it would be preferable to include them both in the control total and in the incomes of those at the top. Suppose we assume that 10% of farmers and 25% of farm income were actually in the income categories over £150—which is probably too high—and that they were distributed across those income categories in the same way as the non-agricultural tax cases and income shown in Table 12.2. This has very little impact on the estimated top income shares for 1938, with for example that of the top 1% increasing only from 17% to 17.3%. In 1943 the impact is slightly greater because farm incomes were so much higher, with the share of the top 1% now rising from 13% to 13.6%. As a consequence, the fall in the top income shares between 1938 and 1943 is slightly less, but the difference is marginal. So including agricultural incomes would mean that the decline in top income shares between 1938 and 1943 was slightly less than shown in Table 12.5 but a substantial decline in top income shares is still seen over the period. Agricultural incomes were only brought comprehensively into the tax net from the 1970s, but would have been on a downward trend as a proportion of total income through the 1950s and 1960s.

From 1943 to the early 1970s we have only fragmentary information but the share of the top 0.1% is seen to decline substantially, followed by a period of stability in this and other top income shares up until the late 1980s/early 1990s. One of the features highlighted by Piketty for other countries during this period, namely sustained high marginal income tax rates from mid-century, certainly does apply to the Irish case. The top marginal income tax rate in the Irish case was 75–80% from the 1930s up to the mid-1970s, then came down to 60%. What is striking in the Irish case is that top income shares do not appear responsive to dramatically different conditions in terms of economic activity. The Irish economy was stagnant in the 1950s, with mass emigration, followed by an opening up to external trade and investment in the 1960s, buoyant economic growth following EEC membership in 1973, a fiscal crisis and slow growth for much of the 1980s, followed by a faltering recovery in the late 1980s.

However the decade of the 1990s saw a marked increase in top income shares as reflected in the income tax statistics, and certainly from the mid-1990s this was in a rapidly changing economic context, with economic growth reaching unprecedented levels in the era of the Celtic Tiger. (The top marginal income tax rate had also come down further, reaching 42% in 2001.) Over this period there is some information available with the published statistics on the composition of top incomes, and also figures based on what the Revenue Commissioners refer to as 'Gross Income' as well as the 'Total Income' figures which were the only ones published for earlier periods and on which we base all our estimates in Table 12.5. While 'total' income is after employee superannuation contributions have been deducted, gross income includes those contributions and is a more comprehensive measure (though still net of for example capital allowances, losses, interest paid and allowable expenses). So we look in Table 12.6 at top income shares estimated from gross income statistics from 1989–90 on (with the income control totals unchanged), to see if that makes any difference to levels or trends when compared with the estimates based on 'total income' presented earlier in Table 12.5. We see that top income shares in gross income are higher, with for example in 1989 the top 1% having 6.4% with total income but 7.2% with gross income. By the end of the decade the gap had widened, with the top 1% having 10.3% with total income but almost 12% with gross income. So the trend over the 1990s is similar with each income measure but the increase in top income shares is more pronounced when the categorization based on 'gross income' is employed.

Turning then to the composition of top incomes, information was published during this period on the breakdown by income range of specific types of taxpayer and on their total income by range.[9] The way in which these groups are defined makes an overall picture of income composition quite difficult to disentangle, because they do not represent an exhaustive and exclusive set—there are overlaps between the groups, with for example 'proprietary directors' being included with the self-employed in some tables but distributed among Schedule D and Schedule E in others. However, as explained in Appendix 12C it is possible to derive a useful

[9] This is available both for 'Gross income' and 'Total income'; here we focus on gross income.

Table 12.6 Top income shares estimated from 'gross incomes', Ireland 1989/90–2000

	Income groups		
	Top 10%	Top 1%	Top 0.5%
1989	33.15	7.15	4.67
1990	34.12	7.59	4.95*
1991	35.53	8.27	5.46*
1992	37.12	8.74	5.70*
1993	36.50	8.48*	
1994	37.60	8.82*	
1995	37.81	9.17	6.14*
1996	37.83	9.58	6.54
1997	38.00	10.14	7.06
1998	38.49	11.18	8.00*
1999	37.75	11.06	7.91
2000	38.79	11.82	8.50*

Source: See Appendix 12A; * = extrapolated into open range.

categorization with some effort, arriving at a three-way breakdown into: (1) self-employed including proprietary directors; (2) those with mainly unearned income taxed under Schedule D; and (3) those with mainly earned income taxed by PAYE under Schedule E. In each case we can either read off or derive the numbers in each income range and their total income from the published figures. Table 12.7 shows the importance of each group in the top, open-ended income category in 1989–90 vs. 2000. The proportion of all the cases in the tax statistics falling into the top range was not of course identical in the two years but it turns out to be quite close at 0.6% vs. 0.8%, so a direct comparison of composition is illuminating.

We see that the self-employed (including proprietary directors) accounted for 54% of those in the top income category in 1989–90, when they had average incomes very similar to the overall mean for that category and thus also accounted for about 54% of the total income accruing to it. Those relying mainly on unearned income were a much smaller group, accounting for only 10% of the top category, but had very much higher incomes on average and thus accounted for 18% of the top group's income. Those with earned incomes paying PAYE accounted for 36% of the cases in the top category but had mean incomes below the other two groups and thus had only 28% of the top category's income.

By 2000, the picture was rather different. We see that the self-employed now account for a substantially higher proportion, 69%, of the cases in the top income category. In addition, their average income is now above the overall average for the top category, so they have even more of the total income at almost three-quarters. By contrast, unearned income is much less important, accounting for less than 4% of the cases in the top income category and a similar share of its total income. PAYE payers have also declined in importance, accounting for less than one-quarter of the income of the top group. So the dramatic increase in the measured share of the top income groups in Ireland over the 1990s was

Table 12.7 Composition of top incomes, Ireland 1989/90 and 2000

	Income groups			
	Self-employed including proprietary directors	Mainly unearned income under Schedule D	Mainly PAYE under Schedule E	All in top category
1989–90: Top income category > £50,000				
% of top income category cases	53.7%	10.0%	36.3%	100% (0.6% of all cases in tax statistics)
Average income	£86,733	£156,387	£65,575	£86,011
% of total income of top category	54.2%	18.2%%	27.7%	100% (5.0% of total income in tax statistics)
2000: Top income category > €150,000				
% of top income category cases	69.3%	3.6%	27.1%	100% (0.8% of all cases in tax statistics
Average income	€335,216	€345,251	€270,660	€318,058
% of total income of top category	73.0%	3.9%	23.1%	100% (10% of total income in tax statistics)

Source: See Appendix 12C.

accompanied by a substantial shift in its composition. The link between these patterns in the income tax statistics and macroeconomic developments including changes in factor shares would clearly merit detailed investigation.

However, while the search for plausible causal explanations and supporting evidence is a priority, one cannot duck the obvious issue in relation to these findings, for Ireland as elsewhere. Can we believe data from tax records as a broadly accurate reflection of reality, or are they so polluted by attempts by the wealthy to evade and avoid tax that they cannot be relied on? This has of course not been ignored in other studies. Piketty (Chapter 3, this volume) for example goes to some length to offer reassurance based on in-depth analysis of the data for France, arguing that tax evasion by the rich is if anything likely to have been more pronounced in earlier years. Similarly Piketty and Saez look in depth at the US data (Chapter 5, this volume), and seek to show that the measurement and taxation of capital gains is not the driving force behind the observed trends. However, this has to be a key challenge for anyone using this source. The similarity in trend across countries offers some comfort here, though in more recent times it is possible that there has been an increasing capacity to move wealth offshore shared across the countries studied. In the Irish case, one would certainly be concerned that changes in the reporting of top incomes to the tax authorities may have played a significant role in the last decade as tax administration has tightened significantly. There have been a variety of high profile public investigations into tax evasion, there has been a sequence of tax amnesties followed by more stringent investigation and application of the tax code. As a result it is commonly believed that reporting behaviour has changed since the late 1980s, though this is by its nature hard to assess. In addition, lower tax rates combined with the availability of various tax avoidance schemes also reduce the incentive to evade—indeed, some recent data from the Revenue Commissioners show that some of the very top income tax filers legitimately paid zero income tax.

It may be useful to employ the 'shares within shares' approach, for example what share of the income of the top 10% goes to the top 1% or what share of the top 1% goes to the top 0.1%, since that will not be affected by the overall control total for income. We can only do this for 1938, 1943, and the years from 1975

Table 12.8 Share of top income groups in top incomes, Ireland 1938–2000

	Share of top 1% as percentage of share of top 10%	Share of top 0.5% as percentage of share of top 1%	Share of top 0.1% as percentage of share of top 1%	Share of top 0.1% as percentage of share of top 0.5%
1938	35.56	73.10	35.14	49.05
1943	36.21	72.26	30.93	42.80
1975	20.82	63.08	21.97	34.83
1976	20.86	62.77	21.81	34.75
1977	20.65	63.17	22.14	35.06
1978	21.84	64.60	23.79	36.83
1979	25.64	70.70	32.98	46.64
1980	21.11	63.27	22.12	34.97
1981	20.63	63.08	21.89	34.70
1982	21.11	63.46	22.43	35.35
1983	21.18	63.56	22.76	35.80
1984	20.59	63.05	22.47	35.64
1985	20.06	62.60	22.39	35.77
1986	20.00	62.00	22.00	35.50
1987	19.71	62.00	21.82	35.20
1988	20.14	62.72	22.40	35.71
1989	20.89	64.37	24.14	37.51
1990	21.38	64.53	23.61	36.59
1991	22.48	66.08		
1992	23.01	65.08		
1993	22.61	64.28		
1994	22.76	64.27		
1995	23.19	65.80		
1996	23.86	66.58		
1997	24.60	67.60		
1998	26.96	69.79		
1999	27.03	69.87		
2000	28.56	70.68		

onwards. Table 12.8 shows that the share of the top 1% or top 0.5% in the total accruing to the top 10% was much higher in the 1930s and 1940s than in 1975. Stability in these shares is then seen until 1989, except for the outlier year of 1979. From 1990 these 'shares within shares' rose, particularly from the mid-1990s, so that the top 1% accounted for 20% of the income of the top 10% at the start of the decade but for 29% by the end of it. The share of the top 0.1% can be tracked only up to 1990, which is most unfortunate given what happened after that date to the shares of the top 0.5% and top 1%, but it was broadly stable between 1975 and 1990 as a proportion of the income of the top 1% or top 0.5%.

12.6 CONCLUSIONS

This chapter has sought to exploit data from income tax records to track changes over time in the shares of top income groups in Ireland. Like the other contributions to this volume, the primary purpose has been to provide a new series on trends in income inequality at the top. Such estimates for Ireland are interesting not only domestically but also comparatively, since Ireland was a predominantly agricultural country in the 1920s when our estimates begin, with industrialization only picking up pace in the 1960s, and with convergence towards the levels of average income seen in the richer countries only coming about in the 1990s—and then very rapidly. Against this background it is very interesting to see top income shares apparently rising in the early 1930s, declining sharply from before the Second World War to the early 1970s, followed by a period of stability, and with a sharp up-turn in these shares in the 1990s. While trying to tease out the underlying factors at work in producing the measured trends, a priority also has to be investigating their reliability in terms of the reporting of incomes to the tax authorities. By its nature that is difficult to do, but this source of data is absolutely critical if we are to capture and understand long-term trends in top income shares.

APPENDIX 12A: SOURCES FOR INCOME TAX AND SURTAX DATA, IRELAND 1938–2000

The sources for the income tax data 1922–2000 are listed in Table 12A.1. The sources for the data on gross incomes 1989–2000 are listed in Table 12A.2.

APPENDIX 12B: NATIONAL INCOME IN THE 1920S AND 1930S

As explained in Section 12.2, official national accounts figures are available for Ireland only for years from 1938 onwards (though some approximation is

Table 12A.1 Source of income data used in deriving 'total' income shares, Ireland 1922–2000

Year	Source
1922	1st Annual Report of the Revenue Commissioners, Year ended 31 March 1924: table 87, p. 85
1923	2nd Annual Report of the Revenue Commissioners, Year ended 31 March 1925: table 99, p. 98
1924	3rd Annual Report of the Revenue Commissioners, Year ended 31 March 1926: table 94, p. 96
1925	4th Annual Report of the Revenue Commissioners, Year ended 31 March 1927: table 92, p. 95
1926	5th Annual Report of the Revenue Commissioners, Year ended 31 March 1928: table 92, p. 94
1927	6th Annual Report of the Revenue Commissioners, Year ended 31 March 1929: table 92, p. 100
1928	7th Annual Report of the Revenue Commissioners, Year ended 31 March 1931: table 93, p. 107
1929	8th Annual Report of the Revenue Commissioners, Year ended 31 March 1931: table 93, p. 107
1930	9th Annual Report of the Revenue Commissioners, Year ended 31 March 1932: table 98, p. 113
1931	10th Annual Report of the Revenue Commissioners, Year ended 31 March 1933: table 117, p. 141
1932	16th Annual Report of the Revenue Commissioners, Year ended 31 March 1939: table 124, p. 193
1933	17th Annual Report of the Revenue Commissioners, Year ended 31 March 1940: table 87, p. 144
1934	18th Annual Report of the Revenue Commissioners, Year ended 31 March 1941: table 82, p. 124
1935	19th Annual Report of the Revenue Commissioners, Year ended 31 March 1942: table 82, p. 127
1936	20th Annual Report of the Revenue Commissioners, Year ended 31 March 1943: table 82, p. 127
1937	21st Annual Report of the Revenue Commissioners, Year ended 31 March 1944: table 81, p. 119
1938(a)	22nd Annual Report of the Revenue Commissioners, Year ended 31 March 1945: table 81, p. 111
1938(b)	Minister for Finance (1946). National Income and Expenditure 1938–1944, Stationery Office: Dublin, Table 6, page 18
1939	23rd Annual Report of the Revenue Commissioners, Year ended 31 March 1946: table 81, p. 119
1940	24th Annual Report of the Revenue Commissioners, Year ended 31 March 1947: table 81, p. 123
1941	25th Annual Report of the Revenue Commissioners, Year ended 31 March 1948: table 77, p. 111
1942	26th Annual Report of the Revenue Commissioners, Year ended 31 March 1949: table 77, p. 109
1943(a)	27th Annual Report of the Revenue Commissioners, Year ended 31 March 1950: table 77, p. 111
1943(b)	Minister for Finance (1946). National Income and Expenditure 1938–1944, Stationery Office: Dublin, Table 6, p. 18
1944	28th Annual Report of the Revenue Commissioners, Year ended 31 March 1951: table 77, p. 118
1945	29th Annual Report of the Revenue Commissioners, Year ended 31 March 1952: table 77, p. 118

(contd.)

Table 12A.1 (*contd.*)

Year	Source
1946	30th Annual Report of the Revenue Commissioners, Year ended 31 March 1953: table 80, p. 119
1947	31th Annual Report of the Revenue Commissioners, Year ended 31 March 1954: table 80, p. 119
1948	32nd Annual Report of the Revenue Commissioners, Year ended 31 March 1955: table 79, p. 119
1949	33rd Annual Report of the Revenue Commissioners, Year ended 31 March 1956: table 79, p. 121
1950	33rd Annual Report of the Revenue Commissioners, Year ended 31 March 1956: table 79, p. 121
1951	33rd Annual Report of the Revenue Commissioners, Year ended 31 March 1956: table 79, p. 121
1952	33rd Annual Report of the Revenue Commissioners, Year ended 31 March 1956: table 79, p. 121
1953	33rd Annual Report of the Revenue Commissioners, Year ended 31 March 1956: table 79, p. 121
1954–63	Data on taxpayers by income range not published
1964	42th Annual Report of the Revenue Commissioners, Year ended 31 March 1965: table 73, p. 144
1965	43th Annual Report of the Revenue Commissioners, Year ended 31 March 1966: table 74, p. 151
1966	44th Annual Report of the Revenue Commissioners, Year ended 31 March 1967: table 75, p. 156
1967	45th Annual Report of the Revenue Commissioners, Year ended 31 March 1968: table 76, p. 152
1968	46th Annual Report of the Revenue Commissioners, Year ended 31 March 1969: table 76, p. 152
1969	47th Annual Report of the Revenue Commissioners, Year ended 31 March 1970: table 77, p. 152
1970	48th Annual Report of the Revenue Commissioners, Year ended 31 March 1971: table 85, pp. 164–5
1971	49th Annual Report of the Revenue Commissioners, Year ended 31 March 1972: table 85, pp. 164–5
1972	50th Annual Report of the Revenue Commissioners, Year ended 31 March 1973: table 85, pp. 162–3
1973	51st Annual Report of the Revenue Commissioners, Year ended 31 March 1974: table 82, pp. 162–3
1974	Data on taxpayers by income range not published
1975	54th Annual Report of the Revenue Commissioners, Year ended 31 December 1976: table 90, pp. 166–7
1976	55th Annual Report of the Revenue Commissioners, Year ended 31 December 1977: table 82, pp. 130–1
1977	56th Annual Report of the Revenue Commissioners, Year ended 31 December 1978: table 84, pp. 132–3
1978	57th Annual Report of the Revenue Commissioners, Year ended 31 December 1979: table 82, pp. 142–3
1979	58th Annual Report of the Revenue Commissioners, Year ended 31 December 1980: table 83, pp. 138–9
1980	59th Annual Report of the Revenue Commissioners, Year ended 31 December 1981: table 84, pp. 144–5

1981	60th Annual Report of the Revenue Commissioners, Year ended 31 December 1982: table 80, pp. 142–3
1982	61th Annual Report of the Revenue Commissioners, Year ended 31 December 1983: table 81, pp. 152–3
1983	63rd Annual Report of the Revenue Commissioners, Year ended 31 December 1985: table 91, pp. 160–1
1984	64th Annual Report of the Revenue Commissioners, Year ended 31 December 1986: table 86, pp. 160–1
1985	65th Annual Report of the Revenue Commissioners, Year ended 31 December 1987: table 86, pp. 150–1
1986	66th Annual Report of the Revenue Commissioners, Year ended 31 December 1988: table 86, pp. 150–1
1987	Statistical Report of the Revenue Commissioners, Year ended 31 December 1989: table 66, pp. 85–6
1988	Statistical Report of the Revenue Commissioners, Year ended 31 December 1990: table 36, pp. 70–1
1989	Statistical Report of the Revenue Commissioners, Year ended 31 December 1991: table 43, pp. 80–1
1990	Statistical Report of the Revenue Commissioners, Year ended 31 December 1992: table 43, pp. 80–1
1991	Statistical Report of the Revenue Commissioners, Year ended 31 December 1993: table 44, pp. 84–5
1992	Statistical Report of the Revenue Commissioners, Year ended 31 December 1994: table IDS7, p. 82
1993	Statistical Report of the Revenue Commissioners, Year ended 31 December 1995: table IDS7, p. 86
1994	Statistical Report of the Revenue Commissioners, Year ended 31 December 1996: table IDS7, p. 76
1995	Statistical Report of the Revenue Commissioners, Year ended 31 December 1997: table IDS8, pp. 76–7
1996	Statistical Report of the Revenue Commissioners, Year ended 31 December 1998: table IDS8, pp. 76–7
1997	Statistical Report of the Revenue Commissioners, Year ended 31 December 1999, Table IDS8, pp. 76–7
1998	Statistical Report of the Revenue Commissioners, Year ended 31 December 2000: table IDS8, p. 77
1999	Statistical Report of the Revenue Commissioners, Year ended 31 December 2001: table IDS8, p. 81
2000	Statistical Report of the Revenue Commissioners, Year ended 31 December 2002: table IDS8, p. 81

required to derive the required control total for the years 1939–43). Prior to 1938 no official national income data was produced, and thus no official series on national income, much less personal sector income, exists. This appendix describes how we estimated national income for each of the years 1922–37, amending the estimates of Duncan (1940*a*, *b*) in the light of subsequent studies, and then interpolating or extrapolating for the years he did not cover.

Duncan (1940*b*) presented the following estimated indices for national income in money terms, 'general prices', and 'real income' for selected years from 1926 to 1940 (see Table 12A.3).

Table12A.2 Source of income data used in deriving 'gross' income shares, Ireland 1989–2000

Year	Source
1989	Statistical Report of the Revenue Commissioners, Year ended 31 December 1991: table 37, pp. 72–3
1990	Statistical Report of the Revenue Commissioners, Year ended 31 December 1992: table 37, pp. 72–3
1991	Statistical Report of the Revenue Commissioners, Year ended 31 December 1993: table 38, pp. 76–7
1992	Statistical Report of the Revenue Commissioners, Year ended 31 December 1994: table IDS1, p. 75
1993	Statistical Report of the Revenue Commissioners, Year ended 31 December 1995: table IDS1, p. 79
1994	Statistical Report of the Revenue Commissioners, Year ended 31 December 1996: table IDS1, p. 69
1995	Statistical Report of the Revenue Commissioners, Year ended 31 December 1997: table IDS1, p. 69
1996	Statistical Report of the Revenue Commissioners, Year ended 31 December 1998: table IDS1, p. 69
1997	Statistical Report of the Revenue Commissioners, Year ended 31 December 1999: table IDS1, p. 68
1998	Statistical Report of the Revenue Commissioners, Year ended 31 December 2000: table IDS1, p. 77
1999	Statistical Report of the Revenue Commissioners, Year ended 31 December 2001: table IDS1, p. 72
2000	Statistical Report of the Revenue Commissioners, Year ended 31 December 2002: table IDS1, p. 81

The pattern of real income growth this suggests is that real GNP grew by about 17% between 1926 and 1938; Kennedy et al. (1988) regarded this as 'plausible enough', but questioned the distribution of that growth across the period (see Kennedy et al. 1988: 53–4, n. 22). Whereas Duncan's figures show real income growing by almost 15% between 1926 and 1931 and only 3% between 1931 and 1936, Kennedy et al. suggest that growth from 1931 to 1936 was probably about 10%, with the increase from 1926 to 1931 correspondingly reduced—which would bring it down to about 6.7%. We have recalculated Duncan's indices for money incomes on this basis, maintaining the price trends he estimated. We then

Table 12A.3 Estimated indices for national income in money terms, 'general prices', and 'real income'

	1926	1929	1931	1933	1936	1938
Money income	95	100	91	83	95	100
General prices	103	100	87	83	87	93
Real income	92	100	105	100	109	108

Note: Indices 1929=100.

Source: Duncan 1940*b*: 141.

took the official national accounts figure for national income in 1938 from the first official national accounts described in the text, and derived national income in nominal terms by applying the index we calculated to this base. This produced national income figures for the selected years for which Duncan made estimates, and we interpolated to fill in the gaps (1927, 1928, 1930, 1932, 1934, and 1935). Since we wished to push the series back to 1922 we also extrapolated back from 1926 to that date, for want of an alternative applying the same annual growth rate as that we estimated in the manner just described from 1926 to 1929.

It is worth comparing the figures this produces with those presented for 1920 by Feinstein in his seminal work which derived estimates of national income and related statistics for the UK from 1855 to 1965 (1972, 1976). Feinstein's estimates cover the UK up to 1920 and Great Britain and Northern Ireland from 1921 onwards, but for 1920 he gives figures for both, so the implied estimates for 'Southern Ireland' can be derived. (I am grateful to Tony Atkinson for bringing this to my attention.) These are that GNP in the South was between £176 million and £240 million depending on whether the income or expenditure approach is used, with a 'compromise' figure of £200 million (see Feinstein 1976 Tables 1, 2 and 4). These are substantially higher than the figure of £146 million for 1922 we have derived here. However, Feinstein's figures for Great Britain and Northern Ireland show a very sharp decline in national income there between 1920 and 1922, with GNP in the latter year only 73% of the 1920 figure. A decline of this order of magnitude in the South, applied to Feinstein's 'compromise' figure for 1920, would produce a figure for 1922 very close to the one being used here. Applied to his lower income based estimate it would produce a lower figure. Given the very specific uncertainties surrounding the 1920–22 period the most that can probably be said is that the national income figures used here are not obviously inconsistent with Feinstein's estimates for 1920.

We then used these national income figures to derive estimates for the income control total we wanted to employ in producing income shares—namely 80% of personal sector income having subtracted transfers and employers social insurance contributions. With no estimates of the components available before the official national accounts began, we simply rely on the relationships that held in 1938, the first year for which they are available. We take personal sector income less transfers and social insurance as a proportion of national income in 1938, apply that proportion to our national income estimates for each year from 1922–37, and take 80% of that figure as our income control total in deriving the income control totals shown in Table 12.4 and the income shares in Table 12.5. The extent of the simplifying assumptions required to produce these estimates, and the uncertainty surrounding the national income figures underlying them, must be emphasized.

APPENDIX 12C: COMPARING THE COMPOSITION OF TOP INCOMES IN 1989–90 AND 2000

In the *Statistical Report of the Revenue Commissioners for 2002*, presenting income tax distribution figures for 1999–2000, the total number of taxpayers above €150,000 is 13,702 and among these the following groups are distinguished in separate tables:

1.	Self-employed including proprietary directors total above €150,000 = 9984	Table IDS2
2.	Mainly earned income assessed under Schedule D total above €150,000 = 5677	IDS3
3.	Mainly unearned income assessed under Schedule D total above €150,000 = 490	IDS4
4.	Mainly PAYE income assessed under Schedule E total above €150,000 = 7535	IDS5
5.	Mainly PAYE income assessed under Schedule E excluding proprietary directors on Schedule E total above €150,000 = 3718	IDS6
6.	Proprietary directors total above €150,000 = 5577	IDS7

However, these are not exhaustive and exclusive categories, with proprietary directors included in 1, 2, and 4, and with 2 included in 1.

Total taxpayers are 2+3+4
[5677+490+7535] = 13,702

Most proprietary directors are in 4, with a minority in 2, but we can calculate how many proprietary directors are in 4 by subtracting 5: [7536–3718] = 3817. We can then calculate how many must be in 2 by subtracting the number in 4 from the total number of proprietary directors 6: [5577–3817] = 1760. So we can derive 2 excluding proprietary directors =7 as [5677–1760] = 3917. We can also categorize total taxpayers as:

7.	Schedule D excluding proprietary directors	3917
3.	Schedule D mainly unearned income	490
5.	Schedule E excluding proprietary directors	3718
6.	Proprietary directors	5577

but there is no table showing the distribution of 7 across income ranges. We can derive the number of self-employed excluding proprietary directors as 1–6: [9984–5577] = 4407. This is 7 plus unearned under Schedule D 3 so includes latter, so an alternative breakdown of total taxpayers is:

1 self-employed including prop directors and unearned Schedule D	9984
[=self-employed excluding proprietary directors (3917) + proprietary directors	(5577)
+ unearned under Schedule D (490)]	
5 PAYE under E excluding proprietary directors	3718

but since we have details in a separate table on 3 unearned under Schedule D, we can also break those out and distinguish 3 groups of interest:

8. Self-employed including proprietary directors but excluding mainly unearned incomes [=1–3, 9984–490]	9494

3. Mainly unearned incomes	490
5. PAYE excluding proprietary directors	3718

We can see the actual income distribution, total income by range, etc. for the second and third of these groups directly in the IDS Tables 4 and 6 respectively. For the first group, we have to calculate these from the table IDS2 for all self-employed including unearned under Schedule D by subtracting the latter—i.e. by subtracting IDS Table 3 from Table 2.

In 1989–90, category 5 is not separately distinguished in a table of its own; however, one can derive 8 (self-employed including proprietary directors) by excluding mainly unearned income as above, and then derive 5 by deducting the other two groups (or equivalently group 1) from the overall total in IDS Table 1.

REFERENCES

Atkinson, A. B. (2005). 'Top incomes in the UK over the 20th century', *Journal of the Royal Statistical Society*, 168(2): 325–43.

Duncan, G. A. (1939). 'The Social Income of the Irish Free State, 1926–38', *Journal of the Statistical and Social Inquiry Society of Ireland* (94th Session, 1940–41), 16: 1–16.

—— (1940). 'The Social Income of Eire, 1938–40', *Journal of the Statistical and Social Inquiry Society of Ireland* (94th Session, 1940–41), 16: 140–1.

Feinstein, C. H. (1972). *National Income, Expenditure and Output of the U.K., 1855–1965*, vol. 6, Studies in the National Income and Expenditure of the United Kingdom. Cambridge: Cambridge University Press.

—— (1976). *Statistical Tables of National Income, Expenditure and Output of the U.K., 1855–1965*. Cambridge: Department of Applied Economics, University of Cambridge and the Royal Economic Society, Cambridge University Press.

Kennedy, K. A. (1994). *Irish National Accounts for the 19th and 20th Centuries* (ESRI Memorandum Series 187). Dublin: ESRI.

—— Giblin, T., and McHugh, D. (1988). *The Economic Development of Ireland in the Twentieth Century*. London: Routledge.

Linehan, T. and Lucey, M. (2000). 'The Compilation of the First Official Set of Irish National Accounts, 1938–44'. Paper for Historical National Accounts Group for Ireland, ESRI, Dublin, 28 January.

Minister for Finance (1946). *National Income and Expenditure, 1938–1944*. Dublin: Stationery Office.

O'Grada, C. (1997). *A Rocky Road: The Irish Economy Since the 1920s*. Manchester: Manchester University Press.

O'Rourke, K. (1995). 'The Costs of International Economic Disintegration: Ireland in the 1930s', *Research in Economic History*, 15: 215–59.

Piketty, T. (2001). *Les hauts revenus en France au 20eme siècle—Inégalités et redistributions, 1901–1998*. Paris: Editions Grasset.

—— (2003). 'Income Inequality in France, 1901–1998', *Journal of Political Economy*, 111: 1004–42.

—— Saez, E. (2003). 'Income Inequality in the United States, 1913–1998', *Quarterly Journal of Economics*, 118: 1–39.

Revenue Commissioners (various years from 1924). *Annual Reports of the Revenue Commissioners*. Dublin: Stationery Office.

—— (various years from 1988). *Statistical Report of the Revenue Commissioners*. Dublin: Stationery Office.

Saez, E. and Piketty, T. (2003). 'The Evolution of High Incomes in Canada, 1920–2000'. Working Paper 9607. Cambridge, MA: NBER.

13

Towards a Unified Data Set on Top Incomes

A. B. Atkinson and T. Piketty

13.1 INTRODUCTION

This chapter brings together the key series on top incomes for the ten countries covered in this volume. Tables 13.1 to 13.10 contain for each of the countries the shares in total income of the top 10%, 5%, 1%, 0.5%, 0.1%, 0.05%, and (where possible) 0.01%, covering as much as possible of the period since 1900. While each of the authors has been careful to provide the full data in their chapters, and in earlier published work, we feel that it is useful to collect them together. We also give a (brief) summary of the main findings; a fuller summary, covering more than twenty countries, will be given in Volume Two.

The establishment of a unified database raises the prospect of comparative analyses making use of a country panel of time series. Data for ten countries, covering most of the twentieth century on a near annual basis, are a rich resource. With such a panel, we can explore common influences on the evolution of top shares and possible interdependencies. As we have already seen, we can learn from cross-country comparisons about common factors. Moreover, the top income recipients in different countries inhabit the same world, and their experiences may well be interdependent. At the same time, the literature on cross-country growth regressions warns us of the possible pitfalls in merging data in this way, without regard to the specificities of both data and reality. Given the differences in systems of income taxation, and of income determination, across OECD countries, we cannot assume that the series are fully homogeneous.

The interpretation of the data depends on the institutional context, which varies from country to country. Some countries are more similar in their background than others. The English-speaking countries studied here in Chapters 4–8, and 12, share a number of common features. Each was once under British rule, and each has a common law legal system. English is the most commonly spoken language in each country, and migration and trade flows between them were high throughout the twentieth century. There may therefore be a case for selecting subsets of countries (see Atkinson and Leigh (2006) for an analysis of five Anglo-Saxon countries). As is suggested by the subtitle of the book, it is interesting to contrast the English-speaking countries and continental Europe.

Before summarizing the main findings in Section 13.3, we therefore consider in Section 13.2 the degree of comparability across countries. The individual chapters have concentrated on comparability over time within each country; here we focus on differences across countries. It has also to be stressed that the series presented here are not necessarily consistent over time in all countries. Considerable efforts have been made to make the series as consistent as possible, but there remain differences in definitions or in measurement. In some cases, as discussed further below, it is possible to link the series or to make adjustments, but in other cases the differences have to be taken into account in the interpretation. For this reason, it is *essential* that anyone using the data set should study the next section.

13.2 COMPARING DIFFERENT STUDIES

The main features of the different estimates are summarized in Table 13.0, so labelled to underline the fact that it should be read before using Tables 13.1–13.10. It should be immediately clear that there are a number of respects in which the estimates differ. Although the authors of individual chapters have modelled their research on Piketty (2001), they have in some cases been unable to follow exactly the same methods and in other cases they have chosen a different approach. Some of these differences in methodology are unlikely to affect the broad conclusions drawn, as has been shown by sensitivity analysis in individual chapters. This applies to the choice of interpolation method, which, at least within intervals (as opposed to extrapolation of an open interval), is not going to have a major impact. The same applies to the choice of age cut-off for the adult population. The studies for Australia, New Zealand, and the UK use persons aged 15 and over, while those for Canada and the US use persons aged 20 and over, which means that the former may give a higher estimate of the share of the top X%. To give some sense of the magnitude of the effect, Atkinson and Leigh (Chapter 7) find for Australia and New Zealand that using persons aged 20 and over would reduce the top 1% share by approximately 0.5 percentage points, and the top 10% share by approximately 2 percentage points.

Other differences are quantitatively more important. Three of the differences seem to us to be of particular significance. The first is the difference in the unit of analysis. For Australia, Canada, New Zealand (since 1953) and the UK (since 1990), the unit is the individual. In the other countries, including all the Continental European countries, the unit of analysis is the 'tax unit' combining the incomes of husbands and wives. In the United States, married women can file tax separate returns, but the number is 'fairly small (about 1% of all returns in 1998)'

Table 13.0 Key features of estimates for ten countries

	France	UK	US	Canada	Australia
Years covered	1900–98 (1900–10 aggregate, 1911–14 missing).	1908–2000 (1961 and 1980 missing).	1913–2002.	1920–2000.	1921–2002 (plus State of Victoria for 1912–23).
Extent of coverage	Initially under 5%.	Initially only top 0.1%.	Initially only around 1%.	Initially around 5%.	Initially around 10%.
Unit of analysis	Tax unit.	Tax unit to 1989; individual from 1990.	Tax unit.	Individual.	Individual.
Population definition	Total number of tax units calculated from number of households and household composition data.	Aged 15 and over; before 1990 total number of tax units calculated from population aged 15 and over minus number of married women.	Total number of tax units calculated from population aged 20 and over minus number of married women.	Aged 20 and over.	Aged 15 and over.
Method of calculating control totals for income	From national accounts.	Addition of estimated income of non-filers.	From 1944, addition of income of non-filers = 20% average income; before 1944 80% (personal income—transfers) from national accounts.	80% (personal income—transfers) from national accounts.	Total income constructed from national accounts.
Income definition	Gross income, net of employee social security contributions.	Prior to 1975 income net of certain deductions; from 1975 total income.	Gross income, adjusted for net income deductions.	Gross income, adjusted for the grossing up of dividend income.	Actual gross income; adjustment made to taxable income prior to 1957.
Treatment of capital gains	Capital gains excluded.	Included where taxable under income tax, prior to introduction of separate Capital Gains Tax.	Capital gains excluded in main series.	Capital gains excluded in main series.	Included where taxable under income tax.

(*contd.*)

Table 13.0 (*Contd.*)

	France	UK	US	Canada	Australia
Breaks in series?		Up to 1920 includes what is now Republic of Ireland; change in income definition in 1975; change to individual basis in 1990.			
Method of interpolation	Pareto	Mean split histogram	Pareto	Pareto	Mean split histogram
Special features		Evidence from super-tax and surtax, and from income tax surveys.			

	New Zealand	Germany	Netherlands	Switzerland	Ireland
Years covered	1921–2002 (1931, 1932, 1941–44 missing).	1891–1918 (annual), 1925–38 (annual or biennial), 1950–98 (triennial).	1914–99 (missing years in 1940s, 1950s, 1960s, 1970s and 1980s).	1933–95/96 (apart from 1933 based on income in 2 years).	1922–2000 (1954–63 missing).
Extent of coverage	Initially less than 10%.	In 1892 Prussia, covered 22%.	In 1914 covered 23%.	In 1933, 14% covered; increases to 33% in 1939 and over 50% from mid-1960s.	Varies; only top 0.1% for much of earlier period; top 0.1% missing in 1990s.
Unit of analysis	Tax unit until 1952, then individual from 1953.	Tax unit.	Tax unit.	Tax unit.	Tax unit
Population definition	Aged 15 and over; before 1953 total number of tax units calculated from population aged 15 and over minus number of married women.	(From 1925) total number of tax units calculated from population aged 21 and over minus number of married couples.	Total number of tax units calculated from population aged 15 and over minus number of married women.	Total number of tax units calculated from population aged 20 and over minus number of married women.	Total number of tax units calculated from population aged 18 and over minus number of married women.

Method of calculating control totals for income	95% of total income constructed from national accounts.	90% of net primary income of households from national accounts minus employers' contributions.	Addition of estimated income of non-filers.	From 1971 20% average income imputed to non-filers; prior to 1971 total income defined as 75% net national income.	80% of (total personal income—state transfers—employers' contributions).
Income definition	Assessable income to 1940; total income from 1945.	After deduction of costs associated with specific income source.	Gross income.	Income before deductions.	Net; also gross from 1989.
Treatment of capital gains	Included where taxable.	Included where taxable.	Not included.	Excluded.	Not included.
Breaks in series?	Assessable income up to 1940; change to individual basis in 1953.	Changes in geographical boundaries.	Three different sources, with breaks in 1950 and 1977.	None indicated.	Different sources: surtax statistics and income tax enquiries.
Method of interpolation	Mean split histogram.	Pareto	Mean split histogram.	Pareto.	Pareto.
Special features		Need to combine *Lohnsteuer* and *Einkommensteuer* data.		Treatment of tax evasion through Swiss accounts.	

(Piketty and Saez 2001: 35).[1] Piketty and Saez therefore treat the data as relating to tax units, although they note that, before the Revenue Act of 1948, a larger number of married women with income in their own right filed separate tax returns (around 5%), and make an adjustment to the earlier years.

As noted in Chapter 2, we cannot predict on a priori grounds the direction of the difference between individual and tax unit based estimates. Consideration of different assumptions about the joint distribution of income suggests that the use of an individual unit rather than a tax unit may lead to higher or lower top shares. Where all rich people are either unmarried or have partners with zero income, and couples are weighted the same as individuals, the share rises on moving to independent assessment, since we have to include a larger number in order to arrive at a given percentage of the population. But if, at the other extreme, all rich tax units consist of couples with equal incomes, then the same amount (and share) of total income is received by a larger fraction of the population, so that the measured share falls. It is not therefore easy to forecast the direction of the difference, and it may well have changed over the century. The growth of female labour force participation means that the joint distribution of earned incomes is now of much greater significance. The ageing of the population means that there are more single elderly persons in the distribution. On the other hand, we can learn from the cases where there was a change. In the case of the US, Piketty and Saez increase the recorded income shares by 'about 2.5%' for the earlier period 1913–47 when there was a degree of separate filing (Piketty and Saez 2001: n.35).[2] In the case of the United Kingdom, the introduction of independent taxation in 1990 was associated with (see Table 13.2) a rise in the share of the top 1% of 13.0% (or 1.1 percentage points), of the top 5% of 8.5% (1.9 percentage points), and of the top 10% of 8.1% (2.75 percentage points). In the case of New Zealand, the introduction of individual taxation in 1953 was associated with (see Table 13.6) an upward jump of around a quarter in the shares of the top 0.1%, 0.5%, and 1%. The share of the top 1% increased by 2 percentage points; the share of the top 5% rose by 4 percentage points. Not all of these changes can necessarily be attributed to the introduction of independent taxation, but it suggests that the difference between individual and tax unit bases needs to be taken into account in interpreting the series for the different countries.

The second significant difference is in the derivation of control totals for income. As described in Chapter 2, there are two main approaches. These are illustrated by those applied in the US at different dates. Piketty and Saez (Chapter 5) for the second half of the period (1944–98) extrapolate from the recorded incomes, imputing to non-filers a fixed fraction of filers' average income

[1] Separate assessment also existed in the UK, but married couples were treated in the statistics as a unit even where the wife elected for separate assessment (see, e.g., Inland Revenue 1963: 81 and 1980: 6).

[2] It should be noted that they use throughout a control total based on tax units, so that separate filing will definitely cause the top share to be understated.

(20% from 1946 to 1998). They note that the resulting total series is a broadly constant percentage (between 77% and 83%) of total personal income recorded in the national accounts if transfers are excluded. They therefore take for the earlier period 1913–43 a control total equal to a constant percentage (80%) of total personal income less transfers. (The estimates for Switzerland involve a similar combination of the two approaches.) As may be seen from Table 13.0, these two methods—estimates of the income of non-filers, and national accounts-based totals—are used to differing degrees in different countries. In Canada, for example, Saez and Veall use throughout (1920–2000) the constant percentage approach, applied to 'total personal income less transfers', basing the percentage (80%) on the experience since the mid-1970s when they feel that filing was close to complete. The estimates for Ireland follow the same method. In the UK, in contrast, the total income of non-filers is constructed from estimates of the different elements of income missing from the tax returns. The resulting total (see Figure 2.4) declines from around 95% to around 85% of total personal income minus transfers recorded in the national accounts. In the Netherlands, a similar approach is followed, with similar implications for the relationship between the control total and total personal income in the national accounts.

The studies for the US and Canada subtract social security transfers on the grounds that they are either partially or totally exempt from tax. This brings us to a third potential problem: the dependence of the estimates on the country-specific features of the income tax legislation that determine the definition of income. In other countries, such as Australia, New Zealand and the UK, the tax treatment of transfers differs, with typically more transfers being brought into taxation over time. The control totals have included transfers for a least part of the century.

The example of transfer payments raises a more general question for income distribution studies. Should the income definition follow the tax law, or should it follow a 'preferred' definition of income? The latter preferred income concept may seek to approximate the Haig–Simons comprehensive definition, including such items as imputed rent, in kind employment benefits, capital gains and losses, and all transfer payments. For a single country study, it may be reasonable to take taxable income, as a concept well understood in that context. Alternatively, one may assume that all taxable incomes differ from the preferred definition by the same percentage, although this does not seem a particularly plausible assumption. In a cross-country comparison, however, there seem good reasons for adopting a definition of income common across countries and that does not depend on the specificities of the tax law in each country.

The adoption of a common definition of income does however pose considerable problems, as illustrated by the treatment of transfers (which have grown very considerably in importance over the century), by capital gains, by the interrelation with the corporate tax system, and by tax deductions. The treatment of capital gains and losses differs across time and across countries. In the US, 'the tax treatment of capital gains and losses has undergone several sweeping revisions since 1913' (Goode 1964: p. 184). Capital gains have been regarded as within the purview of the income tax, but with different treatments regarding the deductibility of losses and the rates of taxation. Piketty and Saez (Chapter 5, this volume) present series for the US both excluding and including realized capital gains. The adjustments have differential effect in different years. In 1949, for instance, the adjustment to exclude capital gains reduced the total by some 2%; 50 years later, in 1999, it reduced the total by some 9%. The same approach is adopted for Canada. In the UK, the approach has been different, with certain gains brought under the regular income tax (and therefore included in the estimates), but most gains excluded from the raw data, since they are taxed under a separate Capital Gains Tax. The latter are not included. Capital gains are not included for Australia nor New Zealand.

The interpretation of the data depends not only on the *personal* tax law, but also on the taxation of *corporations.* One key feature is the extent to which there is an imputation system, under which part of any corporation tax paid is treated as a pre-payment of personal income tax. Payment of dividends can be made more attractive by the introduction of an imputation system, as in the UK in 1973, Australia in 1987 and New Zealand in 1989, in place of a 'classical' system where dividends are subject to both corporation and personal income tax. Insofar as capital gains are missing from the estimates but dividends are covered, a switch towards (away from) dividend payment will increase (reduce) the apparent shares. This needs to be taken into account when interpreting the results.

Income tax systems differ in the extent of their provisions allowing the deduction of such items as interest paid, depreciation, pension contributions, alimony payments, and charitable contributions. Income from which these deductions have been subtracted is often referred to as 'net income'. (We are not referring here to personal exemptions.) The aim is in general to measure gross income before deductions, but this is not always possible. The French estimates show income after deducting employee social security contributions. In a number of countries, the earlier income tax distributions refer to income after these deductions, but the later distributions refer to gross income. In the US, the income tax returns prior to 1944 showed the distribution by net income, after deductions. Piketty and Saez (Chapter 5, this volume) apply adjustment factors to the threshold levels and mean incomes for the years 1913–43 (see Piketty and Saez 2001: 40). As they note, strictly the distribution needs to be re-ranked, but they conclude from examination of the micro-data for 1966–95 that this re-ranking has small effects. In Canada, the tax returns for 1920–45 relate to net income. Deductions were smaller, and Saez and Veall (Chapter 6, this volume) make no adjustment prior to 1929 and for 1929–45 increase all amounts by 2%. In Australia, estimates for 1921–44 are based on taxable rather than total income by ranges of taxable income, while the estimates from 1947–57 are based on the distribution of taxable income by ranges of actual income. Using estimates from overlapping years, adjustments are made to account for these changes. For the UK series in Table 13.2, however, no adjustment is made (there is only one overlap year: 1975). In New Zealand, there is similarly a break in comparability: the tax data from 1921 to 1940 being tabulated by assessable income.

The three areas highlighted above are ripe for further research, as are a number of others. For example, we have not considered differences in the coverage of incomes by composition: in the Netherlands, control totals disaggregated by source of income show that income tax data coverage is much less complete for capital income than for wage income. Further research will undoubtedly allow the database to be made more comparable across countries. At the same time, cross-country differences are likely to remain, and any comparative analysis will need to take these into account. Moreover, there may be a trade-off between improving comparability across countries for recent years and within country comparability over time, particularly where there are micro-data for recent years, but not for the full period.

13.3 SUMMARY OF RESULTS: ENGLISH-SPEAKING COUNTRIES AND CONTINENTAL EUROPE COMPARED

The following graphs contrast the six predominantly English-speaking countries (Australia, Canada, Ireland, New Zealand, UK, and US) with the four Continental European countries studied in this volume (France, Germany, the Netherlands, and Switzerland). In considering these findings, the reader should bear in mind the qualifications set out in the previous section regarding their comparability, both across countries and over time. In the latter case, there are the following breaks in continuity, where those in italics are especially important: Germany (1950), the Netherlands (*1941* and 1977), New Zealand (1945 and *1953*), and UK (1921, 1975, and *1990*). The 1941 break in the Netherlands refers to a major change in the tax regime; the breaks in 1953 for New Zealand and 1990 for the UK refer to the switch from tax unit to individual taxation.

We begin with the shares of the top 10%, which is often regarded as 'the top' income group (many studies of earnings dispersion focus on the top decile). Figure 13.1A shows the shares of the top 10% for the six English-speaking countries. It may be seen that most of the six countries exhibit a U-shape over time, but that they differ considerably. In particular, they differ in the timing of the fall in the share of the top 10%. In all cases, there was a fall in the Second World War, but in both Australia and New Zealand there was an immediate post-war recovery. In Canada and the US, there was limited change in the period 1955–75, whereas Australia, New Zealand, and the UK all exhibited significant peacetime falls in the share of the top 10%. In Ireland, the share was 7 percentage points lower in 1975 than in 1943. We can also see that there is considerable diversity across the six countries, with a range of some 10 percentage points or more. Figure 13.1B shows the shares of the top 10% for the four Continental European countries. (The vertical scale is the same as in

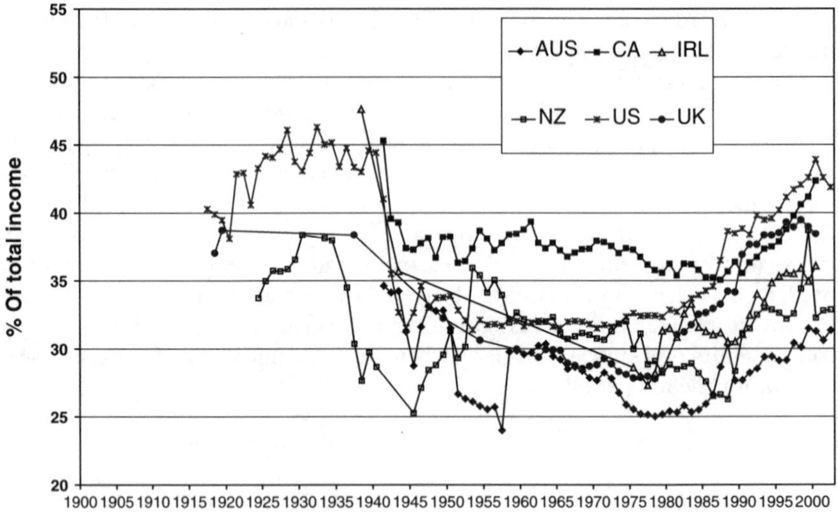

Figure 13.1A Share of top 10% in English-speaking countries

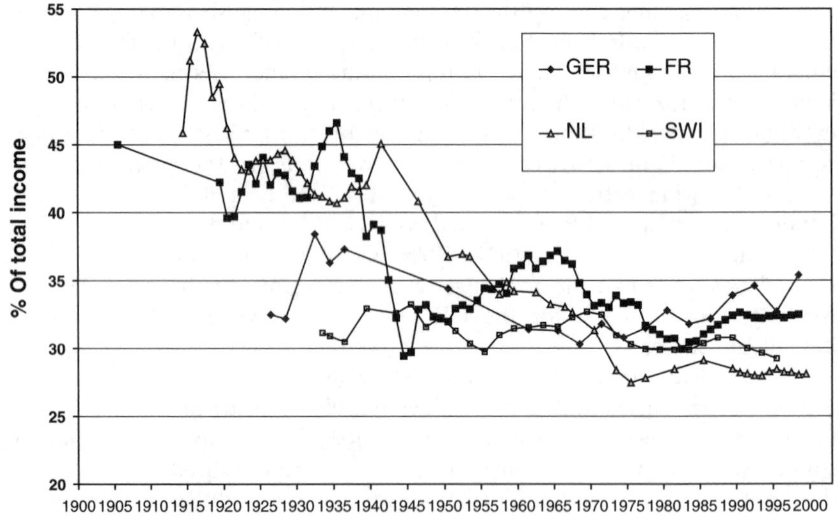

Figure 13.1B Share of top 10% in Continental European countries

Figure 13.1A.) From 1939 the Continental European story is different. As we have seen in Chapter 11, the top income share did not fall in Switzerland during the Second World War, whereas the graph shows that the wartime fall appears to have been greatest in France. (We have to bear in mind the breaks in the series for Germany and the Netherlands; e.g. it is fairly likely that top income shares were smaller in Germany in 1945 than in 1950, when the series

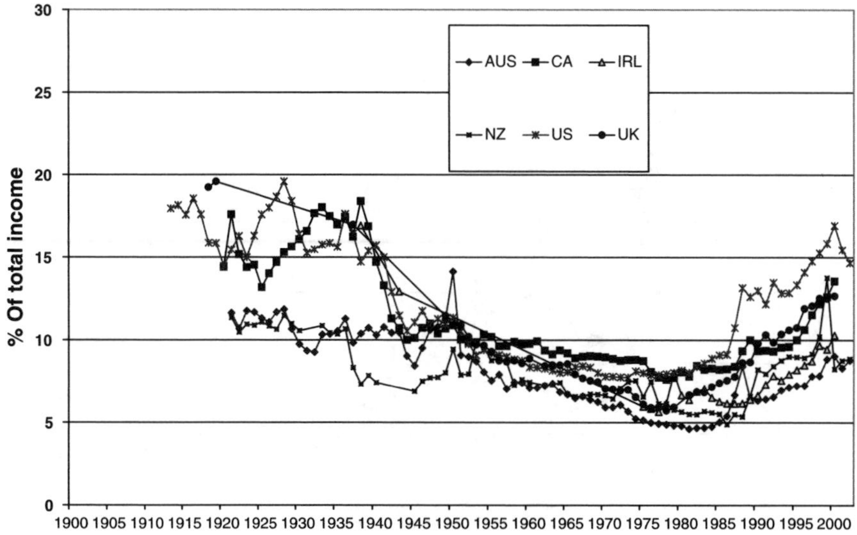

Figure 13.2A Share of top 1% in English-speaking countries

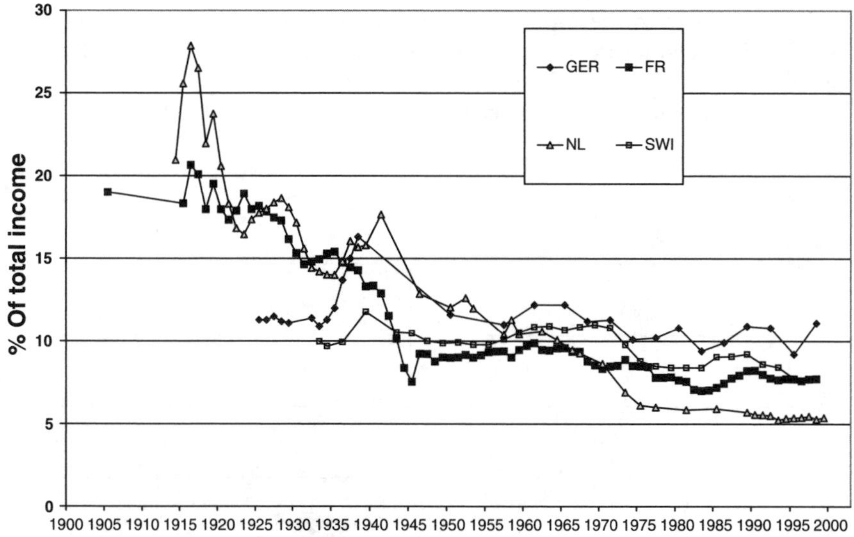

Figure 13.2B Share of top 1% in continental Europe

resume.) There was a period of falling shares in the 1960s and 1970s, except in Germany, but then broad stability over the past 20 years. Most striking is what did not happen: there has not been a U-shaped pattern over the twentieth century.

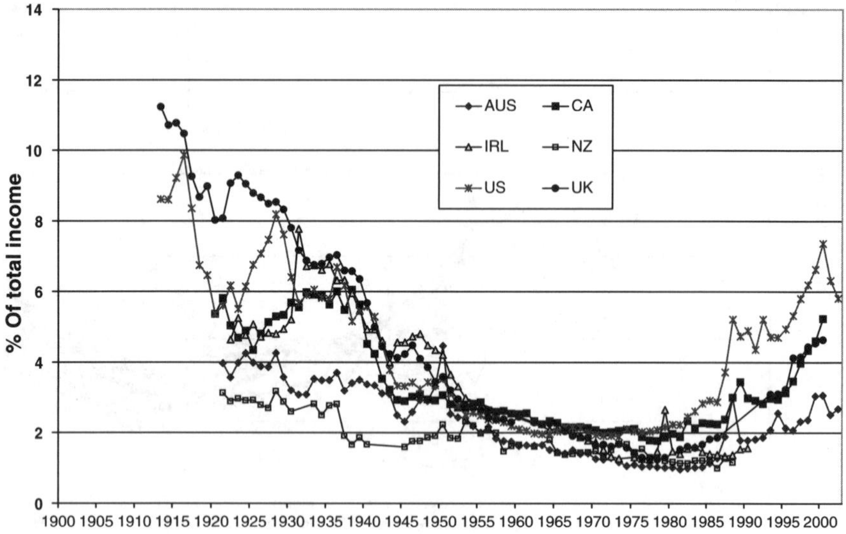

Figure 13.3A Share of top 0.1% in English-speaking countries

We turn now to the top 1%, shown for the English-speaking countries in Figure 13.2A and for the Continental European countries in Figure 13.2B (again on the same scale). The difference between the periods before and after the Second World War is again marked. For France and the Netherlands, there was

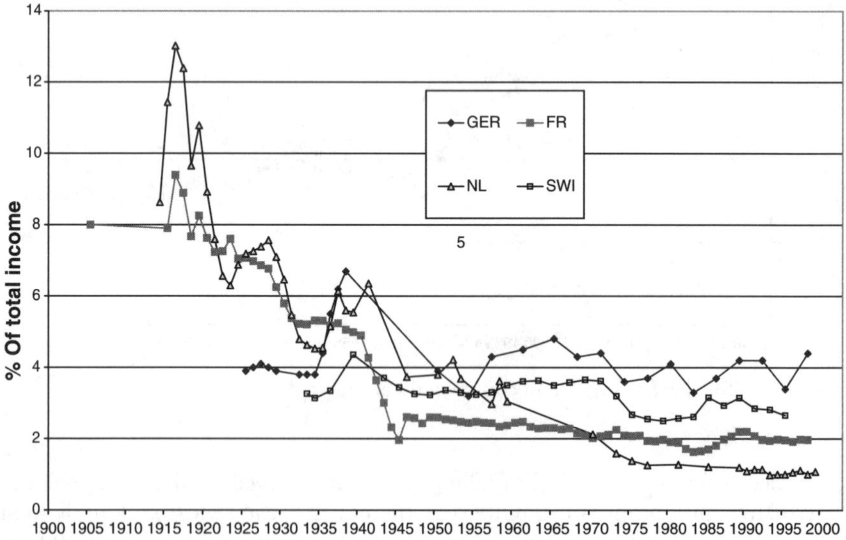

Figure 13.3B Share of top 0.1% in continental European countries

a fall prior to 1939, as in a number of English-speaking countries. But after the Second World War, the picture is more clearly one of stability, with only the Netherlands showing any pronounced reduction (from 1960 to 1975). (It may be noted that the estimated share of the top 1% Germany in the 1990s is twice that in the Netherlands.) In contrast, the six English-speaking countries exhibit a remarkable convergence up to the 1970s. In 1972 the range of the share of the top 1% is from 6.1% in Australia to 7.8% in the US. There was subsequently some divergence, with the share starting to rise in the US but continuing to fall in the other countries. But there is considerable commonality to the rise from the 1980s. (Account has to be taken here of the break in the UK in 1990, with the introduction of independent taxation.)

The share of the top 0.1% is shown in Figures 13.3A and 13.3B. For continental Europe, this again underlines the stability of recent decades, although the preceding period was different in the Netherlands, where there was a distinct fall in the period from the end of the 1950s to the mid-1970s. For the English-speaking there was first convergence to the bottom of the long-run U-shape and then some divergence, but with a general rise in the share of the top 0.1%.

How robust are these findings with respect to the data differences emphasized in the previous section? While the comparison of the *levels* of the shares is likely to be sensitive to the differences, we believe that the *national trends* are more robust. Just to give one example, we have seen that one of the major differences in the methods applied in different countries lies in the estimation of the control totals for income. This does not however affect the estimates of the shares within shares. In Figures 13.4A and 13.4B, we show the share of the

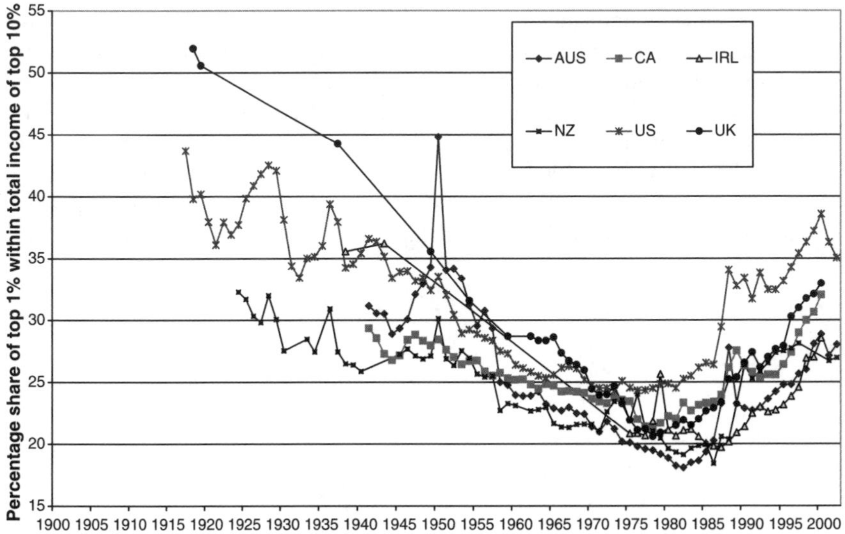

Figure 13.4A Share of top 1% within top 10 English-speaking countries

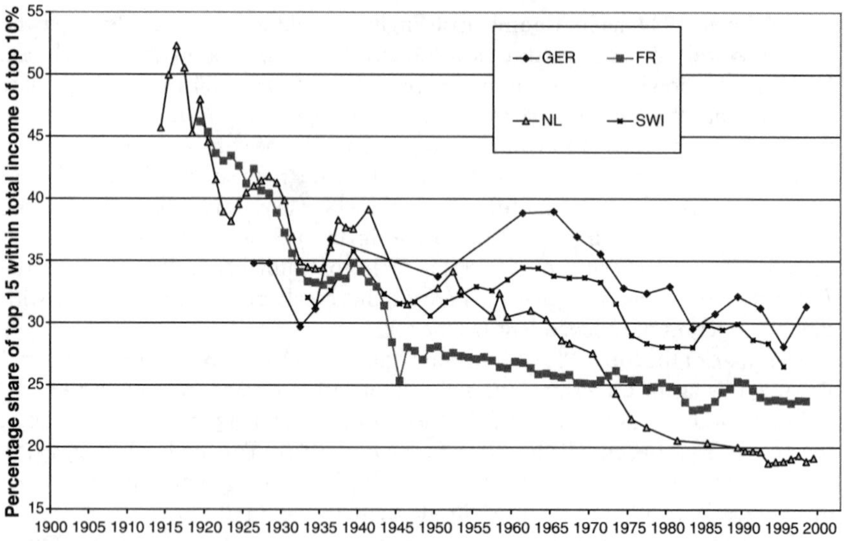

Figure 13.4B Share of top 1% within top 10% continental Europe

top 1% within the top 10%. These results depend on the correct identification of these groups, and hence on the population totals, but not on the income totals. For the English-speaking countries, these show the same U-shape as the values of the shares, with a pattern of convergence and then divergence. Translated into Pareto–Lorenz coefficients (see Chapter 2), there is quite a range in 1975, from 3.30 in Australia to 2.56 in the US. (For the same mean, a lower coefficient indicates more inequality.) Twenty years later, these values had fallen to 2.53 and 1.92 respectively. Interestingly, the coefficients in 1995 for Germany (2.23) and Switzerland (2.36) lie between these values. The coefficient for France (2.66) is higher, as is that for the Netherlands (3.62). It is also interesting to note from Figure 13.4B that the share of the top 1% within the top 10% has fallen from 1960 to the 1990s, even if only modestly in France. For the past quarter century, the contrast remains between the English-speaking upturn and the continental European flatness.

Table 13.1 Shares in total before tax income, France

	Top 10%	Top 5%	Top 1%	Top 0.5%	Top 0.1%	Top 0.05%	Top 0.01%
1900							
1901							
1902							
1903							
1904							
1905	45.00	34.00	19.00	15.00	8.00		3.00
1906							
1907							
1908							
1909							
1910							
1911							
1912							
1913							
1914							
1915			18.31		7.90		3.03
1916			20.65		9.39		3.79
1917			20.09		8.89		3.44
1918			17.95		7.67		2.87
1919	42.25	33.84	19.50		8.26		2.81
1920	39.59	31.41	17.95		7.63		2.86
1921	39.70	31.04	17.32		7.23		2.65
1922	41.54	32.50	17.87		7.26		2.51
1923	43.54	34.15	18.91		7.61		2.61
1924	42.14	32.27	17.96		7.05		2.39
1925	44.07	33.63	18.16		7.07		2.38
1926	42.06	32.34	17.82		6.98		2.41
1927	42.95	32.47	17.45		6.87		2.35
1928	42.75	32.19	17.27		6.77		2.33
1929	41.59	30.90	16.15		6.25		2.16
1930	41.08	30.14	15.31		5.79		1.93
1931	41.12	29.67	14.63		5.37		1.77
1932	43.44	31.06	14.80		5.22		1.67
1933	44.87	31.95	14.95		5.20		1.69
1934	46.01	32.68	15.28		5.31		1.71
1935	46.61	33.10	15.40		5.31		1.74
1936	44.10	31.58	14.74		5.17		1.74
1937	42.90	30.21	14.46		5.24		1.83
1938	42.52	29.79	14.27		5.05		1.75
1939	38.24	27.21	13.30		4.99		1.73
1940	39.11	27.85	13.35		4.90		1.65
1941	38.70	27.37	12.88		4.27		1.30
1942	35.04	24.90	11.53		3.64		1.06
1943	32.26	22.68	10.13		3.01		0.84
1944	29.42	20.18	8.37		2.32		0.61
1945	29.70	19.58	7.54		1.96		0.51
1946	32.87	22.34	9.22		2.61		0.72
1947	33.20	23.05	9.22		2.59		0.68
1948	32.35	21.46	8.75		2.43		0.63
1949	32.20	21.70	9.01		2.61		0.70

(contd.)

Table 13.1 (*contd.*)

	Top 10%	Top 5%	Top 1%	Top 0.5%	Top 0.1%	Top 0.05%	Top 0.01%
1950	31.97	21.62	8.98		2.60		0.70
1951	32.93	22.06	9.00		2.55		0.68
1952	33.19	22.35	9.16		2.53		0.65
1953	32.89	22.10	9.00		2.48		0.65
1954	33.53	22.55	9.14		2.45		0.64
1955	34.42	23.16	9.33		2.48		0.65
1956	34.36	23.11	9.37		2.46		0.65
1957	34.74	23.38	9.37		2.44		0.64
1958	34.05	22.76	9.01		2.34		0.60
1959	35.88	24.14	9.46		2.37		0.60
1960	36.11	24.40	9.71		2.45		0.62
1961	36.82	24.92	9.88		2.48		0.64
1962	35.88	24.16	9.46		2.34		0.58
1963	36.41	24.43	9.43		2.29		0.56
1964	36.84	24.75	9.56		2.30		0.56
1965	37.15	24.94	9.58		2.30		0.56
1966	36.46	24.41	9.36		2.26		0.57
1967	36.21	24.27	9.36		2.29		0.59
1968	34.80	23.08	8.77		2.15		0.56
1969	33.96	22.48	8.55		2.09		0.55
1970	33.14	21.95	8.33		2.02		0.53
1971	33.35	22.10	8.47		2.07		0.53
1972	33.03	21.97	8.52		2.11		0.55
1973	33.90	22.61	8.87		2.26		0.62
1974	33.33	22.09	8.50		2.09		0.53
1975	33.41	22.06	8.48		2.08		0.54
1976	33.19	21.91	8.44		2.08		0.54
1977	31.68	20.71	7.79		1.94		0.51
1978	31.38	20.56	7.80		1.93		0.50
1979	31.03	20.42	7.82		1.97		0.52
1980	30.69	20.11	7.63		1.91		0.50
1981	30.73	20.04	7.55		1.89		0.50
1982	29.93	19.37	7.07		1.72		0.44
1983	30.43	19.53	6.99		1.63		0.40
1984	30.52	19.57	7.03		1.65		0.41
1985	31.05	19.96	7.20		1.70		0.43
1986	31.39	20.30	7.44		1.81		0.46
1987	31.73	20.66	7.75		1.98		0.53
1988	32.09	20.90	7.92		2.06		0.57
1989	32.42	21.31	8.21		2.20		0.62
1990	32.64	21.45	8.23		2.20		0.62
1991	32.44	21.18	7.97		2.07		0.57
1992	32.23	20.90	7.75		1.97		0.54
1993	32.22	20.81	7.65		1.94		0.53
1994	32.37	20.90	7.71		1.98		0.55
1995	32.41	20.93	7.70		1.96		0.54
1996	32.25	20.79	7.59		1.92		0.53
1997	32.42	20.93	7.70		1.98		0.55
1998	32.50	20.98	7.72		1.97		0.55
1999							
2000							

Notes: (1) Figure for 1905 is for 1900–10 averaged.

Source: Table 3A.1.

Table 13.2 Shares in total before tax income, UK

	Top 10%	Top 5%	Top 1%	Top 0.5%	Top 0.1%	Top 0.05%	Top 0.01%
1900							
1901							
1902							
1903							
1904							
1905							
1906							
1907							
1908						8.22	4.04
1909						8.31	4.12
1910						8.37	4.18
1911						8.38	4.19
1912						8.38	4.15
1913					11.24	8.53	4.25
1914					10.71	8.11	4.04
1915					10.77	8.17	4.07
1916					10.47	7.97	4.00
1917					9.26	7.06	3.52
1918	37.03	30.35	19.24	15.46	8.68	6.58	3.21
1919	38.73	31.48	19.59	15.69	8.98	6.79	3.32
1920					8.03	6.06	2.94
1921					8.08	6.04	2.90
1922					9.07	6.78	3.23
1923					9.29	6.95	3.34
1924					9.05	6.74	3.23
1925					8.79	6.53	3.13
1926					8.67	6.42	3.07
1927					8.49	6.28	3.01
1928					8.54	6.34	3.04
1929					8.33	6.15	2.93
1930					7.81	5.74	2.71
1931					7.17	5.24	2.44
1932					6.87	5.00	2.32
1933					6.75	4.91	2.24
1934					6.78	4.92	2.23
1935					6.96	5.08	2.35
1936					7.03	5.12	2.35
1937	38.37	29.75	16.98	13.07	6.59	4.78	2.18
1938					6.57	4.79	2.21
1939					6.35	4.61	2.13
1940					5.67	4.09	1.84
1941					5.00	3.57	1.57
1942					4.44	3.15	1.37
1943				9.04	4.23	2.98	1.28
1944				8.97	4.13	2.90	1.22
1945				9.38	4.23	2.95	1.23
1946				10.00	4.48	3.10	1.27
1947				9.38	4.10	2.81	1.14
1948				8.88	3.86	2.63	1.05
1949	32.25	23.39	11.47	8.12	3.45	2.34	0.94
1950				8.51	3.59	2.42	0.96
1951			10.89	7.69	3.21	2.15	0.85
1952			10.20	7.15	2.95	1.97	0.77

(contd.)

Table 13.2 (*contd.*)

	Top 10%	Top 5%	Top 1%	Top 0.5%	Top 0.1%	Top 0.05%	Top 0.01%
1953			9.72	6.78	2.77	1.84	0.70
1954	30.63	21.22	9.67	6.71	2.72	1.80	0.67
1955			9.30	6.48	2.65	1.77	0.68
1956			8.75	6.03	2.42	1.60	0.61
1957			8.70	5.96	2.37	1.57	0.59
1958			8.76	5.98	2.38	1.57	0.60
1959	29.96	20.26	8.60	5.85	2.30	1.52	0.60
1960			8.87	6.08	2.45	1.63	0.63
1961							
1962	29.37	19.72	8.43	5.76	2.29	1.52	0.58
1963	29.94	20.10	8.49	5.76	2.23	1.47	0.57
1964	29.91	20.07	8.48	5.77	2.26	1.49	0.58
1965	29.88	20.10	8.55	5.79	2.28	1.52	0.62
1966	28.94	19.22	7.92	5.32	2.04	1.37	0.52
1967	28.78	18.99	7.69	5.11	1.91	1.25	0.51
1968	28.55	18.76	7.54	5.00	1.87	1.21	0.47
1969	28.72	18.86	7.46	4.96	1.85	1.22	0.47
1970	28.82	18.65	7.05	4.59	1.64	1.05	0.42
1971	29.29	18.81	7.02	4.56	1.67	1.09	0.40
1972	28.90	18.48	6.94	4.52	1.61	1.04	0.37
1973	28.31	18.18	6.99	4.59	1.68	1.08	0.40
1974	28.10	17.77	6.54	4.29	1.58	1.02	0.37
1975	27.82	17.40	6.10	3.92	1.40	0.91	0.31
1976	27.89	17.33	5.89	3.75	1.30	0.86	0.30
1977	27.96	17.33	5.93	3.75	1.27	0.82	0.28
1978	27.78	17.11	5.72	3.60	1.24	0.79	0.28
1979	28.37	17.57	5.93	3.76	1.30	0.83	0.31
1980							
1981	31.03	19.45	6.67	4.27	1.53	0.99	
1982	31.23	19.65	6.85	4.40	1.61	1.07	
1983	31.76	19.98	6.83	4.36	1.58	1.04	
1984	32.52	20.67	7.16	4.59	1.67	1.10	
1985	32.65	20.75	7.40	4.83	1.82		
1986	32.94	21.04	7.55	4.92	1.86		
1987	33.27	21.38	7.78	5.04			
1988	34.21	22.37	8.63	5.80			
1989	34.15	22.51	8.67	5.90			
1990	36.90	24.43	9.80	6.72			
1991	37.65	25.13	10.32	7.18			
1992	37.64	24.89	9.86	6.74			
1993	38.34	25.51	10.36	7.20	3.09		
1994	38.33	25.62	10.60	7.36	3.10		
1995	38.51	25.80	10.75	7.49	3.24	2.28	
1996	39.30	26.85	11.90	8.59	4.13	3.03	
1997	38.94	26.78	12.07	8.72	4.15	3.02	
1998	39.47	27.42	12.53	9.11	4.44	3.27	
1999	38.97	27.18	12.51	9.15	4.54	3.35	
2000	38.43	27.04	12.67	9.33	4.64	3.37	

Notes: (1) Up to 1920 includes what is now the Republic of Ireland. (2) From 1975, estimates relate to 'total income'; prior to 1975 estimates relate to income net of certain deductions. (3) From 1990, estimates relate to individuals; prior to 1990 estimates relate to tax units.

Source: Table 4.1.

Table 13.3 Shares in total before tax income, US

	Top 10%	Top 5%	Top 1%	Top 0.5%	Top 0.1%	Top 0.05%	Top 0.01%
1900							
1901							
1902							
1903							
1904							
1905							
1906							
1907							
1908							
1909							
1910							
1911							
1912							
1913			17.96	14.73	8.62		2.76
1914			18.16	15.08	8.60		2.73
1915			17.58	14.58	9.22		4.36
1916			18.57	15.60	9.87		4.40
1917	40.29	30.33	17.60	14.23	8.36		3.33
1918	39.90	29.30	15.88	12.39	6.74		2.45
1919	39.48	29.31	15.87	12.23	6.45		2.22
1920	38.10	27.47	14.46	10.95	5.37		1.67
1921	42.86	30.46	15.47	11.60	5.60		1.69
1922	42.95	31.05	16.29	12.38	6.17		2.01
1923	40.59	28.95	14.99	11.32	5.50		1.75
1924	43.26	30.93	16.32	12.42	6.14		2.01
1925	44.17	32.47	17.60	13.41	6.75		2.35
1926	44.07	32.75	18.01	13.75	7.07		2.54
1927	44.67	33.43	18.68	14.33	7.47		2.76
1928	46.09	34.77	19.60	15.17	8.19		3.23
1929	43.76	33.05	18.42	14.21	7.62		3.01
1930	43.07	31.18	16.42	12.42	6.40		2.39
1931	44.40	31.01	15.27	11.32	5.68		2.07
1932	46.30	32.59	15.48	11.55	5.90		1.93
1933	45.03	32.49	15.77	11.78	6.05		2.04
1934	45.16	32.99	15.87	11.80	5.82		1.92
1935	43.39	30.99	15.63	11.67	5.80		1.95
1936	44.77	32.65	17.64	13.37	6.69		2.23
1937	43.35	31.38	16.45	12.42	6.16		2.02
1938	43.00	30.18	14.73	10.82	5.16		1.67
1939	44.57	31.29	15.39	11.37	5.45		1.74
1940	44.43	31.29	15.73	11.66	5.57		1.77
1941	41.02	29.02	15.01	11.15	5.29		1.63
1942	35.49	25.11	12.91	9.60	4.48		1.32
1943	32.67	23.02	11.48	8.43	3.78		0.97
1944	31.55	21.76	10.54	7.60	3.33		0.92
1945	32.64	22.90	11.07	7.87	3.32		0.84
1946	34.62	24.66	11.76	8.28	3.43		0.92
1947	33.02	23.30	10.95	7.71	3.24		0.90
1948	33.72	23.70	11.27	8.03	3.44		0.95
1949	33.76	23.46	10.95	7.77	3.34		0.95
1950	33.87	23.87	11.36	8.14	3.53		0.83

(*contd.*)

Table 13.3 (*contd.*)

	Top 10%	Top 5%	Top 1%	Top 0.5%	Top 0.1%	Top 0.05%	Top 0.01%
1951	32.82	22.67	10.52	7.41	3.12		0.87
1952	32.07	21.85	9.76	6.81	2.76		0.75
1953	31.38	21.01	9.08	6.26	2.51		0.67
1954	32.12	21.56	9.39	6.47	2.57		0.71
1955	31.77	21.38	9.18	6.28	2.49		0.72
1956	31.81	21.35	9.09	6.14	2.38		0.68
1957	31.69	21.17	8.98	6.08	2.36		0.66
1958	32.11	21.26	8.83	5.94	2.29		0.64
1959	32.03	21.02	8.75	5.90	2.19		0.62
1960	31.66	20.51	8.36	5.52	2.10		0.60
1961	31.90	20.91	8.34	5.41	2.05		0.59
1962	32.04	20.94	8.27	5.40	1.98		0.56
1963	32.01	20.90	8.16	5.33	1.96		0.57
1964	31.64	20.62	8.02	5.33	1.97		0.53
1965	31.52	20.70	8.07	5.42	2.04		0.54
1966	31.98	20.99	8.37	5.59	2.15		0.60
1967	32.05	21.07	8.43	5.63	2.16		0.60
1968	31.98	20.98	8.35	5.58	2.15		0.58
1969	31.82	20.68	8.02	5.30	2.00		0.55
1970	31.51	20.39	7.80	5.16	1.94		0.53
1971	31.75	20.50	7.79	5.12	1.91		0.52
1972	31.62	20.37	7.75	5.10	1.92		0.52
1973	31.85	20.57	7.74	5.07	1.89		0.50
1974	32.36	21.04	8.12	5.41	2.11		0.56
1975	32.62	21.03	8.01	5.31	2.04		0.56
1976	32.42	20.85	7.89	5.23	2.02		0.56
1977	32.43	20.83	7.90	5.25	2.04		0.57
1978	32.44	20.86	7.95	5.30	2.08		0.58
1979	32.35	20.83	8.03	5.38	2.16		0.62
1980	32.87	21.17	8.18	5.51	2.23		0.65
1981	32.72	20.97	8.03	5.42	2.23		0.66
1982	33.22	21.40	8.39	5.73	2.45		0.77
1983	33.69	21.79	8.59	5.94	2.61		0.87
1984	33.95	22.10	8.89	6.22	2.83		0.98
1985	34.25	22.38	9.09	6.39	2.91		0.97
1986	34.57	22.59	9.13	6.38	2.87		1.00
1987	36.48	24.49	10.75	7.76	3.73		1.30
1988	38.63	26.95	13.17	9.96	5.21		1.99
1989	38.47	26.66	12.61	9.37	4.74		1.74
1990	38.84	27.05	12.98	9.71	4.90		1.83
1991	38.38	26.43	12.17	8.90	4.36		1.61
1992	39.82	27.88	13.48	10.11	5.21		2.02
1993	39.48	27.41	12.82	9.45	4.72		1.74
1994	39.60	27.50	12.85	9.45	4.70		1.73
1995	40.19	28.11	13.33	9.87	4.94		1.80
1996	41.14	29.15	14.10	10.48	5.32		1.97
1997	41.70	29.83	14.77	11.12	5.80		2.19
1998	42.06	30.31	15.28	11.60	6.19		2.40
1999	42.59	30.91	15.85	12.14	6.63		2.63
2000	43.91	32.15	16.94	13.10	7.37		3.06
2001	42.58	30.61	15.46	11.76	6.31		2.47
2002	41.87	29.75	14.67	11.07	5.81		2.25

Source: Table 6B.1.

Table 13.4 Shares in total before tax income, Canada

	Top 10%	Top 5%	Top 1%	Top 0.5%	Top 0.1%	Top 0.05%	Top 0.01%
1900							
1901							
1902							
1903							
1904							
1905							
1906							
1907							
1908							
1909							
1910							
1911							
1912							
1913							
1914							
1915							
1916							
1917							
1918							
1919							
1920		32.60	14.40	10.49	5.36		2.10
1921		40.58	17.60	12.55	5.81		1.70
1922		34.34	15.17	10.74	5.04		1.63
1923		30.15	14.38	10.22	4.69		1.53
1924		30.65	14.53	10.39	4.89		1.63
1925		29.76	13.18	9.48	4.34		1.32
1926		30.15	14.01	10.22	4.81		1.57
1927		30.70	14.69	10.78	5.13		1.74
1928		31.31	15.32	11.23	5.29		1.75
1929		31.73	15.64	11.47	5.34		1.71
1930		32.74	16.10	11.86	5.68		1.84
1931		36.03	16.60	12.00	5.55		1.72
1932		39.42	17.67	12.72	5.98		1.90
1933		40.88	18.03	12.89	5.91		1.73
1934		39.11	17.50	12.59	5.86		1.84
1935		38.09	16.99	12.19	5.63		1.72
1936		38.35	17.45	12.67	6.00		1.91
1937		35.81	16.26	11.79	5.48		1.54
1938		39.55	18.41	13.31	6.05		1.87
1939		37.23	16.88	12.23	5.63		1.67
1940		33.68	14.71	10.35	4.52		1.53
1941	45.31	30.74	13.30	9.46	4.24		1.29
1942	39.56	26.42	11.30	8.01	3.53		1.06
1943	39.29	25.84	10.72	7.51	3.23		0.92
1944	37.38	24.49	10.01	6.95	2.92		0.82
1945	37.27	24.63	10.12	6.99	2.89		0.78
1946	37.75	25.30	10.72	7.42	3.02		0.79
1947	38.14	25.66	10.99	7.61	3.09		0.82
1948	36.68	24.49	10.39	7.20	2.94		0.71
1949	38.22	25.37	10.69	7.38	2.91		0.69
1950	38.24	25.45	10.88	7.58	3.06		0.74

(*contd.*)

Table 13.4 (*contd.*)

	Top 10%	Top 5%	Top 1%	Top 0.5%	Top 0.1%	Top 0.05%	Top 0.01%
1951	36.31	23.96	10.03	6.94	2.80		0.65
1952	36.44	23.91	9.85	6.75	2.71		0.67
1953	37.36	24.37	9.88	6.75	2.70		0.66
1954	38.68	25.29	10.33	7.10	2.82		0.71
1955	38.08	24.90	10.19	7.00	2.86		0.75
1956	37.22	24.19	9.63	6.57	2.63		0.65
1957	37.76	24.50	9.64	6.54	2.59		0.64
1958	38.39	25.00	9.89	6.68	2.62		0.64
1959	38.44	24.94	9.74	6.55	2.54		0.61
1960	38.78	25.13	9.77	6.56	2.52		0.61
1961	39.35	25.53	9.93	6.63	2.55		0.63
1962	37.77	24.42	9.37	6.23	2.33		0.54
1963	37.37	24.11	9.14	6.06	2.24		0.51
1964	37.77	24.43	9.38	6.24	2.33		0.54
1965	37.23	24.04	9.20	6.12	2.28		0.54
1966	36.76	23.70	8.91	5.88	2.16		0.49
1967	37.06	23.91	9.00	5.93	2.15		0.47
1968	37.31	24.02	9.04	5.96	2.17		0.47
1969	37.34	24.01	9.01	5.91	2.13		0.46
1970	37.92	24.22	8.97	5.87	2.07		0.43
1971	37.83	24.08	8.87	5.79	2.00		0.40
1972	37.55	23.84	8.75	5.74	2.02		0.43
1973	37.02	23.65	8.80	5.78	2.06		0.46
1974	37.38	23.82	8.81	5.76	2.09		0.48
1975	37.28	23.71	8.74	5.73	2.11		0.51
1976	36.74	22.99	8.08	5.21	1.88		0.44
1977	36.18	22.43	7.74	4.98	1.79		0.43
1978	35.77	22.17	7.60	4.90	1.77		0.44
1979	35.57	22.11	7.72	5.06	1.86		0.48
1980	36.23	22.68	8.06	5.27	1.97		0.53
1981	35.39	22.10	7.80	5.08	1.88		0.50
1982	36.24	22.92	8.46	5.66	2.33		0.68
1983	36.19	22.71	8.21	5.44	2.13		0.57
1984	35.78	22.48	8.29	5.55	2.28		0.68
1985	35.25	22.20	8.21	5.51	2.26		0.67
1986	35.22	22.22	8.24	5.52	2.24		0.64
1987	35.05	22.22	8.40	5.69	2.38		0.70
1988	35.66	23.11	9.34	6.54	3.00		1.01
1989	36.36	23.83	10.01	7.15	3.44		1.29
1990	35.54	23.08	9.35	6.55	2.98		1.01
1991	36.31	23.47	9.37	6.51	2.91		0.99
1992	36.72	23.60	9.31	6.44	2.82		0.94
1993	37.31	24.03	9.56	6.64	2.97		0.99
1994	37.49	24.16	9.59	6.65	2.94		0.95
1995	37.85	24.65	10.00	6.99	3.13		1.03
1996	38.77	25.48	10.62	7.53	3.47		1.14
1997	39.78	26.51	11.52	8.32	3.97		1.33
1998	40.61	27.35	12.18	8.87	4.34		1.48
1999	41.17	27.89	12.62	9.25	4.61		1.68
2000	42.34	29.01	13.56	10.11	5.23		1.89
2001							
2002							

Source: Table 6B.1.

Table 13.5 Shares in total before tax income, Australia

	Top 10%	Top 5%	Top 1%	Top 0.5%	Top 0.1%	Top 0.05%	Top 0.01%
1900							
1901							
1902							
1903							
1904							
1905							
1906							
1907							
1908							
1909							
1910							
1911							
1912							
1913							
1914							
1915							
1916							
1917							
1918							
1919							
1920							
1921		19.43	11.63	8.55	3.97	2.80	1.24
1922		17.65	10.68	7.91	3.57	2.45	
1923			11.76	9.08	3.98	2.80	
1924			11.67	8.84	4.25		
1925			11.31	8.58	3.99	2.81	
1926			11.07	8.42	3.88	2.72	
1927			11.68	8.56	3.86	2.64	
1928			11.85	8.92	4.26	3.16	
1929			10.67	7.91	3.58	2.50	
1930			9.75	7.15	3.20	2.22	
1931			9.34	6.93	3.07	2.11	0.85
1932			9.27	6.91	3.08	2.14	0.90
1933			10.32	7.73	3.53	2.46	
1934			10.36	7.79	3.49	2.44	
1935			10.54	7.77	3.49	2.42	
1936			11.28	8.25	3.71	2.56	
1937			9.83	7.17	3.19	2.20	0.89
1938			10.39	7.61	3.41	2.36	0.97
1939		20.71	10.73	7.81	3.50	2.44	1.04
1940		20.57	10.30	7.48	3.37	2.35	0.99
1941	34.61	23.67	10.78	7.68	3.34	2.32	0.94
1942	34.12	23.26	10.43	7.34	3.11	2.12	0.85
1943	34.23	23.42	10.45	7.32	3.09	2.12	0.86
1944	31.25	21.09	9.03	6.22	2.49	1.66	0.64
1945	28.75	19.56	8.44	5.79	2.31	1.55	0.62
1946	31.61	21.76	9.51	6.52	2.59	1.72	0.66
1947	33.10	23.41	10.62	7.31	2.92	1.94	0.73
1948	32.77	23.35	10.80	7.40	2.89	1.96	0.73
1949	32.82	23.66	11.26	7.89	3.31	2.23	
1950	31.53	25.56	14.13	10.22	4.47		

(*contd.*)

Table 13.5 (*contd.*)

	Top 10%	Top 5%	Top 1%	Top 0.5%	Top 0.1%	Top 0.05%	Top 0.01%
1951	26.65	18.87	9.08	6.23	2.53	1.67	
1952	26.31	19.51	8.99	6.11	2.44	1.57	0.55
1953	26.10	18.70	8.71	5.97	2.43	1.58	0.58
1954	25.77	18.10	8.06	5.48	2.19	1.42	0.52
1955	25.53	17.49	7.54	5.10	2.01	1.29	0.48
1956	25.69	17.84	7.91	5.42	2.16	1.39	0.51
1957	23.99	16.33	7.04	4.75	1.84	1.19	0.43
1958	29.77	19.41	7.44	4.86	1.76	1.14	0.41
1959	29.85	19.44	7.39	4.82	1.75	1.12	0.41
1960	29.60	19.14	7.09	4.58	1.62	1.04	0.37
1961	29.71	19.20	7.10	4.58	1.65	1.06	0.40
1962	30.22	19.62	7.23	4.64	1.64	1.04	0.38
1963	30.35	19.84	7.36	4.72	1.65	1.05	0.37
1964	29.45	18.95	6.84	4.37	1.52	0.96	0.34
1965	29.22	18.68	6.69	4.27	1.46	0.92	0.31
1966	28.51	18.19	6.47	4.12	1.41	0.89	0.31
1967	28.66	18.29	6.58	4.23	1.51	0.98	0.38
1968	28.36	17.99	6.38	4.06	1.40	0.89	0.32
1969	27.85	17.61	6.25	4.00	1.42	0.92	0.36
1970	27.65	17.30	5.92	3.74	1.26	0.79	0.27
1971	28.24	17.59	5.92	3.70	1.25	0.78	0.27
1972	27.80	17.50	6.06	3.81	1.29	0.81	0.28
1973	26.74	16.73	5.67	3.54	1.17	0.73	0.24
1974	25.87	15.87	5.22	3.24	1.06	0.65	0.21
1975	25.54	15.65	5.13	3.22	1.10	0.68	0.23
1976	25.20	15.35	4.99	3.11	1.05	0.65	0.21
1977	25.15	15.25	4.92	3.08	1.06	0.67	
1978	25.01	15.14	4.87	3.02	1.03	0.65	
1979	25.17	15.20	4.83	2.97	1.02	0.65	
1980	25.39	15.31	4.79	2.95	1.02	0.66	
1981	25.31	15.15	4.61	2.83	0.96	0.62	
1982	25.82	15.44	4.67	2.87	1.00	0.63	
1983	25.32	15.16	4.68	2.89	1.02	0.66	
1984	25.50	15.25	4.75	2.96	1.03		
1985	25.93	15.63	5.02	3.19	1.14	0.75	0.35
1986	26.61	16.17	5.39	3.48	1.29	0.85	0.36
1987	28.66	17.94	6.67	4.53	1.89	1.41	0.60
1988	30.28	19.84	8.41	6.04	2.99	2.13	0.98
1989	27.64	17.46	6.43	4.29	1.79	1.31	0.51
1990	27.66	17.37	6.34	4.24	1.79	1.33	0.55
1991	28.22	17.70	6.41	4.28	1.81	1.35	0.57
1992	28.52	17.95	6.55	4.38	1.87	1.37	0.57
1993	29.40	18.66	6.96	4.69	2.08	1.46	0.61
1994	29.42	18.87	7.13	5.10	2.56	1.65	0.71
1995	29.13	18.76	7.23	4.95	2.14	1.52	0.73
1996	29.16	18.77	7.24	4.93	2.07	1.44	0.65
1997	30.41	19.73	7.81	5.38	2.32	1.64	0.75
1998	30.11	19.63	7.84	5.43	2.37	1.67	0.76
1999	31.48	20.95	8.84	6.29	3.04	2.15	
2000	31.28	20.98	9.03	6.44	3.06	2.24	
2001	30.61	20.33	8.31	5.75	2.51	1.75	
2002	31.34	20.90	8.79	6.11	2.68	1.87	

Source: Table 7.1.

Table 13.6 Shares in total before tax income, New Zealand

	Top 10%	Top 5%	Top 1%	Top 0.5%	Top 0.1%	Top 0.05%	Top 0.01%
1900							
1901							
1902							
1903							
1904							
1905							
1906							
1907							
1908							
1909							
1910							
1911							
1912							
1913							
1914							
1915							
1916							
1917							
1918							
1919							
1920							
1921		25.39	11.34	7.82	3.13		
1922		23.84	10.47	7.22	2.89		
1923		24.72	10.94	7.54	2.96		
1924	33.73	24.47	10.89	7.51	2.91		
1925	34.97	25.16	11.08	7.60	2.92		
1926	35.73	25.18	10.84	7.36	2.79		
1927	35.69	24.99	10.64	7.20	2.69		
1928	35.85	25.42	11.47	7.98	3.17		
1929	36.54	25.48	10.99	7.48	2.88		
1930	38.38	26.17	10.57	7.06	2.60		
1931							
1932							
1933	38.13	25.99	10.86	7.39	2.81		
1934	37.97	25.64	10.42	6.96	2.49		
1935		24.65	10.36	6.93	2.77		
1936	34.49	24.15	10.66	7.28	2.81		
1937	30.36	20.51	8.33	5.48	1.91		
1938	27.64	18.47	7.32	4.79	1.66		
1939	29.72	19.92	7.85	5.15	1.86		
1940	28.67	19.16	7.42	4.83	1.67		
1941							
1942							
1943							
1944							
1945	25.26	17.08	6.88	4.49	1.60		
1946	27.10	18.54	7.50	4.90	1.76		
1947	28.44	19.54	7.72	5.03	1.77		
1948	28.80	19.67	7.74	5.09	1.87		
1949	29.56	20.32	8.02	5.26	1.92		
1950	31.32	22.59	9.44	6.17	2.23		

(contd.)

Table 13.6 (*contd.*)

	Top 10%	Top 5%	Top 1%	Top 0.5%	Top 0.1%	Top 0.05%	Top 0.01%
1951	29.32	20.11	7.88	5.11	1.85		
1952	30.14	20.59	7.94	5.11	1.83		
1953	35.93	24.83	9.90	6.41	2.33		
1954	35.40	24.29	9.54	6.15	2.20		
1955	34.13	22.89	8.76	5.61	1.98		
1956	35.04	23.53	8.91	5.74	2.10		
1957	33.94	22.69	8.65	5.61	2.00		
1958	31.93	20.66	7.26	4.51	1.48		
1959	32.65	21.37	7.60	4.77	1.63		
1960	32.17	20.93	7.44	4.71	1.66		
1961							
1962	31.97	20.59	7.25	4.60	1.61		
1963	31.98	20.67	7.29	4.63			
1964	32.32	20.85	7.42	4.82	1.80		
1965	31.06	19.69	6.72	4.23	1.43		
1966	30.72	19.30	6.56	4.12	1.38		
1967	30.91	19.39	6.59	4.14	1.41		
1968	31.15	19.59	6.72	4.23	1.44		
1969	31.02	19.47	6.70	4.23	1.45		
1970	30.76	19.11	6.64	4.21	1.48		
1971	30.66	19.01	6.43	4.00	1.31		
1972	31.29	19.90	7.08	4.47	1.52		
1973	31.84	20.35	7.47	4.79	1.69		
1974	32.02	20.38	7.55	4.95	1.68		
1975	29.98	18.70	6.56	4.20	1.45		
1976	31.10	20.36	7.48	4.74	1.55		
1977	28.86	17.89	6.13	3.86	1.31		
1978	29.10	17.99	6.12	3.85	1.29		
1979	28.22	17.29	5.77	3.62	1.21		
1980	28.83	17.51	5.65	3.52	1.18		
1981	28.48	17.15	5.50	3.44	1.14		
1982	28.70	17.24	5.49	3.41	1.14		
1983	28.92	17.52	5.68	3.56	1.22		
1984	28.19	17.09	5.60	3.53	1.22		
1985	27.57	16.74	5.51	3.48	1.19		
1986	26.51	15.85	4.88	3.01	1.00		
1987	26.61	16.29	5.48	3.52	1.27		
1988	26.26	16.08	5.35	3.38	1.16		
1989	28.34	17.97	6.59	4.33			
1990	31.12	20.41	8.21	5.66			
1991	31.48	20.53	7.96	5.37			
1992	32.49	21.32	8.40	5.71			
1993	32.99	21.86	8.76	5.94			
1994	32.86	22.06	9.00	6.12			
1995	32.62	21.97	8.98	6.11			
1996	32.18	21.69	8.92	6.12			
1997	32.57	22.03	9.16	6.32			
1998	34.39	23.58	10.21	7.23			
1999	38.68	27.74	13.77				
2000	32.26	21.20	8.25	5.50			
2001	32.79	21.76	8.76	5.98			
2002	32.86	21.79	8.86	6.09			

Notes: (1) The series up to 1940 relates to assessible income; thereafter it relates to total income. (2) The series up to 1952 relates to tax units; thereafter it relates to individuals.

Source: Table 8.1.

Table 13.7 Shares in total before tax income, Germany

	Top 10%	Top 5%	Top 1%	Top 0.5%	Top 0.1%	Top 0.05%	Top 0.01%
1900							
1901							
1902							
1903							
1904							
1905							
1906							
1907							
1908							
1909							
1910							
1911							
1912							
1913							
1914							
1915							
1916							
1917							
1918							
1919							
1920							
1921							
1922							
1923							
1924							
1925			11.30	8.20	3.90		1.20
1926	32.50	22.10	11.30	8.30	4.00		1.40
1927			11.50	8.50	4.10		1.40
1928	32.20	22.60	11.20	8.20	4.00		1.30
1929			11.10	8.10	3.90		1.30
1930							
1931							
1932	38.40	26.60	11.40	8.30	3.80		1.20
1933			10.90	8.20	3.80		1.20
1934	36.30	25.30	11.30	8.20	3.80		1.30
1935			12.00	8.90	4.40		1.60
1936	37.30	27.00	13.70	10.40	5.50		2.20
1937			15.00	11.50	6.20		2.50
1938			16.30	12.60	6.70		2.60
1939							
1940							
1941							
1942							
1943							
1944							
1945							
1946							
1947							
1948							
1949							
1950	34.40	24.90	11.60	8.20	3.90		1.50
1951							

(*contd.*)

Table 13.7 (*contd.*)

	Top 10%	Top 5%	Top 1%	Top 0.5%	Top 0.1%	Top 0.05%	Top 0.01%
1952							
1953							
1954				6.90	3.20		1.00
1955							
1956							
1957			11.00	7.00	4.30		1.40
1958							
1959							
1960							
1961	31.40	23.40	12.20	9.10	4.50		1.30
1962							
1963							
1964							
1965	31.30	23.10	12.20	9.30	4.80		1.80
1966							
1967							
1968	30.30	21.90	11.20	8.40	4.30		1.60
1969							
1970							
1971	31.80	22.10	11.30	8.50	4.40		1.70
1972							
1973							
1974	30.80	21.60	10.10	7.40	3.60		1.30
1975							
1976							
1977	31.50	21.50	10.20	7.50	3.70		1.30
1978							
1979							
1980	32.80	22.60	10.80	8.10	4.10		1.50
1981							
1982							
1983	31.80	21.30	9.40	6.90	3.30		1.00
1984							
1985							
1986	32.20	21.80	9.90	7.40	3.70		1.30
1987							
1988							
1989	33.90	23.30	10.90	8.20	4.20		1.60
1990							
1991							
1992	34.60	23.60	10.80	8.00	4.20		1.60
1993							
1994							
1995	32.70	21.70	9.20	6.70	3.40		1.40
1996							
1997							
1998	35.40	24.20	11.10	8.30	4.40		1.60
1999							
2000							

Notes: (1) The estimates for Prussia for 1891 to 1918 are not included (see Table 9I.6).
Source: Table 11.2.

Table 13.8 Shares in total before tax income, Netherlands

	Top 10%	Top 5%	Top 1%	Top 0.5%	Top 0.1%	Top 0.05%	Top 0.01%
1900							
1901							
1902							
1903							
1904							
1905							
1906							
1907							
1908							
1909							
1910							
1911							
1912							
1913							
1914	45.87	36.51	20.96	16.34	8.63	6.34	
1915	51.21	42.07	25.58	20.31	11.44	8.58	
1916	53.31	44.18	27.88	22.53	13.02	9.84	
1917	52.47	42.78	26.51	21.34	12.39	9.53	
1918	48.50	38.20	21.95	17.18	9.65	7.40	
1919	49.48	39.34	23.74	19.07	10.79	8.17	
1920	46.23	35.92	20.59	16.30	8.92	6.65	
1921	44.03	33.35	18.29	14.23	7.60	5.65	
1922	43.19	32.13	16.82	12.79	6.57	4.83	
1923	43.08	31.93	16.45	12.40	6.30	4.61	
1924	43.84	32.84	17.34	13.22	6.88	5.09	
1925	43.87	33.04	17.75	13.64	7.19	5.37	
1926	43.87	33.18	17.99	13.82	7.26	5.39	
1927	44.33	33.72	18.37	14.13	7.39	5.47	
1928	44.58	34.01	18.63	14.38	7.57	5.64	
1929	43.85	33.34	18.09	13.86	7.10	5.21	
1930	43.02	32.41	17.15	12.97	6.47	4.69	2.09
1931	42.18	31.11	15.59	11.51	5.47	3.90	1.70
1932	41.33	30.04	14.43	10.46	4.79	3.37	1.44
1933	41.19	29.91	14.20	10.24	4.63	3.24	1.38
1934	40.82	29.62	14.02	10.09	4.53	3.17	1.34
1935	40.69	29.54	14.00	10.10	4.55	3.18	1.33
1936	41.10	30.18	14.83	10.89	5.15	3.70	1.68
1937	41.92	31.23	16.05	12.06	6.13	4.57	2.41
1938	41.60	30.93	15.68	11.63	5.60	4.02	1.81
1939	42.02	31.28	15.79	11.64	5.54	3.93	1.71
1940							
1941	45.07	34.25	17.64	13.06	6.36	4.55	
1942							
1943							
1944							
1945							
1946	40.82	29.08	12.86	8.93	3.74	2.56	1.03
1947							
1948							
1949							
1950	36.74	26.16	12.05	8.59	3.80	2.65	
1951							

(contd.)

Table 13.8 (*contd.*)

	Top 10%	Top 5%	Top 1%	Top 0.5%	Top 0.1%	Top 0.05%	Top 0.01%
1952	36.95	26.45	12.61	9.13	4.22	2.94	
1953	36.76	26.14	11.99	8.44	3.69	2.57	
1954							
1955							
1956							
1957	33.98	23.75	10.39	7.20	2.98		
1958	34.88	24.61	11.29	8.03	3.62		
1959	34.20	23.89	10.43	7.23	3.05		
1960							
1961							
1962	34.12	23.93	10.58	7.39			
1963							
1964	33.25	23.13	10.07	7.00			
1965							
1966	33.05	22.69	9.46	6.44			
1967	32.64	22.30	9.26	6.29			
1968							
1969							
1970	31.34	21.25	8.64	5.76	2.12	1.39	0.57
1971							
1972							
1973	28.37	18.40	6.90	4.48	1.59	1.02	0.36
1974							
1975	27.47	17.40	6.12	3.95	1.38	0.88	0.33
1976							
1977	27.81	17.35	6.01	3.81	1.26	0.77	
1978							
1979							
1980							
1981	28.46	17.57	5.85	3.66	1.28	0.81	
1982							
1983							
1984							
1985	29.10	18.00	5.92	3.65	1.21	0.77	
1986							
1987							
1988							
1989	28.48	17.62	5.70	3.52	1.19	0.78	
1990	28.20	17.33	5.56	3.42	1.09	0.68	
1991	28.11	17.25	5.54	3.41	1.14	0.73	
1992	27.99	17.13	5.50	3.39	1.14	0.73	
1993	27.96	16.97	5.24	3.15	0.98	0.60	
1994	28.28	17.18	5.33	3.21	1.00	0.63	
1995	28.45	17.32	5.37	3.23	1.00	0.61	
1996	28.24	17.22	5.39	3.28	1.06	0.69	
1997	28.21	17.23	5.46	3.34	1.11	0.72	
1998	28.03	17.06	5.29	3.21	1.00	0.61	
1999	28.09	17.13	5.38	3.28	1.08	0.69	
2000							

Notes: (1) Series up to 1946 based on tabulated income tax data. (2) Series from 1950 to 1975 based on tabulated data produced by Central Bureau of Statistics. (3) Series from 1977 based on micro-data Income Panel Survey using tax and other administrative data.

Source: Table 11.2.

Table 13.9 Shares in total before tax income, Switzerland

	Top 10%	Top 5%	Top 1%	Top 0.5%	Top 0.1%	Top 0.05%	Top 0.01%
1900							
1901							
1902							
1903							
1904							
1905							
1906							
1907							
1908							
1909							
1910							
1911							
1912							
1913							
1914							
1915							
1916							
1917							
1918							
1919							
1920							
1921							
1922							
1923							
1924							
1925							
1926							
1927							
1928							
1929							
1930							
1931							
1932							
1933	31.16	21.92	9.98	7.19	3.27		0.94
1934	30.92	21.59	9.69	6.94	3.14		0.91
1935							
1936	30.47	21.46	9.94	7.21	3.35		0.98
1937							
1938							
1939	32.94	23.77	11.78	8.78	4.36		1.52
1940							
1941							
1942							
1943	32.59	22.70	10.54	7.67	3.71		1.43
1944							
1945	33.24	23.36	10.49	7.50	3.44		1.10
1946							
1947	31.58	21.95	10.01	7.15	3.26		1.03
1948							
1949	32.29	22.22	9.88	7.13	3.23		0.96
1950							

(*contd.*)

Table 13.9 (*contd.*)

	Top 10%	Top 5%	Top 1%	Top 0.5%	Top 0.1%	Top 0.05%	Top 0.01%
1951	31.29	21.65	9.91	7.18	3.37		1.07
1952							
1953	30.33	21.16	9.78	7.08	3.30		1.05
1954							
1955	29.72	20.92	9.78	7.06	3.24		0.97
1956							
1957	30.99	21.79	10.11	7.24	3.31		1.03
1958							
1959	31.47	22.35	10.54	7.58	3.51		1.09
1960							
1961	31.56	22.70	10.87	7.85	3.62		1.06
1962							
1963	31.72	22.83	10.91	7.88	3.64		1.12
1964							
1965	31.60	22.60	10.67	7.67	3.50		1.05
1966							
1967	32.29	23.01	10.86	7.81	3.58		1.08
1968							
1969	32.70	23.32	11.00	7.92	3.66		1.14
1970							
1971	32.49	23.03	10.81	7.79	3.62		1.14
1972							
1973	30.96	21.51	9.77	6.98	3.20		1.04
1974							
1975	30.29	20.47	8.79	6.15	2.68		0.83
1976							
1977	29.93	20.12	8.49	5.90	2.56		0.79
1978							
1979	29.89	20.06	8.40	5.82	2.51		0.76
1980							
1981	29.87	20.02	8.40	5.85	2.58		0.84
1982							
1983	29.88	20.00	8.39	5.85	2.62		0.86
1984							
1985	30.35	20.64	9.05	6.48	3.16		1.25
1986							
1987	30.78	20.93	9.07	6.41	2.94		0.96
1988							
1989	30.78	20.96	9.22	6.59	3.15		1.15
1990							
1991	29.99	20.14	8.60	6.09	2.85		1.00
1992							
1993	29.65	19.87	8.42	6.01	2.82		0.98
1994							
1995	29.22	19.27	7.76	5.67	2.67		0.87
1996							
1997							
1998							
1999							
2000							

Notes: (1) For all except 1933, the estimates relate to income averaged over the year shown and the following year.
Source: Table 11.2.

Table 13.10 Shares in total before tax income, Ireland

	Top 10%	Top 5%	Top 1%	Top 0.5%	Top 0.1%	Top 0.05%	Top 0.01%
1900							
1901							
1902							
1903							
1904							
1905							
1906							
1907							
1908							
1909							
1910							
1911							
1912							
1913							
1914							
1915							
1916							
1917							
1918							
1919							
1920							
1921							
1922					4.64		
1923					5.25		
1924					4.77		
1925					5.07		
1926					4.72		
1927					4.83		
1928					4.80		
1929					4.94		
1930					5.21		
1931					7.78		
1932					6.71		
1933					6.74		
1934					6.61		
1935					6.77		
1936					6.31		
1937					6.32		
1938	47.61		16.93	12.38	5.95		
1939					5.46		
1940					4.93		
1941					4.93		
1942					4.61		
1943	35.68		12.92	9.36	4.00		
1944					4.56		
1945					4.56		
1946					4.73		
1947					4.80		
1948					4.48		
1949					4.35		
1950					4.21		

(contd.)

Table 13.10 (*contd.*)

	Top 10%	Top 5%	Top 1%	Top 0.5%	Top 0.1%	Top 0.05%	Top 0.01%
1951					3.65		
1952					3.31		
1953					2.98		
1954							
1955							
1956							
1957							
1958							
1959							
1960							
1961							
1962							
1963							
1964					2.09		
1965				5.46	2.11		
1966				5.57	2.11		
1967					2.02		
1968					1.87		
1969					1.78		
1970					1.73		
1971					1.52		
1972					1.33		
1973				3.51	1.27		
1974							
1975	28.62		5.96	3.76	1.31		
1976	27.96		5.83	3.66	1.26		
1977	27.29		5.64	3.56	1.24		
1978	28.20		6.16	3.98	1.47		
1979	31.32		8.03	5.68	2.65		
1980	31.50		6.65	4.21	1.47		
1981	30.85		6.37	4.02	1.40		
1982	32.57		6.87	4.36	1.55		
1983	33.29		7.05	4.48	1.60		
1984	31.57		6.50	4.10	1.46		
1985	31.28		6.27	3.93	1.40		
1986	31.03		6.15	3.83	1.38		
1987	31.16		6.14	3.81	1.34		
1988	30.51		6.15	3.85	1.37		
1989	30.52		6.38	4.10	1.54		
1990	31.05		6.64	4.28	1.57		
1991	32.46		7.30	4.82			
1992	34.00		7.83	5.09			
1993	33.39		7.55	4.85			
1994	34.84		7.93	5.10			
1995	35.33		8.19	5.39			
1996	35.55		8.48	5.65			
1997	35.51		8.73	5.90			
1998	35.89		9.67	6.75			
1999	34.93		9.44	6.60			
2000	36.07		10.30	7.28			

Notes: (1) Estimates for 1938 and 1943 based on Table 12.2 rather than surtax returns. (2) Estimates from 1975 based on income tax returns.

Source: Table 12.5.

REFERENCES

Atkinson, A. B. and Leigh, A. (2006). 'The Distribution of Top Incomes in Five Anglo-Saxon Countries over the Twentieth Century'. ANU discussion paper.

Goode, R. (1964). *The Individual Income Tax.* Washington, DC: Brookings Institution.

Piketty, T. (2001). *Les hauts revenus en France au 20ème siècle.* Paris: Grasset.

Piketty, T. and Saez, T. (2001). 'Income Inequality in the United States, 1913–1998'. National Bureau of Economic Research Working Paper 8467. Cambridge, MA: NBER.

Index

Index compiled by Frank Pert